## A note about the cover

Is everything *really* an argument? Seeing the images on the cover might make you wonder. The protests from the Arab Spring of 2011, for example, instantly call to mind the very public unrest across Egypt and the Middle East. But what does an image of a beauty pageant tiara say about a person who covets one? How does a smartphone argue for or against the ways that technology is shaping how we communicate with one another? The "99%" sign from an Occupy movement protest, familiar to many who have followed recent political debate, invites you to think about how policy conversations take place, as well as about how demographic information and self-identification shape the American public. And as for the hybrid car and its plug, what's your best call? A plea for us to be more responsible energy consumers? Imposed limits on the freedom that automobiles have afforded us? What's your take?

# everything's an argument/with readings

THE SUN ALSO RISES
ERNEST HEMINGWAY
Unplug.
DiscoverTheForest.org
Shuttle Program 1981 - 2011
Columbia
Challenger
Discovery
Atlantis
Endeavour

Sixth Edition

# EVERYTHING'S AN argument

## *with readings*


Andrea A. Lunsford
Stanford University

John J. Ruszkiewicz
University of Texas at Austin

Keith Walters
Portland State University



BEDFORD / ST. MARTIN'S
Boston ◆ New York

**For Bedford/St. Martin's**

*Senior Developmental Editor:* Adam Whitehurst
*Senior Production Editor:* Ryan Sullivan
*Senior Production Supervisor:* Dennis J. Conroy
*Executive Marketing Manager:* Molly Parke
*Editorial Assistant:* Nicholas McCarthy
*Copy Editor:* Steven Patterson
*Indexer:* Melanie Belkin
*Photo Researcher:* Julie Tesser
*Permissions Manager:* Kalina K. Ingham
*Art Director:* Lucy Krikorian
*Text Design:* Anna Palchik and Graphic World Inc.
*Cover Design:* Billy Boardman
*Cover Photos:* (top to bottom) © Mohammed Huwais/AFP/Getty Images; © Bernhard Lang/Getty Images; © Karen Bleier/AFP/Getty Images; © Fry Design Ltd/Getty Images; © The Image Bank/Getty Images
*Composition:* Graphic World Inc.
*Printing and Binding:* RR Donnelley and Sons

*President, Bedford/St. Martin's:* Denise B. Wydra
*Presidents, Macmillan Higher Education:* Joan E. Feinberg and Tom Scotty
*Editor in Chief:* Karen S. Henry
*Director of Development:* Erica T. Appel
*Director of Marketing:* Karen R. Soeltz
*Production Director:* Susan W. Brown
*Associate Production Director:* Elise S. Kaiser
*Managing Editor:* Shuli Traub



Manufactured in the United States of America.

1 2 3 4 5 6   15 14 13 12

*For information, write:* Bedford/St. Martin's, 75 Arlington Street, Boston, MA 02116   (617-399-4000)

ISBN 978-1-4576-0604-5 (paperback)
ISBN 978-1-4576-3149-8 (hardcover)

***Acknowledgments***

Acknowledgments and copyrights appear at the back of the book on pages 959–69, which constitute an extension of the copyright page. It is a violation of the law to reproduce these selections by any means whatsoever without the written permission of the copyright holder.

# PREFACE

When the first edition of *Everything's an Argument* appeared more than a decade ago, college writing courses that focused on critical reasoning and persuasion were typically second-semester or optional upper-division offerings. Today, influenced by a growing concern that students in college should know how to analyze and make effective arguments, and, perhaps, by the success of *Everything's an Argument* itself, even introductory college writing classes — and many high school Advanced Placement programs — have now adopted the core tenets of this book, summed up by the purposefully controversial title of this text. First, language provides the most powerful means of understanding the world and of using that understanding to help shape lives. Second, arguments seldom if ever have only two sides; rather, they present a dizzying array of perspectives, often with as many "takes" on a subject as there are arguers. As a result, arguments are always in response to other arguments, part of an ongoing conversation that builds throughout our lives. Understanding arguments, then, calls for carefully considering a full range of perspectives and strategies before coming to judgment and joining the conversation. Finally, and most important, all language and symbols are in some way argumentative, pointing in a direction and asking for yet another response, whether it be understanding, identification, or persuasion.

In each previous edition, we have described *Everything's an Argument* as a labor of love for us, and it remains so. Our affection for the book derives in part from knowing that it helps students to make ethical judgments in a world where that ability grows ever more essential. But we have also enjoyed tracking the evolution of argument in our culture and responding to the needs of writers. *Everything's an Argument* first appeared just as new media and technologies were reshaping the ways persuasive writing could be framed and shared. We tried to help writers work creatively in these new environments. Today, students (and instructors) at all levels find themselves overwhelmed by the sheer number of sources technology makes available for their projects; predictably, they want guidance on identifying, evaluating, integrating, and documenting sources for academic projects. Anticipating that need in our previous edition, we offered a chapter on "Academic Arguments." Now, a wholly refreshed version of that material anchors an important six-chapter section on "Research and Arguments," providing writers with an innovative and in-depth guide to serious academic writing. Beginning with a clear explanation of what academic writing actually looks like, the new section illustrates what successful writers do when they build arguments from source materials. And because students read and write in more digital formats than ever, this edition features integrated e-Pages selections available online. These multimodal selections extend the breadth of the examples in *Everything's an Argument with Readings* to include videos, speeches, audio slideshows, an interactive infographic, and more.

In another significant improvement, we have restructured the chapters in Part 2, "Writing Arguments," to offer more clearly sequenced advice for preparing specific types of arguments. Exercises appear throughout these chapters precisely where they are needed (instead of all at the end) to reinforce the concepts under discussion. The chapters also now include a section of specific writing "projects," most of them new to this edition.

Throughout the text, and especially in the chapter "Structuring Arguments," we have given added attention not only to Rogerian rhetoric but to Invitational rhetoric as well, understanding that the need for arguments based on the kind of careful listening and mutual respect that can bring people together has never been greater than it is today. In addition, we've added a discussion of *kairos*, seizing the timely and opportune moment in any argument, in Chapter 1.

So as our audience has grown and culture has made new demands on writers' expectations, our approach has evolved. But we haven't altered our basic approach and attitude. A best-seller in its field since its debut, *Everything's an Argument with Readings* apparently strikes a chord with students and instructors who expect a book on argument to be candid, balanced, and attuned to everyday events. They also have come to expect a stylish and visually striking presentation of issues and concepts. To that end, we have reframed our chapters to deliver their materials more methodically and efficiently, yet in language that we hope is just as welcoming and readable as ever. We use more lists and charts to highlight or summarize key points, but also have made an effort to reduce textual interruptions.

As in previous editions, we offer many fresh arguments, provocative visual images, and multimodal selections to illuminate the ways we all use language to assert our presence in the world. We have tried to balance attention to the critical reading of arguments (*analysis*) with attention to the writing of arguments (*production*), demonstrating both activities with lively—and realistic—examples, on the principle that the best way to appreciate an argument may be to see it in action. Texts of every kind beckon for reactions, from a full reprint of a FactCheck .org study to a student's analysis of the "white lie," from a Netflix screenshot to a novel defense of Wikipedia, from a film trailer that evaluates the media's portrayal of women to an international student's take on the way writing centers deal with international students. The new edition features twelve new full-length essays chosen for their topicality and usefulness as models of argument—on topics ranging from the threats posed by nuclear power to whether people who aren't attractive should receive government benefits to a rhetorical analysis of a David Brooks editorial. We have tried to keep the best and most popular materials from previous editions, but also to search for new examples and arguments—including visual and multimodal ones—that we believe capture the spirit of the times. As always, we want students to page through the book to find the next intriguing argument or to discover one of their own.

After all, our purpose in *Everything's an Argument with Readings* is to present argument as something we do almost from the moment we are born (in fact, an infant's first cry is as poignant a claim as we can imagine)—something as invaluable as good instincts and as worthy of careful attention and practice as any discipline. In pursuing this goal, we try to keep specialized terminology to a minimum. But we also see argument, and want students to regard it, as a craft both powerful and professional. So we have designed *Everything's an Argument with Readings* to be itself a case for civil persuasion, with a voice that aims to appeal to readers cordially but that doesn't hesitate to make demands on them when appropriate.

In selecting themes and arguments for the anthology, we've tried to choose topics of interest and concern to the students we teach as well as issues and texts worth arguing about. In choosing new selections, we've sought readings that will challenge students to consider new perspectives on topics they may feel they already understand and, in particular, to contextualize themselves in a world characterized by increasing globalization and divisive political rhetoric. We have retained several of the chapter topics that have worked especially well in earlier editions—stereotypes in popular culture, bilingualism in America, the cultural and environmental importance of food and water, the meaning of diversity on college campuses, and the links between education and the workforce they will enter upon graduation. In revising these chapters, we have sought to find a balance between including texts that students and teachers found provocative, instructive, and useful, and adding new ones that treat contemporary issues while leading us to think about argumentation in our world in novel, timely ways. For example, what can a news story about a baby whose parents refuse to reveal its sex teach us about the importance we place on gender roles? How is eating "ethically" a complex proposition in a world where factors such as income and food availability force us to think about the ideals versus the realities of our dietary choices? Is it fair to use the metaphor of a bake sale where items are priced according to race and gender to protest affirmative action in education? How does such knowledge help us understand both ourselves and the debates that constitute this society at this moment in human history? And in the sixth edition, we've expanded the scope of these readings to include integrated e-Pages selections online that ask students to analyze videos, audio slideshows, an interactive infographic, and multimedia presentations related to each chapter's theme.

In addition to updating these chapters from the fifth edition, we have added a new chapter on a topic of particular interest to college students. Certainly students today are keenly aware of an entrenched economic downturn that, accompanied by high unemployment, has given rise to an American conversation about one of our dearest principles: opportunity. In "How Do We Define 'Inequality' in American Society?" we have assembled a series of readings that challenge students to think about cultural attitudes toward equality, and we feel that students will be surprised to think about how these deeply felt attitudes have touched off such diverse movements as the Tea Party and Occupy Wall Street.

In choosing new selections for the anthology, in addition to looking for new genres (including multimodal genres) that bring home to students the message conveyed by the book's title, we have tried to reflect the added attention to academic argument in the earlier part of the book. We have searched for examples of research writing that use a range of methodologies, including case studies, quantitative research, and ethnography, with the goal of giving students practice for analyzing the sorts of arguments they will be assigned in their various courses. We have often paired these selections with discussions of the research in the press or other media to encourage students to begin thinking about how knowledge is disseminated and how it moves from books or journal articles to everyday conversation. Finally, we have sought arguments, whether written or visual, that will help students see themselves "among others," to use Clifford Geertz's memorable turn of phrase.

Here is a summary of the key features that continue to characterize *Everything's an Argument with Readings* and of the major new features in this edition:

## Key Features

**Two books in one, neatly linked.** Up front is a brief guide to argument; in the back is a thematically organized anthology of readings. The two parts of the book are linked by cross-references in the margins, leading students from the argument chapters to specific examples in the readings and from the readings to appropriate rhetorical instruction. And both sections refer students to e-Pages selections online that further expand the range of examples that *Everything's an Argument with Readings* is known for.

**An imaginative and winning approach,** going beyond traditional pro/con assumptions to show that argument is everywhere—in essays, music lyrics, news articles, scholarly writing, poems, advertisements, cartoons, posters, bumper stickers, billboards, Web sites, blogs, text messages, and other electronic environments.

**Student-friendly explanations in simple, everyday language,** with many brief examples and a minimum of technical terminology.

**Fresh and important chapter themes that encourage students to take up complex positions.** Readings on topics such as "How Does Popular Culture Stereotype *You*?" "What Should 'Diversity on Campus' Mean and Why?" and "How Do We Define 'Inequality' in American Society?" demand that students explore the many sides of an issue, not just pro/con.

**A real-world, full-color design,** with readings presented in the style of the original publication. Different formats for newspaper articles, magazine articles, essays, writing from the Web (including a time-stamped live blog that reads in reverse chronological order), and other media help students recognize and think about the effect that design and visuals have on written and multimodal arguments, and the full-color design helps bring the many images in the text to life.

## New to This Edition

**A new chapter on inequality that asks "How Do We Define 'Inequality' in American Society?"** From the Tea Party to Occupy Wall Street, Americans are engaged in real-life discussions about opportunity, inequality, and the American Dream. This new chapter illustrates the stakes of this broad-ranging cultural argument for students.

**Sixty new readings** that engage students on a broad range of topics relevant to their lives as citizens and scholars:

- A student newspaper, the *Daily Californian*, live blogs an unfolding real-time argument as conservative students at UC Berkeley host a bake sale designed to protest affirmative action.
- Jim Harper unearths the (huge) common ground between the seemingly opposed Tea Party and Occupy Wall Street movements.
- In e-Pages, the film trailer for *Miss Representation* (available online) criticizes the media's portrayal of women and its effects on young girls' self-esteem and makes a powerful call for change.

**A new six-chapter section on "Research and Arguments"** that provides up-to-date advice for finding, evaluating, using, and documenting research materials in academic arguments. Additions to these chapters include:

- A much-expanded section on exploring the Web for material, with advice on how to use advanced techniques to narrow and focus searches.
- Detailed advice on synthesizing research materials and connecting ideas in sources.
- A clear explanation of "patchwriting," and how to avoid it in research arguments.

**Nine new full-length arguments in Part 2**—on topics ranging from playground safety to the magical appeal of the iPad—that provide engaging, topical new readings for students.

**Exercises** sequenced and distributed throughout the genre chapters in Part 2, supported by new, separate writing project assignments.

**Attention to the goals of invitational argument,** with projects that call for the strategies associated with this form of argument.

**A clear explanation of the ancient rhetorical principle of *kairos*** and of how students can use it in their own writing.

e **e-Pages for *Everything's an Argument with Readings*.** Some aspects of argument are best experienced beyond the printed page. For instance, watching a film trailer on media representations of women demonstrates different strategies for appealing to audiences, and interacting with an infographic on food safety encourages new considerations for organizing evidence. To help extend what students read and learn in this book to the kinds of media they are most familiar with and excited by, we have added compelling multimodal selections to *Everything's an Argument with Readings*. For a complete list of e-Pages, see the book's table of contents. Instructors can also use the free tools accompanying the e-Pages to upload a syllabus, readings, and assignments to share with the class.

You and your students can access the e-Pages from a tab on the *Student Site for Everything's an Argument with Readings* at **bedfordstmartins.com/everythingsanargument/epages**. Students receive access automatically with the purchase of a new book. If the activation code printed on the inside front cover of the student edition does not work, it may be expired. Students can purchase access at the *Student Site*. Instructors receive access information in a separate email for all of the resources on the *Student Site*. You can also log in to request access information.

## You Get More Digital Choices for *Everything's an Argument with Readings*

*Everything's an Argument with Readings* doesn't stop with a book. Online, you'll find both free and affordable premium resources to help students get even more out of the book and your course. You'll also find convenient instructor resources, such as downloadable sample syllabi, classroom activities, and even access to a nationwide community of teachers. To learn more about or order any of the products below, contact your Bedford/St. Martin's sales representative, email sales support (sales_support@bfwpub.com), or visit the Web site at **bedfordstmartins.com**.

### *Student Site for Everything's an Argument with Readings* bedfordstmartins.com/everythingsanargument

Send students to free and open resources, choose flexible premium resources to supplement your print text, or upgrade to an expanding collection of innovative digital content.

**Free and open resources for *Everything's an Argument with Readings*** provide students with easy-to-access reference materials, visual tutorials, and support for working with sources.

- Five free videos of real writers from VideoCentral
- Three free tutorials from *ix visual exercises* by Cheryl Ball and Kristin Arola
- *Bedford Bibliographer,* a tool for collecting source information and making a bibliography in the MLA, APA, and *Chicago* styles

**VideoCentral** is a growing collection of videos for the writing class that captures real-world, academic, and student writers talking about how and why they write. VideoCentral can be packaged with *Everything's an Argument with Readings* for free. An activation code is required. To order VideoCentral packaged with the print book, use ISBN 978-1-4576-4310-1.

***Re:Writing Plus*** gathers all of Bedford/St. Martin's premium digital content for composition into one online collection. It includes hundreds of model documents, the first ever peer-review game, and VideoCentral. *Re:Writing Plus* can be purchased separately or packaged with the print book at a significant discount. An activation code is required. To order *Re:Writing Plus* packaged with the print book, use ISBN 978-1-4576-4308-8.

### i•series

Add more value to your text by choosing one of the following tutorial series, free when packaged with *Everything's an Argument with Readings*. This popular series presents multimedia tutorials in a flexible format, because there are things you can't do in a book. To learn more about package options or any of the products below, contact your Bedford/St. Martin's sales representative or visit **bedfordstmartins.com**.

***ix visualizing composition* 2.0** (available online) helps students put into practice key rhetorical and visual concepts. To order *ix visualizing composition* packaged with the print book, use ISBN 978-1-4576-4307-1.

***i•claim 2.0: visualizing argument*** (available online) offers a new way to see argument—with six multimodal tutorials, an illustrated glossary, more than fifty multimedia arguments, and integrated gradebook reporting. To order *i•claim: visualizing argument* packaged with the print book, use ISBN 978-1-4576-4318-7.

***i•cite: visualizing sources*** (available online as part of *Re:Writing Plus*) brings research to life through an animated introduction, four tutorials, and hands-on source practice. To order *i•cite: visualizing sources* packaged with the print book, use ISBN 978-1-4576-4305-7.

### Bedford e-Book to Go for *Everything's an Argument with Readings*

Students can purchase *Everything's an Argument with Readings* in downloadable e-book formats for computers, tablets, and e-readers. For more details, visit **bedfordstmartins.com/ebooks**.

### Instructor Resources

You have a lot to do in your course. Bedford/St. Martin's wants to make it easy for you to find the support you need—and to get it quickly.

***Instructor's Notes for Everything's an Argument with Readings*** is available both in print and a PDF format that can be downloaded from **bedfordstmartins.com/everythingsanargument/catalog**. *Instructor's Notes* includes chapter overviews, teaching tips, and possible responses and discussion points for the Respond prompts. To order the print version of *Instructor's Notes*, use ISBN 978-1-4576-0926-8.

*TeachingCentral* (**bedfordstmartins.com/teachingcentral**) offers the entire list of Bedford/St. Martin's print and online professional resources in one place. You'll find landmark reference works, sourcebooks on pedagogical issues, award-winning collections, and practical advice for the classroom—all free for instructors.

*Bedford Bits* (**bedfordbits.com**) collects creative ideas for teaching a range of composition topics in an easily searchable blog. A community of teachers—leading scholars, authors, and editors—discuss revision, research, grammar and style, technology, peer review, and much more. Take, use, adapt, and pass the ideas around. Then, come back to the site to comment or share your own suggestions.

**Bedford Coursepacks** allow you to easily integrate our most popular content into your own course management systems. For details, visit **bedfordstmartins.com/coursepacks**.

## Acknowledgments

We owe a debt of gratitude to many people for making *Everything's an Argument with Readings* possible. Our first thanks must go to the thousands of students we have taught in our writing courses over nearly four decades, particularly first-year students at the Ohio State University, Stanford University, and the University of Texas at Austin. Almost every chapter in this book has been informed by a classroom encounter with a student whose shrewd observation or perceptive question sent an ambitious lesson plan spiraling to the ground. (Anyone who has tried to teach claims and warrants on the fly to skeptical first-year students will surely appreciate why we have qualified our claims in the Toulmin chapter so carefully.) But students have also provided the motive for writing this book. More than ever, they need to know how to read and write arguments effectively if they are to secure a place in a world growing ever smaller and more rhetorically challenging.

We are grateful to our editors at Bedford/St. Martin's who contributed their talents to our book, beginning with Joan Feinberg, who has enthusiastically supported the project and provided us with the resources and feedback needed to keep us on track, and continuing with Denise Wydra, who has maintained this invaluable support. With this edition we welcome a new editor, Adam Whitehurst, to *Everything's an Argument with*

*Readings*. He brought new energy to the project and exactly the fresh perspective we needed to decide upon and then execute the improvements, big and small, you will find throughout the sixth edition. We especially appreciate his help in identifying new readings and images and pointing out problems in those we might have relied on for too long.

We are similarly grateful to others at Bedford/St. Martin's who contributed their talents to our book: Shuli Traub, managing editor; Ryan Sullivan, senior project editor; Dennis Conroy, senior production supervisor; Lucy Krikorian, art director; Molly Parke, executive marketing manager; Julie Tesser, art researcher; Margaret Gorenstein, permissions editor; Steven Patterson, copyeditor; and Nicholas McCarthy, editorial assistant.

We'd also like to thank the astute instructors who reviewed the fifth edition: James Allen, College of DuPage; Jordon Crowe, Iowa State University; Linsey Cuti, Kankakee Community College; Sarah Duerden, Arizona State University; Felicia Durden, South Mountain Community College; Nicole Eschen, California State University, Northridge; Robert Ford, Houston Community College, Central; Monika Giacoppe, Ramapo College of New Jersey; Monica Goodell, University of Nebraska–Kearney; Patricia Gott, University of Wisconsin–Stevens Point; Valerie Gray, Harrisburg Area Community College; Dale Hachten, University of Louisville; Helena Hall, Loras College; Rebecca Hewett, California State University, Bakersfield; Rachel Holtz, Purdue University–Calumet; Rachida Jackson, Shaw University; Grace Kessler, California State University, San Marcos; Sean Martin, Duquesne University; Rexann McKinley, Kankakee Community College; Curry Mitchell, California State University, San Marcos; Sharon Mitchell, Wilkes Community College; Gary Montano, Tarrant County College; Lisa Muir, Wilkes Community College; Allison Parker, South Mountain Community College; Jennifer Pecora, Kankakee Community College; Victor Perry, Iowa State University; Mandy Reid, Indiana State University; Iliana Rocha, Arizona State University; Marsha Rutter, Southwestern College; Andrew Scott, Ball State University; and Danielle Sullivan, San Juan College.

Thanks, too, to John Kinkade, who once again has prepared the instructor's notes for this sixth edition, and to Michal Brody for her invaluable help finding (and in some cases transcribing) new reading selections. Finally, we are grateful to the students whose fine argumentative essays appear in our chapters: Rachel Kolb, Claire Liu, Taylor Pearson, Jennifer Pier, Sayoh Mansaray, Jack Chung, Lia Hardin, Sean Kamperman, Manasi

Deshpande, Max Cougar Oswald, and Brian Riady. We hope that *Everything's an Argument with Readings* responds to what students and instructors have said they want and need. And we hope readers of this text will let us know how we've done: please share your opinions and suggestions with us at bedfordstmartins.com/everythingsanargument.

Andrea A. Lunsford
John J. Ruszkiewicz
Keith Walters

# CONTENTS

For readings that go beyond the printed page, see **bedfordstmartins.com/everythingsanargument/epages**.

40/40
40/40
40/40
40/40

keep away from us!
TEXAS

Thanks for leaving your car here last night and not ending my family's lives.
Tara Inskip

IN CONGRESS. July 4, 1776.
The unanimous Declaration of the thirteen united States of America.

LEARNING OUT OF POVERTY

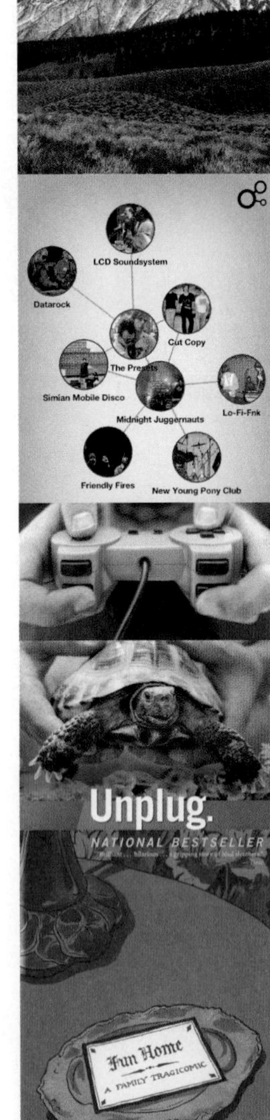
LCD Soundsystem
Datarock
Cut Copy
The Presets
Simian Mobile Disco
Midnight Juggernauts
Lo-Fi-Fnk
Friendly Fires
New Young Pony Club
Unplug.
NATIONAL BESTSELLER
Fun Home
A FAMILY TRAGICOMIC

bedfordstmartins.com/everythingsanargument/epages

## Part 3: Style and Presentation in Arguments 307

 **bedfordstmartins.com/everythingsanargument/epages**

## Part 4: Research and Arguments 365

bedfordstmartins.com/everythingsanargument/epages

**bedfordstmartins.com/everythingsanargument/epages**

## Part 5: Arguments 477

e bedfordstmartins.com/everythingsanargument/epages

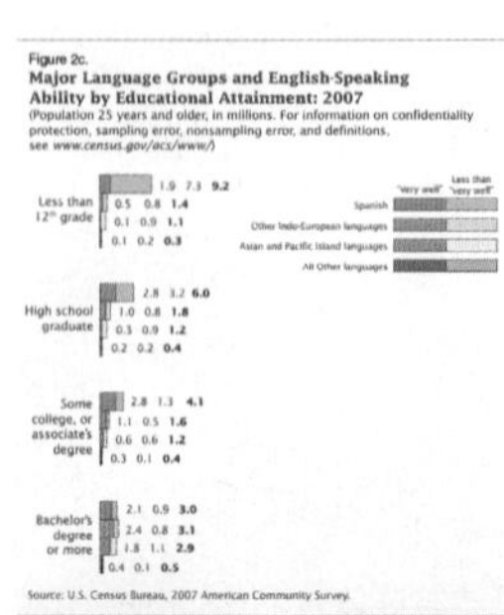

## 23. What's It Like to Be Bilingual in the United States? 568

20 MCNUGGETS $ 4 99
DRIVE THRU OPEN
24 HOURS

## 25. What Should "Diversity on Campus" Mean and Why? 732



e bedfordstmartins.com/everythingsanargument/epages

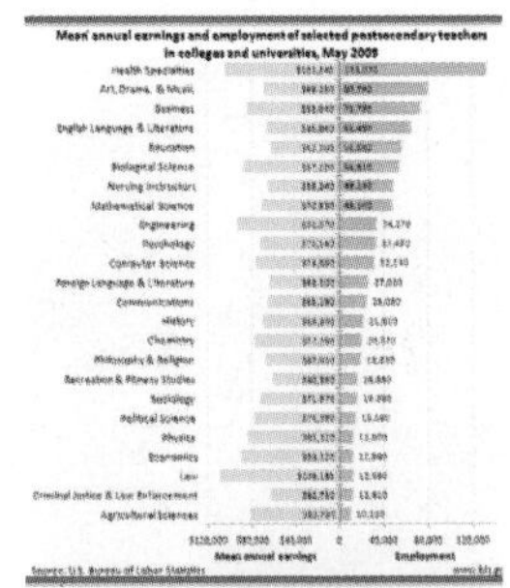

CHECK IT!
self checkout
10
9

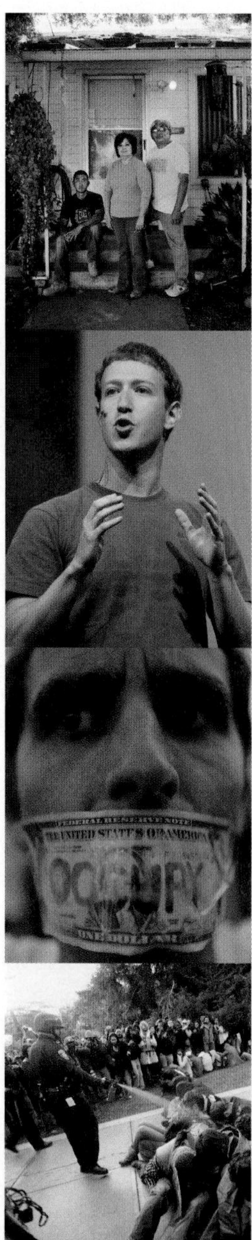




e bedfordstmartins.com/everythingsanargument/epages

# PART 1

# READING AND UNDERSTANDING arguments

# 1 Everything Is an Argument

My wife, Maha, and I have just come from a 45-minute drive, she was the driver through Riyadh streets. #saudi #women2drive #WomenRights

On Friday, June 17, 2011, women in Saudi Arabia took to their cars, defying the law forbidding women to drive and making a defiant argument with their own bodies. Some women were arrested; others eventually relinquished the wheel to husbands or male relatives, but the statement had been made, stirring up a barrage of news coverage and images like the ones above, each of which makes an argument that women should have the freedom to drive.

The "women driving day" in Saudi Arabia was related, in part, to what has been called the "Arab Spring" of 2011. The uprisings began much earlier in the year, after a street vendor in Tunisia, Mohamed Bouazizi, set himself on fire in protest of a government that would not allow him to eke out even the most modest living. Bouazizi's horrifying death inspired others to bring down President Zine el-Abidine Ben Ali.

In late January 2011, huge crowds gathered in Cairo's Tahrir Square, making arguments that eventually forced the ouster of President Hosni Mubarak. Throughout several weeks, protesters tweeted and texted

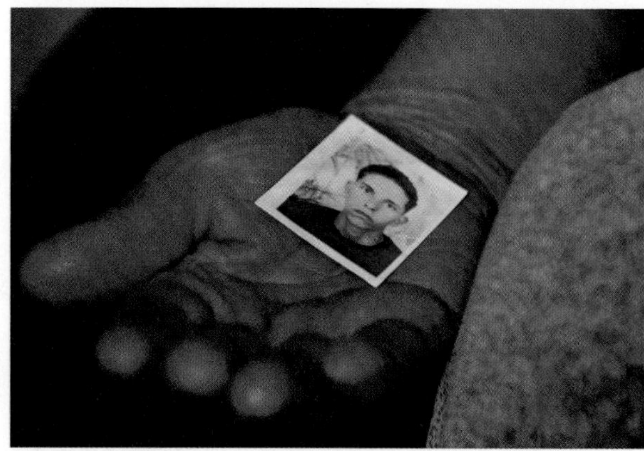

Mohamed Bouazizi

messages and images to tell the world what was happening, like these two sent on January 25 and January 27:

> TravellerWMo-ha-med
> Police throws rocks @ demonstrtrs while we raised our arms.
> We're unarmed, they're in full gear. We are strong, they're weak.
> #25jan#Egypt
> 25 January 2011 16:27:33

> PackafyPakinanAhmed
> after 2 days of protesting, tear gas Is like fresh air, rubber bullets are like raindrops, sticks r like thai massage....
> 27 January 2011 02:03:02

Tweets, blog postings, and images all offered arguments for freedom from repressive regimes, arguments that found voice in music as well. The events in Cairo, for example, inspired the rap "#Jan25," by Omar Offendum, Freeway the Narcicyst, Amir Sulaiman, and Ayah, which went viral on YouTube:

> I heard them say the revolution won't be televised
> Al Jazeera proved them wrong
> Twitter has them paralyzed
> 80 million strong
> And ain't no longer gonna be terrorized
> Organized, mobilized, vocalized . . .

These examples demonstrate one fact of contemporary life in the digital age: anyone, anywhere, with access to a smart phone, can mount an argument that can circle the globe in seconds. The revolutionary arguments advanced in the Middle East were enabled in essential ways by social networking and digital tools increasingly available to all.

We've chosen particularly dramatic examples of arguments (on Twitter, on blogs, on YouTube, on the Web) to open this chapter as a way of introducing our claim that arguments are all around us, in every medium, in every genre, in everything we do. There may be an argument on the T-shirt you put on in the morning, in the sports column you read on the bus, in the prayers you utter before an exam, in the off-the-cuff political remarks of a teacher lecturing, in the assurances of a health center nurse that, "This won't hurt one bit."

The clothes you wear, the foods you eat, and the groups you join make nuanced, sometimes unspoken arguments about who you are and what you value. So an argument can be any text—written, spoken, aural, or visual—that expresses a point of view. In fact, some theorists claim that language is inherently persuasive. When you say, "Hi, how's it going?" in one sense you're arguing that your hello deserves a response. Even humor makes an argument when it causes readers to recognize—through bursts of laughter or just a faint smile—how things are and how they might be different.

More obvious as arguments are those that make a direct claim based on or drawn from evidence. Such writing often moves readers to recognize problems and to consider solutions. Persuasion of this kind is usually easy to recognize:

> **[W]omen unhappy in their marriages often enter full-time employment as an escape. But although a woman's entrance into the workplace does tend to increase the stability of her marriage, it does not increase her happiness.**
>
> **—The Popular Research Institute, Penn State University**

> **We will become a society of a million pictures without much memory, a society that looks forward every second to an immediate replication of what it has just done, but one that does not sustain the difficult labor of transmitting culture from one generation to the next.**
>
> **—Christine Rosen, "The Image Culture"**

**RESPOND•**

Can an argument really be any text that expresses a point of view? What kinds of arguments—if any—might be made by the following items?

a Boston Red Sox cap

a Livestrong bracelet

the "explicit lyrics" label on a best-selling rock CD

the health warning on a package of cigarettes

a belated birthday card

a Rolex watch

## Why We Make Arguments

In the politically divided and entertainment-driven culture of the United States today, the word "argument" may well call up primarily negative images: the angry face or shaking fist of a politician or news "opinionator" who wants to drown out other voices and win at all costs. This is a view of argument we want to explore and challenge in this book. In fact, there are many other ways to argue, including the **invitational arguments** described by researchers Sonja Foss, Cindy Griffin, and Josina Makau. Such arguments are interested in inviting others to join in mutual exploration based on respect. In addition to invitational argument, another kind of argument, called **Rogerian argument** (after psychotherapist Carl Rogers), approaches audiences in nonthreatening ways, finding common ground and establishing trust among those who disagree about issues. Writers who take a Rogerian approach try to see where the other person is coming from, looking for "both/and" or "win/win" solutions whenever possible. (For more on Rogerian strategies, see Chapter 7.)

We have many reasons to argue, then, and not all of them are about winning. In addition to convincing and persuading others, we use arguments to inform, to explore, to make decisions, and even to meditate or pray.

**RESPOND•**

What are your reasons for making arguments? Keep notes for two days about every single argument you make, using our broad definition to guide you. Then identify your reasons: How many times did you aim to persuade? To convince? To inform or explain? To explore? To decide? To meditate?

The risks of Rogerian argument

*"You say it's a win-win, but what if you're wrong-wrong and it all goes bad-bad?"*



Some arguments, of course, *are* aimed at winning, especially those related to politics, business, and law. Two candidates for office, for example, vie for a majority of votes; the makers of one soft drink try to outsell their competitors by appealing to public tastes; and two lawyers try to outwit each other in pleading to a judge and jury. In your college writing, you may also be called on to make an argument that appeals to a "judge" and "jury" (your instructor and classmates). You might, for instance, argue that peer-to-peer music and film file sharing is legal because of the established legal precedent of fair use. In doing so, you may need to defeat your unseen opponents—those who regard such file sharing as theft.

When you argue to win, you are often trying to convince or persuade someone. So what's the difference between these two reasons for arguing? Arguments to convince lead audiences toward conviction, toward agreeing that a claim is true or reasonable or that an action is desirable. Arguments to persuade aim to move others from conviction to *action*. These and other purposes or goals of argument are worth considering in a little more detail, remembering that academic arguments often combine purposes.

## Arguments to Convince

In the excerpt from his book *Disability and the Media: Prescriptions for Change,* Charles A. Riley II intends to convince other journalists to adopt a less stereotypical language for discussing disability.

LINK TO P. 535

Many reports, white papers, and academic articles typically aim to convince rather than persuade their audiences. In a report on the safety record of nuclear plants for a college course, you would likely present evidence to convince general audiences (including an instructor and fellow students) that the issue merited their attention and concern. Even then, the presence of those who might disagree always needs to be considered. In the following passage, controversial political scientist Charles Murray uses intelligence quotient (IQ) correlations to raise questions about higher education that many readers of the *Wall Street Journal*, where his article appeared, may find troubling:

> **There is no magic point at which a genuine college-level education becomes an option, but anything below an IQ of 110 is problematic. If you want to do well, you should have an IQ of 115 or higher. Put another way, it makes sense for only about 15% of the population, 25% if one stretches it, to get a college education.**
>
> **—Charles Murray, "What's Wrong with Vocational School?"**

Murray uses numbers to draw a seemingly objective conclusion about who should attend college, hoping to convince some readers to consider his point. But he's also arguing against those—perhaps a majority of his audience—who prefer to believe that higher education should be encouraged for all.

MOORE MADNESS

Often an image offers an argument intended to convince. On page 8, a cartoonist offers a criticism of well-known activist filmmaker Michael Moore to convince readers that Moore embodies the very qualities he condemns in others.

### Arguments to Persuade

In many situations, writers want not only to convince audiences but to move them to action, whether that involves buying a product, voting for a candidate, or supporting a policy. Advertisements, political blogs, YouTube videos, and newspaper editorials use all the devices of rhetoric to motivate action or produce change. Here Daniel Ben-Ami drives home his argument at the end of an essay on the London-based Web site *Spiked* examining "Why people hate fat Americans":

> By focusing on fat Americans the critics of consumption are saying, implicitly at least, that people should consume less. They are arguing for a world in which Americans become more like those who live in the poorer countries of the world. . . . Yet implementing such a viewpoint is a super-size mistake. Our aspiration for the world should be to give the poor the advantages of affluence enjoyed by those in the

Student protests such as this one could be considered arguments to persuade.

> **West. Living standards in countries such as Ethiopia and Niger should be, at the very least, as high as those in America today. In that sense we should all aim to be fat Americans.**

In this passage, Ben-Ami dramatizes his point by balance and repetition in the structure of his sentences, by reminders in the final paragraph of poverty in Ethiopia and Niger, and by a final ironic call for others to grow as fat as Americans. With these rhetorical moves, he pushes from analysis toward action, which is typical of most persuasive writing.

In your college writing, you can use these same techniques to get your points across and to urge action. You may also use images to help you persuade, perhaps in a college essay arguing that politicians should address the rising costs of attending college.

## Arguments to Inform

The Wikipedia entry titled "Local Food" provides an example of an argument to inform.

LINK TO P. 666

Often, writers argue to inform others, to give information, much like a bumper sticker that simply provides an organization's name and Web address:

***R & L's House of Ribs:***
***www.R&L.com***

A visual argument to inform in Key West, Florida

In fact, a first step in selling anything is to tell customers it exists. The classic poster announcing the first *Batman* film in 1989 carried the iconic image and only two words: "June 23." Many student writers use Twitter to make arguments that inform: a student we know sends weekly Tweets that tell her followers what new Korean film she has seen most recently so that they can check it out for themselves.

## Arguments to Explore

Many important issues today call for arguments to explore them. If there's an "opponent" in such a situation at all (often there is not), it's likely the status quo or a current trend that, for one reason or another, is puzzling. In trying to sort through the extraordinary complexities of the 2011 budget debate, philosophy professor Gary Gutting shows how two distinguished economists—John Taylor and Paul Krugman—draw completely different conclusions from the exact same sets of facts. Exploring how such a thing could occur led Gutting to the conclusion that the two economists were arguing from the same sets of facts, all right, but that they did not have *all* the facts possible; those missing or unknown facts allowed them to fill in the blanks as they could, thus leading them to different conclusions.

Amy Martinez Starke's obituary for Sao Yee Cha explores the Hmong woman's experience as an immigrant in the United States.

LINK TO P. 653

Exploratory arguments can also be personal, such as Zora Neale Hurston's ironic exploration of racism and of her own identity in "How It Feels to Be Colored Me." If you keep a journal or blog, you have no doubt found yourself making arguments to explore issues near and dear to you. Perhaps the essential argument in any such piece is the writer's assertion that a problem exists—and that the writer or reader needs to understand it and respond constructively to it if possible.

## Arguments to Make Decisions

Closely allied to exploratory arguments are arguments that aim to make good, sound decisions, whether about cutting budgets or choosing a career. For college students, choosing a major is a momentous decision, and one way to go about making that decision is to argue your way through several alternatives. By the time you've explored the pros and cons of each alternative, you should be a little closer to a good decision.

Arguments to make decisions occur all the time in the public arena as well. In the summer of 2011, the British tabloid *News of the World* was found to have hacked into the voice messages of a young murder victim as well as relatives of military personnel killed in Afghanistan and Iraq.

Sometimes decisions are not so easy to make.

Dana Summers-Tribune Media Services

These revelations forced Rupert Murdoch, owner of the tabloid (as well as of the much larger News Corporation), and his top advisers to argue their way to a decision, which was to close down *News of the World*. In commenting on Murdoch's decision, the *New York Times* reported that:

Former British Deputy Prime Minister Lord Prescot signs on in support of an inquiry into the *News of the World* phone hacking scandal.

> The move to close *The News of the World* was seen by media analysts as a potentially shrewd decision: jettisoning a troubled newspaper in order to preserve the more lucrative broadcasting deal and possibly expand the company's other British tabloid, *The Sun*, to publish seven days a week.

Murdoch's decision (which ultimately fell through) was hotly debated on all sides throughout Britain, a debate that led others to decide to call for a full public inquiry into phone hacking by the British media, and even by the government.

### Arguments to Meditate or Pray

Sometimes arguments can take the form of prayer or intense meditations on a theme. In such cases, the writer or speaker is most often hoping to transform something in himself/herself or to reach peace of mind. If you know a familiar prayer or mantra, think for a moment of what it "argues" for and how it uses quiet meditation to accomplish that goal. Such meditations don't have to be formal prayers, however. Look, for example, at an excerpt from Michael Lassell's poem "How to Watch Your Brother Die." This poem, which evokes the confusing emotions of a man during the death of his gay brother, uses meditative language that allows readers to understand the speaker and to meditate on life and death themselves:

> Feel how it feels to hold a man in your arms whose arms are used to holding men.
> Offer God anything to bring your brother back.
> Know you have nothing God could possibly want.
> Curse God, but do not abandon Him.
>
> —Michael Lassell, "How to Watch Your Brother Die"

Another sort of meditative argument can be found in the stained-glass windows of churches and other public buildings. Dazzled by a spectacle of light, people pause to consider a window's message longer than they might if the same idea were conveyed on paper.

The Tree of Jesse window in France's Chartres Cathedral

## Occasions for Argument

In an ancient textbook of **rhetoric** (the art of persuasion), the philosopher Aristotle provides an elegant scheme for classifying occasions for argument based on time—past, future, and present. But remember that all classifications overlap to a certain extent, so don't be surprised when arguments about the past have implications for the future or when those about the future bear on the present day.

### Arguments about the Past

Debates about what has happened in the past, or **forensic arguments**, are common in business, government, and academia. The contentious nature of some forensic arguments is evident in this excerpt from a letter to the editor of the *Atlantic Monthly*:

**Occasions for Argument**

| | *Past* | *Future* | *Present* |
|---|---|---|---|
| **What is it called?** | Forensic | Deliberative | Epideictic |
| **What are its concerns?** | What happened in the past? | What should be done in the future? | Who or what deserves praise or blame? |
| **What does it look like?** | Court decisions, legal briefs, legislative hearings, investigative reports, academic studies | White papers, proposals, bills, regulations, mandates | Eulogies, graduation speeches, inaugural addresses, roasts |

> **Robert Bryce's article on the U.S. military's gas consumption in Iraq ("Gas Pains," May *Atlantic*) is factually inaccurate, tactically misguided, and a classic case of a red herring.**
>
> **—Captain David J. Morris**

In replying to this letter, the author of the article, Robert Bryce, disputes Morris's statements, introducing more evidence in support of his original claim.

Forensic arguments rely on evidence and testimony to re-create what can be known about events that have already occurred as well as on precedents (past actions or decisions that influence present policies or decisions) and on analyses of causes and effects. When a housekeeper for a New York hotel accused French politician Dominique Strauss-Kahn of sexual assault, the case depended on exactly what had happened in the past: the prosecution's job was to show beyond a reasonable doubt that sexual assault had occurred while the defense was to offer a different version of the past events. Evidence (including DNA evidence) and testimony will be key constituents in these arguments about the past.

Or consider the ongoing arguments over Christopher Columbus's "discovery" of America: Are his expeditions cause for celebration or unhappy chapters in human history? Or some of both? As these examples suggest, arguments about history are often forensic.

## Arguments about the Future

Debates about what will or should happen in the future—**deliberative arguments**—often establish policies for the future: *Should two people of the same sex be allowed to marry?* and *Should the U.S. Treasury Department bail out failing banks and businesses in times of economic chaos?* are examples of questions that deliberative bodies such as legislatures, congresses, or parliaments answer by making laws or establishing policies.

But arguments about the future can also be speculative, advancing by means of projections and reasoned guesses, as shown in this passage from an essay by *Wired* editor Kevin Kelly, who has argued for several years that "we are headed toward screen ubiquity":

> **As portable screens become more powerful, lighter, and larger, they will be used to view more. . . . Hold an electronic tablet up as you walk along a street, and it will show an annotated overlay of the real street**

> ahead—where the clean restrooms are, which stores sell your favorite items, where your friends are hanging out. Computer chips are so small, and screens so thin and cheap, that in the next 40 years semi-transparent eyeglasses will apply an informational layer to reality. . . . In this way screens will enable us to "read" everything, not just text. Last year alone, five quintillion transistors were embedded into objects other than computers. Very soon most manufactured items, from shoes to cans of soup, will contain a small sliver of dim intelligence, and screens will be the tool we use to interact with this transistorized information.
>
> —Kevin Kelly, "Reading in a Whole New Way"

### Arguments about the Present

Arguments about the present—**epideictic** or **ceremonial arguments**—are usually about contemporary values, that is, widely held beliefs and assumptions that are debated within a society. Often heard at public occasions, they include inaugural addresses, sermons, eulogies, graduation speeches, and civic remarks of all kinds. President Ronald Reagan was a master of ceremonial discourse, and he was particularly adept at defining the core values of the American way of life:

> Ours was the first revolution in the history of mankind that truly reversed the course of government, and with three little words: "We the people." "We the people" tell the government what to do, it doesn't tell us. "We the people" are the driver, the government is the car. And we decide where it should go, and by what route, and how fast.
>
> —Ronald Reagan, "Farewell Address"

More typical than Reagan's impassioned address are values arguments that explore contemporary culture, praising what's admirable and blaming what's not. In the following argument, student Latisha Chisholm looks at rap after Tupac Shakur:

> With the death of Tupac, not only did one of the most intriguing rap rivalries of all time die, but the motivation for rapping seems to have changed. Where money had always been a plus, now it is obviously more important than wanting to express the hardships of Black communities. With current rappers, the positive power that came from the desire to represent Black people is lost. One of the biggest rappers now got his big break while talking about sneakers. Others announce retirement without really having done much for the soul or for Black people's morale. I equate new rappers to NFL players that don't love

Are rappers since Tupac—like Jay-Z—only in it for the money? Many epideictic arguments either praise or blame contemporary culture.

> **the game anymore. They're only in it for the money. . . . It looks like the voice of a people has lost its heart.**
>
> **—Latisha Chisholm, "Has Rap Lost Its Soul?"**

As in many ceremonial arguments, Chisholm here reinforces common values such as representing one's community honorably and fairly.

**RESPOND•**

In a recent magazine, newspaper, or blog, find three editorials—one that makes a forensic argument, one a deliberative argument, and one a ceremonial argument. Analyze the arguments by asking these questions: Who is arguing? What purposes are the writers trying to achieve? To whom are they directing their arguments? Then decide whether the arguments' purposes have been achieved and how you know.

## Kinds of Argument

Yet another way of categorizing arguments is to consider their status or stasis—that is, the *kinds of issues they address*. This system, called **stasis theory**, was used in ancient Greek and Roman civilizations to define questions designed to help examine legal cases. The questions were posed in sequence because each depended on the question(s) preceding it. Together, the questions helped determine the point of contention in an argument. A modern version of those questions might look like the following:

- Did something happen?
- What is its nature?
- What is its quality or cause?
- What actions should be taken?

Each stasis question explores a different aspect of a problem and uses different evidence or techniques to reach conclusions. You can use these questions to explore the aspects of any topic you're considering. We use the stasis issues to define key types of argument in Part 2.

### Did Something Happen? Arguments of Fact

An **argument of fact** usually involves a statement that can be proved or disproved with specific evidence or testimony. For example, the question of pollution of the oceans—is it really occurring?—might seem relatively easy to settle. Either scientific data prove that the oceans are being polluted as a result of human activity, or they don't. But to settle the matter, writers and readers need to ask a number of other questions about the "facts."

- Where did the facts come from?
- Are they reliable?
- Is there a problem with the facts?
- Where did the problem begin and what caused it? (For more on arguments based on facts, see Chapter 4.)

### What Is the Nature of the Thing? Arguments of Definition

One of the most hotly debated issues in American life today involves a question of definition: is a human fetus a human being? If one argues that it is, then a second issue of definition arises: is abortion murder? As

Mark Cadena and Stuart Hata in San Francisco's City Hall after their wedding on November 3, 2008, the day before a California ballot referendum ended several months of legalized marriage ceremonies between same-sex couples in the state. The debate over this issue involves arguments of fact (Does a "civil union" or "domestic partnership" provide the same benefits as a "marriage"?) as well as more basic arguments of definition (Are these forms of legal recognition the same thing? Must "marriage" involve two people of the opposite sex?).

you can see, issues of definition can have mighty consequences, and decades of debate may nonetheless leave the matter unresolved.

Bob Costas used an important definitional distinction to eulogize Mickey Mantle, a great New York Yankee baseball player who had many human faults:

> **In the last year, Mickey Mantle, always so hard upon himself, finally came to accept and appreciate the distinction between a role**

> model and a hero. The first he often was not, the second he always will be.
>
> —Bob Costas, "Eulogy for Mickey Mantle"

But **arguments of definition** can be less weighty than these, though still hotly contested: Is playing video games a sport? Is Batman a tragic figure? Is Mitt Romney a conservative or a moderate? (For more about arguments of definition, see Chapter 9.)

### What Is the Quality or Cause of the Thing? Arguments of Evaluation

**Arguments of evaluation** present criteria and then measure individual people, ideas, or things against those standards. For instance, writer Molly Ivins praises Barbara Jordan by making explicit the qualities and achievements that make someone a "great spirit":

> Barbara Jordan, whose name was so often preceded by the words "the first black woman to . . ." that they seemed like a permanent title, died Wednesday in Austin. A great spirit is gone. The first black woman to serve in the Texas Senate, the first black woman in Congress (she and Yvonne Brathwaite Burke of California were both elected in 1972, but Jordan had no Republican opposition), the first black elected to Congress from the South since Reconstruction, the first black woman to sit on major corporate boards, and so on. Were it not for the disease that slowly crippled her, she probably would have been the first black woman on the Supreme Court—it is known that Jimmy Carter had her on his short list.
>
> —Molly Ivins, "Barbara Jordan: A Great Spirit"

In examining a circumstance or situation, we are often led to wonder what accounts for it: *how did Barbara Jordan achieve what she did, or what happened as a result of her work?* We want to know what shaped the situation she grew up in, what causes led to her development into a "great spirit." (For more about arguments of evaluation, see Chapter 10; for causal arguments, see Chapter 11.)

### What Actions Should Be Taken? Proposal Arguments

**Proposal arguments** present an issue or problem so vividly that readers say *What can we do?* For example, in developing an argument about rising tuition at your college, you might use all the prior stasis questions to

Barbara Jordan addressing fellow members of Congress in 1978

study the issue and establish how much and for what reasons tuition is rising. But the final question—*What actions should be taken?*—will be the most important, since it will lead you to develop proposals for action. In examining a nationwide move to eliminate remedial education in four-year colleges, John Cloud offers a moderate proposal to address the problem:

> **Students age twenty-two and over account for 43 percent of those in remedial classrooms, according to the National Center for Developmental Education. [. . . But] 55 percent of those needing remediation must take just one course. Is it too much to ask them to pay extra for that class or take it at a community college?**
>
> **—John Cloud, "Who's Ready for College?"**

For more about proposal arguments, see Chapter 12.

### STASIS QUESTIONS AT WORK

Suppose you have an opportunity to speak at a student conference on the issue of global warming. You are tentatively in favor of strengthening industrial pollution standards aimed at reducing global warming trends. But to learn more about the issue, you use the stasis questions to get started.

- **Did something happen?** Does global warming exist? *No*, say many in the oil and gas industry; at best, evidence for global warming is inconclusive. *Yes*, say most scientists and governments; global warming is real and has reached serious proportions. To come to your conclusion, you'll weigh the facts carefully and identify problems with opposing arguments.
- **What is the nature of the thing?** Skeptics define global warming as naturally occurring events; most scientists base definitions on human causes. You look at each definition carefully: *How do the definitions foster the goals of each group? What's at stake for each group in defining it that way?*
- **What is the quality or cause of the thing?** Exploring the differing assessments of damage done by climate change leads you to ask who will gain from such analysis: *Do oil executives want to protect their investments? Do scientists want government money for grants? Where does evidence for the dangers of global warming come from? Who benefits if the dangers are accepted as real and present, and who loses?*
- **What actions should be taken?** If global warming is occurring naturally or causing little harm, then arguably *nothing* needs or can be done. But if it is caused mainly by human activity and dangers, action is definitely called for (although not everyone may agree on what such action should be). As you investigate the proposals being made and the reasons behind them, you come closer to developing your own argument.

## Audiences for Arguments

Exploring stasis questions will help you to think about the audience(s) you are addressing, from the flesh-and-blood person sitting across a desk when you negotiate a student loan, to your "friends" on social media, to the "ideal" person you imagine for what you are writing.

Readers and writers in context

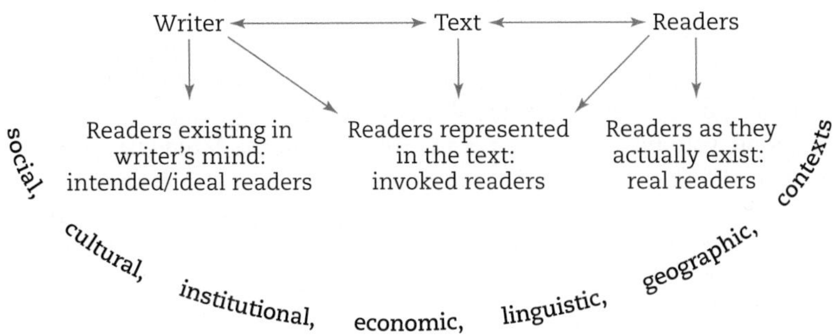


The figure at the top of this page shows just how many dimensions an audience can have as writers and readers negotiate their relationship to a verbal or visual text.

As authors of this book, we are thinking about students like you: you are our intended readers. Though we don't know you personally, we see you in our minds, for we *intend* to write for you. In the same way, the editors of *Rego: The Latino College Magazine* had a clear sense of whom they wanted to reach with their publication. They even offered a graphic to define their audience precisely, identifying it as "the Latino collegiate, postcollegiate, and college-bound demographic."

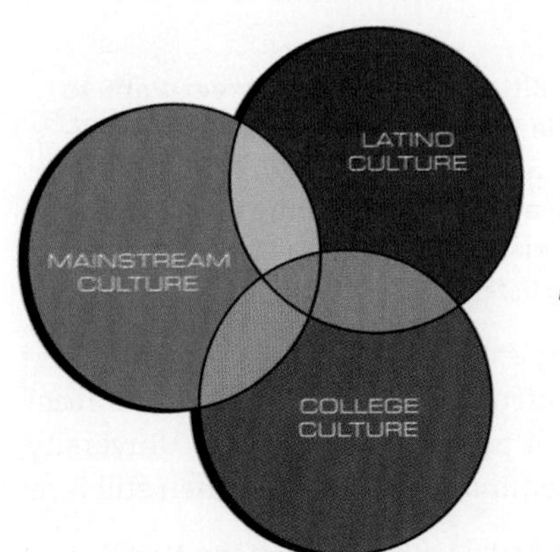


*Rego* defines its audience.

So texts, whether oral, written, or *digital*, have **intended audiences**, those the writer wants to address. But they also have **invoked readers**, those represented in the text itself. (The covers of *Rego*, for example, invoked an audience through representations in the text—of hip Latinos and Latinas.)

In addition to intended and invoked readers, arguments will also have "real" readers who may not be among those a writer originally imagines. You may post something on the Web, for instance, and find that it is read by people you did not address or invoke at all! In the same way, you may read email not sent to you but rather forwarded (sometimes unwittingly) from someone else. As a writer, you want to think carefully about these real readers and to take care with what you post online.

## Considering Contexts

No consideration of audiences can be complete without understanding that reading always takes place in a series of contexts that move outward, from the most immediate situation (the specific circumstance in which the reading occurs) to broader environments (including local and community or institutional contexts like school or church, as well as cultural and linguistic contexts).

When reporter Louise Story of the *New York Times* wrote a front-page story saying that many women attending prestigious colleges planned to abandon their professional careers when they had children, she provoked very different responses from various audiences, depending on their contexts. Jack Schafer of Slate.com, for example, found the story full of evasive qualifying terms, such as *many* and *seems*, that made its claims meaningless:

> While bogus, "Many Women at Elite Colleges Set Career Path to Motherhood" isn't false: It can't be false because it never says anything sturdy enough to be tested. So, how did it get to Page One? Is there a *New York Times* conspiracy afoot to drive feminists crazy and persuade young women that their place is in the home?
>
> —Jack Schafer, "Weasel-Words Rip My Flesh!"

Faculty members at the schools Story examined put the piece in a different context, that of professional women in general. Quoted in a *BU Today* article, Deborah Belle, a professor of psychology at Boston University, found it sadly emblematic of the dilemma professional women still face:

> I think the thing that resonates so badly with me about the *New York Times* article is that the onus is always on the woman, and that's not where it should be. . . . Of course there are superheroes who can do it all, but that's not the point. The point is that none of us should be forced to be in these positions.
>
> —Deborah Belle, qtd. in "The Do-It-All Dilemma"

And female students themselves—from a different generation than their professors—placed the story in their own contexts. Here's Alana Steinhardt from that same *BU Today* article, bringing personal values to bear on the controversy:

> **Why have kids if you can't see them grow up, and be there for the experience? . . . At BU, I'm preparing myself to be a more well-rounded person. That doesn't necessarily mean I have to work.**

As you compose arguments of your own, you need to think carefully about the contexts that surround your readers—and to place your topic in its context as well.

### CULTURAL CONTEXTS FOR ARGUMENT

#### Considering What's "Normal"

If you want to communicate effectively with people across cultures, then learn about the traditions in those cultures and examine the norms guiding your own behavior:

- Explore your assumptions! Most of us regard our ways of thinking as "normal" or "right." Such assumptions guide our judgments about what works in persuasive situations. But just because it may seem natural to speak bluntly in arguments, consider that others may find such aggression startling or even alarming.
- Remember: ways of arguing differ widely across cultures. Pay attention to how people from groups or cultures other than your own argue, and be sensitive to different paths of thinking you'll encounter as well as to differences in language.
- Don't assume that all people share your cultural values, ethical principles, or political assumptions. People across the world have different ways of defining *family*, *work*, or *happiness*. As you present arguments to them, consider that they may be content with their different ways of organizing their lives and societies.
- Respect the differences among individuals *within* a given group. Don't expect that every member of a community behaves—or argues—in the same way or shares the same beliefs. Avoid thinking, for instance, that there is a single Asian, African, or Hispanic culture or that Europeans are any less diverse or more predictable than Americans or Canadians in their thinking. In other words, be skeptical of stereotypes.

## Appealing to Audiences

Aristotle identified three time-tested ways writers can appeal to audiences, and he labeled them *pathos*, *ethos*, and *logos*—appeals that are as effective today as they were in Aristotle's time, though we usually think of them in slightly different terms.

### Emotional Appeals: Pathos

Emotional appeals, or **pathos**, generate emotions (fear, pity, love, anger, jealousy) that the writer hopes will lead the audience to accept a claim. Here is a plea from Doctors without Borders that uses pathos to urge us to contribute to their cause:

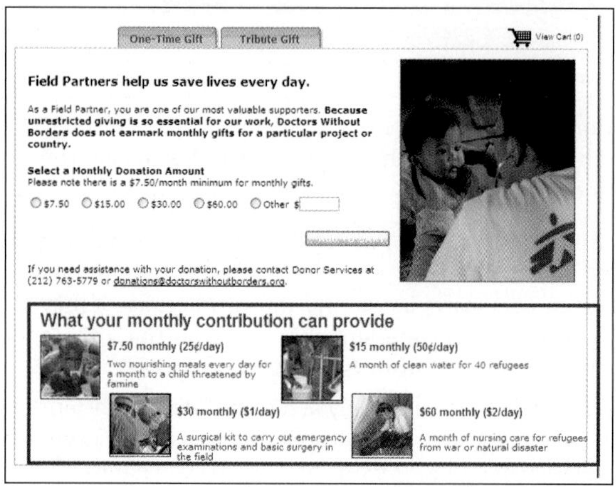


Concrete and descriptive language paints pictures in readers' minds as well, making an emotional appeal that can create a bond between writer and readers. (For more about emotional appeals, see Chapter 2.)

### Ethical Appeals: Ethos

When writers or speakers come across as trustworthy, audiences are likely to listen to and accept their arguments. That trustworthiness (along with fairness and respect) is a mark of **ethos**, or credibility. Showing that you know what you are talking about exerts an ethical appeal, as does emphasizing that you share values with and respect your audience. Visuals can also make strong ethical appeals: think how flags, logos, or even badges convey credibility and authority, as in this Doctors without Borders symbol:

For more about ethical appeals, see Chapter 3.

### Logical Appeals: Logos

Appeals to logic, or **logos**, are often given prominence and authority in U.S. culture: "Just the facts, ma'am," a famous early TV detective on *Dragnet* used to say. Indeed, audiences respond well to the use of reasons and evidence—to the presentation of facts, statistics, credible testimony, cogent examples, or even a narrative or story that embodies a sound reason in support of an argument. (For more about logical appeals, see Chapter 4.)

### *Kairos*: Seizing the Opportune Moment in Arguments

In Greek mythology, Kairos—the youngest son of Zeus—was the god of opportunity. In images, he is most often depicted as running, and his most unusual characteristic is a shock of hair on his forehead. As Kairos dashes by, you have a chance to seize that lock of hair, thereby seizing the opportune moment; once he passes you by, however, you have missed that chance.

Considering your rhetorical situation calls on you to think hard about **kairos**, that is, about the suitable time and place for making an argument and the most opportune ways to make it. Being aware of kairos means being able to understand and take advantage of shifting circumstances and to choose the best (most timely) proofs and evidence for that particular place, situation, and audience.

The effectiveness of many arguments depends on whether or not they are timely. For example, in 2010 Congressional Republicans took advantage of Americans' fears of rising national debt to argue for their agenda to make broad cuts to the federal budget. The timing of their message resonated with the American public, and in the next election they trounced

Democrats, taking control of the House of Representatives (and nearly the Senate as well). By 2011, however, long periods of high unemployment had become Americans' number one concern, and talk of cuts to federal and state budgets lost some of its political clout because such arguments were no longer timely.

In another example, a student was interested in why the tennis match between Billie Jean King and Bobby Riggs (dubbed "The Battle of the Sexes") caused such a sensation: her research led her to identify several key elements that came together in 1973 to create the perfect opportune—or kairotic—moment for a woman to take on a man in tennis, and win.

In your own arguments, thinking about kairos is important early on as you study the context or conversation surrounding your topic and look for opportune moments to get your own point of view into that conversation. It's also important to think about kairos when you analyze your arguments: how can you frame your claims and evidence to resonate with your audience?

**RESPOND.**

What common experiences, if any, do the following objects, brand names, and symbols evoke, and for what audiences in particular? What sorts of appeals do they make: to pathos, ethos, or logos?

a USDA organic label

the golden arches

the Sean John label as seen on its Web site

a can of Coca-Cola

Sleeping Beauty's castle on the Disney logo

Oprah Winfrey

the Vietnam Veterans Memorial

Ground Zero at the World Trade Center site

an AIDS ribbon

## Summing Up Argument: Rhetorical Situations

Thinking about arguments, their contexts, audiences, and appeals brings us to another helpful concept: that of the **rhetorical situation**, a shorthand phrase for the entire set of relationships depicted in the following triangular diagram:

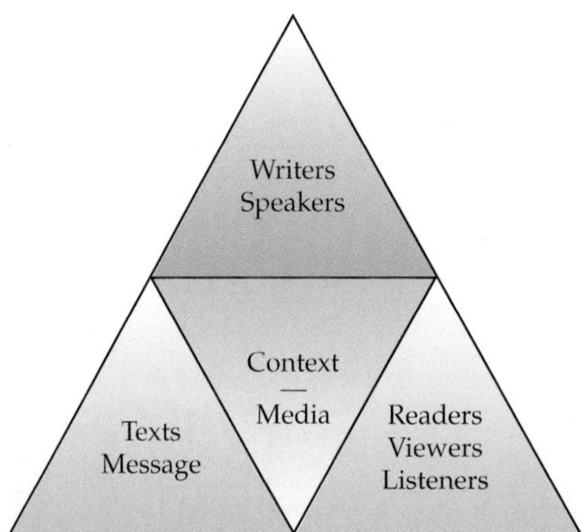


The rhetorical situation

Remember, though, that rhetorical situations are *dynamic*, with all elements affecting one another: for example, a change in audience could affect your handling of the topic and the appeals you use. *Thinking rhetorically* means keeping all these elements in mind, and doing so might even lead you to challenge the title of this text: is everything an argument?

**RESPOND.**

Take a look at the bumper sticker below, and then analyze it. What is its purpose? What kind of argument is it? Which of the stasis questions does it most appropriately respond to? To what audiences does it appeal? What appeals does it make and how?

# 2
# Arguments Based on Emotion: Pathos

Emotional appeals (*appeals to pathos*) are powerful tools for influencing what people think and believe. We all make decisions—even including the most important ones—based on our feelings. That's what the Food and Drug Administration hoped to capitalize on when it introduced nine new warning labels for cigarettes, one of which you see above. One look at the stained, rotting teeth and the lip sore may arouse emotions of fear strong enough to convince people not to smoke.

Editorial cartoonist for *Newsday* Walt Handelsman borrows the emotional strategy of cigarette warning labels to stir up opposition to continuing conflict in Afghanistan. His imaginary "package" (shown above) evokes fear through an iconic image (Death with his sickle) and stirs political anger via an explicit alert: "Prolonged war with no clear objective is harmful to the nation's health!" Yet such labels lead Bob Dorigo Jones, an opponent of lawsuit abuse, in an entirely different direction, publishing a book entitled *Remove Child before Folding: The 101 Stupidest, Silliest, and Wackiest Warning Labels Ever*. His intention is to make us laugh and thereby, perhaps, to question or even doubt the effectiveness of such scary warnings.

The kinds of arguments packed into these three images all appeal to emotion, and modern science has shown us that we often make decisions based on just such appeals. So when you hear that formal or academic arguments should rely solely on facts, remember that facts alone often won't carry the day, even for a worthy cause. The civil rights struggle for gay marriage in the last few years provides a particularly good example of a movement that persuaded people equally by means of the reasonableness and the passion of its claims. Like many debates, the one over gay marriage provoked high emotions on every side, emotions that sometimes led more to divisiveness than progress toward solutions.

Of course, we don't have to look hard for less noble campaigns that are fueled with emotions such as hatred, envy, and greed, campaigns that drive wedges between groups, making them fearful or hateful. For that reason alone, writers should not use emotional appeals casually. (For more about emotional fallacies, see p. 75.)

In "Goodbye, Columbus," Mac McClelland uses emotional appeals to persuade people to pay attention to growing income inequality in the United States.

LINK TO P. 931

## Reading Critically for Pathos

Late on the night of May 1, 2011, the White House blog carried this post: "Tonight, President Obama addressed the Nation to announce that the United States has killed Osama bin Laden, the leader of al Qaeda." Earlier

President Obama addresses the nation. You can see this speech in e-Pages at **bedfordstmartins.com/everythingsanargument/epages.** 

that evening, the president had appeared on TV to deliver that brief address, setting off a barrage of texts, tweets, and YouTube postings as the United States recalled the devastating attacks of September 11, 2001. Ten years later, the president could finally tell the American people that the mastermind of that attack was dead.

The president's address to the nation was very brief—under ten minutes. As he spoke directly to the American people, some fifty-six million people tuned in: the *Huffington Post* announced that some four thousand tweets per second were sent during the nine and a half minutes of the speech. Clearly, the remarks stirred powerful emotions, as in this passage whose concrete and descriptive language brought back vivid memories:

> **The images of 9/11 are seared into our national memory. . . . And yet we know that the worst images are those that were unseen to the world. The empty seat at the dinner table. Children who were forced to grow up without their mother or their father. Parents who would never know the feeling of their child's embrace. Nearly three thousand citizens taken from us, leaving a gaping hole in our hearts.**

Yet as analysts pointed out, the president's speech was also measured. As President George W. Bush had done before him, Obama was careful to say that the United States is not and never has been at war with Islam—but with terrorism. Rather, he simply announced that "a small team of Americans . . . killed Osama bin Laden and took custody of his body." Rather than celebrating or gloating, the president spoke with calm control about American values:

> **So Americans understand the costs of war. Yet as a country, we will never tolerate our security being threatened, nor stand idly by when our people have been killed. We will be relentless in defense of our citizens and our friends and allies. We will be true to the values that make us who we are. And on nights like this one, we can say to those families who have lost loved ones to al Qaeda's terror: Justice has been done.**
>
> **—from whitehouse.gov/blog**

Note that last sentence: "Justice has been done." Using the passive voice puts the emphasis on justice, leaving out who or what had brought that justice. That is just one way in which this passage is understated and calm. Note also the use of words that signal resolve: "we will never tolerate . . . nor stand idly by." We will be "relentless in defense" and "true to the values." Here the president appeals to emotions that he says "make us who we are."

Reactions to the announcement of Osama bin Laden's death

Outside the White House, stronger emotions were on display as crowds celebrated with chants of "USA, USA, USA."

**RESPOND.**

Working with a classmate, make a list of reasons why speakers in highly charged situations like this one (the president speaking on the death of Osama bin Laden) would need to use emotional appeals cautiously, even sparingly. What consequences might heightened emotional appeals lead to? What is at stake for the speaker in such situations, in terms of credibility and ethos?

## Using Emotions to Build Bridges

You may sometimes want to use emotions to connect with readers to assure them that you understand their experiences or, to use President Bill Clinton's famous line, "feel their pain." Such a bridge is especially important when you're writing about matters that readers regard as sensitive. Before they'll trust you, they'll want assurances that you understand the issues in depth. If you strike the right emotional note, you'll

Walter Benn Michaels appeals to his readers' general support for college diversity to build bridges with his audience.

LINK TO P. 809

establish an important connection. That's what Apple founder Steve Jobs does in a 2005 commencement address in which he tells the audience that he doesn't have a fancy speech, just three stories from his life:

> My second story is about love and loss. I was lucky. I found what I loved to do early in life. Woz [Steve Wozniak] and I started Apple in my parents' garage when I was twenty. We worked hard and in ten years, Apple had grown from just the two of us in a garage into a $2 billion company with over four thousand employees. We'd just released our finest creation, the Macintosh, a year earlier, and I'd just turned thirty, and then I got fired. How can you get fired from a company you started? Well, as Apple grew, we hired someone who I thought was very talented to run the company with me, and for the first year or so, things went well. But then our visions of the future began to diverge, and eventually we had a falling out. When we did, our board of directors sided with him, and so at thirty, I was out, and very publicly out. . . .
>
> I didn't see it then, but it turned out that getting fired from Apple was the best thing that could have ever happened to me. The heaviness of being successful was replaced by the lightness of being a beginner again, less sure about everything. It freed me to enter one of the most creative periods in my life. During the next five years I started a company named NeXT, another company named Pixar and fell in love with an amazing woman who would become my wife. Pixar went on to create the world's first computer-animated feature film, *Toy Story*, and is now the most successful animation studio in the world.
>
> —Steve Jobs, "You've Got to Find What You Love, Jobs Says"

In no obvious way is Jobs's recollection a formal argument. But it prepares his audience to accept the advice he'll give later in his speech, at least partly because he's speaking from meaningful personal experiences.

A more obvious way to build an emotional tie is simply to help readers identify with your experiences. If, like Georgina Kleege, you were blind and wanted to argue for more sensible attitudes toward blind people, you might ask readers in the first paragraph of your argument to confront their prejudices. Here Kleege, a writer and college instructor, makes an emotional point by telling a story:

> I tell the class, "I am legally blind." There is a pause, a collective intake of breath. I feel them look away uncertainly and then look back. After all, I just said I couldn't see. Or did I? I had managed to get there on my own—no cane, no dog, none of the usual trappings of blindness. Eyeing me askance now, they might detect that my gaze is not quite

> **focused. . . . They watch me glance down, or towards the door where someone's coming in late. I'm just like anyone else.**
>
> **—Georgina Kleege, "Call It Blindness"**

Given the way she narrates the first day of class, readers are as likely to identify with the students as with Kleege, imagining themselves sitting in a classroom, facing a sightless instructor, confronting their own prejudices about the blind. Kleege wants to put them on edge emotionally.

Let's consider another rhetorical situation: how do you win over an audience when the logical claims that you're making are likely to go against what many in the audience believe? Once again, a slightly risky appeal to emotions on a personal level may work. That's the tack that Michael Pollan takes in bringing readers to consider that "the great moral struggle of our time will be for the rights of animals." In introducing his lengthy exploratory argument, Pollan uses personal experience to appeal to his audience:

> **The first time I opened Peter Singer's *Animal Liberation*, I was dining alone at the Palm, trying to enjoy a rib-eye steak cooked medium-rare. If this sounds like a good recipe for cognitive dissonance (if not**

A visual version of Michael Pollan's rhetorical situation

> **indigestion), that was sort of the idea. Preposterous as it might seem to supporters of animal rights, what I was doing was tantamount to reading *Uncle Tom's Cabin* on a plantation in the Deep South in 1852.**
>
> **—Michael Pollan, "An Animal's Place"**

In creating a vivid image of his first encounter with Singer's book, Pollan's opening builds a bridge between himself as a person trying to enter into the animal rights debate in a fair and open-minded, if still skeptical, way and readers who might be passionate about either side of this argument.

## Using Emotions to Sustain an Argument

You can also use emotional appeals to make logical claims stronger or more memorable. That is the way that photographs and other images add power to arguments. In a TV attack ad, the scowling black-and-white photograph of a political opponent may do as much damage as the claim that he bought his home on the cheap from a financier convicted of fraud. Or the attractive skier in a spot for lip balm may make us yearn for brisk, snowy winter days. The technique is tricky, however. Lay on too much emotion—especially those like outrage, pity, or shame, which make people uncomfortable—and you may offend the very audiences you hoped to convince.

But sometimes a strong emotion such as anger adds energy to a passage, as it does when writer Stuart Taylor and history professor K. C. Johnson react in outrage when Mike Nifong, a prosecutor charged with deliberately lying about evidence in an emotionally charged rape case at Duke University, received only a twenty-four-hour sentence for his misconduct. In an op-ed in the *Washington Post*, the authors review the wider dimensions of the biased prosecution and turn their ire especially on faculty who were too eager to pillory three white student athletes at Duke for an alleged crime against a minority woman that subsequent investigations proved never occurred. As you read the following excerpt, notice how the authors' use of emotional language might lead some readers to share their anger and others to resent it:

> **To be sure, it was natural to assume at first that Nifong had a case. Why else would he confidently declare the players guilty? But many academics and journalists continued to presume guilt months after massive evidence of innocence poured into the public record. Indeed,**

some professors persisted in attacks even after the three defendants were declared innocent in April by North Carolina Attorney General Roy Cooper—an almost unheard-of event.

Brushing aside concern with "the 'truth' . . . about the incident," as one put it, these faculty ideologues just changed their indictments from rape to drunkenness (hardly a rarity in college); exploiting poor black women (the players had expected white and Hispanic strippers); and being born white, male and prosperous.

This shameful conduct was rooted in a broader trend toward subordinating facts and evidence to faith-based ideological posturing. Worse, the ascendant ideology, especially in academia, is an obsession with the fantasy that oppression of minorities and women by "privileged" white men remains rampant in America. Its crude stereotyping of white men, especially athletes, resembles old-fashioned racism and sexism.

—Stuart Taylor and K. C. Johnson, "Guilty in the Duke Case"

In using language this way, writers can generate emotions by presenting arguments in their starkest terms, stripped of qualifications or subtleties. Readers or listeners are confronted with core issues or important choices and asked to consider the consequences.

A sign posted outside the house where the party at the center of the Duke rape case occurred urges prosecutor Mike Nifong to apologize.

It's difficult to gauge how much emotion will work in a given argument. Some issues—such as racism, rape, abortion, and gun control—provoke strong feelings and, as a result, are often argued on emotional terms. But even issues that seem deadly dull—such as funding for Medicare and Social Security—can be argued passionately when proposed changes in these programs are set in human terms: cut benefits and Grandma will have to eat cat food; don't cut benefits and Social Security will surely go broke, leaving nothing for later generations of seniors. Both alternatives might scare people into paying enough attention to take political action.

## Using Humor

Humor has always played an important role in argument, sometimes as the sugar that makes the medicine go down. You can slip humor into an argument to put readers at ease, thereby making them more open to a proposal you have to offer. It's hard to say no when you're laughing. Humor also makes otherwise sober people suspend their judgment and even their prejudices, perhaps because the surprise and naughtiness of wit are combustive: they provoke laughter or smiles, not reflection. That may be why TV shows like *South Park* and *Modern Family* became popular with mainstream audiences, despite their sometimes controversial subjects. Similarly, it's possible to make a point through humor that might not work in more sober writing. Although there were many arguments for and against the repeal of the military's Don't Ask, Don't Tell policy in the fall of 2011, the satirical newspaper *The Onion* printed an article in which it simultaneously celebrated and bemoaned an unconsidered consequence of allowing gay men and women to serve openly, namely gay troops' new vulnerability to being publicly broken up with by their significant others back home:

Michele Bornert jokes throughout her blog in order to connect with her many other deaf readers.

LINK TO P. 638

> Hailed as a monumental step toward equality by gay rights activists, hundreds of Dear John letters reportedly began reaching newly outed troops overseas this week, notifying soldiers for the first time ever that their same-sex partners back home were leaving them and starting a new life with someone else.
>
> According to Pentagon observers, the torrent of brusque, callous letters—which followed Tuesday's repeal of the Don't Ask, Don't Tell policy—has left romantically betrayed homosexuals in every branch of the service grappling with feelings of rejection and despair, a momentous milestone in U.S. military history.

"For too long, gays and lesbians in the armed forces were barred from receiving such letters, leaving them woefully unaware that the person they once called their soul mate had been cheating on them throughout their deployment," said Clarence Navarro of the Human Rights Campaign, an LGBT advocacy group. "But now all troops, regardless of their sexual orientation, are free to have their entire lives ripped out from underneath them in a single short note." "This is a great day for homosexuals," Navarro added. "Even those who now have nothing to return home to."

—*The Onion*, "First-Ever Gay 'Dear John' Letters Begin Reaching U.S. Troops Overseas"

Our laughter testifies to what many people in favor of the repeal had argued all along: that the repeal of Don't Ask, Don't Tell would show that gay troops were just like anyone else in our military, right down to having their hearts broken in a callous manner.

A writer or speaker can use humor to deal with especially sensitive issues. For example, sports commentator Bob Costas, given the honor of eulogizing the great baseball player Mickey Mantle, couldn't ignore problems in Mantle's life. So he argues for Mantle's greatness by admitting the man's weaknesses indirectly through humor:

It brings to mind a story Mickey liked to tell on himself and maybe some of you have heard it. He pictured himself at the pearly gates, met by St. Peter, who shook his head and said, "Mick, we checked the record. We know some of what went on. Sorry, we can't let you in. But before you go, God wants to know if you'd sign these six dozen baseballs."

—Bob Costas, "Eulogy for Mickey Mantle"

Similarly, politicians use humor to admit problems or mistakes they couldn't acknowledge in any other way. Here, for example, is President George W. Bush at the 2004 Radio and TV Correspondents' Dinner discussing his much-mocked intellect:

Those stories about my intellectual capacity do get under my skin. You know, for a while I even thought my staff believed it. There on my schedule first thing every morning it said, "Intelligence briefing."

—George W. Bush

Not all humor is well-intentioned. In fact, among the most powerful forms of emotional argument is ridicule—humor aimed at a particular target. Eighteenth-century poet and critic Samuel Johnson was known for his stinging and humorous put-downs, such as this comment to an aspiring writer: "Your manuscript is both good and original, but the part that is good is not original and the part that is original is not good." Today, even bumper stickers can be vehicles for succinct arguments:

But ridicule is a two-edged sword that requires a deft hand to wield it. Humor that reflects bad taste discredits a writer completely, as does ridicule that misses its mark. Unless your target deserves assault and you can be very funny, it's usually better to steer clear of humor.

## Using Arguments Based on Emotion

You don't want to play puppetmaster with people's emotions when you write arguments, but it's a good idea to spend some time early in your work thinking about how you want readers to feel as they consider your persuasive claims. For example, would readers of your editorial about campus traffic policies be more inclined to agree with you if you made them envy faculty privileges, or would arousing their sense of fairness work better? What emotional appeals might persuade meat eaters to consider a vegan diet—or vice versa? Would sketches of stage props on a Web site persuade people to buy a season ticket to the theater, or would you spark more interest by featuring pictures of costumed performers?

Consider, too, the effect that a story can have on readers. Writers and journalists routinely use what are called *human-interest stories* to give presence to issues or arguments. You can do the same, using a particular incident to evoke sympathy, understanding, outrage, or amusement. Take care, though, to tell an honest story.

**RESPOND.**

1. To what specific emotions do the following slogans, sales pitches, and maxims appeal?

   "Just do it." (ad for Nike)

   "Think different." (ad for Apple computers)

"Reach out and touch someone." (ad for AT&T)

"Yes we can!" (2008 presidential campaign slogan for Barack Obama)

"Country first." (2008 presidential campaign slogan for John McCain)

"By any means necessary." (rallying cry from Malcolm X)

"Have it your way." (slogan for Burger King)

"You can trust your car to the man who wears the star." (slogan for Texaco)

"It's everywhere you want to be." (slogan for Visa)

"Know what comes between me and my Calvins? Nothing!" (tag line for Calvin Klein jeans)

"Don't mess with Texas!" (anti-litter campaign slogan)

"Because you're worth it." (ad for L'Oréal)

2. Bring a magazine to class, and analyze the emotional appeals in as many full-page ads as you can. Then classify those ads by types of emotional appeal, and see whether you can connect the appeals to the subject or target audience of the magazine. Compare your results with those of your classmates, and discuss your findings. For instance, do the ads in news magazines like *Time* and *Newsweek* appeal to different emotions and desires from the ads in publications such as *Cosmopolitan*, *Spin*, *Sports Illustrated*, *Automobile*, and *National Geographic*?

3. How do arguments based on emotion work in different media? Are such arguments more or less effective in books, articles, television (both news and entertainment shows), films, brochures, magazines, email, Web sites, the theater, street protests, and so on? You might explore how a single medium handles emotional appeals or compare different media. For example, why do the comments pages of blogs seem to encourage angry outbursts? Are newspapers an emotionally colder source of information than television news programs? If so, why?

4. Spend some time looking for arguments that use ridicule or humor to make their point: check out your favorite Web sites; watch for bumper stickers, posters, or advertisements; and listen to popular song lyrics. Bring one or two examples to class, and be ready to explain how the humor makes an emotional appeal and whether it's effective.

# 3 Arguments Based on Character: Ethos

Whenever you read anything—whether it's a news article, an advertisement, a speech, or a text message—you no doubt subconsciously analyze the message for a sense of the character and credibility of the sender: *Does this reporter seem biased? Why should I be paying attention to this speaker?* Our culture teaches us to be skeptical of most messages that bombard us with slogans, and that skepticism is a crucial skill in reading and evaluating arguments.

The mottoes associated with various sources of global information aim to "brand" them by helping to establish their character, what ancient rhetors referred to as *ethos*. And sometimes, slogans like "Fair & Balanced," "All the News That's Fit to Print," or "Do No Harm" can be effective: at the very least, if a phrase is repeated often enough, it comes to sound natural and right. Maybe CNN *is* the most trusted name in news!

But establishing character usually takes more than repetition, as marketers of all kinds know. In the auto industry American companies like Ford or GM are trying to reinvent themselves as forward-looking producers of fuel-efficient cars like the Volt, and they have mounted huge campaigns aimed at convincing buyers that their ethos has changed — for the better. Other companies are challenging them: Toyota's third-generation Prius has developed a strong reputation, a "good character" among buyers; the Nissan Leaf—which describes itself as "100% electric. Zero gas. Zero tailpipe"—was named "world car of the year" at the New York International Auto Show as well as a "top safety pick" by the Institute for Highway Safety, thus building an ethos of clean energy and safety. Tata Motors, whose motto is "We care," offers the Nano, the world's cheapest car whose character, they say, can be described as "the people's car." All of these companies know that their success in sales will be directly linked to their ability to establish a convincing and powerful ethos for their products.

If corporations can establish an ethos for themselves and their products, consider how much character matters when we think about people, especially those in the public eye. We'll mention only two very different examples: actor Charlie Sheen and football star Tim Tebow. Despite film credits that include *Platoon* and *Young Guns*, Sheen earned a hard-drinking, womanizing "bad boy" ethos after the questionable behavior of the character he played on TV sitcom *Two and a Half Men*

Charlie Sheen

Tim Tebow

crossed catastrophically into his real life. And though Heisman Trophy–winner Tim Tebow won two NCAA football championships with the Florida Gators before moving into the National Football League, his fame and ethos owe almost as much to unequivocal displays of his Christian faith, signaled on-field by the kneeling gesture now known as Tebowing.

As is often the case, fame brings endorsements. Tebow's "good guy" ethos was on display controversially yet believably in a pro-life Super Bowl ad he made for the Christian group Focus on the Family in 2010. But the athlete is also on the payroll for Nike and for Jockey underwear—usually fully clothed in his ads. And Sheen? What corporation would want to associate its products with such a questionable, and some might say self-destructive, character? In 2012, automaker Fiat hired him to sell Americans on the "Abarth" performance version of its tiny 500 sedan. A TV spot shows him hurling the Abarth at top speed inside a mansion filled with beautiful women: "I love being under house arrest," Sheen muses. In this case, celebrity ethos matches the product perfectly—especially given Fiat's target audience of men.

So you can see why Aristotle treats ethos as a powerful argumentative appeal. Ethos creates quick and sometimes almost irresistible connections between audience and arguments. We observe people, groups, or institutions making and defending claims all the time and inevitably ask ourselves, *Should we pay attention to them? Can we trust them? Do we want to trust them?* Consider, though, that the same questions will be asked about you and your work, especially in academic settings.

In fact, whenever you write a paper or present an idea, you are sending signals about your character and reliability, whether you intend to or not. If your ideas are reasonable, your sources are reliable, and your language is appropriate to the project, you will suggest to academic readers that you're someone whose ideas *might* deserve attention. You can appreciate why even details like correct spelling, grammar, and mechanics will weigh in your favor. And though you might not think about it now, at some point you may need letters of recommendation from instructors or supervisors. How will they remember you? Often chiefly from the ethos you have established in your work. Think about it.

## Understanding How Arguments Based on Character Work

Put simply, arguments based on character (ethos) depend on *trust*. We tend to accept arguments from those we trust, and we trust them (whether individuals, groups, or institutions) in good part because of their reputations. Three main elements—trustworthiness/credibility, authority, and unselfish or clear motives—add up to *ethos*.

To answer serious and important questions, we often turn to professionals (doctors, lawyers, engineers, teachers, pastors) or to experts (those with knowledge and experience) for wise and frank advice. Such people come with some already established ethos based on their backgrounds and their knowledge. Thus, appeals or arguments about character often turn on claims like these:

- A person (or group or institution) is or is not trustworthy or credible on this issue.
- A person (or group or institution) does or does not have the authority to speak to this issue.
- A person (or group or institution) does or does not have unselfish or clear motives for addressing this subject.

## Establishing Trustworthiness and Credibility

Trustworthiness and credibility speak to a writer's honesty, respect for an audience and its values, and plain old likability. Sometimes a sense of humor can play an important role in getting an audience to listen to or "like" you. It's no accident that all but the most serious speeches begin with a joke or funny story: the humor puts listeners at ease and helps them identify with the speaker. When President Obama spoke at the White House Correspondents' Dinner on April 30, 2011, he was coming off escalating attacks by "birthers" claiming that he was not a citizen of the United States. Obama used the opening of his speech to address those claims—in a humorous way aimed at establishing his credibility: To the tune of "I Am a Real American" accompanied by iconic American images interrupted every few seconds by a pulsating copy of his birth certificate, the president opened his remarks with a broad smile, saying "My *fellow* Americans," to loud laughs and cheers. After offering the traditional Hawaiian greeting of "Mahalo," he went on to say that, this week,

> the State of Hawaii released my official long-form birth certificate. Hopefully, this puts all doubts to rest. But just in case there are any lingering questions, tonight I am prepared to go a step further. Tonight, for the first time, I am releasing my official birth *video*.

President Obama tells jokes at the White House Correspondents' Dinner

What followed was a clip from Disney's *The Lion King*, which brought down the house. The president had shown he had a sense of humor, one he could turn on himself, and doing so helped to build credibility: he was, in fact, a "real American." A little self-deprecation like this can endear writers or speakers to the toughest audiences. We'll often listen to people confident enough to make fun of themselves, because they seem clever and yet aware of their own limitations.

But humor alone can't establish credibility. Although a funny anecdote may help dispose an audience to listen to you, you will need to move quickly to make reasonable claims and then back them up with evidence. Showing your authority on a topic is itself a good way to build credibility.

You can also establish credibility by connecting your own beliefs to core principles that are well established and widely respected. This strategy is particularly effective when your position seems to be—at first glance, at least—a threat to traditional values. For example, when conservative author Andrew Sullivan argues in favor of legalizing same-sex marriages, he does so in language that echoes the themes of family-values conservatives:

> **Legalizing gay marriage would offer homosexuals the same deal society now offers heterosexuals: general social approval and specific legal advantages in exchange for a deeper and harder-to-extract-yourself-from commitment to another human being. Like straight marriage, it would foster social cohesion, emotional security, and economic prudence. Since there's no reason gays should not be allowed to adopt or be foster parents, it could also help nurture children.**
>
> **—Andrew Sullivan, "Here Comes the Groom"**

Yet another way to affirm your credibility as a writer is to use language that shows your respect for readers' intelligence. Citing trustworthy sources and acknowledging them properly prove, too, that you've done your homework (another sign of respect) and suggest that you know your subject. So does presenting ideas clearly and fairly. Details matter: helpful graphs, tables, charts, or illustrations may carry weight with readers, as will the visual attractiveness of your text, whether in print or digital form. Even correct spelling counts!

Writers who establish their credibility seem trustworthy. But sometimes, to be credible, you have to admit limitations, too, as the late biologist Lewis Thomas does as he ponders whether scientists

The National Institute of Mental Health boosts its credibility by having a spokesperson acknowledge how difficult it is for an immigrant to admit suffering from depression.

LINK TO P. 611

have overstepped their boundaries in exploring the limits of DNA research:

> Should we stop short of learning some things, for fear of what we, or someone, will do with the knowledge? My own answer is a flat no, but I must confess that this is an intuitive response and I am neither inclined nor trained to reason my way through it.
>
> —Lewis Thomas, "The Hazards of Science"

As Thomas's comments show, a powerful way to build credibility is to acknowledge outright any exceptions, qualifications, or even weaknesses in your argument. For example, a Volkswagen ad from the 1970s with the headline "They said it couldn't be done. It couldn't," shows that pro basketball star Wilt Chamberlain, at seven feet, one inch, tall, just can't fit inside the Bug. This ad is one of a classic series in which

Volkswagen pokes fun at itself and admits to limitations while also promoting the good points about its car. As a result, the company gains credibility in the bargain.

Making such concessions to objections that readers might raise sends a strong signal to the audience that you've looked critically at your own position and can therefore be trusted when you turn to arguing for its merits. Speaking to readers directly, using *I* or *you*, can also help you connect with them, as can using contractions and everyday or colloquial language. In a commencement address, for example, Oprah Winfrey argues that the graduates need to consider how they can best serve others. To build her case, she draws on her own experience—forthrightly noting some mistakes and problems that she has faced in trying to live a life of service:

> I started this school in Africa . . . where I'm trying to give South African girls a shot at a future like yours. And I spent five years making sure that school would be as beautiful as the students. . . . And yet, last fall, I was faced with a crisis. . . . I was told that one of the dorm matrons was suspected of sexual abuse.

Oprah Winfrey in South Africa

> That was, as you can imagine, devastating news. First, I cried—actually, I sobbed. . . . And the whole time I kept asking that question: What is this here to teach me? And, as difficult as that experience has been, I got a lot of lessons. I understand now the mistakes I made, because I had been paying attention to all of the wrong things. I'd built that school from the outside in, when what really mattered was the inside out.
>
> —Oprah Winfrey, Stanford University Commencement Address

In some situations, you may find that a more formal tone gives your claims greater credibility. You'll be making such choices as you search for the ethos that represents you best.

## Claiming Authority

When you read or listen to an argument, you have every right to ask about the writer's authority: *What does he know about the subject? What experiences does she have that make her especially knowledgeable? Why should I pay attention to this writer?*

When you offer an argument, you have to anticipate and be able to answer questions like these, either directly or indirectly. Sometimes the claim of authority will be bold and personal, as it is when writer and activist Terry Tempest Williams attacks those who poisoned the Utah deserts with nuclear radiation. What gives her the right to speak on this subject? Not scientific expertise, but gut-wrenching personal experience:

> I belong to the Clan of One-Breasted Women. My mother, my grandmothers, and six aunts have all had mastectomies. Seven are dead. The two who survive have just completed rounds of chemotherapy and radiation.
>
> I've had my own problems: two biopsies for breast cancer and a small tumor between my ribs diagnosed as a "borderline malignancy."
>
> —Terry Tempest Williams, "The Clan of One-Breasted Women"

At the opening of his radio interview on the Berkeley Bake Sale, host Michael Krasny announces his guests along with their credentials—both are presidents of student political organizations—to establish their ethos.

LINK TO P. 743

We are willing to listen to Williams's claims because she has lived with the nuclear peril she will deal with in the remainder of her essay.

Writers usually establish their authority in less striking ways. Attaching titles to their names, for example, subtly builds authority by saying they hold medical or legal or engineering degrees, or some special certification. Similarly, writers assert authority by mentioning their employers and the number of years they've worked in a given field. As a reader, you'll likely pay more attention to an argument about global warming if it's offered by someone who identifies herself as a professor of atmospheric and oceanic science at the University of Wisconsin, than by your Uncle Sid, who sells tools. But you'll prefer your uncle to the professor when you need advice about a reliable rotary saw.

When your readers may be skeptical of both you and your claim, you may have to be even more specific about your credentials. That's exactly the strategy Richard Bernstein uses to establish his right to speak on the subject of "Asian culture." What gives a New York writer named Bernstein the authority to write about Asian peoples? Bernstein tells us in a sparkling example of an argument based on character:

> The Asian culture, as it happens, is something I know a bit about, having spent five years at Harvard striving for a Ph.D. in a joint program called History and East Asian Languages and, after that, living either as a student (for one year) or a journalist (six years) in China and Southeast Asia. At least I know enough to know there is no such thing as the "Asian culture."
>
> —Richard Bernstein, *Dictatorship of Virtue*

When you write for readers who trust you and your work, you may not have to make such an open claim to authority. But making this type of appeal is always an option.

Authority can also be conveyed through fairly small signals that readers may pick up almost subconsciously. On his blog, writer and media analyst Clay Shirky talks easily about a new teaching job. The italicized words indicate his confidence and authority:

> This fall, I'm joining NYU's journalism program, where, for the first time in a dozen years, I will teach undergraduates. . . . *I could tell* these students that when I was growing up, the only news I read was thrown into our front yard by a boy on a bicycle. They might find this interesting, but only in the way I found it interesting that my father had grown up without indoor plumbing. *What 19 year olds need to know* isn't how it was in Ye Olden Tymes of 1992; *they need to know what we've learned* about supporting the creation and dissemination of news between then and now. Contemplating what I should tell them, *there are only three things I'm sure of*: News has to be subsidized, and it has to be cheap, and it has to be free.
>
> —Clay Shirky, "Why We Need the New News Environment to Be Chaotic"

CULTURAL CONTEXTS FOR ARGUMENT

### Ethos

In the United States, students are often asked to establish authority by drawing on personal experiences, by reporting on research they or others have conducted, and by taking a position for which they can offer strong evidence. But this expectation about student authority is by no means universal.

Some cultures regard student writers as novices who can most effectively make arguments by reflecting on what they've learned from their teachers and elders—those who hold the most important knowledge and, hence, authority. When you're arguing a point with people from cultures other than your own, ask questions like:

- Whom are you addressing, and what is your relationship with that person?
- What knowledge are you expected to have? Is it appropriate or expected for you to demonstrate that knowledge—and if so, how?
- What tone is appropriate? And remember: politeness is rarely, if ever, inappropriate.

## Coming Clean about Motives

When people are trying to sell you something, it's important (and natural) to ask: *Whose interests are they serving? How will they profit from their proposal?* Such suspicions go to the heart of ethical arguments.

Here, for example, someone posting on the Web site Serious Eats, which is "focused on celebrating and sharing food enthusiasm" online, acknowledges—in a footnote—that his attention to Martha Stewart, her Web site, and a *Martha Stewart Living* cookbook may be influenced by his employment history:

> Martha Stewart* has been blipping up on the Serious Eats radar lately.
>
> First it was this astronaut meal she chose for her longtime Microsoft billionaire friend Charles Simonyi, "a gourmet space meal of duck breast confit and semolina cake with dried apricots." Talk about going above and beyond.

Then official word comes that marthastewart.com has relaunched with a fresh new look and new features. The site, which went live in its new form a few weeks before this announcement, is quite an improvement. It seems to load faster, information is easier to find, and the recipes are easier to read—although there are so many brands, magazines, and "omnimedia" on offer that the homepage is a little dizzying at first.

**Full disclosure: I used to work at* Martha Stewart Living *magazine.*

—Adam Kuban, "Martha, Martha, Martha"

Especially in online venues like the one Kuban uses here, writers have to expect that readers will hold diverse views and will be quick to point out unmentioned affiliations as serious drawbacks to credibility. In fact, attacks on such loyalties are common in political circles, where it's almost a sport to assume the worst about an opponent's motives and associations.

But we all have connections and interests that represent the ties that bind us to other human beings. It makes sense that a woman might be concerned with women's issues or that investors might look out for their investments. So it can be good strategy to let your audiences know where your loyalties lie when such information does, in fact, shape your work.

#### Using Ethos in Your Own Writing

- Establish your credibility by connecting to your audience's values, showing respect for them, and establishing common ground where possible. How will you convince your audience you are trustworthy? What will you admit about your own limitations?
- Establish your authority by showing you have done your homework and know your topic well. How will you show that you know your topic well? What appropriate personal experience can you draw on?
- Examine your motives for writing. What, if anything, do you stand to gain from your argument? How can you explain those advantages to your audience?

## RESPOND•

1. Consider the ethos of these public figures. Then describe one or two products that might benefit from their endorsements as well as several that would not.

   Cat Deeley—emcee of *So You Think You Can Dance*

   Margaret Cho—comedian

Johnny Depp—actor

Lady Gaga—singer and songwriter

Bill O'Reilly—TV news commentator

Marge Simpson—sensible wife and mother on *The Simpsons*

Jon Stewart—host of *The Daily Show* on Comedy Central

2. Opponents of Richard Nixon, the thirty-seventh president of the United States, once raised doubts about his integrity by asking a single ruinous question: *Would you buy a used car from this man?* Create your own version of the argument of character. Begin by choosing an intriguing or controversial person or group and finding an image online. Then download the image into a word-processing file. Create a caption for the photo that is modeled after the question asked about Nixon: *Would you give this woman your email password? Would you share a campsite with this couple? Would you eat lasagna that this guy fixed?* Finally, write a serious 300-word argument that explores the character flaws or strengths of your subject(s).
3. Take a close look at your Facebook page (or your page on any other social media site). What are some aspects of your character, true or not, that might be conveyed by the photos, videos, and messages you have posted online? Analyze the ethos or character you see projected there, using the advice in this chapter to guide your analysis.

# 4
# Arguments Based on Facts and Reason: Logos

These three images say a lot about the use and place of logic (*logos*) in Western, and particularly American, culture. The first shows David Caruso as Lt. Horatio Caine in the TV series *CSI: Miami,* in which crime lab investigators use science to determine the facts behind unsolved murder cases. The second refers to an even more popular TV (and film) series, *Star Trek,* whose Vulcan officer, Spock, reasons through logic alone; and the third is a cartoon spoofing a logical argument (nine out of ten prefer X) made so often that it has become something of a joke itself.

These images attest to the prominent place that logic holds: like the investigators on *CSI,* we continue to want access to the facts on the assumption that they will help us make the best arguments. We admire those whose logic is, like Spock's, impeccable, and we respond to implied arguments suggested when they begin, "Nine out of ten doctors recommend . . ." Those are odds that most accept, suggesting overwhelmingly that the next doctor will also agree with the prognosis. But these images also challenge or undercut our reliance on logic alone: Lt. Caine and Spock are characters drawn in broad and often parodic strokes; the "nine out of ten" cartoon directly spoofs such arguments. When the choice is between logic and emotion, however, most of us still say we respect *appeals to logos*—arguments based on facts, evidence, and reason (though we're inclined to test the facts against our feelings and against the ethos of those making the appeal).

## Providing Hard Evidence

Aristotle helps us out in classifying arguments by distinguishing two kinds:

| | | | |
|---|---|---|---|
| **Artistic Proofs** | Arguments the writer/ speaker creates | Constructed arguments | Appeals to reason; common sense |
| **Inartistic Proofs** | Arguments the writer/ speaker is given | Hard evidence | Facts, statistics, testimonies, witnesses, contracts, documents |

We can see these different kinds of logical appeals at work in the most recent attempts of former vice president Al Gore to raise awareness and evoke action on global warming. On September 14, 2011, Gore launched a twenty-four-hour worldwide live-streamed event to introduce the new Climate Reality Project, beginning with a new thirty-minute multimedia presentation shown once an hour for twenty-four hours in every time zone across the globe. The project intends, according to its Web site, to bring

> the facts about the climate crisis into the mainstream and engage the public in conversation about how to solve it. We help citizens around the world reject the lies and take meaningful steps to bring about change.

The project, Gore claims, is guided by "one simple truth":

> The climate crisis is real and we know how to solve it.

Note the emphasis on "the facts about the climate crisis": Gore and his colleagues will have to rely on a lot of hard evidence and inartistic proof in asserting that the "climate crisis is real." In an essay in *Rolling Stone,* Gore summarized some of this evidence, saying that today

> the scientific consensus [for the reality of global warming] is even stronger. It has been endorsed by every National Academy of science of every major country on the planet, every major professional scientific society related to the study of global warming and 98 percent of

"Who Cares about Ice Bears?"

> climate scientists throughout the world. In the latest and most authoritative study by three thousand of the very best scientific experts in the world, the evidence was judged "unequivocal."

Here Gore refers to testimony, statistics, and facts to carry his argument forward. But he also must rely on less "hard" evidence, as when he says:

> Determining what is real can be a challenge in our culture, but in order to make wise choices in the presence of such grave risks, we must use common sense and the rule of reason in coming to an agreement on what is true.

Common sense, Gore tells us, shows us that global warming has got to be true: just look around and see the evidence in the melting ice caps and the rising seas—and a lot more. Gore believes that this artistic appeal will go as far as the hard scientific evidence to convince readers to take action. (Seeing is believing, after all—or is it? See p. 59.) And action is what he's after. At the end of this long essay, he uses another bit of constructed reasoning to show that if everyday Americans make their position clear, the leaders will follow:

> Why do you think President Obama and Congress changed their game on "don't ask, don't tell"? It happened because enough Americans

> delivered exactly that tough message to candidates who wanted their votes. When enough people care passionately enough to drive that message home on the climate crisis, politicians will look at their hole cards, and enough of them will change their game to make all the difference we need.

Will Gore and the Climate Reality Project convince global citizens that they are right about what is "true" about climate change? Not if other powerful voices can help it. A quick Google search for "global warming hoax" will take you to weekly updates providing countervailing studies and testimony. And Gore himself has been an often easy target for attack, especially after some leaked scientific email from Britain evoked charges that climate scientists were "doctoring" the facts, though independent critics eventually determined that the email wording was taken seriously out of context and that the email did not undermine the data on global climate change and its causes.

This cartoon suggests that changing the subject is a fallback strategy when the "facts" are inconvenient.

This ongoing controversy surrounding global warming is a good example of how difficult it can be to distinguish the good evidence from the slanted or fabricated kinds and to decide how to make sound decisions based on it.

## IS SEEING BELIEVING?

Some of the debate over climate change centers on photographs, which may be telling "nothing but the truth"—or not. We have known for decades that all photographs in some way shape or interpret what they show, but in the age of Photoshop readers need to be even more careful about believing what they see, and writers need to be especially careful that the images they use are trustworthy. Whole books have been devoted to "digital fakery" and photographic manipulation, and examples are easy to find. In 2008, Iran was caught red-handed manipulating a photograph of missiles, as you see in the two photographs above: where did the fourth missile (in the right-hand photo) come from? So egregious was this example of manipulation that others like Boing Boing soon got into the act, inviting readers to join in by submitting their own manipulations of the original image on the left.

Today, when we can all slant discussions, cherry-pick examples, and alter images, writers need more than ever to be aware of the ethics of evidence, whether that evidence draws on facts, statistics, survey data, testimony and narratives, or commonsense reasoning.

**RESPOND•**

Discuss whether the following statements are examples of hard evidence or constructed arguments. Not all cases are clear-cut.

1. Drunk drivers are involved in more than 50 percent of traffic deaths.
2. DNA tests of skin found under the victim's fingernails suggest that the defendant was responsible for the assault.
3. A psychologist testified that teenage violence could not be blamed on video games.
4. An apple a day keeps the doctor away.
5. "The only thing we have to fear is fear itself."
6. Air bags ought to be removed from vehicles because they can kill young children and small-frame adults.

## Facts

Gathering factual information and transmitting it faithfully practically define what we mean by professional journalism and scholarship. We'll even listen to people we don't agree with if their evidence is really good. Below, a reviewer for the conservative *National Review* praises William Julius Wilson, a liberal sociologist, because of how well he presents his case:

> In his eagerly awaited new book, Wilson argues that ghetto blacks are worse off than ever, victimized by a near-total loss of low-skill jobs in and around inner-city neighborhoods. In support of this thesis, he *musters mountains of data, plus excerpts from some of the thousands of surveys and face-to-face interviews that he and his research team conducted among inner-city Chicagoans*. It is a book that deserves a wide audience among thinking conservatives.
>
> —John J. Dilulio Jr., "When Decency Disappears" (emphasis added)

When your facts are compelling, they may stand on their own in a low-stakes argument, supported by little more than saying where they come from. Consider the power of phrases such as "reported by the *Wall Street Journal*," or "according to factcheck.org." Such sources gain credibility if they have reported facts accurately and reliably over time. Using such credible sources in an argument can also reflect positively on you.

But arguing with facts can also involve challenging even the most reputable sources if they lead to unfair or selective reporting. In recent years, bloggers and other online critics have enjoyed pointing out the biases or factual mistakes of "mainstream media" (MSM) outlets. These criticisms often deal not just with specific facts and coverage but with the overall way that an issue is presented or "framed." In the following highly rhetorical passage from liberal economist Paul Krugman's blog, he points out what, from his point of view, is a persistent tendency of the mainstream media to claim they are framing issues in "fair and balanced" ways by presenting two opposing sides as if they were equal:

> Watching our system deal with the debt ceiling crisis—a wholly self-inflicted crisis, which may nonetheless have disastrous consequences—it's increasingly obvious that what we're looking at is the destructive influence of a cult that has really poisoned our political system. . . . [T]he cult that I see as reflecting a true moral failure is the cult of balance, of centrism.
>
> Think about what's happening right now. We have a crisis in which the right is making insane demands, while the president and Democrats in Congress are bending over backward to be accommodating—offering plans that are all spending cuts and no taxes, plans that are far to the right of public opinion.
>
> So what do most news reports say? They portray it as a situation in which both sides are equally partisan, equally intransigent—because news reports always do that. And we have influential pundits calling out for a new centrist party, a new centrist president, to get us away from the evils of partisanship.
>
> The reality, of course, is that we already have a centrist president—actually a moderate conservative president. Once again, health reform—his only major change to government—was modeled on Republican plans, indeed plans coming from the Heritage Foundation. And everything else—including the wrongheaded emphasis on austerity in the face of high unemployment—is according to the conservative playbook.
>
> What all this means is that there is no penalty for extremism; no way for most voters, who get their information on the fly rather than doing careful study of the issues, to understand what's really going on.
>
> You have to ask, what would it take for these news organizations and pundits to actually break with the convention that both sides are equally at fault? This is the clearest, starkest situation one can imagine short of civil war. If this won't do it, nothing will.
>
> —Paul Krugman, "The Cult That Is Destroying America"

In an ideal world, good information—no matter where it comes from—would always drive out bad. But you already know that we don't live in an ideal world, so sometimes bad information gets repeated in an echo chamber that amplifies the errors.

Many media have no pretenses at all about being reputable. During the 2008 presidential campaign, the Internet blared statements proclaiming that Barack Obama was Muslim, even after dozens of sources, including many people with whom Obama had worshipped, testified to his Christianity. As a reader and researcher, you should look beyond headlines, bylines, reputations, and especially rumors that fly about the Internet. Scrutinize any facts you collect, and test their reliability before passing them on.

### Statistics

You've probably heard the old saying that "There are three kinds of lies: lies, damned lies, and statistics," and, to be sure, it is possible to lie with numbers, even those that are accurate, because numbers rarely speak for themselves. They need to be interpreted by writers—and writers almost always have agendas that shape the interpretations.

The *New York Times* suggests an argument about bottled water consumption when it offers visual representation of statistical data.

LINK TO P. 723

Of course, just because they are often misused doesn't mean that statistics are meaningless, but it does suggest that you need to use them carefully and to remember that your interpretation of the statistics is very important. Consider an article from the *Atlantic* called "American Murder Mystery" by Hanna Rosin. The "mystery" Rosin writes about is the rise of crime in midsize American cities such as Memphis, Tennessee. The article raised a firestorm of response and criticism, including this analysis of statistical malfeasance from blogger Alan Salzberg:

> The primary statistical evidence given in the article of an association between crime and former Section 8 [housing project] residents, is a map that shows areas with high incidents of crime correspond to areas with a large number of people with Section 8 subsidies (i.e., former residents of housing projects). As convincing as this might sound, it has a fatal flaw: the map looks at total incidents rather than crime rate. This means that an area with ten thousand people and one hundred crimes (and one hundred Section 8 subsidy recipients) will look much worse than an area with one hundred people and one crime (and one Section 8 subsidy recipient). However, both areas have the same rate of crime, and, presumably, the same odds of being a victim of crime. Yet in Betts and Janikowski's analysis, the area with ten thousand people has a higher number of Section 8 subsidy recipients and higher crime, thus "proving" their theory of association.

When relying on statistics in your arguments, make sure you check and double-check them or get help in doing so: you don't want to be accused of using "fictitious data" based on "ludicrous assumptions"!

The text in the cartoon says it all.

*"Now, keep in mind that these numbers are only as accurate as the fictitious data, ludicrous assumptions and wishful thinking they're based upon!"*



**RESPOND.**

Statistical evidence becomes useful only when interpreted fairly and reasonably. Go to the *USA Today* Web site and look for the daily graph, chart, or table called the "USA Today snapshot." Pick a snapshot, and use the information in it to support three different claims, at least two of which make very different points. Share your claims with classmates. (The point is not to learn to use data dishonestly but to see firsthand how the same statistics can serve a variety of arguments.)

## Surveys and Polls

When they verify the popularity of an idea or proposal, surveys and polls provide strong persuasive appeals because they come as close to expressing the will of the people as anything short of an election—the most decisive poll of all. However, surveys and polls can do much more than help politicians make decisions. They can also provide persuasive reasons for action or intervention. When surveys show, for example, that most American sixth-graders can't locate France or Wyoming on a map—not to mention Turkey or Afghanistan—that's an appeal for better instruction in geography. It always makes sense, however, to question poll numbers, especially when they support your own point of view. Ask who commissioned the poll, who is publishing its outcome, who was surveyed (and in what proportions), and what stakes these parties might have in its outcome.

*Cook's Country*'s taste test for chocolate chip cookies gave the surveyors a result they did not expect—homemade cookies didn't place first.

LINK TO P. 726

Are we being too suspicious? No. In fact, this sort of scrutiny is exactly what you should anticipate from your readers whenever you do surveys to explore an issue. You should be confident that you've surveyed enough people to be accurate, that the people you chose for the study were representative of the selected population as a whole, and that you chose them randomly—not selecting those most likely to say what you hoped to hear.

Fathers are more likely than mothers (33% vs. 26%) to say they sometimes play video games with their teens ages 12 to 17.

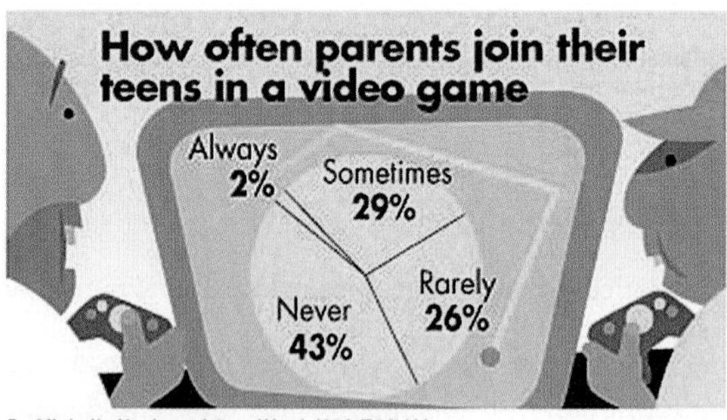


By Michelle Healy and Sam Ward, USA TODAY
Source: Pew Internet & American Life Project

*USA Today* is famous for the tables, pie charts, and graphs it creates to present statistics and poll results. What claims might the evidence in this graph support? How does the design of the item influence your reading of it?

On the other hand, as with other kinds of factual evidence, don't make the opposite mistake by discounting or ignoring polls whose findings are *not* what you had hoped for. In the following excerpts from a column in the *Dallas News*, conservative Rod Dreher forthrightly faces up to the results from a poll of registered Texas voters—results that he finds ominous for his Texas Republican Party:

> The full report, which will be released today, knocks the legs out from under two principles cherished by the party's grassroots: staunch social conservatism and hard-line immigration policies. At the state level, few voters care much about abortion, school prayer and other hot-button issues. Immigration is the only conservative stand-by that rates much mention—and by hitting it too hard, Republicans lose both the Hispanics and independents that make up what the pollster defines as the "Critical Middle." . . .
>
> This is not going to go down well with the activist core of the Texas GOP, especially people like me: a social conservative with firm views on illegal immigration. But reality has a way of focusing the mind, forcing one to realize that political parties are not dogma-driven churches, but coalitions that unavoidably shift over time.
>
> —Rod Dreher, "Poll's Shocking SOS for Texas GOP"

Dreher's frank acknowledgment of findings that did not please him also helps him to create a positive ethos as a trustworthy writer who follows the facts wherever they lead.

The meaning of polls and surveys is also affected by the way that questions are asked. Recent research has shown, for example, that questions about same-sex unions get differing responses according to how they are worded. When people are asked whether gay and lesbian couples should be eligible for the same inheritance and partner health benefits that heterosexual couples receive, a majority of those polled say yes—unless the word *marriage* appears in the question; then the responses are primarily negative. Remember, then, to be very careful in wording questions for any poll you conduct.

Finally, always keep in mind that the date of a poll may strongly affect the results—and their usefulness in an argument. In 2010, for example, nearly 50 percent of California voters supported building more nuclear power plants. Less than a year later, that percentage had dropped to 37 percent after the meltdown of Japanese nuclear power plants in the wake of the March 2011 earthquake and tsunami.

**RESPOND.**

Choose an important issue and design a series of questions to evoke a range of responses in a poll. Try to design a question that would make people strongly inclined to agree, another question that would lead them to oppose the same proposition, and a third that tries to be more neutral. Then try out your questions on your classmates.

## Testimonies and Narratives

Writers can support their arguments with all kinds of human experience presented in the form of narrative or testimony, particularly if that experience is the writer's own. In courts, decisions often take into consideration detailed descriptions and narratives of exactly what occurred. Look at this reporter's account of a court case in which a panel of judges decided, based on the testimony presented, that a man had been sexually harassed by another man. The narrative, in this case, supplies the evidence:

> The Seventh Circuit, in a 1997 case known as *Doe v. City of Belleville*, drew a sweeping conclusion allowing for same-sex harassment cases of many kinds. . . . This case, for example, centered on teenage twin brothers working a summer job cutting grass in the city cemetery of Belleville, Ill. One boy wore an earring, which caused him no end of grief that particular summer—including a lot of menacing talk among his coworkers about sexually assaulting him in the woods and sending him "back to San Francisco." One of his harassers, identified in court documents as a large former marine, culminated a verbal campaign by backing the earring-wearer against a wall and grabbing him by the testicles to see "if he was a girl or a guy." The teenager had been "singled out for this abuse," the court ruled, "because the way in which he projected the sexual aspect of his personality"—meaning his gender—"did not conform to his coworkers' view of appropriate masculine behavior."
>
> —Margaret Talbot, "Men Behaving Badly"

Personal narratives can support a claim convincingly, especially if a writer has earned the trust of readers. In an essay arguing that people should pay very close attention to intuition, regarding it as important as more factual evidence, Suzanne Guillette uses personal narrative to good effect:

> It was late summer 2009: I was walking on a Long Island beach with my boyfriend Mark and some friends. When I saw Mark sit down next

> to his friend Dana on a craggy rock, a sudden electric shock traveled straight up the center of my body. It was so visceral it made me stumble. And then my mind flashed to a recent dream I'd had of Dana sitting on Mark's lap as he rode a bike. *Don't be crazy*, I chided myself, turning to watch the surfers. *They're just friends*. But one night nine months later . . . Mark confessed that he and Dana had had an affair. . . . Each time I had a "flash," I realized that listening to it—or not—had consequences.
>
> —Suzanne Guillette, "Learning to Listen"

This narrative introduction gives readers details to support the claim Guillette is making: we can make big mistakes if we ignore our intuitions. (For more on establishing credibility with readers, see Chapter 3.)

**RESPOND.**

Bring to class a full review of a recent film that you either enjoyed or did not enjoy. Using testimony from that review, write a brief argument to your classmates explaining why they should see that movie (or why they should avoid it), being sure to use evidence from the review fairly and reasonably. Then exchange arguments with a classmate, and decide whether the evidence in your peer's argument helps to change your opinion about the movie. What's convincing about the evidence? If it doesn't convince you, why not?

## Using Reason and Common Sense

If you don't have "hard facts," you can support claims by using reason and common sense. The formal study of reasoning is called *logic*, and you probably recognize a famous example of deductive reasoning, called a syllogism:

**All human beings are mortal.**

**Socrates is a human being.**

**Therefore, Socrates is mortal.**

In valid syllogisms, the conclusion follows logically—and technically—from the premises that lead up to it. Many have criticized syllogistic reasoning for being limited, and others have poked fun at it, as in this cartoon:

**Logic: another thing that penguins aren't very good at.**

But few people use formal deductive reasoning to support claims. Even Aristotle recognized that most people argue perfectly well using informal rather than formal logic. To do so, they rely mostly on habits of mind and assumptions that they share with their readers or listeners.

In Chapter 7, we describe a system of informal logic that you may find useful in shaping credible arguments—**Toulmin argument**. Here, we briefly examine some ways that people use informal logic in their everyday lives. Once again, we begin with Aristotle, who used the term **enthymeme** to describe an ordinary kind of sentence that includes both a claim and a reason but depends on the audience's agreement with an assumption that is left implicit rather than spelled out. Enthymemes can be very persuasive when most people agree with the assumptions they rest on. The following sentences are all enthymemes:

We'd better cancel the picnic because it's going to rain.

Flat taxes are fair because they treat everyone the same.

I'll buy a PC instead of a Mac because it's cheaper.

NCAA football needs a playoff to crown a real national champion.

Sometimes enthymemes seem so obvious that readers don't realize that they're drawing inferences when they agree with them. Consider the first example:

> **We'd better cancel the picnic because it's going to rain.**

Let's expand the enthymeme a bit to say more of what the speaker may mean:

> **We'd better cancel the picnic this afternoon because the weather bureau is predicting a 70 percent chance of rain for the remainder of the day.**

Embedded in this brief argument are all sorts of assumptions and fragments of cultural information that are left implicit but that help to make it persuasive:

> **Picnics are ordinarily held outdoors.**
>
> **When the weather is bad, it's best to cancel picnics.**
>
> **Rain is bad weather for picnics.**
>
> **A 70 percent chance of rain means that rain is more likely to occur than not.**
>
> **When rain is more likely to occur than not, it makes sense to cancel picnics.**

For most people, the original statement carries all this information on its own; the enthymeme is a compressed argument, based on what audiences know and will accept.

But sometimes enthymemes aren't self-evident:

> **Be wary of environmentalism because it's religion disguised as science.**
>
> **iPhones are undermining civil society by making us even more focused on ourselves.**
>
> **It's time to make all public toilets unisex because to do otherwise is discriminatory.**

In these cases, you'll have to work much harder to defend both the claim and the implicit assumptions that it's based on by drawing out the inferences that seem self-evident in other enthymemes. And you'll likely also have to supply credible evidence. A simple declaration of fact won't suffice.

**CULTURAL CONTEXTS FOR ARGUMENT**

### Logos

In the United States, student writers are expected to draw on "hard facts" and evidence as often as possible in supporting their claims: while ethical and emotional appeals are important, logical appeals tend to hold sway in academic writing. So statistics and facts speak volumes, as does reasoning based on time-honored values such as fairness and equity. In writing to global audiences, you need to remember that not all cultures value the same kinds of appeals. If you want to write to audiences across cultures, you need to know about the norms and values in those cultures. Chinese culture, for example, values authority and often indirect allusion over "facts" alone. Some African cultures value cooperation and community over individualism, and still other cultures value religious texts as providing compelling evidence. So think carefully about what you consider strong evidence, and pay attention to what counts as evidence to others. You can begin by asking yourself questions like:

- What evidence is most valued by your audience: Facts? Concrete examples? Firsthand experience? Religious or philosophical texts? Something else?
- Will analogies count as support? How about precedents?
- Will the testimony of experts count? If so, what kind of experts are valued most?

## Providing Logical Structures for Argument

Some arguments depend on particular logical structures to make their points. In the following pages, we identify a few of these logical structures.

### Degree

Arguments based on degree are so common that people barely notice them, nor do they pay much attention to how they work because they seem self-evident. Most audiences will readily accept that *more of a good thing* or *less of a bad thing* is good. In her novel *The Fountainhead*, Ayn Rand

A demonstrator at an immigrants' rights rally in New York City in 2007. Arguments based on values that are widely shared within a society—such as the idea of equal rights in American culture—have an automatic advantage with audiences.

asks: "If physical slavery is repulsive, how much more repulsive is the concept of servility of the spirit?" Most readers immediately comprehend the point Rand intends to make about slavery of the spirit because they already know that physical slavery is cruel and would reject any forms of slavery that were even crueler on the principle that *more of a bad thing is bad*. Rand still needs to offer evidence that "servility of the spirit" is, in fact, worse than bodily servitude, but she has begun with a logical structure readers can grasp. Here are other arguments that work similarly:

Christophe Pelletier's "The Locavore's Dilemma" depends on arguments based on degree as he presents the difficulties involved in the choice to eat only locally grown food.

LINK TO P. 703

> If I can get a ten-year warranty on an inexpensive Kia, shouldn't I get the same or better warranty from a more expensive Lexus?
>
> The health benefits from using stem cells in research will surely outweigh the ethical risks.
>
> Better a conventional war now than a nuclear confrontation later.

## Analogies

**Analogies**, typically complex or extended comparisons, explain one idea or concept by comparing it to something else.

Here, writer and founder of literacy project 826 Valencia, Dave Eggers, uses an analogy in arguing that we do not value teachers as much as we should:

> When we don't get the results we want in our military endeavors, we don't blame the soldiers. We don't say, "It's these lazy soldiers and their bloated benefits plans! That's why we haven't done better in Afghanistan!" No, if the results aren't there, we blame the planners. . . . No one contemplates blaming the men and women fighting every day in the trenches for little pay and scant recognition. And yet in education we do just that. When we don't like the way our students score on international standardized tests, we blame the teachers.
>
> —Dave Eggers and Ninive Calegari, "The High Cost of Low Teacher Salaries"

## Precedent

Arguments from **precedent** and arguments of analogy both involve comparisons. Consider an assertion like this one, which uses a comparison as a precedent:

> If motorists in most other states can pump their own gas safely, surely the state of Oregon can trust its own drivers to be as capable. It's time for Oregon to permit self-service gas stations.

You could tease out several inferences from this claim to explain its reasonableness: people in Oregon are as capable as people in other states; people with equivalent capabilities can do the same thing; pumping gas is not hard, and so forth. But you don't have to because most readers get the argument simply because of the way it is put together.

Here is an excerpt from an extended argument by blogger Neil Warner, in which he argues that the "Arab Spring" of 2011 may not follow the same pattern as its historical precedents:

> ["Arab Spring"] is in many respects a fitting name, one that relates not only to the season in which the unrest really began but also captures perfectly the newfound optimism and youthful determination that seems to have embraced the region. Unfortunately, though, "Spring" as a term for popular movements does not have an encouraging history.
>
> The most comparable event with the same title is the so-called "Spring of the Nations" or "Springtime of the Peoples" of 1848–49. In one of the most stunning international events the world has ever witnessed, a wildfire of liberal revolution spread out across Europe following the

> overthrow of the restored French monarchy in February of 1848. Traditional reactionary regimes fell like dominos and a sense of unity of purpose and hopefulness very comparable in some ways to 2011 in the Arab World embraced the populace, both working class and middle class, of Germany, Italy, the Austrian Empire, and elsewhere. An uprising in November 1848 even forced the Pope to flee Rome.
>
> But by the end of 1849 it had all fizzled out, reactionary forces reassembled and the revolutionaries split, and the old order in Europe settled back down as if nothing had ever happened. . . .
>
> With respect to the Arab world, we can already see the same pattern developing. After an initial panic following the overthrow of Mubarak, the Arab dictatorships of the region have consolidated themselves and clung on for dear life. . . .
>
> —Neil Warner, "The Anatomy of a Spring"

You'll encounter additional kinds of logical structures as you create your own arguments. You'll find some of them in Chapter 5, "Fallacies of Argument," and still more in Chapter 7 on Toulmin argument.

# 5 Fallacies of Argument

*Can we let a shrimp like this run our great country?*

**Vegetarians linked to higher brain power**

AUSTRALIA'S elite high IQ group Mensa has more than its fair share of vegetarians.

That might be more than coincidental, according to new research which suggests that people who choose the vegetarian path are smarter than their carnivorous counterparts.

The study, published in the *British Medical Journal*, traced 8000 people from birth and found that those who

Do the arguments embedded in these three images look a little suspicious to you? Chances are, you recognize them as faulty reasoning of some kind. Such argumentative moves are called **fallacies**, arguments that are flawed by their very nature or structure. The first, a cartoon, represents a move familiar to all who follow political "attack" ads that focus on the character of the person (he's a shrimp!) rather than substance. The second, a protest image, uses scare tactics to compare the Obama administration to the Nazis; and the third, from a news article, illustrates false cause: high IQs could be caused by any number of things, but probably not vegetarianism alone!

Using fallacies can hurt everyone involved, including the person using them, because they make productive argument more difficult. They muck up the frank but civil conversations that people should be able to have, regardless of their differences. But fallacies can be powerful tools, so it's important that you can recognize and point them out in the works of others—and avoid them in your own writing. This chapter aims to help you meet these goals: here we'll introduce you to fallacies of argument classified according to the emotional, ethical, and logical appeals we've discussed earlier (see Chapters 2–4).

## Fallacies of Emotional Argument

Emotional arguments can be powerful and suitable in many circumstances, and most writers use them frequently. However, writers who pull on their readers' heartstrings or raise their blood pressure too often can violate the good faith on which legitimate argument depends.

### Scare Tactics

Politicians, advertisers, and public figures sometimes peddle their ideas by scaring people and exaggerating possible dangers well beyond their statistical likelihood. Such ploys work because it's easier to imagine something terrible happening than to appreciate its rarity.

**Scare tactics** can also be used to stampede legitimate fears into panic or prejudice. People who genuinely fear losing their jobs can be persuaded to fear that immigrants might work for less money. People who are living on fixed incomes can be convinced that minor changes to entitlement programs represent dire threats to their well-being. Such tactics have the effect of closing off thinking because people who are scared often act irrationally. Even well-intended fear campaigns—like those directed against the use of illegal drugs, smoking, or unprotected sex—can misfire if their warnings prove too shrill. People just stop listening.

### *Either-Or* Choices

One way to simplify arguments and give them power is to reduce complicated issues to just two options, one obviously preferable to the other. Here is President Obama speaking to an Associated Press luncheon in 2012 and contrasting his vision of the country with what he wants listeners to believe is his opponents' view:

> **Ask any company where they'd rather locate and hire workers—a country with crumbling roads and bridges, or one that's committed to high-speed Internet and high-speed railroads and high-tech research and development?**

In "The Locavore's Dilemma," how does Christophe Pelletier try to avoid the *either-or* fallacy? Does he succeed? Why or why not?

LINK TO P. 703

Obama is arguing that his economic policies will provide funds for exciting infrastructure developments whereas Republicans are so concerned with deficits that they are willing to allow the country to crumble, literally. A moment's thought, however, suggests that the choices here are too stark to reflect the complexity of the national economy. Yet, like most politicians, Obama can't seem to resist the power of this mode of argument.

***Either-or* choices** can be well-intentioned strategies to get something accomplished. Parents use them all the time ("Eat your broccoli, or you won't get dessert"). But they become fallacious arguments when they reduce a complicated issue to excessively simple terms or when they're designed to obscure legitimate alternatives. For instance, to suggest that renewable power sources such as wind and solar represent the only long-term solution to our energy needs may have rhetorical power, but the choice is too easy and uncomplicated. Energy shortages can be fixed in any number of ways, *including* wind and solar power.

## Slippery Slope

The **slippery slope** fallacy portrays today's tiny misstep as tomorrow's slide into disaster. Some arguments that aim at preventing dire consequences do not take the slippery slope approach (for example, the parent who corrects a child for misbehavior now is acting sensibly to prevent more serious problems as the child grows older). A slippery slope argument becomes wrongheaded when a writer exaggerates the likely consequences of an action, usually to frighten readers. As such, slippery slope arguments are also scare tactics. In recent years, the issue of same-sex marriage has evoked many slippery slope arguments:

> Anyone else bored to tears with the "slippery slope" arguments against gay marriage? Since few opponents of homosexual unions are brave enough to admit that gay weddings just freak them out, they hide behind the claim that it's an inexorable slide from legalizing gay marriage to having sex with penguins outside JC Penney's. The problem is it's virtually impossible to debate against a slippery slope.
>
> —Dahlia Lithwick, "Slippery Slop"

Ideas and actions do have consequences, but they aren't always as dire as writers fond of slippery slope tactics would have you believe.

## Overly Sentimental Appeals

Overly **sentimental appeals** use tender emotions excessively to distract readers from facts. Often, such appeals are highly personal and individual and focus attention on heartwarming or heartwrenching situations that make readers feel guilty if they challenge an idea, a policy, or a proposal. Emotions become an impediment to civil discourse when they keep people from thinking clearly.

Such sentimental appeals are a major vehicle of television news, where tugging at viewers' heartstrings can mean high ratings. For example, when a camera documents the day-to-day sacrifices of parents who are trying to meet their mortgage payments and keep their kids in college in a tough economy, their on-screen struggles can represent the spirit of an entire class of people threatened by callous bankers. But while such individual stories stir genuine emotions, they seldom give a complete picture of a complex social or economic issue.

This image, taken from a gun control protest, is designed to elicit sympathy by causing the viewer to think about the dangers guns pose to innocent children and, thus, support the cause.

### Bandwagon Appeals

**Bandwagon appeals** urge people to follow the same path everyone else is taking. Rather than think independently about where to go, it's often easier to get on board the bandwagon with everyone else.

Many American parents seem to have an innate ability to refute bandwagon appeals. When their kids whine, *Everyone else is going camping without chaperones,* the parents reply, *And if everyone else jumps off a cliff (or a railroad bridge or the Empire State Building), you will too?* The children groan—and then try a different line of argument.

Unfortunately, not all bandwagon approaches are so transparent. In recent decades, bandwagon issues have included the war on drugs, the nuclear freeze movement, the campaign against drunk driving, campaign finance reform, illegal immigration, the defense of marriage, and bailouts for banks and businesses. These issues are all too complex to permit the suspension of judgment that bandwagon tactics require.

Cartoonist Roz Chast's take on bandwagon appeals.

## Fallacies of Ethical Argument

Because readers give their closest attention to authors they respect or trust, writers usually want to present themselves as honest, well-informed, likable, or sympathetic. But not all the devices that writers use to gain the attention and confidence of readers are admirable. (For more on appeals based on character, see Chapter 3.)

### Appeals to False Authority

Many academic research papers find and reflect on the work of reputable authorities and introduce these authorities through direct quotations or citations as credible evidence. (For more on assessing the reliability of sources, see Chapter 18.) **False authority**, however, occurs when writers offer themselves or other authorities as sufficient warrant for believing a claim:

Claim **X is true because I say so.**
Warrant **What I say must be true.**

Claim **X is true because Y says so.**
Warrant **What Y says must be true.**

Though they are seldom stated so baldly, claims of authority drive many political campaigns. American pundits and politicians are fond of citing the U.S. Constitution and its Bill of Rights (Canadians have their Charter of Rights and Freedoms) as ultimate authorities, a reasonable practice when the documents are interpreted respectfully. However, the rights claimed sometimes aren't in the texts themselves or don't mean what the speakers think they do. And most constitutional matters are debatable—as volumes of court records prove. Likewise, religious believers often base arguments on books or traditions that wield great authority in a particular religious community. But the power of such texts is usually limited to that group and less capable of persuading others solely on the grounds of authority.

In short, you should pay serious attention to claims supported by respected authorities, such as the Centers for Disease Control, the National Science Foundation, or the *Globe and Mail*. But don't accept information simply because it is put forth by such offices and agencies. To quote a Russian proverb made famous by Ronald Reagan, "Trust, but verify."

## Dogmatism

Jack Shakley expresses strong opinions about the use of Native American mascots and logos. Is any part of his argument dogmatic? If so, where? If not, why not?

LINK TO P. 520

A writer who asserts or assumes that a particular position is the *only one* that is conceivably acceptable is expressing **dogmatism**, a fallacy of character that undermines the trust that must exist between those who make and listen to arguments. When people write dogmatically, they imply that no arguments are necessary: the truth is self-evident and needs no support.

Some arguments present claims so outrageous that they're unworthy of serious attention: attacks on the historical reality of the Holocaust fall into this category. But few subjects that can be defended with facts, testimony, and good reasons ought to be off the table in a free society. In general, whenever someone suggests that raising an issue for debate is totally unacceptable—whether on the grounds that it's racist, sexist, unpatriotic, blasphemous, insensitive, or offensive in some other way—you should be suspicious.

## *Ad Hominem* Arguments

***Ad hominem*** (Latin for "to the man") **arguments** attack the character of a person rather than the claims he or she makes: when you destroy the credibility of your opponents, you either destroy their ability to present reasonable appeals or distract from the successful arguments they may be offering. Here Christopher Hitchens questions whether former secretary of state Henry Kissinger should be appointed to head an important government commission:

> But can Congress and the media be expected to swallow the appointment of a proven coverup artist, a discredited historian, a busted liar, and a man who is wanted in many jurisdictions for the vilest of offenses?
>
> —Christopher Hitchens, "The Case against Henry Kissinger"

*Ad hominem* tactics like this turn arguments into two-sided affairs with good guys and bad guys, and that's unfortunate, since character often *does* matter in argument. People expect the proponent of peace to be civil, a secretary of the treasury to pay his taxes, and the champion of family values to be a faithful spouse. But it's fallacious to attack an idea by uncovering the foibles of its advocates or by attacking their motives, backgrounds, or unchangeable traits.

### Stacking the Deck

Just as gamblers try to stack the deck by arranging cards so they are sure to win, writers **stack the deck** when they show only one side of the story—the one in their favor. In a Facebook forum on the documentary film *Super Size Me* (which followed a thirty-two-year-old man who ate three meals a day at McDonald's for thirty days with drastic health consequences), one student points out an example of stacking the deck:

> One of the fallacies was stacking the deck. Spurlock stated many facts and gave plenty of evidence of what can happen if you eat fast food in abundunce. Weight gain, decline in health, habit forming, and a toll on your daily life. But he failed to show what could happen if you ate the fast food and participated in daily exercise and took vitamins. The fallacy is that he does not show us both sides of what can happen. Possibly you could eat McDonalds for three meals a day for thirty days and if you engaged in daily exercise and took vitamins maybe your health would be just fine. But we were not ever shown that side of the experiment.
>
> —Heather Tew Alleman, on a Facebook forum

In the same way, reviewers have often been critical of Michael Moore's documentaries, like *Sicko,* that resolutely show only one side of the story (in this case, the evils of American health care). When you stack the deck, you take a big chance that your readers will react like Heather and decide not to trust you: that's one reason it's so important to show that you have considered alternatives in making any argument.

## Fallacies of Logical Argument

You'll encounter a problem in any argument when the claims, warrants, or proofs in it are invalid, insufficient, or disconnected. In theory, such problems seem easy enough to spot, but in practice, they can be camouflaged by a skillful use of words or images. Indeed, logical fallacies pose a challenge to civil argument because they often seem reasonable and natural, especially when they appeal to people's self-interests. Whole industries (such as online psychics) depend on one or more of the logical fallacies for their existence. Political campaigns, too, rely on them in those ubiquitous fifteen-second TV spots.

### Hasty Generalization

A **hasty generalization** is an inference drawn from insufficient evidence: because *my* Honda broke down, then *all* Hondas must be junk. It also forms the basis for most stereotypes about people or institutions: because *a few* people in a large group are observed to act in a certain way, *all* members of that group are inferred to behave similarly. The resulting conclusions are usually sweeping claims of little merit: *Women are bad drivers*; *men are slobs*; *English teachers are nitpicky*; *computer jocks are* . . . , and on and on.

To draw valid inferences, you must always have sufficient evidence (see Chapter 17) and you must qualify your claims appropriately. After all, people do need generalizations to make reasonable decisions in life. Such claims can be offered legitimately if placed in context and tagged

"Google must be anti-American because the company decorates its famous logo for occasions such as the anniversary of *Sputnik*, Earth Day, and Persian New Year but not Memorial Day in the United States." A hasty generalization? Check "doodles" at Google, and decide for yourself.

with appropriate qualifiers—*some, a few, many, most, occasionally, rarely, possibly, in some cases, under certain circumstances, in my limited experience.*

## Faulty Causality

In Latin, this fallacy is known as *post hoc, ergo propter hoc*, which translates as "after this, therefore because of this"—the faulty assumption that because one event or action follows another, the first causes the second. Consider a lawsuit commented on in the *Wall Street Journal* in which a writer sued Coors (unsuccessfully), claiming that drinking copious amounts of the company's beer had kept him from writing a novel.

Some actions do produce reactions. Step on the brake pedal in your car, and you move hydraulic fluid that pushes calipers against disks to create friction that stops the vehicle. In other cases, however, a supposed connection between cause and effect turns out to be completely wrong. For example, doctors now believe that when an elderly person falls and breaks a hip or leg, the injury usually caused the fall rather than the other way around.

That's why overly simple causal claims should always be subject to scrutiny. In summer 2008, writer Nicholas Carr posed a simple causal question in a cover story for the *Atlantic*: "Is Google Making Us Stupid?" Carr essentially answered yes, arguing that "as we come to rely on computers to mediate our understanding of the world, it is our own intelligence that flattens" and that the more one is online the less he or she is able to concentrate or read deeply.

But others, like Jamais Cascio (senior fellow at the Institute for Ethics and Emerging Technologies) soon challenged that causal connection: rather than making us stupid, Cascio argues, Internet tools like Google will lead to the development of "fluid intelligence—the ability to find meaning in confusion and solve new problems, independent of acquired knowledge." The final word on this contentious causal relationship—the effects on the human brain caused by new technology—is still out, and will probably be available only after decades of intense research.

## Begging the Question

Most teachers have heard some version of the following argument: *You can't give me a C in this course; I'm an A student.* A member of Congress accused of taking kickbacks can make much the same argument: *I can't be*

*guilty of accepting such bribes; I'm an honest person.* In both cases, the claim is made on grounds that can't be accepted as true because those grounds themselves are in question. How can the accused bribe taker defend herself on grounds of honesty when that honesty is in doubt? Looking at the arguments in Toulmin terms helps to see the fallacy:

| | |
|---|---|
| Claim | You can't give me a C in this course . . . |
| Reason | . . . because I'm an A student. |
| Warrant | An A student is someone who can't receive Cs. |

| | |
|---|---|
| Claim | Representative X can't be guilty of accepting bribes . . . |
| Reason | . . . because she's an honest person. |
| Warrant | An honest person cannot be guilty of accepting bribes. |

With the warrants stated, you can see why **begging the question**—assuming as true the very claim that's disputed—is a form of circular argument that goes nowhere. (For more on Toulmin argument, see Chapter 7.)

## Equivocation

**Equivocations**—half truths or arguments that give lies an honest appearance—are usually based on tricks of language. Consider the plagiarist who copies a paper word for word from a source and then declares that "I wrote the entire paper myself"—meaning that she physically copied the piece on her own. But the plagiarist is using *wrote* equivocally and knows that most people understand the word to mean composing and not merely copying words. In the first decade of the twenty-first century, critics of the Bush administration said its many denials that *torture* was being used on U.S. prisoners abroad amounted to a

Baseball star Alex Rodriguez admitted that he had taken performance-enhancing drugs during the 2003 season, but said that "I don't know exactly what" and hinted that they may have been legal substances. Some expert observers think that's an equivocation—a dishonest play on the word *know*—since he tested positive for drugs that can't be obtained legally in the United States.

long series of equivocations. What Bush described as the CIA's use of "an alternative set of procedures" was just another equivocal phrase used to cover up what was really going on, which was torture, at least as defined by the Geneva Convention.

### Non Sequitur

A **non sequitur** is an argument whose claims, reasons, or warrants don't connect logically. Children are notably adept at framing non sequiturs like this one: *You don't love me or you'd buy me that bicycle!* Taking a look at the implied warrant shows no connection between love and bikes:

| | |
|---|---|
| Claim | You must not love me . . . |
| Reason | . . . because you haven't bought me that bicycle. |
| Warrant | Buying bicycles for children is essential to loving them. |

A five-year-old might buy that warrant, but no responsible adult would because love doesn't depend on buying bicycles.

Non sequiturs occur when writers omit a step in an otherwise logical chain of reasoning. For example, it's a non sequitur to argue that the poor performance of American students on international math exams means that the country should spend more money on math education. Such a conclusion might be justified if a correlation were known or found to exist between mathematical ability and money spent on education. But the students' performance might be poor for reasons other than education funding alone, so the logical connection fails.

### Straw Man

Those who resort to the **straw man** fallacy attack an argument that isn't really there, often a much weaker or more extreme one than the opponent is actually making. The speaker or writer "sets up a straw man" in this way to create an argument that's easy to knock down, proceeds to do so, and then claims victory over the opponent whose real argument was quite different. In *Arguing with Idiots,* Glenn Beck argues against "the idiot" who says that if we spent as much on education as we do on defense, all would be well, saying that:

> We are all familiar with the bumper stickers pining for the day that the defense budget goes to the schools and the Pentagon has to hold a bake sale, but comparing educational spending with national defense isn't particularly fair, clever, or logical.
>
> First of all, we have to spend money on defense because if we don't defend our country—well, the schools won't matter much. Take the Republic of Georgia, for instance. Do you really think citizens there are worried about standardized test scores or drunk Russian soldiers driving tanks down their streets?

Writing for *Media Matters* about "Glenn Beck and the Great Straw Man Massacre," critic Simon Maloy takes Beck to task for using the strategy in this passage:

> I'm not familiar with those bumper stickers, nor am I familiar with any public education advocates who argue that we stop spending money on national defense. And what does Georgia have to do with any of this? Does anyone begrudge Georgia for spending on its national defense? None of this makes any sense.

By suggesting that those who want to cut defense spending don't want to "defend our country," Beck is setting up a straw man.

### Red Herring

This fallacy gets its name from the old British hunting practice of dragging a dried herring across the path of the fox in order to throw the hounds off the trail. A **red herring** fallacy does just that: it changes the subject abruptly to throw readers or listeners off the trail.

In the highly political item above, from spring 2009, cartoonist William Warren depicts the red herring fallacy when he has President Obama interrupt his Supreme Court nominee Sonia Sotomayor as she replies to a question from a reporter about the Constitution. Obama's words represent what the cartoonist regards as red herring qualifications offered in defense of her appointment. When presented comically like this, red herrings may seem easy to spot. But be on the lookout for them whenever you read, and avoid them in your own writing. If you must resort to red herrings to support an argument, you probably should rethink your claim.

### Faulty Analogy

Comparisons can help to clarify one concept by measuring it against another that is more familiar. Consider how quickly you make a judgment about Britney Spears after reading this comparison with Madonna in a blog posting:

> She's, regardless of how hard she tries, not Madonna. To be fair, Madonna wasn't Madonna at first either, but emulating someone else—even if they're as successful as Madonna—usually doesn't work in the end.
>
> —Erik J. Barzeski, NSLog ( ); (blog)

Does the Berkeley College Republicans' Increase Diversity Bake Sale exhibit characteristics of being based upon a faulty analogy? Why or why not?

LINK TO P. 756

When comparisons are extended, they become *analogies*—ways of understanding unfamiliar ideas by comparing them with something that's already known. But useful as such comparisons are, they may prove false either taken on their own and pushed too far, or taken too seriously. At this point, they become **faulty analogies**—inaccurate or inconsequential comparisons between objects or concepts. An editorial in the *Taipei Times*, for example, found fault with analogies between Egypt and Taiwan in 2011:

> Following weeks of demonstrations in Egypt that ultimately forced former Egyptian president Hosni Mubarak to step down on Friday, some commentators have suggested that events in North Africa could serve as a catalyst for discontent with President Ma Ying-jeou. There are, however, a number of reasons why this analogy is wrongheaded and Taiwanese not only cannot—but should not—go down that road.
>
> For one, the situations in Egypt and Taiwan are very different. Taiwan does not have a radicalized and easily mobilized political opposition such as Egypt's Muslim Brotherhood, which has a long tradition of opposing despotic rule.

This editorial writer goes on to write a lengthy column analyzing the flaws in this analogy.

## RESPOND.

1. Examine each of the following political slogans or phrases for logical fallacies.

   "Resistance is futile." (Borg message on *Star Trek*)

   "It's the economy, stupid." (sign on the wall at Bill Clinton's campaign headquarters)

   "Remember the Alamo." (battle cry)

   "Make love, not war." (antiwar slogan popularized during the Vietnam War)

   "A chicken in every pot." (campaign slogan)

"Guns don't kill, people do." (NRA slogan)

"If you can't stand the heat, get out of the kitchen." (attributed to Harry S. Truman)

"Yes we can." (Obama campaign slogan)

2. Choose a paper you've written for a college class and analyze it for signs of fallacious reasoning. Then find an editorial, a syndicated column, and a news report on the same topic and look for fallacies in them. Which has the most fallacies—and what kind? What may be the role of the audience in determining when a statement is fallacious?
3. Find a Web site that is sponsored by an organization (the Future of Music Coalition, perhaps), business (Coca-Cola, Pepsi), or other group (the Democratic or Republican National Committee), and analyze the site for fallacious reasoning. Among other considerations, look at the relationship between text and graphics and between individual pages and the pages that surround or are linked to them. How does the technique of separating information into discrete pages affect the argument?
4. Political blogs such as DailyKos.com and InstaPundit.com typically provide quick responses to daily events and detailed critiques of material in other media sites, including national newspapers. Study one such blog for a few days to see whether and how the blogger critiques the material he or she links to. Does the blogger point to fallacies in arguments? If so, does he or she explain them or just assume readers understand them? Summarize your findings in an oral report to your class.

# 6
# Rhetorical Analysis

What do Bob Dylan, Lady Gaga, and Kanye West all have in common—beside the fact that all are successful and famous singers? *They all make commercial endorsements*. Lady Gaga's music videos are full of lucrative product placements, and she is now "creative director" for Polaroid, with her own line of "Grey Label" products. Kanye West launched a hangbag line with designer label Fendi. Even counterculture folk legend Bob Dylan—long considered a "virgin," that is, a celebrity who refused to give endorsements—eventually succumbed. In 2004, Dylan took the plunge, making his first-ever commercial—for women's underwear. (Check YouTube for related ads and videos.)

Such endorsements, and the contexts surrounding them, offer strong possibilities for analysis: Do such marketing strategies work? Are they truly effective? Media critic Seth Stevenson, writing in *Slate*, devoted a full column to analyzing Dylan's 2004 TV spot for Victoria's Secret, trying first to figure out why an artist of Dylan's stature would do a commercial endorsement for, of all things, women's lingerie, before turning to another intriguing question—how such ads work their persuasive magic:

> Why would a brand that's about sexiness, youth, and glamour want any connection at all with a decrepit, sixtysomething folksinger? The answer, my friend, is totally unclear. The answer is totally unclear.
>
> Even if Victoria's Secret hopes to bring in more boomer women, do those women want their underwear to exude the spirit and essence of Bob Dylan? Or, conversely, is Bob Dylan the sort of man they're hoping to attract? Even if you're of the belief that men frequently shop at VS for their ladies, I still don't see the appeal of this ad. I, for instance, am a man, and I can assure you that Bob Dylan is not what I'm looking for in a woman's undergarment. (And if I found him there—man, would that be disturbing.)
>
> Victoria's Secret wouldn't return my calls, but media reports say the idea of putting Dylan's face in the ad (they'd been using his song—"Love Sick"—in ads for the past year or so) came straight from corporate chief Les Wexner. To the company's surprise, Dylan accepted their offer. It's at this point that someone at Victoria's Secret should have stopped the madness. Just because you can hire Bob Dylan as the figurehead for your lingerie line, doesn't mean you should. Perhaps no one was willing to say no to the big boss, or perhaps they fully expected Dylan to say no. Joke's on them.
>
> —Seth Stevenson, "Tangled Up in Boobs"

To address the questions, Stevenson performs a brief **rhetorical analysis**—a close reading of a text to find how and whether it persuades. In these few paragraphs from a longer piece, Stevenson considers some of the basic strategies of argument we've explored in earlier chapters: First he identifies the ethos of Victoria's Secret ("sexiness, youth, and glamour") and finds it hard to reconcile with the ethos of the celebrity in the ad ("decrepit, sixtysomething"). He goes on to consider whether the ad might entice older men to buy expensive underwear for women but then rejects that approach: even men who shop for underwear at Victoria's Secret certainly don't want to think about Dylan when they do.

Along the way, Stevenson adds some humor with allusions to Dylan's songs, including his rendition of "Blowin' in the Wind" ("The answer, my friend, is totally unclear") and "Tangled Up in Blue" (the title of his article, "Tangled Up in Boobs"). Then Stevenson takes a step beyond the ad itself to ask whether having a superstar spokesperson like Bob Dylan might seem so cool that the advertisers don't even think about the other messages they might be sending. Stevenson's conclusion? "Joke's on them."

But was it? If Stevenson had dug a little deeper in his analysis, he might have discovered that during a 1960s press conference, when asked which he would choose if he ever decided to "sell out to a commercial interest," Dylan paused, smiled, and said "ladies' garments."[1] This bit of historical context suggests that Stevenson's conclusion ("Joke's on them") may be premature: Might Dylan have simply decided to honor his "promise" from decades earlier? Did someone at Victoria's Secret remember Dylan's comment and see if he would make good on what reporters at the time took as a facetious remark? Had he had this bit of information, Stevenson could have contextualized his analysis and possibly added another layer of irony to it.

As this example suggests, when you begin a rhetorical analysis, be prepared to follow every lead, to dig as deep as you can into the context in which the text you are analyzing exists. Especially when you encounter puzzling, troubling, or very successful appeals, a rhetorical analysis can help you to understand how they work. Begin by asking yourself what strategies the piece employs to move your heart, win your trust, and change your mind—and why it does or doesn't do so. Here's how.

## Composing a Rhetorical Analysis

Exactly how does an iPad ad make you want to buy one immediately? How does an op-ed piece in the *Washington Post* suddenly change your thinking about immigration? A rhetorical analysis might help you understand.

You perform a rhetorical analysis by analyzing how well the components of an argument work together to persuade or move an audience. You can study arguments of any kind—advertisements (as we've seen), editorials, political cartoons, and even songs, movies, or photographs. In every case, you'll need to focus your rhetorical analysis on elements that stand out or make the piece intriguing or problematic. You could begin by exploring issues such as the following:

- What is the purpose of this argument? What does it hope to achieve?
- Who is the audience for this argument?

[1] Thanks to Ryan Ireland of Wright State University for sending us the footage of Dylan's press conference and for noting that "in studying Dylan, one can never mistake a seemingly oddball maneuver for a misfire until significant time has passed."

- What appeals or techniques does the argument use—emotional, logical, ethical?
- What genre of argument is it, and how does the genre affect the argument? (While you might well challenge an argument in an op-ed that lacked sufficient evidence, you wouldn't make the same complaint about a bumper sticker.)
- Who is making the argument? What ethos does it create, and how does it do so? What values does the ethos evoke? How does it make the writer or creator seem trustworthy?
- What authorities does the argument rely on or appeal to?
- What facts, reasoning, and evidence are used in the argument? How are they presented?
- What claims does the argument make? What issues are raised—or ignored or evaded?
- What are the contexts—social, political, historical, cultural—for this argument? Whose interests does it serve? Who gains or loses by it?
- How is the argument organized or arranged? What media does the argument use?
- How does the language or style of the argument work to persuade an audience?

In answering such questions, try to show *how* the key devices in an argument actually make it succeed or fail. Quote freely from a written piece, or describe the elements in a visual argument. (Annotating a visual text is one option.) Show readers where and why an argument makes sense and where it falls apart. If you believe that an argument startles, challenges, insults, or lulls audiences, explain just why that's so, and provide evidence. Don't be surprised when your rhetorical analysis itself becomes an argument. That's what it should be.

## Understanding the Purpose of Arguments You Are Analyzing

To understand how well any argument works, begin with its purpose: Is it to sell running shoes? To advocate for limits to college tuition? To push a political agenda? In many cases, that purpose may be obvious. A conservative blog will likely advance right-wing causes; ads from a baby food company will likely show happy infants delighted with stewed prunes.

But some projects may be indirect about their persuasive intentions. Perhaps you've responded to a mail survey or telephone poll only to discover that the questions are leading you to switch your cell phone service. Does such a stealthy argument succeed? Answering this question provides material for a thoughtful rhetorical analysis in which you measure the strengths, risks, and ethics of such strategies.

## Understanding Who Makes an Argument

Knowing *who* is claiming *what* is key to any rhetorical analysis. That's why persuasive appeals usually have a name attached to them. Remember the statements included in TV ads during the last federal election: "Hello, I'm X—and I approve this ad"? Federal law requires such statements so we can tell the difference between ads a candidate endorses and ones sponsored by groups not even affiliated with the campaigns. Their interests and motives might be very different.

But knowing a name is just a starting place for analysis. You need to dig deeper, and you could do worse than to Google such people or groups to discover more about them. What else have they produced? Who publishes them: the *Wall Street Journal*, the blog DailyKos, or even a LiveJournal celebrity gossip site such as *Oh No They Didn't?* Check out related Web sites for information about goals, policies, contributors, and funding.

Funny, offensive, or both?

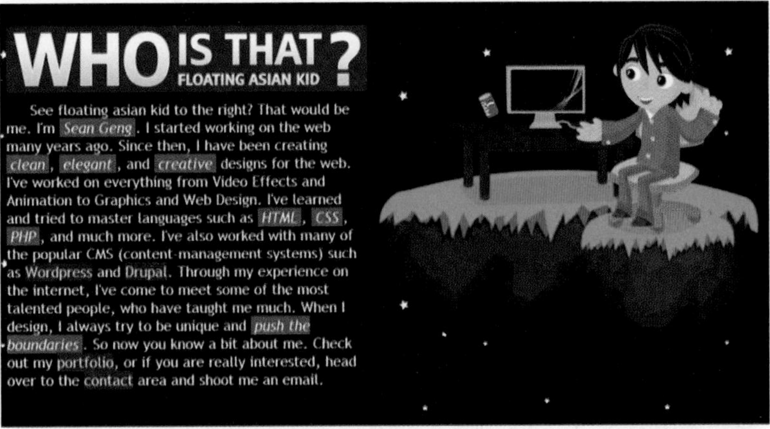


The blogger bio: required reading for rhetorical analysis

**RESPOND•**

Describe a persuasive moment that you can recall from a speech, an editorial, an advertisement, a YouTube clip, or a blog posting. Or research one of the following famous persuasive moments and describe the circumstances—the historical situation, the issues at stake, the purpose of the argument—that make it so memorable.

Abraham Lincoln's "Gettysburg Address" (1863)

Elizabeth Cady Stanton's "Declaration of Sentiments" at the Seneca Falls Convention (1848)

Chief Tecumseh's address to General William Henry Harrison (1810)

Winston Churchill's addresses to the British people during World War II (1940)

Martin Luther King Jr.'s "Letter from Birmingham Jail" (1963)

Ronald Reagan's tribute to the *Challenger* astronauts (1986)

Toni Morrison's speech accepting the Nobel Prize (1993)

Will.i.am and the Black Eyed Peas' "Yes We Can" song/collage on YouTube (2008)

## Identifying and Appealing to Audiences

Most arguments are composed with specific audiences in mind, and their success depends, in part, on how well their strategies, content, tone, and language meet the expectations of that audience. So your rhetorical analysis of an argumentative piece should identify its target readers or viewers (see Audiences for Arguments on pp. 22–25) if possible, or make an educated guess about the audience, since most arguments suggest whom they intend to reach and in what ways.

Both a flyer stapled to a bulletin board in a college dorm ("Why you shouldn't drink and drive") and a forty-foot billboard for Bud Lite might be aimed at the same general population—college students. But each will adjust its appeals for the different moods of that group in different moments. For starters, the flyer will appeal to students in a serious vein, while the beer ad will probably be visually stunning and virtually text-free.

You might also examine how a writer or an argument establishes credibility with an audience. One effective means of building credibility is to show respect for your readers or viewers, especially if they may not agree with you. In introducing an article on problems facing African American women in the workplace, editor in chief of *Essence* Diane Weathers considers the problems that she faced with respecting all her potential readers:

> We spent more than a minute agonizing over the provocative cover line for our feature "White Women at Work." The countless stories we had heard from women across the country told us that this was a workplace issue we had to address. From my own experience at several major magazines, it was painfully obvious to me that Black and White women are not on the same track. Sure, we might all start out in the same place. But early in the game, most sisters I know become stuck—and the reasons have little to do with intelligence or drive. At some point we bump our heads against that ceiling. And while White women may complain of a glass ceiling, for us, the ceiling is concrete.
>
> So how do we tell this story without sounding whiny and paranoid, or turning off our White-female readers, staff members, advertisers and girlfriends? Our solution: Bring together real women (several of them highly successful senior corporate executives), put them in a room, promise them anonymity and let them speak their truth.
>
> —Diane Weathers, "Speaking Our Truth"

Retailers like Walmart build their credibility by simple "straight talk" to shoppers: our low prices make your life better.

Both paragraphs affirm Weathers's determination to treat audiences fairly *and* to deal honestly with a difficult subject. The strategy would merit attention in any rhetorical analysis.

Look, too, for signals that writers share values with readers or at least understand an audience. In the following passage, writer Jack Solomon is clear about one value that he hopes readers have in common—a preference for "straight talk":

> There are some signs in the advertising world that Americans are getting fed up with fantasy advertisements and want to hear some straight talk. Weary of extravagant product claims . . . consumers trained by years of advertising to distrust what they hear seem to be developing an immunity to commercials.
>
> —Jack Solomon, "Masters of Desire: The Culture of American Advertising"

It's increasingly important for writers of novels and film scripts to appeal to more than just a small niche audience. Here Amazon.com reviewer Andi Miller gives her take on Brian Selznick's *The Invention of Hugo*

*Cabret*, which was the inspiration for the recent Martin Scorsese film *Hugo*: "Selznick's creation navigates the grey area between picture book and graphic novel in what certainly constitutes a visual and narrative achievement and a truly original book." After a quick summary, Miller goes on to provide a brief rhetorical analysis that backs up her claim, that *The Invention of Hugo Cabret* is compelling for readers of all ages:

> While the novel largely defies categorization, it closely resembles a silent film in many respects, and fittingly so. In addition to the novel's rich illustrations, Selznick employs photos and movie stills to show the reader his story as opposed to simply telling it. In the tradition of graphic narrative (or sequential art, whatever your term of choice), the illustrations play as integral a role in the overall story as the text. The use of illustrations is hardly gratuitous, for the pictures quite literally take over and carry out the narrative when the text disappears. And, really, who would care if the illustrations were gratuitous? They're gorgeous.
>
> *The Invention of Hugo Cabret* is full of magic—for the child reader, for the adult reader, the film lover, the art lover, for anyone willing to give it a go. If you're scared of the size or the concept, don't be. Open your mind, pour Selznick's creation in, and be reminded of the dream of childhood.

## Examining Arguments Based on Emotion: Pathos

Some emotional appeals are just ploys to win over readers with a pretty face, figurative or real. You've seen ads promising an exciting life and attractive friends if only you drink the right soda or wear a particular brand of clothes. Are you fooled by such claims? Probably not, if you pause to think about them. But that's the strategy—to distract you from thought just long enough to make a bad choice. It's a move worth commenting on in a rhetorical analysis.

Yet emotions can add real muscle to arguments, too, and that's worth noting. For example, persuading people not to drink and drive by making them fear death, injury, or arrest seems like a fair use of an emotional appeal. The public service announcement on page 99 uses an emotion-laden image to remind drivers to think of the consequences.

In a rhetorical analysis, you might note the juxtaposition of image with text, leading readers to connect casual notes left on windshields with the very serious consequences of drunk driving.

How well does the emotional appeal here work?

In analyzing emotional appeals, judge whether the emotions raised—anger, sympathy, fear, envy, joy, or love—advance the claims offered. Consider how columnist and novelist Lionel Shriver uses concrete and graphic language to evoke disgust with SUVs—and anyone who owns one—at a time of soaring gas prices:

> Filling the tank of an SUV in the U.S. has now crossed the psychologically traumatizing $100 mark. The resale value of these monsters is plummeting, and many owners are getting stuck with the things, like holding the Old Maid in cards. I greet this news with sadistic glee. People who bought SUVs were fools and I want them to suffer. Not just because I'm a sanctimonious greenie, but because I'm an aesthete. Sure, SUVs are petro-pigs, and they side-swipe cyclists into the curb. Yes, they emblemize everything about Americans the rest of the world detests: greedy, wasteful, and oblivious to the future. But on top of all that, they're ugly.
>
> —Lionel Shriver, "If the U.S. Election Were a Novel"

Does the use of pathos ("monsters," "petro-pigs") convince you, or does it distract from or undermine the claim that SUVs are ugly? Your task in a rhetorical analysis is to study an author's words, the emotions they evoke, and the claims they support and then to make this kind of judgment.

**RESPOND.**

Browse YouTube or another Web site to find an example of a powerful emotional argument that's made visually, either alone or using words as well. In a paragraph, defend a claim about how the argument works. For example, does an image itself make a claim, or does it draw you in to consider a verbal claim? What emotion does the argument generate? How does that emotion work to persuade you?

## Examining Arguments Based on Character: Ethos

The listener comments that accompany Adriene Hill's radio report frequently raise points that question the ethos of her reporting.

LINK TO P. 696

It should come as no surprise: readers believe writers who seem honest, wise, and trustworthy. So in analyzing the effectiveness of an argument, look for evidence of these traits. Does the writer have the experience or authority to write on this subject? Are all claims qualified reasonably? Is evidence presented in full, not tailored to the writer's agenda? Are important objections to the author's position acknowledged and addressed? Are sources documented? Above all, does the writer sound trustworthy?

When a Norwegian anti-immigration extremist killed seventy-six innocent people in July 2011, Prime Minister Jens Stoltenberg addressed the citizens of Norway (and the world), and in doing so evoked the character or ethos of the entire nation:

> **We will not let fear break us! The warmth of response from people in Norway and from the whole world makes me sure of this one thing: evil can kill a single person, but never defeat a whole people. The strongest weapon in the world—that is freedom of expression and democracy.**

In analyzing this speech, you would do well to look at the way this passage deploys the deepest values of Norway—freedom of expression and democracy—to serve as a response to fear of terrorism. In doing so, Stoltenberg evokes ethical ideals to hold onto in a time of tragedy.

Or take a look at the following paragraph from a blog posting by Timothy Burke, a teacher at Swarthmore College and parent of a preschool child who is trying to think through the issue of homework for elementary school kids:

> So I've been reading a bit about homework, and comparing notes with parents. There is a lot of variation across districts, not just in the amount of homework that kids are being asked to do, but in the kind of homework. Some districts give kids a lot of time-consuming busywork, other districts try to concentrate on having homework assignments be substantive work that is best accomplished independently. Some give a lot from a very early point in K–12 education, some give relatively little. As both a professional educator and an individual with personal convictions, I'd tend to argue against excessive amounts of homework and against assigning busywork. But what has ultimately interested me more about reading various discussions of homework is how intense the feelings are swirling around the topic, and how much that intensity strikes me as a problem in and of itself. Not just as a symptom of a kind of civic illness, an inability to collectively and democratically work through complex issues, but also in some cases as evidence of an educational failure in its own right.

Burke establishes his ethos by citing his reading and his talks with other parents.

Burke considers alternatives (though he then states his tentative preference).

He criticizes immoderate arguments as "a kind of civic illness" (and suggests that he will demonstrate the opposite of such an approach).

In considering the role of ethos in rhetorical analyses, you must pay attention to the details, right down to the choice of words or, in an image, the shapes and colors. The modest, tentative tone that Burke uses in his blog is an example of the kind of choice that can shape an audience's perception of ethos. But these details need your interpretation. Language that's hot and extreme can mark a writer as either passionate or loony. Work that's sober and carefully organized can paint an institution as competent or overly cautious. Technical terms and abstract phrases can make a writer seem either knowledgeable or pompous.

## Examining Arguments Based on Facts and Reason: Logos

In analyzing most arguments, you'll have to decide whether an argument makes a plausible claim and offers good reasons for you to believe it. Not all arguments will package such claims in a single neat sentence, or **thesis**—nor should they. A writer may tell a story from which you have to infer the claim. Visual arguments may work the same way: viewers have to assemble the parts and draw inferences before they get the point.

Some conventional arguments (like those on an editorial page), may be perfectly obvious: writers stake out a claim and then present reasons that you should consider, or they may first present reasons and lay out a case that leads you to accept a claim in the conclusion. Consider the following examples. The first comes from the conclusion of an August 22, 2008, editorial in the *New York Times*; the second from a petition letter for a "nuclear-free California" sponsored by change.org:

> To win the right to host [the Olympic] Games, China promised to honor the Olympic ideals of nonviolence, openness to the world and individual expression. Those promises were systematically broken, starting with this spring's brutal repression in Tibet and continuing on to the ugly farce of inviting its citizens to apply for legal protest permits and then arresting them if they actually tried to do so. . . .
>
> Surely one of the signature events of these Games was the sentencing of two women in their late 70s to "re-education through labor." Their crime? Applying for permission to protest the inadequate compensation they felt they had received when the government seized their homes years ago for urban redevelopment.
>
> A year ago, the I.O.C. predicted that these Games would be "a force for good" and a spur to human-rights progress. Instead, as Human Rights Watch has reported, they became a catalyst for intensified human-rights abuse.
>
> —"Beijing's Bad Faith Olympics," *New York Times*

Ban Nuclear Power Plants in California

Greetings:

The Fukushima, Three Mile Island, and Chernobyl nuclear power disasters have shown us that nuclear power is not safe. As an area prone to frequent earthquakes, California is an especially dangerous place to host a nuclear power plant.

We, the undersigned call for:

—No new nuclear plants.
—Closing existing plants as quickly as safely possible.
—Seeking and implementing greener energy solutions.

[Your Name]

When you analyze explicit claims like these, you look at how they are supported by good reasons and reliable evidence. A lengthy essay may, in fact, contain a series of claims, each developed to support an even larger point. Indeed, every paragraph in an argument may develop a specific and related idea. In a rhetorical analysis, you need to identify all these separate propositions and examine the relationships among them: Are they solidly linked? Are there inconsistencies that the writer should acknowledge? Does the end of the piece support what the writer said (and promised) at the beginning?

You'll also need to examine the quality of the information presented in an argument, assessing how accurately such information is reported, how conveniently it's displayed (in charts or graphs, for

This protester's T-shirt asks you to consider the dangers of nuclear power.

example), and how well the sources cited represent a range of *respected* opinion on a topic. (For more information on the use of evidence, see Chapter 4.)

Knowing how to judge the quality of sources is more important now than ever before because the digital universe is full of junk. In some ways, the computer terminal has become the equivalent of a library reference room, but the sources available online vary widely in quality and have not been evaluated by a library professional. As a consequence, you must know the difference between reliable, firsthand, or fully documented sources and those that don't meet such standards. (For using and documenting sources, see Chapters 18, 19, and 21.)

## Examining the Arrangement and Media of Arguments

Aristotle carved the structure of logical argument to its bare bones when he observed that it had only two parts:

- statement
- proof

You could do worse, in examining an argument, than to make sure that every claim a writer makes is backed by sufficient evidence. Some arguments are written on the fly in the heat of the moment. Most arguments that you read and write, however, will be more than mere statements followed by proofs. Some writers will lay their cards on the table immediately; others may lead you carefully through a chain of claims toward a conclusion. Writers may even interrupt their arguments to offer background information or cultural contexts for readers. Sometimes they'll tell stories or provide anecdotes that make an argumentative point. They'll qualify the arguments they make, too, and often pause to admit that other points of view are plausible.

In other words, there are no formulas or acceptable patterns that fit all successful arguments. In writing a rhetorical analysis, you'll have to assess the organization of a persuasive text on its own merits.

It's fair, however, to complain about what may be *absent* from an argument. Most arguments of proposal (see Chapter 12), for example, include a section that defends the feasibility of a new idea, explaining how it might be funded or managed. In a rhetorical analysis, you might fault an editorial that supports a new stadium for a city without addressing feasibility issues. Similarly, analyzing a movie review that reads like an off-the-top-of-the-head opinion, you might legitimately ask what criteria of evaluation are in play (see Chapter 10).

Rhetorical analysis also calls for you to look carefully at an argument's transitions, headings and subheadings, documentation of sources, and overall tone or voice. Don't take such details for granted, since all of them contribute to the strength—or weakness—of an argument.

Nor should you ignore the way a writer or an institution uses media. Would an argument originally made in a print editorial, for instance, work better as a spoken presentation (or vice versa)? Would a lengthy paper have more power if it included more images? Or do these images distract from a written argument's substance?

Finally, be open to the possibility of new or nontraditional structures of arguments. The visual arguments that you analyze may defy conventional principles of logic or arrangement—for example, making juxtapositions rather than logical transitions between elements or using quick cuts, fades, or other devices to link ideas. Quite often, these nontraditional structures will also resist the neatness of a thesis, leaving readers to construct at least a part of the argument in their heads. Advertisers are growing fond of soft-sell multimedia productions that can seem more like entertainment than what they really are—product pitches. We're asked not just to buy a product but also to live its lifestyle. Is that a reasonable or workable strategy for an argument? Your analysis might entertain such possibilities.

## Looking at Style

Even a coherent argument full of sound evidence may not connect with readers if it's dull, off-key, or offensive. Readers naturally judge the credibility of arguments in part by how stylishly the case is made—even when they don't know exactly what style is. Consider how these simple, blunt sentences from the opening of an argument shape your image of the author and probably determine whether you're willing to continue to read the whole piece:

> **We are young, urban, and professional. We are literate, respectable, intelligent, and charming. But foremost and above all, we are unemployed.**
>
> **—Julia Carlisle, "Young, Privileged, and Unemployed"**

The strong, straightforward tone and the stark juxtaposition of being "intelligent" with "unemployed" set the style for this letter to the editor.

Now consider the humorous and slightly sarcastic tone of the following series of questions that makes an argument about the intelligence of voters in South Florida during the electoral disaster of 2000:

> The question you're asking yourself is: Does South Florida contain the highest concentration of morons in the entire world? Or just in the United States? The reason you're asking this, of course, is South Florida's performance in Tuesday's election.
>
> —Dave Barry, "How to Vote in One Easy Step"

Both styles probably work, but they signal that the writers are about to make very different kinds of cases. Here, style alone tells readers what to expect.

Manipulating style also enables writers to shape readers' responses to their ideas. Devices as simple as sentence length, alliteration, or parallelism can give sentences remarkable power. Consider this passage from a review of *The Other Barack,* about President Obama's father:

> [I]f Obama Sr. were only a jerk, there wouldn't be any reason to read about him, regardless of who his son turned out to be. But there is. Like the president, Obama Sr. was also a brilliant, ambitious idealist who overcame the limited circumstances of his background to attend the best schools in the world, then set out to participate in a movement of vast political promise. That he failed so spectacularly, and that his son succeeded, says a lot about the qualities of character that can distinguish a leader from a lout.
>
> —Andrew Romano, "Who Was Barack Obama's Father?"

In this short passage, Romano uses a very short sentence ("But there is."), alliteration ("a leader from a lout"), and parallelism ("failed so spectacularly" and "succeeded") to paint a complex picture of Barack Obama Sr.

In a rhetorical analysis, you can explore such stylistic choices. Why does a formal style work for discussing one type of subject matter but not another? How does a writer use humor or irony to underscore an important point or to manage a difficult concession? Do stylistic choices, even something as simple as the use of contractions or personal pronouns, bring readers close to a writer, or do technical words and an impersonal voice signal that an argument is for experts only?

To describe the stylistic effects of visual arguments, you may use a different vocabulary and talk about colors, camera angles, editing, balance, proportion, fonts, perspective, and so on. But the basic principle is

This poster, promoting travel to the bicycle-friendly city of Münster, Germany, demonstrates visually the amount of space needed to transport the same number of people by car, bicycle, and bus.

this: the look of an item—whether a poster, an editorial cartoon, or a film documentary—can support the message that it carries, undermine it, or muddle it. In some cases, the look will *be* the message. In a rhetorical analysis, you can't ignore style.

**RESPOND.**

Find a recent example of a visual argument, either in print or on the Internet. Even though you may have a copy of the image, describe it carefully in your paper on the assumption that your description is all readers may have to go on. Then make a judgment about its effectiveness, supporting your claim with clear evidence from the "text."

## Examining a Rhetorical Analysis

On the following pages, well-known political commentator and columnist for the *New York Times*, David Brooks, argues that today's college graduates have been poorly prepared for life after college because of what he sees as a radical excess of supervision. Responding to it with a detailed analysis is Rachel Kolb, a student at Stanford University.

# It's Not about You

## DAVID BROOKS

Over the past few weeks, America's colleges have sent another class of graduates off into the world. These graduates possess something of inestimable value. Nearly every sensible middle-aged person would give away all their money to be able to go back to age 22 and begin adulthood anew.

But, especially this year, one is conscious of the many ways in which this year's graduating class has been ill served by their elders. They enter a bad job market, the hangover from decades of excessive borrowing. They inherit a ruinous federal debt.

More important, their lives have been perversely structured. This year's graduates are members of the most supervised generation in American history. Through their childhoods and teenage years, they have been monitored, tutored, coached and honed to an unprecedented degree.

Yet upon graduation they will enter a world that is unprecedentedly wide open and unstructured. Most of them will not quickly get married, buy a home and have kids, as previous generations did. Instead, they will confront amazingly diverse job markets, social landscapes and lifestyle niches. Most will spend a decade wandering from job to job and clique to clique, searching for a role.

No one would design a system of extreme supervision to prepare people for a decade of extreme openness. But this is exactly what has emerged in modern America. College students are raised in an environment that demands one set of navigational skills, and they are then cast out into a different environment requiring a different set of skills, which they have to figure out on their own.

Worst of all, they are sent off into this world with the whole baby-boomer theology ringing in their ears. If you sample some of the commencement addresses being broadcast on C-Span these days, you see that many graduates are told to: Follow your passion, chart your own course, march to the beat of your own drummer, follow your dreams and find yourself. This is the litany of expressive individualism, which is still the dominant note in American culture.

But, of course, this mantra misleads on nearly every front.

College grads are often sent out into the world amid rapturous talk of limitless possibilities. But this talk is of no help to the central business of adulthood, finding serious things to tie yourself down to. The successful young adult is beginning to make sacred commitments—to a spouse, a community and calling—yet mostly hears about freedom and autonomy.

Today's graduates are also told to find their passion and then pursue their dreams. The implication is that they should find themselves first and then go off and live their quest. But, of course, very few people at age 22 or 24 can take an inward journey and come out having discovered a developed self.

Most successful young people don't look inside and then plan a life. They look outside and find a problem, which summons their life. A relative suffers from Alzheimer's and a young woman feels called to help cure that disease. A young man works under a miserable boss and must develop management skills so his department can function. Another young woman finds herself confronted by an opportunity she never thought of in a job category she never imagined. This wasn't in her plans, but this is where she can make her contribution.

Most people don't form a self and then lead a life. They are called by a problem, and the self is constructed gradually by their calling.

The graduates are also told to pursue happiness and joy. But, of course, when you read a biography of someone you admire, it's rarely the things that made them happy that compel your admiration. It's the things they did to court unhappiness—the things they did that were arduous and miserable, which sometimes cost them friends and aroused hatred. It's excellence, not happiness, that we admire most.

Finally, graduates are told to be independent-minded and to express their inner spirit. But, of course, doing your job well often means suppressing yourself. As Atul Gawande mentioned during his countercultural address last week at Harvard Medical School, being a good doctor often means being part of a team, following the rules of an institution, going down a regimented checklist.

Today's grads enter a cultural climate that preaches the self as the center of a life. But, of course, as they age, they'll discover that the tasks of a life are at the center. Fulfillment is a byproduct of how people engage their tasks, and can't be pursued directly. Most of us are egotistical and most are self-concerned most of the time, but it's nonetheless true that life comes to a point only in those moments when the self dissolves into some task. The purpose in life is not to find yourself. It's to lose yourself.

# Understanding Brooks's Binaries

RACHEL KOLB

Connects article to personal experience to create an ethical appeal.

Provides brief overview of Brooks's argument.

States Brooks's central claim.

As a high school and college student, I was given an incredible range of educational and extracurricular options, from interdisciplinary studies to summer institutes to student-organized clubs. Although today's students have more opportunities to adapt their educations to their specific personal goals, as I did, David Brooks argues that the structure of the modern educational system nevertheless leaves young people ill-prepared to meet the challenges of the real world. In his *New York Times* editorial "It's Not about You," Brooks illustrates excessive supervision and uncontrolled individualistic rhetoric as opposing problems that complicate young people's entry into adult life, which then becomes less of a natural progression than an outright paradigm shift. Brooks's argument itself mimics the pattern of moving from "perversely structured" youth to "unprecedentedly wide open" adulthood: it operates on the basis of binary oppositions, raising familiar notions about how to live one's life and then dismantling them. Throughout the piece, it relies less on factual evidence than on Brooks's own authoritative tone and skill in using rhetorical devices.

Transition sentence.

In his editorial, Brooks objects to mainstream cultural messages that sell students on individuality, but bases his conclusions more on general observations than on specific facts. His argument is, in itself, a loose form of rhetorical analysis. It opens by telling us to "sample some of the commencement addresses being broadcast on C-Span these days," where we will find messages such as: "Follow your passion, chart your own course, march to the beat of your own drummer, follow your dreams and find yourself." As though moving down a checklist, it then scrutinizes the problems with this rhetoric of "expressive individualism." Finally, it turns to Atul Gawande's "countercultural address" about working collectively, en route to confronting the individualism of modern America. C-Span and Harvard Medical School aside, however, Brooks's argument is astonishingly short on external sources. He cites no basis for claims such as "this year's graduates are members of the most supervised generation in American history" or "most successful young people don't look inside and then plan a life," despite the fact that these claims are fundamental to his observations. Instead, his argument persuades through painting a picture—first of "limitless possibilities," then of young men and women called into action by problems that "summon their life"—and hoping that we will find the illustration familiar.

Comments critically on author's use of evidence.

Instead of relying on the logos of his argument, Brooks assumes that his position as a baby boomer and *New York Times* columnist will provide a sufficient enough ethos to validate his claims. If this impression of age and social status did not enter our minds along with his bespectacled portrait, Brooks reminds us of it. Although he refers to the theology of the baby boomer generation as the "worst of all," from the beginning of his editorial he allots himself as another "sensible middle-aged person" and distances himself from college graduates by referring to them as "they" or as "today's grads," contrasting with his more inclusive reader-directed "you." Combined with his repeated use of passive sentence constructions that create a confusing sense of responsibility ("The graduates are sent off into the world"; "the graduates are told"), this sense of distance could be alienating to the younger audiences for which this editorial seems intended. Granted, Brooks compensates for it by embracing themes of "excellence" and "fulfillment" and by opening up his message to "most of us" in his final paragraph, but nevertheless his self-defined persona has its limitations. Besides dividing his audience, Brooks risks reminding us that, just as his observations belong only to this persona, his arguments apply only to a subset of American society. More specifically, they apply only to the well-educated middle to upper class who might be more likely to fret after the implications of "supervision" and "possibilities," or the

Analyzes author's intended audience.

readers who would be most likely to flip through the *New York Times*.

Brooks overcomes his limitations in logos and ethos through his piece's greatest strength: its style. He effectively frames cultural messages in binaries in order to reinforce the disconnect that exists between what students are told and what they will face as full members of society. Throughout his piece, he states one assumption after another, then prompts us to consider its opposite. "Serious things" immediately take the place of "rapturous talk"; "look[ing] inside" replaces "look[ing] outside"; "suppressing yourself" becomes an alternative to being "independent-minded." Brooks's argument is consumed with dichotomies, culminating with his statement "It's excellence, not happiness, that we admire most." He frames his ideas within a tight framework of repetition and parallel structure, creating muscular prose intended to engage his readers. His repeated use of the phrase "but, of course" serves as a metronomic reminder, at once echoing his earlier assertions and referring back to his air of authority.

Closely analyzes Brooks's style.

Brooks illustrates the power of words in swaying an audience, and in his final paragraph his argument shifts beyond commentary. Having tested our way of thinking, he now challenges us to change. His editorial closes with one final binary, the claim that "The purpose in life is not to find yourself" but "to lose yourself." And, although some of Brooks's previous binaries have clanged with oversimplification, this one rings truer. In accordance with his adoption of the general "you," his concluding message need not apply only to college graduates. By unfettering its restrictions at its climax, Brooks liberates his argument. After all, only we readers bear the responsibility of reflecting, of justifying, and ultimately of determining how to live our lives.

Analyzes author's conclusion.

## Work Cited

Brooks, David. "It's Not about You." *Everything's an Argument*. Ed. Andrea A. Lunsford and John J. Ruszkiewicz. 6th ed. Boston: Bedford, 2013, 108–10. Print. Rpt. of "It's Not about You." *New York Times* 30 May 2011.

## GUIDE to writing a rhetorical analysis

### Finding a Topic

A rhetorical analysis is usually assigned: you're asked to show how an argument works and to assess its effectiveness. When you can choose your own subject for analysis, look for one or more of the following qualities:

- a complex verbal or visual argument that challenges you—or disturbs or pleases you
- a text that raises current or enduring issues of substance
- a text that you believe should be taken more seriously

Look for arguments to analyze in the editorial and op-ed pages of any newspaper, political magazines such as the *Nation* or *National Review*, Web sites of organizations and interest groups, political blogs such as DailyKos.com or Powerline.com, corporate Web sites that post their TV ad spots, videos and statements posted to YouTube, and so on.

### Researching Your Topic

Once you've got a text to analyze, find out all you can about it. Use the library or resources of the Web to explore:

- who the author is and what his or her credentials are
- if the author is an institution, what it does, what its sources of funding are, who its members are, and so on
- who is publishing or sponsoring the piece, and what the organization typically publishes
- what the leanings or biases of the author and publisher might be
- what the context of the argument is—what preceded or provoked it and how others have responded to it

### Formulating a Claim

Begin with a hypothesis. A full thesis might not become evident until you're well into your analysis, but your final thesis should reflect the complexity of the piece that you're studying. In developing a thesis, consider questions such as the following:

- How can I describe what this argument achieves?
- What is the purpose, and is it accomplished?
- What audiences does the argument address and what audiences does it ignore, and why?
- Which of its rhetorical features will likely influence readers most: Ethos of the author? Emotional appeals? Style?
- What aspects of the argument work better than others?
- How do the rhetorical elements interact?

Here's the hardest part for most writers of rhetorical analyses: whether you agree or disagree with an argument doesn't matter in a rhetorical analysis. You've got to stay out of the fray and pay attention only to how—and to how well—the argument works.

## Examples of Possible Claims for a Rhetorical Analysis

- Many people admire the vision and eloquence of President Obama; others are put off by his often distant tone and his "professorial" stance. A close look at several of his speeches will illuminate both sides of this debate.
- Today's editorial in the *Daily Collegian* about campus crimes may scare first-year students, but its anecdotal reporting doesn't get down to hard numbers—and for a good reason. Those statistics don't back the position taken by the editors.
- The imageboard 4chan has been called an "Internet hate machine," yet others claim it as a great boon to creativity. A close analysis of its homepage can help to settle this debate.
- The original design of New York's Freedom Tower, with its torqued surfaces and evocative spire, made a stronger argument about American values than its replacement, a fortress-like skyscraper stripped of imagination and unable to make any statement except "I'm 1,776 feet tall."

## Preparing a Proposal

If your instructor asks you to prepare a proposal for your rhetorical analysis, here's a format you might use:

- Provide a copy of the work you're analyzing, whether it's a print text, a photograph, digital image, or URL, for instance.
- Offer a working hypothesis or tentative thesis.
- Indicate which rhetorical components seem especially compelling and worthy of detailed study and any connections between elements. For example, does the piece seem to emphasize facts and logic so much that it becomes disconnected from potential audiences? If so, hint at that possibility in your proposal.
- Indicate background information—about the author, institution, and contexts (political, economic, social, and religious) of the argument—you intend to research.
- Define the audience you'd like to reach. If you're responding to an assignment, you may be writing primarily for a teacher and classmates. But they make up a complex audience in themselves. If you can do so within the spirit of the assignment, imagine that your analysis will be published in a local newspaper, Web site, or blog.
- Suggest the media that you might use. Will a traditional essay work best? Could you use highlighting or other word-processing tools to focus attention on stylistic details? Would it be possible to use balloons, boxes, or other callouts to annotate a visual argument?
- Conclude by briefly discussing the key challenges you anticipate in preparing.

## Thinking about Content and Organization

Your rhetorical analysis is likely to include the following:

- Facts about the text you're analyzing: Provide the author's name; the title or name of the work; its place of publication or its location; the date it was published or viewed.
- Contexts for the argument: Readers need to know where the text is coming from, to what it may be responding, in what controversies it might be embroiled, and so on. Don't assume that they can infer the important contextual elements.
- A synopsis of the text that you're analyzing: If you can't attach the original argument, you must summarize it in enough detail so that a reader can imagine it. Even if you attach a copy of the piece, the analysis should include a summary.

- Some claim about the work's rhetorical effectiveness: It might be a simple evaluative claim or something more complex. The claim can come early in the paper, or you might build up to it, providing the evidence that leads toward the conclusion you've reached.
- A detailed analysis of how the argument works: Although you'll probably analyze rhetorical components separately, don't let your analysis become a dull roster of emotional, ethical, and logical appeals. Your rhetorical analysis should be an argument itself that supports a claim; a simple list of rhetorical appeals won't make much of a point.
- Evidence for every part of the analysis.
- An assessment of alternative views and counterarguments to your own analysis.

## Getting and Giving Response: Questions for Peer Response

If you have access to a writing center, discuss the text that you intend to analyze with a writing consultant before you write the paper. Try to find people who agree with the argument and others who disagree, and take notes on their observations. Your instructor may assign you to a peer group for the purpose of reading and responding to one another's drafts; if not, share your draft with someone on your own. You can use the following questions to evaluate a draft. If you're evaluating someone else's draft, be sure to illustrate your points with examples. Specific comments are always more helpful than general observations.

### *The Claim*

- Does the claim address the rhetorical effectiveness of the argument itself rather than the opinion or position that it takes?
- Is the claim significant enough to interest readers?
- Does the claim indicate important relationships between various rhetorical components?
- Would the claim be one that the creator of the piece would regard as serious criticism?

### *Evidence for the Claim*

- Is enough evidence given to support all your claims? What evidence do you still need?
- Is the evidence in support of the claim simply announced, or are its significance and appropriateness analyzed? Is a more detailed discussion needed?

- Do you use appropriate evidence, drawn from the argument itself or from other materials?
- Do you address objections readers might have to the claim, criteria, or evidence?
- What kinds of sources might you use to explain the context of the argument? Do you need to use sources to check factual claims made in the argument?
- Are all quotations introduced with appropriate signal phrases (such as "As Peggy Noonan points out"), and do they merge smoothly into your sentences?

### *Organization and Style*

- How are the parts of the argument organized? How effective is this organization? Would some other structure work better?
- Will readers understand the relationships among the original text, your claims, your supporting reasons, and the evidence you've gathered (from the original text and any other sources you've used)? If not, what could be done to make those connections clearer? Are more transitional words and phrases needed? Would headings or graphic devices help?
- Are the transitions or links from point to point, sentence to sentence, and paragraph to paragraph clear and effective? If not, how could they be improved?
- Is the style suited to the subject and appropriate to your audience? Is it too formal? Too casual? Too technical? Too bland or boring?
- Which sentences seem particularly effective? Which ones seem weakest, and how could they be improved? Should some short sentences be combined, or should any long ones be separated into two or more sentences?
- How effective are the paragraphs? Do any seem too skimpy or too long? Do they break the analysis at strategic points?
- Which words or phrases seem particularly effective, accurate, and powerful? Do any seem dull, vague, unclear, or inappropriate for the audience or your purpose? Are definitions provided for technical or other terms that readers might not know?

***Spelling, Punctuation, Mechanics, Documentation, and Format***

- Check the spelling of the author's name, and make sure that the name of any institution involved with the work is correct. Note that the names of many corporations and institutions use distinctive spelling and punctuation.
- Get the name of the text you're analyzing right.
- Are there any errors in spelling, punctuation, capitalization, and the like?
- Does the assignment require a specific format? Check the original assignment sheet to be sure.

**RESPOND.**

Find an argument on the editorial page or op-ed page in a recent newspaper. Then analyze it rhetorically, using principles discussed in this chapter. Show how it succeeds, fails, or does something else entirely. Perhaps you can show that the author is unusually successful in connecting with readers but then has nothing to say. Or perhaps you discover that the strong logical appeal is undercut by a contradictory emotional argument. Be sure that the analysis includes a summary of the original essay and basic publication information about it (its author, place of publication, and publisher).

PART 2

# WRITING arguments

# 7 Structuring Arguments

I get hives after eating ice cream.
My mouth swells up when I eat cheese.
Yogurt triggers my asthma.
↓
Dairy products make me sick.

Dairy products make me sick.
Ice cream is a dairy product.
↓
Ice cream makes me sick.

These two sets of statements illustrate the most basic ways in which Western culture structures logical arguments. The first piles up specific examples and draws a conclusion from them: that's **inductive reasoning** and structure. The second sets out a general principle (the major premise of a syllogism) and applies it to a specific case (the minor premise) in order to reach a conclusion: that's **deductive reasoning** and structure. In everyday reasoning, we often omit the middle statement, resulting in what Aristotle called an *enthymeme*: "Since dairy products make me sick, I better leave that ice cream alone." (See p. 68 for more on enthymemes.)

But the arguments you will write in college call for more than just the tight reasoning offered within inductive and deductive reasoning. You will also need to define claims, explain the contexts in which you are offering them, defend your assumptions, offer convincing evidence, deal with those who disagree with you, and more. And you will have to do so using a clear structure that moves your argument forward. This chapter introduces you to three helpful ways to structure arguments. Feel free to borrow from all of them!

## The Classical Oration

The authors of this book once examined a series of engineering reports and found that—to their great surprise—they were generally structured in ways similar to those used by Greek and Roman rhetors two thousand years ago. Thus, this ancient structuring system is alive and well in twenty-first-century culture. The classical oration has six parts, most of which will be familiar to you, despite their Latin names:

*Exordium*: The speaker/writer tries to win the attention and goodwill of an audience while introducing a subject or problem.

*Narratio*: The speaker/writer presents the facts of the case, explaining what happened when, who is involved, and so on. The *narratio* puts an argument in context.

Jonathan Chait provides a *narratio* that establishes a context for his argument when he examines the metaphors surrounding capitalism and the aims of Occupy Wall Street in "Steve Jobs, Occupy Wall Street, and the Capitalist Ideal."

LINK TO P. 927

*Partitio*: The speaker/writer divides up the subject, explaining what the claim is, what the key issues are, and in what order the subject will be treated.

*Confirmatio*: The speaker/writer offers detailed support for the claim, using both logical reasoning and factual evidence.

*Refutatio*: The speaker/writer recognizes and refutes opposing claims or evidence.

*Peroratio*: The speaker/writer summarizes the case and moves the audience to action.

This structure is powerful because it covers all the bases: readers or listeners want to know what your subject is, how you intend to cover it, and what evidence you have to offer. And you probably need a reminder to present a pleasing *ethos* when beginning a presentation and to conclude with enough *pathos* to win an audience over completely. Here, in outline form, is a five-part updated version of the classical pattern, which you may find useful on many occasions:

**Introduction**

- gains readers' interest and willingness to listen
- establishes your qualifications to write about your topic
- establishes some common ground with your audience
- demonstrates that you're fair and evenhanded
- states your claim

**Background**

- presents information, including personal narrative, that's important to your argument

**Lines of Argument**

- presents good reasons, including logical and emotional appeals, in support of your claim

**Alternative Arguments**

- examines alternative points of view and opposing arguments
- notes the advantages and disadvantages of these views
- explains why your view is better than others

**Conclusion**

- summarizes the argument
- elaborates on the implications of your claim
- makes clear what you want the audience to think or do
- reinforces your credibility and perhaps offers an emotional appeal

Not every piece of rhetoric, past or present, follows the structure of the oration or includes all its components. But you can identify some of its elements in successful arguments if you pay attention to their design. Here are the words of the 1776 Declaration of Independence:

> When in the Course of human events, it becomes necessary for one people to dissolve the political bands which have connected them with another, and to assume among the powers of the earth, the separate and equal station to which the Laws of Nature and of Nature's God entitle them, a decent respect to the opinions of mankind requires that they should declare the causes which impel them to the separation.
>
> We hold these truths to be self-evident, that all men are created equal, that they are endowed by their Creator with certain unalienable Rights, that

Opens with a brief *exordium* explaining why the document is necessary, invoking a broad audience in acknowledging a need to show "a decent respect to the opinions of mankind." Important in this case, the lines that follow explain the assumptions on which the document rests.

among these are Life, Liberty, and the pursuit of Happiness—that to secure these rights, Governments are instituted among Men, deriving their just powers from the consent of the governed—That whenever any Form of Government becomes destructive to these ends, it is the Right of the People to alter or to abolish it and to institute new Government, laying its Foundation on such principles and organizing its powers in such form, as to them shall seem most likely to effect their Safety and Happiness. Prudence, indeed, will dictate that Governments long established should not be changed for light and transient causes; and accordingly all experience hath shewn that mankind are more disposed to suffer, while evils are sufferable, than to right themselves by abolishing the forms to which they are accustomed. But when a long train of abuses and usurpations, pursuing invariably the same Object evinces a design to reduce them under absolute Despotism, it is their right, it is their duty, to throw off such Government and to provide new Guards for their future security. —Such has been the patient sufferance of these Colonies; and such is now the necessity which constrains them to alter their former Systems of Government. The history of the present King of Great Britain is a history of repeated injuries and usurpations, all having in direct object the establishment of an absolute Tyranny over these States. To prove this, let Facts be submitted to a candid world.

—Declaration of Independence, July 4, 1776

A *narratio* follows, offering background on the situation: because the government of George III has become destructive, the framers of the Declaration are obligated to abolish their allegiance to him.

Arguably, the *partitio* begins here, followed by the longest part of the document (not reprinted here), a *confirmatio* that lists the "long train of abuses and usurpations" by George III.

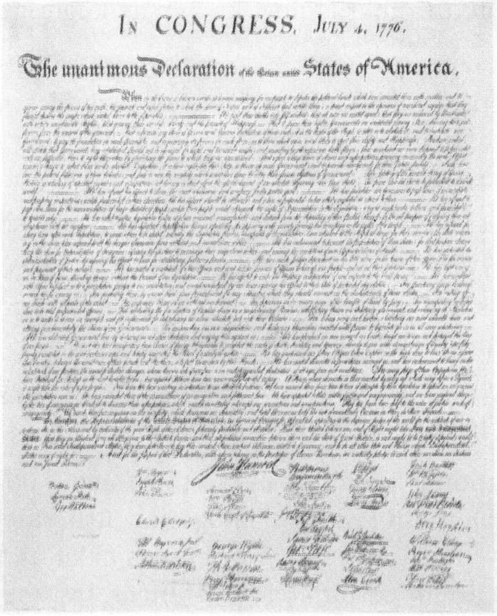

IN CONGRESS, JULY 4, 1776.

The unanimous Declaration [illegible] States of America,

The Declaration of Independence

The authors might have structured this argument by beginning with the last two sentences of the excerpt and then listing the facts intended to prove the king's abuse and tyranny. But by choosing first to explain the purpose and "self-evident" assumptions behind their argument and only then moving on to demonstrate how these "truths" have been denied by the British, the authors forge an immediate connection with readers and build up to the memorable conclusion. The structure is both familiar and inventive—as your own use of key elements of the oration should be in the arguments you compose.

## Rogerian and Invitational Arguments

In trying to find an alternative to confrontational and angry arguments like those that so often erupt in legislative bodies around the world, scholars and teachers of rhetoric adapted the nonconfrontational principles psychologist Carl Rogers employed in personal therapy sessions. In simple terms, Rogers argued that people involved in disputes should not respond to each other until they could fully, fairly, and even sympathetically state the other person's position. Scholars of rhetoric Richard E. Young, Alton L. Becker, and Kenneth L.

Pike developed a four-part structure that is now known as Rogerian argument:

- **Introduction:** The writer describes an issue, a problem, or a conflict in terms rich enough to show that he/she fully understands and respects any alternative position or positions.
- **Contexts:** The writer describes the contexts in which alternative positions may be valid.
- **Writer's position:** The writer states his/her position on the issue and presents the circumstances in which that opinion would be valid.
- **Benefits to opponent:** The writer explains to opponents how they would benefit from adopting his/her position.

Elizabeth Royte employs Rogerian argument as she sorts through the many possible answers to the question of what water we should choose to drink in *Bottlemania.*

LINK TO P. 717

The key to Rogerian argumentation is a willingness to think about opposing positions and to describe them fairly. In a Rogerian structure, you have to acknowledge that alternatives to your claims exist and that they might be reasonable under certain circumstances. In tone, Rogerian arguments steer clear of heated and stereotypical language, emphasizing instead how all parties in a dispute might gain from working together.

In the same vein, feminist scholars Sonja Foss and Cindy Griffin have outlined a form of argument described as "invitational," one that begins with careful attention to and respect for the person or the audience you are in conversation with. Foss and Griffin show that such listening—in effect, walking in the other person's shoes—helps you see that person's points of view more clearly and thoroughly and thus offers a basis for moving together toward new understandings. The kind of argument they describe is what another rhetorician, Krista Ratcliffe, calls "rhetorical listening," which helps to establish productive connections between people and thus especially aids crosscultural communications.

Invitational rhetoric has as its goal not winning over opponents but getting people and groups to work together and identify with each other; it strives for connection, collaboration, and the mutually informed creation of knowledge. You may have opportunities to practice invitational rhetoric in peer-review sessions, when each member of a group listens carefully in order to work through problems and issues. You may also practice invitational rhetoric looking at any contested issue from other people's points of view, taking them into account, and engaging them fairly and respectfully in your own argument. Invitational arguments, then, call up structures that more resemble good two-way conversations or free-ranging dialogues than straight-line marches from thesis to conclusion. Even conventional arguments benefit from invitational strategies by giving space early on to a full range of perspectives, making sure to present them thoroughly and clearly. Remember that in such arguments, your goal is enhanced understanding so that you can open up a space for new perceptions and fresh ideas.

Consider how Frederick Douglass tried to broaden the outlook of his audiences when he delivered a Fourth of July oration in 1852. Most nineteenth-century Fourth of July speeches followed a pattern of praising the Revolutionary War heroes and emphasizing freedom, democracy, and justice. Douglass, a former slave, had that tradition in mind as he delivered his address, acknowledging the "great principles" that the "glorious anniversary" celebrates. But he also asked his (white) listeners to see the occasion from another point of view:

> Fellow-citizens, pardon me, allow me to ask, why am I called upon to speak here today? What have I, or those I represent, to do with your national independence? Are the great principles of political freedom and natural justice, embodied in the Declaration of Independence, extended to us? And am I, therefore, called upon to bring our humble offering to the national altar, and to confess the benefits and express devout gratitude for the blessings resulting from your independence to us? . . . I say it with a sad sense of the disparity between us. I am not included within the pale of this glorious anniversary! Your high independence only reveals the immeasurable distance between us. The blessings in which you, this day, rejoice, are not enjoyed in common. The rich inheritance of justice, liberty, prosperity and independence, bequeathed by your fathers, is shared by you, not by me. The sunlight that brought life

Frederick Douglass

> and healing to you, has brought stripes and death to me. This Fourth of July is yours, not mine. You may rejoice, I must mourn.
>
> —Frederick Douglass, "What to the Slave Is the Fourth of July?"

Although his speech may seem confrontational, Douglass is inviting his audience to recognize a version of reality that they could have discovered on their own had they dared to imagine the lives of African Americans living in the shadows of American liberty. But the solution to the conflict between slavery and freedom, black and white, oppression and justice, was a long time in coming.

It was helped along by the arguments of another African American orator. Speaking at the foot of the Lincoln Memorial in Washington, D.C., on August 28, 1963, Martin Luther King Jr. clearly had Douglass's address (and Abraham Lincoln's Emancipation Proclamation) in mind in the opening of his "I Have a Dream" speech:

Martin Luther King Jr. on the steps of the Lincoln Memorial

> Five score years ago, a great American, in whose symbolic shadow we stand today, signed the Emancipation Proclamation. This momentous decree came as a great beacon light of hope to millions of Negro slaves who had been seared in the flames of withering injustice. It came as a joyous daybreak to end the long night of their captivity.
>
> But one hundred years later, the Negro still is not free. One hundred years later, the life of the Negro is still sadly crippled by the manacles of segregation and the chains of discrimination. One hundred years later, the Negro lives on a lonely island of poverty in the midst of a vast ocean of material prosperity. One hundred years later, the Negro is still languished in the corners of American society and finds himself an exile in his own land.
>
> —Martin Luther King Jr., "I Have a Dream"

King goes on to delineate the many injustices still characteristic of U.S. society. Then, in one of the most brilliant perorations in the history of speechmaking, he invokes a dream of a future in which the United States would live up to the highest ideals of the Declaration of Independence. The outcome he imagines is a Rogerian-style win/win deliverance for all:

> **. . . when we allow freedom to ring, when we let it ring from every village and every hamlet, from every state and every city, we will be able to speed up that day when all of God's children, black men and white men, Jews and Gentiles, Protestants and Catholics, will be able to join hands and sing in the words of the old Negro spiritual: "Free at last! Free at last! Thank God Almighty, we are free at last!"**
>
> **—Martin Luther King Jr., "I Have a Dream"**

Such moments in political life are rare, but in spite of much evidence to the contrary (think of the repeatedly demonstrated effectiveness of political attack ads), the public claims to prefer nonpartisan and invitational rhetoric to one-on-one, winner-take-all battles, suggesting that such an approach strikes a chord in many people, especially in a world that is increasingly open to issues of diversity. The lesson to take from Rogerian or invitational argument is that it makes good sense in structuring your own arguments to learn opposing positions well enough to state them accurately and honestly, to strive to understand the points of view of your opponents, to acknowledge those views fairly in your own work, and to look for solutions that benefit as many people as possible.

**RESPOND •**

Choose a controversial topic that is frequently in the news, and decide how you might structure an argument on the subject, using the general principles of the classical oration. Then look at the same subject from a Rogerian or invitational perspective. How might your argument differ? Which approach would work better for your topic? For the audiences you might want to address?

## Toulmin Argument

In *The Uses of Argument* (1958), British philosopher Stephen Toulmin presented structures to describe the way that ordinary people make reasonable arguments. Because Toulmin's system acknowledges the complications of life—situations when we qualify our thoughts with words such as *sometimes*, *often*, *presumably*, *unless*, and *almost*—his method isn't as airtight as formal logic that uses syllogisms (see p. 123 in this chapter and p. 67 in Chapter 4). But for that reason, Toulmin logic has become a powerful and, for the most part, practical tool for understanding and shaping arguments in the real world. We use his concepts and terminology in subsequent chapters in Part 2.

Toulmin argument will help you come up with ideas and test them and also figure out what goes where in many kinds of arguments. Let's take a look at the basic elements of Toulmin's structure:

| | |
|---|---|
| Claim | **the argument you wish to prove** |
| Qualifiers | **any limits you place on your claim** |
| Reason(s)/ Evidence | **support for your claim** |
| Warrants | **underlying assumptions that support your claim** |
| Backing | **evidence for warrant** |

If you wanted to state the relationship between them in a sentence, you might say:

> **My claim is true, to a qualified degree, because of the following reasons, which make sense if you consider the warrant, backed by these additional reasons.**

These terms—claim, evidence, warrants, backing, and qualifiers—are the building blocks of the Toulmin argument structure. Let's take them one at a time.

## Making Claims

Toulmin arguments begin with **claims**, debatable and controversial statements or assertions you hope to prove.

Many writers stumble when it comes to making claims because facing issues squarely takes thought and guts. A claim answers the question *So what's your point?* or *Where do you stand on that?* Some writers might like to ignore these questions and avoid stating a position. But when you make a claim worth writing about, then it's worth standing up and owning it.

Is there a danger that you might oversimplify an issue by making too bold a claim? Of course. But making that sweeping claim is a logical first step toward eventually saying something more reasonable and subtle. Here are some fairly simple, undeveloped claims:

> The filibuster tactic in the legislatures of both the United States and Canada ought to be abolished.
>
> It's time to legalize the medical use of marijuana.
>
> NASA should launch a human expedition to Mars.
>
> Vegetarianism is the best choice of diet.
>
> Same-sex unions deserve the same protections as those granted to marriage between a man and a woman.

Good claims often spring from personal experiences. You may have relevant work or military or athletic experience—or you may know a lot about music, film, sustainable agriculture, social networking, inequities in government services—all fertile ground for authoritative, debatable, and personally relevant claims.

**RESPOND.**

Claims aren't always easy to find. Sometimes they're buried deep within an argument, and sometimes they're not present at all. An important skill in reading and writing arguments is the ability to identify claims, even when they aren't obvious.

Collect a sample of six to eight letters to the editor of a daily newspaper (or a similar number of argumentative postings from a political blog). Read each item, and then identify every claim that the writer makes. When you've compiled your list of claims, look carefully at the words that the writer or writers use when stating their positions. Is there a common vocabulary? Can you find words or phrases that signal an impending claim? Which of these seem most effective? Which ones seem least effective? Why?

## Offering Evidence and Good Reasons

You can begin developing a claim by drawing up a list of reasons to support it or finding **evidence** that backs up the point.

Evidence and Reason(s) ⟶ So Claim

One student writer wanted to gather good reasons in support of an assertion that his college campus needed more official spaces for parking bicycles. He did some research, gathering statistics about parking-space allocation, numbers of people using particular designated slots, and numbers of bicycles registered on campus. Before he went any further, however, he listed his primary reasons for wanting to increase bicycle parking:

- **Personal experience:** At least twice a week for two terms, he was unable to find a designated parking space for his bike.
- **Anecdotes:** Several of his friends told similar stories. One even sold her bike as a result.
- **Facts:** He found out that the ratio of car to bike parking spaces was 100 to 1, whereas the ratio of cars to bikes registered on campus was 25 to 1.
- **Authorities:** The campus police chief told the college newspaper that she believed a problem existed for students who tried to park bicycles legally.

On the basis of his preliminary listing of possible reasons in support of the claim, this student decided that his subject was worth more research. He was on the way to amassing a set of good reasons and evidence that were sufficient to support his claim.

In shaping your own arguments, try putting claims and reasons together early in the writing process to create enthymemes. Think of these enthymemes as test cases or even as topic sentences:

> Bicycle parking spaces should be expanded because the number of bikes on campus far exceeds the available spots.
>
> It's time to lower the drinking age because I've been drinking since I was fourteen and it hasn't hurt me.
>
> Legalization of the medical use of marijuana is long overdue since it has been proven an effective treatment for symptoms associated with cancer.
>
> Violent video games should be carefully evaluated and their use monitored by the industry, the government, and parents because these games cause addiction and psychological harm to players.

As you can see, attaching a reason to a claim often spells out the major terms of an argument.

Anticipate challenges to your claims.

"I know your type, you're the type who'll make me prove every claim I make."



But your work is just beginning when you've put a claim together with its supporting reasons and evidence—because readers are certain to begin questioning your statement. They might ask whether the reasons and evidence that you're offering really do support the claim: Should the drinking age really be changed just because you've managed to drink since you were fourteen? They might ask pointed questions about your evidence: Exactly how do you know that the number of bikes on campus far exceeds the number of spaces available? Eventually, you've got to address potential questions about the quality of your assumptions and the quality of your evidence. The connection between claim and reason(s) is a concern at the next level in Toulmin argument.

### Determining Warrants

Crucial to Toulmin argument is appreciating that there must be a logical and persuasive connection between a claim and the reasons and data supporting it. Toulmin calls this connection the **warrant**. It answers the question *How exactly do I get from the data to the claim?* Like the warrant in legal situations (a search warrant, for example), a sound warrant in an argument gives you authority to proceed with your case.

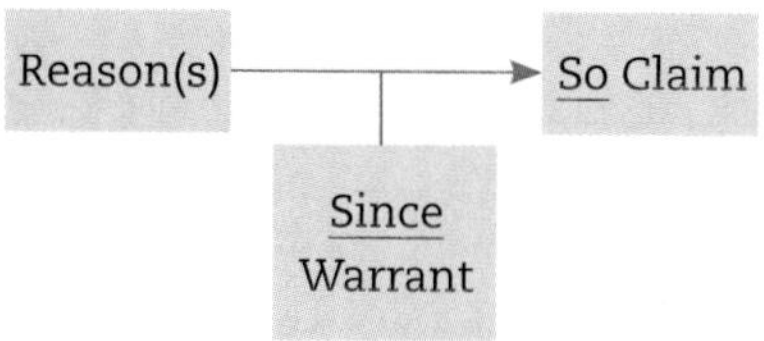


The warrant tells readers what your (often unstated) assumptions are—for example, that any practice that causes serious disease should be banned by the government. If readers accept your warrant, you can then present specific evidence to develop your claim. But if readers dispute your warrant, you'll have to defend it before you can move on to the claim itself.

In Stephanie Hanes's "Little Girls or Little Women?" she interviews blogger and mom Mary Finucane, who believes that girls' princess obsession is harmful to their development as strong women. What warrants lie behind this claim?

LINK TO P. 482

Stating warrants can be tricky because they can be phrased in various ways. What you're looking for is the general principle that enables you to justify the move from a reason to a specific claim—the bridge connecting them. The warrant is the assumption that makes the claim seem believable. It's often a value or principle that you share with your readers. Let's demonstrate this logical movement with an easy example:

**Don't eat that mushroom: it's poisonous.**

The warrant supporting this enthymeme can be stated in several ways, always moving from the reason (*it's poisonous*) to the claim (*Don't eat that mushroom*):

**Anything that is poisonous shouldn't be eaten.**

**If something is poisonous, it's dangerous to eat.**

Here's the relationship, diagrammed:

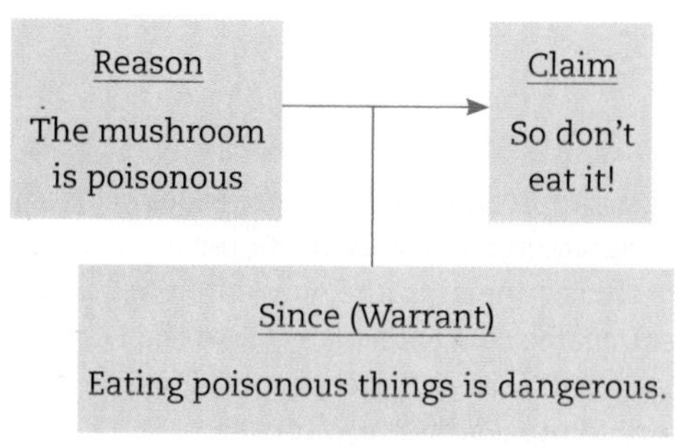

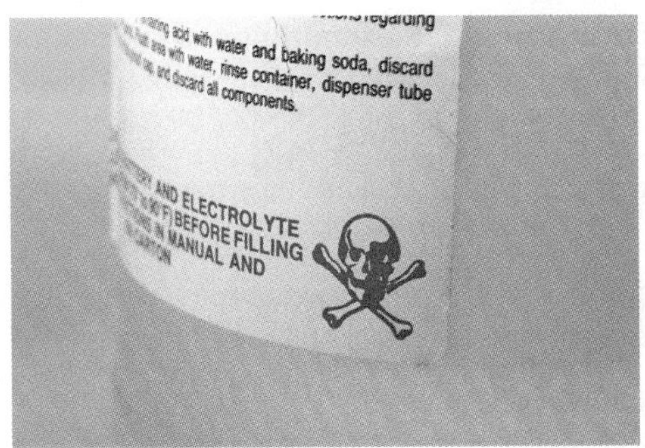


A simple icon—a skull and crossbones—can make a visual argument that implies a claim, a reason, and a warrant.

Perfectly obvious, you say? Exactly—and that's why the statement is so convincing. If the mushroom in question is a death cap or destroying angel (and you might still need expert testimony to prove that it is), the warrant does the rest of the work, making the claim that it supports seem logical and persuasive.

Let's look at a similar example, beginning with the argument in its basic form:

> **We'd better stop for gas because the gauge has been reading empty for more than thirty miles.**

In this case, you have evidence that is so clear (a gas gauge reading empty) that the reason for getting gas doesn't even have to be stated: the tank is almost empty. The warrant connecting the evidence to the claim is also pretty obvious:

> **If the fuel gauge of a car has been reading empty for more than thirty miles, then that car is about to run out of gas.**

Since most readers would accept this warrant as reasonable, they would also likely accept the statement the warrant supports.

Naturally, factual information might undermine the whole argument: the fuel gauge might be broken, or the driver might know that the car will go another fifty miles even though the fuel gauge reads empty. But in most cases, readers would accept the warrant.

Now let's consider how stating and then examining a warrant can help you determine the grounds on which you want to make a case. Here's a political enthymeme of a familiar sort:

> **Flat taxes are fairer than progressive taxes because they treat all taxpayers in the same way.**

Warrants that follow from this enthymeme have power because they appeal to a core American value—equal treatment under the law:

> **Treating people equitably is the American way.**
>
> **All people should be treated in the same way.**

You certainly could make an argument on these grounds. But stating the warrant should also raise a flag if you know anything about tax policy. If the principle is obvious and universal, then why do federal and many progressive state income taxes require people at higher levels of income to pay at higher tax rates than people at lower income levels? Could the warrant not be as universally popular as it seems at first glance? To explore the argument further, try stating the contrary claim and warrants:

> **Progressive taxes are fairer than flat taxes because people with more income can afford to pay more, benefit more from government, and shelter more of their income from taxes.**
>
> **People should be taxed according to their ability to pay.**
>
> **People who benefit more from government and can shelter more of their income from taxes should be taxed at higher rates.**

Now you see how different the assumptions behind opposing positions really are. If you decided to argue in favor of flat taxes, you'd be smart to recognize that some members of your audience might have fundamental reservations about your position. Or you might even decide to shift your entire argument to an alternative rationale for flat taxes:

> **Flat taxes are preferable to progressive taxes because they simplify the tax code and reduce the likelihood of fraud.**

Here, you have two stated reasons that are supported by two new warrants:

> **Taxes that simplify the tax code are desirable.**
>
> **Taxes that reduce the likelihood of fraud are preferable.**

Whenever possible, you'll choose your warrant knowing your audience, the context of your argument, and your own feelings.

**Examples of Claims, Reasons, and Warrants**

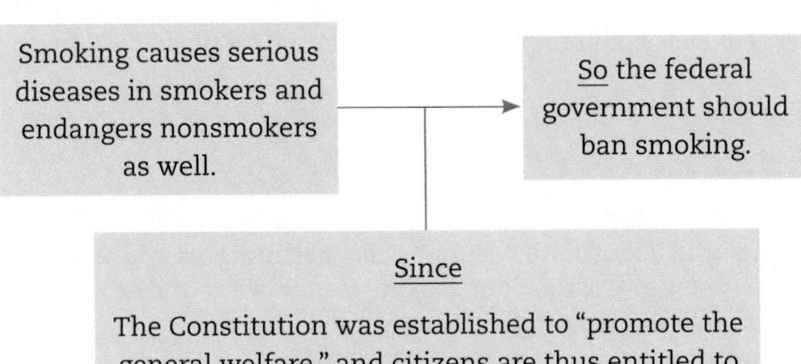


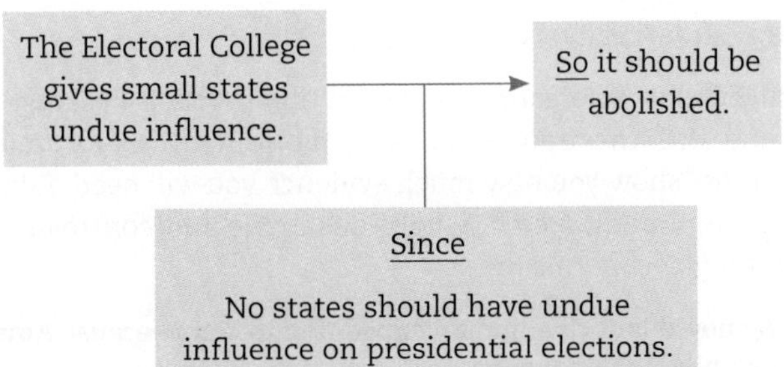


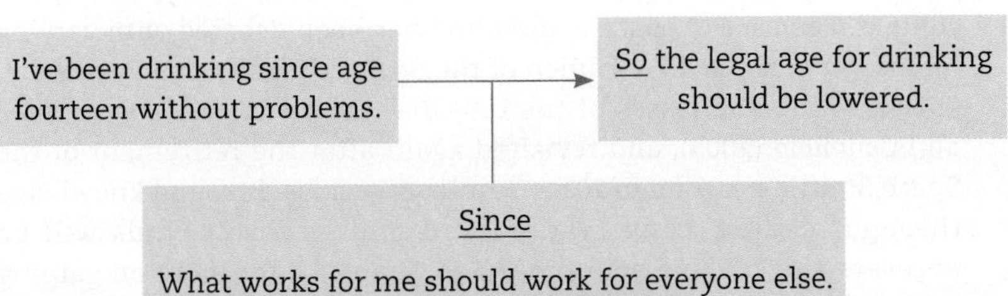

Be careful, though, not to suggest that you'll appeal to any old warrant that works to your advantage. If readers suspect that your argument for progressive taxes really amounts to *I want to stick it to people who work harder than me*, your credibility may suffer a fatal blow.

**RESPOND.**

At their simplest, warrants can be stated as "X is good" or "X is bad." Return to the letters to the editor or blog postings that you analyzed in the exercise on p. 133, this time looking for the warrant that is behind each claim. As a way to start, ask yourself these questions:

> If I find myself agreeing with the letter writer, what assumptions about the subject matter do I share with him/her?
>
> If I disagree, what assumptions are at the heart of that disagreement?

The list of warrants you generate will likely come from these assumptions.

## Offering Evidence: Backing

The richest, most interesting part of a writer's work—backing—remains to be done after the argument has been outlined. Clearly stated claims and warrants show you how much evidence you will need. Take a look at this brief argument, which is both debatable and controversial, especially in tough economic times:

> **NASA should launch a human expedition to Mars because Americans need a unifying national goal.**

Here's one version of the warrant that supports the enthymeme:

> **What unifies the nation ought to be a national priority.**

To run with this claim and warrant, you'd first need to place both in context. The case of space exploration has been debated with varying intensity since the 1957 launch of the Soviet Union's *Sputnik* satellite, sparked after the losses of the U.S. space shuttles *Challenger* (1986) and *Columbia* (2003), and revisited again after the retirement of the Space Shuttle program in 2011. Acquiring such background knowledge through reading, conversation, and inquiry of all kinds will be necessary for making your case. (See Chapter 3 for more on gaining authority.)

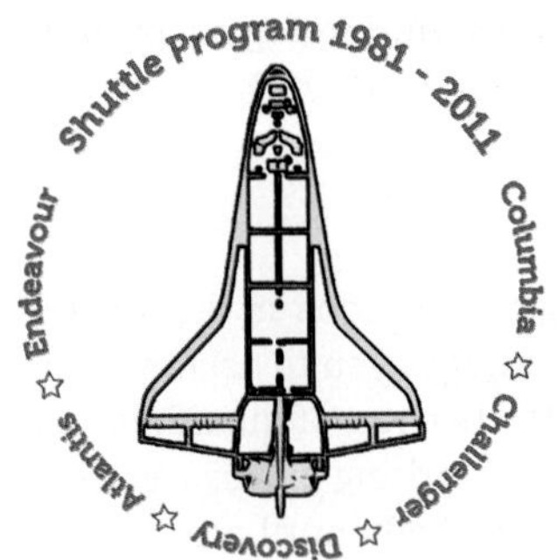


Sticker honoring the retirement of the Space Shuttle program

There's no point in defending any claim until you've satisfied readers that questionable warrants on which the claim is based are defensible. In Toulmin argument, evidence you offer to support a warrant is called **backing**.

**Warrant**

What unifies the nation ought to be a national priority.

**Backing**

Americans want to be part of something bigger than themselves. (Emotional appeal as evidence)

In a country as diverse as the United States, common purposes and values help make the nation stronger. (Ethical appeal as evidence)

In the past, government investments such as the Hoover Dam and the *Apollo* moon program enabled many—though not all—Americans to work toward common goals. (Logical appeal as evidence)

In addition to evidence to support your warrant (backing), you'll need evidence to support your claim:

**Argument in Brief (Enthymeme/Claim)**

NASA should launch a human expedition to Mars because Americans now need a unifying national goal.

**Evidence**

The American people are politically divided along lines of race, ethnicity, religion, gender, and class. (Fact as evidence)

A common challenge or problem often unites people to accomplish great things. (Emotional appeal as evidence)

A successful Mars mission would require the cooperation of the entire nation—and generate tens of thousands of jobs. (Logical appeal as evidence)

A human expedition to Mars would be a valuable scientific project for the nation to pursue. (Appeal to values as evidence)

As these examples show, appeals to values and emotions can be just as appropriate as appeals to logic and facts, and all such claims will be stronger if a writer presents a convincing ethos. In most arguments, appeals work together rather than separately, reinforcing each other. (See Chapter 3 for more on ethos.)

## Using Qualifiers

Even though she finds compelling evidence that television helps cause eating disorders in Fiji, Ellen Goodman qualifies her argument by acknowledging that no one can prove a direct causal link.

LINK TO P. 502

Experienced writers know that qualifying expressions make writing more precise and honest. Toulmin logic encourages you to acknowledge limitations to your argument through the effective use of **qualifiers**. You can save time if you qualify a claim early in the writing process. But you might not figure out how to limit a claim effectively until after you've explored your subject or discussed it with others.

**Qualifiers**

| | | |
|---|---|---|
| few | more or less | often |
| it is possible | in some cases | perhaps |
| rarely | many | under these conditions |
| it seems | typically | possibly |
| some | routinely | for the most part |
| it may be | most | if it were so |
| sometimes | one might argue | in general |

Never assume that readers understand the limits you have in mind. Rather, spell them out as precisely as possible, as in the following examples:

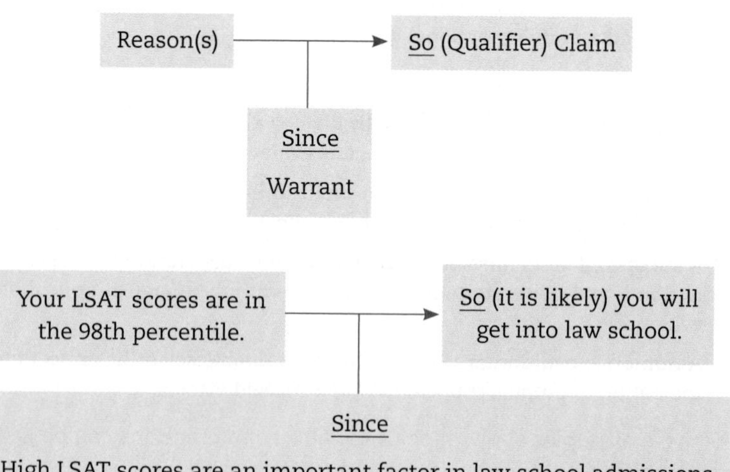

| | |
|---|---|
| Unqualified Claim | People who don't go to college earn less than those who do. |
| Qualified Claim | *In most cases*, people who don't go to college earn less than those who do. |

## Understanding Conditions of Rebuttal

In the Toulmin system, potential objections to an argument are called **conditions of rebuttal**. Understanding and reacting to these conditions are essential to support your own claims where they're weak and also to understand the reasonable objections of people who see the world differently. For example, you may be a big fan of the Public Broadcasting Service (PBS) and the National Endowment for the Arts (NEA) and prefer that federal tax dollars be spent on these programs. So you offer the following claim:

| | |
|---|---|
| Claim | The federal government should support the arts. |

You need reasons to support this thesis, so you decide to present the issue as a matter of values:

| | |
|---|---|
| Argument in Brief | The federal government should support the arts because it also supports the military. |

Now you've got an enthymeme and can test the warrant, or the premises of your claim:

| | |
|---|---|
| Warrant | If the federal government can support the military, then it can also support other programs. |

But the warrant seems frail: you can hear a voice over your shoulder saying, "In essence, you're saying that *Because we pay for a military, we should pay for everything!*" So you decide to revise your claim:

| | |
|---|---|
| Revised Argument | If the federal government can spend huge amounts of money on the military, then it can afford to spend moderate amounts on arts programs. |

Now you've got a new warrant, too:

| | |
|---|---|
| Revised Warrant | A country that can fund expensive programs can also afford less expensive programs. |

This is a premise that you can defend, since you believe strongly that the arts are just as essential as a strong military is to the well-being of the

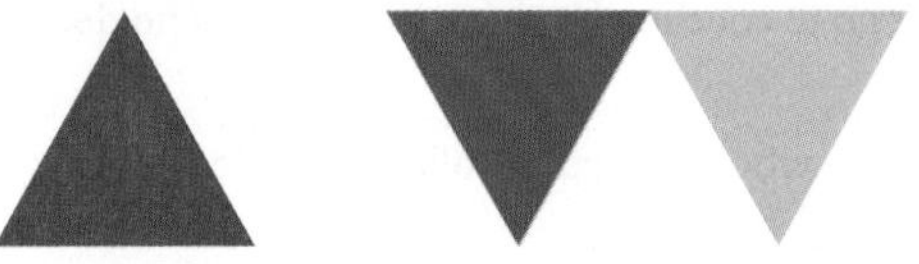


The new NEA logo

country. Although the warrant now seems solid, you still have to offer strong grounds to support your specific and controversial claim. So you cite statistics from reputable sources, this time comparing the federal budgets for the military and the arts. You break them down in ways that readers can visualize, demonstrating that much less than a penny of every tax dollar goes to support the arts.

But then you hear those voices again, saying that the "common defense" is a federal mandate; the government is constitutionally obligated to support a military and support for the arts is hardly in the same league! Looks like you need to add a paragraph explaining all the benefits the arts provide for very few dollars spent, and maybe you should suggest that such funding falls under the constitutional mandate to "promote the general welfare." Though not all readers will accept these grounds, they'll appreciate that you haven't ignored their point of view: you've gained credibility by anticipating a reasonable objection.

Dealing with conditions of rebuttal is an essential part of argument. But it's important to understand rebuttal as more than mere opposition. Anticipating objections broadens your horizons, makes you more open to alternative viewpoints, and helps you understand what you need to do to support your claim.

Within Toulmin argument, conditions of rebuttal remind us that we're part of global conversations: Internet newsgroups and blogs provide potent responses to positions offered by participants in discussions; instant messaging and social networking let you respond to and challenge others; links on Web sites form networks that are infinitely variable and open. In cyberspace, conditions of rebuttal are as close as your screen.

**RESPOND.**

Using a paper that you're writing, do a Toulmin analysis of the argument. When you're done, see which elements of the Toulmin scheme are represented. Are you short of evidence to support the warrant? Have you considered the conditions of rebuttal? Have you qualified your claim adequately? Next, write a brief revision plan: How will you buttress the argument in the places where it is weakest? What additional evidence will you offer for the warrant? How can you qualify your claim to meet the conditions of rebuttal? Then show your paper to a classmate and have him or her do a Toulmin analysis: a new reader will probably see your argument in different ways and suggest revisions that may not have occurred to you.

## Outline of a Toulmin Argument

Consider the claim that was mentioned on p. 139:

| | |
|---|---|
| Claim | The federal government should ban smoking. |
| Qualifier | The ban would be limited to public spaces. |
| Good Reasons | Smoking causes serious diseases in smokers.<br>Nonsmokers are endangered by secondhand smoke. |
| Warrants | The Constitution promises to "promote the general welfare."<br>Citizens are entitled to protection from harmful actions by others. |
| Backing | The United States is based on a political system that is supposed to serve the basic needs of its people, including their health. |
| Evidence | Numbers of deaths attributed to secondhand smoke<br>Lawsuits recently won against large tobacco companies, citing the need for reparation for smoking-related health care costs<br>Examples of bans already imposed in many public places |
| Authority | Cite the surgeon general. |
| Conditions of Rebuttal | Smokers have rights, too.<br>Smoking laws should be left to the states.<br>Such a ban could not be enforced. |
| Responses | The ban applies to public places; smokers can smoke in private. |

The power of the federal government to impose other restrictions on smoking (such as warning labels on cigarettes and bans on cigarette advertisements on television) has survived legal challenges.
The experience of New York City, which has imposed such a ban, suggests that enforcement would not be a significant problem.

## A Toulmin Analysis

You might wonder how Toulmin's method holds up when applied to an argument that is longer than a few sentences. Do such arguments really work the way that Toulmin predicts? In the following short argument, well-known linguist and author Deborah Tannen explores the consequences of a shift in the meaning of one crucial word: *compromise*. Tannen's essay, which originally appeared as a posting on Politico.com on June 15, 2011, offers a series of interrelated claims based on reasons, evidence, and warrants that culminate in the last sentence of the essay. She begins by showing that the word *compromise* is now rejected by both the political right and the political left and offers good reasons and evidence to support that claim. She then moves back to a time when "a compromise really was considered great," and offers three powerful pieces of evidence in support of that claim. The argument then comes back to the present, with a claim that the compromise and politeness of the nineteenth century have been replaced by "growing enmity." That claim is supported with reasoning and evidence that rest on an underlying warrant that "vituperation and seeing opponents as enemies is corrosive to the human spirit." The claims in the argument—that "compromise" has become a dirty word and that enmity and an adversarial spirit are on the rise—lead to Tannen's conclusion: rejecting compromise breaks the trust necessary for a democracy and thus undermines the very foundation of our society. While she does not use traditional qualifying words, she does say that the situation she describes is a "threat" to our nation, which qualifies the claim to some extent: the situation is not the "death" of our nation but rather a "threat." Tannen's annotated essay is on the following page.

## Why Is Compromise Now a Dirty Word?

DEBORAH TANNEN

When did the word "compromise" get compromised?

When did the negative connotations of "He was caught in a compromising position" or "She compromised her ethics" replace the positive connotations of "They reached a compromise"?

Contextual information leading up to initial claim

House Speaker John Boehner said it outright on *60 Minutes* last year. When talking about "compromise," Boehner said, "I reject the word."

"When you say the word 'compromise,'" he explained, ". . . a lot of Americans look up and go, 'Uh-oh, they're gonna sell me out.'" His position is common right now.

In the same spirit, Tony Perkins wrote in a recent CNN.com op-ed piece, "When it comes to conservative principles, compromise is the companion of losers."

The political right is particularly vehement when it comes to compromise. Conservatives are now strongly swayed by the tea party movement, whose clarion call is a refusal to compromise, regardless of the practical consequences.

But the rejection of compromise is more widespread than that. The left regularly savages President Barack Obama for compromising too soon, too much or on the wrong issues. Many who fervently sought universal health coverage, for example, could not celebrate its near accomplishment because the president gave up the public option.

Initial claim

The death of compromise has become a threat to our nation as we confront crucial issues such as the debt ceiling and that most basic of legislative responsibilities: a federal budget. At stake is the very meaning of what had once seemed unshakable: "the full faith and credit" of the U.S. government.

Reason

Evidence

Back when the powerful nineteenth-century senator Henry Clay was called "the great compromiser," achieving a compromise really was considered great. On three occasions, the Kentucky statesman helped the Senate preserve the Union by crafting compromises between the deadlocked slave-holding South and the Northern free states. In 1820, his Missouri Compromise stemmed the spread of slavery. In 1833, when the South was poised to defy federal tariff laws favored by the North and the federal government was about to authorize military action, Clay found a last-minute compromise. And his Compromise of 1850 averted civil war for at least a decade.

It was during an 1850 Senate debate that Clay stated his conviction: "I go for honorable compromise whenever it can be made." Something else he said then holds a key to how the dwindling respect for compromise is related to larger and more dangerous developments in our nation today.

Warrant

"All legislation, all government, all society," Clay said, "is formed upon the principle of mutual concession, politeness, comity, courtesy; upon these, everything is based."

Claim

Concession, politeness, comity, courtesy—none of these words could be uttered now with the assurance of

Reason

listeners' approval. The word "comity" is rarely heard; "concession" sounds weak; "politeness" and "courtesy" sound quaint—much like the contemporary equivalent, "civility."

That Clay lauded both compromise and civil discourse in the same speech reveals the link between, on

Evidence

the one hand, the word "compromise" falling into dispute, and, on the other, the glorification of aggression that I wrote about in my book, *The Argument Culture: Stopping America's War of Words*.

Claim

Today we have an increasing tendency to approach every task—and each other—in an ever more adversarial spirit. Nowhere is this more evident, or more destructive, than in the Senate.

Rebuttal

Though the two-party system is oppositional by nature, there is plenty of evidence that a certain (yes) comity has been replaced by growing enmity. We don't have to look as

Evidence

far back as Clay for evidence. In 1996, for example, an unprecedented fourteen incumbent senators announced that they would not seek reelection. And many, in farewell essays, described an increase in vituperation and partisanship that made it impossible to do the work of the Senate.

Evidence

"The bipartisanship that is so crucial to the operation of Congress," Howell Heflin of Alabama wrote, "especially the Senate, has been abandoned." J. James Exon of Nebraska described an "ever-increasing vicious polarization of the electorate" that had "all but swept aside the former preponderance of reasonable discussion."

But this is not happening only in the Senate. There is a rising adversarial spirit among the people and the press. It isn't only the obvious invective on TV and radio. A newspaper story that criticizes its subject is praised as "tough"; one that refrains from criticism is scorned as a "puff piece." Claim

The notion of "balance" today often leads to a search for the most extreme opposing views—so they can be presented as "both sides," leaving no forum for subtlety, multiple perspectives or the middle ground, where most people stand. Framing issues in this polarizing way reinforces the impression that Boehner voiced: that compromising is selling out. Reason Evidence

Being surrounded by vituperation and seeing opponents as enemies is corrosive to the human spirit. It's also dangerous to our democracy. The great anthropologist Margaret Mead explained this in a 1962 speech. Warrant Claim

"We are essentially a society which must be more committed to a two-party system than to either party," Mead said. "The only way you can have a two-party system is to belong to a party formally and to fight to the death . . ." not for your party to win but "for the right of the other party to be there too." Reason

Today, this sounds almost as quaint as "comity" in political discourse.

Mead traced our two-party system to our unique revolution: "We didn't kill a king and we didn't execute a large number of our people, and we came into our own without the stained hands that have been associated with most revolutions." Reason

With this noble heritage, Mead said, comes "the obligation to keep the kind of government we set up"—where members of each party may "disagree mightily" but still "trust in each other and trust in our political opponents."

Losing that trust, Mead concluded, undermines the foundation of our democracy. That trust is exactly what is threatened when the very notion of compromise is rejected. Conclusion

## What Toulmin Teaches

As Tannen's essay demonstrates, few arguments you read have perfectly sequenced claims or clear warrants, so you might not think of Toulmin's terms in building your own arguments. Once you're into your subject, it's easy to forget about qualifying a claim or finessing a warrant. But remembering what Toulmin teaches will always help you strengthen your arguments:

- Claims should be clear, reasonable, and carefully qualified.
- Claims should be supported with good reasons and evidence. Remember that a Toulmin structure provides the framework of an argument, which you fill out with all kinds of data, including facts, statistics, precedents, photographs, and even stories.
- Claims and reasons should be based on assumptions that readers will likely accept. Toulmin's focus on warrants can be confusing because it asks us to look at the assumptions that underlie our arguments—something many would rather not do. Toulmin pushes us to probe the values that support any argument and to think of how those values relate to particular audiences.
- Effective arguments respectfully anticipate objections readers might offer. Toulmin argument acknowledges that any claim can crumble under certain conditions, so it encourages a complex view that doesn't demand absolute or unqualified positions.

It takes considerable experience to write arguments that meet all these conditions. Using Toulmin's framework brings them into play automatically. If you learn it well enough, constructing good arguments can become a habit.

CULTURAL CONTEXTS FOR ARGUMENT

## Organization

As you think about organizing your argument, remember that cultural factors are at work: patterns that you find persuasive are probably ones that are deeply embedded in your culture. In the United States, many people expect a writer to "get to the point" as directly as possible and to articulate that point efficiently and unambiguously. The organizational patterns favored by many in business hold many similarities to the classical oration—a highly explicit pattern that leaves little or nothing unexplained—introduction and thesis, background, overview of the parts that follow, evidence, other viewpoints, and conclusion. If a piece of writing follows this pattern, American readers ordinarily find it "well organized."

So it's no surprise that student writers in the United States are expected to make their structures direct and their claims explicit, leaving little unspoken. Their claims usually appear early in an argument, often in the first paragraph.

But not all cultures take such an approach. Some expect any claim or thesis to be introduced subtly, indirectly, and perhaps at the end of a work, assuming that audiences will "read between the lines" to understand what's being said. Consequently, the preferred structure of arguments (and face-to-face negotiations, as well) may be elaborate, repetitive, and full of digressions. Those accustomed to such writing may find more direct Western styles overly simple, childish, or even rude.

When arguing across cultures, look for cues to determine how to structure your presentations effectively. Here are several points to consider:

- Do members of your audience tend to be very direct, saying explicitly what they mean? Or are they restrained, less likely to call a spade a spade? Consider adjusting your work to the expectations of the audience.
- Do members of your audience tend to respect authority and the opinions of groups? They may find blunt approaches disrespectful or contrary to their expectations.
- Consider when to state your thesis: At the beginning? At the end? Somewhere else? Not at all?
- Consider whether digressions are a good idea, a requirement, or an element to avoid.

# 8 Arguments of Fact

Many people believe that taking vitamin E daily will prevent heart attacks, cataracts, colon cancer, impotence in men, and wrinkles. Evidence in scientific studies suggests that they are probably wrong.

In the past, female screen stars like Marilyn Monroe could be buxom and curvy, less concerned about their weight than actresses today. Or so the legend goes. But measuring the costumes worn by Monroe and other actresses reveals a different story.

When an instructor announces a tough new attendance policy for her course, a student objects that there is no evidence that students who regularly attend lectures classes perform any better than those who do not. The instructor begs to differ.

## Understanding Arguments of Fact

Factual arguments come in many varieties, but they all try to establish whether something is or is not so, answering questions such as: *Is a historical legend true? Has a crime occurred?* or *Are the claims of a scientist accurate?* At first glance, you might object that these aren't arguments at all but just a matter of looking things up and then writing reports. And you'd be correct to an extent: people don't usually argue factual matters that are settled or undisputed (*The earth orbits the sun*), that might be decided with simple research (*Nelson Mandela was South Africa's first black president*), or that are the equivalent of a rule (*One foot equals 0.3048 meters*). Reporting facts, you might think, should be free of the friction of argument.

Yet facts become arguments whenever they're controversial on their own or challenge people's beliefs and lifestyles. Disagreements about childhood obesity, endangered species, or energy production ought to have a kind of clean, scientific logic to them. But that's rarely the case because the facts surrounding them must be interpreted. Those interpretations then determine what we feed children, where we can build a dam, or how we heat our homes. In other words, serious factual arguments almost always have consequences. *Can we rely on wind and solar power to solve our energy needs? Will the Social Security trust fund really go broke? Is it healthy to eat fatty foods?* People need well-reasoned factual arguments on subjects of this kind to make informed decisions. Such arguments educate the public.

For the same reason, we need arguments to challenge beliefs that are common in a society but held on the basis of inadequate or faulty information. Corrective arguments appear daily in the media, often based on studies written by scientists or researchers that the public would not encounter on their own. Many people, for example, believe that talking on a cell phone while driving is just like listening to the radio. But their intuition is not based on hard data: scientific studies show that using a cell phone in a car is comparable to driving under the influence of alcohol. That's a fact. As a result, some states have banned the use of handheld phones in cars.

Factual arguments also routinely address broad questions about how we understand the past. For example, are the accounts that we have of the American founding—or the Civil War, Reconstruction, or the heroics of the "Greatest Generation" in World War II—accurate? Or

The Internet puts information at our fingertips, but we need to be sure to confirm that information as fact.

do the "facts" that we teach today sometimes reflect the perspectives and prejudices of earlier times or ideologies? The telling of history is almost always controversial and rarely settled: the British and Americans will always tell different versions of what happened in North America in 1776.

It's similarly important to have factual arguments to counterbalance what's narrowly or mistakenly reported—whether by news media, corporations, or branches of government. For good or ill, the words of public figures and the actions of institutions, from churches to news organizations, are now always on record and searchable. Corrective arguments can sometimes play like a game of "Gotcha!" but they broaden readers' perspectives and help them make judgments on the basis of better information. (They also suggest that our institutions are often just as inconsistent, fallible, and petty as the rest of us.)

As you can see, then, arguments of fact do much of the heavy lifting in our world. They report on what has been recently discovered or explore the implications of that new information. They also add interest and complexity to our lives, taking what might seem simple and adding new dimensions to it. In many situations, they're the precursors to other forms of analysis, especially causal and proposal arguments. Before we can explore why things happen as they do or solve problems, we need to know the facts on the ground.

**RESPOND.**

For each topic in the following list, decide whether the claim is worth arguing to a college audience, and explain why or why not.

Hurricanes are increasing in number and ferocity.

Many people die annually of heart disease.

Fewer people would die of colon and prostate cancer each year if they drank more coffee.

Japan might have come to terms more readily in 1945 if the Allies in World War II hadn't demanded unconditional surrender.

Boys would do better in school if there were more men teaching in elementary and secondary classrooms.

The ongoing economic recession will lead drivers to buy more energy-efficient vehicles.

There aren't enough high-paying jobs for college graduates these days.

Hydrogen may never be a viable alternative to fossil fuels because it takes too much energy to change hydrogen into a usable form.

Its opponents have grossly exaggerated the costs of the Patient Protection and Affordable Care Act of 2010.

## Characterizing Factual Arguments

Factual arguments are often motivated by simple human curiosity or suspicion: *Are people who earn college degrees happier than those who don't? If being fat is so unhealthy, why aren't mortality rates rising?* Researchers may notice a pattern that leads them to look more closely at some phenomenon or behavior, exploring questions such as *What if?* or *How come?* Or maybe a writer first notes something new or different or unexpected and wants to draw attention to that fact: *Contrary to expectations, suicide rates are much higher in rural areas than urban ones.*

Such observations can lead quickly to **hypotheses**—that is, toward tentative and plausible statements of fact whose merits need to be examined more closely. *Maybe being a little overweight isn't as bad for people as we've been told? Maybe people in rural areas have less access to mental health services?* To support such hypotheses, writers then have to uncover evidence that reaches well beyond the casual observations that triggered an initial interest—like a news reporter motivated to see whether there's a verifiable story behind a source's tip.

For instance, the authors of *Freakonomics*, Stephen J. Dubner and Steven Levitt, were intrigued by the National Highway Traffic Safety Administration's claim that car seats for children were 54 percent effective in preventing deaths in auto crashes for children below the age of four. In a *New York Times* op-ed column entitled "The Seat Belt Solution," they posed an important question about that factual claim:

> But 54 percent effective compared with what? The answer, it turns out, is this: Compared with a child's riding completely unrestrained.

Their initial question about that claim led them to a more focused inquiry, then to a database on auto crashes, and then to a surprising conclusion: for kids above age twenty-four months, those in car seats were statistically safer than those without any protection but weren't safer than those confined by seat belts (which are much simpler, cheaper, and more readily available devices). Looking at the statistics every which way, the authors wonder if children older than two years would be just as well off physically—and their parents less stressed and better off financially—if the government mandated seat belts rather than car seats for them.

What kinds of evidence typically appear in sound factual arguments? The simple answer might be "all sorts," but a case can be made that factual arguments try to rely on "hard evidence" more than on "constructed" arguments based on logic and reason (see Chapter 4). Even so, some pieces of evidence are harder and more convincing than others.

## Developing a Factual Argument

Entire Web sites are dedicated to finding and posting errors from news and political sources. Some, like Media Matters for America and Accuracy in Media, take overtly partisan stands. Here's a one-day sampling of headlines from Media Matters:

> Glenn Beck's Top 5 Most Inflammatory Moments
>
> Fox Celebrated July 4 by Trying to Debunk Global Warming Again
>
> Fox's Asman Unable to Acknowledge That Reagan Raised Taxes

And here's a listing from Accuracy in Media:

> **FACTS: Obama's Townhall Lacked Them**
>
> **Media Deceptions Support Obama against Israel**
>
> **More Proof That MSNBC Is Working for Obama**

It would be hard to miss the political agendas at work on these sites.

Other fact-checking organizations have better reputations when it comes to assessing the truths behind political claims and media presentations. Though both are routinely charged with bias too, Pulitzer Prize–winning PolitiFact.com and FactCheck.org at least make an effort to be fair-minded across a broader political spectrum. FactCheck, for example, provides a detailed analysis of the claims it investigates in relatively neutral and denotative language, and lists the sources its researchers used—just as if its writers were doing a research paper. At its best, FactCheck.org demonstrates what one valuable kind of factual argument can accomplish.

Any factual argument that you might compose—from how you state your claim to how you present evidence and the language you use—should be similarly shaped by the occasion for the argument and a desire to serve the audiences that you hope to reach. We can offer some general advice to help you get started.

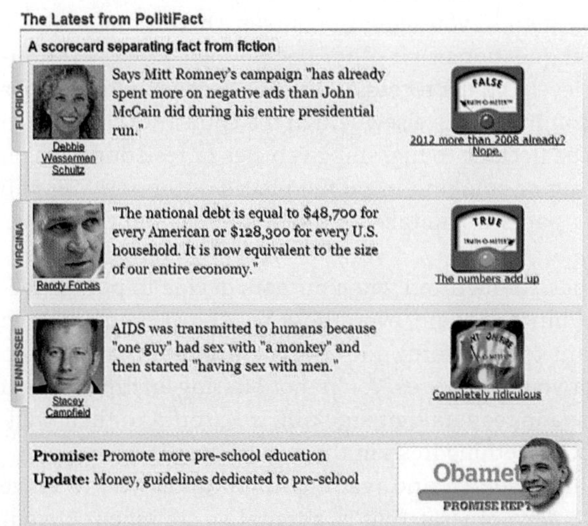


PolitiFact uses a meter to rate political claims from "True" to "Pants on Fire."

**RESPOND •**

The Annenberg Public Policy Center at the University of Pennsylvania hosts FactCheck.org, a Web site dedicated to separating facts from opinion or falsehood in the area of politics. It claims to be politically neutral. Find a case that interests you, either a recent controversial item listed on its homepage or another from its archives. Carefully study the item. Pay attention to the devices that FactCheck uses to suggest or ensure objectivity and the way that it handles facts and statistics. Then offer your own brief *factual* argument about the site's objectivity. A full case from FactCheck.org appears at the end of this chapter as a sample reading.

## Identifying an Issue

In her article "Professors' Liberalism Contagious? Maybe Not," Patricia Cohen offers an argument of fact when she presents the results of recent studies finding that professors do not affect students' political opinions.

LINK TO P. 796

To offer a factual argument of your own, you need to identify an issue or problem that will interest you and potential readers. Look for situations or phenomena—local or national—that seem out of the ordinary in the expected order of things. For instance, you might notice that many people you know are deciding not to attend college. How widespread is this change, and who are the people making this choice?

Or follow up claims that strike you as at odds with the facts as you know them or believe them. Maybe you doubt explanations being offered for your favorite sport team's current slump or for the declining number of minority men in your college courses. Or you might give a local spin to factual questions that other people have already formulated on a national level. Did the recession have as deep an effect on jobs or schools in your community as elsewhere in the country? Do people in your town seem to be flocking to high-mpg vehicles or resisting bans on texting while driving or smoking in public places outdoors? You will likely write a better paper if you take on a factual question that genuinely interests you.

In fact, whole books are written when authors decide to pursue factual questions that intrigue them, even those that have been explored before. But you want to be careful not to argue matters that pose no challenge for you or your audiences. You're not offering anything new if you just try to persuade readers that smoking is harmful to their well-being. So how about something fresh in the area of health?

Quick preliminary research and reading might allow you to move from an intuition to a hypothesis, that is, a tentative statement of your claim: *Having a dog is good for your health.* As noted earlier, factual arguments often provoke other types of analysis. In developing this claim, you'd need to explain what "good for your health" means, potentially an argument of definition. You'd also likely find yourself researching causes of the phenomenon if you can demonstrate that it is factual. As it turns out, your canine hypothesis would have merit if you defined "good for health" as "encouraging exercise." Here's the lead to a *New York Times* story reporting recent research:

> If you're looking for the latest in home exercise equipment, you may want to consider something with four legs and a wagging tail.
>
> Several studies now show that dogs can be powerful motivators to get people moving. Not only are dog owners more likely to take regular walks, but new research shows that dog walkers are more active overall than people who don't have dogs.
>
> One study even found that older people are more likely to take regular walks if the walking companion is canine rather than human.
>
> —Tara Parker-Pope, "Forget the Treadmill. Get a Dog." March 14, 2011

As always, there's another side to the story: what if people likely to get dogs are the very sort already inclined to be more physically active? You could explore that possibility as well (and researchers have), and then either modify your initial hypothesis or offer a new one. That's what hypotheses are for. They are works in progress.

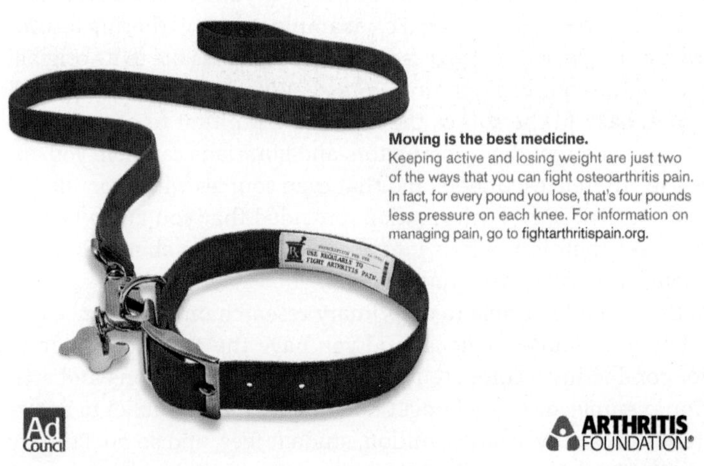


Here's an actual ad based on the claim that exercise (and dog ownership) is good for health.

**RESPOND.**

Working with a group of colleagues, generate a list of twenty favorite "mysteries" explored on cable TV shows, in blogs, or in tabloid newspapers. Here are three to get you started—the alien crash landing at Roswell, the existence of Atlantis, and the uses of Area 51. Then decide which—if any—of these puzzlers might be resolved or explained in a reasonable factual argument and which ones remain eternally mysterious and improbable. Why are people attracted to such topics? Would any of these items provide material for a noteworthy factual argument?

## Researching Your Hypothesis

What kinds of research does Libby Sander rely upon in developing her argument of fact about the increasing number of blue-collar workers returning to college? Could you use similar research in crafting your own factual argument?

LINK TO P. 782

How and where you research your subject will depend, naturally, on your subject. You'll certainly want to review Chapter 17, "Finding Evidence," Chapter 18, "Evaluating Sources," and Chapter 19, "Using Sources," before constructing an argument of fact. Libraries and the Web will provide you with deep resources on almost every subject. Your task will typically be to separate the best sources from all the rest. The word *best* here has many connotations: some reputable sources may be too technical for your audiences; some accessible sources may be pitched too low or be too far removed from the actual facts.

You'll be making judgment calls like this routinely. But do use primary sources whenever you can. For example, when gathering a comment from a source on the Web, trace it whenever possible to its original site, and read the comment in its full context. When statistics are quoted, follow them back to the source that offered them first to be sure that they're recent and reputable. Instructors and librarians can help you appreciate the differences. Understand that even sources with pronounced biases can furnish useful information, provided that you know how to use them, take their limitations into account, and then share what you know about the sources with your readers.

Sometimes, you'll be able to do primary research on your own, especially when your subject is local and you have the resources to do it. Consider conducting a competent survey of campus opinions and attitudes, for example, or study budget documents (often public) to determine trends in faculty salaries, tuition, student fees, and so on. Primary research of this sort can be challenging because even the simplest surveys or polls have to be intelligently designed and executed in a way that samples a representative population (see Chapter 4). But the work could pay off in an argument that brings new information to readers.

### Refining Your Claim

As you learn more about your subject, you might revise your hypothesis to reflect what you've discovered. In most cases, these revised hypotheses will grow increasingly complex and specific. Following are three versions of essentially the same claim, with each version offering more information to help readers judge its merit:

- Americans really did land on the moon, despite what some people think!
- Since 1969, when the *Eagle* supposedly landed on the moon, some people have been unjustifiably skeptical about the success of the United States' *Apollo* program.
- Despite plentiful hard evidence to the contrary—from *Saturn* V launches witnessed by thousands to actual moon rocks tested by independent labs worldwide—some people persist in believing falsely that NASA's moon landings were actually filmed on deserts in the American Southwest as part of a massive propaganda fraud.

The additional details about the subject might also suggest new ways to develop and support it. For example, conspiracy theorists claim that the absence of visible stars in photographs of the moon landing is evidence that it was staged, but photographers know that the camera exposure needed to capture the foreground—astronauts in their bright space suits—would have made the stars in the background too dim to see. That's a key bit of evidence for this argument.

As you advance in your research, your thesis will likely pick up even more qualifying words and expressions, which help you to make reasonable claims. Qualifiers—words and phrases such as *some, most, few, for most people, for a few users, under specific conditions, usually, occasionally, seldom*, and so on—will be among your most valuable tools in a factual argument.

Sometimes it is important to set your factual claim into a context that helps explain it to others who may find it hard to accept. You might have to concede some ground initially in order to see the broader picture. For instance, professor of English Vincent Carretta anticipated strong objections after he uncovered evidence that Olaudah Equiano—the author of

*The Interesting Narrative* (1789), a much-cited autobiographical account of his Middle Passage voyage and subsequent life as a slave—may actually have been born in South Carolina and not in western Africa. Speaking to the *Chronicle of Higher Education*, Carretta explains why Equiano may have fabricated his African origins to serve a larger cause—a growing antipathy to slavery and slave markets:

> **"Whether [Equiano] invented his African birth or not, he knew that what that movement needed was a first-person account. And because they were going after the slave trade, it had to be an account of someone who had been born in Africa and was brought across the Middle Passage. An African American voice wouldn't have done it."**
>
> **—Jennifer Howard, "Unraveling the Narrative"**

Carretta asks readers to appreciate that the new facts that he has discovered about *The Interesting Narrative* do not undermine the work's historical significance. If anything, his research has added new dimensions to its meaning and interpretation.

## Deciding Which Evidence to Use

In this chapter, we've blurred the distinction between factual arguments for scientific and technical audiences and those for the general public (in media such as magazines, blogs, and television documentaries). In the former kind of arguments, readers will expect specific types of evidence arranged in a formulaic way. Such reports may include a hypothesis, a review of existing research on the subject, a description of methods, a presentation of results, and finally a formal discussion of the findings. If you are thinking "lab report," you are already familiar with an academic form of a factual argument with precise standards for evidence.

Less scientific factual arguments—claims about our society, institutions, behaviors, habits, and so on—are seldom so systematic and they may draw on evidence from a great many different media. For instance, you might need to review old newspapers, scan videos, study statistics on government Web sites, read transcripts of Congressional hearings, record the words of eyewitnesses to an event, and so on. Very often, you will assemble your arguments from material found in credible though not always concurring authorities and resources—drawing upon the factual findings of scientists and scholars, but perhaps using their original insights in novel ways.

For example, when the National Endowment for the Arts (NEA) published a study entitled "Reading at Risk" in June 2004 to report "the declining importance of literature to our populace," it reached its pessimistic conclusions by studying a variety of phenomena in a large population:

> **This survey investigated the percentage and number of adults, age eighteen and over, who attended artistic performances, visited museums, watched broadcasts of arts programs, or read literature. The survey sample numbered more than seventeen thousand individuals, which makes it one of the most comprehensive polls of art and literature consumption ever conducted.**
>
> **—National Endowment for the Arts, "Reading at Risk"**

You might ponder the results of this study and wonder whether it defined literature too narrowly if it didn't consider that many people today favor nonprint, nontraditional, and electronic literary forms such as graphic novels or even video games. Your new study might challenge the conclusion of the earlier research by bringing fresh facts to the table.

Often, you may have only a limited number of words or pages in which to make a factual argument. What do you do then? You present your best evidence as powerfully as possible. But that's not difficult. You can make a persuasive factual case with just a few examples: three or four often suffice to make a point. Indeed, going on too long or presenting even good data in ways that make it seem uninteresting or pointless can undermine a claim.

## Presenting Your Evidence

In *Hard Times* (1854), British author Charles Dickens poked fun at a pedagogue he named Thomas Gradgrind, who preferred hard facts before all things human or humane. When poor Sissy Jupe (called "girl number twenty" in his awful classroom) is unable at his command to define *horse*, Gradgrind turns to his star pupil:

> **"Bitzer," said Thomas Gradgrind. "Your definition of a horse."**
>
> **"Quadruped. Graminivorous. Forty teeth, namely twenty-four grinders, four eyeteeth, and twelve incisive. Sheds coat in the spring; in marshy countries, sheds hoofs, too. Hoofs hard, but requiring to be shod with iron. Age known by marks in mouth." Thus (and much more) Bitzer.**
>
> **"Now girl number twenty," said Mr. Gradgrind. "You know what a horse is."**
>
> **—Charles Dickens, *Hard Times***

But does Bitzer? Rattling off facts about a subject isn't quite the same thing as knowing it, especially when your goal is, as it is in an argument of fact, to educate and persuade audiences. So you must take care how you present your evidence.

Factual arguments, like any others, take many forms. They can be as simple and pithy as a letter to the editor (or Bitzer's definition of a horse) or as comprehensive and formal as a senior thesis or even a dissertation. Such a thesis might have just two or three readers mainly interested in the facts you are presenting and the competence of your work. So your presentation can be lean and relatively simple.

But to earn the attention of readers in some more public forum, you may need to work harder to be persuasive. For instance, the National Commission on Adult Literacy's 2008 report, "Reach Higher, America: Overcoming Crisis in the U.S. Workforce," has the design of a formal scientific report, with sixty-five references, ten appendices, and a dozen figures and tables. Like many such studies, it also includes a foreword, an executive summary, and a detailed table of contents. All these elements help readers find the facts they need while also establishing the ethos of the work, making it seem serious, credible, well-conceived, and worth reading.

## Considering Design and Visuals

For an example of how to use design and visuals in factual arguments, see the annotated dollar bills supplied by Occupy George. What are the implications of such an argument? How does design reinforce the argument?

LINK TO P. 921

When you prepare a factual argument, consider how you can present your evidence most effectively. Precisely because factual arguments often rely on evidence that can be measured, computed, or illustrated, they benefit from thoughtful, even artful presentation of data. If you have lots of examples, you might arrange them in a list (bulleted or otherwise) and keep the language in each item roughly parallel. If you have an argument that can be translated into a table, chart, or graph (see Chapter 14), try it. And if there's a more dramatic medium for your factual argument—a Prezi slideshow, a multimedia mash-up, a documentary video posted via a social network—experiment with it, checking to be sure it would satisfy the assignment.

Images and photos—from technical illustrations to imaginative recreations—have the power to document what readers might otherwise have to imagine, whether actual conditions of drought, poverty, or disaster like the earthquake and tsunami that devastated Japan in 2011, or the dimensions of the Roman forum as it existed in the time of

Infographics like this one turn facts and data into arguments.

Julius Caesar. Readers today expect the arguments they read to include visual elements, and there's little reason not to offer this assistance if you have the technical skills to create them.

Consider the rapid development of the genre known as infographics—basically data presented in bold visual form. These items can be humorous and creative, but many, such as "Learning Out of Poverty" on the preceding page, make powerful factual arguments even when they leave it to viewers to draw their own conclusions. Just search "infographics" on the Web to find many examples.

## GUIDE to writing an argument of fact

### Finding a Topic

You're entering an argument of fact when you:

- make a claim about fact or existence that's controversial or surprising: *Climate change is threatening species in all regions by extending the range of non-native plants and animals.*
- correct an error of fact: *The overall abortion rate is not increasing in the United States, though rates are increasing in some states.*
- challenge societal myths: *Many Mexicans fought alongside Anglos in battles that won Texas its independence from Mexico.*
- wish to discover the state of knowledge about a subject or examine a range of perspectives and points of view: *The rationales of parents who homeschool their children reveal some surprising differences.*

### Researching Your Topic

Use both a library and the Web to locate the information you need. A research librarian can be a valuable resource, as are experts or eyewitnesses. Begin research by consulting the following types of sources:

- scholarly books on your subject
- newspapers, magazines, reviews, and journals (online and print)
- online databases
- government documents and reports
- Web sites, blogs, social networking sites, and listservs or newsgroups
- experts in the field, some of whom might be right on your campus

Do field research if appropriate—a survey, a poll, or systematic observation. Or invite people with a stake in the subject to present their interpretations of the facts. Evaluate all sources carefully, making sure that each is authoritative and credible.

## Formulating a Hypothesis

Don't rush into a thesis. Instead, begin with a hypothesis that expresses your beliefs at the beginning of the project but that may change as you learn more. It's OK to start with a question to which you don't have an answer or with a broad, general interest in a subject:

- **Question:** Have higher admissions standards at BSU reduced the numbers of entering first-year students from small, rural high schools?
- **Hypothesis:** Higher admissions standards at BSU are reducing the number of students admitted from rural high schools, which tend to be smaller and less well-funded than those in suburban and urban areas.

- **Question:** Have music sites like Pandora and Spotify reduced the amount of illegal downloading of music?
- **Hypothesis:** Services like Spotify and Pandora may have done more than lawsuits by record companies to discourage illegal downloads of music.

- **Question:** How dangerous is nuclear energy, really?
- **Hypothesis:** The danger posed by nuclear power plants is far less than that attributable to other viable energy sources.

- **Question:** Why can't politicians and citizens agree about the threat posed by the huge federal deficit?
- **Hypothesis:** People with different points of view read different threats into the budget numbers and so react differently.

## Examples of Arguable Factual Claims

- A campus survey that shows that far more students have read *Harry Potter and the Prisoner of Azkaban* than *Hamlet* indicates that our current core curriculum lacks depth.
- Evidence suggests that the European conquest of the Americas may have had more to do with infectious diseases than any superiority in technology or weaponry.
- In the long run, dieting may be more harmful than moderate overeating.

## Preparing a Proposal

If your instructor asks you to prepare a proposal for your project, here's a format that may help:

**State your thesis or hypothesis completely. If you are having trouble doing so, try outlining it in Toulmin terms:**

**Claim:**
**Reason(s):**
**Warrant(s):**

**Alternatively, you might describe the complications of a factual issue you hope to explore in your project, with the thesis perhaps coming later.**

- **Explain why the issue you're examining is important, and provide the context for raising the issue. Are you introducing new information, making available information better known, correcting what has been reported incorrectly, or complicating what has been understood more simply?**
- **Identify and describe those readers you most hope to reach with your argument. Why is this group of readers most appropriate for your project? What are their interests in the subject? How might you involve them in the paper?**
- **Discuss the kinds of evidence you expect to use in the project and the research the paper will require.**
- **Briefly discuss the key challenges you anticipate in preparing your argument.**
- **Describe the format or genre you expect to use: Academic essay? Formal report? Wiki? Infographic? Will you need charts, tables, graphs, other illustrations?**

## Thinking about Organization

The simplest structure for a factual argument is to make a claim and then prove it. But even a basic approach needs an introductory section that provides a context for the claim and a concluding section that assesses the implications of the argument. A factual argument that corrects an error or provides an alternative view of some familiar concept or historical event will also need a section early on explaining what the error or the common belief is. Be sure your opening section answers the *who*, *what*, *where*, *when*, *how*, and (maybe) *why* questions that readers will bring to the case.

Factual arguments offered in some academic fields follow formulas and templates. A typical paper in psychology will include an abstract, a review of literature, a discussion of method, an analysis, and a references list. When you have flexibility in the structure of your argument, it makes sense to lead with a striking example to interest readers in your subject and then to conclude with your strongest evidence. Pay particular attention to transitions between key points.

If you are defending a specific claim, anticipate the ways people with different points of view might respond to your argument. Consider how to address such differences respectfully in the body of your argument. But don't let a factual argument with a persuasive thesis end with concessions or refutations, especially in pieces for the general public. Such a strategy leaves readers thinking about problems with your claim at precisely the point when they should be impressed by its strengths. On the other hand, if your factual argument becomes exploratory, you may find yourself simply presenting a range of positions.

## Getting and Giving Response: Questions for Peer Response

Your instructor may assign you to a group for the purpose of reading and responding to each other's drafts. If not, ask for responses from serious readers or consultants at a writing center. Use the following questions to evaluate a colleague's draft. Since specific comments help more than general observations, be sure to illustrate your comments with examples. Some of the questions below assume a conventional, thesis-driven project, but more exploratory or invitational arguments of fact also need to be clearly phrased, organized, and supported with evidence.

### *The Claim*

- Does the claim clearly raise a serious and arguable factual issue?
- Is the claim as clear and specific as possible?
- Is the claim qualified? If so, how?

### *Evidence for the Claim*

- Is the evidence provided enough to persuade readers to believe your claim? If not, what additional evidence would help? Does any of the evidence seem inappropriate or ineffective? Why?
- Is the evidence in support of the claim simply announced, or do you explain its significance and appropriateness? Is more discussion needed?
- Are readers' potential objections to the claim or evidence addressed adequately? Are alternative positions understood thoroughly and presented fairly?
- What kinds of sources are cited? How credible and persuasive will they be to readers? What other kinds of sources might work better?
- Are all quotations introduced with appropriate signal phrases (such as "As Tyson argues, . . .") and blended smoothly into the writer's sentences?
- Are all visuals titled and labeled appropriately? Have you introduced them and commented on their significance?

### *Organization and Style*

- How are the parts of the argument organized? Is this organization effective, or would some other structure work better?
- Will readers understand the relationships among the claims, supporting reasons, warrants, and evidence? If not, what could be done to make those connections clearer? Are more transitional words and phrases needed? Would headings or graphic devices help?
- How might you use visual elements to make facts you present more readable or persuasive?
- Are there helpful transitions or links from point to point, sentence to sentence, and paragraph to paragraph? If not, how could they be improved?
- Is the style suited to the subject? Is it too formal? Too casual? Too technical? Too bland? How can it be improved?
- Which sentences seem particularly effective? Which ones seem weakest, and how could they be improved? Should some short sentences be combined, or should any long ones be separated into two or more sentences?
- How well constructed are the paragraphs? Do any seem too skimpy or too long? How can they be improved?

- Which words or phrases seem particularly accurate, vivid, and memorable? Do any seem dull, vague, unclear, or inappropriate for the audience or the writer's purpose? Are definitions provided for technical or other terms that readers might not know?

***Spelling, Punctuation, Mechanics, Documentation, and Format***

- Are there any errors in spelling, punctuation, capitalization, and the like?
- Is an appropriate and consistent style of documentation used for parenthetical citations and the list of works cited or references? (See Chapter 21.)
- Does the paper or project follow an appropriate format? Is it appropriately designed and attractively presented? How could it be improved?

## PROJECTS

1. Turn a database of information you find in the library or online into a traditional argument or, alternatively, into an infographic that offers a variety of potential claims. FedStats, a government Web site, provides endless data, but so can the sports or financial sections of a newspaper. Once you find a rich field of study, examine the data and draw your ideas from it, perhaps amplifying your ideas with material from other related sources of information. If you decide to create an infographic, you'll find good examples at VizWorld or Cool Infographics online. Software tools you can use to create infographics include Wordle and Google Public Data. Have fun.
2. Write an argument about one factual matter you are confident —based on personal experience or your state of knowledge—that most people get wrong, time and again. Use your expertise to correct this false impression.
3. Tough economic and political times sometimes reinforce and sometimes undermine cultural myths. With your classmates, generate a list of common beliefs about education, employment, family life, marriage, social progress, technology, and so on that seem to be under unusual scrutiny today. *Does it still pay to invest in higher education? Do two-parent households matter as much as they used to? Can children today expect to do better than their parents?* Pick one area to explore in depth, narrow the topic as much as you can, and then gather facts that inform it by doing research, perhaps working collaboratively to expand your findings. Turn your investigation into a factual argument.
4. Digital and electronic technologies have made still and video cameras cheap, small, and durable. As a result, they are now everywhere—in convenience stores, schools, public streets, subway stations, and so on. They are used by law enforcement and sports officials. And everyone with a cell phone has a camera and video recorder in hand. In all these circumstances, the cameras record what individuals on their own may not see or not remember well, presumably providing a more accurate account of an event.

   Does all this surveillance enhance our society, undermine it in some ways, or have perhaps unforeseen consequences? Study just one type of surveillance, including any others you think of not mentioned here. Read up on the subject in the library or on the Web and consult with a wide range of people interested in the subject, perhaps gathering them together for a discussion or panel discussion. Then offer a factual argument based on what you uncover, reflecting the range of perspectives and opinions you have encountered. For example, you might show whether and how people benefit from the technology, how it's being abused, or both.

Readers will certainly notice the title.

# Why You Should Fear Your Toaster More Than Nuclear Power

TAYLOR PEARSON

A recent nuclear disaster in Japan provides a challenging context for Pearson's claim: we need nuclear energy.

The first person plural point of view (*we*) helps Pearson to connect with his audience.

For the past month or so, headlines everywhere have been warning us of the horrible crises caused by the damaged Japanese nuclear reactors. Titles like "Japan Nuclear Disaster Tops Scale" have fueled a new wave of protests against anything nuclear—namely, the construction of new nuclear plants or even the continued operation of existing plants. However, all this reignited fear of nuclear energy is nothing more than media sensationalism. We need nuclear energy. It's clean, it's efficient, it's economic, and it's probably the only thing that will enable us to quickly phase out fossil fuels.

## Death Toll

First, let's address what is probably everyone's main concern about nuclear energy: the threat it poses to us and the likelihood of a nuclear power plant killing large numbers of people. The actual number of deaths caused by nuclear power plant accidents, even in worst-case scenarios, have been few. Take the Chernobyl accident—the worst and most lethal nuclear incident

---

Taylor Pearson wrote "Why You Should Fear Your Toaster More Than Nuclear Power" while he was a sophomore at the University of Texas at Austin. The assignment asked for a public argument—one good enough to attract readers who could put it down if they lost interest. In other words, a purely academic argument wouldn't work. So Pearson allows himself to exercise his sense of humor. Nor did the paper have to be formally documented. However, Pearson was expected to identify crucial sources the way writers do in magazines and newspapers. The paper provides an example of a factual argument with a clear thesis: "We need nuclear energy."

to date. As tragic as it was, the incident has killed only eighty-two people. More specifically, according to a 2005 release by the World Health Organization, thirty-two were killed in the effort to put out the fires caused by the meltdown and thirty-eight died within months of the accident as a result of acute radiation poisoning. Since the accident occurred in 1986, an additional twelve people have died from the radiation they were exposed to during the accident. Almost all deaths were highly exposed rescue workers. Other nuclear power accidents have been few and never resulted in more than ten deaths per incident. Still think that's too dangerous? To provide some perspective, let's consider an innocuous household appliance, the toaster: over three thousand people died from toaster accidents the first year the appliances were produced and sold in the 1920s, and they still cause around fifty accident-related deaths every year in the United States. So your toaster is far more likely to kill you than any nuclear power plant and subsequently give you a painfully embarrassing epitaph.

Pearson deflates fears by putting deaths caused by nuclear plants in perspective.

In fact, in comparison to the other major means of energy production in the United States, nuclear power is remarkably safe. According the U.S. Department of Labor, coal mining currently causes about sixty-five deaths and eleven thousand injuries per year, while oil drilling is responsible for approximately 125 deaths per year in the United States. Annual death tolls fluctuate depending upon the demand for these resources and the subsequent drilling or mining required, but the human cost is still exponentially more than that of nuclear energy. However, in the decades that nuclear power has been used in the United States, there have been zero deaths caused by nuclear power accidents—none at all. That's much better than the thousands of lives coal, oil, and toasters have cost us. If you care about saving human lives, then you should like nuclear energy.

### RADIATION

Despite nuclear energy causing remarkably few deaths, people are also terrified of another aspect of nuclear power — radiation. Everyone's scared of developing a boulder-size tumor or our apples growing to similar size as a result of the awful radiation given off by nuclear power plants or their potential meltdowns. However, it should comfort you to know (or perhaps not) that you receive more radiation from a brick wall than from a nuclear power plant.

The paper uses technical terms, but makes sure they are accessible to readers.

We live in a radioactive world — nearly everything gives off at least a trace amount of radiation; that includes brick walls. Yes, while such a wall emits about 3.5 millirems of radiation per year, a nuclear power plant gives off about .3 millirems per year. (Millirem is just a unit of radiation dosage.) Of course, this low level of emission is a result of the numerous safeguards set up around the reactors to suppress radiation. So what happens if those safeguards fail? Will everyone surrounding the plant turn into a mutant?

The paper is full of data and statistics from what seem to be reputable authorities and sources.

To answer that question, let's examine the reactor failures in the recent Japanese nuclear crisis following several devastating earthquakes. The damage from the quakes took out the power to several nuclear plants, which caused their core cooling systems to go offline. To prevent reactor meltdowns, workers had to douse the failing reactors in thousands of gallons of seawater to cool the fuel rods, which contain all the radioactive materials. Worries about the resulting radioactive seawater contaminating the ocean and sea life flared as a result. But just how radioactive is the water? Officials from Tokyo Electric Power Company said the water "would have to be drunk for a whole year in order to accumulate one millisievert." People are generally exposed to about 1 to 10 millisieverts each year from background radiation caused by substances in the air and soil. "You would have to eat or drink an awful lot to get any level of radiation that would be harmful," said British nuclear expert Laurence Williams. You get exposed to 5 millisieverts during a coast-to-coast flight across the United States. According to the U.S. Food and Drug Administration, you receive between 5 and 60 millisieverts in a CAT scan, depending on the type. So drinking water for a year that was in direct contact with containers of radioactive material used in those Japanese nuclear plants will expose you to a fifth of the radiation you would get from the weakest CAT scan. How dangerous!

As the paper explores various aspects of nuclear energy, headings keep the reader on track.

### Waste

But even if we have little to fear from nuclear power plants themselves, what about the supposedly deadly byproducts of these plants? Opponents of nuclear energy cite the fact that while nuclear power plants don't emit greenhouse gases, they do leave behind waste that remains radioactive for thousands of years. However, this nuclear waste problem is exaggerated. According to Professor Emeritus of Computer Science at Stanford University, John McCarthy, a 1,000-megawatt reactor produces only 1.5 cubic meters of waste after a year of operation. The current solution is to put the waste in protective containers and store them in caverns cut in granite. At the very least, with such a small amount of waste per reactor, the caverns don't have to be dug very fast.

Pearson strategically concedes a downside of nuclear energy.

Nuclear power plants do produce waste that needs to be kept away from living things, but the actual amount of waste produced is small and therefore manageable. If the United States got all its power from nuclear plants, the amount of waste produced would be equivalent to one pill of aspirin per person, per year—tiny compared to the amount of waste produced by plants that use fossil fuels; the U.S. Energy Information Administration notes that coal alone produces about 1.8 billion metric tons of $CO_2$ emissions per year.

Quantity is not the only factor that has been exaggerated—the amount of time the waste remains dangerously radioactive has also been inflated. After about five hundred years, the fission products' radiation levels drop to below the level at which we typically find them in nature; the thousands of years opponents of nuclear energy refer to are the years the waste will be radioactive, not excessively so. You don't want to stand right next to this material even after those first five hundred years, but if it can exist in nature without doing any noticeable damage, then it doesn't pose any serious threat. Essentially, everything is radioactive; to criticize something for being radioactive without specifying the level of radioactivity means nothing.

### Meeting Our Energy Demands

Although I've done a lot here in an attempt to defend nuclear energy, I still acknowledge it's not perfect. While the nuclear waste problem isn't something to be too worried about, it would still be better if we could satisfy our demand for energy without producing waste, radioactive or otherwise. However, I believe nuclear energy is the only realistic option we have to one day achieve an entirely clean energy reality.

We live in an age dominated by energy—to power our cars, our homes, and our computers. Let's face it: we're not going to give up the lifestyle that energy gives us. But under the current means of energy production—primarily coal in the United States—we're pumping out billions of tons of greenhouse gases that will eventually destroy our planet. So we have a dilemma. While we want to do something about global warming, we don't want to change our high-energy-consumption way of life. What are our options?

The concluding paragraphs compare nuclear power to potential alternatives.

Currently, completely clean sources of energy haven't been developed enough to make them a realistic option to supply all our energy needs. For solar energy to match the energy production of nuclear power plants presently in use, we would have to cover an area the size of New Jersey with solar panels. That's not a realistic option; we're not going to build that many panels just to get ourselves off of our addiction to fossil fuels. The same is true of the other renewable energy sources: wind, geothermal, hydroelectric, etc. The technologies simply aren't mature enough.

However, nuclear power is realistic. We have the means and the technology to make enough nuclear power plants to satisfy our electricity demands. Nuclear plants produce a lot of power with relatively little waste. Moving from coal to nuclear plants could provide us with adequate power until we develop more efficient renewable sources of electricity.

So what's stopping us? Of course, those heavily invested in coal and other fossil fuels lobby the government to keep their industries profitable, but a large source of opposition is also the American public. Because of the atom bombs of World War II, the Cold War, and Chernobyl, we're scared of all things nuclear. Anytime we hear the word "radiation," images of mushroom clouds and fallout enter our minds. But nuclear power plants aren't bombs. No matter what happens to them, they will never explode. Strong as it might be, our fear of nuclear power is overblown and keeping us from using a source of energy that could literally save our planet. We need to stop the fearmongering before we burn our planet to a crisp.

Of course, that's if our toasters don't kill us first.

Pearson ends his argument by asking readers to acknowledge that their fears of nuclear power aren't based in fact.

# Democrats Deny Social Security's Red Ink

BROOKS JACKSON

*February 25, 2011*

*Some claim it doesn't contribute to the federal deficit, but it does.*

**SUMMARY**

Some senior Democrats are claiming that Social Security does not contribute "one penny" to the federal deficit. That's not true. The fact is, the federal government had to borrow $37 billion last year to finance Social Security, and will need to borrow more this year. The red ink is projected to total well over half a trillion dollars in the coming decade.

President Barack Obama was closer to the mark than some of his Democratic allies when he said that Social Security is "not the huge contributor to the deficit that [Medicare and Medicaid] are." That's correct: Medicare and Medicaid consume more borrowed funds than Social Security, and their costs are growing more rapidly. But Obama's own budget director, Jacob Lew, was misleading when he wrote recently that "Social Security benefits are entirely self-financing." That's not true, except in a very narrow, legalistic sense, and doesn't change the fact that Social Security is now a small but growing drain on the government's finances.

Payroll taxes exceeded benefit payments regularly until 2010. But the fact is that Social Security has now passed a tipping point, beyond which the Congressional Budget Office projects that it will permanently pay out more in benefits than it gathers from Social Security taxes. The imbalance is made even larger this year by a one-year "payroll tax holiday" that was

---

"Democrats Deny Social Security's Red Ink" was written by Brooks Jackson, the director of FactCheck.org, which is a project of the Annenberg Public Policy Center. Its mission statement says, "We are a nonpartisan, nonprofit 'consumer advocate' for voters that aims to reduce the level of deception and confusion in U.S. politics. We monitor the factual accuracy of what is said by major U.S. political players in the form of TV ads, debates, speeches, interviews, and news releases. Our goal is to apply the best practices of both journalism and scholarship, and to increase public knowledge and understanding." The site is sponsored by the Annenberg Public Policy Center at the University of Pennsylvania and is not funded by corporations or political groups of any kind. Note that this article does include a list of sources, but they are not listed or cited within the text in any conventional way, such as MLA or APA style.

enacted as part of last year's compromise on extending the Bush tax cuts. The lost Social Security tax revenues are being made up with billions from general revenues that must all be borrowed. The combined effect is to add $130 billion to the deficit in the current fiscal year.

It's important to note that benefit payments are not in immediate danger. Under current law, scheduled benefits can be paid until about 2037, according to the most recent projections. But keeping those benefits flowing is already requiring the use of funds borrowed from the public. So we judge the claim that Social Security is not currently contributing to the deficit to be false.

### Analysis

As always, we take no position on whether Social Security should be changed, either to reduce the deficit or to shore up its troubled finances for future generations. Our job here is simply to establish facts and hold politicians accountable for any misinformation.

We'll start with the basic numbers. The nonpartisan Congressional Budget Office issued its most recent projections for Social Security's income and outgo Jan. 26, along with its twice-yearly "Budget and

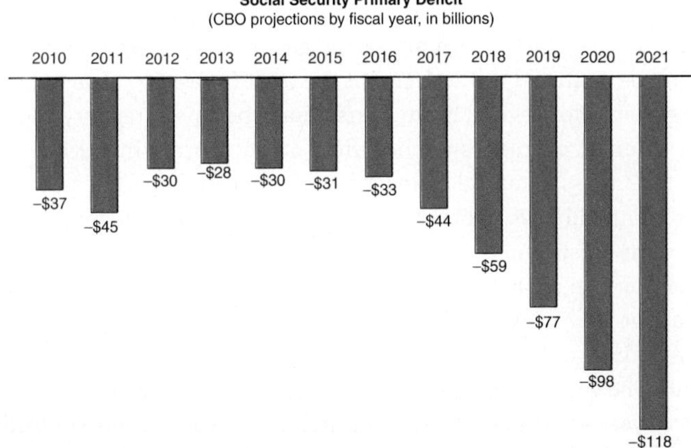


*Source:* CBO "Combined OASDI Trust Funds; January 2011 Baseline." 26 Jan 2011.
*Note:* See "Primary Surplus" line (which is negative, indicating a deficit).

Economic Outlook." What those numbers show is that Social Security ran a $37 billion deficit last year, is projected to run a $45 billion deficit this year, and more red ink every year thereafter.

Matters are even worse than this chart shows. In December, Congress passed a Social Security tax reduction. Workers are temporarily paying 2 percentage points less, from 6.2 percent to 4.2 percent, in Social Security payroll taxes this calendar year. Since the government is making up the shortfall out of general revenues, CBO's deficit projections for the trust funds do not include that. But CBO's figures predict that the "payroll tax holiday" will cost the government's general fund $85 billion in this fiscal year and $29 billion in fiscal year 2012 (which starts Oct. 1, 2011). Since every dollar of that will have to be borrowed, the combined effect of the "tax holiday" and the annual deficits will amount to a $130 billion addition to the federal deficit in the current fiscal year, and $59 billion in fiscal 2012.

Social Security has passed a tipping point. For years it generated more revenue than it consumed, holding down the overall federal deficit and allowing Congress to spend more freely for other things. But those days are gone. Rather than lessening the federal deficit, Social Security has at last—as long predicted—become a drag on the government's overall finances.

As recently as October, CBO was projecting that it would be 2016 before outlays regularly exceed revenues. But Social Security's fiscal troubles are more severe than was thought, and the latest projections show the permanent deficits started several years ahead of earlier predictions.

Don't be confused by the fact that the trust funds are projected to continue growing for several more years. That's because Treasury must still credit interest payments to the funds on the borrowings from earlier years. But unless taxes are increased or other spending is cut severely, the government will have to borrow from the public to pay the interest that it owes to the trust funds.

And don't be misled by those who say the system can pay full benefits until about 2037 without making any changes to the law. That's true, but does not change the fact that Social Security taxes no longer cover those benefits. The government is now borrowing money to pay them, and will do so every year for the foreseeable future. And keep in mind, if nothing is done, when those trust funds are exhausted, benefits would have to be cut by 22 percent in 2037, and more each year after that, according to the most recent report of the system's trustees. By 2084, the system will generate only enough revenue to pay for 75 percent of promised benefit levels.

*Facts vs. Spin*

Those are the facts. But they haven't stopped some Democrats from claiming over and over that Social Security doesn't contribute "one penny" to the deficit. Examples:

Feb. 20, 2011: Sen. Richard Durbin of Illinois, on NBC's *Meet the Press*:

> *Durbin:* Social Security does not add one penny to the deficit. Social Security untouched will make every promised payment for more than 25 years.

Feb. 20, 2011: Sen. Chuck Schumer of New York, on CNN's *State of the Union* with Candy Crowley:

> *Schumer:* Social Security, however, does not contribute one penny to the deficit and won't until 2037.

Feb. 16, Senate Majority Leader Harry Reid of Nevada:

> *Reid:* Social Security has contributed not a single penny to the deficit. So we can talk about entitlements as long as you eliminate Social Security.... Social Security is not part of the problem we have in America with the deficit.

President Barack Obama's budget director, Jacob Lew, doesn't go quite that far. But he did write a Feb. 22 opinion piece in *USA Today* claiming that Social Security "does not cause our deficits" and is "entirely self-financing."

> *Lew:* [L]ooking to the next two decades, Social Security does not cause our deficits. Social Security benefits are entirely self-financing. They are paid for with payroll taxes collected from workers and their employers throughout their careers.

*USA Today*'s editorial writers rebutted Lew and took him to task for making a similar claim earlier, saying, "That would be nice if it were true. It's not." The newspaper stated:

> *USA Today:* Social Security is a cash-in/cash-out program. It went into the red last year, when payroll tax revenue came up about $37 billion short of the benefits paid to retirees.

And as we've shown, *USA Today* is correct.

Interestingly, the president has stopped short of this sort of misleading talk. On Feb. 15, Obama held a White House news conference to defend his budget proposal for fiscal year 2012. And here's what he said about cutting entitlement spending:

> *Obama:* Now, you talked about Social Security, Medicare and Medicaid. The truth is Social Security is not the huge contributor to the deficit that the other two entitlements are.

That's true enough. As Obama concedes, Social Security is a "contributor" to the deficit—$37 billion last year. So how can his fellow Democrats claim that it isn't? When we asked Sen. Schumer's spokesman Brian Fallon, we got this on-the-record response:

> *Brian Fallon:* This is nitpicking to the nth degree. Social Security is a standalone program and is fully solvent. Our deficit problem lies not with Social Security, but with the rest of the budget.

And from Sen. Durbin's spokesman Max Gleischman, we got this:

> *Max Gleischman:* We can argue line items and budget allocations all day—our position is that SS doesn't add to the deficit. Jack Lew and the President agree.

But as we've seen, the president's statement doesn't back up what Durbin said, and Lew chose his words carefully in his *USA Today* article. We agree with Lew that Social Security does not "cause our deficits," at least not by itself. But it already contributes some of the deficit, and that will grow over time unless changes are made somewhere.

When Lew says Social Security is "entirely self-financing," he refers to the trust funds that have built up assets of more than $2.5 trillion over the years. That's what the rest of the government has borrowed and spent on other things. Those trust funds and the future interest payments will keep benefits funded at promised levels for years to come, it's true. But unless the government raises taxes or cuts other spending substantially, the government will need to borrow more from the public to finance its obligations to the trust funds.

In an opinion piece published Dec. 2 on Politico.com, David M. Walker—a former U.S. comptroller general who heads a nonprofit dedicated to reducing the deficit—flatly disagreed with "liberals" who deny Social Security's contribution to the deficit:

> *Walker, Dec. 2:* [C]ontrary to assertions by some liberals, Social Security is now adding to the federal deficit, since it currently pays out more than it

takes in. This negative cash flow position will accelerate and become permanent by 2015.

That was before the CBO's latest projections, which show the negative cash flow has become permanent ahead of schedule.

One of Washington's leading experts on Social Security financing, Eugene Steuerle of the Urban Institute, says that Social Security unambiguously adds to the nation's "fiscal woes" and that quibbling over how trust fund income and expenditures are accounted for is "somewhat silly." In an exchange of e-mails with FactCheck.org, he said:

> *Eugene Steuerle:* I think the right way to phrase the issue is whether an increasing portion of the population receiving benefits and decreasing portions paying taxes adds currently and in the coming years to our fiscal woes. There the answer is an unambiguous, "Yes."

For more on the future effect of Social Security on the budget, see "Social Security and the Budget," a report co-authored by Steuerle for the Urban Institute last May. A figure on page 4 graphically illustrates that Social Security's expenses are projected to outrun its income. The gap is projected to grow to close to 2 percent of the national gross domestic product and remain there for decades, as far in the future as 2080 and beyond.

## Sources

"The 2010 OASDI Trustees Report." Social Security Board of Trustees, 5 Aug 2010.

CNN. "State of the Union with Candy Crowley." Transcript, 20 Feb 2011.

Congressional Budget Office. "CBO's 2010 Long-Term Projections for Social Security: Additional Information." Oct 2010.

Congressional Budget Office. "Combined OASDI Trust Funds, January 2011 Baseline." 26 Jan 2011.

Duggan, James E., and Christopher J. Soares. "Social Security and Medicare Trust Funds and the Federal Budget." U.S. Department of Treasury, Office of Economic Policy, May 2009.

Espo, David. "Reid Wants No Cuts to Social Security." The Associated Press, 16 Feb 2011.

Exchange of emails with Brian Fallon, 23 Feb 2011.

Exchange of emails with Max Gleischman, 22–23 Feb 2011.

Lew, Jacob. "Opposing View: Social Security Isn't the Problem." *USA Today*, 22 Feb 2011.

NBC News. "*Meet the Press* Transcript for Feb. 20, 2011." 20 Feb 2011.

Ohlemacher, Stephen. "CBO: Social Security to Run Permanent Deficits." The Associated Press, 26 Jan 2011.

The Raw Story. "Exclusive: 'Social Security Has Nothing to Do with the Deficit,' Sanders Tells Raw." 19 Jan 2011.

Steuerle, Eugene, and Stephanie Rennane. "Social Security and the Budget." Urban Institute, May 2010.

Telephone interview and exchange of emails with Eugene Steuerle, 23–24 Feb 2011.

*USA Today*. "Our View: Fix Social Security Sooner, Not Later." Editorial, 22 Feb 2011.

The White House. "Press Conference by the President." Transcript, 15 Feb 2011.

# 9
# Arguments of Definition

A student submits a "senior thesis" in history made up almost entirely of music and still images projected onto a wall in a gallery. She wants to redefine current definitions of *thesis*.

A conservative student group accuses the student government on campus of sponsoring a lecture series featuring a disproportionate number of "left-wing" writers and celebrities. A spokesperson for the student government defends its program by questioning the definition of *left-wing* used to classify some of the speakers.

A panel of judges must decide whether computer-enhanced images will be eligible in a contest for landscape photography. At what point is an electronically manipulated image no longer a *photograph*?

## Understanding Arguments of Definition

Definitions matter. Just ask a scientist, a mathematician, an engineer, or a judge. In 2007, the United States Supreme Court decided that the United States Environmental Protection Agency (EPA) had the authority to regulate carbon dioxide ($CO_2$) if it could show that the naturally occurring chemical compound—which humans exhale—met the Clean Air Act's definition of *air pollutant*. Many businesses objected. But Justice John Paul Stevens, writing for the majority in a five to four decision, put it this way:

> **Because greenhouse gases fit well within the Act's capacious definition of "air pollutant," the EPA has statutory authority to regulate emissions of such gases from new motor vehicles.**

As a result, we'll all be driving much different cars and trucks soon in order to reduce $CO_2$ concentrations in the atmosphere.

What the EPA example demonstrates is that arguments of definition aren't abstract academic exercises: they are almost always contentious and often consequential. That's because they wield the power to say what someone or something is or can be. Such arguments can both include or exclude: A wolf in Montana either is an endangered species or it isn't. An unsolicited kiss is or is not sexual harassment. A person merits official political refugee status in the United States or doesn't. Another way of approaching definitional arguments, however, is to think of what falls between *is* and *is not* in a definitional claim. In fact, many definitional disputes occur in that murky realm.

Consider the controversy over how to define *human intelligence*. Some argue that human intelligence is a capacity that is measured by tests of verbal and mathematical reasoning. In other words, it's defined by IQ and SAT scores. Others define *intelligence* as the ability to perform specific practical tasks. Still others interpret *intelligence* in emotional terms as a competence in relating to other people. Any of these positions could be defended reasonably, but perhaps the wisest approach would be to construct a definition of *intelligence* that is rich enough to incorporate all these perspectives—and maybe more.

The fact is that crucial political, social, and scientific terms—such as *intelligence, social justice,* or *war*—are constantly reargued, reshaped, and updated for the times. For instance, in 2011, in order to avoid calling a martial incursion into Libya a "war," the White House defined the strategy as a "kinetic military action." It took heat for the euphemism, but the term makes a useful distinction, as Byron York explains:

> **"Kinetic" is a word that's been used around the Pentagon for many years to distinguish between actions like dropping bombs, launching cruise missiles, or shooting people and newer forms of non-violent fighting like cyber-warfare. At times, it also appears to mean just taking action.**

If you don't like the new expression, you are free to make an argument of definition against it—as many did.

Important arguments of definition can't be decided simply by running to a dictionary. Dictionaries reflect the way that particular groups of people use words at a specified time and place. And like any form of writing, these reference books mirror the prejudices of their makers—as shown, perhaps most famously, in the entries of lexicographer Samuel Johnson (1709–1784), who gave the English language its first great dictionary. Johnson, no friend of the Scots, defined *oats* as "a grain which in England is generally given to horses, but in Scotland supports the people." (To be fair, he also defined *lexicographer* as "a writer of dictionaries, a harmless drudge.") Thus, it's possible to disagree with dictionary definitions or to regard them merely as starting points for arguments.

A cartoonist finds political implications in a euphemism.

**RESPOND.**

Briefly discuss how you might define the italicized terms in the following controversial claims of definition. Compare your definitions of the terms with those of your classmates.

Graphic novels are *serious literature*.

Burning a nation's flag is a *hate crime*.

Matt Drudge and Arianna Huffington aren't *journalists*.

College sports programs have become *big businesses*.

Plagiarism can be an act of *civil disobedience*.

Satanism is a *religion* properly protected by the First Amendment.

Campaign contributions are acts of *free speech* that should never be regulated.

The District of Columbia should not have all the privileges of an American *state*.

Polygamous couples should have the legal privileges of *marriage*.

## Kinds of Definition

Because there are different kinds of definitions, there are also different ways to make a definition argument. Fortunately, identifying a particular type of definition is less important than appreciating when an issue of definition is at stake. Let's explore some common definitional issues.

### Formal Definitions

In "The Locavore's Dilemma," how successfully do you think Christophe Pelletier establishes a formal definition of the term "locavore"? How could he reinforce this definition? In what ways might doing so strengthen his argument?

LINK TO P. 703

**Formal definitions** are what you find in dictionaries. Such definitions place a term in its proper **genus** and **species**—first determining its class and then identifying the features or criteria that distinguish it from other members of that class. That sounds complicated, but a definition will help you see the principle. To define *hybrid car*, you might first place it in a general class—*passenger vehicles*. Then the formal definition would distinguish hybrid cars from other passenger vehicles: *they can move using two or more sources of power, either separately or in combination*. So the full definition might look like this: *a hybrid car is a passenger vehicle* (genus) *that can operate using two or more sources of power, separately or in combination* (species).

Buick LaCrosse: full hybrid or poseur? The big sedan now uses a variety of technologies, including a small electric motor, to get more than thirty-five miles per gallon on the highway. But it cannot run on electricity alone.

Many arguments involve deciding whether an object meets the criteria set by a formal definition. For instance, suppose that you are considering whether a Toyota Prius and a Buick LaCrosse are actually hybrid cars. Both are clearly passenger cars, so the genus raises no questions. But not all vehicles that claim to be hybrids are powered by two sources: some of them are just electrically *assisted* versions of a regular gasoline car. That's the species question. Looking closely, you discover that a Prius can run on either gas or electric power alone. But does the LaCrosse have that flexibility? If not, should it be labeled something other than *hybrid*—perhaps, *mild hybrid*? This definitional question obviously has consequences for consumers concerned about the $CO_2$ emissions discussed earlier.

## Operational Definitions

**Operational definitions** identify an object or idea by what it does or by what conditions create it. For example, someone's offensive sexual imposition on another person may not meet the technical definition of *harassment* unless it is considered *unwanted*, *unsolicited*, and *repeated*. These three conditions then define what makes an act that might be

How does Jennifer Conlin's "The Freedom to Choose Your Pronoun" add complexity to and challenge typical culturally reinforced operational definitions of gender?

LINK TO P. 550

acceptable in some situations turn into harassment. But they might also then become part of a highly contentious debate: were the conditions actually present in a given case? For example, could an offensive act really be harassment if the accused believed sexual interest was mutual and therefore solicited?

As you might imagine, arguments arise from operational definitions whenever people disagree about what the conditions define or whether these conditions have been fulfilled. Here are some examples of those types of questions:

**Questions Related to Conditions**

- Can institutional racism occur in the absence of specific and individual acts of racism?
- Can someone who is paid for their community service still be called a volunteer?
- Does someone who uses steroids to enhance home-run-hitting performance deserve the title Hall of Famer?

**Questions Related to Fulfillment of Conditions**

- Has an institution supported traditions or policies that have led to widespread racial inequities?
- Was the compensation given to a volunteer really "pay" or simply "reimbursement" for expenses?
- Should Player X, who used steroids prescribed for a medical reason, be ineligible for the Hall of Fame?

**RESPOND.**

This chapter opens with several rhetorical situations that center on definitional issues. Select one of these situations, and then, using the strategy of formal definition, set down some criteria of definition. For example, identify the features of a photograph that make it part of a larger class (*art, communication method, journalistic technique*). Next, identify the features that make it distinct from other members of that larger class. Then use the strategy of operational definition to establish criteria for the same object: what does it do? Remember to ask questions related to conditions (*Is a computer-scanned photograph still a photograph?*) and questions related to fulfillment of conditions (*Does a good photocopy of a photograph achieve the same effect as the photograph itself?*).

Prince Charming considers whether an action would fulfill the conditions for an operational definition.

## Definitions by Example

Resembling operational definitions are **definitions by example**, which define a class by listing its individual members. Such definitions can be helpful when it is easier to illustrate or show what related people or things have in common than to explain each one in precise detail. For example, one might define the broad category of *smart phones* by listing the major examples of these products or define *heirloom tomatoes* by recalling all those available at the local farmers' market.

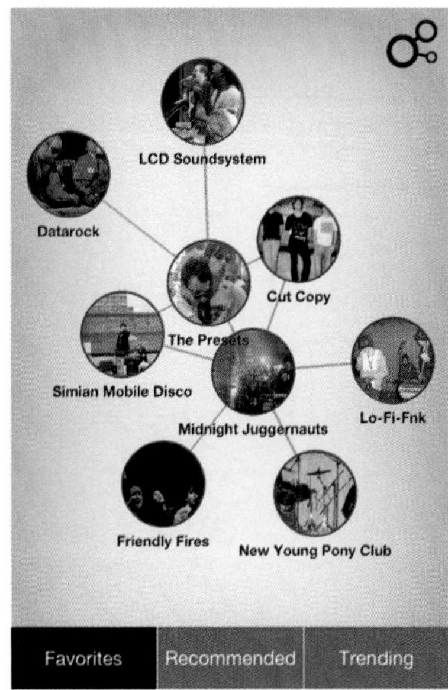


An app like Discovr Music defines musical styles by example when it connects specific artists or groups to others who make similar sounds.

Arguments of this sort may focus on who or what may be included in a list that defines a category—*classic movies*, *worst natural disasters*, *groundbreaking painters*. Such arguments often involve comparisons and contrasts with the items that most readers would agree belong in this list. One could ask why Washington, D.C., is denied the status of a state: how does it differ from the fifty recognized American states? Or one might wonder why the status of planet is denied to asteroids, when both planets and asteroids are bodies that orbit the sun. A comparison between planets and asteroids might suggest that size is one essential feature of the eight recognized planets that asteroids don't meet. (In a recent famous exercise in definition argument, astronomers decided to deny poor Pluto its planetary classification.)

## Developing a Definitional Argument

Definitional arguments don't just appear out of the blue; they often evolve out of daily life. You might get into an argument over the definition of *ordinary wear and tear* when you return a rental car with some soiled upholstery. Or you might be asked to write a job description for a new position to be created in your office: you have to define the job position in a way that doesn't step on anyone else's turf. Or maybe employees on your campus object to being defined as *temporary workers* when they've held their same jobs for years. Or someone derides one of your best friends as *just a nerd*. In a dozen ways every day, you encounter situations that are questions of definition. They're so frequent and indispensable that you barely notice them for what they are.

## Formulating Claims

In addressing a question of definition, you'll likely formulate a *tentative claim*—a declarative statement that represents your first response to such situations. Note that such initial claims usually don't follow a single definitional formula.

### Claims of Definition

A person paid to do public service is not a *volunteer*.

*Institutional racism* can exist—maybe even thrive—in the absence of overt civil rights violations.

*Political bias* has been consistently practiced by the mainstream media.

Theatergoers shouldn't confuse *musicals* with *operas*.

*White lies* are hard to define but easy to recognize.

None of the statements listed here could stand on its own because it likely reflects a first impression and gut reaction. But that's fine because making a claim of definition is typically a starting point, a cocky moment that doesn't last much beyond the first serious rebuttal or challenge. Statements of this sort aren't arguments until they're attached to reasons, data, warrants, and evidence. (See Chapter 7.)

Finding good reasons to support a claim of definition usually requires formulating a general definition by which to explore the subject. To be persuasive, the definition must be broad and not tailored to the specific controversy:

A volunteer is . . .

Institutional racism is . . .

Political bias is . . .

A musical is . . . but an opera is . . .

A white lie is . . .

Now consider how the following claims might be expanded with a general definition to become full-fledged definitional arguments:

**Arguments of Definition**

Someone paid to do public service is not a volunteer because volunteers are people who . . .

Institutional racism can exist even in the absence of overt violations of civil rights because, by definition, institutional racism is . . .

Political bias in the media is evident when . . .

Musicals focus on words while operas . . .

The most important element of a white lie is its destructive nature; the act of telling one hurts both the receiver and the sender.

Notice, too, that some of the issues can involve comparisons between things—such as operas and musicals.

## Crafting Definitions

Imagine that you decide to tackle the concept of *paid volunteer* in the following way:

**Participants in the federal AmeriCorps program are not really volunteers because they receive "education awards" for their public service. Volunteers are people who work for a cause without receiving compensation.**

In Toulmin terms, as explained in Chapter 7, the argument looks like this:

| | |
|---|---|
| Claim | **Participants in AmeriCorps aren't volunteers . . .** |
| Reason | **. . . because they are paid for their service.** |
| Warrant | **People who are compensated for their services are, ordinarily, employees.** |

As you can see, the definition of *volunteers* will be crucial to the shape of the argument. In fact, you might think you've settled the matter with this tight little formulation. But now it's time to listen to the readers over your shoulder (again, see Chapter 7), who are pushing you further. Do the terms of your definition account for all pertinent cases of volunteerism—in particular, any related to the types of public service AmeriCorps members might be involved in? What do you do with unpaid interns: how do they affect your definition of *volunteers*? Consider, too, the word *cause* in your original claim of the definition:

> **Volunteers are people who work for a cause without receiving compensation.**

*Cause* has political connotations that you may or may not intend. You'd better clarify what you mean by *cause* when you discuss its definition in your paper. Might a phrase such as *the public good* be a more comprehensive or appropriate substitute for *a cause*? And then there's the matter of *compensation* in the second half of your definition:

> **Volunteers are people who work for a cause without receiving compensation.**

Aren't people who volunteer to serve on boards, committees, and commissions sometimes paid, especially for their expenses? What about members of the so-called all-volunteer military? They're financially compensated during their years of service, and they enjoy benefits after they complete their tours of duty.

As you can see, you can't just offer up a definition as part of an argument and expect that readers will accept it. Every part of a definition has to be interrogated, critiqued, and defended. So investigate your subject in the library, on the Internet, and in conversation with others, including experts if you can. You might then be able to present your definition in a single paragraph, or you may have to spend several pages coming to terms with the complexity of the core issue.

After conducting research of this kind, you'll be in a better position to write an extended definition that explains to your readers what you believe makes a volunteer a volunteer, how to identify institutional racism, or how to distinguish between a musical and an opera.

## Matching Claims to Definitions

Once you've formulated a definition that readers will accept—a demanding task in itself—you might need to look at your particular subject to see if it fits your general definition. It should provide evidence of one of the following:

- It is a clear example of the class defined.
- It clearly falls outside the defined class.

- It falls between two closely related classes or fulfills some conditions of the defined class but not others.
- It defies existing classes and categories and requires an entirely new definition.

How do you make this key move in an argument? Here's an example from an article by Anthony Tommasini entitled "Opera? Musical? Please Respect the Difference." Early in the piece, Tommasini argues that a key element separates the two musical forms:

> Both genres seek to combine words and music in dynamic, felicitous and, to invoke that all-purpose term, artistic ways. But in opera, music is the driving force; in musical theater, words come first.

His claim of definition (or of difference) makes sense because it clarifies aspects of the two genres.

> This explains why for centuries opera-goers have revered works written in languages they do not speak. . . . As long as you basically know what is going on and what is more or less being said, you can be swept away by a great opera, not just by music, but by visceral drama.
>
> In contrast, imagine if the exhilarating production of Cole Porter's *Anything Goes* now on Broadway . . . were to play in Japan without any kind of titling technology. The wit of the musical is embedded in its lyrics. . . .

But even after having found a distinction so perceptive, Tommasini (like most writers making arguments of definition) still has to acknowledge exceptions.

> Theatergoing audiences may not care much whether a show is a musical or an opera. But the best achievements in each genre . . . have been from composers and writers who grounded themselves in a tradition, *even while reaching across the divide.* [emphasis added]

Where can you locate the key features of a definitional argument in the Wikipedia entry on local food? What features are most effective? Which are least effective?

LINK TO P. 666

If evidence you've gathered while developing an argument of definition suggests that similar limitations may be necessary, don't hesitate to modify your claim. It's amazing how often seemingly cut-and-dry matters of definition become blurry—and open to compromise and accommodation—as you learn more about them. That has proved to be the case as various campuses across the country have tried to define *hate speech* or *sexual harassment*—tricky matters. And even the Supreme Court has never said exactly what *pornography* is. Just when matters seem to be settled, new legal twists develop. Should virtual child pornography created with software be illegal, as is the real thing? Or is a virtual image—even a lewd one—an artistic expression that is protected (as other works of art are) by the First Amendment?

## Considering Design and Visuals

In thinking about how to present your argument of definition, you may find a simple visual helpful, such as the Venn diagram below from Wikimedia Commons that defines *sustainability* as the place where our society and its economy intersect with the environment. Such a visual might even suggest a structure for an oral presentation.

Remember, too, that visuals like photographs, charts, and graphs can also help you make your case. Such items might demonstrate that the conditions for a definition have been met—as the widely circulated and horrific photographs from Abu Ghraib prison in Iraq in 2004 helped to define *torture*. Or you might create a graphic yourself to illustrate a concept you are defining, perhaps through comparison and contrast.

Finally, don't forget that basic design elements—such as boldface and italics, headings, or links in online text—can contribute to (or detract from) the credibility and persuasiveness of your argument of definition.

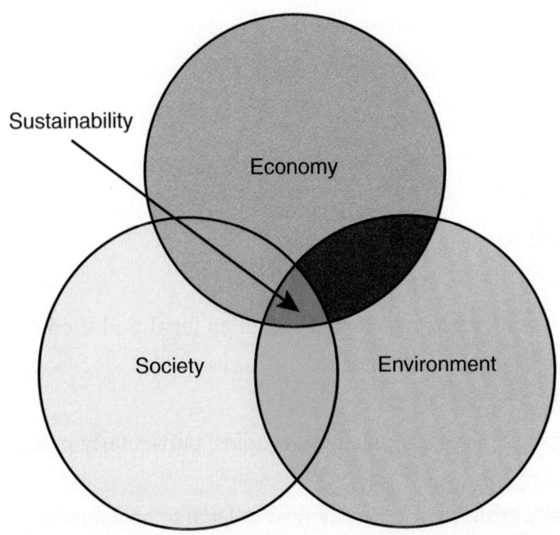

## GUIDE to writing an argument of definition

### Finding a Topic

You're entering an argument of definition when you:

- formulate a controversial or provocative definition: *The American Dream, which once meant a McMansion in a gated community, now has taken on a new definition.*
- challenge a definition: *For most Americans today, the American Dream involves not luxury but the secure pensions, cheap energy costs, and health insurance that workers in the 1950s and 1960s supposedly enjoyed.*
- try to determine whether something fits an existing definition: *Expanding opportunity is* (or is not) *central to the American Dream.*
- seek to broaden an existing definition or create a new definition to accommodate wider or differing perspectives: *In a world where information is easily and freely shared, it may be time to explore alternative definitions of plagiarism.*

Look for issues of definition in your everyday affairs—for instance, in the way that jobs are classified at work, that key terms are used in your academic major, that politicians characterize social issues that concern you, and so on. Be especially alert to definitional arguments that may arise when you or others deploy adjectives such as *true, real, actual,* or *genuine*: *a true patriot, real reform, authentic Mexican food.*

### Researching Your Topic

You can research issues of definition by using the following sources:

- college dictionaries and encyclopedias
- unabridged dictionaries
- specialized reference works and handbooks, such as legal and medical dictionaries
- your textbooks (check their glossaries)
- newsgroups and blogs that focus on particular topics, particularly political ones
- community or advocacy groups that are engaged in legal or social issues

Browse in your library reference room and use the electronic indexes and databases to determine how often disputed or contentious terms or phrases occur in influential online newspapers, journals, and Web sites.

When dealing with definitions, ask librarians about the most appropriate and reliable sources. For instance, to find the definition of a legal term, *Black's Law Dictionary* or a database such as FindLaw may help. Check USA.gov for how the government defines terms.

## Formulating a Claim

After exploring your subject, try to formulate a thesis that lets readers know where you stand or what issues are at stake. Begin with the following types of questions:

- questions related to genus: *Is assisting in suicide a crime?*
- questions related to species: *Is marijuana a harmful addictive drug or a useful medical treatment?*
- questions related to conditions: *Must the imposition of sexual attention be both unwanted and unsolicited to be considered sexual harassment?*
- questions related to fulfillment of conditions: *Has our college kept in place traditions or policies that might constitute racial discrimination?*
- questions related to membership in a named class: *Is any pop artist today in a class with Bob Dylan, the Beatles, Aretha Franklin, or the Rolling Stones?*

If you start with a thesis, it should be a complete statement that makes a claim of definition and states the reasons supporting it. You may later decide to separate the claim from its supporting reasons. But a working thesis should be a fully articulated thought that spells out all the details and qualifications: *Who? What? Where? When? How many? How regularly? How completely?*

However, since arguments of definition are often exploratory and tentative, an initial thesis (if you have one) may simply describe problems in formulating a particular definition: *What we mean by X is likely to remain unsettled until we can agree more fully about Y and Z; The key to understanding what constitutes X may be in appreciating how different groups approach Y and Z.*

## Examples of Definitional Claims

- Assisting a gravely ill person in committing suicide should not be considered *murder* when the motive for the act is to ease a person's suffering and not to benefit from the death.

- Although somewhat addictive, marijuana should not be classified as a *dangerous drug* because it damages individuals and society less than heroin or cocaine and because it helps people with life-threatening diseases live more comfortably.
- Giving college admission preference to all racial minorities can be an example of *class discrimination* because such policies may favor middle- and upper-class students who are already advantaged.
- Attempts to define the concept of *freedom* need to take into account the way the term is historically understood in cultures worldwide, not just in the countries of Western Europe and North America.

## Preparing a Proposal

If your instructor asks you to prepare a proposal for your project, here's a format that may help:

State your thesis or hypothesis completely. If you're having trouble doing so, try outlining it in Toulmin terms:

Claim:

Reason(s):

Warrant(s):

Alternatively, you might describe the complications of a definitional issue you hope to explore in your project, with a thesis perhaps coming later.

- Explain why this argument of definition deserves attention. What's at stake? Why is it important for your readers to consider?
- Identify whom you hope to reach through your argument and why these readers would be interested in it. How might you involve them in the paper?
- Briefly discuss the key challenges that you anticipate in preparing your argument.
- Determine what sources you expect to consult: Web? Databases? Dictionaries? Encyclopedias? Periodicals?
- Determine what visuals to include in your definitional argument.
- Describe the format you expect to use: Research essay? Letter to the editor? Web page?

## Thinking about Organization

Your argument of definition is likely to include some of the following parts:

- a claim involving a question of definition
- a general definition of some key concept
- a careful look at your subject in terms of that general definition
- evidence for every part of the argument, including visual evidence if appropriate
- a careful consideration of alternative views and counterarguments
- a conclusion drawing out the implications of the argument

It's impossible, however, to predict what emphasis each of those parts might receive or what the ultimate shape of an argument of definition will be. Try to account for the ways people with different points of view will likely respond to your argument. Then, consider how to address such differences civilly in the body of your argument.

## Getting and Giving Response: Questions for Peer Response

Your instructor may assign you to a group for the purpose of reading and responding to each other's drafts. If not, ask for responses from serious readers or consultants at a writing center. Use the following questions to evaluate a colleague's draft. Be sure to illustrate your comments with examples; specific comments help more than general observations.

### *The Claim*

- Is the claim clearly an issue of definition?
- Is the claim significant enough to interest readers?
- Are clear and specific criteria established for the concept being defined? Do the criteria define the term adequately? Using this definition, could most readers identify what's being defined and distinguish it from other related concepts?

### *Evidence for the Claim*

- Is enough evidence furnished to explain or support the definition? If not, what kind of additional evidence is needed?

- Is the evidence in support of the claim simply announced, or are its significance and appropriateness analyzed? Is a more detailed discussion needed?
- Are all the conditions of the definition met in the concept being examined?
- Are any objections readers might have to the claim, criteria, evidence, or way the definition is formulated adequately addressed? Have you represented other points of view completely and fairly?
- What kinds of sources are cited? How credible and persuasive will they be to readers? What other kinds of sources might work better?
- Are all quotations introduced with appropriate signal phrases (such as "As Tyson argues, . . .") and blended smoothly into the writer's sentences?

### *Organization and Style*

- How are the parts of the argument organized? Is this organization effective?
- Will readers understand the relationships among the claims, supporting reasons, warrants, and evidence? If not, how might those connections be clearer? Is the function of every visual clear? Are more transitions needed? Would headings or graphic devices help?
- Are the transitions or links from point to point, sentence to sentence, and paragraph to paragraph clear and effective? If not, how could they be improved?
- Is the style suited to the subject? Is it too formal, casual, or technical? Can it be improved?
- Which sentences seem effective? Which ones seem weaker, and how could they be improved? Should short sentences be combined, and any longer ones be broken up?
- How effective are the paragraphs? Too short or too long? How can they be improved?
- Which words or phrases seem effective? Do any seem vague or inappropriate for the audience or the writer's purpose? Are technical or unfamiliar terms defined?

### *Spelling, Punctuation, Mechanics, Documentation, and Format*

- Are there any errors in spelling, punctuation, capitalization, and the like?
- Is the documentation appropriate and consistent? (See Chapter 21.)
- Does the paper or project follow an appropriate format? Is it appropriately designed and attractively presented?

## PROJECTS •

1. Write an argument of definition about a term such as *kinetic military action* (see p. 189) that has suddenly become culturally significant or recently changed in some important way. Either defend the way the term has come to be defined or raise questions about its appropriateness, offensiveness, inaccuracy, and so on. Consider words or expressions such as *terrorism, marriage equality, racist, death panel, enhanced interrogation, tea partier, academic bulimia, occupy anything,* etc.
2. Write an essay in which you compare or contrast the meaning of two related terms, explaining the differences between them by using one or more methods of definition: formal definition, operational definition, definition by example. Be clever in your choice of the intial terms: look for a pairing in which the differences might not be immediately apparent to people unfamiliar with how the terms are used in specific communities. Consider terms such as liberal/progressive, classy/cool, intellectual/egghead, student athlete/jock, and so on.
3. In an essay at the end of this chapter, Jennifer Pier explores the definition of *white lie*, trying to understand not only how it differs from other lies, but also how serious it is. Her conclusion is perhaps startling: "the white lie is the most dangerous form of lying." After reading this selection carefully, respond to Pier's argument in an argument of definition of your own. Or, alternatively, explore a concept similar to *white lie* with the same intensity that Pier brings to her project. Look for a term to define and analyze either from your major or from an area of interest to you.
4. Because arguments of definition can have such important consequences, it helps to develop one by first getting input from lots of "stakeholders," that is, from people or groups likely to be affected by any change in the way a term is defined. Working with a small group, identify a term in your school or wider community that might need a fresh formulation or a close review. It could be a familiar campus word or phrase such as *nontraditional student, diversity, scholastic dishonesty,* or *social justice*; or it may be a term that has newly entered the local environment, perhaps reflecting an issue of law enforcement, safety, transportation, health, or even entertainment. Once you have settled on a significant term, identify a full range of stakeholders. Then, through some systematic field research (interviews, questionnaires) or by examining existing documents and materials (such as library sources, Web sites, pamphlets, publications), try to understand how the term currently functions in your community. Your definitional argument will, in effect, be what you can learn about the meanings that word or phrase has today for a wide variety of people.

# The Reprehensibility of the White Lie

JENNIFER PIER

Opening paragraph defines *white lies* through familiar examples.

The white lie wears many hats, and he is tricky in his disguise. He is hard to define but easy to recognize. Do you like this dress on me? *Of course*. Did you enjoy the party? *It was a blast*. Did you break this vase? *It wasn't me!* This tactic pervades our society, and many times, we don't even notice that we're employing it. The white lie is so enticing and available. It has become almost second nature for people to slip in an untruth that ameliorates a situation. But why do we do this? It's not as if our words actually mean something, as if our lies and truths matter in the grand scheme of things. Perhaps this evasion of responsibility is a sign that they do.

Pier offers a first criterion for *white lie*.

Therein lies the first criterion that defines a white lie. It means something. A listener can deduce a meaning, whether it's the intended one or not, from our words. Take the question that begets the prototypical white lie, a woman asking a man: "Do I look fat in this dress?" Assuming that the dress does indeed make the questioner look fat, what is one to say? If you say that it doesn't, then the woman could technically deduce that she does look fat, but she just happens not to in this dress. Or perhaps she is fat, and she will always look fat?

---

Jennifer Pier wrote this essay for an "Advanced Writing" class during her junior year at the University of Texas at Austin. In her topic proposal, she begins with her sense that "[a] lie is a lie, no matter what color or degree of politeness accompanies it." Then she offered the following as her working thesis: "Although society considers the white lie to be the most benign form of lying, it actually is the most malignant: it meets the criteria for the vilest of lies while also carrying the guise of benevolence (which we bestow upon it through societal convention)." These notions are explored in considerable detail in the final version reprinted here.

So it doesn't matter what type of clothing she dons because in whatever she wears, she will still look fat. Noticing myself going through these conclusions after I've posed the question, I've learned just not to ask it, for my own sanity and for the sanity of the people around me.

Yet white lies, as innocent as they seem, have a meaning behind them. If my sister were to tell me, "Yes, that dress makes you look as hideous and large as the Eiffel Tower," I wouldn't believe her for a second. The absurdity of her statement allows me to see that she is making a gross overstatement. White lies, however, are not so transparent. Within their politeness, they carry a judgment that satisfies a social convention. The liar provides the desired answer to a question or situation because this is his proper role at that moment. When a guest tells his hostess that an obviously lame party was (to him, the hostess, and everyone else there) "Terrific!" he, as well as everyone within hearing range, knows that he is lying. But because it is socially acceptable to tell this type of falsehood, no one passes judgment. The question here shouldn't be whether the guest lied. He did. The ethical issue should be whether in telling this fib his actions are reprehensible. Why is it okay to lie blatantly when one is fulfilling a social convention? It's because his white lie establishes that he is playing by the rules of society: he's being polite.

Pier then explores what makes white lies tolerable.

What is it about the politeness of a white lie that makes it acceptable? I don't think that I can supply a complete answer. But perhaps it is in comparison to the alternative that we tolerate it. Honesty and simplicity don't thrive in our society today. We cling to euphemisms and walk on tiptoes so that we remain politically correct, not allowing ourselves to offend others or hurt ourselves. A painting is art until it offends my culture, free speech exists until it encroaches on my freedoms, and honesty is a virtue only until it gets me into trouble. Nothing can exist by itself as good or bad, right or wrong, without a point of contrast. A white lie is acceptable in comparison

Pier makes a second key distinction here to separate white lies from other types of duplicity: their politeness.

to every other form of lying because, in the short run, it does the least amount of damage.

Over the years, linguists have developed the definition of a paradigmatic lie. Not coincidentally, the formula for a lie mirrors the formula for a mortal sin in the Catholic tradition. Perhaps that makes perfect sense, since one of the Ten Commandments is "you shall not bear false witness against your neighbor." To reach the status of "mortal" sin, an act must go against divine law, the person performing the act must know that the sin is grave, and despite this, he must do it voluntarily. In like manner, to qualify as a lie, a statement must first be false. Then the speaker must know that the statement is false, and finally, in telling someone the statement, the speaker must intend to deceive his audience (Coleman).

The essay now provides an operational definition of *common lying*: three conditions must be in place.

A common "perfect" lie, then, fits all three of these qualifications. What makes a white lie more despicable than the common lie is that a white lie fits all three while carrying with it the duplicity of politeness. Sometimes a person tells a white lie to benefit his audience or to save face. But more often, white lies hide under the ruse of social convention. A white lie is still morally reprehensible—it's still a lie. The innocence associated with a white lie tricks us into looking past its addictive nature. Much like a gateway drug, the white lies we tell initiate a spiral downward into heavier, more serious lies that have lethal effects on our reputations and interpersonal relationships.

The third criterion of a white lie—its destructiveness—is also the most important.

The most important element of a white lie is its destructiveness; the act of telling one hurts both the receiver and the sender. On the surface, it's a handy fix-all for an uncomfortable situation or a loaded question that begs evasion. But a deeper look reveals the disconnect in communication between a speaker and his audience. On one hand, the receiver of the lie is never allowed to hear the truth. Yet, on the other hand, the speaker cannot trust the situation he is in enough to allow himself to speak honestly. Rather than face this vulnerability, he protects himself under the shield of a white lie because, after all, this is a socially acceptable option. But then the speaker grows dependent on this shield. His words lose their truthfulness, and he is conquered by the ease of evasion that the white lie offers.

Going back to the *Do I look fat in this dress?* example, say that this question was asked in the context of a marriage. A wife asks this of her husband as they rush out the door, late for a dinner appointment. The husband, not wanting to waste more time by his wife changing her clothes, says immediately, "No, you look fine." This lie creates a first crack in the foundation of their relationship. As soon as he understands that he's gotten away with this lie, he sees no problem with one or two more. Before long, the foundation will crumble. His wife, perceiving his lies, no matter the severity, begins to doubt any statement or excuse that he makes. Is he really working late, or is he with someone else? What perhaps seemed like a ready and easy answer at the time, in the long run, is only the first step toward the destruction of their marriage.

Pier dramatizes the danger of white lies by describing a slippery slope (see p. 76).

The ease and politeness that we associate with white lies prevents the liar from looking beyond the here-and-now to the problems and consequences that will inevitably arise from its use. This is why the white lie is the most dangerous form of lying. This is why the white lie is morally and ethically reprehensible. I don't mean to condemn those who tell white lies. We all do. Heck, I do—daily. And I don't propose that no one should ever tell a white lie again. Rather, I mean to reveal the white lie for what it truly is and to make us aware of its insidiousness. Perhaps the next time you're grappling between the decision to tell the truth or to slide your way out of confrontation with a white lie, you'll think twice before choosing the latter.

Essay concludes by considering how to deal with white lies.

### Work Cited

Coleman, Linda, and Paul Kay. "Prototypes Semantics: The English Word *Lie*." *Language* 57 (Mar. 1981): 26–44. 14 Apr. 2009. Web.

# The Meaning of Friendship in a Social-Networked World

ALEX PATTAKOS

"What is a friend? A single soul dwelling in two bodies." This quote is attributed to the ancient Greek philosopher Aristotle who wrote extensively about the notion and importance of true friendship as a determinant of *meaningful* living.

Aristotle's view on this matter stands in sharp contrast to what is depicted in the newly-released movie *The Social Network,* destined to become a cult classic, about the founding of the Internet social networking site "Facebook." With the advertising tag line, "You don't get to 500 million friends without making a few enemies," you have to wonder what the definition of "friends" is in this kind of social networking context. And as you watch the relationships depicted in the film, especially that between founder Mark Zuckerberg and his network of "friends," it is obvious that they don't meet the quality standards espoused by Aristotle!

In this connection (no pun intended), computer whiz Zuckerberg and his best friend Eduardo Saverin, also a principal co-founder of Facebook, become embroiled in enough fights, including a nasty legal battle, to establish that there is not a single soul dwelling in their two bodies. The notion of "friend," of course, is used rather loosely in the online world of Facebook. What do you think Aristotle would have to say about the meaning of—and path to—friendship that has come to popularize the new millennium? Have we gone too far in our quest for connection with others in a world that has become increasingly disconnected even if, according to American journalist Thomas Friedman, it is supposedly "flat"?

And in a world of hyper-connectivity driven by technology that knows no bounds, what is happening to true friendship? Is it dying away? Or are

---

Alex Pattakos is a frequent contributor to publications such as *Fast Company* and the *Huffington Post* and the author of the book *Prisoners of Our Thoughts* (2008). He is the founder of the Center for Meaning in Santa Fe, New Mexico.

the various social media "platforms" such as Facebook, Twitter, and LinkedIn simply redefining or transforming our modern-day notion of friendship? If so, what are the implications for life as we know it on this planet? Will we be more happy? Will it promote the kind of meaningful existence that Aristotle was seeking and advocating?

The search for meaning is not only the primary intrinsic motivation of human beings, it is also a megatrend of the twenty-first century. From such a meaning-focused perspective, where does friendship fit in? And how might the social media "advances" referred to here influence, directly and indirectly, the nature of friendships between people and the human quest for meaning?

To be sure, I have more questions than answers, although there are some trends that are worthy of mention on the subject. A recent article in *USA Today* by Mark Vernon, a research fellow at Birkbeck College in London, England, addressed the issue of the social media's influence and concluded, "Just as our daily lives are becoming more technologically connected, we're losing other more meaningful relationships. Yes, we're losing our friends." In other words, the joys of real human contact are being replaced by electronic stimuli and *shallow* friendships, that is, "social connections" rather than the kind of true friendships described and espoused by Aristotle. In our post-modern society, there is evidence that while we have plenty of acquaintances, more and more of us have few individuals to whom we can turn and share our authentic selves, our deep intimacies.

Moreover, according to research published in the *American Sociological Review*, a highly-reputable professional journal, the average American has only two close friends and some twenty-five percent don't have any friends! We're not just "bowling alone," to borrow the title from a book by sociologist Robert Putman, we're effectively *living alone* in the midst of a socially-networked world! Now how ironic is that? Parenthetically, this is an illustration of what I call in my book, *Prisoners of Our Thoughts*, paradoxical intention or working against ourselves. We have become our worst enemy as we seek to navigate the sea of so-called "friends" that we've been promised through Facebook and other social networking sites.

Aristotle once asked his fellow Athenians, "Who would live without friends even if they had every other thing?" Importantly, he believed that good friends were superior to any material possessions one might have. Stop and think, then, for a moment about the quality of friends that we may make online, such as via Facebook, and compare this quality of relationships with other kinds of friends with whom we have actual face-to-face contact—be it infrequent, work-related, social, and intimate, perhaps even loving. Which of these contacts represent meaningful relationships and, by implication, true friendships? Which of these contacts, when all is said and done, really matters the most to you? In addition to feeding your soul, you can feel a single soul dwelling in two bodies?

In his classic work *Ethics*, Aristotle also offered the following ageless wisdom: "The desire for friendship comes quickly. Friendship does not." This is a very profound and perhaps provocative statement, especially in light of the powerful forces behind social networking. ("What do you mean you don't have a Facebook page?") It takes time and effort to build true friendships; relationships through which you are able and willing to disclose your *authentic* self—close thoughts, intimate feelings, and sensitive vulnerabilities including fears. While a social connection on Facebook may be only a click away, cultivating a true friendship is not that easy or straightforward if you believe in and take Aristotle's advice.

Now, in the spirit of full disclosure, I must admit that I'm a "techie" (formerly called a "nerd") and have been for as long as I can remember. Among other things, I was credited by the World Future Society with inventing the concept of the "Electronic Visiting Professor," an innovation in online distance learning when the Information Highway was still a dirt road. I've also been a "Crackberry" (an obsessive-compulsive user of the Blackberry device), and was an early adopter of the iPhone which now keeps me "connected" to family, friends, acquaintances, and others whenever I choose to let it. (Note the "I choose" reference; I am very conscious of the need to manage the technology, not the other way around!) I also regularly use most of the social networking platforms mentioned, explicitly or implicitly, in this blog article. Moreover, I'm very familiar with the propensity among people today to share themselves online with complete strangers-as-friends, presumably feeling safe in the deceptive shadows of cyberspace.

I also recognize that in today's busy, fast-paced world, many people are more likely to tell their hopes and troubles to bartenders, taxi drivers, hair stylists, and therapists than they are to the people who are regularly in their lives. In my opinion, this is a sad commentary on post-modern society for many people seem to have drifted away from true friendships and a sense of "community" and are now living very private, even lonely, lives. It's time to resurrect the meaning and value of authentic relationships with others. It's time to refocus on and allow friendships to flourish in *meaningful* ways, both in our personal and work lives. "A friend is another self," Aristotle also told us. True friendships, which admittedly are a blast from the past, are not simply a manifestation of what is being called "social connectivity" in social networking parlance. No, true friendships are the key to a flourishing, meaningful life, well-being, and a truly-connected society and world. Now would you like to Facebook me?

# 10
# Evaluations

"We don't want to go there for coffee. Their beans aren't fair trade, the drinks are high in calories, and the stuff is *way* overpriced."

Three students who have cochaired the campus Arts Festival for six semesters are all graduating. Their leadership has led to significant improvements in the diversity and quality of cultural activities. So the group calls a special meeting to talk about what qualities it needs in its next leaders to sustain the progress.

Orson Welles's masterpiece *Citizen Kane* is playing at the Student Union for only one more night, but the new *Spider-Man* is featured across the street in THX sound. Guess which movie your roomie wants to see? You intend to set him straight.

## Understanding Evaluations

**Evaluations** are everyday arguments. By the time you leave home in the morning, you've likely made a dozen informal evaluations: You've selected dressy clothes because you have a job interview with a law firm. You've chosen low-fat yogurt and fruit over the pancakes you really love. You've queued up the perfect playlist on your iPod for your hike to campus. In each case, you've applied criteria to a particular problem and then made a decision. That's evaluating on the fly.

Some professional evaluations require more elaborate standards, evidence, and paperwork (imagine an aircraft manufacturer certifying a new jet for passenger service), but they don't differ structurally from the simpler choices that people make all the time. People love to voice their opinions, and they always have. In fact, a mode of ancient rhetoric—called the **ceremonial**, or **epideictic**—was devoted entirely to speeches of praise and blame. (See Chapter 1.)

Today, rituals of praise and blame are a significant part of American life. Adults who would choke at the notion of debating causal or definitional claims will happily spend hours appraising the Oakland Raiders, Boston Red Sox, or Detroit Pistons. Other evaluative spectacles in our culture include awards shows, beauty pageants, most-valuable-player presentations, lists of best-dressed or worst-dressed celebrities, "sexiest people"

Arguments about sports are usually evaluations of some kind.

magazine covers, literary prizes, political opinion polls, consumer product magazines, and—the ultimate formal public gesture of evaluation—elections. Indeed, making evaluations is a form of entertainment in America and generates big audiences (think of *American Idol*) and revenues.

**RESPOND•**

In the last ten years, there has been a proliferation of awards programs for movies, musicians, sports figures, and other categories. For example, before the Academy of Motion Picture Arts and Sciences hands out the Oscars, a half-dozen other organizations have given prizes to the annual crop of films. Write a short opinion piece assessing the merits of a particular awards show or a feature such as *People*'s annual "Sexiest Man Alive" issue. What should a proper event of this kind accomplish? Does the event you're reviewing do so?

## Criteria of Evaluation

Arguments of evaluation can produce simple rankings and winners or can lead to profound decisions about our lives, but they always involve standards. The particular standards we establish for judging anything—whether an idea, a work of art, a person, or a product—are called **criteria of evaluation**. Sometimes criteria are self-evident: a car that gets fifteen miles per gallon is a gas hog, and a piece of fish that smells even a little off shouldn't be eaten. But criteria get complicated when a subject is abstract: *What features make a song a classic? What constitutes a fair wage? How do we measure a successful foreign policy or college career?* Struggling to identify such difficult criteria of evaluation can lead to important insights into your values, motives, and preferences.

Why make such a big deal about criteria when many acts of evaluation seem effortless? We should be suspicious of our judgments especially when we make them casually. It's irresponsible simply to think that spontaneous and uninformed quips should carry the same weight as well-informed and well-reasoned opinions. Serious evaluations always require reflection, and when we look deeply into our judgments, we sometimes discover important questions that typically go unasked, many prefaced by *why*:

- You challenge the grade you received in a course, but you don't question the practice of grading.

- You argue passionately that a Republican Congress is better for America than a Democratic alternative, but you fail to ask why voters get only two choices.
- You argue that buying a hybrid car makes more sense than keeping an SUV, but you don't ask whether taking alternative forms of transportation (like the bus or a bike) makes the most sense of all.

Push an argument of evaluation hard enough, and even simple judgments become challenging and intriguing.

In fact, for many writers, grappling with criteria is the toughest step in producing an evaluation. When you offer an opinion about a topic you know reasonably well, you want readers to learn something from your judgment. So you need time to think about and then justify the criteria for your opinion, whatever the subject.

Do you think, for instance, that you could explain what (if anything) makes a veggie burger good? Though many people have eaten veggie burgers, they probably haven't spent much time thinking about them. But it wouldn't be enough to claim merely that a proper one should be juicy or tasty—such trite claims are not even interesting. The following criteria offered on the *Cook's Illustrated* Web site show what happens when experts give the issue a closer look:

> **We wanted to create veggie burgers that even meat eaters would love. We didn't want them to taste like hamburgers, but we did want them to act like hamburgers, *having a modicum of chew, a harmonious blend of savory ingredients, and the ability to go from grill to bun without falling apart.* [emphasis added]**
>
> —*Cook's Illustrated*

What criteria of evaluation are embedded in this visual argument?

After a lot of experimenting, *Cook's Illustrated* came up with a recipe that met these criteria.

Criteria of evaluation aren't static, either. They differ according to time and audience. Much market research, for example, is designed to find out what particular consumers want now and may want in the future—what their criteria are for buying a product. In good times, people may demand homes with soaring entryways, lots of space, and premium appliances. In tougher times, they may care more about efficient use of space, quality insulation, and energy-efficient stoves and dishwashers. Shifts in values, attitudes, and criteria happen all the time.

**RESPOND.**

Choose one item from the following list that you understand well enough to evaluate. Develop several criteria of evaluation that you could defend to distinguish excellence from mediocrity in the area. Then choose an item that you don't know much about and explain the research you might do to discover reasonable criteria of evaluation for it.

digital cameras
NFL quarterbacks
social networking sites
TV journalists
video games
fashion designers
Navajo rugs
U.S. vice presidents
organic vegetables
hot water heaters
spoken word poetry
athletic shoes
country music bands
hip-hop bands

## Characterizing Evaluation

One way of understanding evaluative arguments is to consider the types of evidence they use. A distinction explored in Chapter 4 between hard evidence and constructed arguments based on reason is helpful here: we defined **hard evidence** as facts, statistics, testimony, and other kinds of arguments that can be measured, recorded, or even found—the so-called smoking gun in a criminal investigation. We defined constructed arguments based on reason as those that are shaped by language, using various kinds of logic.

We can talk about arguments of evaluation the same way, looking at some as quantitative and others as qualitative. **Quantitative arguments** of evaluation rely on criteria that can be measured, counted, or demonstrated in some mechanical fashion (something is taller, faster, smoother, quieter, or more powerful than something else). In contrast, **qualitative arguments** rely on criteria that must be explained through language and media, relying on such matters as values, traditions, and emotions (something is more ethical, more beneficial, more handsome, or more noble than something else). A claim of evaluation might be supported by arguments of both sorts.

## Quantitative Evaluations

At first glance, quantitative evaluations seem to hold all the cards, especially in a society as enamored of science and technology as our own is. Making judgments should be easy if all it involves is measuring and counting—and in some cases, that's the way things work out. *Who's the tallest or heaviest or loudest person in your class?* If your classmates allow themselves to be measured, you could find out easily enough, using the right equipment and internationally sanctioned standards of measurement—the meter, the kilo, or the decibel.

But what if you were to ask, *Who's the smartest person in class?* You could answer this more complex question quantitatively, using IQ tests or college entrance examinations that report results numerically. In fact, almost all college-bound students in the United States submit to this kind of evaluation, taking either the SAT or ACT to demonstrate their verbal and mathematical prowess. Such measures are widely accepted by educators and institutions, but they are also vigorously challenged. What do they actually measure? They predict likely academic success only in college, which is one kind of intelligence.

Quantitative measures of evaluation can be enormously useful, but even the most objective measures have limits. They've been devised by fallible people who look at the world from their own inevitably limited perspectives.

## Qualitative Evaluations

Many issues of evaluation that are closest to people's hearts aren't subject to quantification. *What makes a movie great?* If you suggested a quantitative measure like length, your friends would probably hoot, "Get serious!" But what about box-office receipts, adjusted for inflation? Would films that made the most money—an easily quantifiable measure—be the "best pictures"? That select group would include movies such as *Star Wars, The Sound of Music, Gone with the Wind, Titanic,* and *Avatar*. An interesting group of films—but the best?

To define the criteria for "great movie," you'd more likely look for the standards and evidence that serious critics explore in their arguments, abstract or complicated issues such as their societal impact, cinematic technique, dramatic structures, intelligent casting, and so on. Most of these markers of quality could be defined and identified with some precision but not measured or counted. You'd also have to make your case rhetorically, convincing the audience to accept the markers of quality you are offering and yet appreciating that they might not. A movie reviewer making qualitative judgments might spend as much time defending criteria of evaluation as providing evidence that these standards are present in a particular film. But putting those standards into action can be what makes a review something worth reading. Consider how Roger Ebert, in writing about the classic film *The Godfather*, actually teaches his readers how to find evidence of quality in a great director's choices:

> [Francis Ford] Coppola populates his dark interior spaces with remarkable faces. The front-line actors—Brando, Pacino, Caan, Duvall—are attractive in one way or another, but those who play their associates are chosen for their fleshy, thickly lined faces—for huge jaws and deeply set eyes. Look at Abe Vigoda as Tessio, the fearsome enforcer. The first time we see him, he's dancing with a child at the wedding, her satin pumps balanced on his shoes. The sun shines that day, but

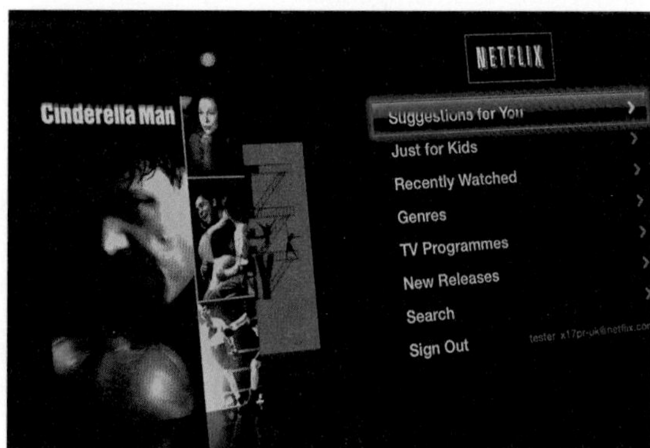


Web sites such as Netflix do offer recommendations for films based on users' past selections and the ratings of other users and critics. Sometimes those judgments are at odds. Then whom do you trust?

never again: He is developed as a hulking presence who implies the possibility of violent revenge. Only at the end is he brightly lit again, to make him look vulnerable as he begs for his life.

**RESPOND.**

For examples of powerful evaluation arguments, search the Web or your library for eulogies or obituaries of famous, recently deceased individuals. Try to locate at least one such item, and then analyze the types of claims it makes about the accomplishments of the deceased. What types of criteria of evaluation hold the obituary or eulogy together? Why should we respect or admire the person?

## Developing an Evaluative Argument

Developing an argument of evaluation can seem like a simple process, especially if you already know what your claim is likely to be. To continue the movie theme for one more example:

> *Citizen Kane* is the finest film ever made by an American director.

Having established a claim, you would then explore the implications of your belief, drawing out the reasons, warrants, and evidence that might support it:

| | |
|---|---|
| Claim | *Citizen Kane* is the finest film ever made by an American director . . . |
| Reason | . . . because it revolutionizes the way we see the world. |
| Warrant | Great films change viewers in fundamental ways. |
| Evidence | Shot after shot, *Citizen Kane* presents the life of its protagonist through cinematic images that viewers can never forget. |

The warrant here is, in effect, an implied statement of criteria—in this case, the quality that defines "great film" for the writer. It may be important for the writer to share that assumption with readers and perhaps to identify other great films that similarly make viewers appreciate new perspectives.

As you can see, in developing an evaluative argument, you'll want to pay special attention to criteria, claims, and evidence.

## Formulating Criteria

Notice how specific the editors of *Cook's Illustrated Magazine* are in establishing their criteria for the ideal chewy chocolate chip cookie.

LINK TO P. 728

Although even casual evaluations (*The band sucks!*) might be traced to reasonable criteria, most people don't defend their positions until they are challenged (*Oh yeah?*). Similarly, writers who address readers with whom they share core values rarely discuss their criteria in great detail. A film critic like Roger Ebert (see p. 220) isn't expected to restate all his principles every time he writes a movie review. Ebert assumes that his readers will—over time—come to appreciate his standards. Still, criteria can make or break a piece.

So spend time developing your criteria of evaluation. What exactly makes a shortstop an all-star? Why is a standardized test an unreliable measure of intelligence? Fundamentally, what distinguishes an inspired fashion designer from a run-of-the-mill one? List the possibilities and then pare the possibilities down to the essentials. If you offer vague, dull, or unsupportable principles, expect to be challenged.

You're most likely to be vague about your beliefs when you haven't thought (or read) enough about your subject. Push yourself at least as far as you imagine readers will. Anticipate readers looking over your shoulder, asking difficult questions. Say, for example, that you intend to argue that anyone who wants to stay on the cutting edge of personal technology will obviously want Apple's latest iPad because it does so many amazing things. But what does that mean exactly? What makes the device "amazing"? Is it that it gives access to email and the Web, has a high-resolution screen, offers an astonishing number of apps, and makes a good e-reader? These are particular features of the device. But can you identify a more fundamental quality to explain the product's appeal, such as an iPad user's experience, enjoyment, or feeling of productivity? (For one answer, see Virginia Postrel's "Why We Prize That Magical Mystery Pad" on p. 240.) You'll often want to raise your evaluation to a higher level of generality like this so that your appraisal of a product, book, performance, or political figure works as a coherent argument, and not just as a list of random observations.

Be certain, too, that your criteria of evaluation apply to more than just your topic of the moment. Your standards should make sense on their own merits and apply across the board. If you tailor your criteria to get the outcome you want, you are doing what is called "special pleading." You might be pleased when you prove that the home team is awesome, but it won't take skeptics long to figure out how you've cooked the books.

**RESPOND.**

Local news and entertainment magazines often publish "best of" issues or articles that catalog their readers' and editors' favorites in such categories as "best place to go on a first date," "best ice cream sundae," and "best dentist." Sometimes the categories are specific: "best places to say 'I was retro before retro was cool'" or "best movie theater seats." Imagine that you're the editor of your own local magazine and that you want to put out a "best of" issue tailored to your hometown. Develop ten categories for evaluation. For each category, list the evaluative criteria that you would use to make your judgment. Next, consider that because your criteria are warrants, they're especially tied to audience. (The criteria for "best dentist," for example, might be tailored to people whose major concern is avoiding pain, to those whose children will be regular patients, or to those who want the cheapest possible dental care.) For several of the evaluative categories, imagine that you have to justify your judgments to a completely different audience. Write a new set of criteria for that audience.

## Making Claims

In evaluations, claims can be stated directly or, more rarely, strongly implied. For most writers, strong statements followed by reasonable qualifications work best. Consider the differences between the following three claims and how much greater the burden of proof is for the first claim:

The most outrageous of them all? Margaret Cho in 2008 lamé mode.

**Margaret Cho is the most shocking comedian ever.**

**Margaret Cho is one of the three or four most outrageous comedians around today.**

**Margaret Cho may come to be regarded as one of the most outspoken comedians of her time.**

Here's a second set of examples demonstrating the same principle, that qualifications generally make a claim of evaluation easier to deal with and smarter:

Malia Wollan tells the story of the globalized poultry market. What claims—either stated or implied—can you find in her reporting on the many ways that parts of chickens are used?

LINK TO P. 708

> No Child Left Behind sure was a dumb idea.
>
> The No Child Left Behind educational reform likely did more harm than good.
>
> While laudable in its intentions to improve American schools, the No Child Left Behind Act of 2001 put so high a premium on testing that it undermined more fundamental aspects of elementary and secondary education.

The point of qualifying a statement isn't to make evaluative claims bland but to make them responsible and reasonable. Consider how Reagan Tankersley uses the criticisms of a musical genre he enjoys to frame a claim he makes in its defense:

> Structurally, dub step is a simple musical form, with formulaic progressions and beats, something that gives a musically tuned ear little to grasp or analyze. For this reason, a majority of traditionally trained musicians find the genre to be a waste of time. These people have a legitimate position. . . . However, I hold that it is the simplicity of dub step that makes it special: the primal nature of the song is what digs so deeply into fans. It accesses the most primitive area in our brains that connects to the uniquely human love of music.
>
> —Reagan Tankersley, "Dub Step: Why People Dance"

Tankersley doesn't pretend that dub step is something it's not, nor does he expect his argument to win over traditionally minded critics. Yet he still makes a claim worth considering.

One tip: Nothing adds more depth to an opinion than letting others challenge it. When you can, use the resources of the Internet or local

Dub step DJs Benga, Artwork, and Skream of Magnetic Man perform.

discussion boards to get responses to your opinions or topic proposals. It can be eye-opening to realize how strongly people react to ideas or points of view that you regard as perfectly normal. Share your claim and, then when you're ready, your first draft with friends and classmates, asking them to identify places where your ideas need additional support, either in the discussion of criteria or in the presentation of evidence.

### Presenting Evidence

Generally, the more evidence in an evaluation the better, provided that the evidence is relevant. For example, in evaluating the performance of two laptops, the speed of their processors would be essential, but the quality of their keyboards or the availability of service might be less crucial yet still worth mentioning. But you have to decide how much detail your readers want in your argument. For technical subjects, you might make your basic case briefly and then attach additional supporting documents at the end—tables, graphs, charts—for those who want more data.

As Heather Mac Donald analyzes the fallout from the "Increase Diversity Bake Sale," what evidence does she see to support its goals to raise awareness of affirmative action in college admissions?

LINK TO P. 765

Just as important as relevance in selecting evidence is presentation. Not all pieces of evidence are equally convincing, nor should they be treated as such. Select evidence that is most likely to influence your readers, and then arrange the argument to build toward your best material. In most cases, that best material will be evidence that's specific, detailed, memorable, and derived from credible sources. The details in these paragraphs from Sean Wilsey's review of *Fun Home: A Family Tragicomic*, a graphic novel by Alison Bechdel, tell you precisely what makes the work "lush," "absorbing," and well worth reading:

> **It is a pioneering work, pushing two genres (comics and memoir) in multiple new directions, with panels that combine the detail and technical proficiency of R. Crumb with a seriousness, emotional complexity, and innovation completely its own. Then there are the actual words. Generally this is where graphic narratives stumble. Very few cartoonists can also write—or, if they can, they manage only to hit a few familiar notes. But *Fun Home* quietly succeeds in telling a story, not only through well-crafted images but through words that are equally revealing and well chosen. Big words, too! In 232 pages this memoir sent me to the dictionary five separate times (to look up "bargeboard," "buss," "scutwork," "humectant," and "perseverated").**
>
> **A comic book for lovers of words! Bechdel's rich language and precise images combine to create a lush piece of work—a memoir where**

> concision and detail are melded for maximum, obsessive density. She has obviously spent years getting this memoir right, and it shows. You can read *Fun Home* in a sitting, or get lost in the pictures within the pictures on its pages. The artist's work is so absorbing you feel you are living in her world.
>
> —Sean Wilsey, "The Things They Buried"

The details in this passage make the case that Alison Bechdel's novel is one that pushes both comics and memoirs in new directions.

In evaluation arguments, don't be afraid to concede a point when evidence goes contrary to the overall claim you wish to make. If you're really skillful, you can even turn a problem into an argumentative asset, as Bob Costas does in acknowledging the flaws of baseball great Mickey Mantle in the process of praising him:

> None of us, Mickey included, would want to be held to account for every moment of our lives. But how many of us could say that our best moments were as magnificent as his?
>
> —Bob Costas, "Eulogy for Mickey Mantle"

**RESPOND•**

Take a close look at the cover of Alison Bechdel's graphic novel *Fun Home: A Family Tragicomic*. In what various ways does it make an argument of evaluation designed to make you want to buy the work? Examinc other books, magazines, or media packages (such as video game or software boxes) and describe any strategies they use to argue for their merit.

## Considering Design and Visuals

Visual components play a significant role in many arguments of evaluation, especially those based on quantitative information. As soon as numbers are involved in supporting a claim, think about ways to arrange them in tables, charts, graphs, or infographics to make the information more accessible to readers. Visual elements are especially helpful when comparing items. Indeed, a visual spread like those in the federal government's "Buy a Safer Car" pamphlet (see p. 228) becomes an argument in itself about the vehicles the government has crash-tested for safety. The facts seem to speak for themselves because they are arrayed with care and deliberation. Similarly, you need to consider how you might present your facts visually to inform and persuade readers.

But don't ignore other basic design features of a text—such as headings for the different criteria you're using or, in online evaluations, links to material related to your subject. Such details can enhance your authority, credibility, and persuasiveness.

# PURCHASING WITH SAFETY IN MIND

| MAKE | MODEL | Body Style | RATINGS: Frontal Crash (Driver) | Frontal Crash (Passenger) | Overall Frontal | Side Barrier (Driver) | Side Barrier (Passenger–Rear Seat) | Side Pole (Driver) | Overall Side | Rollover | Overall Vehicle Score | SAFETY FEATURES: Lane Departure Warning | Forward Collision Warning | Electronic Stability Control |
|---|---|---|---|---|---|---|---|---|---|---|---|---|---|---|
| Cadillac | Escalade RWD | SUV | ★★★★★ | ★★★★ | ★★★★★ | ★★★★★ | ★★★★★ | ★★★★★ | ★★★★★ | ★★★ | ★★★★ | | | S |
| | STS FWD/AWD | 4 DR | NR | NR | NR | NR | NR | NR | NR | ★★★★★ | NR | 0 | 0 | S |
| Chevrolet | Cruze FWD | 4 DR | ★★★★★ | ★★★★★ | ★★★★★ | ★★★★★ | ★★★★★ | ★★★★★ | ★★★★★ | ★★★★ | ★★★★★ | | | S |
| | Equinox AWD | SUV | ★★★★★ | ★★★★ | ★★★★ | ★★★★ | ★★★★★ | ★★★★★ | ★★★★★ | ★★★★ | ★★★★ | | | S |
| | Equinox FWD | SUV | ★★★★★ | ★★★★ | ★★★★ | ★★★★ | ★★★★★ | ★★★★★ | ★★★★★ | ★★★★ | ★★★★ | | | S |
| | Malibu FWD | 4 DR | ★★★★★ | ★★★ | ★★★★ | ★★★★ | ★★★★★ | ★★★★★ | ★★★★★ | ★★★★ | ★★★★ | | | S |
| | Silverado 1500 Crew Cab 4WD | PU | ★★★★ | ★★★★ | ★★★★ | ★★★★★ | ★★★★★ | ★★★★★ | ★★★★★ | ★★★★ | ★★★★ | | | S |
| | Silverado 1500 Crew Cab Hybrid 4WD | PU | ★★★★ | ★★★★ | ★★★★ | ★★★★★ | ★★★★★ | ★★★★★ | ★★★★★ | ★★★★ | ★★★★ | | | S |
| | Silverado 1500 Crew Cab Hybrid RWD | PU | ★★★★ | ★★★★ | ★★★★ | ★★★★★ | ★★★★★ | ★★★★★ | ★★★★★ | ★★★★ | ★★★★ | | | S |
| | Silverado 1500 Crew Cab RWD | PU | ★★★★ | ★★★★ | ★★★★ | ★★★★★ | ★★★★★ | ★★★★★ | ★★★★★ | ★★★★ | ★★★★ | | | S |
| | Silverado 1500 Extended Cab 4WD | PU | ★★★★★ | ★★★★ | ★★★★ | ★★★★★ | ★★★★★ | ★★★★★ | ★★★★★ | ★★★★ | ★★★★ | | | S |
| | Silverado 1500 Extended Cab RWD | PU | ★★★★★ | ★★★★ | ★★★★ | ★★★★★ | ★★★★★ | ★★★★★ | ★★★★★ | ★★★★ | ★★★★ | | | S |
| | Silverado 1500 Regular Cab 4WD | PU | ★★★★★ | ★★★★ | ★★★★ | ★★★★★ | N/A | ★★★★★ | ★★★★★ | ★★★★ | ★★★★ | | | S |
| | Silverado 1500 Regular Cab RWD | PU | ★★★★★ | ★★★★ | ★★★★ | ★★★★★ | N/A | ★★★★★ | ★★★★★ | ★★★★ | ★★★★ | | | S |
| | Tahoe 4WD | SUV | ★★★★★ | ★★★★ | ★★★★★ | ★★★★★ | ★★★★★ | ★★★★★ | ★★★★★ | ★★★ | ★★★★ | | | S |
| | Tahoe Hybrid 4WD | SUV | ★★★★★ | ★★★★ | ★★★★★ | NR | NR | NR | NR | ★★★ | NR | | | S |
| | Tahoe Hybrid RWD | SUV | ★★★★★ | ★★★★ | ★★★★★ | NR | NR | NR | NR | ★★★ | NR | | | S |
| | Tahoe RWD | SUV | ★★★★★ | ★★★★ | ★★★★★ | ★★★★★ | ★★★★★ | ★★★★★ | ★★★★★ | ★★★ | ★★★★ | | | S |
| | Traverse AWD | SUV | ★★★★★ | ★★★★ | ★★★★ | ★★★★★ | ★★★★★ | ★★★★★ | ★★★★★ | ★★★★ | ★★★★★ | | | S |
| | Traverse FWD | SUV | ★★★★★ | ★★★★ | ★★★★ | ★★★★★ | ★★★★★ | ★★★★★ | ★★★★★ | ★★★★ | ★★★★★ | | | S |
| | Volt FWD | 5 HB | ★★★★★ | ★★★★ | ★★★★ | ★★★★★ | ★★★★★ | ★★★★★ | ★★★★★ | ★★★★★ | ★★★★★ | | | S |
| Dodge | Caliber FWD | 5 HB | ★★★★ | ★★★★ | ★★★★ | ★★★ | ★★★★★ | ★ | ★★★ | ★★★★ | ★★★ | | | 0 |
| Ford | Edge AWD | SUV | ★★★ | ★★★ | ★★★ | ★★★★★ | ★★★★★ | ★★★★★ | ★★★★★ | ★★★★ | ★★★★ | | 0 | S |
| | Edge FWD | SUV | ★★★ | ★★★ | ★★★ | ★★★★★ | ★★★★★ | ★★★★★ | ★★★★★ | ★★★★ | ★★★★ | | 0 | S |
| | Escape 4WD | SUV | ★★ | ★★★★ | ★★★ | ★★★ | ★★★ | ★★★★ | ★★★ | ★★★ | ★★★ | | | S |
| | Escape Hybrid 4WD | SUV | ★★ | ★★★★ | ★★★ | ★★★ | ★★★ | ★★★★ | ★★★ | ★★★ | ★★★ | | | S |
| | Escape Hybrid FWD | SUV | ★★ | ★★★★ | ★★★ | ★★★ | ★★★ | ★★★★ | ★★★ | ★★★ | ★★★ | | | S |
| | Escape FWD | SUV | ★★ | ★★★★ | ★★★ | ★★★ | ★★★ | ★★★★ | ★★★ | ★★★ | ★★★ | | | S |

*Code key on page 8*

More Stars. Safer Cars. » 2

This panel uses numerous devices to convey information and make comparisons. How many devices or features can you identify?

## GUIDE to writing an evaluation

### Finding a Topic

You're entering an argument of evaluation when you:

- make a judgment about quality: Citizen Kane *is probably the finest film ever made by an American director.*
- challenge such a judgment: Citizen Kane *is vastly overrated by most film critics.*
- construct a ranking or comparison: Citizen Kane *is a more intellectually challenging movie than* Casablanca.
- explore criteria that might be used in making evaluative judgments: *Criteria for judging films are evolving as the production and audiences of films become ever more international.*

Issues of evaluation arise daily—in the judgments you make about public figures or policies; in the choices you make about instructors and courses; in the recommendations you offer about books, films, or television programs; in the preferences you exercise in choosing products, activities, or charities. Evaluations typically use terms that indicate value or rank—*good/bad, effective/ineffective, best/worst, competent/incompetent, successful/unsuccessful.* When you can choose a topic for an evaluation, write about something on which others regularly ask your opinion or advice.

### Researching Your Topic

You can research issues of evaluation by using the following sources:

- journals, reviews, and magazines (for current political and social issues)
- books (for assessing judgments about history, policy, etc.)
- biographies (for assessing people)
- research reports and scientific studies
- books, magazines, and Web sites for consumers
- periodicals and Web sites that cover entertainment and sports
- blogs for exploring current affairs

Surveys and polls can be useful in uncovering public attitudes: *What books are people reading? Who are the most admired people in the country? What activities or businesses are thriving or waning?* You'll discover that Web sites, newsgroups, and blogs thrive on evaluation. (Ever keep track of who "Likes" what you post on Facebook as evidence of how funny or interesting your Wall is?) Browse these public forums for ideas, and, when possible, explore your own topic ideas there. But remember that all sources need to be evaluated themselves; examine each source carefully, making sure that it is legitimate and credible.

## Formulating a Claim

After exploring your subject, try to draw up a full and specific claim that lets readers know where you stand and on what criteria you'll base your judgments. Come up with a thesis that's challenging enough to attract readers' attention. In developing a thesis, you might begin with questions like these:

- What exactly is my opinion? Where do I stand?
- Can I make my judgment more clear-cut?
- Do I need to narrow or qualify my claim?
- By what standards will I make my judgment?
- Will readers accept my criteria, or will I have to defend them, too? What criteria might others offer?
- What evidence or major reasons can I offer in support of my evaluation?

For a conventional evaluation, your thesis should be a complete statement. In one sentence, make a claim of evaluation and state the reasons that support it. Be sure your claim is specific. Anticipate the questions readers might have: *Who? What? Where? Under what conditions? With what exceptions? In all cases?* Don't expect readers to guess where you stand.

For a more exploratory argument, you might begin (and even end) with questions about the process of evaluation itself. *What are the qualities we seek—or ought to—in our political leaders? What does it say about our cultural values when we find so many viewers entertained by so-called reality shows on television? What might be the criteria for collegiate athletic programs consistent with the values of higher education?* Projects that explore topics like these might not begin with straightforward theses or have the intention to persuade readers.

## Examples of Evaluative Claims

- Though they may never receive Oscars for their work, Tom Cruise and Keanu Reeves deserve credit as actors who have succeeded in a wider range of film roles than most of their contemporaries.

- People are returning to cities because they find life there more civilized than in the suburbs.
- Barack Obama's speech on race, delivered in Philadelphia on March 18, 2008, is the most honest presentation of this issue we have heard since Martin Luther King Jr.'s time.
- Jimmy Carter has been highly praised for his work as a former president of the United States, but history may show that even his much-derided term in office laid the groundwork for the foreign policy and economic successes now attributed to later administrations.
- Because knowledge changes so quickly and people switch careers so often, an effective education today may be one that focuses more on training people how to learn than on teaching them what to know.

## Preparing a Proposal

If your instructor asks you to prepare a proposal for your project, here's a format that may help:

State your thesis completely. If you're having trouble doing so, try outlining it in Toulmin terms:

Claim:

Reason(s):

Warrant(s):

Alternatively, you might describe your intention to explore a particular question of evaluation in your project, with the thesis perhaps coming later.

- Explain why this issue deserves attention. What's at stake?
- Identify whom you hope to reach through your argument and why these readers would be interested in it.
- Briefly discuss the key challenges you anticipate in preparing your argument.
- Determine what research strategies you'll use. What sources do you expect to consult?
- Describe the format you expect to use: Conventional research essay? Letter to the editor? Web page?

## Thinking about Organization

Your evaluation will likely include elements such as the following:

- an evaluative claim that makes a judgment about a person, idea, or object
- the criterion or criteria by which you'll measure your subject
- an explanation or justification of the criteria (if necessary)
- evidence that the particular subject meets or falls short of the stated criteria
- consideration of alternative views and counterarguments

All these elements may be present in arguments of evaluation, but they won't follow a specific order. In addition, you'll often need an opening paragraph to explain what you're evaluating and why. Tell readers why they should care about your subject and take your opinion seriously.

## Getting and Giving Response: Questions for Peer Response

Your instructor may assign you to a group for the purpose of reading and responding to each other's drafts. If not, ask for responses from serious readers or consultants at a writing center. Use the following questions to evaluate a colleague's draft. Be sure to illustrate your comments with examples; specific comments help more than general observations.

### *The Claim*

- Is the claim an argument of evaluation? Does it make a judgment about something?
- Does the claim establish clearly what's being evaluated?
- Is the claim too sweeping? Does it need to be qualified?
- Will the criteria used in the evaluation be clear to readers? Do the criteria need to be defined more precisely?
- Are the criteria appropriate ones to use for this evaluation? Are they controversial? Should they be defended?

### *Evidence for the Claim*

- Is enough evidence provided to show that what's being evaluated meets the established criteria? If not, what additional evidence is needed?
- Is the evidence in support of the claim simply announced, or are its significance and appropriateness analyzed? Is more detailed discussion needed?

- Are any objections readers might have to the claim, criteria, or evidence adequately addressed?
- What kinds of sources are cited? How credible and persuasive will they be to readers? What other kinds of sources might work better?
- Are all quotations introduced with appropriate signal phrases (such as "As Tyson argues, . . .") and blended smoothly into the writer's sentences?

### *Organization and Style*

- How are the parts of the argument organized? Is this organization effective?
- Will readers understand the relationships among the claims, supporting reasons, warrants, and evidence? If not, how might those connections be clearer? Is the function of every visual clear? Are more transitions needed? Would headings or graphic devices help?
- Are the transitions or links from point to point, sentence to sentence, and paragraph to paragraph clear and effective? If not, how could they be improved?
- Are all visuals carefully integrated into the text? Is each visual introduced and commented on to point out its significance? Is each visual labeled as a figure or a table and given a caption as well as a citation?
- Is the style suited to the subject? Is it too formal, casual, or technical? Can it be improved?
- Which sentences seem effective? Which ones seem weaker, and how could they be improved? Should short sentences be combined, and any longer ones be broken up?
- How effective are the paragraphs? Too short or too long? How can they be improved?
- Which words or phrases seem effective? Do any seem vague or inappropriate for the audience or the writer's purpose? Are technical or unfamiliar terms defined?

### *Spelling, Punctuation, Mechanics, Documentation, and Format*

- Are there any errors in spelling, punctuation, capitalization, and the like?
- Is the documentation appropriate and consistent? (See Chapter 21.)
- Does the paper or project follow an appropriate format? Is it attractively designed and presented?

## PROJECTS

1. What kinds of reviews or evaluations do you consult most often or read religiously—those of TV shows, sports stars, video games, fashions, fishing gear, political figures? Try composing an argument of evaluation in your favorite genre: make and defend a claim about the quality of some object, item, work, or person within your area of interest or special knowledge. Let the paper demonstrate an expertise you have gained by your reading. If it helps, model your evaluation upon the work of a reviewer or expert you particularly respect.
2. Prepare a project in which you challenge what you regard as a wrongheaded evaluation, providing sound reasons and solid evidence for challenging this existing and perhaps commonly held view. Maybe you believe that a classic novel you had to read in high school is overrated or that people who criticize video games really don't understand them. Explain why the topic of your evaluation needs to be reconsidered and provide reasons, evidence, and, if necessary, different criteria of evaluation for doing so. For an example of this type of evaluation, see Sean Kamperman's "The Wikipedia Game" on pp. 235–39.
3. Write an evaluation in which you compare or assess the contributions or achievements of two or three notable people working within the same field or occupation. They may be educators, entrepreneurs, artists, legislators, editorial cartoonists, fashion designers, programmers, athletes—you name it. While your first instinct might be to rank these individuals and pick a "winner," this evaluation will work just as well if you can help readers appreciate the different paths by which your subjects have achieved distinction.
4. Within this chapter, the claim is made that criteria of evaluation can change depending on times and circumstances: "In good times, people may demand homes with soaring entryways, lots of space, and premium appliances. In tougher times, they'll likely care more about efficient use of space, quality insulation, and energy-efficient stoves and dishwashers." Working in a group, discuss several scenarios of change and then explore how those circumstances could alter the way we evaluate particular objects, activities, or productions. For example, what impact might global warming have upon the way we determine desirable places to live or vacation? How might a continued economic downturn change the criteria by which we judge successful careers or good educational paths for our children? If people across the globe continue to put on weight, how might standards of personal beauty or fashion alter? If government institutions continue to fall in public esteem, how might we modify our expectations for elected officials? Following the discussion, write a paper or prepare a project in which you explore how one scenario for change might revise customary values and standards of evaluation.

# The Wikipedia Game: Boring, Pointless, or Neither?

SEAN KAMPERMAN

Opening paragraph provides a context and a subtle evaluative thesis: "Wikipedia's usefulness goes far beyond its intended 'encyclopedic' purpose."

When most people think about Wikipedia—the self-styled "free, Web-based, collaborative, multilingual encyclopedia project"—they are likely reminded of the preliminary research they did for that term paper on post-structuralism, or of the idle minutes they may've spent exploring an interesting topic just for the heck of it—the neuroanatomy of purple-striped jellyfish, for example, or *Jersey Shore*. First and foremost a layman's tool, Wikipedia has struggled to find legitimacy alongside more reputable reference sources such as *Encyclopaedia Britannica*, even in spite of the outstanding quality of many of its entries. But fortunately for the makers of the Free Encyclopedia—and for the rest of us—Wikipedia's usefulness goes far beyond its intended "encyclopedic" purpose. Under the right circumstances, it can be as much a source of entertainment as one of knowledge and self-improvement.

WikiHunt is introduced as a cultural phenomenon.

A prime example of this fact is a phenomenon identified as the Wikipedia game—or, as it's now known to users of Apple and Android smart phones, "WikiHunt." WikiHunt is a simple game whose rules draw upon the unique

---

Sean Kamperman wrote "The Wikipedia Game: Boring, Pointless, or Neither?" in spring 2010 for a lower-division course on rhetoric and media at the University of Texas at Austin. In his topic proposal he briefly described Wikipedia games familiar to many students and then indicated what he intended to explore: "A lot of scholars have been very critical of Wikipedia—some going so far as to discourage its use altogether, even for the purpose of gathering background info. Does the fact that games like these use Wikipedia detract from their educational value? Or do the games in some way rebut these criticisms, demonstrating that the practical uses of user-generated online encyclopedias go beyond traditional research and, by extension, considerations of factual correctness?" His paper is the answer to those questions.

architectural features of wikis, in that players perform "moves" by following the links that connect one Wikipedia entry to another. Driven by cultural conditions of dilettantism and the spurts of creativity that tend to come on in times of extreme boredom, dozens if not hundreds of Wikipedia users in high school computer labs, college dormitories, and professional workspaces around the globe have "discovered" the game on their own. Some have even gone so far as to claim sole proprietorship—as in the case of two of my friends, who swear they invented the game while sitting through a lecture on academic dishonesty. Questions of original authorship aside, the Wikipedia game would appear to be a bona fide grassroots phenomenon—and one well worth examining if we consider its possible implications for learning and education.

Understanding that not every reader will know WikiHunt, Kamperman offers a detailed explanation.

If you've never played the Wikipedia game, it's fun—educational—and, for the most part, free; indeed, all you'll need is one or more friends, two computers, and an Internet connection. To begin, navigate to the Wikipedia homepage and click the "Random article" link on the left-hand side of the screen. As advertised, this link will lead you and your friend to two randomly generated Wikipedia articles. The objective from here is to get from your article to your opponent's using nothing but links to other articles. These links, which appear within the text of the articles themselves, are bits of hypertext denoted in blue; click on any of them, and you'll be instantly transported to another article and another set of links. Depending on which version of the rules you're going by, either the player who finishes first or the one who gets to his or her opponent's page using the fewest number of links is the winner. Easy, right?

The paper returns to its thesis when it notes how unexpectedly hard WikiHunt is.

Not exactly. What makes the Wikipedia game hard—and coincidentally, what makes it so much fun—is the vastness of the Web site's encyclopedic content. Click the "Random article" button enough times, and you'll see a pattern emerge: the majority of articles that pop up are short ones covering extremely obscure topics, usually having to do with something related to European club soccer. Entries such as these, labeled "orphans" for their relative paucity of length and links, in fact comprise the majority of Wikipedia articles. So the chances of you or your opponent hitting the randomly-generated-article jackpot and getting a "Jesus" or an "Adolf Hitler"—two pages with tons of links—are pretty slim. Rather, the task at hand usually requires that players navigate from orphan to orphan, as was the case in a game I played just last night with my friends David and Paige. They were unlucky enough to pull up an article on the summer village of Whispering Hills, Alberta, and I was no less unfortunate to get one on "blocking," an old 3D computer animation technique that makes characters and objects look like they're moving. Between these two pages, we were supplied with a total of nineteen links—they had nine doors to choose from, whereas I had ten. That's not a lot to work with. As you can probably surmise, games like this one take more than a few idle minutes—not to mention a heck of a lot of brainpower and spontaneous strategizing.

Indeed, what makes the Wikipedia game interesting is that it welcomes comparison between the players' respective strategies and methods for getting from point A to point B, highlighting differences between their thought processes and respective knowledge sets. To elaborate using the aforementioned example, I initially knew nothing about either Whispering Hills, Alberta, or "Blocking (animation)." What I did know, however, was that in order to get to Canada, I'd have to go through the good old U.S. of A. So I clicked a link at the bottom of the page entitled "Categories: animation techniques," and from there looked for a well-known technique that I knew to be associated with an American software company. Selecting "PowerPoint animation," I was led from there to the article on Microsoft—which, thanks to the company's late '90s monopolistic indiscretions, furnished me with a link to the U.S. Department of Justice. Five clicks later and I was in Alberta, looking for a passageway to Whispering Hills, one

Kamperman uses his own experience to show precisely how WikiHunt tracks users' processes of thought and "knowledge sets."

of the province's smallest, obscurest villages. I finally found it in a series of lists on communities in Alberta—but not before my opponents beat me to the punch and got to my page on "blocking" first. David, a computer science major, had taken a different approach to clinch the win; rather than drawing upon his knowledge of a macroscopic, big-picture subject like geography, he skipped from the article on Canada to a page entitled "Canadian industrial research and development organizations," from which he quickly bored through twelve articles on various topics in the computer sciences before falling on "Blocking (animation)." In his case, specialized knowledge was the key to winning.

But did David and Paige really win? Perhaps—but in the wide world of the Wikipedia game, there are few hard-and-fast rules to go by. Whereas my opponents got to their destination quicker than I, my carefully planned journey down the funnel from big ("United States") to small ("List of summer villages in Alberta") got me to Whispering Hills using two fewer links than they. So in this example, one sees not a clear-cut lesson on how to win the game, but rather a study in contrasting styles. A player can rely on specialized knowledge, linking quickly to familiar domains and narrowing the possibilities from there; or, she/he may choose to take a slower, more methodical approach, employing abstract, top-down reasoning skills to systematically sift through broader categories of information. Ultimately, victory is possible in either case.

Its more casual, entertaining uses aside, Wikipedia gets a bad rap, especially in the classroom. Too many college professors and high school English teachers have simply written it off, some even going so far as to expressly forbid their students from using it while at school. These stances and attitudes are understandable. Teaching students how to find good sources and properly credit them is hard enough without the competing influence of the Wikipedia community, whose definition of an acceptably accurate source seems to extend not only to professionally or academically vetted articles, but to blogs as well, some obviously plagiarized. But to deny Wikipedia a place in the classroom is to deny both students and teachers alike the valuable experience of playing a game that shows us not only what we know, but how we know—how our brains work when posed with the everyday challenge of having to connect ostensibly unrelated pieces of information, and furthermore, how they work differently in that respect.

Acknowledging reservations about Wikipedia, the paper asserts that WikiHunt shows players "how we know."

Knowledge building is a connective or associative process, as the minds behind Wikipedia well know. A casual perusal of any Wikipedia article reveals reams and reams of blue hypertext—bits of text that, when set in isolation, roughly correspond to discrete categories of information about the world. In a sense, the visual rhetoric of Wikipedia invokes the verbal rhetoric of exploration, prompting intrepid Web-using truth seekers to go sailing through a bright blue sea of information that is exciting by virtue of its seeming limitlessness. It should comfort teachers to know that, in quickly navigating through linked knowledge categories to reach their respective destinations, Wikipedia gamers aren't relying too much on their understanding of the articles themselves; rather, what they're relying on is their ability to understand relationships.

Argues that WikiHunt is about learning relationships between ideas.

The fact that so many people have independently found the fun at the heart of Wikipedia should be a heads-up. The Wikipedia game is a grassroots technological innovation that sheds new light on what it means to know—and, perhaps more importantly, one that reminds us that, yes, learning can be fun. It isn't too hard to imagine versions of the game that could be played by kids in school, and how teachers could then use the game to learn more about the stuff of their trade—namely, learning and how it works. So the next time you hear a friend, teacher, or coworker dismiss the Free Encyclopedia as "unreliable" or "unacademic," do knowledge a favor and challenge them to the following:

Defends Wikipedia as supporting a game that proves to be about "learning and how it works."

"Villa of Livia" to "List of Montreal Expos broadcasters" . . .

. . . no click-backs . . .

. . . twenty links or less.

Go.

# Why We Prize That Magical Mystery Pad

## VIRGINIA POSTREL

When Apple introduced the iPad last year, it added a new buzzword to technology marketing. The device, it declared, was not just "revolutionary," a tech-hype cliché, but "magical." Skeptics rolled their eyes, and one Apple fan even started an online petition against such superstitious language.

But the company stuck with the term. When Steve Jobs appeared on stage last week to unveil the iPad 2, which hit stores Friday, he said, "People laughed at us for using the word 'magical,' but, you know what, it's turned out to be magical."

Apple has long had an aura of trend-setting cool, but magic is a bolder—and more provocative—claim. In a promotional video, Jonathan Ive, the company's design chief, explains it this way: "When something exceeds your ability to understand how it works, it sort of becomes magical, and that's exactly what the iPad is." Mr. Ive is paraphrasing the famous pronouncement by Arthur C. Clarke, the science-fiction author and futurist, that "any sufficiently advanced technology is indistinguishable from magic."

So in celebrating the iPad as magical, Apple is bragging that its customers haven't the foggiest idea how the machine works. The iPad is completely opaque. It is a sealed box. You can't see the circuitry or read the software code. You can't even change the battery.

The iPad represents the final repudiation of the original iMacs that in 1998 heralded Mr. Jobs's return to the company. With their translucent, jellybean-colored shells, those machines seemed friendly in part because consumers could see their insides. The iMacs' "translucence celebrates those inscrutable internal components that most of us think of as black magic," wrote the influential design theorists Katherine and Michael McCoy in a 1999 *Fast Company* article. Back then, the challenge was to make technological magic seem benign—white (or Bondi blue) rather than black.

---

Virginia Postrel, author of *The Future and Its Enemies* (1998) and *The Substance of Style* (2003), writes frequently about issues of design and culture. "Why We Prize That Magical Mystery Pad" was published in the *Wall Street Journal* on March 12, 2011.

A closed box offends geeks' tinkering impulse, which demands swappable components and visible source code. But most of us aren't looking to hack our own computers. In fact, the very characteristics that empower enthusiasts tend to frustrate and infantilize ordinary users, making them dependent on the occult knowledge of experts. The techies who so often dismiss Apple products as toys take understandable pride in their own knowledge. They go wrong in expecting everyone to share the same expertise.

Hence Mr. Ive's second boast about the iPad's magic: "I don't have to change myself to fit the product. It fits me." A capable machine makes you feel powerful even if you don't understand it and can't fix it. The perfect tool is invisible, an extension of the user's own will.

With its utterly opaque yet seemingly transparent design, the iPad affirms a little-recognized fact of the supposedly "disenchanted" modern world. We are surrounded by magic. Clarke's Law applies not just to technology from advanced alien civilizations but to the everyday components of our own. We live in a culture made rich by specialization, with enormous amounts of knowledge embedded in the most everyday of artifacts.

Even the "maker ethic" of do-it-yourself hobbyists depends on having the right ingredients and tools, from computers, lasers, and video cameras to plywood, snaps, and glue. Extraordinarily rare even among the most accomplished seamstresses, chefs, and carpenters are those who spin their own fibers, thresh their own wheat, or trim their own lumber—all once common skills. Rarer still is the Linux hacker who makes his own chips. Who among us can reproduce from scratch every component of a pencil or a pencil skirt? We don't notice their magic—or the wonder of electricity or eyeglasses, anesthesia or aspirin—only because we're used to them.

"Between a wish and its fulfillment there is, in magic, no gap," wrote the anthropologist Marcel Mauss in *A General Theory of Magic*. Effortlessly, instantly, the magical alters reality with a tap of the finger or wave of the hand. Sound familiar?

Unfortunately, that magic operates only in the world of bits, where metaphors rule. In the world of atoms, a new iPad won't materialize free.

# 11
# Causal Arguments

Millions of bats in the United States are dying as a result of white-nose syndrome, a bacterial infection that has destroyed entire bat populations. Are spelunkers carrying contaminated equipment spreading it from cave to cave? Some scientists think that's a possibility.

Small business owners and big companies alike seem reluctant to hire new employees. Is it because of complex government regulations, uncertainties about health care costs, worries about debt, improvements in productivity—or all of the above? People needing jobs want to know.

Most state governments use high taxes to discourage the use of tobacco products. But when antismoking campaigns and graphic warning labels convince people to quit smoking, tax revenues decline, reducing support for health and education programs. Will raising taxes even higher restore that lost revenue?

## Understanding Causal Arguments

The eye-catching title image of a *National Geographic* story poses a simple question: "Why Are We So Fat?" You can probably guess that simple questions like this rarely have simple answers. But in this case, the author, Cathy Newman, argues that there are no real surprises:

> [I]n one sense, the obesity crisis is the result of simple math. It's a calories in, calories out calculation. The First Law of Fat says that anything you eat beyond your immediate need for energy, from avocados to ziti, converts to fat. . . . The Second Law of Fat: The line between being in and out of energy balance is slight. Suppose you consume a mere 5 percent over a 2,000-calorie-a-day average. "That's just one hundred calories; it's a glass of apple juice," says Rudolph Leibel, head of molecular genetics at Columbia University College of Physicians and Surgeons. "But those few extra calories can mean a huge weight gain." Since one pound of body weight is roughly equivalent to 3,500 calories, that glass of juice adds up to an extra ten pounds over a year.
>
> —Cathy Newman, "Why Are We So Fat?"

And yet you know that there's more to it than that—as Newman's full story reveals. "Calories in, calories out" may explain the physics of weight gain. But why in recent years have we so drastically shifted the equation

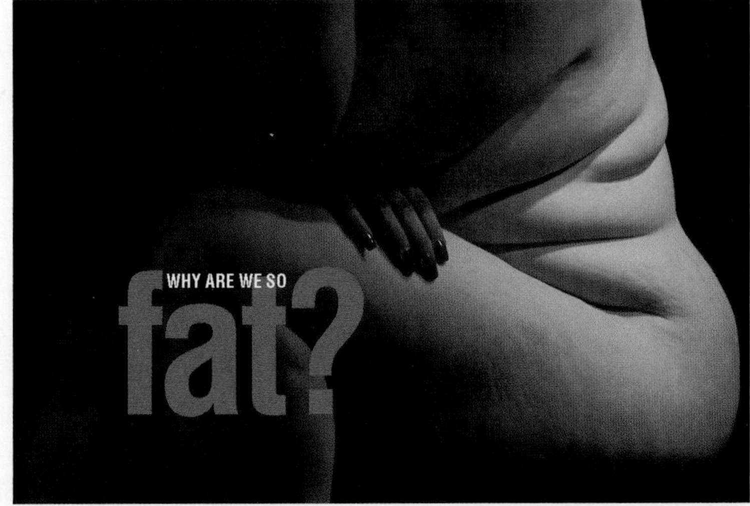


And the answer is . . . ?

from out to in? Because people instinctually crave fatty foods? Because we've grown addicted to giant portions? Because fast-food restaurants and junk-food corner stores are the only ones available in some neighborhoods? Because we walk less? Because we've become Internet or video game addicts? Whatever the reasons for our increased weight, the consequences can be measured by everything from the width of airliner seats to the rise of diabetes in the general population. Many explanations are offered by scientists, social critics, and health gurus, and some are refuted. Figuring out what's going on is a national concern—and an important exercise in cause-and-effect argument.

**Causal arguments**—from the causes of poverty in rural communities to the consequences of ocean pollution around the globe—are at the heart of many major policy decisions, both national and international. But arguments about causes and effects also inform many choices that people make every day. Suppose that you need to petition for a grade change because you were unable to turn in a final project on time. You'd probably enumerate the reasons for your failure—the death of your cat, followed by an attack of the hives, followed by a crash of your computer—hoping that an associate dean reading the petition might see these explanations as tragic enough to change your grade. In identifying the causes of the situation, you're implicitly arguing that the effect (your failure to submit the project on time) should be considered in a new light. Unfortunately, the administrator might accuse you of faulty causality (see p. 83) and judge that failure to complete the project is due more to your procrastination than to the reasons you offer.

Causal arguments exist in many forms and frequently appear as part of other arguments (such as evaluations or proposals). It may help focus your work on causal arguments to separate them into three major categories:

**Arguments that state a cause and then examine its effects**

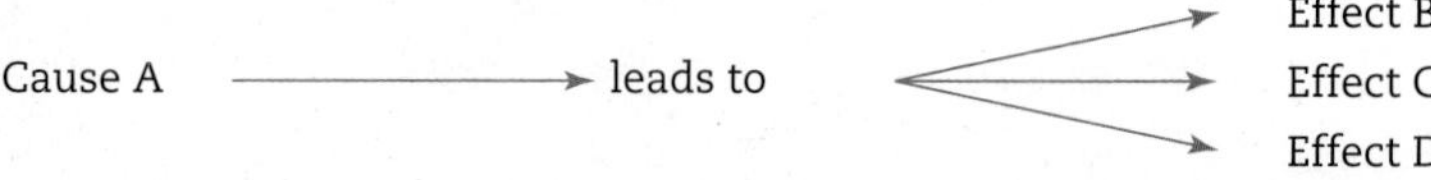


**Arguments that state an effect and then trace the effect back to its causes**

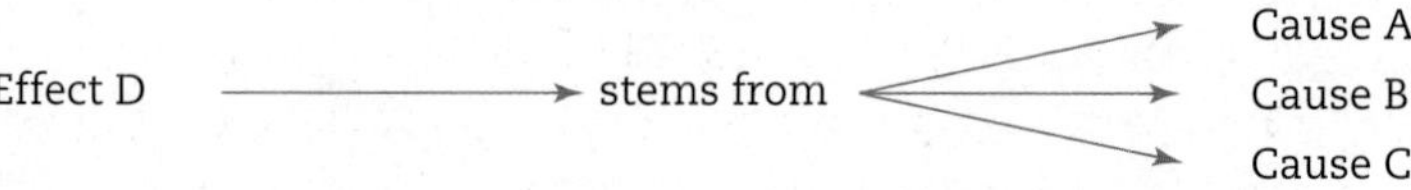

**Arguments that move through a series of links: A causes B, which leads to C and perhaps to D**

Cause A → leads to Cause B → leads to Cause C → leads to Effect D

### ARGUMENTS THAT STATE A CAUSE AND THEN EXAMINE ITS EFFECTS

What would happen if immigration reform suddenly gave millions of people currently already in the United States a legal pathway to citizenship? The possible effects of this "cause" could be examined in detail and argued intensely. Groups on various sides of this hot-button issue would likely present very different scenarios. In this debate, you'd be successful if you could convincingly describe the consequences of this change. Alternatively, you could challenge the causal explanations made by people you don't agree with. But speculation about causes and effects is always risky because life is complicated.

Before he explains how we can better think about our lives, Stewart Friedman argues that the metaphor of "work-life balance" causes people to believe that they have to give up too much in their lives.

LINK TO P. 871

Consider the opening of a May 2007 article from the *Christian Science Monitor* describing possible consequences of then-new U.S. government subsidies to increase the production of ethanol from corn:

> Policymakers and legislators often fail to consider the law of unintended consequences. The latest example is their attempt to reduce the United States' dependence on imported oil by shifting a big share of the nation's largest crop—corn—to the production of ethanol for fueling automobiles.
>
> Good goal, bad policy. In fact, ethanol will do little to reduce the large percentage of our fuel that is imported (more than 60 percent), and the ethanol policy will have ripple effects on other markets. Corn farmers and ethanol refiners are ecstatic about the ethanol boom and are enjoying the windfall of artificially enhanced demand. But it will be an expensive and dangerous experiment for the rest of us.
>
> —Colin A. Carter and Henry I. Miller, "Hidden Costs of Corn-Based Ethanol"

Note that the researchers here begin with a cause—raising the percentage of the corn crop used for ethanol—and then point to the potential effects of that policy change. As it turns out, using corn for fuel did have many unintended consequences, for example, inflating the price not only of corn but of wheat and soybeans as well, leading to food shortages around the globe and even food riots.

Paresh Nath, cartoonist for India's *National Herald*, personifies the causes for a world food crisis in this item from March 2011.

### ARGUMENTS THAT STATE AN EFFECT AND THEN TRACE THE EFFECT BACK TO ITS CAUSES

This type of argument might begin with a specific effect (a catastrophic drop in sales of music CDs) and then trace it to its most likely causes (the introduction of MP3 technology, new modes of music distribution, a preference for single song purchases). Or you might examine the reasons that music executives offer for their industry's dip and decide whether their causal analyses pass muster.

Like other kinds of causal arguments, those tracing effects to a cause can have far-reaching significance. In 1962, for example, the scientist Rachel Carson seized the attention of millions with a famous causal argument about the effects that the overuse of chemical pesticides might have on the environment. Here's an excerpt from the beginning of her book-length study of this subject. Note how she begins with the effects before saying she'll go on to explore the causes:

> [A] strange blight crept over the area and everything began to change. Some evil spell had settled on the community: mysterious maladies swept the flocks of chickens; the cattle and sheep sickened and died. Everywhere was a shadow of death. The farmers spoke of

> much illness among their families. . . . There had been several sudden and unexplained deaths, not only among adults but even among children, who would be stricken suddenly while at play and die within a few hours. The roadsides, once so attractive, were now lined with browned and withered vegetation as though swept by fire. These, too, were silent, deserted by all living things. Even the streams were now lifeless. Anglers no longer visited them, for all the fish had died.
>
> In the gutters under the eaves and between the shingles of the roofs, a white granular powder still showed a few patches; some weeks before it had fallen like snow upon the roofs and lawns, the fields and streams. No witchcraft, no enemy action had silenced the rebirth of new life in this stricken world. The people had done it themselves. . . . What has silenced the voices of spring in countless towns in America? This book is an attempt to explain.
>
> —Rachel Carson, *Silent Spring*

Today, one could easily write a causal argument of the first type about *Silent Spring* and the environmental movement that it spawned.

### ARGUMENTS THAT MOVE THROUGH A SERIES OF LINKS: A CAUSES B, WHICH LEADS TO C AND PERHAPS TO D

In an environmental science class, for example, you might decide to argue that, despite reductions in acid rain, tightened national regulations regarding smokestack emissions from utility plants are still needed for the following reasons:

1. Emissions from utility plants in the Midwest still cause significant levels of acid rain in the eastern United States.
2. Acid rain threatens trees and other vegetation in eastern forests.
3. Powerful lobbyists have prevented midwestern states from passing strict laws to control emissions from these plants.
4. As a result, acid rain will destroy most eastern forests by 2020.

In this case, the first link is that emissions cause acid rain; the second, that acid rain causes destruction in eastern forests; and the third, that states have not acted to break the cause-and-effect relationship that is established by the first two points. These links set the scene for the fourth link, which ties the previous points together to argue from effect: unless X, then Y.

**RESPOND •**

The causes of some of the following events and phenomena are well-known and frequently discussed. But do you understand these causes well enough to spell them out to someone else? Working in a group, see how well (and in how much detail) you can explain each of the following events or phenomena. Which explanations are relatively clear, and which seem more open to debate?

earthquakes/tsunamis

popularity of Lady Gaga or *Jersey Shore*

Cold War

subprime mortgage crisis or GM bankruptcy

AIDS pandemic in Africa

popularity of the *Transformers* films

swelling caused by a bee sting

sharp rise in cases of autism or asthma

climate change

## Characterizing Causal Arguments

Causal arguments tend to share several characteristics.

### THEY ARE OFTEN PART OF OTHER ARGUMENTS.

Many stand-alone causal arguments address questions that are fundamental to our well-being: *Why are juvenile asthma and diabetes increasing so dramatically in the United States? What are the causes of the rise in cases of malaria in Africa, and what can we do to counter this rise? What will happen to Europe if its birthrate continues to decline?*

But causal analyses often work to support other arguments—especially proposals. For example, a proposal to limit the time that children spend playing video games might first draw on a causal analysis to establish that playing video games can have bad results—such as violent behavior, short attention spans, and decreased social skills. The causal analysis provides a rationale that motivates the proposal. In this way, causal analyses can be useful in establishing good reasons for arguments in general.

### THEY ARE ALMOST ALWAYS COMPLEX.

The complexity of most causal relationships makes it difficult to establish causes and effects. For example, in 2011 researchers at Northwestern University reported a startling correlation: youths who participated in church activities were far more likely to grow into obese adults than their counterparts who were not engaged in religious activities. How does one even begin to explain such a peculiar and unexpected finding? Too many church socials? Unhealthy food at potluck meals? More regular social engagement? Perhaps.

Or consider the complexity of analyzing the causes of food poisoning when they strike large populations: in 2008, investigators spent months trying to discover whether tomatoes, cilantro, or jalapeño peppers were the cause of a nationwide outbreak of salmonella. More than seventeen states were affected. But despite such challenges, whenever it is possible to demonstrate convincing causal connections between X and Y, we gain important knowledge and powerful arguments. That's why, for example, great effort went into establishing an indisputable link between smoking and lung cancer. Once proven, decisive legal action could finally be taken to warn smokers.

### THEY ARE OFTEN DEFINITION BASED.

One reason that causal arguments are complex is that they often depend on careful definitions. Recent figures from the U.S. Department of Education, for example, show that the number of high school dropouts is

*"The rise in unemployment, however, which was somewhat offset by an expanding job market, was countered by an upturn in part-time dropouts, which, in turn, was diminished by seasonal factors, the anticipated summer slump, and, over-all, a small but perceptible rise in actual employment."*

Causal arguments can also be confusing.

rising and that this rise has caused an increase in youth unemployment. But exactly how does the study define *dropout*? A closer look may suggest that some students (perhaps a lot) who drop out later "drop back in" and complete high school or that some who drop out become successful entrepreneurs or business owners. Further, how does the study define *employment*? Until you can provide definitions for all key terms in a causal claim, you should proceed cautiously with your argument.

#### THEY USUALLY YIELD PROBABLE RATHER THAN ABSOLUTE CONCLUSIONS.

Because causal relationships are almost always complex or subtle, they seldom can yield more than a high degree of probability. Consequently, they are almost always subject to criticism or open to charges of false causality. (We all know smokers who defy the odds to live long, cancer-free lives.) Scientists in particular are wary when making causal claims.

Even after an event, proving precisely what caused it can be hard. During the student riots of the late 1960s, for example, a commission was charged with determining the causes of riots on a particular campus. After two years of work and almost a thousand pages of evidence and reports, the commission was unable to pinpoint anything but a broad network of contributing causes and related conditions. And how many years is it likely to take to unravel all the factors responsible for the extended recession and economic decline in the United States that began in 2008? After all, serious scholars are still arguing about the forces responsible for the Great Depression of 1929.

In examining the "nuanced and complex" causes behind a decrease in upward mobility, Rana Foroohar confirms that her argument will yield a high degree of probability rather than absolute conclusions.

LINK TO P. 901

To demonstrate that X caused Y, you must find the strongest possible evidence and subject it to the toughest scrutiny. But a causal argument doesn't fail just because you can't find a single compelling cause. In fact, causal arguments are often most effective when they help readers appreciate how tangled our lives and landscapes really are.

## Developing Causal Arguments

### Exploring Possible Claims

To begin creating a strong causal claim, try listing some of the effects—events or phenomena—that you'd like to know the causes of:

- Why do college tuition costs routinely outstrip the rate of inflation?

- Who's really responsible for rises and falls in gasoline prices?
- What has led to recent warnings of contamination along your favorite creek?
- Why has the divorce rate leveled off in recent decades?
- Why do so few younger Americans vote, even in major elections?

Or try moving in the opposite direction, listing some phenomena or causes you're interested in and then hypothesizing what kinds of effects they may produce:

- How will the growing popularity of e-readers change our relationships to books?
- What will happen to health care in the United States as a result of recent legislation?
- What will be the consequences if more liberal (or conservative) judges are appointed to the U.S. Supreme Court?
- What will happen as China and India become dominant industrialized nations?

Read a little about the causal issues that interest you most, and then try them out on friends and colleagues. They might suggest ways to refocus or clarify what you want to do or offer leads to finding information about your subject. After some initial research, map out the causal relationship you want to explore in simple form:

**X might cause (or might be caused by) Y for the following reasons:**

1.
2.
3.

Such a statement should be tentative because writing a causal argument should be an exercise in which you uncover facts, not assume them to be true. Often, your early assumptions (*Tuition was raised to renovate the stadium*) might be undermined by the facts you later discover (*Tuition doesn't fund the construction or maintenance of campus buildings*).

You might even decide to write a wildly exaggerated or parodic causal argument for humorous purposes. Humorist Dave Barry does this when he explains the causes of El Niño and other weather phenomena: "So we see that the true cause of bad weather, contrary to what they have been claiming all these years, is TV weather forecasters, who have also single-handedly destroyed the ozone layer via overuse of hair spray." Most of the causal reasoning you do, however, will take a serious approach to subjects that you, your family, and your friends care about.

**RESPOND.**

Working with a group, write a big *Why?* on a sheet of paper or computer screen, and then generate a list of *why* questions. Don't be too critical of the initial list:

*Why?*

*—do people laugh?*

*—do birds build nests?*

*—do college students binge drink?*

*—do teenagers drive fast?*

*—do babies cry?*

*—do politicians take risks on social media?*

Generate as lengthy a list as you can in fifteen minutes. Then decide which of the questions might make plausible starting points for intriguing causal arguments.

## Defining the Causal Relationships

In developing a causal claim, you can examine the various types of causes and effects in play in a given argument and define their relationship. Begin by listing all the plausible causes or effects you need to consider. Then decide which are the most important for you to analyze or the easiest to defend or critique. The following chart on "Causes" may help you to appreciate some important terms and relationships.

| *Type of Causes* | *What It Is or Does* | *What It Looks Like* |
|---|---|---|
| Sufficient cause | Enough for something to occur on its own | Lack of oxygen is sufficient to cause death<br>Cheating on exam is sufficient to fail a course |
| Necessary cause | Required for something to occur (but in combination with other factors) | Fuel is necessary for fire<br>Capital is necessary for economic growth |

| *Type of Causes* | *What It Is or Does* | *What It Looks Like* |
|---|---|---|
| Precipitating cause | Brings on a change | Protest march ignites a strike by workers<br>Plane flies into strong thunderstorms |
| Proximate cause | Immediately present or visible cause of action | Strike causes company to declare bankruptcy<br>Powerful wind shear causes plane to crash |
| Remote cause | Indirect or underlying explanation for action | Company was losing money on bad designs and inept manufacturing<br>Wind shear warning failed to sound in cockpit |
| Reciprocal causes | One factor leads to a second, which reinforces the first, creating a cycle | Lack of good schools leads to poverty, which further weakens education, which leads to even fewer opportunities . . . |

Even the most everyday causal analysis can draw on such distinctions among reasons and causes. What persuaded you, for instance, to choose the college you decided to attend? *Proximate* reasons might be the location of the school or the college's curriculum in your areas of interest. But what are the *necessary* reasons—the ones without which your choice of that college could not occur? Adequate financial support? Good test scores and academic record? The expectations of a parent?

Once you've identified a causal claim, you can draw out the reasons, warrants, and evidence that can support it most effectively:

**Claim** Certain career patterns cause women to be paid less than men.

**Reason** Women's career patterns differ from men's.

**Warrant** Successful careers are made during the period between ages twenty-five and thirty-five.

**Evidence** Women often drop out of or reduce work during the decade between ages twenty-five and thirty-five to raise families.

**Claim** Lack of community and alumni support caused the football coach to lose his job.

**Reason** Ticket sales and alumni support have declined for three seasons in a row despite a respectable team record.

**Warrant** Winning over fans is as important as winning games for college coaches in smaller athletic programs.

**Evidence** Over the last ten years, coaches at several programs have been sacked because of declining support and revenues.

**RESPOND.**

Here's a schematic causal analysis of one event, exploring the difference among precipitating, necessary, and sufficient causes. Critique and revise the analysis as you see fit. Then create another of your own, beginning with a different event, phenomenon, incident, fad, or effect.

**Event:** Traffic fatality at an intersection

**Precipitating cause:** A pickup truck that runs a red light, totals a Miata, and injures its driver

**Necessary cause:** Two drivers who are navigating Friday rush-hour traffic (if no driving, then no accident)

**Sufficient cause:** A truck driver who is distracted by a cell-phone conversation

## Supporting Your Point

In drafting your causal argument, you'll want to do the following:

- Show that the causes and effects you've suggested are highly probable and backed by evidence, or show what's wrong with the faulty causal reasoning you may be critiquing.
- Assess any links between causal relationships (what leads to or follows from what).
- Show that your explanations of any causal chains are accurate, or identify where links in a causal chain break down.
- Show that plausible cause-and-effect explanations haven't been ignored or that the possibility of multiple causes or effects has been considered.

In other words, you will need to examine your subject carefully and find appropriate ways to support your claims. There are different ways to do that.

For example, in studying effects that are physical (as they would be with diseases or climate conditions), you can offer and test *hypotheses*, or theories about possible causes. That means researching such topics thoroughly because you'll need to draw upon authorities and research articles for your explanations and evidence. (See Chapter 16, "Academic Arguments," and Chapter 17, "Finding Evidence.") Don't be surprised if you find yourself debating which among conflicting authorities make the most plausible causal or explanatory arguments. Your achievement as a writer may be simply that you present these differences in an essay, leaving it to readers to make judgments of their own—as John Tierney does in "Can a Playground Be Too Safe?" at the end of this chapter (see p. 269).

But not all the evidence in compelling causal arguments needs to be strictly scientific or scholarly. Many causal arguments rely on **ethnographic observations**—the systematic study of ordinary people in their daily routines. How would you explain, for example, why some people step aside when they encounter someone head-on and others do not? In an argument that attempts to account for such behavior, investigators Frank Willis, Joseph Gier, and David Smith observed "1,038 displacements involving 3,141 persons" at a Kansas City shopping mall. In results that surprised the investigators, "gallantry" seemed to play a significant role in causing people to step aside for one another—more so than other causes that the investigators had anticipated (such as deferring to someone who's physically stronger or higher in status). Doubtless you've read of other such studies, perhaps in psychology courses. You may even decide to do a little fieldwork on your own—which raises the possibility of using personal experiences in support of a causal argument.

Indeed, people's experiences generally lead them to draw causal conclusions about things they know well. Personal experience can also help build your credibility as a writer, gain the empathy of listeners, and thus support a causal claim. Although one person's experiences cannot ordinarily be universalized, they can still argue eloquently for causal relationships. Listen to Sara Barbour, a recent graduate of Columbia University, as she draws upon her own carefully described experiences to bemoan what may happen when e-readers finally displace printed books:

> In eliminating a book's physical existence, something crucial is lost forever. Trapped in a Kindle, the story remains but the book can no longer be scribbled in, hoarded, burned, given, or received. We may be able to read it, but we can't share it with others in the same way, and its ability to connect us to people, places, and ideas is that much less powerful.
>
> I know the Kindle will eventually carry the day—an electronic reader means no more embarrassing coffee stains, no more library holds and renewals, no more frantic flipping through pages for a lost quote, or going to three bookstores in one afternoon to track down an evasive title. Who am I to advocate the doom of millions of trees when

> the swipe of a finger can deliver all 838 pages of *Middlemarch* into my waiting hands?
>
> But once we all power up our Kindles something will be gone, a kind of language. Books communicate with us as readers—but as important, we communicate with each other through books themselves. When that connection is lost, the experience of reading—and our lives—will be forever altered.
>
> —Sara Barbour, "Kindle vs. Books: The Dead Trees Society," *Los Angeles Times*, June 17, 2011

All these strategies—testing hypotheses, presenting experimental evidence, and offering personal experience—can help you support a causal argument or undermine a causal claim you regard as faulty.

**RESPOND**•

One of the fallacies of argument discussed in Chapter 5 is the *post hoc, ergo propter hoc* ("after this, therefore because of this") fallacy. Causal arguments are particularly prone to this kind of fallacious reasoning, in which a writer asserts a causal relationship between two entirely unconnected events. When Angelina Jolie gave birth to twins in 2008, for instance, the stock market rallied by nearly six hundred points, but it would be difficult to argue that either event is related to the other.

Because causal arguments can easily fall prey to this fallacy, you might find it instructive to create and defend an absurd connection of this kind. Begin by asserting a causal link between two events or phenomena that likely have no relationship: *The enormous popularity of* Jersey Shore *is partially due to global warming.* Then spend a page or so spinning out an imaginative argument to defend the claim. It's OK to have fun with this exercise, but see how convincing you can be at generating plausibly implausible arguments.

## Considering Design and Visuals

You may find that the best way to illustrate a causal relationship is to present it visually. Even a simple bar graph or chart can demonstrate a relationship between two variables that might be related to a specific cause, like the one on the facing page showing the dramatic effects of lowered birthrates. The report that uses this figure explores the effects that such a change would have on the economies of the world.

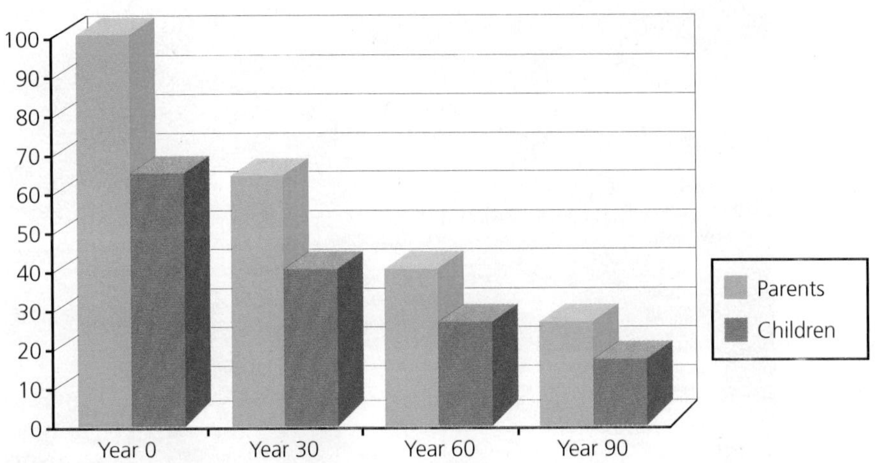


A simple graph can provide dramatic evidence for a causal claim—in this case, the effect of reduced fertility rates on a population.

Or you may decide that the most dramatic way to present important causal information about a single issue or problem is via an infographic, cartoon, or public service announcement. Our arresting example on page 258 is part of a campaign by People for the Ethical Treatment of Animals (PETA). An organization that advocates for animal rights, PETA promotes campaigns that typically try to sway people to adopt vegetarian diets by depicting the practices of the agriculture industry as cruel (many of us have also seen their celebrity antifur campaigns). Their "Meat's Not Green!" campaign, however, attempts to reach an audience that might not buy into the animal rights argument. Instead, it appeals to people who have environmentalist beliefs by presenting data that claims a causal link between animal farming and environmental destruction. How much of this data surprises you?

PETA's ad campaign expands its focus to environmentalists by explaining through causal links why they should consider vegetarian diets.

## GUIDE to writing a causal argument

### Finding a Topic

You're entering a causal argument when you:

- state a cause and then examine its effects: *The ongoing economic downturn has led more people to return to college to enhance their job market credentials.*
- describe an effect and trace it back to its causes: *There has been a recent surge in the hiring of contract workers, likely due to the reluctance of businesses to hire permanent employees who would be subject to new health care regulations.*
- trace a string of causes to figure out why something happened: *The housing and financial markets collapsed in 2008 after government mandates to encourage homeownership led banks to invent questionable financial schemes in order to offer subprime mortgages to borrowers who bought homes they could not afford with loans they could not pay back.*
- explore plausible consequences (intended or not) of a particular action, policy, or change: *The recent ban on incandescent lightbulbs may draw more attention to climate change than any previous government action.*

Spend time brainstorming possibilities for causal arguments. Many public issues lend themselves to causal analysis and argument: browse the homepage of a newspaper or news source on any given day to discover plausible topics. Consider topics that grow from your own experiences.

It's fair game, too, to question the accuracy or adequacy of existing arguments about causality. You can write a strong paper by raising doubts about the facts or assumptions that others have made and perhaps offering a better causal explanation on your own.

### Researching Your Topic

Causal arguments will lead you to many different resources:

- current news media—especially magazines and newspapers (online or in print)
- online databases
- scholarly journals
- books written on your subject (here you can do a keyword search, either in your library or online)
- blogs, Web sites, or social networking sites

In addition, why not carry out some field research? Conduct interviews with appropriate authorities on your subject, create a questionnaire aimed at establishing a range of opinion on your subject, or arrange a discussion forum among people with a stake in the issue. The information you get from interviews, questionnaires, or open-ended dialogue might provide ideas to enrich your argument or evidence to back up your claims.

## Formulating a Claim

For a conventional causal analysis, try to formulate a claim that lets readers know where you stand on some issue involving causes and effects. First, identify the kind of causal argument that you expect to make (see pp. 243–47 for a review of these kinds of arguments) or decide whether you intend, instead, to debunk an existing cause-and-effect claim. Then explore your relationship to the claim. What do you know about the subject and its causes and effects? Why do you favor (or disagree with) the claim? What significant reasons can you offer in support of your position?

End this process by formulating a thesis—a complete sentence that says, in effect, *A causes (or does not cause or is caused by) B*, followed by a summary of the reasons supporting this causal relationship. Make your thesis as specific as possible and be sure that it's sufficiently controversial or interesting to hold a reader's interest. Of course, feel free to revise any such claim as you learn more about a subject.

For causal topics that are more open-ended and exploratory, you may not want to take a strong position, particularly at the outset. Instead, your argument might simply present a variety of reasonable (and possibly competing) explanations and scenarios.

## Examples of Causal Claims

- Right-to-carry gun laws are, in part, responsible for decreased rates of crime in states that have approved such legislation.
- Sophisticated use of social media is now a must for any political candidate who hopes to win.
- The proliferation of images in film, television, and computer-generated texts is changing the way we read and use information.
- Grade inflation is lowering the value of a college education.
- Experts don't yet agree on the long-term impact that sophisticated use of social media will have on American political campaigns, though some effects are already evident.

## Preparing a Proposal

If your instructor asks you to prepare a proposal for your project, here's a format that may help:

**State your thesis or hypothesis completely. If you are having trouble doing so, try outlining it in Toulmin terms:**

**Claim:**

**Reason(s):**

**Warrant(s):**

**Alternatively, you might indicate an intention to explore a particular causal question in your project, with the thesis perhaps coming later.**

- **Explain why this issue deserves attention. What's at stake?**
- **Identify whom you hope to reach through your argument and why this group of readers would be interested in it.**
- **Briefly discuss the key challenges you anticipate in preparing your argument.**
- **Determine what research strategies you'll use. What sources do you expect to consult?**
- **Briefly identify and explore the major stakeholders in your argument and what alternative perspectives you may need to consider as you formulate your argument.**
- **Describe the format you expect to use: Conventional research essay? Letter to the editor? Web page? Press release? Op-ed for the local paper?**

## Thinking about Organization

Your causal argument will likely include elements such as the following:

- a specific causal claim somewhere in the paper—or the identification of a significant causal issue
- an explanation of the claim's significance or importance
- evidence sufficient to support each cause or effect—or, in an argument based on a series of causal links, evidence to support the relationships among the links
- a consideration of other plausible causes and effects, and evidence that you have thought carefully about these alternatives before offering your own ideas

## Getting and Giving Response: Questions for Peer Response

Your instructor may assign you to a group for the purpose of reading and responding to each other's drafts. If not, ask for responses from serious readers or consultants at a writing center. Use the following questions to evaluate a colleague's draft. Be sure to illustrate your comments with examples; specific comments help more than general observations.

### *The Claim*

- Does the claim state a causal argument?
- Does the claim identify clearly what causes and effects are being examined?
- What about the claim will make it appeal to readers?
- Is the claim too sweeping? Does it need to be qualified? How might it be narrowed and focused?
- How strong is the relationship between the claim and the reasons given to support it? How could that relationship be made more explicit?

### *Evidence for the Claim*

- What's the strongest evidence offered for the claim? What, if any, evidence needs to be strengthened?
- Is enough evidence offered to show that these causes are responsible for the identified effect, that these effects result from the identified cause, or that a series of causes and effects are linked? If not, what additional evidence is needed? What kinds of sources might provide this evidence?
- How credible will the sources be to potential readers? What other sources might be more persuasive?
- Is evidence in support of the claim analyzed logically? Is more discussion needed?
- Have alternative causes and effects been considered? Have objections to the claim been carefully considered and presented fairly? Have these objections been discussed?

### *Organization and Style*

- How are the parts of the argument organized? Is this organization effective?
- Will readers understand the relationships among the claims, supporting reasons, warrants, and evidence? If not, how might those connections be clearer? Is the function of every visual clear? Are more transitions needed? Would headings or graphic devices help?

- Are the transitions or links from point to point, sentence to sentence, and paragraph to paragraph clear and effective? If not, how could they be improved?
- Are all visuals carefully integrated into the text? Is each visual introduced and commented on to point out its significance? Is each visual labeled as a figure or a table and given a caption as well as a citation?
- Is the style suited to the subject? Is it too formal, casual, or technical? Can it be improved?
- Which sentences seem effective? Which ones seem weaker, and how could they be improved? Should short sentences be combined, and any longer ones be broken up?
- How effective are the paragraphs? Too short or too long? How can they be improved?
- Which words or phrases seem effective? Do any seem vague or inappropriate for the audience or the writer's purpose? Are technical or unfamiliar terms defined?

### *Spelling, Punctuation, Mechanics, Documentation, and Format*

- Are there any errors in spelling, punctuation, capitalization, and the like?
- Is the documentation appropriate and consistent? (See Chapter 21.)
- Does the paper or project follow an appropriate format? Is it appropriately designed and attractively presented?

## PROJECTS

1. Develop an argument exploring one of the cause-and-effect topics mentioned in this chapter. Just a few of those topics are listed below:

    Declining population of bats in the United States

    Causes of long-term unemployment or declining job markets

    Using the tax code to discourage/encourage specific behaviors (i.e., smoking, eating unhealthy foods, hiring more workers)

    Increasing numbers of obese children and/or adults

    Ramifications of ocean pollution

    Aftermaths of immigration reform

    Repercussions of U.S. ethanol policy

    Effects of declining solar activity

2. Write a causal argument about a subject you know well, even if the topic does not strike you as particularly "academic": *What accounts for the popularity of* The Hunger Games *trilogy? What are the likely consequences of students living more of their lives via social media? How are video games changing the way students you know learn? Why do women love shoes?* In this argument, be sure to separate precipitating or proximate causes from sufficient or necessary ones. In other words, do a deep and revealing causal analysis about your subject, giving readers new insights.

3. John Tierney's essay "Can a Playground Be Too Safe?" (see p. 269) explores some unintended consequences of noble-minded efforts in recent decades to make children's playgrounds safer. After reading the Tierney piece, list any comparable situations you know of where unintended consequences may have undermined the good (or maybe even bad?) intentions of those who took action or implemented some change. Choose the most intriguing situation, do the necessary research, and write a causal argument about it.

4. Lia Hardin's "Cultural Stress Linked to Suicide" on the facing page describes a variety of causal relationships focused on Asian American women in academic environments. Although the newspaper report doesn't make an explicit argument, its implicit message is that specific actions could be taken to lessen the stress the women feel and improve their mental health. In a project of your own, describe a causal situation at your own school, in your community, or at a place of work that is raising issues, problems, or maybe even opportunities that might be addressed. Like Hardin's, your paper need not be overtly persuasive: instead, use it to invite readers to consider a range of plausible causal explanations and relationships.

# Cultural Stress Linked to Suicide

LIA HARDIN

May 31, 2007

Asian American women demonstrate a high rate of suicide when compared with women of other ethnicities, California State–Fullerton researcher Eliza Noh found in a recent empirical study.

The causal claim is introduced: several factors lead to mental health problems. Credentials of researchers are established.

Noh and Stanford mental health professionals Alejandro Martinez, the director of Counseling and Psychological Services (CAPS), and Rona Hu, director of the Acute Inpatient Unit at Stanford Hospital, told *The Daily* that parental pressure, cultural differences between the United States and Asian countries, and avoidance of mental health issues in Asian American families can contribute to the prevalence of mental health problems.

Examples of deaths attributed to the identified factors are given.

Following the death of graduate student Mengyao "May" Zhou earlier this year and the recent revelation that Azia Kim had been squatting in Stanford dorms for eight months despite the fact that she was not a student, suicide and mental health issues in the Asian American community have become widely discussed on the Stanford campus.

Citing the ongoing study, Noh said that the tendency of Asian American women to ignore or deny stress, depression, and other mental health problems can cause the larger anxieties that lead to suicide.

---

Lia Hardin wrote this article as a staff writer for her campus newspaper, the *Stanford Daily*. In it, she explores the factors that contribute to the relatively high rate of suicide among Asian American women. Because she is writing for a newspaper, Hardin does not provide any formal documentation of her sources but simply identifies the three authorities who supplied most of her information.

Expert testimony in support of claim is introduced.

"There are multiple factors that contribute to suicidality," Noh said. "[For Asian American women] there is this pressure to do well in school and that pressure comes from their family members. There is a miscommunication or a lack of communication with their parents. There is a cultural division between them and their parents."

"They are expected to listen to their parents," she said, "to do well in school, not to ask questions and not to talk back."

All those cultural pressures can lead Asian American women to treat mental health issues like an elephant in the room, exacerbating existing problems and generating others.

A second expert researcher is cited.

Hu argued that, for many Asian American women, culturally related issues can contribute directly to mental health problems. She cited young women she knew who had been disowned by their families because of circumstances that parents interpreted as failures.

"The whole concept in the Asian family is that the family is not a democracy," Hu said. "Parents feel entitled to make decisions for their children, including what major or career to choose, or whom to marry. There's a line from a movie where they say, 'There's no word for *privacy* in Chinese.'"

"The sense of shame can be a big part of Asian American culture and that's something that Americans don't understand so much," she added. "If Hugh Grant is caught doing something [shameful,] he apologizes and goes on with his movie career. In Asia, shame can endure for generations. The default Asian coping mechanism is denial."

A third researcher is cited.

Martinez added that differences between education systems in America and Asian countries can lead to misunderstandings within families.

"Specifically in some Asian countries, people have to make career decisions almost when they get to high school," Martinez said. Coming from such a background, parents often misinterpret their children's decision to explore different fields in college.

"If someone did that in their country of origin, it would be a dramatic setback," he said. "They may not be familiar with how much flexibility is possible in the United States."

Martinez cited Korea's suicide rate, which is far higher than the United States.

"The consequences of someone getting a 'B' in a class at Stanford really aren't that great in the context of career decisions and career opportunities," he said. "In other cultures they can be significant."

Noh said that open discussion of mental health issues in the community, along with the availability of resources that can cater specifically to Asian Americans, can be used to counter the problem.

Ways to address the problem are introduced.

"There has to be some serious commitment on the part of the community," Noh said. "[Resources] need to be appropriate for Asian American students. Counselors should be trained in the languages that they speak and have some level of cultural awareness of [students'] backgrounds."

Without those specially tailored resources, she said, Asian American women in her study often chose to reject counseling and therapy altogether.

"The big fear was that they didn't want to go to strangers who didn't know about their situation," she said. "Asian Americans have the lowest rates of utilization of mental health services. There is something about traditional mental health services that doesn't appeal to Asian Americans."

Hu and Martinez said that Stanford has resources for Asian Americans available at campus mental health facilities.

Campus resources for addressing the problem are reviewed.

"We address this in two ways," Martinez said. "An important one is to have diversity on our staff. In addition to that, we do commit some of our resources to making sure that all of our staff have sensitivity to the communities that make up Stanford students."

Hu said that at the Stanford Hospital, some of the attending physicians and residents in psychiatry are Asian and that staff members fluent in Mandarin are available.

Hu and Noh both said that in addition to providing ethnicity-specific resources, fostering discussion of suicide and mental health is important because avoidance of the issue is pervasive in the Asian American community.

"Helping to de-stigmatize things is very helpful," Hu said. "I don't see people disowned so frequently in other cultures."

A final contributing factor to suicide: feeling alone and helpless.

"The number one factor that [study participants] felt in terms of contributing to suicide is that they felt alone and helpless and that they didn't have any place to turn," Noh said. "I've received lots of emails of thanks . . . from people happy that there is dialogue taking place."

# Can a Playground Be Too Safe?

## JOHN TIERNEY

A childhood relic: jungle gyms, like this one in Riverside Park in Manhattan, have disappeared from most American playgrounds in recent decades.

When seesaws and tall slides and other perils were disappearing from New York's playgrounds, Henry Stern drew a line in the sandbox. As the city's parks commissioner in the 1990s, he issued an edict concerning the ten-foot-high jungle gym near his childhood home in northern Manhattan.

"I grew up on the monkey bars in Fort Tryon Park, and I never forgot how good it felt to get to the top of them," Mr. Stern said. "I didn't want to see that playground bowdlerized. I said that as long as I was parks commissioner, those monkey bars were going to stay."

His philosophy seemed reactionary at the time, but today it's shared by some researchers who question the value of safety-first playgrounds. Even if children do suffer fewer physical injuries—and the evidence for

---

John Tierney is a journalist and coauthor of the book *Willpower: Rediscovering the Greatest Human Strength* (2011). He writes the science column "Findings" for the *New York Times*, where this piece was originally published on July 18, 2011.

that is debatable—the critics say that these playgrounds may stunt emotional development, leaving children with anxieties and fears that are ultimately worse than a broken bone.

"Children need to encounter risks and overcome fears on the playground," said Ellen Sandseter, a professor of psychology at Queen Maud University in Norway. "I think monkey bars and tall slides are great. As playgrounds become more and more boring, these are some of the few features that still can give children thrilling experiences with heights and high speed."

After observing children on playgrounds in Norway, England, and Australia, Dr. Sandseter identified six categories of risky play: exploring heights, experiencing high speed, handling dangerous tools, being near dangerous elements (like water or fire), rough-and-tumble play (like wrestling), and wandering alone away from adult supervision. The most common is climbing heights.

"Climbing equipment needs to be high enough, or else it will be too boring in the long run," Dr. Sandseter said. "Children approach thrills and risks in a progressive manner, and very few children would try to climb to the highest point for the first time they climb. The best thing is to let children encounter these challenges from an early age, and they will then progressively learn to master them through their play over the years."

Sometimes, of course, their mastery fails, and falls are the common form of playground injury. But these rarely cause permanent damage, either physically or emotionally. While some psychologists—and many parents—have worried that a child who suffered a bad fall would develop a fear of heights, studies have shown the opposite pattern: A child who's hurt in a fall before the age of nine is less likely as a teenager to have a fear of heights.

By gradually exposing themselves to more and more dangers on the playground, children are using the same habituation techniques developed by therapists to help adults conquer phobias, according to Dr. Sandseter and a fellow psychologist, Leif Kennair, of the Norwegian University for Science and Technology.

"Risky play mirrors effective cognitive behavioral therapy of anxiety," they write in the journal *Evolutionary Psychology*, concluding that this "anti-phobic effect" helps explain the evolution of children's fondness for thrill-seeking. While a youthful zest for exploring heights might not seem adaptive—why would natural selection favor children who risk death before they have a chance to reproduce?—the dangers seemed to be outweighed by the benefits of conquering fear and developing a sense of mastery.

"Paradoxically," the psychologists write, "we posit that our fear of children being harmed by mostly harmless injuries may result in more fearful children and increased levels of psychopathology."

The old tall jungle gyms and slides disappeared from most American playgrounds across the country in recent decades because of parental concerns, federal guidelines, new safety standards set by manufacturers and—the most frequently cited factor—fear of lawsuits.

Shorter equipment with enclosed platforms was introduced, and the old pavement was replaced with rubber, wood chips, or other materials designed for softer landings. These innovations undoubtedly prevented some injuries, but some experts question their overall value.

"There is no clear evidence that playground safety measures have lowered the average risk on playgrounds," said David Ball, a professor of risk management at Middlesex University in London. He noted that the risk of some injuries, like long fractures of the arm, actually increased after the introduction of softer surfaces on playgrounds in Britain and Australia.

"This sounds counterintuitive, but it shouldn't, because it is a common phenomenon," Dr. Ball said. "If children and parents believe they are in an environment which is safer than it actually is, they will take more risks. An argument against softer surfacing is that children think it is safe, but because they don't understand its properties, they overrate its performance."

Reducing the height of playground equipment may help toddlers, but it can produce unintended consequences among bigger children. "Older children are discouraged from taking healthy exercise on playgrounds because they have been designed with the safety of the very young in mind," Dr. Ball said. "Therefore, they may play in more dangerous places, or not at all."

Fear of litigation led New York City officials to remove seesaws, merry-go-rounds, and the ropes that young Tarzans used to swing from one platform to another. Letting children swing on tires became taboo because of fears that the heavy swings could bang into a child.

"What happens in America is defined by tort lawyers, and unfortunately that limits some of the adventure playgrounds," said Adrian Benepe, the current parks commissioner. But while he misses the Tarzan ropes, he's glad that the litigation rate has declined, and he's not nostalgic for asphalt pavement.

"I think safety surfaces are a godsend," he said. "I suspect that parents who have to deal with concussions and broken arms wouldn't agree that playgrounds have become too safe." The ultra-safe enclosed platforms of the 1980s and 1990s may have been an overreaction, Mr. Benepe said, but lately there have been more creative alternatives.

"The good news is that manufacturers have brought out new versions of the old toys," he said. "Because of height limitations, no one's building the old monkey bars anymore, but kids can go up smaller climbing walls and rope nets and artificial rocks."

Still, sometimes there's nothing quite like being ten feet off the ground, as a new generation was discovering the other afternoon at Fort Tryon Park. A soft rubber surface carpeted the pavement, but the jungle gym of Mr. Stern's youth was still there. It was the prime destination for many children, including those who'd never seen one before, like Nayelis Serrano, a ten-year-old from the South Bronx who was visiting her cousin.

When she got halfway up, at the third level of bars, she paused, as if that was high enough. Then, after a consultation with her mother, she continued to the top, the fifth level, and descended to recount her triumph.

"I was scared at first," she explained. "But my mother said if you don't try, you'll never know if you could do it. So I took a chance and kept going. At the top I felt very proud." As she headed back for another climb, her mother, Orkidia Rojas, looked on from a bench and considered the pros and cons of this unfamiliar equipment.

"It's fun," she said. "I'd like to see it in our playground. Why not? It's kind of dangerous, I know, but if you just think about danger you're never going to get ahead in life."

# 12
# Proposals

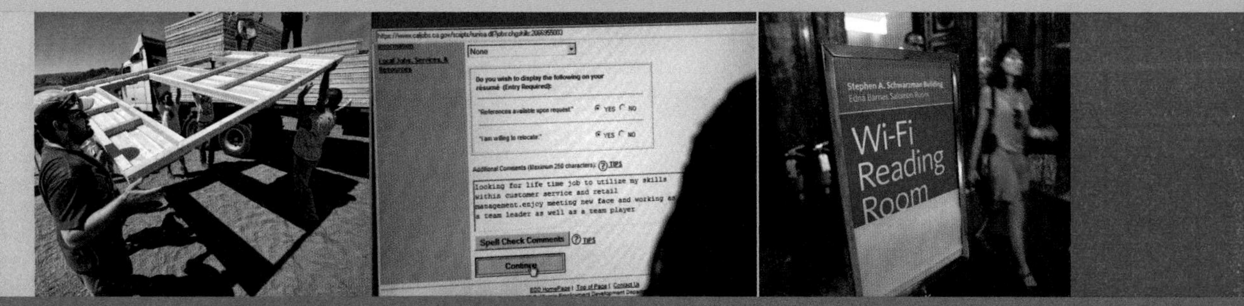


A student looking forward to spring break proposes to two friends that they join a group that will spend the vacation helping to build a school in a Guatemalan village.

The members of a club for undergrad business majors talk about their common need to create informative, appealing résumés. After much talk, three members suggest that the club develop a résumé app especially for business majors looking for a first job.

A project team at a large architectural firm works for three months developing a response to an RFP (request for proposal) to convert a university library into a digital learning center.

## Understanding and Categorizing Proposals

We live in an era of big proposals—complex programs for health care reform, bold dreams to privatize space exploration, multibillion-dollar designs for high-speed rail systems, ceaseless calls to reform education, and so many other such ideas brought down to earth by sobering proposals for budget reform and deficit reduction. As a result, there's often more talk than action because persuading people (or legislatures) to do something—or *anything*!—is always hard. But that's what *proposal arguments* do: they provide thoughtful reasons for supporting or sometimes resisting change.

Such arguments, whether national or local, formal or casual, are important in all of our lives. How many proposals do you make or respond to in one day? A neighbor might suggest that the two of you volunteer to clean up an urban creek bed; a campus group might demand that students get better seats at football games; a supervisor might ask for ideas to improve customer satisfaction at a restaurant; you might offer an ad agency reasons to hire you as a summer intern. In each case, the proposal implies that some action should take place and suggests that there are sound reasons why it should.

Cartoonist Dave Granlund illustrates objections to President Obama's high-speed rail proposal.

In their simplest form, proposal arguments look something like this:

**A should do B because of C.**

A: **Our student government** B: **should endorse the Academic Bill of Rights**

C: **because students should not be punished in their courses for their personal political views.**

Proposals come at us so routinely that it's not surprising that they cover a dizzyingly wide range of possibilities. So it may help to think of proposal arguments as divided roughly into two kinds—those that focus on specific practices and those that focus on broad matters of policy. Here are several examples:

**Proposals about Practices**

- The college should allow students to pay tuition on a month-by-month basis.
- Hotels should once again wash sheets in hot water to curb bedbug infestations.
- The NCAA should not implement a playoff system to determine its Division I football champion.

**Proposals about Policies**

- The college should adopt a policy guaranteeing that students in all majors can graduate in four years.
- The United Nations should make saving the oceans from pollution a global priority.
- The U.S. Congress needs to apply the same fiscal restraints on its spending that state legislatures do.

## RESPOND•

People write proposal arguments to solve problems and to change the way things are. But problems aren't always obvious: what troubles some people might be no big deal to others. To get an idea of the range of problems people face on your campus (some of which you may not even have thought of as problems), divide into groups, and brainstorm about things that annoy you on and around campus, including wastefulness in the cafeterias, 8:00 a.m. classes, and long lines for football or concert tickets. Ask each group to aim for at least a dozen gripes. Then choose three problems, and as a group, discuss how you'd prepare a proposal to deal with them.

## Characterizing Proposals

Proposals have three main characteristics:

- They call for change, often in response to a problem.
- They focus on the future.
- They center on the audience.

In "Is Junk Food Really Cheaper?" Mark Bittman goes to great lengths to expose the myth of cheap fast food. To what extent is his argument also a proposal? How would you characterize it?

LINK TO P. 660

Proposals always call for some kind of action. They aim at getting something done—or sometimes at *preventing* something from being done. Proposals marshal evidence and arguments to persuade people to choose a course of action: *Let's build a completely green house. Let's oppose the latest Supreme Court ruling on Internet privacy. Let's create a campus organization for first-generation college students. Let's resist the proposal for yet another campus outreach program.* But you know the old saying, "You can lead a horse to water, but you can't make it drink." It's usually easier to *convince* audiences what a good course of action is than to *persuade* them to take it (or pay for it). Even if you present a cogent proposal, you may still have work to do.

Proposal arguments must appeal to more than good sense. Ethos matters, too. It helps if a writer suggesting a change carries a certain gravitas earned by experience or supported by knowledge and research. If your word and credentials carry weight, then an audience is more likely to listen to your proposal. So when the commanders of three Apollo moon missions, Neil Armstrong, James Lovell, and Eugene Cernan, wrote an open letter to President Obama expressing their dismay at his administration's decision to cancel NASA's plans for advanced spacecraft and new lunar missions, they won a wide audience:

> For The United States, the leading space faring nation for nearly half a century, to be without carriage to low Earth orbit and with no human exploration capability to go beyond Earth orbit for an indeterminate time into the future, destines our nation to become one of second or even third rate stature. While the President's plan envisages humans traveling away from Earth and perhaps toward Mars at some time in

> the future, the lack of developed rockets and spacecraft will assure that ability will not be available for many years.
>
> Without the skill and experience that actual spacecraft operation provides, the USA is far too likely to be on a long downhill slide to mediocrity. America must decide if it wishes to remain a leader in space. If it does, we should institute a program which will give us the very best chance of achieving that goal.

But even their considerable ethos was not enough to carry the day with the space agency and the man who made the decision.

Yet, as the space program example obviously demonstrates, proposal arguments focus on the future—what people, institutions, or governments should do over the upcoming weeks, months, or, in the NASA moon-mission example, decades. This orientation toward the future presents special challenges, since few of us have crystal balls. Proposal arguments must therefore offer the best evidence available to suggest that actions we recommend will achieve what they promise.

In April 2011, for example, Republican Congressman Paul Ryan, serving as Chair of the House Budget Committee, offered a federal budget plan designed to significantly reduce government spending over the next decade. The title of the seventy-three-page document, "The Path to Prosperity: Restoring America's Plan," emphasized its overtly political mission—to outline a detailed alternative to the spending priorities of

All that remains of the American space program?

Wisconsin Representative Paul Ryan presents "The Path to Prosperity."

the Obama administration. Available online, along with a summary, comparison chart, and response to critics, what quickly became known as the Ryan Plan turned into a political football, embraced by the Republican-dominated House of Representatives and members of the Tea Party, but rejected by the president, many interest groups, and a wide swath of the media. Still, the Ryan Plan did accomplish one implicit goal of many proposal arguments: to put an issue squarely on the table by making specific recommendations. It got people talking and, occasionally, even thinking.

Which raises the matter of audiences. Some proposals are tailored to general audiences; consequently, they avoid technical language, make straightforward and relatively simple points, and sometimes use charts, graphs, and tables to make data comprehensible. You can find such arguments, for example, in newspaper editorials, letters to the editor, and political documents like the Ryan Plan. And such appeals to a broad group make sense when a proposal—say, to finance new toll roads or build an art museum—must surf on waves of community support and financing.

But often proposals need to win the approval of specific groups or individuals (such as financiers, developers, public officials, and legislators) who have the power to make change actually happen. Such arguments will usually be more technical, detailed, and comprehensive than those aimed at the general public because people directly involved with an issue have a stake in it. They may be affected by it themselves and

Proposals have to take audience values into account. Shooting deer, even when they're munching on garden flowers, is unacceptable to most suburbanites.

thus have in-depth knowledge of the subject. Or they may be responsible for implementing the proposal. You can expect them to have specific questions about it and, possibly, formidable objections. So identifying your potential audiences is critical to the success of any proposal. On your own campus, for example, a plan to alter admissions policies might be directed both to students in general and (perhaps in a different form) to the university president, members of the faculty council, and admissions officers.

An effective proposal also has to be compatible with the values of the audience. Some ideas may make good sense but cannot be enacted. For example, many American towns and cities have a problem with expanding deer populations. Without natural predators, the deer are moving closer to homes, dining on gardens and shrubbery, and endangering traffic. Yet one obvious and feasible solution—culling the herds through hunting—is usually not saleable to communities (perhaps too many people remember *Bambi*).

**RESPOND.**

Work in a group to identify about half a dozen problems on your campus or in the local community, looking for a wide range of issues. (Don't focus on problems in individual classes.) Once you have settled on these issues, then use various resources—the Web, the phone book (if you can find one), a campus directory—to locate specific people, groups, or offices whom you might address or influence to deal with the issues you have identified.

## Developing Proposals

In developing a proposal, you will have to do some or all of the following:

- Define a problem that needs a solution or describe a need that is not currently addressed.
- Make a strong claim that addresses the problem or need. Your solution should be an action directed at the future.
- Show why your proposal will fix the problem or address the need.
- Demonstrate that your proposal is feasible.

This might sound easy, but writing a proposal argument can be a process of discovery. At the outset, you think you know exactly what ought to be done, but by the end, you may see (and even recommend) other options.

### Defining a Need or Problem

Stanley Fish proposes a shift from discussions of "equality" to an emphasis on "fairness." How does he argue that such a shift would be more effective?

LINK TO P. 948

To make a proposal, first establish that a need or problem exists. You'll typically dramatize the problem that you intend to fix at the beginning of your project and then lead up to a specific claim. But in some cases, you could put the need or problem right after your claim as the major reason for adopting the proposal:

> **Let's ban cell phones on campus now. Why? Because we've become a school of walking zombies. No one speaks to or even acknowledges the people they meet or pass on campus. Half of our students are so busy chattering to people that they don't participate in the community around them.**

How can you make readers care about the problem you hope to address? Following are some strategies:

- Paint a vivid picture of the need or problem.
- Show how the need or problem affects people, both those in the immediate audience and the general public as well.
- Underscore why the need or problem is significant and pressing.
- Explain why previous attempts to address the issue may have failed.

For example, in proposing that the military draft be restored in the United States or that all young men and women give two years to national service (a tough sell!), you might begin by drawing a picture of a younger generation that is self-absorbed, demands instant gratification, and doesn't understand what it means to participate as a full member of society. Or you might note how many young people today fail to develop the life skills they need to strike out on their own. Or like Congressional Representative Charles Rangel (D–New York), who regularly proposes a Universal National Service Act, you could define the issue as a matter of fairness, arguing that the current all-volunteer army shifts the burden of national service to a small and unrepresentative sample of the American population:

> **The test for Congress . . . is to require all who enjoy the benefits of our democracy to contribute to the defense of the country. . . . The largest segment of our fighting force comes from large urban centers with high unemployment, and from economically depressed small towns. This small portion of the population forces many soldiers to take multiple tours of duty, sometimes as many as six deployments. . . . We make decisions about war without worry over who fights them. Those who do the fighting have no choice; when the flag goes up, they salute and follow orders.**
>
> **—Office of Charles B. Rangel, "Press Release: Rangel Introduces Universal National Service Act," March 17, 2011**

Of course, you would want to cite authorities and statistics to prove that any problem you're diagnosing is real and that it touches your likely audience. Then readers *may* be ready to hear your proposal.

File this cartoon under "anticipate objections to your proposal."

In describing a problem that your proposal argument intends to solve, be sure to review earlier attempts to fix it. Many issues have a long history that you can't afford to ignore (or be ignorant of). For example, if you were arguing for a college football playoff, you might point out that the current bowl championship series represents an attempt—largely unsuccessful—to crown a widely recognized national champion. Understand too that some problems seem to grow worse every time someone tinkers with them. You might pause before proposing any new attempt to reform the current system of financing federal election campaigns when you discover that previous reforms have resulted in more bureaucracy, more restrictions on political expression, and more unregulated money flowing into the system. *"Enough is enough"* can be a potent argument when faced with such a mess.

**RESPOND.**

If you review "Ugly? You May Have a Case" at the end of this chapter, an essay by Daniel S. Hamermesh, a professor at the University of Texas at Austin, you'll discover that he spends most of his essay addressing potential objections to his proposal that we compensate unattractive people for society's prejudicial attitudes toward them. Do you think it makes sense for him to argue this way? Or does Hamermesh need to do more to convince his audience (or you, specifically) that attractive people really do enjoy privileges to such an extent that the government needs to compensate unattractive people in the same ways it protects other disadvantaged groups? What kinds of audience issues does Hamermesh face in making his argument in a newspaper as widely read as the *New York Times*?

## Making a Strong and Clear Claim

After you've described and analyzed a problem, you're prepared to offer a fix. Begin with your claim (a proposal of what X or Y should do) followed by the reason(s) that X or Y should act and the effects of adopting the proposal:

| | |
|---|---|
| Claim | **Communities should encourage the development of charter schools.** |
| Reason | **Charter schools are not burdened by the bureaucracy that is associated with most public schooling.** |

**Effects** Instituting such schools will bring more effective education to communities and offer an incentive to the public schools to improve their programs.

Having established a claim, you can explore its implications by drawing out the reasons, warrants, and evidence that can support it most effectively:

**Claim** In light of a recent U.S. Supreme Court decision that ruled that federal drug laws cannot be used to prosecute doctors who prescribe drugs for use in suicide, our state should immediately pass a bill legalizing physician-assisted suicide for patients who are terminally ill.

**Reason** Physician-assisted suicide can relieve the suffering of those who are terminally ill and will die soon.

Before he proposes a solution, Christophe Pelletier first argues to establish the problems inherent in locavorism as an ideology.

LINK TO P. 703

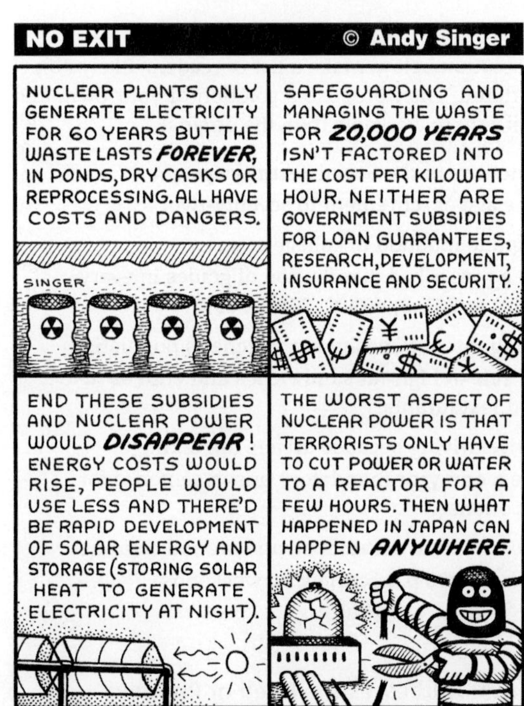


A proposal argument in four panels. You might compare this argument with Taylor Pearson's "Why You Should Fear Your Toaster More Than Nuclear Power" in Chapter 8.

| | |
|---|---|
| Warrant | The relief of suffering is desirable. |
| Evidence | Oregon voters have twice approved the state's Death with Dignity Act, which has been in effect since 1997, and to date the suicide rate has not risen sharply nor have doctors given out a large number of prescriptions for death-inducing drugs. Several other states are considering ballot initiatives in favor of doctor-assisted suicide. |

In this proposal argument, the *reason* sets up the need for the proposal, whereas the *warrant* and *evidence* demonstrate that the proposal is just and could meet its objective. Your actual argument would develop each point in detail.

**RESPOND.**

For each problem and solution below, make a list of readers' likely objections to the solution offered. Then propose a solution of your own, and explain why you think it's more workable than the original.

| | |
|---|---|
| Problem | Future deficits in the Social Security system |
| Solution | Raise the age of retirement to seventy-two. |
| Problem | Severe grade inflation in college courses |
| Solution | Require a prescribed distribution of grades in every class: 10% A; 20% B; 40% C; 20% D; 10% F |
| Problem | Increasing rates of obesity in the general population |
| Solution | Ban the sale of high-fat sandwiches and entrees in fast-food restaurants. |
| Problem | Inattentive driving because drivers are texting |
| Solution | Institute a one-year mandatory prison sentence for the first offense. |
| Problem | Increase in sexual assaults on and around campus |
| Solution | Establish a 10:00 p.m. curfew on weekends. |

## Showing That the Proposal Addresses the Need or Problem

An important but tricky part of making a successful proposal lies in relating the claim to the need or problem that it addresses. Facts and probability are your best allies. Take the time to show precisely how your solution will fix a problem or at least improve upon the current situation. Sometimes an emotional appeal is fair play, too. Here's former NBA player John Amaechi using that approach when he asks superstar Kobe Bryant of the L.A. Lakers not to appeal a $100,000 penalty he received for hurling an antigay slur at a referee:

> Kobe, stop fighting the fine. You spoke ill-advised words that shot out like bullets, and if the emails I received from straight and gay young people and sports fans in Los Angeles alone are anything to go by, you did serious damage with your outburst.
>
> A young man from a Los Angeles public school emailed me. You are his idol. He is playing up, on the varsity team, he has your posters all over his room, and he hopes one day to play in college and then in the NBA with you. He used to fall asleep with images of passing you the ball to sink a game-winning shot. He watched every game you played this season on television, but this week he feels less safe and less positive about himself because he stared adoringly into your face as you said the word that haunts him in school every single day.
>
> Kobe, stop fighting the fine. Use that money and your influence to set a new tone that tells sports fans, boys, men, and the society that looks up to you that the word you said in anger is not OK, not ever. Too many athletes take the trappings of their hard-earned success and leave no tangible legacy apart from "that shot" or "that special game."
>
> —John Amaechi, "A Gay Former NBA Player Responds to Kobe Bryant"

John Amaechi (left) and Kobe Bryant (right)

The paragraph describing the reaction of the schoolboy provides just the tie that Amaechi needs between his proposal and the problem it would address. The story also gives his argument more power.

Alternatively, if you oppose an idea, these strategies work just as well in reverse: if a proposal doesn't fix a problem, you have to show exactly why. Here are a few paragraphs from a column by *Washington Post* writer Robert Samuelson in which he refutes, point by point, a proposal by the federal government to spend $53 billion to develop what might seem like a sensible piece of infrastructure: a national high-speed rail system:

> The reasons why passenger rail service doesn't work in America are well-known: Interstate highways shorten many trip times; suburbanization has fragmented destination points; air travel is quicker and more flexible for long distances (if fewer people fly from Denver to Los Angeles and more go to Houston, flight schedules simply adjust). Against history and logic is the imagery of high-speed rail as "green" and a cutting-edge technology.
>
> It's a triumph of fancy over fact. Even if ridership increased fifteen-fold over Amtrak levels, the effects on congestion, national fuel consumption and emissions would still be trivial. Land use patterns would change modestly, if at all; cutting twenty minutes off travel times between New York and Philadelphia wouldn't much alter real estate development in either. Nor is high-speed rail a technology where the United States would likely lead; European and Asian firms already dominate the market.
>
> Governing ought to be about making wise choices. What's disheartening about the Obama administration's embrace of high-speed rail is that it ignores history, evidence, and logic. The case against it is overwhelming. The case in favor rests on fashionable platitudes. High-speed rail is not an "investment in the future"; it's mostly a waste of money. Good government can't solve all our problems, but it can at least not make them worse.
>
> —Robert Samuelson, "The Enemies of Good Government," *Washington Post*, February 14, 2011

Finally, if your own experience backs up your claim or demonstrates the need or problem that your proposal aims to address, then consider using it to develop your proposal (as John Amaechi does in addressing his proposal to Kobe Bryant). Consider the following questions in deciding when to include your own experiences in showing that a proposal is needed or will in fact do what it claims:

- Is your experience directly related to the need or problem that you seek to address or to your proposal about it?
- Will your experience be appropriate and speak convincingly to the audience? Will the audience immediately understand its significance, or will it require explanation?
- Does your personal experience fit logically with the other reasons that you're using to support your claim?

Be careful. If a proposal seems crafted to serve mainly your own interests, you won't get far.

### Showing That the Proposal Is Feasible

To be effective, proposals must be *feasible*—that is, the action proposed can be carried out in a reasonable way. Demonstrating feasibility calls on you to present evidence—from similar cases, from personal experience, from observational data, from interview or survey data, from Internet research, or from any other sources—showing that what you propose can indeed be done with the resources available. "Resources available" is key: if the proposal calls for funds, personnel, or skills beyond reach or reason, your audience is unlikely to accept it. When that's the case, it's time to reassess your proposal, modify it, and test any new ideas against these revised criteria. This is also when you can reconsider proposals that others might suggest are better, more effective, or more workable than yours. There's no shame in admitting that you may have been wrong. When drafting a proposal, ask friends to think of counterproposals. If your own proposal can stand up to such challenges, it's likely a strong one.

### Considering Design and Visuals

Because proposals often address specific audiences, they can take a number of forms—a letter, memo, Web page, feasibility report, brochure, prospectus, or even an editorial cartoon (see Andy Singer's "No Exit" item on p. 283). Each form has different design requirements. Indeed, the design may add powerfully to—or detract significantly from—the effectiveness of the proposal. Typically, though, proposals are heavy in photographs, tables, graphs, comparison charts, and maps, all designed to help readers understand the nature of a problem and how to solve it. Needless to say, any visual items should be handsomely presented: they contribute to your ethos.

Lengthy reports also usually need headings—or, in an oral report, slides—that clearly identify the various stages of the presentation. Those headings, which will vary, would include items such as Introduction, Nature of the Problem, Current Approaches or Previous Solutions, Proposal/Recommendations, Advantages, Counterarguments, Feasibility, Implementation, and so on. So before you produce a final copy of any proposal, be sure its design enhances its persuasiveness.

A related issue to consider is whether a graphic image might help readers understand key elements of the proposal—what the challenge is, why it demands action, and what exactly you're suggesting—and help make the idea more attractive. That strategy is routinely used in professional proposals by architects, engineers, and government agencies.

For example, the artist rendering on page 289 shows the Bionic Arch, a proposed skyscraper in Taiwan designed by architect Vincent Callebaut. As a proposal, this one stands out because it not only proposes an addition to the city skyline, but it proposes an architectural addition that is self-sufficient and carbon neutral by incorporating solar and wind power as well as bioreactors that purify water and aid in recycling and waste elimination efforts. If you look closely, you'll notice that each floor of the building includes suspended "sky gardens" that, according to the proposal, will help solve the problem of city smog by siphoning away toxic fumes. According to Callebaut, "The skyscraper reduces our ecological footprint in the urban area. It respects the environment and gives a new symbiotic ecosystem for the biodiversity of Taiwan. The Bionic Arch is the new icon of sustainable development." Who wouldn't support a building that looked great *and* helped clean the air?

The Bionic Arch proposes to do more than add retail and office space.

## GUIDE to writing a proposal

### Finding a Topic or Identifying a Problem

You're entering a proposal argument when you:

- make a claim that supports a change in practice: *Water sold in plastic bottles should carry a warning label describing its environmental impact.*
- make a claim that supports a change in policy: *Government workers, especially legislators and administrative officials, should never be exempt from laws or programs imposed on other citizens.*
- make a claim that resists suggested changes in practice or policy: *The surest way to guarantee that HOV lanes on freeways improve traffic flow is not to build any.*
- explore options for addressing existing issues or investigate opportunities for change: *Urban planners need to examine the long-term impact digital technologies may have on transportation, work habits, housing patterns, power usage, and entertainment opportunities in cities of the future.*

Since your everyday experience often calls on you to consider problems and to make proposals, begin your brainstorming for topics with practical topics related to your life, education, major, or job. Or make an informal list of proposals that you would like to explore in broader academic or cultural areas—problems you see in your field or in the society around you. Or do some freewriting on a subject of political concern, and see if it leads to a call for action.

### Researching Your Topic

For many proposals, you can begin your research by consulting the following types of sources:

- newspapers, magazines, reviews, and journals (online and print)
- online databases
- government documents and reports
- Web sites, blogs, social networking sites, listservs, or newsgroups
- books
- experts in the field, some of whom might be right on your campus

Consider doing some field research, if appropriate—a survey of student opinions on Internet accessibility, for example, or interviews with people who have experienced the problem you are trying to fix.

Finally, remember that your proposal's success can depend on the credibility of the sources you use to support it, so evaluate each source carefully (see Chapter 18).

## Formulating a Claim

As you think about and explore your topic, begin formulating a claim about it. To do so, come up with a clear thesis that makes a proposal and states the reasons that this proposal should be adopted. To start formulating a claim, explore and respond to the following questions:

- What do I know about the proposal that I'm making?
- What reasons can I offer to support my proposal?
- What evidence do I have that implementing my proposal will lead to the results I want?

Rather than make a specific proposal, you may sometimes want to explore the range of possibilities for addressing a particular situation or circumstance. In that case, a set of open-ended questions might be a more productive starting point than a focused thesis, suggesting, for instance, what goals any plausible proposal might have to meet.

## Examples of Proposal Claims

- Because Congress has proved itself unable to rein in spending and because debt is threatening the economic stability of the country, increases in federal spending should be capped annually at 2 percent below the rate of inflation in all departments, programs, and entitlements for a decade.
- Every home should be equipped with a well-stocked emergency kit that can sustain inhabitants for at least three days in a natural disaster.
- Congress should repeal the Copyright Extension Act, since it disrupts the balance between incentives for creators and the right of the public to information as set forth in the U.S. Constitution.
- To simplify the lives of consumers and eliminate redundant products, industries that manufacture rechargeable batteries should agree on a design for a universal power adapter.

- People from different economic classes, age groups, political philosophies, and power groups (government, Main Street, Wall Street) all have a stake in reforming current budget and tax policies. But how do we get them to speak and to listen to each other? That is the challenge we face if we hope to solve our national economic problems.

## Preparing a Proposal

If your instructor asks you to prepare a proposal for your project, here's a format that may help:

**State the thesis of your proposal completely. If you're having trouble doing so, try outlining it in Toulmin terms:**

**Claim:**

**Reason(s):**

**Warrant(s):**

**Alternatively, you might describe your intention to explore a particular problem in your project, with the actual proposal (and thesis) coming later.**

- **Explain why this issue deserves attention. What's at stake?**
- **Identify and describe those readers whom you hope to reach with your proposal. Why is this group of readers appropriate? Can you identify individuals who can actually fix a problem?**
- **Briefly discuss the major difficulties that you foresee for your proposal. How will you: Demonstrate that the action you propose is necessary and workable? Persuade the audience to act? Pay for the proposal?**
- **Determine what research strategies you'll use. What sources do you expect to consult?**
- **Describe the format you expect to use: Conventional research essay? Letter to the editor? PowerPoint presentation? Press release? Discussion forum? Op-ed for the local paper?**

## Thinking about Organization

Proposals can take many different forms but generally include the following elements:

- a description of the problem you intend to address or the state of affairs that leads you to propose the action

- a strong and specific proposal, identifying the key reasons for taking the proposed action and the effects that taking this action will have
- a clear connection between the proposal and a significant need or problem
- a demonstration of ways in which the proposal addresses the need
- evidence that the proposal will achieve the desired outcome
- a consideration of alternative ways to achieve the desired outcome and a discussion of why these may not be feasible
- a demonstration that the proposal is feasible and an explanation of how it may be implemented

## Getting and Giving Response: Questions for Peer Response

Your instructor may assign you to a group for the purpose of reading and responding to each other's drafts. If not, ask for responses from serious readers or consultants at a writing center. Use the following questions to evaluate a colleague's draft. Since specific comments help more than general observations, be sure to illustrate your comments with examples. Some of the questions below assume a conventional, thesis-driven project, but more exploratory, open-ended proposal arguments also need to be clearly phrased, organized, and supported with evidence.

### *The Claim*

- Does the claim clearly call for action? Is the proposal as clear and specific as possible?
- Is the proposal too sweeping? Does it need to be qualified? If so, how?
- Does the proposal clearly address the problem that it intends to solve? If not, how could the connection be strengthened?
- Is the claim likely to get the audience to act rather than just to agree? If not, how could it be revised to do so?

### *Evidence for the Claim*

- Is enough evidence furnished to get the audience to support the proposal? If not, what kind of additional evidence is needed? Does any of the evidence provided seem inappropriate or otherwise ineffective? Why?
- Is the evidence in support of the claim simply announced, or are its significance and appropriateness analyzed? Is a more detailed discussion needed?

- Are objections that readers might have to the claim or evidence adequately and fairly addressed?
- What kinds of sources are cited? How credible and persuasive will they be to readers? What other kinds of sources might work better?
- Are all quotations introduced with appropriate signal phrases (such as "As Tyson argues, . . .") and blended smoothly into the writer's sentences?

### *Organization and Style*

- How are the parts of the argument organized? Is this organization effective?
- Will readers understand the relationships among the claims, supporting reasons, warrants, and evidence? If not, how might those connections be clearer? Is the function of every visual clear? Are more transitions needed? Would headings or graphic devices help?
- Are the transitions or links from point to point, sentence to sentence, and paragraph to paragraph clear and effective? If not, how could they be improved?
- Are all visuals carefully integrated into the text? Is each visual introduced and commented on to point out its significance? Is each visual labeled as a figure or a table and given a caption as well as a citation?
- Is the style suited to the subject? Is it too formal, casual, or technical? Can it be improved?
- Which sentences seem effective? Which ones seem weaker, and how could they be improved? Should short sentences be combined, and any longer ones be broken up?
- How effective are the paragraphs? Too short or too long? How can they be improved?
- Which words or phrases seem effective? Do any seem vague or inappropriate for the audience or the writer's purpose? Are technical or unfamiliar terms defined?

### *Spelling, Punctuation, Mechanics, Documentation, and Format*

- Are there any errors in spelling, punctuation, capitalization, and the like?
- Is the documentation appropriate and consistent? (See Chapter 21.)
- Does the paper or project follow an appropriate format? Is it appropriately designed and attractively presented?

## PROJECTS •

1. Identify a proposal currently in the news or one advocated unrelentingly by the media that you *really* don't like. It may be a political initiative, a cultural innovation, a transportation alternative, or a lifestyle change. Spend time studying the idea more carefully than you have before. And then compose a proposal argument based on your deeper understanding of the proposal. You may still explain why you think it's a bad idea. Or you may endorse it, using your new information and your interesting perspective as a former dissenter.
2. The uses and abuses of technology and media—from smart phones to social networks—seem to be on everyone's mind. Write a proposal argument about some pressing dilemma caused by the digital screens that are changing (ruining?) our lives. You might want to explain how to bring traditional instructors into the digital age or establish etiquette for people who walk in traffic using handheld electronic devices. Or maybe you want to keep parents off of social networks. Or maybe you have a great idea for separating professional and private lives online. Make your proposal in some pertinent medium: paper, op-ed, cartoon, photo essay.
3. Write a proposal to yourself diagnosing some minor issue you would like to address, odd behavior you'd like to change, or obsession you'd like to curb. Explore the reasons behind your mania and the problems it causes you and others. Then come up with a plausible proposal to resolve the issue and prove that you can do it. Make the paper hilarious.
4. Working in a group initially, come up with a list of problems—local, national, or international—that seem just about insoluble, from persuading nations to cut down on their $CO_2$ emissions to figuring out how to keep tuition costs in check. After some discussion, focus on just one or two of these matters and then discuss not the issues themselves but the general reasons that the problems have proven intractable. What exactly keeps people from agreeing on solutions? Are some people content with the status quo? Do some groups profit from the current arrangements? Are alternatives to the status quo just too costly or not feasible for other reasons? Do people find change uncomfortable? Following the discussion, work alone or collaboratively on an argument that examines the general issue of *change*: What makes it possible in any given case? What makes it difficult? Use the problems you have discussed as examples to illustrate your argument. Your challenge as a writer may be to make such an open-ended discussion interesting to general readers.

# A Call to Improve Campus Accessibility for the Mobility Impaired

MANASI DESHPANDE

## Introduction

The paper opens with a personal example and dramatizes the issue of campus accessibility.

Wes Holloway, a sophomore at the University of Texas at Austin (UT), never considered the issue of campus accessibility during his first year on campus. But when an injury his freshman year left him wheelchair-bound, he was astonished to realize that he faced an unexpected challenge: maneuvering around the UT campus. Hills that he had effortlessly traversed became mountains; doors that he had easily opened became anvils; and streets that he had mindlessly crossed became treacherous terrain. Says Wes: "I didn't think about accessibility until I had to deal with it, and I think most people are the same way."

Both problem and solution are previewed here, with more details provided in subsequent sections of the paper.

For the ambulatory individual, access for the mobility impaired on the UT campus is easy to overlook. Automatic door entrances and bathrooms with the universal handicapped symbol make the campus seem sufficiently accessible. But for many students and faculty at UT, including me, maneuvering the UT campus in a wheelchair is a daily experience of stress and frustration. Although the University has made a concerted and continuing effort to improve access, students and faculty with physical disabilities still suffer from discriminatory hardship, unequal opportunity to succeed, and lack of independence.

---

Manasi Deshpande wrote a longer version of this essay for a course preparing her to work as a consultant in the writing center at the University of Texas at Austin. We have edited it to emphasize the structure of her complex proposal. Note, too, how she reaches out to a general audience to make an argument that might seem to have a narrow constituency. This essay is documented using MLA style.

The University must make campus accessibility a higher priority and take more seriously the hardship that the campus at present imposes on people with mobility impairments. Better accessibility would also benefit the numerous students and faculty with temporary disabilities and help the University recruit a more diverse body of students and faculty.

The introduction's final paragraph summarizes the argument.

## Assessment of Current Efforts

The current state of campus accessibility leaves substantial room for improvement. There are approximately 150 academic and administrative buildings on campus (Grant). Eduardo Gardea, intern architect at the Physical Plant, estimates that only about nineteen buildings comply fully with the Americans with Disabilities Act (ADA). According to Penny Seay, PhD, director of the Center for Disability Studies at UT Austin, the ADA in theory "requires every building on campus to be accessible." However, as Bill Throop, associate director of the Physical Plant, explains, there is "no legal deadline to make the entire campus accessible"; neither the ADA nor any other law mandates that certain buildings be made compliant by a certain time. Though not bound by specific legal obligation, the University should strive to fulfill the spirit of the law and recognize campus accessibility as a pressing moral obligation.

The author's fieldwork (mainly interviews) enhances her authority and credibility.

## The Benefits of Change

### *Benefits for People with Permanent Mobility Impairments*

The paper uses several layers of headings to organize its diverse materials.

Improving campus accessibility would significantly enhance the quality of life of students and faculty with mobility impairments. The campus at present poses discriminatory hardship on these individuals by making daily activities such as getting to class and using the bathroom unreasonably difficult. Before Wes Holloway leaves home, he must plan his route carefully to avoid hills, use ramps that are easy to maneuver, and enter the side of the building with the accessible entrance. As he

The author outlines the challenges faced by a student with mobility impairment.

goes to class, Wes must go out of his way to avoid poorly paved sidewalks and roads. Sometimes he cannot avoid them and must take an uncomfortable and bumpy ride across potholes and uneven pavement. If his destination does not have an automatic door, he must wait for someone to open the door for him because it is too heavy for him to open himself. To get into Burdine Hall, he has to ask a stranger to push him through the heavy narrow doors because his fingers would get crushed if he pushed himself. Once in the classroom, Wes must find a suitable place to sit, often far away from his classmates because stairs block him from the center of the room.

Accessibility problems are given a human face with examples of the problems that mobility-impaired people face on campus.

Other members of the UT community with mobility impairments suffer the same daily hardships as Wes. According to Mike Gerhardt, student affairs administrator of Services for Students with Disabilities (SSD), approximately eighty students with physical disabilities, including twenty to twenty-five students using wheelchairs, are registered with SSD. However, the actual number of students with mobility impairments is probably higher because some students choose not to seek services from SSD. The current state of campus accessibility discriminates against all individuals with physical disabilities in the unnecessary hardship it imposes and in the ways it denies them independence.

***Benefits for People with Temporary Mobility Impairments***

The author broadens the appeal of her proposal by showing how improved accessibility will benefit everyone on campus.

In addition to helping the few members of the UT campus with permanent mobility impairments, a faster rate of accessibility improvement would also benefit the much larger population of people with temporary physical disabilities. Many students and faculty will become temporarily disabled from injury at some point during their time at the University. They will encounter difficulties similar to those facing people with permanent disabilities, including finding accessible entrances, opening doors without automatic entrances, and finding convenient classroom seating. And, according to Dr. Jennifer

Maedgen, assistant dean of students and director of SSD, about 5 to 10 percent of the approximately one thousand students registered with SSD at any given time have temporary disabilities. By improving campus accessibility, the University would in fact reach out to all of its members, even those who have never considered the possibility of mobility impairment or the state of campus accessibility.

Numbers provide hard evidence for an important claim.

*Benefits for the University*

Better accessibility would also benefit the University as a whole by increasing recruitment of handicapped individuals and thus promoting a more diverse campus. When prospective students and faculty with disabilities visit the University, they might decide not to join the UT community because of poor access. On average, about one thousand students, or 2 percent of the student population, are registered with SSD. Mike Gerhardt reports that SSD would have about 1,500 to 3,000 registered students if the University reflected the community at large with respect to disability. These numbers suggest that the University can recruit more students with disabilities by taking steps to ensure that they have an equal opportunity to succeed.

The author offers a new but related argument: enhanced accessibility could bolster recruitment efforts.

**Counterarguments**

Arguments against devoting more effort and resources to campus accessibility have some validity but ultimately prove inadequate. Some argue that accelerating the rate of accessibility improvements and creating more efficient services require too much spending on too few people. However, this spending actually enhances the expected quality of life of all UT community members rather than just the few with permanent physical disabilities. Unforeseen injury can leave anyone with a permanent or temporary disability at any time. In making decisions about campus accessibility, administrators must realize that having a disability is not a choice and that bad luck

The paper briefly notes possible objections to the proposal.

does not discriminate. They should consider how their decisions would affect their campus experience if they became disabled. Despite the additional cost, the University should make accessibility a priority and accommodate more accessibility projects in its budget.

## Recommendations

### *Foster Empathy and Understanding for Long-Term Planning*

After establishing a case for enhanced campus accessibility, the author offers specific suggestions for action.

The University should make campus accessibility a higher priority and work toward a campus that not only fulfills legal requirements but also provides a user-friendly environment for the mobility impaired. It is difficult for the ambulatory person to empathize with the difficulties faced by these individuals. Recognizing this problem, the University should require the administrators who allocate money to ADA projects to use wheelchairs around the campus once a year. Administrators must realize that people with physical disabilities are not a small, distant, irrelevant group; anyone can join their ranks at any time. Administrators should ask themselves if they would find the current state of campus accessibility acceptable if an injury forced them to use a wheelchair on a permanent basis.

In addition, the University should actively seek student input for long-term improvements to accessibility. The University is in the process of creating the ADA Accessibility Committee, which, according to the office of the Dean of Students' Web site, will "address institutionwide, systemic issues that fall under the scope of the Americans with Disabilities Act." Students should play a prominent and powerful role in this new ADA Accessibility Committee. The Committee should select its student representatives carefully to make sure that they are driven individuals committed to working for progress and representing the interests of students with disabilities. The University should consider making Committee positions paid so that student representatives can devote sufficient time to their responsibilities.

### *Improve Services for the Mobility Impaired*

The University should also work toward creating more useful, transparent, and approachable services for its members with physical disabilities by making better use of online technology and helping students take control of their own experiences.

First, SSD can make its Web site more useful by updating it frequently with detailed information on construction sites that will affect accessible routes. The site should delineate alternative accessible routes and approximate the extra time required to use the detour. This information would help people with mobility impairments to plan ahead and avoid delays, mitigating the stress of maneuvering around construction sites.

The University should also develop software for an interactive campus map. The software would work like MapQuest or Google Maps but would provide detailed descriptions of accessible routes on campus from one building to another. It would be updated frequently with new ADA improvements and information on construction sites that impede accessible routes.

Since usefulness of services are most important for students during their first encounters with the campus, SSD should hold one-on-one orientations for new students with mobility impairments. SSD should inform students in both oral and written format of their rights and responsibilities and make them aware of problems that they will encounter on the campus. Beyond making services more useful, these orientations would give students the impression of University services as open and responsive, encouraging students to report problems that they encounter and assume the responsibility of self-advocacy.

As a continuing resource for people with physical disabilities, the SSD Web site should include an anonymous forum for both general questions and specific complaints and needs. Many times, students notice problems but do not report them because they find visiting or calling SSD time-consuming or because they do not wish to be a burden. The anonymity and immediate feedback provided by the forum would allow for more freedom of expression and provide students an easier way to solve the problems they face.

Services for the mobility impaired should also increase their transparency by advertising current accessibility projects on their Web sites. The University should give its members with mobility impairments a clearer idea of its efforts to improve campus accessibility. Detailed online descriptions of ADA projects, including the cost of each project, would affirm its resolve to create a better environment for its members with physical disabilities.

### Conclusion

Although the University has made progress in accessibility improvements on an old campus, it must take bolder steps to improve the experience of its members with mobility impairments. At present, people with permanent mobility impairments face unreasonable hardship, unequal opportunity to succeed, and lack of independence. To enhance the quality of life of all of its members and increase recruitment of disabled individuals, the University should focus its resources on increasing the rate of accessibility improvements and improving the quality of its services for the mobility impaired.

As a public institution, the University has an obligation to make the campus more inclusive and serve as an example for disability rights. With careful planning and a genuine desire to respond to special needs, practical and cost-effective changes to the University campus can significantly improve the quality of life of many of its members and prove beneficial to the future of the University as a whole.

## Works Cited

Gardea, Eduardo. Personal interview. 24 Mar. 2005.

Gerhardt, Michael. Personal interview. 8 Apr. 2005.

Grant, Angela. "Making Campus More Accessible." *Daily Texan Online*. 14 Oct. 2003. Web. 1 Mar. 2005.

Holloway, Wesley Reed. Personal interview. 5 Mar. 2005.

Maedgen, Jennifer. Personal interview. 25 Mar. 2005.

Office of the Dean of Students, University of Texas at Austin. "ADA Student Forum." 6 Apr. 2005. Web. 23 Apr. 2005.

Seay, Penny. Personal interview. 11 Mar. 2005.

Throop, William. Personal interview. 6 Apr. 2005.

# Ugly? You May Have a Case

## DANIEL S. HAMERMESH

Being good-looking is useful in so many ways.

In addition to whatever personal pleasure it gives you, being attractive also helps you earn more money, find a higher-earning spouse (and one who looks better, too!) and get better deals on mortgages. Each of these facts has been demonstrated over the past twenty years by many economists and other researchers. The effects are not small: one study showed that an American worker who was among the bottom one-seventh in looks, as assessed by randomly chosen observers, earned 10 to 15 percent less per year than a similar worker whose looks were assessed in the top one-third—a lifetime difference, in a typical case, of about $230,000.

Beauty is as much an issue for men as for women. While extensive research shows that women's looks have bigger impacts in the market for mates, another large group of studies demonstrates that men's looks have bigger impacts on the job.

Why this disparate treatment of looks in so many areas of life? It's a matter of simple prejudice. Most of us, regardless of our professed attitudes, prefer as customers to buy from better-looking salespeople, as jurors to listen to better-looking attorneys, as voters to be led by better-looking politicians, as students to learn from better-looking professors. This is not a matter of evil employers' refusing to hire the ugly: in our roles as workers, customers and potential lovers we are all responsible for these effects.

How could we remedy this injustice? With all the gains to being good-looking, you would think that more people would get plastic surgery or makeovers to improve their looks. Many of us do all those things, but as studies have shown, such refinements make only small differences in our beauty. All that spending may make us feel better, but it doesn't help us much in getting a better job or a more desirable mate.

---

Daniel S. Hamermesh is a professor of psychology at the University of Texas at Austin and the author of *Beauty Pays* (2011). This essay originally appeared on August 27, 2011, in the *New York Times*.

A more radical solution may be needed: why not offer legal protections to the ugly, as we do with racial, ethnic and religious minorities, women and handicapped individuals?

We actually already do offer such protections in a few places, including in some jurisdictions in California, and in the District of Columbia, where discriminatory treatment based on looks in hiring, promotions, housing and other areas is prohibited. Ugliness could be protected generally in the United States by small extensions of the Americans With Disabilities Act. Ugly people could be allowed to seek help from the Equal Employment Opportunity Commission and other agencies in overcoming the effects of discrimination. We could even have affirmative-action programs for the ugly.

The mechanics of legislating this kind of protection are not as difficult as you might think. You might argue that people can't be classified by their looks—that beauty is in the eye of the beholder. That aphorism is correct in one sense: if asked who is the most beautiful person in a group of beautiful people, you and I might well have different answers. But when it comes to differentiating classes of attractiveness, we all view beauty similarly: someone whom you consider good-looking will be viewed similarly by most others; someone you consider ugly will be viewed as ugly by most others. In one study, more than half of a group of people were assessed identically by each of two observers using a five-point scale; and very few assessments differed by more than one point.

For purposes of administering a law, we surely could agree on who is truly ugly, perhaps the worst-looking 1 or 2 percent of the population. The difficulties in classification are little greater than those faced in deciding who qualifies for protection on grounds of disabilities that limit the activities of daily life, as shown by conflicting decisions in numerous legal cases involving obesity.

There are other possible objections. "Ugliness" is not a personal trait that many people choose to embrace; those whom we classify as protected might not be willing to admit that they are ugly. But with the chance of obtaining extra pay and promotions amounting to $230,000 in lost lifetime earnings, there's a large enough incentive to do so. Bringing anti-discrimination lawsuits is also costly, and few potential plaintiffs could afford to do so. But many attorneys would be willing to organize classes of plaintiffs to overcome these costs, just as they now do in racial-discrimination and other lawsuits.

Economic arguments for protecting the ugly are as strong as those for protecting some groups currently covered by legislation. So why not go ahead and expand protection to the looks-challenged? There's one legitimate concern. With increasingly tight limits on government resources, expanding rights to yet another protected group would reduce protection for groups that have commanded our legislative and other attention for over fifty years.

We face a trade-off: ignore a deserving group of citizens, or help them but limit help available for other groups. Even though I myself have demonstrated the disadvantages of ugliness in twenty years of research, I nonetheless would hate to see anything that might reduce assistance to groups now aided by protective legislation.

You might reasonably disagree and argue for protecting all deserving groups. Either way, you shouldn't be surprised to see the United States heading toward this new legal frontier.

PART 3

# STYLE AND PRESENTATION IN arguments

# 13
# Style in Arguments

The three images above all reflect strong individual styles: the graceful form of a very distinctive basketball player, the unique drawing style of a well-known graphic narrative artist, and the classic flair of the original iPod ads.

Even scientists, whose work might seem cut-and-dried at first glance, have style—and often lots of it! Five hundred years ago, Johann Bernoulli challenged the greatest mathematicians in the world to solve a problem that had eluded everyone to date. When an anonymous person solved the problem the very day he received it, it didn't matter that he was anonymous: the mathematics world knew that the savant was Isaac Newton. "You can tell the lion," they said, "by his claw." That "claw" was Newton's style.

So we know style when we see it—as in an elegant move in sports or in mathematics, a comic book, an Apple ad—but creating a style of your own is something else. This chapter will help you begin that process. Let's start with looking at how word choice contributes to style.

Sir Isaac Newton

## Style and Word Choice

The words you choose for an argument help define its style—and yours. For most academic arguments, fairly formal language is appropriate. In an article that urges every member of society to care about energy issues, Chevron CEO Dave O'Reilly adopts a formal and serious tone: "We call upon scientists and educators, politicians and policy-makers, environmentalists, leaders of industry, and each one of you to be part of reshaping the next era of energy." Had he written "How 'bout we rally 'round and mix us up a new energy plan?" the effect would have been quite different.

*Slang* and *colloquial terms* may enliven an argument, but they also can bewilder readers. An article about arms-control negotiations that uses terms like *nukes* and *boomers* to refer to nuclear weaponry might confuse readers who assume that the shorthand portrays a flippant attitude toward a serious subject. Be alert, too, to the use of *jargon*, the special vocabulary of members of a profession, trade, or field. Although jargon serves as shorthand for experts, it can alienate readers who don't recognize technical words or acronyms.

Another key to an argument's style is its control of **connotation**, the associations that surround many words. Note the differences among the following three statements:

> **Students from the Labor Action Committee (LAC) carried out a hunger strike to call attention to the below-minimum wages that are being**

> **paid to campus temporary workers, saying, "The university must pay a living wage to all its workers."**
>
> **Left-wing agitators and radicals tried to use self-induced starvation to stampede the university into caving in to their demands.**
>
> **Champions of human rights put their bodies on the line to protest the university's tightfisted policy of paying temporary workers scandalously low wages.**

The style of the first sentence is the most neutral, presenting facts and offering a quotation from one of the students. The second sentence uses loaded terms like *agitators, radicals,* and *stampede* to create a negative image of this event, while the final sentence uses other loaded words to create a positive view. As these examples demonstrate, words matter.

Finally, vivid *concrete* and *specific words* work better in arguments than abstract and general ones. Responding to a claim that American students are falling behind their counterparts in Asia and Europe, Jay Mathews uses memorable language to depict the stereotype:

> **Most commentary on the subject leaves the impression that China and India are going to bury the United States in an avalanche of new technology. Consider, for example, a much-cited *Fortune* article that included the claim that China turned out 600,000 engineers in the previous year, India graduated 350,000, and poor, declining America could manage only 70,000. The cover of *Fortune* showed a buff Chinese beach bully looming over a skinny Uncle Sam. The headline said, "Is the U.S. a 97-Pound Weakling?"**
>
> **—Jay Mathews, "Bad Rap on the Schools"**

Mathews' concrete language (*bury, avalanche,* and *buff Chinese beach bully looming over a skinny Uncle Sam*) creates a style that gets and keeps readers' attention.

## Sentence Structure and Argument

Writers of effective arguments know that "variety is the spice of life" when it comes to stylish sentences. *Varying sentence length* can be especially effective. Here's Mary H. K. Choi introducing the twenty-third season of *The Simpsons*:

> **Let's make a pact. The next person who whines about how *The Simpsons* sucks gets flung in a well. The rest of us can tailgate. Spare us your blustery, pedantic indignation. There's nothing to add. No**

> petition long enough, no outcry loud enough. Winter is coming, and so is the Fox series' twenty-third season and 500th episode. If this really upsets you . . . Just. Quit. Watching.
>
> —Mary H. K. Choi

Choi opens with a dramatic first sentence, followed by one a little longer and then a series of short, staccato statements that lead up to the compound *Winter is coming, and so is. . . .* And note the special effects she creates by dividing up the last sentence for emphasis: *Just. Quit. Watching.*

Variety in the way sentences open can also help create a subtly pleasing style. Here is Lisa Miller writing about the spread of "Tiger Mom" tactics in child raising:

> Happy Rogers, age eight, stands among her classmates in the schoolyard at dismissal time, immune, it seems, to the cacophonous din. A poised and precocious blonde, Hilton Augusta Parker Rogers, nicknamed Happy, would be at home in the schoolyard of any affluent American suburb or big-city private school. But here, at the elite, bilingual Nanyang Primary School in Singapore, Happy is in the minority, her Dakota Fanning hair shimmering in a sea of darker heads. This is what her parents have traveled halfway around the world for. While her American peers are feasting on the idiocies fed to them by junk TV and summer movies, Happy is navigating her friendships and doing her homework entirely in Mandarin.
>
> —Lisa Miller, "How to Raise a Global Kid"

**RESPOND.**

Work with a classmate to revise Miller's paragraph, making sure that every sentence begins the same way, with the subject first. Then read the passage aloud and see if it sounds much less effective and memorable. It's the variety in sentence openings that does the trick!

**Parallel structures** in sentences also help create style. In a review of a biography of writer Henry Roth, Jonathan Rosen includes the following description:

> His hands were warped by rheumatoid arthritis; the very touch of his computer keyboard was excruciating. But he still put in five hours a day, helped by Percocet, beer, a ferocious will, and the ministrations of several young assistants.
>
> —Jonathan Rosen, "Writer, Interrupted"

In the first sentence, Rosen chooses parallel clauses, with the first one about Roth's arthritic hands balanced by the next one describing the results of putting those hands on a keyboard. In the second sentence, Rosen also uses a series of parallel specific nouns and noun phrases (*Percocet, beer, the ministrations*) to build up a picture of Roth as extremely persistent.

**RESPOND.**

Turn to something you read frequently—a blog, a sports or news magazine, or a friend's page on Twitter—and look closely at the sentences. What seems distinctive about them? Do they vary in terms of their length and the way that they begin? If so, how? Do they use parallel structures or other structural devices to good effect? How easy to read are they, and what accounts for that ease?

## Punctuation and Argument

In a memorable comment, actor and director Clint Eastwood said, "You can show a lot with a look. . . . It's punctuation." Eastwood is right about punctuation's effect, and it is important that as you read and write

"You can show a lot with a look. . . . It's punctuation."

arguments, you consider punctuation closely. Here are some ways in which punctuation helps to enhance style.

The *semicolon* signals a pause that is stronger than a comma but not as strong as a period. Semicolons often connect two independent clauses that are linked by one idea. See how Romesh Ratnesar describes the results of the infamous "Stanford Prison Experiment" in which students were either "guards" or "prisoners":

> Some of [the "prisoners"] rebelled violently; others became hysterical or withdrew into despair.
>
> —Romesh Ratnesar, "The Menace Within"

Using a semicolon gives Ratnesar's sentence an abrupt rhythmic shift, in this case from rebellion to despair.

Writers also use end punctuation to create stylistic effects. Although the *exclamation point* can be irritating if overused (think of those Facebook status updates that bristle with them), it can be helpful for creating tone if used sparingly. In an argument about the treatment of prisoners at Guantanamo, consider how Jane Mayer evokes the sense of desperation in some of the suspected terrorists:

> As we reached the end of the cell-block, hysterical shouts, in broken English, erupted from a caged exercise area nearby. "Come here!" a man screamed. "See here! They are liars! . . . No sleep!" he yelled. "No food! No medicine! No doctor! Everybody sick here!"
>
> —Jane Mayer, "The Experiment"

While sometimes used interchangeably, the *dash* and the *colon* create different stylistic effects. Dashes offer a great way to call attention to a relevant detail that isn't itself necessary information in the sentence you're writing. Here are dashes used to insert such information in the opening of Philip Womack's London *Telegraph* review of *Harry Potter and the Deathly Hallows, Part 2*:

> *Harry Potter and the Deathly Hallows, Part 2*—the eighth and final film in the blockbusting series—begins with our teenage heroes fighting for their lives, and for their entire world.

The review continues with a sentence that makes good use of a colon, which often introduces explanations or examples:

> The first scene of David Yates's film picks up where his previous installment left off: with a shot of the dark lord Voldemort's noseless face in triumph as he steals the most powerful magic wand in the world from the tomb of Harry's protector, Professor Dumbledore.

And Womack concludes his review with a powerful *question mark* that signals not only the evaluation of the entire film but a prediction for the future:

> **This is not an end. How could it be?**
>
> **—Philip Womack**

As these examples suggest, punctuation is often key to creating the rhythm of an argument. Take a look at how Maya Angelou uses a dash along with another punctuation mark—ellipsis points—to indicate a pause or hesitation, in this case one that builds anticipation:

> **Then the voice, husky and familiar, came to wash over us—"The winnah, and still heavyweight champeen of the world . . . Joe Louis."**
>
> **—Maya Angelou, "Champion of the World"**

Creating rhythms can be especially important in online communication when writers are trying to invest their arguments with emotion or emphasis. Some writers still use asterisks in online communication to convey emphasis the way that italic or boldface type creates in print texts: "You *must* respond to this message today!" Others use emoticons or other new characters to establish a particular rhythm, tone, and style. In an argument where the stakes are high, though, most writers use conventional style. The use of asterisks and emoticons is so common in online communication that many chat and comments programs automatically convert type enclosed in asterisks to bold, or emoticons to graphics.

**RESPOND•**

Try writing a brief movie review for your campus newspaper, experimenting with punctuation as one way to create an effective style. See if using a series of questions might have a strong effect, whether exclamation points would add or detract from the message you want to send, and so on. When you've finished the review, compare it to one written by a classmate, and look for similarities and differences in your choices of punctuation.

## Special Effects: Figurative Language and Argument

Any magazine or Web site will show how figurative language works in arguments. When a reviewer of new software that promises complete filtering of ads on the Web refers to the product as "a weedwhacker for the Web," he's using figurative language (in this case, metaphor) to advance an argument about the nature and function of that product. When a writer calls Disney World a "smile factory," she begins a stinging critique of the way pleasure is "manufactured" there.

Figurative language, which is indispensable to writers, brings two major strengths to arguments. First, it helps us understand things by drawing parallels between an unknown and a known. For example, to describe DNA, scientists Watson and Crick used the figures of a helix (spiral) and a zipper to help people understand this new concept.

Figures of speech are usually classified into two main types: **tropes** involve a change in the ordinary meaning of a word or phrase, and **schemes** involve a special arrangement of words. Here is a brief listing—with examples—of some of the most familiar kinds.

## Tropes

### METAPHOR

Marjorie Agosín acknowledges the power of metaphor by replacing the proverbial phrase "translators are traitors" with the metaphor of translators as "splendid friends" in the last sentence of her essay. What other metaphors can you find in her essay?

LINK TO P. 599

A bedrock of our language, **metaphor** implies a comparison between two things and thereby clarifies and enlivens many arguments. Columnist David Brooks depends on metaphors in an essay arguing that such figures are "at the very heart of how we think":

> Even the hardest of sciences depend on a foundation of metaphors. To be aware of metaphors is to be humbled by the complexity of the world, to realize that deep in the undercurrents of thought there are thousands of lenses popping up between us and the world, and that we're surrounded at all times by what Steven Pinker of Harvard once called "pedestrian poetry."
>
> —David Brooks, "Poetry for Everyday Life"

In the following passage, novelist and poet Benjamin Sáenz uses several metaphors to describe his relationship to the southern border of the United States:

> It seems obvious to me now that I remained always a son of the border, a boy never quite comfortable in an American skin, and certainly not comfortable in a Mexican one. My entire life, I have lived in a liminal space, and that space has both defined and confined me. That liminal space wrote and invented me. It has been my prison, and it has also been my only piece of sky.
>
> —Benjamin Sáenz, "Notes from Another Country"

In another example from Andrew Sullivan's blog, he quotes an 1896 issue of *Munsey's Magazine* that uses a metaphor to explain what, at that time, the bicycle meant to women and to clarify the new freedom it gave women who weren't accustomed to being able to ride around on their own:

> To men, the bicycle in the beginning was merely a new toy, another machine added to the long list of devices they knew in their work and play. To women, it was a steed upon which they rode into a new world.

### SIMILE

A **simile** uses *like* or *as* to compare two things. Here's a simile from an essay on cosmology from the *New York Times*:

> Through his general theory of relativity, Einstein found that space, and time too, can bend, twist, and warp, responding much as a trampoline does to a jumping child.
>
> —Brian Greene, "Darkness on the Edge of the Universe"

And here is a series of similes, from an excerpt of a *Wired* magazine review of a new magazine for women:

> Women's magazines occupy a special niche in the cluttered infoscape of modern media. Ask any *Vogue* junkie: no girl-themed Web site or CNN segment on women's health can replace the guilty pleasure of slipping a glossy fashion rag into your shopping cart. Smooth as a pint of chocolate Häagen-Dazs, feckless as a thousand-dollar slip dress, women's magazines wrap culture, trends, health, and trash in a single, decadent package. But like the diet dessert recipes they print, these slick publications can leave a bad taste in your mouth.
>
> —Tiffany Lee Brown, "En Vogue"

Here, three similes—*smooth as a pint of chocolate Häagen-Dazs* and *feckless as a thousand-dollar slip dress* in the third sentence and *like the diet dessert recipes* in the fourth—add to the image of women's magazines as a mishmash of "trash" and "trends."

On Michael Krasny's radio program, guests discuss whether an "Increase Diversity Bake Sale" is a sound analogy for criticizing college affirmative action admissions policies.

LINK TO P. 743

### ANALOGY

**Analogies** compare two things, often point by point, either to show similarity or to argue that if two things are alike in one way, they are probably alike in other ways as well. Often extended in length, analogies can

This cartoon mocks the Republican presidential nominating process by using a familiar analogy.

clarify and emphasize points of comparison. In an argument about the failures of the aircraft industry, a writer uses an analogy for potent contrast:

> If the aircraft industry had evolved as spectacularly as the computer industry over the past twenty-five years, a Boeing 767 would cost five hundred dollars today, and it would circle the globe in twenty minutes on five gallons of fuel.
>
> —*Scientific American*

To be effective, analogies have to hold up to scrutiny. In reflecting on the congressional debacle of July 2011 that took the United States close to default, columnist Joe Nocera draws an analogy:

> You know what they say: Never negotiate with terrorists. It only encourages them. These last few months, much of the country has watched in horror as the Tea Party Republicans have waged jihad on the American people. Their intransigent demands for deep spending cuts, coupled with their almost gleeful willingness to destroy one of America's most invaluable assets, its full faith and credit, were incredibly irresponsible. But they didn't care. Their goal, they believed, was worth blowing up the country for, if that's what it took.
>
> —Joe Nocera

CULTURAL CONTEXTS FOR ARGUMENT

### Levels of Formality and Other Issues of Style

At least one important style question needs to be asked when arguing across cultures: what level of formality is most appropriate? In the United States, a fairly informal style is often acceptable and even appreciated. Many cultures, however, tend to value formality. If in doubt, err on the side of formality:

- Take care to use proper titles as appropriate (*Ms.*, *Mr.*, *Dr.*, and so on).
- Don't use first names unless you've been invited to do so.
- Steer clear of slang and jargon. When you're communicating with members of other cultures, slang may not be understood, or it may be seen as disrespectful.
- Avoid potentially puzzling pop cultural allusions, such as sports analogies or musical references.

When arguing across cultures or languages, another stylistic issue might be clarity. When communicating with people whose native languages are different from your own, analogies and similes almost always aid in understanding. Likening something unknown to something familiar can help make your argument forceful—and understandable.

Nocera's comparison between Tea Partiers and terrorists offended many, who wrote to condemn the tone of the piece and to note that the analogy doesn't hold. Here's Michael from New York City, who says:

> **I am not a tea partier, or a Republican, but I just have to comment on the tone of this article. Comparing tea partiers to terrorists now . . . interesting. They are not terrorists, they are citizens who banded together to push for what they believe in.**

#### OTHER TROPES

*Signifying*, in which a speaker or writer cleverly and often humorously needles another person, is a distinctive trope found extensively in African American English. In the following passage, two African American men (Grave Digger and Coffin Ed) signify on their white supervisor (Anderson), who has ordered them to discover the originators of a riot:

> **"I take it you've discovered who started the riot," Anderson said.**
> **"We knew who he was all along," Grave Digger said.**
> **"It's just nothing we can do to him," Coffin Ed echoed.**
> **"Why not, for God's sake?"**
> **"He's dead," Coffin Ed said.**
> **"Who?"**
> **"Lincoln," Grave Digger said.**
> **"He hadn't ought to have freed us if he didn't want to make provisions to feed us," Coffin Ed said. "Anyone could have told him that."**
>
> **—Chester Himes, *Hot Day, Hot Night***

Coffin Ed and Grave Digger demonstrate the major characteristics of effective signifying—indirection, ironic humor, fluid rhythm, and a surprising twist at the end. Rather than insulting Anderson directly by pointing out that he's asked a dumb question, they criticize the question indirectly by ultimately blaming a white man (and not just any white

In these *Boondocks* strips, Huey signifies on Jazmine, using indirection, ironic humor, and two surprising twists.

man, but one they're supposed to revere). This twist leaves the supervisor speechless, teaching him something and giving Grave Digger and Coffin Ed the last word—and the last laugh.

Take a look at the example of signifying from a *Boondocks* cartoon (see opposite page). Note how Huey seems to be sympathizing with Jazmine and then, in two surprising twists, reveals that he has been needling her all along.

**Hyperbole** is the use of overstatement for special effect, a kind of fireworks in prose. The tabloid gossip magazines that scream at you in the checkout line are champions of hyperbole. Everyone has seen these overstated arguments and perhaps marveled at the way they sell.

Hyperbole is also the trademark of serious writers. In a column arguing that men's magazines fuel the same kind of neurotic anxieties about appearance that have long plagued women, Michelle Cottle uses hyperbole and humor to make her point:

> **My affection for *Men's Health* is driven by pure gender politics. . . . With page after page of bulging biceps and Gillette jaws, robust hairlines and silken skin, *Men's Health* is peddling a standard of male beauty as unforgiving and unrealistic as the female version sold by those dewy-eyed pre-teen waifs draped across covers of *Glamour* and *Elle*.**
>
> —Michelle Cottle, "Turning Boys into Girls"

How does this cartoon make light of the frequent use of hyperbole in sports broadcasting?

As you might imagine, hyperbole can easily backfire. Blogging on the *Robinson Post*, Matthew Robinson deplores the use of hyperbole on both the right and the left:

> Glenn Beck, in a discussion on his show about some Americans' distaste for the recent healthcare overhaul, compared the U.S. government to pedophilic rapist Roman Polanski, and the American people to a thirteen-year-old girl. . . . Maureen Dowd compared her own experience as a Catholic woman to that of the subjugated women of Saudi Arabia, calling the Catholic Church, "an inbred and wealthy men's club cloistered behind walls and disdaining modernity . . . an autocratic society that repress[es] women and ignore[s] their progress in the secular world."
>
> —Matthew Robinson, "Sticks and Stones: How Hyperbole Is Hurting America"

**Understatement** uses a quiet message to make its point. In her memoir, Rosa Parks—the civil rights activist who made history in 1955 by refusing to give up her bus seat to a white passenger—uses understatement so often that it becomes a hallmark of her style. She refers to Martin Luther King Jr. simply as "a true leader," to Malcolm X as a person of "strong conviction," and to her own lifelong efforts as just a small way of "carrying on."

Understatement can be particularly effective in arguments that might seem to call for its opposite. When Watson and Crick published their first article on the structure of DNA, they felt that they had discovered the secret of life. (Imagine what a Fox News or MSNBC headline might have been for this story!) Yet in an atmosphere of extreme scientific competitiveness, they closed their article with a vast understatement: "It has not escaped our notice that the specific pairing we have postulated immediately suggests a possible copying mechanism for the genetic material." A half century later, considering the profound developments in genetics, the power of this understatement still resonates strongly.

**Rhetorical questions**, which we use frequently, don't really require answers. When you say "Who cares?" or "How should I know?" you're using such questions. Rhetorical questions also show up in arguments. In reviewing a book on power in the Disney dynasty, Linda Watts uses a series of rhetorical questions to introduce part of her argument:

> If you have ever visited one of the Disney theme parks, though, you have likely wondered at the labor—both seen and unseen—necessary to maintain these fanciful environments. How and when are the

> **grounds tended so painstakingly? How are the signs of high traffic erased from public facilities? What keeps employees so poised, meticulously groomed, and endlessly cheerful?**
>
> **—Linda S. Watts, review of *Inside the Mouse***

And Erin Biba asks a potent rhetorical question in her analysis of Facebook "friending":

> **So if we're spending most of our time online talking to people we don't even know, how deep can the conversation ever get?**
>
> **—Erin Biba, "Friendship Has Its Limits"**

**Antonomasia** is probably most familiar to you from sports coverage: "His Airness" still means Michael Jordan, "The Great One," Wayne Gretzky. But it's also used in fields like politics, sometimes neutrally (Arnold Schwarzenegger as "The Governator"), sometimes as a compliment (Ronald Reagan as "The Great Communicator"), and sometimes as a crude and sexist put-down (Sarah Palin as "Caribou Barbie") or in the entertainment industry (as in calling Owen Wilson "The Butterscotch Stallion"). Such nicknames can pack arguments into just one phrase. What does calling Jordan "His Airness" argue about him?

**Irony** uses words to convey a meaning in tension with or opposite to their literal meanings to create special effects in argument. One of the most famous sustained uses of irony in literature occurs in Shakespeare's *Julius Caesar* as Antony punctuates his condemnation of Brutus with the repeated ironic phrase, "But Brutus is an *honourable* man." Publications such as the *Onion* and the online *Ironic Times* are noted for their satiric treatment of politics and popular culture, scoring points while provoking a chuckle.

**RESPOND•**

Use online sources (such as American Rhetoric's Top 100 Speeches at http://www.americanrhetoric.com/top100speechesall.html) to find the text of an essay or a speech by someone who uses figures of speech liberally. Pick a paragraph that is rich in figures and rewrite it, eliminating every bit of figurative language. Then read the original and your revised version aloud to your class. Can you imagine a rhetorical situation in which your pared-down version would be appropriate?

## Schemes

**Schemes**, figures that depend on word order, can add stylistic "zing" to arguments. Here are ones that you're likely to see most often.

**Parallelism** involves the use of grammatically similar phrases or clauses for special effect:

> For African Americans, the progress toward racial equality over the last half century was summed up in a widely quoted sequence: "Rosa sat so that Martin could walk. Martin walked so that Obama could run. Obama ran so that our children could fly."

**Antithesis** is the use of parallel structures to mark contrast or opposition:

> Marriage has many pains, but celibacy has no pleasures.
>
> —Samuel Johnson

> Those who kill people are called murderers; those who kill animals, sportsmen.

**Inverted word order**, in which the parts of a sentence or clause are not in the usual subject-verb-object order, can help make arguments particularly memorable:

> Into this grey lake plopped the thought, I know this man, don't I?
>
> —Doris Lessing

> Hard to see, the dark side is.
>
> —Yoda

**Anaphora**, or effective repetition, can act like a drumbeat in an argument, bringing the point home. In an argument about the future of Chicago, Lerone Bennett Jr. uses repetition to link Chicago to innovation and creativity:

> [Chicago]'s the place where organized Black history was born, where gospel music was born, where jazz and the blues were reborn, where the Beatles and the Rolling Stones went up to the mountaintop to get the new musical commandments from Chuck Berry and the rock'n'roll apostles.
>
> —Lerone Bennett Jr., "Blacks in Chicago"

And speaking of the Rolling Stones, here's Dave Barry using repetition comically in his comments on their 2002 tour:

> Recently I attended a Rolling Stones concert. This is something I do every two decades. I saw the Stones in the 1960s, and then again in the 1980s. I plan to see them next in the 2020s, then the 2040s, then the 2060s, at their 100th anniversary concert.
>
> —Dave Barry, "OK, What Will Stones Do for 100th Anniversary?"

**Reversed structures** for special effect have been used widely in political argumentation.

> Ask not what your country can do for you; ask what you can do for your country.
>
> —President John F. Kennedy, 1961 Inaugural Address

> The Democrats won't get elected unless things get worse, and things won't get worse until the Democrats get elected.
>
> —Jeane Kirkpatrick

> Your manuscript is both good and original. But the part that is good is not original, and the part that is original is not good.
>
> —Samuel Johnson

**RESPOND**

Identify the figurative language used in the following slogans:

"Energy drink with attitude." (Red Eye)

"Open happiness." (Coca-Cola)

"Melts in your mouth, not in your hands." (M&M's)

"Be all that you can be." (U.S. Army)

"Breakfast of champions." (Wheaties)

"America runs on Dunkin'." (Dunkin' Donuts)

"Got milk?" (America's Milk Processors)

# 14 Visual and Multimedia Arguments

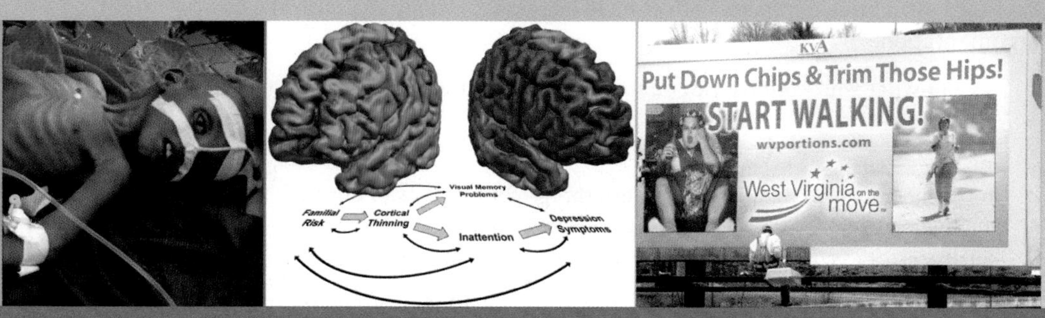


We don't need to be reminded that visual and multimedia images have clout. The images above, for example, all make powerful arguments—about the face of malnutrition in Somalia today, about how psychiatric drugs combat depression, about the need to confront and hopefully conquer obesity. Of course, some images are so iconic that they become part of our cultural memory. Just think of the first images you saw of planes slamming into the World Trade Center towers. Or the photographs of Japanese cities after the 2011 earthquake and tsunami. Or maybe you recall YouTube video of President Obama standing at the end of a long hall announcing the death of Osama bin Laden, or the dramatic opening ceremonies of the 2012 Summer Olympics in London. Images like these stick in our memories.

## The Power of Visual Arguments

Yet even in mundane moments, images—from T-shirts to billboards to animated films and computer screens—influence us. Media analyst Kevin Kelly remarks on the "ubiquity" of screens and their images in our lives:

> Everywhere we look, we see screens. The other day I watched clips from a movie as I pumped gas into my car. The other night I saw a movie on the backseat of a plane. We will watch anywhere. Screens playing video pop up in the most unexpected places—like ATM machines and supermarket checkout lines and tiny phones; some movie fans watch entire films in between calls. These ever-present screens have created an audience for very short moving pictures, as brief as three minutes, while cheap digital creation tools have empowered a new generation of filmmakers, who are rapidly filling up those screens. We are headed toward screen ubiquity.
>
> —Kevin Kelly, "Becoming Screen Literate"

As technology makes it easier for us to create and transmit images, those images become more compelling than ever, brought to us via Blu-ray and high-definition television on our smartphones and computers, on our walls, in our pockets, in our cars. But visual arguments weren't invented by YouTube, and they've always had power. The pharaohs of Egypt lined the banks of the Nile River with statues of themselves to assert their authority, and over thirty thousand years ago, people in the south of France created magnificent cave paintings to celebrate and to communicate.

Still, the ease and speed with which all of us can create and share images seems unprecedented. Beginning with the introduction of personal computers with image-controlled interfaces in the 1980s, slowly and then with the force of a tsunami, these graphic computers (the only kind that people use now) moved society further away from an age of print into an era of electronic, image-saturated communications.

Most of us have adjusted to a world of seamless, multichannel, multimedia connections. The prophet of this time was Marshall McLuhan, who nearly fifty years ago proclaimed that "the medium is the massage," with the play on *message* and *massage* intentional. As McLuhan says, "We shape our tools and afterwards our tools shape us. . . . All media works us over completely."

Marshall McLuhan

**RESPOND.**

Find an advertisement, either print or digital, that uses both verbal and visual elements. Analyze its argument by answering some of the questions on pages 329–33. Then switch ads with a classmate, and analyze his or her argument. Compare your responses to the two ads. If they're different—and they probably will be—how do you account for the differences? What effect does the audience have on the argument's reception? What differences appear between your own active reading and your classmate's?

## Shaping the Message

Images make arguments of their own. A photograph, for example, isn't a faithful representation of reality; it's reality shaped by the photographer's point of view. That's probably one reason why so many Facebook users change their photos so often—to present themselves at their very best.

Those who produce images fashion the messages that those images convey, but those who "read" those images are by no means passive. To some extent, we actively shape what we see and have learned to see things according to their meanings within our culture. People don't always see things the same way, which explains why eyewitnesses to a particular event often report it differently. Even instant replays don't always solve disputed calls on football fields. The visual images that surround us today and compete for our attention, time, and money are designed to invite, perhaps even coerce, us into seeing them in a specific way. But we all have our own frames of reference and can resist such pressures—if we are sharp!

## Analyzing Visual Elements of Arguments

To figure out how a visual or multimedia argument works, start by examining its key components:

- the creators and distributors
- the medium it uses
- the viewers and readers it hopes to reach
- its content and purpose
- its design

Following are brief analyses of several visual arguments, along with questions to explore when you encounter similar texts.

### The Creators and Distributors

This image from Amnesty International calls on viewers to help "Abolish the use of child soldiers worldwide," noting that "Children have the right to be children." This group, a nongovernmental organization with three million members in 150 countries around the globe, has as its mission to end "grave abuses of human rights." Amnesty International has carried out many campaigns, including Stamp Out Torture, Stop Violence against Women, and Demand Dignity. How does this information help you "read" the image above? Why might the organization have chosen this image to support their campaign? How well does it achieve its purpose?

**Questions about Creators and Distributors**

- Who created this visual or multimedia text? Who distributed it?
- What can you find out about these people and other work that they have done?
- What does the creator's attitude seem to be toward the image(s)?
- What do the creator and the distributor intend its effects to be? Do they have the same intentions?

## The Medium

During February 2011, protesters occupied Cairo's Tahrir Square and used their mobile devices as tools to let the world know what was happening. They tweeted and texted and sent cell phone pictures documenting police atrocities, and newspapers around the world printed tweets rather than formal reports from their journalists, like this one sent to London's *Globe and Mail*: "What's worse than being detained three hours by Egyptian army? Watching a four-year-old girl being detained with you even longer." Protesters kept their phones alive by hacking streetlamps to keep them charged. During this period, the medium was indeed a big part of the message. The photo above shows graffiti painted by protesters to promote the use of social media, including Facebook, to share information about the protests. What message is the graffiti sending? More importantly, how does media play a role in sending such a message?

#### Questions about the Medium

- Which media are used for this visual text? Images only? Words and images? Sound, video, animation, graphs, charts—and in what ways are they interactive?
- How are the media used to communicate words and images? How do various media work together?
- What effect does the medium have on the message of the text? How would the message be altered if different media were used?
- What role do words—if there are words—play in the visual text? How do they clarify, reinforce, blur, or contradict the image's message?

### The Viewers and Readers

#### Questions about Viewers and Readers

- What does the visual text assume about its viewers and what they know and agree with?
- What overall impression does the visual text create in you?
- What positive or negative feelings about individuals, scenes, or ideas does the visual intend to evoke in viewers?

In 1977, Paul Davis created this poster celebrating Native American political activist Leonard Crowdog. The poster uses simple language and a strong image to express solidarity among Native Americans (and their political allies) and to affirm Crowdog's call for renewal of Native American traditions. In what ways can visual arguments invoke their audiences or even become a part of their cultural histories? With what similar visual items (such as posters or CD art) do you identify?

Take a close look at this photograph taken during the 2008 presidential campaign: is your eye drawn first to the earnest face in the middle, the one with a pink John McCain T-shirt on? If so, pull back and take in the whole photo: what's with that pair of legs? An Associated Press photographer took this photo of Sarah Palin, causing a flap: was the photo sexist and prurient, or was it upbeat and emblematic of a new kind of feminism? What was the photographer's purpose in taking the shot? How do you read its message?

## The Content and Purpose

### Questions about Content and Purpose

- What purpose does the visual text convey? What is it designed to convey?
- What cultural values does the visual evoke? The good life? Love and harmony? Sex appeal? Adventure? Power? Resistance? Freedom?
- Does the visual reinforce these values or question them? How does the visual strengthen the argument?
- What emotions does the visual evoke? Are these the emotions that it intends to evoke?

## The Design

### Questions about Design

- How is the visual text composed? What's your eye drawn to first? Why?
- What's in the foreground? In the background? What's in or out of focus? What's moving? What's placed high, and what's placed low? What's to the left, in the center, and to the right? What effect do these placements have on the message? If the visual text is interactive, how well does that element work and what does it add?
- Is any information (such as a name, face, or scene) highlighted or stressed to attract your attention?
- How are light and color used? What effects are they intended to create? What about video? Sound? Animation?

This is the central image on the Web site of Wikipedia, a collaborative nonprofit encyclopedia project. Since its launch (as Nupedia) in 2000, Wikipedia has grown to include 21 million articles in 282 languages, all of them authored by volunteers around the world. This central image acts as a logo, a portal to access the site's content, and, in a way, a mission statement for the organization. How does your eye construct this logo? What do you notice first, and how do your eyes move around the page? Do the parts make sense when you put them together?

- What details are emphasized? What details are omitted or deemphasized? To what effect? Is anything downplayed, ambiguous, confusing, distracting, or obviously omitted? Why?
- What, if anything, is surprising about the design of the visual text? What do you think is the purpose of that surprise?
- Is anything in the visual repeated, intensified, or exaggerated? Is anything presented as "supernormal" or idealistic? What effects do these strategies intend to create? What effects do they have on you? How do they clarify or reinforce (or blur or contradict) the message?
- How are you directed to move within the argument? Are you encouraged to read further? Click on a link? Scroll down? Fill out a form? Provide your email address? Place an order?

**RESPOND•**

Find three or four Web pages that exemplify good visual design, and then find three or four that don't. When you've picked the good and bad designs, draw a rough sketch of each page's physical layout. Where are the graphics? Where is the text? What are the size and position of text blocks relative to graphics? How is color used? Can you discern common design principles among the pages, or does each good page work well in its own way? Write up your findings, focusing on how the visual arguments influence audiences.

## Using Visuals in Your Own Arguments

It's easy today to use images and multimedia in your own writing. In fact, many college classes now call for projects to be posted on the Web, which almost always involves the use of images. Other courses invite or require students to make multimedia presentations or to create arguments in the form of videos, photo collages, comics, or other combinations of media.

### Using Images and Multimedia to Appeal to Emotion

Many of the photos taken during police intervention during Occupy Wall Street protests raised powerful emotional arguments about the proper use of police force.

LINK TO P. 921

Many advertisements, YouTube videos, political documentaries, rallies, marches, and even church services use images and multimedia to trigger emotions. You can't flip through a magazine, watch a video, or browse the Web without being cajoled or seduced by images of all kinds—most of them designed in some way to attract your eye and attention and many of them linked to other media or using animation or some sort of interactive element.

#### CHOOSE IMAGES CAREFULLY

You want to take advantage of technology to appeal effectively to your readers' emotions. To do so, think first of the purpose of your writing: you want every image or use of multimedia to carry out that purpose. Look at the famous *Apollo 8* photograph of our planet as a big blue marble hanging above the horizon of the moon. You could use this image to introduce an argument about the need for additional investment in the space program. Or it might become part of an argument about the need to preserve our frail natural environment, or an argument against nationalism: *From space, we are one world*. You could make any of these claims without the image, but the photograph—like most images—will probably touch members of your audience more powerfully than words alone could.

A striking image, like this *Apollo 8* photograph of the earth shining over the moon, can support many different kinds of arguments.

### REMEMBER THE POWER OF COLOR

As the photo of the earth demonstrates, color can have great power: the blue earth floating in deep black space carries a message of its own. Our response to color is part of our biological and cultural makeup. So it makes sense to consider what colors are compatible with the kinds of arguments you're making.

In most situations, you can be guided in your selection of colors by your own good taste, by designs you admire, or by the advice of friends or helpful professionals. Some design and presentation software will even help you choose colors by offering dependable "default" shades or an array of pre-existing designs and compatible colors (for example, of presentation slides). To be emotionally effective, the colors you choose for a design should follow certain commonsense principles. If you're using background colors on a political poster, Web site, or slide, the contrast between words and background should be vivid enough to make reading easy. For example, white letters on a yellow background are not usually legible. Similarly, any bright background color should be avoided for a long document because reading is easiest with dark letters against a light or white background. Avoid complex patterns; even though they might look interesting and be easy to create, they often interfere with other more important elements of a presentation.

When you use visuals in your college projects, test them on prospective readers. That's what professionals do because they appreciate how delicate the choices of visual and multimedia texts can be. These responses will help you analyze your own arguments and improve your success with them.

## Using Images and Multimedia to Appeal to Character

Careful use of images and multimedia can help to establish the character and credibility of your text as well as your own ethos as a writer. If you are on Facebook, LinkedIn, or other social networking sites, you will know how images especially create a sense of who you are and what you value. It's no accident that employers have been known not to hire people because of the images they find on their Facebook pages—or just the opposite: we know one person whose Facebook page use of images and multimedia so impressed a prospective employer that she got the job on the spot. So whether you are using images and multimedia on your personal pages or in your college work, it pays to attend to how they shape your ethos.

### USE IMAGES AND MULTIMEDIA TO REINFORCE YOUR CREDIBILITY AND AUTHORITY

Just like the Red Cross, the Department of Homeland Security, and the Canadian Olympic Committee, you want to use images and multimedia that will build your trustworthiness and authority. For a Web site about a

Take a look at these three images, each of which intends to convey credibility and authority. Do they accomplish their goals? Why or why not?

group or organization you belong to or represent, you might display its logo or emblem because such images can provide credibility. An emblem or a logo can also convey a wealth of cultural and historical implications. That's why university Web sites often include the seal of the institution somewhere on the homepage or why the president of the United States travels with a presidential seal to hang on the speaker's podium. Other kinds of media can also enhance ethos. For an essay on safety issues in competitive biking, you might include a photo of yourself in a key race, embed a video showing how serious accidents often occur, or include an audio file of an interview with an injured biker. The photo shows that you have personal experience with biking, while the video and audio files show that you have done research and know your subject well, thus helping to affirm your credibility.

### CONSIDER HOW DESIGN REFLECTS YOUR CHARACTER

Almost every design element sends signals about character and ethos. For example, the type fonts that you select for a document can mark you as warm and inviting or as efficient and contemporary. The warm and inviting fonts often belong to a family called *serif*. The serifs are those little flourishes at the ends of the strokes that make the fonts seem handcrafted and artful:

warm and inviting (Bookman Old Style)

warm and inviting (Times New Roman)

warm and inviting (Georgia)

Cleaner, modern fonts go without those little flourishes and are called *sans serif*. These fonts are cooler, simpler, and, some argue, more readable on a computer screen (depending on screen resolution):

efficient and contemporary (Helvetica)

efficient and contemporary (Verdana)

efficient and contemporary (Comic Sans MS)

Other typographic elements shape your ethos as well. The size of type can make a difference. If your text or headings are in boldface and too large, you'll seem to be shouting:

**LOSE WEIGHT! PAY NOTHING!***

Tiny type, on the other hand, might make you seem evasive:

> *Excludes the costs of enrollment and required meal purchases. Minimum contract: 12 months.

Your choice of *color*—especially for backgrounds—can make a statement about your taste, personality, and common sense. For instance, you'll create a bad impression with a Web page whose dark background colors or busy patterns make reading difficult. If you want to be noticed, you might use bright colors—the same sort that would make an impression in clothing or cars. But subtle background shades are a better choice in most situations.

Don't ignore the power of *illustrations* and *photographs*. Because they reveal what you visualize, images can communicate your preferences,

Olympic champion Michael Phelps learned a quick lesson about ethos when a drug-related incident tarnished his reputation, costing him an endorsement deal with Kellogg's. His photograph had already appeared on boxes of Kellogg's Corn Flakes and Wheaties.

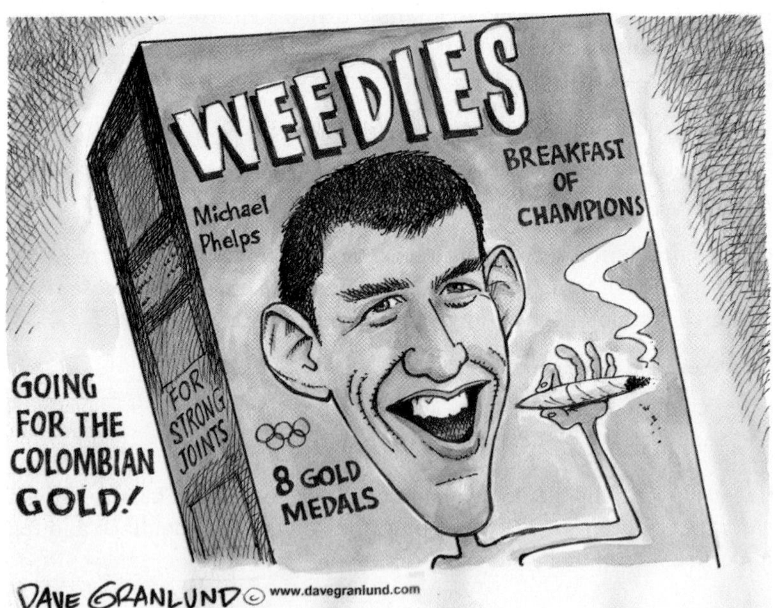

sensitivities, and inclusiveness. Conference planners, for example, are careful to create brochures that represent all participants, and they make sure that the brochure photos don't show only women, only men, or only members of one racial or ethnic group.

Even your choice of *medium* says something important about you. Making an appeal on a Web site sends signals about your technical skills, contemporary orientation, and personality. If you direct people to a Facebook or Flickr page, be sure that the images and items there present you in a favorable light.

**RESPOND.**

Choose a project or essay you have written recently and examine it for how well it establishes your credibility and how well it is designed. Ask a classmate or friend to look at it and tell you how effectively it is designed and how well it represents you. Then go back to the drawing board with a memo to yourself about how you might use images and multimedia to improve it.

You should also be careful that any *handouts* you use during a presentation or any slides you may show work to build your ethos and authority as well. And remember that you don't always have to be high-tech to be effective: when reporting on a children's story that you're writing, the most effective medium of presentation might be cardboard and paper made into an oversized book and illustrated by hand.

### FOLLOW DESIGN CONVENTIONS

Many kinds of writing have required design conventions. When that's the case, follow them to the letter. It's no accident that lab reports for science courses are sober and unembellished. Visually, they reinforce the professional ethos of scientific work. The same is true of a college research paper. You might resent the tediousness of placing page numbers in the appropriate corner, aligning long quotations just so, and putting footnotes in the right place, but these visual details help convey your competence. So whether you're composing a term paper, résumé, film, animated comic, or Web site, look for competent models and follow them.

## Visual Arguments Based on Facts and Reason

The *New York Times* offers an argument on bottled water that is based on facts and reason and that is created mostly by visual elements.

LINK TO P. 721

Not that long ago, media critics ridiculed the colorful charts and graphs in newspapers like *USA Today*. Now, comparable features appear in even the most traditional publications because they work: they convey information efficiently. We now expect information to be presented graphically, to see multiple streams of data on our screens, and to be able to interact with many of these presentations.

### ORGANIZE INFORMATION VISUALLY

Graphic presentation calls for careful design, which can help readers and viewers look at an item and understand what it does. A brilliant, much-copied example of such an intuitive design is a seat adjuster invented many years ago by Mercedes-Benz (see below). It's shaped like a tiny seat. Push any element of the control, and the real seat moves in that direction—back and forth, up and down. No instructions are necessary.

Good visual design can work the same way in an argument by conveying information without elaborate instructions. Titles, headings, subheadings, enlarged quotations, running heads, and boxes are some common visual signals.

- Use headings to guide your readers through your print or electronic document. For long and complex pieces, use subheadings as well, and make sure they are parallel.
- Use type font, size, and color to show related information within headings.
- Plan how text should be arranged on a page by searching for relationships among items that should look alike.
- Use a list or a box to set off information that should be treated differently from the rest of the presentation or for emphasis. You can also use shading, color, and typography for emphasis.
- Place your images and illustrations carefully: what you position front and center will appear more important than items in less conspicuous places. On a Web site, key headings should usually lead to subsequent pages on the site.

Mercedes-Benz's seat adjuster

Remember, too, that design principles evolve and change from medium to medium. A printed text or an overhead slide, for example, ordinarily works best when its elements are easy to read, simply organized, and surrounded by restful white space. But some types of Web pages thrive on visual clutter that attracts attention by packing a wide variety of information onto a relatively limited screen. Look closely, and you'll probably find the logic in these designs.

### USE VISUALS TO CONVEY DATA EFFICIENTLY

Words are powerful and capable of precision and subtlety. But some information is conveyed more efficiently by charts, graphs, drawings, maps, or photos. When making an argument, especially to a large group, consider what information should be delivered in nonverbal form.

The Pew Research Center organizes its information in graphs and charts to help readers make sense of the large amount of data that it is presenting.

LINK TO P. 888

A *pie chart* is an effective way of comparing parts to the whole. You might use a pie chart to illustrate the ethnic composition of your school, the percentage of taxes paid by people at different income levels, or the consumption of energy by different nations. Pie charts depict such information memorably, as the one on p. 342 shows.

A *graph* is an efficient device for comparing items over time or according to other variables. You could use a graph to trace the rise and fall of test scores over several decades or to show college enrollment by sex, race, and Hispanic origin, as in the bar graph on p. 342.

*Diagrams* or *drawings* are useful for drawing attention to details. Use drawings to illustrate complex physical processes or designs of all sorts. After the 2001 attack on the World Trade Center, for example, engineers prepared drawings and diagrams to help citizens understand precisely what led to the total collapse of the buildings.

You can use *maps* to illustrate location and spatial relationships—something as simple as the distribution of office space in your student union or as complex as the topography of Utah. Such information would be far more difficult to explain in words alone. And you can now use tools like UMapper to customize maps.

*Timelines* allow you to represent the passage of time graphically, and online tools like Dipity can help you create them for insertion into your documents.

Web pages can also make for valuable illustrations. Programs like ShrinkTheWeb let you create snapshots of Web sites that can then be inserted easily into your writing.

**Portrait of America**

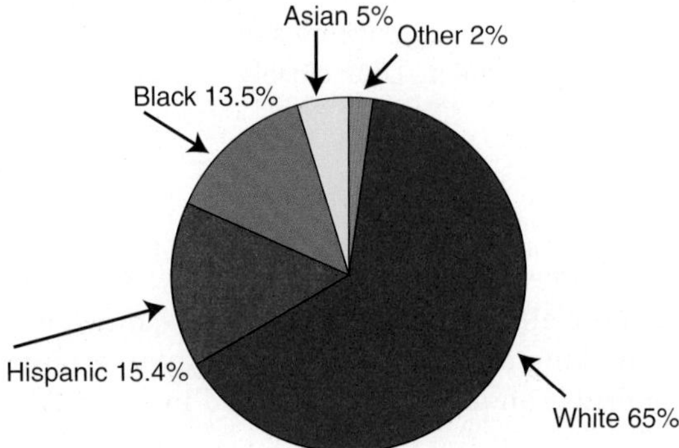


Source: Census Bureau

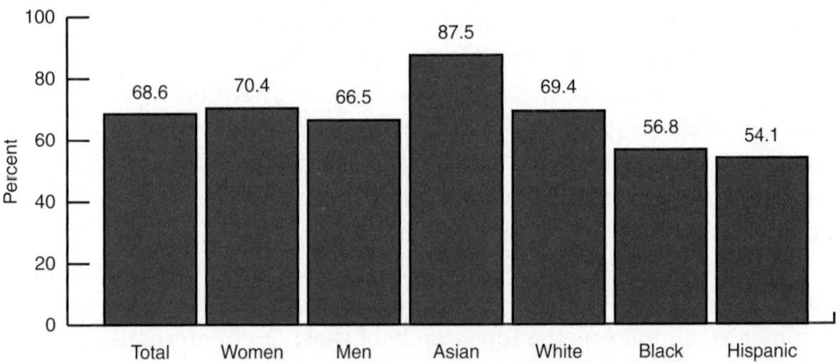


**College enrollment of year 2005 high school graduates, by sex, race, and Hispanic origin**

### FOLLOW PROFESSIONAL GUIDELINES FOR PRESENTING VISUALS

Charts, graphs, tables, illustrations, timelines, snapshots of Web sites, and video clips play such an important role in many fields that professional groups have come up with guidelines for labeling and formatting these items. You need to become familiar with those conventions as you advance in a field. A guide such as the *Publication Manual of the American Psychological Association* (6th edition) or the *MLA Handbook for Writers of Research Papers* (7th edition) describes these rules in detail. See also Chapter 15, "Presenting Arguments."

### REMEMBER TO CHECK FOR COPYRIGHTED MATERIAL

You also must be careful to respect copyright rules when using visual items that were created by someone else. It's relatively easy these days to download visual texts of all kinds from the Web. Some of these items—such as clip art or government documents—may be in the *public domain*, meaning that you're free to use them without requesting permission or paying a royalty. But other visual texts may require permission, especially if you intend to publish your work or use the item commercially. And remember: anything you place on a Web site is considered "published." (See Chapter 20 for more on intellectual property.)

# 15
# Presenting Arguments

Sometimes you won't have a choice about how to present an argument: your instructor will say, "Write a report," or "Design a Web page." But often you'll be the one to decide what kind of presentation best fits your topic, purpose, and audience, just as the writers above chose a face to face oral presentation (Josette Sheeran's talk at a conference on World Food Security), the student site that contains additional materials linked to this text (accessible via the QR code provided), or a Web-based presentation (Lawrence Lessig's use of slides and Web tools to talk about Internet and wireless gambling).

## Print Presentations

For many arguments that you make in college, print is still a major mode of delivery. Print texts are more permanent than most Web-based materials, they're inexpensive and easy to produce, and they offer a precise way to express abstract ideas or to set down complicated chains of reasoning. In making arguments in print today, though, you have an embarrassment of riches. What used to be confined to black print on 8½ x 11" white paper read left to right, top to bottom, today can be designed in a dizzying array of shapes, sizes, and colors.

As you think about presenting print-based arguments, try answering these questions:

- What overall tone do you want to create in this written argument? What's the purpose of your argument, and to whom is it addressed?
- What format will get your message across most effectively? A formal report? A newsletter? A triple-fold brochure? A poster? Whatever you choose, follow the conventions of that format by looking at good examples.
- What fonts will make your argument most readable? Will varying the font or type size help guide readers through your text? Will it draw attention to what's most important?
- Will you use subheads as another guide? If so, what size type will you select? Will you use all caps, boldface, or italics? In any case, be consistent in the style and the structure of subheads (all nouns, for example, or all questions).
- Should you use colors other than black ink and white paper in presenting your argument? What colors best evoke your tone and purpose? What colors will be most appealing?
- How will you use white or blank space in your argument? To give readers time to pause? To establish a sense of openness or orderliness?
- Will you use visuals in your print argument? If so, how will you integrate them smoothly into the text? (For more on the role of visuals in arguments, see Chapter 14.)

**RESPOND•**

Choose a print presentation that you find particularly effective. Study it carefully, noting how its various elements—format, type sizes, typefaces, color, white space, visuals, and overall layout—work to deliver its message. If you find a particularly ineffective print presentation, carry out the same analysis to figure out why it's bad. Finally, prepare a five-minute presentation of your findings to deliver in class.

## F2F Oral and Multimedia Presentations

You are probably being asked to make oral presentations in your classes, but you may be given few if any instructions in how to do so effectively. And students returning from summer internships say their employers expect them to be good at delivering arguments orally—and at accompanying their presentations with well-designed slides or illustrations.

It's hard to generalize here, but capable presenters attribute their success to several crucial elements:

- They have thorough knowledge of their subjects.
- They pay attention to the values, ideas, and needs of their listeners.
- They use structures and styles that make their spoken arguments easy to follow.
- They realize that oral arguments are interactive. (Live audiences can argue back!)
- They appreciate that most oral presentations involve visuals, and they plan accordingly.
- They practice, practice—and then practice some more.

### Oral Arguments in Discussions

You are arguing all the time, whether exploring the meaning of a poem in English class, arguing against a writer's interpretation of an economics phenomenon, or speaking against a student government policy on funding political organizations. You can improve your performance in such situations by observing effective speakers and by joining conversations whenever you can. The more that you participate in lively discussions, the more comfortable you'll be with speaking your mind. Here are some tips to help you do so:

- Do the required reading so that you know what you're talking about.
- Listen carefully and purposefully, and jot down important points.
- Speak briefly to the point under discussion so that your comments are relevant. Don't do all the talking.
- Ask questions about issues that matter to you: others probably have the same thoughts.
- Occasionally offer brief summaries of points that have already been made to make sure that everyone is "on the same page."

CULTURAL CONTEXTS FOR ARGUMENT

### Speaking Up in Class

Speaking up in class is viewed as inappropriate or even rude in some cultures. In the United States, however, doing so is expected and encouraged. Some instructors even assign credit for such class participation.

- Respond to questions or comments by others in specific rather than vague terms.
- Try to learn the names of people in the discussion, and then use them.
- When you are already part of a discussion, invite others to join in.

## Formal Oral and Multimedia Presentations

When asked to make a formal presentation in class or on the job, consider the context carefully. Note how much time you have to prepare and how long the presentation should be: never infringe on the time of other speakers. Consider also what visual aids, slides, or handouts might make the presentation successful. Will you need an overhead projector, a flip chart, a whiteboard? What presentation software, if any, will you use?

Check out where your presentation will take place. In a classroom with fixed chairs? A lecture or assembly hall? An informal sitting area? Will you have a lectern? Other equipment? Will you sit or stand? Remain in one place or move around? What will the lighting be, and can you adjust it?

Sometimes oral presentations are group efforts. When that's the case, plan and practice accordingly. The work will need to be divvied up, and you will need to work out who speaks when. Finally, note any criteria for evaluation: how will your live oral argument be assessed?

In addition to these logistical matters, consider these rhetorical elements whenever you make a formal presentation:

**Purpose.** Determine your major argumentative purpose. Is it to inform? To convince or persuade? To explore? To make a decision? To entertain? Something else?

**Audience.** Who is your audience? An interested observer? A familiar face? A stranger? What will be the mix of age groups, of gender, etc.? Are you a peer of the audience members? Think carefully about what they know about your topic and what opinions they're likely to hold.

**Structure.** Structure your presentation so that it's easy to follow. Plan an introduction that gets the audience's attention and a conclusion that makes your argument memorable. You'll find more help with structure on p. 349.

## Arguments to Be Heard

Amy Tan's "Mother Tongue" is a speech that is a fully written-out script. What features can you identify that establish this text as an argument to be heard?

LINK TO P. 622

Even if you deliver a live presentation from a printed text, be sure to compose a script that is to be *heard* rather than *read*. Such a text—whether in the form of note cards, an overhead list, or a fully written-out script—should feature a strong introduction and conclusion, an unambiguous structure with helpful transitions and signposts, concrete diction, and straightforward syntax.

### STRONG INTRODUCTIONS AND CONCLUSIONS

Like readers, listeners remember beginnings and endings best. Work hard, therefore, to make these elements of your spoken argument especially memorable. Consider including a provocative or puzzling statement, opinion, or question; a memorable anecdote; a powerful quotation; or a vivid visual image. If you can refer to the interests or experiences of your listeners in the introduction or conclusion, then do so.

Look at the introduction to Toni Morrison's acceptance speech to the Nobel Academy when she won the Nobel Prize for Literature:

> **"Once upon a time there was an old woman. Blind but wise." Or was it an old man? A guru, perhaps. Or a griot soothing restless children. I have heard this story, or one exactly like it, in the lore of several cultures. "Once upon a time there was an old woman. Blind. Wise."**
>
> **—Toni Morrison**

Here, Morrison uses a storytelling strategy, calling on the traditional "Once upon a time" to signal to her audience that she's doing so. Note also the use of repetition and questioning. These strategies raise interest and anticipation in her audience: how will she use this story in accepting the Nobel Prize?

Toni Morrison accepting the Nobel Prize for Literature in 1993

## CLEAR STRUCTURES AND SIGNPOSTS

For a spoken argument, you want your organizational structure to be crystal clear. So offer an overview of your main points toward the beginning of the presentation, and make sure that you have a sharply delineated beginning, middle, and end. Throughout the report or lecture, remember to pause between major points and to offer *signposts* to mark your movement from one topic to the next. They can be transitions as obvious as *next*, *on the contrary*, or *finally*. Such words act as memory points in your spoken argument and thus should be explicit and concrete: *The second crisis point in the breakup of the Soviet Union occurred hard on the heels of the first,* rather than *The breakup of the Soviet Union came to another crisis*. You can also keep listeners on track by repeating key words and concepts and by using unambiguous topic sentences to introduce each new idea.

## STRAIGHTFORWARD SYNTAX AND CONCRETE DICTION

Avoid long, complicated sentences and use straightforward syntax (subject-verb-object, for instance, rather than an inversion of that order). Remember, too, that listeners can hold onto concrete verbs and nouns more easily than they can grasp a steady stream of abstractions.

How does Adriene Hill's radio report on ethical eating take advantage of the medium of radio interviews and reports in order to explain a complex issue?

LINK TO P. 696

When you need to deal with abstract ideas, illustrate them with concrete examples.

Take a look at the following text that student Ben McCorkle wrote about *The Simpsons*, first as he prepared it for an essay and then as he adapted it for a live oral and multimedia presentation:

**Print Version**

> The Simpson family has occasionally been described as a *nuclear* family, which obviously has a double meaning: first, the family consists of two parents and three children, and, second, Homer works at a nuclear power plant with very relaxed safety codes. The overused label "dysfunctional," when applied to the Simpsons, suddenly takes on new meaning. Every episode seems to include a scene in which son Bart is being choked by his father, the baby is being neglected, or Homer is sitting in a drunken stupor transfixed by the television screen. The comedy in these scenes comes from the exaggeration of commonplace household events (although some talk shows and news programs would have us believe that these exaggerations are not confined to the madcap world of cartoons).
>
> —Ben McCorkle, "*The Simpsons:* A Mirror of Society"

**Oral Version (with a visual illustration)**

> What does it mean to describe the Simpsons as a *nuclear* family? Clearly, a double meaning is at work. First, the Simpsons fit the dictionary meaning—a family unit consisting of two parents and some children. The second meaning, however, packs more of a punch. You see, Homer works at a nuclear power plant [pause here] with *very* relaxed safety codes!
>
> Still another overused family label describes the Simpsons. Did everyone guess I was going to say *dysfunctional*? And like *nuclear*, when it comes to the Simpsons, *dysfunctional* takes on a whole new meaning.
>
> Remember the scene when Bart is being choked by his father?
>
> How about the many times the baby is being neglected?
>
> Or the classic view—Homer sitting in a stupor transfixed by the TV screen!
>
> My point here is that the comedy in these scenes often comes from double meanings—and from a lot of exaggeration of everyday household events.

Note that the second version presents the same information as the first, but this time it's written to be *heard*. The revision uses simpler syntax, so the argument is easy to listen to, and employs signposts, repetition, a list, and italicized words to prompt the speaker to give special emphasis where needed.

Homer Simpson in a typical pose

## Arguments to Be Remembered

Some oral and multimedia arguments have power just because they stick in the memory—the way catchy song lyrics do. For instance, people who don't even know what the slogan means still recognize James Polk's 1844 rallying cry: "Fifty-Four Forty or Fight!" Or consider the impact of a song lyric like Lorrie Morgan's "What part of *no* don't you understand?"—which is a riff on an even simpler women's rights argument: "No means *no*."

More recently, Republican presidential hopeful Herman Cain used deliberate repetition and parallel structure to fashion a tax reform plan people might notice. Called simply 9-9-9, Cain proposed a 9 percent

Some arguments are memorable in part because they offer repetition.

personal income tax rate, 9 percent corporate tax rate, and 9 percent national sales tax. Even though economists criticized his idea roundly, Cain enjoyed a momentary boost in the polls in 2011 before his campaign foundered over other issues. (See Chapter 13 for more on using figurative language to make arguments vivid.)

**RESPOND.**

Take three or four paragraphs from an essay that you've recently written. Then, following the guidelines in this chapter, rewrite the passage to be heard by a live audience. Finally, make a list of every change that you made.

### REPETITION, PARALLELISM, AND CLIMACTIC ORDER

Whether they're used alone or in combination, repetition, parallelism, and climactic order are especially appropriate for spoken arguments that sound a call to arms or that seek passionate engagement from the audience. Perhaps no person in the twentieth century used them more effectively than Martin Luther King Jr., whose sermons and speeches helped to spearhead the civil rights movement. Standing on the steps of the Lincoln Memorial in Washington, D.C., on August 23, 1963, with hundreds of thousands of marchers before him, King called on the nation to make good on the "promissory note" represented by the Emancipation Proclamation.

Look at the way that King uses repetition, parallelism, and climactic order in the following paragraph to invoke a nation to action:

> It is obvious today that America has defaulted on this promissory note insofar as her citizens of color are concerned. Instead of honoring this sacred obligation, America has given the Negro people a bad *check* which has come back marked "*insufficient funds.*" But *we* refuse to believe that the bank of justice is bankrupt. *We* refuse to believe that there are *insufficient funds* in the great vaults of opportunity of this nation. So *we have come* to cash this *check*—a *check* that will give us upon demand the riches of freedom and the security of justice. We *have also come* to this hallowed spot to remind America of the fierce urgency of now. There is no time to engage in the luxury of cooling off or to take the tranquillizing drug of gradualism. *Now* is the time *to rise* from the dark and desolate valley of segregation to the sunlit path of racial justice. *Now* is the time *to open* the doors of opportunity to all of God's children. *Now* is the time *to lift* our nation from the quicksands of racial injustice to the solid rock of brotherhood.
>
> —Martin Luther King Jr., "I Have a Dream" (emphasis added)

The italicized words highlight the way that King uses repetition to drum home his theme and a series of powerful verb phrases (*to rise, to open, to lift*) to build to a strong climax. These stylistic choices, together with the vivid image of the "bad check," help to make King's speech powerful, persuasive—and memorable.

You don't have to be as highly skilled as King to take advantage of the power of repetition and parallelism. Simply repeating a key word in your argument can impress it on your audience, as can arranging parts of sentences or items in a list in parallel order.

## The Role of Visuals in Oral and Multimedia Arguments

Visual materials—chart, graphs, posters, and presentation slides—are major tools for conveying your message and supporting your claims. In many cases, a picture can truly be worth a thousand words. (For more about visual argument, see Chapter 14.)

Be certain that any visuals that you use are large enough to be seen by all members of your audience. If you use slides or overhead projections, the information on each frame should be simple, clear, and easy to process. For slides, use 24-point type for major headings, 18 point for subheadings, and at least 14 point for other text. The same rule of clarity and simplicity holds true for posters, flip charts, and whiteboards.

And remember not to turn your back on your audience while you refer to these visuals. If you prepare supplementary materials (such as bibliographies or other handouts) for the audience, don't distribute them until the audience actually needs them. Or wait until the end of the presentation so that they don't distract listeners from your spoken argument.

If you've watched many PowerPoint presentations, you're sure to have seen some bad ones. But nothing is more deadly than a speaker who stands up and reads from each screen. It is fine to use presentation slides to furnish an overview for a presentation and to give visual signposts to listeners. But never read the slides word for word—or even put much prose on a screen. You'll just put your audience to sleep.

For an oral and multimedia presentation, Sach Wickramasekara used the PowerPoint slides shown on p. 356 to compare Frank Miller's graphic novel *Sin City* and its movie adaptation. Notice that the student uses text minimally, letting the pictures do the talking.

His choices in layout and font size also aim for clarity but without sacrificing visual appeal. The choice of white on a black background is appropriate for the topic—a stark black-and-white graphic novel and its shades-of-gray movie version. But be aware that light writing on a dark background can be hard to read and that dark writing on a white or cream-colored background is almost always a safer choice. Sach is not reading from his slides; rather the slides illustrate the point he is making orally. In this case, the words and the images work together beautifully.

(Note that if your presentation shows or is based on source materials—either text or images—your instructor may want you to include a slide that lists the sources at the end of the presentation.)

The best way to test the effectiveness of any images, slides, or other visuals is to try them out on friends, family members, classmates, or roommates. If they don't get the meaning of the visuals right away, revise and try again.

Remember, finally, that visuals and accompanying media tools can help make your presentation accessible but that some members of your audience may not be able to see your presentation or may have trouble seeing or hearing them. Here are a few key rules to remember:

- Use words to describe projected images. Something as simple as *That's Franklin Roosevelt in 1944* can help even sight-impaired audience members appreciate what's on a screen.
- Consider providing a written handout that summarizes your presentation or putting the text on an overhead projector—for those who learn better by reading *and* listening.
- If you use video, take the time to label sounds that might not be audible to audience members who are hearing impaired. (Be sure your equipment is caption capable and use the captions; they can be helpful to everyone when audio quality is poor.)

## Oral and Multimedia Presentation Strategies

In spite of your best preparation, you may feel some anxiety before a live presentation. This is natural. (According to one Gallup poll, Americans often identify public speaking as a major fear—scarier than possible attacks from outer space.) Experienced speakers say that they have strategies for dealing with anxiety, and even that a little nervousness—and accompanying adrenaline—can act to a speaker's advantage.

The most effective strategy seems to be thoroughly knowing your topic and material. Confidence in your own knowledge goes a long way toward making you a confident speaker. In addition to being well prepared, you may want to try some of the following strategies:

- Practice a number of times, running through every part of the presentation. Leave nothing out, even audio or video clips. Work with the equipment you intend to use so that you are familiar with it. It also may help to visualize your presentation, imagining the scene in your mind as you run through your materials.
- Time your presentation to make sure you stay within your allotted slot.
- Tape yourself (video, if possible) at least once so that you can listen to your voice. Tone of voice and body language can dispose audiences for—or against—speakers. For most oral arguments, you want to develop a tone that conveys commitment to your position as well as respect for your audience.

## Introduction

A frame from the *Sin City* graphic novel.

"Instead of trying to make it [*Sin City*] into a movie which would be terrible, I wanted to take cinema and try and make it into this book."

- Robert Rodriguez, DVD Interview

The same scene from the *Sin City* movie.

## Technology

Right: The original scene from the graphic novel.

Left: The scene is filmed with live actors on a green screen set.

Right: The final version of the scene, after the colors have been changed to shades of black and white. Notice the sapphire shade of the convertible, and how it stands out from the background.

[Opening Slide: Title]

Hi, my name is Sach.

[Change Slide: Introduction]

Take a look at this pair of scenes. Can you tell which one's from a movie and which one's from a graphic novel? How can two completely different media produce such similar results? Stay tuned; you're about to hear how.

[Pause]

[Change Slide: Technology]

Part of what makes *Sin City* so innovative is the technology powering it. The movie captures the look of the graphic novel so well by filming actors on a green screen and using digital imagery to put detailed backdrops behind them. Computer technology also turns the movie's visuals into shades of black and white with rare dashes of color splashed in, reproducing the noir feel of the original novels. Thus, scenes in *Sin City* have a photorealistic yet stylized quality that differentiates them from both the plain black-and-white images of the comics and the real sets used in other movies.

- Think about how you'll dress for your presentation, remembering that audience members usually notice how a speaker looks. Dressing for an effective presentation depends on what's appropriate for your topic, audience, and setting, but most experienced speakers choose clothes that are comfortable, allow easy movement, and aren't overly casual. Dressing up a little indicates that you take pride in your appearance, have confidence in your argument, and respect your audience.
- Get some rest before the presentation, and avoid consuming too much caffeine.
- Relax! Consider doing some deep-breathing exercises. Then pause just before you begin, concentrating on your opening lines.
- Maintain eye contact with members of your audience. Speak to them, not to your text or to the floor.
- Interact with the audience whenever possible; doing so will often help you relax and even have some fun.
- Most speakers make a stronger impression standing than sitting, so stand if you have that option. Moving around a bit may help you maintain good eye contact.
- When using presentation slides, stand to the side so that you don't block the view. Look at the audience rather than the slide.
- Remember to allow time for audience responses and questions. Keep your answers brief so that others may join the conversation.
- Finally, at the very end of your presentation, thank the audience for its attention to your arguments.

### A Note about Webcasts: Live Presentations over the Web

This discussion of live oral and multimedia presentations has assumed that you'll be speaking before an audience that's in the same room with you. Increasingly, though—especially in business, industry, and science—the presentations you make will be live, but you won't be in the same physical space as the audience. Instead, you might be in front of a camera that will capture your voice and image and relay them via the Web to attendees who might be anywhere in the world. In another type of Webcast, participants can see only your slides or the software that you're demonstrating, using a screen-capture relay without cameras, and you're not visible but still speaking live.

In either case, as you learn to adapt to Webcast environments, most of the strategies that work in oral and multimedia presentations for an audience that's physically present will continue to serve you well. But there are some significant differences:

- Practice is even more important in Webcasts, since you need to be able to access online any slides, documents, video clips, names, dates, and sources that you provide during the Webcast.
- Because you can't make eye contact with audience members, it's important to remember to look into the camera (if you are using one), at least from time to time. If you're using a stationary Webcam, perhaps one mounted on your computer, practice standing or sitting without moving out of the frame and yet without looking stiff.
- Even though your audience may not be visible to you, assume that if you're on camera, the Web-based audience can see you. If you slouch, they'll notice. Assume too that your microphone is always live. Don't mutter under your breath, for example, when someone else is speaking or asking a question.

**RESPOND**

Attend a presentation on your campus, and observe the speaker's delivery. Note the strategies that the speaker uses to capture and hold your attention (or not). What signpost language and other guides to listening can you detect? How well are visuals integrated into the presentation? What aspects of the speaker's tone, dress, eye contact, and movement affect your understanding and appreciation (or lack of it)? What's most memorable about the presentation, and why? Finally, write up an analysis of this presentation's effectiveness.

## Web-Based Presentations

Even without the interactivity of Webcasts, most students have enough access to the Web to use its powers for effective presentations, especially in Web sites and blogs.

The Web site for the band Moonlight Social.

## Web Sites

You may already have created a Web site for a class or an extracurricular group or project. Take a look at a site designed by Jeremy Burchard and specifically at the "About" page, shown above, for the band he is part of, Moonlight Social. Note that this page design is simple and clear, with a menu bar across the top and three images on the left balanced by a block of text on the right. Also note that it allows a free download and that the entire page makes an argument that we should listen to their music.

In planning any Web site, you'll need to pay careful attention to your rhetorical situation—the purpose of your site, its intended audience, and the overall impression that you want to make. To get started, you may want to visit several sites that you admire, looking for effective design ideas and ways of organizing navigation and information. Creating a map or storyboard for your site will help you to think through the links from page to page.

Experienced Web designers cite several important principles for Web-based presentations. The first of these is *contrast*, which is achieved through the use of color, icons, boldface, and so on; contrast helps guide readers through the site. The second principle, *proximity*, calls on you to keep together the parts of a page that are closely related, again for ease of reading. *Repetition* means using a consistent design throughout the site for the elements (such as headings and links) that help readers move smoothly through the environment. Finally, designers concentrate on an *overall impression* or mood for the site, which means that the colors and visuals on the pages should help to create that impression rather than challenge or undermine it.

Here are some additional tips that may help you design your site:

- The homepage should be eye-catching, inviting, and informative. Use titles and illustrations to make clear what the site is about.
- Think carefully about two parts of every page—the navigation area (menus or links) and the content areas. You want to make these two areas clearly distinct from one another. And make sure you *have* a navigation area for every page, including links to the key sections of the site and a link back to the homepage. Ease of navigation is one key to a successful Web site.
- Either choose a design template that is provided by Web-writing tools or create a template of your own that ensures that the elements of each page are consistent.
- Remember that some readers may not have the capacity to download heavy visuals or to access elements like Flash. If you want to reach a wide audience, stick with visuals that can be downloaded easily.
- Remember to include Web contact information on every page, but not your personal address or phone number.

### Videos

When is a video the best medium for delivering a message? When it fits well with the purpose of the message and enables the writer to reach a wider audience than a live presentation can. And students today have opportunities to make arguments using this influential medium.

When Max Oswald became concerned that online communication was separating people rather than bringing them together in the way that face-to-face communication can, he decided that the best way to get his message across was through a short film. Called "Progress," the video features Max talking directly with his viewers about the distancing effects of online communication. We also see Max moving around a room as he

Max Cougar Oswald speaks in "Progress," the video he created for his writing class. You can see this presentation in e-Pages at **bedfordstmartins.com/everythingsanargument/epages**.

speaks, gesturing to slides that underscore the points he is making. At the end of the clip, however, Max steps into camera range and we realize he has been standing aside throughout. He looks at the audience and says he will end not with the video, which he argues has distanced us from him, but by talking to us face-to-face. The effect of the shift was a dramatic instantiation of the point his video was making.

### Wikis

To make working on group projects easier, many classes have begun to use wikis, which are Web-based sites that enable writers to collaborate in the creation of a single project or database. The most famous group effort of this kind is, of course, Wikipedia, but software such as DokuWiki, MediaWiki, or Tiki Wiki helps people to manage similar, if less ambitious, efforts of their own, whether it be exploring questions raised in academic courses or examining and supporting needs within a community. Wiki projects can be argumentative in themselves, or they might furnish raw data and evidence for subsequent projects.

If asked to participate in a wiki, you should, naturally, learn how to use the assigned software and follow course or project guidelines for entering and documenting the material you contribute. Just as you will expect your colleagues to use reliable sources or make accurate observations, they will depend on you to do your part in shaping the project. Of course, within the wiki, participants will be able to draw upon each other's strengths and, ideally, to compensate for any weaknesses. So take your responsibilities seriously.

## Blogs

No Web texts have captured the public imagination more swiftly than blogs, which are now too numerous to count as well as thoroughly interactive.

In many ways, these blogs offer an alternative to traditional newspapers, TV networks, and periodicals: blogs often break important news stories as well as give more breadth to the political spectrum. As such, blogs create an ideal space for building communities, engaging in arguments, and giving voice to views and opinions of ordinary, everyday folks. We seldom see these people writing or being written about in major print media—many of which now sponsor blogs themselves as part of their electronic versions.

The *Daily Californian*'s live blog about UC Berkeley's "Increase Diversity Bake Sale" is, like many live blogs, printed in reverse chronological order, with more recent posts added at the top of the page. How does this help an audience follow an event in real time?

LINK TO P. 756

The Web site for Moonlight Social contains a blog. Take a look at this posting from February 8, 2011:

> Hi there
> It looks like you've stumbled upon a blog! But why is Moonlight Social blogging? Well, people like to talk about themselves . . . and bands like to talk about themselves even more. But more importantly, we want to keep you, the fans, in the loop. So here's what you can expect: quick updates, some responses to questions from the comments posted in the contact section, and maybe a musical thought or three. We'll keep it brief, and you let us know if you like it enough to keep it around!
>
> Music update: You can officially expect to hear two new songs at our next show.
>
> HOW EXCITING!
>
> Response to Jessica: Glad you like the music player! The song you're talking about is called "Even If"—the third song in the rotation. Click the little arrows under the play/pause button until it pops up.
>
> Response to Mango: The song you're referring to is called "The Idea of Me," and it is certainly on the docket to be recorded. A video of a live version may pop up some time soon too, so keep an eye out. And we can't wait for the next show either!
>
> Speaking of the next show, it's Feb. 17th at New World Deli at 8:30—see you there!

Wonkette

HOT AIR

TPM

Political blogs Wonkette, Hot Air, and Talking Points Memo are well-known for their lively comments sections.

Note that the Moonlight Social blog is direct and personable and that it allows for readers to comment. The bloggers then respond to comments, thus setting up a dialogue with their fans.

Of course, like everything else, blogs can have downsides: they are idiosyncratic, can be self-indulgent and egoistic, and can distort issues by spreading misinformation very quickly. If you're a fan of blogs, be sure to read carefully. The information on blogs hasn't been critically reviewed in the way that traditional print sources edit their stories. But also remember that blogs have reported many instances of the mainstream media's failure to live up to their own standards.

Political blogs get plenty of attention, and you can easily join in on the conversation there, bringing your arguments to bear on issues they raise. If you do blog, or comment on blogs, remember to follow commonsense good manners: be respectful and think carefully about what you are saying and about the impression you want to leave with those who read you.

**RESPOND.**

Go to a blog that you admire or consult frequently. Then answer the following questions:

Why is a blog—a digital presentation—the best way to present this material?

What advantages over a print text or a live oral and multimedia presentation does the blog have?

How could you "translate" the argument(s) of this site into print or live oral format? What might be gained or lost in the process?

PART 4

# RESEARCH AND arguments

# 16
# Academic Arguments

Much of the writing you will do in college (and some of what you may do later in your professional work) is called **academic discourse** or **academic argument**. Although this kind of writing has many distinctive features, in general it shares these characteristics:

- It is based on research and uses evidence that can be documented.
- It is written for a professional, academic, or school audience likely to know something about its topic.
- It makes a clear and compelling point in a formal, objective, and often technical style.
- It follows agreed-upon conventions of format, usage, and punctuation.
- It is documented, using some professional citation style.

Academic writing is serious work, the kind you are expected to do whenever you are assigned a term paper, research paper, or capstone project. Manasi Deshpande's proposal "A Call to Improve Campus Accessibility for the Mobility Impaired" in Chapter 12 is an example of an academic argument of the kind you may write in college. You will find other examples of such work throughout this book.

## Understanding What Academic Argument Is

**Academic argument** covers a wide range of writing. But its hallmarks are an appeal to reason and a faith in research. As a consequence, such arguments cannot be composed quickly, casually, or off the top of one's head. They require careful reading, accurate reporting, and a conscientious commitment to truth. Academic pieces do not entirely tune out appeals to ethos or emotions: such arguments often convey power and authority through their impressive lists of sources and their formal style. But an academic argument simply crumbles if its facts are skewed or its content proves to be unreliable.

Look, for example, how systematically a communications scholar presents facts and evidence in an academic argument about privacy and social networking in the United States:

> According to three 2005 Pew Reports (Lenhart, 2005; Lenhart, et al., 2005; Lenhart and Madden, 2005), 87 percent of American teens aged 12–17 are using the Internet. Fifty-one percent of these teenagers state that they go online on a daily basis. Approximately four million teenagers or 19 percent say that they create their own weblogs (personal online journals) and 22 percent report that they maintain a personal Web page (Lenhart and Madden, 2005). In blogs and on personal Web sites, teenagers are providing so much personal information about themselves that it has become a concern. Today, content creation is not only sharing music and videos; it involves personal diaries.
>
> —Susan B. Barnes, "A Privacy Paradox: Social Networking in the United States"

Note, too, that this writer draws her material from reports produced by the Pew Research Center, a well-known and respected organization. Chances are you immediately recognize that this paragraph is an example of a researched academic argument.

Hyon B. Shin and Robert A. Kominski's report on language use in the United States meets all of the criteria for academic argument listed here and provides a potential model for your own writing.

LINK TO P. 571

You can also identify academic argument by the way it addresses its audiences. Some academic writing is clearly aimed at specialists in a field who are familiar with both the subject and the terminology that surrounds it. As a result, the researchers make few concessions to general readers unlikely to encounter or appreciate their work. You see that single-mindedness in this abstract of an article about migraine headaches in a scientific journal: it quickly becomes unreadable to nonspecialists.

> **Abstract**
>
> Migraine is a complex, disabling disorder of the brain that manifests itself as attacks of often severe, throbbing head pain with sensory sensitivity to light, sound and head movement. There is a clear familial tendency to migraine, which has been well defined in a rare autosomal dominant form of familial hemiplegic migraine (FHM). FHM mutations so far identified include those in CACNA1A (P/Q voltage-gated Ca(2+) channel), ATP1A2 (N(+)-K(+)-ATPase) and SCN1A (Na(+) channel) genes. Physiological studies in humans and studies of the experimental correlate—cortical spreading depression (CSD)—provide understanding of aura, and have explored in recent years the effect of migraine preventives in CSD. . . .
>
> —Peter J. Goadsby, "Recent Advances in Understanding Migraine Mechanisms, Molecules, and Therapeutics," *Trends in Molecular Medicine*, Vol. 13, No. 1, pp. 39–44 (January 2007)

Yet this very article might later provide data for a more accessible argument in a magazine such as *Scientific American*, which addresses a broader (though no less serious) readership. Here's a selection from an article on migraine headaches from that more widely read journal (see also the infographic on p. 370):

> At the moment, only a few drugs can prevent migraine. All of them were developed for other diseases, including hypertension, depression and epilepsy. Because they are not specific to migraine, it will come as no surprise that they work in only 50 percent of patients—and, in them, only 50 percent of the time—and induce a range of side effects, some potentially serious.
>
> Recent research on the mechanism of these antihypertensive, antiepileptic and antidepressant drugs has demonstrated that one of their effects is to inhibit cortical spreading depression. The drugs' ability to prevent migraine with and without aura therefore supports the school of thought that cortical spreading depression contributes to both kinds of attacks. Using this observation as a starting point, investigators have come up with novel drugs that specifically inhibit cortical spreading depression. Those drugs are now being tested in migraine sufferers with and without aura. They work by preventing gap junctions, a form of ion channel, from opening, thereby halting the flow of calcium between brain cells.
>
> —David W. Dodick and J. Jay Gargus, "Why Migraines Strike," *Scientific American* (August 2008)

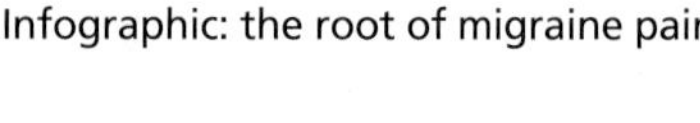

Infographic: the root of migraine pain

Such writing still requires attention, but it delivers important and comprehensible information to any reader seriously interested in the subject and the latest research on it.

Even when academic writing is less technical and demanding, its style will retain a noticeable formality—maybe even stiffness. To some extent in academic arguments, the authors seem to disappear, the tone is objective and dispassionate, the language avoids highly connotative expressions, and all the *i*'s are dotted and *t*'s crossed. Here's an abstract for an academic paper on the Burning Man phenomenon, demonstrating those qualities:

> Every August for more than a decade, thousands of information technologists and other knowledge workers have trekked out into a barren stretch of alkali desert and built a temporary city devoted to art, technology, and communal living: Burning Man. Drawing on extensive archival research, participant observation, and interviews, this paper explores the ways that Burning Man's bohemian ethos supports new forms of production emerging in Silicon Valley and especially at Google. It shows how elements of the Burning Man world—including the building of a socio-technical commons, participation in project-based artistic labor, and the fusion of social and professional interaction—help shape and legitimate the collaborative manufacturing processes driving the growth of Google and other firms. The paper thus develops the notion that Burning Man serves as a key cultural infrastructure for the Bay Area's new media industries.
>
> —Fred Turner, "Burning Man at Google: A Cultural Infrastructure for New Media Production"

A scene from Burning Man.

You might imagine a different and far livelier way to tell a story about the annual Burning Man gathering in Nevada, but this piece respects the conventions of its academic field.

Another way you likely identify academic writing—especially term papers—is by the way it draws upon sources and builds arguments from research done by experts and reported in journal articles and books. Using an evenhanded tone and dealing with all points of view fairly, such writing brings together multiple voices and intriguing ideas. You can see these moves in just one paragraph from a heavily documented student essay examining the comedy of Chris Rock:

> The breadth of passionate debate that [Chris] Rock's comedy elicits from intellectuals is evidence enough that he is advancing discussion of the foibles of black America, but Rock continually insists that he has no political aims: "Really, really at the end of the day, the only important thing is being funny. I don't go out of my way to be political" (qtd. in Bogosian 58). His unwillingness to view himself as a black leader triggers Justin Driver to say, "[Rock] wants to be caustic and he wants to be loved" (32). Even supporters wistfully sigh, "One wishes Rock would own up to the fact that he's a damned astute social critic" (Kamp 7).
>
> —Jack Chung, "The Burden of Laughter: Chris Rock Fights Ignorance His Way"

Readers can quickly tell that author Jack Chung has read widely and thought carefully about how to present his argument.

As you can see even from these brief examples, academic arguments cover a broad range of topics and appear through a variety of media—as a brief note in a journal like *Nature*, for example, a poster session at a conference on linguistics, a short paper in *Physical Review Letters*, a full research report in microbiology, or an undergraduate honors thesis in history. Moreover, scholars today are pushing the envelope of traditional academic writing in some fields. Physicians, for example, are using narrative more often in medicine to communicate effectively with other medical personnel.

What do all these projects have in common? One professor we know defines academic argument as "carefully structured research," and that seems to us to be a pretty good definition.

## Developing an Academic Argument

In your first years of college, the academic arguments you make will probably include the features and qualities we've discussed above—and which you see demonstrated in the sample academic arguments at the end of this chapter. In addition, you can make a strong academic argument by following some time-tested techniques.

**Choose a topic you want to explore in depth.** Unless you are assigned a topic (and remember that even assigned topics can be tweaked to match your interests), look for a subject that intrigues you—one you *want* to learn more about. One of the hardest parts of producing an academic argument is finding a topic narrow enough to be manageable in the time you have to work on it but also rich enough to sustain your interest over the same period. Talk with friends about possible topics and explain to them why you'd like to pursue research on this issue. Browse through books and articles that interest you, make a list of potential subjects, and then zero in on one or two top choices.

**Get to know the conversation surrounding your topic.** Once you've chosen a topic, expect to do even more reading and browsing—a lot more. Familiarize yourself with what's been said about your subject and especially with the controversies that currently surround it. Where do scholars agree, and where do they disagree? What key issues seem to be at stake? You can start by exploring the Internet, using key terms that are associated with your topic. But you may be better off searching the more specialized databases at your library with the assistance of a librarian who can help you narrow your search and make it more efficient. Library databases will also give you access to materials not available via Google or other online search engines—including, for example, full-text versions of journal articles. For much more on identifying appropriate sources, see Chapter 17, "Finding Evidence."

**Assess what you know and what you need to know.** As you read about your topic and discuss it with others, keep notes on what you have learned, including what you already know about it. Such notes should soon reveal where the gaps are in your knowledge. For instance, you may discover a need to learn about legal issues and thus end up doing research in a law school library. Or perhaps talking with experts about your topic might be helpful. Instructors on your campus may have the knowledge you need, so explore your school's Web site to find faculty or staff to talk with. Make an appointment to visit them during office hours and bring the sorts of questions to your meeting that show you've done basic work on the subject.

Mack D. Mariani and Gordon J. Hewitt include a discussion section in their academic journal article that reviews previous research on their topic. Providing this background information helps academic writers clarify areas for further exploration that their own arguments will address.

LINK TO P. 801

**Come up with a claim about your topic.** The chapters in Part 2, "Writing Arguments," offer instruction in formulating thesis statements, which most academic arguments must have. Chapters 8–12, in particular, explain how to craft claims tailored to individual projects ranging from arguments of fact to proposals. Remember here, though, that good claims are controversial. After all, you don't want to debate something that everyone already agrees upon or accepts.

In addition, your claim needs to say something consequential about an important or controversial topic and be supported with strong evidence and good reasons (see Chapter 17). Here, for example, is the claim that Brian Riady defends in his research argument on problems writing centers face when helping international students (reprinted at the end of this chapter): "Non-directive tutoring fails non-native English speakers for the exact reason that it so effectively assists native English speakers: *culture*." Each piece of evidence that Brian presents after stating his thesis develops that claim and leads to the specific recommendations with which he ends his paper.

**Consider your rhetorical stance and purpose.** Once you have a claim, ask yourself where you stand with respect to your topic and how you want to represent yourself to those reading your argument.

- You may take the stance of a reporter: you review what has been said about the topic; analyze and evaluate contributions to the conversation surrounding it; synthesize the most important strands of that conversation; and finally draw conclusions based on them.
- You may see yourself primarily as a critic: you intend to point out the problems and mistakes associated with some view of your topic.
- You may prefer the role of an advocate: you present research that strongly supports a particular view on your topic.

Whatever your perspective, remember that in academic arguments you want to come across as fair and evenhanded, especially when you play the advocate. Your stance will always be closely tied to your purpose, which in most of your college writing will be at least twofold: to do the best job in fulfilling an assignment for a course and to support the claim you are making to the fullest extent possible. Luckily, these two purposes work well together.

**Think about your audience(s).** Here again, you will often find that you have at least two audiences—and maybe more. First, you will be writing to the instructor who gave you the project, so take careful notes when the assignment is given and, if possible, set up a conference to nail down your teacher's expectations: what will it take to convince this audience that you have done a terrific job of writing an academic argument? Beyond your instructor, you should also think of your classmates as an audience—informed, intelligent peers who will be interested in what you have to say. Again, what do you know about these readers, and what will they expect from your project?

Finally, consider yet another audience—people who are already discussing your topic. These will include the authors whose work you have read and the larger academic community of which they are now a part. If your work appears online or in some other medium, you could reach more people than you initially expect.

**Concentrate on the material you are gathering.** Any academic argument is only as good as the evidence it presents to support its claims. Give each major piece of evidence (a lengthy article, say, that addresses your subject directly) careful scrutiny:

- Summarize its main points.
- Analyze how those points are pertinent.
- Evaluate the quality of the supporting evidence.
- Synthesize the results of your analysis and evaluation.
- Summarize what you think about the article.

In other words, test each piece of evidence and then decide which to keep—and which to throw out. But do not gather only materials that favor your take on the topic. You want, instead, to look at all legitimate perspectives on your claim, and in doing so, you may even change your mind. That's what good research for an academic argument can do: remember the "conscientious commitment to truth" we mentioned earlier? Keep yourself open to discovery and change. (See Chapter 18, "Evaluating Sources," and Chapter 19, "Using Sources.")

Give visual and nonprint materials the same scrutiny you would to print sources since these days you will likely be gathering or creating such materials in many fields. Remember that the graphic representation of data always involves an interpretation of that material: numbers can lie and pictures distort. (For more information on evaluating visuals, see Chapter 14.)

**Take special care with documentation.** As you gather materials for your academic argument, record where you found each source so that you can cite it accurately. For print sources, develop a working bibliography either on your computer or in a notebook you can carry with you. For each book, write the name of the author, the title of the book, the city of publication, the publisher, the date of publication, and the place that you found it (the section of the library, for example, and the call number for the book). For each article, write the name of the author, the title of the article, the title of the periodical, and the volume, issue, and exact page numbers. Include any other information you may later need in preparing a works cited list or references list.

For electronic sources, keep a careful record of the information you'll need in a works cited list or references list. Write the author and title information, the name of the database or other online site where you found the source, the full electronic address (URL), the date the document was first produced, the date it was published on the Web or most recently updated, and the date you accessed and examined it. The simplest way to ensure that you have this information is to print a copy of the source, highlight source information, and write down any other pertinent information.

Remember, too, that different academic fields use different systems of documentation, so if your instructor has not recommended a style of documentation to you, ask in class about it. Scholars have developed these systems over long periods of time to make research in an area reliable and routine. Using documentation responsibly shows that you understand the conventions of your field or major and that you have paid your dues, thereby establishing your position as a member of the academic community. (For more detailed information, see Chapter 21, "Documenting Sources.")

**Think about organization.** As you review the research materials you have gathered, you are actually beginning the work of drafting and designing your project. Study the way those materials are organized, especially any from professional journals. You may need to include in your own argument some of the sections or features you find in professional research:

- Does the article open with an abstract, summarizing its content?
- Is there a formal introduction to the subject or a clear statement of a thesis or hypothesis?
- Does the article begin with a "review of literature," summarizing recent research on its topic?
- Does the piece describe its methods of research?
- How does the article report its results and findings?
- Does the article use charts and graphs to report data?
- Does the piece use headings and subheadings?
- How does the work summarize its findings or make recommendations?
- Does the essay offer a list of works cited or references?

Anticipate some variance in the way materials are presented from one academic field to another.

As you organize your own project, check with your instructor to see if there is a recommended pattern for you to follow. If not, create a scratch outline or storyboard to describe how your essay will proceed. In reviewing your evidence, decide which pieces support specific points in the argument. Then try to position your strongest pieces of evidence in key places — near the beginning of paragraphs, at the end of the introduction, or toward a powerful conclusion. In addition, strive to achieve a balance between, on the one hand, your own words and arguments, and on the other hand, the sources that you use or quote in support of the argument. The sources of evidence are important props in the design, but they shouldn't overpower the structure of your argument itself.

And remember that your organization needs to take into account the placement of visuals — charts, tables, photographs, and so on. (For specific advice on structuring arguments, review the "Thinking about Organization" sections in the "Guides to Writing" for Chapters 8–12.)

**Consider style and tone.** Most academic argument adopts the voice of a reasonable, fair-minded, and careful thinker who is interested in coming as close to the truth about a topic as possible. A style that achieves that tone may have some of the following features:

- It strives for clarity and directness, though it may tolerate jargon.
- It favors denotative rather than connotative language.
- It is usually impersonal, avoiding "I" and using the third person.
- In some fields, it may use the passive voice routinely.
- It uses technical language, symbols, and abbreviations for efficiency.
- It avoids colloquialisms, slang, and even contractions.

Anne E. Becker's study of body image and identity in Fiji exemplifies a clear, direct academic style. Even though she makes a complex argument, her writing remains straightforward and readable.

LINK TO P. 505

The examples at the end of this chapter demonstrate traditional academic style, though there is, as always, a range of possibilities in its manner of expression.

**Consider design and visuals.** Most college academic arguments look more like articles in professional journals than those one might find in a glossier periodical like *Scientific American*—that is, they are usually black on white, use a traditional font size and type (like 11-point Times New Roman), and lack any conscious design other than inserted tables or figures. But such conventions are changing as more students gain access to software that allows for more sophisticated design elements.

Indeed, student writers today may now go well beyond print, creating digital documents that can integrate a variety of media and array data in strikingly original ways. But always consider what kinds of design best suit your topic, purpose, and audience and then act accordingly. As you think about the design possibilities for your academic argument, you may want to consult your instructor—and to test your ideas and innovations on friends or classmates.

In choosing visuals to include for your argument, be sure each one makes a strong contribution to your message and is appropriate and fair to your topic and your audience. Treat visuals as you would any other sources and integrate them into your text. Like quotations, paraphrases, and summaries, visuals need to be introduced and commented on in some way. In addition, label and number ("Figure 1," "Table 2," and so on) all visuals, provide a caption that includes source information and describes the visual, and cite the source in your references page or works cited list. Even if you create a visual (such as a bar graph) by using information from a source (the results, say, of a Gallup poll), you must cite the source. If you use a photograph you took yourself, cite it as a personal photograph.

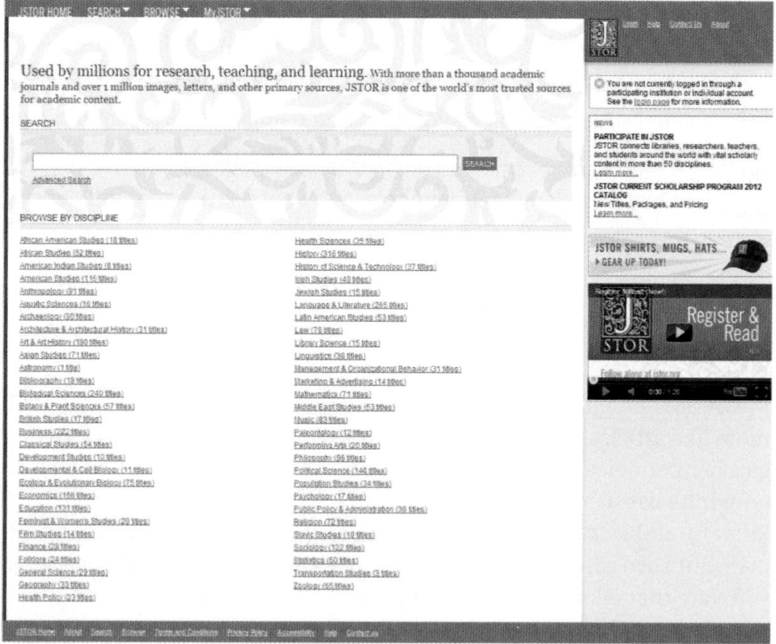


JSTOR is a database for journal articles in many disciplines. Such articles are important to academic arguments.

**Reflect on your draft and get responses.** As with any important piece of writing, an academic argument calls for careful reflection on your draft. You may want to do a "reverse outline" to test whether a reader can pull a logical and consistent pattern out of the paragraphs or sections you have written. In addition, you can also judge the effectiveness of your overall argument, assessing what each paragraph contributes and what may be missing. Turning a critical eye to your own work at the draft stage can save much grief in the long run. Be sure to get some response from classmates and friends too: come up with a set of questions to ask them about your draft and push them for honest responses. Find out what is confusing or unclear to others in your draft, what needs further evidence, and so on.

**Edit and proofread your text.** Proofread an academic argument at least three times. First review it for ideas, making sure that all your main points and supporting evidence make sense and fit nicely together. Give special attention to transitions and paragraph structure and the way you have arrayed information, positioned headings, and captioned graphic items. Make sure the big picture is in focus.

Then read the text word by word to check spelling, punctuation, quotation marks, apostrophes, abbreviations—in short, all the details that can go wrong simply because of a slip in attention. To keep their focus at this level, some readers will even read an entire text backwards. Notice too where your computer's spelling and grammar checkers may be underlining particular words and phrases. Don't ignore these clear signals.

Finally, check that every source mentioned in the academic argument appears in the references list and that every citation is correct. This is also the time to make any final touchups to your overall design. Remember that how the document looks is part of what establishes its credibility.

## RESPOND•

1. Look closely at the following five passages, each of which is from an opening of a published work, and decide which ones provide examples of academic argument. How would you describe each one, and what are its key features? Which is the most formal and academic? Which is the least? How might you revise them to make them more—or less—academic?

During the Old Stone Age, between thirty-seven thousand and eleven thousand years ago, some of the most remarkable art ever conceived was etched or painted on the walls of caves in southern France and northern Spain. After a visit to Lascaux, in the Dordogne, which was discovered in 1940, Picasso reportedly said to his guide, "They've invented everything." What those first artists invented was a language of signs for which there will never be a Rosetta stone; perspective, a technique that was not rediscovered until the Athenian Golden Age; and a bestiary of such vitality and finesse that, by the flicker of torchlight, the animals seem to surge from the walls, and move across them like figures in a magic-lantern show (in that sense, the artists invented animation). They also thought up the grease lamp—a lump of fat, with a plant wick, placed in a hollow stone—to light their workplace; scaffolds to reach high places; the principles of stenciling and Pointillism; powdered colors, brushes, and stumping cloths; and, more to the point of Picasso's insight, the very concept of an image. A true artist reimagines that concept with every blank canvas—but not from a void.

—Judith Thurman, "First Impressions," *The New Yorker*

I stepped over the curb and into the street to hitchhike. At the age of ten I'd put some pretty serious mileage on my thumb. And I knew how it was done. Hold your thumb up, not down by your hip as though you didn't much give a damn whether you got a ride or not. Always hitch at a place where a driver could pull out of traffic and give you time to get in without risking somebody tailgating him.

—Harry Crews, "On Hitchhiking," *Harper's*

Coral reef ecosystems are essential marine environments around the world. Host to thousands (and perhaps millions) of diverse organisms, they are also vital to the economic well-being of an estimated 0.5 billion people, or 8% of the world's population who live on tropical coasts (Hoegh-Guldberg 1999). Income from tourism and fishing industries, for instance, is essential to the economic prosperity of many countries, and the various plant and animal species present in reef ecosystems are sources for different natural products and medicines. The degradation of coral reefs can therefore have a devastating impact on coastal populations, and it is estimated that between 50% and 70% of all reefs around the world are currently threatened (Hoegh-Guldberg). Anthropogenic influences are cited as the major cause of this degradation, including sewage, sedimentation, direct trampling of reefs, over-fishing of herbivorous fish, and even global warming (Umezawa et al. 2002; Jones et al. 2001; Smith et al. 2001).

—Elizabeth Derse, "Identifying the Sources of Nitrogen to Hanalei Bay, Kauai, Utilizing the Nitrogen Isotope Signature of Macroalgae," *Stanford Undergraduate Research Journal*

While there's a good deal known about invertebrate neurobiology, these facts alone haven't settled questions of their sentience. On the one hand, invertebrates lack a cortex, amygdala, as well as many of the other major brain structures routinely implicated in human emotion. And unsurprisingly, their nervous systems are quite minimalist compared to ours: we have roughly a hundred thousand bee brains worth of neurons in our heads. On the other hand, some invertebrates, including insects, do possess the rudiments of our stress response system. So the question is still on the table: do they experience emotion in a way that we would recognize, or just react to the world with a set of glorified reflexes?

—Jason Castro, "Do Bees Have Feelings?" *Scientific American*

From the richest high school to the poorest high school in America, students are being told that employment in the computer industry is nothing less than salvation from the indignities of the jobs those others have to do to survive. If you don't learn your computer skills well, if by some chance you're bored sitting in front of that screen, day after day under buzzing fluorescents, pecking at a vanilla keyboard, clicking a mouse, it's your problem, and there will be no excuse for your fate in this new economy: you will be doomed to menial, manual labor. That dirty, anybody-can-do-that work. Poor income, low prestige. *Pues, así va la vida, compa,* that's life if you don't get your stuff right.

—Dagoberto Gilb, "Work Union," *Gritos*

2. Working with another student in your class, find examples from two or three different fields of academic arguments that strike you as being well written and effective. Spend some time looking closely at them. Do they exemplify the key features of academic arguments discussed in this chapter? What other features do they use? How are they organized? What kind of tone do the writers use? What use do they make of visuals? Draw up a brief report on your findings (a list will do), and bring it to class for discussion.

3. Read the following three paragraphs, and then list changes that the writer might make to convert them into an academic argument:

The book—the physical paper book—is being circled by a shoal of sharks, with sales down 9 percent this year alone. It's being chewed by the e-book. It's being gored by the death of the bookshop and the library. And most importantly, the mental space it occupied is being eroded by the thousand Weapons of Mass Distraction that surround us all. It's hard to admit, but we all sense it: it is becoming almost physically harder to read books.

In his gorgeous little book *The Lost Art of Reading—Why Books Matter in a Distracted Time*, the critic David Ulin admits to a strange feeling. All his life, he had taken reading as for granted as eating—but then, a few years ago, he "became aware, in an apartment full of books, that I could no longer find within myself the quiet necessary to read." He would sit down to do it at night, as he always had, and read a few paragraphs, then find his mind was wandering, imploring him to check his email, or Twitter, or Facebook. "What I'm struggling with," he writes, "is the encroachment of the buzz, the sense that there's something out there that merits my attention."

> I think most of us have this sense today, if we are honest. If you read a book with your laptop thrumming on the other side of the room, it can be like trying to read in the middle of a party, where everyone is shouting to each other. To read, you need to slow down. You need mental silence except for the words. That's getting harder to find.
>
> —Johann Hari, "How to Survive the Age of Distraction"

4. Choose two pieces of your college writing, and examine them closely. Are they examples of strong academic writing? How do they use the key features that this chapter identifies as characteristic of academic arguments? How do they use and document sources? What kind of tone do you establish in each? After studying the examples in this chapter, what might you change about these pieces of writing, and why?
5. Go to a blog that you follow, or check out one like the *Huffington Post* or *Ricochet*. Spend some time reading the articles or postings on the blog, and look for ones that you think are the best written and the most interesting. What features or characteristics of academic argument do they use, and which ones do they avoid?

# A Directive Approach toward ESL/EFL Writers

BRIAN RIADY

Opening paragraph explains the context for this academic argument.

Since its origin in Stephen North's "The Idea of a Writing Center" and Jeff Brooks's "Minimalist Tutoring," a non-directive approach has become firmly embedded in writing center methodology (Clark 33). The premise of the non-directive approach is that minimizing direct instruction at a writing center will simultaneously improve student learning, keep student writers accountable, and make students feel more comfortable about seeking writing help. At the same time, non-directive tutoring lets students retain ownership of their work, while circumventing potential problems with plagiarism. This approach, which was initially accepted precisely because its collaborative methods rejected the dominant top-down, current traditional pedagogy of its time, persists as a fundamental element of American writing center culture today.

But in recent years, a dramatic increase in ESL [English as a Second Language] consultations at writing centers, caused mainly by escalating admission rates for international students, has led writing center faculty to reevaluate the effectiveness of this non-directive pedagogy. In an attempt to adapt traditional conferencing strategies to the ESL writer, writing center faculty have found that the non-directive approach—which has been hailed as a writing center "bible" (Shamoon and Burns 135), writing

---

Brian Riady wrote this research argument for a course at the University of Texas at Austin that prepares undergraduates to work as tutors at the Undergraduate Writing Center. Brian's topic reflects his own status as an international student from Singapore majoring in Communication Studies, Rhetoric and Writing, and Economics. The paper uses MLA documentation.

Second paragraph ends with a thesis sentence.

center "dogma" (Clark 34), and a writing center "mantra" (Blau 1)—does not effectively assist ESL writers. Nondirective tutoring fails non-native English speakers for the exact reason that it so effectively assists native English speakers: culture.

Culture is at the heart of the ESL student's struggle with writing because culture informs writing. Every culture defines effective writing—and the means to achieving it—differently. Most ESL students understand what good writing looks and sounds like in their own culture, but because good writing is culturally constructed, these students have difficulty understanding what good writing is in standardized, academic American English. Hence, writing that appears to be effective to the non-native English speaker may seem illogical or nonsensical to the native speaker.

Explains how culture defines writing, quoting from experts.

Take Arabic, for instance. In Arabic, good language is decorative, ornate, and intentionally pleasing (Zinsser). "It's all proverbs," writes William Zinsser. "Arabic is full of courtesy and deference, some of which is rooted in fear of the government." And because Arabic is a historically oral culture, Arabs emphasize a balanced sound and "prefer symmetry to variety" (Thonus 19). What constitutes effective Arabic, then, is a result of a combination of cultural, historical, and in some countries, political factors. But what Arabs consider good writing—ornate, proverbial, symmetrical prose—would be the ruin of someone trying to write good English.

Provides evidence that Arabic and Japanese cultures define "good writing" differently.

The same is true of Japanese. Persuasive rhetoric in Japanese follows the *ki-shoo-ten-ketsu* form (Thonus 18). *Ki-shoo-ten-ketsu* form begins with *ki-shoo*, or the full development of an argument; then proceeds with *ten*, an indirectly related subtheme; before ending with *ketsu*, or the conclusion or thesis (Thonus 18). Transitions are rarely if ever present, because the Japanese believe that it is the reader's responsibility to connect the various parts of the essay. Thonus notes that this "deviates from western argumentation in that the *ten* subtheme departs from the topic, while the thesis . . . is withheld until the final paragraph" (18). When the *ki-shoo-ten-ketsu* rhetorical form is used in English, writing often sounds foreign and is more descriptive than persuasive.

When ESL writers of Japanese or Arabic or any other foreign descent attempt to learn English, they are hampered not only by their "limited backgrounds in the rhetoric of written English but also by their learned patterns as educated writers of their own languages" (Powers 41). Such writers deal simultaneously with an unfamiliar culture and an unfamiliar language. For them, learning to write effectively in English is not merely transferring the rules of "good writing" from their native language and applying them to English; rather it is learning a new set of cultural assumptions of what "good writing" is altogether. Such writers often struggle to deviate from their instinctive cultural assumptions and fail to think about writing in a new way.

Consequently, when writing center tutors and ESL student writers collaborate for a writing consultation, the traditional non-directive model of writing center consultations falls short. Non-directive consulting works well with native English speakers precisely because consultant and writer share certain cultural notions of "good writing." By asking the right questions, an experienced consultant can unobtrusively lead a writer to discover ways to improve his own writing (Powers 41). In this sense, a writing consultant can actually direct "the conference through the use of questions, much as Socrates determined the direction of the Platonic dialogues" (Clark 35).

But when tutor and writer come into a consultation with different sets of cultural assumptions, the routine technique of Socratic, non-directive questioning often does not work. Leading questions can only lead a student writer to discover his own mistakes if he has a basic grasp of how his writing should be. Non-directively asking an ESL student to consider his audience is inherently problematic if the ESL student is unfamiliar with what his audience knows and expects. Similarly, a writer will fail to discover his own mechanical errors by reading his work out loud if he does not understand how "correct" writing should sound (Powers 41–42). As Powers puts it: "[to] merely take the [non-directive] techniques we use with native-speaking writers and apply them to ESL writers may fail to assist the writers we intend to help" (41).

Hence, Powers argues, "successful assistance to ESL writers may involve more intervention in their writing processes than we consider appropriate with native-speaking writers" (44). ESL writers struggle with an unfamiliar culture, audience, and rhetoric, and what they need from writing consultants is knowledge of how an American academic audience will respond to their work. To best assist the ESL writer, a consultant must be directive insofar as she becomes a "cultural informant about American academic expectations" (Powers 41). A writing consultant must in other words be directive in teaching an ESL student what constitutes "good writing" and how to accomplish "good writing" in the culture of American academia.

Argues for using more directive tutoring of international students.

This is not to say that consultants should completely disregard the non-directive approach; consultants should still refrain from acting as a one-stop proofreading service. In "Tutors as Teachers: Assisting ESL/EFL Students in the Writing Center," Terese Thonus advises consultants to avoid the tendency to merely correct surface-level errors in ESL writing, even if such errors may seem overwhelming. Most ESL students demonstrate basic proficiency of English vocabulary and grammar by passing the TOEFL, and may be able to isolate mechanical problems and self-correct with a little guidance. But emphasizing correctness in a directive, current traditional manner, and demanding a correct product of ESL writers "will engender frustration and even the loss of confidence, just as does demanding perfect native-like English pronunciation" (Kobayashi 107). Rather,

Qualifies his argument, citing several experts.

consultants must find a balance between directive teaching and non-directive tutoring that is most effective for ESL students.

Learning to be more directive with ESL students poses an especially tricky problem for writing tutors accustomed to non-directive consulting. Non-directive consulting is so firmly embedded in the culture of writing centers that it is "hard for practitioners to accept possible tutoring alternatives as useful or compelling" (Shamoon and Burns 135). Directive tutoring when measured against this predominant writing center culture is seen as a failure. Consequently, a consultant who does engage in directive tutoring may feel that she has betrayed the non-directive philosophy when in fact she has successfully met the needs of the ESL student writer.

Acknowledges difficulties in implementing his proposal.

What needs to occur is a significant paradigm shift in the culture of writing centers. The existing writing center culture assumes that there is one correct standard for writing, and a one-size-fits-all approach to assisting writers in consultations. Writing centers and their staff must first reassess their own cultural assumptions, and realize that their way is but a single option amongst myriad equally "correct" alternatives. They must in other words recognize that the non-directive methodology is not the right method in an absolute sense, but a helpful method that must be appropriately adapted to assist writers with different needs.

Such a paradigm shift will not be easy, but as writing centers move forward and prepare to meet the challenges of the future, it will be necessary. Improving the methods of writing instruction at writing centers is a continuous process: it began with the conception of the writing center, proceeded with a rejection of the current traditional pedagogy for the non-directive approach, and must continue on with an enhanced cultural sensitivity and awareness for ESL student writers.

Concludes by asserting the need for greater cultural awareness.

## Works Cited

Blau, Susan. "Issues in Tutoring Writing: Stories from Our Center." *The Writing Lab Newsletter* 19.2 (1992): 1–4. Web. 10 Apr. 2011.

Clark, Irene L. "Perspectives on the Directive/Non-Directive Continuum in the Writing Center." *The Writing Center Journal* 22.1 (2001): 33–50. Web. 11 Apr. 2011.

Kobayashi, Toshihiko. "Native and Nonnative Reactions to ESL Compositions." *TESOL Quarterly* 26.1 (1992): 81–112. Web. 6 Apr. 2011.

Powers, Judith K. "Rethinking Writing Center Conferencing Strategies for the ESL Writer." *The Writing Center Journal* 13.2 (1993): 39–47. Web. 6 Apr. 2011.

Shamoon, Linda K., and Deborah H. Burns. "A Critique of Pure Tutoring." *The Writing Center Journal* 15.2 (1995): 134–151. Print.

Thonus, Terese. "Tutors as Teachers: Assisting ESL/EFL Students in the Writing Center." *The Writing Center Journal* 13.2 (1993): 13–22. Web. 10 Apr. 2011.

Zinsser, William. "Writing English as a Second Language." *The American Scholar* (2009): Web. 11 Apr. 2011.

# China: The Prizes and Pitfalls of Progress

LAN XUE

**Abstract**

Pushes to globalize science must not threaten local innovations in developing countries, argues Lan Xue.

Developing countries such as China and India have emerged both as significant players in the production of high-tech products and as important contributors to the production of ideas and global knowledge. China's rapid ascent as a broker rather than simply a consumer of ideas and innovation has made those in the "developed" world anxious. A 2007 report by UK think tank Demos says that "U.S. and European pre-eminence in science-based innovation cannot be taken for granted. The centre of gravity for innovation is starting to shift from west to east."[1]

But the rapid increase in research and development spending in China—of the order of 20% per year since 1999—does not guarantee a place as an innovation leader. Participation in global science in developing

This article was written by Lan Xue, a faculty member in the School of Public Policy and Management and the director of the China Institute for Science and Technology Policy, both at Tsinghua University in Beijing, China. It was published in the online edition of *Nature* in July 2008.

Illustrations by D. Parkins.

countries such as China is certainly good news for the global scientific community. It offers new opportunities for collaboration, fresh perspectives, and a new market for ideas. It also presents serious challenges for the management of innovation in those countries. A major discovery in the lab does not guarantee a star product in the market. And for a country in development, the application of knowledge in productive activities and the related social transformations are probably more important than the production of the knowledge itself. By gumming the works in information dissemination, by misplacing priorities, and by disavowing research that, although valuable, doesn't fit the tenets of modern Western science, developing countries may falter in their efforts to become innovation leaders.

### VICIOUS CIRCLE

China's scientific publications (measured by articles recorded in the Web of Science) in 1994 were around 10,000, accounting for a little more than 1% of the world total. By 2006, the publications from China rose to more than 70,000, increasing sevenfold in 12 years and accounting for almost 6% of the world total (see graph, next page). In certain technical areas, the growth has been more dramatic. China has been among the leading countries in nanotechnology research, for example, producing a volume of publications second only to that of the United States.

The publish-or-perish mentality that has arisen in China, with its focus on Western journals, has unintended implications that threaten to obviate the roughly 8,000 national scientific journals published in Chinese. Scientists in developing countries such as China and India pride themselves on publishing articles in journals listed in the Science Citation Index (SCI) and the Social Science Citation Index (SSCI) lists. In some top-tier research institutions in China, SCI journals have become the required outlet for research.

A biologist who recently returned to China from the United States was told by her colleague at the research institute in the prestigious Chinese Academy of Sciences (CAS) that publications in Chinese journals don't really count toward tenure or promotion. Moreover, the institute values only those SCI journals with high impact factors. Unfortunately, the overwhelming majority of the journals in SCI and SSCI lists are published in developed countries in English or other European languages. The language requirement and the high costs of these journals mean that few researchers in China will have regular access to the content. Thus as China spends more and publishes more, the results will become harder to

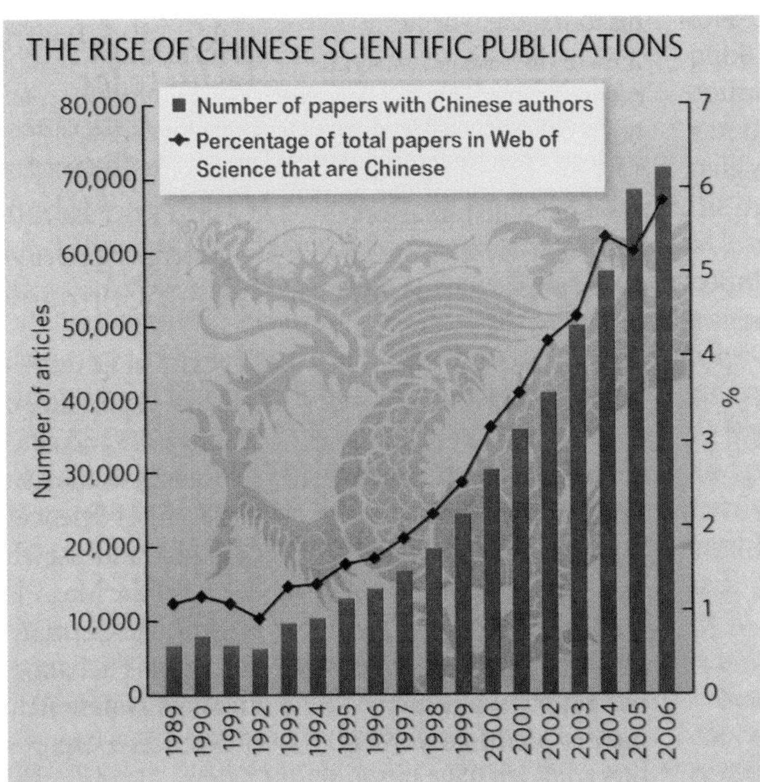


find for Chinese users. This trend could have a devastating impact on the local scientific publications and hurt China's ability to apply newly developed knowledge in an economically useful way.

Several members of the CAS expressed their concerns on this issue recently at the 14th CAS conference in Beijing. According to Molin Ge, a theoretical physicist at the Chern Institute of Mathematics, Nankai University, Tianjin, as more high-quality submissions are sent to overseas journals, the quality of submissions to local Chinese journals declines, which lowers the impact of the local Chinese journals. This becomes a vicious circle because the lower the impact, the less likely these local journals are to get high-quality submissions.[2]

**Setting Agendas**

Research priorities in developing countries may be very different from those in developed nations, but as science becomes more globalized, so too do priorities. At the national level, developing countries' research priorities increasingly resemble those of the developed nations, partly as a result of international competitive pressures. For example, after the United States announced its National Nanotechnology Initiative (NNI) in 2001, Japan and nations in Europe followed suit, as did South Korea, China, India, and Singapore. According to a 2004 report by the European Union,[3] public investment in nanotechnology had increased from €400 million (U.S. $630 million) in 1997 to more than €3 billion in 2004.

Part of the pressure to jump on the international bandwagon comes from researchers themselves. Scientists in the developing world maintain communications with those elsewhere. It is only natural that they want to share the attention that their colleagues in the developed Western world and Japan are receiving by pursuing the same hot topics. The research is exciting, fast-moving, and often easier to publish. At the same time, there are many other crucial challenges to be met in developing countries. For example, public health, water and food security, and environmental protection all beg for attention and resources. If people perceive these research areas as less intellectually challenging and rewarding, the issues will fail to receive the resources, support, and recognition they require. Without better agenda-setting practices, the scientific community will continue to face stinging criticism. It can send a satellite to Mars but not solve the most basic problems that threaten millions of lives in the developing world.

The introduction of Western scientific ideals to the developing world can generate an environment that is hostile to the indigenous research that prima facie does not fit those ideals. The confrontation between Western medicine and traditional Chinese medicine dates back to the early days of the twentieth century when Western medicine was first introduced in China. The debate reached a peak last year when a famous actress, Xiaoxu Chen, died from breast cancer. She allegedly insisted on treatment by Chinese traditional medicine, raising the hackles of some who claimed it to be worthless. Many Chinese still support traditional medicine and say that the dominance of Western medicine risks endangering China's scientific and cultural legacy.

A similar row erupted around earthquake prediction. In the 1960s and 1970s, China set up a network of popular earthquake-prediction stations, using simple instruments and local knowledge. For the most part, the network was decommissioned as China built the modern earthquake-monitoring system run by the China Earthquake Administration. When the system failed to predict the recent Sichuan earthquake, several people claimed that non-mainstream approaches had predicted its imminence. Scientists in the agency have tended to brush off such unofficial and individual predictions. To many this seems arrogant and bureaucratic.

It would be foolish and impossible to stop the globalization of science. There are tremendous benefits to science enterprises in different countries being integrated into a global whole. One should never think of turning back the clock. At the same time, it is possible to take some practical steps to minimize the harmful effects of this trend on local innovation.

### PRIORITIZING FOR THE PEOPLE

First of all, there is a need to re-examine the governance of global science in recognition of the changing international geography of science. Many international norms and standards should be more open and accommodating to the changing environment in developing countries. For example, there is a need to re-evaluate the SCI and SSCI list of journals to include quality journals in the developing countries. In the long run, the relevant scientific community could also think about establishing an international panel to make decisions on the selection of journals for these indices, given their important influence. The recent move by Thomson Reuters, the parent company of ISI, to expand its coverage of the SCI list by adding 700 regional academic journals, is a step in the right direction.[4]

English has become the de facto global language of science. Developing countries should invest in public institutions to provide translation services so that global scientific progress can be disseminated quickly. Developing countries can learn from Japan, a world leader in collecting scientific information and making it available to the public in the local language. At the same time, there should also be international institutions to provide similar services to the global science community so that "results and the knowledge generated through research should be freely accessible to all," as advocated by Nobel Laureates John Sulston and Joseph Stiglitz.[5]

When setting agendas, governments in developing countries must be careful in allocating their resources for science to achieve a balance between following the science frontier globally and addressing crucial domestic needs. A balance should also be struck between generating knowledge and disseminating and using knowledge. In addition, the global science community has a responsibility to help those developing countries that do not have adequate resources to solve problems themselves.

Finally, special efforts should be made to differentiate between pseudoscience and genuine scientific research. For the latter, one should tolerate or even encourage such indigenous research efforts in developing countries even if they do not fit the recognized international science paradigm. After all, the real advantage of a globalized scientific enterprise is not just doing the same research at a global scale, but doing new and exciting research in an enriched fashion.

## References


1. Leadbeater, C. & Wilsdon, J. *The Atlas of Ideas: How Asian Innovation Can Benefit Us All* (Demos, 2007).
2. Xie, Y. et al. *Good submissions went overseas—Chinese S&T journals could not keep up with their overseas peers*, Chinese Youth Daily, 25 June 2008.
3. http://ec.europa.eu/nanotechnology/pdf/nano_com_en_new.pdf
4. http://scientific.thomsonreuters.com/press/2008/8455931/
5. Sulston, J. & Stiglitz, J. *Science is being held back by outdated laws, The Times* (5 July 2008).

# 17
# Finding Evidence

In making and supporting claims for academic arguments, writers use all kinds of evidence — data from journal articles, scholarly books, records from archives, personal observations, fieldwork and surveys, and so on. But such evidence doesn't exist in a vacuum. Instead, the quality of evidence — how it was collected, by whom, and for what purposes — may become part of the argument itself. Evidence may be persuasive in one time and place but not in another; it may convince one kind of audience but not another; it may work with one type of argument but not the kind you are writing. The point is that finding "good" evidence for a research project is rarely a simple matter.

## Considering the Rhetorical Situation

To be most persuasive, evidence should match the time and place in which you make your argument—that is to say, your rhetorical situation. For example, arguing that government officials in the twenty-first century should use the same policies to deal with economic troubles that were employed in the middle of the twentieth might not be convincing on its own. After all, almost every aspect of the world economy has changed in the past fifty years. In the same way, a writer may achieve excellent results by citing a detailed survey of local teenagers as evidence for education reform in her rural hometown, but she may have less success using the same evidence to argue for similar reforms in a large inner-city community.

College writers also need to consider the fields that they're working in. In disciplines such as experimental psychology or economics, **quantitative data**—the sort that can be observed and counted—may be the best evidence. In many historical, literary, or philosophical studies, however, the same kind of data may be less appropriate or persuasive, or even impossible to come by. As you become more familiar with a discipline, you'll gain a sense of what it takes to support a claim. The following questions will help you understand the rhetorical situation of a particular field:

- What kinds of data are preferred as evidence? How are such data gathered and presented?
- How are definitions, causal analyses, evaluations, analogies, and examples used as evidence?
- How does the field use firsthand and secondhand sources as evidence? What kinds of data are favored?
- How are statistics or other numerical information used and presented as evidence? Are tables, charts, or graphs commonly used? How much weight do they carry?
- What or who counts as an authority in this field? How are the credentials of authorities established?
- What weight do writers in the field give to **precedence**—that is, to examples of similar actions or decisions made in the past?
- Is personal experience allowed as evidence? When?
- How are quotations used as part of evidence?
- How are images used as part of evidence, and how closely are they related to the verbal parts of the argument being presented?

As these questions suggest, evidence may not always travel well from one field to another. Nor does it always travel easily from culture to culture. Differing notions of evidence can lead to arguments that go nowhere fast. For instance, when Italian journalist Oriana Fallaci interviewed Ayatollah Khomeini, Iran's supreme leader, in 1979, she argued in a way that's common in North American and Western European cultures: she presented claims that she considered to be adequately backed up with facts ("Iran denies freedom to people. . . . Many people have been put in prison and even executed, just for speaking out in opposition"). In response, Khomeini relied on very different kinds of evidence—analogies ("Just as a finger with gangrene should be cut off so that it will not destroy the whole body, so should people who corrupt others be pulled out like weeds so they will not infect the whole field") and, above all, the authority of the Qur'an. Partly because of these differing beliefs about what counts as evidence, the interview ended

The need for evidence depends a lot on the rhetorical situation.

unsuccessfully. In arguing across cultural divides, whether international or more local, you need to think carefully about how you're accustomed to using evidence—and about what counts as evidence to other people (without surrendering your own intellectual principles).

## Using Data and Evidence from Research Sources

The evidence you will use in most academic arguments—books, articles, films, documents, photographs—will likely come from sources you locate in libraries, databases, or online. How well you can navigate these complex territories will determine the success of many of your academic and professional projects. Research suggests that most students overestimate their ability to manage these tools and, perhaps more important, don't seek the help they need to find the best materials for their projects. We can't cover all the nuances of doing academic research here, but we can at least point you in the right directions.

**Explore library resources: printed works and databases.** Your college library has printed materials (books, periodicals, reference works) as well as terminals that provide access to its electronic catalogs, other libraries' catalogs via the Internet, and numerous proprietary databases (such as Academic Search Complete, Academic OneFile, JSTOR) not available publicly on the Web. Crucially, libraries also have librarians whose job it is to guide you through these resources, help you identify reputable materials, and show you how to search for materials efficiently. The best way to begin a serious academic argument then is often with a trip to the library or a discussion with your professor or librarian. Also be certain that you know your way around the library. If not, ask the staff there to help you locate the following tools: general and specialized encyclopedias; biographical resources; almanacs, yearbooks, and atlases; book and periodical indexes; specialized indexes and abstracts; the circulation computer or library catalog; special collections; audio, video, and art collections; and the interlibrary loan office.

At the outset of a project, determine what kinds of sources you will need to support your project. (You might also review your assignment to see whether you're required to consult different kinds of sources.) If you'll use print sources, find out whether they're readily available in your library or whether you must make special arrangements (such as an interlibrary loan) to acquire them. For example, your argument for a senior thesis might benefit from material available mostly in old newspapers and magazines: access to them might require time and ingenuity. If you need to locate other nonprint sources (such as audiotapes, videotapes, artwork, or photos), find out where those are kept and whether you need special permission to examine them.

Most academic resources, however, will be on the shelves or available electronically through databases. Here's when it's important to understand the distinction between library databases and the Internet/Web. Your library's computers hold important resources that aren't on the Web or aren't available to you except through the library's system. The most important of these resources is the library's catalog of its holdings (mostly books), but college libraries also pay to subscribe to *scholarly databases*—guides to journal and magazine articles, the LexisNexis database of news stories and legal cases, and compilations of statistics, for example—that you can use for free.

You should consult these electronic sources through your college library, perhaps even before turning to the Web. But using these professional databases isn't always easy or intuitive, even when you can reach them on your own computer. You likely need to learn how to focus and narrow your searches (by date, field, types of material, and so on) so that you don't generate unmanageable lists of irrelevant items. That's when librarians or your instructor can help, so ask them for assistance. They expect your questions.

For example, librarians can draw your attention to the distinction between subject headings and keywords. The Library of Congress Subject Headings (LCSH) are standardized words and phrases that are used to classify the subject matter of books and articles. Library catalogs and databases usually use the LCSH headings to index their contents by author, title, publication date, and subject headings. When you do a subject search of the library's catalog, you're searching only one part of the electronic record of the library's books, and you need to use the exact wording of the LCSH. These subject headings are available in your library.

On the other hand, searches with *keywords* use the computer's ability to look for any term in any field of the electronic record. Keyword searching is less restrictive than searching by subject headings, but it requires you to think carefully about your search terms to get usable results. In addition, you need to learn techniques to limit (or expand) your search. These include combining keywords with *and*, *or*, *not*, parentheses, and quotation marks or using similar procedures that are built into the catalog's or database's search mechanism.

Determine, too, early on, how current your sources need to be. If you must investigate the latest findings about, say, a new treatment for HIV/AIDS, check very recent periodicals, medical journals, and the Web. If you want broader, more detailed coverage and background information, look for scholarly books. If your argument deals with a specific time period, newspapers, magazines, and books written during that period may be your best assets.

How many sources should you consult for an academic argument? Expect to look over many more sources than you'll end up using, and be sure to cover all major perspectives on your subject. Read enough sources to feel comfortable discussing it with someone with more knowledge than you. You don't have to be an expert, but your readers should sense that you are well informed.

**Explore online resources.** Chances are your first instinct when you need to find information is to do a quick keyword search on the Web. Even a smartphone app may suffice when you want simple data—like the names of the actors in a recent film. But if you intend to support a serious academic argument, you need to approach the Web more professionally. Like library catalogs and databases, the Internet offers two ways to search for sources related to an argument—one using subject categories and one using keywords.

A subject directory organized by categories (such as you might find at Yahoo! Directory) allows you to choose a broad category like "Entertainment" or "Science," and then click on increasingly narrow categories like "Movies" or "Astronomy," and then "Thrillers" or "The Solar System," until you reach a point where you're given a list of Web sites or the opportunity to do a keyword search.

With the second kind of Internet search option, a search engine, you start right off with a keyword search—filling in a blank, for example, on Google's opening screen. Because the Internet contains vastly more material than even the largest library catalog or database, exploring it with a search engine requires careful choices and combinations of keywords. For an argument about the fate of the antihero in contemporary films, for example, you might find that *film* and *hero* produce far too many possible matches, or hits. You might further narrow the search by adding a third keyword—say, *American* or *current*. In doing such searches, you'll need to observe the search logic that is followed by a particular database. Using *and* between keywords (*movies and heroes*) usually indicates that both terms must appear in a file for it to be called up. Using *or* between keywords usually instructs the computer to locate every file in which either one word or the other shows up, and using *not* tells the computer to exclude files containing a particular word from the search results (*movies not heroes*).

More crucially with a tool like Google is to discover how the resources of the site itself can refine your choice or direct you to works better suited to academic argument. When you search for any term, you can click "Advanced Search" at the bottom of the results page and bring up a full screen of options to narrow your search in important ways.

But that's not the end of your choices. With an *academic* argument, you might want to explore your topic in either Google Books or Google Scholar. Both resources send you to the level of materials you might need for a term paper or professional project. And Google offers other

Google offers many kinds of research tools like this "Advanced Search" page. Explore them from the "More" and "Even More" menus on search pages.

### SEARCHING ONLINE OR IN DATABASES

- Don't rely on simple Web searches only.
- Find library databases targeted to your subject.
- Use advanced search techniques to focus your search.
- Learn the difference between *subject heading* and *keyword* searches.
- Understand the differences between academic and popular sources.
- Admit when you don't know how to find material.
- *Routinely* ask for help from librarians and instructors.

options as well: it can direct you to images, photographs, blogs, and so on. The lesson is simple. If your current Web searches typically involve no more than using the first box that a search engine offers, you aren't close to using all the power available to you. Explore that tool you use all the time and see what it can really do.

## Collecting Data on Your Own

Not all your supporting materials for an academic argument must come from print or online sources. You can present research that you have carried out or been closely involved with; this kind of research usually requires that you collect and examine data. Here, we discuss the kinds of firsthand research that student writers do most often.

**Perform experiments.** Academic arguments can be supported by evidence you gather through experiments. In the sciences, data from experiments conducted under rigorously controlled conditions are highly valued. For other kinds of writing, more informal experiments may be acceptable, especially if they're intended to provide only part of the support for an argument.

If you want to argue, for instance, that the recipes in *Bon Appétit* magazine are impossibly tedious to follow and take far more time than the average person wishes to spend preparing food, you might ask five or six people to conduct an experiment—following two recipes from a recent issue and recording and timing every step. The evidence that you gather from this informal experiment could provide some concrete support—by way of specific examples—for your contention.

But such experiments should be taken with a grain of salt (maybe organic in this case). They may not be effective with certain audiences. And if your experiments can easily be attacked as skewed or sloppily done ("The people you asked to make these recipes couldn't cook a Pop-Tart"), then they may do more harm than good.

**Make observations.** "What," you may wonder, "could be easier than observing something?" You just choose a subject, look at it closely, and record what you see and hear. But trained observers say that recording an observation accurately requires intense concentration and mental agility. If observing were easy, all eyewitnesses would provide reliable accounts. Yet experience shows that when several people observe the same phenomenon, they generally offer different, sometimes even contradictory, accounts of those observations. For instance, when TWA Flight 800 exploded off the coast of New York in 1996, eyewitnesses gave various accounts, some even claiming that they saw a missile streaking toward the passenger jet. The official report found that an internal electrical short likely ignited vapors in a fuel tank.

Before you begin an observation yourself, decide exactly what you want to find out, and anticipate what you're likely to see. Do you want to observe an action that is repeated by many people—perhaps how people behave at the checkout line in a grocery store? Or maybe you want to study a sequence of actions—for instance, the stages involved in student registration, which you want to argue is far too complicated. Or maybe you are motivated to examine the interactions of a notoriously contentious campus group. Once you have a clear sense of what you'll analyze and what questions you'll try to answer through the observation, use the following guidelines to achieve the best results:

- Make sure that the observation relates directly to your claim.
- Brainstorm about what you're looking for, but don't be rigidly bound to your expectations.
- Develop an appropriate system for collecting data. Consider using a split notebook or page: on one side, record the minute details of your observations; on the other, record your thoughts or impressions.

- Be aware that the way you record data will affect the outcome, if only in respect to what you decide to include in your observational notes and what you leave out.
- Record the precise date, time, and place of the observation(s).

You may be asked to prepare systematic observations in various science courses, including anthropology or psychology, where you would follow a methodology and receive precise directions. But observation can play a role in other kinds of arguments and use various media: a photo essay, for example, might serve as an academic argument in some situations.

Twin Cities Public Television made extensive use of interviews in their exploration of efforts to revive the Ojibwe language. Why do you think this kind of evidence is important?

LINK TO P. 628

**Conduct interviews.** Some evidence is best obtained through direct interviews. If you can talk with an expert—in person, on the phone, or online—you might obtain information you couldn't have gotten through any other type of research. In addition to an expert opinion, you might ask for firsthand accounts, biographical information, or suggestions of other places to look or other people to consult. The following guidelines will help you conduct effective interviews:

- Determine the exact purpose of the interview, and be sure it's directly related to your claim.
- Set up the interview well in advance. Specify how long it'll take, and if you wish to record the session, ask permission to do so.
- Prepare a written list of both factual and open-ended questions. (Brainstorming with friends can help you come up with good questions.) Leave plenty of space for notes after each question. If the interview proceeds in a direction that you hadn't expected but that seems promising, don't feel that you have to cover every one of your questions.
- Record the subject's full name and title, as well as the date, time, and place of the interview.
- Be sure to thank those people whom you interview, either in person or with a follow-up letter or email message.

A serious interview can be eye-opening when the questions get a subject to reveal important experiences or demonstrate their knowledge or wisdom.

The Pew Research Center demonstrates in its report on perceptions of income inequality how complex and wide-ranging a survey must be to produce useful data.

LINK TO P. 888

**Use questionnaires to conduct surveys.** Surveys usually require the use of questionnaires. Questions should be clear, easy to understand, and designed so that respondents' answers can be easily analyzed. Questions that ask respondents to say "yes" or "no" or to rank items on a scale (1 to 5, for example, or "most helpful" to "least helpful") are particularly easy to tabulate. Because tabulation can take time and effort, limit the number of questions you ask. Note also that people often resent being asked to answer more than about twenty questions, especially online.

A key requirement of survey questions is that they be easy to understand.

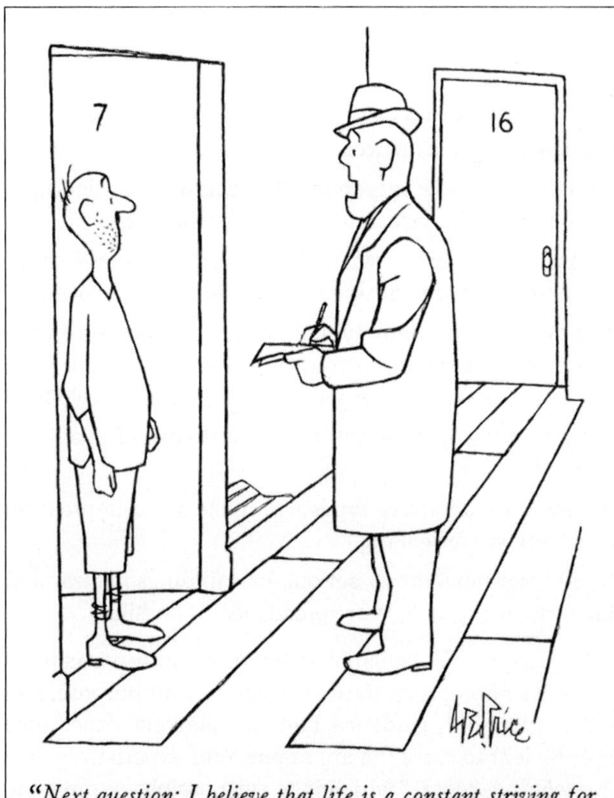

Here are some other guidelines to help you prepare for and carry out a survey:

- Write out your purpose in conducting the survey, and make sure that its results will be directly related to your purpose.
- Brainstorm potential questions to include in the survey, and ask how each relates to your purpose and claim.
- Figure out how many people you want to contact, what the demographics of your sample should be (for example, men in their twenties or an equal number of men and women), and how you plan to reach these people.
- Draft questions that are as free of bias as possible, making sure that each calls for a short, specific answer.
- Think about possible ways that respondents could misunderstand you or your questions, and revise with these points in mind.
- Test the questions on several people, and revise those questions that are ambiguous, hard to answer, or too time-consuming to answer.
- If your questionnaire is to be sent by mail or email or posted on the Web, draft a cover letter explaining your purpose and giving a clear deadline. For mail, provide an addressed, stamped return envelope.
- On the final draft of the questionnaire, leave plenty of space for answers.
- Proofread the final draft carefully. Typos will make a bad impression on those whose help you're seeking.
- After you've done your tabulations, set out your findings in clear and easily readable form, using a chart or spreadsheet if possible.

**Draw upon personal experience.** Personal experience can serve as powerful evidence when it's appropriate to the subject, to your purpose, and to the audience. If it's your only evidence, however, personal experience usually won't be sufficient to carry the argument. Your experiences may be regarded as merely "anecdotal," which is to say possibly exceptional, unrepresentative, or even unreliable. Nevertheless, personal experience can be effective for drawing in listeners or readers, as N'Gai Croal does in the following example arguing that the video games with the greatest potential are those that appeal to the nongeek:

> I still get questions every now and then from people looking for advice on how to get their hands on a Nintendo Wii. But more and more, I'm hearing stories from people who've already scored one and are still

Personal experience provides evidence for the popularity of Wii bowling (at least among humans).

rhapsodizing about it months after taking possession of the slim white console. The gushing comes from some of the most unexpected people. The grill man at my favorite New York burger joint told me last week that in his household, he mows down zombies in Resident Evil 4, his wife works out using Wii Fit, and he's introducing his son to the classic games of his youth via the Wii's download service. Similarly, a cardiologist friend of mine and his medical-resident girlfriend use Wii Golf to unwind; when they have friends over on the weekends, the same relaxing game turns into a fierce competition.

As someone who covers videogames for *Newsweek*, I've marveled at how quickly the tastes of nontraditional players have moved from the margins of the industry toward the center. This is happening at the same time that geek tastes have taken center stage in other areas of pop culture: witness the summer movie schedule, which looks like new-release Wednesdays at your local comic-book shop.

—N'Gai Croal, "You Don't Have to Be a Nerd"

**RESPOND.**

1. The following is a list of general topic ideas from the Yahoo! Directory's "Issues and Causes" page. Narrow one or two of the items down to a more specific subject by using research tools in the library or online

such as scholarly books, journal articles, encyclopedias, magazine pieces, and/or informational Web sites. Be prepared to explain how the particular research resources influenced your choice of a more specific subject within the general subject area. Also consider what you might have to do to turn your specific subject into a full-blown topic proposal for a research paper assignment.

| | |
|---|---|
| Age discrimination | Multiculturalism |
| Climate change | Pornography |
| Cloning | Poverty |
| Corporal punishment | Racial profiling |
| Drinking age | Social Security reform |
| Drugs and sports | Tax reform |
| Factory farming | Urban sprawl |
| Global warming | Video games |
| Immigration reform | Weight and nutrition |
| Media ethics and accountability | Zoos |

2. Go to your library's online catalog page and locate its list of research databases. You may find them presented in various ways: by subject, by field, by academic major, by type—even alphabetically. Try to identify three or four databases that might be helpful to you either generally in college or when working on a specific project, perhaps one you identified in the previous exercise. Then explore the library catalog to see how much you can learn about each of these resources: What fields do they cover? What kinds of data do they offer? How do they present the content of their materials (by abstract, by full text)? What years do they cover? What search strategies do they support (keyword, advanced search)? To find such information, you might look for a help menu or an "About" link on the catalog or database homepages. Write a one-paragraph description of each database you explore and, if possible, share your findings via a class discussion board or wiki.
3. What counts as evidence depends in large part on the rhetorical situation. One audience might find personal testimony compelling in a given case, whereas another might require data that only experimental studies can provide. Imagine that you want to argue that advertisements should not include demeaning representations of chimpanzees and that the use of primates in advertising should be banned. You're encouraged to find out that a number of companies such as Honda and Puma have already agreed to such a ban, so you decide to present your argument to other companies' CEOs and advertising officials. What kind of evidence would be most compelling to this group? How

would you rethink your use of evidence if you were writing for the campus newspaper, for middle schoolers, or for animal-rights group members? What can you learn about what sort of evidence each of these groups might value—and why?

4. Finding evidence for an argument is often a discovery process. Sometimes you're concerned not only with digging up support for an already established claim but also with creating and revising tentative claims. Surveys and interviews can help you figure out what to argue, as well as provide evidence for a claim.

   Interview a classmate with the goal of writing a brief proposal argument about the career that he or she should pursue. The claim should be something like *My classmate should be doing X five years from now.* Limit yourself to ten questions. Write them ahead of time, and don't deviate from them. Record the results of the interview (written notes are fine; you don't need to tape the interview). Then interview another classmate with the same goal in mind. Ask the same first question, but this time let the answer dictate the next nine questions. You still get only ten questions.

   Which interview gave you more information? Which one helped you learn more about your classmate's goals? Which one better helped you develop claims about his or her future?

# 18
# Evaluating Sources

As many examples in this text have shown, the effectiveness of an argument often depends on the quality of the sources that support or prove it. You'll need to carefully evaluate and assess all your sources, including those that you gather in libraries, from other print sources, in online searches, or in your own field research.

Remember that different sources can contribute in different ways to your work. In most cases, you'll be looking for reliable sources that provide accurate information or that clearly and persuasively express opinions that might serve as evidence for a case you're making. At other times, you may be seeking material that expresses ideas or attitudes—how people are thinking and feeling at a given time. You might need to use a graphic image, a sample of avant-garde music, or a controversial YouTube clip that doesn't fit neatly into categories such as "reliable" or "accurate" yet is central to your argument. With any and all such sources and evidence, your goals are to be as knowledgeable about them and as responsible in their use as you can be and to share honestly what you learn about them with readers.

When might a tattle-tale actually be a reliable source—and how would you know?

"I'm *not* being a tattle-tale! —
I'm being a reliable source!"



You don't want to be naïve in your use of any source material. Most of the evidence that is used in arguments on public issues—even material from influential and well-known sources—comes with considerable baggage. Scientists and humanists alike have axes to grind, corporations have products to sell, politicians have issues to promote, journalists have reputations to make, publishers and media companies have readers, listeners, viewers, and advertisers to attract and to avoid offending. All of these groups produce and use information to their own benefit, and it's not (usually) a bad thing that they do so. You just have to be aware that when you take information from a given source, it will often carry with it at least some of the preferences, assumptions, and biases (conscious or not) of the people who produce and disseminate it. Teachers and librarians are not exempted from this caution.

To correct for these biases, draw on as many reliable sources as you can handle when you're preparing to write. You shouldn't assume that all arguments are equally good or that all the sides in a controversy can be supported by the same weight of evidence and good reasons. But you want to avoid choosing sources so selectively that you miss essential issues and

CNN's Nancy Grace, a former prosecutor, has been accused of allowing her pro-prosecution bias to influence her commentary.

perspectives. That's easy to do when you read only sources that agree with you or when the sources that you read all seem to carry the same message.

Especially when writing on political subjects, be aware that the sources you're reading or citing almost always support particular beliefs and goals. That fact has been made apparent in recent years by bloggers—from all parts of the political spectrum—who put the traditional news media under daily scrutiny, exposing errors, biases, and omissions. Even so, these political bloggers (mostly amateur journalists, although many are professionals in their own fields) have their own agendas and so must be read with caution themselves.

## Assessing Print Sources

Since you want information to be reliable and persuasive, it pays to evaluate each potential source thoroughly. The following principles can help you evaluate print sources:

- **Relevance.** Begin by asking what a particular source will add to your argument and how closely the source is related to your argumentative claim. For a book, the table of contents and the index may help you decide. For an article, look for an abstract that summarizes its content. If you can't think of a good reason for using the source, set it aside. You can almost certainly find something better.
- **Credentials of the author.** Sometimes the author's credentials are set forth in an article, in a book, or on a Web site, so be sure to look for them. Is the author an expert on the topic? To find out, you can gather

information about the person on the Internet using a search engine like Yahoo! or Ask.com. Another way to learn about the credibility of an author is to search Google Groups for postings that mention the author or to check the Citation Index to find out how others refer to this author. If you see your source cited by other sources you're using, look at how they cite it and what they say about it that could provide clues to the author's credibility.

- **Stance of the author.** What's the author's position on the issue(s) involved, and how does this stance influence the information in the source? Does the author's stance support or challenge your own views?
- **Credentials of the publisher or sponsor.** If your source is from a newspaper, is it a major one (such as the *Wall Street Journal* or the *Washington Post*) that has historical credentials in reporting, or is it a tabloid? Is it a popular magazine like O: *The Oprah Magazine* or a journal sponsored by a professional group, such as the *Journal of the American Medical Association*? If your source is a book, is the publisher one you recognize or that has its own Web site? When you don't know the reputation of a source, ask several people with more expertise: a librarian, an instructor, or a professional in the field.
- **Stance of the publisher or sponsor.** Sometimes this stance will be obvious: a magazine called *Save the Planet!* will take a pro-environmental stance, whereas one called *America First!* will probably take a conservative stance. But other times, you need to read carefully between the lines to identify particular positions and see how the stance affects the message the source presents. Start by asking what the source's goals are: what does the publisher or sponsoring group want to make happen?
- **Currency.** Check the date of publication of every book and article. Recent sources are often more useful than older ones, particularly in the sciences. However, in some fields (such as history and literature), the most authoritative works are often the older ones.
- **Accuracy.** Check to see whether the author cites any sources for the information or opinions in the article and, if so, how credible and current they are.
- **Level of specialization.** General sources can be helpful as you begin your research, but later in the project you may need the authority or currency of more specialized sources. Keep in mind that highly specialized works on your topic may be difficult for your audience to understand.

Note the differences between the cover of *Popular Science* and that of a physics journal.

- **Audience.** Was the source written for a general readership? For specialists? For advocates or opponents?
- **Length.** Is the source long enough to provide adequate details in support of your claim?
- **Availability.** Do you have access to the source? If it isn't readily accessible, your time might be better spent looking elsewhere.
- **Omissions.** What's missing or omitted from the source? Might such exclusions affect whether or how you can use the source as evidence?

## Assessing Electronic Sources

You'll probably find working with new media both exciting and frustrating, for even though these tools (the Web, social networks, Twitter, and so on) are enormously useful, they offer information of widely varying quality. Because Web sources are mostly open and unregulated, careful researchers look for corroboration before accepting evidence they find online, especially if it comes from a site whose sponsor's identity is unclear.

In such an environment, you must be the judge of the accuracy and trustworthiness of particular electronic sources. In making these judgments, rely on the same criteria and careful thinking that you use to assess print sources. In addition, you may find the following questions helpful in evaluating online sources:

- Who has posted the document or message or created the site/medium? An individual? An interest group? A company? A government agency? For Web sites, does the URL offer any clues? Note especially the final suffix in a domain name—*.com* (commercial), *.org* (nonprofit organization), *.edu* (educational institution), *.gov* (government agency),

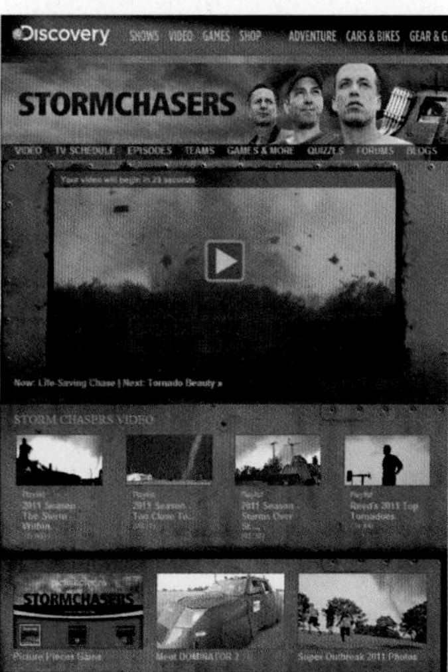


What are the kinds and levels of information available on these Web sites—a federal site on tornadoes and severe weather, a personal site about tornadoes and storm chasing, and a commercial site about the TV show *Storm Chasers*?

*.mil* (military), or *.net* (network). Also note the geographical domains that indicate country of origin—as in *.ca* (Canada) or *.ar* (Argentina). Click on some links of a Web site to see if they lead to legitimate and helpful sources or organizations.

- What can you determine about the credibility of the author or sponsor? Can the information in the document or site be verified in other sources? How accurate and complete is it? On a blog, for example, look for a link that identifies the creator of the site (some blogs are managed by multiple authors).
- Who can be held accountable for the information in the document or site? How well and thoroughly does it credit its own sources? On a wiki, for example, check its editorial policies: who can add to or edit its materials?
- How current is the document or site? Be especially cautious of undated materials. Most reliable sites are refreshed or edited regularly.
- What perspectives are represented? If only one perspective is represented, how can you balance or expand this point of view? Is it a straightforward presentation, or could it be a parody or satire?

## Assessing Field Research

If you've conducted experiments, surveys, interviews, observations, or any other field research in developing and supporting an argument, make sure to review your results with a critical eye. The following questions can help you evaluate your own field research:

- Have you rechecked all data and all conclusions to make sure they're accurate and warranted?
- Have you identified the exact time, place, and participants in all your field research?
- Have you made clear what part you played in the research and how, if at all, your role could have influenced the results or findings?
- If your research involved other people, have you gotten their permission to use their words or other materials in your argument? Have you asked whether you can use their names or whether the names should be kept confidential?

**RESPOND.**

1. The chapter claims that "most of the evidence that is used in arguments on public issues . . . comes with considerable baggage" (p. 411). Find an article in a journal, newspaper, or magazine that uses evidence to support a claim of some public interest. It might be a piece about traffic safety, funding of public schools, dietary recommendations for school children, proposals for air-quality regulation, and so on. Identify several specific pieces of evidence, information, or data presented in the article and then evaluate the degree to which you would accept, trust, or believe those statements. Be prepared to explain specifically why you would be inclined to trust or mistrust any claims based on the data.
2. *The Chronicle of Higher Education* routinely publishes a list called "What They're Reading on College Campuses." Locate one such list either by consulting the journal itself in the library or searching the feature's title on the Web. Then choose one of the listed books, preferably a work of nonfiction, and analyze it by using as many of the principles of evaluation for printed books listed in this chapter as you can without actually reading the book: Who is the author and what are his/her credentials? Who is the publisher and what is its reputation? What can you find out about the book's relevance and popularity: why might the book be on the list? Who is the primary audience for the book? How lengthy is it? How difficult? Finally, consider how likely it is that the book you have selected would be used in an academic paper. If you do choose a work of fiction, might the work be studied in a literature course?
3. Choose a news or information Web site that you visit routinely. Then, using the guidelines discussed in this chapter, spend some time evaluating its credibility. You might begin by comparing it with Google News or Arts & Letters Daily, two sites that have a reputation for being reliable.

# 19
# Using Sources

You may gather an impressive amount of evidence on your topic—from firsthand interviews, from careful observations, and from intensive library and online research. But until that evidence is woven into the fabric of your own argument, it's just a stack of details. You still have to turn that data into information that will be persuasive to your intended audiences.

## Building a Critical Mass

Throughout the chapters in Part 4, "Research and Arguments," we've stressed the need to discover as much evidence as possible in support of your claim. If you can find only one or two pieces of evidence—only one or two reasons or illustrations to back up your thesis—then you may be on unsteady ground. Although there's no definite way of saying how much evidence is enough, you should build toward a critical mass by having several pieces of evidence all pulling in the direction of your claim.

Casey Anthony at trial

And remember that **circumstantial evidence** (that is, indirect evidence that *suggests* that something occurred but doesn't prove it directly) may not be enough if it is the only evidence that you have. Many Americans were outraged in July 2011 when a jury acquitted defendant Casey Anthony of the murder of her two-year-old daughter Caylee. But in its case the prosecution had presented no direct evidence for Anthony's guilt to the jury—no eyewitness, confession, or murder weapon; it could point only to highly suspicious situations and behavior. And, as Jennifer Dearborn, editor of the *Rutgers Law Record*, explains, citing Kevin Jon Heller:

> The problem with relying on mostly circumstantial evidence . . . is that it can "simultaneously [be] evidence of guilt and innocence." Thus, the evidence presented in the Anthony trial, when taking everything into account, did not particularly point in one direction or another.

If your evidence for a claim relies solely on circumstantial evidence, on personal experience, or on one major example, you should extend your search for additional sources and good reasons to back up your claim—or modify the argument. Your initial position may simply have been wrong.

## Synthesizing Information

As you gather information, you must find a way to make all the facts, ideas, points of view, and quotations you have encountered work with and for you. The process involves not only reading information and recording data carefully, but also pondering and synthesizing it—that is, figuring out how what you've examined supports your specific claims.

You typically begin by paraphrasing or summarizing sources so that you understand exactly what they offer and which ideas are essential to your project. You also decide which, if any, sources offer materials you want to quote directly or reproduce (such as an important graph or table). Then you work to introduce or frame such borrowed materials so that readers grasp their significance and see important relationships. Throughout this review process, ask questions such as the following:

- Which sources help to set the context for your argument? In particular, which items present new information or give audiences an incentive for reading your work?
- Which items provide background information that is essential for anyone trying to understand your argument?
- Which items help to define, clarify, or explain key concepts of your case? How can these sources be presented or sequenced so that readers appreciate your claims as valid or, at a minimum, reasonable?
- Which of your sources might be used to illustrate technical or difficult aspects of your subject? Would it be best to summarize such technical information to make it more accessible, or would direct quotations be more authoritative and convincing?
- Which sources (or passages within sources) furnish the best support or evidence for the claims within your argument? How can these materials be presented or arranged most effectively?
- Which materials do the best job outlining conflicts or offering counterarguments to claims within a project? Which sources might help you to address any important objections or rebuttals?

Remember that yours should be the dominant and controlling voice in an argument. You are like the conductor of an orchestra, calling upon separate instruments to work together to create a rich and coherent sound. The worst kinds of academic papers are those that mechanically walk through a string of sources—often just one item per paragraph—without ever getting all these authorities to talk to each other or with the author. Such papers go through the motions, but don't get anywhere. You can do better.

**Paraphrase sources you will use extensively.** In a **paraphrase**, you put an author's ideas—including major and minor points—into your own words and sentence structures, following the order the author has given them in the original piece. You usually paraphrase sources that you expect to use

"Who is the fairest one of all, and state your sources!"

Backing up your claims with well-chosen sources makes almost any argument more credible.

heavily in a project. But if you compose your notes well, you may be able to use much of the paraphrased material directly in your paper (with proper citation) because all of the language is your own. A competent paraphrase proves you have read material or data carefully: you demonstrate not only that you know what a source contains, but that you also appreciate what it means. There's an important difference.

Here are guidelines to help you paraphrase accurately and effectively in an academic argument:

- Identify the source of the paraphrase, and comment on its significance or the authority of its author.
- Respect your sources. When paraphrasing an entire work or any lengthy section of it, cover all its main points and any essential details, following the same order the author uses. If you distort the shape of the material, your notes will be less valuable, especially if you return to them later.
- If you're paraphrasing material that extends over more than one page in the original source, note the placement of page breaks since it is

highly likely that you will use only part of the paraphrase in your argument. You will need the page number to cite the specific page of material you want to cite.

- Make sure that the paraphrase is in your own words and sentence structures. If you want to include especially memorable or powerful language from the original source, enclose it in quotation marks.
- Keep your own comments, elaborations, or reactions separate from the paraphrase itself. Your report on the source should be clear, objective, and free of connotative language.
- Collect all the information necessary to create an in-text citation as well as an item in your works cited list or references list. For online materials, be sure you know how to recover the source later.
- Label the paraphrase with a note suggesting where and how you intend to use it in your argument.
- Recheck to make sure that the words and sentence structures are your own and that they express the author's meaning accurately.

Following is a paraphrase of "A Directive Approach toward ESL/EFL Writers," a research essay by Brian Riady reprinted in Chapter 16 on p. 383.

> In "A Directive Approach toward ESL/EFL Writers," Brian Riady argues that the tutoring method used most often in writing centers, called "non-directive," may not work for ESL students because it does not deal with the cultural differences of non-native students. Riady explains that Arabic and Japanese students, for example, think differently about style and argument than do American writers. Unfortunately, non-directive tutoring—which uses questions to get students to understand their writing problems—does not help when foreign students do not recognize what good writing in a culture is. So ESL students usually need more help and advice than writing center tutors trained in non-directive methods are comfortable giving. Riady cites research suggesting that writing centers need to adapt their methods to the needs of writers, understanding that no single approach to tutoring works for everyone.
>
> **Note:** This source gains credibility because Riady is himself an international student who works as a tutor in a writing center.

**Summarize all sources that you examine.** Unlike a paraphrase, a **summary** records just the gist of a source or a key idea—that is, only enough information to identify a point you want to emphasize. Once again, this much-shortened version of a source puts any borrowed ideas into your own words. At the research stage, summaries help you identify key points you want to make and, just as important, provide a record of what you have read. In a project itself, a summary helps readers understand the sources you are using.

Here are some guidelines to help you prepare accurate and helpful summaries:

- Identify the thesis or main point in a source and make it the heart of your summary. In a few detailed phrases or sentences, explain to yourself (and readers) what the source accomplishes.
- If your summary includes a comment on the source (as it might in the summaries used for annotated bibliographies), be sure that you won't later confuse your comments with what the source itself asserts.
- When using a summary in an argument, identify the source, state its point, and add your own comments about why the material is significant for the argument that you're making.
- Include just enough information to recount the main points you want to cite. A summary is usually much shorter than the original. When you need more information or specific details, you can return to the source itself or prepare a paraphrase.
- Use your own words in a summary and keep the language objective and denotative. If you include any language from the original source, enclose it in quotation marks.
- Collect all the information necessary to create an in-text citation as well as an item in your works cited list or references list. For online sources without page numbers, record the paragraph, screen, or other section number(s) if available.
- Label the summary with a note that suggests where and how you intend to use it in your argument.
- Recheck the summary to make sure that you've captured the author's meaning accurately and that the wording is entirely your own.

Following is a summary of "A Directive Approach toward ESL/EFL Writers," a research essay by Brian Riady. Notice how much shorter it is than the paraphrase of the same article on p. 422.

> In "A Directive Approach toward ESL/EFL Writers," Brian Riady argues that because the tutoring method used most often in writing centers, called "non-directive," may not work for non-native students, alternative and more straightforward forms of instruction need to be considered.

**Use quotations selectively and strategically.** To support your argumentative claims, you'll want to quote (that is, to reproduce an author's precise words) in at least three kinds of situations:

- when the wording expresses a point so well that you cannot improve it or shorten it without weakening it,
- when the author is a respected authority whose opinion supports your own ideas powerfully, and/or
- when an author or authority challenges or seriously disagrees with others in the field.

Consider, too, that charts, graphs, and images may also function like direct quotations, providing convincing evidence for your academic argument.

In an argument, quotations from respected authorities will establish your ethos as someone who has sought out experts in the field. Just as important sometimes, direct quotations (such as a memorable phrase in your introduction or a detailed eyewitness account) may capture your readers' attention. Finally, carefully chosen quotations can broaden the appeal of your argument by drawing on emotion as well as logic, appealing to the reader's mind and heart. A student who is writing on the ethical issues of bullfighting, for example, might introduce an argument that bullfighting is not a sport by quoting Ernest Hemingway's comment that "the formal bull-fight is a tragedy, not a sport, and the bull is certain to be killed" and then accompany the quotation with an image such as the one on the facing page.

The following guidelines can help you quote accurately and effectively:

- Quote or reproduce materials that readers will find especially convincing, purposeful, and interesting. You should have a specific reason for every quotation.
- Don't forget the double quotations marks [" "] that must surround a direct quotation in American usage. If there's a quote within a quote, it is surrounded by a pair of single quotation marks [' ']. British usage does just the opposite, and foreign languages often handle direct quotations much differently.
- When using a quotation in your argument, introduce its author(s) and follow the quotation with commentary of your own that points out its significance.
- Keep quoted material relatively brief. Quote only as much of a passage necessary to make your point while still accurately representing what the source actually said.

A tragedy, not a sport?

- If the quotation extends over more than one page in the original source, note the placement of page breaks in case you decide to use only part of the quotation in your argument.
- In your notes, label a quotation you intend to use with a note that tells you where you think you'll use it.
- Make sure you have all the information necessary to create an in-text citation as well as an item in your works cited list or references list.
- Copy quotations carefully, reproducing the punctuation, capitalization, and spelling exactly as they are in the original. If possible, copy the quotation from a reliable text and paste it directly into your project.
- Make sure that quoted phrases, sentences, or passages fit smoothly into your own language. Consider where to begin the quotation to

make it work effectively within its surroundings or modify the words you write to work with the quoted material.

- Use square brackets if you introduce words of your own into the quotation or make changes to it ("And [more] brain research isn't going to define further the matter of 'mind'").
- Use ellipsis marks if you omit material ("And brain research isn't going to define . . . the matter of 'mind'").
- If you're quoting a short passage (four lines or less in MLA style; forty words or less in APA style), it should be worked into your text, enclosed by quotation marks. Longer quotations should be set off from the regular text. Begin such a quotation on a new line, indenting every line one inch or ten spaces (MLA) or a half inch or five to seven spaces (APA). Set-off quotations do not need to be enclosed in quotation marks.
- Never distort your sources when you quote from them, or present them out of context. Misusing sources is a major offense in academic arguments.

**Frame all materials you borrow with signal words and introductions.** Because source materials are crucial to the success of arguments, you need to introduce borrowed words and ideas carefully to your readers. Doing so usually calls for using a signal phrase of some kind in the sentence to introduce or frame the source. Often, a signal phrase will precede a quotation. But you need such a marker whenever you introduce borrowed material, as in the following examples:

> According to noted primatologist Jane Goodall, the more we learn about the nature of nonhuman animals, the more ethical questions we face about their use in the service of humans.
>
> The more we learn about the nature of nonhuman animals, the more ethical questions we face about their use in the service of humans, according to noted primatologist Jane Goodall.
>
> The more we learn about the nature of nonhuman animals, according to noted primatologist Jane Goodall, the more ethical questions we face about their use in the service of humans.

In each of these sentences, the signal phrase tells readers that you're drawing on the work of a person named Jane Goodall and that this person is a "noted primatologist."

Now look at an example that uses a quotation from a source in more than one sentence:

> In *Job Shift*, consultant William Bridges worries about "dejobbing and about what a future shaped by it is going to be like." Even more worrisome, Bridges argues, is the possibility that "the sense of craft and of professional vocation . . . will break down under the need to earn a fee" (228).

The signal verbs *worries* and *argues* add a sense of urgency to the message Bridges offers. They also suggest that the writer either agrees with—or is neutral about—Bridges's points. Other signal verbs can have a more negative slant, indicating that the point being introduced by the quotation is open to debate and that others (including the writer) might disagree with it. If the writer of the passage above had said, for instance, that Bridges *unreasonably contends* or that he *fantasizes*, these signal verbs would carry quite different connotations from those associated with *argues*.

In some cases, a signal verb may require more complex phrasing to get the writer's full meaning across:

> Bridges recognizes the dangers of changes in work yet refuses to be overcome by them: "The real issue is not how to stop the change but how to provide the necessary knowledge and skills to equip people to operate successfully in this New World" (229).

As these examples illustrate, the signal verb is important because it allows you to characterize the author's or source's viewpoint as well as your own—so choose these verbs with care.

**Some Frequently Used Signal Verbs**

| | | | |
|---|---|---|---|
| acknowledges | claims | emphasizes | remarks |
| admits | concludes | expresses | replies |
| advises | concurs | hypothesizes | reports |
| agrees | confirms | interprets | responds |
| allows | criticizes | lists | reveals |
| argues | declares | objects | states |
| asserts | disagrees | observes | suggests |
| believes | discusses | offers | thinks |
| charges | disputes | opposes | writes |

Mac McClelland depends heavily on quotations in her article "Ohio's War on the Middle Class." How many different signal verbs can you find? How do these choices help shape her argument?

LINK TO P. 931

Note that in APA style, these signal verbs should be in the past tense: *Blau (1992) claimed*; *Clark (2001) concluded*.

**Connect the sources in a project with your own ideas.** The best academic arguments often have the flavor of a hearty but focused intellectual conversation. Scholars and scientists create this impression by handling research materials strategically and selectively. Here's how some college writers use sources to achieve specific goals within an academic argument.

- **Establish a context.** Brian Riady, whose full essay appears in Chapter 16, sets the context for his thesis statement by offering it only after he first cites three scholars who take a contrary view. Even if you know nothing about methods of tutoring in a writing center, you immediately understand that Riady's thesis is controversial and potentially significant just from the individual words he selects from those sources to describe the kind of instruction he intends to challenge:

> In an attempt to adapt traditional conferencing strategies to the ESL writer, writing center faculty have found that the non-directive approach—which has been hailed as a writing center "bible" (Shamoon and Burns 135), writing center "dogma" (Clark 34), and a writing center "mantra" (Blau 3)—does not effectively assist ESL writers. Non-directive tutoring fails non-native English speakers for the exact reason that it so effectively assists native English speakers: culture.

When using Web sources, take special care to check authors' backgrounds and credentials.

The brief quotations also have the interesting rhetorical effect of undermining the traditional view by making it seem hardened and doctrinaire.

- **Review the literature on a subject.** You will often need to tell readers what authorities have already written about your topic. So, in a paper on the effectiveness of peer editing, Susan Wilcox does a very brief "review of the literature" on her subject, pointing to three authorities who support using the method in writing courses. She quotes from the authors and also puts some of their ideas in her own words:

> Bostock cites one advantage of peer review as "giving a sense of ownership of the assessment process" (1). Topping expands this view, stating that "peer assessment also involves increased time on task: thinking, comparing, contrasting, and communicating" (254). The extra time spent thinking over the assignment, especially in terms of helping someone else, can draw in the reviewer and add a greater importance to taking the process seriously, especially since the reviewer knows that the classmate is relying on his advice. This also adds an extra layer of accountability for the student; his hard work—or lack thereof—will be seen by peers, not just the instructor. Cassidy notes, "students work harder with the knowledge that they will be assessed by their peers" (509): perhaps the knowledge that peer review is coming leads to a better-quality draft to begin with.

The paragraph is straightforward and useful, giving readers an efficient overview of the subject. If they want more information, they can find it by consulting Wilcox's works cited page.

- **Introduce a term or define a concept.** Quite often in an academic argument, you may need to define a term or explain a concept. Relying on a source may make your job easier *and* enhance your credibility. That is what Laura Pena achieves in the following paragraph, drawing upon two authorities to explain what teachers mean by a "rubric" when it comes to grading student work.

> To understand the controversy surrounding rubrics, it is best to know what a rubric is. According to Heidi Andrade, a professor at SUNY-Albany, a rubric can be defined as "a document that lists criteria and describes varying levels of quality, from excellent to poor, for a specific assignment" ("Self-Assessment" 61). Traditionally, rubrics have been used primarily as grading and evaluation tools (Kohn 12), meaning that a rubric was not used until after students handed their papers in to their teacher. The teacher would then use a rubric to evaluate the students' papers according to the criteria listed on the rubric.

Note that the first source provides the core definition while information from the second offers a detail important to understanding when and how rubrics are used—a major issue in Pena's paper. Her selection of sources here serves her thesis while also providing readers with necessary information.

- **Present technical material.** Sources can be especially helpful, too, when material becomes technical or difficult to understand. Writing on your own, you might lack the confidence to handle the complexities of some subjects. While you should challenge yourself to learn a subject well enough to explain it in your own words, there will be times when a quotation from an expert serves both you and your readers. Here is Natalie San Luis dealing with some of the technical differences between mainstream and Black English:

  > The grammatical rules of mainstream English are more concrete than those of Black English; high school students can't check out an MLA handbook on Ebonics from their school library. As with all dialects, though, there are certain characteristics of the language that most Black English scholars agree upon. According to Samy Alim, author of *Roc the Mic Right,* these characteristics are the "[h]abitual *be* [which] indicates actions that are continuing or ongoing. . . . Copula absence. . . . Stressed *been*. . . . *Gon* [indicating] the future tense. . . . *They* for possessive. . . . Postvocalic *–r*. . . . [and] *And* and *ang* for 'ink' and 'ing'" (115). Other scholars have identified "[a]bsence of third-person singular present-tense *s*. . . . Absence of possessive *'s*," repetition of pronouns, and double negatives (Rickford 111–24).

  Note that using ellipses enables San Luis to cover a great deal of ground. Readers not familiar with linguistic terms may have trouble following the quotation, but remember that academic arguments often address audiences comfortable with some degree of complexity.

- **Develop or support a claim.** Even academic audiences expect to be convinced and one of the most important strategies for a writer is to use sources to amplify or support a claim. Here's Brian Riady again, combining his voice (as an international student himself) with that of two scholars to warn against making writing centers seem like editing services for international students for whom English is a second or foreign language (ESL/EFL):

  > This is not to say that consultants should completely disregard the non-directive approach; consultants should still refrain from acting as a one-stop proofreading service. In "Tutors as Teachers: Assisting ESL/EFL Students in the

> Writing Center," Terese Thonus advises consultants to avoid the tendency to merely correct surface-level errors in ESL writing, even if such errors may seem overwhelming. Most ESL students demonstrate basic proficiency of English vocabulary and grammar by passing the TOEFL, and may be able to isolate mechanical problems and self-correct with a little guidance. But emphasizing correctness in a directive, current traditional manner, and demanding a correct product of ESL writers "will engender frustration and even the loss of confidence, just as does demanding perfect native-like English pronunciation" (Kobayashi 107). Rather, consultants must find a balance between directive teaching and non-directive tutoring that is most effective for ESL students.

- **Highlight differences or counterarguments.** The sources you encounter in developing a project won't always agree with each other or you. In academic arguments, you don't want to hide such differences, but instead point them out honestly and let readers make judgments based upon actual claims. Here is a paragraph in which Laura Pena again presents two views on the use of rubrics as grading tools:

> Some naysayers, such as Alfie Kohn, assert that "any form of assessment that encourages students to keep asking, 'How am I doing?' is likely to change how they look at themselves and what they're learning, usually for the worse." Kohn cites a study that found that students who pay too much attention to the quality of their performance are more likely to chalk up the outcome of an assignment to factors beyond their control, such as innate ability, and are also more likely to give up quickly in the face of a difficult task (14). However, Ross and Rolheiser have found that when students are taught how to properly implement self-assessment tools in the writing process, they are more likely to put more effort and persistence into completing a difficult assignment and may develop higher self-confidence in their writing ability (sec. 2). Building self-confidence in elementary-age writers can be extremely helpful for when they tackle more complicated writing endeavors in the future.

In describing Kohn as a "naysayer," Pena may tip her hand and lose some degree of objectivity. But her thesis has already signaled her support for rubrics as a grading tool, so academic readers will probably not find the connotations of the term inappropriate.

These examples suggest only a few of the ways that sources, either summarized or quoted directly, can be incorporated into an academic argument to support or enhance a writer's goals. Like these writers, you should think of sources as your copartners in developing and expressing ideas. But you are still in charge.

- **Avoid "patchwriting."** When using sources in an argument, someone accustomed to working online may be tempted to do what Professor Rebecca Moore Howard termed "patchwriting." **Patchwriting** is the process of stitching a paper together from Web or online materials that have been copied or only lightly reworked; in addition, these materials are usually presented with little or no documentation. Here, for example, is a patchwork paragraph about the dangers wind turbines pose to wildlife:

  Scientists are discovering that technology with low carbon impact does not mean low environmental or social impacts. That is the case especially with wind turbines, whose long massive fiberglass blades have been chopping up tens of thousands of birds that fly into them, including golden eagles, red-tailed hawks, burrowing owls and other raptors in California. Turbines are also killing bats in great numbers. The 420 wind turbines now in use across Pennsylvania killed more than 10,000 bats last year—mostly in the late summer months, according to the State Game Commission. That's an average of 25 bats per turbine per year, and the Nature Conservancy predicts as many as 2,900 turbines will be set up across the state by 2030. It's not the spinning blades that kill the bats; instead, their lungs effectively blow up from the rapid pressure drop that occurs as air flows over the turbine blades. But there's hope we may figure out solutions to these problems because, since we haven't had too many wind turbines heretofore in the country, we are learning how to manage this new technology as we go.

  The paragraph reads well and is full of details. But it would be considered plagiarized (see Chapter 20) because it fails to identify its sources and because most of the material has simply been lifted directly from the Web. How much is actually copied? We've highlighted the borrowed material:

  Scientists are discovering that technology with low carbon impact does not mean low environmental or social impacts. That is the case especially with wind turbines, whose long massive fiberglass blades have been chopping up tens of thousands of birds that fly into them, including golden eagles, red-tailed hawks, burrowing owls and other raptors in California. Turbines are also killing bats in great numbers. The 420 wind turbines now in use across Pennsylvania killed more than 10,000 bats last year—mostly in the late summer months, according to the State Game Commission. That's an average of 25 bats per turbine per year, and the Nature Conservancy predicts as many as 2,900 turbines will be set up across the state by 2030. It's not the spinning blades that kill the bats; instead, their lungs effectively blow up from the rapid pressure drop that occurs as air flows over the turbine blades. But there's hope we may figure out solutions to these problems because, since we haven't had too many wind turbines heretofore in the country, we are learning how to manage this new technology as we go.

But here's the point. An academic writer who has gone to the trouble of finding so much information will gain more credit and credibility just by properly identifying, paraphrasing, and quoting the sources used. The resulting paragraph is actually more impressive because it demonstrates how much reading and synthesizing the writer has actually done:

Scientists like George Ledec of the World Bank are discovering that technology with low carbon impact "does not mean low environmental or social impacts" (Tracy). That is the case especially with wind turbines. Their massive blades spinning to create pollution-free electricity are also killing thousands of valuable birds of prey, including eagles, hawks, and owls in California (Rittier). Turbines are also killing bats in great numbers (Thibodeaux). The *Pittsburgh Post-Gazette* reports that 10,000 bats a year are killed by the 420 turbines currently in Pennsylvania. According to the state game commissioner, "That's an average of 25 bats per turbine per year, and the Nature Conservancy predicts as many as 2,900 turbines will be set up across the state by 2030" (Schwartzel). It's not the spinning blades that kill the animals; instead, *DiscoveryNews* explains, "the bats' lungs effectively blow up from the rapid pressure drop that occurs as air flows over the turbine blades" (Marshall). But there's hope that scientists can develop turbines less dangerous to animals of all kinds. "We haven't had too many wind turbines heretofore in the country," David Cottingham of the Fish and Wildlife Service points out, "so we are learning about it as we go" (Tracy).

Works Cited

Marshall, Jessica. "Wind Turbines Kill Bats without Impact." *DiscoveryNews.com*. Discovery Communications, 25 Aug. 2008. Web. 11 Dec. 2011.

Rittier, John. "Wind Turbines Taking Toll on Birds of Prey." *USA Today*. Gannett, 4 Jan. 2005. Web. 10 Dec. 2011.

Schwartzel, Erich. "Pa. Wind Turbines Deadly to Bats, Costly to Farmers." *Post-Gazette.com*. PG Publishing, 17 July 2011. Web. 12 Dec. 2011.

Thibodeaux, Julie. "Bats Getting Caught in Texas Wind Turbines." *PegasusNews.com*. PanLocal Media, 9 Nov. 2011. Web. 10 Dec. 2011.

Tracy, Ryan. "Wildlife Slows Wind Power." *WallStreetJournal.com*. Dow Jones, 10 Dec. 2011. Web. 10 Dec. 2011.

**RESPOND.**

1. Select one of the essays from Chapters 8–12 or 16. Following the guidelines in this chapter, write a paraphrase of the essay that you might use subsequently in an academic argument. Be careful to describe the essay accurately and to note on what pages specific ideas or claims are located. The language of the paraphrase should be entirely your own—though you may include direct quotations of phrases, sentences, or longer passages you would likely use in a paper. Be sure these quotations are introduced and cited in your paraphrase: *Pearson claims that nuclear power is safe, even asserting that "your toaster is far more likely to kill you than any nuclear power plant" (175)*. When you are done, trade your paraphrase with a partner to get feedback on its clarity and accuracy.
2. Summarize three readings or fairly lengthy passages from Parts 1–3 of this book, following the guidelines in this chapter. Open the item with a correct MLA or APA citation for the piece (see Chapter 21). Then provide the summary itself. Follow up with a one- or two-sentence evaluation of the work describing its potential value as a source in an academic argument. In effect, you will be preparing three items that might appear in an annotated bibliography. Here's an example:

   Pearson, Taylor. "Why You Should Fear Your Toaster More Than Nuclear Power." In *Everything's an Argument* by Andrea A. Lunsford and John J. Ruszkiewicz. Boston: Bedford, 2013. 174–79. Print. Argues that since the dangers of nuclear power (death, radiation, waste) are actually less than those of energy sources we rely on today, nuclear plants represent the only practical way to generate the power we need and still reduce greenhouse gases. The journalistic piece provides many interesting facts about nuclear energy, but is informally documented and so does not identify its sources in detail or include a bibliography.

3. Working with a partner, agree upon an essay that you will both read from Chapters 8–12 or 16, examining it as a potential source for a research argument. As you read it, choose about a half-dozen words, phrases, or short passages that you would likely quote if you used the essay in a paper and attach a frame or signal phrase to each quotation. Then compare the passages you selected to quote with those your partner culled from the same essay. How do your choices of quoted material create an image or ethos for the original author that differs from the one your partner has created? How do the signal phrases shape a reader's sense of the author's position? Which set of quotations best represents the author's argument? Why?

4. Select one of the essays from Chapters 8–12 or 16 to examine the different ways an author uses source materials to support claims. Begin by highlighting the signal phrases you find attached to borrowed ideas or direct quotations. How well do they introduce or frame this material? Then categorize the various ways the author actually uses particular sources. For example, look for sources that provide context for the topic, review the scholarly literature, define key concepts or terms, explain technical details, furnish evidence, or lay out contrary opinions. When you are done, write a paragraph assessing the author's handling of sources in the piece. Are the borrowed materials integrated well with the author's own thoughts? Do the sources represent an effective synthesis of ideas?

# 20 Plagiarism and Academic Integrity

In many ways, "nothing new under the sun" is more than just a cliché. Most of what you think or write is built on what you've previously read or experienced. Luckily, you'll seldom be called on to list every influence on your life. But you do have responsibilities in school and professional situations to acknowledge any intellectual property you've borrowed when you create arguments of your own. If you don't, you may be accused of **plagiarism**—claiming as your own the words, research, or creative work of others.

What is intellectual property? It's complicated. But, for academic arguments in Western culture, it is the *expression* of ideas you find in works produced by others that you then use to advance and support your own claims. You have to document not only when you use or reproduce someone's exact words, images, music, or other creations (in whole or in part), but also when you borrow the framework others use to put ideas together in original or creative ways. Needless to say, intellectual property rights have always been contentious, but never more so than

The FBI has warned consumers for decades about the penalties for violating copyright. Your school no doubt has its own policies for handling violations such as plagiarism.

today, when new media make it remarkably easy to duplicate and share all sorts of materials. Accustomed to uploading and downloading files, cutting and pasting passages, you may be comfortable working with texts day-to-day in ways that are considered dishonest in school.

So it is essential that you read and understand any policies on academic integrity that your school has set down. In particular, pay attention to how those policies define, prosecute, and punish cheating, plagiarism, and collusion. Some institutions recognize a difference between intentional and unintentional plagiarism, but you don't want the honesty of anything you write to be questioned. You need to learn the rules and understand that the penalties for plagiarism are severe not only for students but for professional writers as well.

Fortunately there's an upside to handling borrowed materials responsibly. When you give full credit to your sources, you enhance your ethos in academic arguments—which is why "Academic Integrity" appears in this chapter's title. Audiences will applaud you for saying thanks to those who've helped you. Crediting your sources also proves that you have shown "due diligence": you demonstrate that you understand what others have written about the topic and encourage others to join the intellectual conversation. Finally, citing sources reminds you to think critically about how to use the evidence you've collected. Is it timely and reliable? Have you referenced authorities in a biased or overly selective way? Have you double-checked all quotations and paraphrases? Thinking through such questions helps to guarantee the integrity of your academic work.

In the nineteenth century, before patents applied to living organisms, beautiful lithographs like this hand-colored illustration of the Red Astrachan apple were published to establish the claims that breeders of new fruit species had to their intellectual property.

Wikipedia is commonly attacked as an unreliable source. Take a look at the entry for *Local Food*, paying special attention to how the article acknowledges sources and how Wikipedia alerts readers that articles may contain unreliable or uncredited information. Do you think this material is accurately sourced and cited?

LINK TO P. 666

Proper acknowledgment of sources is crucial in academic writing. Check out Mack D. Mariani and Gordon J. Hewitt's extensive notes for an example of how to do it right.

LINK TO P. 801

## Acknowledging Your Sources Accurately and Appropriately

The basic principles for documenting materials are relatively simple. Give credit to all source materials you borrow by following these three steps: (1) placing quotation marks around any words you quote directly, (2) citing your sources according to the documentation style you're using, and (3) identifying all the sources you have cited in a list of references or works cited. Materials to be cited in an academic argument include all of the following:

- direct quotations
- facts that are not widely known
- arguable statements
- judgments, opinions, and claims that have been made by others

- images, statistics, charts, tables, graphs, or other illustrations that appear in any source
- collaboration—that is, the help provided by friends, colleagues, instructors, supervisors, or others

However, three important types of evidence or source material do not need to be acknowledged or documented. They are the following:

- common knowledge, which is a specific piece of information most readers in your intended audience will know (that Barack Obama won the 2008 presidential election, for instance)
- facts available from a wide variety of sources (that the Japanese bombed Pearl Harbor on December 7, 1941, for example)
- your own findings from field research (observations, interviews, experiments, or surveys you have conducted), which should be clearly presented as your own

For the actual forms to use when documenting sources, see Chapter 21.

Of course, the devil is in the details. For instance, you may be accused of plagiarism in situations like the following:

- if you don't indicate clearly the source of an idea you obviously didn't come up with on your own
- if you use a paraphrase that's too close to the original wording or sentence structure of your source material (*even* if you cite the source)
- if you leave out the parenthetical in-text reference for a quotation (*even* if you include the quotation marks themselves)

And the accusation can be made even if you didn't intend to plagiarize.

Online, you will encounter materials that obviously remix or parody images and ideas that belong to others. But intellectual property is treated much differently in school: clear guidelines apply whenever you use source materials. So you must learn to document sources accurately and fully and not be careless about this very important procedure.

Here, for example, is the first paragraph from an essay by Russell Platt published in the *Nation*:

> **Classical music in America, we are frequently told, is in its death throes: its orchestras bled dry by expensive guest soloists and greedy musicians unions, its media presence shrinking, its prestige diminished, its educational role ignored, its big record labels dying out or merging into faceless corporate entities. We seem to have too many**

> **well-trained musicians in need of work, too many good composers going without commissions, too many concerts to offer an already satiated public.**
>
> —Russell Platt, "New World Symphony"

To cite this passage correctly in MLA documentation style, you could quote directly from it, using both quotation marks and some form of note identifying the author or source. Either of the following versions would be acceptable:

> Russell Platt has doubts about claims that classical music is "in its death throes: its orchestras bled dry by expensive guest soloists and greedy musicians unions" ("New World").
>
> But is classical music in the United States really "in its death throes," as some critics of the music scene suggest (Platt)?

You might also paraphrase Platt's paragraph, putting his ideas entirely in your own words but still giving him due credit by ending your remarks with a simple in-text note:

> A familiar story told by critics is that classical music faces a bleak future in the United States, with grasping soloists and unions bankrupting orchestras and classical works vanishing from radio and television, school curricula, and the labels of recording conglomerates. The public may not be willing to support all the talented musicians and composers we have today (Platt).

All of these sentences with citations would be keyed to a works cited entry at the end of the paper that would look like the following in MLA style:

> Platt, Russell. "New World Symphony." *The Nation*. The Nation, 3 Oct. 2005. Web. 15 Oct. 2009.

How might a citation go wrong? As we indicated, omitting either the quotation marks around a borrowed passage or an acknowledgment of the source is grounds for complaint. Neither of the following sentences provides enough information for a correct citation:

> But is classical music in the United States really in its death throes, as some critics of the music scene suggest, with its prestige diminished, its educational role ignored, and its big record labels dying (Platt)?
>
> But is classical music in the United States really in "its death throes," as some critics of the music scene suggest, with "its prestige diminished, its educational role ignored, [and] its big record labels dying"?

Just as faulty is a paraphrase such as the following, which borrows the words or ideas of the source too closely. It represents plagiarism, despite the fact that it identifies the source from which almost all the ideas—and a good many words—are borrowed:

> In "New World Symphony," Russell Platt observes that classical music is thought by many to be in bad shape in America. Its orchestras are being sucked dry by costly guest artists and insatiable unionized musicians, while its place on TV and radio is shrinking. The problem may be that we have too many well-trained

A *Doonesbury* cartoon on intellectual property pokes fun at best-selling historian and presidential biographer Stephen Ambrose, who was found to have plagiarized passages from at least twelve authors in at least six of his books—and in his doctoral dissertation.

**DOONESBURY** **BY GARRY TRUDEAU**

> musicians who need employment, too many good composers going without jobs, too many concerts for a public that prefers *Desperate Housewives*.

Even the fresh idea not taken from Platt at the end of the paragraph doesn't alter the fact that the paraphrase is mostly a mash-up of Platt's original words, lightly stirred.

## Using Copyrighted Internet Sources

If you've done any surfing on the Internet, you know that it opens the door to worldwide collaborations: you can contact individuals and groups around the globe and have access to whole libraries of information. As a result, writing (especially online writing) often is made up of materials woven from many sources. But when you gather information from Internet sources and use it in your own work, it's subject to the same rules that govern information gathered from other types of sources.

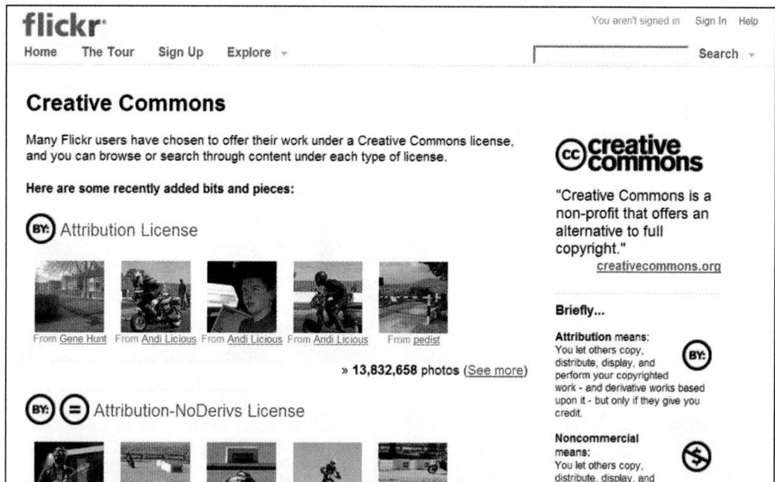


A growing number of works, such as photographs, music, and video, are published online under the so-called Creative Commons license, which often eliminates the need to request permission. These works—marked with a Creative Commons license at Flickr, for example—are made available to the public under this alternative to copyright, which grants blanket permission to reuse or remix work under certain terms if credit is given to the work's creator.

Even if the material does not include a copyright notice or symbol ("© 2013 by Andrea A. Lunsford and John J. Ruszkiewicz," for example), it's likely to be protected by copyright laws, and you may need to request permission to use part or all of it. Although they're currently in flux, "fair-use" legal precedents still allow writers to quote brief passages from published works without permission from the copyright holder if the use is for educational or personal, noncommercial reasons and if full credit is given to the source. For blog postings or any serious professional uses (especially online), however, you should ask permission of the writer before you include any of his or her material in your own argument. For graphics, photos, or other images that you wish to reproduce in your text, you should also request permission from the creator or owner if the text is going to be disseminated beyond your classroom—again, especially if it's going to appear on the Web.

If you do need to make a request for permission, here are some examples:

From: sanchez.32@stanford.edu
To: litman@mindspring.com
CC: lunsford.2@stanford.edu
Subject: Request for permission

Dear Professor Litman:

I am writing to request permission to quote from your essay "Copyright, Owners' Rights and Users' Privileges on the Internet: Implied Licenses, Caching, Linking, Fair Use, and Sign-on Licenses." I want to quote some of your work as part of an article I am writing for the *Stanford Daily* to explain the complex debates over ownership on the Internet and to argue that students at my school should be participating in these debates. I will give full credit to you and will cite the URL where I first found your work (msen.com/~litman/dayton/htm).

Thank you very much for considering my request.

Raul Sanchez

From: fox.360@stanford.edu
To: fridanet@aol.com
CC: lunsford.2@stanford.edu
Subject: Request for permission

Dear Kimberley Masters:

I am a student at Stanford University writing to request your permission to download and use a photograph of Frida Kahlo in a three-piece suit (fridanet/suit.htm#top) as an illustration in a project about Kahlo that I and two other students are working on in our composition class. This project will be posted on a school Web site. In the report on our project, we will cite members.aol.com/fridanet/kahlo.htm as the URL, unless you wish for us to use a different source.

Thank you very much for considering our request.

Jennifer Fox

## Acknowledging Collaboration

Many newspaper articles, regardless of who is listed as the author, use reporting that has been gathered collaboratively. How does the *Daily Californian* credit the many student reporters who gathered information for their live blog on the "Increase Diversity Bake Sale"?

LINK TO P. 756

Writers generally acknowledge all participants in collaborative projects at the beginning of the presentation, report, or essay. In print texts, the acknowledgment is often placed in a footnote or brief prefatory note.

The seventh edition of the *MLA Handbook for Writers of Research Papers* (2009) calls attention to the growing importance of collaborative work and gives the following advice on how to deal with issues of assigning fair credit all around:

> Joint participation in research and writing is common and, in fact, encouraged in many courses and in many professions. It does not constitute plagiarism provided that credit is given for all contributions. One way to give credit, if roles were clearly demarcated or were unequal, is to state exactly who did what. Another way, especially if roles and contributions were merged and shared, is to acknowledge all concerned equally. Ask your instructor for advice if you are not certain how to acknowledge collaboration.

**RESPOND•**

1. Not everyone agrees that intellectual material is property that should be protected. The slogan "information wants to be free" has been showing up in popular magazines and on the Internet, often with a call to readers to take action against protection such as data encryption and further extension of copyright.

   Using a Web search engine, look for pages where the phrase "free information" appears. Find several sites that make arguments in favor of free information, and analyze them in terms of their rhetorical appeals. What claims do the authors make? How do they appeal to their audience? What's the site's ethos, and how is it created? After you've read some arguments in favor of free information, return to this chapter's arguments about intellectual property. Which arguments do you find most persuasive? Why?

2. Although this book is concerned principally with ideas and their written expression, other forms of intellectual property are also legally protected. For example, scientific and technological developments are protectable under patent law, which differs in some significant ways from copyright law.

   Find the standards for protection under U.S. copyright law and U.S. patent law. You might begin by visiting the U.S. copyright Web site (http://copyright.gov). Then imagine that you're the president of a small high-tech corporation and are trying to inform your employees of the legal protections available to them and their work. Write a paragraph or two explaining the differences between copyright and patent, and suggest a policy that balances employees' rights to intellectual property with the business's needs to develop new products.

3. Define *plagiarism* in your own terms, making your definition as clear and explicit as possible. Then compare your definition with those of two or three other classmates, and write a brief report on the similarities and differences you noted in the definitions. You might research terms such as *plagiarism*, *academic honesty*, and *academic integrity* on the Web. Also be certain to check how your own school defines the words.

4. Spend fifteen or twenty minutes jotting down your ideas about intellectual property and plagiarism. Where do you stand, for example, on the issue of music file sharing? On downloading movies free of charge? Do you think these forms of intellectual property should be protected under copyright law? How do you define your own intellectual property, and in what ways and under what conditions are you willing to share it? Finally, come up with your own definition of *academic integrity*.

# 21
# Documenting Sources

What does documenting sources have to do with argument? First, the sources that a writer chooses form part of any argument, showing that he or she has done some research, knows what others have said about the topic, and understands how to use these items as support for a claim. Similarly, the list of works cited or references makes a statement, saying, "Look at how thoroughly this essay has been researched" or "Note how up-to-date I am!"

Even the choice of documentation style makes an argument in a subtle way. You'll note in the instructions that follow, for example, that the Modern Language Association (MLA) style requires putting the date of publication of a print source at or near the end of a works cited list entry, whereas the American Psychological Association (APA) style places that date near the beginning of a reference list citation. Pay attention to such fine points of documentation style, always asking what these choices suggest about the values of scholars and researchers who use a particular system of documentation.

## MLA Style

Documentation styles vary from discipline to discipline, with one format favored in the social sciences and another in the natural sciences, for example. Widely used in the humanities, MLA style is fully described in the *MLA Handbook for Writers of Research Papers* (7th edition, 2009). In this discussion, we provide guidelines drawn from the *MLA Handbook* for in-text citations, notes, and entries in the list of works cited.

### In-Text Citations

MLA style calls for in-text citations in the body of an argument to document sources of quotations, paraphrases, summaries, and so on. For in-text citations, use a signal phrase to introduce the material, often with the author's name (*As LaDoris Cordell explains, . . .*). Keep an in-text citation short, but include enough information for readers to locate the source in the list of works cited. Place the parenthetical citation as near to the relevant material as possible without disrupting the flow of the sentence, as in the following examples.

#### 1. Author Named in a Signal Phrase

Ordinarily, use the author's name in a signal phrase to introduce the material, and cite the page number(s) in parentheses.

> Loomba argues that Caliban's "political colour" is black, given his stage representations, which have varied from animalistic to a kind of missing link (143).

#### 2. Author Named in Parentheses

When you don't mention the author in a signal phrase, include the author's last name before the page number(s) in the parentheses.

> Oil from shale in the western states, if it could be extracted, would be equivalent to six hundred billion barrels, more than all the crude so far produced in the world (McPhee 413).

#### 3. Two or Three Authors

Use all authors' last names.

> Gortner, Hebrun, and Nicolson maintain that "opinion leaders" influence other people in an organization because they are respected, not because they hold high positions (175).

#### 4. Four or More Authors

The MLA allows you to use all authors' last names or to use only the first author's name with *et al.* (in regular type, not italicized). Although either format is acceptable when applied consistently throughout a paper, in an argument it is better to name all authors who contributed to the work.

> Similarly, as Goldberger, Tarule, Clinchy, and Belenky note, their new book builds on their collaborative experiences (xii).

#### 5. Organization as Author

Give the full name of a corporate author if it's brief or a shortened form if it's long.

> In fact, one of the leading foundations in the field of higher education supports the recent proposals for community-run public schools (Carnegie Corporation 45).

#### 6. Unknown Author

Use the full title of the work if it's brief or a shortened form if it's long.

> "Hype," by one analysis, is "an artificially engendered atmosphere of hysteria" ("Today's Marketplace" 51).

#### 7. Author of Two or More Works

When you use two or more works by the same author, include the title of the work or a shortened version of it in the citation.

> Gardner presents readers with their own silliness through his description of a "pointless, ridiculous monster, crouched in the shadows, stinking of dead men, murdered children, and martyred cows" (*Grendel* 2).

#### 8. Authors with the Same Last Name

When you use works by two or more authors with the same last name, include each author's first initial in the in-text citation.

> Father Divine's teachings focused on eternal life, salvation, and socioeconomic progress (R. Washington 17).

#### 9. Multivolume Work

Note the volume number first and then the page number(s), with a colon and one space between them.

> Aristotle's "On Plants" is now available in a new translation edited by Barnes (2: 1252).

**10. Literary Work**

Because literary works are often available in many different editions, you need to include enough information for readers to locate the passage in any edition. For a prose work such as a novel or play, first cite the page number from the edition you used, followed by a semicolon; then indicate the part or chapter number (114; ch. 3) or act or scene in a play (42; sc. 2).

> In *The Madonnas of Leningrad*, Marina says, "she could see into the future" (7; ch. 1).

For a poem, cite the stanza and line numbers. If the poem has only line numbers, use the word *line(s)* in the first reference (lines 33–34) and the number(s) alone in subsequent references.

> On dying, Whitman speculates, "All that goes onward and outward, nothing collapses, / And to die is different from what any one supposed, and luckier" (6.129-30).

For a verse play, omit the page number, and give only the act, scene, and line numbers, separated by periods.

> Before he takes his own life, Othello says he is "one that loved not wisely but too well" (5.2.348).

> As *Macbeth* begins, the witches greet Banquo as "Lesser than Macbeth, and greater" (1.3.65).

**11. Works in an Anthology**

For an essay, short story, or other short work within an anthology, use the name of the author of the work, not the editor of the anthology; but use the page number(s) from the anthology.

> In the end, if the black artist accepts any duties at all, that duty is to express the beauty of blackness (Hughes 1271).

**12. Sacred Text**

To cite a sacred text, such as the Qur'an or the Bible, give the title of the edition you used, the book, and the chapter and verse (or their equivalent), separated by a period. In your text, spell out the names of books. In a parenthetical reference, use an abbreviation for books with names of five or more letters (for example, *Gen.* for Genesis).

> He ignored the admonition "Pride goes before destruction, and a haughty spirit before a fall" (*New Oxford Annotated Bible*, Prov. 16.18).

### 13. Indirect Source

Use the abbreviation *qtd. in* to indicate that what you're quoting or paraphrasing is quoted (as part of a conversation, interview, letter, or excerpt) in the source you're using.

As Catherine Belsey states, "to speak is to have access to the language which defines, delimits and locates power" (qtd. in Bartels 453).

### 14. Two or More Sources in the Same Citation

Separate the information for each source with a semicolon.

Adefunmi was able to patch up the subsequent holes left in worship by substituting various Yoruba, Dahomean, or Fon customs made available to him through research (Brandon 115-17; Hunt 27).

### 15. Entire Work or One-Page Article

Include the citation in the text without any page numbers or parentheses.

The relationship between revolutionary innocence and the preservation of an oppressive postrevolutionary regime is one theme Milan Kundera explores in *The Book of Laughter and Forgetting*.

### 16. Work without Page Numbers

If the work isn't numbered by page but has numbered sections, parts, or paragraphs, include the name and number(s) of the section(s) you're citing. (For paragraphs, use the abbreviation *par.* or *pars.*; for section, use *sec.*; for part, use *pt.*)

Zora Neale Hurston is one of the great anthropologists of the twentieth century, according to Kip Hinton (par. 2).

Describing children's language acquisition, Pinker explains that "what's innate about language is just a way of paying attention to parental speech" (Johnson, sec. 1).

### 17. Electronic or Nonprint Source

Give enough information in a signal phrase or parenthetical citation for readers to locate the source in the list of works cited. Usually give the author or title under which you list the source.

In his film version of *Hamlet*, Zeffirelli highlights the sexual tension between the prince and his mother.

## Explanatory and Bibliographic Notes

The MLA recommends using explanatory notes for information or commentary that doesn't readily fit into your text but is needed for clarification, further explanation, or justification. In addition, the MLA allows bibliographic notes for citing several sources for one point and for offering thanks to, information about, or evaluation of a source. Use a superscript number in your text at the end of a sentence to refer readers to the notes, which usually appear as endnotes (with the heading *Notes*, not underlined or italicized) on a separate page before the list of works cited. Indent the first line of each note five spaces, and double-space all entries.

### TEXT WITH SUPERSCRIPT INDICATING A NOTE

Stewart emphasizes the existence of social contacts in Hawthorne's life so that the audience will accept a different Hawthorne, one more attuned to modern times than the figure in Woodberry.[3]

### NOTE

[3] Woodberry does, however, show that Hawthorne was often unsociable. He emphasizes the seclusion of Hawthorne's mother, who separated herself from her family after the death of her husband, often even taking meals alone (28). Woodberry seems to imply that Mrs. Hawthorne's isolation rubbed off on her son.

## List of Works Cited

A list of works cited is an alphabetical listing of the sources you cite in your essay. The list appears on a separate page at the end of your argument, after any notes, with the heading *Works Cited* centered an inch from the top of the page; don't underline or italicize it or enclose it in quotation marks. Double-space between the heading and the first entry, and double-space the entire list. (If you're asked to list everything you've read as background—not just the sources you cite—call the list *Works Consulted.*) The first line of each entry should align on the left; subsequent lines indent one-half inch or five spaces. See p. 464 for a sample works cited page.

## BOOKS

The basic information for a book includes four elements, each followed by a period:

- the author's name, last name first (for a book with multiple authors, only the first author's name is inverted)
- the title and subtitle, italicized
- the publication information, including the city followed by a colon, a shortened form of the publisher's name (such as Harvard UP) followed by a comma, and the publication date
- the medium of publication (*Print*)

### 1. One Author

Skloot, Rebecca. *The Immortal Life of Henrietta Lacks*. Waterville: Thorndike, 2010. Print.

### 2. Two or More Authors

Jacobson, Sid, and Ernie Colón. *The 9/11 Report: A Graphic Adaptation*. New York: Hill, 2006. Print.

### 3. Organization as Author

American Horticultural Society. *The Fully Illustrated Plant-by-Plant Manual of Practical Techniques*. New York: American Horticultural Society and DK, 1999. Print.

### 4. Unknown Author

*National Geographic Atlas of the World*. New York: Natl. Geographic, 2004. Print.

### 5. Two or More Books by the Same Author

List the works alphabetically by title. Use three hyphens for the author's name for the second and subsequent works by that author.

Lorde, Audre. *A Burst of Light*. Ithaca: Firebrand, 1988. Print.

---. *Sister Outsider*. Trumansburg: Crossing, 1984. Print.

### 6. Editor

Rorty, Amelie Oksenberg, ed. *Essays on Aristotle's Poetics*. Princeton: Princeton UP, 1992. Print.

### 7. Author and Editor

Shakespeare, William. *The Tempest*. Ed. Frank Kermode. London: Routledge, 1994. Print.

**8. Selection in an Anthology or Chapter in an Edited Book**

List the author(s) of the selection or chapter; its title; the title of the book in which the selection or chapter appears; *Ed.* and the name(s) of the editor(s); the publication information; and the inclusive page numbers of the selection or chapter.

Brown, Paul. "'This thing of darkness I acknowledge mine': *The Tempest* and the Discourse of Colonialism." *Political Shakespeare: Essays in Cultural Materialism*. Ed. Jonathan Dillimore and Alan Sinfield. Ithaca: Cornell UP, 1985. 48-71. Print.

**9. Two or More Works from the Same Anthology**

Include the anthology itself in the list of works cited.

Gates, Henry Louis, Jr., and Nellie McKay, eds. *The Norton Anthology of African American Literature*. New York: Norton, 1997. Print.

Then list each selection separately by its author and title, followed by a cross-reference to the anthology.

Karenga, Maulana. "Black Art: Mute Matter Given Force and Function." Gates and McKay 1973-77.

Neal, Larry. "The Black Arts Movement." Gates and McKay 1960-72.

**10. Translation**

Hietamies, Laila. *Red Moon over White Sea*. Trans. Borje Vahamaki. Beaverton: Aspasia, 2000. Print.

**11. Edition Other Than the First**

Lunsford, Andrea A., John J. Ruszkiewicz, and Keith Walters. *Everything's an Argument with Readings*. 6th ed. Boston: Bedford, 2013. Print.

**12. One Volume of a Multivolume Work**

Byron, Lord George. *Byron's Letters and Journals*. Ed. Leslie A. Marchand. Vol. 2. London: Murray, 1973-82. Print. 12 vols.

**13. Two or More Volumes of a Multivolume Work**

Byron, Lord George. *Byron's Letters and Journals*. Ed. Leslie A. Marchand. 12 vols. London: Murray, 1973-82. Print.

**14. Preface, Foreword, Introduction, or Afterword**

Kean, Thomas H., and Lee H. Hamilton. Foreword. *The 9/11 Report: A Graphic Adaptation*. By Sid Jacobson and Ernie Colón. New York: Hill, 2006. ix-x. Print.

### 15. Article in a Reference Work

Kettering, Alison McNeil. "Art Nouveau." *World Book Encyclopedia*. 2002 ed. Print.

### 16. Book That Is Part of a Series

Include the series title and number after the publication information.

Moss, Beverly J. *A Community Text Arises*. Cresskill: Hampton, 2003. Print. Language and Social Processes Ser. 8.

### 17. Republication

Scott, Walter. *Kenilworth*. 1821. New York: Dodd, 1996. Print.

### 18. Government Document

United States. Cong. House Committee on the Judiciary. *Impeachment of the President. 40th Cong.,* 1st sess. H. Rept. 7. Washington: GPO, 1867. Print.

### 19. Pamphlet

*An Answer to the President's Message to the Fiftieth Congress*. Philadelphia: Manufacturer's Club of Philadelphia, 1887. Print.

### 20. Published Proceedings of a Conference

Edwards, Ron, ed. *Proceedings of the Third National Folklore Conference*. 26-27 Nov. 1988. Canberra, Austral.: Australian Folk Trust, 1988. Print.

### 21. Title within a Title

Tauernier-Courbin, Jacqueline. *Ernest Hemingway's* A Moveable Feast*: The Making of a Myth*. Boston: Northeastern UP, 1991. Print.

## PERIODICALS

The basic entry for a periodical includes four elements, each followed by a period:

- the author's name, last name first
- the article title, in quotation marks
- the publication information, including the periodical title (italicized), the volume and issue numbers (if any, not italicized), the date of publication, and the page number(s)
- the medium of publication (*Print*)

For works with multiple authors, only the first author's name is inverted. Note that the period following the article title goes inside the closing quotation mark. Finally, note that the MLA omits *the* in titles such as *The New Yorker*.

### 22. Article in a Journal

Give the issue number, if available.

Anderson, Virginia. "'The Perfect Enemy': Clinton, the Contradictions of Capitalism, and Slaying the Sin Within." *Rhetoric Review* 21 (2002): 384-400. Print.

Radavich, David. "Man among Men: David Mamet's Homosocial Order." *American Drama* 1.1 (1991): 46-66. Print.

### 23. Article That Skips Pages

Seabrook, John. "Renaissance Pears." *New Yorker* 5 Sept. 2005: 102+. Print.

### 24. Article in a Monthly Magazine

Lelyveld, Joseph. "What 9/11 Wrought." *Smithsonian* Sept. 2011: 58-64. Print.

### 25. Article in a Weekly Magazine

Reed, Julia. "Hope in the Ruins." *Newsweek* 12 Sept. 2005: 58-59. Print.

### 26. Article in a Newspaper

Friend, Tim. "Scientists Map the Mouse Genome." *USA Today* 2 Dec. 2002: A1. Print.

### 27. Editorial or Letter to the Editor

Posner, Alan. "Colin Powell's Regret." Editorial. *New York Times* 9 Sept. 2005: A20. Print.

### 28. Unsigned Article

"Court Rejects the Sale of Medical Marijuana." *New York Times* 26 Feb. 1998, late ed.: A21. Print.

### 29. Review

Wildavsky, Ben. "Bad Educations." Rev. of *Academically Adrift: Limited Learning on College Campuses*, by Richard Arum and Joseph Roksa. *Wilson Quarterly* 35.2 (2011): 98-99. Print.

## ELECTRONIC SOURCES

Most of the following models are based on the MLA's guidelines for citing electronic sources in the *MLA Handbook* (7th edition, 2009), as well as on up-to-date information available at its Web site (http://mla.org). The MLA no longer requires the use of URLs but assumes that readers can locate a source by searching the author, title, and other publication information given in the citation. The basic MLA entry for most electronic sources should include the following elements:

- name of the author, editor, or compiler
- title of the work, document, or posting
- information for print publication, if any
- information for electronic publication
- medium of publication (e.g., *Web*, *CD-ROM*, etc.)
- date of access

### 30. Document from a Professional Web Site

When possible, include the author's name; the title of the document, in quotations; the name of the Web site, italicized; the sponsor or publisher; the date of publication; the medium consulted (*Web*); and the date you accessed the site.

"Fair Use and Short Form Media." *Critical Commons: For Fair & Critical Participation in Media Culture*. USC Institute for Multimedia Literacy, 23 Nov. 2010. Web. 3 Sept. 2011.

### 31. Entire Web Site

Include the name of the person or group who created the site, if relevant; the title of the site, italicized, or (if there is no title) a description such as *Home page*, not italicized; the publisher or sponsor of the site; the date of publication or last update; the medium consulted (*Web*); and the date of access.

*Kotaku*. Gawker Media, 12 Jan. 2011. Web. 30 Aug. 2011.

Mitten, Lisa. *Native American Sites*. Lisa A. Mitten, 16 Sept. 2008. Web. 3 Dec. 2008.

### 32. Course, Department, or Personal Web Site

For a course Web site, include the instructor's name; the title of the site, italicized; a description of the site (such as *Course home page*, *Dept. home page*, or *Home page*—not italicized); the sponsor of the site (academic department and institution); dates of the course or last update to the page; the medium; and date of access. For an academic department, list the name of the department; a description; the academic institution; the date the page was last updated (use *n.d.* for no date, not italicized); the medium (*Web*); and the date of access.

Dept. of English. Home page. Amherst Coll., n.d. Web. 5 Apr. 2007.

Lunsford, Andrea A. Home page. Stanford U, 27 Mar. 2003. Web. 10 Sept. 2011.

Lunsford, Andrea A. *Memory and Media*. Course home page. Dept. of English, Stanford U, Sept.-Dec. 2002. Web. 13 Mar. 2006.

### 33. Online Book

Cite an online book as you would a print book. After the print publication information (if any), give the title of the Web site or database in which the book appears, italicized; the medium (*Web*); and the date of access.

Riis, Jacob A. *How the Other Half Lives: Studies among the Tenements of New York*. Ed. David Phillips. New York: Scribner's, 1890. *The Authentic History Center*. Web. 26 Mar. 2009.

Treat a poem, essay, or other short work within an online book as you would a part of a print book. After the print publication information (if any), give the title of the Web site or database, italicized; the medium (*Web*); and the date of access.

Dickinson, Emily. "The Grass." *Poems: Emily Dickinson*. Boston: Roberts Brothers, 1891. *Humanities Text Initiative American Verse Project*. Web. 6 Jan. 2008.

### 34. Article in an Online Journal

For an article in an online journal, cite the same information that you would for a print journal. If the online article does not have page numbers, use *n. pag.* (not italicized). Then add the medium consulted (*Web*) and the date of access.

Edwards, Chris. "A Wealth of Opportunity: An Undergraduate Consultant's Look into the Benefits of Working at a Writing Center." *Praxis: A Writing Center Journal* 7.2 (2010): n. pag. Web. 28 May 2011.

### 35. Article in an Online Magazine or Newspaper

For an article in an online magazine or newspaper, cite the author; the title of the article, in quotation marks; the name of the magazine or newspaper, italicized; the sponsor of the Web site; the date of publication; the medium (*Web*); and the date you accessed the article.

Broad, William J. "In Ancient Fossils, Seeds of a New Debate on Warming." *New York Times*. New York Times, 7 Nov. 2006. Web. 12 Jan. 2009.

McIntosh, Jill. "First Drive: 2013 Audi Q5 Hybrid." *Canadian Driver*. CanadianDriver Communications, 20 June 2011. Web. 15 Aug. 2011.

#### 36. Posting to a Discussion Group

Begin with the author's name; the title of the posting, in quotation marks (if there is no title, use the description *Online posting*, not italicized); the name of the Web site, italicized; the sponsor or publisher of the site (use *N.p.*, not italicized, if there is no sponsor); the date of the posting; the medium; and the date of access.

Kent, Robert. "Computers Legalized, Net Still Banned for Cubans." *Freenet Chat*. The Free Network Project, 5 May 2008. Web. 15 Nov. 2008.

#### 37. Work from an Online Database or a Subscription Service

For a work from an online database, list the author's name; the title of the work, in quotation marks; any print publication information; the name of the database, italicized; the medium consulted (*Web*); and the date of access.

"Bolivia: Elecciones Presidenciales de 2002." *Political Database of the Americas*. Web. 12 Nov. 2006.

Penn, Sean, and Jon Krakauer. "*Into the Wild* Script." *Internet Movie Script Database*. Web. 12 June 2011.

For a work from an online service to which your library subscribes, include the same information as for an online database. After the information about the work, give the name of the database, italicized; the medium; and the date you accessed the work.

"Breaking the Dieting Habit: Drug Therapy for Eating Disorders." *Psychology Today* Mar. 1995: 12+. *ProQuest*. Web. 30 Nov. 2010.

If you're citing an article from a subscription service to which you subscribe (such as AOL), use the following model:

Weeks, W. William. "Beyond the Ark." *Nature Conservancy* Mar.-Apr. 1999. *America Online*. Web. 30 Nov. 2008.

### 38. Email Message

Include the writer's name; the subject line, in quotation marks; *Message to [recipient's name]* (not italicized); the date of the message; and the medium of delivery (*E-mail*). (Note that MLA style is to hyphenate *e-mail*.)

Moller, Marilyn. "Seeing Crowns." Message to Beverly Moss. 3 Jan. 2003. E-mail.

### 39. Computer Software or Video Game

Include the title, italicized; the version number (if given); publication information; and the medium. If you are citing material downloaded from a Web site, include the title and version number (if given), but instead of publication information, add the publisher or sponsor of the Web site; the date; the medium (*Web*); and the date of access.

*The Sims* 3. Vers. 1.24. Redwood City: Electronic Arts, 2009. CD-ROM.

*Web Cache Illuminator*. Vers. 4.02. NorthStar Solutions, n.d. Web. 12 Nov. 2007.

### 40. CD-ROM, Diskette, or Magnetic Tape, Single Issue

McPherson, James M., ed. *The American Heritage New History of the Civil War*. New York: Viking, 1996. CD-ROM.

### 41. Periodically Revised CD-ROM

Include the author's name; publication information for the print version of the text (including its title and date of publication); the medium (CD-ROM); the title of the database (italicized); the name of the company producing it; and the publication date of the database (month and year, if possible).

Heyman, Steven. "The Dangerously Exciting Client." *Psychotherapy Patient* 9.1 (1994): 37-46. CD-ROM. *PsycLIT*. SilverPlatter. Nov. 2006.

### 42. Multidisc CD-ROM

*The 1998 Grolier Multimedia Encyclopedia*. Danbury: Grolier Interactive, 1998. CD-ROM. 2 discs.

## OTHER SOURCES (INCLUDING ONLINE VERSIONS)

### 43. Unpublished Dissertation

Fishman, Jenn. "'The Active Republic of Literature': Performance and Literary Culture in Britain, 1656–1790." Diss. Stanford U, 2003. Print.

### 44. Published Dissertation

Baum, Bernard. *Decentralization of Authority in a Bureaucracy*. Diss. U of Chicago, 1959. Englewood Cliffs: Prentice, 1961. Print.

### 45. Article from a Microform

Sharpe, Lora. "A Quilter's Tribute." *Boston Globe* 25 Mar. 1989: 13. Microform. *NewsBank*: Social Relations 12 (1989): fiche 6, grids B4-6.

### 46. Personal, Published, or Broadcast Interview

For a personal interview, list the name of the person interviewed, the label *Personal interview* (not italicized), and the date of the interview.

Mullin, Joan. Personal interview. 2 Sept. 2010.

For a published interview, list the name of the person interviewed and the title (if any), or if there is no title, use the label *Interview by [interviewer's name]* (not italicized); then add the publication information, including the medium.

Marshall, Andrew. "The Marshall Plan." Interview by Douglas McGray. *Wired*. CondéNet, Feb. 2003. Web. 17 Mar. 2010.

Taylor, Max. "Max Taylor on Winning." *Time* 13 Nov. 2000: 66. Print.

For a broadcast interview, list the name of the person interviewed, and the label *Interview* (not italicized), and the name of the interviewer (if relevant); then list information about the program, the date of the interview, and the medium.

Fairey, Shepard. "Spreading the Hope: Street Artist Shepard Fairey." Interview by Terry Gross. *Fresh Air*. Natl. Public Radio. WBUR, Boston. 20 Jan. 2009. Radio.

If you listened to an archived version online, after the site's sponsor (if known), add the interview date, medium (*Web*), and date of access.

Fairey, Shepard. "Spreading the Hope: Street Artist Shepard Fairey." Interview by Terry Gross. *Fresh Air*. Natl. Public Radio. 20 Jan. 2009. Web. 13 Feb. 2009.

### 47. Letter

Treat a published letter like a work in an anthology, but include the date of the letter.

Jacobs, Harriet. "To Amy Post." 4 Apr. 1853. *Incidents in the Life of a Slave Girl*. Ed. Jean Fagan Yellin. Cambridge: Harvard UP, 1987. 234-35. Print.

**48. Film**

Jenkins, Tamara, dir. *The Savages*. Perf. Laura Linney and Philip Seymour Hoffman. 2007. Fox Searchlight. Web. 4 Mar. 2008.

*The Lord of the Rings: The Return of the King*. Dir. Peter Jackson. Perf. Elijah Wood, Ian McKellen. New Line Cinema, 2003. Film.

**49. Television or Radio Program**

"Baelor." *Game of Thrones*. Dir. Alan Taylor. Writ. David Benioff and D. B. Weiss. Perf. Sean Bean, Emilia Clarke, and Kit Harington. HBO. 9 June 2011. Television.

Schorr, Daniel. "Week in Review with Daniel Schorr." *Weekend Edition*. Natl. Public Radio. KQED, San Francisco. 20 Dec. 2008. Radio.

**50. Sound Recording**

Black Rebel Motorcycle Club. "Howl." *Howl*. RCA Records, 2005. CD.

Brandon Flowers. "Crossfire." *Flamingo*. Island, 2010. MP3.

**51. Work of Art or Photograph**

List the artist or photographer; the work's title, italicized; the date of composition (if unknown, use *n.d.*); and the medium of composition (*Oil on canvas*, *Bronze*, *Photograph*, etc.). Then cite the name of the museum or other location and the city.

Ulmann, Doris. *Man Leaning against a Wall*. 1930. Photograph. Smithsonian American Art Museum, Washington, DC.

To cite a reproduction in a book, add the publication information.

*General William Palmer in Old Age*. 1810. Oil on canvas. National Army Museum, London. *White Mughals: Love and Betrayal in Eighteenth-Century India*. William Dalrymple. New York: Penguin, 2002. 270. Print.

To cite artwork found online, omit the medium of composition, and after the location add the title of the database or Web site, italicized; the medium consulted (*Web*); and the date of access.

Chagall, Marc. *The Poet with the Birds*. 1911. Minneapolis Inst. of Arts. *Artsmia .org*. Web. 6 Oct. 2003.

**52. Lecture or Speech**

Jobs, Steve. Baccalaureate Address. Stanford University, Stanford, CA. 18 June 2005. Address.

### 53. Performance

*Anything Goes*. By Cole Porter. Perf. Klea Blackhurst. Shubert Theatre, New Haven. 7 Oct. 2003. Performance.

### 54. Map or Chart

*World Political Map (Classic)*. Washington: Natl. Geographic, 2007. Print.

### 55. Cartoon

Ramirez, Michael. "The Phoenix." Cartoon. *Investors.com*. Investor's Business Daily. 10 Sept. 2011. Web. 11 Sept. 2011.

### 56. Advertisement

Banana Republic. Advertisement. *Wired* Sept. 2009: 13. Print.

On p. 463, note the formatting of the first page of a sample essay written in MLA style. On p. 464, you'll find a sample works cited page written for the same student essay.

## Sample First Page for an Essay in MLA Style

Lesk 1

Emily Lesk

Professor Arraéz

Electric Rhetoric

15 November 2008

Red, White, and Everywhere

America, I have a confession to make: I don't drink Coke. But don't call me a hypocrite just because I am still the proud owner of a bright red shirt that advertises it. Just call me an American. Even before setting foot in Israel three years ago, I knew exactly where I could find one. The tiny T-shirt shop in the central block of Jerusalem's Ben Yehuda Street did offer other designs, but the one with a bright white "Drink Coca-Cola Classic" written in Hebrew cursive across the chest was what drew in most of the dollar-carrying tourists. While waiting almost twenty minutes for my shirt (depicted in Fig. 1), I watched nearly every customer ahead of me ask for "the Coke shirt, *todah rabah* [thank you very much]."

Fig. 1. *Hebrew Coca-Cola T-shirt*. Personal photograph. Despite my dislike for the beverage, I bought this Coca-Cola T-shirt in Israel.

At the time, I never thought it strange that I wanted one, too. After having absorbed sixteen years of Coca-Cola propaganda through everything from NBC's Saturday morning cartoon lineup to the concession stand at Camden Yards (the Baltimore Orioles' ballpark), I associated the shirt with singing along to the "Just for the Taste of It" jingle and with America's favorite pastime, not with a brown fizzy beverage I refused to consume.

## Sample List of Works Cited for an Essay in MLA Style

Lesk 7

Works Cited

Coca-Cola Santa pin. Personal photograph by the author. 9 Nov. 2008.

"The Fabulous Fifties." *Beverage Industry* 87.6 (1996): 16. *General OneFile*. Web. 2 Nov. 2008.

"Fifty Years of Coca-Cola Television Advertisements." *American Memory*. Motion Picture, Broadcasting and Recorded Sound Division, Lib. of Cong. 29 Nov. 2000. Web. 5 Nov. 2008.

"Haddon Sundblom and Coca-Cola." *Thehistoryofchristmas.com*. 10 Holidays, 2004. Web. 2 Nov. 2008.

Hebrew Coca-Cola T-shirt. Personal photograph by the author. 8 Nov. 2008.

Ikuta, Yasutoshi, ed. *'50s American Magazine Ads*. Tokyo: Graphic-Sha, 1987. Print.

Pendergrast, Mark. *For God, Country, and Coca-Cola: The Definitive History of the Great American Soft Drink and the Company That Makes It*. 2nd ed. New York: Basic, 2000. Print.

## APA Style

*The Publication Manual of the American Psychological Association* (6th edition, 2010) provides comprehensive advice to student and professional writers in the social sciences. Here we draw on the *Publication Manual*'s guidelines to provide an overview of APA style for in-text citations, content notes, and entries in the list of references.

### In-Text Citations

APA style calls for in-text citations in the body of an argument to document sources of quotations, paraphrases, summaries, and so on. These in-text citations correspond to full bibliographic entries in the list of references at the end of the text.

#### 1. Author Named in a Signal Phrase

Generally, use the author's name in a signal phrase to introduce the cited material, and place the date, in parentheses, immediately after the author's name. For a quotation, the page number, preceded by *p.* (neither underlined nor italicized), appears in parentheses after the quotation. For electronic texts or other works without page numbers, paragraph numbers may be used instead, preceded by the abbreviation *para.* For a long, set-off quotation, position the page reference in parentheses one space after the punctuation at the end of the quotation.

> According to Brandon (1993), Adefunmi opposed all forms of racism and believed that black nationalism should not be a destructive force.

> As Johnson (2005) demonstrated, contemporary television dramas such as *ER* and *Lost* are not only more complex than earlier programs but "possess a quality that can only be described as subtlety and discretion" (p. 83).

#### 2. Author Named in Parentheses

When you don't mention the author in a signal phrase, give the name and the date, separated by a comma, in parentheses at the end of the cited material.

> *The Sopranos* has achieved a much wider viewing audience than ever expected, spawning a cookbook and several serious scholarly studies (Franklin, 2002).

### 3. Two Authors

Use both names in all citations. Use *and* in a signal phrase, but use an ampersand (&) in parentheses.

> Associated with purity and wisdom, Obatala is the creator of human beings, whom he is said to have formed out of clay (Edwards & Mason, 1985).

### 4. Three to Five Authors

List all the authors' names for the first reference. In subsequent references, use just the first author's name followed by *et al.* (in regular type, not underlined or italicized).

> Lenhoff, Wang, Greenberg, and Bellugi (1997) cited tests that indicate that segments of the left brain hemisphere are not affected by Williams syndrome whereas the right hemisphere is significantly affected.

> Shackelford (1999) drew on the study by Lenhoff et al. (1997).

### 5. Six or More Authors

Use only the first author's name and *et al.* (in regular type, not underlined or italicized) in every citation, including the first.

> As Flower et al. (2003) demonstrated, reading and writing involve both cognitive and social processes.

### 6. Organization as Author

If the name of an organization or a corporation is long, spell it out the first time, followed by an abbreviation in brackets. In later citations, use the abbreviation only.

| | |
|---|---|
| **First Citation** | (Federal Bureau of Investigation [FBI], 2002) |
| **Subsequent Citations** | (FBI, 2002) |

### 7. Unknown Author

Use the title or its first few words in a signal phrase or in parentheses (in the example below, a book's title is italicized).

> The school profiles for the county substantiate this trend (*Guide to secondary schools*, 2003).

#### 8. Authors with the Same Last Name

If your list of references includes works by different authors with the same last name, include the authors' initials in each citation.

G. Jones (1998) conducted the groundbreaking study of retroviruses, whereas P. Jones (2000) replicated the initial trials two years later.

#### 9. Two or More Sources in the Same Citation

List sources by the same author chronologically by publication year. List sources by different authors in alphabetical order by the authors' last names, separated by semicolons.

While traditional forms of argument are warlike and agonistic, alternative models do exist (Foss & Foss, 1997; Makau, 1999).

#### 10. Specific Parts of a Source

Use abbreviations (*p.*, *pt.*, and so on) in a parenthetical citation to name the part of a work you're citing. However, *chapter* is not abbreviated.

Pinker (2003, p. 6) argued that his research yielded the opposite results.

Pinker (2003, Chapter 6) argued that his research yielded the opposite results.

#### 11. Online Document

To cite a source found on the Internet, use the author's name and date as you would for a print source, and indicate the chapter or figure of the document, as appropriate. If the source's publication date is unknown, use *n.d.* ("no date"). To document a quotation, include paragraph numbers if page numbers are unavailable. If an online document has no page or paragraph numbers, provide the heading of the section and the number of the paragraph that follows.

Werbach argued convincingly that "despite the best efforts of legislators, lawyers, and computer programmers, spam has won. Spam is killing email" (2002, p. 1).

#### 12. Email and Other Personal Communication

Cite any personal letters, email messages, electronic postings, telephone conversations, or personal interviews by giving the person's initial(s) and last name, the identification, and the date. Do not list email in the references list, and note that APA style uses a hyphen in the word *e-mail.*

E. Ashdown (personal communication, March 9, 2003) supported these claims.

## Content Notes

The APA recommends using content notes for material that will expand or supplement your argument but otherwise would interrupt the text. Indicate such notes in your text by inserting superscript numerals. Type the notes themselves on a separate page headed *Footnotes* (not underlined, italicized, or in quotation marks), centered at the top of the page. Double-space all entries. Indent the first line of each note five to seven spaces, and begin subsequent lines at the left margin.

#### TEXT WITH SUPERSCRIPT INDICATING A NOTE

Data related to children's preferences in books were instrumental in designing the questionnaire.[1]

#### NOTE

[1]Rudine Sims Bishop and members of the Reading Readiness Research Group provided helpful data.

## List of References

The alphabetical list of sources cited in your text is called *References*. (If your instructor asks you to list everything you've read as background—not just the sources you cite—call the list *Bibliography*.) The list of references appears on a separate page or pages at the end of your paper, with the heading *References* (not underlined, italicized, or in quotation marks) centered one inch from the top of the page. Double-space after the heading, and begin your first entry. Double-space the entire list. For print sources, APA style specifies the treatment and placement of four basic elements—author, publication date, title, and publication information. Each element is followed by a period.

- **Author:** List all authors with last name first, and use only initials for first and middle names. Separate the names of multiple authors with commas, and use an ampersand (&) before the last author's name.
- **Publication date:** Enclose the publication date in parentheses. Use only the year for books and journals; use the year, a comma, and the month or month and day for magazines and newspapers. Do not abbreviate the month. If a date is not given, put *n.d.* ("no date," not italicized) in the parentheses. Put a period after the parentheses.

- **Title:** Italicize titles and subtitles of books and periodicals. Do not enclose titles of articles in quotation marks. For books and articles, capitalize only the first word of the title and subtitle and any proper nouns or proper adjectives; also capitalize the first word following a colon. Capitalize all major words in the title of a periodical.
- **Publication information:** For a book published in the United States, list the city of publication and state abbreviation. For books published outside the United States, identify city and country. Provide the publisher's name, dropping *Inc.*, *Co.*, or *Publishers*. If the state is already included within the publisher's name, do not include the postal abbreviation for the state. For a periodical, follow the periodical title with a comma, the volume number (italicized), the issue number (if provided) in parentheses and followed by a comma, and the inclusive page numbers of the article. For newspaper articles and for articles or chapters in books, include the abbreviation *p.* ("page") or *pp.* ("pages").

The following APA style examples appear in a "hanging indent" format, in which the first line aligns on the left and the subsequent lines indent one-half inch or five spaces.

## BOOKS

### 1. One Author

Jones, L. H. (2004). *William Clark and the shaping of the West*. New York, NY: Hill and Wang.

### 2. Two or More Authors

Steininger, M., Newell, J. D., & Garcia, L. (1984). *Ethical issues in psychology*. Homewood, IL: Dow Jones-Irwin.

### 3. Organization as Author

Use the word *Author* (neither underlined nor italicized) as the publisher when the organization is both the author and the publisher.

Linguistics Society of America. (2002). *Guidelines for using sign language interpreters*. Washington, DC: Author.

### 4. Unknown Author

*National Geographic atlas of the world.* (2004). Washington, DC: National Geographic Society.

#### 5. Book Prepared by an Editor

Hardy, H. H. (Ed.). (1998). *The proper study of mankind*. New York, NY: Farrar, Straus.

#### 6. Selection in a Book with an Editor

Villanueva, V. (1999). An introduction to social scientific discussions on class. In A. Shepard, J. McMillan, & G. Tate (Eds.), *Coming to class: Pedagogy and the social class of teachers* (pp. 262-277). Portsmouth, NH: Heinemann.

#### 7. Translation

Perez-Reverte, A. (2002). *The nautical chart* (M. S. Peaden, Trans.). New York, NY: Harvest. (Original work published 2000)

#### 8. Edition Other Than the First

Wrightsman, L. (1998). *Psychology and the legal system* (3rd ed.). Newbury Park, CA: Sage.

#### 9. One Volume of a Multivolume Work

Will, J. S. (1921). *Protestantism in France* (Vol. 2). Toronto, Canada: University of Toronto Press.

#### 10. Article in a Reference Work

Chernow, B., & Vattasi, G. (Eds.). (1993). Psychomimetic drug. In *The Columbia encyclopedia* (5th ed., p. 2238). New York, NY: Columbia University Press.

If no author is listed, begin with the title.

#### 11. Republication

Sharp, C. (1978). *History of Hartlepool.* Hartlepool, United Kingdom: Hartlepool Borough Council. (Original work published 1816)

#### 12. Government Document

U.S. Bureau of the Census. (2001). *Survey of women-owned business enterprises*. Washington, DC: Government Printing Office.

#### 13. Two or More Works by the Same Author

List the works in chronological order of publication. Repeat the author's name in each entry.

Rose, M. (1984). *Writer's block: The cognitive dimension*. Carbondale: Southern Illinois University Press.

Rose, M. (1995). *Possible lives: The promise of public education in America.* Boston, MA: Houghton Mifflin.

### PERIODICALS

#### 14. Article in a Journal Paginated by Volume

Bowen, L. M. (2011). Resisting age bias in digital literacy research. *College Composition and Communication, 62*, 586-607.

#### 15. Article in a Journal Paginated by Issue

Carr, S. (2002). The circulation of Blair's Lectures. *Rhetoric Society Quarterly, 32*(4), 75-104.

#### 16. Article in a Monthly Magazine

Baker, C. (2008, September). Master of the universe. *Wired, 16*(9), 134-141.

#### 17. Article in a Newspaper

Nagourney, A. (2002, December 16). Gore rules out running in '04. *The New York Times*, pp. A1, A8.

#### 18. Letter to the Editor or Editorial

Erbeta, R. (2008, December). Swiftboating George [Letter to the editor]. *Smithsonian, 39*(9), 10.

#### 19. Unsigned Article

Guidelines issued on assisted suicide. (1998, March 4). *The New York Times*, p. A15.

#### 20. Review

Avalona, A. (2008, August). [Review of the book *Weaving women's lives: Three generations in a Navajo family*, by L. Lamphere]. *New Mexico, 86*(8), 40.

#### 21. Published Interview

Shor, I. (1997). [Interview with A. Greenbaum]. *Writing on the Edge, 8*(2), 7-20.

#### 22. Two or More Works by the Same Author in the Same Year

List two or more works by the same author published in the same year alphabetically by title (excluding *A*, *An*, or *The*), and place lowercase letters (*a*, *b*, etc.) after the dates.

Murray, F. B. (1983a). Equilibration as cognitive conflict. *Developmental Review, 3*, 54-61.

Murray, F. B. (1983b). Learning and development through social interaction. In L. Liben (Ed.), *Piaget and the foundations of knowledge* (pp. 176-201). Hillsdale, NJ: Erlbaum.

### ELECTRONIC SOURCES

The following models are based on the *APA's Publication Manual* (6th edition). A change for handling electronic sources involves the use of a digital object identifier (DOI) when available (instead of a URL) to locate an electronic source. The DOI is a unique number assigned to an electronic text (article, book, or other item) and intended to give reliable access to it. A second change is that a date of retrieval is no longer necessary unless a source changes very frequently. The basic APA entry for most electronic sources should include the following elements:

- name of the author, editor, or compiler
- date of electronic publication or most recent update
- title of the work, document, or posting
- publication information, including the title, volume or issue number, and page numbers
- the DOI (digital object identifier) of the document, if one is available
- a URL, only if a DOI is not available, with no angle brackets and no closing punctuation.

#### 23. World Wide Web Site

To cite a whole site, give the address in a parenthetical reference. To cite a document from a Web site, include information as you would for a print document, followed by a note on its retrieval. Provide a date of retrieval only if the information is likely to change frequently.

American Psychological Association. (2000). DotComSense: Commonsense ways to protect your privacy and assess online mental health information. Retrieved from http://helping.apa.org/dotcomsense

Mullins, B. (1995). Introduction to Robert Hass. Readings in contemporary poetry at Dia Center for the Arts. Retrieved from http://www.diacenter.org/prg/poetry/95_96/intrhass.html

#### 24. Article from an Online Periodical

For an article you read online, provide either a DOI or the URL of the periodical's home page preceded by *Retrieved from*.

Lambert, N. M., Graham, S. M., & Fincham, F. D. (2009). A prototype analysis of gratitude: Varieties of gratitude experiences. *Personality and Social Psychology Bulletin, 35,* 1193-1207. doi:10.1177/0146167209338071

Palmer, K. S. (2000, September 12). In academia, males under a microscope. *The Washington Post*. Retrieved from http://www.washingtonpost.com

### 25. Article or Abstract from a Database

For an article you find on a database, provide a DOI if one is available. If the online article does not have a DOI, locate the homepage for the journal in which the article appears and provide that URL. You need not identify the database you have used.

Kennedy, C., & Covell, K. (2009). Violating the rights of the child through inadequate sexual health education. *International Journal of Children's Rights, 17*(1), 143-154. doi:10.1163/092755608X278939

Hayhoe, G. (2001). The long and winding road: Technology's future. *Technical Communication, 48*(2), 133-145. Retrieved from http://www.stc.org/pubs/techcommGeneral01.asp

### 26. Software or Computer Program

OSX Lion (Version 10.7) [Computer operating system]. (2011). Cupertino, CA: Apple, Inc.

### 27. Online Government Document

Cite an online government document as you would a printed government work, adding the date of access and the URL. If you don't find a date, use *n. d.*

Finn, J. D. (1998, April). *Class size and students at risk: What is known? What is next?* Retrieved from United States Department of Education website http://www.ed.gov/pubs/ClassSize/title.html

### 28. Posting to a Discussion Group

Include an online posting in the references list only if you're able to retrieve the message from a mailing list's archive. Provide the author's name; the date of posting, in parentheses; and the subject line from the posting. Include any information that further identifies the message in square brackets. For a listserv message, end with the retrieval statement, including the name of the list and the URL of the archived message.

Troike, R. C. (2001, June 21). Buttercups and primroses [Msg 8]. Message posted to the American Dialect Society's ADS-L electronic mailing list, archived at http://listserv.linguistlist.org/archives/ads-1.html

### 29. Newsgroup Posting

Include the author's name, the date and subject line of the posting, the access date, and the name of the newsgroup.

Wittenberg, E. (2001, July 11). Gender and the Internet [Msg 4]. Retrieved from news://comp.edu.composition

### 30. Email Message or Synchronous Communication

Because the APA stresses that any sources cited in your list of references must be retrievable by your readers, you shouldn't include entries for email messages or synchronous communications (MOOs, MUDs); instead, cite these sources in your text as forms of personal communication (see p. 467). And remember that you shouldn't quote from other people's email without asking their permission to do so.

## OTHER SOURCES

### 31. Technical or Research Reports and Working Papers

Kinley-Horn and Associates. (2011). *ADOT bicycle safety action plan* (Working Paper No. 3). Phoenix: Arizona Department of Transportation.

### 32. Unpublished Paper Presented at a Meeting or Symposium

Welch, K. (2002, March). *Electric rhetoric and screen literacy*. Paper presented at the meeting of the Conference on College Composition and Communication, Chicago.

### 33. Unpublished Dissertation

Seward, D. E. (2008). *Civil voice in Elizabethan parliamentary oratory: The rhetoric and composition of speeches delivered at Westminster in 1566* (Unpublished doctoral dissertation). University of Texas at Austin, Austin, TX.

### 34. Poster Session

Mensching, G. (2002, May). *A simple, effective one-shot for disinterested students*. Poster session presented at the National LOEX Library Instruction Conference, Ann Arbor, MI.

### 35. Motion Picture, Video, or DVD

Bigelow, K. (Director). (2009). *The hurt locker*. [Motion picture]. United States: Summit Entertainment.

### 36. Television Program, Single Episode

Imperioli, M. (Writer), & Buscemi, S. (Director). (2002, October 20). Everybody hurts [Television series episode]. In D. Chase (Executive producer), *The Sopranos*. New York, NY: Home Box Office.

### 37. Sound Recording

Begin with the writer's name, followed by the date of copyright. Give the recording date at the end of the entry (in parentheses, after the period) if it's different from the copyright date.

Ivey, A., Jr., & Sall, R. (1995). Rollin' with my homies [Recorded by Coolio]. On *Clueless* [CD]. Hollywood, CA: Capitol Records.

**RESPOND•**

1. The MLA and APA styles differ in several important ways, both for in-text citations and for lists of sources. You've probably noticed a few: the APA lowercases most words in titles and lists the publication date right after the author's name, whereas the MLA capitalizes most words and puts the publication date at the end of the works cited entry. More interesting than the details, though, is the reasoning behind the differences. Placing the publication date near the front of a citation, for instance, reveals a special concern for that information in the APA style. Similarly, the MLA's decision to capitalize titles isn't arbitrary: that style is preferred in the humanities for a reason. Working in a group, find as many consistent differences between the MLA and APA styles as you can. Then, for each difference, speculate about the reasons these groups organize or present information in that way. The MLA and APA style manuals themselves may be of help. You might also begin by determining which academic disciplines subscribe to the APA style and which to the MLA.
2. Working with another person in your class, look for examples of the following sources: an article in a journal, a book, a film, a song, and a TV show. Then make a references page or works cited entry for each one, using either MLA or APA style.

PART 5

# arguments

# 22 How Does Popular Culture Stereotype *You*?

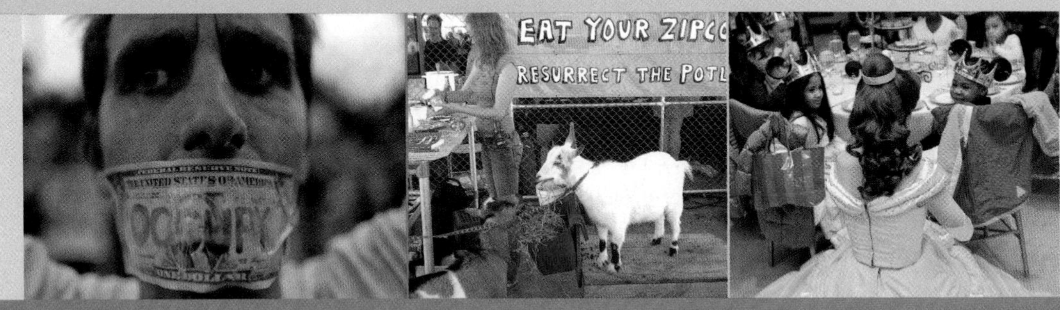


If you check the dictionary, you'll learn that the term *stereotype* originally referred to a printing plate cast in metal from the mold of a page of set type. English borrowed the word from French, but its parts are ultimately of Greek origin: *stereo* means "solid" or "three-dimensional," while *type* means "model." By extension, the word has come to mean a widely held image that is fixed and allows for little individuality among a group's members. Ironic, isn't it, that a term that originally referred to a three-dimensional printing plate has come to refer to a one-dimensional representation of an entire group?

The selections in this chapter focus on stereotyping in popular culture, including the media, challenging you to analyze what many would consider to be unsavory or unfair stereotypes of various groups found there. The chapter opens with two selections about stereotypes and little girls. A 2011 article about the "Disney Princess Effect" examines the ways that once little girls discover Disney Princesses, a line of dolls, their interests and their understanding of themselves often change in ways many parents and social scientists find troubling. The second selection takes a critical look at beauty pageants for little girls and the many, often contradictory messages they are sending.

Next come a pair of readings—an op-ed piece by syndicated columnist Ellen Goodman and an excerpt from a scholarly research article by Anne E. Becker—on a related topic. Both authors explore the arrival of American television in the South Pacific island of Fiji and its consequences for young Fijian women and their changing body image. Not only do these women now reject traditional local notions of beauty by striving to be thin, but they also have very particular reasons for doing so that are linked to images of women in American television programs. Goodman first learned about the research she writes about during an oral presentation by Becker at an academic conference; the excerpt of the research article we reprint here later appeared in print.

The next selection examines evictions at a sorority house at DePauw University. Many on campus, including some of the sorority's members, noticed that, interestingly, those who were evicted did not fit most Americans' stereotype of a sorority sister. Not surprisingly, a debate ensued about what had happened and why. It is followed by discussions of a long-unsettled debate in American society, whether or not Indian mascots are a good thing and why, and of a reality TV show about American Muslims that contains especially insightful observations about media and stereotypes.

The chapter's selection focusing on making a visual argument examines stereotypes that are simultaneously mocked and perpetuated in cartoons. As you study these cartoons carefully, give some thought to the ways that humorous arguments of the sorts used in cartoons permit our society to deal indirectly with certain controversial issues. You will likewise want to consider the stereotypes that don't show up in these cartoons, whether they are simply too potentially explosive or whether the editors may not have felt comfortable reproducing them for fear of unwanted controversy.

The preface to a book by Charles A. Riley II focuses passionately on how people with disabilities are—and aren't—represented in the media and popular culture. In addition to his take on these problems, we include a set of guidelines from the National Center on Disability and Journalism that offers advice about how media might do a better job than they currently do in this regard.

The following two selections remind us of the investment we all have in being able to put everyone we meet into boxes labeled MALE or FEMALE. Patricia J. Williams's column considers why there was such an uproar when the parents of newly born Storm Stocker refused to tell anyone other than Storm's siblings whether Storm is a girl or a boy. Jennifer Conlin examines the question of our investment in the gender binary as she documents the ways that some adolescents are now "choosing their pronouns," that is, making choices about how they represent themselves to others as they struggle—or play with—that binary.

Closing the chapter is the introduction to Claude M. Steele's important 2010 book *Whistling Vivaldi and Other Clues to How Stereotypes Affect Us*. Steele, a well-known psychologist, examines what researchers term "the stereotype threat," the way that our fear of being stereotyped often influences our actions.

Originally, stereotypes were part of a printer's trade, enabling the printer to disseminate information quickly and cheaply. No less a part of popular culture today, stereotypes of a different sort still disseminate information. You'll have to evaluate how much that information is worth.

For additional material related to this chapter, visit the e-Pages for *Everything's an Argument with Readings* online at **bedfordstmartins.com/everythingsanargument/epages**.

▼ *Stephanie Hanes, a freelance journalist, has written for a number of U.S. publications, including the* Christian Science Monitor, *where this article first appeared,* Smithsonian Magazine, *and* USA Today. *She also lived for four years in South Africa and continues to write frequently about topics related to southern Africa and areas in the developing world where there are crises of various sorts. In this cover story from the* Christian Science Monitor *published October 3, 2011, Hanes examines in some detail a trend that many find disturbing: the growing sexualization of very young girls. As you read, pay special attention to the kinds of evidence that Hanes uses to support her analysis and to the ways she uses statistics in particular. (By the way, if you're not already familiar with the Disney Princesses, take the time to Google the term; what you learn will be especially useful background as you read the article.)*

# Little Girls or Little Women? The Disney Princess Effect

STEPHANIE HANES

*In today's highly sexualized environment—where 5-year-olds wear padded bras—some see the toddlers-and-tiaras Disney Princess craze leading to the preteen pursuit of "hot" looks. Do little girls become little women too soon?*

*Mary Finucane and her daughter, dressed like a princess*

A few years ago, Mary Finucane started noticing changes in the way her 3-year-old daughter played. The toddler had stopped running and jumping, and insisted on wearing only dresses. She sat on the front step quietly—waiting, she said, for her prince. She seemed less imaginative, less spunky, less interested in the world.

Ms. Finucane believes the shift began when Caoimhe (pronounced Keeva) discovered the Disney Princesses, that omnipresent, pastel packaged franchise of slender-waisted fairy-tale heroines. When Finucane mentioned her suspicions to other parents, they mostly shrugged.

"Everyone seemed to think it was inevitable," Finucane says. "You know, it was Disney Princesses from [ages] 2 to 5, then Hannah Montana, then

*High School Musical*. I thought it was so strange that these were the new trajectories of female childhood."

She decided to research the princess phenomenon, and what she found worried her. She came to believe that the $4 billion Disney Princess empire was the first step down a path to scarier challenges, from self-objectification° to cyberbullying to unhealthy body images. Finucane, who has a background in play therapy, started a blog—"Disney Princess Recovery: Bringing Sexy Back for a Full Refund"—to chronicle her efforts to break the grip of Cinderella, Belle, Ariel, et al. on her household.

5 Within months she had thousands of followers.

"It was validating, in a sense, that a lot of parents were experiencing it," she says. "It was this big force entering our lives so early, with such strength. It concerned me for what was down the road."

Finucane's theory about Disney Princesses is by no means universal. Many parents and commentators defend Happily Ever After against what some critics call a rising "feminist attack," and credit the comely ladies with teaching values such as kindness, reading, love of animals, and perseverance.

If there's any doubt of the controversy surrounding the subject, journalist Peggy Orenstein mined a whole book (*Cinderella Ate My Daughter*) out of the firestorm she sparked in 2006 with a *New York Times* essay ("What's Wrong With Cinderella?").

Disney, for its part, repeated to the *Monitor* its standard statement on the topic: "For 75 years, millions of little girls and their parents around the world have adored and embraced the diverse characters and rich stories featuring our Disney princesses. . . . [L]ittle girls experience the fantasy and imagination provided by these stories as a normal part of their childhood development."

10 And yet, the Finucane and Orenstein critique does resonate with many familiar with modern American girlhood as "hot" replaces pretty in pink, and getting the prince takes on a more ominous tone. Parents and educators regularly tell researchers that they are unable to control the growing onslaught of social messages shaping their daughters and students.

"Parents are having a really hard time dealing with it," says Diane Levin, an early childhood specialist at Wheelock College in Boston who recently co-wrote the book *So Sexy So Soon*. "They say that things they used to do aren't working; they say they're losing control of what happens to their girls at younger and younger ages."

It only takes a glance at some recent studies to understand why parents are uneasy:

- A University of Central Florida poll found that 50 percent of 3- to 6-year-old girls worry that they are fat.
- One-quarter of 14- to 17-year-olds of both sexes polled by The Associated Press and MTV in 2009 reported either sending naked pictures of themselves or receiving naked pictures of someone else.
- The marketing group NPD Fashionworld reported in 2003 that more than $1.6 million is spent annually on thong underwear for 7- to 12-year-olds.
- Children often come across Internet pornography unintentionally: University of New Hampshire researchers found in 2005 that one-third of Internet users ages 10 to 17 were exposed to unwanted sexual material, and a London School of Economics study in 2004 found that 60 percent of children who use the Internet regularly come into contact with pornography.

And on, and on. It's enough, really, to alarm the most relaxed parent.

But as Professor Levin, Finucane, and Orenstein show, there is another trend today, too—one that gets far less press, but is much more hopeful.

Trying to make a safer, healthier environment for girls, an ever-stronger group of educators, parents, institutions, and girls themselves are pushing back against growing

***self-objectification:*** turning one's self into an object, seeing oneself through the eyes of others.

*More and more girls begin wearing eye makeup early in life.*

marketing pressure, new cyberchallenges, and sexualization, which the American Psychological Association (APA) defines in part as the inappropriate imposition of sexuality on children.

Many are trying to intervene when 15
girls are younger, like Finucane, who doesn't advocate banning the princesses but taking on the ways that they narrow girls' play (advocating more color choices, suggesting alternative story plotlines). Some tap into the insight and abilities of older girls—with mentoring, for example. Still others take their concerns into the public sphere, lobbying politicians and executives for systemic change such as restricting sexualized advertising targeting girls.

Together, they offer some insights for how, as Finucane says, to bring sexy back for a refund.

## Soccer Heading Makes a Bad Hair Day

The first step, some say, is to understand why any of this matters.

By many measures, girls are not doing badly. According to the Washington-based Center on Education Policy, high school girls perform as well as boys on math and science tests and do better than their male peers in reading. Three women now graduate from college for every 2 men. Far more women play sports, which is linked to better body image, lower teen pregnancy rates, and higher scholastic performance.

And opportunities for girls today are much broader than 50 years ago when, for example, schools didn't even allow girls to wear pants or to raise and lower the flag, notes Stephanie Coontz, co-chair of the nonprofit Council on Contemporary Families. "It is important to keep all of this in perspective," she says.

Still, there are signs of erosion of 20
the progress in gender equity. Take athletics.

"Girls are participating in sports at a much increased level in grade school," says Sharon Lamb, a professor of education and mental health at the University of Massachusetts, Boston. But, she adds, they start to drop out of sports at the middle school level when they start to believe that sports are unfeminine and unsexy.

The Women's Sports Foundation found that 6 girls drop out of sports for every 1 boy by the end of high school, and a recent Girl Scout study found that 23 percent of girls between the ages of 11 and 17 do not play sports because they do not think their bodies look good doing so.

And looking good, Ms. Lamb says, is increasingly tied to what it means to play. Star female athletes regularly pose

---

***second-wave feminist:*** feminism associated with the period from the 1960s until the early 1990s in contrast to first-wave feminism (nineteenth and early twentieth century), which focused on getting the vote for women, or third-wave feminism (feminism since the mid-1980s), which is much more international and much more concerned with the diversity of experiences among women from different backgrounds within a society.

naked or seminaked for men's magazines; girls see cheerleaders (with increasingly sexualized routines) on TV far more than they see female basketball players or other athletes.

The effects are felt in academia as well. Earlier this year, a Princeton University study found a growing leadership gap among male and female undergraduates. Nannerl Keohane, who chaired the Princeton steering committee, wrote in an e-mail interview that "the climate was different in the late 1990s and the past decade." And she linked the findings to shifts in popular culture such as "the receding of second-wave feminist° excitement and commitment, a backlash in some quarters, a reorientation of young women's expectations based on what they had seen of their mothers' generation, a profound reorientation of popular culture which now glorifies sexy babes consistently, rather than sometimes showing an accomplished woman without foregrounding her sexuality."

*Girls' shoes increasingly resemble those worn by adult women.*

25 This "sexy babes" trend is a big one.

"For young women, what has replaced the feminine mystique is the hottie mystique," Ms. Coontz says. "Girls no longer feel that there is anything they must not do or cannot do because they're female, but they hold increasingly strong beliefs that if you are going to attempt these other things, you need to look and be sexually hot."

In television shows, for instance, women are represented in far more diverse roles—they are lawyers, doctors, politicians. But they are always sexy. A woman might run for high political office, but there is almost always analysis about whether she is sexy, too.

In 2010, the APA released a report on the sexualization of girls, which it described as portraying a girl's value as coming primarily from her sexual appeal. It found increased sexualization in magazines, by marketers, in music lyrics, and on television—a phenomenon that includes "harm to the sexualized individuals themselves, to their interpersonal relationships, and to society."

Sexualization, it reported, leads to lower cognitive performance and greater body dissatisfaction. One study cited by the report, for instance, compared the ability of college-age women to solve math problems while trying on a sweater (alone in a dressing room) with that of those trying on swimsuits. Sweater wearers far outperformed the scantily dressed.

30 Research also connects sexualization to eating disorders, depression, and physical health problems. Even those young women—and experts say there are growing numbers of them—who claim that it is empowering to be a sex object often suffer the ill effects of sexualization.

"The sexualization of girls may not only reflect sexist attitudes, a society tolerant of sexual violence, and the exploitation of girls and women but may also contribute to these phenomena," the APA said.

Objectifying women is not new, of course.

"What's different is just the sheer amount of messaging that girls are getting, and the effective way that these images are used to market to younger and younger girls," says Lyn Mikel Brown, an education professor at Colby College in Waterville, Maine. "They're getting it relentlessly. And in this busy world it's somehow harder for parents to stop and question it. It's like fish in water—it's the water. It's in the air. It's easy for it to get by us."

### Help Girls to See the Problem

So what to do? To start, girls can become media critics, says Professor Brown's high school–age daughter, Maya Brown. The younger Brown serves on the Girls' Advisory Board of Hardy Girls Healthy Women, an organization based in Maine that develops girl-friendly school curricula and runs a variety of programs for girls.

"There are so many images of girls, and they are always objectifying—it's hard to make that go away," Maya says. "What you really need is for the girls to be able to see it."

She knows this firsthand. Her mother would regularly pause television shows or movies to talk about female stereotypes; when she read to Maya, she would often change the plotlines to make the female characters more important. (It was only when Maya got older that she realized that Harry Potter was far more active than Hermione.)

"It would get kind of annoying," Maya, now 16, says with a laugh. "When we were watching a movie and she'd pause it and say, 'You know, this isn't a good representation,' I'd be like, 'Yeah, yeah, yeah, I caught that. Can we watch our show now?'"

Professor Brown had many opportunities to intervene. According to the Kaiser Family Foundation, the percentage of television shows with sexual content—from characters talking about their sexual exploits to actual intercourse—increased from 54 percent in 1998 to 70 percent in 2005.

In her book, Levin says that the numbers would be even higher if advertisements were included. And reality television, which has ballooned during the past decade, is particularly sexualizing. Scholars point out that the most popular reality shows either have harem-style plots, with many women competing to please one man, or physical-improvement goals.

Young girls get similarly sexualizing messages in their own movies and television shows. The Geena Davis Institute on Gender and Media found recently that fewer than 1 in 3 speaking characters (animal or human) in G-rated family films are female, and even animated female characters tend to wear sexualized attire: Disney's Jasmine, for instance, has a sultry off-the-shoulder look, while even Miss Piggy shows cleavage.

Given this backdrop, many child development experts say the best way to handle the media onslaught for younger girls is for parents to simply opt out.

The American Academy of Pediatrics recommends no screen time—television, movies, and Internet—for infants under 2 years of age; for older children, the AAP suggests only one to two hours a day. This would be a significant change for most American families. In 2003, the Kaiser Family Foundation found that 36 percent of children under 6 live in a house where the TV is on all or almost all of the time; 43 percent of children ages 4 to 6 have a TV in their bedroom. In 2010 the foundation reported that, on average, children ages 8 to 18 consume 10 hours, 45 minutes' worth of screen media content a day.

Even if parents limited TV and movies, though, the sexualization of women would still get through on the radio, in magazines at grocery store checkout lines, on billboards, and in schools, not to mention on the all-powerful Internet. Those images, as in television, have become far more sexualized.

In one recent study, University of Buffalo sociologists Erin Hatton and Mary Nell Trautne examined the covers of *Rolling Stone* magazine between 1967 and 2009. They found a "dramatic increase in hypersexualized° images of women," to the point that by 2009, nearly every woman to grace the magazine's cover was conveyed in a blatantly sexual way, as compared with 17 percent of the men. (Examples include a tousled-haired Jennifer Aniston lying naked on a bed, or a topless Janet Jackson with an unseen man's hands covering her breasts.)

With no way to get away from the sexualized images, Maya says, it's better to recognize and co-opt them.

She and other young women helped develop the website powered bygirl.org on which girls blog, comment, and share ideas about female sexualization in the media. The site includes an app that lets users graffiti advertisements and then post the altered images—one recent post, for instance, takes a Zappos magazine advertisement showing a naked woman covered only by the caption "more than shoes!" and adds, "Yet no creativity" to the slogan.

"Once it's brought to light in a satirical way, it loses its power," says Jackie Dupont, the programs director at Hardy Girls Healthy Women. "The ridiculousness about what the advertisements are trying to say about women becomes more apparent."

### Sexy's Not about Sex, It's about Shopping

Media images, though, are only a part of the sexualization problem. More invasive, Levin and others say, is marketing.

Since the deregulation movement of the 1980s, the federal government has lost most oversight of advertising to children. This has encouraged marketers to become increasingly brazen, says Levin. Marketers are motivated to use the sexualization of women to attract little girls, or violence to attract little boys, because developmentally children are drawn to things they don't understand, or find unnerving, Levin says.

In this context, she says, sexy is not about sex, but about shopping. If girls can be convinced to equate "sexy" with popularity and girlness itself, and if "sexy" requires the right clothes, makeup, hairdo, accessories, and shoes, then marketers have a new bunch of consumers.

"Age compression," the phenomenon of younger children adopting patterns once reserved for older youths, helps with sales. If girls start wearing lip gloss when they are 6 years old (as almost half of them do, according to Experian Simmons national consumer research) and mascara when they are 8 (the percentage of 8- to 12-year-olds wearing mascara doubled between 2007 and 2009, to almost 1 in 5, according to market research from the NPD Group), then it's clearly better for cosmetic companies. This is also why, Levin speculates, thong underwear is now sold to 7-year-olds, and padded bras show up on the racks for 5-year-olds.

Meanwhile, there are deepening gender divisions in toys, clothing, and play activities. Orenstein explores in *Cinderella Ate My Daughter* how the color pink has become increasingly ubiquitous to the point where many young girls police each other with a pink radar—if that tricycle, for instance, isn't pink, well then, you shouldn't be riding it.

*A Disney Princess hosting a tea party*

Brown points out in her book that there is no pink equivalent for boys. Although the color blue, sports equipment, and fire engines grace much of their décor, boys still have far more options of how to define themselves.

"In unprecedented levels, girls are being presented with a very narrow image of girlhood," Brown says.

One of the best ways to keep girls from falling into rigid gender roles is to broaden their horizons.

"If we are bombarded with thousands of images a day that give the illusion of choice, but are in fact really simplistic and repetitive, it's important to not just say girls can do anything, but to give them the actual experience," said Ms. Dupont from Hardy Girls Healthy Women, where the Adventure Girls program for second- to sixth-graders connects girls with women who have excelled in nontraditional fields, from construction and rugby to chemistry and dog-sledding.

This is what Finucane tried to do with her daughter. She did not want to crush Caoimhe's fantasies, but she also wanted her to see more of the possibilities open to girls. So although Caoimhe wanted to read only Disney Princess books—titles such as *Cinderella: My Perfect Wedding*—Finucane insisted on sharing stories about Amelia Earhart° and other powerful women. She bought native American dress-up clothes and a Princess Presto outfit to go with the frothy pink Disney gowns.

### Trying to Stay One Step Ahead

Finucane says that Caoimhe, now 5, is pretty much free of the princess obsession. These days she is entranced

---

***hypersexualized:*** extremely or excessively sexualized.

***Amelia Earhart (1897–1937):*** famous American pilot and author who disappeared over the Pacific Ocean while trying to fly around the world. Earhart, the first woman to fly across the Atlantic, set a number of aviation records. She was also the first woman to receive the Distinguished Flying Cross.

by *James and the Giant Peach* and *The Wizard of Oz*.

"I try to stay maybe one step ahead," Finucane says. "The grip they had is lost. She's still into characters and theatrical production, but she no longer believes that you can't leap if you're a princess, or female."

60 Parents' involvement is key, Levin says, but they do not have to act alone. Over the past few years, a growing group of advocacy organizations have formed to help fight against marketing pressure and sexualization.

Levin and others have campaigned for new regulations on how advertisers can approach children; groups such as truechild.org and Campaign for a Commercial Free Childhood have also pushed for marketing restrictions and have held summits about countering the consumer culture and sexualization. The organization TRUCE—Teachers Resisting Unhealthy Children's Entertainment—publishes media and play guides in which they review toys, check marketers' claims, and recommend age-appropriate activities. Recently, actress Geena Davis joined Sen. Kay Hagan (D) of North Carolina and Rep. Tammy Baldwin (D) of Wisconsin to lobby for a bill that would support efforts to improve the image of women and girls in the media.

Girls themselves have joined different advocacy efforts, including organizing and participating in the SPARK (Sexualization Protest: Action, Resistance, Knowledge) Summit in New York City, a gathering of girls and adults who hold forums on media awareness, sexuality, and fighting stereotypes.

Schools can also share the burden. Catherine Steiner-Adair, a therapist and educational consultant, has worked with school systems across the country for 30 years to develop curriculum that will increase social and emotional intelligence among boys and girls. She says that programs where girls are encouraged to create and then delve into their own projects are often successful.

"Girls discover what it means to take their own interests seriously and to pursue them deeply and vigorously," she says. She says that schools that can start focusing on these issues earliest have the best success. In a four-year study published in 2007 by the Collaborative for Academic, Social, and Emotional Learning, researchers found that students who participate in these sorts of programs show more empathy, self-confidence, and more academic success than their peers without social-emotional curriculum.

65 "Given today's culture and the access people have and the lack of boundaries between home and school and between people and technology, you have to begin this work in first grade," she says. "The schools that are doing it in first grade are very different cultures—they're kinder, they're more respectful, they're less bullying."

### Girls Stuck in the Social-Feedback Loop

Ms. Steiner-Adair's point about technology is the elephant in the chat room.

In any conversation about the sexualization of girls, the Internet is always mentioned as a huge new challenge. Not only does the Web allow easy—and often unwanted—access to sexual images (in terms of numbers of websites and views, porn is king of the Web), it offers a social-feedback loop that is heavy on appearance and superficiality, and low on values that scholars say might undermine sexualization, such as intelligence and compassion.

Girls—and boys—encourage each other to embrace sexualization. Teens who post sexy pictures of themselves on Facebook, for instance, are rewarded with encouraging comments. Educator and author Rachel Simmons, who recently rereleased *Odd Girl Out*, her book about girl aggression, with new chapters on the Internet, tells of a 13-year-old who posted a photo of herself in tight leggings, her behind lifted toward the camera.

"She posts it on Facebook and gets 10 comments underneath it telling her how great her butt looks," Ms. Simmons says.

70 "Girls are using social media to get feedback in areas that they've been told by the culture that they need to express or work on. That's not girls being stupid. . . . Many girls post or send provocative images because they're growing up in a culture that places a lot of value in their sexuality."

The answer is not for parents to cancel the Wi-Fi, Simmons and others say. There are many ways that girls can use the Internet and social media for good. But the technology does require monitoring—and self-evaluation.

It's hard to criticize a girl for delving into social media, for instance, when her parents are constantly checking their own iPhones.

"We can't sit there and say, 'Oh, the kids are so messed up,'" she says. "We have to look at ourselves."

**RESPOND**

1. As Hanes represents the "Disney Princess Effect," what is it, and why does it matter? What other cultural trends is it related to? According to Hanes's characterization of the situation, who or what might be responsible for the increasing sexualization of little girls?
2. In its online form, the original article included a link to an online photo gallery: http://bit.ly/t8qkxP. Examine these photos and their captions. Do they merely illustrate the article, or are they providing particular kinds of support for the claims it makes? Which photo(s) and caption(s) do you find most effective? Why? (Chapter 14, which discusses visual arguments, may help you think systematically about these questions.)
3. Hanes uses statistics along with other kinds of evidence in interesting ways to support her claims. (Often arguments about this topic in the media rely primarily on personal experience or analyses of a few cases.) Find three or four statistics Hanes cites that gave you pause—that surprised you a bit—and be prepared to share these, to talk about your response, and to explain the value of using statistics effectively when discussing topics that are often discussed only in terms of personal experience.
4. Visit Mary Finucane's blog, "Disney Princess Recovery: The Aging 8-Year-Old": http://bit.ly/gIwa2H. Pay special attention to the "Welcome" information on the right-hand side of the page. How accurately has Hanes characterized and represented Finucane's stance or position toward sexualization? What evidence can you provide for your evaluation?
5. Another especially interesting aspect of this article is the process by which Hanes defines the notion *sexualization*. Rather than giving a single definition at the first mention of the term, she builds up a definition across the course of the article. Skim the article again, noting every place that she provides or more indirectly suggests a definition for *sexualization*. Once you have collected and listed these instances of definition, **write a formal definition** of the sort you might use in a paper on this topic. Then **create an operational definition** of the term. Finally, give a **definition by example**. (See Chapter 9 for information on kinds of definitions. To complete this assignment, you may decide that you need to consult other sources; if you do, be sure to credit them properly, using information provided in Chapter 21.)

*Skip Hollandsworth (1957– ) is the pen name of Walter Ned Hollandworth, an award-winning journalist who is currently one of the executive editors of the* Texas Monthly. *Born in North Carolina, Hollandsworth graduated from Texas Christian University, where he was a sportswriter for the school paper. Several of Hollandsworth's articles for the* Texas Monthly *have become the basis for television programs or movies. In this article, which first appeared in* Good Housekeeping, *in August 2011, he reports on child beauty pageants, which were originally especially popular in the South as well as California, but are apparently now as American as apple pie. As you read this article, consider how its subject relates to the previous selection by Stephanie Hanes, "Little Girls or Little Women? The Disney Princess Effect."*

# Toddlers in Tiaras

SKIP HOLLANDSWORTH

It's 6:30 on a Saturday morning at the Southfork Hotel in Plano, TX, just north of Dallas, and in Room 326, 6-year-old Eden Wood is perched on a stool, quietly staring at herself in a lighted mirror, waiting for the transformation to begin. First, a stylist applies layers of foundation, blush, eye shadow, mascara, lipliner, and hot-pink lipstick. Then she turns to Eden's hair—except it's not Eden's hair. A long blond fall, full of curly ringlets, is attached to the back of the little girl's head, and using a brush and curling iron, the stylist teases all the hair, real and synthetic, until it looks as if it's going to float away. Finally, she runs a cloth over Eden's already manicured fingernails and adds a touch of bronzer to her spray-tanned arms and legs.

"OK, sweet girl, let's get after it," declares Eden's mother, Mickie, a congenial, determined-looking 46-year-old who's wearing glasses with hot-pink frames and a matching pink coat over a black pantsuit. Eden jumps off the stool and steps into a $3,000 hand-sewn bubble gum–pink dress covered with sequins and edged with lace that billows out, tutu-like, just below her waist.

Mickie helps her put on white ankle socks and unblemished white patent leather Mary Janes. Finally, she snaps faux diamond earrings onto Eden's ears and fastens a glittery rhinestone necklace around her neck. After an hour and 30 minutes, her daughter has become part Barbie, part Madame Alexander° doll, and part Las Vegas showgirl.

Eden, who's from Taylor, AR, is about to participate with 90 or more other girls in a beauty pageant put on by Texas-based Universal Royalty Beauty Pageant, one of the country's best-known children's beauty pageant organizers. All around the conference room and adjoining hallways that serve as the pre-contest prep area, little girls do the pageant version of suiting up. Some are having fake eyelashes applied; others sit quietly as their parents insert dental prosthetics called "flippers" into their mouths to cover the gaps where baby teeth have fallen out. A few are already on the stage, doing one final run-through of the formal "beauty walks" that they will later perform, acts that require the girls to cross one foot over the other and slowly pivot in a semicircle while keeping their shoulders back and their eyes locked on the judges.

5 "Remember, honey, step, then turn, then give those judges a big wink," one mother says encouragingly, holding a brush in one hand and a mirror in the other. *"Your job is to make them love you."*

JonBenet Ramsey,° who would have turned 21 this month had she not been brutally murdered, remains the most famous pageant girl in the world. All one has to do is say her name and the images come flooding back—not those from photos of her home in Boulder, CO, where she was found in the basement on December 26, 1996, but those of the 6-year-old pixie strutting across pageant stages, looking like a baby Marilyn Monroe with makeup more suited to a woman several times her age.

Rayanna DeMatteo, a 22-year-old student at Samford University in Birmingham, AL, regularly competed at events with JonBenet. "I remember playing hide-and-seek with her," she says. "We used to jump into the hotel pools together after competition." DeMatteo remembers that increasingly, as she grew older, being part of the pageant world was something she wanted to hide. "I don't tell people my secret about what I did back in the day," she says. "I don't want people to know that I was a pageant girl."

Before JonBenet, most Americans didn't know such beauty pageants existed, and they were shocked at what they saw. Karen Steinhauser, Denver's chief deputy district attorney at the time, bluntly told reporters, "It's impossible to look at these photos and not see a terribly exploited little girl." *CBS Evening News* anchor Dan Rather° compared the video footage of JonBenet at pageants to "kiddie porn." Given the force of what, at the time, felt like national outrage, one would think that child pageants would have faded away. But, in fact, the opposite is true. Though beauty pageants for adult women seem to be disappearing from the landscape (even the Miss America pageant no longer draws respectable television ratings), kiddie pageants are flourishing. Fueled by a reality TV show, an estimated 250,000 American girls participate in more than 5,000 beauty pageants every year.

The promise of a tiara has always been a fast, easy sell to young girls who pine to be princesses—just ask

---

***Madame Alexander:*** a brand of collectible doll dating from the 1920s. Madame Alexander dolls have often been based on licensed characters from movies or novels or famous women, living or dead.

***JonBenet Ramsey (1990–1996):*** a six-year-old girl murdered on Christmas Day in her home under suspicious circumstances. The much-publicized case has never been solved. Part of its notoriety came from the fact that Ramsey was a frequent contestant in child beauty pageants.

***Dan Rather (1931– ):*** anchor for the *CBS Evening News* from 1981 to 2005. Rather also contributed to *60 Minutes*, and he now serves as anchor of *Dan Rather Reports* on HDNet. In an earlier era, when the evening news was a trusted source of information, Rather's comments carried great weight with many viewers.

Disney, which reportedly makes approximately $4 billion annually from its more than 26,000 princess-related retail items. The connection between princesses and pageants exploded in 1954 with the first televised broadcast of the Miss America pageant; 27 million viewers tuned in. Six years later, Miami played host to Little Miss Universe, the first official beauty pageant for children. Soon, kiddie pageants emerged all over the U.S., particularly in the South and in California. "It was the thing to do if you had a halfway cute kid," says Nicole Eggert, 39, who was crowned Miss Universe, Petite Division, in 1976, when she was 4. That pageant led to a lucrative shampoo commercial and the launch of a decades-long acting career. Eggert went on to starring roles in popular 1980s and 1990s television shows such as *Baywatch* and *Charles in Charge*. She remembers the child pageant world as decidedly low-key. "None of the kids had their hair done, no one had makeup on; no one had custom-made gowns—it was a party dress from a store," says Eggert. "I remember it being sort of a joke [that I won] because my mom had a hard time getting me to brush my hair."

10 Although some of today's contests are now promoted as "natural pageants," in which girls compete in off-the-rack togs and little or no makeup, it's the glitz pageants that remain the most popular. While prizes are relatively small, the investment can be enormous. Parents, many of whom have only modest incomes, pay for high-glitz coaches ($50 to $100 an hour), high-glitz photographers ($300 per session, with $150 for retouching), high-glitz wig makers ($150 to $175 a pop), and high-glitz spray tanners ($25 per pageant). One company goes so far as to offer parents a "breakthrough Pageant Preparation System" with this promise: "No more drives home with tears! No more disappointing pageants, missed opportunities, and humiliating moments."

"When we talk high-glitz, we mean the glitzier the better, and we make no apologies for it," says Universal Royalty Beauty Pageant owner Annette Hill, who puts on about 12 to 15 high-glitz pageants a year, culminating in a national pageant that pays out $75,000 in cash and prizes, including $10,000 to the winner. "We love the beautiful dresses and the big hairstyles. We love the bling and makeup. We love our girls showing lots and lots of style, and we love seeing them sparkle."

After JonBenet's death, a few journalists and commentators went so far as to suggest that her tricked-up pageant look could have been the reason for her murder. Perhaps, they said, she had become the target of a pedophile who lurked around pageants. "The way people were talking, you would have thought we were all going to be murdered by child molesters," says Brooke Breedwell, who was 7 at the time. A recent graduate of the University of Tennessee, Knoxville, Breedwell was one of the country's most famous child contestants during the JonBenet era. For Breedwell, JonBenet's murder was more than a tragedy—it was a little girl's worst nightmare. "I remember thinking when she got killed, I was going to get killed. I was convinced it was a serial killer going after pageant girls. I would hide under my covers, terrified, at night."

Stacy Dittrich, a former detective in Ashland, OH, who specialized in sex crimes and who is now a true-crime author and media analyst, says, "I found, in the course of my work, pedophiles who had gone to great lengths to obtain videos of little girls walking around provocatively, pulling their shirts down off their shoulders and smiling at the camera." Even though Dittrich never worked on a case in which a pedophile stalked a child from a pageant, she did have experience with pedophiles who lurked at football games to snap pictures of young kids. "I arrested one guy who sat at his window and took photographs of the neighborhood girls playing in a sprinkler," she remembers. "When I see pageants on TV, I think, *These are the types of videos those pedophiles would watch*." While Dittrich isn't totally against pageants, she thinks air-ing them on television is irresponsible: "On TV, they are not only giving out the names of these children, but they also tell you what towns these little girls live in," she says. "It would not be difficult whatsoever for an obsessive pedophile to track these children down."

There is scant documented evidence to suggest that pageants put little girls in danger, yet many psychologists believe that developmental and emotional problems can stem from the pressure and value system that pageants embody. A 2007 report issued by the American Psychological Association Task Force on the Sexualization of Girls claims that parents who put their daughters in pageants can contribute "in very direct and concrete ways" to "the precocious° sexualization" of their daughters. "These pageant girls are taught from a very early age that what is most critically important in life is their physical appearance along with a superficial and eroticized charm. They are presented in a hypersexualized manner that is completely inappropriate to their ages," says Mary E. Doheny, Ph.D., of the Family Institute at Northwestern University. Doheny says, "Also, for the mothers, their whole focus is imparting the critical importance of physical beauty, and along with that is the mothers' implicit criticism of their girls' own unembellished beauty. They are always applying makeup to their girls' faces, dressing them up, and dyeing their hair. They are hypervigilant about diet and posture. And so the message these little girls take away is that natural beauty isn't enough—that their self-esteem and sense of self-worth only comes from being the most attractive girl in the room, not from being smart or resourceful or tough or creative."

15 "These little girls are being trained to look and act like sexual bait," says Nancy Irwin, Psy.D., a Los Angeles–based psychotherapist who specializes in working with sexually abused clients, particularly teenage girls. "And what's really disturbing is that so many of these girls seem to be tools of their mothers, who think this is the way for the girls to get fame and attention." Raised in Atlanta, Irwin herself competed in pageants when she was a teenager and a young adult. "I did them in hopes of getting college scholarship money. I worry that these girls are just doing it because they are being ordered to do it—and if they don't win, many times their mothers let them have it," she says.

A small 2005 study, published in *Eating Disorders: The Journal of Treatment & Prevention*, that involved 22 women, half of whom had participated in child beauty pageants, concluded that there were "no significant differences" between the two groups on measures of bulimia, body perception, depression, and self-esteem. But it did find that the former pageant girls scored significantly higher on "body dissatisfaction, interpersonal distrust, and impulse dysregulation [an inability to resist performing actions that would be harmful to themselves or others]."

It is difficult to ignore the link between the flirtatious behavior exhibited by pint-size contestants in heavy makeup (it's not uncommon for toddlers to be encouraged to wink or blow kisses at the judges) and the naive sexuality that is becoming increasingly blatant among elementary school girls. Author and journalist Peggy Orenstein, who wrote about child beauty pageants in her latest book, *Cinderella Ate My Daughter: Dispatches from the Front Lines of the New Girlie-Girl Culture*, believes that pageant girls are being taught to see themselves as objects of others' pleasure. "I'm not saying that when they wiggle their hips and wink at judges at the age of 4 or 5, they have any idea that what they're doing is a highly eroticized,

---

***precocious:*** developing prematurely.

seductive gesture," she says. "But pageant girls are definitely learning that if they act in a very sexualized way, they will get attention. The risk is that as they become adult women, they will continue to see their sexuality as a performance and not something connected to their own true feelings."

Whether it's a 5-year-old strutting down the pageant runway in lipstick and false eyelashes or the 7-year-olds who became a YouTube sensation for a sexy Beyoncé "Single Ladies (Put a Ring on It)" dance routine, the fact that these young girls don't mean to be sexual is actually part of the problem. When very young girls learn to disconnect sexy motions from the thoughts and feelings behind them, it's hard for them to integrate all of those elements as they get older. Deborah Tolman, Ed.D., a professor at Hunter College and author of *Dilemmas of Desire: Teenage Girls Talk about Sexuality,* says, "From *Toddlers & Tiaras* to *America's Next Top Model,* reality TV takes away a lot of what we know is good for girls. Focusing so much on how you look is problematic. Instead of focusing on how she feels—which is an important skill growing up—a girl learns to sexualize herself. Your body is a compass, and premature sexuality takes the arrow out of the compass."

"In 1996, when JonBenet was murdered, it was shocking for us to see a 6-year-old wearing lipstick and eye shadow," says Orenstein. "Now, market research studies have found nearly half of today's 6- to 9-year-olds are already using lipstick or lip gloss. Walmart launched a makeup line just for girls 8 to 12. Abercrombie & Fitch marketed a padded push-up bikini top for 8-year-olds. It's easy to slam pageants, but maybe that's because no one wants to deal with the bigger picture, which is the day-to-day sexualization of all our daughters."

20 Perhaps it's precisely because sexy dress-up has gone mainstream that *Toddlers & Tiaras*, the TLC network's hit reality show about child pageants, draws 1.4 million viewers per week. *Toddlers & Tiaras* made Eden Wood a star. The chubby-cheeked 6-year-old has more than 15,000 fans on her Facebook page, and there are nearly 700 YouTube videos of her posing, prancing, or performing one of her talent routines: a song-and-dance act in which she struts and swaggers, swings her hips, flips her hair, coyly sticks her fingers in her dimpled cheeks, and belts out lyrics in her untrained but very enthusiastic voice.

The demands of pageant life can be relentless. Many of the girls start competing as babies; some, like Eden, are homeschooled and spend Fridays making all-day trips to pageants. The time devoted to pageants is a developmental concern, says Northwestern's Doheny: "On the most benign level, the girls who participate in pageants truly limit the time they get to engage in playtime and other creative endeavors, or to learn and practice other competencies, like sports or personal relationships with peers." The top girls on the pageant circuit not only have hair and makeup stylists; they also have "beauty walk" consultants and "talent" coaches.

Eden has her own agent, Heather Ryan, a Des Moines, IA, mom who, after entering her oldest daughter in pageants, realized there was money to be made representing the country's top glitz contestants. Ryan is the agent for 34 girls, and while she won't discuss dollar figures, she says none come close to making the money that Eden does. So far, with Eden's parents' approval, Ryan has produced an Eden look-alike doll, a book about Eden's life entitled *From Cradle to Crown*, Eden's first single ("Cutie Patootie," which Ryan wrote), and T-shirts that feature a photo of Eden in a showgirl-style pink costume and matching headdress along with a slogan that reads "I'm Tanned and Ready for the Stage!" All of Eden's merchandise is sold on her website, littleedenwood.com. But it is her TV appearances that have given Eden such a massive profile. Fans turn out in droves at her mall appearances to see her sing and to have her autograph a CD or poster. Only days before the Plano pageant, the agent announced that later this summer, Eden and a couple of other pageant contestants would do an eight-city tour of the Midwest, billed as "The Glamour Girls Starring Eden Wood." Eden is even taking her show abroad as a special celebrity guest at Universal Royalty's first-ever pageant in Australia this summer, signing autographs, posing for photos, and singing songs such as "Cutie Patootie." Even as Eden walks into the Southfork Hotel ballroom, she's got her pageant smile on: teeth clenched, lips unmoving. Many contestants gape at her, awestruck. One holds out a sheet of paper for Eden to autograph. "Thank you!" Eden says, signing her name in big block letters. Another tells Eden that she owns two blond-haired dolls, both of which are named—that's right—Eden. "Yay!" says Eden cheerfully.

"It's simply amazing," says Mickie, who's renowned in pageant circles for her level of prep, even bringing along a portable spray-tan machine to pageants. "Eden's now got fan clubs in Europe and Australia. Strangers come up to her and ask for her autograph. They call her America's sweetheart. I'm telling you, for a family from a poor little town in Arkansas, this is like a fairy tale come true."

Not all child pageant participants come from modest means, but it's hard not to see the material aspirations reflected in the paste-jewelry crowns that sparkle atop the heads of little girls like Eden. Melissa Harris-Perry, Ph.D., a professor of political science at Tulane University, says, "We tend to think that we're very class-mobile in America, that anybody can do anything. But the fact is, we're not. Most working-class girls born into working-class families are going to die working-class. These pageants are a time for them and their moms to have the Kate Middleton° moment. These moms want to live the princess story and, more, to feel like they've captured it for their daughters—this instant of extreme specialness. If you think about the royal wedding, it really was like a pageant in that way. Kate Middleton was praised during the ceremony for the same things these girls are praised for: 'Look how she can stand so still and self-possessed and smiling while people take photographs of her.'"

25 When Mickie Wood compares Eden's pageant career to a fairy tale, the question is, for whom? For Brooke Breedwell, pageants were a potent symbol of her mother's ambition. When she was 3 months old, her mother began entering her in pageants; Breedwell left the circuit, at her own insistence, when she was 8. "I had to quit soccer, and I couldn't go to certain school events or friends' birthday parties, all because my mom wanted to spend thousands and thousands of dollars so I could win $500 and a trophy," she says. "I ended up having a very tense relationship with her because she was always nitpicking at me, pushing me to be perfect. One day I got so mad I threw a curling iron at her, and I finally quit because of the stress. And you know what I hate? All these years later, I've still got this anxiety about feeling like I have to be perfect."

Breedwell says if she ever has a daughter, she'll never let her do pageants. But in the next breath, she says, "I did love performing; I will say that. I miss the feeling of being onstage."

If you were to come across Eden in Taylor, a town of 566 people that is a few miles north of the Arkansas-Louisiana line, you would think she was just another

---

***Kate Middleton (1982– ):*** Catherine, Duchess of Cambridge, since her April 2011 marriage to Prince William, Duke of Cambridge, who is second in line to the throne of the British Commonwealth. She is the first person who was not a member of a royal family or of the aristocracy to marry an heir to the throne in over three and a half centuries. Thus, the British press has characterized her as a "commoner" who has married a prince.

country girl, cute but not particularly beautiful, with her hair in pigtails and the knees of her blue jeans scuffed and dirty. She lives in a small brown brick house with her father, Louis, a welder and full-time farmer, and Mickie, a music and drama teacher at the local public school. One day, when a visitor arrives, Eden is outside, riding her bicycle with training wheels past a truck in the driveway that's on blocks with the transmission pulled out, then past the backyard chicken coop, whose roof is held down by two tires.

When she heads inside the house, Eden walks down a dimly lit hallway filled with mounted deer heads, her father's hunting trophies. She opens the door to her bedroom—and the contrast is breathtaking. The walls are lavender, and painted on the closet doors, like a coat of arms, are the initials "E" and "W." Her bed is set inside an oversize pink dollhouse that reaches to the ceiling. At least 300 trophies line the floor, many taller than Eden herself, and custom-made shelves hold a seemingly endless array of glittery crowns and sashes.

Throughout the room are photos of Eden in pageant costumes. While spray tans rule the pageant stage, in photos the look is pure porcelain doll. Many of them have been retouched to make her hair blonder, her face creamy white, her eyes bigger and rounder, and her lips larger than life. It is nearly impossible to recognize that the child in the pictures is the same girl who is standing in the room.

30 Mickie was raised on a farm not far from Taylor, and as a young teenager and college student, she entered a couple of local beauty pageants and sang with country music bands. She quit the pageant world a few years before she married Louis. After years of trying to get pregnant, she gave birth to Eden at age 40. When Eden was 14 months old, Mickie entered her in the infant division of the Miss Lumberjack pageant in a nearby town—"People told me my baby was too pretty to keep hidden at home," she recalls—where Eden won for best hair. Mickie then entered Eden in a pageant in Shreveport, LA, "and a judge told me I had a star on my hands." As Eden got older, Mickie began driving her to pageants around the South in her red pickup truck, keeping a curling iron plugged into the cigarette lighter. By the age of 3, Eden was winning trophies in some of the bigger high-glitz pageant circuits—Darling Dolls of America, Tiny Miss America, Ultimate Dream Queen, and International Fresh Faces, among others.

*Toddlers & Tiaras* began featuring Eden in 2009, when she was 4. In one commercial promoting the show, there's a shot of Eden sweeping across the stage as the announcer says, "A toddler's greatest fear. Two little words: Eden Wood." Soon, she was being interviewed on such shows as *Good Morning America* and *Entertainment Tonight.* Reporters couldn't get enough of this chubby-cheeked, hip-wiggling girl whose original song "Cutie Patootie" included the refrain "I'm a cutie, cutie patootie. Rockin' out the pageant stage and shakin' my booty."

Predictably, there was plenty of criticism. After Eden performed "Cutie Patootie" on *The Talk,* CBS's afternoon talk show, cohost Sharon Osbourne, clearly dismayed, said that Mickie needed to let Eden be a normal little girl. "Seriously, do people believe I'd be so cruel as to force my only child to do all this if she didn't like doing it?" Mickie says at their home, making Eden a peanut butter sandwich. "When Eden gets to a pageant, it's like someone has flipped a switch in her. She shines with this bubbly joy. And my husband and I have always made it clear to her that the minute she wants to quit, then we'll quit, no questions asked."

"But I don't want to quit," Eden chimes in as she happily munches on her sandwich. "I want to be a star!" Nevertheless, in an episode of *Toddlers & Tiaras*, as Mickie walks Eden to the stage, she is caught on tape telling the little girl, "It's on you, the whole thing. All the work, all the money—it's all on you."

Eden is one of the rare money-makers in the child beauty pageant world: She's earned about $40,000 worth of cash, prizes, and endorsements during her very short career. Yet, since she's been competing from babyhood, her cash winnings are actually less than $10,000 a year. Mickie admits that she and her husband have probably spent $100,000 on Eden's pageant life, which includes the cost of dresses, coaches, stylists, retouched photos, entry fees (which run up to $2,000 at the bigger national pageants), and travel expenses.

35 "Some of these families spend $75,000 a year on pageants; they could do a lot more in terms of expanding their daughters' horizons and sense of possibilities with that money," says author Orenstein. "They could take their daughters around the world, and these little girls would get a lot more out of it than they would dressing up and parading across a stage." But just as you can't tell someone how to raise their kid, you can't tell them how to spend their cash. "We have money in the bank, and we see what we spend on Eden as an investment in her future," says Mickie with a shrug. "Pageants have given her something I've never gotten—a chance to experience life outside of Taylor. And who knows what this will lead to—maybe Hollywood."

Despite her enthusiasm, the trophies, the merchandise, and the tours, Eden's chances of becoming a child star in Hollywood are, at best, slim. "The entertainment industry doesn't go for girls who are trained to be fake and manipulative, and I'm sorry, but high-glitz girls are like trained monkeys," says Keith Lewis, the former owner of a Southern California talent agency that specialized in child models and child actors. Lewis, ironically, now codirects the Miss New York USA and Miss California USA pageants. He says he always turns away potential contestants from the high-glitz world. "Even grown-up, they still look and act like mannequins."

Adjusting to life without a tiara can be tough on former pageant girls. "Oh, listen, I had huge withdrawal pains after my career was over," says University of Texas at Austin student Thumper Gosney, who reluctantly stopped doing most pageants when she was 14 and about to enter high school. "I would go back and look at videos of myself as a kid in pageants, and feel numb because my entire identity was gone," she says.

Gosney gave away some of her pageant trophies to the Special Olympics organization to be reused at its contests, but she still keeps some around to remind her of what her life was like once. "I actually told a friend of mine the other day how I wish I could go back and do pageants," she says. Gosney, who is majoring in theater and dance, hopes she can someday be on a stage again. She pauses for a moment, her mind sifting through the memories. "It's difficult to just be a regular girl."

In the packed hotel ballroom, Annette Hill walks to the podium next to the stage, grabs a microphone, and shouts, "Are you ready for your girls to shine?" The crowd roars. Almost all of the audience is made up of contestants and their families from Texas and adjoining states, but a few have traveled from as far away as Wisconsin and North Carolina. Like the Woods, most of them appear to come from modest backgrounds. Yet they, too, have spent thousands of dollars to make sure their daughters are perfectly coiffed and dressed.

40 Hill announces that the overall winner, known in Universal Royalty parlance as the Ultimate Grand Supreme Winner (the terminology in pageants is as hyperbolic° as the makeup), will receive a beautiful "pink Princess Canopy Bed" that retails for $1,000. The girls bounce excitedly up and down on their toes while the parents are all aflutter.

---

***hyperbolic:*** given to hyperbole, or exaggeration.

"You can do it, Mia!" shouts one mother, Marina Spargo, as her 4-year-old daughter heads for the stage to do her beauty walk. The blue-eyed Mia is wearing a giant blond fall, false eyelashes, and a powdery-blue off-the-shoulder sequined dress that is so puffy, she has to hold her arms out to the sides. It looks as if she might fall over. Yet she calmly hits her marks on the stage and executes all her turns, her smile never cracking. "She's very facial," one mother murmurs admiringly—"facial" being a high-glitz term to describe a girl's beauty. "And look at how she does her pretty feet [a reference to the way a girl stands]. She's the total package."

When Mia finishes, the 38-year-old Marina, who's wearing orange drawstring sweatpants and a black T-shirt, grabs the arm of her husband, Ray, a strapping man who works in the maintenance department of a demolition company near Lake Jackson, TX, a town south of Houston. In 2004, looking for a wife, Ray used the Internet to contact Marina, a pretty blond Russian who lived a thousand miles north of Moscow. He flew to meet her, proposed to her in Moscow's Red Square at the end of his two-week visit, and, seven months later, brought her to Texas, where they married. In December 2006, Marina gave birth to Mia, "but she felt so isolated and alone, barely knowing any English, that I thought she might move back to Russia," recalls the 53-year-old Ray. "I saw a newspaper ad for a children's beauty pageant at a local mall, and I signed us up, thinking, *Maybe this will give Marina something to do.*"

Marina, who had never before been to a beauty pageant—she was a cross-country skier in Russia—put Mia in a new dress, stood onstage, and held her before the judges, who started smiling. "I said to my husband, 'Let's do this again,'" recalls Marina in a thick Russian accent. "We did it again, and we almost won. I was very excited. I thought, *So this is America!*"

Now Mia is one of the up-and-comers on the high-glitz circuit. She practices every day on a little plywood stage her father built for her in the backyard and often sits with her mother in front of a computer, studying videos of Eden and other high-glitz stars. At the Universal Royalty pageant, there's buzz around the ballroom that Mia has a shot at beating Eden. And she is genuinely charming when she later comes back for her talent act, pretending to be a Russian doll who escapes from her dollhouse to dance to Russian music.

45 But then Eden hits the stage, and she's so preternaturally° poised doing her beauty walk, the entire room goes silent. For her talent presentation, she performs "Underpuppy," an original song written to strike back at her critics. There's even a reference to Sharon Osbourne, who had implied to Mickie Wood that the pageant mom was a bad parent:

*They said I would never be anything*
*but pageant queen.*
*They said no matter how good,*
*you won't get to Hollywood.*
*Jealousy, hypocrisy,*
*Why you gotta be so mean? . . .*
*Root for me, cheer for me.*
*'Cause I'm the underpuppy . . .*
*You sneered when I sang "Cutie"*
*Why you got to be so snooty?*
*Not everyone is Ozzy's groupie . . .*
*Your judgment makes me stronger.*
*Listen—that's my career,*
*getting longer.*

Although her untrained voice is a little screechy, with a barnyard twang, Eden sings with such enthusiasm while dancing all over the stage that the crowd

---

***preternaturally:*** unusually, unnaturally, supernaturally.

gives her a standing ovation. "Get it, girl!" shouts Mickie, who has planted herself right behind the judges. "Smile, girl!"

By the end of the day, many of the younger girls are asleep on their parents' shoulders as they await the results. Some have to be roused to go up and claim their trophies. And everyone does get a trophy from Hill, who graciously refers to each loser as "one of our finalists" or "a future winner."

Finally, it's time to announce the Ultimate Grand Supreme Winner. The girls who got the highest scores from the judges, including Eden and Mia, are called to the stage. Almost shaking with nervousness, Marina puts her hands to her mouth.

Hill reads the judges' final tally and announces that Mia scored highest in her age group, 0 to 5, and is a runner-up. Tears spring from Marina's eyes as Mia gets a sash, a crown, a trophy, and a teddy bear. Then comes a surprise: Eden scored highest in her age group, 6 and up, and is also a runner-up. The winner is Alex Howe, an 11-year-old girl from Louisiana. Despite the diversity of kids in the room, all three finalists are blond and blue-eyed.

50 Eden tearfully runs out of the ballroom. "I wanted to win the pink princess bed and sleep in it tonight," she blurts out to Mickie. But in the hotel room, her tears are soon gone. Mickie later tells her that the bed manufacturer wants to create a special Eden Wood Edition of the Princess Canopy Bed that will have Eden's picture on the pillows and her signature on the footboard. "And Eden, honey, they'll give you a bed for free," Mickie says.

"Yay!" Eden shouts, and soon she's in her bathing suit, headed to the hotel pool to swim with the other girls.

After Marina, Ray, and Mia pack up for the ride back to Lake Jackson, Mia climbs into the backseat, next to her trophy. Someone asks her what she's going to do when she gets home.

"Go outside and practice on my stage for my next pageant," she says. "That's my girl," says Marina with a laugh. "That's my beautiful girl."

## RESPOND•

1. What argument(s) is Hollandsworth making in this article? How clear and explicit is his own stance or position toward the pageants he describes? What evidence can you give to support your responses?
2. Consider this article and the previous selection, Stephanie Hanes's "Little Girls or Little Women? The Disney Princess Effect." Both treat similar sets of issues and even use some of the same sources of evidence, for example, the work of journalist Peggy Orenstein. Are there other similarities? How do the two articles differ with respect to tone, kinds of evidence cited, and arguments made? To what degree might intended audience help account for these differences? *Good Housekeeping* is characterized as a women's magazine, and the path to the online version of this article is HOME > FAMILY & RELATIONSHIPS > PARENTING TIPS while the *Christian Science Monitor* is generally seen as an online newspaper that presents objective and, as one source terms it, "nonhysterical" coverage of the topics it discusses. (See Chapter 6 for a discussion of the notion of audience.)

3. One of the most interesting affordances of the new media is the fact that they give the reader the possibility of talking back. At the time this textbook is being written, one comment has been posted about this article, and the commenter is Rayanna DeMatteo, who is quoted in the article with respect to her memories of JonBenet Ramsey and her own participation in child beauty pageants. Here is the comment DeMatteo posted:

   > I want to clear something up. The way the article presents the quote isn't exactly how I said it or what I said. I said that I didn't want to tell anyone because I didn't want my friends to be my friends just because I was in pageants and had won all the money I did. I said I wanted my friends to like me for me not for what I could offer them. All girls can be a little fake and materialistic and I just wanted to have some girlfriends that wanted to be my friend for who I was. And not for the fact that I was in pageants. I was never embarrassed or ashamed that I did pageants. If anything they let me come out of my shell. They gave a lot of confidence. I loved doing them. I just wanted to clear the air.

   How should we interpret this comment? Should we assume that DeMatteo recalls exactly what she said or the context in which she said it? Should we assume that Hollandsworth misinterpreted or misrepresented DeMatteo's exact words or what they meant in context? If we take DeMatteo's comments at face value, assuming that her version of what she said represents what she said during the interview, how might that influence our evaluation of the article? Of Hollandsworth's credibility? What might this example teach us about the challenges of working with sources generally, especially those from interviews we conduct? (See Chapters 18 and 19 for information on evaluating and using sources.)

4. This article's title is obviously an allusion to the TLC reality television program *Toddlers & Tiaras*, which Hollandsworth discusses. Visit the program's website—http://bit.ly/eM5KN4—or look for YouTube videos related to the program (or child beauty pageants more broadly). For example, http://bit.ly/pZd9ja shows a video of a child doing an impression of Dolly Parton, the well-known Country and Western singer. Use what you see in the the video(s) you watch as evidence as you **write an essay** in which you evaluate some aspect of the hypersexualization of young girls in America. You may want to evaluate the videos as evidence for claims made by Hollandsworth, Hanes, or both; you may wish to evaluate whether hypersexualization or child beauty pageants are necessarily causes for alarm; or you may find some other feature of this topic that you can evaluate using the videos as evidence. Obviously, you'll need to include a description of the videos you rely on as well as the URL for them in your essay.

5. "So this is America!" Hollandsworth quotes Marina Spargo, the mother of Mia and an immigrant to the United States from Russia, as saying (paragraph 43). Which particular aspects of Mia's and Marina's experiences might Marina be thinking of when she made this remark? **Write an essay** in which you define what is particularly American about child beauty pageants. In other words, which positive and not-so-positive aspects of American culture do we see manifest in these pageants? Your essay will likely take the form of an argument of definition or an evaluative argument. (See Chapters 9 and 10 for discussions of these two categories of arguments.)

*Until her retirement in 2010, Ellen Goodman, a Pulitzer Prize–winning journalist, wrote a regular column for the* Boston Globe, *where this article first appeared in May 1999, a few days after many newspapers had featured a news story about how adolescent Fijian girls' self-image was affected by watching American TV. Goodman's column generally appeared on the op-ed pages of newspapers across the country. As you read, consider how she uses a discussion of a scientific study and the evidence it cites to make a claim about what she sees as a larger social problem. Keep in mind that Goodman wrote this article shortly after the shootings at Columbine High School in Colorado, where two male students killed and wounded a number of other students and teachers.*

# The Culture of Thin Bites Fiji

ELLEN GOODMAN

First of all, imagine a place women greet one another at the market with open arms, loving smiles, and a cheerful exchange of ritual compliments:

"You look wonderful! You've put on weight!"

Does that sound like dialogue from Fat Fantasyland? Or a skit from fat-is-a-feminist-issue satire? Well, this Western fantasy was a South Pacific fact of life. In Fiji, before 1995, big was beautiful and bigger was more beautiful—and people really did flatter one another with exclamations about weight gain.

In this island paradise, food was not only love, it was a cultural imperative. Eating and overeating were rites of mutual hospitality. Everyone worried about losing weight—but not the way we do. "Going thin" was considered to be a sign of some social problem, a worrisome indication the person wasn't getting enough to eat.

5 The Fijians were, to be sure, a bit obsessed with food; they prescribed herbs to stimulate the appetite. They were a reverse image of our culture. And that turns out to be the point.

Something happened in 1995. A Western mirror was shoved into the face of the Fijians. Television came to the island. Suddenly, the girls of rural coastal villages were watching the girls of *Melrose Place* and *Beverly Hills 90210*, not to mention *Seinfeld* and *E.R.*

Within 38 months, the number of teenagers at risk for eating disorders more than doubled to 29 percent. The number of high school girls who vomited for weight control went up five times to 15 percent. Worse yet, 74 percent of the Fiji teens in the study said they felt "too big or fat" at least some of the time and 62 percent said they had dieted in the past month.

This before-and-after television portrait of a body image takeover was drawn by Anne Becker, an anthropologist and psychiatrist who directs research at the Harvard Eating Disorders Center. She presented her research at the American Psychiatric Association last week with all the usual caveats. No, you cannot prove a direct causal link° between television and eating disorders. Heather Locklear° doesn't cause anorexia. Nor does Tori Spelling° cause bulimia.

Fiji is not just a Fat Paradise Lost. It's an economy in transition from subsistence agriculture° to tourism and its entry into the global economy has threatened many old values.

10 Nevertheless, you don't get a much better lab experiment than this. In just 38 months, and with only one channel, a television-free culture that defined a fat person as robust has become a television culture that sees robust as, well, repulsive.

All that and these islanders didn't even get *Ally McBeal*.°

"Going thin" is no longer a social disease but the perceived requirement for getting a good job, nice clothes, and fancy cars. As Becker says carefully, "The acute and constant bombardment of certain images in the media are apparently quite influential in how teens experience their bodies."

Speaking of Fiji teenagers in a way that sounds all too familiar, she adds, "We have a set of vulnerable teens consuming television. There's a huge disparity between what they see on television and what they look like themselves—that goes not only to clothing, hairstyles, and skin color, but size of bodies."

In short, the sum of Western culture, the big success story of our entertainment industry, is our ability to export insecurity: We can make any woman anywhere feel perfectly rotten about her shape. At this rate, we owe the islanders at least one year of the ample lawyer Camryn Manheim° in *The Practice* for free.

15 I'm not surprised by research showing that eating disorders are a cultural byproduct. We've watched the female image shrink down to Calista Flockhart at the same time we've seen eating problems grow. But Hollywood hasn't been exactly eager to acknowledge the connection between image and illness.

Over the past few weeks since the Columbine High massacre, we've broken through some denial about violence as a teaching tool. It's pretty clear that boys are literally learning how to hate and harm others.

Maybe we ought to worry a little more about what girls learn: To hate and harm themselves.

*Calista Flockhart in 1998*

---

***causal link:*** a justified claim that X causes Y. Scientific research based on statistics, as is the Becker study that Goodman refers to, cannot demonstrate causality; instead, it demonstrates correlation, a mathematical link between two (or more) phenomena that is likely not chance or accidental in nature. Prolonged exposure to direct sunlight is correlated with higher rates of skin cancer, but this fact does not mean that playing tennis in Arizona year-round causes skin cancer.

***Heather Locklear (1961– ):*** American actress best known for her television roles, including Amanda Woodward in *Melrose Place*.

***Tori Spelling (1973– ):*** American actress and best-selling author.

***subsistence agriculture:*** a model of farming focused on growing enough to keep one's own family and animals fed, in contrast to growing food to sell or large-scale commercial farming.

**Ally McBeal:** an award-winning Fox television series that aired from 1997 until 2002 and featured Calista Flockhart—whose thin figure was often the subject of comment—as a young attorney working in Boston.

***Camryn Manheim (1961– ):*** an actress known for playing Ellenor Frutt on *The Practice*, an ABC legal drama that aired from 1997 until 2004.

Chapter 11 notes that causal arguments are often included as part of other arguments. Goodman's article reports on Anne Becker's research (an excerpt of which is reprinted in the following selection, beginning on page 505) to support a larger argument.

LINK TO P. 243

*A Fijian woman—before 1995*

## RESPOND.

1. What is Goodman's argument? How does she build it around Becker's study while not limiting herself to that evidence alone? (Consider, especially, paragraphs 15–17.)
2. What knowledge of popular American culture does Goodman assume that her *Boston Globe* audience has? How does she use allusions to American TV programs to build her argument? Note, for example, that she sometimes uses such allusions as conversational asides—"All that and these islanders didn't even get *Ally McBeal*," and "At this rate, we owe the islanders at least one year of the ample lawyer Camryn Manheim in *The Practice* for free"—to establish her ethos. (For a discussion of ethos, see Chapter 3.) In what other ways do allusions to TV programs contribute to Goodman's argument? Would you have understood this article without the glosses to *Ally McBeal* and *The Practice* that the editors have provided? What does this situation teach you about the need to consider your audience and their background knowledge as you write? (See Chapter 6 for a discussion of audience.)
3. At least by implication, if not in fact, Goodman makes a causal argument about the entertainment industry, women's body image, and the consequences of such an image. What sort of causal argument does she set up? (For a discussion of causal arguments, see Chapter 11.) How effective do you find it? Why?
4. Many professors would find Goodman's conversational style inappropriate for most academic writing assignments. Choose several paragraphs of the text that contain information appropriate for an argumentative academic paper. Then **write a few well-developed paragraphs** on the topic. (Paragraphs 4–8 could be revised in this way, though you would put the information contained in these five paragraphs into only two or three longer paragraphs. Newspaper articles often feature short paragraphs of one or two sentences, which is generally an inappropriate length for paragraphs in academic writing.)

▼ *Anne E. Becker received her MD and PhD in anthropology as well as her ScM in epidemiology from Harvard University. Currently, she is vice-chair of the Department of Global Health and Social Medicine, where she holds the Maude and Lillian Pressley Professorship; she also serves as an associate professor of psychiatry at Harvard Medical School, where she directs the Social Sciences MD-PhD Program. Throughout her career, Becker has conducted fieldwork in Fiji on teenage girls and eating disorders, which is sometimes referred to as "disordered eating" in research on this topic. This selection presents three sections of one of Becker's research articles, "Television, Disordered Eating, and Young Women in Fiji," which originally appeared in a special 2004 issue of the academic journal* Culture, Medicine, and Psychiatry *devoted to global eating disorders. The sections presented are "Abstract," "Discussion," and "Conclusions"; if you are familiar with research articles, you can immediately guess that the missing sections are those between the abstract and the discussion section that review earlier research on the topics of the paper, state the research questions to be investigated, describe the methods used to investigate the research questions, and report the results of the study. As you read the sections reprinted here, consider how writing about research for other researchers (as Becker has done here) differs from writing about research for a popular audience (as Ellen Goodman does in the previous selection, "The Culture of Thin Bites Fiji," which relies on an earlier oral presentation of Becker's research as a starting point for Goodman's discussion).*

# Television, Disordered Eating, and Young Women in Fiji: Negotiating Body Image and Identity during Rapid Social Change

ANNE E. BECKER

**ABSTRACT** Although the relationship between media exposure and risk behavior among youth is established at a population level, the specific psychological and social mechanisms mediating the adverse effects of media on youth remain poorly understood. This study reports on an investigation of the impact of the introduction of television to a rural community in Western Fiji on adolescent ethnic Fijian girls in a setting of rapid social and economic change. Narrative data were collected from 30 purposively selected ethnic Fijian secondary school girls via semi-structured, open-ended interviews.° Interviews were conducted in 1998, 3 years after television was first broadcast to this region of Fiji. Narrative data were analyzed for content relating to response to television and mechanisms that mediate self and body image in Fijian adolescents. Data in this sample suggest that media imagery is used in both creative and destructive ways by adolescent Fijian girls to navigate opportunities and conflicts posed by the rapidly changing social environment. Study respondents indicated their explicit modeling of the perceived positive attributes of characters presented in television dramas, but also the beginnings of weight and body shape preoccupation, purging behavior to control weight, and body disparagement.° Response to television appeared to be shaped by a desire for competitive social positioning during a period of rapid social transition. Understanding vulnerability to images and values imported with media will be critical to preventing disordered eating and, potentially, other youth risk behaviors in this population, as well as other populations at risk.

***narrative data . . . semi-structured, open-ended interviews:*** data resulting from oral interviews during which the girls answered questions covering a range of topics and told stories about their experiences rather than simply answering the sorts of questions you find on questionnaires where the ordering of questions is fixed and the choices of answers are given and forced (e.g., Yes/No; Strongly Agree/Agree/Disagree/Strongly Disagree).

***disparagement:*** speaking about something in a negative way.

**KEY WORDS:** body image, eating disorders, Fiji, modernization

## DISCUSSION

Minimally, and at the most superficial level, narrative data reflect a shift in fashion among the adolescent ethnic Fijian population studied. A shift in aesthetic ideals is remarkable in and of itself given the numerous social mechanisms that have long supported the preference for large bodies. Moreover, this change reflects a disruption of both apparently stable traditional preference for a robust body shape and the traditional disinterest in reshaping the body (Becker 1995).

Subjects' responses to television in this study also reflect a more complicated reshaping of personal and cultural identities inherent in their endeavors to reshape their bodies. Traditionally for Fijians, identity had been fixed not so much in the body as in family, community, and relationships with others, in contrast to Western-cultural models that firmly fix identity in the body/self. Comparatively speaking, social identity is manipulated and projected through personal, visual props in many Western social contexts, whereas this was less true in Fiji. Instead, Fijians have traditionally invested themselves in nurturing others—efforts that are then concretized in the bodies that one cares for and feeds. Hence, identity is represented (and experienced) individually and collectively through the well-fed bodies of others, not through one's own body (again, comparatively speaking) (Becker 1995). In addition, since Fiji's economy has until recently been based in subsistence agriculture, and since multiple cultural practices encourage distribution of material resources, traditional Fijian identity has also not been represented through the ability to purchase and accumulate material goods.

More broadly than interest in body shape, however, the qualitative data demonstrate a rather concrete identification with television characters as role models of successful engagement in Western, consumeristic lifestyles. Admiration and emulation of television characters appears to stem from recognition that traditional channels are ill-equipped to assist Fijian adolescents in navigating the landscape of rapid social change in Fiji. Unfortunately, while affording an opportunity to develop identities syntonic° with the shifting social context, the behavioral modeling on Western appearance and customs appears to have undercut traditional cultural resources for identity-making (Becker et al. 2002). Specifically, narrative data reveal here that traditional sources of information about self-presentation and public comportment have been supplanted by captivating and convincing role models depicted in televised programming and commercials.

*syntonic:* emotionally responsive to one's environment.

It is noteworthy that the interest in reshaping the body differs in subtle 5
but important ways from the drive for thinness observed in other social contexts. The discourse° on reshaping the body is, indeed, quite explicitly and pragmatically focused on competitive social positioning—for both employment opportunities and peer approval. This discourse on weight and body shape is suffused with moral as well as material associations (i.e., that appear to be commentary on the social body). That is, repeatedly expressed sentiment that excessive weight results in laziness and undermines domestic productivity may reflect a concern about how Fijians will "measure up" in the global economy. The juxtaposition of extreme affluence depicted on most television programs against the materially impoverished Fijians associates the nearly uniformly thin bodies and restrained appetites of television characters with the (illusory) promise of economic opportunity and success. Each child's future, as well as the fitness of the social body, seems to be at stake.

*discourse:* here, the kinds of comments young girls made about a particular topic during the interviews.

In this sense, disordered eating among the Fijian schoolgirls in this study appears to be primarily an instrumental means of reshaping body and identity to enhance social and economic opportunities. From this perspective, it may be premature to comment on whether or not disordered eating behaviors share the same meaning as similar behaviors in other cultural contexts.

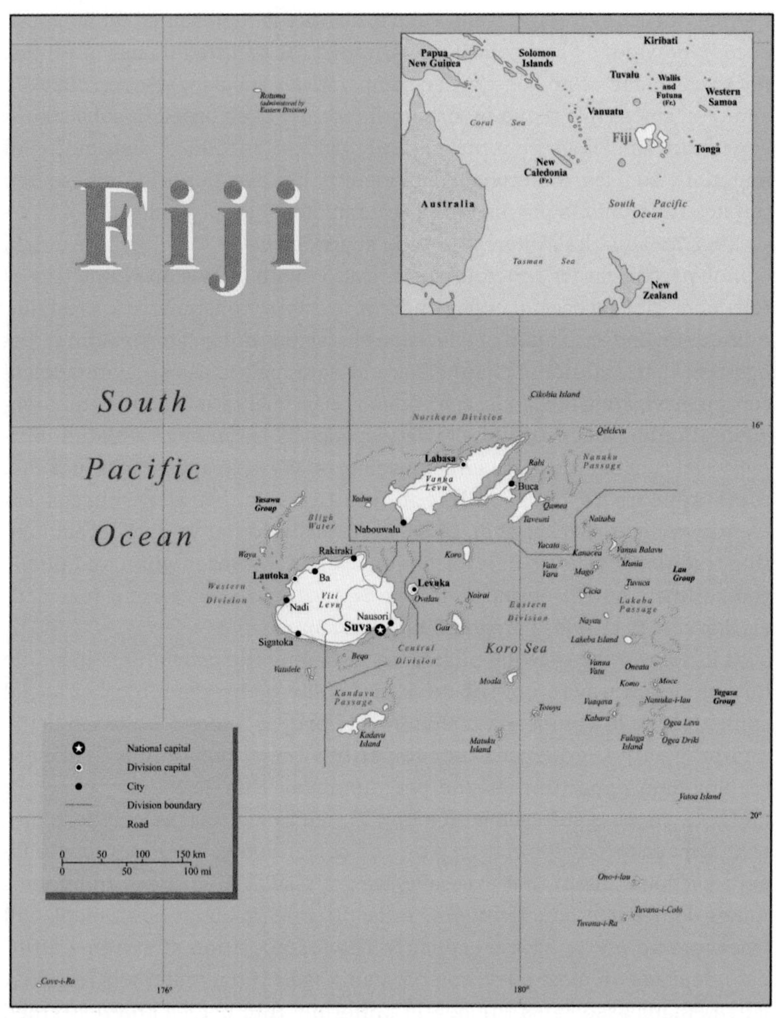


It is also premature to say whether these behaviors correspond well to Western nosologic° categories describing eating disorders. Regardless of any differences in psychological significance of the behaviors, however, physiologic risks will be the same. Quite possibly—and this remains to be studied in further detail—disordered eating may also be a symbolic embodiment of the anxiety and conflict the youth experience on the threshold of rapid social

***nosologic:*** relating to diseases.

change in Fiji and during their personal and collective navigation through it. Moreover, there is some preliminary evidence that the disordered eating is accompanied by clinical features associated with the illnesses elsewhere and eating disorders may be emerging in this context. Finally, television has certainly imported more than just images associating appearance with material success; it has arguably enhanced reflexivity° about the possibility of reshaping one's body and life trajectory and popularized the notion of competitive social positioning.

*reflexivity:* self-reflection.

The impact of imported media in societies undergoing transition on local values has been demonstrated in multiple societies (e.g., Cheung and Chan 1996; Granzberg 1985; Miller 1998; Reis 1998; Tan et al. 1987; Wu 1990). As others have argued in other contexts, ideas from imported media can be used to negotiate "hybrid identities" (Barker 1997) and otherwise incorporated into various strategies for social positioning (Mazzarella 2003) and coping with modernization (Varan 1998). Likewise and ironically, here as elsewhere in the world (see Anderson-Fye 2004), Fijian youth must craft an identity which adopts Western values about productivity and efficiency in the workplace while simultaneously selling their Fijian-ness (an essential asset to their role in the tourist industry). Self-presentation is thus carefully constructed so as to bridge and integrate dual identities. That these identities are not consistently smoothly fused is evidenced in the ambivalence in the narratives about how thin a body is actually ideal.

Becker uses survey and interview data to support her argument about eating disorders in Fiji. Chapter 4 offers examples of "hard evidence" used in arguments based on fact.

LINK TO P. 56

The source of the emerging disordered eating among ethnic Fijian girls thus appears multifactorial and multidetermined.° Media images that associate thinness with material success and marketing that promotes the possibility of reshaping the body have supported a perceived nexus° between diligence (work on the body), appearance (thinness), and social and material success (material possessions, economic opportunities, and popularity with peers). Fijian self-presentation has absorbed new dimensions related to buying into Western styles of appearance and the ethos of work on the body. A less articulated parallel to admiration for characters, bodies, and lifestyles portrayed on imported television is the demoralizing perception of not comparing favorably as a population. It is as though a mirror was held up to these girls in which they perhaps saw themselves as poor and overweight. The eagerness they express in grooming themselves to be hard workers or perhaps obtain competitive jobs perhaps reflects their collective energy and anxiety about how they, as individuals, and as a Fijian people, are going to fare in a globalizing world. Thus preoccupation with weight loss and the restrictive eating and purging certainly reflect pragmatic strategies to optimize social and economic success. At the same time, they surely contribute

*multifactorial and multidetermined:* created by many factors and caused by many forces.

*nexus:* a point of convergence or intersection.

to body- and self-disparagement and reflect an embodied distress about the uncertainty of personal future and the social body.

*ata:* data, likely
, concerning the
pread, and control of
ases.

Epidemiologic data° from other populations confirm an association between social transition (e.g., transnational migration, modernization, urbanization) and disordered eating among vulnerable groups (Anderson-Fye and Becker 2004). In particular, the association between upward mobility and disordered eating across diverse populations has relevance here (Anderson-Fye 2000; Buchan and Gregory 1984; Silber 1986; Soomro et al. 1995; Yates 1989). Exposure to Western media images and ideas may further contribute to disordered eating by first promoting comparisons that result in perceived economic and social disadvantage and then promoting the notion that efforts to reshape the body will enhance social status. It can be argued that girls and young women undergoing social transition may perceive that social status is enhanced by positioning oneself competitively through the informed use of cultural symbols—e.g., by bodily appearance and thinness (Becker and Hamburg 1996). This is comparable to observations that children of immigrants to the U.S. (for whom the usual parental "map of experience" is lacking) substitute alternative "cultural guides" from the media as resources for negotiating successful social strategies (Suarez-Orozco and Suarez-Orozco 2001). In both scenarios, adolescent girls and young women assimilating to new cultural standards encounter a ready cultural script for comportment and appearance in the media.

## Conclusions

> "I've wondered how television is made and how the actress and actors, I always wondered how television, how people acted on it, and I'm kind of wondering whether it's true or not." (S-48)

The increased prevalence of disordered eating in ethnic Fijian schoolgirls 10
is not the only story—or even the most important one—that can be pieced together from the respondents' narratives on television and its impact.[1] Nor are images and values transmitted through televised media singular forces in the chain of events that has led to an apparent increase in disordered eating attitudes and behaviors. The impact of media coupled with other sweeping economic and social change is likely to affect Fijian youth and adults in many ways. On the other hand, this particular story allows a window into the powerful impact and vulnerability of this adolescent female population. This story also allows a frame for exploring resilience and suggesting interventions for future research.

In some important ways, Fiji is a unique context for investigating the impact of media imagery on adolescents. In Fiji in particular, the evolving and multiple—and potentially overlapping or dissonant—social terrain presents novel challenges and opportunities for adolescents navigating their way in the absence of guidance from "conventional" wisdom and social hierarchies that may have grown obsolete in some respects. Doubtless the profound ways in which adolescent girls are influenced by media imagery extend beyond the borders of Fiji and the ways in which young women in Fiji consume and reflect on televised media may suggest mechanisms for its impact on youth in other social contexts. This study, therefore, allows insight into the ways in which social change intersects with the developmental tasks of adolescence to pose the risk of eating disorders and other youth risk behaviors.

Adolescent girls and young women in this and other indigenous, small-scale societies may also be especially vulnerable to the effects of media exposure for several key reasons. For example, in the context of rapid social change, these girls and young women may lack traditional role models for how to successfully maneuver in a shifting economic and political environment. Moreover, in societies in which status is traditionally ascribed° rather than achieved,° girls and women may feel more compelled to secure their social position through a mastery of self-presentation that draws heavily from imported media. It is a logical and frightening conclusion that vulnerable girls and women across diverse populations who feel marginalized from the locally dominant culture's sources of prestige and status may anchor

***ascribed status:*** status that one is granted by others, often on the basis of external qualities (for example, being a firstborn son in a society that values male children and pays attention to birth order).

***achieved status:*** status that one somehow wins or attains (for example, placing first in a competition).

*Singer-songwriter Jill Scott plays Precious Ramotswe, owner of the No. 1 Ladies' Detective Agency, in the television miniseries about Alexander McCall Smith's fictional sleuth, set in Botswana. Ramotswe frequently reflects on her status as a "traditionally built" African woman in a society where standards of female attractiveness are rapidly changing.*

their identities in widely recognized cultural symbols of prestige popularized by media-imported ideas, values, and images. Further, these girls and women have no reference for comparison of the televised images to the "realities" they portray and thus to critique and deconstruct the images they see compared with girls and women who are "socialized" into a culture of viewership. Without thoughtful interventions[2]—yet to be explored with the affected communities—the unfortunate outcome is likely to be continued increasing rates of disordered eating and other youth risk behaviors in vulnerable populations undergoing rapid modernization and social transition.

## Notes

1. For example, the increased incidence of suicide and other self-injury in Fiji (Pridmore et al. 1995) may index social distress related to rapid social change.
2. Prevention efforts that might be useful include psychoeducational information about the psychological and medical risks associated with bingeing, purging, and self-starvation as well as media literacy programs that assist youth in critical and informed viewing of televised programming and commercials.

## References


Anderson-Fye, E.P.
2000 Self-Reported Eating Attitudes Among High School Girls in Belize: A Quantitative Survey. Unpublished Qualifying Paper. Department of Human Development and Psychology, Harvard University, Cambridge, MA.

Anderson-Fye, E.
2004 A "Coca-Cola" Shape: Cultural Change, Body Image, and Eating Disorders in San Andrés, Belize. Culture, Medicine and Society 28: 561–595.

Anderson-Fye, E., and A.E. Becker
2004 Socio-Cultural Aspects of Eating Disorders. *In* Handbook of Eating Disorders and Obesity. J.K. Thompson, ed., pp. 565–589. Wiley.

Barker, C.
1997 Television and the Reflexive Project of the Self: Soaps, Teenage Talk and Hybrid Identities. British Journal of Sociology 48: 611–628.

Becker, A.E.
1995 Body, Self, Society: The View from Fiji. Philadelphia: University of Pennsylvania Press.

Becker, A.E., and P. Hamburg
1996 Culture, the Media, and Eating Disorders. Harvard Review of Psychiatry 4: 163–167.

Becker, A.E., R.A. Burwell, S.E. Gilman, D.B. Herzog, and P. Hamburg
2002 Eating Behaviors and Attitudes Following Prolonged Television Exposure Among Ethnic Fijian Adolescent Girls. British Journal of Psychiatry 180: 509–514.

Buchan, T., and L.D. Gregory
1984 Anorexia Nervosa in a Black Zimbabwean. British Journal of Psychiatry 145: 326–330.

Cheung, C.K., and C.F. Chan
1996 Television Viewing and Mean World Value in Hong Kong's Adolescents. Social Behavior and Personality 24: 351–364.

Granzberg, G.
1985 Television and Self-Concept Formation in Developing Areas. Journal of Cross-Cultural Psychology 16: 313–328.

Mazzarella, W.
2003 Shoveling Smoke: Advertising and Globalization in Contemporary India. Durham, NC: Duke University Press.

Miller, C.J.
1998 The Social Impacts of Televised Media Among the Yucatec Maya. Human Organization 57: 307–314.

Pridmore, S., K. Ryan, and L. Blizzard
1995 Victims of Violence in Fiji. Australian and New Zealand Journal of Psychiatry 29: 666–670.

Reis, R.
1998 The Impact of Television Viewing in the Brazilian Amazon. Human Organization 57: 300–306.

Silber, T.J.
1986 Anorexia Nervosa in Blacks and Hispanics. International Journal of Eating Disorders 5: 121–128.

Soomro, G.M., A.H. Crisp, D. Lynch, D. Tran, and N. Joughin
1995 Anorexia Nervosa in "Non-White" Populations. British Journal of Psychiatry 167: 385–389.

Suarez-Orozco, C., and M.M. Suarez-Orozco
2001 Children of Immigration. Cambridge, MA: Harvard University Press.

Tan, A.S., G.K. Tan, and A.S. Tan
1987 American TV in the Philippines: A Test of Cultural Impact. Journalism Quarterly 64: 65–72, 144.

Varan, D.
1998 The Cultural Erosion Metaphor and the Transcultural Impact of Media Systems. Journal of Communication 48: 58–85.

Wu, Y.K.
1990 Television and the Value Systems of Taiwan's Adolescents: A Cultivation Analysis. Dissertation Abstracts International 50: 3783A.

Yates, A.
1989 Current Perspectives on the Eating Disorders: I. History, Psychological and Biological Aspects. Journal of the American Academy of Child and Adolescent Psychiatry 28(6): 813–828.

## RESPOND •

1. How does Becker link exposure to Western media to the changing notions young Fijian women have of their own bodies? Why does Becker claim these women now want to be thin? How are these changes linked to other social changes occurring in Fiji, to adolescence, and to gender, especially in small-scale societies?
2. As Becker notes, she relies on qualitative data—specifically, interview data—to support her arguments. Why are such data especially appropriate, given her goals of understanding the changing social meanings of body image for young Fijian women as part of other rapid social changes taking place in Fiji? (For a discussion of firsthand evidence, see Chapter 17.)
3. Throughout the "Discussion" and "Conclusions" sections, Becker repeatedly qualifies her arguments to discourage readers from extending them further than she believes her data warrant. Find two cases where she does so, and explain the specific ways that she reminds readers of the limits of her claims. (For a discussion on qualifying claims and arguments, see Chapter 7.)
4. These excerpts from Becker's article represent research writing for an academic audience. What functions does each of the reprinted sections serve for the article's readers, and why is each located where it is? Why, for example, is an abstract placed at the beginning of an article? Why are key words a valuable part of an abstract?
5. In paragraph 3, in the "Discussion" section of her article, Becker compares and contrasts how Westerners (which would include Americans) and Fijians understand identity, especially as it relates to the body. **Write an essay** in which you evaluate Becker's characterization of Western notions of identity. (For a discussion of evaluative arguments, see Chapter 10.) Unless you have detailed knowledge of a culture very different from Western cultures (Fiji, for example), you may want to begin by trying to demonstrate that Becker's assessment is correct, at least to some degree, rather than claiming that she misunderstands the West. Once you've conceded that there's at least some truth in her assessment, you may be able to cite cases of American subcultures that don't "firmly fix identity in the body/self."

*Sam Dillon currently works as a national education correspondent for the* New York Times, *writing often on issues relating to education in the United States. Earlier in his career, he reported from various Latin American countries. His journalistic writing has garnered several prestigious awards, including two Pulitzer Prizes. The* New York Times *broke this story about the Delta Zeta sorority at DePauw University in its February 25, 2007, edition, setting off a widely discussed controversy that eventually led to the closure of the sorority on the university's campus. As you read this article, consider the ways in which stereotyping might have played a role in what happened—and what didn't.*

# Evictions at Sorority Raise Issue of Bias

SAM DILLON

GREENCASTLE, Ind.—When a psychology professor at DePauw University here surveyed students, they described one sorority as a group of "daddy's little princesses" and another as "offbeat hippies." The sisters of Delta Zeta were seen as "socially awkward."

Worried that a negative stereotype of the sorority was contributing to a decline in membership that had left its Greek-columned house here half empty, Delta Zeta's national officers interviewed 35 DePauw members in November, quizzing them about their dedication to recruitment. They judged 23 of the women insufficiently committed and later told them to vacate the sorority house.

The 23 members included every woman who was overweight. They also included the only Korean and Vietnamese members. The dozen students allowed to stay were slender and popular with fraternity men—

*Women at DePauw University who either were asked to leave the Delta Zeta house or resigned in protest hold a sorority photo.*

women the ald attract new e 12 were so infuri- .

ly everyone who didn't fit a sorority member archetype° told to leave," said Kate Holloway, senior who withdrew from the chapter during its reorganization.

"I sensed the disrespect with which this was to be carried out and got fed up," Ms. Holloway added. "I didn't have room in my life for these women to come in and tell my sisters of three years that they weren't needed."

Ms. Holloway is not the only angry one. The reorganization has left a messy aftermath of recrimination and tears on this rural campus of 2,400 students, 50 miles southwest of Indianapolis.

The mass eviction battered the self-esteem of many of the former sorority members, and some withdrew from classes in depression. There have been student protests, outraged letters from alumni° and parents, and a faculty petition calling the sorority's action unethical.

DePauw's president, Robert G. Bottoms, issued a two-page letter of reprimand to the sorority. In an interview in his office, Dr. Bottoms said he had been stunned by the sorority's insensitivity.

"I had no hint they were going to disrupt the chapter with a membership reduction of this proportion in the middle of the year," he said. "It's been very upsetting."

The president of Delta Zeta, which has its headquarters in Oxford, Ohio, and its other national officers declined to be interviewed. Responding by e-mail to questions, Cynthia Winslow Menges, the executive director, said the sorority had not evicted the 23 women, even though the national officers sent those women form letters that said: "The membership review team has recommended you for alumna status. Chapter members receiving alumnae status should plan to relocate from the chapter house no later than Jan. 29, 2007."

Ms. Menges asserted that the women themselves had, in effect, made their own decisions to leave by demonstrating a lack of commitment to meet recruitment goals. The sorority paid each woman who left $300 to cover the difference between sorority and campus housing.

The sorority "is saddened that the isolated incident at DePauw has been mischaracterized," Ms. Menges wrote. Asked for clarification, the sorority's public relations representative e-mailed a statement saying its actions were aimed at the "enrichment of student life at DePauw."

This is not the first time that the DePauw chapter of Delta Zeta has stirred controversy. In 1982, it attracted national attention when a black student was not allowed to join, provoking accusations of racial discrimination.

---

***archetype:*** here, a model or perfect example.

***alumni:*** the masculine plural form of *alumnus*, a (male) graduate. The feminine singular form is *alumna*, and the feminine plural is *alumnae*. These plural forms are retained from Latin, their language of origin. As sometimes continues to be the case in English, a masculine form—here, *alumni*—is used to refer to both females and males.

Earlier this month, an Alabama lawyer and several other DePauw alumni who graduated in 1970 described in a letter to *The DePauw*, the student newspaper, how Delta Zeta's national leadership had tried unsuccessfully to block a young woman with a black father and a white mother from joining its DePauw chapter in 1967.

Despite those incidents, the chapter appears to have been home to a diverse community over the years, partly because it has attracted brainy women, including many science and math majors, as well as talented disabled women, without focusing as exclusively as some sororities on potential recruits' sex appeal, former sorority members said.

"I had a sister I could go to a bar with if I had boy problems," said Erin Swisshelm, a junior biochemistry major who withdrew from the sorority in October. "I had a sister I could talk about religion with. I had a sister I could be nerdy about science with. That's why I liked Delta Zeta, because I had all these amazing women around me."

But over the years DePauw students had attached a negative stereotype to the chapter, as evidenced by the survey that Pam Propsom, a psychology professor, conducts each year in her class. That image had hurt recruitment, and the national officers had repeatedly warned the chapter that unless its membership increased, the chapter could close.

At the start of the fall term the national office was especially determined to raise recruitment because 2009 is the 100th anniversary of the DePauw chapter's founding. In September, Ms. Menges and Kathi Heatherly, a national vice president of the sorority, visited the chapter to announce a reorganization plan they said would include an interview with each woman about her commitment. The women were urged to look their best for the interviews.

*Elizabeth Haneline, who was among those evicted, said, "The Greek system hasn't changed at all, but instead of racism, it's image now."*

The tone left four women so unsettled that they withdrew from the chapter almost immediately.

Robin Lamkin, a junior who is an editor at *The DePauw* and was one of the 23 women evicted, said many of her sisters bought new outfits and modeled them for each other before the interviews. Many women declared their willingness to recruit diligently, Ms. Lamkin said.

A few days after the interviews, national representatives took over the house to hold a recruiting event. They asked most members to stay upstairs in their rooms. To welcome freshmen downstairs, they assembled a team that included several of the women eventually asked to stay in the sorority, along with some slender women invited from the sorority's chapter at Indiana University, Ms. Holloway said.

"They had these unassuming freshman girls downstairs with these plastic women from Indiana University, and 25 of my sisters hiding upstairs," she said. "It was so fake, so completely dehumanized. I said, 'This calls for a little joke.'"

Ms. Holloway put on a wig and some John Lennon rose-colored glasses, burst through the front door and skipped around singing, "Ooooh! Delta Zeta!" and other chants.

The face of one of the national representatives, she recalled, "was like I'd run over her puppy with my car."

...resentatives ...sions in the form ...n Dec. 2, which said ...a intended to increase ...p to 95 by the 2009 anni-..., and that it would recruit ...g a "core group of women."

Elizabeth Haneline, a senior computer science major who was among those evicted, returned to the house that afternoon and found some women in tears. Even the chapter's president had been kicked out, Ms. Haneline said, while "other women who had done almost nothing for the chapter were asked to stay."

At least part of the disagreement behind this conflict lies in different criteria for evaluating who makes a good member of a sorority. See Chapter 10 for more on how to develop criteria for evaluation arguments.

LINK TO P. 216

25 Six of the 12 women who were asked to stay left the sorority, including Joanna Kieschnick, a sophomore majoring in English literature. "They said, 'You're not good enough' to so many people who have put their heart and soul into this chapter that I can't stay," she said.

In the months since, Cynthia Babington, DePauw's dean of students, has fielded angry calls from parents, she said. Robert Hershberger, chairman of the modern languages department, circulated the faculty petition; 55 professors signed it.

"We were especially troubled that the women they expelled were less about image and more about academic achievement and social service," Dr. Hershberger said.

30 During rush activities this month, 11 first-year students accepted invitations to join Delta Zeta, but only three have sought membership.

On Feb. 2, Rachel Pappas, a junior who is the chapter's former secretary, printed 200 posters calling on students to gather that afternoon at the student union. About 50 students showed up and heard Ms. Pappas say the sorority's national leaders had misrepresented the truth when they asserted they had evicted women for lack of commitment.

"The injustice of the lies," she said, "is contemptible."

### Correction: March 2, 2007

An article on Sunday about the eviction at DePauw University of members of the Delta Zeta sorority by the national organization referred incorrectly to a woman identified only as a black member of the sorority. Although the woman, Leah Souder, was not in fact one of 35 sorority members interviewed by the national organization, nor was she among the 23 of those 35 who received eviction letters, she says she has not heard from the national office since its reorganization of the DePauw chapter and assumes she is no longer a member.

## RESPOND •

1. What examples of stereotyping do you find discussed in this article? Who is being stereotyped? What or who, do you believe, are the sources of the stereotypes? What evidence is there in the article of people who are criticizing or contesting stereotypes? Who are they, and how are they calling stereotypes into question?
2. Paragraphs 13–14 provide historical background about the Delta Zeta sorority on the DePauw campus. Is this information necessary to the article? If so, how? If not, why not? What is the relationship between paragraphs 13–14 and paragraphs 15–16? What is the role of these two latter paragraphs in the article?
3. In printed newspapers, corrections appear several days after the original article is printed, but someone doing research might well not notice them. In contrast, a correction posted on an electronic source will always be available to future readers. In some cases, the correction is incorporated into the original article rather than being noted separately at the end of the article. The correction that appears at the end of this article reminds us that even award-winning journalists sometimes make errors. How serious, in your opinion, was the error in Dillon's original article? Does this correction influence how you read or evaluate the article? Does it influence how you evaluate the ethos of the writer? (For a discussion of ethos, see Chapter 3.)
4. As the headnote on p. 515 implies, this article set off a national controversy. For information about what happened, read the entry entitled "DePauw University Delta Zeta Discrimination Controversy" on Wikipedia. As is common with Wikipedia entries, especially those about fairly recent events, all the references cited are electronic sources. Thus, you can inspect the sources that were used in writing the entry. Choose three of the articles used as sources, and **write an evaluative argument** focusing on the support that they provide for the claims they make. (For a discussion of evaluative arguments, see Chapter 10.)
5. One way to analyze the situation at DePauw is to consider it as an argument of definition: Did stereotyping occur in the Delta Zeta sorority? **Write an argument of definition** considering the situation described in this article and the Wikipedia entry on the "DePauw University Delta Zeta Discrimination Controversy." You'll need to formulate a definition of stereotyping and demonstrate why the events at DePauw did or did not constitute stereotyping.

ɀley is former chair of the Los Angeles City/County Native mmission as well as president emeritus of the California ɀy Foundation (CCL), a local nonprofit philanthropic organization ɔrts "transformative change" in the region and the larger world. ɀrved as president of the CCL from 1980 until 2004. (Emeritus is ɔf honor granted in the business world upon retirement to someone ɔ has made important contributions to a company, corporation, or foun- ɀation over a long period of time. This rank is also conferred on some professors at the time of their retirement.) Shakley is currently a member of the Board of Advisors of the Center on Philanthropy and Public Policy at the University of Southern California. This article appeared in August 2011 on the op-ed page of the LA Times. (Traditionally, in U.S. newspapers, readers found pieces expressing opinions on various timely subjects and written by syndicated columnists or by writers who did not work for the newspaper on the page opposite the editorial page, hence, the name "op-ed.") As you read, note the kinds of evidence Shakley uses to support his position as well as important concessions he makes to those who would argue that teams should not bother to get rid of Native American mascots.

Shakley begins his argument with a personal anecdote. How does the use of personal experience help focus his argument? For more on using personal experience as evidence, see Chapter 17.

LINK TO P. 405

# Indian Mascots—You're Out!

JACK SHAKLEY

*Removing Native American names and mascots from college and professional teams is the right thing to do.*

I got my first lesson in Indians portrayed as sports team mascots in the early 1950s when my father took me to a Cleveland Indians–New York Yankees game. Dad gave me money to buy a baseball cap, and I was conflicted. I loved the Yankees, primarily because fellow Oklahoman Mickey Mantle had just come up and was being touted as rookie of the year. But being mixed-blood Muscogee/Creek,° I felt a (misplaced) loyalty to the Indians. So I bought the Cleveland cap with the famous Chief Wahoo logo on it.

When we got back to Oklahoma, my mother took one look at the cap with its leering, big-nosed, bucktoothed redskin caricature just above the brim, jerked it off my head and threw it in the trash. She had been fighting against Indian stereotypes all her life, and I had just worn one home. I was only 10 years old, but the look of betrayal in my Creek mother's eyes is seared in my memory forever.

So maybe I shouldn't have been surprised when half a century later, a *Los Angeles Times* editorial about legislators in North Dakota struggling over whether the University of North Dakota should be forced to change its team name and mascot from the Fighting Sioux provoked such a strong reaction. It was an irritant, like a long-forgotten piece of shrapnel° working its way to the surface.

Most stories about sports teams and their ethnic mascots are treated like tempests in a teacup. The *Times'* editorial writer, however, while noting that the solons° probably had better things to do, understood the sensitivity and pain that can accompany such a seemingly trivial subject. It is a small matter, perhaps, but far from trivial.

Many of the fights over team names 5
and mascots cover familiar territory.

*Respect or racism?*

Usually the team name in question has been around so long as to lose a good bit of its meaning. The University of Illinois' Fighting Illini, for example, refers to an Indian nation, but now that its Chief Illiniwek mascot has been abandoned, few people make the connection. Nor do they think twice about what the Atlanta Braves or Edmonton Eskimos or Florida State Seminoles represent other than sports franchises. But that doesn't necessarily make the brands benign. And the irony that the football team in our nation's capital is called the Redskins is not lost on a single Native American.

The controversy over changing ethnocentric° mascot names is not a simple matter of stodgy white alums holding onto college memories. Indians, too, are conflicted. In a 2002 study on the subject, *Sports Illustrated* reported that 84% of Native Americans polled had no problem with Indian team names or mascots. Although the methods used by the magazine to reach these figures were later criticized, that misses the point. If 16% of a population finds something offensive, that should be enough to signal deep concern. There are many things in this country that are subject to majority rule; dignity and respect are not among them.

And it is dignity and respect we are talking about. Since the creation of the National Coalition on Racism in

*What does the word* savages *connote for you?*

Sports and Media in 1991, that group of Native American organizations has been protesting negative portrayals of Indians, hammering away at what's behind our discomfort with Indian

***Muscogee/Creek:*** a Native American tribe originally from the Southern part of the United States.

***shrapnel:*** here, fragments from an exploding shell or grenade that penetrate a soldier's or civilian's skin and flesh during wartime. Shrapnel wounds are often fatal or severely debilitating. In cases where the wounded individual survives, the fragments sometimes cannot be surgically removed and remain inside the body.

***solon:*** legislator; as used in the United States today, the word often carries at least some negative connotations. Historically, Solon was an ancient Athenian statesman and reformer whose work helped create the conditions that gave rise to democracy in Athens.

***ethnocentric:*** assuming the superiority of a single ethnic group, generally one's own, and seeing the world from that perspective.

sports mascots. Many of these mascots—maybe most of them—act like fools or savage cutthroats.

When I went to an Atlanta Braves game in the 1970s, the Braves name wasn't the biggest problem. It was that cringe-worthy Chief Noc-A-Homa who came stomping and war-dancing his way out of a tepee in center field every time the Braves hit a home run that got to me. He was dressed in a Plains Indian chief's eagle bonnet and acted like a village idiot. To their credit, the Braves retired Chief Noc-A-Homa and his girlfriend Princess Win-A-Lot in 1983, amid assertions by the Braves' home office that the protesters were over-dramatizing the issue.

Few people complain about Florida State University calling itself the Seminoles. But its war-painted and lance-threatening mascot Chief Osceola is intended to be menacing, and that's the take-away many children will have. Such casual stereotyping can breed callousness. In the "only good Indian" category, in 1999 the *New York Post* entitled an editorial about the pending New York–Cleveland baseball playoffs, "Take the Tribe and Scalp 'Em."

10 It isn't easy or inexpensive to remove ethnic and racial stereotypes from college and professional sports. When Stanford University changed from the Indians to the Cardinal in 1972, recriminations were bitter. Richard Lyman, a friend of mine, was president of Stanford at the time. He said the university lost millions of alumni dollars in the short run, but it was the right thing to do.

In 21st century America, to name a sports team after an African American, Asian or any other ethnic group is unthinkable. So why are Native Americans still fair game? As benign as monikers like Fighting Sioux and Redskins or mascots like Chief Osceola may seem, they should take their place with the Pekin, Ill., Chinks° and the Atlanta Black Crackers° in the dust bin of history. It is the right thing to do.

---

***Pekin Chinks:*** name of the high school sports teams in Pekin, IL, from 1930 until 1980, when the teams became the Dragons. The school mascots were a male and female student dressed in traditional Chinese attire; the origin of the mascots was the similarity between the town's name and the name *Peking*, the earlier English spelling of Beijing, the capital of China. Chinese Americans had sought a name change as early as 1975, but the change occurred only in 1980 despite protests.

***Atlanta Black Crackers:*** a professional African American baseball team that existed from 1919 until 1952, five years after Jackie Robinson broke the color barrier in major league baseball.

## RESPOND •

1. What argument is Shakley making about stereotypes in the media and popular culture? What sorts of claims does he make to support his position? What concessions does he make to those who might disagree with him? (See paragraphs 5, 6, and 11 in particular.) How does he use these concessions to strengthen his own position?
2. What kinds of evidence does Shakley use to support his argument? How effective are his historical examples? In other words, what response did you have when you read about the Braves' mascots of the 1970s, for example, or the two examples cited in the final paragraph? Why might Shakley have chosen these examples? How do they represent pathetic appeals? (See Chapter 2 for a discussion of pathos and pathetic appeals.)
3. The case of the Florida Seminoles is an interesting one because Florida State University (FSU) and the Seminole Tribe of Florida have reached an agreement, albeit a controversial one, that permits FSU to continue using their mascot, Chief Osceola, and the team name, the Seminoles. They were prompted to do so following a 2005 ruling by the National Collegiate Athletic Association outlawing "mascots, nicknames, or images deemed hostile or abusive in terms of race, ethnicity, or national origin." Investigate this specific case to find out about the details of the agreement and debates surrounding it. (One resource is "Bonding over a Mascot," by Joe Lapointe, which appeared in the *New York Times* in December 2006, http://nyti.ms/Okvsow. As you read that article, pay careful attention to the ways in which stereotypes are themselves part of the terms of the agreement.) Based on what you learn, be prepared to discuss how Shakley would likely critique the Seminole Tribe's agreement with FSU beyond what he says in this essay.
4. Shakley refers to the National Coalition on Racism in Sports and Media (NCRSM), an American Indian organization formed in 1991. Visit the organization's Web site, http://bit.ly/7wrjxg, to learn more about this organization and its efforts to fight what it sees as negative stereotyping. In what ways does NCRSM seek to fight the common argument by supporters of the status quo, that is, that Native American mascots, nicknames, and images are used to honor American Indians and their culture and should be taken as compliments rather than as insults?

5. In concluding his essay, Shakley asks, "So why are Native Americans still fair game?" (His choice of metaphors here is surely not accidental: he is arguing, of course, that American culture is treating Native Americans as prey much as the American government and white settlers did during the nineteenth century in particular.) **Write an essay** in which you seek to respond to Shakley's question. As he notes, we cannot imagine naming a sports team after some other ethnic group or keeping such a name at this point in the history of American culture. Why should Native Americans be an exception? Depending on the way you approach this assignment, you may find yourself creating an argument that focuses largely on issues of definition or evaluation or a causal argument. (See Chapters 9, 10, and 11, respectively, for information on these three categories of argument.) Note that this assignment does not require that you state your own position with respect to this topic; however, you may wish to do so if doing so would be helpful to you.

*Porochista Khakpour (1979– ) is an Iranian-born American reared in California. Her 2007 novel* Sons and Other Flammable Objects *about fathers and sons of Iranian origin in the United States following the events of 9/11 received critical acclaim, winning several awards. Prior to becoming a novelist, Khakpour was a journalist writing about arts and entertainment for a number of newspapers and magazines. She has taught creative writing and literature at institutions in the United States and in Europe, and she is currently a member of the creative writing faculty in the MFA program at Fairfield University, Connecticut. This selection, "Reality TV Goes Where Football Meets the Hijab," first appeared in the* New York Times *in November 2011. As you read, pay careful attention to the ways that Khakpour simultaneously invokes an audience with intimate knowledge of American popular culture, especially reality TV, while mockingly using her status as an outsider—a freak—to critique media stereotypes in the United States in nonthreatening ways.*

# Reality TV Goes Where Football Meets the Hijab°

POROCHISTA KHAKPOUR

If anything made me an American, it was television. I learned English from soap operas—after kindergarten, curled up Mommy-side—and then beyond, the many hours she abandoned the sofa for the kitchen when I alternated between after-school cartoons and adult crime dramas. English came to me, and with it so many questions about what was happening on TV. But one that never hit home was why the people on the screen did not resemble my family. I suppose when your daily life involves acute consciousness of being a foreigner, you lack that sense of entitlement; self-identification with a popular representation of America was a luxury this newly transplanted Iranian immigrant didn't even know to lust for.

At school in suburban Los Angeles we took TV show residue and dumped it on the playground, recreating sitcoms and cartoon plots during recess. I was always typecast by the director, myself. I played only villains, Catra of *She-Ra*, the Misfits of *Jem*, Nellie of *Little House on the Prairie*. When the fifth grade put on a production of *The Wizard of Oz*, I tried out for the Wicked Witch, knowing I'd settle on Flying Monkey (the other brown girl, the class's sole South Asian, was immediately cast as Toto°) and was

***hijab:*** the head covering worn by some Muslim women, generally as a sign of their piety. Most often the hijab covers all the hair as well as the neck, leaving only the face visible.

***Toto:*** Dorothy's dog in the novel and the movie *The Wizard of Oz.*

*Sisters Suehaila Amen (left), who is wearing a hijab, and Shadia Amen-McDermott discuss their show* All-American Muslim.

crushed when I became a Kansan extra. I knew by then that heroines and ingénues◦ were "fair," as fairy tale convention dictated. Darkness—dark hair, dark eyes, dark skin—always equaled trouble, as if it actually implied a dark side. This expanded as I evolved into a teenage thespian◦ of school drama festival circuits, where, if not Medea◦ or Antigone,◦ I could be the comic relief: the zany psycho at worst and the wisecracking best friend at best.

In other words, part of assimilation was a crash course in sober self-awareness. I gravitated toward the freak, the outsider, the antagonist,◦ the one who did not belong in the protagonist's◦ vision, not because I had low self-esteem but because conditions couldn't have allowed for normal self-esteem. A bottle of water bobbing in an ocean doesn't contemplate its wetness, after all. I knew my place. I was a freak, and I consoled myself with one thought: Of all places, America was a pretty O.K. place for freakdom.

And that's one message sent by our culture of reality TV. Well-intentioned efforts like the new *All-American Muslim* aside, it's the realm of the freak—think of Puck from *The Real World*, the Osbournes at the dinner table, Kris Jenner accompanying her daughter on a Playboy shoot, Somethin of *Flavor of Love* defecating on the floor during a no-pun-intended elimination ceremony. The reality show theorem is a simple one: Propose a basic niche, and then go about a set of proofs that, with simple variations on a theme, repetitively reinforce it. The show

---

***ingénue:*** a common character type in literature, theater, and film; most often, an innocent, naïve, unsophisticated, and pure young woman or girl.

***thespian:*** actor.

***Medea:*** mythological ancient Greek enchantress who, according to Euripides's play of the same name, killed her two children when their father, Jason, betrayed her with another woman.

***Antigone:*** a virtuous character in Greek mythology. According to Sophocles's tragedy of the same name, Antigone's two brothers died fighting each other for the throne of Thebes, plunging the city into civil war. The city's new ruler declared that one of the brothers would have a state funeral while the other's body would be left outside the city walls to rot, the worst possible fate in ancient Greece. By night, Antigone rescued her brother's body and gave it a proper burial. She was captured. During her trial, she argued that her behavior was more ethical than the ruler's, and the ruler decreed that she would be buried alive in a cave.

masterminds might even pledge to prop up a people—designers! cooks! the Amish! dwarf grooms!—by raising awareness, perhaps pursuing the idea that exposure in itself is a type of service, but the world of toddlers and their tiaras, and sister-wives and bridalplasty is the all-for-profit evil twin of Documentary Land. Its value lies in sensation and so, more often than not, we are watching the shows the same way we rubberneck a car crash. Or we file its so-bad-it's-goodness under "guilty pleasure," along with Hostess products° and bummed smokes and other things that will eventually kill us.

5 And this becomes more culturally problematic when you throw ethnocentric° reality shows in the mix. The most famous one set a false precedent by getting away with it. While Snooki and the Situation even managed to irk some Italian-Americans in the end, *Jersey Shore* escaped citation from the political-correctness police, since we don't live in a time of mass marginalization of Italian-Americans.

Cable channels have been trying their hand at the ethnocentric reality lottery ever since, from Russians (*Russian Dolls*) to Chinese (*Family Restaurant*) to even Iranians. Over the summer Bravo announced *The Shahs of Sunset*, and one can imagine that that Iranian-American venture, produced by Ryan Seacrest, will be a manic mash-up of much Jersey Shoring in the kingdom of Kardashia.

Mr. Seacrest's announcement seemed mired in flash and trash: "Armed with chromed-out cars, logo-ridden purses and designer outfits, they've got it, and they're not afraid to flaunt it. But while these young socialites know how to spend money—they also know the value of family and tradition. It's a part of Los Angeles culture and lifestyle that definitely has to be seen to be believed." That implied adherence to Reality 101 spectacle has got my inner-child-freak losing it over what might happen to my native Tehrangelenos.°

Compare that reality take on a Middle Eastern people with a news release about *All-American Muslim*, the latest from TLC (the channel behind *Sarah Palin's Alaska*), starting Sunday night: "Through these families and their diverse experiences, we will explore how they blend their values and traditions with everyday life in America." The author Reza Aslan, whose media entertainment company, BoomGen Studios, has been helping TLC with publicity, calls it "a groundbreaking, intimate look inside the lives of a group of Muslim families in Dearborn, Mich., who are struggling with the everyday issues that all families deal with." He adds, "Except they are doing it at a time of unprecedented anti-Muslim hysteria in America."

Everyday. There is a reason that word keeps coming up. There is absolutely nothing extraordinary about *All-American Muslim*, and that's the point.

10 Enter the Midwest's Little Mideast: Dearborn, "America's Muslim Capital," is over 30 percent Arab. It's also home to the Islamic Center of America, the largest mosque in the country. The show focuses on five families in this enclave. You have the newlyweds Nawal and Nader, on the verge of having a baby; Mike, the deputy police chief; Foaud, the head coach of the high school football team; Nina, the platinum-blond businesswoman; and the heavily tattooed and pierced Shadia, who marries an Irish-Catholic.

The most maxi-Muslim predicaments in the first few episodes? Foaud switching the nearly all-Muslim football team's practice to nocturnal hours

---

***antagonist:*** briefly, the "bad guy" in a story, play, or film.

***protagonist:*** briefly, the "good guy" in a story, play, or film.

***Hostess products:*** baked goods produced by Hostess Brands, most famously Hostess Twinkies, CupCakes, Ding Dongs, and other snacks.

***ethnocentric:*** assuming the superiority of a single ethnic group, generally one's own, and seeing the world from that perspective.

***Tehrangelenos:*** Iranians living in Los Angeles (from Tehran, the capital of Iran, and Angelenos, residents of Los Angeles).

*Dearborn's Islamic Center of America*

because of Ramadan fasting°; Shadia's groom-to-be's conversion to Islam (it involves the uttering of a single holy phrase before Shadia's relaxed, wisecracking family); and Shadia's sister Samira's donning of the hijab in order to enhance her fertility by appearing pious in God's eyes. And that's about it.

The ground is breaking, as Mr. Aslan implies, but ever so demurely. In a January article in the *Chicago Tribune* in which I was quoted, the columnist Clarence Page° examined Katie Couric's answer to Islamophobia°: "*The Cosby Show*° did so much to change attitudes about African-Americans in this country, and I think sometimes people are afraid of things they don't understand," he quoted her as saying. Mr. Page, in calling Muslims the "new 'Negroes,'" also felt the Cosby characters served a great purpose in showing "the American Dream is not for whites only." But if patiently viewed by the gladiatorial-combat-hungry masses, *All-American Muslim* might achieve much more at first by taking on less: showing people that Arab Muslims are Americans. Then maybe we can move on to American Dreaming.

I admit, as I watched preview episodes, the lessons seemed not for me at first; I drifted a bit, mildly entertained by superficial peripherals like Midwestern accents on Middle Eastern people. The show's affable educationality reminded me of high school cultural exchange videos in language class. I caught myself longing for a drunken brawl, someone in the bed of someone they shouldn't be with, some pretty girl's big stink on a spiral staircase.

But then I realized the freak was there. For many Americans just a woman in a hijab is a red alert on the freak meter. Voyeurism is the draw here, but it's voyeurism with a silver lining. Between the Islamophobe and Islamist there are the simply curious who may catch on that assumptions about a certain other's freakdom are sorely misplaced. "Muslims: they're just

---

**Ramadan fasting:** During the lunar month of Ramadan, devout Muslims avoid food, beverage, tobacco, and sexual activity from before dawn (the time one can tell a black thread from a white thread) until sundown.

**Clarence Page (1947– ):** Pulitzer Prize–winning syndicated columnist who writes for the *Chicago Tribune*, broadcast journalist, and author. An African American, Page often examines issues related to race.

**Islamophobia:** fear of Islam or Muslims.

**The Cosby Show:** award-winning prime-time NBC sitcom focusing on the Huxtable family, starring Bill Cosby as Cliff Huxtable, an obstetrician, and Phyllis Rashad as his wife, Clair, an attorney, which ran from 1984 to 1992. One of the biggest hits of the decade, the program was the first to represent an affluent, professional African American family on prime-time television, though race as a topic was rarely explicitly addressed.

like you and me" seems like an embarrassing message for us to be grappling with in 2011, but our ever-fearing "never-forgetting" has created a forever-post-Sept. 11 era whose only antidote might be a normalcy verging on mundanity.°

15 It would be nice to pretend that the straightness of *All-American Muslim* is part of reality TV's sobering up, a sort of noble resurrection after death by trashiness, but more likely the matteing° of the glossy-exotic here is entirely measured. Some of us might miss the spectacle of the freak—I can even see the confused child in me scouring the women of the cast for my hot mess of choice and coming up empty-handed—but even the most jaded of us Middle Eastern Americans might come out with a valuable lesson.

Seasons ago, before I knew of any potential reality hits on anything close to my ethnicity, I decided to embark on a novel about two of my worst nightmares: the first Iranian-American reality television family and war with Iran. Insanity ensues, of course, but once I walked away from *All-American Muslim* and back to my desk, I found my instincts challenged a bit. Maybe that stranger-than-fiction dream my kiddie self and my adult writer self would never have indulged could happen: for once, maybe the freaks took off their masks, and people liked what they saw.

---

***mundanity:*** the condition of being boring or everyday.

***matte:*** to finish with a flat (in contrast to shiny or glossy) surface.

## RESPOND •

1. What arguments is Khakpour making about how stereotyping works in American society and especially in the media? In what ways is she arguing for the benefits of reality TV, an often-maligned genre of popular media?
2. Khakpour's discussion of television and popular media reflects themes common in the writing of recent generations of the children of immigrants to the United States. As she notes in the selection's opening line, "If anything made me an American, it was television." What, specifically, did television teach Khakpour about how Americans see the world? At the same time, as Khakpour also notes, she never saw her own family—or families like hers—represented on television. What lessons did she learn from that fact?
3. Humor is always a two-edged sword, and misused, it does far more damage than good. Yet Khakpour uses humor quite effectively. How, specifically, does she use humor? Who or what are the targets of her humor? How does her use of humor enable her to critique American society without putting readers who are different from her on the defensive?
4. From a different perspective, we might claim that Khakpour uses aspects of Rogerian argumentation as discussed in Chapter 7, specifi-

cally the ways that she finds common ground with readers whose lives may be different from hers in many regards. In addition to humor (see question 3), what other techniques does Khakpour use in discussing Muslims in America at a time when suspicion of Muslims continues to run high?

5. In December 2011, *All-American Muslim* became the subject of controversy when it was condemned by the Florida Family Association for representing Muslims in a positive light; the FFA led a campaign to get sponsors to drop their sponsorship of this program and succeeded in some cases. Investigate this controversy, and **write a rhetorical analysis** of the arguments used by the FFA to argue for their position or by those who took issue with the FFA's campaign. (Chapter 6 provides information about rhetorical analyses.)
6. As noted, Khakpour contends that reality television can serve very useful roles in a society like ours. **Write an essay** in which you evaluate the positive and negative ways that reality television deals with or perpetuates stereotypes in American society. You will likely want to select a single reality television program and analyze it (and perhaps a single episode of that program) in some detail rather than choosing examples from many different programs. (See Chapter 10 on evaluative arguments.)

**Andy Singer, *Bicycle Gun Racks***
Singer has been a self-syndicated cartoonist for more than two decades, and his work appears in many publications here and abroad. (His Web site is andysinger.com.) In this cartoon, NRA refers to the National Rifle Association, of course, and Singer assumes readers share certain stereotypes about who NRA members are—and likely aren't.

## Making a Visual Argument: Cartoons and Stereotypes

▲ *A well-known anthropologist claims that if he were dropped into a strange culture and had only an afternoon to figure out the nature of social organization there, he'd ask local people to tell him jokes because jokes ultimately reveal the fault lines in a society; that is, they indirectly indicate where the social divisions are. Jokes frequently treat topics that are taboo or nearly so; thus, they likewise reveal perspectives on controversial issues as understood within a given society. Of course, jokes are a genre of the spoken language while cartoons are their multimodal print equivalent. By combining image and text in some way, cartoons present arguments that critique some aspect of the social order, whether a controversy that has simmered for quite a while or some recent event that was the talk of yesterday's talk shows and Twitter feeds. The arguments cartoons present, often mocking in nature, are profoundly local. A major reason humor, including jokes and cartoons, doesn't translate well is that the things each society (and subgroups within any given society) considers funny and the topics it considers appropriate to make light of vary widely. As you study the cartoons in this selection, examine each from these perspectives. Is the cartoon concerned with a long-standing controversy or some specific event or situation? What social divisions in American society does the cartoon acknowledge, and what is the basis for those divisions—political affiliation, age, ethnicity, sex or gender, sexual identity, region of birth, or some combination of these? As noted in the introductory note to the chapter, you will also want to consider which common stereotypes you don't see represented in these cartoons and whether it is because they are too potentially incendiary or explosive to find their way into print in mainstream publications or in textbooks like this one. In other words, what social taboos can't be violated, at least not in these contexts, when the medium is cartoons? Finally, think about the cultural knowledge required to understand each of these cartoons; as you'll see, in some cases, that knowledge is quite complex.*

**Matthew Diffee, *Whack-a-Yankee***
Matthew Diffee, a graduate of Bob Jones University, grew up in Texas and North Carolina. In addition to being a cartoonist, he's the creator of several volumes in the "Rejection Collection" series, in which he gathers cartoons that were rejected by the *New Yorker* along with interviews with the cartoonists. The most recent volume in this series is *The Best of the Rejection Collection: 293 Cartoons That Were Too Dumb, Too Dark, or Too Naughty for the* New Yorker (2011). In this cartoon, which, in fact, appeared in the *New Yorker*, Diffee gives new life to a long-standing regional rivalry in the United States. If you're not familiar with the game "Whack-a-Mole," check out the Wikipedia entry on it, paying attention to colloquial usage of the phrase; you'll need that information to understand this cartoon.

**Eric Allie, *Get a Job***
Eric Allie is a cartoonist for the *St. Paul Pioneer Press*, and his work is syndicated by Cagle Cartoons. This cartoon came in response to a remark made during the 2012 presidential primaries by Democratic strategist Hilary Rosen, who stated that Anne Romney, wife of Republican presidential candidate Mitt Romney, "hasn't worked a day in her life." Republicans were quick to capitalize on these remarks by appealing to stereotypes of liberals as disrespectful of the values of conservative women who stay home to raise families. (Romney had stayed home to rear her five sons, and as she responded, "Believe me, it was hard work.")

**Rob Tornoe, *Gay Marriage in New Jersey***
Rob Tornoe is a political cartoonist who lives in Delaware. His Web site is robtornoe.com. This cartoon appeared in January 2010, shortly after the New Jersey Senate voted against gay marriage; the Iowa Supreme Court had upheld the right to gay marriage in April 2009. How does this cartoon trade on regional stereotypes about progressive politics in New Jersey versus Iowa?

**Jen Sorensen, *The Hoodie: Apparel of Peril!***
Jen Sorensen, the creator of *Slowpoke*, considers herself an alternative cartoonist who focuses on current events. Her Web site is slowpokecomics.com. As she notes on the site, she didn't go to art school, but she wore a lot of black in high school. This cartoon appeared early in 2012, during the controversy surrounding the shooting of Trayvon Martin, an unarmed, seventeen-year-old African American man, by George Zimmerman, a twenty-eight-year-old multiracial Hispanic who was a community watch coordinator in a gated community in Sanford, Florida. Rivera is a well-known media personality of Puerto Rican and Jewish ancestry who frequently appears on Fox television.

**RESPOND**

1. How would you state the argument each cartoon is making? In particular, what position or stance is the cartoonist taking with respect to the topic of the cartoon? What evidence can you cite for your claim?
2. Cartoonists who create single-panel cartoons like these face great challenges: they have limited resources and space to make their argument clear, and they must do so in a humorous way. A key way they succeed is by paying careful attention to visual and verbal detail. Choose two of these cartoons you think are especially effective in this regard, and be prepared to explain to your classmates how the cartoonists have used visual images and words effectively in ways that support each cartoon's argument.
3. A common source of humor is the juxtaposition of things that normally do not occur together. Where do we see evidence of this strategy in each of these cartoons?
4. How does each cartoonist rely on stereotypes to make his or her point? In other words, which stereotypes common in American society do we see represented in these cartoons, and how does each cartoonist represent them so that they are immediately identifiable by readers?
5. As noted in the introduction to this selection, understanding humor requires a great deal of local contextual information. Imagine that a newly arrived international student asked you to explain one of these cartoons to her or him. In several healthy paragraphs, **write a description and explanation** of the cartoon you find most interesting. Begin by describing what readers see when they read the cartoon; then move on to explain what the cartoon means. Be sure to deal with the issues raised in questions 1–4. Conclude by explaining what Americans would likely find humorous about the cartoon and what the cartoon tells us about American society.

▼ *Charles A. Riley II is a professor of journalism at Baruch College, part of the City University of New York. He also served as editor in chief of WE, a now-defunct national bimonthly magazine that focused on disability issues. During his career, he has received several awards for his writing on issues relating to disability. (Riley is able-bodied, a fact that he believes has important consequences for his writing on these issues.) Among his books are* Aristocracy and the Modern Imagination *(1980);* Disability and Business: Best Practices and Strategies for Inclusion *(1980);* Color Codes: Modern Theories of Color in Philosophy, Painting and Architecture, Literature, Music, and Psychology *(1995);* Small Business, Big Politics: What Entrepreneurs Need to Know to Use Their Growing Political Power *(1996); and* The Jazz Age in France *(2004). The selections featured here come from* Disability and the Media: Prescriptions for Change *(2005). These selections include the opening pages of Riley's "Preface" as well as an appendix created by the National Center on Disability and Journalism in 2002 that offers guidelines for portraying people with disabilities in the media. As you read, note ways in which Riley marshals evidence to demonstrate a need for change and the appendix constitutes a set of proposals to create that change.*

# Disability and the Media: Prescriptions for Change

CHARLES A. RILEY II

Every time Aimee Mullins sees her name in the papers she braces herself for some predictable version of the same headline followed by the same old story. Paralympian, actress, and fashion model, Mullins is a bilateral, below-the-knee amputee, who sprints a hundred meters in less than sixteen seconds on a set of running prostheses called Cheetahs because they were fashioned after the leg form of the world's fastest animal. First, there are the headlines: "Overcoming All Hurdles" (she is not a hurdler, although she is a long jumper) or "Running Her Own Race," "Nothing Stops Her," or the dreaded overused "Profile in Courage." Then come the clichés and stock scenes, from the prosthetist's office to the winner's podium. Many of the articles dwell on her success as the triumph of biomechanics, a "miracle of modern medicine,"

*Aimee Mullins at the sixth annual L'Oréal Paris Women of Worth awards ceremony in 2011*

turning her fairy tale into a *Coppélia*° narrative (or a *Six Million Dollar Woman*° movie sequel). From the local paper where she grew up (Allentown, Pennsylvania), to national exposure in *Esquire* and *People* and guest spots on *Oprah*, Mullins's "inspiring" saga is recycled almost verbatim by well-meaning journalists for audiences who never seem to get enough of its feel-good message even if they never actually find out who Mullins is.

This is the patronizing, trivializing, and marginalizing ur-narrative° of disability in the media today. The mainstream press finds it irresistible, but this steady diet of sugar has its dangers. The cliché has excluded the mature, fully realized coverage that people with disabilities have long deserved. For Mullins, it has translated into well over her Warholian° fifteen minutes of fame, bringing her the financial rewards of sponsorships, motivational speaking gigs, and modeling contracts at the expense of being turned into a latter-day poster child.° Stories about her rarely get around to mentioning that she was a Pentagon intern while making the dean's list as an academic star in history and diplomacy at Georgetown, or that she is one of the actresses in Matthew Barney's avant-garde *Cremaster* film series.

Mullins is not the only celebrity with a disability to be steamrolled out of three-dimensional humanity into allegorical° flatness. All the branches of the

**Coppélia:** a nineteenth-century French comic and sentimental opera in which Dr. Coppélius creates a dancing doll that is so lifelike that a young man falls in love with her.

**Six Million Dollar Woman:** an allusion to *Six Million Dollar Man*, a late 1970s ABC television program about an astronaut who was "rebuilt" after a crash to become a cyborg, part human and part machine.

***ur-narrative:*** the prefix *ur-* refers to the earliest, original, or most primitive or basic. Hence, the ur-narrative is the source narrative on which all others are based.

***Warholian:*** a reference to Andy Warhol (1928–1987), American avant-garde artist who commented in 1968, "In the future, everyone will be famous for fifteen minutes," a critique of how modern media create instant celebrities.

*Early examples of poster children*

***poster child:*** a perfect representative. The source of the phrase is the image of a disabled child or one with a visible medical condition whose photo is used on posters to elicit sympathy and donations.

***allegorical:*** the adjectival form of *allegory*, a moral story in which the characters, always one-dimensional in nature, suggest a meaning beyond the story. Thus, in Aesop's fable about the ant and the grasshopper, listeners are to understand that the wise person prepares for future needs, as the ant did, rather than wasting time, as did the grasshopper.

Before he offers his proposal, Riley first explains how stereotyping causes problems for the disabled. For more on causal arguments, see Chapter 11.

LINK TO P. 242

media considered here, from print to television, radio and the movies (including advertisements) to multimedia and the Internet, are guilty of the same distillation of stories to meet their own, usually fiscal, ends. For example, even though her autobiography is remarkably ahead of its time in its anticipation of disability culture, by the time Helen Keller° had been sweetened for movie audiences in Patty Duke's° version of her life, little was left out of the fiery trailblazer. In much the same way, Christopher Reeve° and Michael J. Fox° have been pigeonholed by print and television hagiographers° as lab experiments and tragic heroes. Packaged to raise philanthropic or advertising dollars, they perform roles no less constrained than the pretty-boy parts they played on screen earlier in their lives.

What is wrong with this picture? By jamming Mullins and the others into prefabricated stories—the supercrip, the medical miracle, the object of pity—writers and producers have outfitted them with the narrative equivalent of an ill-fitting set of prostheses. Each of these archetypal narratives has its way of reaching mass audiences, selling products (including magazines and movie tickets), and financially rewarding both the media outlet and the featured subject. In some ways, as optimists point out, this represents an improvement. We have had millennia of fiction and nonfiction depicting

*Helen Keller (1880–1968):* the first American who was both deaf and blind to graduate from college, Keller was an author and activist for progressive causes.

*Patty Duke (1946– ):* an American actress who played Helen Keller in the 1959 play *The Miracle Worker* and in the 1962 film version of the story.

*Christopher Reeve (1952–2004):* an American actor who is best known for his four Superman films. In 1995, he was paralyzed in a riding accident and used a wheelchair for the rest of his life. After his accident, he became an activist for public issues related to spinal-cord injuries and stem-cell research.

*Michael J. Fox (1961– ):* an award-winning Canadian-born actor. Diagnosed with Parkinson's disease in 1991, he revealed the condition to the public in 1998 and partially retired in 2000.

*hagiographer:* technically, one who studies saints. Here, hagiography is used to refer to the ways in which able-bodied individuals often portray people with disabilities as saints, thereby refusing to let them be fully human.

*Patty Duke (center) as Helen Keller in* The Miracle Worker

*Michael J. Fox, an actor and Parkinson's disease activist*

angry people with disabilities as villains, from Oedipus° to Ahab° to Dr. Strangelove.° The vestigial° traces of that syndrome still occasionally recur, although with far less frequency, in current movies or television series and in journalists' fixation on the mental instability of violent criminals. However, today's storytellers, including those in the disability media, are more likely to make people with disabilities into "heroes of assimilation," to borrow a phrase from Erving Goffman's° seminal work on disability, *Stigma: Notes on the Management of Spoiled Identity*.

As Goffman knew too well, just as the stigmatization of the villain had its 5
dilatory effects° on societal attitudes, so too does relentless hagiography, particularly by transforming individuals into symbols and by playing on an audience's sympathy and sense of superiority. Those who labor in the field of disability studies point out that disability culture and its unique strengths are absent from this story of normalization. Others would simply note that the individual is lost in the fable, an all-American morality tale that strikes one of the most resonant chords in the repertoire: redemption. Like the deathless Horatio Alger° tale, the story of the hero of assimilation emphasizes many of the deepest values and beliefs of the Puritan tradition, especially the notion that suffering makes us stronger and better. An able-bodied person falls from grace (often literally falling or crashing, as in the case of many spinal cord injuries), progresses through the shadows of rehabilitation and

***Oedipus:*** the mythical Greek king who unknowingly fulfills a prophecy that he will kill his father and marry his mother. After realizing what he has done, he blinds himself.

***Ahab:*** the captain of the whaling ship in Herman Melville's 1851 novel *Moby-Dick*. After losing a leg in an earlier effort to kill the whale Moby-Dick, Ahab is obsessed with harpooning the creature. His actions lead to the loss of the ship and the lives of all onboard with the exception of Ishmael, whose narrative opens the novel.

*Ahab from* Moby-Dick

***Dr. Strangelove:*** the title character in the 1964 film comedy *Dr. Strangelove or: How I Learned to Stop Worrying and Love the Bomb*. Strangelove, played by Peter Sellers, uses a wheelchair and suffers from alien hand syndrome. He is often used to represent the stereotype of a "mad scientist."

***vestigial:*** adjectival form of *vestige*, a more basic or rudimentary structure that no longer has any useful function; therefore, a useless leftover.

***Erving Goffman (1922–1982):*** a highly influential Canadian-born sociologist who taught in the United States. His work was much concerned with the nature of the social organization of everyday life.

***dilatory effects:*** effects that delay or cause delay, here of positive changes in societal attitudes.

***Horatio Alger Jr. (1832–1899):*** the prolific author of popular "rags to riches" tales in which hardworking, virtuous poor boys rise to stable and productive lives at the lower edges of the middle class.

depression, and by force of willpower along with religious belief pulls through to attain a quality of life that is less disabled, more normal, basking in the glow of recognition for beating the odds.

This pervasive narrative can be found in print, on television, in movies, in advertisements, and on the Web. Its corrosive effect on understanding and attitudes is as yet unnoticed. It is impossible to know the full degree of damage wreaked by the demeaning and wildly inaccurate portrayal of people with disabilities, nor is it altogether clear whether much current progress is being made. Painful as it is for me as an advocate to report the bad news, I cannot help but point out that the "movement" has slowed to a crawl in terms of political and economic advancement for 54 million Americans. The stasis° that threatens is at least partly to be blamed on a reassuring, recurring image projected by the media that numbs nondisabled readers and viewers into thinking that all is well.

***stasis:*** here, inactivity or lack of movement.

This study aims to expose the extent of the problem while pinpointing how writers, editors, photographers, filmmakers, advertisers, and the executives who give them their marching orders go wrong, or occasionally get it right. Through a close analysis of the technical means of representation, in conjunction with the commentary of leading voices in the disability community, I hope to guide future coverage to a more fair and accurate way of putting the disability story on screen or paper. Far from another stab at the political correctness target, the aim of this content analysis° of journalism, film, advertising, and Web publishing is to cut through the accumulated clichés and condescension to find an adequate vocabulary that will finally represent the disability community in all its vibrant and fascinating diversity. Nothing like that will ever happen if the press and advertisers continue to think, write, and design as they have in the past.

***content analysis:*** a family of research methodologies used in the humanities and social sciences that focus on the content of "messages"—books, articles, movies, paintings, research interviews—to study recurring themes or patterns across time or at a given time. For example, we could use content analysis to trace the shift from the use of *crippled* to *disabled* in newspaper articles or the ways that people with disabilities were portrayed in early twentieth-century American novels.

## Appendix A

### Guidelines for Portraying People with Disabilities in the Media

Fear of the unknown. Inadequate experience. Incorrect or distorted information. Lack of knowledge. These shape some of the attitudinal barriers that people with disabilities face as they become involved in their communities.

People working in the media exert a powerful influence over the way people with disabilities are perceived. It's important to the 54 million Americans with disabilities that they be portrayed realistically and that their disabilities are explained accurately.

Awareness is the first step toward change. 10

### Tips for Reporting on People with Disabilities

- When referring to individuals with disabilities use "disability," not "handicapped."
- Emphasize the person, not the disability or condition. Use "people with disabilities" rather than "disabled persons," and "people with epilepsy" rather than "epileptics."
- Omit mention of an individual's disability unless it is pertinent to the story.
- Depict the typical achiever with a disability, not just the super-achiever.
- Choose words that are accurate descriptions and have non-judgmental connotations.
- People with disabilities live everyday lives and should be portrayed as contributing members of the community. These portrayals should:
  - Depict people with disabilities experiencing the same pain/pleasure that others derive from everyday life, e.g., work, parenting, education, sports and community involvement.
  - Feature a variety of people with disabilities when possible, not just someone easily recognized by the general public.
  - Depict employees/employers with disabilities working together.
- Ask people with disabilities to provide correct information and assistance to avoid stereotypes in the media.
- Portray people with disabilities as people, with both strengths and weaknesses.

### *Appropriate Words When Portraying People with Disabilities*

**Never Use**

**victim**—use: person who has/experienced/with.
**[the] cripple[d]**—use: person with a disability.
**afflicted by/with**—use: person has.
**invalid**—use: a person with a disability.
**normal**—most people, including people with disabilities, think they are.
**patient**—connotes sickness. Use: person with a disability.

**Avoid Using**

**wheelchair bound/confined**—use: uses a wheelchair or wheelchair user.
**homebound employment**—use: employed in the home.

### Use with Care

**courageous, brave, inspirational** and similar words routinely used to describe persons with disabilities. Adaption to a disability does not necessarily mean someone acquires these traits.

## *Interviewing People with Disabilities*

When interviewing a person with a disability, relax! Conduct your interview as you would with anyone. Be clear and candid in your questioning and ask for clarification of terms or issues when necessary. Be upfront about deadlines, the focus of your story, and when and where it will appear.

### Interviewing Etiquette

- Shake hands when introduced to someone with a disability. People with limited hand use or artificial limbs do shake hands.
- Speak directly to people with disabilities, not through their companions.
- Don't be embarrassed using such phrases as "See you soon," "Walk this way" or "Got to run." These are common expressions, and are unlikely to offend.
- If you offer to help, wait until the offer is accepted.
- Consider the needs of people with disabilities when planning events.
- Conduct interviews in a manner that emphasizes abilities, achievements and individual qualities.
- Don't emphasize differences by putting people with disabilities on a pedestal.

This appendix offers a set of clear guidelines but sometimes does not explain the reasoning behind particular guidelines. Practice identifying the warrants, as described in Chapter 7, that lie behind these claims.

LINK TO P. 135

### When Interviewing People with Hearing Disabilities

- Attract the person's attention by tapping on his or her shoulder or waving.
- If you are interviewing someone with a partial hearing loss, ask where it would be most comfortable for you to sit.
- If the person is lip-reading, look directly at him/her and speak slowly and clearly. Do not exaggerate lip movements or shout. Do speak expressively, as facial expressions, gestures and body movements will help him/her understand you.
- Position yourself facing the light source and keep hands and food away from your mouth when speaking.

### When Interviewing People with Vision Disabilities

- Always identify yourself and anyone else who might be present.
- When offering a handshake, say, "Shall we shake hands?"
- When offering seating, place the person's hand on the back or arm of the seat.
- Let the person know if you move or need to end the conversation.

### When Interviewing People with Speech Disabilities

- Ask short questions that require short answers when possible.
- Do not feign understanding. Try rephrasing your questions, if necessary.

### When Interviewing People Using a Wheelchair or Crutches

- Do not lean on a person's wheelchair. The chair is part of his/her body space.
- Sit or kneel to place yourself at eye level with the person you are interviewing.
- Make sure the interview site is accessible. Check for:
  Reserved parking for people with disabilities
  A ramp or step-free entrance
  Accessible restrooms
  An elevator if the interview is not on the first floor
  Water fountains and telephones low enough for wheelchair use

Be sure to notify the interviewee if there are problems with the location. Discuss what to do and make alternate plans.

### Writing about Disability

One of the first and most significant steps to changing negative stereotypes and attitudes toward people with disabilities begins when we rethink the way written and spoken images are used to portray people with disabilities. The following is a brief, but important, list of suggestions for portraying people with disabilities in the media.

People with disabilities are not "handicapped," unless there are physical or attitudinal barriers that make it difficult for them to participate in everyday activities. An office building with steps and no entry ramp creates a "handicapping" barrier for people who use wheelchairs. In the same way, a hotel that does not have a TTY/telephone (teletypewriter) creates a barrier for someone who is hearing disabled. It is important to focus on the person, not necessarily the disability. In writing, name the person first and then, if necessary, explain his or her disability. The same rule applies when speaking. Don't focus on someone's disability unless it's crucial to the point being made.

In long, written materials, when many references have been made to persons with disabilities or someone who is disabled, it is acceptable for later references to refer to "disabled persons" or "disabled individuals."

15 Because a person is not a condition or a disease, avoid referring to someone with a disability by his or her disability alone. For example, don't say someone is a "post-polio" or a "C.P." or an "epileptic." Refer instead to someone who has post-polio syndrome, or has cerebral palsy, or has epilepsy.

Don't use "disabled" as a noun because it implies a state of separateness. "The disabled" are not a group apart from the rest of society. When writing or speaking about people with disabilities, choose descriptive words and portray people in a positive light.

Avoid words with negative connotations:

- Avoid calling someone a "victim."
- Avoid referring to people with disabilities as "cripples" or "crippled." This is negative and demeaning language.
- Don't write or say that someone is "afflicted."
- Avoid the word "invalid" as it means, quite literally, "not valid."
- Write or speak about people who use wheelchairs. Wheelchair users are not "wheelchair-bound."
- Refer to people who are not disabled as "non-disabled" or "able-bodied." When you call non-disabled people "normal," the implication is that people with disabilities are not normal.
- Someone who is disabled is only a patient to his or her physician or in a reference to medical treatment.
- Avoid cliches. Don't use "unfortunate," "pitiful," "poor," "dumb," "crip," "deformed," "retard," "blind as a bat" or other patronizing and demeaning words.
- In the same vein, don't glamorize or make heroes of people with disabilities simply because they have adapted to their disabilities.

Your concerted efforts to use positive, non-judgmental respectful language when referring to people with disabilities in writing and in everyday speaking can go a long way toward helping to change negative stereotypes.

## RESPOND •

1. In what ways does Riley contend that the media and popular culture wrongly stereotype people with disabilities? What negative consequences follow from this stereotyping for such people? For those who do not have disabilities? Why?
2. How convincingly has Riley defined a problem or need, which is the first step in a proposal argument? (For a discussion of proposal arguments, see Chapter 12.)
3. What is your response to "Appendix A: Guidelines for Portraying People with Disabilities in the Media"? Are you familiar with the practices that these guidelines seek to prevent? Do you find the guidelines useful or necessary? Why or why not? What justification might be offered for why specific guidelines are important? (Here, you will want to choose three or four of the guidelines and make explicit the arguments in support of each of them.)
4. Look for some specific representations of people with disabilities in current media and popular culture—in advertisements, television programs, or movies. To what extent do these representations perpetuate the stereotypes that Riley discusses, "the supercrip, the medical miracle, the object of pity" (paragraph 4)? **Write an argument of fact** in which you present your findings. (For a discussion of arguments of fact, see Chapter 8.) If you do not find representations of people with disabilities in various media or in popular culture, that absence is significant and merits discussion and analysis.
5. **Write an evaluative essay** in which you assess the value of these guidelines. In other words, if the media follow these guidelines, what will the consequences be for the media? For society at large? To what extent will following these guidelines likely influence negative stereotypes about people with disabilities? (For a discussion of evaluative arguments, see Chapter 10.)

*Aimee Mullins practices her jumps.*

▼ *Patricia J. Williams (1951– ) writes monthly for the* Nation, *a weekly magazine known for its liberal perspectives on culture and politics. Williams's column, "Diary of a Mad Law Professor," examines issues related to law and culture in the United States, Britain, and France. She is most widely known as a legal scholar whose work focuses on understanding legal theory from perspectives that acknowledge the experience of people from different racial and ethnic groups. Currently, she holds the James L. Dohr Professorship of Law at Columbia University. The author of four books, she was the recipient of a MacArthur Foundation Fellowship (often referred to as the Genius Awards) in 2000. In this essay, which appeared in June 2011, Williams's focus is not race or ethnicity but stereotypes related to gender, using the example of Storm Stocker, a child whose parents and siblings have decided not to reveal Storm's biological sex. Thus, people aren't sure whether to refer to Storm as* he, she, *or* it. *As Williams notes, when this item made the news in English-speaking countries, it created quite a storm—no pun intended! Contrary to some speculation, Storm is not intersexed, that is, the baby does not display both male and female genitalia; instead, Storm is biologically male or female. At the time we are writing this headnote, December 2011, nonfamily members (except for a midwife and a few other medical professionals) do not know which. As you read this essay, consider the ways in which language, and more specifically, pronouns, can encourage us to think in terms of stereotypes.*

# Are We Worried about Storm's Identity—or Our Own?

PATRICIA J. WILLIAMS

When my son was 2, he went to a nursery school where he often played with a cheerful little girl I'll call Jessie. Jessie's parents dropped her off earlier than most of the other kids, and she was in the habit of standing by the door as others arrived, taking their lunchboxes and helpfully lining them up in the classroom's big old refrigerator. As my son and Jessie became better friends, he began to imitate her every move. Every morning Jessie would stand on the right-hand side of the door taking lunchboxes; my son would stand on the left-hand side taking lunchboxes; and they would take turns running to and from the large, battered fridge.

I remember this ritual of theirs, however, not just because they were so gosh-darned adorable. I remember it because one morning the classroom teacher smiled warmly as they went through their identical paces and said, "Your son is such a sturdy little security guard! And Jessie, she's our mini-hostess with the mostest!"

That story came to mind when I read about Storm, the 5-month-old baby who has become the center of an international controversy because the child's parents have refused to reveal Storm's sex. Kathy Witterick and David Stocker sent an e-mail to their circle of friends, saying, "We've decided not to share Storm's sex for now—a tribute to freedom and choice in place of limitation." In no time, that message went viral, showing up on *The Huffington Post* as well as radio, TV and in newspapers throughout North America.

The public response has been overwhelmingly negative. Although Kathy Witterick's follow-up letter in the *Ottawa Citizen* made clear that Storm's immediate family knows the sex, and that there are no secrets withheld from Storm's siblings, most people have found it strange, "creepy" or "freakish." On *The View*, Elisabeth Hasselbeck called it "a social experiment." Others called for the couple's children to be removed by social services.

While it seems to me that "not sharing Storm's sex 5
for now" is hardly a full-fledged commitment to lifelong gender suppression or neutered identity, I will leave to mental health experts the propriety of Storm's parents' stance. As a purely philosophical matter, however, the situation is intriguing. After all, it is a much under-interrogated° political truism° that "we're all just people," or "we're all equal" or "it doesn't matter what your religion is" or "I don't see race." Who cares about anything else if "we're all American citizens"?

Yet when some intrepid souls actually follow such identity-erasing truisms to their logical, uncomfortable ends—refusing altogether to engage in the conventions of gendered identity, as with baby Storm—it is profoundly unsettling. We're not supposed to talk—to think—about difference based on gender, race, ethnicity, religion et al. But that supposition holds only when the marks, the phenotypes,° the stigmas,° are

*Storm, often incorrectly referred to as "the genderless baby"*

***under-interrogated:*** rarely examined or questioned.

***truism:*** a statement assumed to be true; a frequently uttered statement that is ultimately meaningless or nearly so.

***phenotype:*** someone's physical appearance, often in terms of apparent racial or ethnic background, in contrast to *genotype*, or the genetic makeup of an individual.

clear—indeed so clear that all conversation coagulates around the dynamics of denial: "I didn't notice you were black—what a reverse racist you are for labeling yourself!" "Why can't you be like everyone else instead of flaunting your religion by wearing that khimar,° that yarmulke,° that bindi?"° "If women want equality in the workplace, they should stop demanding womb-based privilege."

Where, however, there is ambiguity, a switch gets flipped. If race or ethnicity is at all indeterminate, the first question is "What are you?" Where gender is not instantly discernible, anxiety or even rage ensues. We want our boxes, our neat cabinets of thought. When crowing over a newborn and asking, "Is it a boy or a girl?" what we really are seeking is the satisfaction of our own eagerness to assign gender. The instant we know, we run out to buy blue rather than pink or dolls rather than trucks. The pitch of our cooing goes up or down accordingly. Gender, rather than sex, is a social response, embedded in our language, culture, education, ideology, vision. When my son and his friend Jessie went through exactly the same motions, it was gender assignment that led their teacher to describe them in such unconsciously distinct ways.

Our anxiety in response to Witterick and Stocker's decision reveals a tension in our culture between the insistence on pinning down unknown aspects of another's identity and the assumption that we don't need to know anything about anyone except that they're human. Indeed, if there is "a social experiment" being done, it surely also tests those of us beyond the Witterick-Stocker household. Spoken or unspoken, assigning identity is something we are always doing—in fact, we need to do so as to order our world. Yet we almost always do so without giving one whit of thought to all the underlying histories of assortment we imply; perhaps taking the occasional time out to review is not a bad thing.

And so we must find some way to speak of this child. If we don't want to call Storm "it"—and really,

Chapter 9 offers different types of definitions that writers use in developing arguments of definition. On which, if any, does Williams's argument depend?

LINK TO P. 190

---

*stigma:* a distinguishing mark. While the term can be used in reference to a mark on the skin that indicates a disease (e.g., measles, leprosy), here, it is used figuratively to mean a stain on one's identity caused by membership in a group that society views in a negative way.

*khimar:* one of the many kinds of head covering worn by some observant Muslim women around the world. Generally, a khimar covers the hair, neck, and shoulders, and falls down the wearer's back, often to the waist or lower; thus, only the wearer's face is revealed.

*yarmulke:* the small, round headcap made of cloth and worn by Orthodox Jewish men to keep their head covered at all times in fulfillment of a requirement of religious law. Another common term for *yarmulke* is *kippa*.

*bindi:* a forehead decoration, often a red dot, worn by some South and Southeast Asian women and women of South or Southeast Asian descent. While it was originally a Hindu custom, the practice of wearing a bindi has spread to women of many religious backgrounds in or from these parts of the world.

we don't—we have to call Storm, well, um, Storm. All the time. No shortcuts. In English, there is no adequately humanizing yet universal pronoun,° no general reference to common humanity; in order to speak comfortably, we automatically must yield to the partitions of him, of her, of gender. In the absence of pronouns, address necessarily becomes specific, individual, even intimate.

10 What would it mean if we were forced to hold in abeyance° that foundering loss we feel when we encounter the limits of the known? What if we had to sit—just "for now"—with the uncertainty that exists beyond the bounds of the normative,° the easily colloquial?° What if we had to greet one another with such boundary-muddling specificity that the hostess in the security guard and the security guard in the hostess were made manifest?° Perhaps we should bring less panic to that moment of liminality° and instead hold ourselves open to the wealth of possibilities.

---

***universal pronoun:*** a third-person singular pronoun that has a single form rather than forms that require distinguishing between males (*he*) and females (*she*) and/or humans and inanimate objects (*he* and *she* versus *it*). In many languages of the world, there is such a pronoun, although the biological gender of a person being spoken about may be indicated in many other ways.

***to hold in abeyance:*** to postpone or stop temporarily.

***normative:*** relating to, conforming to, or prescribing norms or standards, that is, the way things should or must be.

***colloquial:*** the language of everyday, familiar conversation.

***manifest:*** apparent or obvious; easily observed.

***liminality:*** being on the threshold between two places or, figuratively, as here, between two ways of seeing or experiencing a situation.

**RESPOND •**

1. Rather than passing judgment on the decision Storm's parents have made not to reveal their baby's biological sex, Williams uses the case of Storm to pose what she terms a "philosophical" question (paragraph 5), although the question is not posed until later in the article. What specific philosophical question is Williams posing? Can you put the question in your own words? In light of her comments, how is this question and the accompanying discussion an argument? What kind of argument is it—one of fact, of definition, of evaluation, of cause, or a proposal? Why? (See Chapters 8–12 for discussions for these categories of argument.)

2. In presenting her argument, Williams uses a very common strategy, especially among writers and speakers in the humanities. She opens with an anecdote, a short account of something that happened (paragraphs 1–2), and then returns briefly to the anecdote as she concludes her remarks (paragraph 10). Read these three paragraphs; then, reread the entire essay. In what ways does this anecdote contribute to the essay? (If you're having trouble with this question, imagine what the essay would be like without the anecdote.)
3. What does Williams mean by the title, "Are We Worried about Storm's Identity—or Our Own?" Obviously, at this point in Storm's life, the baby cannot appreciate what it means to be female or male or to be so labeled repeatedly. In what sense, then, does a concern with Storm's identity provide evidence that we all have a great deal invested in "our boxes, our neat cabinets of thought" (paragraph 7) and that we are profoundly uncomfortable when we can't fit people into them?
4. Particularly if you found question 3 difficult, you should Google "Storm Stocker" and read the comments posted on various media Web sites in response to Storm's parents' decision. As you'll see, commenters generally responded very negatively to the story and gave strong evidence that they had much invested in a world where everyone is either male or female and unambiguously so. Choose three or four comments that you find especially interesting in terms of the argument(s) they are making, and be prepared to share them with your classmates and to explain the assumptions the arguments make as well as the reasons you find them interesting. (If you need help analyzing arguments, you might consult Chapter 7, especially the section on Toulmin argumentation.)
5. Like many scholars who write about issues of gender, Williams assumes a clear distinction between sex and gender. Reread the selection, noting down every instance of either of these words, whether alone or in phrases (e.g., *gender assignment*, paragraph 7). Once you have made this list, **write a definitional essay** in which you distinguish between these two concepts, demonstrating how they are not the same and why it is useful to be able to distinguish between them. (See Chapter 9 for information on essays of definition.) You may wish to use resources from the Internet as you consider this assignment, especially if you find it difficult to distinguish between these concepts on the basis of Williams's work alone. Remember that if you consult other sources, you will need to give them appropriate credit. (See Chapter 19 on using sources and Chapter 21 on documenting sources.)

*Jennifer Conlin, who majored in English at the University of Michigan, has been a journalist since the mid-1980s. She spent twenty years of her career living in Europe and the Middle East, returning to the United States in 2010. She currently lives in the Detroit area. In this article, which appeared in the* New York Times *in September 2011, Conlin examines some of the issues raised by the previous selection, Patricia J. Williams's "Are We Worried about Storm's Identity—or Our Own?" pushing them further in several ways. First, her focus is adolescents, who can speak for themselves, not a child whose sex we don't know. Second, she raises questions about the complex links between biological sex, gender identity, and sexual orientation or identity. As you read, pay special attention to how those quoted in the article sometimes conflate two or more of these categories.*

# The Freedom to Choose Your Pronoun

**JENNIFER CONLIN**

Katy, a high school junior in Ann Arbor, Mich., first encountered "other" as a gender option at a meeting of Lesbian, Gay, Bisexual, Transgender,° Queer, Questioning and Allies (LGBTQQA) in seventh grade. "For those of us in the nonconforming gender community, it is great to see Google make the option more mainstream," she said.

Though Google created the "other" option for privacy reasons rather than as a transgender choice, young supporters of preferred gender pronouns (or P.G.P.'s as they are called) could not help but rejoice. Katy is one of a growing number of high school and college students who are questioning the gender roles society assigns individuals simply because they have been born male or female.

"You have to understand, this has nothing to do with your sexuality and everything to do with who you feel like inside," Katy said, explaining that at the start of every LGBTQQA meeting, participants are first asked if they would like to share their P.G.P.'s. "Mine are 'she,' 'her' and 'hers' and sometimes 'they,' 'them' and 'theirs.'"

P.G.P.'s can change as often as one likes. If the pronouns in the dictionary don't suffice, there are numerous made-up ones now in use, including "ze," "hir" and "hirs," words that connote both genders because, as Katy explained, "Maybe one day you wake up and feel more like a boy."

5 Teenagers are by nature prone to rebellion against adult conventions, and as the gender nonconformity movement gains momentum among young people, "it is about rejecting the boxes adults try to put kids in by assuming their sexual identity labels their personal identity," said Dr. Ritch

***transgender:*** identifying with or expressing a gender identity differing from the one associated with one's biological sex at birth.

C. Savin-Williams, director of the Cornell University Sex and Gender Lab. "These teens are fighting the idea that your equipment defines what it means for you to be a boy or girl. They are saying: 'You don't know me by looking at me. Assume nothing.'"

Dr. Savin-Williams, who is also the author of the book *The New Gay Teenager*, went on to list some of the new adjectives young people use to describe themselves: "bi-curious," "heteroflexible,"° "polyamorous"° and even "wiggly."

The semantic° variations are part of a nascent° effort worldwide to acknowledge some sort of neutral ground between male and female, starting at the youngest ages. Last year, a preschool in Sweden, appropriately called Egalia, opened with the goal of eliminating all gender bias by referring to the children as "friends," instead of girls and boys, as well as avoiding all gender-specific pronouns.

Australia last month issued new passport guidelines allowing citizens to give their official gender as male, female or indeterminate. In Britain, the Home Office is also considering a third gender category on passports, according to reports.

In the United States, the transgender movement is beginning to find advocates in high schools. There are now nearly 5,000 Gay-Straight Alliance Clubs, high school organizations offering support to teenagers, registered with the Gay, Lesbian and Straight Education Network, a national organization whose mission is "to assure that each member of every school community is valued and respected regardless of sexual orientation or gender identity/expression."

10 "More students today than ever are thinking about what gender means and are using this language to get away from masculine and feminine gender assumptions," said Eliza Byard, the network's executive director.

Some colleges, too, are starting to adopt nongender language. Last month, students at Pomona College in Claremont, Calif., voted to edit the student constitution so that it contains only gender-neutral language. And in 2009, the University of Michigan Student Assembly passed a resolution eliminating gender-specific pronouns from the Statement of Student Rights and Responsibilities.

From an early age, it was obvious to Loan Tran, 16 (whose P.G.P.'s are "he, him and his," and "they, them and theirs"), that his "assigned"° gender did not align with the roles society prescribed. "If I don't state my P.G.P.'s, people assume I am a 'she, her, hers,' from my high-pitched voice," said Loan, who is president of the Gay-Straight Alliance at his high school in Charlotte, N.C.

When told that because of the nature of his name and the fact that the interview was being conducted over the phone, I now actually had no idea if Loan was born a boy or girl, Loan replied, "Awesome."

It was only toward the end of the conversation that Loan revealed that he was "assigned female" at birth.

15 Loan said he grew up in a traditional Vietnamese family, where men's and women's roles are strictly defined. "At first it made my parents angry that I was not this perfect extension of them," Loan said. "But now they are trying to learn more about the community."

Loan is a student ambassador for the Gay, Lesbian and Straight Education Network. "Today more people are O.K. with the gay and lesbian community than the gender-neutral community, which feels more threatening, I suppose, because it impacts a greater portion of society," Loan said. "But the important thing is we have a safe meeting place as teens to express our P.G.P.'s and show our true selves to one another."

---

***heteroflexible:*** predominantly but not exclusively heterosexual.

***polyamorous:*** being involved in more than one significant sexual relationship at any given time.

***semantic:*** relating to meaning.

***nascent:*** being born, coming into being.

***assigned:*** here, emphasizing the fact that someone else—medical personnel and/or family—assigned the speaker, Loan, an identity based on apparent biological sex.

## RESPOND •

1. What argument(s) might supporters of preferred gender pronouns (PGP's) claim to be making and why? What is your response to such arguments? Why, in your opinion, do you respond as you do?
2. Supporters of PGP's are making complex assumptions about language—specifically, pronouns—on the one hand and identity categories, whether those related to biological sex, gender identity, or sexual orientation or identity, on the other. Using the discussion of Toulmin argumentation presented in Chapter 7, seek to make as explicit as possible the argument(s) PGP supporters are making about language and identity categories.
3. Comments posted in response to articles are often interesting places to see examples of critical reading and evaluation, especially in certain publications like the *New York Times*. If you can, you may wish to read the comments posted in response to this article on the *New York Times* site, especially those labeled as "Highlights," a label indicating that the editors see these remarks as among the most thought provoking of those posted. Some commenters were critical of Dr. Savin-Williams because of the way in which, at least as represented here, he seemed to confuse issues of gender identity and sexual orientation or identity. Why might they make such a claim? Why is keeping complex categories like these distinct especially important when constructing arguments? (Chapter 9 on arguments of definition may prove useful in answering this question.)
4. Another critique of the article was that some of the students quoted seemed to be prisoners of language and of stereotypes themselves. As one commenter, cyncytee, who claimed to be posting in Cincinnati, wrote on October 1:

   Put me in the relatively intolerant column on this one. English pronouns distinguish male from female by "equipment," as the story puts it. That is not repressive. Over several generations, society has come to accept that physical gender does not—or should not, at least—determine one's life roles. That's for the better. Denying physical realities because of how one feels in the morning is ridiculous. How 'bout we just learn that hims and hers come with all sorts of vocal pitches and outward accouterments and that invoking old, gender-specific traditions doesn't make one that gender.

   What responses might the supporters of PGP's offer to this critique of their assumptions and actions?

5. Many of the selections in this chapter, especially this one and the previous one by Patricia J. Williams about Storm Stocker, provide evidence of the way American culture is struggling with the stereotyped gender roles and the fear that they are in many ways like prisons from which we can't escape. **Write an evaluative essay** in which you examine this claim; in so doing, you may wish to support, reject, or modify it. As you write, you'll likely want to refer to one or more of the selections you've read and perhaps quote it or them. When doing so, remember that you'll need to incorporate your sources and credit them properly. (See Chapter 10 for information about evaluative arguments and Chapters 19 and 21 for incorporating and documenting sources.)

*Claude M. Steele (1946– ) is currently dean of the School of Education at Stanford, where he earlier served as professor of psychology. Steele is a social psychologist, that is, a psychologist whose research focuses on the ways in which other people influence us: these other people may be people we know or those we imagine, and their influence on us can shape what we think, what we feel, or how we behave. An example might be our fears about how others—our best friends or strangers on the street—might respond to something we wear or say or do. Steele is best known for his work on what is called the stereotype threat, the topic of this selection. In fact, this selection is the opening chapter of Steele's 2010 book,* Whistling Vivaldi and Other Clues to How Stereotypes Affect Us, *which appeared in the very important series of books* Issues of Our Times. *You'll immediately note that Steele is not writing for other psychologists; rather, he is writing for a general educated audience. Thus, the kinds of evidence he uses are not limited to the kinds of evidence—quantitative data from experiments—that he would use in a research article intended for other social psychologists. As you read, pay attention to the kinds of evidence Steele uses to support his argument; likewise pay close attention to your own response to his claims about how stereotypes ultimately affect us all.*

# An Introduction: At the Root of Identity, from *Whistling Vivaldi and Other Clues to How Stereotypes Affect Us*

CLAUDE M. STEELE

1.

I have a memory of the first time I realized I was black. It was when, at seven or eight, I was walking home from school with neighborhood kids on the last day of the school year—the whole summer in front of us—and I learned that we "black" kids couldn't swim at the pool in our area park, except on Wednesday afternoons. And then on those summer Wednesdays, with our swimming suits wrapped tightly in our towels, we filed, caravan-style, out of our neighborhood toward the hallowed pool in the adjoining white neighborhood. It was a strange weekly pilgrimage. It marked the racial order of the time and place—Chicagoland, the 1950s and early 1960s. For me it was what the psychologist William Cross calls an "encounter"—with the very fact that there was a racial order. The implications of this order for my life seemed massive—a life of swimming only on Wednesday afternoons? Why? Moreover, it turned out to be a portent of things to come. I next found out that we black kids—who, by the way, lived in my neighborhood and who had been, until these encounters, just kids—couldn't go to the roller rink, except on Thursday nights. We could be regular people but only in the middle of the week? These segregations were hard to ignore. And mistakes were costly, as when, at thirteen, after arriving at six in the morning, I waited all day to be hired as a caddy at an area golf course, only to be told at the end of the day that they didn't hire Negroes. This is how I became aware I was black. I didn't know what being black meant, but I was getting the idea that it was a big deal.

With decades of hindsight, I now think I know what was going on. I was recognizing nothing less than a condition of life—most important, a condition of life tied to my race, to my being black in that time and place. The condition was simple enough: *if* I joined the caravan and went to the pool on Wednesday afternoons *then* I got in; *if* I went to the pool any other time, *then* I didn't get in. To my seven- or eight-year-old self, this was a bad condition of life. But the condition itself wasn't the worst of it. For example, had my parents imposed it on me for not taking out the garbage, I wouldn't have been so upset. What got me was that it was imposed on me because I was black. There was nothing I could do about that, and if being black was reason enough to restrict my swimming, then what else would happen because of it?

In an interview many years later, a college student . . . would describe for me an experience that took a similar form. He was one of only two whites in an African American political science class composed of mostly black and other minority students. He, too, described a condition of life: if he said something that revealed an ignorance of African American experience, or a confusion about how to think about it, then he could well be seen as racially insensitive, or . . . worse; if he said nothing in class, then he could largely escape the suspicion of his fellow students. His condition, like my swimming pool condition, made him feel his racial identity, his whiteness, in that time and place—something he hadn't thought much about before.

From experiences like these, troubling questions arise. Will there be other conditions? How many? In how many areas of life? Will they be about important things? Can you avoid them? Do you have to stay on the lookout for them?

When I encountered my swimming pool restriction, it mystified me. 5
Where did it come from? Conditions of life tied to identity like that still mystify me. But now I have a working idea about where they come from. They come from the way a society, at a given time, is organized around an identity like race. That organization reflects the history of a place, as well as the ongoing individual and group competition for opportunity and the good life. The way Chicagoland was organized around race in the late 1950s and early 1960s—the rigid housing segregation, the de facto° school segregation, the employment discrimination, and so on—meant that black people in that time and place had many restrictive conditions of life tied to their identity, perhaps the least of which was the Wednesday afternoon swimming restriction that so worried my seven- or eight-year-old self.

***de facto:*** a Latin expression meaning "concerning fact"; in modern English, it refers to something that is the case because of practice, that is, because of what people do. It stands in contrast to *du jure*, which means "concerning law." Steele's point is that even though school segregation may not have been legal, it was the day-to-day reality for schoolchildren at that time with rare exception.

This book is about what my colleagues and I call *identity contingencies*—the things you have to deal with in a situation because you have a given social identity, because you are old, young, gay, a white male, a woman, black, Latino, politically conservative or liberal, diagnosed with bipolar disorder, a cancer patient, and so on. Generally speaking, contingencies are circumstances you have to deal with in order to get what you want or need in a situation. In the Chicagoland of my youth, in order to go swimming I had to restrict my pool going to Wednesday afternoons. That's a contingency. In his African American political science class, my interviewee had the added pressure that his ignorance could cause him serious disapproval. That, too, is a contingency. What makes both of these contingencies identity contingencies is that the people involved had to deal with them because they had a particular social identity in the situation. Other people in the situation didn't have to deal with them, just the people who had the same identity he had. This book examines the role these *identity contingencies* play in our lives, in the broader society, and in some of society's most tenacious problems.

Now, of course, ours is an individualistic society. We don't like to think that conditions tied to our social identities have much say in our lives, especially if we don't want them to. We have a creed. When barriers arise, we're supposed to march through the storm, picking ourselves up by our bootstraps. I have to count myself a subscriber to this creed. But this book offers an important qualification to this creed: that by imposing on us certain conditions of life, our social identities can strongly affect things as important as our performances in the classroom and on standardized tests, our memory capacity, our athletic performance, the pressure we feel to prove ourselves, even the comfort level we have with people of different groups—all things we typically think of as being determined by individual talents, motivations, and preferences.

The purpose of this book is nothing less than to bring this poorly understood part of social reality into view. I hope to convince you that ignoring it—allowing our creed of individualism, for example, to push it into the shadows—is costly, to our own personal success and development, to the quality of life in an identity-diverse society and world, and to our ability to fix some of the bad ways that identity still influences the distribution of outcomes in society.

How do identity contingencies influence us? Some constrain our behavior down on the ground, like restricted access to a public swimming pool. Others, just as powerful, influence us more subtly, not by constraining behavior on the ground but by putting a threat in the air.

## 2.

At the center of this book is a particular kind of identity contingency, that of 10
stereotype threat. I believe stereotype threat is a standard predicament of life. It springs from our human powers of intersubjectivity—the fact that as members of society we have a pretty good idea of what other members of our society think about lots of things, including the major groups and identities in society. We could all take out a piece of paper, write down the major stereotypes of these identities, and show a high degree of agreement in what we wrote. This means that whenever we're in a situation where a bad stereotype about one of our own identities could be applied to us—such as those about being old, poor, rich, or female—we know it. We know what "people could think." We know that anything we do that fits the stereotype could be taken as confirming it. And we know that, for that reason, we could be judged and treated accordingly. That's why I think it's a standard human predicament. In one form or another—be it through the threat of a stereotype about having lost memory capacity or being cold in relations with others—it happens to us all, perhaps several times a day.

It is also a threat that, like the swimming pool restriction, is tied to an identity. It is present in any situation to which the stereotype is relevant. And this means that it follows members of the stereotyped group into these situations like a balloon over their heads. It can be very hard to shake.

Consider the experience of Brent Staples, now a columnist for the *New York Times*, but then a psychology graduate student at the University of Chicago, a young African American male dressed in informal student clothing walking down the streets of Chicago's Hyde Park° neighborhood. In his own words:

> I became an expert in the language of fear. Couples locked arms or reached for each other's hand when they saw me. Some crossed to the other side of the street. People who were carrying on conversations went mute and stared straight ahead, as though avoiding my eyes would save them. . . .
>
> I'd been a fool. I'd been walking the streets grinning good evening at people who were frightened to death of me. I did violence to them by just being. How had I missed this . . .
>
> I tried to be innocuous but didn't know how. . . . I began to avoid people. I turned out of my way into side streets to spare them the sense that they were being stalked. . . . Out of nervousness I began to whistle and discovered I was good at it. My whistle was pure and sweet—and also in tune. On the street at night I whistled popular tunes from the Beatles and Vivaldi's° *Four Seasons*. The tension drained from people's bodies when they heard me. A few even smiled as they passed me in the dark. (pp. 202–3)

Staples was dealing with a phantom, a bad stereotype about his race that was in the air on the streets of Hyde Park—the stereotype that young African American males in this neighborhood are violence prone. People from other groups in other situations might face very different stereotypes—about lacking math ability rather than being violence prone for example—but their predica-

***Hyde Park:*** the affluent neighborhood where the University of Chicago and several other educational institutions are located on the South Side of the city. It is adjacent to some of Chicago's poorest neighborhoods, which are overwhelmingly African American.

***Antonio Vivaldi (1678–1741):*** prolific Italian Baroque composer, violinist, and priest. Among the best known of his works is a set of four violin concertos, *The Four Seasons*, each of which tries to paint a sound picture of the season it represents.

*The Algonquin Apartments in Hyde Park, Chicago, in a 1951 photo*

ments would be the same. When they were in situations where those stereotypes could apply to them, they understood that one false move could cause them to be reduced to that stereotype, to be seen and treated in terms of it. That's stereotype threat, a contingency of their identity in these situations.

Unless, as Staples discovered, they devised a way to deflect it. Staples whistled Vivaldi, by his own account a very good version of it. What would that do for him? Would it improve his attitude toward others on the street, make him more understanding? Probably not. What it did for sure was change the situation he was dealing with. And how it did this illustrates nicely the nature of stereotype threat. In a single stroke, he made the stereotype about violence-prone African American males less applicable to him personally. He displayed knowledge of white culture, even "high white culture." People on the street may not have recognized the Vivaldi he was whistling, but they could tell he was whistling classical music. This caused him to be seen differently, as an educated, refined person, not as a violence-prone African American youth. Such youths don't typically walk down the street whistling classical music. While hardly being aware of it, people drop the stereotype of violence-proneness as the lens through which they see him. He seems less threatening. People don't know who he is; but they know he isn't someone to fear. Fear fades from their demeanor.° Staples himself relaxes. The stereotype in the air that threatened him is fended off. And the change in the behavior of those on the street, and in his own behavior, reveals the power that a mere stereotype—floating in the air like a cloud gathering the nation's history—was having on everyone all along.

***demeanor:*** behavior or appearance.

*Whistling Vivaldi* is about the experience of living under such a cloud—an 15
experience we all have—and the role such clouds play in shaping our lives and society.

### 3.

Suppose you are invited into a psychology laboratory and asked to play ten holes of golf on a miniature course that has been set up in a small room. Suppose also that you are a white college student, reasonably athletically inclined. Now suppose that just as you are getting the feel of the golf clubs, you are told that the golf task is part of a standardized sports psychology measure called the Michigan Athletic Aptitude Test (MAAT), which measures "natural athletic ability." How well do you think you'd do? Would being told that the golf task measures natural athletic ability make a difference?

A group of social psychologists at Princeton University led by Jeff Stone did exactly this experiment several years ago. They found something very interesting: white students who were told the golf task measured natural athletic ability golfed a lot worse than white students who were told nothing about the task. They tried just as hard. But it took them, on average, three strokes more to get through the course.

What was it about thinking of the task as a measure of natural athletic ability that so strikingly undermined their performance?

Jeff and his colleagues reasoned that it had something to do with their being white. In the terms I have been using, it had to do with a contingency of white identity that comes to bear in situations where natural athletic ability is being evaluated. This contingency comes from a broadly known stereotype in this society that, compared with blacks at least, whites may have less natural athletic ability. Participants in Jeff's experiment would know this stereotype simply by being members of this society. They might not believe it. But being told that the golfing task measured the very trait their group was stereotyped as lacking, just before they began the task, could put them in a quandary: their frustration on the task could be seen as confirming the stereotype, as a characterization both of themselves and of their group. And this, in turn, might be upsetting and distracting enough to add an average of three strokes to their scores.

20 The stereotype about their group, and the threatening interpretation of their golf frustration that it posed, is not a contingency like the swimming pool restriction of my youth that directly affected behavior. It imposed no extra restrictions on their golfing, or any material° impediments. But it was nonetheless a contingency of their identity during the golf task. *If* they experienced frustration at golf, *then* they could be confirming, or be seen to be confirming, the unsavory stereotype. *If* they didn't experience frustration at golf, *then* they didn't confirm the racial stereotype. This was an extra pressure they had to deal with during the golfing task, for no other reason than that they were white. It hung over them as a threat in the air, implying that one false move could get them judged and treated as a white kid with no natural athletic ability. (You will learn later in the book how my colleagues and I came to call this kind of threat in the air simply *stereotype threat*.)

***material:*** here, concrete or actual (in contrast to psychological or imagined).

With this reasoning in tow, Jeff and colleagues started asking more questions.

If the mere act of telling white Princeton students that their golfing measured natural athletic ability had caused them to golf poorly by distracting them with the risk of being stereotyped, then telling black Princeton students the same thing should have no effect on their golfing, since their group isn't stereotyped in that way. And it didn't. Jeff and his colleagues had put a

*How do what Steele calls* stereotype threats *show how stereotypes about groups of people are culturally ingrained?*

group of black Princeton students through the same procedure they'd put the white students through. And, lo and behold, their golfing was unaffected. They golfed the same whether or not they'd been told the task measured natural athletic ability.

Here was more evidence that what had interfered with white students' golfing, when it was seen to measure natural athletic ability, was a distracting sense of threat arising from how whites are stereotyped in the larger society.

But Jeff and his research team weren't satisfied. They devised a still cleverer way to make their argument.

They reasoned that if group stereotypes can really set up threats in the 25
air that are capable of interfering with actions as concrete as golfing for entire groups of people—like the stereotype threat Staples had to contend with on the streets of Hyde Park—then it should be possible to set up a stereotype threat that would interfere with black students' golfing as well. All they'd have to do was represent the golfing task as measuring something related to a bad stereotype of blacks. Then, as black participants golfed, they'd have to fend off, like whites in the earlier experiment, the bad stereotype about their group. This added pressure might hurt their golfing.

They tested this idea in a simple way. They told new groups of black and white Princeton students that the golf task they were about to begin was a measure of "sports strategic intelligence." This simple change of phrase had a powerful effect. It now put black students at risk, through their golfing, of confirming or being seen to confirm the ancient and very bad stereotype of blacks as less intelligent. Now, as they tried to sink their putts, any mistake could make them feel vulnerable to being judged and treated like a less intelligent black kid. That was a heavy contingency of identity in this situation indeed, which might well cause enough distraction to interfere with their golfing. Importantly, this same instruction freed white students of stereotype threat in this situation, since whites aren't stereotyped as less intelligent.

The results were dramatic. Now the black students, suffering their form of stereotype threat during the golfing task, golfed dramatically worse than the white students, for whom this instruction had lifted stereotype threat. They took, on average, four strokes more to get through the course.

Neither whites, when the golfing task was represented as a test of natural athletic ability, nor blacks, when it was represented as a test of sports strategic intelligence, confronted a directly interfering contingency of identity in these experiments—nothing that directly affected their behavior like a swimming pool restriction. The contingencies they faced were threats in the air—the threat that their golfing could confirm or be seen to confirm a bad group stereotype as a characterization of their group and of themselves. Still, it was a threat with a big effect. On a course that typically took between twenty-two and twenty-four strokes to complete, it led whites to take three more strokes to complete it, and blacks to take five more strokes to complete it.

At first glance, one might dismiss the importance of something "in the air" like stereotype threat. At second glance, however, it's clear that this threat can be a tenacious force in our lives. Staples had to contend with it every time he walked down the streets of his own neighborhood. White athletes have to contend with it in each competition, especially against black athletes. Think of the white athlete in a sport with heavy black competition. To reach a high level of performance, say, to make it into the National Basketball Association, which is dominated by black players, the white athlete would have to survive and prosper against a lifelong gauntlet° of performance situations loaded with this extra race-linked threat. No single good athletic performance would put the stereotype to rest. The effort to disprove it would be Sisyphean,° reemergent at each important new performance.

The aim of this book is not to show that stereotype threat is so powerful 30
and persistent that it can't be overcome. Quite the contrary. Its goal is to show how, as an unrecognized factor in our lives, it can contribute to some of

***gauntlet:*** an earlier military punishment where the solider punished had to run between a row of soldiers who struck him from either side as he passed.

***Sisyphean:*** endless and futile; the term comes from Greek mythology, where Sisyphus, a king of Corinth who had repeatedly sought to outsmart the gods, was condemned in the afterlife to roll a large boulder up a steep hill, only to watch it roll to the bottom of the hill again, at which point Sisyphus had to begin the task again. The image below represents Sisyphus rolling the stone.

our most vexing personal and societal problems, but that doing quite feasible things to reduce this threat can lead to dramatic improvements in these problems.

4.

Now suppose it wasn't miniature golf that you were asked to perform when you arrived at a psychology experiment, and suppose it wasn't your group's athletic ability that was negatively stereotyped in the larger society. Suppose it was difficult math problems that you were asked to solve on a timed standardized test, and suppose that it was your group's math ability that was negatively stereotyped in the larger society. In other words, suppose you were an American woman showing up for an experiment involving difficult math.

Would the stereotype threat that is a contingency of your gender identity in math-related settings be enough to interfere with your performance on the test? Would you be able to just push through this threat of being seen stereotypically and perform well anyway? Or would the very effort to push hard on a timed test be distracting enough to impair your performance despite the extra effort? Would you experience this threat, this contingency of identity, every time you tried difficult math in settings with males around? Would this contingency of identity in math settings become frustrating enough to make you avoid math-related college majors and careers? Would women living in a society where women's math ability is not negatively stereotyped experience this threat? Would their scores be better?

Or suppose the test you were asked to take wasn't the Michigan Athletic Aptitude Test but was the SAT, and suppose the negative stereotype about your group wasn't about athletic ability, or even about math ability, alone, but about scholastic ability in general. Again, would the stereotype threat you experience as a contingency of your identity in scholastic settings be enough to interfere with your performance on this test? Does the threat cause this interference by diverting mental resources away from the test and onto your worries? Would the stereotype threat you experience in scholastic settings affect other experiences as well, such as your classroom performance and your comfort interacting with teachers, professors, teaching assistants, and even other students not in your group? Would this contingency of identity make these settings so frustrating for you that you might try to avoid them in choosing a walk of life?

The purpose of this book is to describe the journey that my colleagues and I have taken in formulating these and related questions and then in systematically trying to answer them over the past twenty years. The experience has been like trying to solve a mystery. And the approach of the book is to give you an over-the-shoulder view of how that mystery has unfolded, of the progression of ideas and revelations, often from the research itself, about the surprising ways that stereotypes affect us—our intellectual functioning, our stress reactions, the tension that can exist between people from different groups, and the sometimes very surprising strategies that alleviate these effects and thereby help solve some of society's worst problems. And because science is rarely a solitary activity anymore—something long true for me—the story also describes many of the people who have done this research, as well as how they work. You will also meet many interesting people who have experienced this threat—including a famous journalist, an African American expatriate in Paris, a person who rose from sharecropping to wealth in rural North Carolina, students at some of America's most elite universities, and students in some of America's most wanting K through 12 schools.

35 Although the book deals with issues that can have a political charge, neither it nor the work it reports is propelled by an ideological orientation—to the best of my and my colleagues' ability. One of the first things one learns as a social psychologist is that everyone is capable of bias. We simply are not, and cannot be, all knowing and completely objective. Our understandings and views of the world are partial, and reflect the circumstances of our particular lives. This is where a discipline like science comes in. It doesn't purge us of bias. But it extends what we can see and understand, while constraining bias. That is where I would stake my claim, at any rate. The constant back-and-forth between ideas and research results hammers away at bias and, just as important, often reveals aspects of reality that surpass our original ideas and insights. When that has happened—and it has—that is the direction our research goes in. I would like to see my strongest convictions as arising from that kind of revelation, not from prior belief, and I hope you will get a view of that experience as you read along.

Arising this way, several general patterns of findings have persistently emerged in this research. Seeing these patterns, more than any ideas or hunches I began this research with, has convinced me of the importance of identity contingencies and identity threat in our lives.

The first pattern is that despite the strong sense we have of ourselves as autonomous individuals, evidence consistently shows that contingencies tied to our social identities do make a difference in shaping our lives, from the way we perform in certain situations to the careers and friends we choose. As the white world-class sprinter takes the starting blocks in the 100-meter dash at the Olympic trials, he is as autonomous an individual as the black sprinters next to him. And they all face precisely the same 100 meters of free and open track. Nonetheless, in order to do well in that situation, research suggests that he may have to surmount a pressure tied to his racial identity that the black sprinters don't face.

The second dimension of reality, long evident in our research, is that identity threats—and the damage they can do to our functioning—play an important role in some of society's most important social problems. These range from the racial, social class, and gender achievement gaps that persistently plague and distort our society to the equally persistent intergroup tensions that often trouble our social relations.

Third, also coming to light in this research is a general process—involving the allocation of mental resources and even a precise pattern of brain activation—by which these threats impair a broad range of human functioning. Something like a unifying understanding of how these threats have their effect is emerging.

Finally, a set of things we can do as individuals to reduce the impact of 40
these threats in our own lives, as well as what we as a society can do to reduce their impact in important places like schools and workplaces, has come to light. There is truly inspirational news here: evidence that often small, feasible things done to reduce these threats in schools and classrooms can dramatically reduce the racial and gender achievement gaps that so discouragingly characterize our society.

These findings have convinced me of the importance of understanding identity threat to our personal progress, in areas of great concern like achivement and better group relations, and to societal progress, in achieving the identity-integrated civil life and equal opportunity that is a founding dream of this society. This book presents the journey that my colleagues and I have taken in getting to this conviction.

Let's begin the journey where it began—Ann Arbor, Michigan, 1987.

## References

Staples, B. Black men and public space. (1986, December). *Harper's Magazine*.

Stone, J., Lynch, C. I., Sjomeling, M., & Darley, J. M. (1999). Stereotype threat effects on Black and White athletic performance. *Journal of Personality and Social Psychology*, *77*, 1213–1227.

## RESPOND •

1. How does Steele define stereotype threat and its importance for all of us? What specific conclusions does he draw from his research and that of others on stereotype threat and stereotypes more broadly?
2. What specific functions does the lengthy quotation from an essay by Brent Staples (paragraph 12) play in Steele's argument? Why could Steele simply not paraphrase or summarize Staples's discussion? What value is there for Steele in using a first-person example here? In using an example from someone else, rather than using another example of his own? If Steele had been writing an essay of 500 words, how might he have used this quotation or information from it? Why? (See Chapter 19 for a discussion of using sources.)
3. As noted in the headnote, if Steele were writing only for social psychologists, his primary support would come from quantitative evidence based on experiments. Here, however, Steele uses many sorts of evidence. What kinds of evidence does he use to support his claims? (See Chapter 17 for information on what counts as evidence.) How effective are they and why? (For example, is any of his evidence particularly memorable? What makes it so?)
4. Steele also uses definitions in very interesting and effective ways. Explain how Steele goes about defining the following abstract notions: *encounter* (paragraph 1), *condition of life* (paragraph 2), *contingency* (paragraph 6), *threats in the air* (paragraph 9), and *intersubjectivity* (paragraph 10). (We've listed the first occurrence of each term; you may need to track a term's recurrence throughout the piece to understand how Steele works to define it. You may want to consult Chapter 9 on arguments of definition to get a clear picture of how writers can go about offering definitions.) How does each of these definitions contribute to the effectiveness of Steele's selection?
5. Even though Steele is writing for a general audience, he is adamant that he is writing as a social scientist, and one of the major arguments of the selection is the importance of scientific ways of creating knowledge. In this regard, he sees himself as constructing an argument based on facts. Study the selection from this perspective, paying special attention to his discussions of qualifications to our society's creed (paragraph 7), how psychologists develop hypotheses and then refine them by doing additional experiments (paragraph 22 and following), and the value of science (paragraph 37). **Write an argument of fact** based on Steele's understanding of the value of science, specifically how and why science is necessary if we are to understand what it means to be human. (Chapter 8 discusses arguments of fact in detail.)

6. The selections in this chapter have focused on how society stereotypes you in ways you may not even have been aware of. This chapter adds an additional notion—the stereotype threat—to our discussion. **Write an essay** in which you apply this notion to your own life or that of someone you know well. The essay could take any of several forms; for example, it could be primarily factual, definitional, evaluative, or causal in nature, or it might make a proposal. (Chapters 8–12 treat these categories of arguments.)

# 23
# What's It Like to Be Bilingual in the United States?

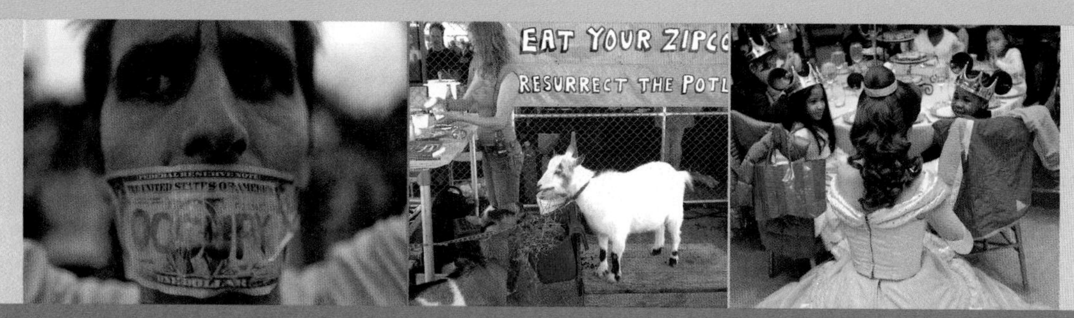


At home and abroad, the United States is often portrayed as a monolingual country where a single language, English, reigns supreme—and always has. Is the truth so simple? The selections in this chapter offer you the opportunity to learn about languages other than English in the United States through the eyes (and ears) of Americans who are bilingual or who study bilingualism professionally.

The opening selection by Hyon B. Shin and Robert A. Kominski presents information from the most recent national study of language use in the United States, conducted in 2007. You'll likely be surprised to learn how many Americans report speaking a language other than English at home as well as the percentage among them who claim to speak English very well.

The following two selections offer two very different perspectives on bilingualism with a focus on the relationship between Spanish and English. The narrator in Sandra Cisneros's short story "Bien Pretty" argues that if you haven't made love in Spanish with a native speaker of the language, you can't imagine what you've missed. Marjorie Agosín, a professor, writer, human rights activist, and political refugee from Chile, explains in prose and poetry why she "writes in Spanish and lives in translation." The fourth selection, "The 'F Word'" by Firoozeh Dumas, an Iranian immigrant married to a French immigrant, examines how Americans deal and don't deal with foreign names.

The fifth and sixth selections present public service announcements in languages other than English or in a bilingual format. These visual arguments stand as evidence that the linguistic landscape in the country isn't monolingual while challenging you to consider the possible advantages of such announcements from the perspective of audience: the language you choose influences who likely can or can't understand your message.

The next two selections give us insights from writers whose first languages are Vietnamese and Chinese, respectively. The protagonist in a chapter from *Monkey Bridge*, a novel by law professor Lan Cao, describes the situation of a refugee, an adolescent Vietnamese girl, who, because she absorbs English and comes to understand American culture easily, must parent her mother, who finds things like supermarkets disorientingly foreign. Award-winning novelist Amy Tan reframes the issue of bilingualism in broader terms, focusing on the varieties of English she and her mother use.

Selections nine and ten examine bilingualism that most Americans often ignore. A transcript and video segments from Twin Cities Public Television examine the efforts of the Ojibwe community in Minnesota to bring their language back to life and ensure that it does not disappear, a struggle going on in almost all Native American communities that have not already lost their languages. In a very different context, Michele J. Bornert's blog postings examine bilingualism—and life—for those who use American Sign Language as their primary means of interaction but who are literate in English and may have the ability to read lips or, in some cases, speak.

By examining several instances where immigrants have arrived in the United States and managed to become highly successful entrepreneurs without mastering English, Kirk Semple challenges the frequently heard claim that you have to have English to survive in the United States. At the same time, these cases are clearly exceptions that "prove the rule" in the original sense of that saying—where *prove* meant "try" or "test"—though in the end, the rule still stands.

The chapter closes with Amy Martinez Starke's obituary written for Sao Yee Cha, a Hmong woman who moved to Portland, Oregon, after two years of living in a refugee camp in Thailand, where she had fled during the Vietnam War. In describing her life, it comments on her struggles with English and reminds us that Americans who speak languages other than English came to be here in many ways.

If you grew up speaking two or more languages, these readings give you a chance to think about how your experiences compare to those of other Americans who are like you in some significant way. If you don't already speak a second language, there's still time: monolingualism isn't a terminal disease, a favorite bumper sticker argues. Even as English plays an increasingly important role in the world, learning another language changes the way you see yourself and the world. In the meantime, these readings offer you the chance to learn about the lives of a growing number of Americans—even people sitting in your classroom—that you might otherwise never know.

For additional material related to this chapter, visit the e-Pages for *Everything's an Argument with Readings* online at **bedfordstmartins.com/everythingsanargument/epages**.

▼ *This selection, "Language Use in the United States: 2007," is a 2010 U.S. Census Bureau report written by Hyon B. Shin and Robert A. Kominski, both of whom are demographic statisticians employed by the Census Bureau. (A demographer is someone who studies the characteristics of populations—topics like population size and density, birth and death rates, and changes over time, using quantitative data; hence, a demographic statistician is a statistician who specializes in analyzing demographic data.) Like reports from the Census Bureau generally, this document provides the most complete and readily accessible presentation of data about some topic relating to the U.S. population. As this selection explains, the data on which this report are based come from the 2007 American Community Survey, an ongoing survey of the U.S. population that complements and supplements the U.S. census, which is conducted every ten years. The relevant questions here are those that deal with the reported use of a language other than English at home and the reported ability of individuals aged five or older to speak English. As you read this report, seek to determine the kinds of arguments it makes—factual, definitional, evaluative, causal, or proposal—and why. Likewise, pay attention to the information that is presented about the geographic area in which you live or areas in which you have lived. After all, the report is documenting social changes that have occurred in your lifetime.*

# Language Use in the United States: 2007

HYON B. SHIN AND ROBERT A. KOMINSKI

## Introduction

This report provides information on the number and characteristics of people in the United States in 2007 who spoke a language other than English at home. While the vast majority of the population 5 years old and over in the United States spoke only English at home (80 percent), the population speaking a language other than English at home has increased steadily for the last three decades. The number of speakers increased for many non-English languages, but not all. This changing landscape of speakers of non-English languages in the United States is highlighted in this report.

Figure 1.
**Reproduction of the Questions on Language From the 2007 American Community Survey**

**13** **a. Does this person speak a language other than English at home?**
☐ Yes
☐ No → *SKIP to question 14*

**b. What is this language?**

*For example: Korean, Italian, Spanish, Vietnamese*

**c. How well does this person speak English?**
☐ Very well
☐ Well
☐ Not well
☐ Not at all

Source: U.S. Census Bureau, 2007 American Community Survey.

***decennial:*** occurring every ten years; the last U.S. census was conducted in 2010.

Data from the 2007 American Community Survey (ACS) are used to describe the language use of the U.S. population aged 5 and over. Responses to language and English-speaking ability questions that were historically collected once every 10 years in the decennial° census are now captured every year in the ACS. As Appendix A (at the end of this report) shows, questions about language have varied greatly over time. Since the 1980 decennial census, however, the same series of three questions has been used in U.S. Census Bureau data collections (see Figure 1). The first question pertains to everyone 5 years old and over. It asks if the person speaks a language other than English at home. A person who responds "yes" to this question is then asked to report the language. The Census Bureau codes these responses into 381 detailed languages. The third question asks "how well" that person speaks English, with answer categories of "very well," "well," "not well," and "not at all."

Data on speakers of languages other than English and on their English-speaking ability provide more than just an interesting portrait of a changing nation. Routinely, these data are used in a wide variety of legislative, policy, and research applications. Legal, financial, and marketing decisions regarding language-based issues all rely on information that begins with data on non-English language use and English-speaking ability.[1]

## Four Major Language Groups

**Spanish** includes Spanish, Spanish Creole, and Ladino.

**Other Indo-European languages** include most languages of Europe and the Indic languages of India. These include the Germanic languages, such as German, Yiddish, and Dutch; the Scandinavian languages, such as Swedish and Norwegian; the Romance languages, such as French, Italian, and Portuguese; the Slavic languages, such as Russian, Polish, and Serbo-Croatian; the Indic languages, such as Hindi, Gujarati, Punjabi, and Urdu; Celtic languages; Greek; Baltic languages; and Iranian languages.

**Asian and Pacific Island languages** include Chinese; Korean; Japanese; Vietnamese; Hmong; Khmer; Lao; Thai; Tagalog or Pilipino; the Dravidian languages of India, such as Telugu, Tamil, and Malayalam; and other languages of Asia and the Pacific, including the Philippine, Polynesian, and Micronesian languages.

**All Other languages** include Uralic languages, such as Hungarian; the Semitic languages, such as Arabic and Hebrew; languages of Africa; native North American languages, including the American Indian and Alaska native languages; and indigenous languages of Central and South America.

Table 1 provides some basic information from the 2007 ACS about speakers of non-English languages and their English-speaking ability. Of 281.0 million people aged 5 and over, 55.4 million people (20 percent of this population) spoke a language other than English at home. While the Census Bureau codes 381 detailed languages, data tabulations are not generally available for all of these detailed groups. Instead, the Census Bureau collapses languages into smaller sets of "language groups." The simplest collapse uses four major groups: Spanish; Other Indo-European languages; Asian and Pacific Island languages; and All Other languages. These four groups are further explained in the text box.

Of the 55.4 million people who spoke a language other than English at 5
home, 62 percent spoke Spanish (34.5 million speakers), 19 percent spoke an Other Indo-European language (10.3 million speakers), 15 percent spoke an Asian and Pacific Island language (8.3 million speakers), and 4 percent spoke an Other language (2.3 million speakers). The majority of speakers across all

Table 1.
**Population 5 Years and Older Who Spoke a Language Other Than English at Home by Language Group and English-Speaking Ability: 2007**
(For information on confidentiality protection, sampling error, nonsampling error, and definitions, see *www.census.gov/acs/www/*)

| Characteristic | Total people | English-speaking ability | | | |
|---|---|---|---|---|---|
| | | Very well | Well | Not well | Not at all |
| NUMBER | | | | | |
| Population 5 years and older | 280,950,438 | (X) | (X) | (X) | (X) |
| Spoke only English at home | 225,505,953 | (X) | (X) | (X) | (X) |
| Spoke a language other than English at home | 55,444,485 | 30,975,474 | 10,962,722 | 9,011,298 | 4,494,991 |
| Spoke a language other than English at home | 55,444,485 | 30,975,474 | 10,962,722 | 9,011,298 | 4,494,991 |
| Spanish or Spanish Creole | 34,547,077 | 18,179,530 | 6,322,170 | 6,344,110 | 3,701,267 |
| Other Indo-European languages | 10,320,730 | 6,936,808 | 2,018,148 | 1,072,025 | 293,749 |
| Asian and Pacific Island languages | 8,316,426 | 4,274,794 | 2,176,180 | 1,412,264 | 453,188 |
| Other languages | 2,260,252 | 1,584,342 | 446,224 | 182,899 | 46,787 |
| PERCENT | | | | | |
| Population 5 years and older | 100.0 | (X) | (X) | (X) | (X) |
| Spoke only English at home | 80.3 | (X) | (X) | (X) | (X) |
| Spoke a language other than English at home | 19.7 | 55.9 | 19.8 | 16.3 | 8.1 |
| Spoke a language other than English at home | 100.0 | 55.9 | 19.8 | 16.3 | 8.1 |
| Spanish or Spanish Creole | 62.3 | 52.6 | 18.3 | 18.4 | 10.7 |
| Other Indo-European languages | 18.6 | 67.2 | 19.6 | 10.4 | 2.8 |
| Asian and Pacific Island languages | 15.0 | 51.4 | 26.2 | 17.0 | 5.4 |
| Other languages | 4.1 | 70.1 | 19.7 | 8.1 | 2.1 |

(X) Not applicable.

Note: Margins of error for all estimates can be found in Appendix Table 1 at <www.census.gov/population/www/socdemo/language/appendix.html>. For more information on the ACS, see <www.census.gov/acs/www/>.

Source: U.S. Census Bureau, 2007 American Community Survey.

four of these major language groups reported speaking English "very well." The percentage of these groups reporting an English-speaking ability of "very well" ranged from around 50 percent of Asian and Pacific Island language speakers to 70 percent of speakers in the Other language group.

People speaking at a level below the "very well" category are thought to need English assistance in some situations.[2] Around 24.5 million people reported their English-speaking ability as something below "very well" (that is, "well," "not well," or "not at all"). Higher percentages of people needing English assistance were present for speakers of Spanish (47 percent) and Asian and Pacific Island languages (49 percent) than among Other Indo-European languages (33 percent) or Other languages (30 percent).

## Findings

### Characteristics of People Speaking a Language Other Than English at Home

While the majority of people spoke only English at home, important differences exist across some social characteristics. Figures 2a to 2c show the number of people speaking a language other than English at home for the

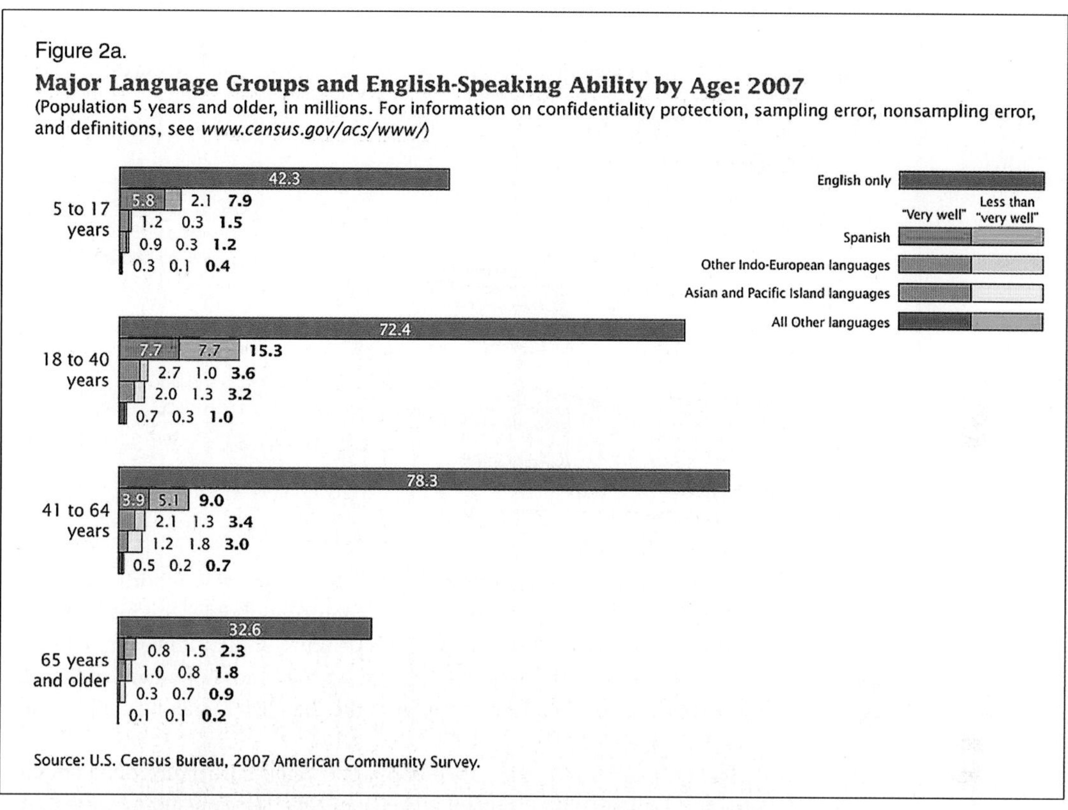


Figure 2a.

**Major Language Groups and English-Speaking Ability by Age: 2007**

(Population 5 years and older, in millions. For information on confidentiality protection, sampling error, nonsampling error, and definitions, see *www.census.gov/acs/www/*)

Source: U.S. Census Bureau, 2007 American Community Survey.

four major language groups by English-speaking ability by age, nativity,° and educational attainment. Figure 2a shows that the group aged 41 to 64 had the largest number of English-only speakers (78.3 million), compared to 42.3 million speakers aged 5 to 17, 72.4 million speakers aged 18 to 40, and 32.6 million speakers aged 65 and over. Conversely, foreign-language speakers numbered 10.9 million (21 percent) among 5 to 17 year olds, 23.1 million (24 percent) among 18 to 40 year olds, 16.1 million (17 percent) among 41 to 64 year olds, and 5.3 million (14 percent) among older people.

*nativity:* here, place of birth—whether born in or outside the United States.

Across the four major language groups, a disproportionately large number and proportion of all people who spoke a language other than English at home were those aged 18 to 40 who spoke Spanish. Among all 55.4 million speakers of non-English languages, 15.3 million (28 percent) met this description.

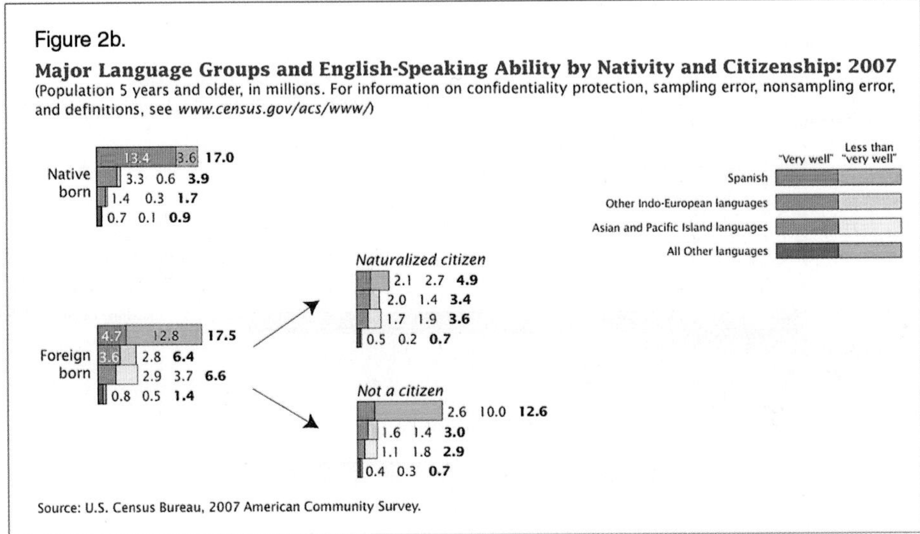


Figure 2b.
**Major Language Groups and English-Speaking Ability by Nativity and Citizenship: 2007**
(Population 5 years and older, in millions. For information on confidentiality protection, sampling error, nonsampling error, and definitions, see *www.census.gov/acs/www/*)

Source: U.S. Census Bureau, 2007 American Community Survey.

About half of speakers of non-English languages also reported that they did not speak English "very well." The proportion of older Spanish speakers who reported lower levels of English-speaking ability, however, was even higher—57 percent of people 41 to 64 years old and 65 percent of Spanish speakers 65 years old and over reported their English-speaking ability as less than "very well."

Figure 2b focuses on the native-born and foreign-born status of individuals. 10
This figure shows that among Spanish speakers, nearly as many were native born as foreign born (17.0 million compared to 17.5 million). This is not the case for the other three language groups—all three had more foreign born.

Spanish speakers who were foreign born were more likely to speak English less than "very well" than native-born Spanish speakers (73 percent compared to 21 percent). Among the remaining three groups, the foreign-born Asian and Pacific Island language group was the only one where those speaking English less than "very well" outnumbered those speaking "very well."

Of those speakers of a non-English language who were foreign-born, 12.6 million were citizens and 19.3 million were noncitizens. Foreign-born Spanish speakers were more likely to be noncitizens than any of the three other groups (72 percent compared to 46 percent of Other Indo-European speakers, 45 percent of Asian and Pacific Island speakers, and 51 percent of All Other speakers). In addition, a much larger number and proportion of foreign-born Spanish speakers who were not citizens reported speaking English less than "very well" (79 percent), more than any other language group, whether citizen or not.

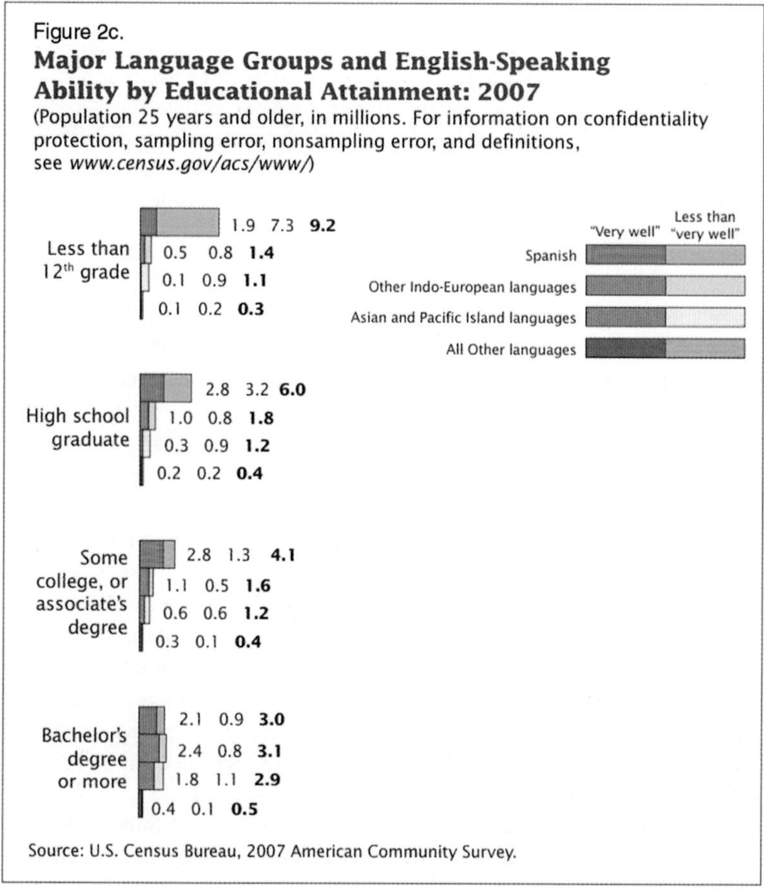


Figure 2c.
**Major Language Groups and English-Speaking Ability by Educational Attainment: 2007**
(Population 25 years and older, in millions. For information on confidentiality protection, sampling error, nonsampling error, and definitions, see *www.census.gov/acs/www/*)

Source: U.S. Census Bureau, 2007 American Community Survey.

Figure 2c shows the four major language groups and the English-speaking ability of their members by four levels of educational attainment for the population 25 years old and over: less than a 12th grade education, high school graduate, some college experience, and a bachelor's degree or more. Most Spanish speakers 25 years old and over had not completed high school (41 percent)—a larger percentage than for the other three major language groups (15 percent for Other Indo-European language and 17 percent for both Asian and Pacific Island language speakers and for Other language speakers). Conversely, while the college completion level (bachelor's degree or more) for the three non-Spanish language groups ranged from 34 to 45 percent, only 14 percent of the Spanish-speaking population attained this level of education.

For all four language groups, those who had not completed high school had larger proportions of speakers with limited English-speaking ability than for those who reported speaking English "very well." In addition, individuals who were high school graduates and also spoke Asian and Pacific Island languages had a higher proportion speaking English less than "very well."[3]

## Languages Spoken in the United States: A Historical Look

As Appendix A shows, census questions about language have varied over the 15
years. In some censuses, questions were asked of "mother tongue" (the language spoken in the household when the respondent was growing up) or were asked only of the foreign-born population. Since the 1980 census, however, the same three questions have been asked of everyone aged 5 and over in the household.

Table 2 provides a detailed list of 17 different languages spoken in the home for the period 1980 to 2007.[4] This list provides data for only those languages that were available in all four time periods.

Table 2 shows the growth of some languages since 1980 as well as the real and relative decline of others. In 1980, 23.1 million people spoke a language other than English at home, compared to 55.4 million people in 2007 (a 140 percent increase, during which the U.S. population grew 34 percent). The largest numeric increase was for Spanish speakers (23.4 million more in 2007 than in 1980). Vietnamese speakers had the largest percentage increase (511 percent). Eight languages more than doubled during the period, including four that had fewer than 200,000 speakers in 1980: Russian, Persian, Armenian, and Vietnamese.

Some languages declined since 1980. Italian, the second-most frequently spoken non-English language in 1980 (after Spanish), had a net decline of about 800,000 speakers (50 percent decline). It is now the ninth-ranked language on the list of languages other than English spoken at home. Other languages, such as Polish, Yiddish, and Greek, also had large proportionate decreases. While increased immigration led to gains for some language groups, other groups experienced aging populations and dwindling migrant flows into the United States.

## Languages Spoken in the United States

Most of the detailed language information the Census Bureau provides uses a list of 39 individual languages and language groups. These 39 languages and the respective English-speaking ability of their speakers are detailed in Table 3. In 2007, seven of these languages had more than a million speakers.

Table 2.

**Languages Spoken at Home: 1980, 1990, 2000, and 2007**

(For information on confidentiality protection, sampling error, nonsampling error, and definitions, see *www.census.gov/acs/www/*)

| Characteristic | 1980 | 1990 | 2000 | 2007 | Percentage change 1980–2007 |
|---|---|---|---|---|---|
| Population 5 years and older | 210,247,455 | 230,445,777 | 262,375,152 | 280,950,438 | 33.6 |
| Spoke only English at home | 187,187,415 | 198,600,798 | 215,423,557 | 225,505,953 | 20.5 |
| Spoke a language other than English at home[1] | 23,060,040 | 31,844,979 | 46,951,595 | 55,444,485 | 140.4 |
| | | | | | |
| Spoke a language other than English at home[2] | 23,060,040 | 31,844,979 | 46,951,595 | 55,444,485 | 140.4 |
| Spanish or Spanish Creole | 11,116,194 | 17,345,064 | 28,101,052 | 34,547,077 | 210.8 |
| French (incl. Patois, Cajun, Creole) | 1,550,751 | 1,930,404 | 2,097,206 | 1,984,824 | 28.0 |
| Italian | 1,618,344 | 1,308,648 | 1,008,370 | 798,801 | –50.6 |
| Portuguese or Portuguese Creole | 351,875 | 430,610 | 564,630 | 687,126 | 95.3 |
| German | 1,586,593 | 1,547,987 | 1,383,442 | 1,104,354 | –30.4 |
| Yiddish | 315,953 | 213,064 | 178,945 | 158,991 | –49.7 |
| Greek | 401,443 | 388,260 | 365,436 | 329,825 | –17.8 |
| Russian | 173,226 | 241,798 | 706,242 | 851,174 | 391.4 |
| Polish | 820,647 | 723,483 | 667,414 | 638,059 | –22.2 |
| Serbo-Croatian | 150,255 | 70,964 | 233,865 | 276,550 | 84.1 |
| Armenian | 100,634 | 149,694 | 202,708 | 221,865 | 120.5 |
| Persian | 106,992 | 201,865 | 312,085 | 349,686 | 226.8 |
| Chinese | 630,806 | 1,319,462 | 2,022,143 | 2,464,572 | 290.7 |
| Japanese | 336,318 | 427,657 | 477,997 | 458,717 | 36.4 |
| Korean | 266,280 | 626,478 | 894,063 | 1,062,337 | 299.0 |
| Vietnamese | 197,588 | 507,069 | 1,009,627 | 1,207,004 | 510.9 |
| Tagalog | 474,150 | 843,251 | 1,224,241 | 1,480,429 | 212.2 |

[1] The languages highlighted in this table are the languages for which data were available for the four time periods: 1980, 1990, 2000, and 2007.

[2] The total does not match the sum of the 17 languages listed in this table because the total includes all the other languages that are not highlighted here.

Note: Margins of error for all estimates can be found in Appendix Table 2 at <www.census.gov/population/www/socdemo/language/appendix.html>. For more information on the ACS, see <www.census.gov/acs/www/>.

Source: U.S. Census Bureau, 1980 and 1990 Census, Census 2000, and 2007 American Community Survey.

With 34.5 million speakers, Spanish was by far the most commonly spoken non-English language. Chinese was the only other detailed language with at least 2 million speakers. Even at this detailed level, however, there were still five other specific languages with over a million speakers: French, Tagalog, Vietnamese, German, and Korean.

The English-speaking ability of the speakers of these specific language 20
groups varied greatly; in some cases, certain groups reported speakers with higher levels of English-speaking ability, while other groups had speakers who were less adept with English. Some groups, such as Spanish, Russian, Chinese, and Vietnamese, showed higher proportions of those speaking English less than "very well" while other languages, such as French, German,

Table 3.
**Detailed Languages Spoken at Home by English-Speaking Ability for the Population 5 Years and Older: 2007**
(For information on confidentiality protection, sampling error, nonsampling error, and definitions, see *www.census.gov/acs/www/*)

| Characteristic | Number of speakers | Percentage of speakers of a non-English language | English-speaking ability | | | |
|---|---|---|---|---|---|---|
| | | | Very well | Well | Not well | Not at all |
| Population 5 years and older | 280,950,438 | (X) | (X) | (X) | (X) | (X) |
| Spoke only English at home | 225,505,953 | (X) | (X) | (X) | (X) | (X) |
| Spoke a language other than English at home | 55,444,485 | 100.0 | 55.9 | 19.8 | 16.3 | 8.1 |
| Spoke a language other than English at home | 55,444,485 | 100.0 | 55.9 | 19.8 | 16.3 | 8.1 |
| Spanish or Spanish Creole | 34,547,077 | 62.3 | 52.6 | 18.3 | 18.4 | 10.7 |
| Other Indo-European languages | 10,320,730 | 18.6 | 67.2 | 19.6 | 10.4 | 2.8 |
| French | 1,355,805 | 2.5 | 78.2 | 14.5 | 6.8 | 0.4 |
| French Creole | 629,019 | 1.1 | 56.7 | 24.3 | 14.8 | 4.3 |
| Italian | 798,801 | 1.4 | 71.8 | 17.2 | 9.6 | 1.4 |
| Portuguese | 687,126 | 1.2 | 56.6 | 22.0 | 14.9 | 6.4 |
| German | 1,104,354 | 2.0 | 82.8 | 12.6 | 4.4 | 0.3 |
| Yiddish | 158,991 | 0.3 | 70.3 | 18.3 | 9.5 | 1.9 |
| Other West Germanic languages | 270,178 | 0.5 | 76.2 | 19.7 | 3.4 | 0.7 |
| Scandinavian languages | 134,925 | 0.2 | 86.4 | 11.3 | 2.2 | 0.1 |
| Greek | 329,825 | 0.6 | 73.0 | 16.5 | 9.6 | 1.0 |
| Russian | 851,174 | 1.5 | 49.8 | 25.2 | 18.2 | 6.7 |
| Polish | 638,059 | 1.2 | 56.8 | 24.0 | 15.2 | 4.1 |
| Serbo-Croatian | 276,550 | 0.5 | 58.4 | 24.4 | 14.3 | 2.9 |
| Other Slavic languages | 312,109 | 0.6 | 61.6 | 23.0 | 12.5 | 2.9 |
| Armenian | 221,865 | 0.4 | 55.1 | 21.7 | 14.9 | 8.2 |
| Persian | 349,686 | 0.6 | 61.7 | 22.6 | 12.4 | 3.3 |
| Gujarati | 287,367 | 0.5 | 64.1 | 21.5 | 10.6 | 3.9 |
| Hindi | 532,911 | 1.0 | 79.6 | 15.3 | 4.0 | 1.1 |
| Urdu | 344,942 | 0.6 | 70.1 | 19.1 | 8.3 | 2.4 |
| Other Indic languages | 616,147 | 1.1 | 61.4 | 24.4 | 10.2 | 4.0 |
| Other Indo-European languages | 420,896 | 0.8 | 62.5 | 22.9 | 11.5 | 3.2 |
| Asian and Pacific Island languages | 8,325,886 | 15.0 | 51.4 | 26.2 | 17.0 | 5.4 |
| Chinese | 2,464,572 | 4.5 | 44.4 | 25.7 | 19.6 | 10.3 |
| Japanese | 458,717 | 0.8 | 53.8 | 29.1 | 15.7 | 1.4 |
| Korean | 1,062,337 | 1.9 | 41.8 | 29.3 | 24.2 | 4.7 |
| Mon-Khmer, Cambodian | 185,056 | 0.3 | 46.3 | 25.6 | 21.4 | 6.7 |
| Hmong | 181,069 | 0.3 | 52.9 | 24.1 | 15.5 | 7.4 |
| Thai | 144,405 | 0.3 | 48.4 | 34.8 | 14.7 | 2.1 |
| Laotian | 149,045 | 0.3 | 51.1 | 23.5 | 19.9 | 5.4 |
| Vietnamese | 1,207,004 | 2.2 | 39.3 | 29.0 | 25.2 | 6.5 |
| Other Asian languages | 634,608 | 1.1 | 70.1 | 20.2 | 7.5 | 2.2 |
| Tagalog | 1,480,429 | 2.7 | 69.0 | 23.8 | 6.5 | 0.6 |
| Other Pacific Island languages | 358,644 | 0.7 | 63.1 | 26.0 | 10.0 | 0.8 |
| Other languages | 2,250,792 | 4.1 | 70.1 | 19.7 | 8.1 | 2.1 |
| Navajo | 170,717 | 0.3 | 75.3 | 14.4 | 7.3 | 2.9 |
| Other Native American languages | 200,560 | 0.4 | 86.4 | 10.0 | 3.2 | 0.4 |
| Hungarian | 91,297 | 0.2 | 71.6 | 20.0 | 7.3 | 1.0 |
| Arabic | 767,319 | 1.4 | 66.2 | 22.1 | 9.7 | 2.0 |
| Hebrew | 213,576 | 0.4 | 81.6 | 14.7 | 3.1 | 0.5 |
| African languages | 699,518 | 1.3 | 66.2 | 22.6 | 8.8 | 2.3 |
| All other languages | 107,805 | 0.2 | 62.3 | 19.0 | 11.6 | 7.0 |

(X) Not applicable.

Note: Margins of error for all estimates can be found in Appendix Table 3B at <www.census.gov/population/www/socdemo/language/appendix.html>. For more information on the ACS, see <www.census.gov/acs/www/>.

Source: U.S. Census Bureau, 2007 American Community Survey.

Scandinavian, and Hebrew, reported higher than average levels of speaking English "very well."

As the number of languages spoken rises and falls over time, to some degree these patterns reflect historical immigration and settlement patterns, along with other unique situations. For example, English is routinely taught in Scandinavian schools, and many speakers of Native American languages were born and raised in the United States and have routinely interacted with English their entire lives. Nevertheless, Table 3 demonstrates that English-speaking ability varied widely across different language communities.

### Language Concentration in States

Languages spoken at home are not evenly distributed throughout the nation. Some areas have high percentages of speakers of non-English languages, while others have lower levels. Table 4 shows the proportion of people who spoke a language other than English at home across the 50 states and the District of Columbia, as well as the English-speaking ability levels in those states.

As can be seen in Table 4 and Figure 3, the percentage of people who spoke a language other than English at home varied substantially across states; just 2 percent of West Virginians 5 years old and over reported speaking a language other than English at home, while 43 percent of people in California reported the same. Moreover, Figure 3 shows that relatively high levels of other language speakers were common in the Southwest and in the larger immigrant gateway states of the East, such as New York, New Jersey, and Florida. With the exception of Illinois, relatively lower levels of foreign-language speakers prevail in most of the Midwest and in the South.

Similarly, levels of English-speaking ability were also different across states. Figure 4 shows the percentage of foreign-language speakers who reported their English-speaking ability was less than "very well." In Montana, a relatively small percentage of foreign-language speakers (19 percent) reported having diffculty speaking English. In Arkansas, however, about half of all people speaking another language at home (51 percent) reported they had trouble with English.

25 Quite often, concentrations of specific language groups were found in certain areas of the country. In the short term, the factors creating these concentrations include points of entry into the United States and family connections facilitating chain migration° (Palloni et al. 2003).[5] In the longer term, internal migration streams, employment opportunities, and other family situations help to facilitate the diffusion of language groups within the country.

***chain migration:*** pattern of migration in which new immigrants come to a location in the receiving country where earlier groups of immigrants from the same region of the home country now live.

Table 4.

**Population 5 Years and Older Speaking a Language Other Than English at Home by English-Speaking Ability by State: 2007**

(For information on confidentiality protection, sampling error, nonsampling error, and definitions, see *www.census.gov/acs/www/*)

| State | Population 5 years and older | Spoke a language other than English at home | Percent who spoke a language other than English at home | English-speaking ability | | | |
|---|---|---|---|---|---|---|---|
| | | | | Very well | Well | Not well | Not at all |
| United States..... | 280,950,438 | 55,444,485 | 19.7 | 55.9 | 19.8 | 16.3 | 8.1 |
| Alabama ........... | 4,318,848 | 183,831 | 4.3 | 53.6 | 16.6 | 20.4 | 9.3 |
| Alaska ............. | 632,806 | 100,508 | 15.9 | 60.6 | 25.7 | 11.7 | 2.0 |
| Arizona ............ | 5,839,788 | 1,662,549 | 28.5 | 55.8 | 17.7 | 15.5 | 11.0 |
| Arkansas ........... | 2,637,847 | 167,962 | 6.4 | 48.8 | 21.2 | 20.7 | 9.2 |
| California ......... | 33,891,325 | 14,441,651 | 42.6 | 53.2 | 19.8 | 17.2 | 9.8 |
| Colorado ........... | 4,512,195 | 755,749 | 16.7 | 55.3 | 19.0 | 17.9 | 7.8 |
| Connecticut ......... | 3,290,325 | 639,586 | 19.4 | 60.5 | 21.0 | 13.7 | 4.8 |
| Delaware ........... | 805,602 | 96,929 | 12.0 | 62.7 | 17.6 | 15.5 | 4.3 |
| District of Columbia ... | 551,980 | 80,195 | 14.5 | 68.6 | 15.8 | 11.4 | 4.2 |
| Florida ............. | 17,105,241 | 4,465,787 | 26.1 | 54.1 | 19.8 | 16.5 | 9.5 |
| Georgia ............ | 8,818,349 | 1,056,615 | 12.0 | 51.9 | 21.1 | 18.9 | 8.1 |
| Hawaii ............. | 1,195,661 | 305,212 | 25.5 | 57.1 | 25.8 | 14.7 | 2.3 |
| Idaho .............. | 1,382,539 | 135,893 | 9.8 | 59.5 | 17.5 | 17.0 | 6.0 |
| Illinois.............. | 11,961,769 | 2,603,244 | 21.8 | 54.8 | 21.5 | 17.1 | 6.6 |
| Indiana............. | 5,903,675 | 437,434 | 7.4 | 60.0 | 19.9 | 14.5 | 5.6 |
| Iowa................ | 2,790,906 | 183,743 | 6.6 | 59.8 | 19.9 | 15.4 | 5.0 |
| Kansas............. | 2,580,638 | 256,109 | 9.9 | 56.1 | 18.6 | 18.1 | 7.2 |
| Kentucky ........... | 3,963,318 | 164,024 | 4.1 | 55.3 | 21.1 | 18.4 | 5.1 |
| Louisiana........... | 3,996,750 | 328,041 | 8.2 | 68.2 | 17.4 | 10.9 | 3.5 |
| Maine.............. | 1,247,427 | 92,291 | 7.4 | 74.8 | 16.5 | 7.3 | 1.4 |
| Maryland ........... | 5,243,703 | 775,267 | 14.8 | 59.5 | 21.1 | 14.6 | 4.9 |
| Massachusetts....... | 6,072,036 | 1,228,856 | 20.2 | 57.3 | 21.5 | 14.5 | 6.7 |
| Michigan ........... | 9,435,733 | 850,865 | 9.0 | 62.0 | 19.9 | 13.6 | 4.5 |
| Minnesota .......... | 4,844,316 | 464,630 | 9.6 | 58.2 | 20.9 | 15.3 | 5.7 |
| Mississippi.......... | 2,705,640 | 91,779 | 3.4 | 59.0 | 16.0 | 15.8 | 9.2 |
| Missouri............ | 5,484,696 | 316,838 | 5.8 | 61.0 | 20.2 | 14.1 | 4.7 |
| Montana............ | 898,614 | 37,055 | 4.1 | 80.9 | 12.6 | 5.4 | 1.0 |
| Nebraska........... | 1,645,880 | 148,297 | 9.0 | 57.0 | 19.8 | 15.6 | 7.6 |
| Nevada ............ | 2,371,632 | 650,338 | 27.4 | 52.9 | 23.0 | 16.6 | 7.5 |
| New Hampshire...... | 1,240,806 | 98,008 | 7.9 | 69.8 | 18.5 | 10.7 | 1.0 |
| New Jersey ......... | 8,130,371 | 2,262,008 | 27.8 | 58.2 | 20.5 | 15.5 | 5.8 |
| New Mexico......... | 1,828,867 | 652,880 | 35.7 | 72.9 | 14.0 | 8.6 | 4.5 |
| New York ........... | 18,097,578 | 5,229,102 | 28.9 | 54.3 | 20.9 | 17.4 | 7.4 |
| North Carolina....... | 8,429,207 | 814,645 | 9.7 | 51.8 | 19.2 | 20.3 | 8.7 |
| North Dakota........ | 599,205 | 35,387 | 5.9 | 73.5 | 15.7 | 9.4 | 1.3 |
| Ohio............... | 10,727,127 | 646,477 | 6.0 | 64.7 | 20.3 | 11.8 | 3.2 |
| Oklahoma .......... | 3,357,386 | 276,163 | 8.2 | 54.8 | 19.4 | 18.7 | 7.1 |
| Oregon............. | 3,511,093 | 504,621 | 14.4 | 53.4 | 19.1 | 18.7 | 8.8 |
| Pennsylvania........ | 11,703,178 | 1,107,017 | 9.5 | 62.1 | 20.1 | 13.8 | 4.0 |
| Rhode Island........ | 996,158 | 207,071 | 20.8 | 56.2 | 18.9 | 16.6 | 8.3 |
| South Carolina....... | 4,113,842 | 241,144 | 5.9 | 54.5 | 20.8 | 17.8 | 6.9 |
| South Dakota........ | 740,248 | 46,384 | 6.3 | 75.9 | 14.6 | 7.6 | 1.8 |
| Tennessee.......... | 5,750,581 | 335,560 | 5.8 | 54.6 | 20.6 | 18.0 | 6.9 |
| Texas.............. | 21,924,924 | 7,437,834 | 33.9 | 56.6 | 17.6 | 15.6 | 10.1 |
| Utah............... | 2,392,633 | 331,682 | 13.9 | 57.0 | 19.1 | 16.4 | 7.5 |
| Vermont............ | 588,849 | 30,174 | 5.1 | 76.5 | 14.8 | 6.5 | 2.1 |
| Virginia............ | 7,201,765 | 956,248 | 13.3 | 59.7 | 20.8 | 14.7 | 4.8 |
| Washington ......... | 6,046,464 | 1,012,440 | 16.7 | 54.0 | 22.5 | 16.5 | 7.1 |
| West Virginia ........ | 1,707,922 | 39,153 | 2.3 | 69.2 | 15.8 | 13.5 | 1.6 |
| Wisconsin .......... | 5,245,596 | 428,790 | 8.2 | 60.7 | 19.5 | 15.1 | 4.7 |
| Wyoming ........... | 487,399 | 30,419 | 6.2 | 68.1 | 16.0 | 10.9 | 5.0 |

Note: Margins of error for all estimates can be found in Appendix Table 48 at <www.census.gov/population/www/socdemo/language/appendix.html>. For more information on the ACS, see <www.census.gov/acs/www/>.

Source: U.S. Census Bureau, 2007 American Community Survey.

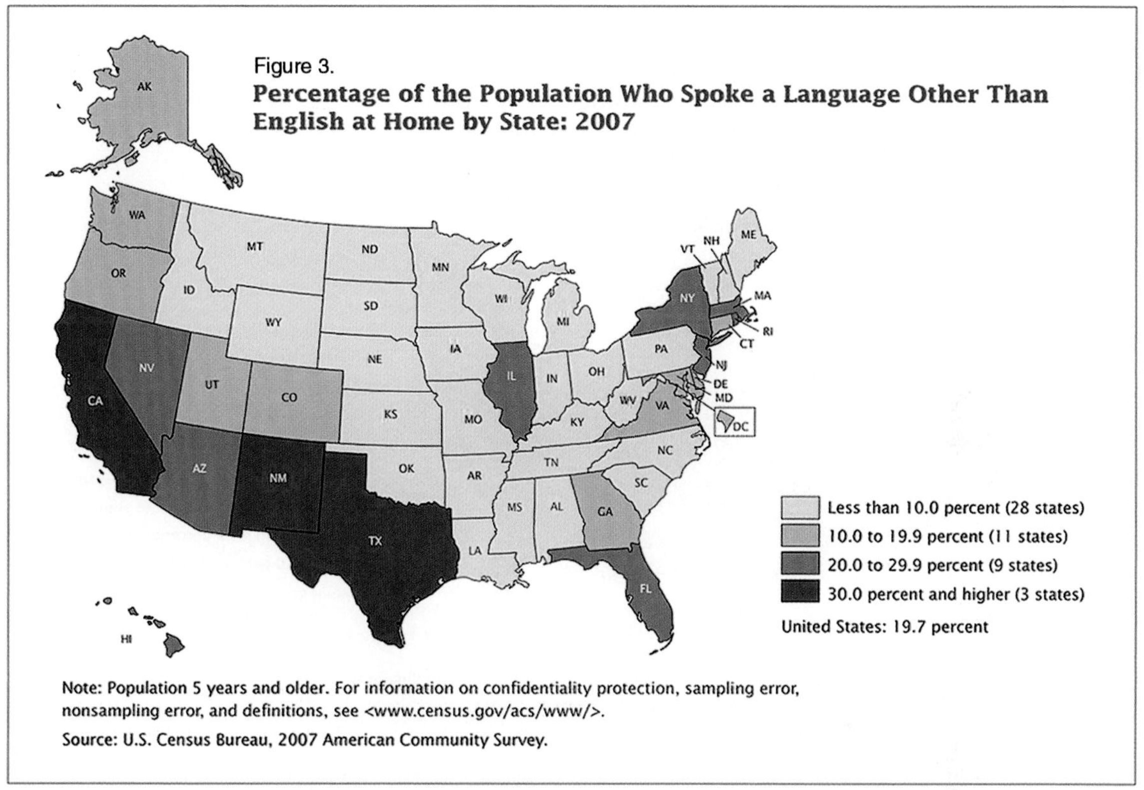


Figure 3.
**Percentage of the Population Who Spoke a Language Other Than English at Home by State: 2007**

Note: Population 5 years and older. For information on confidentiality protection, sampling error, nonsampling error, and definitions, see <www.census.gov/acs/www/>.

Source: U.S. Census Bureau, 2007 American Community Survey.

Figures 5a to 5h are a series of maps that show the geographic distribution of the most commonly spoken languages in the United States.[6] These maps show the percentage of people 5 years old and over in each state who spoke Spanish, French, German, Slavic languages, Korean, Chinese, Vietnamese, and Tagalog.[7] The intervals shown on each map are determined by dividing the range of values for each language into four equal intervals. For Spanish speakers, three states (Texas, California, and New Mexico)[8] were in the highest interval, but the southwest corridor of the United States also had a sizable percentage of the population speaking Spanish (see Figure 5a). Louisiana and Maine had the highest percentage of French speakers, but Florida and many states in the Northeast had a substantial percentage as well. The presence of French Creole speakers in Louisiana and of Haitian Creole speakers in Florida contributed to the higher levels of French speakers in these states (see Figure 5b).

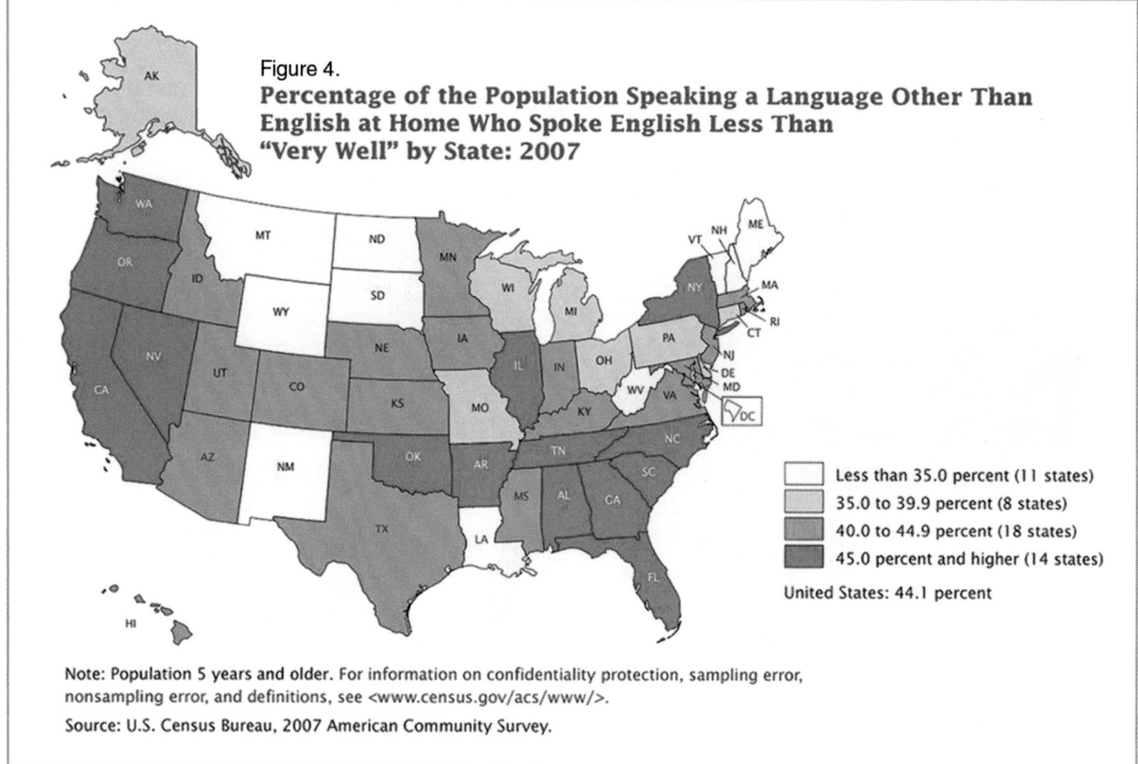


Figure 4.
**Percentage of the Population Speaking a Language Other Than English at Home Who Spoke English Less Than "Very Well" by State: 2007**

Note: Population 5 years and older. For information on confidentiality protection, sampling error, nonsampling error, and definitions, see <www.census.gov/acs/www/>.

Source: U.S. Census Bureau, 2007 American Community Survey.

Figure 5c shows German speakers spanning the Canadian border of the United States, with the highest percentages in the Dakotas.[9] Pennsylvania had a sizable number of speakers of Pennsylvania Dutch, which is a West Germanic language. Indiana, with a relatively large number of people of German ancestry, also had a high percentage of German speakers.[10] Slavic languages, which include Russian, Polish, and Serbo-Croatian, had the highest percentage of speakers in Illinois, New York, New Jersey, and Connecticut.[11] A substantial level of Slavic speakers also was found in the West Coast states (see Figure 5d).

Figure 5e shows Hawaii having the highest concentration of Korean speakers, followed by California and New Jersey. California and New York housed the highest percentage of Chinese speakers, followed by Hawaii and Massachusetts (see Figure 5f).

Figures 5a-5d.
**Percentage of the Population 5 Years and Older Speaking Specified Languages by State: 2007**

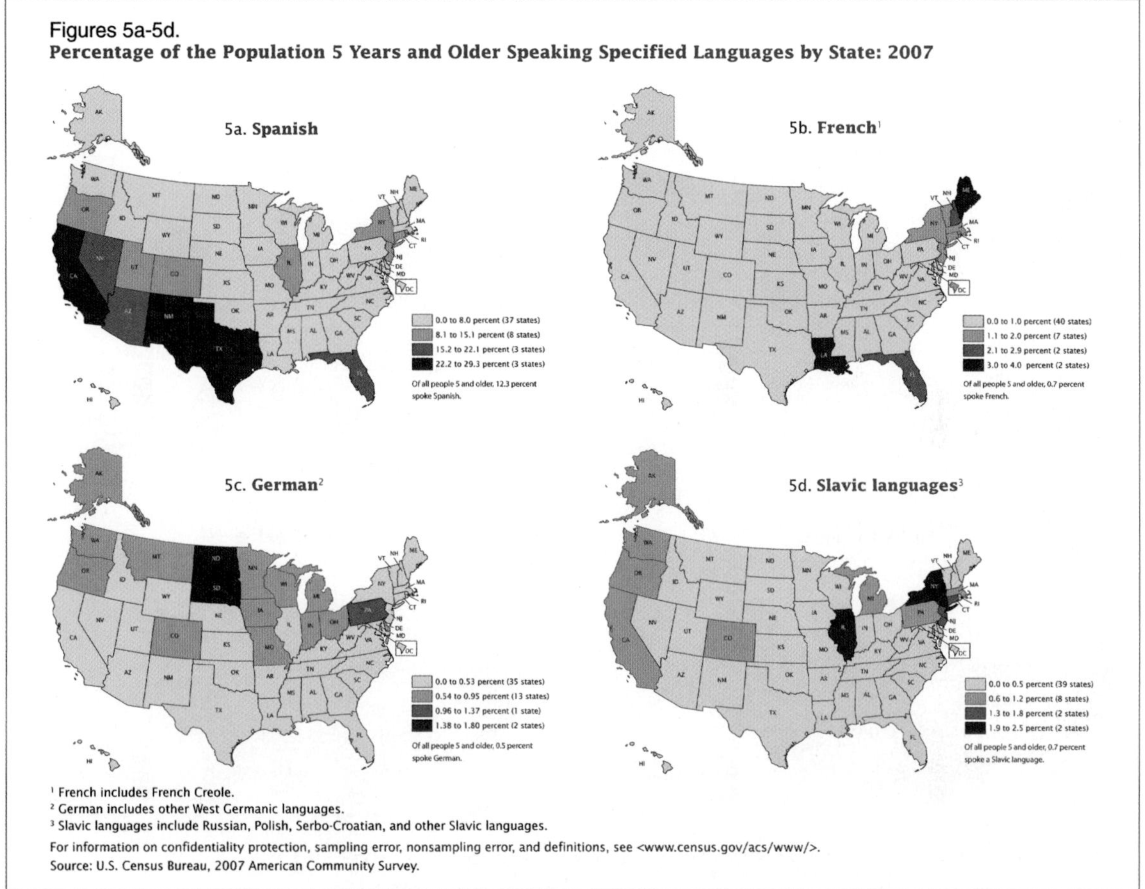


[1] French includes French Creole.
[2] German includes other West Germanic languages.
[3] Slavic languages include Russian, Polish, Serbo-Croatian, and other Slavic languages.
For information on confidentiality protection, sampling error, nonsampling error, and definitions, see <www.census.gov/acs/www/>.
Source: U.S. Census Bureau, 2007 American Community Survey.

As with Korean speakers, higher levels of Vietnamese speakers were evident throughout the country rather than a large concentration among contiguous states. California had the highest percentage of Vietnamese speakers, followed by Hawaii, Washington, and Texas (see Figure 5g).[12] Tagalog, a language of the Philippines, had its highest percentage of speakers in Hawaii. Alaska, California, and Nevada also had high levels, but not as high as Hawaii.[13]

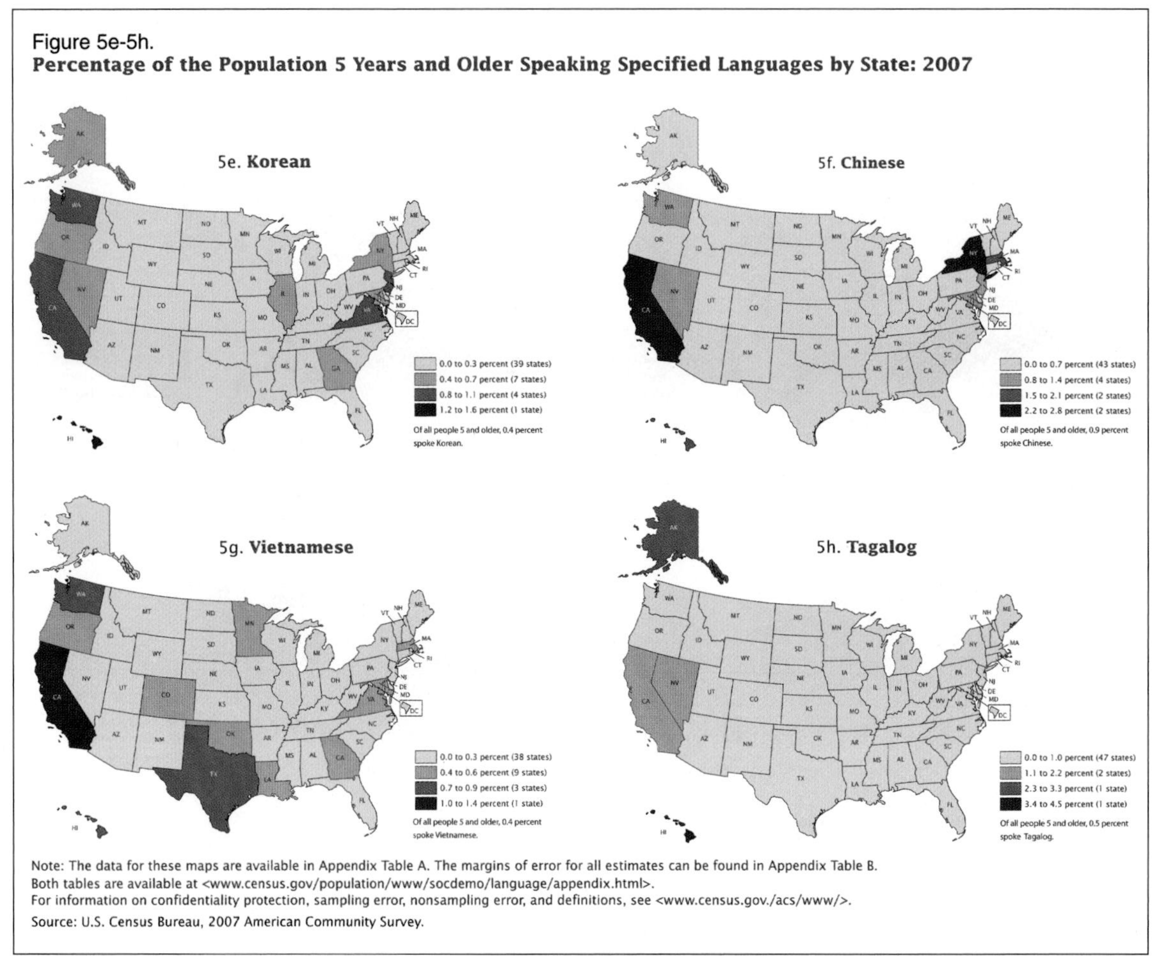


Figure 5e-5h.
**Percentage of the Population 5 Years and Older Speaking Specified Languages by State: 2007**

Note: The data for these maps are available in Appendix Table A. The margins of error for all estimates can be found in Appendix Table B. Both tables are available at <www.census.gov/population/www/socdemo/language/appendix.html>.
For information on confidentiality protection, sampling error, nonsampling error, and definitions, see <www.census.gov./acs/www/>.
Source: U.S. Census Bureau, 2007 American Community Survey.

## Language Concentration in Metropolitan and Micropolitan Areas

Just as languages were dispersed unevenly across states, metropolitan 30
and micropolitan statistical areas also displayed similar effects. Large metro areas such as New York, Los Angeles, and Chicago generally had large proportions of foreign-language speakers because of the economic opportunities in these places or because they act as gateway points of entry into the

Table 5.

**Distribution of Speakers of Specific Non-English Languages Across Metropolitan and Micropolitan Statistical Areas: 2007**

(For information on confidentiality protection, sampling error, nonsampling error, and definitions, see *www.census.gov/acs/www/*)

| Detailed language | Metropolitan and micropolitan statistical areas with the largest proportion of speakers of specified language[1,2] | | | | | | | | | | |
|---|---|---|---|---|---|---|---|---|---|---|---|
| | Total number of speakers of non-English languages | Percent | 1st metro or micro area[1] | Percent | 2nd metro or micro area[2] | Percent | 3rd metro or micro area | Percent | 4th metro or micro area | Percent | Percent in all other areas |
| Spanish | 34,547,077 | 100.0 | Los Angeles | 12.8 | New York | 9.5 | Miami | 5.6 | Chicago | 4.3 | 67.8 |
| French | 1,355,805 | 100.0 | New York | 10.1 | Washington | 4.5 | Boston | 4.1 | Miami | 4.1 | 77.2 |
| French Creole | 629,019 | 100.0 | Miami | 35.9 | New York | 28.1 | Boston | 6.5 | Orlando | 4.2 | 25.2 |
| Italian | 798,801 | 100.0 | New York | 32.7 | Boston | 5.2 | Chicago | 4.9 | Philadelphia | 3.9 | 53.2 |
| Portuguese | 687,126 | 100.0 | New York | 18.9 | Providence | 14.9 | Boston | 12.4 | Miami | 7.4 | 46.4 |
| German | 1,104,354 | 100.0 | New York | 5.8 | Chicago | 3.6 | Los Angeles | 3.2 | Washington | 2.1 | 85.4 |
| Yiddish | 158,991 | 100.0 | New York | 76.0 | Poughkeepsie | 6.2 | Miami | 3.8 | Los Angeles | 2.2 | 11.9 |
| Scandinavian | 134,925 | 100.0 | Los Angeles | 6.2 | New York | 6.1 | Seattle | 5.4 | Minneapolis | 3.4 | 79.0 |
| Greek | 329,825 | 100.0 | New York | 26.1 | Chicago | 13.6 | Boston | 6.0 | Philadelphia | 3.1 | 51.2 |
| Russian | 851,174 | 100.0 | New York | 29.5 | Los Angeles | 6.3 | Chicago | 4.6 | San Francisco | 3.8 | 55.9 |
| Polish | 638,059 | 100.0 | Chicago | 31.3 | New York | 22.8 | Hartford | 3.6 | Detroit | 3.3 | 39.0 |
| Serbo-Croatian | 276,550 | 100.0 | New York | 11.9 | Chicago | 11.4 | St. Louis, MO-IL | 4.6 | Phoenix | 4.5 | 67.6 |
| Armenian | 221,865 | 100.0 | Los Angeles | 71.8 | New York | 4.6 | Fresno, CA | 2.5 | Boston | 2.4 | 18.6 |
| Persian | 349,686 | 100.0 | Los Angeles | 29.3 | New York | 9.1 | Washington | 7.2 | San Francisco | 6.1 | 48.2 |
| Gujarati | 287,367 | 100.0 | New York | 22.5 | Chicago | 11.2 | Los Angeles | 5.3 | Philadelphia | 4.9 | 56.2 |
| Hindi | 532,911 | 100.0 | New York | 16.4 | San Francisco | 6.6 | Chicago | 5.7 | Los Angeles | 5.0 | 66.3 |
| Urdu | 344,942 | 100.0 | New York | 23.4 | Chicago | 10.4 | Houston | 8.6 | Washington | 7.4 | 50.1 |
| Chinese | 2,464,572 | 100.0 | New York | 20.6 | Los Angeles | 15.4 | San Francisco | 12.4 | San Jose | 4.9 | 46.7 |
| Japanese | 458,717 | 100.0 | Los Angeles | 16.8 | Honolulu, HI | 9.7 | New York | 8.7 | San Francisco | 4.9 | 60.0 |
| Korean | 1,062,337 | 100.0 | Los Angeles | 22.8 | New York | 15.0 | Washington | 6.0 | Chicago | 4.2 | 52.0 |
| Mon-Khmer, Cambodian | 185,056 | 100.0 | Los Angeles | 18.5 | Boston | 9.3 | Stockton, CA | 5.1 | Seattle | 4.6 | 62.5 |
| Hmong | 181,069 | 100.0 | Minneapolis | 25.2 | Sacramento | 13.4 | Fresno, CA | 11.6 | Milwaukee | 5.2 | 44.6 |
| Thai | 144,405 | 100.0 | Los Angeles | 15.7 | New York | 6.3 | San Francisco | 4.8 | Washington | 4.4 | 68.9 |
| Laotian | 149,045 | 100.0 | Minneapolis | 5.1 | Fresno, CA | 4.6 | Nashville | 4.5 | Los Angeles | 4.5 | 81.3 |
| Vietnamese | 1,207,004 | 100.0 | Los Angeles | 17.0 | San Jose | 9.3 | Houston | 6.1 | Dallas | 4.6 | 63.0 |
| Tagalog | 1,480,429 | 100.0 | Los Angeles | 17.5 | San Francisco | 11.0 | New York | 9.1 | San Diego | 5.8 | 56.6 |
| Navajo | 170,717 | 100.0 | Farmington, NM | 16.5 | Gallup, NM[2] | 12.0 | Flagstaff, AZ | 10.3 | Albuquerque, NM | 5.4 | 55.9 |
| Hungarian | 91,297 | 100.0 | New York | 20.1 | Los Angeles | 5.8 | Cleveland | 4.9 | Chicago | 3.9 | 65.3 |
| Arabic | 767,319 | 100.0 | New York | 14.6 | Detroit | 11.2 | Los Angeles | 7.0 | Chicago | 5.7 | 61.6 |
| Hebrew | 213,576 | 100.0 | New York | 38.8 | Los Angeles | 11.6 | Miami | 8.4 | Boston | 3.4 | 37.9 |

[1] The Office of Management and Budget's statistical area definitions (for metropolitan and micropolitan statistical areas) are those issued by that agency in December 2006. Each metropolitan or micropolitan statistical area with a state abbreviation after its name in the table indicates that the full title of that area is displayed. Below are the full titles of metropolitan statistical areas that are abbreviated in the table:

Boston – Boston-Cambridge-Quincy, MA-NH
Chicago – Chicago-Naperville-Joliet, IL-IN-WI
Cleveland – Cleveland-Elyria-Mentor, OH
Dallas – Dallas-Fort Worth-Arlington, TX
Detroit – Detroit-Warren-Livonia, MI
Hartford – Hartford-West Hartford-East Hartford, CT
Houston – Houston-Sugar Land-Baytown, TX
Los Angeles – Los Angeles-Long Beach-Santa Ana, CA
Miami – Miami-Fort Lauderdale-Pompano Beach, FL
Milwaukee – Milwaukee-Waukesha-West Allis, WI
Minneapolis – Minneapolis-St. Paul-Bloomington, MN-WI
Nashville – Nashville-Davidson–Murfreesboro–Franklin, TN
New York – New York-Northern New Jersey-Long Island, NY-NJ-PA
Orlando – Orlando-Kissimmee, FL
Philadelphia – Philadelphia-Camden-Wilmington, PA-NJ-DE-MD
Phoenix – Phoenix-Mesa-Scottsdale, AZ
Poughkeepsie – Poughkeepsie-Newburgh-Middletown, NY
Providence – Providence-New Bedford-Fall River, RI-MA
Sacramento – Sacramento–Arden-Arcade–Roseville, CA
San Diego – San Diego-Carlsbad-San Marcos, CA
San Francisco – San Francisco-Oakland-Fremont, CA
San Jose – San Jose-Sunnyvale-Santa Clara, CA
Seattle – Seattle-Tacoma-Bellevue, WA
Washington – Washington-Arlington-Alexandria, DC-VA-MD-WV

[2] Gallup, NM, is the only micropolitan statistical area in this table. The other areas displayed in the table are metropolitan statistical areas.

Note: Margins of error for all estimates can be found in Appendix Table 5 at <www.census.gov/population/www/socdemo/language/appendix.html>. For more information on the ACS, see <www.census.gov/acs/www/>.

Source: U.S. Census Bureau, 2007 American Community Survey.

country. Not all of the high levels of language clustering occurred in these three metro areas, however. Table 5 presents the metro or micro areas in which 30 of the 39 detailed languages had the largest number of speakers.[14]

As Table 5 shows, some languages were widely distributed across areas, while other languages had a large proportion of their speakers in just one or two areas. Of these languages, Yiddish is an extreme example of language concentration—76 percent of all its speakers lived in the New York metro area, with another 6 percent in the Poughkeepsie metro area, 4 percent in the Miami metro area, and 2 percent in the Los Angeles metro area. This means that 88 percent of all Yiddish speakers lived in just one of these four metro areas. The remaining 12 percent of Yiddish speakers were spread throughout the rest of the country.

In other similar cases, the two or three largest concentrations account for a large overall proportion of the total number of speakers. Polish, for example, had 31 percent of its speakers in the Chicago metro area, with another 23 percent in the New York metro area. Among Hmong speakers, the Minneapolis-St. Paul (25 percent), Sacramento (13 percent), and Fresno (12 percent) metro areas accounted for half of all speakers of this language in the United States.[15]

By contrast, speakers of Laotian were much more widely dispersed throughout the country. The Minneapolis-St. Paul, Fresno, Nashville, and Los Angeles metro areas each had about 5 percent of all Laotian speakers, leaving the remaining 81 percent of speakers spread throughout the rest of the country.

This high degree of dispersion was actually more common among languages that have long been a part of the nation's history. German, a language spoken by many immigrants to the United States over the last few centuries, was highly dispersed. The four largest concentrations in the United States account for just 15 percent of all German speakers in the country. Similar high levels of dispersion are seen for languages such as French (77 percent outside the four largest metro concentrations) and Scandinavian languages (79 percent).

### Summary

This report provides illustrative evidence of the continuing and growing role 35
of non-English languages as part of the national fabric. Fueled by both long-term historic immigration patterns and more recent ones, the language diversity of the country has increased over the past few decades. As the nation continues to be a destination for people from other lands, this pattern

of language diversity will also likely continue. Given the patterns of location and relocation over time, local areas may see specific or diverse changes in the languages spoken in any given locality.

## Source of the Data and Accuracy of the Estimates

### The American Community Survey

Many of the findings presented in this report were based on the American Community Survey (ACS) data collected in 2007. These data were based on the population living in either households or group quarters (which include correctional facilities, nursing homes, college dormitories, group homes, and overnight shelters) that were included in the ACS sample. The U.S. Census Bureau is both the sponsor and the collector of the American Community Survey.

The 2007 ACS is based on a sample of just under 3 million housing unit addresses and a separate sample of just under 200 thousand people living in group quarters. ACS figures are estimates based on this sample and approximate the actual figures that would have been obtained by interviewing the entire household and group quarters populations using the same methodology. The estimates from the 2007 ACS sample may also differ from estimates based on other survey samples of housing units and group quarters and the people living within those housing units and group quarters.

### The Decennial Census

Other findings presented in this report that were not derived from the 2007 ACS were collected from previously published findings based on data from each decennial census conducted by the Census Bureau since 1980. In general, the decennial censuses collected data from the population living in households as well as those living in group quarters such as those described above.

### Sampling and Nonsampling Error

Sampling error occurs when the characteristics of a sample are measured instead of those of the entire population (as from a census). Note that sample-based estimates will vary depending on the particular sample selected from the population, but all attempt to approximate the actual figures. Measures of the magnitude of sampling error reflect the variation in the estimates over all possible samples that could have been selected from the population using the same sampling, data collection, and processing methods.

Estimates of the magnitude of sampling errors are provided in the form of 40
margins of error for all key ACS estimates included in this report. The Census Bureau recommends that data users incorporate this information into their analyses, as sampling error in survey estimates could impact the conclusions drawn from the results. All comparative statements in this report have undergone statistical testing, and comparisons are significant at the 90 percent confidence level° unless noted otherwise. This means the 90 percent confidence interval for the difference between the estimates being compared does not include zero.

***significant at the 90 percent confidence level:*** that is, the chances that the statements in the report are valid are 90 out of 100. (Because the data used are based on a sample of the population rather than the entire population, these statistics are estimates; the issue here is how accurate these estimates are. A 90 percent confidence level is the level used for much demographic research.)

In addition to sampling error, nonsampling errors may be introduced during any phase of data collection or processing. For example, operations such as editing, reviewing, or keying data from questionnaires may introduce error into the estimates. The primary source of nonsampling error and the processes instituted to control error in the 2007 ACS are described in further detail in the 2007 ACS Accuracy of the Data document.

Title 13, U.S. Code, Section 9, prohibits the Census Bureau from publishing results from which the identity of an individual survey respondent could be determined. For more information on how the Census Bureau protects the confidentiality of data, see the 2007 ACS Accuracy of the Data document.

## For More Information

Further information from the 2007 ACS is available from the American FactFinder on the Census Bureau's Web site, at http://factfinder.census.gov/home/saff/main.html?_lang=en.

Measures of ACS quality—including sample size and number of interviews, response and nonresponse rates, coverage rates, and item allocation rates—are available at www.census.gov/acs/www/UseData/sse/.

Additional information about language use is available on the Census 45
Bureau's Web site.

## Contact

For additional information on these topics, please call 1-866-758-1060 (toll free) or visit www.census.gov.

### Suggested Citation

Shin, Hyon B., and Robert A. Kominski. 2010. Language Use in the United States: 2007, American Community Survey Reports, ACS-12. U.S. Census Bureau, Washington, DC.

### User Comments

The Census Bureau welcomes the comments and advice of users of our data and reports. Please send comments and suggestions to:

Chief, Housing and Household
Economic Statistics Division
U.S. Census Bureau
Washington, DC 20233-8500

### Appendix A

## Language Questions Used in Decennial Censuses

**2000:** *(Collected for all ages: retained for persons 5 years old and over)*

Does this person speak a language other than English at home?

What is this language?

How well does this person speak English (very well, well, not well, not at all)?

**1990:** *(For persons 5 years old and over)*

Does this person speak a language other than English at home?

What is this language?

How well does this person speak English (very well, well, not well, not at all)?

**1980:** *(For persons 3 years old and over; tabulated for 5 years old and over)*

Does this person speak a language other than English at home?

What is this language?

How well does this person speak English (very well, well, not well, not at all)?

**1970:** *(No age for question; tabulations limited)*

What language, other than English, was spoken in this person's home when he was a child? (Spanish, French, German, Other [specify] _______, None—English only)

**1960:** *(For foreign-born persons)*

What language was spoken in his home before he came to the United States?

**1950:** *(Not asked)*

**1940:** *(For persons of all ages; asked under the category of "Mother Tongue [or Native Language]")*

Language spoken at home in earliest childhood.

**1930:** *(For foreign-born persons; asked under the category of "Mother Tongue [or Native Language] of Foreign Born")*

Language spoken in home before coming to the United States.

**1920:** *(For foreign-born persons)*

Place of birth and mother tongue of person and each parent.

Whether able to speak English.

**1910:** *(Mother tongue was collected for all foreign-born persons, to be written in with place of birth; also collected for foreign-born parents. Specific instructions on correct languages to write in and a list of appropriate European languages were provided to the enumerator. Similar instructions may have carried over to 1920.)*

Whether able to speak English; or, if not, give language spoken.

**1900:** *(For all persons 10 years old and over)*

"Can speak English" was asked after the two questions "Can read" and "Can write."

**1890:** *(For all persons 10 years old and over)*

"Able to speak English. If not, the language or dialect spoken" was asked after the questions "Able to Read" and "Able to Write."

**1790–1880:** *(No evidence of language questions or English-ability questions)*

Note: The universe used for data collection may not be the same as in tabulations. In some cases, data were tabulated for foreign-born only or White foreign-born only. Consult publications.

## Notes

1. Self-reported data on English-speaking ability have demonstrated the measure to be highly reliable and usable. See "How Good Is How Well? An Examination of the Census English-Speaking Ability Question," http://www.census.gov/population/www/socdemo/lang_use.html.
2. For example, the Voting Rights Act of 1965 uses these criteria to determine the need for bilingual election materials.

3. For people 25 years old and over who were not high school graduates, those who spoke Other Indo-European languages "very well" (38.9 percent) were not statistically different from those who spoke All Other languages "very well" (37.6 percent). Reciprocally, those who spoke less than "very well" for both languages were not statistically different from each other (61.1 percent and 62.4 percent, respectively).
4. Data from 1980, 1990, and 2000 are from decennial censuses, whereas the data from 2007 come from the 2007 American Community Survey. For more information about language use and English-speaking ability differences between the census and the American Community Survey, read "Comparison of the Estimates on Language Use and English-Speaking Ability from the ACS, the C2SS, and Census 2000 (Report)." This report can be accessed at http://www.census.gov/acs/www/Downloads/Language_Comparison_Report_2008-03.doc. Corresponding tables are accessible at http://www.census.gov/acs/www/Downloads/Language_Comparison_Tables_2008-03.xls.
5. Palloni, A.; D.S. Massey; M. Ceballos; K. Espinosa; and M. Spittel. 2001. "Social Capital and International Migration: A Test Using Information on Family Networks." *American Journal of Sociology*, Vol. 106, No. 5: 1262–1298.
6. Figures 5a to 5h illustrate the proportions of these languages by state, but many of the percentages of speakers in each state are relatively small comparable to the total population of the state. The percentages for these maps can be found in Appendix Table A at www.census.gov/population/www/socdemo/language/appendix.html.
7. French includes French Creole; German includes other West Germanic languages; and Slavic languages include Russian, Polish, Serbo-Croatian, and other Slavic languages.
8. The percentage of Spanish speakers living in California (28.5 percent) was not statistically different from the percentage of Spanish speakers living in New Mexico (28.2 percent).
9. The percentages of German speakers living in North Dakota (1.8 percent) and in South Dakota (1.5 percent) were not statistically different from each other.
10. For more information on ancestry, visit the Ancestry Web site at www.census.gov/population/www/ancestry/index.html.
11. The percentage of Slavic speakers living in New Jersey (1.8 percent) was not statistically different from the percentage of Slavic speakers living in Connecticut (1.7 percent).
12. The percentages of Vietnamese speakers in Hawaii (0.9 percent), Washington (0.9 percent), and Texas (0.7 percent) were not statistically different from one another.
13. The percentages of Tagalog speakers in Alaska (2.3 percent), California (2.2 percent), and Nevada (2.2 percent) were not statistically different from one another.
14. The nine languages that are not on this list are those languages that are aggregated or are groups of languages, such as Other West Germanic languages or All Other languages.
15. The percentages of Hmong speakers in Sacramento (13 percent) and in Fresno (12 percent) were not statistically different from each other.

## RESPOND •

1. How would you characterize the argument made by this selection overall? Is it an argument of fact, an argument of definition, an argument of evaluation, a causal argument, or a proposal? What evidence would you give for your claim? At the same time, can you find short passages that represent other kinds of arguments in this selection? Give several examples. (For a discussion of kinds of arguments, see Chapter 1.)
2. How does this report give us insight into the changing nature of bilingualism in the United States—not only the languages and groups involved, but also the places where languages other than English are likely found and reasons why? Why, according to the report, are data such as those presented here useful and even necessary?
3. This report is produced by the U.S. Census Bureau. In what ways does that fact represent an ethical appeal (or should it)? For example, how might it influence your evaluation of the credibility of this report as a source you might use in constructing an academic argument? How does the section entitled "Source of the Data and Accuracy of the Estimates" (p. 589) represent an ethical appeal? (For a discussion of ethical appeals, see Chapter 3. For a discussion of evaluating sources, see Chapter 18.)
4. Compare the information given in Table 4 and Figure 3. Both present information about the population aged 5 or older who were reported to speak a language other than English at home by state in 2007. What information do both present? What additional information is presented in Table 4? What does the presentation in Figure 3 make evident that the presentation in Table 4 cannot show us? What do these two presentations of the data—and in some cases, the same data—remind us about the nature of visual arguments? (For a discussion of visual arguments, see Chapter 14.)
5. Study Appendix A (p. 591) carefully. As noted, it provides the questions that have been used about language in the U.S. census as far back as 1890, when the first questions were asked. As should be clear, the questions have not been consistent, and many decades, no questions were asked about language at all. What problems does this situation create for researchers who wish to understand changing patterns of language use in this country? What consequences does it have for the country as a whole?

6. Although you might have impressions and perhaps some experiential knowledge of the social changes going on in the communities where you've lived, we bet that you've learned some things from this report. Use this information as a starting point to **write an investigation** of your own. In all cases, you will be composing what is primarily an argument based on facts. (See Chapters 4 and 8 for additional information.) You might, for example, (a) interview older people in your community (or a community you've lived in) about how, based on their impressions, the demographics of the community have changed over the past ten, twenty, or thirty years with respect to the presence of people who speak a language other than English; (b) use this report and information from the references it cites (census data or other reports) to provide a detailed, factual argument about how the community you now live in (or one you have lived in) has changed with respect to the presence of other languages there; or (c) propose another topic that uses these data as a starting point.

▼ *Born in Chicago in 1954, Sandra Cisneros is a Mexican American writer who lives and writes in San Antonio, Texas, where she has long been involved in supporting Chicana/o writers and the local artistic community. She is the author of novels, short stories, and poetry about the Mexican American experience, particularly that of Mexican American women, including most recently the novel* Caramelo *(2002) and the collection* Vintage Cisneros *(2004). Cisneros has been the recipient of numerous important awards, including a MacArthur Foundation Fellowship. In this excerpt from the short story "Bien Pretty," which appeared in* Woman Hollering Creek and Other Stories *(1991), Cisneros helps readers understand how bilinguals experience the languages they know. As you read, note how Cisneros's narrator uses careful description to make her argument.*

***bien:*** very.

# From "Bien° Pretty"

## SANDRA CISNEROS

***Luis Buñuel (1900–1983):*** a Spanish filmmaker, famous for his often bizarre, surrealist visual imagery.

***la Alhambra:*** from an Arabic phrase meaning "the red palace"; a palace, citadel, and gardens in Grenada in southern Spain, home of the Nasrid sultans in the thirteenth and fourteenth centuries and famous for its detailed Islamic carving and tilework.

I'd never made love in Spanish before. I mean not with anyone whose *first* language was Spanish. There was crazy Graham, the anarchist labor organizer who'd taught me to eat jalapeños and swear like a truck mechanic, but he was Welsh and had learned his Spanish running guns to Bolivia.

And Eddie, sure. But Eddie and I were products of our American education. Anything tender always came off sounding like the subtitles to a Buñuel° film.

But Flavio. When Flavio accidentally hammered his thumb, he never yelled "Ouch!" he said "¡Ay!" The true test of a native Spanish speaker.

¡Ay! To make love in Spanish, in a manner as intricate and devout as la Alhambra.° To have a lover sigh *mi vida, mi preciosa, mi chiquitita,* and whisper things in that language crooned to babies, that language murmured by grandmothers, those words that smelled like your house, like flour tortillas, and the inside of your daddy's hat, like everyone talking in the kitchen at the same time, or sleeping with the windows open, like sneaking cashews from the crumpled quarter-pound bag Mama always hid in her lingerie drawer after she went shopping with Daddy at the Sears.

*That* language. That sweep of palm leaves and fringed shawls. That star- 5
tled fluttering, like the heart of a goldfinch or a fan. Nothing sounded dirty or hurtful or corny. How could I think of making love in English again? English with its starched *r*'s and *g*'s. English with its crisp linen syllables. English crunchy as apples, resilient and stiff as sailcloth.

But Spanish whirred like silk, rolled and puckered and hissed. I held Flavio close to me, in the mouth of my heart, inside my wrists.

Incredible happiness. A sigh unfurled of its own accord, a groan heaved out from my chest so rusty and full of dust it frightened me. I was crying. It surprised us both.

"My soul, did I hurt you?" Flavio said in that other language.

I managed to bunch my mouth into a knot and shake my head "no" just as the next wave of sobs began. Flavio rocked me, and cooed, and rocked me. *Ya, ya, ya*. There, there, there.

I wanted to say so many things, but all I could think of was a line I'd read 10
in the letters of Georgia O'Keeffe° years ago and had forgotten until then. Flavio . . . did you ever feel like flowers?

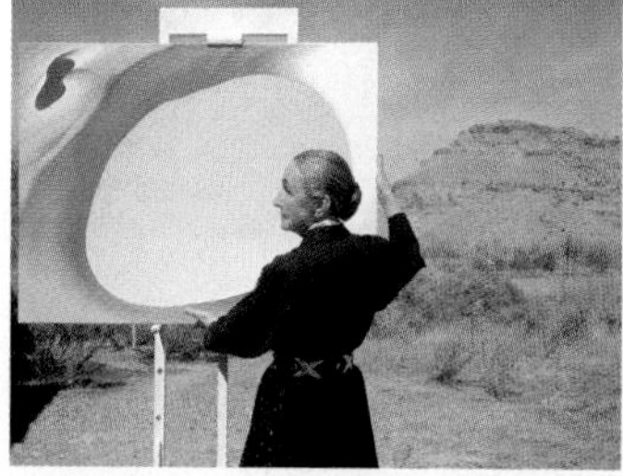

***Georgia O'Keeffe (1887–1986):*** the most famous American woman painter of the twentieth century. Among the best known of her paintings are large canvases of flowers or parts of flowers, which many viewers continue to experience as quite sensual.

## RESPOND •

1. For Cisneros—and one can likely claim it for all bilinguals—in some sense the languages she knows aren't equal. Rather, each language is associated with different worlds of experience. What does Spanish connote for the narrator in Cisneros's text? What does English connote? Where would such connotations come from?
2. One resource that bilingual writers have is codeswitching—switching between the languages they know. In this excerpt, we see the simple noun phrase "la Alhambra" (paragraph 4) from Spanish, which we can correctly understand even if we know no Spanish. We also see the phrase "*Ya, ya, ya*" (paragraph 9), which is followed immediately by the English equivalent, "There, there, there." Yet we also find the phrases "*mi vida, mi preciosa, mi chiquitita*" (paragraph 4), which we may not be able to figure out the meanings of. (In fact, the phrases translate literally as "my life, my precious [one], my dearest little [one]"—things native speakers of English wouldn't normally say to one another, even when being intimate. Such phrases are perfectly normal among speakers of Spanish.) Why might writers purposely create texts that include parts readers may not be able to understand? Why would such a strategy be especially effective when talking about intimacies like making love?

What tropes does Cisneros use in her essay? See descriptions of the different types of figurative language in Chapter 13 to help you figure out your answer.

LINK TO P. 315

3. All humans probably have an emotional attachment to one or more languages or language varieties, most often one associated with childhood. **Create a text** in which you explore and define the meaning of some language or language variety—a regional, social, or ethnic variety of English, for example—for you. Your text can take the form of an essay, or you may wish to create a sketch more like Cisneros's (though you needn't write about anything so intimate as lovemaking!). In it, seek to help readers—both those who know that language variety and those who don't—understand its meanings and significance for you.

*Marjorie Agosín (1955– ) is a professor of Spanish at Wellesley College in Massachusetts; she has written and edited more than eighty books. She has been honored with numerous awards for both her writing and her human rights activism, which she has focused on the situation of women, especially Latin American women. She was reared in Chile, the country to which her grandparents had moved early in the twentieth century at a time when Jews faced persecution in parts of Europe. Her family moved to the United States in the 1970s, after a right-wing military coup overthrew the Chilean government. In this essay, which originally appeared in* Poets & Writers *in 1999 and was translated by Celeste Kostopulos-Cooperman, Agosín explains why she, as a political exile, "writes in Spanish and lives in translation." In the poem that follows it, "English," translated by Monica Bruno, Agosín compares and contrasts English and Spanish. As you read, consider how the experiences of an exile might differ from those of immigrants who come to the United States for other reasons, particularly with regard to language.*

# Always Living in Spanish

MARJORIE AGOSÍN

## Recovering the Familiar, through Language

In the evenings in the northern hemisphere, I repeat the ancient ritual that I observed as a child in the southern hemisphere: going out while the night is still warm and trying to recognize the stars as it begins to grow dark silently. In the sky of my country, Chile, that long and wide stretch of land that the poets blessed and dictators abused, I could easily name the stars: the three Marias, the Southern Cross, and the three Lilies, names of beloved and courageous women.

But here in the United States, where I have lived since I was a young girl, the solitude of exile makes me feel that so little is mine, that not even the sky has the same constellations, the trees and the fauna the same names or sounds, or the rubbish the same smell. How does one recover the familiar? How does one name the unfamiliar? How can one be another or live in a foreign language? These are the dilemmas of one who writes in Spanish and lives in translation.

Since my earliest childhood in Chile I lived with the tempos and the melodies of a multiplicity of tongues: German, Yiddish,° Russian, Turkish, and many Latin songs. Because everyone was from somewhere else, my relatives laughed, sang, and fought in a Babylon° of languages. Spanish was reserved for matters of extreme seriousness, for commercial transactions, or for illnesses, but everyone's mother tongue was always associated with the memory of spaces inhabited in the past: the shtetl,° the flowering and vast Vienna avenues, the minarets of Turkey, and the Ladino° whispers of Toledo. When my paternal grandmother sang old songs in Turkish, her voice and body assumed the passion of one who was there in the city of Istanbul, gazing by turns toward the west and the east.

Destiny and the always ambiguous nature of history continued my family's enforced migration, and because of it I, too, became one who had to live and speak in translation. The disappearances, torture, and clandestine deaths in my country in the early seventies drove us to the United States, that other America that looked with suspicion at those who did not speak English and especially those who came from the supposedly uncivilized regions of Latin America. I had left a dangerous place that was my home, only to arrive in a dangerous place that was not: a high school in the small town of Athens, Georgia, where my poor English and my accent were the cause of ridicule and insult. The only way I could recover my usurped country and my Chilean childhood was by continuing to write in Spanish, the same way my grandparents had sung in their own tongues in diasporic° sites.

5 The new and learned English language did not fit with the visceral emotions and themes that my poetry contained, but by writing in Spanish I could recover fragrances, spoken rhythms, and the passion of my own identity. Daily I felt the need to translate myself for the strangers living all around me, to tell them why we were in Georgia, why we ate differently, why we had fled, why my accent was so thick, and why I did not look Hispanic. Only at night, writing poems in Spanish, could I return to my senses, and soothe my own sorrow over what I had left behind.

This is how I became a Chilean poet who wrote in Spanish and lived in the southern United States. And then, one day, a poem of mine was translated and published in the English language. Finally, for the first time since I had left Chile, I felt I didn't have to explain myself. My poem, expressed in another language, spoke for itself . . . and for me.

Sometimes the austere sounds of English help me bear the solitude of knowing that I am foreign and so far away from those about whom I write. I must admit I would like more opportunities to read in Spanish to people whose language and culture is also mine, to join in our common heritage and in the feast

***Yiddish:*** a Germanic language, much influenced by Hebrew and Aramaic and spoken by Ashkenazi Jews in Central and Eastern Europe and their descendants. In the nineteenth century, it was found in most of the world's countries with an Ashkenazi population, including the United States. Yiddish is written in the Hebrew alphabet.

***Babylon:*** here, confusion, associated with the Old Testament story of the Tower of Babel, where God "confounded the language" spoken by all the earth's inhabitants so that they could not understand one another. (The Biblical Hebrew word for "to confuse" is *bilbél*.)

***shtetl:*** a small Jewish village or town in Eastern Europe (originally, a Yiddish word meaning "little town").

***Ladino:*** a nearly extinct Romance language based on archaic Castilian Spanish and spoken by Sephardic Jews in the Balkans, North Africa and the Middle East, Turkey, and Greece. It originated in Spain (the Toledo that Agosín refers to is a city in Spain) and was carried elsewhere by the descendants of Jews exiled from there during the Inquisition.

***diasporic:*** relating to a diaspora, or dispersion of a group of people across a large geographic area to which they aren't native.

of our sounds. I would also like readers of English to understand the beauty of the spoken word in Spanish, that constant flow of oxytonic° and paraoxytonic° syllables (*Vérde qué té quiéro vérde*),° the joy of writing—of dancing—in another language. I believe that many exiles share the unresolvable torment of not being able to live in the language of their childhood.

I miss that undulating and sensuous language of mine, those baroque° descriptions, the sense of being and feeling that Spanish gives me. It is perhaps for this reason that I have chosen and will always choose to write in Spanish. Nothing else from my childhood world remains. My country seems to be frozen in gestures of silence and oblivion. My relatives have died, and I have grown up not knowing a young generation of cousins and nieces and nephews. Many of my friends were disappeared,° others were tortured, and the most fortunate, like me, became guardians of memory. For us, to write in Spanish is to always be in active pursuit of memory. I seek to recapture a world lost to me on that sorrowful afternoon when the blue electric sky and the Andean cordillera° bade me farewell. On that, my last Chilean day, I carried under my arm my innocence recorded in a little blue notebook I kept even then. Gradually that diary filled with memoranda, poems written in free verse, descriptions of dreams and of the thresholds of my house surrounded by cherry trees and gardenias. To write in Spanish is for me a gesture of survival. And because of translation, my memory has now become a part of the memory of many others.

Translators are not traitors, as the proverb says, but rather splendid friends in this great human community of language.

*Cordillera in Torres del Paine National Park, Chile*

To conclude her essay, Agosín defines translators as "splendid friends." What other argument of definition can you find in this piece? Chapter 9 details the variety and power of arguments of definition.

LINK TO P. 187

***oxytonic:*** with the main stress on the final or single syllable of a word.

***paraoxytonic:*** with the main stress on the next-to-last syllable of a word.

**Vérde qué té quiéro vérde** (stressed syllables marked, translation, "Green. How I want you green"): the opening line of a famous poem by Federico García Lorca and an illustration of stress falling on oxytonic and paraoxytonic syllables.

***baroque:*** extremely ornate or flowery.

***were disappeared:*** although *disappear* is generally an intransitive verb that cannot take a direct object or be used in the passive voice, Chileans and Spanish speakers from other countries with repressive political regimes began using this "incorrect" grammatical construction to refer to individuals who disappeared and were presumed dead after being taken into custody by the authorities, often for no valid reason. The expression is now used in many languages, including English.

***cordillera:*** mountain ranges consisting of more or less parallel chains of peaks.

# English

MARJORIE AGOSÍN Translated by Monica Bruno

*Don Quijote after a failed joust with a windmill. Standing at his side is his faithful servant, Sancho Panza.*

**windmills:** an allusion to Don Quijote (see note on next page), who tilted at windmills with his lance, imagining them to be giants.

## I

I discovered that English
is too skinny,
functional,
precise,
too correct,
meaning
only one thing.
Too much wrath,
too many lawyers and sinister policemen,
too many deans at schools for small females,
in the Anglo-Saxon language.

## II

In contrast Spanish
has so many words to say come with me friend,
make love to me on
the *césped,* the *grama,* the *pasto.*[1]
Let's go party,[2]
at dusk, at night, at sunset.
Spanish
loves
the unpredictable, it is
dementia,
all windmills° and velvet.

## III

Spanish
is simple and baroque,

---

[1]All three words mean "grass" in English.

[2]The Spanish version of this poem uses two phrases that mean "to party": *de juerga* and *de fiesta.*

a palace of nobles and beggars,
it fills itself with silences and the breaths of dragonflies.
Neruda's° verses
saying "I could write the saddest verses
tonight,"
or Federico° swimming underwater through the greenest of greens.

**IV**

Spanish
is Don Quijote° maneuvering,
Violeta Parra° grateful
spicy, tasty, fragrant
the rumba, the salsa, the cha-cha.
There are so many words
to say
naive dreamers
and impostors.
There are so many languages in our
language: Quechua,° Aymará,° Rosas chilensis,° Spanglish.°

***Pablo Neruda (1904–1973):*** the pen name of the Nobel Prize–winning Chilean poet, politician, and diplomat, considered by many the finest Latin American poet of the twentieth century.

***Federico García Lorca (1898–1936):*** a Spanish poet and playwright. A sympathizer with leftist causes and a homosexual, Lorca was executed by a Nationalist firing squad in the Spanish Civil War. He wrote *"Verde que te quiero verde,"* cited by Agosín in her essay.

---

***Don Quijote (also spelled Quixote):*** the hero of Miguel de Cervantes's satiric novel of the same name, originally published in two volumes in 1605 and 1615. Quijote is a knight who, after reading too many courtly romances, goes off to find adventure. Quijote's name and the adjective *quixotic* are often applied to someone who, inspired by high (but often false) ideals, pursues an impossible task.

***Violeta Parra (1917–1967):*** a Chilean folksinger most often associated with "La Nueva Canción," a style of Latin American popular music much influenced by folk traditions. Her best-known work is perhaps "Gracias à la vida" ("Thanks to Life").

***Quechua:*** the language of the former Inca empire and the major indigenous language of the central Andes today.

***Aymará:*** one of the major indigenous languages of Bolivia.

***Rosas chilensis:*** Latin species name for a rose indigenous to Chile.

***Spanglish:*** a popular label for the practice of switching between Spanish and English within a conversation or sentence, as many bilingual Hispanics do when they speak with other bilinguals.

V

I love the imperfections of
Spanish,
the language takes shape in my hand:
the sound of drums and waves,
the Caribbean in the radiant foam of the sun,
are delirious upon my lips.
English has fallen short for me,
it signifies business,
law
and inhibition,
never the crazy, clandestine,
clairvoyance of
love.

**RESPOND**

1. Why does Agosín write only in Spanish? How do her reasons for using Spanish compare with those of Cisneros? How does she regard using Spanish as relating to her ancestry as a Jew?
2. What sort of experiences did Agosín have while trying to learn English? How typical do you think her experiences were? In other words, how do Americans who are native speakers of English treat non-native speakers of English? How did Spanish represent a source of strength and consolation to Agosín during the period when she was learning English?
3. What does Spanish represent for Agosín? Why would it represent these things for her?
4. As the selections by Cisneros and Agosín make clear, for many Americans whose ancestors can be traced somehow to the Spanish-speaking world, to lose Spanish would be to lose a fundamental part of their identity as individuals and as members of larger groups. Using these texts, perhaps personal experience, and perhaps discussions you have with people who claim to be bilingual or bidialectal (that is, to speak a dialect of English other than Standard English, the variety expected and rewarded at school), **write an essay** in which you seek to define the role of language(s) in the creation of individual and group identity. (For a discussion of arguments of definition, see Chapter 9.)

▼ *Firoozeh Dumas (1965– ) is an Iranian American writer who moved to California at age seven, later returned to Iran for several years, and finally reimmigrated to the United States. Her first book,* Funny in Farsi: A Memoir of Growing up Iranian in America *(2003), from which this selection comes, offers a hilarious account of what happens when languages and cultures come in contact and collide as they inevitably do in immigrant families. (By the way, Farsi is another name for Persian, the most widely spoken language in Iran.) When she married a Frenchman, she took his family name; hence, her last name, Dumas. Dumas is also author of* Laughing without an Accent: Adventures of an Iranian American, at Home and Abroad *(2008). In "The 'F Word,'" Dumas describes how Americans in general deal (or fail to deal) with names from languages unfamiliar to them. She explains how dealing with this situation is part of the immigrant experience for those from many language backgrounds. As you read, note how she employs humor and figurative language, using the latter even as a device to help structure her essay.*

# The "F Word"

FIROOZEH DUMAS

My cousin's name, Farbod, means "Greatness." When he moved to America, all the kids called him "Farthead." My brother Farshid ("He Who Enlightens") became "Fartshit." The name of my friend Neggar means "Beloved," although it can be more accurately translated as "She Whose Name Almost Incites Riots." Her brother Arash ("Giver") initially couldn't understand why every time he'd say his name, people would laugh and ask him if it itched.

All of us immigrants knew that moving to America would be fraught with challenges, but none of us thought that our names would be such an obstacle. How could our parents have ever imagined that someday we would end up in a country where monosyllabic names reign supreme, a land where "William" is shortened to "Bill," where "Susan" becomes "Sue," and "Richard" somehow evolves into "Dick"? America is a great country, but nobody without a mask and a cape has a z in his name. And have Americans ever realized the great scope of the guttural sounds° they're missing? Okay, so it has to do with linguistic roots, but I do believe this would be a richer country if all

***gutteral sounds:*** consonants articulated at the back of the throat and considered by speakers of English to be harsh or unpleasant sounding.

Americans could do a little tongue aerobics and learn to pronounce "kh," a sound more commonly associated in this culture with phlegm, or "gh," the sound usually made by actors in the final moments of a choking scene. It's like adding a few new spices to the kitchen pantry. Move over, cinnamon and nutmeg, make way for cardamom° and sumac.°

*cardamom:* a spice commonly used in the Middle East, South Asia, and East Asia.

*sumac:* a dark red, sour-tasting spice used in many Middle Eastern cuisines.

Exotic analogies aside, having a foreign name in this land of Joes and Marys is a pain in the spice cabinet. When I was twelve, I decided to simplify my life by adding an American middle name. This decision serves as proof that sometimes simplifying one's life in the short run only complicates it in the long run.

My name, Firoozeh, chosen by my mother, means "Turquoise" in Farsi. In America, it means "Unpronounceable" or "I'm Not Going to Talk to You Because I Cannot Possibly Learn Your Name and I Just Don't Want to Have to Ask You Again and Again Because You'll Think I'm Dumb or You Might Get Upset or Something." My father, incidentally, had wanted to name me Sara. I do wish he had won that argument.

5 To strengthen my decision to add an American name, I had just finished fifth grade in Whittier, where all the kids incessantly called me "Ferocious." That summer, my family moved to Newport Beach, where I looked forward to starting a new life. I wanted to be a kid with a name that didn't draw so much attention, a name that didn't come with a built-in inquisition as to when and why I had moved to America and how was it that I spoke English without an accent and was I planning on going back and what did I think of America?

My last name didn't help any. I can't mention my maiden name, because:

"Dad, I'm writing a memoir."

"Great! Just don't mention our name."

Suffice it to say that, with eight letters, including a z, and four syllables, my last name is as difficult and foreign as my first. My first and last name together generally served the same purpose as a high brick wall. There was one exception to this rule. In Berkeley, and only in Berkeley, my name drew people like flies to baklava. These were usually people named Amaryllis or Chrysanthemum, types who vacationed in Costa Rica and to whom lentils described a type of burger. These folks were probably not the pride of Poughkeepsie, but they were refreshingly nonjudgmental.

10 When I announced to my family that I wanted to add an American name, they reacted with their usual laughter. Never one to let mockery or good judgment stand in my way, I proceeded to ask for suggestions. My father suggested "Fifi." Had I had a special affinity for French poodles or been considering a career in prostitution, I would've gone with that one. My mom suggested

"Farah," a name easier than "Firoozeh" yet still Iranian. Her reasoning made sense, except that Farrah Fawcett was at the height of her popularity and I didn't want to be associated with somebody whose poster hung in every postpubescent boy's bedroom. We couldn't think of any American names beginning with F, so we moved on to *J*, the first letter of our last name. I don't know why we limited ourselves to names beginning with my initials, but it made sense at that moment, perhaps by the logic employed moments before bungee jumping. I finally chose the name "Julie" mainly for its simplicity. My brothers, Farid and Farshid, thought that adding an American name was totally stupid. They later became Fred and Sean.

That same afternoon, our doorbell rang. It was our new next-door neighbor, a friendly girl my age named Julie. She asked me my name and after a moment of hesitation, I introduced myself as Julie. "What a coincidence!" she said. I didn't mention that I had been Julie for only half an hour.

Thus I started sixth grade with my new, easy name and life became infinitely simpler. People actually remembered my name, which was an entirely refreshing new sensation. All was well until the Iranian Revolution,° when I found myself with a new set of problems. Because I spoke English without an accent and was known as Julie, people assumed I was American. This meant that I was often privy to their real feelings about those "damn I-raynians." It was like having those X-ray glasses that let you see people undressed, except that what I was seeing was far uglier than people's underwear. It dawned on me that these people would have probably never invited me to their house had they known me as Firoozeh. I felt like a fake.

***Iranian Revolution:*** the series of events, beginning in 1979, that transformed Iran from a constitutional monarchy to a populist Islamic theocracy, first ruled by Ayatollah Khomeini. Americans associate the revolution with the holding of sixty-six American hostages at the U.S. embassy in Tehran for a period of 444 days (1979–1981).

When I went to college, I eventually went back to using my real name. All was well until I graduated and started looking for a job. Even though I had graduated with honors from UC–Berkeley, I couldn't get a single interview. I was guilty of being a humanities major, but I began to suspect that there was more to my problems. After three months of rejections, I added "Julie" to my résumé. Call it coincidence, but the job offers started coming in. Perhaps it's the same kind of coincidence that keeps African Americans from getting cabs in New York.

Once I got married, my name became Julie Dumas. I went from having an identifiably "ethnic" name to having ancestors who wore clogs. My family and non-American friends continued calling me Firoozeh, while my coworkers and American friends called me Julie. My life became one big knot, especially when friends who knew me as Julie met friends who knew me as Firoozeh. I felt like those characters in soap operas who have an evil twin. The two, of course, can never be in the same room, since they're played by the same person, a struggling actress who wears a wig to play one of the twins and dreams of moving on to bigger and better roles. I couldn't blame my mess on a screenwriter; it was my own doing.

I decided to untangle the knot once and for all by going back to my real 15
name. By then, I was a stay-at-home mom, so I really didn't care whether people remembered my name or gave me job interviews. Besides, most of the people I dealt with were in diapers and were in no position to judge. I was also living in Silicon Valley, an area filled with people named Rajeev, Avishai, and Insook.

Humor unites this book excerpt. How does Dumas use humor to increase the appeal of her argument? See Chapter 2 for a discussion of how humor works in argument.

LINK TO P. 38

Every once in a while, though, somebody comes up with a new permutation and I am once again reminded that I am an immigrant with a foreign name. I recently went to have blood drawn for a physical exam. The waiting room for blood work at our local medical clinic is in the basement of the building, and no matter how early one arrives for an appointment, forty coughing, wheezing people have gotten there first. Apart from reading *Golf Digest* and *Popular Mechanics*, there isn't much to do except guess the number of contagious diseases represented in the windowless room. Every ten minutes, a name is called and everyone looks to see which cough matches that name. As I waited patiently, the receptionist called out, "Fritzy, Fritzy!" Everyone looked around, but no one stood up. Usually, if I'm waiting to be called by someone who doesn't know me, I will respond to just about any name starting with an F. Having been called Froozy, Frizzy, Fiorucci, and Frooz and just plain "Uhhhh . . . ," I am highly accommodating. I did not, however, respond to "Fritzy" because there is, as far as I know, no *t* in my name. The receptionist tried again, "Fritzy, Fritzy DumbAss." As I stood up to this most linguistically original version of my name, I could feel all eyes upon me. The room was momentarily silent as all of these sick people sat united in a moment of gratitude for their own names.

Despite a few exceptions, I have found that Americans are now far more willing to learn new names, just as they're far more willing to try new ethnic foods. Of course, some people just don't like to learn. One mom at my children's school adamantly refused to learn my "impossible" name and instead settled on calling me "F Word." She was recently transferred to New York where, from what I've heard, she might meet an immigrant or two and, who knows, she just might have to make some room in her spice cabinet.

## RESPOND •

1. How might you summarize Firoozeh Dumas's argument? What is its subject—the importance of names, the ways in which Americans have traditionally responded to unfamiliar names, the immigrant experience, or all of these?
2. Carefully reread paragraph 12, in which Dumas explains how having an "American" name and speaking English without a foreign accent was like having "X-ray glasses." Is Dumas's portrayal of Americans in this passage and elsewhere in the essay flattering? Humorous? Honest? Dumas notes that "people assumed I was American." What definition of "American" must she (and those she writes about) be assuming? Is such a definition valid, given evidence she presents elsewhere in the essay and the fact that the United States is often called a nation of immigrants? At what point does an immigrant become an American?
3. How would you describe Dumas's use of humor? Find three examples that you especially like, and explain how the humor helps the author achieve her goals. In what ways does Dumas's argument represent satire, with the simultaneous goals of ridiculing and remedying a problematic situation? (For a discussion of the uses of humor in argumentation, see Chapter 2.)
4. How does Dumas use the repeated metaphor of the spice cabinet to help structure her argument? Why is this metaphor an appropriate one, given her topic? How does the metaphor permit her to critique the mother who called her "F Word" (paragraph 17)?
5. **Write a rhetorical analysis** of Dumas's argument that focuses on evaluating the contribution of humor to its overall effect. One way to think about the role of humor is to imagine what the essay might have been like if Dumas had tried to write about this subject in a straightforward, serious manner. (For a discussion of how to do a rhetorical analysis, see Chapter 6.)

*Here, we present two public service announcements (PSAs) in Spanish that are ultimately comments on bilingualism in the United States. The first, "En la comunidad latina tenemos una cultura de silencio," was created by the National Institute of Mental Health (NIMH), part of the U.S. Department of Health and Human Services. NIMH focuses on supporting research about mental and behavioral disorders, advocating for people who suffer from them, and raising awareness of them in the general population. This poster was part of a 2005 campaign to raise awareness about depression in men. In addition to this poster, NIMH produced public service announcements for broadcast media, print publications, and the Web. By the time we put together this edition of the textbook, the ad had become part of a slightly different campaign directed toward men generally, and this image is one of several depicting men from different ethnic backgrounds who have struggled with depression. For the Spanish-language Web page on this campaign, visit http://1.usa.gov/mOXAZ6; for some of the same information in English, visit http://1.usa.gov/d5Pn0e. A news release at http://1.usa.gov/sIMMth provides information about NIMH's motivations for creating a campaign that focused on depression targeted at men who are speakers of Spanish.*

*The second PSA focuses on the role of Latino parents in encouraging their children to attend college. It was prepared by the Hispanic Scholarship Fund and Grupo Gallegos. The Hispanic Scholarship Fund is currently engaged with the Vidal Partnership, working with the Ad Council. The Council, a private, nonprofit organization, seeks to use the talents and resources of those in communication and advertising to create PSAs for various media. This ad campaign was listed among "Current Work" in December 2011. The Web page reproduced here, http://bit.ly/syFlcR, provides an overview of the campaign as well as two broadcast PSAs (one for television and one for radio), two print ads, and links to the sites TusPalabrasDeHoy.org and YourWordsToday.org, created by the Hispanic Scholarship Fund. On this Web site, the pull-down menus for La Campaña/The Campaign provide additional information about the campaign and its goals.*

*As you study these visual arguments, consider how language choice stands as evidence of someone's intended and invoked audience and how complex and multilayered Web sites are as arguments.*

# Making a Visual Argument: Public Service Announcements in Spanish

# “En la comunidad latina tenemos una cultura de silencio”.

—Rodolfo Palma-Lulión, Estudiante Universitario

**Real Men. Real Depression.**
**Estos hombres son reales.**
**La depresión también.**

“Nadie tiene depresión en la comunidad latina. En la comunidad latina tenemos una cultura de silencio en ciertos aspectos de nuestra vida. Especialmente como inmigrantes trabajamos duro. Eso es lo que se espera. Y decir que uno tiene depresión es como dejar que la vida te gane”. La depresión es una enfermedad real que se puede tratar con éxito. Para más información, llame al 1-866-227-6464, visite www.nimh.nih.gov, o contacte a su médico.

**Hay que tener valor para solicitar ayuda. Rodolfo lo hizo.**

***Idiomatic translation:***
“In the Latino community, we have a culture of silence.”
—Rodolfo Palma-Lulión, University Student

These men are real. So is depression.

“No one in the Latino community suffers from depression. In the Latino community, we have a culture of silence about certain aspects of our life. Especially, as immigrants, we work hard. That’s what’s expected. And to say that you’re depressed is like letting life defeat you.” Depression is a real illness that can be treated successfully. For more information, call 1-866-227-6464, visit www.nimh.nih.gov, or contact your doctor.

You have to be brave to ask for help. Rodolfo did it.

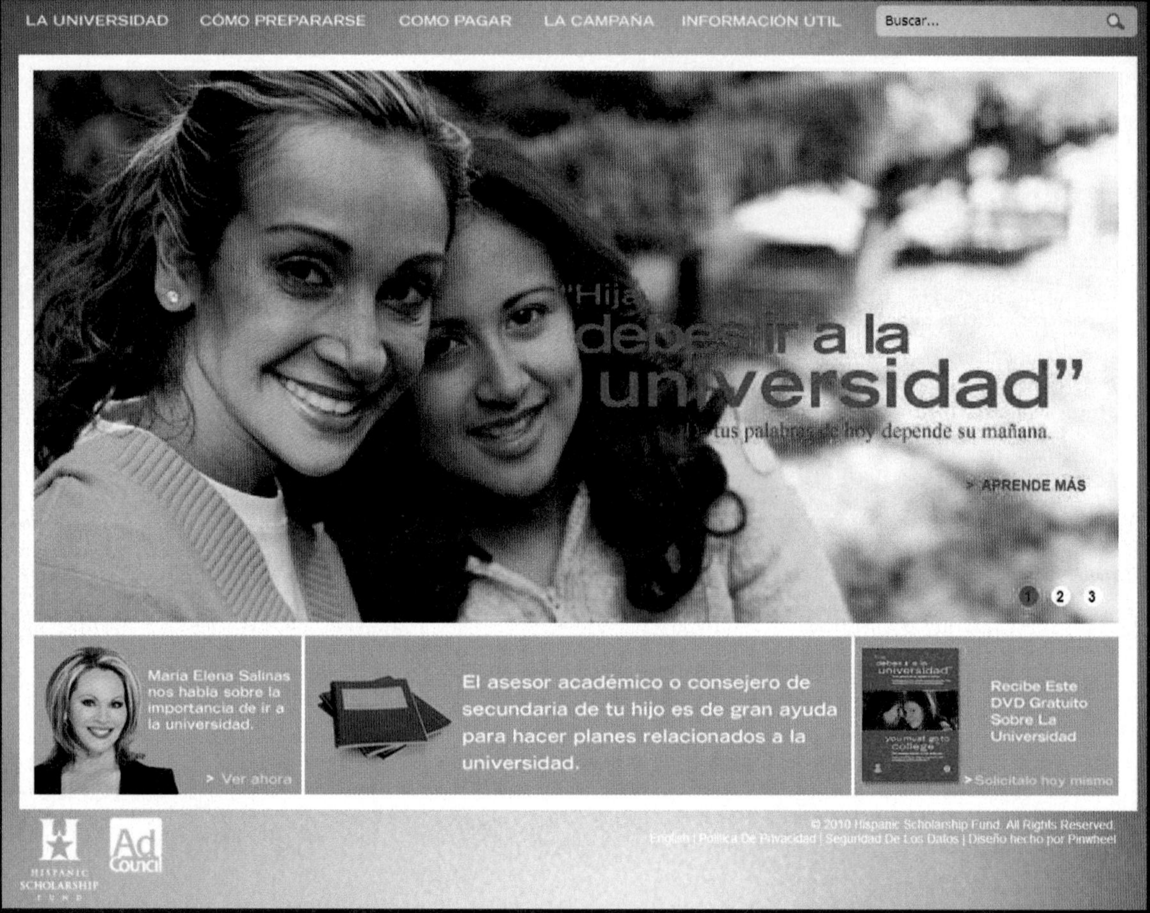

LA UNIVERSIDAD CÓMO PREPARARSE COMO PAGAR LA CAMPAÑA INFORMACIÓN UTIL Buscar...

"Hija, debes ir a la universidad"

De tus palabras de hoy depende su mañana.

> APRENDE MÁS

1 2 3

Maria Elena Salinas nos habla sobre la importancia de ir a la universidad.

> Ver ahora

El asesor académico o consejero de secundaria de tu hijo es de gran ayuda para hacer planes relacionados a la universidad.

Recibe Este DVD Gratuito Sobre La Universidad

> Solicítalo hoy mismo

Ad Council


English | Política De Privacidad | Seguridad De Los Datos | Diseño hecho por Pinwheel

***Idiomatic translation:***
"Hija, you must go to college"

Their tomorrow depends on your words

## RESPOND •

1. These ads appear in English and Spanish versions. (In fact, the ad about depression includes the tag line "Real Men. Real Depression" in English, an example of codeswitching of a sort one wouldn't likely see if these ads were in a country where Spanish is the major or official language.) How do language choice and intended or invoked audience interact in these advertisements? Many U.S. Latinos are highly bilingual, although some of them prefer English, some prefer Spanish, and others have no preference. On the other hand, some Hispanic Americans speak little or no English, and still others speak little or no Spanish. How does this situation complicate efforts to create advertisements that target this community?
2. Evaluate "En la comunidad latina tenemos una cultura de silencio" as an arugment. What role does the personal testimony of Rodolfo Palma-Lulión play in the PSA? Does it matter that he is a university student? Why or why not? Why might the phrase "Real Men. Real Depression" appear in English?
3. Evaluate one or more of the ads created for the "Hispanic College Preparation" campaign as arguments. How do the images, sounds, and/or words work together to make an argument? How well is the argument motivated, given the justification that is cited for creating the campaign?
4. Some might criticize U.S. government agencies or the Ad Council for producing advertisements in any language other than English. What arguments might they use for such criticisms? What costs, direct or indirect, might there be if the U.S. government or the Ad Council does not produce PSAs in languages other than English?
5. Bilingualism is once again part of daily life in a growing number of public places in the United States, much as it was in many places during the periods before World War I in particular. Thus, we find billboards, signs, flyers, and ads in magazines that are partially or fully in a language other than English. Find two such advertisements, and **write an evaluative essay** in which you offer a rhetorical analysis of the ads, comparing them and evaluating which is more

effective for its intended audience, which you'll need to define. (It's worth remembering that Spanish-language billboards advertising a particular brand of Mexican beer near many college campuses may be targeted more at students who know no Spanish other than *cerveza* than they are at those fluent in the language.) If your skills in other languages are limited, you may need to seek a classmate's help in translating the ads. (Don't rely on online translation Web sites!) Be sure to include a copy of the ads you analyze with your essay. (For discussions of rhetorical analyses and evaluative arguments, see Chapters 6 and 10, respectively.)

# The Gift of Language

LAN CAO

*Lan Cao is currently a Boyd fellow and a professor of law at the Marshall-Wythe School of Law at the College of William and Mary. She's the author of* Monkey Bridge *(1997), the semiautobiographical novel from which this excerpt comes. (A monkey bridge is a spindly bamboo bridge used by Vietnamese peasants.) The novel recounts the experiences of a young woman who, like Lan Cao, came to the United States fleeing the Vietnam War. Cao herself arrived here in 1975.*

*At this point in the novel the narrator, an adolescent girl, and her mother have moved to the United States, having had to leave behind the girl's maternal grandfather—their only other living relative. The girl had arrived before the mother and had stayed with an American colonel her family had befriended while he was in Vietnam. He and his wife are the Uncle Michael and Aunt Mary referred to in the text. This excerpt begins with a comparison of American and Asian markets but quickly moves to more complex topics. As you read, try to put yourself in Lan Cao's position. For some readers, it will be an all too familiar one; for others, it may be almost unimaginable.*

I discovered soon after my arrival in Falls Church that everything, even the simple business of shopping the American way, unsettled my mother's nerves. From the outside, it had been an ordinary building that held no promises or threats beyond four walls anchored to a concrete parking lot. But inside, the A&P brimmed with unexpected abundance. Built-in metal stands overflowed with giant oranges and grapefruits meticulously arranged into a pyramid. Columns of canned vegetables and fruits stood among multiple shelves as people well rehearsed to the demands of modern shopping meandered through the fluorescent aisles. I remembered the sharp chilled air against my face, the way the hydraulic door made a sucking sound as it closed behind.

My first week in Connecticut with Uncle Michael and Aunt Mary, I thought Aunt Mary was a genius shopper. She appeared to have the sixth sense of a bat and could identify, record, and register every item on sale. She was skilled in the art of coupon shopping—in the American version of Vietnamese haggling, the civil and acceptable mode of getting the customers to think they had gotten a good deal.

The day after I arrived in Farmington, Aunt Mary navigated the cart—and me—through aisles, numbered and categorized, crammed with jars and cardboard boxes, and plucked from them the precise product to match the coupons she carried. I had been astonished that day that the wide range of choices did not disrupt her plan. We had a schedule, I discovered, which Aunt Mary mapped out on a yellow pad, and which we followed, checking off item after item. She called it the science of shopping, the ability to resist the temptations of dazzling packaging. By the time we were through, our cart would be filled to the rim with cans of Coke, the kinds with flip-up caps that made can openers obsolete, in family-size cartons. We had chicken and meat sealed in tight, odorless packages, priced and weighed. We had fruits so beautifully polished and waxed they looked artificial. And for me, we had mangoes and papayas that were still hard and green but which Aunt Mary had handed to me like rare jewels from a now extinct land.

But my mother did not appreciate the exacting orderliness of the A&P. She could not give in to the precision of previously weighed and packaged food, the bloodlessness of beef slabs in translucent wrappers, the absence of

*Saigon:* the former name of what is today officially Ho Chi Minh City, though many Vietnamese, especially older ones from the region, continue to use the city's earlier name. Saigon served as the capital of South Vietnam from 1955 until North and South Vietnam were reunited in 1975 at the end of the Vietnam War.

carcasses and pigs' heads. In Saigon,° we had only outdoor markets. "Sky markets," they were called, vast, prosperous expanses in the middle of the city where barrels of live crabs and yellow carps and booths of ducks and geese would be stacked side by side with cardboard stands of expensive silk fabric from Hong Kong. It was always noisy there—a voluptuous mix of animal and human sounds that the air itself had assimilated and held. The sharp acrid smell of gutters choked by the monsoon rain. The unambiguous odor of dried horse dung that lingered in the atmosphere, partially camouflaged by the fat, heavy scent of guavas and bananas.

My mother knew the vendors and even the shoppers by name and would 5
take me from stall to stall to expose me to her skills. They were all addicted to each other's oddities. My mother would feign indifference and they would inevitably call out to her. She would heed their call and they would immediately retreat into sudden apathy. They knew my mother's slick bargaining skills, and she, in turn, knew how to navigate with grace through their extravagant prices and rehearsed huffiness. Theirs had been a mating dance, a match of wills.

Toward the center of the market, a man with a spotted boa constrictor coiled around his neck stood and watched day after day over an unruly hodgepodge of hand-dyed cotton shirts, handkerchiefs, and swatches of white muslin; funerals were big business in Vietnam. To the side, in giant paper bags slit with round openings, were canaries and hummingbirds which my mother bought, one hundred at a time, and freed, one by one, into our garden; it was a good deed designed to generate positive karma for the family. My mother, like the country itself, was obsessed with karma. In fact, the Vietnamese word for "please," as in "could you please," means literally "to make good karma." "Could you please pass the butter" becomes "Please make good karma and pass me the butter." My mother would cup each bird in her hand and set it on my head. It was her way of immersing me in a wellspring of karmic charm, and in that swift moment of delight when the bird's wings spread over my head as it contemplated flight, I believed life itself was utterly beautiful and blessed.

*black market:* smuggled in, so as to avoid import taxes and laws against importing foreign goods.

Every morning, we drifted from stack to stack, vendor to vendor. There were no road maps to follow—tables full of black market° Prell and Colgate were pocketed among vegetable stands one day and jars of medicinal herbs the next. The market was randomly organized, and only the mighty and experienced like my mother could navigate its patternless paths.

But with a sense of neither drama nor calamity, my mother's ability to navigate and decipher simply became undone in our new life. She preferred the improvisation of haggling to the conventional certainty of discount cou-

*Bilingual outreach worker helping Vietnamese shoppers in the United States*

pons, the primordial° messiness and fishmongers' stink of the open-air market to the aroma-free order of individually wrapped fillets.

*primordial:* original, in the sense of the first created that gave rise to things more developed or organized.

Now, a mere three and a half years or so after her last call to the sky market, the dreadful truth was simply this: we were going through life in reverse, and I was the one who would help my mother through the hard scrutiny of ordinary suburban life. I would have to forgo the luxury of adolescent experiments and temper tantrums, so that I could scoop my mother out of harm's way and give her sanctuary. Now, when we stepped into the exterior world, I was the one who told my mother what was acceptable or unacceptable behavior.

All children of immigrant parents have experienced these moments. 10
When it first occurs, when the parent first reveals the behavior of a child, is a defining moment. Of course, all children eventually watch their parents' astonishing return to the vulnerability of childhood, but for us the process begins much earlier than expected.

"We don't have to pay the moment we decide to buy the pork. We can put as much as we want in the cart and pay only once, at the checkout counter." It took a few moments' hesitation for my mother to succumb to the peculiarity of my explanation.

And even though I hesitated to take on the responsibility, I had no other choice. It was not a simple process, the manner in which my mother relinquished motherhood. The shift in status occurred not just in the world but in the safety of our home as well, and it became most obvious when we entered the realm of language. I was like Kiki, my pet bird in Saigon, tongue untwisted and sloughed of its rough and thick exterior. According to my mother, feeding the bird crushed red peppers had caused it to shed its tongue in successive layers and allowed it to speak the language of humans.

Every morning during that month of February 1975, while my mother paced the streets of Saigon and witnessed the country's preparation for imminent defeat, I followed Aunt Mary around the house, collecting words like a beggar gathering rain with an earthen pan. She opened her mouth, and out came a constellation of gorgeous sounds. Each word she uttered was a round stone, with the smoothness of something that had been rubbed and polished by the waves of a warm summer beach. She could swim straight through her syllables. On days when we studied together, I almost convinced myself that we would continue that way forever, playing with the movement of sound itself. I would listen as she tried to inspire me into replicating the "th" sound with the seductive powers of her voice. "Slip the tip of your tongue between your front teeth and pull it back real quick," she would coax and coax. Together, she and I sketched the English language, its curious cadence and rhythm, into the receptive Farmington landscape. Only with Aunt Mary and Uncle Michael could I give myself an inheritance my parents never gave me: the gift of language. The story of English was nothing less than the poetry of sound and motion. To this day, Aunt Mary's voice remains my standard for perfection.

Cao uses the personal experience of the narrator to build her story. In what ways can this experience be considered evidence? Chapter 17 examines varieties of evidence, including personal experience.

LINK TO P. 395

My superior English meant that, unlike my mother and Mrs. Bay, I knew the difference between "cough" and "enough," "bough" and "through," "trough" and "thorough," "dough" and "fought." Once I made it past the fourth or fifth week in Connecticut, the new language Uncle Michael and Aunt Mary were teaching me began gathering momentum, like tumbleweed in a storm. This was my realization: we have only to let one thing go—the language we think in, or the composition of our dream, the grass roots clinging underneath its rocks—and all at once everything goes. It had astonished me, the ease with which continents shift and planets change course, the casual way in which the earth goes about shedding the laborious folds of its memories. Suddenly, out of that difficult space between here and there, English revealed itself to me with the ease of thread unspooled. I began to understand the levity and weight of its sentences. First base, second base, home run. New terminologies were not difficult to master, and gradually the possibility of perfection began edging its way into my life. How did those numerous Chinatowns and Little Italys sustain the will to maintain a distance, the desire to inhabit the edge and margin of American life? A mere eight weeks into Farmington, and the American Dream was exerting a sly but seductive pull.

15 By the time I left Farmington to be with my mother, I had already created for myself a different, more sacred tongue. Khe Sanh,° the Tet Offensive,° the Ho Chi Minh Trail°—a history as imperfect as my once obviously imperfect English—these were things that had rushed me into the American melting pot. And when I saw my mother again, I was no longer the same person she used to know. Inside my new tongue, my real tongue, was an astonishing new power. For my mother and her Vietnamese neighbors, I became the keeper of the word, the only one with access to the light-world. Like Adam, I had the God-given right to name all the fowls of the air and all the beasts of the field.

***Khe Sanh:*** a remote U.S. Marine base in Vietnam. On January 21, 1968, troops from the North Vietnamese army attacked the base, starting an eleven-week battle that was one of the most brutal of the Vietnam War.

***Tet Offensive:*** a surprise attack on over a hundred South Vietnamese cities and towns by the North Vietnamese army in 1968 during the truce declared to celebrate Tet, the Vietnamese New Year. Although many of the 70,000 North Vietnamese troops died and their military was left unstable, the offensive is often considered a public relations defeat for the United States because it made North Vietnam's military seem stronger than many had believed and reduced the American public's willingness to continue the war.

***Ho Chi Minh Trail:*** a complex network of paths, roads, and jungle trails leading from the panhandle of northern Vietnam through Laos and Cambodia and into southern Vietnam. The trail was used throughout the Vietnam War to resupply the North Vietnamese military with food and weaponry, to transport soldiers into South Vietnam, and to launch close-range attacks on South Vietnam.

The right to name, I quickly discovered, also meant the right to stand guard over language and the right to claim unadulterated authority. Here was a language with an ocean's quiet mystery, and it would be up to me to render its vastness comprehensible to the newcomers around me. My language skill, my ability to decipher the nuances of American life, was what held us firmly in place, night after night, in our Falls Church living room. The ease with which I could fabricate wholly new plot lines from TV made the temptation to invent especially difficult to resist.

And since my mother couldn't understand half of what anyone was saying, television watching, for me, was translating and more. This, roughly, was how things went in our living room:

The Bionic Woman had just finished rescuing a young girl, approximately my age, from drowning in a lake where she'd gone swimming against her mother's wishes. Once out of harm's way, Jaime made the girl promise she'd be more careful next time and listen to her mother.

Translation: the Bionic Woman rescued the girl from drowning in the lake, but commended her for her magnificent deeds, since the girl had heroically jumped into the water to rescue a prized police dog.

20 "Where's the dog?" my mother would ask. "I don't see him."

"He's not there anymore, they took him to the vet right away. Remember?" I sighed deeply.

"Oh," my mother said. "It's strange. Strong girl, Bionic Woman."

The dog that I convinced her existed on the television screen was no more confusing than the many small reversals in logic and the new identities we experienced her first few months in America.

"I can take you in this aisle," a store clerk offered as she unlocked a new register to accommodate the long line of customers. She gestured us to "come over here" with an upturned index finger, a disdainful hook we Vietnamese use to summon dogs and other domestic creatures. My mother did not understand the ambiguity of American hand gestures. In Vietnam, we said "Come here" to humans differently, with our palm up and all four fingers waved in unison—the way people over here waved goodbye. A typical Vietnamese signal beckoning someone to "come here" would prompt, in the United States, a "goodbye," a response completely opposite from the one desired.

"Even the store clerks look down on us," my mother grumbled as we 25
walked home. This was a truth I was only beginning to realize: it was not the enormous or momentous event, but the gradual suggestion of irrevocable and protracted change that threw us off balance and made us know in no uncertain terms that we would not be returning to the familiarity of our former lives.

It was, in many ways, a lesson in what was required to sustain a new identity: it all had to do with being able to adopt a different posture, to reach deep enough into the folds of the earth to relocate one's roots and bend one's body in a new direction, pretending at the same time that the world was the same now as it had been the day before. I strove for the ability to realign my eyes, to shift with a shifting world and convince both myself and the rest of the world into thinking that, if the earth moved and I moved along with it, that motion, however agitated, would be undetectable. The process, which was as surprising as a river reversing course and flowing upstream, was easier said than done.

**RESPOND •**

1. What's your initial response to this excerpt from Cao's novel? Given the mother's cultural expectations, which she has brought from Vietnam, is it logical for her to respond as she does? In what senses is Cao forced to parent her mother?
2. How does Cao construct the argument she makes here? What sorts of evidence does she rely on? How does she use language effectively to convey her ideas? (Chapters 7, 17, and 13, respectively, will help you answer these questions.)
3. The tale that Cao tells has been told many times in the writings of immigrants, especially those who arrive in the United States as children with parents who speak little or no English. What are the consequences for family life? How does language become a source of power for the child? How does this power disrupt traditional patterns of family life?

4. Cao, like many immigrant children, lost much of her native language—Vietnamese—as well as French, another language widely spoken by educated Vietnamese at that time. (France had colonized Vietnam for many years prior to the war.) The decline in her ability to use these languages had negative repercussions for her relationship with her parents. As she commented in an interview given while she was a visiting law professor at Duke University, "The more educated I became, the more separate I was from my parents. I think that is a very immigrant story." Even native speakers of English often report similar situations in their own lives. Should such separation from one's home community be a necessary consequence of education for native or non-native speakers of English in the United States? Why or why not? Might there be ways to prevent it? Are there benefits to preventing it? Should such efforts be made? Why? **Write an essay** in which you tackle these questions. Your essay will likely include features of evaluative, causal, and proposal arguments. (For discussions of these, see Chapters 10, 11, and 12, respectively.) If the situation described is unfamiliar to you, you might make a point of interviewing people who know about it firsthand.

*Amy Tan (1952– ), best known for her novels* The Joy Luck Club *(1989) and* The Kitchen God's Wife *(1991), writes most often about relationships between Chinese American daughters and their mothers and about each group's struggles with generational and cultural differences. Her work is often praised for its sensitive and realistic rendering of dialogue. During her adolescence, Tan lost her father and her brother to brain tumors. As she recounts, she went on to study English at San Jose State University rather than becoming a neurosurgeon, as her mother had hoped. Tan began as a technical writer but started writing fiction after reading a novel by Louise Erdrich, a Native American writer. This text is a talk Tan gave as part of a panel entitled "Englishes: Whose English Is It Anyway?" at a language symposium in San Francisco in 1989. As you read, try to imagine hearing Tan deliver this speech.*

# Mother Tongue

## AMY TAN

I am not a scholar of English or literature. I cannot give you much more than personal opinions on the English language and its variations in this country or others.

I am a writer. And by that definition, I am someone who has always loved language. I am fascinated by language in daily life. I spend a great deal of my time thinking about the power of language—the way it can evoke an emotion, a visual image, a complex idea, or a simple truth. Language is the tool of my trade. And I use them all—all the Englishes I grew up with.

Recently, I was made keenly aware of the different Englishes I do use. I was giving a talk to a large group of people, the same talk I had already given to half a dozen other groups. The nature of the talk was about my writing, my life, and my book, *The Joy Luck Club*. The talk was going along well enough, until I remembered one major difference that made the whole talk sound wrong. My mother was in the room. And it was perhaps the first time she had heard me give a lengthy speech—using the kind of English I have never used with her. I was saying things like, "The intersection of memory upon imagination" and "There is an aspect of my fiction that relates to thus-and-thus"—a speech filled with carefully wrought grammatical phrases, burdened, it suddenly seemed to me, with nominalized forms, past perfect tenses, conditional phrases—all the forms of standard English that I had learned in school and through books, the forms of English I did not use at home with my mother.

Just last week, I was walking down the street with my mother, and I again found myself conscious of the English I was using, the English I do use with her. We were talking about the price of new and used furniture and I heard myself saying this: "Not waste money that way." My husband was with us as well, and he didn't notice any switch in my English. And then I realized why. It's because over the twenty years we've been together I've often used that same kind of English with him, and sometimes he even uses it with me. It has become our language of intimacy, a different sort of English that relates to family talk, the language I grew up with.

So you'll have some idea of what this family talk I heard sounds like, I'll 5
quote what my mother said during a recent conversation which I videotaped and then transcribed. During this conversation, my mother was talking about

a political gangster in Shanghai who had the same last name as her family's, Du, and how the gangster in his early years wanted to be adopted by her family which was rich by comparison. Later, the gangster became more powerful, far richer than my mother's family, and one day showed up at my mother's wedding to pay his respects. Here's what she said in part:

"Du Yusong having business like fruit stand. Like off the street kind. He is Du like Du Zong—but not Tsung-ming Island people. The local people call putong, the river east side, he belong to that side local people. That man want to ask Du Zong father take him in like become own family. Du Zong father wasn't look down on him, but didn't take seriously, until that man big like become mafia. Now important person, very hard to inviting him. Chinese way, came only to show respect, don't stay for dinner. Respect for making big celebration, he shows up. Mean gives lots of respect. Chinese custom. Chinese social life that way. If too important won't have to stay too long. He come to my wedding. I didn't see, I heard it. I gone to boy's side, they have YMCA dinner. Chinese age I was 19."

Tan's open, informal style may make you feel as if you're part of a conversation among friends, but her text is carefully prepared in ways that casual conversation is not. See Chapter 13 to learn some of the techniques that Tan uses so effectively.

LINK TO P. 309

You should know that my mother's expressive command of English belies how much she actually understands. She reads the *Forbes* report, listens to *Wall Street Week*, converses daily with her stockbroker, reads all of Shirley MacLaine's books with ease—all kinds of things I can't begin to understand. Yet some of my friends tell me they understand fifty percent of what my mother says. Some say they understand eighty to ninety percent. Some say they understand none of it, as if she were speaking pure Chinese. But to me, my mother's English is perfectly clear, perfectly natural. It's my mother tongue. Her language, as I hear it, is vivid, direct, full of observation and imagery. That was the language that helped shape the way I saw things, expressed things, made sense of the world.

Lately, I've been giving more thought to the kind of English my mother speaks. Like others, I have described it to people as "broken" or "fractured" English. But I wince when I say that. It has always bothered me that I can think of no way to describe it other than "broken," as if it were damaged and needed to be fixed, as if it lacked a certain wholeness and soundness. I've heard other terms used, "limited English," for example. But they seem just as bad, as if everything is limited, including people's perception of the limited English speaker.

I know this for a fact, because when I was growing up, my mother's "limited" English limited my perception of her. I was ashamed of her English. I believed that her English reflected the quality of what she had to say. That is, because she expressed them imperfectly her thoughts were imperfect. And I had plenty of empirical evidence to support me: the fact that people in department stores, at banks, and at restaurants did not take her seriously, did not give her good service, pretended not to understand her, or even acted as if they did not hear her.

10 My mother has long realized the limitations of her English as well. When I was fifteen, she used to have me call people on the phone to pretend I was she. In this guise, I was forced to ask for information or even to complain and yell at people who had been rude to her. One time it was a call to her stockbroker in New York. She had cashed out her small portfolio and it just so happened we were going to go to New York the next week, our very first trip outside California. I had to get on the phone and say in an adolescent voice that was not very convincing, "This is Mrs. Tan."

And my mother was standing in the back whispering loudly, "Why he don't send me check, already two weeks late. So mad he lie to me, losing me money."

And then I said in perfect English, "Yes, I'm getting rather concerned. You had agreed to send the check two weeks ago, but it hasn't arrived."

Then she began to talk more loudly, "What he want, I come to New York tell him front of his boss, you cheating me?" And I was trying to calm her down, make her be quiet, while telling the stockbroker, "I can't tolerate any more excuses. If I don't receive the check immediately, I am going to have to speak to your manager when I'm in New York next week." And sure enough, the following week there we were in front of this astonished stockbroker, and I was sitting there redfaced and quiet, and my mother, the real Mrs. Tan, was shouting at his boss in her impeccable broken English.

We used a similar routine just five days ago, for a situation that was far less humorous. My mother had gone to the hospital for an appointment, to find out about a benign brain tumor a CAT scan had revealed a month ago. She said she had spoken very good English, her best English, no mistakes. Still, she said, the hospital did not apologize when they said they had lost the CAT scan and she had come for nothing. She said they did not seem to have any sympathy when she told them she was

*Author Amy Tan and her mother*

anxious to know the exact diagnosis since her husband and son had both died of brain tumors. She said they would not give her any more information until the next time and she would have to make another appointment for that. So she said she would not leave until the doctor called her daughter. She wouldn't budge. And when the doctor finally called her daughter, me, who spoke in perfect English—lo and behold—we had assurances the CAT scan would be found, promises that a conference call on Monday would be held, and apologies for any suffering my mother had gone through for a most regrettable mistake.

15 I think my mother's English almost had an effect on limiting my possibilities in life as well. Sociologists and linguists probably will tell you that a person's developing language skills are more influenced by peers. But I do think that the language spoken in the family, especially in immigrant families which are more insular, plays a large role in shaping the language of the child. And I believe that it affected my results on achievement tests, IQ tests, and the SAT. While my English skills were never judged as poor, compared to math, English could not be considered my strong suit. In grade school, I did moderately well, getting perhaps Bs, sometimes B+s in English, and scoring perhaps in the sixtieth or seventieth percentile on achievement tests. But those scores were not good enough to override the opinion that my true abilities lay in math and science, because in those areas I achieved As and scored in the ninetieth percentile or higher.

This was understandable. Math is precise; there is only one correct answer. Whereas, for me at least, the answers on English tests were always a judgment call, a matter of opinion and personal experience. Those tests were constructed around items like fill-in-the-blank sentence completion, such as "Even though Tom was ________, Mary thought he was ________." And the correct answer always seemed to be the most bland combinations of thoughts, for example, "Even though Tom was shy, Mary thought he was charming," with the grammatical structure "even though" limiting the correct answer to some sort of semantic opposites, so you wouldn't get answers like "Even though Tom was foolish, Mary thought he was ridiculous." Well, according to my mother, there were very few limitations as to what Tom could have been, and what Mary might have thought of him. So I never did well on tests like that.

The same was true with word analogies, pairs of words, in which you were supposed to find some sort of logical, semantic relationship—for example, "sunset" is to "nightfall" as ________ is to ________. And here, you would be presented with a list of four possible pairs, one of which showed the same kind of relationship: "red" is to "stoplight," "bus" is to "arrival," "chills" is to "fever," "yawn" is to "boring." Well, I could never think that way. I knew what the tests were asking, but I could not block out of my mind the images already created by the first pair, "sunset is to nightfall"—and I would see a burst of colors against a darkening sky, the moon rising, the lowering of a curtain of stars. And all the other pairs of words—red, bus, stoplight, boring—just threw up a mass of confusing images, making it impossible for me to sort out something as logical as saying: "A sunset precedes nightfall" is the same as "a chill precedes a fever." The only way I would have gotten that answer right would have been to imagine an associative situation, for example, my being disobedient and staying out past sunset, catching a chill at night, which turns into feverish pneumonia as punishment, which indeed did happen to me.

I have been thinking about all this lately, about my mother's English, about achievement tests. Because lately I've been asked, as a writer, why there are not more Asian-Americans represented in American literature. Why are there few Asian-Americans enrolled in creative writing programs? Why do so many Chinese students go into engineering? Well, these are broad sociological questions I can't begin to answer. But I have noticed in surveys—in fact, just last week—that Asian students, as a whole, always do significantly better on math achievement tests than in English. And this makes me think that there are other Asian-American students whose English spoken in the home might also be described as "broken" or "limited." And perhaps they also have teachers who are steering them away from writing and into math and science, which is what happened to me.

Fortunately, I happen to be rebellious in nature, and enjoy the challenge of disproving assumptions made about me. I became an English major my first year in college after being enrolled as pre-med. I started writing nonfiction as a freelancer the week after I was told by my former boss that writing was my worst skill and I should hone my talents toward account management.

But it wasn't until 1985 that I finally began to write fiction. And at first I 20
wrote using what I thought to be wittily crafted sentences, sentences that would finally prove I had mastery over the English language. Here's an example from the first draft of a story that later made its way into *The Joy Luck Club*, but without this line: "That was my mental quandary in its nascent state." A terrible line, which I can barely pronounce.

Fortunately, for reasons I won't get into today, I later decided I should envision a reader for the stories I would write. And the reader I decided upon was my mother, because these were stories about mothers. So with this reader in mind—and in fact, she did read my early drafts—I began to write stories using all the Englishes I grew up with: the English I spoke to my mother, which for lack of a better term might be described as "simple"; the English she used with me, which for lack of a better term might be described as "broken"; my translation of her Chinese, which could certainly be described as "watered down"; and what I imagined to be her translation of her Chinese if she could speak in perfect English, her internal language, and for that I sought to preserve the essence, but not either an English or a Chinese structure. I wanted to capture what language ability tests can never reveal: her intent, her passion, her imagery, the rhythms of her speech and the nature of her thoughts.

Apart from what any critic had to say about my writing, I knew I had succeeded where it counted when my mother finished reading my book and gave me her verdict: "So easy to read."

## RESPOND•

1. How have Tan's attitudes toward her mother's English changed over the years? Why? In what ways does Tan describe a situation that probably is faced by most children of immigrants? In what ways is this situation like or unlike the embarrassment that children generally feel about their parents at some point in their growing up?
2. Why is Tan suspicious of language ability tests? What are her complaints? What sorts of evidence does she offer? Do you agree or disagree with her argument? Why?
3. Tan's text was written to be read aloud by the author herself. In what ways might this fact be important? (For a discussion of the features of arguments to be heard, see Chapter 15.) What would it be like, for example, to have heard Tan deliver this text? How would such an experience have been different from reading it on the page? Had Tan written the piece to be read silently by strangers—as her novels are, for example—how might she have altered it? Why?
4. What does Tan mean when she claims that she uses "all the Englishes [she] grew up with" (paragraph 2)? What are these Englishes? What are her problems in giving them labels? Do you agree with Tan's implied argument that we should use all our Englishes and use them proudly? Why or why not? Are there any limits to this position? If so, what are they? **Write an essay** evaluating Tan's position. (In preparing for this assignment, you might think about the Englishes that you know and use. Do they all have recognizable names or convenient labels? Do you associate them with certain people or places or activities? What does each represent to you? About you? Do you have ambivalent feelings about any of them? Why? For a discussion of evaluative arguments, see Chapter 10.)

*Discussions of languages other than English in the United States most often focus on Spanish—a language that was spoken in what is today the United States before English was spoken here—or on the languages of other more recent groups of immigrants. Rarely, however, do these discussions consider the languages of the first peoples to settle this continent, Native Americans. There were some 300 languages spoken north of Mexico when Europeans first came to this continent; at the end of the twentieth century, some 175 indigenous languages were still spoken in the United States, and about a third of those were spoken by only a handful of elderly speakers.*

*As this selection demonstrates, however, some Native communities are seeking to keep their language alive in a context where English is the dominant language of the larger society. It includes transcripts from three segments from* First Speakers: Restoring the Ojibwe Language, *an award-winning television program produced by Dianne Steinbach, Stephanie Mosher, and John Whitehead for Twin Cities Public Television. The program was first broadcast on November 26, 2010. You can view these and additional segments of the program at http://bit.ly/a6gPH9. In addition to watching the program, when you visit the Web site, you'll see that there are other informative resources available. In this regards, this Web site represents a multimedia argument (see Chapter 14). As you read the transcripts and especially as you watch these excepts, consider the complexity of multimedia arguments; also give thought to what it might mean for a culture to lose its language and to how it must make the elders who appear in the program feel to hear children freely speaking the language—something they have not heard for a while.*

# First Speakers: Restoring the Ojibwe Language

TWIN CITIES PUBLIC TELEVISION

---

**A note on the transcript:** Content spoken in Ojibwe and subtitled on the screen is shown here in parentheses. Content spoken in Ojibwe and not subtitled is not transcribed. Additional information has been provided in curly brackets ({ }). Where possible, speakers have been identified based on names given in screen captions. After first mention, they are referred to by initials. Other speakers are identified as "Man" or "Woman" based on apparent male or female voice quality.

Here is a list of speakers who speak more than once, all Ojibwe, and information given about them.

Keller Paap (KP), teacher

Anton Treuer (AT), historian

Brenda Child (BC), historian

Adrian Liberty (AL), teacher, Niigaane School

Anna Gibbs (AG), Ponemah elder

Larry Stillday (LS), Ponemah elder

Louise Erdrich (LE), author

Kim Anderson (KA), teacher

Leslie Harper (LH), director, Niigaane School

Susan Johnson (SJ), Ponemah elder

**Part 1, Introduction (7:11)**

Keller Paap: The most valuable intellectual treasure we have is our . . . are our languages.

Anton Treuer: We're at a make-or-break time for the future of the Ojibwe language.

Brenda Child: Something that many of us took for granted when we were younger people is now disappearing.

Adrian Liberty: (I am going to talk to you why our language and religion are of extreme importance.)

AT: To lose the language is to lose the medium we have for conducting most of 5
our ceremonies. There's *a lot* at stake.

Anna Gibbs: (Our language was almost lost. Even now it's almost lost.)

Larry Stillday: Language is life. We don't call it a language; we live it. It's a living thing.

David Bisonette: What's really important to understand about Ojibwe language is how it captures the way that Ojibwe people see the world.

Louise Erdrich: And it's a treasure. It's every bit as much a treasure as any very, very ancient artifact.

{TITLE: *First Speakers: Restoring the Ojibwe Language*, Narrated by Louise Erdrich}

*Using puppets to teach Ojibwe to adults*

LE: While many Americans are familiar with the loss of biodiversity, the problem of shrinking habitats and endangered species, fewer are aware of the accelerating pace of human cultural loss. According to a recent UNESCO study, of the approximately six thousand languages currently spoken in the world, only half are expected to survive this century. A language dies every fourteen days. The Ojibwe language is one of those endangered tongues.°

***endangered tongue (or language):*** a language that will disappear unless some action is taken because there has been a break in its transmission across generations. Because some generations did not learn the community language when they were children, they cannot pass it on to their children. Therefore, the spoken language will disappear unless efforts are made to keep it from dying.

AT: I feel that we're at a make-or-break time for the future of the Ojibwe language, at least as it's spoken in the United States.

LE: Ojibwe is spoken across a wide swath of North America, from eastern Canada through the Great Lakes region, and as far west as Montana. While fluency rates° remain high in some remote parts of Canada, the language is in decline in the United States.

***fluency rates:*** the degree to which members of a community speak a language and are able to speak it for a range of functions.

AT: Especially on the U.S. side, we're very worried about the future of the language.

BC: When I was growing up, my mother and all her siblings spoke Ojibwe. My grandmother spoke Ojibwe. My grandfather did not speak English; he spoke Ojibwe exclusively. And what we're noticing as kind of older generations of Ojibwe people pass away, and a new generation coming up, they don't have that experience of Ojibwe as the older generation had.

AT: We have around a thousand speakers left; most of them are in Minnesota, 15
on the Red Lake Reservation, with another pocket of strength in Mille Lacs.

KP: Most people who are functional speakers,° I would say, are above seventy years old. So, in places you may only have a handful of remaining speakers.

*functional speakers:* speakers who can speak a language well enough to use it in their daily lives, though they do not have complete mastery of the language's vocabulary or grammar.

LE: Late nineteenth-century boarding schools and other assimilationist policies° were the leading causes of the language's decline. But now proponents of language revitalization° are attempting to write a new chapter in the history of Indian education, one filled with hope for the future. A new generation of Ojibwe scholars and educators are racing against time, working with the remaining fluent elders, the so-called "first speakers," to preserve Ojibwe language and culture, and to produce the next generation of speakers. But even as programs in Minnesota and Wisconsin begin to bear fruit, some parents and educators remain skeptical.

*assimilationist policies:* policies that directly or indirectly require members of a group to give up aspects of their group identity to become more like members of a dominant or more powerful group.

*language revitalization:* efforts by individuals, communities, or governments to give an endangered language new life—to make it *vital* or living—again.

LE: I think what people who are looking at this from the outside always wonder is why—well, if there's not that many speakers, why save it? I get this question all the time. It's not a language that is of economic use, people say. And what my answer is, is, Is everything economic? Is everything based on a system of economics? Do we really want three languages in the whole world?

AG: (I will help you parents talk to your baby so that he'll hear the Ojibwe language before it's lost.)

BC: I look at it as part of our cultural heritage in Minnesota that we all should 20
be invested in because what's unique about Ojibwe and Dakota is that they are the indigenous° languages of the place we live. So it makes it very different than Somali, it's different than Swedish, because those are sometimes languages that have been spoken in Minnesota, but they're not the indigenous languages of our region.

*indigenous:* referring to the first or original settlers of a place.

LE: It's every bit as much a treasure as any very, very ancient artifact that we preserve with immense care in a glass case in a museum somewhere. How much more vital is it to have a living, breathing language that tells us how life evolved here on this very continent?

### Part 3, Immersion° 1 (9:19)

*immersion:* a method used for language teaching where the language to be learned is also used as a medium of instruction; thus, academic subjects are taught in the language.

{Archie Mosay, 1901–1996}

LE: Archie Mosay came of age at a time when speaking Ojibwe was a liability. Today's elders are still scarred by their early school experiences.

*An Ojibwe language study group at the University of Michigan, Ann Arbor*

EUGENE STILLDAY, PONEMAH ELDER: I think the extent of my English at the time I entered school was about two or three words of "hello," "good-bye," whatever it was. And we were forbidden to speak our language at school.

MARLENE STATELY, NIIGAANE ELDER: When we went to school we had braids, and the teachers lined up all the Native children and they cut our braids off, so we went home looking like little Dutch boys, y'know?

DORA MOSAY AMMANN, ST. CROIX TRIBAL ELDER: I remember as a little girl, my parents 25
couldn't . . . they were required that we either go to church and go to school, or we were forced with the idea that they would come and take us away so that they could teach us these things. And this was when all these {Native American} kids were put in foster homes, and we had to . . . we weren't allowed to speak our language, so we lost our language.

LE: Many of the parents and grandparents of today's elders were sent away as children to the U.S. government-run boarding schools.

AT: They would take children, usually very young first-grade children, age six, and they would remove them from their communities and home and place them in a residential school. They would have their hair cut and their traditional clothes burned up, and get uniforms, marched to class.

BC: Children could not speak their tribal language. They had to speak English. They were supposed to attend Christian church services.

AT: It was designed to assimilate. Captain Richard Henry Pratt, the superintendent of the first Indian boarding school in the U.S. said, "Our goal is to kill the Indian in order to save the man." And he really felt that it was doing a favor to Native people to kind of rub out their culture and their language. The damage was tremendous, to individuals and to the entire community.

{Children and teachers in a classroom speaking Ojibwe}

KIM ANDERSON, TEACHER: (Who are you?)

CHILD: (Namanjiins. I'm Makwa [Bear] Clan.)

LE: If government boarding schools are the dark past of Indian education, then schools like this are the future.

CHILD AT BLACKBOARD, READING: (Twenty-eight, sixty-two.)

KP, TEACHER: (That's right.)

AT: I feel very hopeful. We see the beginning efforts at a significant language revitalization effort ongoing right now.

LE: Much of that hope lies with language immersion programs. Immersion schools in Minnesota and Wisconsin were influenced by the success of these programs elsewhere.

{Teachers and children in Hilo, Hawaii, singing in Hawaiian}

AT: The experience of indigenous groups like the Hawaiian Islanders and the Maori° of New Zealand has proven that language immersion programs work.

*Maori:* the indigenous people of New Zealand, who are of Polynesian origin.

LE: Hawaiians went from five hundred speakers to around 15,000, and probably the most exciting thing there is that about three thousand of them are first language speakers, so it's the first language that they're learning in the home.

{Chorus of children in New Zealand, singing}

LE: The Maori also had a lot of success, and in varying degrees other tribes in the United States have, too, such as the Blackfeet° and the Mohawk.°

*Blackfeet:* an Algonquian Indian tribe located today in Montana and Alberta, Canada.

*Mohawk:* an Iroquois Indian tribe located today in upstate New York and in Ontario and Quebec, Canada.

AT: Brooke Ammann is the former education director for the St. Croix Band of Chippewa. She and her husband, Sean Fahrlander, spent a year studying immersion programs in Hawaii and several other states. If the boarding schools of old divided families, she says the new immersion schools are bringing them together.

BROOKE AMMANN, LANGUAGE ADVOCATE: In a lot of the cases for the immersion programs is that there's a family involved, a family who wants their children to have this opportunity. That was something that was everyplace that we visited, these Native parents saying, "We want something different."

{Teacher and children in park area of a reservation, speaking Ojibwe}

AL, TEACHER: [OK, when you hear two whistles, what do you do?]

LE: The Niigaane School, on the Leech Lake Reservation fits the pattern.

AL, TEACHER: [When I pull it back . . . I pull it back to the same spot. Is that right?]

LE: It was founded by a team that included Leslie Harper and Adrian Liberty. 45

AL: My son has been in the program from the beginning, and his mom is the director of the program, and I'm his teacher, and I've been his teacher for a few years. And we're divorced, we've been divorced for a number of years now. And we do the best we can, I think we do pretty good, so I'm actually pretty proud of it.

LESLIE HARPER: We both knew as parents, this was how we wanted to raise our son and that we wanted our son to go to school here. It was something for our son, but also for other kids.

SEAN FAHRLANDER, LANGUAGE ADVOCATE: It was Leslie's legwork; she busted her butt. She pulled it together and said, let's do this, a school within a school. And they got an outbuilding at Bug-O-Nay-Ge-Shig School, which is a BIA° charter school, and out of it sprang Niigaane.

*BIA:* Bureau of Indian Affairs, a federal agency that is currently part of the U.S. Department of the Interior; one of its divisions oversees tribal schools. The earlier mention of "U.S. government-run boarding schools" was a reference to BIA schools.

LH: I'm the director of the program here, {showing film crew around the facility} but we also have three elders who work with us, and they're our real bosses. We've got Gerri Howard, Leona Wakanabo, and Marlene Stately. And we designed it so that we would make sure we have a first speaker of Ojibwe in all our classrooms. We go from kindergarten through fifth grade, and we have multiage classrooms. So this first classroom is *baanajaanh wadiswan*, it's our little baby bird nest,° and *gimiwan*, Dustin Burnette, is teamed up primarily with Marlene.

*(language) nest:* an immersion-based program for revitalizing languages developed in New Zealand among Maori communities; the method involves having older, fluent speakers participate actively in elementary classrooms, serving as language models and as resources of important cultural knowledge. As in the example here, curricula are designed as much as possible around events significant to the indigenous community, such as maple sugar camp.

{Teacher addressing children in Ojibwe}

AL, TEACHER: [What's been put here inside the pail?] 50

LH: *Nenookaasi wadiswan*, that's our grades two and three classroom; that's our hummingbird nest.

KA, TEACHER: [How many?]

CHILDREN: [Five]

KA, TEACHER: [Is that it?]

LH: That's Kim Anderson, and she's paired primarily with Leona Wakonabo.

AL, TEACHER: [But maybe you should do this one.]

LH: And then we've got *Baapaasi wadiswan,* our little woodpecker nest.

AL, TEACHER: [You used a little more. Is that right? Good.]

LH: That's our grades four and five classroom, and that's where Naabek teaches, Adrian, and he's paired primarily with Gerri, with Gerri Howard.

AL, TEACHER: [You should help him. What is that called?]

LH: {Outside with teachers and students} We're just getting to the tail end of our maple sugar, our maple sap run. We've been going out pretty much every day for the last couple of weeks to the maple sugar camp. So we made sure that that was an integral part of curriculum here, when we come back and do any of our reading, our math, any of our social kind of stuff.

AL, TEACHER: [What do they use to make firewood?]

STUDENT: [An axe.]

AL: I love working with the kids. When you see a student just kind of light up, "Oh, yeah, that's how you say that!" {Addressing students} [*Makoons!* High five!] It's just so worth it because I know what it's like to not know; I know what it's like to not know yourself and have questions and stuff. And I also know what it's like to start having understandings of who you are and who we're meant to be.

## PART 5, PONEMAH (4:36)

{Voices of children}

ROSE TAINTER: I'm Rose Tainter, I'm from the Red Lake Reservation. I was born in Ponemah, Minnesota. I grew up talking Ojibwe.

LE: It's no accident that Rose Tainter and Eugene Stillday both grew up here in Ponemah, Minnesota. Located on the Red Lake Reservation, about an hour north of Bemidji, this small community is home to a disproportionately large population of fluent Ojibwe speakers.

*allotment:* U.S. government policy in effect from 1887 until 1934 whereby a reservation's land, which had been held as the property of all its members, was divided and given to individual Indians, any remainder being sold to non-Indians. Historians see the results of allotment as having been extremely negative for Indians living on reservations.

AT: Ponemah's a very special place, as is all of the Red Lake Reservation. Unlike all of the other reservations in Minnesota, and unlike most in the country, Red Lake has never gone through the process of allotment,° so the entire reservation is owned by the tribe. The land is held in what's called *federal trust*, no individual people own land there. So the concept and relationship that people have to the land is different. The relationship with one's ancestors is also conceived of and thought of in daily practice very differently. So, there are no church burials in Ponemah.

SUSAN JOHNSON, PONEMAH ELDER: {Walking in large yard, accompanied by film crew} Yeah. This is my mother's grave.

AT: People bury their dead right in their front yard.

SJ: I got my mother, my uncle, my uncle and my sister.

*tenacious:* strong or tight.

AT: So there's a very tenacious° hold to culture, custom, practice, and because of that, the language is also very strong there.

LS: {Driving} Over here on the right is my mother's parents' homestead. And so we had to walk all the way over here.

*fluent speaker:* in contrast to a functional speaker, a speaker who has mastered fully the vocabulary and grammar of a language.

LE: Larry Stillday is a typical Ponemah fluent speaker.° Raised in a bilingual home, he still speaks Ojibwe. A Vietnam veteran and recovering alcoholic, Larry runs a chemical dependency treatment center here. Most days he takes lunch here, at the local nutritional center.

LAVONNE WHITEFEATHER: [C'mon, hurry up!]

LS: [What for?! You better start smiling!] {Both laugh} [So, what ya doing here?]

AT: Pretty much everybody who's fifty or older is a speaker, which is in far better shape than all of the other Ojibwe communities in the United States. And there's a sense of pride that's very, very evident. You drive into the reservation, and there's a sign that says "Ponemah, home of the Ojibwe language."

LS: {With woman, inside nutritional center, opening Styrofoam food container} [What is it?] Soup. [Did you eat?]

SJ: [Not yet.]

LS: [See how good it goes when we speak Ojibwe?]

SJ: {Nods and vocalizes affirmation}

LS: [That's why we remember it.]

SJ: Yeah. [My grandma taught me.] My grandma.

LS: Oh. That's the nature of our language. [We remember . . . what happened.]

AT: They're proud of the fact that the language is alive there, and that's a source of pride for everybody, whether they're a speaker or not.

## RESPOND•

1. What argument(s) is each section of this program making? What functions does each serve independently? As part of the program as a whole? (For information on the functions arguments serve, see "Why We Make Arguments" in Chapter 1.)
2. Based on the information from readings in this chapter, how does the bilingualism found in Native American communities differ from that found in communities of recent immigrants? In what ways is it similar? How is this community, in particular, responding to language endangerment?
3. What different sorts of testimonies and narratives do you see in the segments of this selection? What roles do different kinds of speakers play as they provide information that becomes part of the program? (See Chapter 4 for a discussion of testimonies and narratives as evidence.) Is it relevant that all of the participants are Ojibwe? Why or why not? In what ways is their ethnicity an ethical appeal? It is important to remember in this context that a few decades ago, there would not have been a group of Native American scholars focusing on these questions from an Indian perspective. (See Chapter 3 on ethical appeals.)
4. The primary audience for this program is obviously not people who speak Ojibwe. In what ways have the program's creators accommodated those of us who do not speak the language and who may know nothing about Ojibwe culture without overwhelming us?
5. **Write a rhetorical analysis** of one of the segments of *First Speakers*, of the entire program, or of the Twin Cities Public Television site dedicated to the program as visual or multimedia arguments. (See Chapter 6 for information on rhetorical analyses and Chapter 14 for help in analyzing visual and multimedia arguments.) You may well wish to include visual images as part of your analysis. Obviously, your responses to the previous four questions should help you with this assignment.

*The selection that opened this chapter, which is based on data collected by the U.S. census, does not include at least one important source of bilingualism in the United States today, American Sign Language (ASL), a manual language used by people who are deaf and by those who interact regularly with them. In discussions of deafness, you'll see a distinction made between people who are deaf and those who are Deaf. People who are deaf are unable to hear—an audiological condition—and they communicate with hearing people in a range of ways: speaking English (depending on when they became deaf) and speech reading (also called lip reading), using some form of manual communication and an intrerpreter, or writing in English. People who are Deaf sign ASL and identify with the Deaf community. (There have been debates about whether someone who is hearing can truly be Deaf; an important category of individuals involved here is composed of CODAs—children of Deaf adults—who signed before they spoke and are completely at home in both the hearing and Deaf communities.) People who use ASL and who have received any education at all (and nearly all have) will be bilingual to at least some degree because they will read and write English, but they will sign ASL, a language whose structure is very, very different from that of spoken English (or even British Sign Language).*

*Here we present three blog entries from "Deaf Expressions," a blog created by Michele J. Bornert. In addition to blogging, Bornert is a Deaf artist, an ASL teacher, an actress, a freelance writer, and a wife and mother; she lives in Grand Rapids, Michigan. She was born partially deaf and lost her hearing completely during adolescence after she'd discovered her love of theater. Although she can speak English with no problem, ASL is her preferred method of communication, partly because, as she reports, she has no facility with speech reading at all. The mother of three, she is married to a man who hears and signs, and her children all sign. In fact, she reports that hers is a signing household. She and her husband have started a company, Deaf Expressions (deafexpressions.net), to provide training in ASL as well as make presentations about deafness, the Deaf community, and hearing loss to hearing audiences. As you read these three entries, consider how bilingualism in the American households where ASL is used is similar to and different from the other examples of bilingualism you've read about in this chapter.*

# Three Blog Postings from *Deaf Expressions*

MICHELE J. BORNERT

*Thursday, January 6, 2011*

## TELL ME YOUR SECRETS—A DEAF PERSON'S LACK OF PRIVACY

The Deaf Community is a tight-knit group in which deaf and hearing alike can get together and socialize. The hearies in this group consist of many different people, not the least of which are the interpreters in any given area.

As a member of the Deaf Community, I often find myself friends with the very people who provide interpretation for my appointments, entertainment, education, etc. That, in and of itself, is great! Any person I can get to tolerate me enough to have a conversation, is more than welcome to come my way! And there are some awesome interpreters around here. Oh, don't get me wrong; there are a few doozies. . . .

In her blog, Bornert writes for an audience that might have varying degrees of understanding about issues or obstacles facing the Deaf community. How does her use of humor help bridge that gap in understanding?

LINK TO P. 33

I once went to see a doctor and the interpreter couldn't understand my signing or keep up with the doctor's speaking. The doc and me ended up writing back and forth while the 'terp sat there and watched/read. Wow! And she got paid for that?? But that's another blog entry all together. . . .

Anyway, it seems to me a little unfair and awkward that interpreters in my area know so much about my private life via 'terping for my appointments. And, believe me, my private life is frightening at times. Heck, *I'm* frightening at times.

But there's one particular aspect of my life that I don't really want to share. 5
But, because this is a blog of my experiences, I'm just going to open myself up here to say that I am disabled because of a severe mental illness. Yes, I'm stone deaf, too, but that doesn't strike me as a disability when compared to what I have to go through because of a brain disorder.

So, this morning, I wasn't doing very well. OK. I was doing terribly! I had an emergency appointment to see my psychiatrist and there was, of course, an interpreter scheduled. I definitely have a first choice in interpreters, but sometimes that person isn't available and, today, that was the case.

One of the effects of my condition is that it becomes difficult for me to show expression in my face. My voice becomes monotone and quiet (so I'm told), too. It's a total 180 from what people usually see in me. Usually I'm full of zest and friendly and chatty. I usually take care of my appearance, wear clean clothes, and put on makeup when I have an appointment. But, because I'm relapsing, I did none of that today—well, this week, in fact.

I shuffled (literally) into the office lobby, registered, and sat down. My interpreter arrived about two minutes after I did and I could tell she was in a good mood and ready to talk about our latest adventures. But I couldn't do it. I couldn't even look at her. I just sat there, husband beside me, staring into space. Barbie (the 'terp) was a little put back. However, I will say she was totally professional and kind about the situation.

*Hearing students learning to sign*

When it came time for me to talk with my doctor for a medicine change, I had to relay information about my condition and recent experiences to him. This is something very personal and that holds a great amount of stigma. I haven't shared my disorder with anyone except my immediate family (husband and children). And I certainly didn't want someone whom I love hanging out with at Deaf events, finding out how sick I am by listening to me ramble on to my doctor.

It just doesn't seem right for an interpreter to know everything personal 10
about me, because they've been at the appointments; and yet I only know what they've felt comfortable opening up and telling me about them. Why do *they* get to know it all?

I guess it's a dilemma that will go on forever. We deafies need interpreters and, in order to understand, someone has to sit in and listen to our private thoughts and problems. Professionally, I have yet to meet an interpreter who has taken that knowledge and done something disrespectful (that I know of). Actually, that's not true. But I'll save that for another post, too.

However, **interpreters are only human**. You sit in and listen to someone talk psychotically and it's going to affect you. You're going to have feelings about what you're hearing. I'm not saying everyone will harbor those feelings, but everyone will *have* some. 'Terps included.

So, here I sit in my living room. After spilling my beans, my life, and my secrets, I sit here naked (metaphorically—the other option is just plain old creepy), knowing that Barbie knows my soul is warped. I'm not afraid she'll go off and tell people. I know she won't. But I hate the fact that she knows now and there weren't a lot of options to stop her (or someone who was called to interpret) from knowing.

Perhaps video interpreting will become popular and I'll have 'terps from around the country—not people down the street that have a potluck on Memorial Day. But until then, I need to figure out how to accept that my secrets won't always be my secrets. If I get an STD (I won't—don't worry), there's going to be at least one person out there in the Deaf Community who knows, because they interpreted the appointment. And if I'm crazy, there's going to be someone out there who knows that, too. Check.

*Tuesday, September 7, 2010*

## "MOM'S DEAF—LET'S PARTY!!!"

"But I *was* home on time, Mom! I've been in the bathroom!" 15

Now, how was I supposed to know if he was telling the truth? No one else was in the house and he's usually pretty honest . . . as far as I know. So, I let it go. After all, he was home safe and sound. But how was I supposed to set the standards high when the kids have an advantage over me in that area?

Fact is, once they're out of my sight, there's simply no way to know what's happening. They can tell me how obedient they've been, but how do I really know? I can follow them around and check on them incessantly, but what mother wants to have to do that?

Being a CODA (Child of Deaf Adults) isn't always easy, but you gotta admit, there's a lot they can get away with because Mom and/or Dad's ears don't pick up the way other parents' do. And it's hard for me, as a mother, to accept this.

However, as frustrating as the situation may be, it isn't completely without humor. . . .

Saturday, I had a family come to our home in regard to their homeschooled 20
daughter taking an American Sign Language class from me. They arrived right on time. I sat them on the big couch; my interpreting husband sat on the little couch; and I sat across from everyone in a chair.

Now this is a business, so I'm doing my darndest to ensure that the meeting and interview go as professionally as possible. I've told the children to stay in their rooms. I had everything written up and tried to explain what exactly the course entailed. All the while this was happening, the mother, seated at the far end of the couch, kept glancing off to the side, wide-eyed, and looking a bit disturbed. I chalked it up to nerves and continued on.

It wasn't until later that night, when my husband made a remark that the family had probably thought we were animal torturers, that I found out just what the mother's disturbed looks were for.

See, my 10-year-old daughter had a friend over. Her room is right next to our living room. Seems that, while I was trying hard to look all professional and confident, these two rugrats were in her room, playing target practice with the cat!

"Get her! Go that way and stop her!"

"Ouch! She just scratched me!" 25

"Quick, throw a pillow at her!"

And the entire time, the cat was mewing and screeching, calling for help.

So there you have it. As a Deaf parent of hearing kids, I have to face the fact that there will be times when I'm out of the loop or oblivious to their actions. And this is with a 13-, 11-, and 10-year-old. Just wait till they're all teenagers!!!

*Saturday, July 31, 2010*

## LEARNING AMERICAN SIGN LANGUAGE TAKES TIME

As an ASL teacher and as a deaf person in general, I've found that almost all of the people I encounter who are wanting to learn American Sign Language go into it with unrealistic expectations. They all expect to take a series of classes and then be able to venture out into the Deaf community and converse in sign with little or no effort. And this goes both ways, meaning they expect to be able to relay their messages in sign language and they expect to be able to comprehend all of the messages relayed to them in the signed response.

For a while I thought that the only reason for this was that people assumed 30
that learning sign language would be easier than learning a new spoken

language. Many think of sign as simply drawing pictures in the air. Sure, they'll admit there's some things you must know the formal sign for, but that should be easy to pick up, right? It's a primitive language—ones cavemen used—and, therefore, should be self-explanatory and easier to pick up than, say, German.

A lot of people actually believe that. I think that's because many people generally view ASL as mime or gesturing being the main point, so, I mean, how hard can it really be? It's like this grand game of charades. When they then go in and decide they're going to learn it "formally," it's hard for them to realize that they've had the wrong idea.

I had thought that the idea of thinking that learning a new language would be easy was only usually applied to learning sign language, but then I asked my husband. He said that it often applied to spoken languages as well. When he decided to learn Spanish so that he could readily interact with the people he encountered at the airport (where he works), he signed up for a community class—excited by the prospect of being able to chat with other Spanish-speaking people when the class was finished. He believed that he would have a basic grasp of the language by the end of the class. And when the class ended and he took what he learned with him to work, he was frustrated that he still struggled to interact with the Spanish-speaking community.

I think it's human nature. People want to know what they want to know and they want to know it at that very moment. Whether it's how to speak a language, how to play a sport, or how to work the new computer or television, people (generally speaking) don't have a whole lot of patience. So, when they get the notion to learn a new language, they don't expect it to be as difficult as it really is.

One common tendency is to take the new vocabulary words you've learned and put them in a sentence using the word order of the language you already know . . . such as the common method of signing American Sign Language signs in English word order. It's one factor of language learning that truly is a challenge—learning new grammatical rules and sentence structure.

Another struggle is understanding that there is no one way of expressing 35
something. In English when you want to say something, there are many ways to word it. For example:

*"I can't believe that stupid guy over there is giving me a dirty look!"*

*"There is an annoying man sitting over there who keeps giving me a dirty look and it's ticking me off!"*

*"Why is he glaring at me? It's bugging me!"*

*"If that guy doesn't stop staring at me, I'm going to get very upset!"*

You get the idea. 40

Just as English ideas can be phrased various ways and get the same point across, so, too, can ASL. There is no one specific way things absolutely must be worded. You're learning a language; you're not taking a biology class. There is no one answer that is the only right answer. There are nuances that you can only learn through interaction and practice.

Yes, of course you can be taught the vocabulary and grammatical structure. And if you study daily and immerse yourself with other signers (preferably native speakers), you can get a very good grasp of the language in about two years. They say fluency comes around seven to ten years of serious study. But you will always be learning. Always. That goes for any language you learn. Heck, even native English speakers take English courses throughout school, attend workshops on the use of English, and major in English in college. We're always learning. There is no point where you can say, "OK. Now I know it all." (Although I do know many people who think they do.)

So try to be patient. Don't expect so much so fast. It's a language. It's not a skill like dancing, where you learn how to step ball change and then never need to learn that again. It's an ongoing venture. But, and this is a big but, it's a journey that will lead you through many wonderful experiences.

Don't be hard on yourself if you're not able to fully converse with a deaf signer after, say, one 10-week class. That's unrealistic. There's simply too much to learn to accomplish it all in one course. You might want to have every possible bit of information crammed into every minute of each class in order to feel you've gotten your money and time's worth. But you have to think about this in a mature manner. Use what you learn. Every day. Go where the signers are (and please remember to go where the skilled signers are and not just a bunch of students who are also just learning). Interact in the Deaf Culture. Become involved. There's no point in learning a new language if you won't have anyone to share it with. Man, oh, man! How many students I've worked with who have said that they don't want to go to a Deaf event because they're scared they won't be able to communicate. But, you have to. It's scary, but you have to. Besides, why are you learning it anyway if you're not going to actually use it with people who need it?

So, will you learn American Sign Language in a few months' time? No, you 45
won't. Don't expect that. Will you find, in a group of 5 teachers, that they all teach how to say something in exactly the same way? No. There is no one exact way. But will all of your work be worth it in the end? Absolutely. It's worth it.

But do me one favor: Once you learn it, put it to good use. That's all I ask.

## RESPOND •

1. How would you characterize the argument made by each of these blog entries? Which do you find most interesting? Most compelling? Why? In what way does each entry present some aspect of bilingualism in the United States?
2. How is the bilingualism described in these entries like or unlike the bilingualism described in other selections in this chapter? What accounts for the similarities? The differences?
3. In what ways does Bornert use humor in creating her arguments? How effectively does she do so? How does her use of humor contribute to the ethos that she creates? (See Chapter 2 for a discussion of humor in arguments and Chapter 3 for a discussion of ethos.)

4. Like most blog entries, Bornert's postings tend to be written in an informal style. What features of blogging encourage writers to be informal as they create blog entries? If you visit Bornert's blog, you'll see that she also tweets. What features of tweeting shape those messages? Why?
5. As noted in question 4, Bornert's style is quite informal; it is certainly too informal for an academic essay. At the same time, her discussion of privacy in the first posting or her analysis of why language learning is challenging for adults could easily be relevant to an academic essay you might write. **Summarize each of these postings** as you might if you wished to include a discussion of them in an academic essay you were writing on each of these topics. In your treatment of each entry, be sure to include summary, paraphrase, and quotations, and document your source properly. (See Chapter 16 for a discussion of academic arguments, Chapter 19 for a discussion of using sources, and Chapter 21 for a discussion of documenting sources.)

*Kirk Semple (1966– ) has written for the* New York Times *since 2003 with assignments at the United Nations, in Haiti, and in Iraq. He currently focuses on immigration issues. Prior to writing for the* Times, *he was a foreign correspondent in Colombia and worked for several papers in the United States. Jeffrey E. Singer also contributed reporting for this article. As you read this selection, which appeared in November 2011, pay attention to the way that Semple situates the article with respect to debates about the need for English as an official language, on the one hand, and the ways technology is changing daily life, on the other.*

# Moving to U.S. and Amassing a Fortune, No English Needed

**Kirk Semple**

More than 40 years after arriving in New York from Mexico uneducated and broke, Felix Sanchez de la Vega Guzman still can barely speak English. Ask him a question, and he will respond with a few halting phrases and an apologetic smile before shifting back to the comfort of Spanish.

Yet Mr. Sanchez has lived the great American success story. He turned a business selling tortillas on the street into a $19 million food manufacturing empire that threaded together the Mexican diaspora° from coast to coast and reached back into Mexico itself.

Mr. Sanchez is part of a small class of immigrants who arrived in the United States with nothing and, despite speaking little or no English, became remarkably prosperous. And while generations of immigrants have thrived despite language barriers, technology, these days, has made it easier for such entrepreneurs to attain considerable affluence.

Many have rooted their businesses in big cities with immigrant populations large enough to insulate them from everyday situations that demand English. After gaining traction in their own communities, they have used the tools of modern communication, transportation and commerce to tap far-flung resources and exploit markets in similar enclaves around the country and the world.

5 "The entire market is Hispanic," Mr. Sanchez said of his business. "You don't need English." A deal, he said, is only a cheap long-distance phone call or a few key strokes on the computer away. "All in Spanish," he added.

Mr. Sanchez, 66, said he always wanted to learn English but had not had time for lessons.

"I couldn't concentrate," he said in a recent interview, in Spanish. "In addition, all the people around me were speaking in Spanish, too."

In New York City, successful non-English-speaking entrepreneurs like Mr. Sanchez have emerged from the largest immigrant populations, including those from China, South Korea and Spanish-speaking countries.

***diaspora:*** the dispersion of a group of people across a large geographic region to which they aren't native.

*Felix Sanchez de la Vega Guzman, 66, turned selling tortillas on the street into a $19 million food business.*

Among them is Zhang Yulong,° 39, who emigrated from China in 1994 and now presides over a $30-million-a-year cellphone accessories empire in New York with 45 employees.

Kim Ki Chol, 59, who arrived in the United States from South Korea in 1981, opened a clothing accessories store in Brooklyn and went on to become a successful retailer, real estate investor and civic leader in the region's Korean diaspora.

In the United States in 2010, 4.5 million income-earning adults who were heads of households spoke English "not well" or "not at all," according to the Census Bureau; of those, about 35,500 had household incomes of more than $200,000 a year.

Nancy Foner, a sociology professor at the City University of New York who has written widely on immigration, said it was clear that modern technology had made a big difference in the ability of immigrant entrepreneurs with poor or no English skills to expand their companies nationally and globally.

"It wasn't impossible—but much, much harder—for immigrants to operate businesses around the globe a hundred years ago, when there were no jet planes, to say nothing of cellphones and computers," Ms. Foner said.

Advocates for the movement sometimes known as Official English have long pressed for legislation mandating English as the official language of government, arguing that a common language is essential for the country's cohesion and for immigrant assimilation and success.

But stories like Mr. Sanchez's, though certainly unusual, seem to suggest that an entrepreneur can do just fine without English—especially with the aid of modern technology, not to mention determination and ingenuity.

For Mr. Sanchez, who became an American citizen in 1985, one anxious moment came when he had to pass his naturalization test. The law requires that applicants be able to read, write and speak basic English.

But Mr. Sanchez and other entrepreneurs said that the test, at least at the time they took it, had been rudimentary and that they had muddled through it.

Mr. Sanchez immigrated to the United States in 1970 from the Mexican state of Puebla with only a

***Zhang Yulong/Kim Ki Chol:*** Note that as is often the case with personal names from East Asia, the family name is given first; thus, Semple later refers to Mr. Zhang and Mr. Kim.

*Zhang Yulong, 39, has a $30-million-a-year cellphone accessories company.*

fifth-grade education. He held a series of low-paying jobs in New York, including washing dishes in a Midtown restaurant. The Mexican population in the New York region was small back then, but it soon began growing, as did the demand for authentic Mexican products.

In 1978, Mr. Sanchez and his wife, Carmen, took $12,000 in savings, bought a tortilla press and an industrial dough mixer in Los Angeles, hauled the machinery back to the East Coast and installed it in a warehouse in Passaic, N.J. Mr. Sanchez spent his days driving a forklift at an electrical-equipment factory and spent his evenings and nights making tortillas and selling them door-to-door in Latino neighborhoods around New York City.

His company, Puebla Foods, grew with the Mexican population, and he was soon distributing his tortillas and other Mexican products, like dried chilies, to bodegas° and restaurants throughout the Northeast. At its peak, his enterprise had factories in cities all across North America, including Los Angeles, Miami, Pittsburgh, Toronto and Washington. It has since been buffeted by competition and by the economy, and he has scaled back.

He has relied heavily on a bilingual staff, which at times has included his three children, born and raised in New Jersey.

Mr. Zhang, the cellphone accessories entrepreneur, said his lack of English had not been a handicap. "The only obstacle I have is if I get too tired," said Mr. Zhang, who also owns a property development company and an online retail firm.

In 2001, Mr. Zhang set up a wholesale business in cellphone accessories in Manhattan. He then raised money from relatives and investors in China to open a manufacturing plant there to make leather cellphone cases for export to the United States, Canada and Latin America.

His business boomed, and he opened warehouses in Los Angeles, New York City and Washington, controlling his international manufacturing, supply and retail chain from his base in New York.

Mr. Zhang now lives in a big house in Little Neck, Queens, with his wife, three daughters and parents, and drives a Lexus S.U.V. He has not applied for citizenship, preferring to remain a legal permanent resident and maintain his Chinese citizenship, which spares him the bother of securing a Chinese visa when he goes to China for business.

While he can speak rudimentary English—he rates his comprehension at 30 percent—he conducts nearly his entire life in Chinese. His employees

***bodega:*** a small neighborhood grocery shop that generally includes wine among the items for sale. In some places, the term is used only for shops that sell Hispanic food items (the word is of Spanish origin) while in New York City, it has come to be used to refer to convenience stores generally.

speak the languages of trading partners: English, Spanish, Creole, Korean and French, not to mention multiple Chinese dialects.

Over the course of a lengthy interview, he gamely tried on several occasions to converse in English, but each time he ran into roadblocks and, with a shrug of resignation, resumed speaking through a translator in Mandarin.

Mr. Kim, the Korean retailer, recalled that when he opened his first store in Brooklyn, nearly his entire clientele was Afro-Caribbean and African-American, and his customers spoke no Korean.

"You don't have to have a big conversation," he recalled. "You can make gestures."

*Kim Ki Chol, 59, from South Korea, is a successful retailer, real estate investor, and civic leader.*

While his holdings have grown, he 30
has also formed or led associations and organizations that focus on empowering the Korean population in the United States. As in business, modern communication has made it much easier for him to raise his profile throughout the Korean diaspora well beyond New York.

"The success of my life is not only that I make a lot of money," he said, "but that I make a lot of Korean people's lives better."

Yet he admitted that he was embarrassed by his inability to speak English. He has gone so far as to buy some English-tutorial computer programs, but for years, they have gone mostly unused.

**RESPOND•**

1. What argument(s) is Semple making in this selection, specifically with regard to the necessity of immigrants to master English? What particular factors have enabled the three men who are profiled here to succeed in the United States? What challenges have they overcome? How have they been able to do so? How representative do you think the experiences of these three men might be? Why?
2. How successful is Semple at constructing an argument based on fact? Use the suggestions in the "Guide to Writing an Argument of Fact" in Chapter 8 as the basis for your evaluation.
3. Once you've completed question 2, check out the comments readers made in response to Semple's article (http://nyti.ms/MBL2Id), especially those listed as "Highlights" and those listed as "Readers' Recommendations" to see whether those posting comments would

Semple's article relies primarily on evidence collected through interviewing his subjects. Review Chapter 17 and consider what other types of evidence he might have included to enhance his argument.

LINK TO P. 395

likely agree with your assessment. Do the comments you find there lead you to reassess Semple's success at creating an argument based on fact? Why or why not? (By the way, you'll notice that many of the comments refer to the Occupy Wall Street movement, which was taking place when this article was published.)

4. As you may be aware, journalists rarely get to write the titles for their articles. In fact, this article appeared with two slightly different titles, and it has been given a third title elsewhere on the *New York Times'* Web site. In the national edition of the *Times*, the article appeared with the title used here: "Moving to U.S. and Amassing a Fortune, No English Needed." The version of the article that appeared in the New York City edition was entitled "Moving to U.S. and Prospering, without English." Finally, in the "Times Topics" section of the paper's Web page that archives Semple's articles, the piece is listed as "Immigrant Entrepreneurs Succeed without English" (http://nyti.ms/tYWLNh). In what sense does each title make a slightly different argument about the article that follows? Which of the titles sticks most closely to the facts? Which might be said to contain additional emotional appeals? (See Chapter 2 for a discussion of arguments based on emotions.)

5. An interesting aspect of this article is the way that it offers three similar rags-to-riches stories very appealing to Americans in terms of how we like to view the opportunities the country offers to those who work hard, yet it contradicts another commonly held view of the country as a place where success for immigrants depends on mastering English. (If you are not familiar with the genre of "rags to riches" stories, you might look for information about it on the Internet; Wikipedia is a good place to start.) **Write an essay** in which you evaluate the claim that English is necessary for success for immigrants to the United States, especially as technology enables people around the world to be in touch in ways that were not possible just a few short years ago. You may wish to do some research before beginning your essay. A good place to get ideas about perspectives on this issue is the reader comments referred to in question 3. You will likely find that your response will be a qualified one, rather than full support for or rejection of the claim. Be sure to consider what might be gained or lost for the immigrant, his/her family, his/her local community, and the country if English is or is not learned. (For help with qualifying claims, see Chapter 7, and for help with evaluative arguments, see Chapter 10.)

*This selection documents the life of Sao Yee Cha, a Hmong woman who moved to Portland, Oregon, in 1978 after spending two years in a refugee camp in Thailand following the Vietnam War. The Hmong are a Southeast Asian ethnic group that traditionally lived as farmers in isolated mountainous regions of Laos. Early in the 1960s, the U.S. Central Intelligence Agency recruited many Hmong men to fight in what later became known as "The Secret War" against Communists in neighboring Vietnam. (Between 12,000 and 40,000 Hmong are estimated to have died in these efforts. The name of the war derives from the fact that the United States did not officially acknowledge its role in the Laotian civil war until later, in 1995.) Following the U.S. withdrawal from Vietnam in 1975 and the Communist takeover of Laos, the Hmong were targeted for persecution. Many were evacuated through CIA efforts, but some 40,000 managed to get to refugee camps in Thailand by walking overland and crossing the Mekong River. Today, the United States is home to the largest Hmong community outside of Asia.*

*This article appeared in September 2008 in the Portland newspaper* The Oregonian *in its weekly series "Life Story," which reports on the life of an everyday person from the local community who has recently passed away. It was written by Amy Martinez Starke, a staff writer for the paper. As you read this selection, ask yourself what sort of argument an obituary represents. Also consider how Sao Yee Cha's experiences of bilingualism were similar to and different from those recounted by other writers in this chapter.*

Starke does not rely on a great deal of figurative language, but her obituary is gracefully and stylishly written. Take a look at the discussion of sentence structure and punctuation in Chapter 13 for more on how to use style in argument.

LINK TO P. 311

# Hmong Elder Didn't Forget the Old Ways

AMY MARTINEZ STARKE

By 7, she was fetching water from the river. By 14, she was married, and by 21, she was raising livestock, harvesting rice, and raising three small children while her husband was off with other Hmong recruits waging guerrilla war against the Viet Cong.

For years, Sao Yee Cha cared alone for their farm and children. She considered this her duty as wife to Sua Lee as he rose through the ranks to captain.

When the Communists seized power and with her husband marked for execution, the family, now including seven surviving children, set out for a refugee camp on foot through the jungle.

They spent more than two years in a squalid north Thailand camp with thousands of other refugees. In 1978, when Sao Yee was 40 and pregnant with her last child, a church in Portland offered to sponsor the family.

Sao Yee foresaw one big problem: 5
She had heard there was no rice in America, only bread. When the family got off the plane and Coke and sandwiches were placed in front of them, their worst fears were confirmed. "How can we live without rice?" Sao Yee cried.

She was stunned at the sight of so many blue eyes and had to learn how to ride an escalator in her long Laotian skirt.

The woman who had been able to navigate minefields in Laos found she

*Sao Yee Cha in a Thai refugee camp*

faced still more challenges resettling in an apartment near Roosevelt High School.

It was a cold November when they arrived. They had to learn how to turn on the stove and how to use a shower and a Western toilet.

She gave birth to her last child and named him Emanuel° for the hospital where he was born in Portland.

Fred Meyer° took the place of their 10
farm, and she was relieved to learn that there was rice in America. But learning to shop for that rice was difficult.

Then she had to sit in a classroom studying English. Sao Yee had never been to school.

Within four months of their arrival, her husband, a highly decorated veteran, clan elder, shaman° and traditional healer, got a job at the Hilton Portland. Sao Yee got a job picking strawberries, green beans and cucumbers. She sewed bags for potatoes and onions, and she made water hoses.

She saw her children through Portland public schools and through eight marriages to fellow Hmong; she paid four dowries° and collected four dowries.

She tried to learn to drive. But that ended quickly after she hit a telephone pole. She grew to like the Tri-Met° bus system, which brought her independence. Although she could barely read, she could describe the way to Value Village° by visual landmarks.

In 1984, Sao Yee insisted the family 15
buy a house on Southeast Woodstock and 57th instead of renting.

In 1997, they moved to a 10-acre farm in Woodburn.° Sao Yee—now known as Grandma—could raise cows and pigs, silkie chickens and Muscovy ducks, long green beans, hot peppers and green mustard. Grandma and her husband lived with their oldest son's family.

Each morning early, Grandma got up early to cook, pack lunches and do laundry. Men weren't allowed in her kitchen.

"This is my role; this is what I do," she insisted.

She used her cell phone to call friends. For hours, she and those friends were glued to the TV watching Hmong DVDs she bought by the dozens. They were mostly love stories and soap opera dramas, always with Hmong folk songs.

And ever since arriving in Port- 20
land, she followed pro wrestling; she got to go to Wrestlemania in Seattle once. She liked Las Vegas and Spirit

---

***Emanuel:*** Legacy Emanuel Hospital and Health Center, a private hospital in Portland, Oregon, founded in 1912 by Lutherans.

***Fred Meyer:*** a grocery and department store founded in 1922 in Portland, Oregon, and now a division of the Kroger Company.

***shaman:*** in many traditional belief systems, an individual who has the knowledge and power to serve as intermediary between this world and the spirit world.

***dowry:*** in many traditional societies, the money, property, or goods that a bride brings to her husband. The American custom of having the bride's family pay for the wedding developed from this practice.

***Tri-Met:*** The Tri-Country Metropolitan Transportation District of Oregon, Portland's public transportation system.

***Value Village:*** a for-profit chain of secondhand thrift stores.

***Woodburn:*** an agricultural community 30 miles south of Portland.

Sao Yee Cha and one of her grandchildren

Sao Yee Cha in traditional Hmong dress

Sao Yee Cha at home in America

Mountain,° but would gamble no more than $30.

She flew to Minnesota to visit two daughters and took the Greyhound to California to visit another daughter, fretting about the housework left undone back home.

At first, she thought the family's stay in America might be temporary. But gradually she realized this was home and was glad to be here.

Still, 30 years in this country did not dim her dismay at seeing her young ones growing up with new ways of thinking.

The tiny woman who had borne so much now had to bear the burden of enforcing the old ways.

She lectured her daughters and daughters-in-law to respect their husbands' authority. When they resisted and told her of the new ways, she cried.

It hurt her to see her grandchildren accept American culture. "Girls don't court boys!" she cried. "In our tradition, we don't do that! Don't disgrace your family!"

She lamented the loss of a world in which all knew their place, their role according to age and gender and clan.

Grandma Sao Yee, who suffered from several health problems, died suddenly at age 70, two weeks after visiting her daughters in Minneapolis, where she took in the Mall of America.

She never went back to Laos.

At the traditional Hmong mourning ritual, shamans, through ancient words and tunes, retraced her life's journey and guided her soul back to the spot where her placenta° was buried, there to be reunited with her ancestors and then to be reborn.

---

***Spirit Mountain:*** a casino in Grande Ronde, Oregon, operated by the Confederated Tribes of the Grand Ronde Community of Oregon.

***placenta:*** an internal organ that connects the developing fetus with its mother's body; it is expelled shortly after the birth of the child. The placenta is generally incinerated in the West, but in many of the world's cultures is thought to have special powers or value and thus may be buried or disposed of in a special, often ceremonial, fashion.

## RESPOND •

1. How is Sao Yee Cha's bilingualism like and unlike that of others whose experiences have been described in this chapter?
2. What sort of occasion gives rise to an obituary—forensic, deliberative, or epideictic? (The answer may be more complex than it seems. For a discussion of occasions for argument, see Chapter 1.)
3. In what ways do the illustrations that accompany this selection form part of the argument? What do they contribute to the force of the argument? (For a discussion of visual arguments, see Chapter 14.)
4. **Write an essay** in which you compare and contrast bilingualism in America as experienced by two or more of the individuals whose lives, real or fictional, are recounted in this chapter. You may wish to compare the lives of those who were or might have been exiles or refugees, to focus on two or more individuals who discuss childhood memories tied to bilingualism or a language other than English, to examine the challenges faced by two or more as they sought to be part of life in a country that generally identifies itself as being monolingual, or to explore another topic. This essay may employ aspects of factual, definitional, evaluative, and causal arguments as well as rhetorical analysis. (For discussions of these, see Chapters 8–11 and 6, respectively.)
5. Based on what you have learned from readings in this chapter or from other experiences that you have had, interview one or more bilinguals, and **write an essay** in which you analyze their experiences. (Chapter 17 presents information on interviews, and Chapter 18 presents information on using sources from field research.) As in the previous questions, this essay may employ aspects of factual, definitional, evaluative, and causal arguments as well as rhetorical analysis. (For discussions of these, see Chapters 8–11 and 6, respectively.)

# 24
# Why Worry about Food and Water?

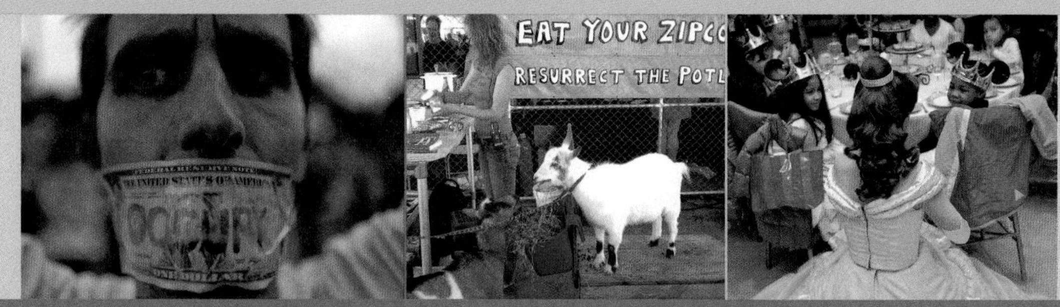


A major change in American culture over the past decade or so has been a growing interest in (and, many would say, obsession with) food and water. Until the economic downturn of 2008, at least, Americans increasingly ate meals in restaurants, bought take-out or prepared food at grocery stores, or had food delivered, and increasingly, they became concerned with where their food comes from, whether and how it is processed, and how it is prepared. Turn on cable television at any hour of the day or night, and you can find someone demonstrating how to prepare food—generally on several different channels.

During the same period, bottled water became ubiquitous in American life. Everywhere you go, people are likely to be carrying bottles of water, whether disposable bottles or bottles designed to be refilled, something that simply didn't happen not so long ago. How might we understand these changes?

In the chapter's opening selection, award-winning cookbook writer and blogger Mark Bittman questions whether junk food really is cheaper than "good food," offering arguments that led some readers to cry foul. Next we present the entries on "Local Food" and "Farm-to-Table" from Wikipedia, the collaboratively created online reference work. Launched in 2001, Wikipedia heralded a major shift in the creation and diffusion of information about nearly everything in over 282 languages. (Given its importance, we figure you should examine an entry from the perspective of argument despite the fact that some professors refuse to let students cite it as a source. If you're like most of us, it's the first source you go to for quick information.) As you're likely aware, the local food movement argues that food grown near you is better for you, the environment, and the world than is food from far away. As you'll see, not everyone agrees. In a largely visual argument, illustrator Claire Ironside compares and contrasts the carbon footprint associated with eating apples and oranges where she lives, demonstrating the challenges of understanding carbon footprints or what it means to claim local food is good food—or even better food.

The next four selections examine the food industry, especially local food, from a range of perspectives. Eric Mortenson writes about how the owners of a small farm have gone organic and are diversifying in their efforts to remain local. In a radio feature for *Marketplace*, Adriene Hill examines the complexity of eating ethically, and listeners who posted comments fear she got it all wrong. In his blog posting, "The Locavore's Dilemma," Christophe Pelletier examines the same issue with much more nuance than Hill does. Malia Wollan's article from a magazine with the provocative name of *Meatpaper* documents "how globalization kills chickens for their parts," reminding us that at the same time there is a push for eating locally, there is also a growing globalization of food distribution. In this particular case, global distribution is clearly working against local food in sub-Saharan Africa. After reading this article, you may never think of chicken in quite the same way.

The next two selections focus on water, specifically the bottled kind. Mark Coleman's review of *Bottlemania: How Water Went on Sale and Why We Bought It* offers an evaluative argument about Elizabeth Royte's 2008 book while the following selection comes from the concluding chapter of the book itself. As you'll see, Royte appreciates the complex reasons to buy bottled water—and to avoid doing so. Along with the excerpt, a visual argument from the *New York Times* helps you visualize the number of plastic bottles created by the bottled water craze in the United States.

The final two selections in the chapter come from *Cook's Country* and *Cook's Illustrated* magazines. The first is an evaluation of ready-to-bake dough for chocolate chip cookies, potentially useful information for the next time you make a grocery store snack raid late in the evening. The second is at once a recipe and an argument for making the real thing from scratch. We did, and our students agreed that folks at *Cook's Illustrated* know what they're talking about when they give advice. Never imagined that a chocolate chip cookie could be an argument? Think again.

For additional material related to this chapter, visit the e-Pages for *Everything's an Argument with Readings* online at **bedfordstmartins.com/everythingsanargument/epages**.

▼ *Although not formally trained in the field, Mark Bittman (1950– ) came to food through journalism and now focuses professionally on cooking at home. He is the author of several award-winning cookbooks, has appeared in several PBS series about cooking, and writes regularly on food for the* New York Times, *where this article appeared in late September 2011. The past few years have seen his concerns turn to the politics of food, including global warming, obesity, and the costs—environmental and personal—of consuming a diet rich in meat. His Web site is markbittman.com. In this selection, a feature, Bittman makes the argument that contrary to received wisdom, junk food is not cheaper in terms of the actual costs. As you read, seek to find places where Bittman might have strengthened his argument by qualifying his claims. As you'll see, those posting comments about the article had no trouble finding places where they'd contend he overstated his case.*

# Is Junk Food Really Cheaper?

MARK BITTMAN

The "fact" that junk food is cheaper than real food has become a reflexive° part of how we explain why so many Americans are overweight, particularly those with lower incomes. I frequently read confident statements like, "When a bag of chips is cheaper than a head of broccoli . . ." or "It's more affordable to feed a family of four at McDonald's than to cook a healthy meal for them at home."

This is just plain wrong. In fact it isn't cheaper to eat highly processed food: a typical order for a family of four—for example, two Big Macs, a cheeseburger, six chicken McNuggets, two medium and two small fries, and two medium and two small sodas—costs, at the McDonald's a hundred steps from where I write, about $28. (Judicious ordering of "Happy Meals" can reduce that to about $23—and you get a few apple slices in addition to the fries!)

In general, despite extensive government subsidies, hyperprocessed food remains more expensive than food cooked at home. You can serve a roasted chicken with vegetables along with a simple salad and milk for about $14, and feed four or even six people. If that's too much money, substitute a meal of rice and canned beans with bacon, green peppers and onions; it's easily enough for four people and costs about $9. (Omitting the bacon, using dried beans, which are also lower in sodium, or substituting carrots for the peppers reduces the price further, of course.)

Another argument runs that junk food is cheaper when measured by the calorie, and that this makes fast food essential for the poor because they need cheap calories. But given that half of the people in this country (and a higher percentage of poor people) consume too many calories rather than too few, measuring food's value by the calorie makes as much sense as measuring a drink's value by its alcohol content. (Why not drink 95 per-

***reflexive:*** automatic or unthinking.

*Always available, easy, and fairly cheap. Is that the problem?* © Daniel Borris for the *New York Times* Multimedia

cent neutral grain spirit, the cheapest way to get drunk?)

5 Besides, that argument, even if we all needed to gain weight, is not always true. A meal of real food cooked at home can easily contain more calories, most of them of the "healthy" variety. (Olive oil accounts for many of the calories in the roast chicken meal, for example.) In comparing prices of real food and junk food, I used supermarket ingredients, not the pricier organic or local food that many people would consider ideal. But food choices are not black and white; the alternative to fast food is not necessarily organic food, any more than the alternative to soda is Bordeaux.°

The alternative to soda is water, and the alternative to junk food is not grass-fed beef and greens from a trendy farmers' market, but anything other than junk food: rice, grains, pasta, beans, fresh vegetables, canned vegetables, frozen vegetables, meat, fish, poultry, dairy products, bread, peanut butter, a thousand other things cooked at home—in almost every case a far superior alternative.

"Anything that you do that's not fast food is terrific; cooking once a week is far better than not cooking at all," says Marion Nestle, professor of food studies at New York University and author of *What to Eat*. "It's the same argument as exercise: more is better than less and some is a lot better than none."

The fact is that most people can afford real food. Even the nearly 50 million Americans who are enrolled in the Supplemental Nutrition Assistance Program (formerly known as food stamps) receive about $5 per person per day, which is far from ideal but enough to survive. So we have to assume that money alone doesn't guide decisions about what to eat. There are, of course, the so-called food deserts, places where it's hard to find food: the Department of Agriculture says that more than two million Americans in low-income rural areas live 10 miles or more from a supermarket, and more than five million households without access to cars live more than a half mile from a supermarket.

Still, 93 percent of those with limited access to supermarkets do have access to vehicles, though it takes them 20 more minutes to travel to the store than the national average. And after a long day of work at one or even two jobs, 20 extra minutes—plus cooking time—must seem like an eternity.

10 Taking the long route to putting food on the table may not be easy, but for almost all Americans it remains a choice, and if you can drive to McDonald's you can drive to Safeway. It's cooking that's the real challenge. (The real challenge is not "I'm too busy to cook." In 2010 the average American, regardless of weekly earnings, watched no less than an hour and a half of television per day. The time is there.)

The core problem is that cooking is defined as work, and fast food is both a pleasure and a crutch. "People really are stressed out with all that they have to do, and they don't want to cook," says Julie Guthman, associate professor of community studies at the University of California, Santa Cruz, and author of the forthcoming *Weighing In: Obesity, Food Justice, and the Limits of Capitalism*. "Their reaction is, 'Let me enjoy what I want to

---

***Bordeaux:*** here, a wine from the well-known Bordeaux region of France.

*Comparison shopping and comparing nutritional value*

eat, and stop telling me what to do.' And it's one of the few things that less well-off people have: they don't have to cook."

It's not just about choice, however, and rational arguments go only so far, because money and access and time and skill are not the only considerations. The ubiquity,° convenience and habit-forming appeal of hyperprocessed foods have largely drowned out the alternatives: there are five fast-food restaurants for every supermarket in the United States; in recent decades the adjusted for inflation price of fresh produce has increased by 40 percent while the price of soda and processed food has decreased by as much as 30 percent; and nearly inconceivable resources go into encouraging consumption in restaurants: fast-food companies spent $4.2 billion on marketing in 2009.

Furthermore, the engineering behind hyperprocessed food makes it virtually addictive. A 2009 study by the Scripps Research Institute indicates that overconsumption of fast food "triggers addiction-like neuroaddictive° responses" in the brain, making it harder to trigger the release of dopamine.° In other words the more fast food we eat, the more we need to give us pleasure; thus the report suggests that the same mecha-

***ubiquity:*** being present everywhere.

***neuroaddictive:*** "neuro" (of the nervous system) + "addictive."

nisms underlie drug addiction and obesity.

This addiction to processed food is the result of decades of vision and hard work by the industry. For 50 years, says David A. Kessler, former commissioner of the Food and Drug Administration and author of *The End of Overeating,* companies strove to create food that was "energy-dense, highly stimulating, and went down easy. They put it on every street corner and made it mobile, and they made it socially acceptable to eat anytime and anyplace. They created a food carnival, and that's where we live. And if you're used to self-stimulation every 15 minutes, well, you can't run into the kitchen to satisfy that urge."

15 Real cultural changes are needed to turn this around. Somehow, no-nonsense cooking and eating—roasting a chicken, making a grilled cheese sandwich, scrambling an egg, tossing a salad—must become popular again, and valued not just by hipsters in Brooklyn or locavores° in Berkeley. The smart campaign is not to get McDonald's to serve better food but to get people to see cooking as a joy rather than a burden, or at least as part of a normal life.

As with any addictive behavior, this one is most easily countered by educating children about the better way. Children, after all, are born without bad habits. And yet it's adults who must begin to tear down the food carnival.

The question is how? Efforts are everywhere. The People's Grocery in Oakland secures affordable groceries for low-income people. Zoning laws in Los Angeles restrict the number of fast-food restaurants in high-obesity neighborhoods. There's the Healthy Food Financing Initiative, a successful Pennsylvania program to build fresh food outlets in underserved areas, now being expanded nationally. FoodCorps and Cooking Matters teach young people how to farm and cook.

As Malik Yakini, executive director of the Detroit Black Community Food Security Network, says, "We've seen minor successes, but the food movement is still at the infant stage, and we need a massive social shift to convince people to consider healthier options."

How do you change a culture? The answers, not surprisingly, are complex. "Once I look at what I'm eating," says Dr. Kessler, "and realize it's not food, and I ask 'what am I doing here?' that's the start. It's not about whether I think it's good for me, it's about changing how I feel. And we change how people feel by changing the environment."

20 Obviously, in an atmosphere where any regulation is immediately labeled "nanny statism,"° changing "the environment" is difficult. But we've done this before, with tobacco. The 1998 tobacco settlement limited cigarette marketing and forced manufacturers to finance anti-smoking campaigns—a negotiated change that led to an environmental one that in turn led to a cultural one, after which kids said to their parents, "I wish you didn't smoke." Smoking had to be converted from a cool habit into one practiced by pariahs.°

Chapter 7 discusses the importance of understanding conditions of rebuttal. How well do you think Bittman anticipates rebuttals to his argument? Where should he anticipate additional rebuttals?

LINK TO P. 143

***dopamine:*** hormone produced by the brain that stimulates the "reward circuit," which works to increase pleasurable feelings. Addictive drugs, among other substances, trigger the release of dopamine, flooding the reward circuit, which, over time, requires greater doses of the drug to achieve the same level of effect.

***locavores:*** people who make a point of eating food produced locally.

***nanny statism:*** a term that originated in Britain to criticize governmental policies that are seen as overly interventionist, that is, policies that seek to control people's lives in various ways. A nanny is, of course, a person who takes care of someone else's children for pay.

***pariahs:*** social outcasts.

*Where Chicken McNuggets come from*

A similar victory in the food world is symbolized by the stories parents tell me of their kids booing as they drive by McDonald's.

To make changes like this more widespread we need action both cultural and political. The cultural lies in celebrating real food; raising our children in homes that don't program them for fast-produced, eaten-on-the-run, high-calorie, low-nutrition junk; giving them the gift of appreciating the pleasures of nourishing one another and enjoying that nourishment together.

Political action would mean agitating to limit the marketing of junk; forcing its makers to pay the true costs of production; recognizing that advertising for fast food is not the exercise of free speech but behavior manipulation of addictive substances; and making certain that real food is affordable and available to everyone. The political challenge is the more difficult one, but it cannot be ignored.

What's easier is to cook at every opportunity, to demonstrate to family and neighbors that the real way is the better way. And even the more fun way: kind of like a carnival.

**RESPOND.**

1. What is Bittman's argument? How would you characterize it? Is it an argument of fact? Of definition? Of evaluation? A causal argument? A proposal? (See Chapters 8–12 for a discussion of these kinds of arguments.) However you characterize it, find examples of the other kinds of argument in Bittman's article as well.
2. Interestingly, Bittman admits that "rational arguments go only so far" (paragraph 12), a major assumption of this textbook. By this point in the selection, what rational arguments has Bittman presented for his claims? Following this concession, what arguments does he offer in discussing why rational arguments are insufficient to change the situation he is criticizing?
3. What sort of ethos does Bittman create for himself in this essay? Based on this article, what sort of person do you think he might be? Why? (See Chapter 3 for a discussion of ethos and arguments based on character.)
4. Study the visual feature carefully. How is it designed to make an argument? How does it contribute support to Bittman's article? What design features make it especially effective? (See Chapter 14 for a discussion of visual and multimedia arguments.)

5. As Chapter 7 explains, effective writers qualify their claims in order to represent the complexity of reality, on the one hand, and in order to make their task simpler, on the other—after all, it is generally much easier to provide sufficient support for a qualified claim than for one that is not qualified in some way. How does Bittman qualify his claims? Make a list of places in the article where he qualifies a claim and/or acknowledges a counterargument before seeking to demonstrate that his perspective is the better one.
6. Readers of the *Times* posting comments about this article did not always think that Bittman had qualified his claims sufficiently or that he had considered all of the relevant facts he should have. Examine the comments at http://nyti.ms/vmNlme, noting criticisms of Bittman's position or the arguments he offered in support of his position. Although you may wish to read all the comments, the "Highlights" represent comments the editors find most insightful while "Readers' Recommendations" show how frequently other readers voted for (or "liked") a comment. Once you have studied these comments, **write an evaluative essay** in which you evaluate Bittman's argument and his claims. As you write, you will likely wish to refer to comments you read on the *Times* Web site, so you will need to document these as sources. (See Chapter 10 for a discussion of evaluative arguments and Chapters 19 and 21 on using and documenting sources. You may find Chapter 5 on fallacies useful if you find that commenters directly or indirectly contend that Bittman has made fallacious arguments.)

*This selection comprises two related entries downloaded from Wikipedia on December 29, 2011. It is no exaggeration to claim that Wikipedia has changed the way many people think about the nature of, the creation of, and access to knowledge. The opening paragraph of the entry for "Wikipedia" (at least in late December 2011, when this headnote was written) explains that the site was launched in 2001, that volunteers create the entries for the site, that it is the most consulted general electronic reference work, and that there are editions of the site in 282 languages with the English-language site being the largest by far. The site's name is what linguists term a* portmanteau, *a word that blends parts of two other words to create a new word: here,* wiki, *the Hawaiian word for "fast," and* -pedia *from* encyclopedia. *Given the importance of this new research tool (one used by nearly everyone, whether it is admitted or not!), it is appropriate that we include entries from Wikipedia in a text entitled* Everything's an Argument *and ask you to evaluate them. Read these entries on two levels—as a source of information (a factual argument) about local food and about the farm-to-table movement, on the one hand, and as an argument about collaboration and collaboratively created knowledge, on the other.*

# Local Food

## FROM WIKIPEDIA, THE FREE ENCYCLOPEDIA

This article **is written like a personal reflection or essay rather than an encyclopedic description of the subject.** Please help improve it by rewriting it in an encyclopedic style. *(February 2011)*

It has been suggested that *Farm-to-table* be merged into this article or section. (Discuss) *Proposed since January 2011.*

**Local food** or the **local food movement** is a "collaborative effort to build more locally based, self-reliant food economies—one in which sustainable food production, processing, distribution, and consumption is integrated to enhance the economic, environmental, and social health of a particular place."[1] It is part of the concept of local purchasing and local economies; a preference to buy locally produced goods and services rather than those produced by corporatized institutions.

*The Marylebone farmers' market in London, United Kingdom*

It is not solely a geographical concept. A United States Department of Agriculture publication explains local food as "related to the distance between food producers and consumers," as well as "defined in terms of social and supply chain characteristics."[2]

## Contents



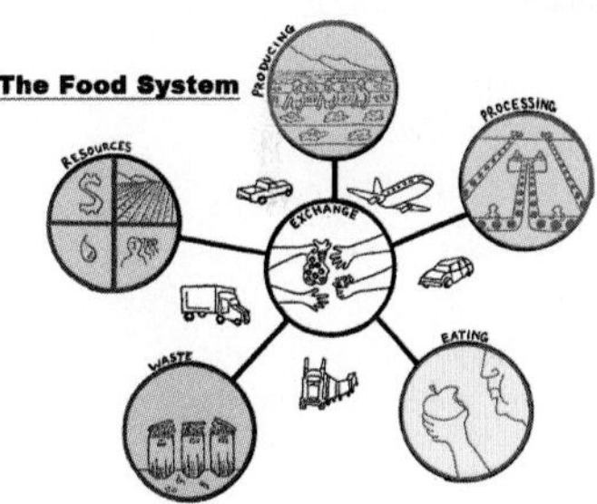

*Local food system diagram*

## Local Food Systems

The term "Food System" refers to how food is produced and reaches consumers, and why we eat what we do. It subsumes the terms "food chain" and "food economy," which are both too narrowly linear and/or economic. The food system can be broken down to three basic components: Biological, Economic/political, and Social/cultural. The Biological refers to the organic processes of food production; the Economic/political refers to institutional moderation of different groups' participation in and control of the system, and the Social/cultural refers to the "personal relations, community values, and cultural relations which affect people's use of food."[3]

Local food systems are an alternative to the global corporate models where producers and consumers are separated through a chain of processors/manufacturers, shippers, and retailers. They "are complex networks of relationships between actors including producers, distributors, retailers, and consumers grounded in a particular place. These systems are the unit of measure by which participants in local food movements are working to increase food security and ensure the economic, ecological, and social sustainability of communities."[4]

## Definitions of "Local"

There is no single definition of "local" or "local food systems" in terms of the 5
geographic distance between production and consumption. But defining "local" based on marketing arrangements, such as farmers selling directly to consumers at regional farmers' markets or to schools, is well recognized.[5] There are "a number of different definitions for local [that] have been used or recorded by researchers assessing local food systems [and] most [are] informed by political or geographic boundaries. Among the more widely circulated and popular defining parameters is the concept of food miles, which has been suggested for policy recommendations."[6] In 2008 Congress passed H.R.2419, which amended the Consolidated Farm and Rural Development Act. In the amendment "locally" and "regionally" are grouped together and are defined as

> (I) the locality or region in which the final product is marketed, so that the total distance that the product is transported is less than 400 miles from the origin of the product; or (II) the State in which the product is produced.
>
> —Bill Text—110th Congress (2007–2008)—THOMAS (Library of Congress [http://thomas.loc.gov/cgi-bin/query/z?c110:h2419])

In May 2010 the USDA acknowledged this definition in an informational leaflet.[7]

The concept of "local" is also seen in terms of ecology, where food production is considered from the perspective of a basic ecological unit defined by its climate, soil, watershed, species, and local agrisystems, a unit also called an ecoregion or a foodshed. The concept of the foodshed is similar to that of a watershed; it is an area where food is grown and eaten.

## Contemporary Local Food Market

The USDA included statistics about the growing local food market in the leaflet released in May 2010. The statistics are as follows; "Direct-to-consumer marketing amounted to $1.2 billion in current dollar sales in 2007, according to the 2007 Census of Agriculture, compared with $551 million in 1997. Direct-to-consumer sales accounted for 0.4 percent of total agricultural sales in 2007, up from 0.3 percent in 1997. If nonedible products are excluded from total agricultural sales, direct-to-consumer sales accounted for 0.8 percent of agricultural sales in 2007. The number of farmers' markets rose to 5,274 in 2009, up from 2,756 in 1998 and 1,755 in 1994, according to USDA's Agricultural Marketing Service. In 2005, there were 1,144 community-supported agriculture organizations (CSAs) in operation, up from 400 in 2001 and 2 in 1986, according to a study by the nonprofit, nongovernmental organization National Center for Appropriate Technology. In early 2010, estimates exceeded 1,400, but the number could be much larger. The number of farm to school programs, which use local farms as food suppliers for school meals programs, increased to 2,095 in 2009, up from 400 in 2004 and 2 in the 1996–97 school year, according to the National Farm to School Network. Data from the 2005 School Nutrition and Dietary Assessment Survey, sponsored by USDA's Food and Nutrition Service, showed that 14 percent of school districts participated in farm to school programs, and 16 percent reported having guidelines for purchasing locally grown produce."[8]

*A cheesemaking workshop with goats at Maker Faire 2011. The sign declares, "Eat your Zipcode!"*

Networks of local farmers and producers are now collaborating together in the UK, in Europe as well as in Canada and in the U.S. to provide an online farmers market to customers. In this way, more consumers can now buy locally even online when they cannot attend a local farmers market. This also provides local farmers and producers another route to market and keeps overheads low as website costs are shared.

Examples of this are: Tastes of Anglia (http://www.tastesofanglia.com) in the UK, BALLE (http://www.livingeconomics.org) (Business Alliance for Local Living Economies), and the 30 Mile Meal Project (http://www.athensohio.com/30mile) in the U.S.

Supermarkets are beginning to tap into the local foods market as well. 10
Walmart announced plans in 2008 to spend $400 million during that year on locally grown produce.[9] Wegman's, a 71-store chain across the northeast, has purchased local foods for over 20 years as well. In their case, the produce manager in each store controls the influx of local foods—the relationships with the local farms are not centrally controlled.[10] A recent study led by Miguel Gomez, a professor of Applied Economics and Management at Cornell University and supported by the Atkinson Center for a Sustainable Future found that in many instances, the supermarket supply chain did much better in terms of food miles and fuel consumption for each pound compared to farmers markets. It suggests that selling local foods through supermarkets may be more economically viable and sustainable than through farmers markets.[11]

### Locavore and Invasivore

Those who prefer to eat locally grown/produced food sometimes call themselves **locavores** or **localvores**.[12] This term began circulation around August 2005 in the San Francisco area when a number of "foodies" launched a website, Locavores.com, after being inspired by the book *Coming Home to Eat* by ecologist Gary Paul Nabham.

More recently, an "invasivore" movement has emerged as a subset of the locavore movement, which encourages the consumption of nonindigenous invasive species with the intent of controlling harmful populations.[13][14]

### Local Food Campaigns

#### North Carolina 10% Campaign

Launched in late 2009, North Carolina's 10% campaign is aimed at stimulating economic development, creating jobs, and promoting North Carolina's agricultural offerings.[15] The campaign is a partnership between the Center for Environmental Farming Systems (CEFS), with support from N.C. Cooperative Extension and the Golden LEAF Foundation. More than 4,400 individuals and 427 businesses, including 76 restaurants, have signed on to the campaign through the website (http://www.nc10percent.com/) as they have pledged to spend 10 percent of their food budget on locally sourced foods. Participants receive weekly emails prompting them to record how much they have spent on local food that week. Currently the campaign reports that more than $10 million has been recorded by participants. "The $10 million mark is a true testament to the commitment of our agricultural community and the quality of North Carolina–grown products."[16]

The North Carolina Center for Environmental farming estimates that if all North Carolinians allocated 10% of their food expenditures on locally produced food, then $3.5 billion would be generated for the state's economy. Brunswick, Cabarrus, Chatham, Guilford, Forsyth, Onslow, and Rockingham counties have adopted resolutions in support of the campaign. Stores are advertising local products with buy-local food labels. CEFS co-director, Nancy Creamer, explains the following: "North Carolina is uniquely positioned to capitalize on the increased consumer demand for locally produced foods. . . . Agriculture is the backbone of our economy. The state's climate, soils, and coastal resources support production of a wide variety of produce, meats, fish, and seafood."[17]

## See Also

- Ark of Taste
- Community-based economics
- Community-supported agriculture
- The Declaration for Healthy Food and Agriculture
- Fallen Fruit
- Farm to fork
- Keep Austin Weird
- Local Food Plus
- Localism (politics)
- Low carbon diet
- Slow Food
- Slow Money
- Sustainable agriculture
- Sustainable Table
- Terra Madre
- Terroir
- The 100-Mile Diet
- The Omnivore's Dilemma
- Vertical farming
- Wild farming
- WWOOF

## References

1. ^ Feenstra, G. (2002) "Creating space for sustainable food systems: Lessons from the field." *Agriculture and Human Values*. 19(2). 99–106.
2. ^ Martinez, Steve. "Local Food Systems Concepts, Impacts, and Issues" (http://permanent.access.gpo.gov/lps125302/ERR97/.pdf). Economic Research Service. Retrieved 10 May 2011.

3. ^ Tansey, Geoff; Worsley, Tony (1995). "Food System—A Guide." Earthscan. Online version available at: http://www.knovel.com.lp.hscl.ufl.edu/web/portal/browse/display?_EXT_KNOVEL_DISPLAY_bookid=2284&VerticalID=0

4. ^ Dunne, Jonnie B.; Chambers, Kimberlee J.; Giombolini, Katlyn J.; Schlegel, Sheridan A. "What does 'local' mean in the grocery store? Multiplicity in food retailers' perspectives on sourcing and marketing local foods" (http://journals.cambridge.org.proxy.libraries.rutgers.edu/download.php?file=%2FRAF%2FRAF26_01%2FS1742170510000402a.pdf&code=53cc6732d2c77ece589a28152cc6112a). *Renewable Agriculture and Food Systems.* pp. 46–59. doi:10.1017/S1742170510000402 (http://dx.doi.org/10.1017%2FS1742170510000402).

5. ^ Martinez, Steve. "Local Food Systems Concepts, Impacts, and Issues" (http://permanent.access.gpo.gov/lps125302/ERR97.pdf). Economic Research Service. Retrieved 10 May 2011.

6. ^ Dunne, Jonnie B.; Chambers, Kimberlee J.; Giombolini, Katlyn J.; Schlegel, Sheridan A. "What does 'local' mean in the grocery store? Multiplicity in food retailers' perspectives on sourcing and marketing local foods" (http://journals.cambridge.org.proxy.libraries.rutgers.edu/download.php?file=%2FRAF%2FRAF26_01%2FS1742170510000402a.pdf&code=53cc6732d2c77ece589a28152cc6112a). *Renewable Agriculture and Food Systems.* pp. 46–59. doi:10.1017/S1742170510000402 (http://dx.doi.org/10.1017%2FS1742170510000402).

7. ^ "Consumer demand for food that is locally produced, marketed, and consumed . . ." (http://www.ers.usda.gov/Publications/ERR97/ERR97_ReportSummary.pdf), Local Food Systems: Concepts, Impacts, and Issues," by Steve Martinez, Michael Hand, Michelle Da Pra, Susan Pollack, Katherine Ralston, Travis Smith, Stephen Vogel, Shellye Clark, Luanne Lohr, Sarah Low, and Constance Newman, May 2010, ERS (Economic Research Service) Report Summary, U.S. Department of Agriculture.

8. ^ Martinez, Steve. "Local Food Systems Concepts, Impacts, and Issues" (http://permanent.access.gpo.gov/lps125302/ERR97.pdf). Economic Research Service. Retrieved 10 May 2011.

9. ^ Burros, Marian (6 August 2008). "Supermarket Chains Narrow Their Sights" (http://www.nytimes.com/2008/08/06/dining/06local.html). *New York Times.* Retrieved 20 July 2011.

10. ^ Burros, Marian (6 August 2008). "Supermarket Chains Narrow Their Sights" (http://www.nytimes.com/2008/08/06/dining/06local.html). *New York Times*. Retrieved 20 July 2011.

11. ^ Prevor, Jim (1 October 2010). "Jim Prevor's Perishable Pundit" (http://www.perishablepundit.com/index.php?date=10/01/10&pundit=1). Retrieved 20 July 2011.

12. ^ Roosevelt, M. (2006) "The Lure of the 100-Mile Diet" (http://www.time.com/time/magazine/article/0,9171,1200783,00.html). *Time*. Sunday, June 11, 2006. Accessed on Nov. 1, 2007, at 10:35 am PDT.

13. ^ "A Diet for an Invaded Planet." *New York Times*, January 2, 2011 (http://www.nytimes.com/2011/01/02/weekinreview/02gorman.html).

14. ^ invasivore.org (http://invasivore.org/2011/01/welcome-to-invasivore-org).

15. ^ http://www.cefs.ncsu.edu.libproxy.lib.unc.edu/A.

16. ^ "North Carolina campaign promoting locally grown food." Southeast Farm Press (Online Exclusive), 22 Nov. 2011. General OneFile. Web. 11 Dec. 2011.

17. ^ "10% campaign off to a strong start." (2011, January). *NC Farm Bureau Magazine*. Retrieved from http://www.ncfbmagazine.org/2011/01/10-campaign-off-to-strong-start.

## External Links

- Tasting Food, Tasting Sustainability: Defining the Attributes of an Alternative Food System with Competent, Ordinary People. (http://findarticles.com/p/articles/mi_qa3800/is_200007/ai_n8899894) Human Organization 59:2 (July): 177–186.
- Global List of Local Food Systems Related Organizations on WiserEarth (http://www.wiserearth.org/organization/limitToMasterid/339/limitToType/aof).
- Moseley, W. G. 2007. "Farmers in developing world hurt by 'eat local' philosophy in U.S." *San Francisco Chronicle*. November 18. pg. E5. (http://articles.sfgate.com/2007-11-18/opinion/17270262_1_fair-trade-organic-food-organic-farming).
- *The Ontario Table is a local culinary guide, character study of a soil, a region, a terrain, a people, a cuisine, even of a place in time. (http://www.ontariotable.com).

Retrieved from "http//en.wikipedia.org/w/index.php&title=Local_food&oldid=470356762"

Categories: Food politics | Rural community development | Sustainable food system

- This page was last modified on 9 January 2012 at 01:12.
- 

# Farm-to-Table

## FROM WIKIPEDIA, THE FREE ENCYCLOPEDIA

This article **needs additional citations for verification.** Please help improve this article by adding citations to reliable sources. Unsourced material may be challenged and removed. *(January 2011)*

It has been suggested that this article or section be merged into *Local food*. (Discuss) *Proposed since January 2011.*

**Farm-to-table** (or **farm-to-fork**) refers to, in the food safety field, the stages of the production of food: harvesting, storage, processing, packaging, sales, and consumption.[1] Farm-to-table also refers to a movement concerned with producing food locally and delivering that food to local consumers. Linked to the local food movement, the movement is promoted by some in the agriculture, food service, and restaurant communities. It may also be associated with organic farming initiatives, sustainable agriculture, and community-supported agriculture.

Many farm-to-table advocates cite the works of Wendell Berry, Wes Jackson, Michael Pollan, John Jeavons, Alice Waters, Joel Salatin, and others in their preference for the freshest ingredients and in their attempts to educate their customers about the link between farmers, farm communities, ancient food-production practices, and the food we eat. Increasingly, the public backlash against genetically modified organisms in our food supply has added a note of political activism to what had been, until recently, a largely aesthetic movement. Farm-to-table restaurants may buy their produce directly from farmers, usually local. In a few cases, the restaurants and farms may be owned and operated by the same people. Restaurants who choose to buy from local food producers regularly yield healthier, better quality meals for their customers.[2] The farm-to-table movement has arisen more or less concurrently with recent changes in attitude about food safety, food freshness, food seasonality, and small-farm economics. Advocates and practitioners of the farm-to-table model frequently cite as their motivations the scarcity of fresh, local ingredients; the poor flavor of ingredients shipped from afar; the poor nutritional integrity of shipped ingredients; the encroachment of genetically modified foods into the food economy; the disappearance of small family farms; the disappearance of heirloom and open-pollinated fruits and vegetables; and the dangers of a highly centralized food-growing and distribution system.

Among the first vocal and influential farm-to-table businesses were: Alice Waters' Chez Panisse restaurant in Berkeley, California; Jerry Traunfeld's Herbfarm in Washington; Blake Spalding and Jen Castle's Hell's Backbone Grill in Boulder, Utah; and Stone Barns restaurant outside New York City. In the last few years the number of farm-to-table operations has grown rapidly.

Recently, some food and agriculture writers have begun to describe a philosophical divide among chefs: the "food-as-art," or, in some cases, "molecular gastronomy" camp, including Ferran Adrià and Grant Achatz have increasingly focused on "food made strange," in which the ingredients are so transformed as to be surprising and even unrecognizable in the final food product. The farm-to-table chefs, on the other hand, have increasingly come to rely upon extremely fresh ingredients that have been barely modified, sometimes presented raw just a few feet from where they grew. Generally, the farm-to-table chefs rely on traditional farmhouse cooking, and may refer to their preparations as "vernacular food" or "peasant food," with its emphasis on freshness, seasonality, local availability, and simple preparations.

## See Also

- Food miles
- Low carbon diet
- Organic farming
- Sustainable agriculture
- Kitchen garden

## References

1. ^ Sari Edelstein, *Food and nutrition at risk in America: Food insecurity, biotechnology, food safety, and bioterrorism* (2009), p. 72.
2. ^ Parish, L. (2011). "Farm-to-table trends." *Journal of Business* (10756124), 26(17), 11.

### External Links

- Center for Environmental Farming Systems (http://www.cefs.ncsu.edu/)
- USDA article "Food Safety: From Farm to Fork" (http://www.ars.usda.gov/is/pr/2006/061023.htm)
- Stone Barns restaurant website (http://www.bluehillfarm.com/food/blue-hill-stone-barns)
- Biointensive gardening website (http://www.growbiointensive.org/)
- Blake Spalding and Jen Castle's Hell's Backbone Grill website (http://www.hellsbackbonegrill.com/)
- Alice Waters' Chez Panisse restaurant website (http://www.chezpanisse.com/)
- Adrian Ferrà's elBulli restaurant website (http://www.elbulli.com/)
- Grant Achatz's Alinea restaurant website (http://www.alinea-restaurant.com/pages/staff/staff_top.html)
- New Mexico Farm to Table website (http://www.farmtotablenm.org/)
- [1] (http://ehis.ebscohost.com/eds/pdfviewer/pdfviewer?sid=5451feba-6f7b-44cd-b8e6-62d176f3d074%40sessionmgr112&vid=3&hid=101)

Retrieved from "http://en.wikipedia.org/w/index.php?title=Farm-to-table&oldid=452890611"

Categories: Sustainable food system

- This page was last modified on 28 September 2011 at 15:46.
- 

### RESPOND

1. In what ways is an encyclopedia article, including one in a collaborative, online reference work like Wikipedia, an argument? What kind of argument is it or should it be? What evidence can you cite for your claims?
2. The audiences for encyclopedia entries are always multiple. On the one hand, people with no background in a given subject should be able to read an entry and get a clear picture of the state of knowledge on that

subject, including current debates about it. On the other hand, experts on a topic should be able to read an entry, nodding approvingly as they move through the article and finding that the relevant information has been presented clearly and faithfully. Did you find that the creators of these articles wrote appropriately for someone with your level of knowledge on the subject? Why or why not? How does your response compare to those of your classmates, who may have read the articles with different amounts or kinds of background knowledge?

3. An interesting part of Wikipedia is the way in which it makes the collaborative process visible to those who wish to participate in it or understand it. For example, at the top of entries, readers often see tabs labeled "Article," "Discussion" or "Read" (which discusses aspects of the entry), "Edit" (which permits authorized users to post editorial changes), and "View History" (which keeps track of all changes made and the person making them). As the notes at the beginning of each of these entries indicate, there was a suggestion that the second entry be merged into the first, a suggestion that was ultimately rejected. To what extent do you see the two entries as overlapping? To what extent do you see them as different? Should they be merged? (You may want to consult the "Discussion" on these entries; if the archive on this discussion is still available, it may give you some additional ideas about the links between the two entries.)
4. Some of the contributors to and editors of entries are not happy with the "Local Food" entry, as noted at the beginning of the article. Consult the Wikipedia entry on "Encyclopedia Style" to get a clear idea of the criteria by which contributors and editors evaluate entries. Do you agree that the "Local Food" entry does not meet these criteria? Why or why not? What revisions might you suggest to improve the entry? In response to this question, you may either **write an essay** in which you propose a set of changes to the entry or you may **rewrite the entry** so that it conforms to Wikipedia's standards. (Truth be told, your professor may make the choice for you! If you need help with proposals, see Chapter 12.)
5. Investigate the local food movement in your own town or in a nearby town or city. What forms does it take? Is it a new phenomenon, or is it part of the way that people have already eaten there? (You may need to interview some older people to gather such information.) If there is little or no evidence for a local food movement where you live, try to discover why. If you find strong evidence of such a movement, what can you discover about its origins? About how it has changed? **Write an essay** in which you report your results. The essay may be primarily factual in nature, or it may be definitional, evaluative, or causal, or it may be a proposal. (For a discussion of these types of essays, see Chapters 8–12.)

Claire Ironside is an instructor of illustration at Sheridan College School of Animation, Art, and Design in Ontario, Canada, where she teaches in the applied illustration program. With training in environmental and communication design studies, she is especially interested in issues of social engagement and activism as well as sustainability. This selection, "Apples to Oranges," uses primarily visual means to make its argument. Its title plays on an everyday expression that is used when two things are compared unfairly because they are fundamentally different in one or more ways. We found this selection in Food, a 2008 book edited by John Knechtel. It appears in the Alphabet City series, copublished by Alphabet City Media and the MIT Press. Each volume focuses on a single theme and brings together artists and writers from diverse perspectives to encourage readers to question their basic assumptions about the topic. As you study this selection, think about what it would take to translate Ironside's argument into words alone and whether doing so is even possible. (By the way, to convert kilometers to miles, multiply the number of kilometers by .62 to get a rough equivalent.)

# Making a Visual Argument: Apples to Oranges

CLAIRE IRONSIDE

The Big Apple
Colborne, Ontario

photo: Claire Ironside

# apples to oranges

claire ironside

The Orange Julep
Montreal, Quebec

photo: Adrian Black

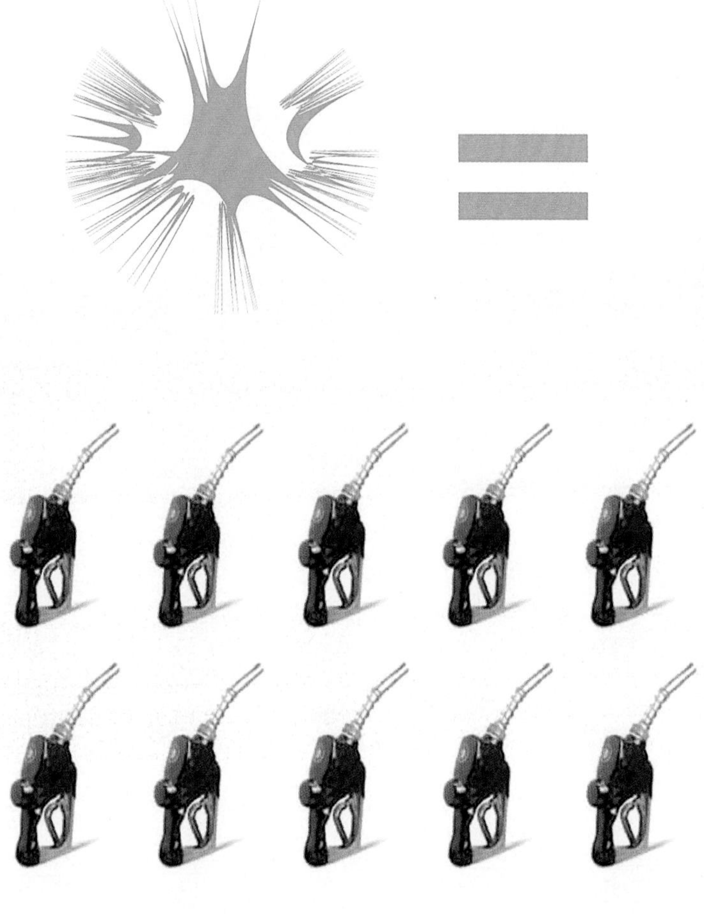

**Your food travels an average distance of 2,414 kilometers to get to your plate, which is a large part of the reason every calorie you eat takes an average of 10 fossil fuel calories to produce.***

**A look at the fossil fuel inputs of a locally grown, organic apple, and a California orange, both destined for the Toronto market, reveals the difference.**

* Dr. Joseph Pimentel, Cornell University professor of ecology and agricultural science.

# Colborne to Toronto
# 178 km

# Orange County to Toronto
# 5,632 km

# Fossil fuel inputs of a local, organic apple

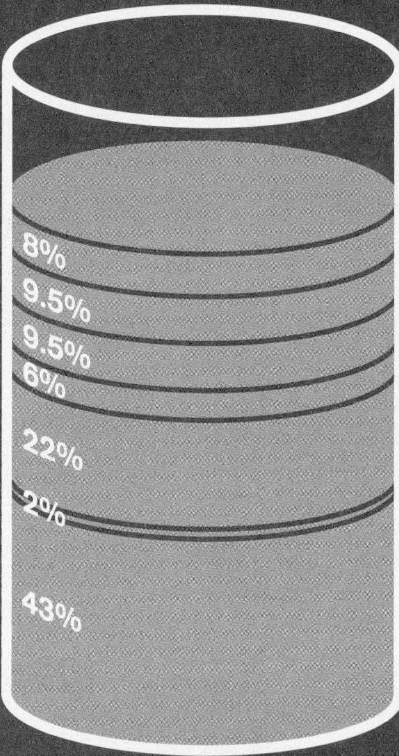

# Fossil fuel inputs of a Californian orange

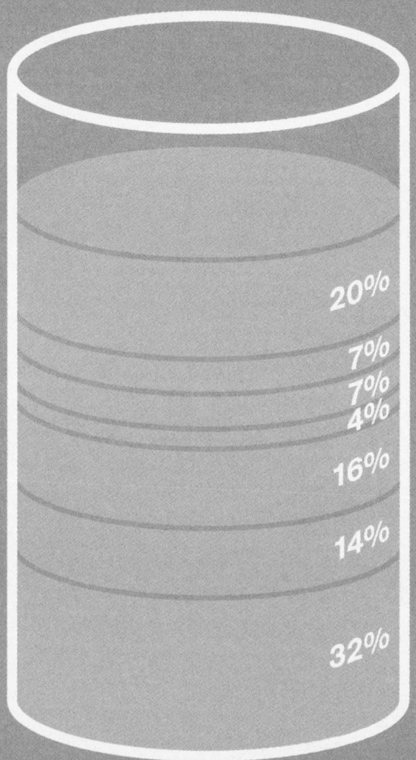

# Total fossil fuel footprint of a local, organic apple compared with average

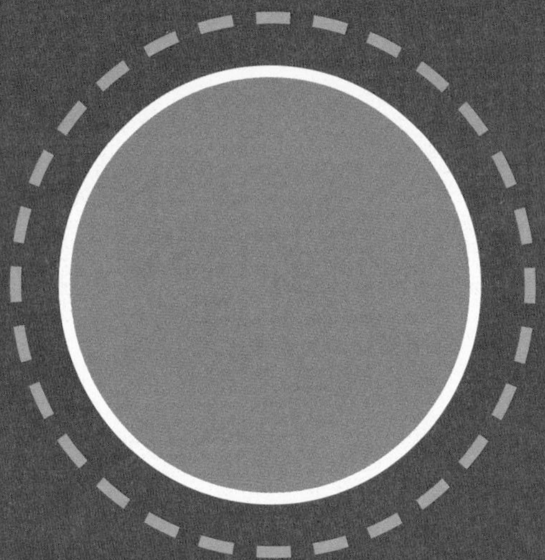

APPLE FOSSIL FUEL FOOTPRINT

1:8

# Total fossil fuel footprint of a Californian orange compared with average

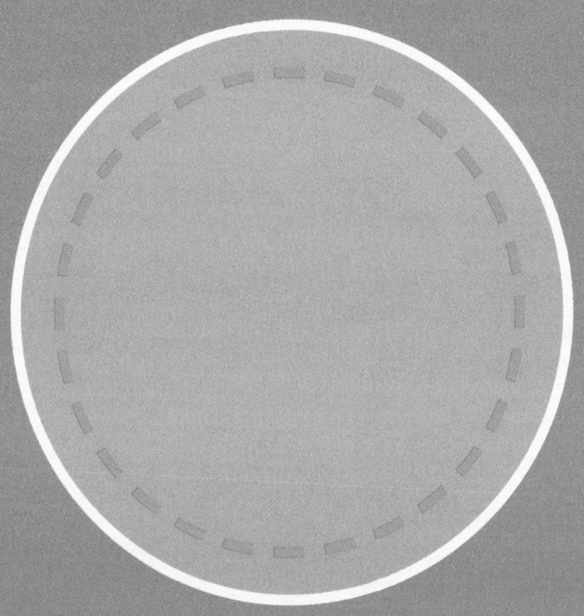

ORANGE FOSSIL FUEL FOOTPRINT

1:12

## RESPOND •

1. What is Ironside's explicit argument? What kind of argument is it (for example, of fact or definition)? Might she be making an implicit argument? What would that argument be? And what kind of argument is it?
2. Analyze each pair of pages in Ironside's argument. What does each juxtaposition contribute to her argument? How would you characterize the purpose of the comparison related to fossil-fuel inputs? What value might there be in the details given? What sorts of conclusions might we draw from this juxtaposition?
3. Evaluate the visual aspects of Ironside's argument, including her choice of colors.
4. Ironside's argument is part of a larger debate about carbon footprints. As this book goes to press, there are many Internet sites where you can calculate your own footprint. One is the Nature Conservancy's "What's My Carbon Footprint?" (http://www.nature.org/initiatives/climatechange/calculator). After you've calculated your footprint at this site, visit others, and compare the calculations you get there. **Write an essay** in which you report your findings and discuss the factors that might account for any discrepancies. (For a discussion of arguments of fact and definition, see Chapters 8 and 9, respectively.)
5. Ironside takes a single fact (about the relationship between each calorie you consume and the fossil-fuel calories that are required to produce it) and illustrates this fact in a complex and sophisticated way. She compares two examples and demonstrates the nature of the average by showing an example that is above average and one that is below average. Choose a single fact about food and think of a visual argument that can illustrate it (as Ironside has here). You can either create the visual argument or describe it in words by discussing aspects of design (color, shape, images, and so on). (For a discussion of visual argument, see Chapter 14.)

*Eric Mortenson has been a reporter in Oregon since 1980, working for both the* Eugene Register-Guard *and the* Oregonian, *the daily newspaper of the Portland metropolitan area, where this selection first appeared in September 2011. At the* Oregonian, *Mortenson writes regularly about issues related to the environment, land use, agriculture, and forestry. In an email to one of the authors of this textbook, he reports that he grew up in Hood River, Oregon, surrounded by orchards, and that his summer jobs involved picking fruit, operating combines, plowing, and driving wheat trucks. His older brother has spent his career working for a timber company. He hopes that these experiences give him a better understanding of the issues he writes about than someone who has not had these opportunities might have.*

*As is often the case with newspapers that have print and online editions, this article appeared with two different titles. The online edition uses the title that we use below, while the print edition carried the title "Family Pulls In, Branches Out: Tom and Barbara Boyer Adapted Their 400 Acres to Fit a Changing Market, Lifestyle." As you read this article, consider which title you think is more appropriate; also pay attention to what this article teaches about the complexities of eating locally as well as the questions it raises about sustainability.*

# A Diversified Farm Prospers in Oregon's Willamette Valley by Going Organic and Staying Local

**ERIC MORTENSON**

McMINNVILLE°—To hear Tom Boyer explain it, farming has a proper pace to it. He shakes his head at farmers who get too big too fast. The ones who get out ahead of themselves in terms of acreage, bank loans or expensive equipment. In their haste, those fellows are "right next to stumbling," he says.

Sometimes, of course, every farmer races from chore to chore, hustles to beat the weather and scrambles to solve the latest tractor breakdown. "It keeps you high-stepping to keep on top of it," Boyer says.

On their 400 acres° a mile south of McMinnville, Boyer and his wife, Barbara, face the challenge common to Oregon's 38,800 farmers: How do

***McMinnville:*** county seat of Yamhill County, OR, located about thirty-five miles southwest of Portland. It is the center of Oregon's wine industry and produces grains, timber, and tree-grown fruits as well as horticultural and dairy products.

***acre:*** unit of surface measure commonly used in the United States, about 44,000 square feet, or about 90% of a standard American football field (not counting the end zones). It is about 40% of a hectare, the unit of surface measure used in the metric system.

you keep your balance when markets change, costs increase and regulations crank?

How do you mesh what you love with the complications of water, fuel, fertilizer and financing? What about consumer expectations? What if traffic is so thick and fast you're scared to move bulky equipment to your next field down the highway? What if the neighbor sells out and plants condos instead of crops?

How do you adapt, hold on and prosper?

This is one farm's walk. The Boyers found their pace by going organic and sticking local. By scaling back while reaching out, and by dialing in and diversifying.

Tom Boyer is 54, the fourth generation to farm in Oregon and the third on this ground, which hugs the curving contour of the South Yamhill River. He's a jacket and jeans guy, wears his cap to the dinner table and calls his wife Babs. He's bald, stocky, keeps a droopy 1970s mustache and is a central casting font° of laconic° country expressions.

Which can be misleading. He gets by on four hours sleep a night, and spends his time, when the house is quiet, reading and researching. "You're constantly fine-tuning," he says. "If you're not fine-tuning, you're out of business."

"I call him my Einstein," Barbara Boyer says.

She's 44, a Connecticut girl with a plant science degree who never imagined she'd end up an Oregon farmwife. She's dark-haired, gregarious and a natural organizer. She won election to the board of the Yamhill County Soil & Water Conservation District and in November will take a seat on the Oregon Board of Agriculture.

She co-founded and now manages the McMinnville Farmer's Market. She's leaning on the county's school districts to add local fruit and vegetables to lunch menus. A "no brainer" in such a fine agricultural county, she says.

The Boyer farm, under Tom's father and grandfather and in his first years, grew grain, multiple varieties of grass seed, and turnips, radish and mustard for seed. That changed after a seed marketing company folded and left him holding several million pounds of vegetable seed. Never again, he vowed, would he let a middleman control his destiny.

## Diversify and Prosper

The Boyers set out to establish five "profit centers" at the farm—five ways to make money.

At the heart of it is their "Gourmet Hay."

The Boyers have always grown grass hay—some fields have produced 30 years running—but they began marketing to the many hobby farms and ranches in the area, people with a few horses, goats or cattle to feed. Although international demand has pushed the price of Oregon hay to $220 a ton or more, the Boyers sell for $130 to $160 a ton. Couldn't look customers in the eye if they gouged them, they say.

They produce 30,000 to 40,000 87-pound bales annually and deliver to about 450 regular customers. They restrict deliveries to a 50-mile radius. Haul beyond that, Tom Boyer says, and you're a trucker instead of a farmer.

They use organic techniques. Instead of chemical fertilizer, the Boyers buy 300 to 500 tons of pomace—grape skins and seeds left over from pressing at local wineries—and mix it with manure. They spread it on the hay fields in the fall. Tom Boyer calls it "trail mix" for earthworms, whose work makes for rich, healthy, well-drained soil. "Our worm count is way high," he says.

A second profit center emerged in 2004 from a conservation project along the South Yamhill River. Working with the federal Farm Service Agency, the Boyers and various community groups planted 10,000 trees over seven years. The Boyers estimate they gave up 24 acres of cropland by planting trees in a buffer zone stretching 180 feet from the riverbank, and the FSA pays them $6,000 annually as compensation. That's less than what they could earn if the land was kept in production, but the restored riparian° buffer cools the river and controls erosion.

"We want to have as nice a river to swim in as I did when I was a kid," Tom Boyer says.

---

***font:*** literally, a container, usually made of stone, for holding the water used in baptism in a Christian church; here, figuratively, a reservoir or source.

***laconic:*** using few words; brief.

***riparian:*** located on a river bank.

Third is a Community Supported Agriculture° operation, in which subscribers pay for weekly boxes of fresh vegetables. The Boyers converted 1.5 acres of hay field into a garden, and grow tomatoes, carrots, beans, kale, cabbage, squash and other edibles.

They plan to expand the garden by another quarter acre and continue enriching it with the pomace treatment.

"If you caress a garden it will produce a third more," Tom Boyer says. "That's how you do it."

The fourth profit center is Barbara Boyer's job at McMinnville Farmer's Market, which pays $5,000 a year.

The fifth is a work in progress. They're fixing up the original farmhouse, a two-story, 1909 beauty, and plan to rent it to vacationers who want to experience a working farm. People ought to know, Tom Boyer says, there are "land rich, pocket poor" family farmers who are "out there busting their butts."

The restoration has a proper pace, as well. They pick one major project each year: replaced the roof in 2009, rebuilt the front porch last year and this fall will add stone steps, front and back.

Tom Boyer sees the house rental as a way to "keep the story alive."

His son, Ted, lives nearby and is beginning to show interest in returning to the farm. And Ted's young daughter, Josi, loves every aspect.

"If heritage were not important, why not just sell it and coast?" Tom asks.

His smile is his answer.

"I think it's worth punishing a few more generations," he says.

### There's More

The Boyers have farmed up to 1,000 acres by leasing land, but found themselves "highway farmers" moving from field to field. They're scaling back to the home place, and believe they can maintain hay production with additional irrigation.

Even that comes with complications, however. The Boyers hold the oldest water rights on the South Yamhill. If they increase their take, some newcomer to the fast-growing county might get bumped off. They don't relish the prospect.

But farming is tough. There are testy times during harvest, when rain threatens the hay and the baler or stacker breaks down, when Tom Boyer says he has "a regular Jesus moment" and questions why he does it.

The answer lies deep. Farming, he says with a laugh, "gets in your blood and then you're screwed."

But good moments overcome bad. Delivering hay to somebody you like, he says, is like going to meet a friend.

Perspective and energy also arrive with the farm's idealistic "woofers," unpaid interns who come to the farm through a program called Worldwide Opportunities on Organic Farms.° In the past three years, the Boyers have hosted 79 woofers for two-week stays, putting them up in their basement. The current intern, Meghan Bender, was a waitress in Manhattan before arriving to pick beans and tomatoes and push a wheelbarrow for the first time.

"I spend most of the day in the garden," Bender says with a broad smile. "It feels really right."

That goes both ways.

"Maybe we are doing something right," Tom Boyer says. "These kids are coming from across the country to be here."

The Boyers have worked only two Sundays in 18 years; once when they had to catch up on the harvest after a friend's funeral on a Saturday, another time to help a friend whose equipment had broken down. Otherwise, Sundays are for spiritual recharge. Time to find that proper pace. Stay on the steady.

A reminder, Tom Boyer says, "That there's some sort of life other than on a tractor."

---

***Community Supported Agriculture (CSA):*** movement that began in Japan and Germany in the 1960s and came to the United States in the 1980s. The weekly boxes that subscribers receive contain whatever is ripe at the time and thus change seasonally.

***Worldwide Opportunities on Organic Farms (WWOOF):*** movement begun in England in the early 1970s to give individuals the opportunity to work on organic farms in rural areas or another country in exchange for room and board. There are about 50 national WWOOF organizations that form a loose network around the world.

## RESPOND

1. What arguments is Mortenson making in this article? In what ways does the information here help you understand the challenges of being an independent farmer in the United States at this historical moment? In what ways does it give you useful information about the relationship many Americans have with the food they consume?
2. What sorts of hard evidence does Mortenson use in this selection? How effectively does he use them? (You might imagine what the article would be like if he had not used these sources of evidence. For a discussion of hard evidence, see Chapter 4.)
3. As is often the case in such newspaper articles, Mortensen seeks to create the Boyers as three-dimensional characters by describing them in some detail. Watch the video posted with this article (http://bit.ly/u42a67). In what ways has Mortensen captured aspects of each of the Boyers' personality? Are there other details he might have added? How do such details serve as arguments based on emotion, ethos, or fact? (See Chapters 2–4 on these arguments.)
4. This article received two posted comments, which are reproduced here as written:

   ecohumanist October 02, 2011 at 8:48AM
   I am really glad that this farm in the willamette valley stayed local. It would be sad to see another farm move to mexico or china.

   It's time to have a serious discussion about sustainability. These "local" and "organic" farms that cater to wealthy limousine liberals are NOT PART OF A GLOBAL SOLUTION!

   ruonboard October 02, 2011 at 8:59AM
   Great story. These people are enjoying success and happiness through a positive use of their land. The bonus is the fact that their efforts also help others in the community. This is a great example of the benefits of doing things right and free market capitalism. Kudos.

   Even though Portland has a reputation of being an especially liberal city, neither of these comments is especially liberal in its stance. The first criticizes "wealthy limousine liberals," just the sort of folks who are often seen as supporting the local food or farm-to-table movement described in the Wikipedia entries in an earlier selection while the second interprets the Boyers' actions as evidence of what happens when "free market capitalism" is allowed to work. On the other hand, we can imagine many liberal supporters of the local food movement (not just "wealthy limousine liberal" folk) who find much to like in the article as well. What does this situation remind us about the complexities of audience? (For a discussion of audience, see Chapter 6.) What does it teach us about the ways that a single source can be used by people with very different sets of values to support very different claims? (For a discussion of making claims, see Chapter 7.)

5. **Write an essay** in which you explore some topic related to local independent farms in the area where you study or an area where you live. Using this article as a starting point, you might investigate the challenges independent farmers face generally; to tackle this topic, you'll want to do some research on the Internet or interview people knowledgeable about these issues, including farmers themselves. You could write an essay about WWOOF, Worldwide Opportunities on Organic Farms, using information you get from its Web site or elsewhere on the Internet, from interviews with farmers in your area who participate in WWOOF, or from people who have been WWOOF volunteers. From a different perspective, you might check local news sources, especially newspapers, to discover issues currently relevant on topics related to independent farmers, farmers' markets, or the local food supply.

*Adriene Hill is a multimedia reporter for* Marketplace*, a radio program produced by American Public Media in association with the University of Southern California and focusing on business and the economy. It is the most popular business program in America, surpassing all the business programming on television in terms of listeners/viewers. In her reporting, Hill focuses on sustainability, specifically, the ways individuals understand sustainability as it relates to the environment and sustainability in relationship to consumers. This radio feature, "Eating Ethically—It's Complicated," aired on Friday, September 23, 2011, during a segment of the program entitled "Marketplace Money," which is hosted by Tess Vigeland. You can listen to this feature at http://bit.ly/tnAbnq. We've also included the comments that were posted about the feature. Thanks to the affordances of the new media, listeners or readers can now engage in interactions with broadcasters or writers and with other listeners or readers. As you listen to this radio segment, study the transcript and read the comments, then consider how the new media have created contexts for public debate and argument that did not exist a few short years ago.*

# Eating Ethically—It's Complicated (and Listener Comments)

ADRIENE HILL

---

### Transcript

HOST TESS VIGELAND: Buying local is trendy these days. Really trendy. And it's not just hipsters looking to score locally grown lemon oregano. People have all sorts of reasons for spending their food budget close to home. Support the local economy. Help out the environment—fewer miles traveled means less pollution, right? It turns out, like so many things, it is complicated. From the Marketplace Sustainability desk, Adriene Hill reports.

ADRIENE HILL: Pity the potato. It's a long haul from the soiled hands of the farm worker to the shiny, misty shelves at the grocery store.

Food, like our potato, travels an average of 1,500 miles before it realizes its life purpose on the end of a fork. That's about the distance from Omaha to Los

*The Wednesday farmers' market in Pershing Square in downtown Los Angeles features local fruits and vegetables from surrounding areas.*

Angeles. And it's enough of a trek—involving enough gas and pollution—to get some people all worked up about "food miles."°

*food miles:* the distance in miles that food is transported from the place where it is grown to the place where it is consumed. Food miles are one measure that can be used in quantifying the impact of food on the environment, including the issues related to climate change. On its Web site, *Marketplace* provided a link to the International Institute for the Environment and Development as a source of information on food miles: http://bit.ly/rHbX8f.

Want to reduce that number? Try your local farmer's market.

{At farmers' market. Farmer shouting.}

HILL: I wanted to know how far these potatoes have traveled.

ALEX WEISER: They have traveled around 110 miles, 115 miles.

HILL: And are they good travelers? 5

WEISER: Yeah, they travel well.

HILL: Apparently, they don't fuss in the back seat. Alex Weiser runs Weiser Family Farms. He's got a table of beautiful heirloom potatoes.

WEISER: I think people want food that is grown locally, and is grown for flavor, and has great nutritional value and is not wasting resources.

HILL: Kathleen Merrigan is the U.S. deputy secretary of agriculture. She says there are all sorts of reasons farmers are good neighbors. Local farms help people eat better by making fresh, healthy foods more available. And buying local can help support local economies.

KATHLEEN MERRIGAN: All wonderful stuff. 10

HILL: Today, when it's so hard to figure out how to spend our food budget responsibly, and ethically and sustainably, food miles can seem like an easy indicator. But it's not quite that simple. For one, food miles are not the best way to judge how much pollution food is responsible for.

MERRIGAN: We know from our studies that the fuel use per unit of product delivered to consumers may be higher or lower.

HILL: Transportation only accounts for about 10 percent of the pollution created by the food we eat. And "local" doesn't say anything about how the food was grown; just imagine the energy it takes to grow a tomato in the winter in a heated greenhouse.

CHUCK NICHOLSON: If they are trying to minimize energy usage, there have been a number of studies that have shown it's probably better changing your diet than it is to think about buying local.

HILL: Chuck Nicholson is a professor at Cornell and Cal Poly. According to one 15
study, cutting red meat and dairy out of your diet one day a week has the same environmental impact as eating local. Nicholson has studied the impact of reducing food miles in the dairy industry—research he says that points to a broader issue with the local food movement.

NICHOLSON: Your local decisions can have effects on people farther away.

HILL: If you and I and our neighbors start buying local, whole systems of food production will be affected. Which isn't always a good thing, especially if you're the farmer far away.

GAWAIN KRIPKE: There are other issues to be concerned about in the sourcing of our food, including social justice.

HILL: Gawain Kripke is policy director at OxFam in Washington, D.C. His colleagues worked on an analysis of the global food market to show how dependent farmers in poorer countries are on the food dollars of developed countries. One tidbit from the study: UK food-supply chains support one to one and a half million farm workers in sub-Saharan Africa.

KRIPKE: We don't want to exclude small food producers, for instance, in poor 20
countries just because they are distant from us, because we're using this distance measure.

HILL: The basic idea is that if you buy your broccoli from your local farmer, you're not buying it at the grocery store. Which means that the broccoli farmer in another part of the world that sells to your grocery store, won't have a market for it and won't make a living.

It's a bit of a conundrum. How do you feed yourself and your family in a way that's good for them and everybody else and the planet?

According to the experts, it boils down to something like this: Buy fruits and veggies in season. Look for fair-trade labels on international foods. Buy local, when it makes sense. Waste less. And, eat less meat.

I feel like I always wind up saying that.

**Comments Posted by Listeners**

Thomas Wallace—Sep 24, 2011

I was somewhat incensed at the commentaries made as to why one should not eat local. The examples given were that the energy used by a locally grown hot house tomato, or that buying local detracts from the livelihood of a farmer in some other country. The hothouse tomato is a really bad example. Most local food is grown seasonally outside. Furthermore hothouses can be heated with wood waste which is a locally produced carbon neutral fuel unlike jet fuel or diesel. Why should we be so worried about the foreign farmer when we already have shipped off most of our manufacturing jobs which were the backbone of rural economies? Growing local food is about the only thing we can do, and the money spent on it stays in the local economy. And now we should feel guilty of growing our own food??? The idea that somehow eating local deprives farmers somewhere in the world of a livelihood is utterly laughable. The global food industry consists of large corporations who receive almost all the benefits of the trade. The people in third world countries who work in these industries cannot afford to buy the very food they help produce. I am reminded of a picture in *National Geographic* where people in Kenya working in the processing plants for Nile Perch could only afford to buy the fish carcasses from the fish they processed. I have listened to Public Radio for thirty years and can honestly say that I have never heard such nonsensical baseless drivel as I heard on this segment of Marketplace.

Oliver Owen—Sep 24, 2011

I'm so cheesed with the sloppy Marketplace Money report about the ethics of local agriculture. If there's more than one variable to consider when discussing a subject, does that mean you headline with "it's complicated"? And, use of words like trendy and hipster are so negative and confining. You might want to consider being more conservative with the use of cheap catch phrases, lousy dialogue, and divisive language, unless of course, you want to turn people off from local agriculture. This piece didn't help at all to clarify matters for people on the fence about where to spend their food budget. The final message may have been alright, albeit a "complicated" and uninspired local version of Michael Pollan's° "Eat food, not too much, mostly plants," but the path you took to get there was befuddling.

Claudia Ruffle—Sep 25, 2011

Thank you, Thomas Wallace, for your CRITICALLY RELEVANT, IMPORTANT commentary. I believe Marketplace did enough of a disservice with this story that they should do a follow-up story which includes all of the problems with it that T. Wallace has pointed out.

Daniel DeAngelo—Sep 25, 2011

Agree with other commenters. This story really rung hollow in my ears with its 25
not very thorough reporting. Talk to Michael Pollan, talk to Alice Waters,° talk to Will Allen° who is empowering truly local food for poorer inner city residents. And why can't the farmers in sub-Saharan Africa produce food for their OWN local communities? Why can't we cut out red meat one day a week (or more) AND eat locally? It's not an either/or dilemma. Marketplace, please redo this story with more depth and insight. We listeners expect more depth and nuance from our public radio.

Pat Krueger—Sep 25, 2011

Saying that eating less meat and dairy products won't affect the economy. How do expect the beef and dairy industries to survive? They deserve to make a living also.

Adriane Tish—Sep 26, 2011

I was with you on a light, interesting, mulling-type article until the "we don't want to exclude small producers in poor countries" defense. What the? That came out of left field. One of the main incentives for going local is, in fact, to support your own community, your own farmer, instead of the one far away. Your own local farmer is most likely also a small producer. And last time I checked, America wasn't "poor" but we certainly have our share of deficiencies to overcome. I know the farmer at my local market isn't driving up in a Porsche or making a ConAgra°

***Michael Pollan (1955– ):*** American journalist and activist who has been dubbed a "liberal food intellectual"; he is the author of several recent important books about food, including *The Omnivore's Dilemma: A Natural History of Four Meals* (2006).

***Alice Waters (1944– ):*** American chef, author, and activist; the owner of Chez Panisse restaurant in Berkeley, California, which was among the first to use locally grown, organic ingredients. Waters created the Edible Schoolyard program at an elementary school in Berkeley and has worked tirelessly to improve the quality of public school meals, especially in poorer areas, by encouraging the use of healthy and organic ingredients.

***Will Allen (1949– ):*** CEO of Growing Power, a farm and community center in Milwaukee, Wisconsin. The son of sharecroppers, a former professional basketball player, and a recipient of a MacArthur Foundation Fellowship, Allen is an expert in urban agriculture and a recognized authority on agriculture and food policy, especially in urban areas.

***ConAgra Foods, Inc.:*** a large American packaged food company that provides products to supermarkets and restaurants.

executive-level salary . . . For me it's easy—buy everything I can locally and anything I need/want that isn't available can be filled in with externals.

Margaret Thompson—Sep 26, 2011

Maybe one of the reasons the story was sloppy is that "sustainable" is not defined. Buying locally is the ultimate in creating a sustainable community because it keeps money circling locally and creates relationships between producer and consumer. Locally pastured cows and chickens maximize renewable resources with minimal waste. The main inputs are sunshine, grass, and water. The main "output" is recycled to grow more grass. The chickens also provide labor in distributing the manure and improve hygiene by eating the larval pests that grow in the cow flops. Add a bull and a rooster, and you can create materials for next year. Think of the wasteful inputs and outputs that go into canned organic beans shipped. Besides, the price of grass fed beef makes sure you eat it infrequently and savor every bite. As for sustainable on a worldwide scale, why don't American and European relief organizations purchase food grown in sub-Saharan Africa to feed displaced people in other parts of Africa rather than sending food grown by US farmers to refugee camps? (I know, it's political, not economics.) As for me, since Israeli produce is the only food that I've seen in Philadelphia that was grown anywhere near Africa, I'm not depriving sub-Saharan farmers when I buy produce grown on my food co-op's farm. South American farmers, maybe.

Joan J—Sep 26, 2011

Ooof . . . really? My bulk purchases of tomatoes and peppers and eggplants from my local farmer's market all summer and fall (to make my own sauce and roasted veggies to freeze for use all winter) is somehow depriving poor farmers elsewhere in the world? Give me a break! I'm still spending money, still consuming—I'm just spending it with my local farmers. I guess I cut out the middle actors—chain stores and large-scale processors—but I don't think I'm leaving families on the edge with my purchasing habits. In fact, I know exactly who receives my money, and they aren't exactly living large off their earnings. This was an incredibly disappointing piece: did Monsanto° or ADM° underwrite it?

Kristina Klingbeil—Sep 27, 2011

Thanks for the interesting follow-up. I found the story rather lax and lopsided 30
as well. Perhaps the show could find a "sustainability" commentator each week from some organization like Sierra Club. . . .

***Monsanto:*** a multinational corporation specializing in biotechnology and agriculture. Its headquarters is in Missouri. It produces 90 percent of the genetically engineered seeds used in the United States. This and other facts about its practices have often made it a target of environmental and antiglobalization activists.

***ADM (Archer Daniels Midland):*** a multinational conglomerate with headquarters in Illinois. Its plants around the world convert grains into a range of products. *Fortune* magazine has named it the most admired food production company in the country several times in recent years.

**RESPOND.**

1. What was your response to Hill's audio feature before you read the comments? After you read them?
2. As noted, the focus of *Marketplace* is business and the economy. Hence, we can assume that listeners to the program share those interests or are interested in learning about those perspectives on the news of the day. How do we see those concerns reflected in the comments posted about this feature?
3. Which part or parts of Hill's features did those commenting find most problematic? (Here, you may need to reread the transcript carefully and note the sections of it about which commenters posted remarks.) From the perspective of Toulmin, Hill and one of the experts she interviewed seem to have assumed a warrant that was not shared by listeners who posted comments on this topic. How could this warrant be stated? Might Hill have prepared her listeners in some way for the information that was presented in this section of the feature by making the warrant explicit or qualifying the claims made? (See Chapter 7 for discussions of Toulmin argumentation, warrants, and qualifying claims.)
4. Are all the criticisms made of Hill's feature valid? (In other words, should you trust a commenter any more than you trust Hill?) For example, investigate Thomas Wallace's claim about whether most local food is grown seasonally outside. Is this claim valid anywhere in the United States? Everywhere? A trip to the grocery store might give you some idea about whether it is, although you'll likely need to do a bit more research to determine the extent to which this claim is valid. And what of his argument about tomatoes grown in hothouses? After all, it may be true that wood waste could be used to heat hothouses, but what is the likelihood that it is or will be?
5. As noted, Hill focuses on issues related to sustainability, a word that was not so commonly used only a few years ago. **Write an essay** in which you seek to define sustainability. You will obviously need to rely on other sources, whether those found on the Internet or in the library or interviews with individuals who have more knowledge than you do of this topic. (See Chapter 9 for a discussion of definitional arguments.)

# The Locavore's Dilemma

CHRISTOPHE PELLETIER

*Christophe Pelletier created* The Food Futurist *(http://hfgfoodfuturist.com/), a blog that promises "independent and critical thinking about the future of food and farming" in May 2009. He is also author of* Future Harvests: The Next Agricultural Revolution *(2010) and owns a consulting firm that specializes in issues related to all aspects of food production. Educated at the Institut National Agronomique in France, he speaks five languages; currently, he lives and works in Vancouver, British Columbia. This selection, "The Locavore's Dilemma," appeared on his blog in December 2010. As you read it, you will see that he takes a very different stance toward the issue of ethical eating than Adriene Hill did in the previous selection, "Eating Ethically—It's Complicated." Think about the ways that Pelletier's argument is a proposal.*

There is a growing trend, or at least a growing noise in favor of eating locally produced food. The "locavores" as they are called, claim that 100-mile food is the way to a more sustainable agriculture and consumption. Is this approach realistic and could it be the model for the future?

This movement is rather popular here in Vancouver, British Columbia. The laid-back residents who support the local food paradigm certainly love their cup of coffee and their beer. Wait a minute! There is no coffee plantation anywhere around here. There is not much barley produced around Vancouver, either. Life should be possible without these two beverages, should it not? The disappearance of coffee—and tea—from our households will make the lack of sugar beets° less painful. This is good because sugar beets are not produced in the region. At least, there is no shortage of water.

But this is not all. There is no cocoa plantation around here, and believe me, there are many people who are addicted to chocolate. British Columbia does not produce citrus or other warm climate fruit. If we are to become locavores, we must say goodbye to orange juice, to lemons, to bananas. Even the so popular sushi must disappear because of the lack of rice. There are no rice fields in this area, and neither are there wheat fields. The Asian population certainly would have a hard time eliminating rice from their diet. The lack of wheat means no flour; and no flour means no bread, no pastries, and no cookies. The carbohydrate supply is going to be tough. If we must consume local, our lifestyle is going to change dramatically. Potatoes and cabbage is the way of the future. But before going all local food, the local locavores must realize that British Columbia produces only 48% of all the food its inhabitants consume. One out of two locavores would have to starve. Going exclusively local would also affect deeply the source of animal protein. Most of the animal feed is made of ingredients that come from much farther than 100 miles. The chickens and eggs would become less available. Farmed salmon, BC's° largest agricultural export, could not use the type of feed they currently use, as fishmeal and fish oil come from Peru and vegetable oil comes from farms located far away. There would go many jobs with very little alternatives. If we look beyond food, other agricultural products such as cotton and wool would not be an option anymore. Cars would disappear, because the main component of

***sugar beets:*** a major source of processed sugar.

***BC:*** abbreviation for British Columbia.

Pay attention to how much space Pelletier devotes in his argument to describing potential problems with his proposal. How does thinking about his topic as complex make his proposal more or less feasible?

LINK TO P. 287

tires, rubber, is not produced under this climate. The 100-mile rule will solve traffic problems. If local consumption is the rule for food, should it not be the rule for everything as well? China would probably have different views about this. Not only would their manufacturing collapse, but also if they have to produce food within 100 miles of the consumer, they would have to give up importing agricultural commodities. For them, a true locavore system would mean famine. The same would be true here in British Columbia. When people are hungry, they are not so picky about the distance from the producing farm.

***ideology:*** set of beliefs that form a comprehensive vision regarding a person's goals and actions.

***pragmatically:*** practically.

The problem with concepts such as local consumption is that the basic idea has some value, but the idea quickly evolves into an ideology,° and ideologies tend to make their followers stop thinking pragmatically.° Today, the idea of eating locally in a place like Vancouver is possible because supply easily meets demand, thanks to the 3,000-mile foods. This is ironical. If the distance to market has to be within 100 miles, farmers in low population density areas, such as many regions of North America, South America and Central Europe, would have a different type of problem. They would produce an abundance of food, but because there are not enough people to consume it locally, the law of supply and demand tells us that the price of agricultural commodities would plummet, food would stay in storage and farmers would go out of business, while people in China, and in British Columbia, would suffer hunger. Clearly, the 100-mile diet needs some amendments.

***shelf life:*** the amount of time a food item remains edible; lettuce has a shorter shelf life than sweet potatoes, which have a shorter shelf life than canned goods.

5 Intuitively, it sounds logical that locally produced food has a lower carbon footprint than food that comes from 2,000 to 10,000 miles away. However, this is only partly true. The means of transportation affects the carbon footprint. The environmental impact of transport is much higher for road transport than it is for rail transport, which is also higher than water transport. The type of transport also depends on the type of commodity brought to market. Perishables need to reach consumers as quickly as possible for shelf life° reasons, while dry goods, such as for instance grains and oilseeds, do not face the same kind of deadline. The quality of the logistics is also crucial to reduce the carbon footprint. A fully loaded truck is much more efficient than a local truck dropping small quantities in many places, thus driving around most of the time with empty space in the trailer.

The emphasis should not be so much on local as it should be about the search for efficient and low environmental impact. More than the distance from the farm to the consumer, it would be more useful to provide consumers with information about the actual carbon footprint of the products they buy. They would have the possibility to make the right choices. Retailers, too, would be able to make decisions about their sourcing strategies. Clean products and clean producers need to be rewarded for doing a good job. Here in Vancouver, local food products are more expensive than similar offerings from California, Mexico, Ecuador or Chile. How do you convince families with a tight budget to spend more for local products that look pretty much the same? This problem needs to be addressed. Currently, farmers markets are much about marketing. They sell the experience as much as their production methods. Only a wealthy minority can afford to buy at these markets. The prices are not based on production costs plus farmers' income. They are as high as possible, because the farmers can ask these prices. The wealthy city dwellers are willing to pay a substantial premium above what they can buy from the local supermarket. In this relation farmer-consumer, price bargaining does not take place. If these farmers were to try to sell to a grocery retail chain, they would never get the prices they get from the consumers who will not haggle about the price. This is why more farmers try to sell directly to consumers: they make more money that way. However, this might change in the future. A number of retailers are working towards offering "farmers market" products in their store. This already makes market farmers nervous.

Is local production for local markets the way of the future? My answer is that it partly will be and it partly will not. I do expect a shift of the location of production for perishables. Consumer habits will change, too. In the West, consumers have been spoiled. They can eat anything from anywhere at any time of the year. This luxury probably will not be affordable for long anymore. The superfluous° will naturally be eliminated.

***superfluous:*** unnecessary.

As the economics of energy, and therefore of food, will change, producers will increasingly locate their operations closer to cities; and even inside cities. Urban farming is a growing activity. Although it started mostly in poor neighborhoods as a way of having a small patch of land for personal consumption, more sophisticated and efficient systems are being developed. My expectation is that production, and consumption, of vegetables and fragile fruit (for instance strawberries) will gradually become more integrated in the urban landscape than they are now. I also think that we will see animal productions, such as fresh dairy, poultry meat, and eggs, relocate closer to consumer markets. An interesting development is aquaponics, the combination of greenhouse produce with fish production in tanks. The production of non-perishables will not relocate. It does not have to. What will probably change is the transportation infrastructure in many areas where these commodities are produced. This is good news for coffee drinkers and chocolate addicts. After all, transport of commodities over long distance is not just the result of cheap oil. The Silk Road° and the spice trade by the Dutch° took place before mankind even knew about oil. Trade has always been a force of progress for humanity. It helps an increasing number of people to have access to goods that make their lives better. The rules of trade may not always be fair, but like all human activities, it is a work in progress. Limiting our food supply to 100 miles would be a regression.° Subsistence agriculture has not demonstrated that it could feed the world. Most of the people suffering of hunger live in subsistence agriculture areas.

***Silk Road:*** interlocking trade routes connecting East, South, and West Asia with Europe and part of North and East Africa. While originally used as early as the second century BCE for the Chinese silk trade, they were expanded and widely used until the late medieval period. These trade routes played major roles in the development of several ancient civilizations, including those of China, India, Persia, Arabia, and Rome.

***spice trade by the Dutch:*** Beginning in the late 1500s, the Dutch began trading with Southeast Asia as a source of spices, including tea. The Dutch East India Company was set up in 1602, and the seventeenth century saw trade with and colonization of Asia by the British, the Portuguese, and the French.

***regression:*** here, a move backwards.

**RESPOND.**

1. What is Pelletier's argument? How well does he support it? How is it similar to yet different from Hill's argument in the previous selection, "Eating Ethically—It's Complicated"? What, for Pelletier, is the problem with the notion of eating locally? Do you think he is concerned about the ethics of our eating patterns?
2. We expect proposal arguments to have an evaluative component. What specifically does Pelletier evaluate and critique? What criteria does he use for making his evaluative claims? (See Chapter 10 for a discussion of evaluative arguments and Chapter 12 for a discussion of proposal arguments.)
3. In the closing paragraphs of the blog posting, Pelletier offers a proposal: his predictions about local production and local markets in the future. What specific predictions does he make? How well do you think he has supported them? How do you think the experts quoted in Hill's radio feature and those posting comments on that feature might respond to Pelletier's predictions? Why?
4. What sort of ethos does Pelletier create for himself? Do you think he is someone you would like? Why or why not? In particular, how do you respond to his use of humor—at least mild sarcasm—in the opening paragraphs of this blog posting when he is criticizing British Columbians who love coffee, beer, chocolate, and other foodstuffs, on the one hand, but might claim to be committed locavores, on the other? Is this an effective way of making these arguments? (Chapter 3 provides a discussion of ethos.)

5. **Write a rhetorical analysis** of Pelletier's blog posting, paying special attention to the kinds of arguments he uses (or does not use). To the extent that you can, link the way he constructs his argument to the content of the argument and the ideology or ideologies that Pelletier himself subscribes to. Here, you'll obviously need to study the posting carefully in order to deduce the beliefs and values that underlie Pelletier's view of the world. As you'll see, they are not that difficult to tease out: for example, at the beginning of paragraph 6, he writes, "The emphasis should not be so much on local as it should be about the search for efficient and low environmental impact." In this sentence, we see an explicit statement that he values efficiency as well as practices that will have a relatively low environmental impact, all things considered. (Chapter 6 offers information about rhetorical analyses.)

▼ *Malia Wollan, who lives in Berkeley, California, contributes regularly to the* New York Times, *and her work has appeared on National Public Radio, on PBS's* Frontline, *and in the* Wall Street Journal. *In 2008, she held a Fellowship in Environmental Journalism at Middlebury College, and in 2011, she blogged and tweeted about Occupy Oakland for the* Times. *She identifies as a "dark meat eater" and is one of the editors of* Meatpaper, *the magazine where this selection first appeared in June 2008. As the homepage for the magazine notes, meat is "polarizing"—"divisive and universal, delicious and disturbing, funny and dead-serious"—and the magazine seeks to understand its subject in all its complexity. While many of us are aware of globalization as a force in many industries, we're probably not aware of what that might mean when it comes to the meat those of us who are carnivores eat. As you read this selection, consider why issues of globalization and the food supply are more complex than you had ever imagined.*

# Migration, on Ice: How Globalization Kills Chickens for Their Parts

MALIA WOLLAN

In a colossal cold storage warehouse in Ghana's port city of Tema, a boyish-faced 27-year-old named Bilal Saffieddine had something to show me. He pointed into the dark. "All that is poultry leg quarters," he said. Outside, the temperature blistered. Inside, thin men dressed in wool scarves and heavy coats climbed over house-sized stacks of boxed dark chicken meat. Their breath formed white puffs of condensed air. Saffieddine is a manager and financial controller for Silver Platter Ltd., the largest importer of U.S. poultry products into Ghana. "Ghana is a leg quarter country, not a whole chicken country," he told me.

> *"A woman eating a salad at a Wendy's in Maine could be ingesting the breast of the same chicken whose gizzard flavors a chicken stew in Togo and whose thigh is served with borscht in Moscow and whose excess fat will soon go to a ConocoPhillips refinery in Texas to make synthetic diesel fuel."*

Like the mass of frozen chicken he imports, Saffieddine is the product of the globalized market. Born in Lebanon, he left for South Africa to import canned goods after graduating from university. But he found it too dangerous. His first day on the job, one of his truck drivers was shot in the head by thugs. He moved to Ghana, where he drives his Mercedes SUV without fear of highwaymen and where the market for imported meat is booming. When Saffieddine considers the continent, everything is big and bright—the profits, the ships, the quantities. "Look at how much Tyson° takes to Russia!" he said. "In Africa the numbers are still small but they'll go up. Guaranteed!" Indeed, more than 35.5 million pounds of frozen chicken arrived in Ghana's ports in 2007, nearly 70 times what Ghana imported in 1999.

Silver Platter Ltd., Saffieddine's employer, is a subsidiary of import giant the Tajideen Group, a maze of limited-liability corporations based in Beirut and operating throughout Africa. In Ghana, Tajideen employs over 1,000 people and has an exclusive import partnership with Tyson Foods. Once a month, a cargo ship arrives in Tema's port from New Orleans carrying up to 4.4 million pounds of frozen chicken. In normal weather conditions the trip takes between 12 and 15 days. At port, it takes Saffieddine's swarm of employees between five and seven days just to unload the boxes of leg quarters from the ship.

In the global poultry market, a nation is a dark meat country or a light meat country, a leg quarter country or a whole chicken country. A country's place on the meat color spectrum is determined in large part by economic preferences, but taste matters, too. Most Ghanaians I spoke with said they liked the flavor and texture of dark meat better than white meat. Africa has seen a surge in poultry imports over the last several years since the U.S. poultry industry took notice of the continent. "There are a lot of hungry mouths to feed in Africa," Toby Moore, of the industry trade group Poultry & Egg Export Council, told me. "And we've got a lot of low-cost protein to ship."

*A poultry warehouse in Tema, Ghana*

5 Globalization and the rising demand for animal protein have turned the chicken into the world's most mobile and abundant migratory bird. This modern migration isn't one of whole birds, but rather of dismembered parts—wings in one direction, breasts in another.

The hue of a chicken's meat depends on the type of movement the muscle makes during the bird's lifetime. Repeated, constant muscle motion requires more oxygen, which is stored in a dark-colored

***Tyson:*** Tyson Foods International, a multinational corporation headquartered in Arkansas; it is the largest producer of meat products in the United States.

protein called myoglobin. Since chickens live much of their lives standing, their leg muscles are full of myoglobin and thick with veins. A confined bird is flightless, resulting in breast and wing meat lighter in color, more uniform in texture, and lower in fat and calories. It's easier to eat white meat and forget that what's being masticated was once an animal.

Americans and western Europeans, on the whole, tend to favor white meat. So what happens to all those leftover chicken legs, wings, hearts, livers, feet, and gizzards?

They go to places like Cuba, Iraq, Maldova, and Ghana. In 2007, the United States exported $2.7 billion in mostly dark meat poultry to countries across the globe. Huge international corporations like Tyson Foods have created a global food chain wherein nearly every part of a slaughtered chicken finds a market, often many thousands of miles from where it originally hatched from its egg. In 2007, for example, the majority of chicken feet were shipped to China, while offal—known in layperson's parlance as guts—went to China, Mexico, and Jamaica. Russia got the lion's share of leg quarters, followed by Lithuania, Ukraine, and Angola. In this globalized market, a woman eating a salad at a Wendy's in Maine could be ingesting the breast of the same chicken whose gizzard flavors a chicken stew in Togo and whose thigh is served with borscht in Moscow and whose excess fat will soon go to a ConocoPhillips refinery in Texas to make synthetic diesel fuel.

In Ghana, it is cheaper to buy frozen Tyson chicken parts shipped across the Atlantic Ocean in temperature-controlled cargo containers than it is to buy a freshly slaughtered chicken from the neighbor down the street. I located Ghana's meat shops by their awnings, decorated with hand-drawn pictures of bright pink chicken parts. Inside these shops, Tyson leg quarters, per pound, sell for approximately one-sixth the price of Ghana-grown chicken. "With Tyson we don't have to advertise," importer Saffieddine told me cheerily. "The price promotes the product."

10 But that low-cost, foreign chicken makes many African poultry producers angry. Even in a "leg quarter country," chickens hatch from eggs as whole birds and must be raised and slaughtered as such.

*"In America, poultry farmers get corn and soybeans for below the cost of production. Here, humans are competing with chickens for corn. How can Ghana possibly compete?"*

William Awuku Ahiadormey is 42, with a broad face and a rare but bright smile. He is the farm manager at Sydals Limited, one of the largest poultry producers in Ghana. The farm sits on a stretch of red ground surrounded by scraggly shrubs in a tiny town called Adjie Kojo, outside Tema. Armed men patrol the dusty road to protect the cows, sheep, and more than 100,000 chickens from thieves.

"Trade policy here kicks Ghanaian people out of the market," Ahiadormey told me in his tiny office, decorated with posters featuring chicken breeds, chicken feed, and chicken eggs. "Everybody in Ghana who should be benefiting from the poultry industry is going out of business." Ahiadormey has a master's degree in agricultural economics from the University of Ghana. His thesis attempted to decipher how Ghanaian poultry producers might become competitive with foreign imports. Given his line of work, the topic seemed as much a plea as an academic inquiry. Ahiadormey showed me reams of data and endless PowerPoint slides chronicling everything from high interest rates on business loans to exorbitant feed costs. "In America, poultry farmers get corn and soybeans for below the cost of production," he told me. "Here, humans are competing with chickens for corn. How can Ghana possibly compete?"

Economic trade theory suggests that when it comes to poultry, Ghanaians probably shouldn't even try. "The way Ghana competes is to keep its domestic markets flexible," said Larry Karp, professor of agricultural and resource economics at the University of California, Berkeley. "So Ghana can move into the sectors where it is more efficient." That means that if poultry farmers can't be efficient enough to compete on the global free market, they should either adjust wages and cut costs or move into another economic sector—say, cacao° production—where they can be competitive.

But Ahiadormey is a chicken farmer, not a cacao farmer. Strolling though the red dust fields between the barns, Ahiadormey relaxed a little. He swung open the gate to a huge barn brimming with young chicks, and cocked his head sideways in paternal fondness. "These are local chicks from a local producer," he said and then stood quietly, listening to the persistent peeping, seemingly oblivious to the reek of chicken manure.

15 As inevitable as the global trade in chicken parts seems, it is actually remarkably tenuous°—particularly when factors like disease, rising grain prices, the cost of oil, war, and climate change are thrown into the mix. Last year it took just a single event to reveal the fragility of the free market chicken trade.

In May 2007, the deadly avian bird virus H5N1 broke out in Ghana, just as it had in 2006 in other countries in West Africa and Southeast Asia. Chickens from infected farms were incinerated. Saffieddine's frozen inventory remained in the warehouses. Chicken sales dropped. People everywhere were afraid to eat poultry regardless of its origin.

In response to bird flu fears, the USA Poultry & Egg Export Council launched an ongoing marketing campaign to assuage° health concerns and tout the inexpensive tastiness of the U.S. poultry flooding the African market. The first campaign sent a man in a brightly colored chicken costume to dance in the streets of Accra,° giving out free prizes and chicken coupons to passersby. The promotional push was run by one of Africa's largest marketing agencies, Exp (whose tag line is "Activating Demand"). Exp continues to pass out DVDs of the chicken gyrating in the sweltering heat, wearing its USA POULTRY apron. Inexplicably, the video's soundtrack features the song "Barbie Girl" by Scandinavian pop group Aqua, whose less-than-appetizing lyrics include, "I'm a Barbie girl, in the Barbie world! Life in plastic, it's fantastic!"

Inside Exp's austere office in Accra's suburbs, the air conditioning blew at temperatures almost as cold as Saffieddine's freezer warehouse. I asked Abdul-Aziz Amankwa, Exp's young and impeccably dressed director, how the dancing-chicken costume went over with Ghanaians. He laughed, and said the company has moved on to more targeted campaigns. The new USA poultry marketing campaign, Amankwa explained, focuses on women and mothers, tapping into Ghana's highly organized women's groups, which have long established themselves around churches, businesses, and community centers. "The woman plays a critical role in the consumption of chicken," he explained. "Mothers get their communities and families to eat USA chicken. They become the advocates." Exp staff organized cook-offs and recipe competitions where women win boxes of frozen USA chicken as prizes.

---

*cacao:* the tree whose seeds give us cocoa and chocolate.

*tenuous:* here, unstable.

*assuage:* calm or relieve.

*Accra:* city of over two million inhabitants that is the capital of the West African nation of Ghana.

In a country where more than 30 percent of the population lives in poverty, cheap protein is both a blessing and a curse. On the one hand, it provides affordable nutrition. On the other, it eliminates livelihoods. Ghanaians I spoke with disagree about how much foreign chicken should be allowed into their country. But they tend to agree that frozen dark meat chicken doesn't taste as good as fresh. Many refer to it as "mortuary chicken" for the malodorous° smell common during defrosting. In Ghana, power outages are a daily ritual, and it is difficult to keep products from partially defrosting during transport or blackouts. One effective method for masking the smell is to fry the chicken, a culinary trick used by the multitude of street food vendors.

On my last day in Ghana I'd skipped dinner. I was hungry. Leaving the fan whirring in my hotel room, I walked out into the night, careful to avoid the raw sewage running in a ditch along the curbside. I found 25-year-old Nicholas Brenyah standing under a bare lightbulb frying chicken. He told me he was the "boss" of Christ Castle Fast Food, a plywood and corrugated metal shack on the side of a busy road. Though it was midnight, a line of taxi drivers and graveyard shifters waited impatiently for their food. Brenyah's type of business is known in Ghana as *check check*—a nocturnal, makeshift stand selling fried chicken and rice. I placed my order and watched the oil spit and pop in the wok. I asked Brenyah what cut of chicken he cooked, and he smiled, "Leg quarter!"

And from what company?

"Tyson!"

Why?

"It's cheap!"

He bundled my chicken and rice in newsprint and tied it with twine. I carried the little poultry packet toward the next check check stand and asked the question again. The answer was the same, "Tyson!"

"Tyson!"

"Tyson!"

All the way down the road.

---

***malodorous:*** smelly.

**RESPOND •**

1. What sort of responses do you have to Wollan's essay? What is your rational response—the response that focuses on facts and reason? What sort of affective or emotional response do you have? If you eat chicken—and truth be told, similar stories can likely be told not only about other kinds of meat but about many other foods as well—what sort of response did you find yourself having as you read the selection?
2. How would you characterize Wollan's argument? Is it an argument of fact? Of definition? Of evaluation? A causal argument? A proposal? What evidence can you give for your claim? Once you've decided which of these kinds of arguments best characterizes the selection as a whole, look for sections of the article that represent other kinds of arguments. (Chapters 8–12 discuss each of these kinds of arguments in turn.)
3. The headnote explains that *Meatpaper*, the magazine where this article first appeared, assumes that meat is "polarizing"—"divisive and universal, delicious and disturbing, funny and dead-serious"—and it seeks to understand its subject in all its complexity. How well did Wollan's article succeed in helping the magazine reach its goal? Why and how?

4. To what extent does the information presented in this selection (and perhaps in some of the earlier readings) provide evidence for the claim that the local food movement is the concern of "wealthy limousine liberals" and those who generally do not have to struggle to survive, whether we think about issues of social class in this country or the global situation more broadly? As you'll recall, "wealthy limousine liberals" is a phrase that occurs in a comment posted in response to Mortenson's feature on the Boyers, "A Diversified Farm Prospers in Oregon's Willamette Valley by Going Organic and Staying Local," earlier in this chapter. (In the name of full disclosure, at least one of the authors of this textbook is a strong supporter of the local farmers' markets in his city.)
5. This article, like the previous selection, Pelletier's blog posting, "The Locavore's Dilemma," demonstrate the tensions between the global and the local. It is easy to see why many Americans, especially younger ones and Americans of means, might have an idealistic commitment to supporting the local in terms of food production and consumption for any number of reasons, yet the reality of the matter is that, as Pelletier points out, most of us like our coffee, chocolate, tea, or rice, along with many other things that can't be produced locally. **Write an essay** in which you explore these tensions—or even contradictions. You may seek to define them in novel ways, to evaluate them, to describe their causes, or to propose a way of making peace with them (if you believe that can be done). (Chapters 9–12 provide information about each of these kinds of essays.)

▼ *The selections thus far in this chapter have focused on food, but water (particularly bottled water) also has been part of these discussions for several reasons. In this selection, which appeared in June 2008 in the* Los Angeles Times, *Mark Coleman reviews a book that deals with these issues,* Bottlemania: How Water Went on Sale and Why We Bought It *by Elizabeth Royte. (The next selection is an excerpt from Royte's book.) As you read Coleman's selection, consider book reviews as a subcategory of evaluative arguments, and learn as much as you can about the arguments that Royte presents about bottled water.*

# Review of *Bottlemania: How Water Went on Sale and Why We Bought It*

MARK COLEMAN

In 2006, Americans consumed, per capita,° more than 25 gallons of bottled water—twice as much as in 1997 and almost five times as much as in 1987. And what ignites Elizabeth Royte's reportorial spark in *Bottlemania*—at least initially—is the ecological cost of all those plastic empties: We discard between 30 billion and 40 billion bottles of Poland Spring, the most popular brand, in a year.

Like her previous book, *Garbage Land: On the Secret Trail of Trash*, this tautly paced volume more closely resembles a travel narrative than a tree-hugging° jeremiad.° Royte doesn't traffic in platitudes,° moral certainties or oversimplification; she's unafraid of ambiguity. Seamlessly blending scientific explanation and social observation, she pursues the course of Poland Spring back to its source in Fryeburg, Maine.

"Fryeburg is tied up in fits," she writes. "Its abundance of fine water has cast its unwitting residents into the middle of a social, economic, and environmental drama." Her mordant° wit comes in handy: "It's easier to picture kids guzzling beer out here than deer nuzzling around mossy springs," she notes. "But Fryeburg, for all its out-of-season torpor,° once bustled with economic activity: sawmills and timber operations, a shoe manufacturing plant, a couple of machine shops, corn shops, and dozens of thriving dairy farms. Now, it has the water-extraction business, which contributes nothing to the town's long-term economic welfare."

What drives this obsessive thirst—this compulsion to pay for something we can essentially get for free? Royte characterizes the nationwide craving for bottled water, "in a country where more than 89 percent of tap water meets or exceeds federal health and safety regulations," as both an outra-

***per capita:*** (Latin, "per head") per person.

***tree-hugging:*** strongly environmentalist, often implying criticism of such a stance.

***jeremiad:*** an extended complaint, usually sad or mournful in nature.

***platitudes:*** trite, often meaningless, statements.

***mordant:*** biting or sarcastic.

***torpor:*** lethargy or inactivity.

geous marketing coup° and an unparalleled social phenomenon. Beginning in the late 1970s with Orson Welles'° high-toned television pitches for Perrier, bottled water has been promoted for its snob appeal as much as its health benefits. Jennifer Aniston's° recent spots for Smartwater strike Royte as typically absurd. "Some ads depict her naked and others place her, clad, in an elegant restaurant, where her plastic water bottle looks, to someone with my peculiar mindset, like litter amid the crystal stemware."

5 Royte's "peculiar mindset" is that of an unabashed tap-water enthusiast who savors the irony that "purified" water from municipal sources—Dasani and Aquafina, as opposed to bottled spring water or mineral water, like Perrier—accounts for 44% of U.S. bottled-water sales. If her personal disavowal of bottled water borders on the puritanical, it also comes across as pragmatic: "Foie gras° tastes better than chopped liver. That doesn't mean I'm going to buy it. I don't need to spoil myself. I don't want to get used to expensive things . . . that might . . . disrupt the social and environmental order."

Like any good travel writer, Royte possesses an intellectual curiosity that continually lures her off the beaten path. The second half of *Bottlemania* takes a sharp turn, upending many of the author's previous assumptions about tap water.

"I decide to visit Kansas City," she writes, "where the public utility sucks from the Missouri River something that resembles chocolate Yoo-Hoo° and turns it into water so good that national magazines shower it with awards and even the locals buy it in bottles." All along the Missouri and the Mississippi, cities drink from and discharge into the same river. Visiting a municipal water-treatment plant, Royte is alternately impressed and appalled: "[T]he filtering process mimics, in a supercondensed time frame, the purifying processes of nature. It's the same ecosystem service provided for free in such places as Fryeburg, Maine, by glacier-made beds of sand and gravel."

Royte knows when not to intrude, when to let a devastating quote or damning exchange stand on its own:

"What do you do with the atrazine [an herbicide] once you filter it out?"

"We put it back in the river." 10

It seems that because of oil spills, industrial discharges, agricultural runoff, animal waste and sewage (both treated and raw), tap water is far from risk-free. Suddenly, the stainless-steel extraction pipes of Poland Spring don't seem quite so redundant,° and Royte admits that after her tap-water investigations, "I'm not immune to the appeal of springwater." Yet the conclusion of *Bottlemania* is more thoughtful than despairing, even though much of what we've learned isn't comforting. If our future really does include drinking reclaimed or "repurified" wastewater, Royte is willing to hold her nose and remain philosophical. "As bad as toilet-to-tap sounds," she concludes, "I have to remind myself: all water is recycled."

Chapter 10 notes that evaluation arguments always depend upon evaluative criteria, such as those Coleman makes explicit when he notes how Elizabeth Royte succeeds as a writer.

LINK TO P. 216

*coup:* a clever accomplishment or triumph.

*Orson Welles (1915–1985):* an American actor, director, producer, and writer perhaps best known for his film *Citizen Kane* (1941).

*Jennifer Aniston (1969– ):* an American film and television actress perhaps best known for her role in the television series *Friends*.

*foie gras:* (French, "fatty liver") an appetizer that usually is made of goose liver. Because the geese are generally force fed, this food has been boycotted by those concerned with animal rights.

*Yoo-Hoo:* a bottled chocolate drink.

*redundant:* unnecessary or useless because it duplicates something that already exists.

**RESPOND.**

1. How would you characterize Mark Coleman's evaluation of Elizabeth Royte's book? Do you think that he likes the book? How well? Why? What evidence can you cite for your characterization of his evaluation?
2. A review of a book (or movie or DVD or concert) is, by definition, an evaluative argument. What criteria does Coleman use in evaluating Royte's book? Do these criteria seem appropriate and sufficient to the task? Why or why not? (For a discussion of evaluative arguments, see Chapter 10.)
3. Coleman contends that as a writer, "Royte doesn't traffic in platitudes, moral certainties or oversimplification; she's unafraid of ambiguity" (paragraph 2). What evidence do you find for these claims in his review? Should you find any?
4. Examine Coleman's use of quotations from Royte's book. What functions do they serve in Coleman's own argument? (In answering this question, you may wish to make a list of all the quotations to examine their functions carefully.)
5. Using the discussion of evaluative arguments in Chapter 10, **write an evaluation** of Coleman's review of Royte's book. In other words, formulate criteria for evaluating a review, and then apply them to this review. An interesting way to complete this assignment would be to locate other reviews of this book, determine how they are similar to and different from Coleman's, and use this knowledge as you formulate your criteria. Consider the kinds of information, evaluations, and evidence that you, as a reader, would hope to find in a review.

▼ *This selection consists of two parts. The first is an excerpt from the closing chapter of the book reviewed in the previous selection, Elizabeth Royte's* Bottlemania: How Water Went on Sale and Why We Bought It. *The second is a graphic from the July 2007* New York Times *that is now posted as part of a "Times Topics" Web page on "Bottled Water" (http://nyti.ms/jrxrs).*

*The selection from Royte's final chapter helps to conclude her book by responding to two of its motivating questions: what kind of water should we be drinking and why? In addition to* Bottlemania, *published in 2008, Royte is also the author of* The Tapir's Morning Bath: Solving the Mysteries of the Tropical Rain Forest *(2002) and* Garbage Land: On the Secret Trail of Trash *(2005). The graphic "Satisfying the National Thirst . . . With Lots of Bottles" from the* New York Times *makes arguments about one of the controversies surrounding bottled water in overwhelmingly visual ways. As you read the excerpt from* Bottlemania, *pay attention to the ways that Royte gives us signs that she is coming to the end of her book's argument. As you study the* New York Times *graphic, consider how its arguments complement those that Royte uses.*

# Excerpt from *Bottlemania: How Water Went on Sale and Why We Bought It*

---

ELIZABETH ROYTE

For now, what should we be drinking? The EPA° tells us that the Untied States has one of the safest water supplies in the world. "I wouldn't hesitate to drink tap water anywhere in the country," Cynthia Dougherty, director of the EPA's Office of Groundwater and Drinking Water, says. Drink a glass of water in any city in the United States, Dr. Ronald B. Linsky of the National Water Research Institute said in *Avoiding Rate Shock: Making the Case for Water Rates*, a report published by the American Water Works Association, and you "have a very, very high assurance of safe, high-quality drinking water." If you fall into no risk category, says the NRDC,° you can drink most cities' tap water without a problem.

***EPA:*** the U.S. Environmental Protection Agency, a government agency that is charged with protecting the country's environment.

***NRDC:*** the National Resources Defense Council, a nongovernmental organization that contends that it is "the nation's most effective environmental action group."

Statements like these confirm my personal bias: that water should be locally sourced, delivered by energy-efficient, publicly owned pipes, generate close to zero waste, and cost, for eight glasses a day, about forty-nine cents a year. Buy that water in bottles and you'd be spending $1,400.

But it isn't that simple: if it were, 20 percent of Americans wouldn't drink only bottled water. In 2006, 89.3 percent of the nation's nearly fifty-three thousand community water systems were in compliance with more than ninety EPA standards. That left 29.8 million people with water that missed the mark on either health or reporting standards, or both. (Many in this group live on Indian lands, and many drink from small systems, which have the most trouble meeting regulations.) Moreover, neither the EPA nor your water utility has anything to say about the condition of the pipes in your house. And then there are those risk categories.

"Right to know" reports advise the very young, the pregnant, the very old, or the immunocompromised° (for example, people who are HIV-positive or undergoing chemotherapy) to consult with their doctors before drinking tap water, even in communities where water gets high marks. Some scientists define the at-risk population even more broadly, to include not just babies but children and teens, lactating° women, and anyone over fifty-five. "Look at your annual report, then decide, based on your personal situation, if you need to do anything different," Dougherty says.

5 What's the big concern? It depends whom you ask; when you're a hammer, everything looks like a nail. Scientists who study lead worry about lead. Scientists who study the connections between chemicals and cancer worry about disinfection by-products.° Microbiologists worry about tiny bugs.

Studies by epidemiologists° indicate that at least seven million Americans experience gastrointestinal° illnesses from waterborne microbes each year, of whom a thousand die. "Different people react to the same environment in different ways," says Ronnie D. Levin, a longtime EPA employee who is also a visiting scientist in the water and health program at the Harvard School of Public Health. "There is no bright golden line° that says there's no risk." Seven million is too many, Levin says. "I did a cost-benefit analysis and I think we can do better than that, without increasing the amount of disinfectants in the water."

Levin is wary of using more chlorine and other disinfectants because they generate disinfection by-products, "none of which are good." Her solution? Require utilities that rely on surface water to filter it first, to remove organic contaminants, and then to disinfect, instead of the other way around.

Until those utilities retrofit, I ask Levin, what about bottled water?

***immunocompromised:*** having a compromised or not fully functional immune system to fight disease.

***lactating:*** producing milk.

***disinfection by-products:*** the results of chemical interactions between the organic material in the water to be treated and the chemicals used to treat the water.

***epidemiologists:*** scientists who study how diseases are spread and controlled.

***gastrointestinal:*** involving the stomach and intestines.

***bright golden line:*** a clear marker distinguishing between two categories (here, with risk and without risk).

There is uncertainty about that too, she says. "It really comes down to your comfort level. Bottled water's monitoring and enforcement aren't good." Because we don't know the results of plants' inspections, "it's a crapshoot what you're getting."

So what do you drink? 10

"You've got to go with what you've got." Tap, in other words.

Do you filter?

"I do the right thing," she says, which I take to mean yes.

By this point I've spoken to enough scientists and environmental experts to believe my countertop Brita° is giving me more psychological than physical benefit, and that anyone with good reason to be suspicious of her tap water should invest in a point-of-use filter—the kind of gizmo you install on your faucet or under your sink. (Of pour-through filters, Levin says, "If there's nothing to filter out of your water, they are fine.") But not everyone is at high risk of illness, not everyone can afford a point-of-use filter and its maintenance (if they're not changed regularly, filters can put contaminants *into* water), and the money might better be spent on other preventive health measures.

To smooth out equity issues (under-the-sink filters can cost a couple hun- 15
dred dollars to buy and plumb), Robert D. Morris, the epidemiologist, suggests that utilities help pay for, install, and maintain point-of-use devices. In that way, water utilities could have confidence, he writes in *The Blue Death*, "that occasional occurrences of accidental, incidental, or intentional contamination would have little if any consequence." What would that cost? I ask him. "About a third of the utility's annual cost," he says, "but it's onetime only. You'd amortize° that cost, and you'd recycle the filters. There are economies of scale in buying a lot of them. But, yes, the consumer will ultimately pay for it."

All these caveats° beg the question: how do I know if I should be suspicious of my water? The EPA says, "Read your annual water report." But those documents—written by the utility—can be flawed, and some are essentially propaganda. (And again, they say nothing about the condition of your pipes.) They report yearly averages over time and, with some contaminants, over multiple locations within a system, which can obscure spikes. They don't necessarily list contaminants that aren't regulated (such as perchlorate,° radon,° and MTBE°), and their reporting periods close long before data reach customers. Reports may state that finished water has no cryptosporidium,° but the protozoan° parasite is notoriously difficult to detect.

When the NRDC studied the water-quality reports of nineteen cities in 2001, it gave five of them a poor or failing grade for burying, obscuring, and omitting findings about health effects of contaminants in city water

***Brita:*** a commercial brand of water filter.

***amortize:*** in accounting or budgeting, to spread the cost of something over the period when it will be used rather than treating the entire cost as a onetime expense.

***caveats:*** warnings.

***perchlorate:*** a potentially dangerous water contaminant. The degree of danger is debated.

***radon:*** a radioactive chemical element that occurs as a gas in the atmosphere and in some spring water.

***MTBE:*** methyl tertiary butyl ether, a chemical compound that is used as an additive to gasoline. It easily pollutes groundwater supplies.

***cryptosporidium:*** a protozoan that causes human diarrhea.

***protozoan:*** relating to a single-cell microorganism.

*Which is the greater problem, the water or the plastic bottle it comes in?*

supplies, printing misleading statements, and violating a number of right-to-know requirements, such as the rule that says reports must identify known sources of pollutants in city water. What's a devotee of the tap to do? Read your report carefully, learn about the health effects of contaminants, call your utility with questions, then test your water yourself.

Drinking the waters of the Ashokan and other upstate reservoirs, here in New York City, my husband and I fall into no obvious risk category, but could eight-year-old Lucy fight off cryptosporidiosis?° (Treatment with ultraviolet light hasn't yet started.) And while disinfection by-products worry me a little (I live far from where the chlorine goes in, which gives trihalomethanes° a longer time to build up), do they worry me enough to spend another hundred bucks a year on filters?

*cryptosporidiosis:* an infection caused by cryptosporidium and characterized by chronic diarrhea.

*trihalomethanes:* chemical compounds in solvents and refrigerants.

*manganese:* a chemical element that is necessary in trace levels for all life but that may destroy the central nervous system when people are overexposed to it.

To settle the question, I order my own tests. I fill four different containers with unfiltered tap water and mail them on ice to a certified lab in Ypsilanti, Michigan. When I rip open the envelope in two weeks, I'm relieved: I've got no lead, no coliform, no nitrates, and my total trihalomethanes are well within federal limits (at least on this November day: they may be higher in the heat of summer). But my manganese°—of all things—is 40 percent higher than the federal standard (though still 5.7 times lower than that tasty

Gerolsteiner° I drank in Bryant Park). My Brita won't remove the mineral, but according to experts, this level presents no health risk to either children or adults. Steven Schindler, my water-testing guru at the Department of Environmental Protection, says the city never exceeded the state's limit of 0.3 parts per million in 2007. (The federal limit is 0.05 parts per million, but it's a "secondary level," which means utilities aren't required to test for it; the contaminant affects only the aesthetics of the water. At long last, the mystery of the reddish fuzz in the bottom of my Brita appears to be solved.) If manganese is my only problem, I'm happy. Like the vast majority of Americans, I can keep drinking tap water without worry.

***Gerolsteiner:*** a naturally carbonated mineral water from Germany.

I come away from my investigations with at least one certainty: not all tap 20
water is perfect. But it is the devil we know,° the devil we have standing to negotiate with and to improve. Bottled-water companies don't answer to the public, they answer to shareholders. As Alan Snitow and Deborah Kaufman write in *Thirst*, "If citizens no longer control their most basic resource, their water, do they really control anything at all?"

Chapter 7 explains that in classical rhetoric, the *peroratio* summarized the speaker's case and moved the audience to action. Note how Royte here begins reviewing her argument and exploring future actions her readers should take.

LINK TO P. 124

Bottled water does have its place—it's useful in emergencies and essential for people whose health can't tolerate even filtered water. But it's often no better than tap water, its environmental and social price is high, and it lets our public guardians off the hook for protecting watersheds, stopping polluters, upgrading treatment and distribution infrastructure, and strengthening treatment standards.

***the devil we know:*** an allusion to the expression "Better the devil we do know than the one we don't." It means that something known (and possibly problematic) should be chosen over something unknown that could turn out to be much worse.

Certainly, nearly everything humans do has an environmental impact—biking to work, recycling newspapers, and drinking tap water included. But understanding that impact is the first step toward reducing it. It's true that the impact of bottled water looks minuscule next to other water uses—growing beef, say, or manufacturing cars. But try telling that to someone who lives on a springwater truck route or who drinks from a well that shares an aquifer° with a commercial pump. As Lucy sings out when I try to tell her that some problem of hers is trivial in the larger scheme of things, "Not for me-eeee."

***aquifer:*** a permeable underground layer of soil, rock, or sand that stores and yields water.

If someday I find myself wanting to buy bottled water, I will do it as an informed consumer, someone who knows that the images on the label may not reflect an ecological reality, that part of its sticker price may be landing in the pockets of lawyers and PR° flacks,° that profits probably aren't benefiting those who live near the source, and that the bottle and its transportation have a significant carbon footprint. And then I will try to drink with the fullest pleasure; pleasure that, to quote Wendell Berry° on the pleasure of eating, "does not depend on ignorance."

***PR:*** public relations.

***flacks:*** spokespeople, especially those who can turn a potential disadvantage into an advantage.

***Wendell Berry (1934– ):*** a Kentucky-born writer, critic, and farmer.

### Works Cited

*Avoiding rate shock: Making the case for water rates.* 2004. Denver: American Water Works Association.

Morris, Robert D. 2007. *The blue death: Disease, disasters, and the water we drink.* New York: HarperCollins.

Snitow, Alan, Deborah Kaufman, and Michael Fox. 2007. *Thirst: Fighting the corporate theft of our water.* San Francisco: Jossey-Bass.

## Satisfying the National Thirst ...

*Beverage Digest*, which tracks trends in the industry, reports that the amount of liquid consumed by the average American holds steady at an estimated 182.5 gallons per year. Bottled water's share is growing, while almost everything else is in decline.

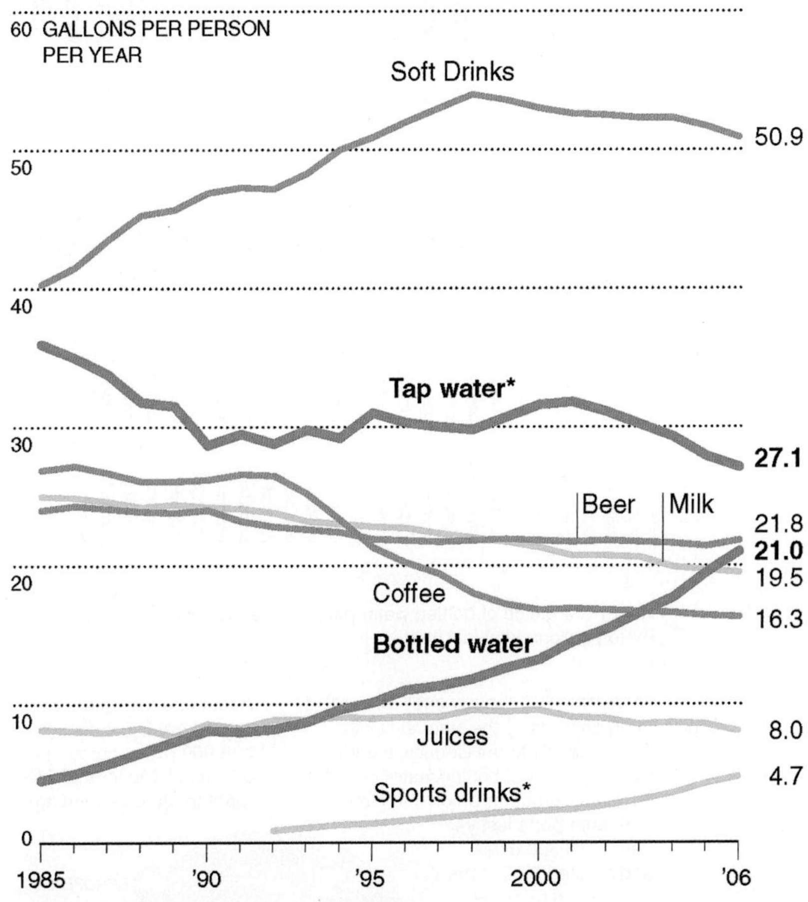


**Tap water figures include small quantities of other beverages; they included sports drinks until 1992.*

## ... With Lots of Bottles

This is what an average American's yearly consumption of bottled water looks like (in one of many possible combinations of bottles). It was 21 gallons — or 79.5 liters — in 2006.

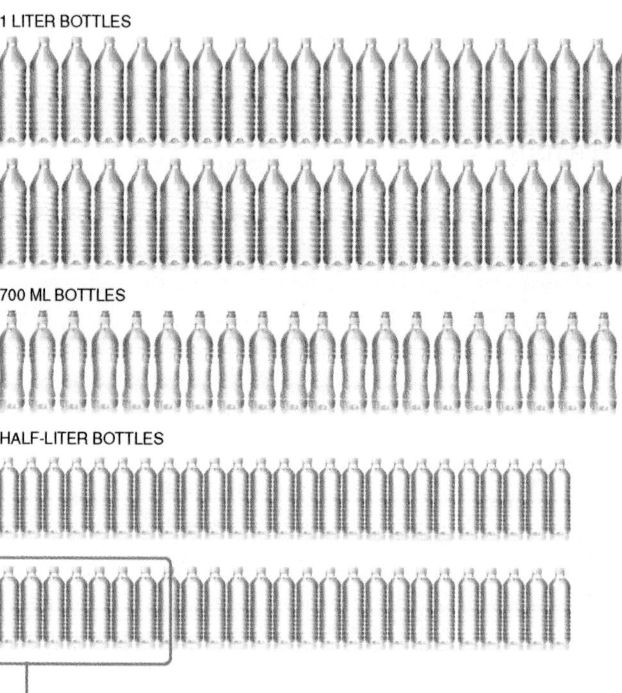


About one gallon of bottled water per American is imported — 300 million gallons total last year.

**ESTIMATING THE CARBON COST** According to an analysis by the Natural Resources Defense Council, the 43 million gallons of bottled water imported from the European Union into New York area ports last year traveled 3,500 miles and created 3,800 tons of carbon dioxide — equivalent to 660 cars running for a year.

About one million gallons came from Fiji, a distance of 8,000 miles, creating an additional 190 tons of $CO_2$ (another 30 cars running).

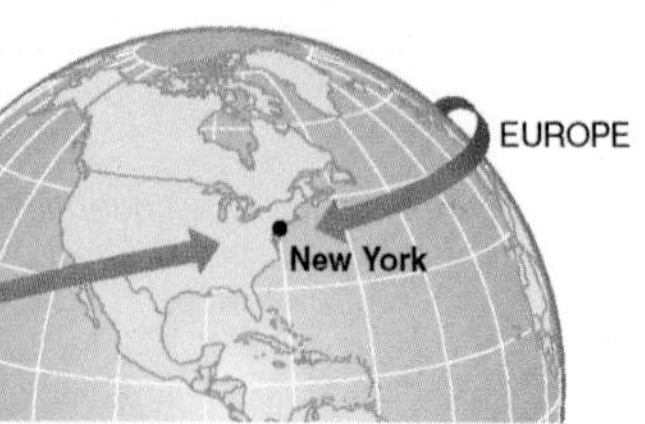

## RESPOND •

1. Briefly summarize Royte's response to the question with which she begins this excerpt. How well does she support her conclusions?
2. Summarize the arguments that are made by the *New York Times* graphic on pp. 723–24, and describe several contexts in which it could conceivably be used. Evaluate the graphic's effectiveness as a visual argument. (You may wish to locate the *Times* article with which this graphic originally appeared and use that information as part of your evaluation. For a discussion of evaluative arguments, see Chapter 10. For a discussion of visual arguments, see Chapter 14.)
3. In paragraph 2 of the previous selection, Mark Coleman's review of Royte's book, Coleman claims that "Royte doesn't traffic in platitudes, moral certainties or oversimplification; she's unafraid of ambiguity." What evidence for his evaluation do you see in this excerpt from Royte's book?
4. One of the ways that readers know that Royte is writing for a popular audience rather than an academic one is that she does not use footnotes or precise references (for example, page numbers) for quotations. She includes a list of works entitled "Selected Bibliography and Further Reading" at the end of the book, although it is not comprehensive, as we discovered tracking down the references for the three works that she cited in this excerpt (which we have presented as a Works Cited list). What are the advantages and disadvantages of using footnotes and explicit citations from a writer's point of view? A reader's? A publisher's? How does the absence of footnotes and explicit citations influence your evaluation of her text? Does it make it less formal and more inviting? Does it weaken Royte's ethos as a credible, trustworthy author? Why?
5. What is the current state of public debates about issues of water—tap versus bottled, local versus imported, natural versus flavored, plastic bottles and the carbon footprint? A good place to start may be to see if there have been arguments on your campus about the sale of bottled water or alternatives to bottled water. Investigate recent debates about water, and **construct an academic argument** that treats one of these topics. The argument may be factual, evaluative, or causal in nature. (For a discussion of academic argument, see Chapter 16. For a discussion of factual, evaluative, and causal arguments, see Chapters 8, 10, and 11, respectively.)

*We end this chapter on food and water with two common genres of argument among people who take food seriously—an evaluative argument about which brand of ready-to-bake chocolate chip cookie dough is best and a recipe for homemade chocolate chip cookies. Both* Cook's Country Magazine *and the related* Cook's Illustrated Magazine *provide what they term "foolproof" recipes for home cooks as well as evaluations of cooking equipment and ingredients. Both publications pride themselves on not being glossy, advertising-laden magazines created by "food stylists"; rather, the recipes published have been tested and retested many times in the same test kitchen that is used for the public television program* America's Test Kitchen. *Thus, these magazines represent another aspect of the current American interest with food—cooking programs on television that are linked to magazines and cookbooks, all of which have a presence on the Internet.*

*Unlike some magazines, however, these do not accept advertising, a fact that they use as an ethical appeal when they promote their "unbiased" and "objective" stance in evaluating cookware or ingredients. Rather than focusing on preparing food according to traditional recipes, these magazines try to develop recipes that take a minimum of time and effort while offering consistent high-quality results. Many cooks now subscribe to the magazines' Web sites, which grant them access to over two decades of recipes and videos. "Ready-to-Bake Chocolate Chip Cookies" appeared in the April 2005 issue of* Cook's Country, *and "The Perfect Chocolate Chip Cookie" appeared in the May 2009 issue of* Cook's Illustrated. *As you read these two selections, analyze each in ways that you likely never have looked at recipes and "best of" lists—as arguments.*

# Ready-to-Bake Chocolate Chip Cookies

*COOK'S COUNTRY MAGAZINE*

**List of Products Tested**

Homemade Cookies (with Nestlé Toll House Semi-Sweet Morsels)
Nestlé Toll House Chocolate Chip Cookie Dough
Nestlé Toll House Refrigerated Chocolate Chip Cookie Dough Bar

To determine if we could cheat and buy ready-to-bake cookie dough, we baked up cookies from homemade dough, cookie dough sold in the traditional log shape, and the new dough bars.

Nothing beats a good homemade cookie straight from the oven, right? Or can you cheat and buy ready-to-bake cookie dough? To find out if our tasters could tell the difference, we baked up three batches of cookies: one homemade recipe taken from the back of a bag of semisweet chips; one refrigerator dough sold in the traditional log shape; and one from a new product sold as a dough bar. No need to slice or measure the dough—it's already been cut into individual pieces. Just break off as many as you like and bake.

Our results were, well, surprising: The homemade batch didn't win? It seems that when it comes to chocolate chip cookies, the number of chips per cookie is what counts. Both types of ready-to-bake cookies were chock full of tiny chips, and one (the winner) had more chips than our homemade cookies. While tasters praised the homemade cookies for being light and chewy and having great butterscotch flavor, they criticized their sparse dotting of chips. Granted, the chips were larger than those in the ready-to-bake doughs, but tasters wanted more chocolate bite-for-bite. Of course, this problem can be easily remedied by adding more chips or by switching to the mini-chips used in the other doughs.

Of the two types of ready-to-bake cookies, the slice-and-bake (or more accurately, scoop and bake, from a log of dough) won not only for having the most chips but also for their more natural, craggy appearance. (Because the soft dough is hard to slice, the cookies look better if you scoop the dough.) The break-and-bake cookies were a little too flat and uniform to suggest homemade.

How much does the convenience of ready-made 5
dough cost? The break-and-bake cookies and the slice-and-bake cookies each cost $3.59 and give you between 20 and 24 cookies (made from 18 ounces of dough). The ingredients for our homemade cookies cost about $4.50, but the recipe makes at least four dozen cookies—certainly a better value.

If extra money (and artificial ingredients) is not a deterrent, the log of prepared cookie dough (not the break-and-bake variety) is your best bet. Personally, we'd rather save some money and make our own cookies. We'll just add more chips next time.

**WINNER:** Nestlé Toll House Chocolate Chip Cookie Dough

These cookies are "loaded with chips" and have "nice craggy top and crisp edges."

| | PRODUCT TESTED | PRICE* |
|---|---|---|
| RECOMMENDED | Nestlé Toll House Chocolate Chip Cookie Dough "Loaded with chips," "nice craggy top and crisp edges." | $3.69 for about 2 dozen cookies |
| RECOMMENDED | Homemade Cookies (with Nestlé Toll House Semi-Sweet Morsels) "Crunchy and chewy with the best flavor," but "low chip-to-cookie ratio." | $4.50 for about 4 dozen cookies |
| NOT RECOMMENDED | Nestlé Toll House Refrigerated Chocolate Chip Cookie Dough Bar "Flat and compact," and "too uniform." | $3.69 for 20 cookies |

*Prices subject to change.

*What kind of argument might freshly baked chocolate chip cookies be?*

# Solving the Mystery of the Chewy Chocolate Chip Cookie

*COOK'S ILLUSTRATED MAGAZINE*

After testing 40 variations, we discover how to make a thick, chewy gourmet shop cookie at home.

### The Problem

We tried innumerable published recipes claiming to produce thick, chewy cookies but were disappointed batch after batch.

### The Goal

The quest began simply enough: We wanted to duplicate, at home, the big, delicious, chewy chocolate chip cookies bought in the trendy specialty cookie shops. For us, first and foremost, this genre of home-baked chocolate chip drop cookie had to look and taste like the ultimate, sinful cookie: thick (½ inch high), jumbo (3 inches in diameter), and bursting with chocolate. It also had to have a mouthwatering, uneven surface texture with rounded edges and be slightly crispy but tender on the outside and rich, buttery, soft, and chewy on the inside.

### The Solution

One key element in achieving this cookie was melting the butter. According to food scientist Shirley Corriher, when butter is melted, free water and fat separate. When this melted butter is combined with flour, the proteins in the flour grab the water and each other to immediately form elastic sheets of gluten. This creates a product with a chewy texture. At the same time, the sugars and fats are working to inhibit gluten formation, which prevents the cookies from getting too tough. After numerous tests, varying the type of flour, the proportion of flour to butter, and sifting and not sifting, we decided that the best cookie resulted from unsifted, bleached, all-purpose flour, which has a lower protein content than unbleached. Also, the problem of the cookie hardening after several hours was eliminated by the addition of a single egg yolk; the added fat acts as a tenderizer.

## Thick and Chewy Chocolate Chip Cookies

*Makes 1½ dozen 3-inch cookies.*

These truly chewy chocolate chip cookies are delicious served warm from the oven or cooled. To ensure a chewy texture, leave the cookies on the cookie sheet to cool. You can substitute white, milk chocolate, or peanut butter chips for the semi- or bittersweet chips called for in the recipe. In addition to chips, you can flavor the dough with one cup of nuts, raisins, or shredded coconut.

### Ingredients

**2⅛** cups bleached all-purpose flour (about 10½ ounces)
**½** teaspoon table salt
**½** teaspoon baking soda
**12** tablespoons unsalted butter (1½ sticks), melted and cooled slightly
**1** cup brown sugar (light or dark) (7 ounces)
**½** cup granulated sugar (3½ ounces)
**1** large egg
**1** large egg yolk
**2** teaspoons vanilla extract
**1–2** cups chocolate chips or chunks (semi- or bittersweet)

### Instructions

1. Heat oven to 325 degrees. Adjust oven racks to upper- and lower-middle positions. Mix flour, salt, and baking soda together in medium bowl; set aside.
2. Either by hand or with electric mixer, mix butter and sugars until thoroughly blended. Mix in egg, yolk, and vanilla. Add dry ingredients; mix until just combined. Stir in chips.
3. Following illustrations on the next page, form scant ¼ cup dough into ball. Holding dough ball using fingertips of both hands, pull into two equal halves. Rotate halves ninety degrees and, with jagged surfaces exposed, join halves together at their base, again forming a single cookie, being careful not to smooth dough's uneven surface. Place formed dough onto one of two parchment paper–lined 20-by-14-inch lipless cookie sheets, about nine dough balls per sheet. Smaller cookie sheets can be used, but fewer cookies can be baked at one time and baking time may need to be adjusted. (Dough can be refrigerated up to 2 days or frozen up to 1 month—shaped or not.)
4. Bake, reversing cookie sheets' positions halfway through baking, until cookies are light golden brown and outer edges start to harden yet centers are still soft and puffy, 15 to 18 minutes (start checking at 13 minutes). (Frozen dough requires an extra 1 to 2 minutes baking time.) Cool cookies on cookie sheets. Serve or store in airtight container.

**STEP-BY-STEP**

Shaping Thick Chocolate Chip Cookies

1. *Creating a jagged surface on each dough ball gives the finished cookies an attractive appearance. Start by rolling a scant ¼ cup of dough into a smooth ball.*

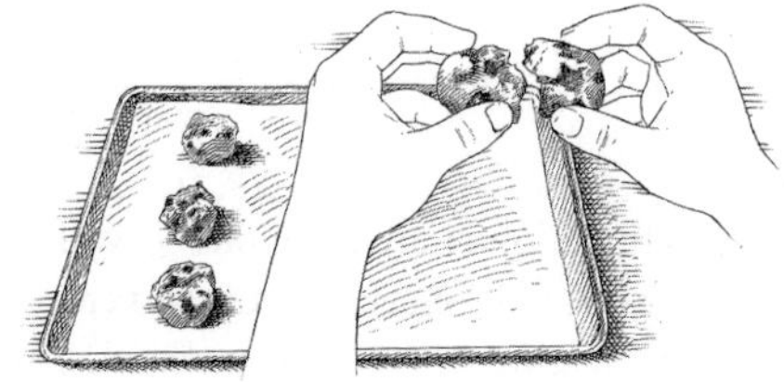

2. *Holding the dough ball in the fingertips of both hands, pull the dough apart into two equal halves.*

3. *Each half will have a jagged surface where it was ripped from the other. Rotate each piece 90 degrees so that the jagged edge faces up.*

4. *Jam the halves back together into one ball so that the top surface remains jagged.*

As Chapter 3 explains, authors can increase their authority by detailing their experience with the subject and by appealing to specialized knowledge, two strategies that we can see the author of this article employing.

LINK TO P. 50

## RESPOND•

1. What kind of argument is the first section of "Ready-to-Bake Chocolate Chip Cookies"? (For example, an argument of fact or of definition?) The list of recommended products? What kind of argument is "Solving the Mystery of the Chewy Chocolate Chip Cookie"? The recipe? What evidence can you provide for your claims?
2. Examine carefully the first section of "Ready-to-Bake Chocolate Chip Cookies" and the first section of "Solving the Mystery of the Chewy Chocolate Chip Cookie." What sorts of ethical appeals do you find in each? What sorts of appeal to emotion? To facts and reason? (For a discussion of kinds of appeals, see Chapters 2, 3, and 4.)
3. As described in the headnote to the selections, *Cook's Country* and *Cook's Illustrated* are distinct magazines, each with a Web site (http://www.cookscountry.com and http://www.cooksillustrated.com). Visit both of these sites to see how their intended audiences are similar and different. In making your assessment, you will want to consider all the available evidence, including visual layout, kinds of recipes given, and language used. **Write an essay** in which you describe your findings. (For a discussion of factual arguments, see Chapter 8. For a discussion of definitional arguments—and you may be defining each audience—see Chapter 9. Chapter 1 discusses intended audiences.)
4. Agree to the proposal argument that the recipe offers: bake the cookies. Or, if you don't like thick and chewy chocolate chip cookies or this particular recipe for them, find another recipe for a dish that you do like, and follow it meticulously. **Write an essay** in which you evaluate the recipe that you used and the resulting food that you prepared. This assignment will be most fun if you and friends do the cooking—or at least the tasting—together. You may even want to taste the cookies as a class. (For a discussion of evaluative arguments, see Chapter 10.)
5. If you are especially interested in food issues and in doing research, research the carbon footprint of the cookies discussed here. (As you may recall, question 4 about Claire Ironside's "Apples to Oranges" reading earlier in this chapter discusses the notion of carbon footprint.) This task will require a trip or two to the grocery store, careful reading of labels, and research on the Internet. (In fact, a group of students might take on this project together. If there are several groups, each could focus on a different cookie recipe or different category of recipe.) After you have completed the necessary research, **write a factual argument** about what you discovered. (For a discussion of arguments of fact, see Chapter 8.)

# 25
# What Should "Diversity on Campus" Mean and Why?

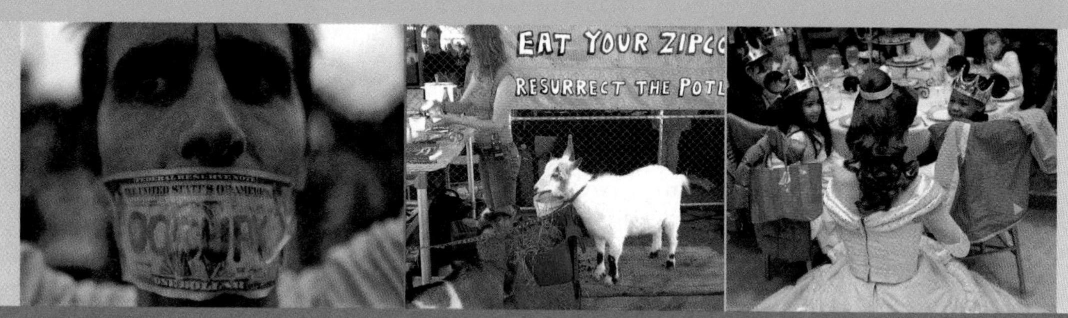


Visit your school's homepage, and look for information about diversity; if there isn't a link from the homepage, use the search function to see how long it takes to get information about diversity on your campus. We predict that it won't take long. If your school is like most, you might conclude that *diversity* has a meaning that is narrower than the *Oxford English Dictionary*'s definition of the term: "the condition or quality of being diverse, different, or varied; difference, unlikeness." (For linguists, cases of semantic narrowing like this one often stand as evidence that social change of one sort or another is taking place in the community where the narrowing occurs.) The arguments in this chapter challenge you to think about the meaning of *diversity* on your own campus—what it might mean, what it should mean, and whether it's relevant at all.

The chapter opens with a portfolio of visual arguments, award-winning posters in an annual competition with the theme of diversity at Western Washington University, each of which serves as a definitional argument of sorts.

The next four selections focus on a now-common event on campuses that always makes the papers: a bake sale sponsored by a conservative student organization where pricing is based on the buyer's ethnic background, gender, or some other demographic characteristic. Such a sale at Berkeley in September 2011 made the national news for days, and we ask you to examine such public arguments here. On his radio program, Michael Krasny of KQED interviewed two students, one on either side of this issue, the day before the sale occurred. Krasny and those who called or emailed comments helped demonstrate the complexity of such bake sales as arguments. The next selection presents the live blog from the *Daily Californian*, the Berkeley student newspaper; this new genre exists only because of the technology that supports it. These accounts of the event are followed by two evaluative treatments of it: Heather Mac Donald's "Half Baked: UC Berkeley's Diversity Machine Loses Its Mind over Cupcakes" and Tina Korbe's "Remember the Racist Cupcakes? Fordham University Fights Back with Its Own Bake Sale" focus on different aspects of such bake sales—and diversity on campus—though both writers identify themselves as conservatives.

The next two selections continue this discussion with a particular focus on the ratio of females to males in applicant pools and on college campuses. In a much-discussed article, "To All the Girls I've Rejected," Jennifer Delahunty Britz writes as an admissions officer at a private college and a mother, seeking to explain the reality of the gender gap and its consequences for female applicants. In his more provocatively titled online article, "Affirmative Action for Men," Scott Jaschik examines legal and ethical issues in admissions in light of this gender gap.

The following two selections examine categories of students often overlooked in discussions of diversity on campus. In "Blue-Collar Boomers Take Work Ethic to College," Libby Sander considers the potential consequences of older Americans' returning to college in times of economic downturn. Likewise, Edward F. Palm offers some advice to those already on campus about the growing number of students who are veterans from the wars in Afghanistan and Iraq.

Two selections then consider issues of what is sometimes termed "ideological diversity" on campus. Patricia Cohen asks if professors' liberalism is contagious, and based on the available evidence, she concludes that it likely is not. Among the research studies her article mentions is one by Mack D. Mariani and Gordon J. Hewitt, "Indoctrination U.? Faculty Ideology and Changes in Student Political Orientation," an excerpt from which we present here to give you some idea of what research shows on this topic.

The chapter closes with an excerpt from the introduction to Walter Benn Michaels's book *The Trouble with Diversity: How We Learned to Love Identity and Ignore Inequality*. Michaels argues that our discussions of diversity, especially when focused on ethnic or racial diversity, are simply on the wrong track. Such discussions may keep us occupied, but they conveniently prevent us from dealing with deeper, more serious issues that we all work hard to avoid.

For additional material related to this chapter, visit the e-Pages for *Everything's an Argument with Readings* online at **bedfordstmartins.com/everythingsanargument/epages**.

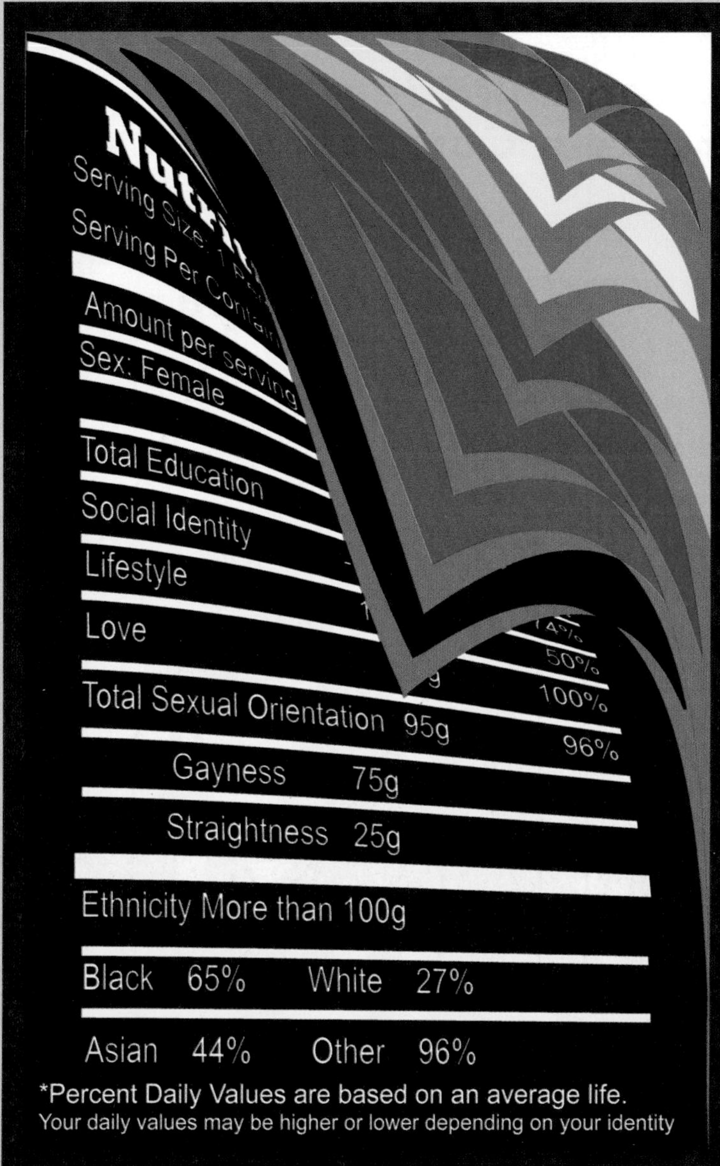


Joseph Wagner, *Peeling Off Labels,* 2009

# Making a Visual Argument: Student-Designed Diversity Posters

◀ *Since 1997, the Office of University Residences at Western Washington University in Bellingham, Washington, has sponsored an annual poster contest in which students are invited to submit posters about the year's theme, always some aspect of diversity, and to submit a written statement describing how the poster design relates to that theme. As the University's Web page about the poster contests explains, "Historically, the poster contest has served to offer students an opportunity to visually display how diversity impacts their lives based on a specific theme identified by a student committee. Artists are encouraged to capture the look, feel, and character of diversity. While the structure for how winners are selected has changed with technology, the overall winner's design is published by University Residences and displayed around campus." To learn more about the contest, visit http://bit.ly/sf4OAn. As you study these winning designs, consider the definition each directly or indirectly offers of diversity.*

Through Our Identities
We Create a Community of

CELEBRATE DIVERSITY EVERY DAY

University Residences

2011 Diversity Poster Contest
Grand Prize Winner:
**Anthony Jackson**

**Anthony Jackson, *Through Our Identities We Create a Community of Diversity*, 2011**

Bailey Jones, *Speak Out about Diversity,* 2010

Stephanie Heyman, *Everyone a Part, No One Apart,* 2003

**Melanie Frost, *Embracing Diversity in University Residences,* 1998**

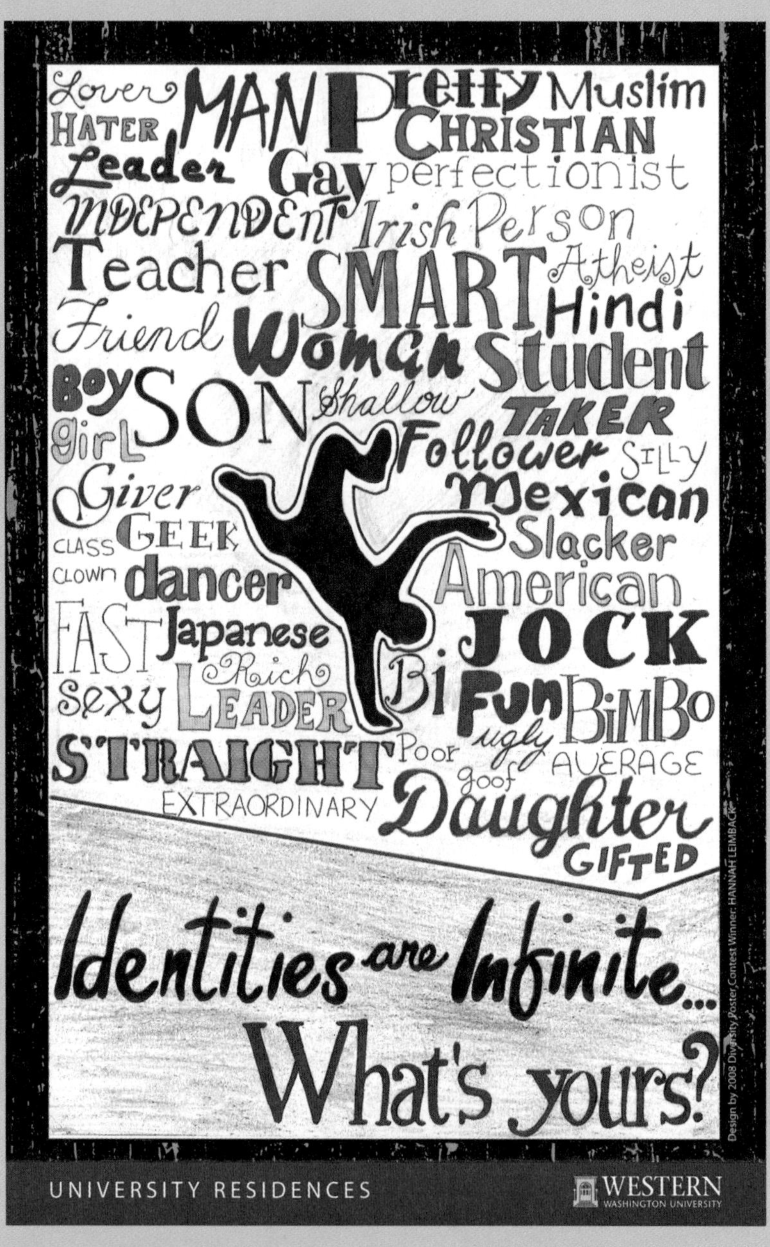


Hannah Leimback, *Identities Are Infinite . . . What's Yours?*, 2008

Megan Stampfli, *Embrace Diversity*, 2004

## RESPOND •

1. Which of these visual arguments do you find most appealing? Least appealing? Why?
2. Analyze the relationship between text (the words used) and the visual images and layout in each of the posters. What's the interaction between the text, on the one hand, and the visual images and layout, on the other, in each one? Which poster is most effective in this regard? Why?
3. If you take each of these posters to be a definitional argument, defining diversity in some way, what argument is each making? In other words, how does each poster define *diversity*? (For a discussion of definitional arguments, see Chapter 9.)
4. In defining and commenting on the notion of diversity, these posters range from approaching the topic in a didactic fashion (that is, seeking to teach a moral lesson) to approaching it much more vaguely. (Note the evaluative—and potentially negative—connotations the labels "didactic" and "vague" carry.) Choose the posters that you find most explicitly didactic and those that you find vaguer in their approach to the topic. Justify your choices. Which approach do you prefer? Why? Which do you believe is more effective in situations like this one? Why?
5. **Write an essay** in which you evaluate two of these posters, commenting on the definition of diversity presented or assumed (question 3); the relationship between text, on the one hand, and visual images and layout, on the other (question 2); and the artists' approach to the subject (question 4). (For a discussion of evaluative arguments, see Chapter 10.)
6. **Write a definitional essay** in which you define the notion of diversity as it might or should be understood on American college campuses today or your campus specifically. (For a discussion of definitional arguments, see Chapter 9.)

▼ *In late September 2011, the Berkeley College Republicans announced that they would be sponsoring a campus bake sale where the costs of cupcakes would depend on the sex and race or ethnicity of the customer as a way of protesting what they saw as the unfairness of California Senate Bill 185, dealing with affirmative action, which Governor Jerry Brown later vetoed. People teaching on university campuses for very long had seen such bake sales before; in fact, some version of them pops up every few years on campuses here or there, but this one gained considerable national attention. This selection and the next three—the* Daily Californian*'s live blog about the event, a commentary by Heather Mac Donald, "Half Baked," and a blog posting by Tina Korbe, "Remember the Racist Cupcakes? Fordham University Fights Back with Its Own Bake Sale"—examine the bake sale from several perspectives. To give you some background on the issue, we present a transcript of an award-winning KQED radio program,* Forum, *featuring Michael Krasny, a former professor of English and an author, as moderator and two guests, Andy Nevis, the executive director of the Berkeley College Republicans, and Vishalli Loomba, president of the Associated Students of the University of California. We'd encourage you to listen to this part of the radio program, which aired on September 27, 2011, as you read by going to http://bit.ly/r6TQqp. As you listen and read, think about the issues being debated on two levels. The first is the controversial topic of affirmative action, while the second is a rhetorical one: when, if ever, is satire inappropriate as a form of argument about a controversial issue?*

# The Berkeley Bake Sale

MICHAEL KRASNY AND GUESTS

---

Host: Michael Krasny (MK)

Guests: Andy Nevis, executive director of the Berkeley College Republicans (AN)

Vishalli Loomba, president of the Associated Students of the University of California (VL)

**0:00**

MK: From KQED, public radio in San Francisco, I'm Michael Krasny. Coming up on *Forum* this morning in our first half hour, we'll hear from both sides on a controversy that has erupted on the UC Berkeley campus over the Campus Republican Club's planned bake sale for today, which features lower prices for non-whites and women. Then, at 9:30, we hear all about new research out of UC Berkeley which allows scientists literally to see what is inside of minds. Brave New World? *Forum* is next, after this.

**1:00**

MK: From KQED, public radio in San Francisco, I'm Michael Krasny. Good morning and welcome to this morning's *Forum* program. California Senate Bill 185, which is being considered by Governor Jerry Brown, would authorize public universities to consider race, gender, ethnicity, and national and geographic origin in the admissions process. In reaction to that bill, and as a counter to a campus event in support of it, UC Berkeley Republican Club created a controversy by setting up a bake sale for today which features a sliding scale based on race and gender. The group has said its intent is satire, but it has created a good deal of anger and even some threats, and we want to talk about it in this first *Forum* half-hour segment. Joining us to do that this morning, from the Berkeley campus are, well, Andy Nevis, who is executive director of the Berkeley College Republicans. Good morning. Welcome to the program.

**1:45**

AN: Hey, thanks for having me, Michael.

MK: Glad to have you. And, also glad to have Vishalli Loomba, who is president of the Associated Students of the University of California—they're elected representatives of the UC Berkeley student body, and a molecular and cell biology major. Vishalli Loomba joins us from the campus, welcome.

VL: Thank you, good morning, Michael. 5

MK: Good morning to you. Andy Nevis, let me begin with you. I know that this has really from the group's perspective been touted as being satiric, and for publicity, and really to highlight what *you* think of as . . . what your group thinks of as racism. What about . . . though . . . the fact that many, including Ms. Loomba's organization and the Chancellor, have said that this is hurting people, that it's causing a great deal of pain?

**2:28**

AN: Well, I think, y'know, when you have an event, any kind of free speech event, you sometimes have to do things that are going to warrant attention. I mean, I've heard a lot of criticism that we should have had a Town Hall, y'know, we should have had some kind of discussion on this, but the fact of the matter is sometimes you have to have some visual image to get people's attention before you can have a good discussion about it. And so I think, y'know, we certainly don't intend to . . . actually, we *do* intend to offend people, but we intend to offend people the same way they should be offended about race-based admission. It's discriminatory here, and it's also discriminatory in that case. So, we actually hope that people feel uncomfortable, because that's our goal. That's part of, y'know, free speech. Free speech isn't always comfortable, but at the same time we want to make very clear we don't intend to, y'know, threaten anybody, we don't intend to make anybody feel unwelcome on campus. We are more than happy to discuss this issue with anyone that would like to; it's all about starting a dialogue.

**3:30**

MK: Well, freedom of speech is certainly something that the Berkeley campus has been identified with since the Mario Savio° days, but the Chancellor said, looking at his statement here, "Freedom of speech is not properly exercised without taking responsibility for its impact." In other words, he is promoting the idea that you need to think of civility, and you need to think of people's feelings, I guess. I want to hear your response to that, but also, you mentioned threats. Your group has alleged threats as a result of this bake sale?

***Mario Savio (1942–1996):*** a leader of the Berkeley Free Speech movement in the mid-1960s in support of student free speech and the right to engage in political activity on campus. The Free Speech Movement is often seen as marking the beginning of the student political activism that characterized the late 1960s and 1970s and is linked in complex ways to the civil rights movement, the women's movement, the gay rights movement, and the movement to end the Vietnam War.

**3:56**

AN: Yes, we've had a number of threats made against our organization. People have said, including, sadly, other Berkeley students, have said, y'know, they're going to come by and flip over the table, they're gonna throw cupcakes at us, just a lot of really, really disturbing things have been said about our organization. That's really disappointing. Now to get to your first point about the Chancellor's comment, I think that, y'know, we're definitely, as I said, we're trying to start a dialogue, and I just don't see how having a bake sale necessarily hurts other students. I would hope that it would start a dialogue with them. As I said, it might make them feel uncomfortable, but that's the whole point of free speech. If you can't make people feel uncomfortable, then the whole notion of free speech is kind of worthless. That's the whole goal, is to try to impart some kind of emotional response in the individuals that will be seeing our bake sale today.

**4:57**

MK: Andy Nevis, again, with us by phone, executive director of the Berkeley 10
College Republicans, and Vishalli Loomba, president the Associated Students of the University of California. They have already put out a statement that this is contrary to the principles of community. Let's talk about why this isn't just good dialogue or free speech, as we're hearing from Mr. Nevis. Vishalli Loomba?

**5:20**

VL: So, I think I completely value the members of BCR for coming forward and wanting to express their opinions; I think that's important, and that we should be having constructive dialogue on the issues of SB 185 or any other legislation, but I think this tactic is not constructive, and it's creating a very divisive environment. And it's really important, I know that Andy mentioned that free speech has to make people uncomfortable in order to mean something, and, I mean, I don't necessarily agree with that, and I think that when you're creating a dialogue—and I know that this has received a lot of media attention—and I think something important to look at is what is too far? And when do you, when do you realize that you crossed the line? And when you begin to compromise on respecting your peers and making them feel unwelcome and unwanted on their own campus, I think that's taking it a little too far in the name of free speech. And you really need to think critically. Like, if your intent is truly just to educate other students on your opinion on the issue, there are much more constructive ways to do that.

**6:22**

MK: So you've been hearing from a lot of students that they are hurt by this and that it's had this kind of effect?

VL: Yeah, yeah, right from the outset on Thursday night, when the event was posted, from then, I've been hearing from many, many students from all different campus communities, who are very upset and feel extremely offended, and hurt, and disrespected and unwelcome on campus.

MK: Well, you've talked about getting the sponsorship of the Republican Club revoked, and they've said, "You'll find yourself in court if you do that. It's unconstitutional." Is the Associated Students Group planning on some kind of litig . . . uh, move toward revocation of their charter?

**7:00**

VL: No, I don't think so. The Student Government, the senators, met on Sunday 15
in a special meeting, and discussed student group conduct in general, and just sort of discussed what the responsibility of student groups should be to the campus climate and the environment, and respecting their peers and other students, and other organizations, and holding events to make sure that they're not creating an environment that's divisive and that's making students feel uncomfortable, but I don't think at this point there would be anything as drastic as removing funding.

**7:32**

MK: Vishalli Loomba again is president of the Associated Students of the University of California. I'm going to open up the phone lines. I know there are many of you who have strong opinions on this or have questions you'd like to raise, and we'd certainly like to hear from you. You can join us now toll-free, and this is a half-hour segment, so if you'd like to register your thoughts or join us, the time to do so would be now. The toll-free number to join us at is 866-733-6786, and we do welcome your calls. Again, you can join us toll-free now at 866-733-6786. You can also send an email to forum@kqed.org, or you can post a question or comment on our Web site, simply by going to kqed dot org slash forum and clicking on the segment. A group of Republican students, again, at UC Berkeley under fire for planning to hold a bake sale today where the cost of the cookie is based on the race of the person buying, and the group says it's meant as a satire of legislation on the Governor's desk that would allow California universities to consider race and gender in college admissions. We're taking up that issue, and finding out your thoughts about whether you think it's offensive or not, or just political commentary, and really starting dialogue. As Andy Nevis is saying—Andy Nevis is executive director of the Berkeley College Republicans, and I guess there's some concern on your part, isn't there, that, well, there's a kind of chipping away at 209, Mr. Nevis . . .

**8:47**

AN: Yeah, absolutely. We think that the will of the voters was made extremely clear, y'know, when they passed Proposition 209, and to me, this is an attempt, essentially, to overturn that proposition by legislative action, which we think is completely unconstitutional, and not to mention that Governor Brown likes to talk a lot about how he respects the will of the people, how he wants, y'know, the people to be able to vote on, like, tax measures, tax increases. Well, I would ask him, you know, please respect the will of the voters and the will of the people on this issue. They've already spoken. If you want to overturn, if you want to re-allow affirmative action, then go back to the ballot and try to convince people otherwise.

**9:31**

MK: Did you have on your original event page—I just want to get this on the record, I think you took it down, but "if you don't come to the bake sale, you're a racist"?

AN: Yes, that was on the original page.

MK: . . . and decided, I think probably advisedly, to take it down. Let me go to 20
this question of 209, Vishalli Loomba, with you, that *was* the will of the people; it was a ballot measure that essentially got rid of affirmative action, and I suppose those who think there should be a meritocracy or are opposed to affirmative action see this as a threat, and you would say what to them?

**10:02**

*UC:* University of California.

VL: SB 185 is *not* affirmative action. It allows the UC° system to consider race, gender, and other factors in the entire holistic admissions process. It's not, by any means, affirmative action, or putting affirmative action . . . it's not doing that. So I don't see how that's a valid argument. It's completely different.

MK: But it is, perhaps, as Mr. Nevis said, moving in that direction or chipping away at 209?

*CSU:* California State University.

VL: I think that's an opinion, I don't think so. The Senate bill, it authorizes the UC system and the CSU° to consider race and gender along with other relevant factors. And so I don't think that it's chipping away at 209, and it's in no way even close to affirmative action, so I don't see that as a valid argument. And I think with the issue of the bake sale, it's, that's a valid argument, if you're against SB 185, that's fine, speak out against it but in a constructive manner. Putting on something like an event, like this bake sale where you have, um, different prices, differential pricing based on race, is offensive. And it's not as . . . if you want to make a tangible difference, then you can do a phone bank, like the people in support of SB 185, students in support of SB 185, today on campus will be holding a phone bank to Governor Jerry Brown's office to encourage him to sign the bill into law. And if students really were against this, and they wanted to talk and have a constructive conversation about SB 185, that would be a much more constructive event, in my opinion, than holding an event like this that is just making students feel extremely uncomfortable and creating a divisive environment.

**11:43**

MK: The bake sale was, according to the Berkeley College Republicans, a response to the phone bank, but we want to go to our phone bank and get your calls in here. I want to mention, by the way, that this essentially identical kind of bake sale was done eight years ago on the Berkeley campus, it's not new, but let me go to our callers and let's bring them in, and, Michael, you're first, good morning.

**11:59**

MICHAEL: Yeah, a quick question—so Vishalli is against the bake sale, but to me 25
it would seem that any argument that could be made against the bake sale could also be made against the new law. I'd love to hear her comments about that.

**12:14**

MK: I think that's you, Ms. Loomba.

VL: I'm sorry, what was the question?

MK: He said the same kind of arguments against the bake sale, I think the caller is saying, could be made against the new law that's on Governor Brown's desk.

VL: I mean, I don't think that the same arguments can be made. SB 185, I don't see how that directly . . . I don't see how that's offensive to people, where the bake sale is directly offending students who are on this campus, and coming to, and like, to attend this school, where they feel like, where they feel uncomfortable in their campus environment, even coming to school and attending their classes because they feel like there are students on campus who are racist and who are participating in this sort of event. And so, I don't think that the same criticism can really be applied to the legislation.

**13:00**

30 MK: Well, let me ask Andy Nevis, are you offended by 186?

AN: Yes, I think it's offensive . . .

MK: 185, pardon me.

AN: Yes, 185, I think treating people differently based on race, I mean, we can beat around the bush as to whether it's affirmative action or not, but the bottom line is the will of the voters in Prop. 209, was that race should not be a factor in admissions. This would make race a factor in admissions, and I think the people of California and certainly the Berkeley College Republicans think that's offensive. And we also think, by the way, that charging people different prices at a bake sale is also offensive, but we see the two issues as equivalent, and so we're trying to make that point today. As I said, we are trying . . . you know, sometimes you have to have something somewhat controversial in order to start a discussion. I also mentioned, I talked to another student group, one of the nonpartisan student groups last night, and they're now interested in having a forum on this issue. That probably would not have happened had we not had this event, so I think this is a first step towards having that constructive dialogue. And furthermore, I'd just like to say, that if there are any Berkeley students listening that feel offended by our event, y'know, come and stop by and talk with us about it. I'd be happy to talk with anybody; in fact, I talked to many friends already who were a little bit uncomfortable at the beginning, but I had a chance to talk with them, and I think at the very least, even if they don't agree with us, that they understand what we're doing and why we're doing it. So I think that would be much more constructive than passing resolutions and, y'know, just condemning us based on our speech.

**14:32**

MK: Well, there have been students who have condemned you and have expressed anger and disgust, but there has been some levity, too. I read where one African American student said his white friends are asking him to buy cupcakes for them so he can get a lower price. Let me go to more of your calls. Jesús joins us, good morning.

35 JESÚS: Hey. Yeah, I'm typically for 185 here, I protested 209 when I was in college more than ten years ago, but I think what the Republican group did is actually pretty clever, and I think the other side of it, this group over here is kind of playing right into their hands. So, y'know, to say that it's offensive is . . . it's

a stretch, they're doing satire. It's kind of funny, and I think it's working for them, so, y'know, I'll take my comments off the air here.

**15:24**

MK: All right, well, thank you for your comments. Here's a listener, Eleanor, who writes from a different perspective and says, "What the white Republican group neglects is the quality of treatment has been different between the groups over all these years; that is, are the cheap cupcakes made out of tainted ingredients? Are the white cupcakes made out of Belgian imported chocolate? The point being, you cannot equate racism with a bake sale. It is a deeply rooted and complete issue. To gloss over it like this shows insensitivity and a lack of understanding of the issue, and as a white female, I find this bake sale offensive and ignorant." And Mark writes, "I'd just like to say that everyone raising concerns about this is giving the BCR exactly what they want—attention." And we'll give attention to more of your calls. Bill, join us, you're on.

**16:04**

Bill: Yes. I have a question for the College Republicans. I'm wondering, exactly what prices are you charging? How many different race-based prices do you have and what are they?

AN: OK, so, basically, first of all, I should clarify that we are *not* actually going to be enforcing these prices as it is. It is strictly political theater, people can pay, y'know, whatever they want for a cupcake or a cookie. But the prices that we have, for display, is . . . we have Caucasian students are two dollars, Asian Americans are a dollar fifty, I believe Hisp . . . Latino students are a dollar, African Americans seventy-five cents, and Native Americans twenty-five cents, and all women are twenty-five cents off. I could be wrong on a few of those numbers; I don't have them right in front of me, but they're something like that.

MK: I think that's right, actually.

Bill: How did you come up with those prices? 40

**17:00**

AN: Well, basically, y'know, we weren't as concerned with coming up with a specific value for each, y'know, group as opposed to the overall message that this is discriminating based on race. So I can't tell you that there's a specific reason why African Americans are seventy-five cents as opposed to a dollar, or what the case may be. The pricing structure, the specific pricing structure, is somewhat beside the point. The overall point is that it's treating people differently based on race and gender, and we believe that that is wrong whether it's in a bake sale or in university admissions.

MK: I notice, though, Vishalli Loomba, that the campus Democratic club said that what's being done here is essentially a mocking of the struggles of people of color. Do you agree with that?

**17:49**

VL: Yeah, I do agree with that because I think you can't dismiss it and say the pricing structure is beside the point. That's precisely the point. To rank people in a differential price structure according to their races, I mean, that is obviously a discussion that needs to be had. Like, why are Asian Americans one fifty? Why are African Americans seventy-five cents? What thought was put into that? That, in and of itself, is so offensive and inherently racist. I mean, you can't just dismiss that fact; it's a huge factor of why students are feeling so uncomfortable with this and why people feel so offended.

MK: Well, we're getting a lot of responses, as you listeners might imagine. Here's Christopher who says, "Free speech is a legitimate defense of the legality of this bake sale. It is not a defense of its morality. The fact is that while the BCR has every legal right to make the argument they're making, the argument is faulty and offensive. Considering race in college admissions is in service of legitimate social goals, fostering diversity, and righting past injustices. Equating the right of those who have historically been discriminated against to an education with discount on a cupcake trivializes these goals, and is racially insensitive." Angela writes, "Good for the Republican club for standing up for themselves. It is a shame that the Associated Student Body president would talk about making everyone feel comfortable on campus, but infringe upon the rights of these students to peacefully protest against laws they find unjust." And a listener from San Jose, Eric, says, "Michael, it is sad that some Berkeley students wish to shut down a bake sale, and in so doing silence valid protest. This is not open and free-spirited Berkeley of past decades." Let me go to more of your calls, and we'll go to San Jose. Aaron, you're on the air.

**19:24**

AARON: Hi, so, my question is: Doesn't the UC system already give weight to high 45
school applicants that come from neighborhoods where they have strug-

gling schools, for example, a struggling school in L.A.? A student from there is going to be given, um, weight, in the application process because of the neighborhood and the socioeconomic conditions surrounding that school versus a student who's applying from, say, Cupertino, in the Bay Area, where they're coming from, y'know, a lot of advantages.

MK: In fact, Andy Nevis, there may be in place a kind of an under-the-radar admissions system.

**20:02**

AN: Yeah, well, basically, the Berkeley College Republicans, at least, doesn't really have a problem with taking into account an individual's challenges they've faced during their life, whether that be socioeconomic or any other challenges that they've had that may have made it more difficult for them to achieve academically than another student. We just don't think that it's appropriate to blanketly say that somebody's race has caused them more difficulty than someone else's race. I think race is an incredibly complex issue. Every person's experience with the issue of race is different. So, to say that just because you're a certain ethnicity, you're going to get a preference . . . We think that every case should be considered on its merits, individually, based on the challenges that that person has faced.

MK: Vishalli Loomba, since Andy Nevis has singled out race here, I'd like you to comment on that.

VL: I think that's absolutely ridiculous. You really don't think that race has played a factor for your entire childhood, since you've been brought up? I think you're dismissing a huge issue, and just completely dismissing race and saying it's not a factor.

MK: Well, just a question to you, Vishalli Loomba, on that point. Would say . . . 50
we get back to a lot of the old arguments about affirmative action, but would a student from a wealthy background who happens to be Native American or African American or Latino, as opposed to, say, a working-class poor white kid, should there be a preference there?

**21:31**

VL: Well, that's why it's part of a holistic process. You look at everything. And race is a part of that, and you can't dismiss it and say that it's not a part of everything else. And your race, your ethnicity, your heritage, your socioeconomic status are all factors that play into this process, and play into your upbringing, and I think that you can't just dismiss it and say it's invalid.

**22:00**

Many of the callers to Krasny's radio show are testing the limits of the UC Berkeley College Republicans' bake sale analogy. After reading these questions, do you think the bake sale represents a faulty analogy?

LINK TO P. 87

MK: Well, here's a listener who says, "I find it odd that there is so much protest about the bake sale but not about SB 185. I think that the bake sale is clearly a great stunt, which is why it's the topic for today's show," and that's from William, and we'll go to Eva, who's calling us from UC Berkeley. Hi, Eva.

Eva: Hi. So, I wanted to find out, why aren't you discounting the bake sale for men. I mean, men are the ones, there's a growing trend, that guys are getting . . . there are fewer and fewer guys compared to girls on campuses, so shouldn't there be affirmative action towards men in schools? So why wouldn't you be discounting cookies . . .

MK: You're leaving out your own gender here, Andy Nevis?

AN: Well, I think in this case, we're looking at what historically has been the 55
trend. Historically, when there has been affirmative action or consideration of gender in college admissions, it has been geared towards giving advantage towards females. Of course, that could change, but we don't know that for sure. So, it's based on the historical practices of colleges and universities.

MK: Final word from you, Vishalli Loomba.

**23:16**

VL: Yeah, I was just going to say that I think it's a sexist mentality. It's absolutely ridiculous, and if you look at the real world, women are still making, what, seventy-five cents to the dollar? So, it's extremely offensive to post things like that on the Internet and say, and hold an event like that. And I'd also like to add that I think there are a couple of comments that said that I'm silencing BCR and I don't want them to protest. That's completely incorrect. I fully support the ideas that members of BCR should be expressing their views. I encourage dialogue, and I love that we're . . .

MK: That'll have to be the final word here; we've come to the break. You can continue talking about this on our Web site, KQED dot org slash forum. Click on the segment. I'm Michael Krasny.

## RESPOND •

1. How would you characterize the issues raised by California Senate Bill 185 for the College Republicans and for the Associated Students of the University of California? What arguments does each side offer in favor of the stance it has taken? Which arguments do you find most convincing? (Note: This isn't a question about which side you most agree with. In fact, work hard to separate your own value commitments from your evaluation of the argument each side offers.) Why?
2. Not surprisingly, Krasny, a former professor of English, understood the Berkeley College Republicans' Bake Sale as a case of satire. What specifically is being satirized? How? In fact, Krasny was careful to note that "the group has said its intent is satire," but he continues by acknowledging that "it has created a good deal of anger and even some threats." How effective do you find this act of "political theater," as Andy Nevis termed it? Why?
3. How well does Krasny moderate the interview? Do you perceive that he is balanced in his approach to the topic? That he is fair to those he is interviewing or receiving comments from? Why or why not? In what senses is he modeling a rhetorical analysis, as discussed in Chapter 6?
4. Live interview programs, especially those involving more than one interviewee and more particularly those that include comments from callers or online comments, are improvisational in nature. Even the host, who is ostensibly in charge, cannot be sure where the program will end or how it will get there. The host must also monitor the passing of time. How do the constraints of this rhetorical context influence the messages or arguments that can be offered? (Chapter 1 considers rhetorical situations.) Based on studying this transcript and perhaps your own experience, what kinds of responses to questions from interviewees or comments by listeners are most effective? Which are least effective? What can you learn about shaping effective arguments from considering these questions?
5. Using the example of the Berkeley Bake Sale, **write an essay** in which you evaluate the uses and possible limits of satire as critique when dealing with emotionally charged issues like the ones at stake here, including affirmative action, racism, sexism, and free speech, especially at an institution that has quite a history of public debate about each. Are there situations in which satire is inappropriate or at least ill-advised? What might they be and why? What role, if any, might or should the intent of the satirists play in responding to these questions? Is it relevant? Why or why not? What would it mean for satirists to take responsibility for their actions, as the chancellor of the university has claimed they should (paragraph 8)? (Chapter 10 considers evaluative arguments.)

▼ *Here, we present the live blog from the Increase Diversity Bake Sale sponsored by the Berkeley College Republicans on September 27, 2011. Jordan Bach-Lombardo and Leslie Toy, reporters for the* Daily Californian, *the Berkeley campus newspaper, are listed as the "authors" of the live blog with Chloe Hunt, Nicholas Luther, Curan Mehra, JD Morris, Annie Sciacca, Alex Sklueff, Amruta Trivedi, Christopher Yee, and Mihir Zaveri listed as reporting from the field. In addition, the live blog used the work of staff photographers, who are credited with their photos in the post. You'll recall from an earlier selection, Michael Krasny's* Forum *radio discussion before this event took place, the two major groups involved are the Berkeley College Republicans (BCR) and the Associated Students of the University of California (ASUC), the student government at UC Berkeley. The term* blog *wasn't coined until the late 1990s, but the practice began earlier in the decade. Of course, diaries were precursors to blogs, but the assumed audiences are quite different: diarists are writing for themselves (perhaps with an eye toward future publication) while bloggers hope for the largest readership possible. Live blogs represent an additional stage in the genre's evolution. In this selection, you'll find short entries linked to the time an event occurred often along with a photo of the event. Obviously, anyone with Internet access could have followed the events as they unfolded. If you're used to reading live blogs, you'll know that you begin at the end of the text and read backward—a consequence of available technology. As you read this entry, consider how technology shapes what is possible in argumentation and what might be gained (or perhaps lost) by being able to capture complex events like the ones reported on here as they unfold. You can visit the original posting at http://bit.ly/nDff3B.*

# Live Blog: "Increase Diversity Bake Sale"

*DAILY CALIFORNIAN*

### Most Recent Posts

- Legal forum on affirmative action in education held at UC Berkeley
- A tale of two protests

- Campus hypocrisy during bake sale
- Let conversation rise
- Fiat Lux

Amid a national media storm and an outcry of racism, the Berkeley College Republicans are holding their "Increase Diversity Bake Sale," which sets a tiered price system for baked goods based on race and sex. The sale today is intended to satirically protest SB 185—affirmative action–like legislation that is currently awaiting Gov. Jerry Brown's signature. However, campus student leaders and administrators have condemned the event, which was first announced on Facebook Thursday night.

*Opponents of the Berkeley College Republicans' Increase Diversity Bake Sale stand on Upper Sproul Plaza.*
Carli Baker/Staff

**Go here for a collection of our previous coverage of the controversy surrounding the Berkeley College Republicans' "Increase Diversity Bake Sale."**

*Chloe Hunt, Nicholas Luther, Curan Mehra, JD Morris, Annie Sciacca, Alex Sklueff, Amruta Trivedi, Christopher Yee, and Mihir Zaveri of the* Daily Californian *reporting from the field.*

**3:25 p.m.**

"The Coalition," a newly formed cross-cultural, cross-gender group, held a press conference in the Cesar Chavez Student Center to present demands of the campus, administration and state government. The press conference lasted approximately 15 minutes and the coalition did not take questions after reading its statement.

5 "We are a united body of students that are working to transform the public higher education system," said Naomi Wilson, a member of the coalition, at the press conference. "The Coalition's demonstration today, known as 'The Affirmation,' is our beginning action. We will no longer allow the university to pacify us by minimally addressing these issues."

*Former UC Regent Ward Connerly sits at the Increase Diversity Bake Sale table on Upper Sproul Plaza.*
Ashley Chen/Staff

**2:27 p.m.**

The Berkeley College Republicans have cleaned up their table and are walking off of Sproul Plaza.

**2:02 p.m.**

As the scale of demonstrations has diminished, political debates have sparked up at the Berkeley College Republicans table. Topics include affirmative action and the distribution of wealth in American society.

**1:48 p.m.**

BAMN° representatives at the bake sale table in Sproul Plaza have issued a challenge to the Berkeley College Republicans to debate affirmative action. If the campus Republicans agree, BAMN has said that it will book Pauley Ballroom for the event.

***BAMN (By Any Means Necessary):*** shortened form of the name of a national activist left-wing organization promoting civil rights, most often by public demonstrations and intervention through court cases. Its full name is Coalition to Defend Affirmative Action, Integration & Immigrant Rights, and Fight for Equality By Any Means Necessary. "By any means necessary" is an allusion to a line from a 1965 speech by Malcolm X (1925–1965), the African American Muslim activist who said, "We declare our right on this earth to be a man, to be a human being, to be respected as a human being, to be given the rights of a human being in this society, on this earth, in this day, which we intend to bring into existence *by any means necessary*." The "we" in these lines referred to African Americans. At the time, "by any means necessary" was assumed to include violence, in contrast to Dr. Martin Luther King's nonviolent approach to gaining civil rights for African Americans.

**1:25 p.m.**

The "Conscious Cupcake Giveaway" has wrapped up its distribution of over 200 baked goods.

"We didn't set up closer to [the Berkeley College Republicans] because this 10
wasn't about confrontation," said Damaris Olaechea, who gave away cupcakes. "It is a forum for many voices, not a screaming match."

**1:11 p.m.**

According to members of the "black out" protest, the protest finished early because of the heat.

**1:10 p.m.**

Members of Cloyne have given away thousands of sugary snacks on the plaza.

"We gave away about 2000 baked goods, now we're giving out free hugs," said Haley Kitchens, a third-year UC Berkeley student. "We're arguing against the way they went about this in a discriminatory and hateful way."

**1:06 p.m.**

A little after 1:00 p.m., the "black out" protesters stood up on Sproul Plaza and chanted, "It is our duty to fight for our freedom." They are now dispersing and leaving Sproul Plaza.

**1:02 p.m.**

15 BAMN is no longer protesting in front of the campus Republicans' table. The area of the table does not have protesters directly in front of it, except for anti–SB 185 demonstrators.

The campus Republicans' has sold out of cupcakes. Cookies are still available. People at the Republicans' table said that most people who took baked goods were willing to pay for them.

**12:42 p.m.**

In response to BAMN's chants directly at the Berkeley College Republicans, Derek Zhou, vice president of the group, said "it's free speech."

"They have just as much of a right as us," he added.

**12:31 p.m.**

Protesters against SB 185 have formed a human barrier around the back of the bake sale table.

**12:28 p.m.**

20 Members of the group known as By Any Means Necessary (BAMN) are chanting directly in front of the bake sale: "Affirmative action is a must. We won't go to the back of the bus" and "Hey hey, ho ho, this racist bake sale's got to go."

**12:19 p.m.**

Compared to other events currently occurring, there is not much to report from the ASUC phone bank.

"It's quiet here because of all the spectacle over there," said Nolan Pack, sustainability coordinator in the ASUC Office of the External Affairs Vice President. "We're being serious about making a difference while they're over there using a cheap gimmick to get attention."

**12:08 p.m.**

Protesters are still lying down.

*Former ASUC Senator Stefan Montouth protested along with hundreds of other students and community members in opposition to the Increase Diversity Bake Sale.*
Shirin Ghaffary/Staff

*Members of the co-op community also sold baked goods on Upper Sproul Plaza today.*
Kevin Hahn/Staff

*Opponents of the Increase Diversity Bake Sale raise their fists and cheer on Upper Sproul Plaza.*
Randy Adam Romero/Staff

"I hope it's comfortable for them," said Ward Connerly,° a former UC Regent and a driving force behind Proposition 209 who is working with the Berkeley College Republicans at the bake sale.

*Ward Connerly (1939– ):* former Regent of the UC California (1993–2005) who was the driving force behind California's Proposition 209, a referendum that outlawed preferential treatment based on gender or race/ethnicity in state government, including university admissions in the state's public universities. Part of the controversy surrounding the proposition was the fact that Connerly is African American.

**12:02 p.m.**

As the clock struck twelve, the line of protesters lay down on Upper Sproul Plaza. 25

"The Republicans' basic message is that people of color and women would benefit most from SB 185," said Lou Brown, a volunteer at the Revolution Bookstore who is protesting in front of the bake sale. "But Governor Brown's weak-ass bill doesn't even come close to making amends for hundreds of years of slavery and exploitation."

*A member of the Berkeley College Republicans sells a baked good to a patron on Upper Sproul Plaza during the Increase Diversity Bake Sale.*
Derek Remsburg/Staff

**11:59 a.m.**

Meanwhile, business is continuing at the bake sale as members of the Berkeley College Republicans discuss SB 185 with customers.

"In order to move society forward, we've got to look past race," said Derek Zhou, vice president of the group.

**11:55 a.m.**

The roughly 300 people are all beginning to face Sproul Hall and join hands.

**11:48 a.m.**

The line of approximately 300 protesters dressed in black has now moved to Upper Sproul Plaza. Participants are not talking to reflect their silent protest. 30

*Berkeley College Republicans and supporters hold signs for the Increase Diversity Bake Sale.*
Giana Tansman/Staff

**11:43 a.m.**

The group dressed in black who were formerly gathered at Lower Sproul Plaza have stopped moving at Bancroft Way and Telegraph Avenue. Several are carrying signs with messages that include "Don't UC Us" and "UC Us Now."

"We're committed," said Salih Muhammad, chair of the campus Black Student Union, addressing the crowd. "We're ready to make change on this campus."

### 11:33 a.m.

Vice Chancellor Harry LeGrande said that, although he has no opinion on SB 185, today's bake sale is about freedom of speech in the university. LeGrande added that he hopes to see healthy, peaceful discourse among students.

*Students and members of the public protest the Berkeley College Republicans' Increase Diversity Bake Sale on Upper Sproul Plaza.*
Randy Adam Romero/Staff

### 11:24 a.m.

Students including members of the Black Student Union have started a march from Lower Sproul Plaza to the bake sale on Upper Sproul Plaza. They plan to peacefully protest by lying on their backs for two hours, starting at noon.

### 11:21 a.m.

35 The group gathered on Lower Sproul Plaza has started chanting: "It's our duty to fight for our freedom," "We have nothing to lose but our chains" and "It is our duty to win."

*Hundreds of students and community members were lying down on Upper Sproul Plaza in opposition to the Increase Diversity Bake Sale.*
Anna Vignet/Senior Staff

Meanwhile, Haitian-American Andre Louis, an ex-Berkeley student, joined in the protest on the side of the Berkeley College Republicans, helping them hold signs. He is not officially affiliated with the BCR.

"[UC Berkeley] demonstrates on a daily basis that it cares much more about politics, political correctness and demagoguery than either free inquiry or education, which is what I stand here defending," he said. "I don't see how the means [of the BCR bake sale] are offensive. Satire is a much used and successful political tactic historically."

### 11:16 a.m.

UC Berkeley Vice Chancellor for Equity and Inclusion Gibor Basri said that members of the Berkeley College Republicans do not reflect complete understanding of the issue in their bake sale.

*Students dressed in black were lying down on Upper Sproul Plaza to oppose the Increase Diversity Bake Sale.*
Anna Vignet/Senior Staff

"They've misread SB 185," he said. "It would not overturn prop. 209."

### 11:00 a.m.

40 Meanwhile, the ASUC phone bank in support of SB 185—the event that triggered the campus Republicans' bake sale, which in turned sparked the

*Students and community members dressed in black and holding signs joined hands in protest against the Increase Diversity Bake Sale.*
Carli Baker/Staff

campus racism debate and the national media attention—has seen about 50 people sign up to make calls, according to Beatrice Montenegro, a UC Student Association field organizer.

**10:56 a.m.**

A BAMN protest has lined up across from the Berkeley College Republicans' table, where members of the campus Republicans' group are standing with signs protesting SB 185.

Across from them, Ronald Cruz, an attorney with BAMN, is still talking through his megaphone.

"They have not answered the opposition or called for debate," he said.

**10:46 a.m.**

UC Berkeley Vice Chancellor for Equity and Inclusion Gibor Basri spoke in an interview on Sproul Plaza: "We'd be ready for race-blind admissions if, when you looked through the K–12 system and the academic performance indexes for the different races, you saw no correlation. Currently we are not there."

**10:39 a.m.**

UCPD Lt. Marc DeCoulode said that there are "several" officers in Sproul Plaza 45
monitoring the bake sale.

Meanwhile, a group of around 100 people dressed in all black are gathering in Lower Sproul Plaza.

Thirty-five cupcakes have been sold so far.

**10:34 a.m.**

Elia Kritz, dressed as a Native American, said the bake sale is offensive because it trivializes the issue of affirmative action.

"If [the Berkeley College Republicans] were serious about the issue, they would have done something serious," she said.

*Opponents of the Increase Diversity Bake Sale stand in a line on Upper Sproul Plaza.*
Giana Tansman/Staff

UC Berkeley junior Byron Hunt also took issue with the event.

"I think this bake sale is pretty counterproductive," he said. "They could have sent their message without causing such a controversy."

*Members of the affirmation prepare for a counterprotest of the Berkeley College Republicans' Increase Diversity Bake Sale.*

Kevin Foote/Staff

**10:26 a.m.**

Ronald Cruz, an attorney working to restore affirmative action, spoke to the gathering crowd in Sproul Plaza.

"Let's not let this event be unprotested, speak out for equality today," he said.

BAMN has also arrived at the plaza.

Liana Mulholland, who graduated from the University of Michigan in 2009, said she was protesting with BAMN because "they work to restore affirmative action."

"It is the key to defending public education at all levels," she said.

*Ward Connerly, a driving force behind Proposition 209, in Sproul Plaza.*

Jan Flatley-Feldman/Staff

**10:17 a.m.**

Ward Connerly, a former UC Regent and a driving force behind Proposition 209, has come to UC Berkeley to help the Berkeley College Republicans sell cupcakes.

**10:00 a.m.**

UC Berkeley Professor of political science Wendy Brown tried to buy all the baked goods at the Republicans' sale, but they did not allow her to do so.

"I thought the Republicans were free enterprise, but they won't let me buy all the cupcakes," she said.

*Shawn Lewis of the Berkeley College Republicans stands behind the Increase Diversity Bake Sale table on Upper Sproul Plaza.*

Randy Adam Romero/Staff

**9:45 a.m.**

The Berkeley College Republicans have begun to set up their table. Police and media outnumber other attendees at this point.

Affirmative Action, bake sale, Berkeley College Republicans, Increase Diversity Bake Sale

**RESPOND.**

1. In what ways can we think of live blogs as arguments? Would you categorize this live blog as an argument of fact? Of definition? Of evaluation? A causal argument? A proposal? (Chapters 8–12 discuss these categories of arguments.) What would need to change for this live blog to become a category of argument other than the one it is?
2. What are the advantages and disadvantages of live blogs as records of complex historical events like the bake sale and responses to it? In what ways are live blogs necessarily incomplete? How is reading a live blog as an event unfolds different from reading the blog after the event is completed?
3. How do the photos included as part of the blog contribute to its effectiveness? To the argument(s) it makes?
4. While there was no violence at the Berkeley event, the sorts of arguments that were taking place were by no means examples of Rogerian argumentation as discussed in Chapter 7. Is it possible to engage in Rogerian argumentation about topics as heated as those at stake in the debates at Berkeley? Must both sides agree to use Rogerian argumentation? Why or why not? What might a Rogerian argument look like in this case if you contend that form of argumentation is possible here?
5. Choose one of the photos that you find interesting and **write a description** of the sort that might be used in a factual essay on the bake sale. You will need to describe the contents of the photo, but you will also need to link the description explicitly to some aspect of the event being described.
6. **Write an essay** examining some aspect of this controversy—affirmative action, racism, sexism, freedom of speech, or perhaps another topic. Obviously, you'll be writing about the past, so in some sense your text will be evaluative. In addition to the information presented here, you'll likely want to check out the *Daily Californian*'s full coverage of this controversy at http://bit.ly/nQ10be for additional information. The essay may take many forms: defining what the issues were (or weren't), evaluating whether the bake sale was a good tactic for making a point, examining the events that led one side or the other to respond at it did (a causal argument), or proposing how public universities or American society might deal with one or more of the issues involved in the controversy. (Chapters 8–12 discuss these categories of argument.)

▼ *Heather Mac Donald is a John M. Olin Fellow at the Manhattan Institute and serves as a contributing editor to its quarterly magazine,* City Journal. *The Institute, now in its fourth decade, is a think tank known for its support of conservative and free-market-oriented ideas on a range of issues. Trained as an attorney, Mac Donald has made a reputation as one of the most interesting and provocative of American political commentators, particularly on various urban problems. She has also distinguished herself by being a proponent of what she terms secular conservatism, arguing that conservatism in no way needs to assume or require religious belief. This article was posted on the* City Journal *Web site on September 28, 2011, at http://bit.ly/p14iIe. As you read it, consider the audience she invokes.*

# Half Baked: UC Berkeley's Diversity Machine Loses Its Mind over Cupcakes

HEATHER MAC DONALD

Tuesday's now infamous affirmative-action bake sale at the University of California at Berkeley is unlikely to dissuade Governor Jerry Brown from signing a bill that would reintroduce race and gender preferences into the state's public universities. It has nevertheless served one useful function: it has clarified just what Berkeley's vice chancellor for equity and diversity does for his whopping $194,000 annual salary.

Berkeley's College Republicans wanted their "Increase Diversity Bake Sale" to serve as a counterweight to a phone bank erected on the campus's main thoroughfare, where students could call Brown and urge him to sign the preference-reinstating legislation, Senate Bill 185. Like other anti-affirmative-action bake sales on college campuses over the last decade, the College Republicans' sale priced items according to the race and gender of the customer: whites paid $2 for a pastry, with Latinos paying $1 and blacks 75 cents, while women got a 25-cent discount on all items.

And like all such previous bake sales, it triggered a storm of ludicrously clueless outrage. Student Devonte Jackson told the *San Francisco Chronicle* that the sale was inappropriate and hurtful, "attacking underrepresented communities by reducing their communities to a cheaply priced good." The president of Berkeley's student government, which sponsored the pro–SB 185 phone bank, explained to CNN that the bake sale "humorized and mocked the struggles of people of color on this campus." Another student government officer professed dismay at such a shocking insult to students of color. "We were really taken aback and, frankly, disgusted," Joey Freeman informed the *Los Angeles Times*. Capping off this outpouring of what one can only hope is willful misreading, the student senate passed an emergency resolution on Sunday condemning "the use of discrimination whether it is in satire or in seriousness by any student group."

Gibor Basri, Berkeley's vice chancellor for equity and diversity, could have served a valuable role here by pointing out that the bake sale was obviously a parody of racial and gender preferences, not a criticism of students themselves. Whatever one thinks about the issue of preferences, he might have said, such political theater belongs to Berkeley's once-revered tradition of free speech. Instead, Basri chose to stoke the melodramatic self-pity of today's college students. "A lot of students, especially students of color, read [the bake sale] as placing a higher value on white students," Basri told the *New York Times*. Basri, in other words, obeyed the ironclad script for all such minor perturbations in the otherwise unbroken reign of campus political correctness. That script requires that the massive campus-diversity bureaucracy treat the delusional claims of hyperventilating students with utter seriousness. Students in the ever-expanding roster of official campus victim groups flatter themselves that by attending what is in fact the most caring, protective, and opportunity-rich institution in the history of the world, they are braving unspeakable threats to their ego and even to their physical safety. (Indeed, so desirable is this alleged threatened status that a gender and women's studies major held a sign during Tuesday's protest of the bake sale decrying the exclusion of "queer people" from the Republicans' pricing structure.)

5 This supposedly toxic "campus climate" has engendered a nauseating rhetoric about the need for "creating safe spaces" for various endangered groups, who would otherwise risk utter obliteration in the tsunami of hatred and bias that daily washes over them. Reality check: no adult on today's college campuses wishes for anything more than to see females and minority students succeed to the utmost of their capacities. The overwhelming majority of students, meanwhile, are indifferent to race and gender and simply want to get along. It is hard not to attribute bad faith to Basri for his stupendously misguided interpretation of the bake sale as "placing a higher value on white students." If he really is incapable of understanding such a simple satire, he does not belong in an institution of higher learning—or at least what used to pass for one. One might think that a college administrator's mission would be to work for enlightenment, diffusing whatever tensions may arise from ignorance and misunderstanding. Basri has, after all, been granted an enormous piece of taxpayer largesse, commanding an expensive office of 17 staffers.

But like all such campus diversocrats, Basri is in fact a partisan in the crusade for unending identity politics, stoking tensions rather than calming them. The University of California is already wasting millions of dollars on these ever-expanding diversity sinecures.° (And UC Berkeley itself has gone into the business of diversity activism, sponsoring a student-run, credit-bearing course in how to agitate for racial preferences.) If Governor Brown signs SB 185 into law (likely violating the state's constitution, which, after Proposition 209, forbids granting preferential treatment on the basis of race, sex, or ethnicity), the diversity bureaucracy and its political supporters in Sacramento will have scored another victory and ensured the diversocracy's future growth—as students admitted for their race, not their academic qualifications, provide the pretext for yet more vice chancellors for equity and diversity.

***sinecure:*** Latin for "without care"; a position that requires little or no work but provides great benefits.

Mac Donald characterizes the Increase Diversity Bake Sale as an act of parody, which would seek to make an argument by portraying a situation in a humorous light. How effective is this strategy?

LINK TO P. 38

## RESPOND

1. Did you get new information from this selection about the bake sale at Berkeley that had not been included in the previous selections on that topic? What information is new? How does it help you understand the bake sale and the ensuing protests?
2. Mac Donald's argument is obviously evaluative in nature. What specifically is she evaluating? (She has at least several targets.) What evaluative criteria is she using? Which are explicitly stated and which are implicitly stated or assumed? (Chapter 10 presents information about evaluative arguments.)
3. How does Mac Donald use the behavior of the gender and women's studies major at the bake sale to support her claims (paragraph 4)? What specific claims is she making with this example?
4. Describe Mac Donald's invoked audience. Is it likely that she will persuade anyone who does not already agree with her position to change theirs? Why or why not? Note at least a half-dozen particular word choices that will surely appeal to those who already agree with her but that will likely alienate those who do not. How do such word choices function as arguments based on emotion? As arguments based on character? (Chapter 6 discusses audience, while Chapters 2 and 4 discuss arguments based on pathos and logos, respectively.)
5. Chapter 19 discusses using sources. Imagine that you are using this source in a factual essay about the bake sale held at Berkeley. **Write a two-to-three-paragraph summary** of this article in which you describe and characterize Mac Donald's position on the issue. You will surely want to use some direct quotations, but you will also want to pay careful attention to the verbs that you use to introduce those quotations, especially the signal verbs you use, as well as the words you choose to characterize the stance or position she takes. If you succeed at your task, your readers will not be able to tell exactly what your own stance on the bake sale is, but they will have a very clear picture of what Mac Donald's is. Be sure to add the appropriate citation for this article in two forms: as if you had gotten the information from the original Web site and as if you had taken it from this book.

▶ *Tina Korbe is a rising star among conservative bloggers and commentators. Educated at the University of Arkansas, she then became a staff member at the Heritage Foundation, a conservative think tank in Washington, D.C. In this selection, a blog entry that was posted on October 7, 2011, she describes another response to the Berkeley sale: fighting satire with satire. In her mid-twenties, Korbe blogs for Hot Air, which claims to be "the leading conservative blog for breaking news and commentary covering the Republican primary, the 2012 election, politics, media, and culture." You can see the original posting at http://bit.ly/pcF8Bx. As you read this selection, consider how the motivations for the Fordham bake sale complicate questions of diversity on college and university campuses.*

# Remember the Racist Cupcakes? Fordham University Fights Back with Its Own Bake Sale

TINA KORBE

Interesting. About a week ago, when the University of California–Berkeley College Republicans hosted a bake sale with a pricing structure based on common college admissions practices, opponents of the sale cried "racism." That's because the pricing structure dramatically revealed that some minority students have an easier time obtaining admission to universities, thanks to affirmative action—and critics of the bake sale didn't like that the publicity stunt revealed that truth. Surprisingly, most of the backlash *didn't* come from the white students who were charged $2 a cupcake as Asians were charged $1.50, Hispanics $1.00, blacks $0.75, and Native Americans $0.25.

Now, Fordham University students plan to host a bake sale in response to the Cal-Berkeley event. Dubbed "The REAL Affirmative Action Bake Sale," the sale's pricing structure will take all admissions factors—including family income, legacy status, and athletic ability—into account. The results? Children of the very wealthy will have to pay just $0.25 for a cupcake and athletes will have to pay just $0.50. Legacies and under-represented minorities will pay $1.00 while general admission will be $1.30 for women and $1.25 for men.

Mark Naison, professor of African and African American Studies at Fordham, explains why this structure is actually more reflective of what drives the college admissions process:

> According to James Shulman and William Bowen, in their book *The Game of Life: College Sports and Educational Values*, recruited male athletes, in the 1999 cohort, received a 48 percent admissions advantage, as compared to 25 percent for legacies, and 18 percent for minorities (the comparable figures for women athletes were 54 percent, 24 percent, and 20 percent, respectively). Not only do athletes get a larger admissions advantage, Bowen and Shulman report; they constitute a larger portion of the student population than under-represented minorities at the nation's top colleges, averaging 20 percent at the Ivy League colleges and 40 percent at Williams. And the vast majority of the recruited athletes at those colleges who get those admissions advantages are white, including participants in sports like men's and women's lacrosse, golf, tennis, and sailing, which few minorities play in.

> But it was not the material in *The Game of Life* which most outraged my students; it was the analysis offered in a book I used in my course for the first time, Peter Schmidt's *Color and Money: How Rich White Kids Are Winning the War over College Affirmative Action*. According to Schmidt, higher education has become a plutocracy, where "a rich child has about 25 times as much chances as a poor one of someday enrolling in a college rated as highly selective or better." In the last twenty years, Schmidt claims, universities have quietly given significant admissions advantages to students whose parents can pay full tuition, make a donation to the school, or have ties to influential politicians. Schmidt's statistics, showing 74 percent of students in the top two tiers of universities come from families making over $83,000, as compared to 3 percent come from families making under $27,000 a year, enraged my students.

Frankly, the Fordham bake sale sounds awesome. It reflects that underrepresented minorities receive advantages—but it also points out all the ways the college admissions process isn't exactly an academics-based meritocratic one. Instead, it reflects all the ways college has become about so much more—and so much less—than education. Personally, as much as I love college sports and all the other traditional trappings of "the college experience" from rec centers to on-campus concerts, I wonder whether that might not be a shame. I'm inclined to agree with American Enterprise Institute scholar Charles Murray, who writes that the elevation of the bachelor degree to an almost-entitlement for middle class kids does a disservice to individuals who might not be academically minded but who offer other abilities to society. Instead of making those individuals feel like they *have* to go to college to have a job worth working, we ought to offer them opportunities to develop their nonacademic abilities and provide them with ways to use those abilities to contribute to society. In effect, college sports do that for athletes who might not otherwise go to college (and, arguably, from an academic perspective, *shouldn't* go to college)—but that they're *tied* to educational institutions is misleading. Murray proposes to abolish the B.A. as a right-of-passage piece of paper and bring back *true* universities, centers to cultivate research and thought. That's dramatic and controversial, but well worth considering. In the meantime, both the Berkeley and Fordham bake sales did what they were designed to do—spur discussion.

**RESPOND.**

1. What arguments is the Fordham bake sale making? In what ways is it a critique and parody of the bake sale at Berkeley? What motivated the Fordham bake sale?
2. If we analyze the Fordham bake sale as a Toulmin argument, what form would it take? (Chapter 7 discusses the structure of Toulmin arguments.)
3. How does the Fordham bake sale complicate your efforts to understand diversity on college and university campuses, especially as it relates to matters of admissions? What might it teach us about satire and controversial issues?
4. Korbe is known as a political conservative, and she posted this blog entry on a Web site that identifies itself as conservative. What particular aspects of the blog posting, if any, reflect conservative thinking? How?
5. While lengthy quotations like the one Korbe uses show up in blog entries, they almost never occur in academic writing, especially in the sorts of papers you will be writing for courses. Working with the quoted material given here, **rewrite the text using paraphrasing and direct quotations** so that it that would be acceptable for you to use in a research paper on bake sales as responses to debates about affirmative action on college and university campuses. (Chapters 19–21 will help you with this task.)

▼ *Few columns on the op-ed page of the* New York Times *receive the continuing attention that "To All the Girls I've Rejected" has. If you Google the author's name, you'll see that writers at the time the piece appeared in late March 2006 and even now refer to or cite this piece, often for its frankness and for the complicated issues that it raises. Jennifer Delahunty Britz is the dean of admissions and financial aid at Kenyon College, a private school in Gambier, Ohio. Her undergraduate degree was in history, and she holds an MFA in creative nonfiction. She has served as director of admissions at three private colleges and worked as a consultant with the Lawlor Group, a major marketing firm in higher education. In this selection, she writes about how her office seeks to deal with what is often termed the "gender gap" on U.S. campuses as more and more young women and fewer and fewer young men apply to college. As you read this piece, try to anticipate the sorts of responses it got then and gets now, responses we'll examine in the questions on this selection and in the next selection.*

# To All the Girls I've Rejected

JENNIFER DELAHUNTY BRITZ

A few days ago I watched my daughter Madalyn open a thin envelope from one of the five colleges to which she had applied. "Why?" was what she was obviously asking herself as she handed me the letter saying she was waitlisted.

Why, indeed? She had taken the toughest courses in her high school and had done well, sat through several Saturday mornings taking SAT's and the like, participated in the requisite number of extracurricular activities, written a heartfelt and well-phrased essay and even taken the extra step of touring the campus.

She had not, however, been named a National Merit finalist, dug a well for a village in Africa, or climbed to the top of Mount Rainier. She is a smart, well-meaning, hard-working teenage girl, but in this day and age of swollen applicant pools that are decidedly female, that wasn't enough. The fat acceptance envelope is simply more elusive for today's accomplished young women.

I know this well. At my own college these days, we have three applicants for every one we can admit. Just three years ago, it was two to one. Though Kenyon was a men's college until 1969, more than 55 percent of our applicants are female, a proportion that is steadily increasing. My staff and I carefully read these young women's essays about their passion for poetry, their desire to discover vaccines and their conviction that they can make the world a better place.

5 I was once one of those girls applying to college, but that was 30 years ago, when applying to college was only a tad more difficult than signing up for a membership at the Y. Today, it's a complicated and prolonged dance that begins early, and for young women, there is little margin for error: A grade of C in Algebra II/Trig? Off to the waitlist you go.

Rest assured that admissions officers are not cavalier in making their decisions. Last week, the 10 officers at my college sat around a table, 12 hours every day, deliberating the applications of hundreds of talented young men and women. While gulping down coffee and poring over statistics, we heard about a young woman from Kentucky we were not yet ready to admit outright. She was the leader/president/editor/captain/lead actress in every activity in her school. She had taken six advanced placement

To All the Girls I've Rejected

© Gail Anderson and Sam Eckersley

courses and had been selected for a prestigious state leadership program. In her free time, this whirlwind of achievement had accumulated more than 300 hours of community service in four different organizations.

Few of us sitting around the table were as talented and as directed at age 17 as this young woman. Unfortunately, her test scores and grade point average placed her in the middle of our pool. We had to have a debate before we decided to swallow the middling scores and write "admit" next to her name.

Had she been a male applicant, there would have been little, if any, hesitation to admit. The reality is that because young men are rarer, they're more valued applicants. Today, two-thirds of colleges and universities report that they get more female than male applicants, and more than 56 percent of undergraduates nationwide are women. Demographers predict that by 2009, only 42 percent of all baccalaureate degrees awarded in the United States will be given to men.

We have told today's young women that the world is their oyster; the problem is, so many of them believed us that the standards for admission to today's most selective colleges are stiffer for women than men. How's that for an unintended consequence of the women's liberation movement?

10 The elephant that looms large in the middle of the room is the importance of gender balance. Should it trump the qualifications of talented young female applicants? At those colleges that have reached what the experts call a "tipping point," where 60 percent or more of their enrolled students are female, you'll hear a hint of desperation in the voices of admissions officers.

Beyond the availability of dance partners for the winter formal, gender balance matters in ways both large and small on a residential college campus. Once you become decidedly female in enrollment, fewer males and, as it turns out, fewer females find your campus attractive.

What are the consequences of young men discovering that even if they do less, they have more options? And what messages are we sending young women that they must, nearly 25 years after the defeat of the Equal Rights Amendment, be even more accomplished than men to gain admission to the nation's top colleges? These are questions that admissions officers like me grapple with.

In the meantime, I'm sending out waitlist and rejection letters for nearly 3,000 students. Unfortunately, a majority of them will be female, young women just like my daughter. I will linger over letters, remembering individual students I've met, essays I loved, accomplishments I've admired. I know all too well that parents will ache when their talented daughters read the letters and will feel a bolt of anger at the college admissions officers who didn't recognize how special their daughters are.

Yes, of course, these talented young women will all find fine places to attend college—Maddie has four acceptance letters in hand—but it doesn't dilute the disappointment they will feel when they receive a rejection or waitlist offer.

15 I admire the brilliant successes of our daughters. To parents and the students getting thin envelopes, I apologize for the demographic realities.

## RESPOND •

1. What were your responses to this selection? Were you aware of the issue it deals with? What were your intellectual responses, that is, those based on reason or knowledge? What were your affective responses, that is, those based on feelings or attitudes?
2. What arguments is Britz making in this essay? Are her arguments focused primarily on the past, the future, or the present? Why? Who are Britz's audiences? Consider here not only her title but also how she frames her comments. To whom does she seem to be writing? (See Chapter 1 for a discussion of occasions for argument and Chapter 6 for a discussion of audience.)
3. How does Britz use personal experience in this essay to create arguments based on emotion, character, and facts and logic? A useful way to think about this question will be to consider the different roles that Britz has now and in the past with respect to the issues she is discussing. (Chapters 2–4 discuss arguments based on pathos, ethos, and logos, respectively.)
4. Explain the humor in the visual illustration that appeared with this column when it was first published. How does the visual play-on-words contribute to its humor? How is it relevant to the argument the article is making?
5. This column continues to be mentioned or cited in debates about the gender gap on campus and what has come to be termed "affirmative action for men" in higher education, the topic of the following selection. In short, it continues to cause quite a stir, and it has had interesting consequences, including two Web pages on the Kenyon College Web site, "Frank Answers to Questions about Gender and Kenyon Admissions" (http://bit.ly/tqDhYA) and "A Personal Statement from Jennifer Delahunty Britz" (http://bit.ly/thN2dt). Why do you imagine the college has posted these two pages on its "New Room" site? **Write a rhetorical analysis** of these two Web pages as a response to Britz's original article. Given the complex rhetorical situation in which she is writing, you may wish to consider whether Britz's statement employs aspects of Rogerian argumentation and why it might do so. In your rhetorical analysis, be sure to comment on how the two Web pages work together to function as a response to concerns individuals might have about Britz's original article. (On rhetorical analyses, see Chapter 6. For information on rhetorical situations, consult Chapter 1, and on Rogerian argumentation, consult Chapter 7.)

*Approximately a week after Jennifer Delahunty Britz published the previous selection, "To All the Girls I've Rejected," Scott Jaschik posted this selection in March 2006 on* Inside Higher Ed, *an online publication founded in 2004 that is devoted to colleges and universities. Jaschik is one of the founders of the publication, having served as an editor at the* Chronicle of Higher Education. *As you read this selection, note that even though he and Britz treat the same topic, the balance of arguments based on emotion, character, and facts and reason in the two selections is very, very different.*

# Affirmative Action for Men

## SCOTT JASCHIK

When admissions officers gather to create a freshman class, there is a large elephant in the room, wrote Jennifer Delahunty Britz, in the *New York Times*[1] last week: the desire to minimize gender imbalance in their classes. Britz, the admissions dean at Kenyon College, wrote that her institution gets far more applications from women than from men and that, as a result, men are "more valued applicants." Britz discussed a female candidate who was considered borderline by the Kenyon team but who—had she been a he—would have been admitted without hesitation.

Why is it important to favor male applicants? "Beyond the availability of dance partners for the winter formal, gender balance matters in ways both large and small on a residential college campus. Once you become decidedly female in enrollment, fewer males and, as it turns out, fewer females find your campus attractive," Britz wrote.

The gender gap in undergraduate enrollments is, of course, no secret in academe. Women are solidly in the majority (about 57 percent nationally) and their percentages are only expected to increase[2] in the years ahead. The gender gap first started to show up—more than a decade ago—at liberal arts colleges, with educators guessing that men preferred larger institutions or the engineering and business programs more prevalent at universities. But recently, the gap has started to show up at flagship public universities, too: Some board members at the University of North Carolina at Chapel Hill were so stunned in May to learn that this year's freshman class would be 58 percent female that they asked if it was time to institute affirmative action for men.[3]

Chapel Hill isn't going that route, but Kenyon is. And while Britz's column stunned many applicants and parents and frustrated many advocates for women, its substance didn't surprise admissions officers. While few admissions officers wanted to talk publicly about the column, the private reaction was a mix of "of course male applicants get some help" along with "did she have to share that information with the world?"

### Is It Legal?

5 Lawyers who work on higher education law were also intrigued by issues raised by the column, but most wanted to talk on background° and more than one asked a variation of the question "did her president know she was going to write that?"

***talk on background:*** to talk off the record; in other words, experts talking on background know that they will not be named or quoted directly and that the purpose of the conversation is to help educate the reporter or writer about the topic.

The reality is, however, that Kenyon is unlikely to face any legal problems for its policies—although if Chapel Hill took the advice of those trustees who wanted to adopt a pro-testosterone° admissions policy, it would be in trouble. Title IX of the Education Amendments of 1972[4] bars gender discrimination in all education programs at institutions receiving federal funds (all but a handful of colleges). But Title IX has an important exemption: On admissions decisions, the statute covers all vocational, graduate and professional programs, but for undergraduate admissions, it applies only to public institutions. Kenyon, as a private institution, isn't covered.

***pro-testosterone:*** since testosterone is the principle sex hormone associated with males, this coinage obviously means "favoring males."

Private institutions are covered in terms of how they treat students once they are admitted, and that includes athletics. That could be relevant to the admissions issue because one reason cited by advocates for affirmative action for men in admissions (although not cited by the Kenyon dean) is that a lopsided gender ratio in enrollments can make it more difficult to comply with Title IX in athletics. That's because the most straightforward way to comply with Title IX's rules for athletics participation is to demonstrate "proportionality"—that the percentage of female athletes is roughly the same as the proportion of female undergraduates. Institutions that are majority female and that have a football team often find proportionality daunting.

Several lawyers familiar with Title IX said on background that they found intriguing and potentially illegal the scenario where a private institution favored male applicants (in theory legal) to build male enrollments so that sports programs for men could be protected over programs for women (potentially illegal).

The Education Department's Office for Civil Rights is charged with enforcing Title IX, and released written answers to questions prompted by the Kenyon column. At a public institution, the department said, regulations "prohibit treating individuals differently on the basis of sex, including giving preferences on the basis of sex." The only exception to this, the department said, would be "affirmative action to overcome the effects of conditions that resulted in limited participation in the recipient's education program by persons of one sex."

10 The Supreme Court has never ruled on the use of gender-based affirmative action in higher education. But the OCR statement noted that in the Supreme Court's 1996 decision[5] finding that Virginia Military Institute, as a public institution, could not deny admission to women, the justices said that under the Constitution, any public institution using gender-based distinctions in admissions needed an "exceedingly persuasive justification" that was "substantially related" to an "important government interest." While trying to read the minds of Supreme Court justices is risky, it seems hard to imagine that Justice Ruth Bader Ginsburg, author of the decision, was thinking about a good ratio of dance partners as such a government interest.

In 1999, the University of Georgia was sued by a white woman for its use of an admissions formula that gave extra points for being male and/or a minority applicant. Had the woman been a black man, the extra points for race and gender would have put her above the admissions cutoff level, but she was instead rejected. Even before a federal judge rejected Georgia's system as unconstitutional, the university stopped awarding the extra points to men, although it tried without success to defend the way it was using race in admissions.

Affirmative action in college admissions has been subject to much litigation, but the focus has been on race and ethnicity. In the landmark decision in 2003 upholding the right of colleges to use race in admissions,[6] Justice Sandra Day O'Connor wrote that limited use of affirmative action was justified to create a critical mass in a student body, because of the educational value of such diversity. But her decision stressed the limited way race was used by the law school at the University of Michigan, and the Supreme Court at the same time rejected a system used in undergraduate admissions at Michigan that relied more heavily on race and ethnicity.

Some lawyers cautioned against viewing gender and race in admissions in the same legal terms because the Supreme Court has generally subjected racial distinctions to the highest scrutiny. But others—especially critics of affirmative action—said that if the O'Connor standards were applied to gender, public colleges could be in trouble for favoring men, since no one is suggesting that there isn't a critical mass of men in higher education.

Roger Clegg, president and general counsel of the Center for Equal Opportunity, a group opposed to affirmative action, said policies like Kenyon's "should not be legal." He said that O'Connor was apparently swayed by educators' arguments that if they didn't reach some figure—say 5 percent—in terms of black enrollment, qualified black students would enroll elsewhere. "But there's no way you can say that without affirmative action for men, you wouldn't have some minimum level," he said.

## Is It Right?

Just because private colleges appear to have the legal right to favor men in 15
admissions, that doesn't mean that they should necessarily do so. But many admissions officials say that policies like that at Kenyon are entirely appropriate.

Joyce Smith, executive director of the National Association for College Admission Counseling, said that the uproar over the Kenyon column misses the reality that admissions officers favor all kinds of groups. "Institutions want to have a diverse class and you want all kinds of representation," she said. Smith noted that many colleges have outreach programs for women in math and science programs, and said that the social realities of a college class are a real factor.

"If you have a dance, you have to have enough folks to dance with," she said.

At Kenyon, while there is a gap, dancing is probably still possible. The college currently has 770 men and 870 women—a gap of under 5 percent. But the gap is larger in applications (1,848 from men and 2,400 from women). In terms of applicant quality, female admitted students topped male applicants on the verbal portion of the SAT, 705 to 681, while men bested the women on the math section by a smaller margin, 675 to 665.

To the extent that Kenyon is favoring male applicants, that poses both personal and professional concerns for Jocelyn Samuels. She is vice president for education and employment at the National Women's Law Center and has a daughter who is waiting to find out if Kenyon has admitted her for the fall.

Samuels said that she believes strongly in the value of diversity, and that 20
one reason that it was important to have a critical mass of students from different genders or races or ethnicities is so that no one single black person or female or male student must speak for all—as any one person couldn't do, given the diversity within genders, races, etc. But Samuels noted that the arguments being put forward by colleges—about social life and student perceptions of campuses as too female—weren't educational in nature.

"I think stereotyping of any sort is a dangerous business and saying that men won't come to a campus that is dominated by females is the kind of stereotypical thinking that Title IX was intended to prohibit," she said. She said that she found it "legally problematic" and "missing the point of the educational reasons that the Supreme Court has authorized schools to take race and gender into account" for colleges to be justifying discrimination by saying "we want to make sure our students can get dates."

Katha Pollitt, a columnist for *The Nation*, was so angry when she read the column in the *Times* that she fired off e-mail messages to Kenyon's president and a women's studies listserv, and posted comments on *The Nation*'s blog.[7] In an interview, she called the male favoritism "scandalous," and said people would never stand for the equivalent logic about other groups. "Boys won't apply to schools that are too majority female? What about whites? What about Christians applying to schools where there are so many Jews? It's saying that the market place forces [admissions officers] to discriminate. I think it's shameful."

Pollitt also said that these policies debase affirmative action, which she strongly supports. "Affirmative action is intended to remedy past discrimination. There is no past discrimination against white males," she said. She also sees these policies as defining the college experience as social, not educational. "Is this an intellectual endeavor or the prom committee?"

Others were bothered by the column for other reasons.

Barmak Nassirian, associate executive director of the American Asso- 25
ciation of Collegiate Registrars and Admissions Officers, said that he definitely sees "consciousness within the profession" about the gender gap in applications, and that the gap has grown large enough at some institutions to cause real concern. But he questioned whether there is

really as much unfairness as many people assume because of the Kenyon article. If colleges were so willing to favor men, Nassirian said, there are still enough men applying to college that institutions would be 50–50 on enrollment, and they're not.

More broadly, he said that the discussion is reinforcing a false sense about college admissions—a sense that is always more of a problem in this time of year, as students await answers from colleges. People have an "idealized image of admissions" in which all the applicants are lined up in some kind of precise, merit-based order and when an admissions dean has lined up her class, she figures out how many slots she has, walks down the line to the appropriate place, and admits everyone on one side and rejects the rest.

"There is no line, and there's no real consensus on merit," he said. "If everyone at the top of this imagined line is a cello player majoring in nursing, you will skip over the next cello player wanting to be a nurse," he said. Nassirian noted that there are colleges with strong math-science programs and weaker humanities programs, so would-be poets might have an edge over an engineer. It's all about context, he says, but now the public will again think there is a magic formula, benefiting men.

For her part, Pollitt hopes that not just women, but men will be angered by policies like that described at Kenyon. "I wouldn't apply there," said Pollitt (who was admitted from an all-female applicant pool at Radcliffe College), "and the flip side is that if I was a boy, I wouldn't want to apply either. Now we know that the boys who go there are stupid."

**Links**

[1] http://www.nytimes.com/2006/03/23/opinion/23britz.html

[2] http://www.insidehighered.com/news/2005/09/12/projections

[3] http://www.insidehighered.com/news/2005/06/03/gender

[4] http://www.dol.gov/oasam/regs/statutes/titleix.htm

[5] http://www.law.cornell.edu/supct/html/94-1941.ZS.html

[6] http://www.law.cornell.edu/supct/html/02-241.ZS.html

[7] http://www.thenation.com/blogs/notion?bid=15&pid=71886

**RESPOND.**

1. What arguments is Jaschik making in this article? How does he begin with Britz's column, the previous selection, "To All the Girls I've Rejected," using it as a springboard for discussing a range of related issues? What do we learn from Jaschik's article about the complex nature of the issues involved as various groups and individuals understand them?
2. Jaschik discusses his topic from two perspectives, a legal one and an ethical one. What relationship, if any, is there between these two perspectives? Why is this an interesting way to treat the topic, given the likely audience of *Inside Higher Ed*?
3. Comments in paragraphs 4 and 5 of this article make clear that some groups were surprised that Britz had spoken publicly about the issue of admissions and the gender gap on campus. Which groups were surprised? How does their surprise offer readers insight into the issue itself? Why might one group have wanted to talk on background about the topic?
4. As is often the case in online contexts, Jaschik's article received many comments. Here is an interesting one by someone who identifies himself as "Joe Counselor":

   I am an admission counselor at a "highly selective" small, residential, liberal arts college, similar to Kenyon. In reading the postings, I felt the need to chime in with a few points

   . . . "Name withheld upon request" offered a great point in an earlier post. S/he said, "The vast majority (I'd say upwards of 85%) of the applicants we received were 'qualified' to do the work at the college." This is the case at my institution, as I'm sure it is at a lot of other institutions. Most of our applicants are extremely bright, receive great grades, and test very well. We received 3,588 applications for a total of 265 spots, so how are we to differentiate between applicants? You advocated using a system where SATs and grades are the only factors. As idealistic and nice as that is, you completely overlook differences between high schools. I speak not just of the differences between the "haves" and the "have-nots" but also, for example, certain elite private schools are notorious for grade deflation.° You cited AP and IB credits. . . . What about high schools that do not offer AP or IB designated classes? I realize one could prepare on their own for the exam, but by now, hopefully my point comes across clearly—there is no objective "be all, end all" solution available.

   A second issue that was not discussed is institutional priorities. Colleges are businesses. Students and their parents are paying customers. I often get asked the question, "What is the difference between your college and X college?" Parents want to know why they should pay 30K–40K a

***grade deflation:*** in contrast to grade inflation, where students' GPAs continue to rise, as they have in most U.S. high schools and colleges over the past few decades, deflation occurs when students' GPAs go down. In other words, grading standards at these schools continue to rise so that there are fewer and fewer high grades, regardless of the quality of student work.

year to send Junior to my institution. Differentiation is a simple reality and colleges seek a diverse crop of students not just for the potential to improve their campus life and discussion, etc., but for other bonuses. A 50/50 male female balance is good for campus dynamics AND parents like hearing that during information sessions. They like hearing 70/30 in-state/out-of-state ratio, or that 36% of our students are students of color because Junior will be exposed to students with different backgrounds. Like most colleges and universities, our President and Board of Trustees have given us a few things to think about while reading. Obviously, our chief goal is to admit a great academic class, but we're also charged with shaping a class that offers more than just 265 academic all-stars. We need quarterbacks, dancers, pianists, etc. . . . And then the development office° likes to weigh in from time to time with "special cases" . . . after all, who doesn't want a new science building or athletic facility on campus?

In short, let's not go crucifying Ms. Britz for what she wrote. At a school that looks to fill 441 spots from a pool of 3,929, all the while appeasing the president, the development office, the alums, the coaches, and (apparently) the masses, she does a pretty great job.

How do Joe Counselor's remarks complicate an already complicated situation? In other words, what new relevant information does he add to our understanding of the set of issues being addressed? What sorts of arguments does Joe Counselor offer? Are his arguments based on emotion, character, or facts and reasons? How do they compare with the sorts of arguments often made in comments posted online in response to articles?

5. *Framing* refers to the perspective from which a person views or discusses an issue. To use an example from the last decade, immediately after the events of September 11, 2001, the White House framed what had happened as crimes, a frame that sets into motion ideas like locating the individual criminals and bringing them to justice. Within hours, however, the White House began to speak of a War on Terror, a very different frame that brings to mind an enemy (usually a country or group of countries), military response, and special powers for the president. In short, the way a topic is framed can greatly influence how it is perceived—for example, whether it is seen as a problem, what kind of problem or whose problem it might be, and what sorts of solutions might exist, if any. What are the consequences of framing the problem Britz discusses in the previous selection, "To All the Girls I've Rejected," as affirmative action for men? **Write an essay** in which you evaluate the frame of affirmative action as a way of discussing this issue or explore the consequences of this frame (this would be a causal argument). In planning for this assignment, you may wish to consider alternative framings of the issue as well as the debates about the positive and negative aspects of affirmative action.

***development office:*** the office on a college and university campus that focuses on fund-raising, including courting donors in the hope of getting sizable donations from them in the short term or in their wills.

▼ *Unlike people in many other countries, Americans can take college classes at any point in their life (if they can pay for them), and a growing number of older Americans are going to college for the first time or returning to school for any number of reasons. In this selection, Libby Sander, a staff reporter at the* Chronicle of Higher Education, *a newspaper that covers all aspects of postsecondary education, examines some of the consequences of this phenomenon. Her focus in this January 2008 article is older Americans who are returning to community colleges. The economic downturn beginning late in 2008 and continuing at the time this edition is being written in 2012 has resulted in increased unemployment, which often encourages adults to return to school to gain additional education and skills. As you read this selection, think about the extent to which students at your school represent what this article terms "the traditional student . . . fresh out of high school" and the extent to which age is part of diversity on your campus.*

# Blue-Collar° Boomers Take Work Ethic to College

LIBBY SANDER

For 16 years, Russell Kearney awoke at 1:30 a.m. to hoist boxes of Wonder bread and Hostess cakes onto a truck and deliver them along a 120-mile route through eastern North Carolina.

After a decade, lifting and pushing thousands of pounds of bread—sometimes as much as 10 tons a day—he ruptured a disk in his back, making it feel "like my spine was cut in half," Mr. Kearney says. But he continued to work for five more years, until finally, "I just couldn't get out of the chair," he says. "I just couldn't do it anymore."

And so, at age 53, after a lifetime of working in heavy-labor jobs, Mr. Kearney took an unexpected detour from the delivery route he figured he'd be driving until retirement. This new road led straight to the classroom, a setting he hadn't seen since graduating from high school in 1968. At nearby Lenoir Community College, he trained for a new kind of job, one that did not involve such strain on his body—a job, he hoped, that would give him a steady paycheck through the rest of his 50s and well into his 60s.

Mr. Kearney's journey to college is becoming a common one among workers in the baby-boomer° generation who are old enough to feel the strain of decades of physical labor, but too young to retire.

5 With the help of community colleges, some baby boomers are changing gears and retraining for new jobs that are less physically taxing. In doing so, these workers are among those who are redefining the tradi-

***blue-collar:*** working-class. Blue-collar jobs involve physical labor and are usually paid by the hour, in contrast to white-collar jobs, for which employees receive salaries.

***baby boomer:*** someone born between 1946 and the early 1960s. After the end of World War II, the birthrate increased rapidly as soldiers returned home, and it began dropping sharply by the mid-1960s.

*The median age of the graduating class at many colleges continues to rise.*

tional notion of retirement by working much later in life. And they are also leaving their mark on community colleges, many of which are fine-tuning their programs and making them more accessible to older adults.

"There's this image that older students are only coming to college for life enrichment, to take this and that course for their own personal enjoyment," says Jan Abushakrah, a sociology professor at Portland Community College, in Oregon, and director of its gerontology program. But in a recent survey of older students at her college, Ms. Abushakrah says, more than three-quarters said they came back to school to find a job or a new skill to keep a current job. "The older students are serious about using the college experience to get the skills that they need."

Mr. Kearney's days of loading the bread truck may be over, but his desire to work is not. Now 57, he spends his days in the operating room at Wayne Memorial Hospital, in his hometown of Goldsboro, N.C., where he is a surgical technologist. He assists surgeons in everything from routine procedures to 2 a.m. Caesarean sections, which he says he finds exciting.

"A lot of older people think they're not as useful, as productive as they used to be," Mr. Kearney says. "But I see older people who could work rings around younger people. Just because you got a few years on you, you can do it."

### Working Longer

The image of aging boomers as prosperous preretirees eager to repair to the golf course belies a much more complicated portrait. A sizable demographic° of people will require some sort of retraining in order to keep working and keep the paychecks coming in.

"It is a story that's just unfolding," 10
says Susan Porter Robinson, vice president for lifelong learning at the American Council on Education. "It's really a mosaic. If you look at them proportionately, yes, baby boomers are very well educated in terms of their predecessors. . . . But you have to then dig deeper to look at those who've been disenfranchised° from those opportunities."

Of the nearly 80 million baby boomers born between 1946 and 1965 who will reach retirement age over the next 20 years, many are expected to keep working well into their 60s or even their 70s.

By 2014, 41 percent of adults aged 55 and older will still be in the work-

***demographic:*** a group of people who are alike with respect to some social characteristic (such as age, social class, or ethnicity).

***disenfranchised:*** not granted full rights or opportunities.

Sander offers both inartistic proofs, such as statistical evidence, and artistic proofs, those based on reason and common sense, to buttress her claims. For more on using logos in arguments, see Chapter 4.

LINK TO P. 55

place, according to recent estimates by the Bureau of Labor Statistics. And in a 2005 survey of adults between the ages of 50 and 59 by the MetLife Foundation and Civic Ventures, 66 percent said they planned to keep working in some fashion during their retirement years. Of that 66 percent, 15 percent said they would never retire.

David Cox, an electrician in Soap Lake, Wash., expects to work into his 60s. He spent years crawling on his stomach to run wires through confined spaces before deciding, at age 53, that he much preferred the idea of young electricians doing the crawling while he ran the business.

"I'm getting old for this kind of stuff," says Mr. Cox, who suffered a back injury last spring that brought his wire-running days to an abrupt end. But, he says, "I refuse to sit around the house and do nothing because I can't work." So Mr. Cox, who is now 54, enrolled in the industrial electrical-technology program at Big Bend Community College, in nearby Moses Lake. There, he is studying toward an associate degree that would give him the credentials he says he needs to start such a business.

15 The wave of baby boomers returning to school is expected to crest in coming years, and administrators say it will do more than just alter the typical notion of retirement. Those boomer students will further challenge the outdated notion of what constitutes a "traditional" student.

That traditional student—fresh out of high school and able to take four years or more to complete a bachelor's degree—"just doesn't exist anymore," says Ms. Abushakrah. "Many colleges still assume that that's the typical student and all other people are exceptions. But the exceptions are becoming the rule."

For those workers who never finished college or skipped it altogether, the transition to a second or third career can be difficult, especially if their previous jobs involved little or no interaction with the technology that is the bedrock of many occupations. Community colleges play a key role in reaching out to these kinds of students, determining their needs, helping them decide which new career path to pursue, and giving them the proper schooling to do it.

But even community colleges, which, by definition, serve their communities, are finding that they need to revamp some of their policies to fulfill this mission.

"The colleges are going to have to adapt to serve this population," says George Boggs, president of the American Association of Community Colleges. "Community colleges have been the most adaptable institutions around. They offer classes on the weekends, in the evenings, in shopping centers and churches. They're very flexible in trying to meet the needs of students, so I think they're going to be very flexible in reaching these students as well."

### Ready for a Change

20 As colleges adapt to older students, they must consider the needs of those like Dannie Hill. Mr. Hill gave college a try decades ago after graduating from high school in Brooklyn. But taking classes while working full time at a fast-food restaurant to support his mother and two younger siblings proved to be too much, he says. So he dropped out. After a few years working as a messenger on Wall Street and in the purchasing department of a major financial-services company, he went into construction.

For the 20 or so years that Mr. Hill worked in construction, in New York City and Pennsylvania, he grew accustomed to wearing seven layers of clothing in the winter, lifting lumber or Sheetrock, framing walls, and lugging heavy materials around a work site. And though he took pride in working with his hands and seeing the buildings he helped construct, it exhausted him, and he didn't want to do it forever.

"It's hard on your back, hard on your joints, especially in the wintertime," says Mr. Hill, of Bethlehem, Pa. "It's four months of you against Mother Nature, just trying to get the job done."

Mr. Hill, who is 46, decided last year that he wanted a change—and that he needed a college education to make it happen.

"Unless I have certain training, I'm not going to be able to walk into an office," Mr. Hill says. "I want a job sitting down, at the computer, in the cubicle. Show me what papers to push. After being out in the field for so many years, I would like a sit-down job."

25 A single parent of a 14-year-old son, Mr. Hill recently completed his first semester at Northampton Community College, in Pennsylvania, where he took courses in philosophy and psychology two nights a week. He attends Northampton as part of Act 101, a state-funded program that

assists lower-income adults going back to school.

The most difficult part of being back in school, Mr. Hill says, is the technology. "Kids are saying, 'Just download it here and put it on your MP3 player to your iPod to your flash drive.' . . . Oh, my goodness," he laughs, "there's just so much stuff you don't get into unless you're a student."

Despite the challenges that computers present, Mr. Hill says his most important tool still works just fine. "The most rewarding thing, I have to admit, was actually realizing that the brain has not stopped working and that you can obtain new knowledge even in this modern, technical world," he says. "And when I got my first A, that really said to me, wow, I can do this."

But the joy of high marks is tempered by a certain sense of urgency, he adds: "I don't have time to fail the class, because I don't have time to make it up. I have to get it right the first time."

**Changes Ahead**

Older students like Mr. Kearney, Mr. Hill, and Mr. Cox are emblematic of the no-nonsense approach that many adult students bring to their college experience, says Bernie Ronan, acting president of Mesa Community College, in Mesa, Ariz.

"They do not have the luxury nor 30
the interest in going back to college for two or three or four years," Mr. Ronan says. "They need something they can get quick. So what that says to institutions like mine is that the traditional 16-week semester needs to be modified significantly so that individuals can come in and maximize learning in blocks that are more intense and more tailored."

Older students ask for flexible class schedules, credit for prior learning or work experience, and thorough career-placement counseling when the time comes to look for a job. They want the learning experience to create a seamless transition into a new career.

To achieve that, degree programs have to be a fair reflection of the job opportunities in a region, making partnerships between institutions, industry groups, and local economic-development agencies essential, says Mr. Ronan, whose college near Phoenix is one of the largest in the country.

Although community colleges are relatively nimble and responsive to the regions they serve, Mr. Ronan says, they have still been slow to react. But that is changing.

The sheer size of the baby-boomer cohort,° Mr. Ronan says, means that changes in curriculum and support services are mandatory. Simply tweaking a course offering here or there is not going to satisfy the demands of older students.

"The buzz that's created around 35
this population is growing," Mr. Ronan says. "These people are just flowing out of one kind of employment and into another every day. The more that happens, the more you have to pay attention to it."

Many educators predict that the changes in curriculum and support services triggered by the baby boomers' arrival will benefit all students, regardless of their age. By responding to the needs of baby boomers now, they say, community colleges will have the opportunity to engage in institutionwide makeovers that will help them educate future generations more efficiently.

For Mr. Hill, the "honest concern" that administrators at his college have shown him makes all the difference, he says. "A person at my age has a lot of different boundaries when they start making decisions and changes in their lives," he says. "You really kind of need a program that's going to open their arms and roll out the red carpet and show them the way.

"Nobody is spoon-feeding me," he hastens to add. "But they make it accessible."

---

***cohort:*** a group of individuals who belong to a particular demographic category. The term is often used with respect to age (for example, the baby boomers).

## RESPOND •

1. What argument(s) is Libby Sander making in this selection? What factors account for the situation that she is describing? To what extent are these older Americans becoming students as a matter of choice? As a matter of necessity? As Sander describes the situation, in what ways does social class intersect with the values that these students bring to school with them?
2. As noted, this article was written before the economic downturn of 2008. How has the economic situation in the United States changed since that time? Do you believe that these changes have had any influence on who is attending college or why? What evidence might you offer for your position?
3. What sorts of evidence does Sander present to support her claims? How might her article have been different if she had relied only on, let's say, statistics? How would the tone of the article, for example, have been different? (For a discussion of kinds of evidence, see Chapter 4 on logical appeals and Chapter 17 on what counts as evidence.)
4. How does the presence of older Americans on campus change the nature of college life? How might the life experiences of people like Russell Kearney, David Cox, and Dannie Hill influence their behavior as students? How might they influence the nature or content of class discussions, for example? What advantages might there be to having a student population that is not all of a single age cohort?
5. Conduct some research on the age demographics of the school you attend. You might, for example, investigate statistics about whether the average age of the student population has changed over the past few years or even decades. You might further try to determine whether the age of students is statistically related to their sex or to other demographic variables like ethnicity or social class. (All of the cases Sander discusses are men.) Another option for this assignment would be to interview two or more older students, asking what led them to come or return to school and what sorts of experiences they have had. If you are such a student, you may wish to document your own experiences or to interview similarly situated students to see how representative your experiences have been. An interesting issue with regard to this group of students is how schools refer to them; common labels are "returning students," "students older than average," or "nontraditional students." You might analyze the arguments made by each of these labels and others you collect from visiting the Web sites of various colleges and universities. Finally, you could document how your school seeks to welcome and accommodate these students. Here,

you might wish to interview staff members who focus on assisting them. Depending on what you have discovered and your own goals, in reporting your findings you may wish to **create a factual argument, an evaluation, or a proposal**, to name some possibilities. (For discussions of these categories of argument, see Chapters 8, 10, and 12, respectively.) Don't limit your options to a traditional written argument: creating a video based on interviews with several students might be an effective choice for this assignment.

*Edward F. Palm is a retired dean for social sciences and humanities at Olympic College, a two-year community college in Bremerton, Washington, who now teaches full-time online for Strayer University, a for-profit institution. He served with the U.S. Marines in the Vietnam War. In this essay, posted in September 2008 on insidehighered.com, a Web site devoted to issues in postsecondary education, Palm offers advice to those who work as administrators, faculty, and staff at colleges and universities about how to help today's veterans integrate into college life and be successful students. The essay opens with two lines from "Tommy," a poem by the British writer Rudyard Kipling (1865–1936), who was awarded the Nobel Prize for Literature in 1907. "Tommy" was a term commonly used to refer to a British soldier, and the poem bitterly criticizes the way that British civilians dealt with enlisted soldiers at the time it was written. The phrase "thin red 'eroes" refers to especially heroic British soldiers from a particular battle in the Crimean War in 1854, while "blackguards,"* pronounced blaggards, *refers to the then-common stereotype of British enlisted soldiers as vagabonds and criminals. As you read this selection, note the many ways that Palm establishes a credible and trustworthy ethos, and pay attention to how he structures this proposal argument.*

# The Veterans Are Coming! The Veterans Are Coming!

## EDWARD F. PALM

> We aren't no thin red 'eroes, nor we aren't no blackguards too,
> But single men in barracks, most remarkable like you.
> —"Tommy," Rudyard Kipling (1892)

***Parris Island:*** a U.S. Marine base near Beaufort, South Carolina, that trains enlisted soldiers.

***mess:*** military jargon referring to meals and the preparation of food.

Picture it: Marine Corps boot camp, Parris Island,° summer, circa 1965.

Five weeks into the program, two Marine recruits find themselves on mess° duty, assigned to the pot shack, a small detached building out behind the mess hall proper. For the first time since arriving on the island, these two are out from under the watchful eyes of drill instructors and able to talk freely to one another. Up until then, a strict code of silence had been enforced, with recruits allowed to speak only to their drill instructors, and even then, only when spoken to.

*Marines at Parris Island*

As they dutifully scrub a never-ending series of pots large enough to cook missionaries in, they take advantage of their new-found freedom to compare notes about how they are enjoying their stay in this semi-tropical paradise.

"I'm glad I'm going to be out of here next week!" one of the recruits remarks, his voice echoing out from the bottom of the pot he was leaning into.

"Whadaya mean?" the other asks, reminding his comrade in suds that they 5
had three weeks to go until graduation.

"I know, but I'm only sixteen, and I turned myself in last week." [The minimum enlistment age has always been seventeen, with a parent's consent; eighteen-year-olds can enlist with or without a parent's blessing.]

"They said they'd have me out within a couple weeks," he adds, "in time to begin my senior year back at my old high school." "I got in so much trouble and was generally such a pain in the ass," he explains, "that my mother finally offered to lie about my age and sign the papers if I would go in the service. So that's what I did."

"You know," he admits, "I used to think school was the worst thing that ever happened to me. But when I get back in that classroom, they're going to have to beat me out with a stick!"

I was the other recruit, the one who was of age and who had no Get-Out-of-Parris-Island-Free card. I've often wished I had made a note of that underage recruit's name and hometown. He was almost a high school drop-out, and I would bet that he went on to become a doctor, lawyer, teacher, or some other sort of professional.

I too would emerge from the Marine Corps reborn as a serious student, but my 10
road to Damascus° lasted about four years and included a side trip to Vietnam. As one who has spent a good bit of his subsequent life in academic circles, I have often wished that we could treat many of today's high-school juniors to summer camp at Parris Island. If nothing else, these campers would certainly come back with the material for wondrous essays on how they spent their summer vacations. But, like my young friend in the pot shack, many would come back with a new-found appreciation for the opportunity to get an education.

***road to Damascus:*** an unexpected experience that causes one's life to change course. The allusion is to the New Testament narrative of Saul, who persecuted Christians until, while traveling to Damascus, he had an experience that led to his sudden conversion to Christianity, after which he took the name Paul and became the faith's greatest advocate.

*Former soldiers stock up on textbooks and other academic supplies in 1945. Up to $500 in tuition, fees, books, and materials for each academic year was provided free to veterans under the World War II GI Bill.*

Palm offers a story about his past in the military and mentions his long-standing connection to academic life as ways of enhancing his authority to speak about how campuses should treat veterans. For more on building an ethos, see Chapter 3.

LINK TO P. 42

Would that it were possible! But the good news is that today's colleges and universities are soon to enjoy a great influx of academically born-again,° highly motivated students. War, as I can personally attest, has a way of reordering one's priorities and values, and today's veterans will soon have access to the best education benefits available since the World War II GI Bill.° This new GI Bill, in fact, is even more generous than its "Good War"° predecessor. Veterans of the wars in Iraq and Afghanistan, as well as any veteran who just manages to get discharged honorably, will not only get tuition, fees, books, and a living allowance. They will also be able to transfer their educational benefits to their spouses or children. Either way, we in academe° stand to gain. The question is, are we really ready to welcome today's veterans into our midst?

We do, in fact, have an unfortunate history to overcome. Not everyone in America's ivory towers° was eager to roll out the red carpet for that first wave of government subsidized veterans. The prevailing fear was that the democratization of higher education would inevitably result in the debasement of higher education. Academic standards have indeed slipped since World War II

***born-again:*** having had a conversion experience (like Paul).

***GI Bill:*** any act of Congress that provides support for veterans returning to civilian life. Such bills generally include scholarship support for vocational or higher education.

***Good War:*** a phrase that sometimes is used to refer to World War II, an example of antonomasia (see Chapter 13).

***academe:*** higher education.

***ivory towers:*** a phrase that sometimes is used to refer to colleges and universities, an example of antonomasia (see Chapter 13). It often carries strong negative connotations.

but for a whole host of cultural and societal reasons and not simply as a result of our efforts to accommodate returning GI's.

By the time I started college in the late '60s, the snobbery of the late '40s seemed to have been largely forgotten, but some older professors still seemed to feel the need to apologize for their predecessors. My own adviser, for instance, upon learning that I had been in Vietnam, hastened to assure me that he had been very much in favor of welcoming veterans to campus and that he felt we had "a lot to contribute." His reassurance seemed gratuitous° at the time. Vietnam veterans were facing a very different sort of suspicion. We were being repeatedly portrayed in the media as psychologically maimed and socially debilitated and, therefore, potentially dangerous. I cannot say that I directly and knowingly suffered from this stigma, but then again, I stopped volunteering the information that I had been in Vietnam.

***gratuitous:*** uncalled for or unjustified.

Of course, popular support for the military is much stronger now than it was then, and today's veterans need not fear being viewed as objects of suspicion on campus. Or do they?

15 I have been concerned recently in finding promotional literature on upcoming symposia° that seem to link the need for "Threat Assessment" or "Behavior Intervention" teams with "serving" or "integrating" returning veterans. What next?

***symposia:*** the plural of *symposium*, a formal word for a lecture or lecture series.

Should we expect to hear administrators sounding the alarm? *"The veterans are coming, the veterans are coming! Lock up the women and the livestock!"* Frankly, I worry that this is how certain right-wing critics of academe are going to interpret the linkage of threat assessment and veterans.

In all fairness, I have no doubt that these symposia are worthwhile, and I will take it on faith that the organizers are not viewing a potential influx of veterans as a threat to campus safety and simply want to be prepared to offer non-academic psychological counseling to any veteran who may need and want it. Most faculty and administrators, I would hope, realize that, of all the horrific campus shootings we have heard about in recent years, not one of the perpetrators was a military veteran.

This is not to dispute the need itself. In light of recent events, any campus that does not have an appropriately qualified team poised to intervene in cases of troubling or threatening behavior is putting itself at great risk. But to connect this need to the anticipated influx of veterans could prove to be a public relations nightmare and could actually provoke some of the very behavior we seek to avoid. One of the paradoxes of military history is that countries that have prepared for war have generally gotten it. Individual human nature can be equally paradoxical. People who are unjustly treated as objects of suspicion, out of anger and resentment, sometimes act out in ways that justify that suspicion. But that is the worst case scenario. *Rambo*° was only a figment of novelist David Morrell's imagination. The great majority of veteran students who feel mistrusted and misjudged will not act out violently; they will simply drop out.

**Rambo:** a novel by David Morrell about a Vietnam War veteran. It inspired a series of movies starring Sylvester Stallone.

This is likewise not to deny that many of today's combat veterans suffer from Post-traumatic Stress Disorder° or that campuses should not make counseling and other support services available to them. I can personally attest that a little combat goes a long way. But, again, the great majority of PTSD sufferers are not disruptive or violent and should not be viewed as such until or unless they provide reasonable cause. As for offering counseling, the advice of many a wise piano teacher regarding when to start children on lessons would seem to apply here as well: "when they ask for them."

***Post-traumatic Stress Disorder (PTSD):*** a persistent severe anxiety following an extremely psychologically stressful experience. It often seriously disrupts a person's life.

How then should we view and treat today's returning veterans? A little sensitivity training may be in order. I am not a psychologist or a counselor myself, but as a veteran, I think I can offer five pieces of common sense advice that would go a long way toward striking the right tone as a veteran-friendly school. 20

**First, treat veterans as you would any other student.** Do not single them out for special attention. Individualized mailings or special meetings to explain the V.A.'s policies and the school's certification requirements may be in order, but guard against any suggestion that veterans will need any more special attention than any of today's students who may or may not be academically or culturally prepared for college. Remember that the average veteran has proven his or her ability to adapt to strange surroundings and to navigate his or her way through a more complicated bureaucracy than the average academic could endure.

**Second, do not thank veterans you don't know for their service.** Most people who have served had mixed motives for enlisting in the first place and complicated feelings about the experience of having served, especially in combat. If my own post-Vietnam experience is any indication—and I think it is—it takes many veterans a long time to sort out how they feel about what they've been through and whether it was worthwhile—especially if the country remains divided about whether the cause was noble and the war necessary. To thank a veteran you don't know for his or her service is to put that veteran on the spot. It assumes an ideological and political kinship that may or may not exist. I know it makes me uncomfortable. Keep in mind as well that some will doubt your sincerity, wondering if what you're really saying is, "I'm glad you went so that I [or my son or daughter] didn't have to go." Wait until you know a veteran well—including how he or she really feels about having served—before deciding to offer your thanks.

**Third, do not shy away from any political or social issues appropriate to your class.** While they may have conformed to military discipline long enough and well enough to earn honorable discharges, veterans are not monolithic° in their attitudes, ideals, and values. Expect them to be just as open-minded and diverse in their opinions and viewpoints as any other group of today's students. Conversely, expect them to resent unfounded assumptions about their politics and personal beliefs.

***monolithic:*** uniform and rigid, like a large block of stone.

By the same token, if you have never been in the military, do not assume that you really know what it is like and what it is all about. Even more important, reserve judgment about whether academe really is the superior institution. Having been both a military officer and an academic, I have learned two things: First, academics are no more open-minded than anyone else; they are just better at articulating and defending their prejudices. Second, I have known Marine colonels who are more collegial and collaborative than commanding, and I have known college presidents who are more commanding than collegial and collaborative. Do not approach today's veterans as "people who were lost and now are found."

***ineffable:*** unable to be captured or expressed in words.

**Fourth, when it comes to what they did in the war, don't ask; wait for 25
them to decide if and when they want to tell.** The experience of combat is largely ineffable.° It cannot be adequately expressed or shared with people who have not experienced it, and most who have are conflicted about it. If they do choose to share, do not judge. Remember that those who have not been there do not share the same frame of reference. Hemingway° had a phrase for it: "a way you'll never be." Remember as well that a pretentious moral empathy can be just as infuriating as an uninformed disapproval. In general, veterans prefer to let other veterans do the listening. They know they'll understand.

***(Ernest) Hemingway (1899–1961):*** an American writer and Nobel Prize winner.

**Finally, expect veterans to do well.** Just as the expectation that someone will behave badly can create a self-fulfilling prophecy, greeting someone with the expectation that he or she will excel can achieve the desired result. That same undergraduate adviser who puzzled me with his patronizing comment about supporting the first G.I. Bill more than redeemed himself later by soliciting my comments in class when we were discussing a story set in a World War II training camp, Philip Roth's° "Defender of the Faith." I was able to clarify some of the military practices and customs on which the story turns, and my professor stoked my self-confidence by telling the class that "he speaks from an interesting perspective; he was in the military himself."

*Philip Roth (1933– ):* an American writer and Pulitzer Prize winner. "Defender of the Faith" involves a Jewish military officer who tries to avoid being manipulated by another Jewish soldier into giving him special treatment because of their shared ethnicity.

Such made-to-order opportunities to bring a particular student in, admittedly, do not come along every day. And, with older students in general, instructors always need to guard against appearing to be patronizing or condescending. But, in general, we should expect veterans to be as highly motivated and appreciative of getting a second chance at an education as was that underage Marine back in the pot shack.

## RESPOND

1. In what ways is Palm's essay a proposal argument? What does he propose? What situation leads him to offer his proposal? How appropriate do you find Palm's advice? (For a discussion of proposal arguments, see Chapter 12.)
2. The first half of Palm's essay is based on personal experiences. In what ways does Palm use these experiences to construct logical arguments? Ethical arguments? Emotional arguments? (For a discussion of these kinds of arguments, see Chapters 4, 3, and 2, respectively.) An interesting way to think about this question would be to consider what the essay would be like if it began with paragraph 15.
3. One resource that writers of arguments have is their readers' knowledge of earlier texts, events, and situations. By referring to specific things that readers know, writers communicate more than they explicitly say. (*Intertextuality* is the technical label for this relationship, especially when it involves relationships between written texts or text-like things, such as films.) Palm takes advantage of this fact throughout this essay. How, for example, does an understanding of the allusion in the title, the poem by Kipling, the New Testament story of Paul, the *Rambo* novel and the movies it inspired, and the Roth short story strengthen and enrich Palm's argument? How does the use of such intertextuality

contribute to Palm's ethos? What is missed by readers who do not have knowledge of these texts, events, or situations?

4. Giving advice to others, especially people you do not know well, is always a challenging rhetorical task. How well does Palm do? Consider the tone that he uses in the final third of the essay, where he gives "five pieces of common sense advice" (paragraph 20). How would you characterize it? Do you find the tone effective? Why or why not?
5. Track down Palm's original essay on the Internet, and read the comments that readers posted in response to it. Choose two that you find especially effective—that make clear, appropriate arguments in a concise fashion—and **write a rhetorical analysis** of them in which you explain and demonstrate why they represent effective arguments. (For a discussion of rhetorical analyses, see Chapter 6.)
6. Do research on veterans and higher education. Depending on your interest and the school that you attend, this research could take several forms—historical research into how the original GI Bill affected American society, including its class system; interviews of veterans of different generations who returned to school after completing military service or veterans from the Iraq and Afghanistan wars who currently attend your school; interviews of school staff or administrators who help veterans return to school; or research about how your school helps returning veterans. **Write an essay** in which you present your findings.

▼ *This selection and the following one, an excerpt from Mack D. Mariani and Gordon J. Hewitt's research article, "Indoctrination U.? Faculty Ideology and Changes in Student Political Orientation," examine a controversy that has raged for the past few decades among some faculty and public commentators: whether liberals, who are overrepresented on college and university faculties with respect to their number in the general population, especially at elite private and large public institutions, turn their students into liberals. The term "intellectual diversity," referring to a range of intellectual and academic perspectives among faculty, especially those in the humanities, social sciences, and fine arts, is sometimes used in these debates. The author of this selection, Patricia Cohen, writes for the* New York Times *on issues related to education, ideas, and intellectual life. As you read the selection, which first appeared in the* Times *in November 2008, you'll see that some critics of American higher education who are concerned about these issues argue that this debate is asking the wrong question. Seek to figure out what diversity, and especially intellectual diversity, means for them.*

# Professors' Liberalism Contagious? Maybe Not

PATRICIA COHEN

An article of faith among conservative critics of American universities has been that liberal professors politically indoctrinate their students. This conviction not only fueled the culture wars but has also led state lawmakers to consider requiring colleges to submit reports to the government detailing their progress in ensuring "intellectual diversity," prompted universities to establish faculty positions devoted to conservatism and spurred the creation of a network of volunteer watchdogs to monitor "political correctness" on campuses.

Just a few weeks ago Michael Barone, a fellow at the conservative American Enterprise Institute, warned in the *Washington Times* against "the liberal thugocracy," arguing that today's liberals seem to be taking "marching orders" from "college and university campuses."

But a handful of new studies have found such worries to be overwrought. Three sets of researchers recently concluded that professors have virtually no impact on the political views and ideology of their students.

If there has been a conspiracy among liberal faculty members to influence students, "they've done a pretty bad job," said A. Lee Fritschler, a professor of public policy at George Mason University and an author of the new book *Closed Minds? Politics and Ideology in American Universities* (Brookings Institution Press).

5 The notion that students are induced to move leftward "is a fantasy," said Jeremy D. Mayer, another of the book's authors. (Bruce L. R. Smith is the third co-author of the book.) When it comes to shaping a young person's political views, "it is really hard to change the mind of anyone over 15," said Mr. Mayer, who did extensive research on faculty and students.

"Parents and family are the most important influence," followed by the news media and peers, he said. "Professors are among the least influential."

A study of nearly 7,000 students at 38 institutions published in the current *PS: Political Science and Politics*, the journal of the American Political Science Association, as well as a second study that has been accepted by the journal to run in April 2009, both reach similar conclusions. "There is no evidence that an instructor's views instigate political change among students," Matthew Woessner and April Kelly-Woessner, a husband-and-wife team of political scientists who have frequently conducted research on politics in higher education, write in that second study.

Their work is often cited by people on both sides of the debate, not least because Mr. Woessner describes himself as politically conservative.

No one disputes that American academia is decidedly more liberal than the rest of the population, or that there is a detectable shift to the left among students during their college years. Still, both studies in the peer-reviewed° *PS*, for example, found that changes in political ideology could not be attributed to proselytizing professors but rather to general trends among that age group. As Mack D. Mariani at Xavier University and Gordon J. Hewitt at Hamilton College write in the current issue, "Student political orientation does not change for a majority of students while in college, and for those that do change there is evidence that other factors have an effect on that change, such as gender and socioeconomic status."

10 That may be, said Daniel Klein, an economist at George Mason, but those results don't necessarily mean there isn't a problem. Mr. Klein, whose research has shown that registered Democrats vastly outnumber Republicans among faculty in the humanities and social sciences at American colleges and universities, maintains that the focus on the liberal-conservative split is misdirected. Such terms are vague and can be used to describe everything from attitudes about religion and family to the arts and lifestyles, he said.

The real issue, said Mr. Klein, who calls himself a libertarian,° is that social democratic ideas dominate universities—ideas that play down the importance of the individual and promote government intervention.

Such "academic groupthink" means that the works of such thinkers are not offered enough, he argues. "A major tragedy is that they're not getting exposed to the good stuff," he said, citing the works of John Stuart Mill,° Adam Smith,° Friedrich Hayek° and Milton Friedman.°

---

***peer-reviewed:*** evaluated by fellow researchers. During the process of peer review of articles being considered for publication in scholarly journals, neither the authors nor the reviewers know the identity of the other parties. This system helps to ensure that evaluation is fair because the research, rather than the person who conducted it, is evaluated. In academic fields, the most prestigious publications are those that have gone through the process of peer review.

***libertarian:*** a political philosophy that works to minimize the role of government in order to maximize the freedom of individuals.

***John Stuart Mill (1806–1873):*** a British philosopher and economist. As an economist, he was a supporter of free markets; as a philosopher, he is best known for his writings on the nature of liberty and on utilitarianism, the philosophy that the good is whatever creates happiness for the greatest number of people.

***Adam Smith (1723–1790):*** a Scottish moral philosopher who is considered to be the father of modern economics. His *An Inquiry into the Nature and Causes of the Wealth of Nations* (1776) presents an argument for free markets that continues to influence economic theories.

***Friedrich Hayek (1899–1992):*** an Austrian-born philosopher and economist who shared the Nobel Prize for economics in 1974. His work staunchly defends classical liberalism, which emphasizes individual freedom, limited government, and free-market capitalism.

***Milton Friedman (1912–2006):*** an American economist, public intellectual, and 1976 Nobel Prize winner in economics. Friedman taught at the University of Chicago for over thirty years. A strong opponent of government control or intervention in markets, he is considered one of the most influential economists of the last half century.

"Even if we had hard, definite evidence that students weren't influenced by their professors, there is still reason for great concern about the composition of the faculty," Mr. Klein added.

K. C. Johnson, a historian at the City University of New York, characterizes the problem as pedagogical, not political. Entire fields of study, from traditional literary analysis to political and military history, are simply not widely taught anymore, Mr. Johnson contended: "Even students who want to learn don't have the opportunity because there are no specialists on the faculty to take courses from."

15 "The conservative critics are inventing a straw man that doesn't exist and are missing the real problem that does," he added.

Anne Neal, the president of the American Council of Trustees and Alumni, which closely follows this issue, agrees that "it is not about left and right."

Many researchers and critics also agree that a better grounding in American history and politics is important. "It wasn't too long ago that schools and universities required civic education and American history," Mr. Fritschler noted. "Almost all of those requirements have evaporated."

A number of organizations that have a large base of conservative supporters, like Ms. Neal's council and the National Association of Scholars, have been promoting a return to traditional courses in western civilization and American history.

Mr. Fritschler said that perhaps the most insidious° side effect of assumptions about liberal influence has been an overall disengagement on campus from civic and political affairs, and a reluctance to promote serious debate of political issues. If anything, he added, the problem is not too much politics, but too little.

This article has been revised to reflect the following correction:

Correction: November 6, 2008

An article on Monday about research that has found that professors have virtually no impact on the political views and ideology of their students omitted the name of a co-author of the book *Closed Minds? Politics and Ideology in American Universities*, two of whose authors were quoted in the article. In addition to A. Lee Fritschler and Jeremy D. Mayer, Bruce L. R. Smith is a co-author of the book.

---

***insidious:*** harmful in a subtle and often almost hidden way.

K. C. Johnson argues that conservative critics of academic life have employed an argument based on a fallacy. For more on the straw man argument and other fallacies, see Chapter 5.

LINK TO P. 74

## RESPOND

1. The first half of this article contends that an "article of faith" among certain critics of American higher education may, in fact, be false. What is the article of faith, and what arguments and evidence does Cohen cite that may undercut it?
2. The second half of this article takes a different turn, arguing that there is, indeed, a problem on American campuses but a problem of a very different nature. According to this section of the article, what is the real problem? Cohen closes this article by indirectly quoting A. Lee Fritschler: "If anything . . . the problem is not too much politics, but too little" (paragraph 19). What does Fritschler mean by this statement? What would you imagine Fritschler's own political values and commitments to be? Why?
3. In paragraph 15, Cohen quotes K. C. Johnson: "The conservative critics are inventing a straw man that doesn't exist and are missing the real problem that does." What does Johnson mean? What is a straw man when one is discussing arguments? Does it involve ethical, emotional, or logical appeals? Why? What is the specific straw man that Johnson contends is being created in this situation? (For a discussion of fallacies of argument, including a straw man argument, see Chapter 5.)
4. Cohen mentions the American Council of Trustees and Alumni (paragraph 16) and the National Association of Scholars (paragraph 18). Do some research on these two organizations to discover their positions and the values to which they are committed. In light of this research, evaluate Anne Neal's claim that "it is not about left and right." In other words, based on your research, would you expect that most of the members of these two organizations are politically conservative and therefore affiliated with the right or politically liberal and therefore affiliated with the left? Why? Is this information relevant to Neal's claim? Why or why not?
5. In paragraph 17, A. Lee Fritschler is quoted as claiming that "almost all" of the requirements involving civic education and American history have disappeared from college campuses. Investigate the situation on your own campus. How have the requirements for graduation shifted over the past several decades? Does your school require fewer courses in civic education and American history than it used to? Does it require different courses in these areas? Has it added new requirements? What is their nature? To answer these questions, you will have to visit your school's library. Although an electronic catalog lists the

requirements for your current academic year, the catalogs from previous years probably exist only in paper format. **Write an essay** in which you document and evaluate the changes in graduation requirements at your institution. (For a discussion of arguments of fact, see Chapter 8; for a discussion of evaluative arguments, see Chapter 10.) One way to complete this assignment would be to work in groups, with each group surveying a five- to ten-year period going back several decades. Each group would then write an essay on its findings, and then all groups together could evaluate what the changes in requirements might mean.

▼ *In the previous selection, "Professors' Liberalism Contagious? Maybe Not," Patricia Cohen cites several empirical studies that had been conducted on the question of whether professors' reported political attitudes affect those of their students. Here, we present two sections of one of the studies Cohen discusses—"Indoctrination U.? Faculty Ideology and Changes in Student Political Orientation." The selection comprises the article's introduction, or opening section, and the discussion, or closing section. (Omitted are the review of previous research on this topic; the presentation of the research questions, data collected, and methodology used to collect them; and the reporting of the quantitative results and analysis of them.) The article was published in October 2008 in* PS: Political Science & Politics, *a journal of the American Political Science Association that focuses on political science, teaching, and contemporary politics. Mack D. Mariani is assistant professor of political science at Xavier University in Cincinnati while Gordon J. Hewitt is assistant dean of the Faculty for Institutional Research at Hamilton College in Clinton, New York. As you read this selection, consider how arguments based on quantitative evidence, like this one, differ from those based on political convictions without such hard evidence. Likewise, note the ways that Mariani and Hewitt seek to demonstrate that their research is unbiased, fair, and accurate.*

# Indoctrination U.? Faculty Ideology° and Changes in Student Political Orientation (Excerpt)

*ideology:* set of beliefs that form a comprehensive vision regarding a person's goals and actions.

MACK D. MARIANI AND GORDON J. HEWITT

In the provocatively titled *Indoctrination U.*,° David Horowitz argues that radical members of college faculties have "intruded a political agenda into the academic curriculum," engaging in propaganda rather than scholarship and indoctrinating students rather than teaching them (Horowitz 2007, xi). Although allegations of liberal bias in academia are nothing new, the issue has gained increased attention as the result of efforts by Horowitz and the Center for the Study of Popular Culture (CSPC) to promote the Academic Bill of Rights for American colleges and universities.[1]

*indoctrination:* the teaching of people to accept and believe things uncritically, often with the connotation of brainwashing.

According to Horowitz, the goal of the Academic Bill of Rights is to inspire college officials "to enforce the rules that were meant to ensure the fairness and objectivity of the college classroom" (Horowitz 2007, 2).[2] Supporters argue that an Academic Bill of Rights is needed to "protect students from one-sided liberal propaganda . . . [and] to safeguard a student's right to get an education rather than an indoctrination."[3] Opponents of the initiative, including the American Association of University Professors, have characterized the Academic Bill of Rights as an assault on academic freedom (Jacoby 2005; Schrecker 2006) that is based on exaggerated claims of anti-conservative bias (Ehrlich and Colby 2004; Wiener 2005; Jacobson 2006a; 2006d; Jaschik 2006b).[4]

Although a growing body of social science research indicates that college faculties are disproportionately liberal and Democratic, at least when compared with the population in general (Brookings 2001; HERI 2002; Klein and Western 2005; Jaschik 2005; Klein and Stern 2005a; 2005b; 2006; Rothman, Lichter, and Nevitte 2005), there has been very little systematic research on whether faculty members' political leanings actually affect the ideological views of the students they teach. If students' political views are being changed by a left-leaning professoriate, we should be able to see evidence of that influence; indeed, we would expect that changes in political orientation would be most dramatic among students at more ideologically liberal institutions.

This study utilizes empirical° evidence from the CIRP Freshman Survey,° the College Student Survey,° and the Higher Education Research Institute (HERI) Faculty Survey° to assess the effect of faculty ideology on the political attitudes of undergraduate students over the course of a four-year college career (2001–2005). Our analysis of 38 private colleges and 6,807 student respondents indicates that, consistent with a number of previous studies, faculty members are predominantly liberal and Democratic. We find little evidence, however, that faculty ideology is associated with changes in students' ideological orientation. The students at colleges with more liberal faculties were not statistically° more likely to move to the left than students at other institutions.

## Discussion

The goal of this study is to assess whether faculty political orientation is associ- 5
ated with changes in student political orientation. The findings presented here suggest that faculty political orientation at the institutional level does not significantly° influence student political orientation. The descriptive data also indicate that while faculty orientation is overwhelmingly liberal, student orien-

***empirical:*** derived from observation; here, drawing conclusions based on the statistical analysis of survey data (in contrast to drawing conclusions based on a theory).

***CIRP Freshman Survey:*** the Cooperative Institutional Research Program Freshman Survey. It is administered annually to over 40,000 freshmen at 700 two-year colleges, four-year colleges, and universities.

***College Student Survey:*** an exit survey of college seniors at four-year institutions across the country much like the CIRP survey of freshmen. Since 2006, it has been called the College Senior Survey.

***Higher Education Research Institute (HERI) Faculty Survey:*** a survey of faculty at two- and four-year institutions that is conducted every three years by the Higher Educational Research Institute, which is home to the Cooperative Institutional Research Program.

***statistically:*** based on the use of tests of statistical significance. The findings represent an actual relationship between variables rather than a chance occurrence.

***significantly:*** in quantitative studies, this word has a technical meaning, specifically, systematically in a way that is demonstrably unlikely due to chance.

tation when leaving college is not significantly different than the population at large. Our analysis did find that other institutional and personal characteristics, including institutional control, gender and socio-economic status, have an effect on changes in student political ideology. It should be noted that neither of the regression models° had a high level of predictive value ($R^2 = .002$, $R^2 = .006$),° but they did show which key variables were significantly correlated with change in student political orientation.

The finding that institutional control is correlated with change in political orientation is not surprising. Students at religiously controlled institutions were less likely to move to the left during their college career and we believe that this is most likely due to self-selection.° Students with strong religious beliefs are probably more likely to attend religiously controlled institutions. Institutional culture may also play a part, as both the freshman and faculty surveys indicate higher levels of conservatism among peers and faculty members at religious institutions.

Our results show that female college students are more likely than men to move to the left during the course of their college careers. It is well established that in the general population women are more liberal than men and according to Dey (1997) and data from the ANES° that is also the case for college-aged women.[5] Our results also indicate that higher socioeconomic status (as measured by estimated parental income) is associated with changes in political orientation toward the right. The finding that more wealthy students are more likely to move to the right during the course of their college careers (and vice versa) may reflect increasing student awareness about political parties and ideologies and where they stand on issues related to wealth, taxes, and government assistance for lower-income Americans (see for instance Stonecash, Brewer, and Mariani 2002).

Though we are hopeful that this study contributes to ongoing debates about faculty ideology and indoctrination, there are some limitations to this study that should be taken into account by other researchers. We are mindful, for instance, that our finding that students move leftward during college is not, by itself, evidence of indoctrination. Students may move to the left as a result of other factors, such as shared cultural influences, a common stage in personal development, or as a reaction to peer pressure, current events, or political developments. We have tried to deal with this problem by controlling for faculty ideology; if faculty ideology has an impact on student ideology then changes in student ideology should be more pronounced at institutions with more liberal faculty members and vice versa. We find little evidence that this is the case. Of course, this finding does not necessarily mean that

***regression models:*** statistical tools that enable researchers to predict one variable when they know the value of another variable (or variables).

***R:*** Pearson's coefficient of regression or the coefficient of determination. It shows how statistically useful the model is in predicting what will occur in the future. As the authors note, the predictive value of the two models was low (two cases out of 1,000 and six out of 1,000), but the analysis demonstrates which variables are correlated (related) from a statistical point of view.

***self-selection:*** in research, situations in which individuals make choices that influence the makeup of social groups. For example, we would not be surprised to find that Catholic institutions have a higher percentage of Catholic students than do public institutions generally, not because Catholic institutions give Catholic applicants preference (although some may) but because Catholic students choose to apply to Catholic institutions in large numbers.

***ANES:*** the American National Election Study. The reference for this 2004 study is in the list of references.

professors act fairly or without ideological bias in their teachings, subject matter, or selection of reading materials. Professors could, after all, be *failing* to indoctrinate students despite their concerted efforts to do so! Regardless of any biases (intentional or unintentional) that professors bring to their teaching, the findings presented here may help alleviate the concern that students, on a widespread basis, are adopting the political positions of their liberal professors.

Why are explicit summaries helpful to readers of academic arguments? What tips can you pick up from studying this one? For more on academic arguments, see Chapter 16.

LINK TO P. 367

Another limitation of this paper is that it focuses on institutions and, in doing so, it does not tell us much of anything about a student's individual experiences or the ideological views of the particular professors a student interacted with during their college career. While it would be preferable to take into account the ideology of the faculty members who actually taught each particular student, privacy laws make it very difficult to gather the data without running into considerable problems with regard to sample size and representativeness. In addition there are some advantages to our approach of looking at overall faculty ideology. Part of the argument is that students are being indoctrinated not just in class, but from the general climate created by faculty members that pervades their teaching, scholarship, and outside of the classroom activities. The indoctrination argument is, in large part, about what goes on in the classroom. But what goes on in the classroom is affected by the broader campus culture and vice versa. Thus, the overall faculty ideology of the institution is likely to influence all students in some way.

10 Though the number of students examined here is considerable (6,807), the number of institutions remains relatively small (38). We were limited by the fact that relatively few institutions participate in all three of the surveys needed to account for faculty ideology and changes in student ideology over time. There are no public universities in the sample, and large percentages are selective liberal arts colleges. Though this is a limitation, many of the conservative critiques focus in particular on elite and private colleges, so it is not entirely without merit to use this sample as a test of the indoctrination argument. It should also be noted that students at these institutions who take longer than four years to complete their programs are unlikely to be included in the senior year surveys used in this study (and were therefore likely to be dropped from the dataset).

A final limitation of this study relates to the potential impact of an exogenous° shock—the September 11 terrorists attacks. The college students in our sample began college in the fall of 1999 and finished in the spring of 2003. For the students in this sample, the terrorist attacks of September 11, 2001, took place at the start of their junior year in college, roughly midway through their college careers. Clearly, the September 11 attacks have the

***exogenous:*** outside. Here, a variable was external to the study, and its impact could not be controlled or determined.

potential to impact this cohort of students' political viewpoints. For this reason, further research is needed to assess whether similar changes occur for other groups of students whose college careers occurred under different historical circumstances.

To summarize, there are four important findings here related to questions about faculty ideology and fears that liberal faculty members are indoctrinating students to adopt a liberal ideology. First, it is very clear that faculty members tend to be liberal and are much more liberal than the general population. Second, there is evidence that there is a degree of self-selection going on among students when they choose a college. Students tend to enroll at institutions that have a faculty orientation makeup more similar to their own. This area is ripe for further research, for there may be other institutional factors at play, such as campus culture or history. Third, students whose ideology changes while in college tend to change to the left, but that movement is within the normal orientation range of 18–24-year-olds in the general population. Fourth, and most important, there is no evidence that faculty ideology at an institutional level has an impact on student political ideology. Student political orientation does not change for a majority of students while in college, and for those that do change there is evidence that other factors have an effect on that change, such as gender and socioeconomic status. Based on the data presented in this study, college students appear to be more firm in their political beliefs than conventional wisdom suggests. Though students' political ideology is not set in stone, it does not appear to change as a result of faculty ideology, at least at an institutional level.

## Notes

*We wish to thank John Pryor of the Higher Education Research Institute at UCLA, Daniel Klein at GMU, and our colleagues at Hamilton College and Xavier University for their support and assistance on this project. Given that this is a study of faculty ideology, it seems reasonable to be open about our own ideological dispositions. We come from divergent political and ideological perspectives. One author is conservative and has worked extensively for Republican candidates and officeholders, while the other is liberal and active in Democratic politics at the local level.

1. The Center for the Study of Popular Culture was launched by Horowitz in 1988. In 2006, the center was renamed the David Horowitz Freedom Center. See David Horowitz Freedom Center, "About Us." www.horowitzfreedomcenter.org/FlexPage.aspx?area=aboutus (June 8, 2007).
2. The full text of the Academic Bill of Rights is available at www.studentsforacademicfreedom.org. A print version can be found in Horowitz (2007, 129–132). See also Horowitz 2004, Hegel 2004, and Klein 2004.

3. Rep. Jack Kingston (R-GA), as cited in Alyson Klein (2004). See also Horowitz 2004. Note too that there are those on the right who have voiced their opposition to the Academic Bill of Rights; see for instance Beck 2005.
4. In 2005 and 2006, the Academic Bill of Rights was introduced in Congress and at least 21 state legislatures. It resulted in a series of highly contentious state legislative hearings (Schrecker 2006; Jacobson 2006a) but little concrete legislative action. See, for instance, Jacobson 2005, 2006a, 2006b, 2006c, 2006d, and Jaschik 2006a. For a state by state roundup on the status of legislation related to the Academic Bill of Rights, see the Free Exchange Coalition's "Legislative Tracker" at www.freeexchangeoncampus.org/index.php?option=come_content&task=section&id=5&Itemid=61 (September 24, 2007). Note that the AAUP, which strongly opposes the Academic Bill of Rights, is a member of the Free Exchange Coalition.
5. According to the American National Election Study of 2004, 29.6% of females of all ages self-identified as left-of-center (slightly liberal, liberal, or extremely liberal), compared to 20.7% of males. Among 18–24-year-olds, 38.9% of females identified themselves as left-of-center, compared to 33.3% of males (ANES 2004).

## References

The American National Election Studies. 2004. Ann Arbor, MI: University of Michigan, Center for Political Studies.

Beck, Stefan. 2005. "Time in the Trenches: Campus Conservatives Need to Toughen Up." *National Review Online*, April 13. www.nationalreview.com/comment/beck200504130758.asp (June 8, 2007).

Brookings Institution. 2001. "National Survey on Government Endeavors." www.brook.edu/comm/reformwatch/rw04_surveydata.pdf (June 8, 2007).

Dey, Eric L., 1997. "Undergraduate Political Attitudes: Peer Influence in Changing Social Context." *The Journal of Higher Education* 68 (4): 398–413.

Ehrlich, Tom, and Anne Colby. 2004. "Political Bias in Undergraduate Education." *Carnegie Perspectives: The Carnegie Foundation for the Advancement of Teaching* 90 (3). www.carnegiefoundation.org/perspectives/sub.asp?key=245&subkey=1135 (June 8, 2007).

Hebel, Sara. 2004. "Patrolling Professors' Politics." *Chronicle of Higher Education*, February 13. http://chronicle.com/weekly/v50/i23/23a01801.htm (June 8, 2007).

Higher Education Research Institute (HERI). 2002. "The American College Teacher: National Norms for 2001–2002: UCLA Study Finds Growing Gap in Political Liberalism between Male and Female Faculty." Press release. www.gseis.ucla.edu/heri/act_pr_02.html (May 29, 2007).

Horowitz, David. 2007. *Indoctrination U.: The Left's War on Academic Freedom*. New York: Encounter Books.

———. 2004. "In Defense of Intellectual Diversity." *Chronicle of Higher Education*, February 13. http://chronicle.com/weekly/v50/i23/23b01201.htm (June 8, 2007).

Jacobson, Jennifer. 2006a. "Pa. Lawmakers Get Mixed Message on Fixing Perceived Liberal Bias in Academe." *Chronicle of Higher Education*, April 7. http://chronicle.com/weekly/v52/i31/31a03701.htm (June 8, 2007).

———. 2006b. "Tilting at Academe." *Chronicle of Higher Education*, March 24. http://chronicle.com/weekly/v52/i29/29a02501.htm (June 8, 2007).

———. 2006c. "Political-Bias Bill Passes S.D. House." *Chronicle of Higher Education*, February 17. http://chronicle.com/weekly/v52/i24/24a03201.htm (June 8, 2007).

———. 2006d. "Conservative Activist Admits Lack of Evidence for Some Allegations of Faculty Bias." *Chronicle of Higher Education*, January 20. http://chronicle.com/weekly/v52/i20/20a03301.htm (June 8, 2007).

———. 2005. "Pennsylvania Lawmakers Hold Hearings on Political Bias in College Classrooms." *Chronicle of Higher Education*, November 25. http://chronicle.com/weekly/v52/i14/14a03201.htm (June 8, 2007).

Jacoby, Russell. 2005. "So Universities Hire Liberal Faculty—This Is News?" History News Network, George Mason University, March 28. http://hnn.us/article/10836.html (June 8, 2007).

Jaschik, Scott. 2006a. "Grading Edge for Conservative Students." *Inside Higher Ed.*, March 30.

———. 2006b. "Retractions from David Horowitz." *Inside Higher Ed.*, January 11.

———. 2005. "Leaning to the Left." *Inside Higher Ed.*, March 30. http://insidehighered.com/news/2005/03/30/politics (June 8, 2007).

Klein, Alyson. 2004. "Worried on the Right and the Left." *Chronicle of Higher Education*, July 9. http://chronicle.com/weekly/v50/i44/44a02101.htm (June 8, 2007).

Klein, Daniel B., and Charlotta Stern. 2006. "Sociology and Classical Liberalism." *The Independent Review: A Journal of Political Economy* 11 (1): 37–52.

———. 2005a. "Political Diversity in Six Disciplines." *Academic Questions* 18 (1): 40–52.

———. 2005b. "Professors and Their Politics: The Policy Views of Social Scientists." *Critical Review: An Interdisciplinary Journal of Politics and Society* 17 (3 & 4): 257–303.

Klein, Daniel B., and Andrew Western. 2005. "Voter Registration of Berkeley and Stanford Faculty." *Academic Questions* 18 (1): 53–65.

Rothman, Stanley, S. Robert Lichter, and Neil Nevitte. 2005. "Politics and Professional Advancement among College Faculty." *The Forum* 3 (1).

Schrecker, Ellen. 2006. "Worse Than McCarthy." Point of View. *Chronicle of Higher Education*, February 10. http://chronicle.com/weekly/v52/i23/23b02001.htm (June 8, 2007).

Stonecash, Jeff, Mark Brewer, and Mack Mariani. 2002. *Diverging Parties: Realignment, Social Change, and Political Polarization*. Boulder, CO: Westview.

Wiener, Jon. 2005. "When Students Complain about Professors, Who Gets to Define the Controversy?" *Chronicle of Higher Education*, March 13. http://chronicle.com/weekly/v51/i36/36b01201.htm (May 25, 2006).

## RESPOND

1. One purpose of this research was to use the statistical analysis of data gathered from students to test a claim commonly made by conservative critics of American universities. What claim is being tested? State this claim as a Toulmin argument. (For a discussion of Toulmin argumentation, see Chapter 7.)
2. What did Mariani and Hewitt find when they tested the claim discussed in question 1? What is the difference between a purely logical argument (as discussed in question 1) and one based on empirical data (as is the case in this research)?
3. Briefly outline the "Discussion" section of this selection to get a clear idea of how it is structured. In outlining, you are looking for the major topic of each paragraph and the way that the paragraphs work together to conclude the article. Based on this particular "Discussion" section, how would you characterize the functions of a discussion section of a research article? In other words, how is this section structured and why?
4. A particularly interesting aspect of this article and one that empirical researchers very much appreciate is the way that it qualifies claims, as discussed in Chapter 7. Analyze paragraph 8 in this regard by first copying the paragraph and then underlining any language that can be seen as a qualification of a claim. Compare your results with those of a classmate. Likewise, discuss why the qualified claims made here are ultimately stronger and less subject to criticism than are unqualified claims.
5. A large part of the "Discussion" section describes the limitations of the research. How does this discussion contribute to the researchers' ethos? In what ways does an acknowledgment of the limitations of a research study function like qualifiers in an argument? How does the authors' note—the unnumbered endnote indicated by an asterisk—contribute to their ethos? (For a discussion of ethos, see Chapter 3. For a discussion of qualifiers, see Chapter 7.)
6. A common task in academic and professional writing is summarizing in one or two paragraphs an aspect of an empirical study like this one. **Write a summary** of the limitations of the study discussed by the authors, and **write a summary** of the findings of the study. Summaries can be seen as a category of factual arguments. (For a discussion of arguments of fact, see Chapter 8.)

▼ *Walter Benn Michaels is currently a professor of English at the University of Illinois at Chicago, where he teaches literary theory and American literature. His influential essay "Against Theory," coauthored with Steven Knapp, was published in 1982, and his books include* The Shape of the Signifier: 1967 to the End of History *(2004). This selection is an excerpt from the introduction to his most recent book,* The Trouble with Diversity: How We Learned to Love Identity and Ignore Inequality *(2006). Michaels begins this selection with an extended discussion of a literary text, F. Scott Fitzgerald's* The Great Gatsby, *one of the most famous American novels, which was published in 1925. Its central character, Jay Gatsby, seeks to win back Daisy Buchanan, a beautiful woman whom he had courted years earlier when he was a poor soldier but who had married a man fron an "old money" background like her own. After meeting her, Gatsby had changed his name to cover up his German immigrant roots at a time when people of most immigrant backgrounds were not fully accepted in elite society. He had also become wealthy, but his money was "new money"; though readers never learn exactly where it comes from, its sources are clearly disreputable and likely illegal. Many scholars now see* The Great Gatsby *as one of the best literary depictions and critiques of American life and values. While you read this selection, consider why we chose to end a chapter on diversity with this selection.*

# The Trouble with Diversity: How We Learned to Love Identity and Ignore Inequality

WALTER BENN MICHAELS

"The rich are different from you and me" is a famous remark supposedly made by F. Scott Fitzgerald to Ernest Hemingway,° although what made it famous—or at least made Hemingway famously repeat it—was not the remark itself but Hemingway's reply: "Yes, they have more money." In other words, the point of the story, as Hemingway told it, was that the rich really aren't very different from you and me. Fitzgerald's mistake, he thought, was that he mythologized or sentimentalized the rich, treating them as if they were a different kind of

***Ernest Hemingway (1899–1961):*** an American writer and Nobel Prize winner. His first novel was *The Sun Also Rises* (1926).

person instead of the same kind of person with more money. It was as if, according to Fitzgerald, what made rich people different was not what they *had*—their money—but what they *were*, "a special glamorous race."

To Hemingway, this difference—between what people owned and what they were—seemed obvious, and it was also obvious that the important thing was what they were. No one cares much about Robert Cohn's° money in *The Sun Also Rises*, but everybody feels the force of the fact that he's a "race-conscious" "little kike."° And whether or not it's true that Fitzgerald sentimentalized the rich and made them more glamorous than they really were, it's certainly true that he, like Hemingway, believed that the fundamental differences—the ones that really mattered—ran deeper than the question of how much money you had. That's why in *The Great Gatsby*, the fact that Gatsby has made a great deal of money isn't quite enough to win Daisy Buchanan back. Rich as he has become, he's still "Mr. Nobody from Nowhere," not Jay Gatsby but Jimmy Gatz. The change of name is what matters. One way to look at *The Great Gatsby* is as a story about a poor boy who makes good, which is to say, a poor boy who becomes rich—the so-called American dream. But *Gatsby* is not really about someone who makes a lot of money; it is instead about someone who tries and fails to change who he is. Or, more precisely, it's about someone who pretends to be something he's not; it's about Jimmy Gatz pretending to be Jay Gatsby. If, in the end, Daisy Buchanan is very different from Jimmy Gatz, it's not because she's rich and he isn't (by the end, he is) but because Fitzgerald treats them as if they really do belong

***Robert Cohn:*** a Jewish character in *The Sun Also Rises* who develops an inferiority complex as a result of his outsider status.

***kike:*** an ethnic slur referring to Jews that was widely used in the early twentieth century.

*Robert Redford played the lead in the 1974 film* The Great Gatsby.

to different races, as if poor boys who made a lot of money were only "passing" as rich. "We're all white here," someone says, interrupting one of Tom Buchanan's racist outbursts. Jimmy Gatz isn't quite white enough.

What's important about *The Great Gatsby*, then, is that it takes one kind of difference (the difference between the rich and the poor) and redescribes it as another kind of difference (the difference between the white and the not-so-white). To put the point more generally, books like *The Great Gatsby* (and there have been a great many of them) give us a vision of our society divided into races rather than into economic classes. And this vision has proven to be extraordinarily attractive. Indeed, it's been so attractive that the vision has survived even though what we used to think were the races have not. In the 1920s, racial science° was in its heyday; now very few scientists believe that there are any such things as races. But many of those who are quick to remind us that there are no biological entities called races are even quicker to remind us that races have not disappeared; they should just be understood as social entities instead. And these social entities have turned out to be remarkably tenacious, both in ways we know are bad and in ways we have come to think of as good. The bad ways involve racism, the inability or refusal to accept people who are different from us. The good ways involve just the opposite: embracing difference, celebrating what we have come to call diversity.

Indeed, in the United States, the commitment to appreciating diversity emerged out of the struggle against racism, and the word *diversity* itself began to have the importance it does for us today in 1978 when, in *Bakke v. Board of Regents*,° the Supreme Court ruled that taking into consideration the race of an applicant to the University of California (in this case, it was the medical school at UC Davis) was an acceptable practice if it served "the interest of diversity." The point the Court was making here was significant. It was not asserting that preference in admissions could be given, say, to black people because they had previously been discriminated against. It was saying instead that universities had a legitimate interest in taking race into account in exactly the same way they had a legitimate interest in taking into account what part of the country an applicant came from or what his or her nonacademic interests were. They had, in other words, a legitimate interest in having a "diverse student body," and racial diversity, like geographic diversity, could thus be an acceptable goal for an admissions policy.

5 Two things happened here. First, even though the concept of diversity was not originally connected with race (universities had long sought diverse student bodies without worrying about race at all), the two now came to be firmly associated. When universities publish their diversity statistics today, they're not talking about how many kids come from Oregon. My university—

***racial science:*** the scientific investigation of and debate about matters related to race. The field often attracts those who are seeking to find evidence for the existence of distinct races and for ranking them in a hierarchy, though many scientists studying these issues disavow both aims.

**Bakke v. Board of Regents:** *Regents of the University of California v. Bakke*, a 1978 U.S. Supreme Court decision. Bakke, a white man, claimed that he had been discriminated against in violation of federal and state laws when he was not admitted to the UC-Davis medical school in 1973 and 1974 even though nonwhite candidates with significantly lower test scores were. In a 5–4 decision, the court ruled that quota systems for admissions are illegal but that schools can consider race as one of many factors in admissions decisions. (Subsequent Supreme Court decisions have largely maintained this position.) Bakke was later admitted to and graduated from the UC-Davis medical school; his name and this case continue to be associated with the notion of reverse discrimination.

the University of Illinois at Chicago—is ranked as one of the most diverse in the country, but well over half the students in it come from Chicago. What the rankings measure is the number of African Americans and Asian Americans and Latinos we have, not the number of Chicagoans.

And, second, even though the concept of diversity was introduced as a kind of end run° around the historical problem of racism (the whole point was that you could argue for the desirability of a diverse student body without appealing to the history of discrimination against blacks and so without getting accused by people like Alan Bakke of reverse discrimination against whites), the commitment to diversity became deeply associated with the struggle against racism. Indeed, the goal of overcoming racism, which had sometimes been identified as the goal of creating a "color-blind" society, was now reconceived as the goal of creating a diverse, that is, a color-conscious, society.[1] Instead of trying to treat people as if their race didn't matter, we would not only recognize but celebrate racial identity. Indeed, race has turned out to be a gateway drug for all kinds of identities, cultural, religious, sexual, even medical. To take what may seem like an extreme case, advocates for the disabled now urge us to stop thinking of disability as a condition to be "cured" or "eliminated" and to start thinking of it instead on the model of race: we don't think black people should want to stop being black; why do we assume the deaf want to hear?[2]

*end run:* a football play in which the person carrying the ball tries to run around the end of the opposing team's line. As a figure of speech, it is any action that tries to get around opponents or difficulties without confronting them directly, often through the use of trickery.

The general principle here is that our commitment to diversity has redefined the opposition to discrimination as the appreciation (rather than the elimination) of difference. So with respect to race, the idea is not just that racism is a bad thing (which of course it is) but that race itself is a good thing. Indeed, we have become so committed to the attractions of race that (as I've already suggested above [. . .]) our enthusiasm for racial identity has been utterly undiminished by scientific skepticism about whether there is any such thing. Once the students in my American literature classes have taken a course in human genetics, they just stop talking about black and white and Asian races and start talking about black and European and Asian cultures instead. We love race, and we love the identities to which it has given birth.

The fundamental point of this book is to explain why this is true. The argument, in its simplest form, will be that we love race—we love identity—because we don't love class.[3] We love thinking that the differences that divide us are not the differences between those of us who have money and those who don't but are instead the differences between those of us who are black and those who are white or Asian or Latino or whatever. A world where some of us don't have enough money is a world where the differ-

Michaels offers several different arguments, but perhaps the richest and most complex is his causal argument that traces the effects of our traditional thinking about diversity. For more on how causal arguments work, see Chapter 11.

LINK TO P. 242

ences between us present a problem: the need to get rid of inequality or to justify it. A world where some of us are black and some of us are white—or biracial or Native American or transgendered—is a world where the differences between us present a solution: appreciating our diversity. So we like to talk about the differences we can appreciate, and we don't like to talk about the ones we can't. Indeed, we don't even like to acknowledge that they exist. As survey after survey has shown, Americans are very reluctant to identify themselves as belonging to the lower class and even more reluctant to identify themselves as belonging to the upper class. The class we like is the middle class.

But the fact that we all like to think of ourselves as belonging to the same class doesn't, of course, mean that we actually do belong to the same class. In reality, we obviously and increasingly don't. "The last few decades," as *The Economist*° puts it, "have seen a huge increase in inequality in America."[4] The rich *are* different from you and me, and one of the ways they're different is that they're getting richer and we're not. And while it's not surprising that most of the rich and their apologists on the intellectual right are unperturbed by this development, it is at least a little surprising that the intellectual left has managed to remain almost equally unperturbed. Giving priority to issues like affirmative action and committing itself to the celebration of difference, the intellectual left has responded to the increase in economic inequality by insisting on the importance of cultural identity. So for thirty years, while the gap between the rich and the poor has grown larger, we've been urged to respect people's identities—as if the problem of poverty would be solved if we just appreciated the poor. From the economic standpoint, however, what poor people want is not to contribute to diversity but to minimize their contribution to it—they want to stop being poor. Celebrating the diversity of American life has become the American left's way of accepting their poverty, of accepting inequality.

**The Economist:** a weekly newsmagazine based in London and focusing on international affairs. Its target audience is affluent and highly educated.

I have three goals in writing this book. The first is to show how our current 10
notion of cultural diversity—trumpeted as the repudiation of racism and biological essentialism°—in fact grew out of and perpetuates the very concepts it congratulates itself on having escaped. The second is to show how and why the American love affair with race—especially when you can dress race up as culture—has continued and even intensified. Almost everything we say about culture (that the significant differences between us are cultural, that such differences should be respected, that our cultural heritages should be perpetuated, that there's a value in making sure that different cultures survive) seems to me mistaken, and this book will try to show why. And the third goal

***essentialism:*** the assumption that all members of a category are alike or share similar, if not identical, characteristics. Essentialist arguments take the form of "All X's are Y" and often appear in arguments about social difference. Examples include claims that gay men aren't athletic, straight men aren't empathetic, and people from a specific ethnic group are (or are not) intelligent.

is—by shifting our focus from cultural diversity to economic equality—to help alter the political terrain of contemporary American intellectual life.

## Notes

1. Consciousness of color was, it goes without saying, always central to American society insofar as that society was a committedly racist one. The relevant change here—marked rather than produced by *Bakke*—involved (in the wake of both the successes and failures of the civil rights movement) the emergence of color consciousness as an antiracist position. The renewed black nationalism in the 1960s is one standard example of this transition, but the phenomenon is more general. You can get a striking sense of it by reading John Okada's *No-No Boy*, a novel about the Japanese Americans who answered no to the two loyalty questions on the questionnaire administered to them at the relocation centers they were sent to during World War II. The novel itself, published in 1957, is a pure product of the civil rights movement, determined to overcome race (and ignore class) in the imagination of a world in which people are utterly individualized—"only people." It began to become important, however, as an expression of what Frank Chin, in an article written in 1976 and included as an appendix to the current edition, calls "yellow soul," and when it's taught today in Asian American literature classes, reading it counts toward the fulfillment of diversity requirements that Okada himself would not have understood.
2. Simi Linton, *Claiming Disability* (New York: New York University Press, 1998), 96.
3. The relations between race and class have been an important topic in American writing at least since the 1930s, and in recent years they have, in the more general form of the relations between identity and inequality, been the subject of an ongoing academic discussion. Some of the more notable contributions include *Culture and Equality* (2000) by Brian Barry, *Redistribution or Recognition* (2003), an exchange between Nancy Fraser and Axel Honneth, and *The Debate on Classes* (1990), featuring an important essay by Erik Olin Wright and a series of exchanges about that essay. And in my particular field of specialization, American literature, Gavin Jones is about to publish an important and relevant book called *American Hunger*. I cite these texts in particular because, in quite different ways, they share at least some of my skepticism about the value of identity. And I have myself written in an academic context about these issues, most recently in *The Shape of the Signifier* (2004). *The Trouble with Diversity* is in part an effort to make some of the terms of the discussion more vivid to a more general audience. More important, however, it is meant to advance a particular position in that discussion, an argument that the concept of identity is incoherent and that its continuing success is a function of its utility to neoliberalism.
4. *The Economist*, December 29, 2004.

## RESPOND •

1. What, for Walter Benn Michaels, is the real issue that American society needs to confront? How, for him, does defining *diversity* in terms of a celebration of difference, especially ethnic difference, prevent Americans from both seeing the real issue and doing anything about it? In what ways does our society's focus on ethnic and cultural diversity necessarily perpetuate racism and biological essentialism (paragraph 10)?
2. Why and how are these issues relevant to discussions of diversity on campus in general? On the campus you attend?
3. Later in this introduction, Michaels, a liberal, points out ways in which both conservatives and liberals in American public life, first, focus on racial or ethnic differences rather than issues of social inequality and, second, benefit from doing so. In a 2004 essay, "Diversity's False Solace," he notes:

   > [W]e like policies like affirmative action not so much because they solve the problem of racism but because they tell us that racism is the problem we need to solve. . . . It's not surprising that universities of the upper middle class should want their students to feel comfortable [as affirmative action programs enable and encourage them to do]. What is surprising is that diversity should have become the hallmark of liberalism.

   Analyze the argument made in this paragraph as a Toulmin argument. (For a discussion of Toulmin argumentation, see Chapter 7.)
4. How would you characterize Michaels's argument? In what ways is it an argument of fact? A definitional argument? An evaluative argument? A causal argument? A proposal? (For a discussion of these kinds of arguments, see Chapters 8–12.)
5. This chapter has provided many perspectives on an issue that is hotly debated on American campuses and in American society at large—diversity. Should diversity be something that schools strive for? If so, what kinds of diversity? What should a diverse campus look like, and why? **Write a proposal essay** in which you define and justify the sort(s) of diversity, if any, that your school should aim for. Seek to draw widely on the perspectives that you've read in this chapter—in terms of topics discussed and also approaches to those or other topics that you might consider. If you completed the assignment in question 6 for the first selection in this chapter (p. 742), you will surely want to reread your essay, giving some thought to how and why your understanding of diversity has or has not changed as you have read the selections in this chapter. (For a discussion of proposals, see Chapter 12.)

# 26
# What Are You Working For?

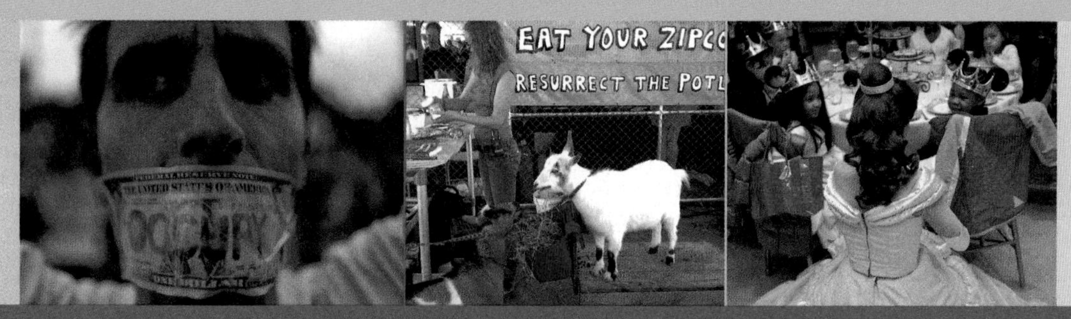


If you're reading this introduction, odds are that you have clear reasons for doing so and much broader motivations for being in school in the first place. Your family and friends assume that you're working toward something—perhaps a grade, a diploma, or ultimately a job. This chapter's selections encourage you to engage in deliberative arguments with your classmates and yourself about your long-term motivations and expectations. You'll examine the goals that you are working to reach after you leave college and enter a world where work—in the narrow sense of making a living—will be one of your primary activities.

The chapter opens with two stories from StoryCorps, a project that records narratives from the lives of different Americans; each deals with work in a different way. Both narrators link experiences from youth to the work they later chose. Next, Lisa W. Foderaro reports on the effect of the economic downturn of 2008 on teenagers, especially those of well-to-do parents, many of whom reduced allowances and encouraged their children to do what previously had been unthinkable: get a part-time job. In "Learning by Degrees" and an online live chat with the author, Rebecca Mead examines the increasingly common claim that perhaps college isn't worth the cost after all.

The next three selections consider this discussion by investigating whether and how education might pay off in the future. The U.S. Bureau of Labor Statistics shows that it does, but in a blog posting, Laurence Shatkin cries, "Not so fast!" and explains why the department's statistics don't tell the entire story. In "The Major and the Job Market, the Dream and the Reality," Mark Bauerlein encourages his fellow academics to do research about the job market before they give advice about possible career paths to the undergraduates they teach.

In "Our Unpaid, Extra Shadow Work," Craig Lambert discusses a disappearing service economy that passes extra work onto each and every one of us.

Thomas L. Friedman's "The Start-Up of You" and reader responses to it give you a chance to examine common assumptions about what the American workplace will be like in the future and to decide what sort of workplace you believe American students should be preparing themselves for. As he often does, Friedman offers an appealing vision of the future, but, as readers point out, one that may be flawed in important ways. The final selection in the chapter, an excerpt from Stewart D. Friedman's book *Total Leadership: Be a Better Leader, Have a Richer Life* and a transcript of an Amazon.com video about it, argues that folks who think in terms of a balance between work and life commit a serious logical fallacy. Friedman proposes a different way of defining the problem and finding a solution, one that we hope is useful to you now and in the future.

Students are in college for a variety of reasons, and your immediate focus may not be the world of work that awaits you after graduation. Yet as the selections in this chapter remind you, many employers and researchers who study higher education see college as preparation for work. You are learning useful information, but you are also developing habits of work and mind that should serve you well in the future—everything from showing up on time to the ability to think outside the box to the ability to write well. With luck, these selections may help you define your own goals so that you'll know exactly what you're working for now and later.

e For additional material related to this chapter, visit the e-Pages for *Everything's an Argument with Readings* online at **bedfordstmartins.com/everythingsanargument/epages**.

*We open this chapter on education and work with two stories that were part of the StoryCorps Project, an award-winning effort to record the stories of everyday Americans talking to someone inside the mobile StoryCorps booth. Two CDs are created for each story told, one for the storyteller and one for the American Folklife Center at the Library of Congress, so that future generations will be able to hear contemporary Americans talk about things that matter to them. Some 10,000 stories had been collected by 2007, and excerpts from forty-nine of them were chosen for the 2007 volume* Listening Is an Act of Love: A Celebration of American Life from the StoryCorps Project, *edited by Dave Isay, the founder of StoryCorps and its parent company, Sound Portraits Productions. The two interviews included here are from the chapter "Work and Dedication." The first, recorded in July 2005 in New Town, North Dakota, is an interview with Monica Mayer, a physician who is a family practitioner on the Fort Berthold Reservation in New Town. The interviewer is Dr. Mayer's cousin, Spencer Wilkinson Jr., who is also her patient. The second interview was recorded in Pittsburgh in June 2006 and features Ken Kobus, who is telling his friend Ron Baraff about his working life in a steel mill. Both of these interviews tell stories of parents' influence on their children's choice of career. Give some thought to how your parents or caregivers have influenced the hopes that you have for your working life.*

# Dr. Monica Mayer, 45, Interviewed by Her Cousin and Patient, Spencer Wilkinson Jr., 39

## DAVE ISAY, EDITOR

*Dr. Monica Mayer and Spencer Wilkinson Jr.*

***half-breed:*** an offensive term describing someone who is of mixed ethnic heritage, especially someone with one American Indian parent and one parent of European origin.

### Recorded in New Town, North Dakota

*Spencer Wilkinson Jr.:* What made you choose to pursue a career in medicine?

*Dr. Monica Mayer:* My father was full-blood German, and my mother was full-blood Indian, and it was pretty tough in the sixties growing up half-breed,° so to speak. My father didn't have any sons, so he raised us like little boys. And I must have been in about seventh grade, and I wasn't doing well in school. In fact, I was maybe getting Cs, and I'm the oldest of three girls. So my dad packed us up in his pickup truck and took us out to his old homestead land, which is about eighteen miles north of New Town, in the middle of nowhere. Well, New Town's kind of in the middle of nowhere, but, I mean, this is *really* in the middle of nowhere. And he packed us some lunches and some water. He dropped us off out there at seven or eight in the morning and said he wanted all the rocks picked up and put in the northwest corner in one big pile and that he'd come back that night to pick us up, and it had better be done.

So there we were, working hard all day, and then he comes back. And we're dirty, stinky, sweaty, sore muscles, crying. My dad pulls up, and he gets out of the pickup. And we must have been a sight to see. I looked at him and said, since I was the oldest—my two younger sisters are hiding behind me—"Dad, we don't think this is fair we have to work this hard." And I remember him saying, "Is that right? Well, do you think I like working like this every day?" "No." He said, "You know, your mother said you girls don't like school and you're not doing very well. So I talked to Momma, and we decided that you're going to come out here and work like this so your hind ends will get used to how your life's going to be when you get older." So I said, "Well, if we got good grades, do we have to come out here and work this hard?" And he said, "No. That's the deal."

These personal narratives about work are appealing in part because of the bridges they build through emotional arguments. For more about how pathos works in arguments, see Chapter 2.

LINK TO P. 30

Well, he didn't have to bust my head twice up against the brick wall. My two younger sisters and I were laughing about that, because they remember that particular day exactly the way I remembered it. One day of hard labor changed everything.

*July 29, 2005*

*Today, Monica Mayer practices family medicine on the Fort Berthold reservation in New Town, North Dakota. Her sister Holly is the Director of Public Health Nurses on the reservation, and her sister Renee is Tribal Social Services Director.*

## Ken Kobus, 58, Tells His Friend Ron Baraff, 42, about Making Steel

DAVE ISAY, EDITOR

RECORDED IN PITTSBURGH, PENNSYLVANIA

*Ken Kobus:* Both of my grandfathers worked in the mill. My father started in 1937. I started about twenty-nine years later, in 1966, at the same plant. I was always enthralled with steel from the time I was a very young person. I always wanted to go into the mill, but I was always too young to go. And finally when I turned sixteen, I told my dad that he had to take me—and I bugged him until he did.

You look at it from his point of view, he was a union guy. And for him to come to the mill on his day off, he had to take a bit of harassment for it:

*Ken Kobus (left) and Ron Baraff (right)*

"What the heck are you doing here?" My dad had straight dark black hair; his nickname was Crow. When we finally got into the mill, they said, "Crow, what are you doing here? It's your day off! Are you crazy?" At the same time, though, he was very proud. He thought enough to bring his son into the place that he worked.

When I went into the shop, I was actually a little bit frightened. All these things were moving back and forth, and I was afraid I was going to get run over and didn't know where to move. My dad just walked straight through like nothing was going on. Steelmaking is just beautiful. It's unimaginable beauty. When you're charging a furnace, you get all these sparkles off of the iron, and so you just see thousands and thousands of sparkles.

We proceeded into the plant, and my dad went over and talked to the boss of the shop. I found out that they were going to tap a furnace. I remember it like yesterday, although it's now forty-two years later. We went over to the furnace, and I found out that they were going to let me tap the furnace. When we went over, a lot of the guys started gathering around. Even though I was sixteen, I recognized that something was strange. This probably is not the way it is normally done. But I didn't really care because I was going to get to tap the furnace, and if these guys want to watch, fine with me.

5 There was a battery box with a switch and a little button that you used to set off the dynamite charge and the foreman said, "When I tell you to, flip the switch; and when I tell you to tap, press the button." And my dad came to me and says, "I don't care what you do," he says, "don't let go of that battery box."

So came time and they blew the siren for "all clear" and then waited a little bit just to make sure that nobody's below, because when the steel lets loose, sparks go everywhere. It came time to flip the switch, and then it came time to press the button. The dynamite blew up and made such a god-awful sound, and there was smoke and fire and sparks everywhere. And then the steel started running into the spout, and there were flames shooting up and out of the spout, and I jumped up in the air. I must have jumped three, four feet in the air, I was so scared. And then I knew why all these guys were around. They started laughing, because it was such a sight to see somebody so scared. I was the show for that day, and they had their good laugh on me.

But it was spectacular. The steel started running and went into the ladle. When it hits the bottom of the ladle, it goes *splunch* and makes all kinds of different sounds that you never expect. What do you think happens when 2,900-degree steel hits finely powdered coal that's lying in the bottom of the ladle? Well, it creates a fire that you just can't imagine. The fire almost hit the roof of the shop, and it was eighty feet above you, and you're standing right beside this ladle of running steel. And the supervisor is not telling the guys to run away; he's telling them, "Throw some bags here" and "Throw some this there." There's all these people moving around, and there's all this heat, and it's just an unforgettable experience.

Two years later I started working in the mills. I worked in the foundry. I was the third helper on the electric furnace, and I worked various jobs in the steel foundry.

*Ron Baraff:* If you could choose any job in the steel mill, what would it be?

*Ken:* Oh, I'd choose my dad's job. He was a first helper, in charge of an 10
open-hearth furnace. To face a furnace is just—it's hard to describe because when you open a door of the furnace, it's at over 3,000 degrees, and your whole body's standing in front of a door opened to hell. It has effects on your body; it stretches your skin. And you watch cold steel, scrap metal, being put into there, and you just watch it become more and more red and red and red, and then it just sort of like disappears and falls apart. You see huge, huge boiling steel—it's not water, it's steel. And you see these bubbles and these balls flopping out and it's just like a volcano. You're looking in a volcano.

I know it stuck with my father for all his life. I mean, when he was dying, he couldn't talk. He had throat cancer, and so they took his voice box out—and he was in a lot of pain. I was in the hospice, and I was watching him in the bed once and the doctor came in. He saw that I was looking at my dad, and my dad was lying on his back and his hands up in the air, and he was turning and manipulating. The doctor says, "I wonder what the heck he's doing." Because, you know, he did it all the time. He would be lying on his back, and he would be doing this stuff, and they had no clue as to what he was doing. I said, "He's making steel." I could see what he was doing. He was opening furnace doors, and he was adjusting the gas on the furnace and the draft. I could see. The doctor was amazed. To the day he died that's what he lived: steelmaking. And that's quite an impression. And it's made an impression on me, too. I could always recommend to somebody to watch steel being born. It's just fantastic. It's a spectacle that is unreal.

I've been working for forty years, and it's just long, hard work. A lot of times I can't imagine how the men bear up against it. The guys knew how to work and could face up to the job and just were so strong. I was proud to be around many guys that could do that, that wanted to do that, and had pride in doing that. They took pride in what they did. And they knew that people looked at them with honor. They made steel.

*June 20, 2006*

## RESPOND •

1. Although we generally don't think of stories as arguments, they all express points of view. (In fact, everything is an argument, if we believe the title of this book.) Summarize the arguments made by each of these narratives.
2. What does each of these narratives teach us about work and dedication?
3. In her interview, does Monica Mayer sound like a doctor as she talks? Why or why not? Is her language appropriate to the context and audience? Why or why not? Would her story have been different if she had used more formal language? Would it have been as effective? Why or why not? (For a discussion of style in arguments, see Chapter 13.)
4. One of Ken Kobus's arguments is that "steelmaking is just beautiful" (paragraph 3). Was such a claim surprising for you? Why? What evidence does Kobus offer? For him, what is the nature of the beauty of steelmaking? (It is, for example, not like the beauty of flowers in spring or a child's face.) In what ways is his discussion of this issue a definitional argument? (For a discussion of definitional arguments, see Chapter 9.)
5. Interview someone you know about the job that they hold or hope to hold. One of the appendices to *Listening Is an Act of Love*, "Favorite StoryCorps Questions," lists these questions under the heading "Work":

   What do you do for a living?
   Tell me about how you got into your line of work.
   Do you like your job?
   What did you want to be when you grew up?
   What lessons has your work life taught you?
   Do you plan on retiring? If so, when? How do you feel about it?
   Do you have any favorite stories about your work life?

   These questions may help you get started. You might interview a family member or someone else who has been influential in your own thinking about your career goals, or you might interview someone who has a job that you think you'd never want. After you've completed the interview, **write an essay** in which you present what you learned, creating a portrait of the person from the perspective of her or his work life (or the goals that she or he has for work in the future). Parts of the argument will likely be factual, and others will be definitional, evaluative, or causal. The shape of the argument will depend on what you learn in the interview and your own goals in writing. Remember that Chapter 17 offers some additional tips on interviews.

▼ *The economic downturn that began in the middle of 2008 had far-reaching consequences for nearly all Americans, rich or poor, who found that their lives had changed in a very short period of time. Predictions as we write in early 2012 assume that even as the economy begins to stabilize and improve in some regard, the consequences of the downturn will be with us in many ways for a long time. This article, which appeared in the* New York Times *in December 2008, explores the effects of the downturn on teenagers in terms of changes in their lives at the time and in their future options. Lisa W. Foderaro has written for the* Times *for over two decades. She frequently writes about issues related to higher education and to the New York City metropolitan area. (This article appeared in the "New York" section of the national edition of the* Times.*) As you read, think back to late 2008, and reflect on what your life and the lives of your family and friends were like, whether things have gotten better or worse, and what the consequences of the economic situation have been or will be for your working future.*

# The Well-to-Do Get Less So, and Teenagers Feel the Crunch

LISA W. FODERARO

Jodi Hamilton began her senior year of high school in Woodcliff Lake, N.J., this fall on the usual prosperous footing. Her parents were providing a weekly allowance of $100 and paying for private Pilates classes, as well as a physics tutor who reported once a week to their 4,000-square-foot home.

But in October, Jodi's mother lost her job managing a huge dental practice in the Bronx, then landed one closer to home that requires more hours for less money. Pilates was dropped, along with takeout sushi dinners, and Jodi's allowance, which covers lunch during the week, slipped to $60. Instead of having a tutor, Jodi has become a tutor, earning $150 a week through that and baby-sitting.

"I just thought it would be responsible to get a job and have my own money so my parents didn't have to pay for everything," said Jodi, who is 17. "I always like to be saving up for something that I have my eye on—a ring, a necklace, a handbag."

It is impossible to quantify how many affluent parents have trimmed allowances in recent months—or how many of their offspring, in turn, have sought either formal employment or odd jobs. But interviews with dozens of teenagers, parents, educators, and employers suggest that many youngsters from well-to-do families seem to have found a new work ethic as the economic crisis that has jeopardized their parents' jobs and investments has also led to less spending money for Saturday night movies or binges at Abercrombie & Fitch.

After focusing on studies and 5
résumé-polishing extracurricular activities in recent years, these teenagers are job-seeking at the worst possible time, however, with employment of 16- to 19-year-olds at its lowest level in 61 years as out-of-work adults compete for low-paying positions.

"We have the Mall at Short Hills a stone's throw away, and there are a load of kids who applied," said Nancy Siegel, head counselor at Millburn High School in New Jersey. "But they are not finding the market welcoming."

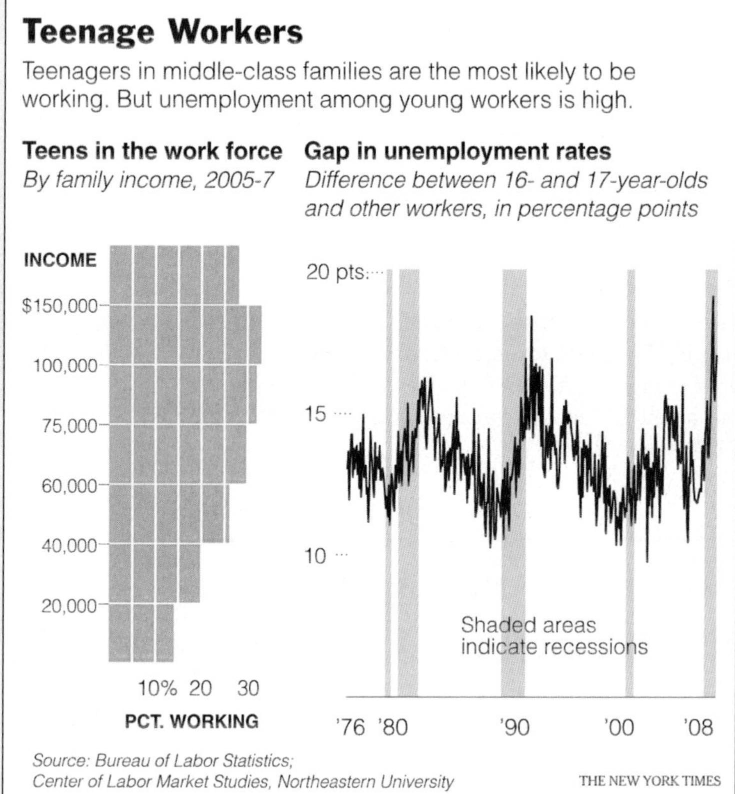


At the marble-sheathed Westchester Mall in White Plains, job applications have increased at stores including Origins, Tommy Hilfiger and the Gap, where job queries from teenagers are up 30 percent over last fall.

Julia Stark, a senior at Packer Collegiate Institute, a top private school in Brooklyn, said that this fall she and her friends are "all trying to work as much as we can" to pay for weekend restaurant dinners, a welcome break from a heavy course load and college applications.

In Greenwich, Conn., a Web-based program that connects high school students with nearby job opportunities has attracted 100 seekers each month since September, up from 40 to 60 a month last fall.

"I didn't want to bug my parents for extra cash over the long weekend," said Christian Rosier, a junior, who found a job on the Greenwich Student Employment Service the week before Thanksgiving that paid $50 for a few hours of moving furniture. "I like the one-shot jobs because I can do it on a Friday afternoon and still have time to hang out with my friends on the weekend."

Teenagers from working- and middle-class families are, of course, feeling similar—if not more acute—pressure. Sumit Pal, 17, a senior at Information Technology High School in Queens, said his parents cut his $5 weekly allowance two months ago after the deli where his father works started to lose business. Sumit was interviewed two weeks ago for a job at a company that sponsors rock bands.

"I don't mind losing my allowance," he said. "It goes toward other things, like groceries."

Teenage participation in the national labor force has fallen steadily since 1979, when 49 percent of all 16- and 17-year-olds had some kind of work; last year, the figure was 30 percent.

A recent study by the Center for Labor Market Studies at Northeastern University showed that teenage employment from 2005 to 2007 rose with household incomes that go up to $150,000 a year: 14 percent of teenagers from families earning less than $20,000 a year work, as do 26 percent of those whose families make $60,000, 32 percent of those earning $80,000, and 33 percent of those between $120,000 and $150,000.

Over $150,000, it drops to 28 percent. "Research shows that the bigger allowance you get from Mom and Dad," explained Andrew M. Sum,

*Since her allowance was cut to $60 a week from $100, Jodi Hamilton, 17, right, has taken up tutoring. Her pupil here is Sigourney Barman, 12.*

director of Northeastern's center, "the less likely you are to work."

Since the 1990s, many affluent children seeking admission to selective colleges have been discouraged from paid work and steered instead toward volunteer service projects. Rebuilding homes in New Orleans or teaching English in developing countries, seemingly better résumé fodder, supplanted after-school or summer jobs scooping ice cream or answering phones.

"There's been such a push to demonstrate to colleges that they're involved with activities and charities that it's almost too pedestrian° to say that work is part of what I do," said William S. Miron, the principal at Millburn High School.

Brent A. Neiser of the National Endowment for Financial Education, a group based in Colorado that offers financial literacy programs, said parents tend to "shortchange the benefits of scut° work" but that even ho-hum employment can be valuable—and impress admissions officers.

"Dress codes, rules, punctuality, and being teachable is enrichment in itself," Mr. Neiser said. "You're contributing to the economy, you're contributing to your personal economy, and you're picking up skill sets and habits that will prepare you for your full-time employment."

Michael Pollack, a vice president 20
of CBS, said that he was happy to see his 14-year-old son, Zachary, get a job at a veterinary hospital in Scarsdale, N.Y., in September, because Zachary was learning some basic lessons about money.

"I really want him to feel it and save it and spend it so he knows that money goes away," Mr. Pollack said. "If he wants to treat all his friends to a movie, that's great. But he needs to see that it bottoms out. Where else are they going to get that experience?"

Zachary, who earns $80 a weekend for 11 hours feeding and caring for animals, said that he was glad to "help my parents with our financial situation."

"Things I need, they'll buy," he said, "and things I want, I'll buy."

Jill Tipograph, who lives in Bergen County and owns Everything Summer, a company that advises parents on camp, travel, and work opportunities, said she sent her son to college in Boston this fall with a lump sum in his bank account that was supposed to last the semester. "But he went through the money like water," she said.

---

***pedestrian:*** here, ordinary or not worth mentioning.

***scut:*** tedious, menial.

25 So Ms. Tipograph and her husband decided to deposit a set amount once a week and told their son to use the prepaid meal plan more often. "We also said that if you feel you can't live on the allowance we're giving you, then please look for a part-time job," she added.

He seems to be getting the message, choosing a 10-hour bus ride over a train or plane for a recent visit to a friend in Washington.

Kat Rosier, a single mother of boys ages 12 and 17 in Greenwich, has resisted the idea of a job for her older son, Christian, who plays hockey and rows on the crew team, even as her interior design business has suffered.

"Here's my dilemma," she explained. "His time is so limited, and I would hate for his grades to fall this year so he could make $100 a week and then for him to not get into as good a college as he wants."

Still, having recently lost a job sprucing up the second home of a client who works in finance, Ms. Rosier said her family might need to adjust some habits. "The other night Christian had eight friends over and I spent $110 on pizza," she said. "I don't mind doing that, but he's got to know that the pizza budget is not $500 a month."

30 Christian said he was otherwise cutting back: "If I'm hungry, I won't drive to McDonald's. I'll just eat something at home instead of spending $10 on lunch."

Jodi Hamilton's mother, Jill, said she had been impressed by her daughter's determination to earn, noting that "she sent out a massive e-mail for baby-sitting and tutoring, and she got so many offers there aren't enough hours in the week."

Suddenly, the tables are turned: Two weeks ago, Ms. Hamilton borrowed $640 from Jodi.

Foderaro's article explores the effects of an economic downturn on teenagers from different economic classes. For more on how causal arguments work, see Chapter 11.

LINK TO P. 242

## RESPOND

1. What challenges did the economic downturn present to the teenagers who are discussed in Lisa W. Foderaro's article? In what ways were teenagers from different social classes similarly affected? In what ways were the effects different? Were the differences purely quantitative (that is, different degrees of the same effects), or were they qualitative (that is, different kinds of effects)? How and why?
2. The article discusses the ways that high school students are expected to create a particular kind of ethos as college applicants. What consequences, if any, do you think the economic downturn might have on this application process and these expectations? Why?
3. The graphic "Teenage Workers" did not appear in the print version of this article but was included in the online version. Are there aspects of the graphic that you find surprising? These figures are for teens who did paid work outside the home. Work that is not paid officially (taxed by the government) is not included. Thus, work done around the house, on most farms, or in a family business was not shown on this graphic. What information does the graphic contribute to the article that is not already included in the written text? The graph on the left, "Teens in the work force," is discussed in some detail in the article, but the graph on the right, "Gap in unemployment rates," is not. **Write a paragraph** in which you describe this graphic as you would if you were using it to construct an argument of your own.

4. Not all readers were happy with the topic or content of Foderaro's article. In addition to the *Times*' "Readers' Comments" (which you can access at nyti.ms/wrASAz), the article was the subject of a snarky posting on the *NYTPicker*, a blog devoted to the *Times* (which can be found at bit.ly/wvhKqu). Check out one or more of these sources. Then **write an evaluative essay** in which you evaluate some aspects of the responses to the article. As you'll note, there are many topics worthy of investigation—for example, emotionally charged responses based on the economic status or social class of the writer or narratives about the writer's own experiences with work or money growing up. In considering the electronic replies to the article, you may wish to start by examining the Editors' Selections or the Readers' Recommendations. An interesting topic might be the relationship—or lack of a relationship—between the replies that are favored by readers and those favored by the editors. (For a discussion of evaluative arguments, see Chapter 10.)
5. As the headnote to this selection states, the United States—and indeed the world—fell into an economic downturn in 2008, and whatever the "new normal" will end up being continues to be defined. How has the downturn affected your life or the lives of people you know? **Write a factual essay** in which you treat some aspect of this topic. You may have vivid and even painful memories of changes that took place—a family member's losing a job and not being able to find another one, losing a home to foreclosure, giving up long-held dreams—or you may be less consciously aware of the changes that may have taken place. Especially in the latter case, you may wish to interview family members or friends about how they understand what has happened to them and the country over the past few years. If writing about your own experience is simply too challenging at this point, then interview a friend not in your class about how the downturn has affected his/her life. Work hard to report the information you collect in a factual argument (in contrast to, say, an evaluative argument or one that focuses on causes). Especially if you found the attitudes of some of the people quoted in the article offensive because they seemed so out of touch with the lives of most Americans, as did the commenters at *NYTPicker* referenced in question 4, give special attention to issues related to audience. (See Chapter 6 for a discussion of identifying and appealing to audience.)

▼ *This selection has two parts: a short article, "Learning by Degrees," by Rebecca Mead, which was first published in the* New Yorker *in June 2010, and an online live chat with her about the cost of college. Mead, who was educated at Oxford University in England and at New York University, has been a staff writer for the* New Yorker *since 1997; she writes stories for an especially popular section of the magazine, "Talk of the Town," where this article appeared. The* New Yorker *is a weekly magazine with a readership that extends far beyond the boundaries of the city for which it is named or even the Northeast, thanks largely to the high quality of its writing; it is known for its cultural commentary, the short stories and poetry it publishes, and its cartoons. Like many publications, it seeks to incorporate the best of current technology like online live chats with its authors: readers are invited to log on and send questions or comments to an author at a specified time. The magazine then posts transcripts of these interactions on its Web site. Misleadingly, comments are always labeled "Question from [screen name]" when, in fact, what is posted is often a comment rather than a query.*

*The topic of both these texts is one that continues to be a hot one, especially in light of the 2008 economic downturn, namely, the value of or even need for a college education, particularly one that focuses on the liberal arts—disciplines like literature, languages, philosophy, history, and the social sciences—in contrast to fields like business or engineering, that is, professional programs that prepare students directly for particular kinds of jobs. (The term "liberal arts" comes from ancient Greek and Roman times, when free men studied grammar, rhetoric, and logic as part of their preparation for participating in governing their societies; during the Middle Ages, mathematics, geometry, astronomy, and music were added to the curriculum. These seven subjects became the curriculum in Europe's earliest universities.) As you read the article and the transcript of the live chat, look for evidence of Mead's position in this debate, and particularly as you read the live chat, notice how Mead's responses to posters' comments create an ethos of professionalism.*

# "Learning by Degrees" and Live Chat with the Author

REBECCA MEAD

A member of the Class of 2010—who this season dons synthetic cap and gown, listens to the inspirational words of David Souter° (Harvard), Anderson Cooper° (Tulane), or Lisa Kudrow° (Vassar), and collects a diploma—need not be a statistics major to know that the odds of stepping into a satisfying job, or, indeed, any job, are lower now than might have been imagined four long years ago,

***David Souter (1939– ):*** former Associate Justice of the U.S. Supreme Court, having served from 1990 to 2009.

***Anderson Cooper (1967– ):*** American journalist and television personality. He is the anchor for the CNN news program *Anderson Cooper 360* and host of the syndicated talk show *Anderson*.

***Lisa Kudrow (1963– ):*** American actor best known for her role as Phoebe in the sitcom *Friends*.

when the first posters were hung on a dorm-room wall, and having a .edu e-mail address was still a novelty. Statistically speaking, however, having an expertise in statistics may help in getting a job: according to a survey conducted by the National Association of Colleges and Employers, graduates with math skills are more likely than their peers in other majors to find themselves promptly and gainfully employed.

The safest of all degrees to be acquiring this year is in accounting: forty-six percent of graduates in that discipline have already been offered jobs. Business majors are similarly placed: forty-four percent will have barely a moment to breathe before undergoing the transformation from student to suit. Engineers of all stripes—chemical, computer, electrical, mechanical, industrial, environmental—have also fared relatively well since the onset of the recession: they dominate a ranking, issued by Payscale.com, of the disciplines that produce the best-earning graduates. Particular congratulations are due to aerospace engineers, who top the list, with a starting salary of just under sixty thousand dollars—a figure that, if it is not exactly stratospheric,° is twenty-five thousand dollars higher than the average starting salary of a graduate in that other science of the heavens, theology.°

Economics majors aren't doing badly, either: their starting salary averages about fifty thousand a year, rising to a mid-career median° of a hundred and one thousand. Special note should be taken of the fact that if you have an economics degree you can, eventually, make a living proposing that other people shouldn't bother going to college. This, at least, is the approach of Professor Richard K. Vedder, of Ohio University, who is the founder of the Center for College Affordability and Productivity. According to the *Times*, eight out of the ten job categories that will add the most employees during the next decade—including home-health aide, customer-service representative, and store clerk—can be performed by someone without a college degree. "Professor Vedder likes to ask why fifteen percent of mail carriers have bachelor's degrees," the paper reported.

The argument put forth by Professor Vedder (Ph.D., University of Illinois) is, naturally, economic: of those overly schooled mail carriers, he said, "Some of them could have bought a house for what they spent on their education." Another economist, Professor Robert I. Lerman, of American University (Ph.D., M.I.T.), told the *Times* that high schools, rather than readying all students for college, should focus on the acquisition of skills appropriate to the workplace. According to the *Times*, these include the ability to "solve problems and make decisions," "resolve conflict and negotiate," "cooperate with others," and "listen actively."

---

***stratospheric:*** the region of the earth's atmosphere that extends from about seven miles to about thirty miles above the planet's surface; here, the term is used in its more common figurative meaning, at the extreme end of a scale.

***theology:*** the academic discipline devoted to the study of religion or specific religions and their influence as well as the nature of religious belief more generally.

***median:*** in statistics, the middle number in a series arranged from lowest to highest (or vice versa). We use the median (in contrast to the average, or the mean) when we know that the series of numbers we are analyzing is not equally distributed. Here, for example, a few very high salaries might influence the average salary and mislead us if we consider the average salary; if, however, we take the middle salary, we will have a clearer point of comparison for looking across time or across salaries for people with different majors.

It may be news that the academy° is making a case for the superfluity° of the academy, but skepticism about the value of college, and of collegians, is hardly novel. Within the sphere of business, a certain romance attaches to the figure of the successful college dropout, like Steve Jobs, who was enrolled at Reed° for only a semester, or Bill Gates, who started at Harvard in 1973 but didn't get his degree until it was granted, honorarily,° thirty-four years later. On the political stage, too, having spent excessive hours in seminar rooms and libraries is widely regarded as a liability. *Vide*° Peggy Noonan's° celebration, during the 2004 Presidential campaign, of George W. Bush's lack of cerebration.° "He's not an intellectual," Noonan wrote in the *Wall Street Journal.* "Intellectuals start all the trouble in the world."

The candidates' education, or the insufficiency thereof, came up again during the most recent Presidential election. Sarah Palin told Katie Couric that she was "not one of those who maybe came from a background of, you know, kids who perhaps graduate college and their parents get them a passport and give them a backpack and say go off and travel the world"—even though Palin evidently considered college impor-
5 tant enough to have tried out five different ones within three years. Meanwhile, Barack Obama's degrees from prestigious universities were, to his critics, evidence of his unfitness for office. "The last thing we need are more pointy-headed intellectuals running the government," the political scientist Charles Murray (B.A., Harvard; Ph.D., M.I.T.) said during the closing months of the campaign. As President, Obama has rightly noted that too many Americans are already skipping college or dropping out, even without economists having advised them to do so; within weeks of the Inauguration, he pledged to increase the national graduation rate, which is significantly lower than that of many other developed nations, including Canada, Japan, and Korea.

The skip-college advocates' contention—that, with the economic downturn, a college degree may not be the best investment—has its appeal. Given the high cost of attending college in the United States, the question of whether a student is getting his or her money's worth tends to loom large with whoever is paying the tuition fees and the meal-plan bills. Even so, one needn't necessarily be a liberal-arts graduate to regard as distinctly and speciously° utilitarian° the idea that higher educa-

***academy:*** higher education, often with mild to strong negative connotations.

***superfluity:*** irrelevance, excessiveness; the opposite of *necessity*.

***Reed College:*** an elite private liberal arts college in Portland, Oregon.

***honorary degree:*** a degree, often a doctorate, that a college or university bestows on an individual who has made important contributions to society in some way without the person's having taken the courses, exams, etc., normally required for a degree.

***vide:*** Latin abbreviation meaning "see"; generally used to refer readers to a specific section of a text.

***Peggy Noonan (1950– ):*** American political writer best known for having served as President Ronald Reagan's speechwriter. She also assisted President George H. W. Bush in this role. Currently, she is a columnist for the *Wall Street Journal* and a commentator on news programs.

***cerebration:*** a rarely used word meaning "thinking."

***speciously:*** initially appealing but ultimately false or misleading.

***utilitarian:*** having usefulness as its ultimate goal in contrast to other possible goals.

tion is, above all, a route to economic advancement. Unaddressed in that calculus is any question of what else an education might be for: to nurture critical thought; to expose individuals to the signal accomplishments of humankind; to develop in them an ability not just to listen actively but to respond intelligently.

All these are habits of mind that are useful for an engaged citizenry, and from which a letter carrier, no less than a college professor, might derive a sense of self-worth. For who's to say in what direction a letter carrier's thoughts might, or should, turn, regardless of the job's demands? Consider Stephen Law, a professor of philosophy at the University of London, who started his working life delivering mail for the British postal service, began reading works of philosophy in his spare time, decided that he'd like to know more, and went on to study the discipline at City University, in London, and at Oxford University. (A philosophy graduate in the Class of 2010, by the way, stands to earn an average starting salary of forty thousand dollars a year, rising to a lifetime median of seventy-six thousand. Not exactly statistician money, but something to think about.) Indeed, if even a professionally oriented college degree is no longer a guarantee of easily found employment, an argument might be made in favor of a student's pursuing an education that is less, rather than more, pragmatic.° (More theology, less accounting.) That way, regardless of each graduate's ultimate path, all might be qualified to be carriers of arts and letters,° of which the nation can never have too many.

---

***pragmatic:*** here, practical or directed toward a goal, specifically, employment.

***arts and letters:*** the fine arts and the humanities (or the liberal arts more broadly), excluding mathematics, the sciences, and technical fields.

## *May 31, 2010*

## Ask the Author Live: Rebecca Mead

***Posted by the* New Yorker**

In this week's Comment, Rebecca Mead writes about the cost of college. Today, Mead answered readers' questions in a live chat. A transcript of their discussion follows.

Compare the level of commentary in Mead's article to what is offered in the live chat. How do they differ as possible sources you might use in your own writing? How would you use them?

LINK TO P. 828

***Rebecca Mead:*** Hello, everyone, Rebecca Mead here. Looking forward to our chat. 10

***Question from Sarina:*** As a senior in high school who is set to graduate in two weeks, I know many, including myself, who have had to forgo their top-choice schools because of the price. Is it worth it to enroll in a cheaper state college than a more expensive private university? Do the opportunities really diminish?

***Rebecca Mead:*** Hi Sarina, I'm not an education expert, but my sense is that there are many, many state schools where you can get an excellent education—and where you will find many classmates who, like you, are highly motivated, which counts for a great deal in a peer group. Good luck with wherever you go!

***Question from Evelyn:*** I know some people who aren't academically cut out for college, but as even simple jobs such as janitorial work now require bachelor's degrees, should we still push everyone through college?

***Rebecca Mead:*** Thanks, Evelyn. Of course we all know people who aren't cut out for college, but I know it's a mistake to think of education only as a route to a better career. Reading books, studying history—all these things contribute to making us better citizens, too.

***Question from Alexander P. Grimsdall:*** I don't think US college is worth 15
what you pay, but as a Brit, I wish we had to pay more for our universities here as all but the top ones have very limited facilities . . .

***Rebecca Mead:*** Full disclosure: I'm British, too, and did my undergraduate degree in England. I came to America to do a Master's degree, and here I still am.

***Question from Jean:*** Great article in *Wash Post* recently by Jay Matthews re how parents can influence/sway their child's decision when the in-state tuition/private choice becomes an issue.

***Rebecca Mead:*** Must take a look. I agree with the responder above that state/public schools can be a great choice, with many excellent professors.

***Question from Mike:*** As far as writing goes, is there any value to getting a University degree? Or would time be better spent just writing?

***Rebecca Mead:*** The best education for a writer, I think, is to read a lot— 20
college can be a good place to do that.

***Question from Ike:*** Hi Rebecca, I'm a soon-to-graduate college student. I think I may be one of those who were convinced to attend without much consideration of the reality of the situation. I picked a Russian major almost randomly, and I'm still not sure what I'd like to "do with it" (which is something people ask me a lot). People often have told me that employers will like the fact that I have a degree at all, regardless of the field. Do you find that this is true and that I won't have tooooo much trouble finding a job that doesn't have to do with Russian translation or teaching?

***Rebecca Mead:*** Hey, Ike, congratulations on your soon-to-graduate status. I'm not sure you have to end up "doing" anything with your Russian expertise. And I would think the fact that you chose to study Russian would stand you in good stead with employers looking for graduates who are broad-minded and interested in the world. Good luck. Just to add for

Ike—you should read Elif Batuman's wonderful new book about studying Russian. It's (indirectly) a wonderful work of advocacy for studying what interests you, not what you think employers are going to be looking for.

***Question from D. Jones:*** I am surprised at the self-serving individualism that launched and pervades both this discussion, all media stories, and American culture. I'd rather have answers to: Is education worthwhile for society? How much education is necessary for a civil society? What kind? If more people are well-educated is a place better in which to live? etc. A quote attributed to Derek Bok° is, "If you think education is expensive, try ignorance." I think he was talking about a society, especially a democracy where voters need a measure of intelligence.

*Derek Bok (1930– ):* American law professor and former president of Harvard University; Bok is the author of nine books.

***Rebecca Mead:*** Could not agree more.

25 ***Question from Jessica:*** Well, I think that the "self-serving individualism" nevertheless captures current trends (as well as longer term ones) that relate to education, you're just hearing them in a name-contextualized context. In response to Sarina: I attend classes at two Universities—one public state school, one "southern ivy" and I can attest to the fact that BOTH institutions offer a fantastic academic, extracurricular, athletic and networking buffet of opportunities—so Sarina, I think you might find that your state college education will surprise you. (And you can always hit up another top-choice school for grad school, possibly!)

***Question from Louis T.:*** I have a philosophy final in a couple hours. Wish me luck?

***Rebecca Mead:*** Log off!

***Question from Michel:*** Which is more valuable: a master's degree, or work experience?

***Rebecca Mead:*** I'm sure it depends on the discipline. My master's degree was in journalism, but everything important I ever learned about being a journalist I learned on the job. (It was a great way to move to New York City, though.)

30 ***Question from Jessica:*** I have a philosophy degree in a few years. Wish me luck?

***Rebecca Mead:*** Luck!

***Question from Alexander P. Grimsdall:*** The way politicians on both sides of the pond° seem to think, the more who get to go to college, the better, but there is a limit surely . . . In the UK there is a vast number of university graduates who have massive debts and cannot get a job due to the glut of those in a similar position. That is bad enough, but this must be even more acute in the US due to the higher cost of a US college education. My instinct is that in the US there is a tradition of a "college fund," but is the penny

*both sides of the pond:* a colloquial expression used to refer to the United States and the United Kingdom, the "pond" being the Atlantic Ocean.

starting to drop that a college degree buys you nothing, unless it is from an Ivy League college and even then, nothing is guaranteed? I graduate next year, and I find myself sifting through internship in politics/IR° etc. as I know my degree won't set me apart from the crowd. And as for D. Jones . . . I agree education is important, but I think there needs to be an end to the idea that college is the golden ticket, and also, is it good for society to have a mass of disillusioned debt-ridden graduates?

***IR:*** international relations.

***Rebecca Mead:*** Alexander—sorry to hear you're so pessimistic. But "a college degree buys you nothing"—must we only think of an education as a form of economic currency? I appreciate that it is costly to go to college in the states (and even now, to a lesser extent, in the UK) but I think it's a terrible mistake to only think in terms of a degree "buying" you something.

***Question from Mike:*** Sarina, looking back, I wish I'd gone to a public university. My bills for my private education are weighing heavily on me now. That's not to say the job market won't turn around in the future. But it's something to think about.

***Question from Betty:*** There's been quite a bit of chatter about shortening 35
the college degree to three years (*NY Times* article written by Trachtenberg and Kauvar° which garnered quite a few replies from academics and students alike). What's your take on this idea—could it actually help students with loans in the long run, does this help university enrollments, and lastly would a three-year degree hurt the perceived professional legitimacy of a college job applicant? Thanks!

***Trachtenberg and Kauvar:*** the reference is to "A Degree in Three" by Stephen Joel Trachtenberg and Gerald Kauvar, which appeared on May 24, 2010, on the op-ed page of the *Times*; see http://nyti.ms/yvbHUR.

***Rebecca Mead:*** I don't know the ins and outs of this but it looks like an intriguing idea.

***Question from John:*** Just wanted to respond to Mike's question about whether employers are likely to look favorably on his having an undergraduate degree. My experience has been that the skills (critical thinking, communication, etc.) are a strength that employers value.

***Question from Josephine:*** In talking to my younger sister's age group (10 years younger) it seems that their opinion is that many people go to college/university, pay the money, and just get the pass through. Meaning they go through the motions where nothing is learnt. Finland, on the other hand, has a fantastic education system even before you factor in the cost:value.

***Rebecca Mead:*** That's too bad about your sister and her friends. I don't know anything about the Finnish education system (beyond the fact that they all seem to emerge speaking better English than we do).

***Question from Jan:*** I am a teacher in a huge school district where we are 40
encouraged (required?) to encourage all students to be a part of the "College-Bound Culture" that the district is espousing. College will not be the best

choice for many of our students. It is frustrating to constantly tell students that they should prepare themselves for college, when I don't believe it myself. It's ludicrous! The value of an education—of any type—is to prepare oneself to be a successful and useful citizen. Our district should be preparing students for a variety of careers that will not require college.

***Rebecca Mead:*** A successful and useful citizen, yes. And also one able to think critically.

***Question from Alexander P. Grimsdall:*** I'm not pessimistic about a college degree at all . . . I think the experience is extremely valuable for anyone, broadens the mind etc., and I don't think it is all about economic value. I am so happy I have had the experience. I'm just not sure that the idea that "everyone should get a degree" is exactly realistic. It is difficult as I don't think anyone should be able to stand in the way of someone's aspirations. Are you saying that the more people go to college the better . . . even if there are no jobs for them when they come out?

***Rebecca Mead:*** Sorry to have misrepresented you! I'm not a policy expert—I am only arguing that there is more to an education than an economic ticket.

***Question from Corey:*** As someone who will be beginning an English Ph.D. in the Fall, I was wondering if you get the sense that humanities Ph.D.s are worse off than people who just stop with B.A.s? (Or, will I be the homeless guy spouting lines of Pope° at passersby?)

*Alexander Pope (1688–1744):* a widely quoted eighteenth-century British poet famous not only for his poetry but also for his translation of Homer.

45 ***Rebecca Mead:*** Pope!

***Question from Jan:*** Our school district does something to help combat the ever-rising cost of college. There are several campuses that offer early-college programs. Students spend 5 years on the high school campus using a "compacted" curriculum. After the 5th year, they emerge from high school with an "Associate's Degree" and two years of college already finished paid by the district. They can then apply to complete their studies at a 4-year institution, if they want.

***Rebecca Mead:*** Sounds interesting!

***Question from Steve Burks:*** Should colleges have the responsibility of ensuring that their majors correspond with viable job markets? And if not, should colleges offer more pronounced disclaimers, e.g., "Students might not find work with these degrees"? I ask because, frankly, some people go to college so they can get a job, not because they love to learn, and college marketing plays into the employment expectation. Maybe it isn't false advertising, but perhaps something loosely akin? Thanks.

***Rebecca Mead:*** Hey, Steve, I'm amused/horrified by your suggestion of an academic disclaimer. But I would have thought that one of the things one should learn from college is that nothing is guaranteed. Even if you study something as vocational as accountancy, you still may end up not getting a job as an accountant.

***Question from Jess:*** Also, what is the penalty for not having an under- 50
graduate degree? How many opportunities does it cut off, and are those the very opportunities which pave a path to influence, financial stability, etc.? Are there any writers there at the *New Yorker*, for example, that don't have a degree?

***Rebecca Mead:*** Interesting question to which I don't know the answer—but I am pretty sure that none of us were hired because of the degree we got. Though we might well have been hired because of the education we got—in the larger sense of education.

***Question from Tony Zucker:*** The accounting prof at Columbia took a few minutes one day in 1969 to compare the learning potential of a college prof vs. a sewer worker for the NYC. One finishes HS, goes to and pays for Columbia, gets grants for an MA and gets thru a PhD without any real income. Finally he gets on the faculty and starts up the ladder. The other person quits HS at 16 and gets on the NYC payroll. The break even point where the academic finally matches the sewer worker in combined gross income was in his 50s.

***Rebecca Mead:*** But I bet he didn't then advise his own children to forget about college and go and become sewer workers.

***Question from Jessica:*** Sorry—not sure if my computer is cooperating, so I'll compile my questions: I'm curious if you could offer any tips to aspiring journalists (I'm studying Philosophy but am interested in the industry) and also: I think the networking opportunities (ultimately it's these that do a great job of well, leading to jobs) afforded students by an institution (alumni network, general resources, even just learning how to connect and communicate etc.) that become just as important as the education itself, if you're looking at college with a "where is my return in investment" type of mentality.

***Rebecca Mead:*** Hey, Jessica, thanks for your questions. Best qualification 55
for an aspiring journalist is curiosity, so philosophy sounds promising . . .

***Question from Patrick:*** Universities in America, as you may know, are about 10 times more expensive than those in the UK at which the fees are about £4000.° Can the somewhat-excessive fees of American universities, as some put it, be justified? Do you feel that there is a real reason? For it certainly isn't the quality of education; Cambridge, Oxford° and Imperial often rank among the top universities in the world.

***Rebecca Mead:*** It would take a greater expert than me to answer this one, but I can certainly say from personal experience of both systems that the

***£4000:*** on the day of this live chat, 4,000 British pounds equaled $5,776. Higher education in Britain has traditionally been much, much less expensive—until recently, it was free—than in the United States because it was paid for by the government; it is also worth noting that a far lower percentage of British young people attend college than do American young people.

***Cambridge and Oxford:*** the two oldest and most prestigious universities in England.

***Colorado College:*** a small, private liberal arts college in Colorado Springs, Colorado, known for its unusual scheduling system—students study eight courses per year, each in intensive three-and-a-half-week blocks; tuition (without room, board, or other fees) for 2011–12 was nearly $40,000.

knowledge of how much a class is costing—and how high that price is—makes a dramatic difference to the way in which one metabolizes it intellectually.

***Question from B. Vandal:*** I find the whole discussion today far too traditional. The bottom line is that the higher the degree you have, the more earning potential you have. Having said that, there is no reason for people to pursue their education so that they complete their education by age 22 (or 26) for a graduate degree. More than ever, people are earning degrees later in life either by choice or because their skills have become outdated. With people living and working longer, we should never say a college degree is not possible for some—but that the paths students choose can be very different.

***Question from Kalani R. Man:*** The American higher-ed system is uniquely capitalistic: indeed, that's why they're the best. In the UK, you lords go to Cambridge & Oxford; in France, half the students will end up with a vocational degree; in Germany, you'll get some awesome specializations from more recent academic fields like travel literature and philology; however, in America, you can study anything you want as long as you pay for it (see: liberal arts colleges, especially those like Colorado College° and Evergreen°). Personally, I can't afford the education I'd like (CC), but I have the benefit of great friends who can pass their knowledge on to me. Still, Web 2.0 allows college students (and "pre"-college students) a chance to interact with people from around the world. The problem with getting such a global education (that is, a free one from the Internet, rather than, say, college) is that no one will take you seriously besides the people with whom you can communicate effectively. And since communication is a legit skill for practically any job, with such a worldly, albeit virtual, education, you'll be prepared to note threads on a more international scale, and have job opportunities around the world once you "graduate." American universities are great, but only if you plan on staying in America. After all, Plato reminds us the goal of an educational system is to make good citizens while Homi Bhabha° tells us the nation-state° is so, like, 1846.°

***Rebecca Mead:*** Interesting argument—though your characterization of 60
Oxford and Cambridge is about 100 years out of date. Sorry!

***Question from Jess:*** Rebecca, I think the days of leaving university and walking into a guaranteed job are well and truly over. However, it is more like an essential basic qualification—employers will certainly expect more, but they will expect an undergrad degree at the least.

***Rebecca Mead:*** You may be right. And a short anecdote to end up with—a few years ago I took my US driver's test, and had a few driving lessons to

***Evergreen:*** Evergreen State College in Olympia, Washington, a public liberal arts college known for its nontraditional, interdisciplinary approach to education; tuition (without room, board, or other fees) for 2011–12 ranged from $6,900 for Washington residents to $18,090 for nonresidents.

***Homi K. Bhabha (1949– ):*** Anne F. Rothenberg Professor of English and American Literature and Language at Harvard and a key figure in postcolonial studies, a field that seeks to understand the consequences of European and American colonialism and imperialism for both the colonized and the colonizers.

***nation-state:*** a political entity (a state) that corresponds to a cultural and/or ethnic entity (a nation). Today, we often think of the world as being composed of nation-states whereas in earlier periods, it was generally composed of empires.

***1846:*** representing the era before 1848, when revolutions broke out in France, Germany, Italy, Austria, Brazil, and other countries demanding a more participatory government and a greater concern for the needs of the working classes. This upheaval, though not immediately successful in many regards, is linked to the rise of the contemporary nation-state in Europe and elsewhere.

brush up on my (woefully limited) driving skills. The teacher said to me, "I could just teach you how to pass the test—but why don't I teach you to drive as well?" So my point would be, if you're getting a degree, why not also get an education at the same time? Thanks to everyone, and sorry I couldn't get to all your questions.

## RESPOND •

1. Characterize Mead's argument in "Learning by Degrees." What is her central claim? What evidence does she provide for her position? How does she deal with potential criticisms of her position or alternative positions on the issues she is discussing? In what ways does she qualify her claims? How does doing so strengthen her argument? (See Chapter 7 for information on structuring arguments.)
2. What sorts of evidence does Mead use in presenting information in "Learning by Degrees"? Make a list of all the kinds of evidence she uses as well as the sources she provides for that information. How do her use and presentation of evidence contribute to her ethos? (See Chapters 7 and 17 on evidence and Chapter 3 on ethos in arguments.)
3. Try to summarize the arguments that are being made by the people posting comments in the live chat with Mead. If you read carefully, you've already noticed some people besides Mead posted more than once. (Here, it may be easiest to begin by listing the main point of each comment or question that is posted and then to try to group those points into categories. You may end up with a visual diagram that lists the major arguments and shows the relationships among them using spatial arrangement and conventions like arrows.) Do you find this task easy or challenging? Why might this be the case?
4. How do such electronically mediated interactions permit new kinds of arguments to take place in the public arena? How might we characterize such interactions? How, for example, are they like or not like face-to-face interactions?
5. What sort of ethos does Mead create, especially in the live chat interaction? What evidence can you offer for your claims? **In an essay, seek to describe this ethos**—an argument of fact and/or definition—**and to evaluate its effectiveness** in light of the goals the magazine and Mead might have for participating in the live chat and of the constraints created by the technology participants are using. (Obviously, you'll need to specify what you see those goals and constraints as being. Chapters 8–10 will help you with issues of arguments of fact, definitional arguments, and evaluations.)

*The U.S. Bureau of Labor Statistics, part of the government's Department of Labor, is tasked with collecting and disseminating statistical information on topics related to labor economics. One of its major concerns is, not surprisingly, impartiality in data collection and reporting. In other words, the bureau seeks to produce trustworthy data that can become the basis for arguments based on fact as well as other kinds of argument. (If you visit the URL for this site—http://1.usa.gov/9SIzUC—you can click on links that will take you to pages showing the actual data on which the figures are based as well as the sources of those data.) In this selection from September 2010, the bureau provides statistical information about a range of topics relating to higher education. For each topic, a short summary and a figure are presented. As you study the information—textual and visual—for each topic, consider how it might be used as evidence in constructing arguments about a range of topics from the value of higher education to educational inequities to U.S. competitiveness in the global marketplace.*

# Making a Visual Argument: Spotlight on Statistics: Back to College

U.S. BUREAU OF LABOR STATISTICS

Whether you're a bright-eyed freshman, an experienced upper-classman, a faithful alumnus,° an educated professor, a capable administrator, or even a college-sports enthusiast, you are probably familiar with some of the numerous public and private colleges and universities spread across the United States. The establishment and growth of these institutions, and their contributions to the nation, have long been one of the most notable aspects of U.S. history.

The first institutions of higher learning in colonial North America were founded to supply the demand for clergy and school teachers. In recent decades, colleges and universities have trained the workers that put men on the moon and created the Internet age.

In 2009, there were over 10,000 establishments (places of employment, whether campuses, offices, research facilities, or other locations) operated by colleges and universities in the United States. This Spotlight presents BLS data related to college and university students and graduates, as well as colleges and universities as an industry and place of employment.

---

***alumnus:*** a graduate of an institution, especially a college or university. English continues to use this Latin word as well as other forms of the word used in Latin. Thus *alumnus* is the masculine singular form; *alumna*, the feminine singular; *alumni*, the masculine plural as well as the form used when a group includes females and males; and *alumnae*, the feminine plural. The shortened forms, *alum* and *alums*, are also frequently used, especially in contexts that are not formal.

# For the College Educated: Increasing Employment . . .

All of the increase in employment over the past two decades has been among workers who have taken at least some college classes or who have associate or bachelor's degrees—and mostly among workers with bachelor's degrees. The number of these college-educated workers has increased almost every year. Over the 1992–2009 period, the number of college-educated workers increased from 27 million to 44 million. In contrast, the number of employed people with only a high school diploma or without a high school diploma has remained steady or decreased.

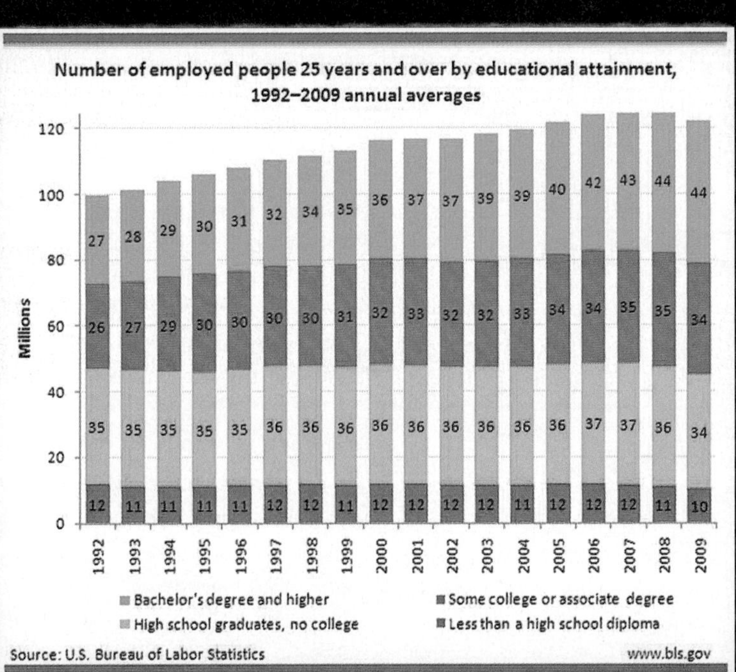

## . . . Lower Unemployment . . .

Business cycles run their course and the economy goes from expansion to recession—but regardless of whether the economy is booming or contracting, an inverse relationship exists between education and unemployment: more education is associated with less unemployment. In 2009, the unemployment rate for workers with college degrees was 4.6 percent. The rate for workers without a high school diploma was 10 points higher.

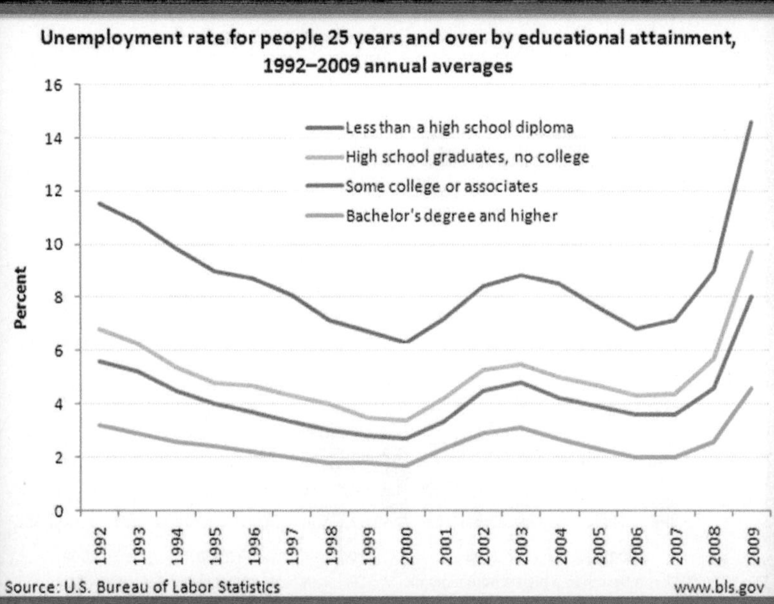

# . . . and Higher Earnings

If you think what people say about higher education leading to higher earnings is a cliché, you might want to consider that sometimes clichés are true. In 2009, the median° weekly earnings of workers with bachelor's degrees were $1,137. This amount is 1.8 times the average amount earned by those with only a high school diploma, and 2.5 times the earnings of high school dropouts.

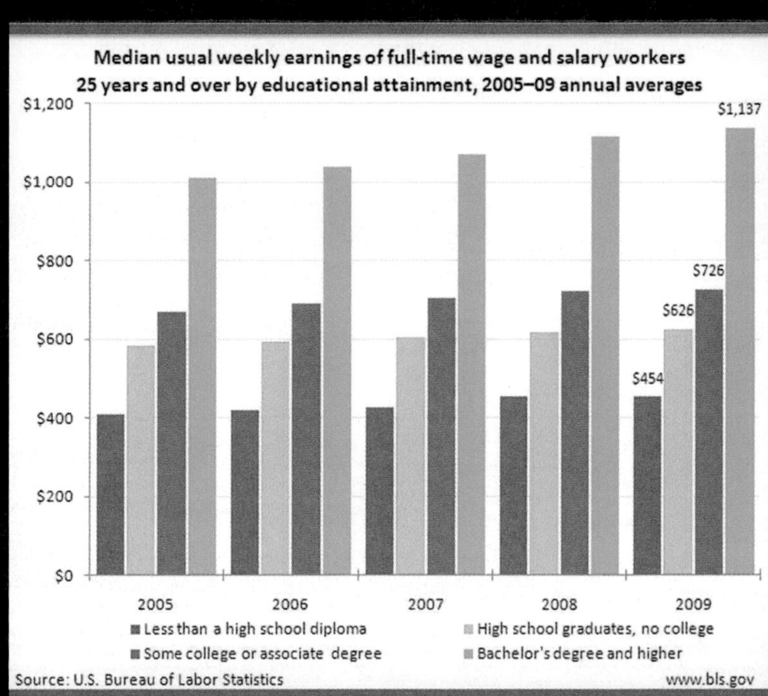


***median:*** in statistics, the middle number in a series arranged from lowest to highest (or vice versa). We use the median (in contrast to the average, or the mean) when we know that the series of numbers we are analyzing is not equally distributed. Here, for example, a few very high salaries might influence the average salary and mislead us if we consider the average salary; if, however, we take the middle salary, we will have a clearer point of comparison when looking across time or across salaries for people who work different jobs.

# Degree Attainment by Age 22

In October when they were 22 years old, 9.7 percent of young adults had bachelor's degrees and 27.0 percent were enrolled in college during the 2002–2007 period. Young women were more likely to have finished their degrees or be enrolled than young men.

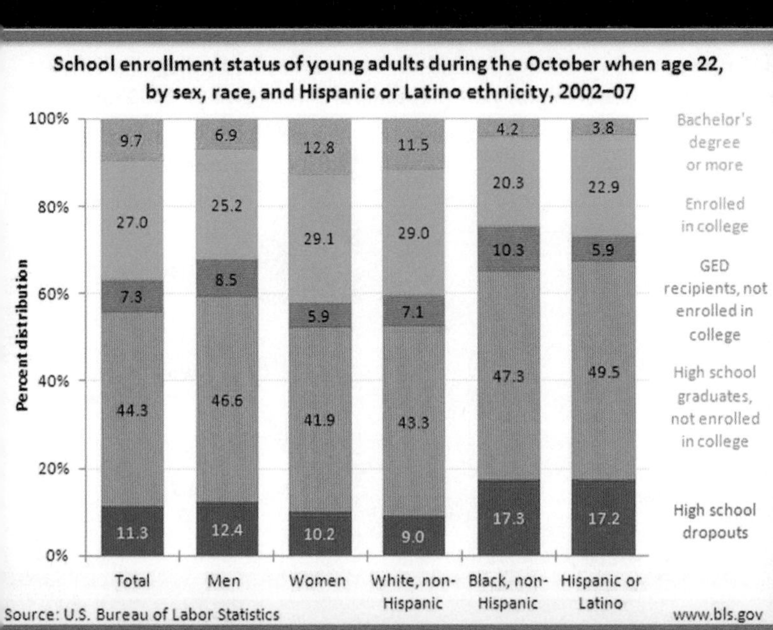

## Time to Sleep, Learn, and Play

On average, college students slept 8.4 hours, engaged in educational activities (such as attending classes or studying) for 3.6 hours, and enjoyed leisure and sports activities for 3.5 hours on a typical weekday during the school year over the 2005–2009 period.

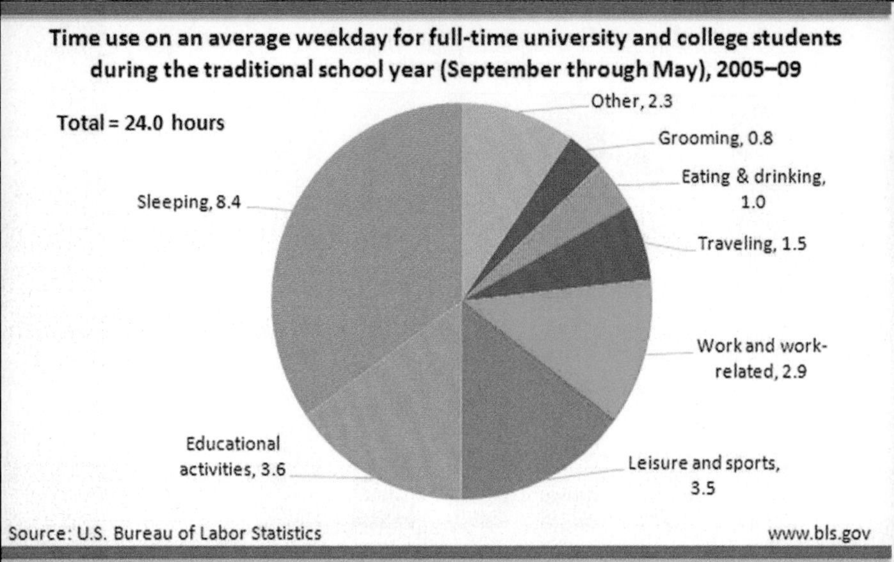

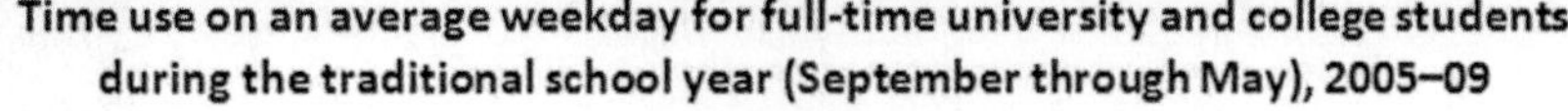


NOTE: Data include individuals, ages 15 to 49, who were enrolled full time at a university or college. Data include non-holiday weekdays and are averages for the traditional school year (September through May), 2005–09.

## Around the World

In the United States, 40 percent of adults between the ages of 25 and 64 had bachelor's degrees in 2007. In Canada, 48 percent had bachelor's degrees.

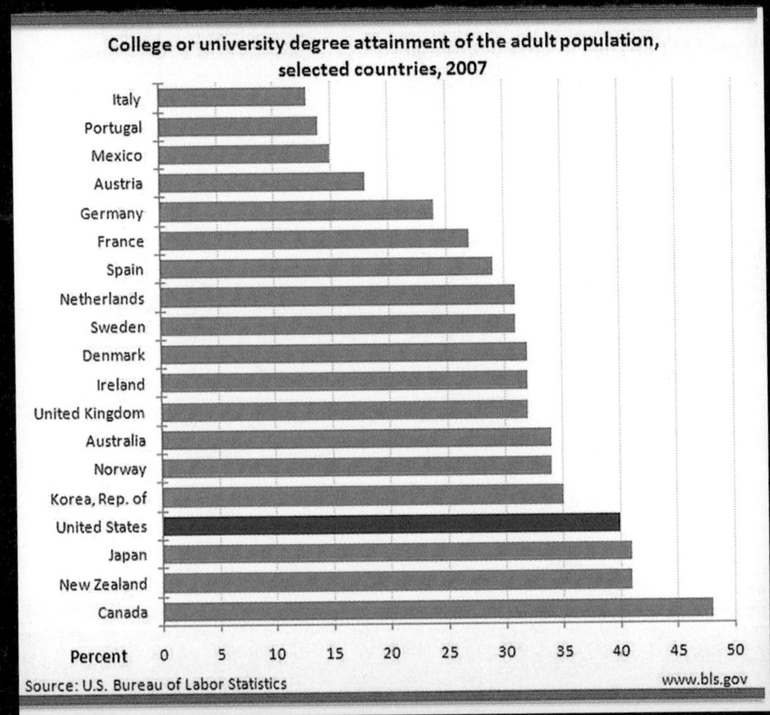

# The Price of Tuition

Since 1981, the cost of college tuition has consistently increased faster than the overall inflation rate.

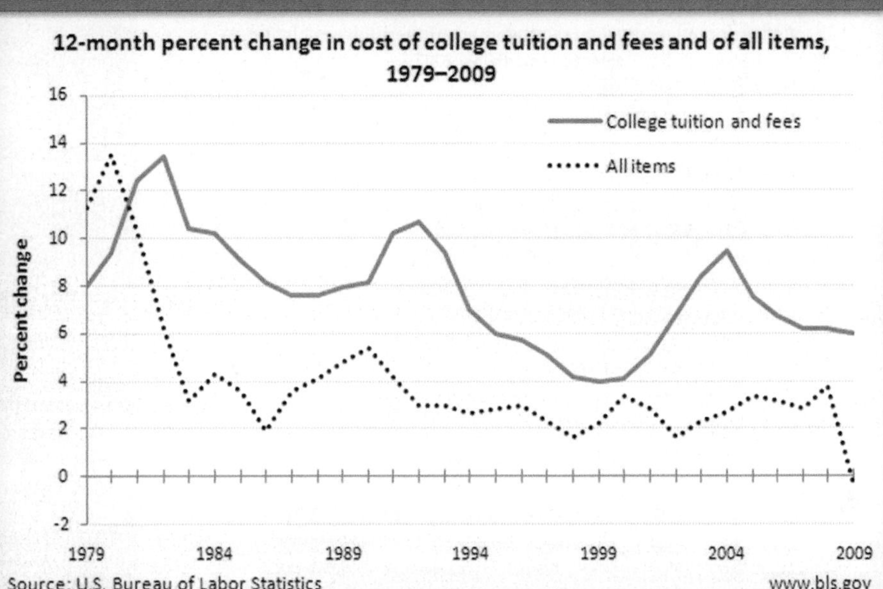

# College and University Employment Increasing . . .

Over the past five decades, college and university employment—both in terms of absolute numbers and as a percentage of total employment—has increased significantly. In 1960, about 850,000 people were employed in colleges and universities; in 2009 the number was over 3.9 million. Over the same period, the percentage of all workers who were employed by colleges and universities has doubled, increasing from 1.5 percent in 1960 to 3.0 percent in 2009.

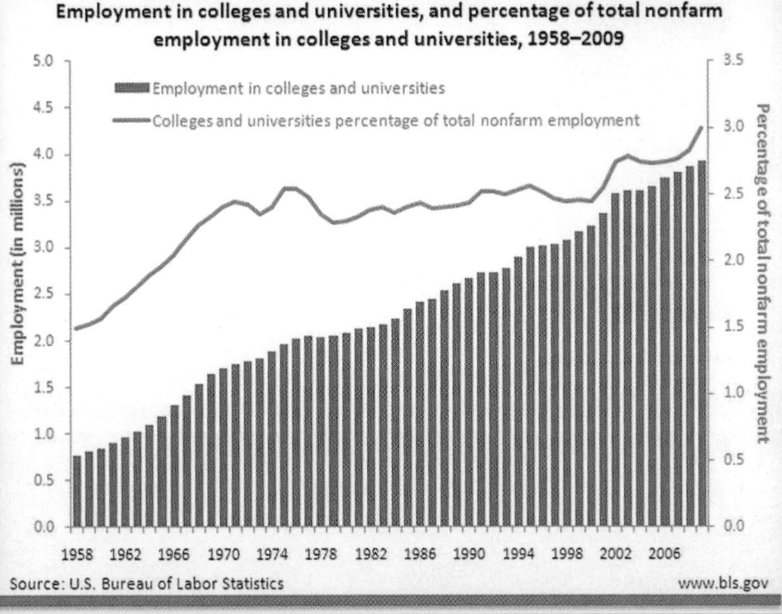


NOTE: Employment in colleges and universities is the sum of private sector employment in colleges and universities and state government employment in education. Federal and local government college and university employment, which is relatively small, is not included. State employment in education may include some employees that are not employed in colleges and universities.

## . . . And Expected to Continue Increasing

In 2008, about 1.7 million of the people employed on campus were postsecondary teachers (that is, college professors and instructors). Their number is projected to increase to over 1.9 million—an increase of over 15 percent—from 2008 to 2018. Over the same period, employment in all occupations is projected to increase about 10 percent.

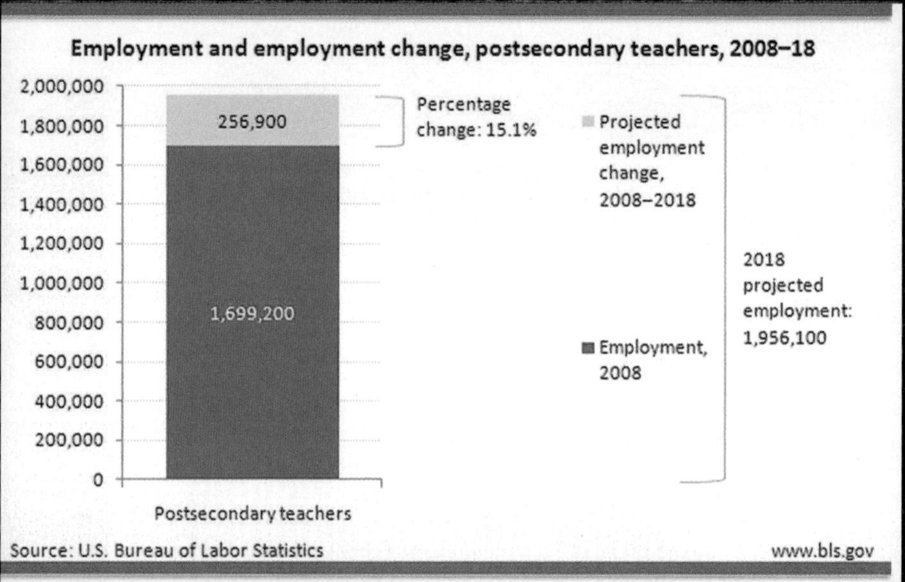

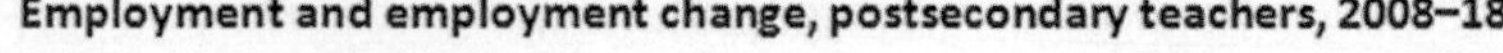

## College Compensation Costs

Employer costs for employee compensation averaged $44.82 per hour worked for colleges and universities in the civilian sector in March 2010. Of this amount, $31.12 went towards wages and salaries, and $13.70 for benefits.

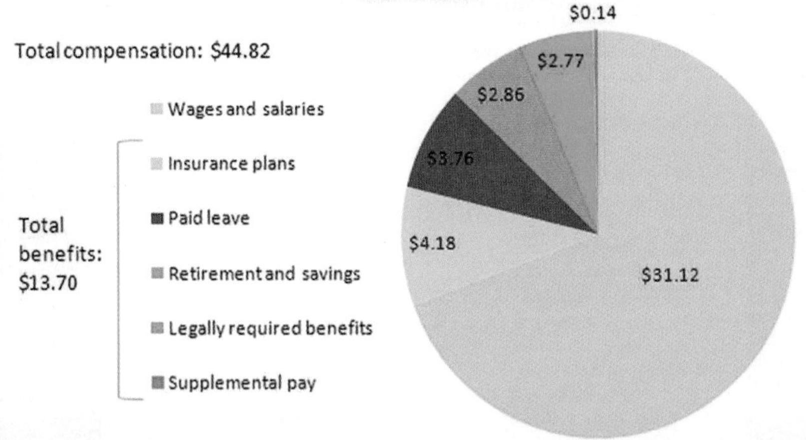

# Professor Pay

The earnings of postsecondary teachers, and the number employed, varied by subject and specialty. Health specialties° teachers, with employment of over 130,000 in May 2009, were more numerous than any other type of college or university postsecondary teacher. The number of postsecondary health specialties teachers is more than 10 times greater than the number of physics, economics, law, criminal justice and law enforcement, or agricultural science teachers. Law teachers and health specialties teachers were the highest paid postsecondary teachers; both had average annual earnings over $100,000 in 2009.

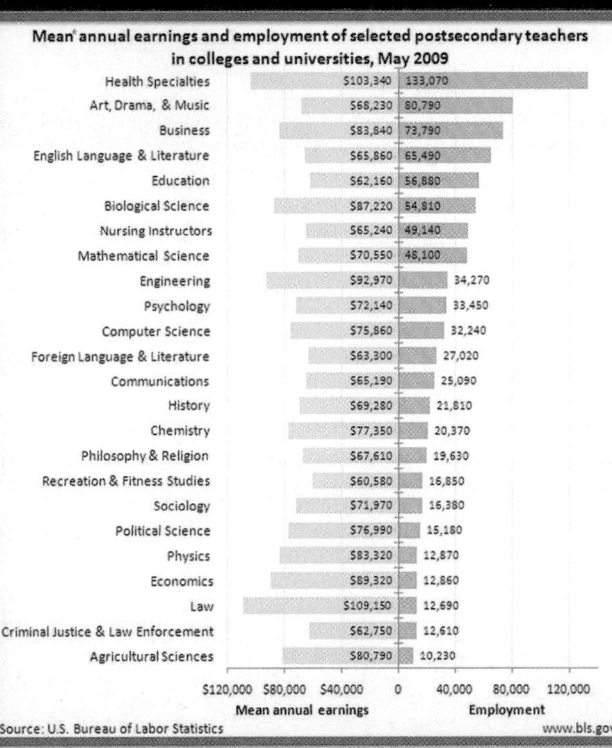

# Worker Safety

Colleges and universities are relatively safe workplaces. In 2008, the incidence rate of nonfatal occupational injuries and illnesses involving days away from work (per 10,000 full-time workers) was 64.5 in colleges and universities, compared with 113.3 in all private industry. The three most common events or exposures that caused injuries—fall on the same level, contact with object or equipment, and overexertion—were the same in both colleges and universities and private industry, albeit in different order.

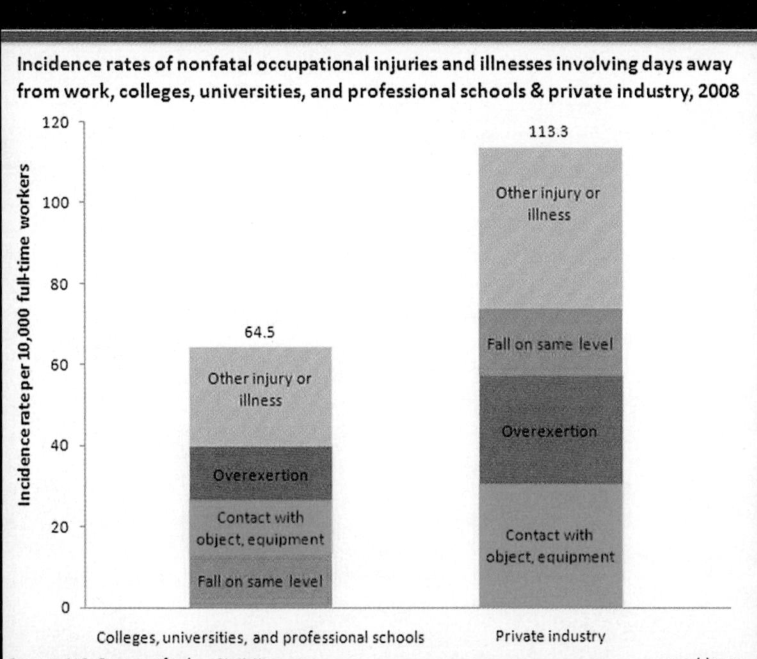

1. In what ways might we read the information provided about each of the topics as an argument? Do these arguments work together to form an argument or several arguments at some more abstract level? (Consider, for example, why the topics are arranged in the order that they are. Their ordering doesn't seem to be haphazard or random. Does there appear to be some sequence to the arrangement of at least some of the topics?)
2. Were you surprised by the information presented about any of these topics? Which one(s) and why?
3. How could these figures be used to support arguments about the value of education and especially higher education? Which specific figures would be most useful? What claims could they be used to support?
4. Examine closely the figure "Mean Annual Earnings and Employment of Selected Postsecondary Teachers in Colleges and Universities, May 2009." Although there is no reason to doubt the accuracy of these data, many professors—including yours—would likely argue that they are misleading for several reasons. First, they combine information from colleges, universities, and professional schools; junior colleges; technical and trade schools; general medical and surgical hospitals; and business schools and computer and management training—very different kinds of institutions with very different pay scales. Second, they ignore regional differences: 2011 data from the U.S. Bureau of Statistics show that the average wage in these fields in Massachusetts was $120,170 while for the nonmetropolitan regions of Southeast Iowa, it was $45,760. (Of course, the cost of living in those two locations is quite different as well, but those differences alone would not account for such disparities in wages.) Third, as the Bureau of Labor Statistics Web site notes in a footnote to one of the charts providing data on this topic, the data assume year-round full-time employment, though most professors with full-time jobs at four-year institutions have nine-month contracts and, increasingly, institutions use part-time faculty as a cost-saving measure. While other observations could be made, it should be clear that these data, though accurate, are, in some basic sense, misleading or potentially misleading. What does this situation demonstrate about the need to understand thoroughly the context(s) in which statistics you might wish to use in constructing arguments were collected as well as the limitations of those statistics?
5. Choose a figure that you find especially interesting or effective, and in a paragraph, **explain why you find it an interesting or effective way to present information**. You may want to begin by comparing the information presented in the short summary of the figure with all the information presented in the figure itself.

6. A skill that many students have difficulty mastering is writing effectively about figures or tables. (In fact, a major complaint from professors in the social and natural sciences about their students' writing is that students find it challenging to write about charts, tables, and figures.) Working with a classmate, discuss the following questions and work together to **write a paragraph** that could accompany one of the figures in this selection. Be sure that your paragraph doesn't merely repeat the information in the text—that would be plagiarism!—but instructs readers about the information provided and about what they should see in the figure as they study it. Obviously, your paragraph will be a factual argument of sorts. (Chapter 8 discusses factual arguments, while Chapter 14 discusses visual arguments.)

   Questions to consider: When you focus on the figure alone, ignoring the commentary, what is the major pattern that you see? Do you see patterns across the various cohorts or years? Reading your discussion of the figure, do you think readers will understand what is being quantified, how it is being quantified (percentages, wages [in dollars], millions of people employed by degree category), and what the major and minor patterns are in the distribution of data?

*The third figure in the previous selection, "Median Usual Weekly Earnings of Full-Time Wage and Salary Workers 25 Years and Over by Educational Attainment, 2005–09 Annual Averages" (p. 842), can easily be used to support the argument that education pays, but as Rebecca Mead notes in "Learning by Degrees," some researchers are not so quick to accept that argument hook, line, and sinker—or, indeed, to accept it at all. One such critic is Laurence Shatkin, an author and specialist in career information as well as a senior product developer for JIST, a publishing company that focuses on the fields of job searches, career exploration, and occupational information, among others. In the blog posting "Education Pays, but Perhaps Less Than You Thought," on FastCompany.com in October 2008, Shatkin explains why the U.S. Bureau of Labor Statistics doesn't tell the whole story. As you read the blog posting, consider the potential pitfalls of statistics, especially those you might find on the Internet. Likewise, give some thought to his final claim.*

# Education Pays, but Perhaps Less Than You Thought

LAURENCE SHATKIN

If you Google the phrase "education pays," the very first hit you'll get is a page at the Bureau of Labor Statistics that features a chart representing the median weekly earnings in 2007 of people with various levels of education. The higher the level of education, the higher the income. For example, high school graduates earned $604 per week, compared to $987 for those with a bachelor's degree and $1,497 for those with a doctoral degree. The figures are derived from the Current Population Survey.

The chart makes a compelling case and is probably popular with guidance counselors. My daughter, who teaches a GED° class for Spanish-speakers at a community college, has used the figures from this chart in a brochure aimed at recruiting students. I have used the figures in a book for JIST. A related fact that is often quoted is that the advantage of a college degree has been growing in recent years.

But this week I came across a study that qualifies the information in this chart. The article, "Real Wage Inequality," by Enrico Moretti of U.C. Berkeley,

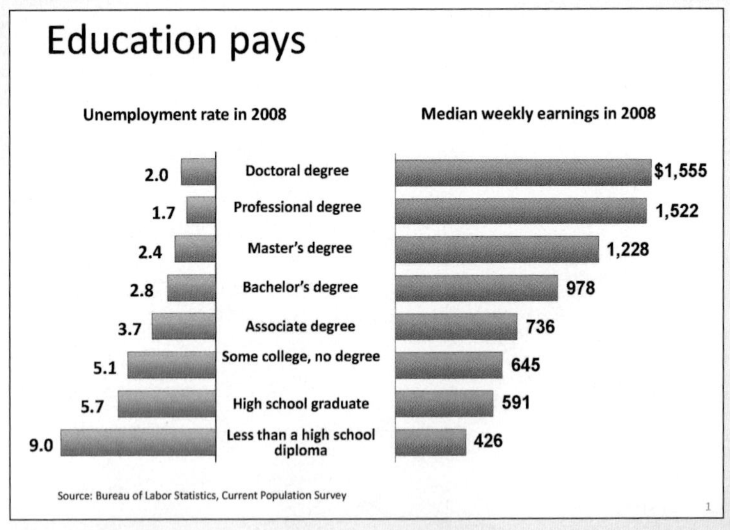

does not refute the "Education Pays" figures, but it points out that earnings are just one factor in the equation of well-being. Moretti notes that, from 1980 to 2000, college graduates have tended to concentrate in cities, especially in cities where the cost of housing is higher and has increased rapidly during this period. (The differences in housing costs do not seem to be related to housing quality. That is, college grads do not seem to live in a more expensive style of housing; rather, they live where the same kind of housing simply costs more.) As a result, the advantage of the college degree in terms of spending cash is not as great as the chart might suggest.

***GED:*** General Education Development tests, which are given in the United States and Canada. Certificates of passing the tests are often used as the equivalent of a high school diploma.

Specifically, Moretti found that half of the college wage advantage disappears when one accounts for the difference in housing costs. For example, in 2000 the college graduates were earning about 60% more but were enjoying an actual advantage of only 37%–43%. He also found that the increase in the advantage of a college degree between 1980 and 2000, often said to be about 20%, actually is between 8% and 10% when housing costs are factored in.

5 It's interesting to consider the question of *why* college graduates are concentrating in these high-rent cities. Moretti evaluates two possible explanations. The demand-pull hypothesis assumes that high-skilled workers are more productive in these cities, and therefore job opportunities are attracting college grads there. The supply-pull hypothesis assumes that college graduates are flocking to high-rent cities because they are attracted by amenities° other than employment, and their presence in these cities is driving up rents. Moretti argues for the demand-pull hypothesis, noting that as college graduates crowd into cities, their relative wages also get a boost, indicating their greater productivity. However, he does not rule out that a supply-pull phenomenon may also be occurring.

***amenities:*** things that make life comfortable, enjoyable, or pleasant. Shatkin is likely thinking about the fact that urban areas, in contrast to rural areas, provide a wider range of restaurants, stores, and leisure-time opportunities.

Moretti bases his comparisons on pre-tax earnings, but he notes that taxation causes further erosion of the college advantage. Because the federal income tax is progressive, college grads in expensive cities may have higher pre-tax earnings, but this comes with a larger tax bite in addition to the rent bite already noted. Furthermore, he notes, the tax codes in California and in New England coastal states are also progressive,° meaning an additional tax bite for college grads there.

***progressive:*** imposing higher rates of taxation on higher amounts of income.

Shatkin's analysis of the data demonstrates that statistics don't always tell the whole story. For more on arguments based on facts and reason, see Chapter 4.

LINK TO P. 55

Would these findings change my advice to a young person? Not at all. Education may not produce as great an increment in spending cash as the BLS chart suggests, but it still provides an advantage. It also provides many nonmonetary satisfactions that economists rarely measure.

## RESPOND

1. Take Shatkin's challenge, and Google "education pays." (If the Bureau of Labor Statistics [BLS] isn't the first hit you get, look down the list until you find the most recent BLS statistics on this topic.) How do current data compare with those from 2008? Why, for Shatkin, are these statistics at least partially misleading? (Be careful here: there is more than one step to the argument.)
2. What might account for the concentration of college graduates in urban areas, according to Enrico Moretti? Which hypothesis does he prefer? The fact that Moretti does not rule out one of the two hypotheses likely means that he does not have adequate data to draw a conclusion. Do you favor one hypothesis over the other on the basis of your life experiences? Which one and why? Why might Moretti, as an economist, not be willing to trust his life experience in answering this question?
3. Does Moretti's study or Shatkin's discussion of taxes mean that the Bureau of Labor Statistics is wrong? Why or why not?
4. Chapter 4 discusses statistics as examples of hard evidence or what Aristotle termed "inartistic appeals." What does this selection remind us about the nature and limitations of so-called hard evidence?
5. Shatkin closes his blog posting by stating that despite the research he discusses, he would not change his advice to young people to get an education because it pays both in actual monetary terms and in "many nonmonetary satisfactions that economists rarely measure" (paragraph 7). Do you agree with this advice? If so, would you agree if there were no monetary benefit? Why or why not? What sorts of "nonmonetary satisfactions," if any, have you gotten or do you hope to get from your education? **Write an essay** in which either you define and evaluate these satisfactions or you explain why you believe that your education has not provided them. You may also wish to speculate about whether economists could find ways of measuring these satisfactions. (For a discussion of definitional and evaluative essays, see Chapters 9 and 10, respectively.)

# The Major and the Job Market, the Dream and the Reality

MARK BAUERLEIN

*Mark Bauerlein is a professor of English at Emory University in Atlanta; he also served as director of the Office of Research and Analysis at the National Endowment for the Arts from 2003 until 2005. In addition to his scholarly writing, he also writes for a number of popular daily or weekly newspapers. This selection first appeared in October 2011 on* Brainstorm: Ideas and Culture, *a blog that is part of the* Chronicle of Higher Education's *Web site. (You can see the original blog entry at http://bit.ly/vCw1Si.)* The Chronicle *comprises the Web site, which is updated weekdays, and a weekly print edition; it is the major source of information about higher education in the United States for college and university administrators, faculty, and staff. As you read this selection, consider who Bauerlein's intended audience is and how you know; also give some thought to the argument he is making about what you should be working for.*

I took out a student loan when I was an undergraduate back in 1980, but it was only for a few thousand dollars. I could have borrowed more and lived better, but I was scared to pile up any more debt than I had to in order to pay enrollment fees and pick up the rent for the next couple of months. Back then, tuition in the University of California system was still only around $1,000 a year, and I could cover much of it with the part-time job I had for all five years (it took me 15 quarters and three summer-school sessions to graduate).

I can't imagine racking up the student debt that one hears about these days—not because of any moral superiority to today's borrowers, but precisely because of the fear I would have had of doing so at age 22. The *Los Angeles Times* portrays one of those big borrowers [http://lat.ms/wvLdJR] in a story on the Occupy Wall Street gatherings. He's a recent graduate of Ithaca College, and he owes $90,000 (!) to the banks. His case is one of sheer stupidity, and he knows it. He left high school as an honor student, and he was offered a full scholarship at one of the public universities in New York State, but a program at Ithaca College attracted him away, a special sequence in film directing in the communications department. He enrolled, but "became disenchanted with the program" and switched to English. After graduation, he couldn't find any steady job that would cover the bills. He now lives with his parents and mows lawns.

He's a good kid, though, and you can't knock him as a whiner or having an entitlement mentality. He wants to work, and he's contemplating entering the military (which has a program to cut $60,000 [!] from his debt). But one can't help but wonder about the lack of forethought, the unreality, of his prior decisions. You give up a free education at a SUNY school to study film directing at a cost of $35,000+ a year (that's what Ithaca College charges now)? What does the Bureau of Labor Statistics say about job prospects for film directing in its *Occupational Outlook Handbook* (http://www.bls.gov/oco/)? What was he thinking each time he received a loan check? What did he think was going to happen when he graduated? Had he heard too many "follow your dreams" and "pursue your passion" exhortations° in high school?

***exhortation:*** emphatic encouragement.

He looks upon the others at the protests with an innocent, skeptical eye. Here's the final section of the story:

> "College makes you cynical," he said quickly. "I guess I'm proud of my degree. I just don't see where it gets me."
>
> Cynical, perhaps, but when he read on the Internet about the rumblings down near Wall Street, he decided to join the fray.
>
> "I kept seeing posts that everyone there was upper-middle-class and while their hearts are in the right place, they're trying to represent something they don't know," said Grant, who hitched a ride the two hours to Manhattan on Thursday.
>
> His first day at Zuccotti Park, he seemed baffled by some of the flakier characters around him.
>
> "'I choose compassion,'" he said, reading a sign near him. "What the heck does that mean?"
>
> He figured he was seeing "my generation's hippies. . . . At least they're better than hipsters. We don't like them."
>
> The longer Grant spent perusing this poor man's Olympic Village, the more he became intrigued by the variety of grievances and the spirit. At one point, a chorus of protesters called people over, announcing, "The think tank is going to be discussing corporate personhood. Right here, right now."
>
> Grant looked interested. But before he could say anything, a man who said he was from New Hampshire photographed Grant's sign and bellowed at him: "Lame, you're lame. . . . Stop complaining. Get a job."
>
> Grant had been mostly silent the last few days, but this time he fired back: "That's why we're here, buddy. We can't get jobs."
>
> By Tuesday, Grant had found work with the organizers running a camera—something he learned in college. It won't pay, but he said it felt good to have purpose.
>
> "I've gotten a job with the movement," he texted. "It's eating up all of my time."

5 I spoke with a student yesterday who was wavering between a program in communications and one in speech therapy. I typed a few words into Google and the first site that came up was a 2009 story in *Forbes* with the headline: "Where the Jobs Are: Speech Pathologist." The subheading was, "It's a caring profession that can't get enough people working for it." I passed it along to her and advised her to think about it.

In fact, I urge every professor who advises students to have the *Occupational Outlook Handbook* on his or her desk, ever ready to show to uncertain students.

## RESPOND •

1. What argument(s) is Bauerlein making? What sort of evidence does he offer for the claims he makes? To what degrees are his arguments based on emotion? On character? On facts and reason? (See Chapters 2–4 for discussions of these kinds of arguments.) What is your response to his argument(s)?
2. Who is Bauerlein's invoked audience? His intended audience? What is the relationship between them? What evidence can you give for your claims?
3. Why might Bauerlein have begun his blog posting with a personal anecdote rather than with the claim that he makes in the opening line of paragraph 2? Would the posting have been more or less effective if he had begun by clearly stating his position rather than by telling a story? Why might this anecdote be especially effective given his intended audience? (See Chapter 4 on the value of testimonies and narratives.)
4. Because of the blog posting's final paragraph, we can easily claim that this selection represents a proposal. What proposal is Bauerlein making? To what extent is his proposal well developed, according to the criteria given in Chapter 12? Do you believe that Bauerlein's proposal is a judicious one?
5. As is not uncommon in blog postings, Bauerlein quotes at length from another source, here an article from the *Los Angeles Times* about the Occupy Wall Street movement, after commenting on it. Why might he have included the passage after he has commented on it? How would the blog be different if he had quoted the passage first and then commented on it?
6. The sort of lengthy quotation discussed in question 5 would not be appropriate in nearly all academic writing. Instead, the writer would have to summarize, paraphrase, and quote from the text, using quotations sparingly. **Write a summary** of this lengthy quotation, using paraphrasing and quotations, that could replace the text reproduced here; in other words, you should be able to replace the quotation with the summary your write without detracting from Bauerlein's message. You'll likely want to read the source article from the *Los Angeles Times* in its entirety before beginning this task. (See Chapter 19 for a discussion of using sources and Chapter 21 for a discussion of documenting sources.)

*Craig Lambert is an editor and staff writer at the* Harvard Magazine, *the alumni magazine of Harvard University. He has also written for* Sports Illustrated *and* Town and Country. *A competitive sculler, he is author of* Mind over Water: Lessons on Life from the Art of Rowing. *In this selection, which appeared in the "Week in Review" section of the Sunday edition of the* New York Times *in October 2011, Lambert examines one of the most fundamental ways that life in America has changed over the past few decades: customers are now expected to do for themselves tasks that employees used to be paid to do. In examining this increasingly common but rarely analyzed phenomenon, Lambert provides us with insights into the ways that economic pressures on the service economy are changing how Americans understand the notion of work.*

# Our Unpaid, Extra Shadow Work

CRAIG LAMBERT

The other night at the supermarket I saw a partner at a downtown law firm working as a grocery checker, scanning bar codes. I'm sure she earns at least $300,000 per year. Even so, she was scanning and bagging her purchases in the self-service checkout line. For those with small orders, this might save time spent waiting in slower lines. Nonetheless, she was performing the unskilled, entry-level jobs of supermarket checker and bagger free of charge.

This is "shadow work," a term coined 30 years ago by the Austrian philosopher and social critic Ivan Illich, in his 1981 book of that title. For Dr. Illich, shadow work was all the unpaid labor—including, for example, housework—done in a wage-based economy.

In a subsistence economy, work directly answers the needs of life: gathering food, growing crops, building shelters and fires. But once money comes into play, a whole range of tasks arises that do not address basic needs. Instead, such work may enable one to earn money and buy both necessities and, if possible, luxuries.

To do the work requires extra jobs, like commuting. The commuter often has to own, insure, maintain and fuel a car—and drive it—just to get to work and back. These unpaid activities ancillary° to earning one's wages are examples of shadow work.

5 In the industrialized world, few of us live in a subsistence mode, so shadow work is ubiquitous°: shopping, paying bills, housework. Digital technology—with its spam, e-mail, texting, smartphones and so on—is steadily ramping up the burden of shadow work for all whose lives revolve around its magnetic field.°

Science fiction novels of a half-century ago dramatized conflicts between humans and robots, asking if

***ancillary:*** here, secondary or expected in addition.

***ubiquitous:*** found everywhere.

***magnetic field:*** the space (or field) around a magnetic force in which the power of the force can be detected; here, used metaphorically, to describe the attraction that digital technology has for us and the power it exerts on our lives.

Lambert begins his article by providing a definition of "shadow work." How does this definition help him structure the argument that follows?

LINK TO P. 187

*Who saves money when you use the self-checkout?*

people were controlling their technologies, or if the machines were actually in charge. A few decades later, with the digital revolution in juggernaut° mode, the verdict is in. The robots have won. Although the automatons° were supposedly going to free people by taking on life's menial, repetitive tasks, frequently, technological innovation actually offloads such jobs onto human beings.

The conventional wisdom is that America has become a "service economy,"° but actually, in many sectors, "service" is disappearing. There was a time when a gas station attendant would routinely fill your tank and even check your oil and clean your windshield and rear window without charge, then settle your bill. Today, all those jobs have been transferred to the customer: we pump our own gas, squeegee our own windshield, and pay our own bill by swiping a credit card. Where customers once received service from the service station, they now provide "self-service"—a synonym for "no service." Technology enables this sleight of hand, which lets gas stations cut their payrolls, having co-opted their patrons into doing these jobs without pay.

Examples abound, helping drive unemployment rates. Airports now have self-service check-in kiosks that allow travelers to perform the jobs of ticket agents. Travel agents once unearthed, perused and compared fares, deals and hotel rates. Shadow-working travelers now do all of this themselves on their computer screens. Medical patients are now better informed than ever—as a result of hours of online shadow work. In 1998, the Internal Revenue Service estimated that taxpayers spent six billion hours per year on "tax compliance activities." That's serious shadow work, the equivalent of three million full-time jobs.

Once upon a time, retail stores had employees who were not cashiers but roamed the floor, assisting customers. Go into a Walmart or Target or Staples and find someone to help you locate and choose a product. Good luck. You're on your own, left to wander the aisles in search of an unoccupied staff person. (Meanwhile, you might stumble on and purchase some item you hadn't planned on buying.) Here, it's not technology, but a business tactic that cuts payroll expenses by trimming the service provided to customers—and prolongs the time those customers spend rambling around inside the

---

***juggernaut:*** an overpowering force, often one that demands total devotion.

***automaton:*** robot.

***service economy:*** an economy based on providing service to customers (in contrast, say, to one based on manufacturing, which creates goods to be sold).

store. Regardless, the result is still more shadow work, as customers take on the job that retail salespeople once did.

10 Shadow work isn't always unpaid; sometimes it shows up at one's salaried job in the form of new tasks covertly added to one's responsibilities. Not long ago, human resources departments kept track of employees' vacation, personal and sick days. In many organizations, employees now enter their own data into absence management software.

One nostalgic appeal of the *Mad Men* television series is the way it evokes memories of certain amusingly dated aspects of business life, like "support staff," and even "secretaries." Support staff is becoming a quaint, antiquarian° concept, a historical curiosity like typewriters, stenography° and executive washrooms. We all have our own computers, of course, and we type and print our own letters, copy our own reports and mail our own missives.° Even those in senior management perform these humdrum jobs.

Of course, these shadow chores never appear in one's job description, let alone justify any salary increase. Shadow work is just covertly added to our daily duties. As robotic devices replace human workers, end-users like customers and employees are taking on the remnant of the transaction that still requires wetware—a brain. New waves of technology change how things are done, and we docilely° adapt—unavoidably so, as there's usually no alternative. Running a business without e-mail is hardly a viable option, but with e-mail comes spam to be evaluated and deleted—more shadow work.

To be sure, shadow work has its benefits. Bagging one's own groceries or pumping one's own gas can save time. Shadow work can increase autonomy and enlarge our repertoire of skills and knowledge. Research on the "Ikea effect," named for the Swedish furniture manufacturer whose products often require home assembly, indicates that customers value a product more highly when they play a role in constructing it.

Still, doctors routinely observe that one of the most common complaints today is fatigue; a 2007 study pegged its prevalence in the American work force at 38 percent. This should not be surprising. Much of this fatigue may result from the steady, surreptitious° accumulation of shadow work in modern life. People are simply doing a huge number of tasks that were once done for them by others.

15 Doing things for one another is, in fact, an essential characteristic of a human community. Various mundane jobs were once spread around among us, and performing such small services for one another was even an aspect of civility. Those days are over. The robots are in charge now, pushing a thousand routine tasks onto each of our backs.

---

***antiquarian:*** outdated.

***stenography:*** shorthand; prior to improvements in recording devices and later the creation of desktop computers, secretaries had often been trained to take dictation from supervisors using a shorthand system permitting them to write as quickly as the supervisor spoke.

***missive:*** a letter, technically one that is formal or official in nature.

***docilely:*** obediently, easily managed.

***surreptitious:*** secret or hidden, often with the connotation of being improper or unauthorized.

## RESPOND •

1. What argument(s) is Lambert making? To what extent are they stated explicitly (that is, in a clear statement), and to what extent are they implicit (that is, implied but never made explicit)?

2. There is much evidence that Lambert is offering a causal argument, but which of the kinds of causal arguments discussed in the "Understanding Causal Arguments" section of Chapter 11 is it? Once you're decided which kind it is, diagram the argument using the illustrations in this section of Chapter 11 as a model.
3. Lambert is especially effective in the way that he creates and uses definitions. Not only does he use them to define a term in a specific way, but he also uses them to advance the argument he is making. Examine in detail how he defines "shadow work" (paragraph 2), "subsistence economy" (paragraph 3), and "wetware" (paragraph 12). How does each of these definitions serve to help Lambert's readers understand a key concept while advancing his argument?
4. Another characteristic of this selection is its ample use of examples as evidence. Take two or three paragraphs of the essay that contain examples you find particularly convincing or interesting, make a list of all the examples that occur in these paragraphs, and determine the specific function for which Lambert uses them. Would the essay have been less convincing with fewer examples? With more examples? How can a writer determine how many examples are needed to create a persuasive argument?
5. In a profound sense, Lambert is commenting on the consequences of a shift in the American economy from a manufacturing economy to a service economy combined with advances in technology and the desire of merchants to remain competitive by keeping costs as low as possible. He makes explicit some of the results of this shift: "no service" for customers in many contexts, fewer service jobs (which have traditionally been held by people with less education or fewer skills), and a shifting of the burden for this work onto the consumer (or the employee, when it occurs in one's place of employment). Explore some aspect of the consequences of this shift **in an evaluative or causal essay**. For example, you might ask whether society is best served by having attorneys who make over $300,000 per year scan their own groceries. Is this the best use of the attorneys' time? Would their lives and society be better if the grocery store hired additional checkers, a move that would surely increase food costs and reduce competitiveness unless other grocers made the same move? From a very different perspective, you might consider the consequences of the growth in shadow work and the likely shape of the future labor market. What sorts of jobs will there be? How much or what kind of education will they require? You will likely want to do research on the topic you decide to pursue so that you can write with some authority. (See Chapters 10 and 11 for information on evaluative and causal arguments. If you consult outside sources, check out Chapters 18, 19, and 21 on evaluating sources, using them, and documenting them.)

*In this selection, we present a column by the popular and influential journalist and author Thomas L. Friedman (1953– ) as well as reader responses to the column—the two letters to the editor that appeared in the print edition of the* New York Times *and were later archived on the paper's Web site as well as several of the 307 comments posted by readers on the* Times *Web site. Friedman's column appeared in July 2011.*

*Friedman has an advanced degree in Middle Eastern studies from Oxford University in England and often writes about the Middle East. His last few books, all best sellers, have sought, however, to understand the consequences of globalization. He has won three Pulitzer Prizes for his news coverage. As you read Friedman's column, pay attention to the assumptions Friedman is making about the future of the American workplace. In case you have trouble finding them, the reader comments will help you in that task.*

# "The Start-Up of You" and Readers' Responses

## THOMAS L. FRIEDMAN

The rise in the unemployment rate last month to 9.2 percent has Democrats and Republicans reliably falling back on their respective cure-alls. It is evidence for liberals that we need more stimulus and for conservatives that we need more tax cuts to increase demand. I am sure there is truth in both, but I do not believe they are the whole story. I think something else, something new—something that will require our kids not so much to find their next job as to invent their next job—is also influencing today's job market more than people realize.

Look at the news these days from the most dynamic sector of the U.S. economy—Silicon Valley. Facebook is now valued near $100 billion, Twitter at $8 billion, Groupon at $30 billion, Zynga at $20 billion and LinkedIn at $8 billion. These are the fastest-growing Internet / social networking companies in the world, and here's what's scary: You could easily fit all their employees together into the 20,000 seats in Madison Square Garden, and still have room for grandma. They just don't employ a lot of people, relative to their valuations, and while they're all hiring today, they are largely looking for talented engineers.

Indeed, what is most striking when you talk to employers today is how many of them have used the pressure of the recession to become even more productive by deploying more automation technologies, software, outsourcing, robotics—anything they can use to make better products with reduced head count and health care and pension liabilities. That is not going to change. And while many of them are hiring, they are increasingly picky. They are all looking for the same kind of people—people who not only have the critical thinking skills to do the value-adding jobs that technology can't, but also people who can invent, adapt and reinvent their jobs every day, in a market that changes faster than ever.

Today's college grads need to be aware that the rising trend in Silicon Valley is to evaluate employees every quarter, not annually. Because the merger of globalization and the IT° revolution means new products are

*IT:* information technology.

being phased in and out so fast that companies cannot afford to wait until the end of the year to figure out whether a team leader is doing a good job.

5 Whatever you may be thinking when you apply for a job today, you can be sure the employer is asking this: Can this person add value every hour, every day—more than a worker in India, a robot or a computer? Can he or she help my company adapt by not only doing the job today but also reinventing the job for tomorrow? And can he or she adapt with all the change, so my company can adapt and export more into the fastest-growing global markets? In today's hyperconnected world, more and more companies cannot and will not hire people who don't fulfill those criteria.

But you would never know that from listening to the debate in Washington, where some Democrats still tend to talk about job creation as if it's the 1960s and some Republicans as if it's the 1980s. But this is not your parents' job market.

This is precisely why LinkedIn's founder, Reid Garrett Hoffman, one of the premier starter-uppers in Silicon Valley—besides co-founding LinkedIn, he is on the board of Zynga, was an early investor in Facebook and sits on the board of Mozilla—has a book coming out after New Year called *The Start-Up of You*, co-authored with Ben Casnocha. Its subtitle could easily be: "Hey, recent graduates! Hey, 35-year-old midcareer professional! Here's how you build your career today."

Hoffman argues that professionals need an entirely new mind-set and skill set to compete. "The old paradigm of climb up a stable career ladder is dead and gone," he said to me. "No career is a sure thing anymore. The uncertain, rapidly changing conditions in which entrepreneurs start companies is what it's now like for all of us fashioning a career. Therefore you should approach career strategy the same way an entrepreneur approaches starting a business."

To begin with, Hoffman says, that means ditching a grand life plan. Entrepreneurs don't write a 100-page business plan and execute it one time; they're always experimenting and adapting based on what they learn.

10 It also means using your network to pull in information and intelligence about where the growth opportunities are—and then investing in yourself to build skills that will allow you to take advantage of those opportunities. Hoffman adds: "You can't just say, 'I have a college degree, I have a right to a job, now someone else should figure out how to hire and train me.'" You have to know which industries are working and what is happening inside them and then "find a way to add value in a way no one else can. For entrepreneurs it's differentiate or die—that now goes for all of us."

Finally, you have to strengthen the muscles of resilience. "You may have seen the news that [the] online radio service Pandora went public the other week," Hoffman said. "What's lesser known is that in the early days [the founder] pitched his idea more than 300 times to VC's° with no luck."

## Letters to the Editor: Ways to Succeed in Today's Job Market

To the Editor:

In "The Start-Up of You" (column, July 13), Thomas L. Friedman has (again) hit the nail squarely on the head: job seekers need an entrepreneurial mind-set to compete.

The dramatic shift in work—away from the tradition of a 40-hour workweek and toward individuals' building of "bodies of work" (and maybe companies?) with lifestyles to match—is happening because of the pressure on organizations to innovate and increase productivity, but also because of the increasing preference of people to work for themselves.

No doubt, the economic downturn was a factor in the rush to independent

***VC:*** venture capitalist: someone who invests money ("capital") in a new company.

contractor and freelance status, yet no one should expect all those folks to go meekly back into the cubicles of giant corporations anytime soon.

This trend should put new pressure on educational aspirations at every level. Our future depends on having this generation of workers and the next well prepared for lifelong learning, adaptation to continuous change and a level of global awareness most of us can only begin to imagine.

Kathy Tunheim
Minneapolis, July 13, 2011
The writer is senior adviser on jobs creation to Gov. Mark Dayton of Minnesota.

To the Editor:

Thomas L. Friedman and Reid Garrett Hoffman, whose coming book *The Start-Up of You* is cited in the column, are no doubt correct about the changing landscape of employment in the United States.

They portray 35-year-old workers as being in "midcareer," tell us that tech companies want "talented engineers" and advise workers to invest in themselves because they don't "have a right to a job."

Couple all that with the likelihood that the eligibility age for Social Security will almost certainly be raised in coming years, the continuing practice of offshoring jobs and the continuing loss of jobs to technology, and we are staring at a real problem down the road: what to do with those "late career" employees, those obsolete 40-, 50- and 60-year-olds who don't match the profile?

Not everyone is a ballerina or a golf pro. And not everyone is an entrepreneur. An economy that requires entrepreneurial skills of all workers is headed for real trouble.

Clay Bonnyman Evans
Niwot, Colo., July 13, 2011

## Comments Posted about the Article on the *Times* Web Site

8.
C Wolfe
Bloomington, IN
July 13th, 2011
7:31 am

It seems to me that what we're seeing is a change in how we determine value, and not in a good way. People enjoy using Facebook, but if it ceased to exist tomorrow, so what? It isn't as if people would starve, or we'd suddenly lack water or fuel or clothes to wear or clean air to breathe. People wouldn't stop sharing their experiences with each other, they'd just find another way to do it. And relatively few people would even be out of work. The economic value of Facebook is pure illusion. Ditto Twitter; the people who use it would miss it, but its existence doesn't solve the real problems confronting us, nor would its disappearance create new problems.

The supposed value of social networking companies, or internet companies that serve as mere conduits for what others create, is precisely what's wrong with the economy. They're valued in absurd disproportion to what they actually contribute to society. It's all perception and no substance. I'd feel much better if you told me that the fastest growing companies were developing new energy sources. We need to think strategically for the long term, and not simply react like infatuated teenagers to the sensation of the moment.

Recommended by 848 Readers

26.
harry
michigan
July 13th, 2011
8:47 am

Silicon Valley is not going to lead this country out of the economic funk we are in today. This article is meaningless in today's climate. Our leaders have sold this country out to the lowest bidder so the elites can get even richer. The real question is will we ever employ people in manufacturing again. Not everyone can be a software designer or engineer. We still need people to build widgets. Tariffs on all imported worthless stuff is my answer.

Recommended by 326 Readers

27.
Melanie
Wisconsin
July 13th, 2011
8:48 am

My father who just turned 100 in June was told by his immigrant step-father that he'd amount to nothing because he wasn't pursuing a trade, but going to the High School of Commerce and pursuing a business career. Dad was being judged by 19th Century standards, but he was a 20th Century man. He did well following a business career, even with just a high school diploma and entered the middle class, raising a daughter who went to college. In the same way, we can't give students and young people today strategies that worked in the 20th Century and expect them to thrive in the 21st Century. This is a fabulous article—can't wait to read the book Mr. Friedman mentions.

Recommended by 39 Readers

55.
Dave
Florida
July 13th, 2011
10:37 am

I'm nearing 50, and have been fortunate enough to have had some of the professional risks I've taken over the years work out well to the positive side of the ledger. But to really insist that this way of life constitutes the minimum bar for personal success requires glossing over a few other realities of life: (a) not having kids—my path toward success didn't make room for them, and in retrospect, I was incredibly fortunate that my second wife brought three teenage kids into my life who accepted me with love and as an additional guidepost in their lives, (b) celebrating creativity and real-time adaptability over all else is really just Darwinism° on steroids, and (c) this path is the surest possible way forward toward a world in which income inequality becomes even more pronounced and entrenched. Having spent a few years in Silicon Valley a long time ago, I thoroughly understand this mindset. For the best and the brightest, it must be ever thus. For the rest of the population, including some of my nieces and nephews, I genuinely fear for the social repercussions.

Recommended by 321 Readers

56.
Fred
New York, NY
July 13th, 2011
10:39 am

30 years ago, during a group study session in college, one student stood up and walked around our table saying, "Study hard, there are thousands of students in China, Japan and Korea who are committed to studying harder than us and we're competing with them." Most everyone at the table laughed and told him to shut up, but I thought that he was saying something useful and true. He's a specialist in Artificial Intelligence now and what he said then remains true. We forget that at our peril.

Recommended by 78 Readers

59.
H.B.Esbin, PhD
Toronto
July 13th, 2011
10:40 am

At the heart of your cogent° piece is a prescription for education transformation. The goal of increasing student mastery of STEM skills [science, technology, engineering, and mathematics] is good. However these skills are not sufficient to drive invention and innovation. A complementary set of skills are also needed. For example, creativity and collaboration. For creativity, one needs imagination. For collaboration, one needs good social and emotional skills like self awareness and empathy. The imaginative faculty is simply given short shrift in education. In other words, the critical thinking skills you refer to and the ability to invent and adapt may be in demand but they are not being developed purposefully or consistently. For example, only 40% of US public schools provide social and emotional skills development.* There is therefore a gap between what employers want and the kinds of employees they are getting. The way to close the gap is "upstream" in elementary and secondary school. Thankfully this is underway due to leadership of organizations like Partners for 21C Learning.

[*Study—"The Impact of Enhancing Students' Social and Emotional Learning: A Meta-Analysis of School-Based Universal Interventions"]

Recommended by 36 Readers

***Darwinism:*** here, the notion of the survival of the fittest.

***cogent:*** convincing or well argued.

64.
Hi USA
Georgia, USA
July 13th, 2011
10:52 am

This article by Friedman is a reminder for those seeking employment: the job market is smaller, more critical, and can pick and choose. But Mr. Friedman missed an important point about companies and the changing times, a point that never goes away: management style and treatment of employees. It is not just about getting in, landing the job. Companies need to reinvent themselves in order to keep the talent they so desperately need. It works both ways, and believe me, companies that forget how to say thanks lose good people. A paycheck is not what everyone seeks in life.

Recommended by 50 Readers

143.
Dave F.
South of Chicago, IL
July 13th, 2011
11:46 am

This article sums up what has been in my thoughts for the last six months or so. When my employer put me at 4 days a week starting in 2009, I figured it might last a year—two tops. Well into my third year of four-day weeks, I have come to the realization (belatedly, I admit) that I may NEVER go back to 5 days a week, and therefore need to start using the skills I have to make up some of the lost income presently, and be prepared for potential lost income in the future by having another avenue to make money.

I took a big step on that path yesterday by purchasing a component necessary to make my new enterprise a reality. Mr. Friedman's article gives me further confidence that I did the right thing. Don't wait for someone to "give" you a job; go make one. Even if it doesn't pay you much right now, it could be something big in the future. Start building now, keep updating, keep adapting.

Mr. Friedman is probably right—do you want to be sitting there three years later (like I did) saying, "I should have done this sooner"? I was fortunate enough to have a job to get my family through; what I'm doing now on my "off day" will now help us thrive again, instead of being hunkered down in survival mode.

Recommended by 27 Readers

170.
David Andrews
Middlebury, VT
July 13th, 2011
12:50 pm

I just watched *The Social Network*,° with all of its moral ambiguity and its depiction of a world much like the one Friedman describes here. I find myself totally depressed about the prospects for the 95 percent of Americans who don't manage to grasp these scarcer and scarcer brass rings and hold on for 50+ years, justifying their value every few months. As others point out, this vision of economic life basically leads to a small number of very successful, very rich people who have the brains and chutzpah (and luck and power) to make things happen, or get in early with venture capital investments in support of these folks and their projects. The banquet table spread in this vision may be splendid, but there will be a lot of people missing at the feast.

A lot of Americans, the vast majority, will be left in the dust with declining standards of living, as the less "creative" jobs are eliminated or outsourced. The gap between rich and poor, already extreme, can only get worse in this scenario. Unless rich and successful people are willing to pay MUCH higher taxes, there will be lots of misery among the underemployed poor and middle class.

Recommended by 63 Readers

206.
Sharon Reagan
Williams, Oregon
July 13th, 2011
1:19 pm

This new job market will be great for the exceptional few; but what about the 99.9% of the rest of us who are ordinary?

Recommended by 31 Readers

---

**The Social Network:** a 2010 film about the controversies surrounding the creation of the social networking site Facebook.

***prototype machine:*** a machine that builds prototypes, models that can be used to demonstrate to executives or venture capitalists that a proposed product is worth investing time and money in.

279.
DK
Simi Valley
July 13th, 2011
3:46 pm

Let's see: you are employed by a corporation as a writer for a newspaper. What do you know about starting a business first hand?

Do you realize the combination of skill, knowledge, capital, luck and a complete commitment of your time? Very few people possess these elements, and that is why most businesses fail within a few years. Most people can and do find contentment in their lives and careers by being an employee. Look at companies like Google. Look at the giant, General Electric—the resources these types of companies have cannot be matched in most fields. For example, my company has a million dollars invested in a rapid-prototype machine°—something I couldn't imagine doing on my own.

Friedman: you don't know of what you write here.

Recommended by 35 Readers

## RESPOND•

1. What arguments is Friedman making? What consequences might these arguments have for you as you think about your future in the workplace, whether you plan to work in the United States or internationally?
2. Before what is often termed Web 2.0—the version of the Internet we are all familiar with now, one that encourages participation by permitting users to post comments, photos, and videos; create blogs; and interact with other users in novel ways—newspapers encouraged debate by publishing letters to the editor on their editorial pages: a few selected letters appeared, generally offering a limited range of responses to the original article. Obviously, the commenting function so common in Web 2.0 has changed the nature of responding to arguments publicly since anyone with Internet access and the desire to do so can respond—and frequently they do. One tip for how to learn about the complexity of a topic and the range of opinions surrounding it is to read the comments posted about an article on the topic in papers like the *New York Times*. (In smaller papers, the comments sections often become shouting matches full of snarky comments that provide little or no evidence for the claims made. For whatever reasons, readers of the *Times* generally provide at least some evidence for their claims.) Study the letters and comments reprinted in this selection, noting the number of people who support Friedman's argument(s) in some way and those who are critical of them or some part of them. Be sure to note down the evidence offered by those who support or critique his positions.
3. Once you have completed question 2, turn your attention to those who critique Friedman's position in particular. In many cases, their critiques assume or claim that Friedman has made faulty assumptions or has committed some of the fallacies of argument discussed in

Chapter 5. (After all, making faulty assumptions can generally be analyzed as evidence of fallacious thinking.) Which particular fallacies might they claim Friedman has engaged in? Which category of fallacy—those of emotional argument, ethical argument, or logical argument—do these fall into?

4. Comment 206 by Sharon Reagan could be tweeted. Would it be an effective argument as a tweet? What are some of the features of an effective tweet? How do tweets differ rhetorically from longer arguments of the sorts represented by the other comments posted here?
5. Not surprisingly, several of the posted comments address the same issue—that is, they offer the same support for or criticism of Friedman's position. Working with a classmate, choose a group of comments (including one of the letters if you like) that take a similar position, and determine which is most effective and why.
6. **Write a definitional essay** in which you try to describe (and define, of course) the consequences for you of the new workplace as Friedman describes it, given your current understanding of your career plans in the short and long terms. (Chapter 9 treats arguments of definition.) As you plan your essay, give some thought to the sort(s) of definition that will be most effective for your essay.

*We close this chapter with two related texts by Stewart D. Friedman, an award-winning teacher who is founding director of the Leadership Program and the Work/Life Integration Project at the Wharton School of the University of Pennsylvania. (Wharton was founded in 1881 as the first U.S. college-affiliated school of business.) Much of Friedman's research and publishing focuses on how people integrate work into their lives. The first text is a transcript of a short video that appears on Amazon.com's Web site selling Friedman's 2008 book,* Total Leadership: Be a Better Leader, Have a Richer Life. *For Friedman, total leadership is a vision of leadership that is informed by a person's core values, which are reflected in all aspects of his or her life. It contrasts with notions of leadership that focus only on the workplace. Such a redefinition of leadership is currently going on at many business schools across the United States and around the world. (Information on Friedman's approach, including training workshops and testimonials from former participants, can be found at http://www.totalleadership.org.)*

*The second text is a chapter from Friedman's book. Like much writing for members of the professional classes, it assumes an educated reader whose job includes supervising other people. It likewise assumes that the reader wants to do a better job of supervising than she or he currently is able to do. Although this selection is based on research in management, business, and psychology, it is not written like a textbook that presents a great deal of detailed information. In some ways, its frequent exercises and questions to reflect on make it seem like a self-help book. Finally, it makes an argument that is distinct from the arguments of other similar books: the writer hopes to sell books and likely tickets to training workshops. As you watch the video, study the transcript, read the chapter, and do the exercises, reflect on the many things that Friedman has mastered about how to construct effective arguments. At the same time, reflect on what you're working for and the likelihood that it will help you to be a better leader and have a richer life.*

# The Fallacy of "Work-Life Balance"

STEWART D. FRIEDMAN

Compare Friedman's short video presentation with his written chapter. In what ways does the presentation, as an argument to be heard, differ from the written chapter? For more on oral arguments, see Chapter 15.

LINK TO P. 346

**Transcript of the Video on Amazon.com for the Book *Total Leadership***

http://www.amazon.com/gp/mpd/permalink/m39ac1ujq5dhud

Harvard Business Publishing
*Total Leadership: Be a Better Leader, Have a Richer Life*

Stewart D. Friedman, Author

A lot of people talk about work-life balance, many more people today than when I first started addressing this issue twenty years ago when my first son was born. And it's become a very present issue in many different sectors of our society and abroad. And there's a lot of important reasons for that. But balance is the wrong metaphor. Balance is the wrong metaphor because it implies trade-offs. It implies that you've got to give up one part of your life to have success in another part. And what I want to encourage people to do is to see the possibility of what I call "four-way wins," which requires that you use leadership to better integrate the different parts of your life, all four: work, home, community, and self.

Please email feedback to:
video@harvardbusiness.org
Harvard Business Publishing is an affiliate of Harvard Business School

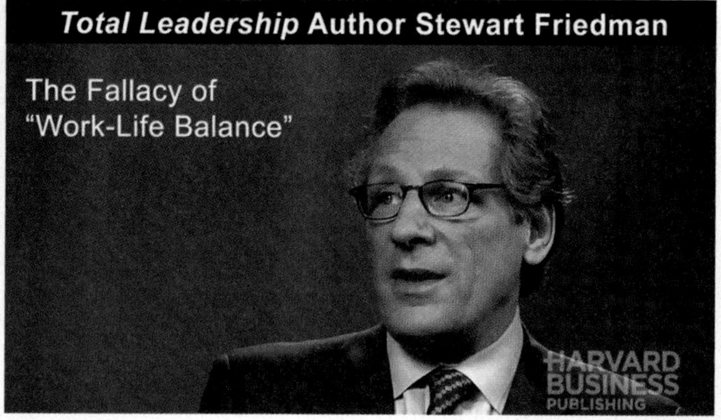

# Take the Four-Way View

STEWART D. FRIEDMAN

Now that you've thought about your core values° and your vision of the kind of world you want to create, we're ready to go deeper into what it means for you to act with authenticity by exploring the relative importance of the four domains of your life, the attention you give them, whether the goals you pursue in each one are in sync with the others, and how satisfied you are with how things are going, in each area and altogether. Like Kerry,° Lim Chang did all this too.

*core values:* the values that you hold "most dear and are willing to strive or even fight for." In an earlier chapter of his book, Friedman asks his readers to complete an exercise in which they come up with a list of five to nine core values and to explain the importance of each in one to two sentences. To get them started, he provides a list of forty-two values (such as "achievement, advancement, adventure, aesthetics, affluence, authority") along with short definitions, all based on the work of other researchers.

*Kerry (Tanaka):* a person whom Friedman discusses as an example in an earlier chapter.

Lim's five-foot-ten-inch body barely contains his infectious energy. His jet-black hair contrasts sharply with the pearly-white teeth that shine brightly through his smile. Lim is the "rah-rah" guy on the soccer team who is always screaming to pump up his teammates. The son of a physician father and a homemaker mother, Lim, thirty-four, and his wife have a two-year-old son and another on the way. From offices in Orange County, he and the dozen people directly reporting to him manage West Coast operations of a national retail design firm. Although he works fifty-five to sixty hours each week, he makes it a point not to work on weekends.

He runs marathons for fun, though when I first met him, Lim was finding it quite difficult to keep up his exercise regimen. The issues that motivated his interest in my Total Leadership course were not unlike those many people confront. He was having a hard time achieving what at first he called "balance" between the different areas of his life. Here's what he wrote about his early efforts in the program, about two years after having completed it:

> One of the exercises in the initial push to clarify what was important was a chart that showed the level of importance of each of my four life domains and the time I was devoting to each. It became clear that I was paying a disproportionate amount of attention to my career and that I wasn't spending nearly enough time on developing my mind, body, and spirit.
>
> But it wasn't just about how I was spending my time, as I saw when I drew four circles representing what I really cared about in each of the four domains. I asked myself, did the circles line up as they do in the center of a tree, or were they disconnected, like random puddles all over the place? Was I being the person (the strong, centered "tree") I really wanted to be? The short answer: no. This made me feel uncomfortable.
>
> I rated how happy I was with the different aspects of my life, and I was surprised. If someone had simply asked me how satisfied I was in each

> domain, the answers would not have matched that chart. By assessing the importance, time, and energy I gave to each domain, and the give-and-take among them, I was able to more realistically evaluate my overall satisfaction. It turned out that I was much more satisfied with work and family than with my community and self—that was not my intuition going into the exercise.
>
> I started asking . . . What changes could I make to pay more attention to what really mattered to me—and less to what didn't? What was it that I was doing at work and at home that made me feel good about how things were going there? Was it that my behavior at work and at home was more consistent with my core values? What would people at work and home say made me most successful? If I could answer these questions, I might find new ways of using what I already knew about producing satisfaction at work and at home to improve my community and self areas.

Just as Lim did, in this chapter you're going to learn to take the four-way view. By looking closely at the different domains of your life—work, home, community, and self—you'll clarify what's important to you and see your life from a fresh perspective. You'll also begin to explore what it means for you to act with integrity by recognizing the whole person.

The exercises you'll do in this chapter will help you to discover whether 5
you're being real: are you paying attention to what you care about most, acting in ways that are consistent with the person you want to be, going after goals that matter, and achieving happiness in all the parts as well in your life as a whole?

### Define Your Domains

Start by defining your four domains. This is a subjective process, so you must define your domains in whatever way makes the most sense for you. For most people, the work domain is your job: what you do for a living or, if you're between jobs, what you're aiming to do next. If you're in school, whether or not you have a job as well, then school is part of your work domain. To fully grasp what your work domain comprises, think beyond just the hours you sit in your cubicle, office, or whatever your work space is, and consider the wide array of things you do as part of your career. This might include taking classes, traveling, participating in trade associations, talking to mentors about your career, or doing research on future entrepreneurial opportunities.

Then there's the home, or family, domain. Again, it's a subjective judgment you'll make here. This domain can include the people (or animals) you live with, your family of origin (parents, siblings, and others), or your family of creation (spouse, significant other, children, and others).

Likewise, the net you cast around your community or society domain can be as wide as you like, including friends, neighbors, social groups, religious institutions, charitable activities, political committees, membership in non-profit organizations, or anything that bears on your impact on the world beyond your work and your family.

Finally, there is the domain of yourself. This includes your emotional health, intellectual knowledge, physical health, leisure, and spiritual life.

### The Four-Way Attention Chart

The next step in understanding your four life domains is to examine your 10
choices about the focus of your attention to them in light of their relative importance to you. Completing the four-way attention chart fills in an essential part of the picture of how things stand today. It shows how you manage the allocation of your time and energy—the amount of attention you pay to the various people and projects in your life—and so helps you assess whether you're actually doing what you care about doing.

This chart doesn't, however, address the other part of the picture: whether or not your actions and your goals for each domain—the how and the why—are in harmony with the others. We'll explore that later in this chapter. Together, these two assessments give a full picture of whether you're demonstrating authenticity and being real in all domains of your life. And painting it is a crucial step forward in your thinking about the experiments you might try to improve your satisfaction and performance in all domains.

Keep in mind, as you do this exercise, that your subjective judgment is all that matters here. For instance, your involvement in community and society is whatever this means to you, and not what others want of you. So it may be about giving money to charity, helping your friends, cleaning up your neighborhood, or getting involved in targeted campaigns to make the world a better place. And remember that this chart indicates only how you see things now. When you complete this chart again, after your experiments, your numbers will probably be different, if you're like most people who've done this. As you progress through the book—as you learn more about how to demonstrate authenticity, integrity, and creativity—the relationships among work, home, community, and self will change.

#### Victor's° Four-Way Attention Chart

*Victor (Gardener):* a person whom Friedman discusses as an example in an earlier chapter.

Victor assessed the importance of the four major areas of his life by assigning these percentages in the first column: 35, 35, 10, and 20. At the same time

**The Four-Way Attention Chart**

One way of being real is to grasp the connection between the importance of each part of your life and what you actually pay attention to every day. The chart below is another window through which to see what's important to you. In the first column, consider the relative importance of each major area of your life *today*. Assign a percentage to each and make sure they add up to 100. If you place as much importance on work/career/school as you do on the other three areas of your life combined, put "50%" in that cell on the chart. If, as another example, all four domains are of equal importance to you, then put "25%" in each cell of the first column.

In the second column, consider how much time and energy you actually focus on each domain in a typical week. Assign a percentage to each. Make sure these numbers, too, add up to 100.

| Domain | Importance | Focus of time and energy |
|---|---|---|
| Work/Career/School | % | % |
| Home/Family | % | % |
| Community/Society | % | % |
| Self: mind, body, spirit | % | % |
| | 100% | 100% |

After you've completed the chart, write notes in response to the following questions:

1. What are the consequences of the current choices you make about your focus of time and energy spent at work, at home, in the community, and for yourself?
2. As you look at these eight numbers, are there any adjustments you'd like to make—either in what's important or in where you focus your attention—to change any of these numbers?
3. What would it take to actually make these adjustments in your life?

he started the Total Leadership program, Victor's work domain included being an IT director in a major bank *and* being a student in a full-time executive MBA program that convened for classes every other weekend and for longer stretches in the summer. This part, he observed, was equal in weight to his family domain, which comprised his wife, two children, and parents. His community domain, he noted, comprised a few friends and just a bit more. Of the four domains, he was unapologetic about this being the least important to him. Finally, his interest in his own personal fulfillment was less important to him than his work and his family, but more important than his involvement in community and society.

Victor then distributed percentages to indicate how much time and energy he actually spent in each area, in a typical week, in the second column: 65, 20, 5, and 10. In a demonstration of an obvious mismatch—which most people report when they do this exercise—he overemphasized work compared with the other domains. Everyone's chart is unique, of course. But what typically transpires over the course of the Total Leadership program is a noticeable move toward a closer fit between what's important and where you devote your attention. Here's some of what Victor said about his four-way attention chart:

> What I care about and what I do with my time are not very well aligned. The mismatch with my family really bothers me. I make an effort to spend time at either end of the day to be around our kids by taking them to school, or just trying to get home before they go to bed, but our interactions aren't going that well at the moment—probably because I'm so preoccupied with work and school. My wife's started to refer to herself as a "single mom."
>
> I just don't care much about my community domain right now. I try to keep up with my friends and do a small amount of volunteering and charitable giving. It's all I can do. And as for my self domain, I'm probably in the worst physical and spiritual shape ever. But I feel that I need to defer doing anything about this right now.
>
> I'm just trying to do everything—and succeeding at little. It's imperative that I find ways of having the different parts of my life create more positive impact on each other. Otherwise, I don't see how I can keep dissatisfaction in one area of my life from spilling over into other areas.

15 The self-awareness Victor developed through this exercise was an important step. By thinking about his responses to his four-way attention chart, Victor started asking new questions about where he might find opportunities for constructive change in how he wove together his work and the rest of his life. Was there a way, for example, for him to make adjustments that would make his wife feel less like a "single mom" that would, at the same time, inspire him to bring greater enthusiasm to his work? Was it possible for him to give more attention to improving his physical well-being and, in doing so, produce benefits not only for his health but also for his employer, his family, and his community?

These questions helped him to start thinking about some changes. But there was more to do still in finding gaps between the current state of things and what he really wanted in his life.

### Your Four Circles

Once you have completed your four-way attention chart, you're ready to draw a graphical representation of the four domains that will help you perceive whether or not they are in harmony. The attention chart is especially useful for getting you to look squarely at the issue of your choices about the allocation of your attention—your time and energy. Drawing the four circles asks you to consider a different question: are you the same person wherever you go?

### The Four Circles

Are the four domains of your life compatible or in conflict? Before you draw anything, there are two choices to make as you think about the pattern of your four circles.

- **Consider size.** The first choice you've already made; that is, the *size* of the circles. The size of each circle corresponds to the importance you assigned to it in the first column of the four-way attention chart. If, for example, "Work" was 30 percent and "Home" was 40 percent, then the "Home" circle would be about one-third bigger than the "Work" circle. In this case, work is less important than home.
- **Think about relative location.** The second choice is each circle's *location in relation to the others*: do they overlap or are they separate? Where you place your four circles, how much they overlap represents your best estimate of how compatible or incompatible the domains are with each other. Complete *harmony* between any two domains—which exists when the aims in one domain, and your way of achieving them, fit perfectly with the other domain—would be represented by complete overlap of the two representative circles. Complete incompatibility, or *conflict*, between any two domains—when your actions and their results in one are antagonistic to the other—would be shown by representative circles that have no overlap at all.

Now you are ready to draw your circles. Take a piece of paper, or find a digital file, or go to www.totalleadership.org, and draw four circles, each representing one of the four domains: work, home, community, and self. Write the name of each domain in or around the corresponding circle.

Begin to write down your thoughts. One way to think about achieving greater authenticity is to imagine what you would have to do to have a life illustrated by four completely overlapping circles. Keep in mind that few people have completely overlapping circles; this is an image to aim for. What are your ideas for how you might pursue goals in such a way as to achieve greater overlap, or compatibility, and to reduce conflict among domains?

Here, it's not a matter of how much attention you're devoting to the different parts of your life but, rather, how the interests you are serving in one domain relate to your interests in the other domains. Are you being the person you want to be, no matter where you are in life?

We'll use your four circles as another tool for gaining a deeper understanding of what's important to you in the different roles you play in life, how they affect each other, and where there are gaps between domains that you can close.

## Imagine the Perfect Center of a Tree

Complete overlap of all four domains is, of course, extraordinarily rare. It's hard to conceive of a real life in which the goals you seek and the way you act in all aspects of your life are in pure harmony. The best examples might be those of great religious leaders—the likes of Buddha, Christ, Mohammed, the Dalai Lama, and Moses. In the lives of these exemplars, the purposes pursued by the private person were essentially the same as those sought in the context of their work, family, and society.

But since you're human, not divine, don't worry if your four circles don't line up exactly. Indeed, if you drew your circles to look like the perfect center of a strong tree's trunk, with all four domains concentric around a common core, then please return this book immediately and contact me to arrange an interview! Consider that complete incompatibility between any two domains—circles that have no common area at all—is not uncommon. There is almost always some conflict, in the real world, between who you are in one part of your life and who you are in the other parts.

It's useful to identify areas of compatibility, as well as of discord, among life domains, for this helps you to see the harmony that already exists, and so give you ideas for expanding it. You'll start to ask, "If I can do it here, why not there . . . and there?"

This picture serves as an instrument to help you think about the relationships among the different parts of your life. The center of a tree is an ideal to strive for, and the contrast between it and your current picture, the one you just drew, can lead you to new ideas for taking action to increase your authenticity. The closer you can get to entirely overlapping domains, in other words, the more likely you're being the person you want to be, wherever you are and in whatever role you're in at that moment.

### Learning from the Four Circles

We read what Victor thought about when he examined his responses to the four-way attention chart. Now let's look at how he drew his four circles, shown in figure 3-1.

This image painfully revealed to Victor that there was no overlap whatso- 25
ever between his work and family domains.

> Work is pretty much out there on its own. There is some overlap with my self domain, as I get a good feeling about myself from having a successful working life. But that's pretty much it. I find this rather distressing! And there is not much overlap between my self and family domains at the moment. I really must do something about this.

What Victor realized when analyzing the picture he drew of his four circles is that, among other things, the person he is at work—the goals and interests he pursues as an IT director at an investment bank—is entirely

*Figure 3-1. Victor's four circles*

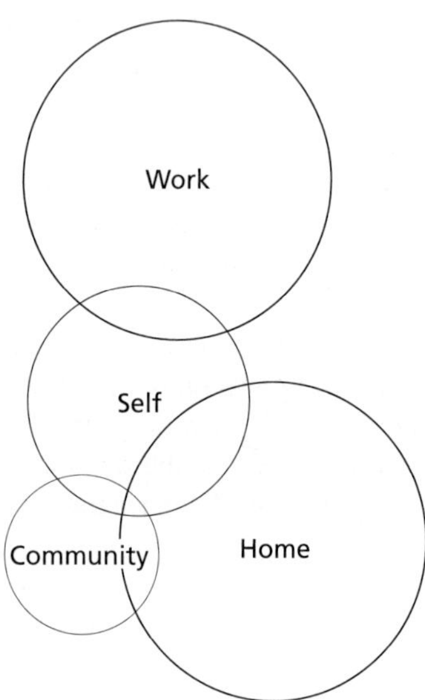


different from the father and husband he wants to be at home. In Victor's leadership vision, . . . he wrote about having his children engaged in his work and also about applying skills he developed teaching his children music to his managerial responsibilities at work. There was some overlap between work and home domains in that leadership vision, but there were none that he could see in his current life circumstances. What Victor learned was discouraging to him, but it was a wake-up call, a seed of transformation. Already, Victor had clarified what's important to him. He began to create new insights about possible four-way wins.

One goal of the Total Leadership process is to create change in order to produce harmony among your four domains. You can learn, in other words, from your four circles by asking what you would have to do to have them overlapping. You might start by looking, for example, at your work. Would you have to change your career entirely to bring it closer to the person you are in your family? Or, instead, would you have to change how you think about what you do at work as it relates to your family, your role in society, and your mind, body, and spirit? Another way to approach this issue is to ask about the purpose of your career: is it to earn money to keep you and your loved ones fed and sheltered, to enjoy the material things in life, or is there something about it that makes you feel proud about the impact you're having on the world through your work? And if so, how does this feeling affect how your friends and family see you? Further, what would you have to change to make this feeling grow and be more a part of your everyday experience of your work and career? Would you have to *act* differently, or would you have to *think* differently about what you're accomplishing through your work?

Now let's consider questions about your home and family. What changes would you have to make to bring this part of your life into harmony with the other parts? Let's say you're a student just about to graduate college, for example. Would you have to change the level of dependence you now have on your parents? If so, how might you do this in a way that would be good for them and for you? Or let's say you're living in an intimate relationship with someone who has different values from yours and doesn't support the role you're playing in society. Should you end the relationship? Less drastically, perhaps, is there a way to change how she sees this other part of your life so that she becomes more supportive of it?

Pondering such questions as you look at your four circles generates ideas for specific things you might do to achieve greater compatibility and less conflict.

Roxanne's drawing of her four circles (see figure 3-2) was quite different 30
from Victor's.

Even though there is no overlap between Roxanne's self and work domains—in other words, her professional life just isn't in sync with what she wants for her self in promoting a healthy mind, body, and spirit—there is quite a lot of overlap otherwise. For instance, through her roles as a mother and as a business professional, she feels she's making valuable contributions

*Figure 3-2. Roxanne's four circles*

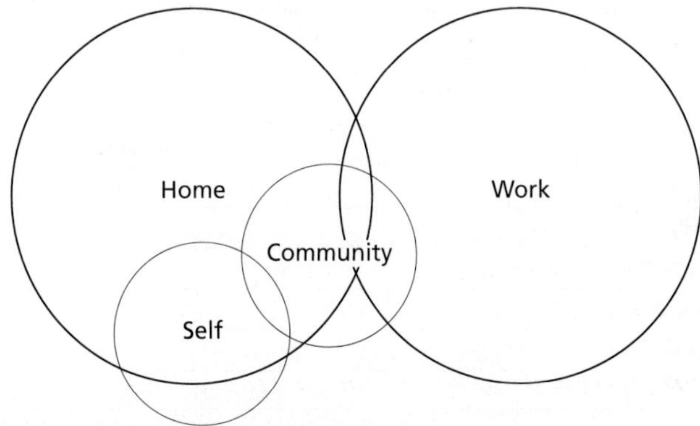

to society in raising her children and in selling chemical products that improve health care.

In studying her four circles, Roxanne began to have some thoughts about things she could do to produce even greater overlap.

> I tend to work at home on the weekends, mainly because, I'm embarrassed to admit, I've just not been creative enough to find something more engaging to do with my family that's good for all of us. I guess I've been driven by the belief that all my investments in work will free up my time to do other things later—and it's always *later*—when something more important is planned for our family.
>
> Maybe I can plan some things to do now with my family—like golf, tennis, swimming—that are also things that I want to do for myself. Or I can plan family activities that support what I'd like to be doing for our local community. Or I can become involved with already existing work activities that support the community, such as the United Way.

Just as it was for Roxanne, the picture you draw of your four circles is another tool for stimulating your thinking about how *you* might create better harmony among your life domains. But we're not quite done with the four-way view of your life's domains.

### Domain Satisfaction: Your Four-Way Happiness Rating

Now assess whether or not you're satisfied with each domain, and with your life as a whole. In other words, are you happy with how things are going?

**Domain Satisfaction—The Four-Way Happiness Rating**

Indicate how satisfied you are presently with how things are going in each domain, and for your life as a whole, by writing a number from 1 to 10, where 1 = not satisfied and 10 = fully satisfied, in the appropriate column.

| Domain | Satisfaction |
|---|---|
| Work/Career/School | |
| Home/Family | |
| Community/Society | |
| Self: mind, body, spirit | |
| Life as a whole | |
| | |

## Just a Matter of Time?

So what is it about the relationship among the four domains that affects 35
whether you feel satisfied? How you spend your time matters, of course. But, it turns out that, surprising as it might seem, managing your time is *not* the major factor. In a study described in *Work and Family—Allies or Enemies?* Jeff Greenhaus and I found that while the "time bind" so often cited in the literature on work/family conflict is no doubt very real, there is a more subtle and pervasive problem that reduces satisfaction in the different domains of life: psychological interference between them.[1] That's when your mind is pulled to somewhere other than where your body is. This happens to all of us. There may even be times when you've been reading this book and your eyes are on the page but your mind has drifted off. You aren't focused. Put differently, there are times when you might be physically present but psychologically absent—something people can usually tell because it affects your ability to connect with them.

If you reduce psychological interference, you increase your ability to focus on *what* matters *when* it matters, and you minimize the destructive impact conflicts can cause between, for instance, work and family. A main premise of this book is that it takes leadership skill to manage the boundaries between the different areas of your life—not just the physical boundaries of time and space, but the psychological boundaries of focus and attention—and to integrate them well for mutual gain.

Being real by demonstrating authenticity is a necessary first step. You must assess the relationship between what's important and where you devote your time. But you must also understand the implications of what your four circles mean to you. André, the married father of two young children and product manager for a global software developer, had this to say about what he learned from his analysis of the relationships among his four domains:

> When I first thought about creating the four circles, I realized that I had been looking at my life domains as separate wedges of a pie rather than as circles that could overlap. In other words, I was viewing my life—and its different parts—as a zero-sum game where to give to one part, I had to take from somewhere else. And where did it get me? When I took actions to make things better in one domain, it always meant decreasing my satisfaction in another domain.
>
> I believe this is why I find it so difficult to be fully engaged in the different domains. So often, I just feel as if I'm being pulled in different directions. When I try to prioritize things, I end up failing to meet expectations and do what people legitimately expect of me. That makes me dissatisfied.

> Looking at the domains this way has helped me realize that I have to change my thought process and find new ways to integrate the different areas of my life. They do overlap, and they need to overlap. They're not separate pieces of the pie.

Is it possible to have your pie and eat it too? The evidence I've seen convinces me that it is—certainly more so than most people believe. Getting there means taking steps to ensure that the goals you're pursuing in each domain of your life are mutually enriching *and* consistent with your core values and aspirations. Does this mean you need to change how you spend your time? Probably, and it might also mean change in how you think about what you're doing with the time you're spending.

Clarifying what's important enhances your sense of authenticity, of being who you want to be. You can take control and create for yourself a life where you do not always have to trade success and satisfaction in one domain for success and satisfaction in another.

When you've clarified what's important to you, you become more of a 40
leader who acts with authenticity, whose values and actions are aligned. When you lead with authenticity, it's easier to get support from the important people in your life. This book is not about striking a balance between work and the rest of life. It is about identifying your values—what's important to you—and making them come alive in your everyday actions at work, at home, in the community, and for your self.

Having done all this soul searching, looking within, you'll now look outward in the next steps on this journey.

**Pause and Reflect on Your Four-Way View**

**Here are things to keep in mind as you synthesize what you've done in chapter 3 before moving on to chapter 4. Read through your responses to the exercises in this chapter. Consider the following questions. Write about them and then, if possible, talk about them with your coach.**

1. **What are the main ideas you take away from what you've just read?**
2. **What is the biggest disconnect in the relationship among your four domains?**
3. **What changes might you make to bring the four domains of your life into greater harmony?**
4. **How would such changes affect your happiness ratings?**

## Note

1. Stewart D. Friedman and Jeffrey H. Greenhaus, *Work and Family—Allies or Enemies? What Happens When Business Professionals Confront Life Choices* (New York: Oxford University Press, 2000).

## RESPOND •

1. What argument is Stewart D. Friedman making in the video from the Amazon.com Web site? In what ways is it a definitional argument? (In addition to the features of definitional argument discussed in Chapter 9, note that a common strategy in a definitional argument is saying what something is *not*, as Friedman does here.) How is ethos created in this short video? (Consider not only what is said but also how it is packaged.)
2. Focus on the structure of the chapter from *Total Leadership*. (You may wish to list the titles of the sections and exercises in the order in which they occur to help you analyze the chapter's structure.) To what extent and in what ways is this chapter organized according to the principles of stasis theory (which are discussed in Chapter 1) or the categories of argument that are presented in the text (arguments of fact, arguments of definition, arguments of evaluation, causal arguments, and proposals)? Why is such an organization appropriate, given Friedman's goals?
3. How does Friedman use the extended examples of Victor and Roxanne to advance his argument? Would his argument be less effective without these examples? Why? What specific roles do they play in the argument?
4. What role do the activities in the chapter play in Friedman's argument? What did you learn from doing them, for example? (If you didn't complete them, do so now.) How are these activities indicated in the text? How effective is the layout of the text in this regard? What roles do Figures 3-1 and 3-2 play in Friedman's argument? What are the benefits of including two such figures, rather than simply relying on one?
5. What are you working for? Using the tools that Friedman provides in this chapter, **write an essay** in which you discuss your own efforts to understand the life that you seek, balancing commitments to work, home, community, and self. This essay may draw on any of the categories of argument that are presented in the text. You may wish to use a chart illustrating your four circles. In writing, you may draw on other readings in this chapter, other reading that you have done on this topic, and thoughts that you've had about these issues.

# 27
# How Do We Define "Inequality" in American Society?

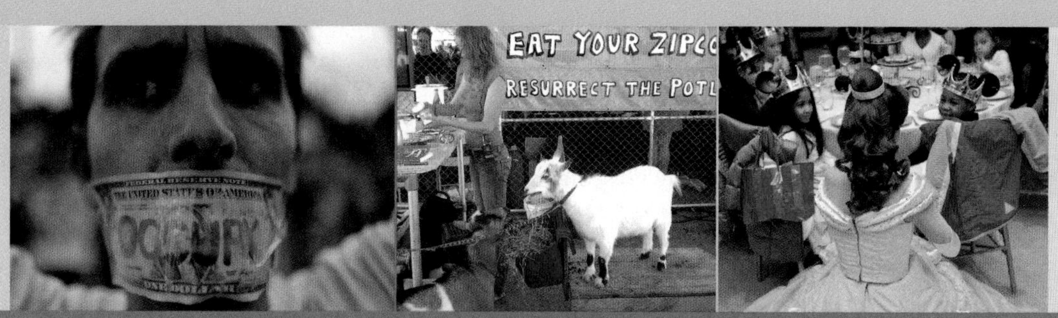


Late in 2011, the Occupy Wall Street Movement focused public attention on the difference between what it termed the 99% and the 1% as well as issues of income inequality in the United States, sparking similar movements around the world. Participants in the Occupy movement saw direct links between their actions and recent protest movements such as the Arab Spring earlier in 2011 facilitated by the new media. Though criticized for its lack of a central message, Occupy clearly struck a nerve with Americans generally as they continued to struggle with the consequences of the economic downturn of 2008. In this chapter, we present readings that try to understand debates at that time about issues related to social inequality in American society. Given America's history, we'd contend that these debates are the latest instantiation of arguments that have taken place in one form or another since before our country's founding.

The chapter opens with a January 2012 report from the Pew Research Center, "Rising Share of Americans See Conflict between Rich and Poor," a factual argument reporting the results of opinion polls showing changes in public attitudes toward the income differential. The second selection, Rana Foroohar's "What Ever Happened to Upward Mobility?" provides important background information for thinking about inequality in the United States by presenting historical context, on the one hand, and an international perspective, on the other.

A blog posting from CATO@LIBERTY offers a visual analysis of the similarities and differences between two groups usually seen as sharing disdain for one another—those participating in the Occupy protests and those supporting the Tea Party. Like several other selections in the chapter, this one demonstrates the ways that deep discontent with certain aspects of American life cuts across political lines. John Marsh's article "Why Education Is Not an Economic Panacea" questions a commonplace of American life, the assumption that education alone will solve our problems, but his reasons for this claim distinguish him clearly from most who argue for this position. The fifth selection presents six visual arguments from the Occupy movement. (Perhaps because this movement has relied on new media from its inception, we should expect visual arguments to play an important role in these debates.)

The following selection is a blog posting. In "Steve Jobs, Occupy Wall Street, and the Capitalist Ideal," Jonathan Chait takes on both conservatives and the leadership of the Occupy movement for their allegiance to brittle and extreme understandings of capitalism. In an interesting way, he seeks to stake out a position on middle ground between the ready-made extremes that characterize much U.S. political discourse.

Mac McClelland returns to Columbus, Ohio, to discover that you can't go home again, especially given the country's current economic situation. In "Goodbye, Columbus: Ohio's War on the Middle Class," she documents in painful detail the practical consequences of this situation on the thirtysomethings of her generation.

The final two selections challenge you to step back and reflect on the chapter's other readings. Andrew Kohut, president of the Pew Research Center, which issued the report that opens the chapter, reframes the findings of that study in "Don't Mind the Gap" while Stanley Fish, a noted literary theorist and legal scholar, argues that those who focus on equality as a response to income inequality are missing the point; as he argues in "Fair Is Fair," our goal should be fairness, not equality.

Odds are you'll recall some of these debates. As several of these writers remind us, we will continue to struggle with these issues for some time.

For additional material related to this chapter, visit the e-Pages for *Everything's an Argument with Readings* online at **bedfordstmartins.com/everythingsanargument/epages**.

*When this report from Richard Morin of the Pew Social & Demographic Trends Project was issued in January 2012, it made national headlines, and in the following weeks, it was frequently referred to by media commentators as evidence of changes in how Americans perceive issues of economic equality. The Pew Social & Demographic Trends Project investigates the attitudes of Americans on a range of topics "by combining original public opinion survey research with social, economic and demographic data analysis." In short, it seeks to create trustworthy factual arguments that will be of use to multiple audiences. The Project is part of the larger Pew Research Center, a nonpartisan think tank based in Washington, D.C., and funded by the Pew Charitable Trusts, an independent not-for-profit organization that works "to improve public policy, inform the public and stimulate civic life." (You can inspect the original report at http://bit.ly/Ar1htK.) As you read, note the ways that the report's authors work to establish a nonpartisan ethos, that is, one that avoids taking sides but focuses instead on creating fair, factual reports that can be trusted by readers who might make widely different political assumptions.*

# Rising Share of Americans See Conflict between Rich and Poor

RICHARD MORIN, PEW RESEARCH CENTER

The Occupy Wall Street movement no longer occupies Wall Street, but the issue of class conflict has captured a growing share of the national consciousness. A new Pew Research Center survey of 2,048 adults finds that about two-thirds of the public (66%) believes there are "very strong" or "strong" conflicts between the rich and the poor—an increase of 19 percentage points since 2009.

Not only have perceptions of class conflict grown more prevalent; so, too, has the belief that these disputes are intense. According to the new survey, three-in-ten Americans (30%) say there are "very strong conflicts" between poor people and rich people. That is double the proportion that offered a similar view in July 2009 and the largest share expressing this opinion since the question was first asked in 1987.

As a result, in the public's evaluations of divisions within American society, conflicts between rich and poor now rank ahead of three other potential sources of group tension—between immigrants and the native born; between blacks and whites; and between young and old. Back in 2009, more survey respondents said there were strong conflicts between immigrants and the native born than said the same about the rich and the poor.[1]

Virtually all major demographic groups now perceive significantly more class conflict than two years ago. However, the survey found that younger adults, women, Democrats and African Americans are somewhat more likely than older people, men, Republicans, whites or Hispanics to say there are strong disagreements between rich and poor.

While blacks are still more likely than whites to see serious class conflicts, 5
the share of whites who hold this view has increased by 22 percentage points, to 65%, since 2009. At the same time, the proportion of blacks (74%) and Hispanics (61%) sharing this judgment has grown by single digits (8 and 6 points, respectively).

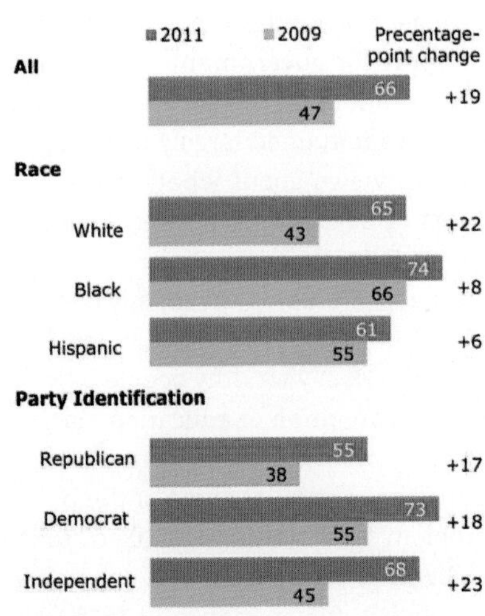


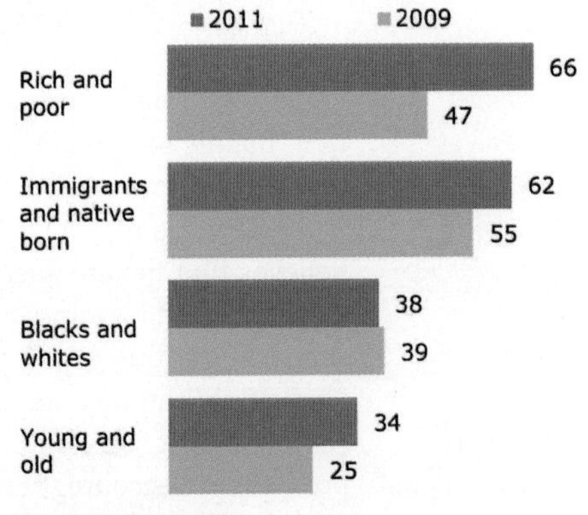

The biggest increases in perceptions of class conflicts occurred among political liberals and Americans who say they are not affiliated with either major party. In each group the proportion who say there are major disagreements between rich and poor Americans increased by more than 20 percentage points since 2009.

These changes in attitudes over a relatively short period of time may reflect the income and wealth inequality message conveyed by Occupy Wall Street protesters across the country in late 2011 that led to a spike in media attention to the topic. But the changes may also reflect a growing public awareness of underlying shifts in the distribution of wealth in American society.[2]

According to the most recent U.S. Census Bureau data, the proportion of overall wealth—a measure that includes home equity, stocks and bonds and the value of jewelry, furniture and other possessions—held by the top 10% of the population increased from 49% in 2005 to 56% in 2009.

**Why the Rich Are Rich**

*Most rich people are wealthy because ...*

**... they know the right people or were born into wealthy families**

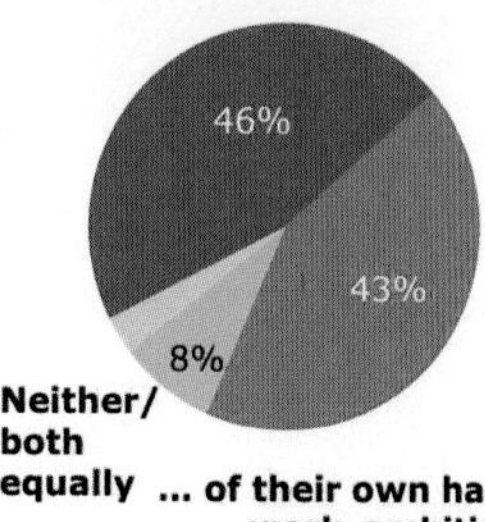


Note: Share of "Don't know/refused" and other responses shown but not labeled

PEW RESEARCH CENTER

### Perceptions of the Wealthy

While the survey results show a significant shift in public perceptions of class conflict in American life, they do not necessarily signal an increase in grievances toward the wealthy. It is possible that individuals who see more conflict between the classes think that anger toward the rich is misdirected. Nor do these data suggest growing support for government measures to reduce income inequality. In fact, other questions in the survey show that some key attitudes toward the wealthy have remained largely unchanged. For example, there has been no change in views about whether the rich became wealthy through personal effort or because they were fortunate enough to be from wealthy families or have the right connections.

A 46% plurality believes that most rich people "are wealthy mainly because 10
they know the right people or were born into wealthy families." But nearly as many have a more favorable view of the rich: 43% say wealthy people became rich "mainly because of their own hard work, ambition or education," largely unchanged from a Pew survey in 2008.

Moreover, a recent Gallup survey found that a smaller share of the public believes that income inequality is a problem "that needs to be fixed" today than held that view in 1998 (45% vs. 52%). And when asked to rate the importance of various alternative federal policies, fewer than half (46%) say "reduc[ing] the income and wealth gap between the rich and the poor" is "extremely" or "very" important. In contrast, more than eight-in-ten (82%) say policies that encourage economic growth should be high priorities.

***nationally representative sample:*** one that mirrors the population of the entire nation with respect to variables like race/ethnicity, age, and sex.

***oversample:*** a sampling technique used with regard to one or more variables in order to yield a representative sample.

**About the Survey**

This report is based on findings from a Pew Research Center telephone survey conducted with a nationally representative sample° of 2,048 adults ages 18 and older living in the continental United States, including an oversample° of 808 adults ages 18 to 34. A total of 769 interviews were completed with respondents contacted by landline telephone and 1,279 with those contacted on their cellular phone. The data are weighted to produce a final sample that is representative of the general population of adults in the continental United States. Survey interviews were conducted under the direction of Princeton Survey Research Associates International, in English and Spanish.

- Interviews conducted December 6–19, 2011
- 2,048 interviews
- Margin of sampling error° is plus or minus 2.9 percentage points for results based on the total sample and 4.4 percentage points for adults ages 18 to 34 at the 95% confidence level.°

## Social Conflict in American Life

About two-thirds of the public say there are strong conflicts between the rich and the poor, and nearly half of these (30%) say these conflicts are "very strong." An additional 36% say these differences are "strong," while 23% view them as "not very strong." Only 7% say there are no conflicts between rich and poor Americans, while the remainder does not offer an opinion.

Three other historic social divisions are viewed as less pervasive or contentious. About six-in-ten (62%) say there are strong conflicts between immigrants and the native born, including 24% who characterize these disagreements as "very strong."

That represents a major change from the Pew Research Center survey conducted in 2009. At that time, a larger share of Americans believed that there were more strong conflicts between immigrants and the native born than between rich and poor people (55% vs. 47%). Today, even though perceptions of disagreements between immigrants and the native born have increased by 7 percentage points in the past two years, this social divide now ranks behind rich-poor conflicts in the public's hierarchy of social flashpoints.

15 Two other social divides are viewed as less pervasive or intense. Fewer than four-in-ten (38%) say there are serious conflicts between blacks and whites, including 10% who see these conflicts as being "very strong." About a third say there are similar disagreements between the young and old (34%, a 9-point increase since 2009).

***sampling error:*** the likely possible amount of error that can occur when a researcher assumes that a sample is, in fact, identical to the population it presents. Here, for the total sample, the sampling error is plus or minus 2.9 percentage points; thus, the response for the entire national population likely falls somewhere in the range between 2.9 percentage points below the stated response and 2.9 percentage points above it. (For example, if 46% of the respondents in the sample replied "agree" to a question, we can assume that between 43.1% and 48.9% of the national population would reply to the same question with a response of "agree.") The sampling error for adults 18–24 is larger at 4.4 percentage points; in this case, the actual response for this group at the national would fall between 4.4% below the given response and 4.4% above it. The lowest possible sampling error yields the most trustworthy data.

***95% confidence level:*** in statistical reasoning, the likelihood that a calculation represents an actual relationship rather than an accidental one. In this case, odds are 95 out of 100 that the reported percentages are accurate for the national population as a whole; in only 5 cases out of 100 would these data not be accurate.

### Income and Perceptions of Class Conflict

The perception that strong and growing conflicts exist between the economic classes is broadly held. Not only do those at the bottom rungs of the income scale agree that there are serious disagreements between the economic classes, but even those who are relatively well-off hold that belief.

Nearly two-thirds (64%) of all adults with family incomes of less than $20,000 a year report serious conflicts between the rich and poor—a view shared by 67% of those earning $75,000 a year or more.

Moreover, the perceptions of class conflicts have grown in virtual lock step across all income groups since 2009, rising by 17 percentage points among those earning less than $20,000 and by 18 points among those making $75,000 or more.

The increase is slightly larger among middle-income Americans earning between $40,000 and $75,000. Among this group, the share who say there are strong class conflicts increased by 24 points, from 47% in 2009 to 71% in the latest survey.

**Rich vs. Poor**

*Q. In America how much conflict is there between poor people and rich people?*

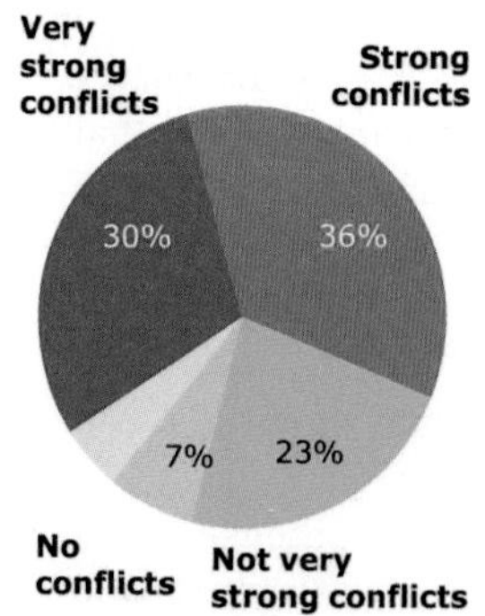


Note: Share of "Don't know/refused" and "Can't choose" responses shown but not labeled

PEW RESEARCH CENTER

**Perception of Class Conflict Rises In All Income Levels**

*% in each group who say there are "very strong" or "strong" conflicts between rich and poor*

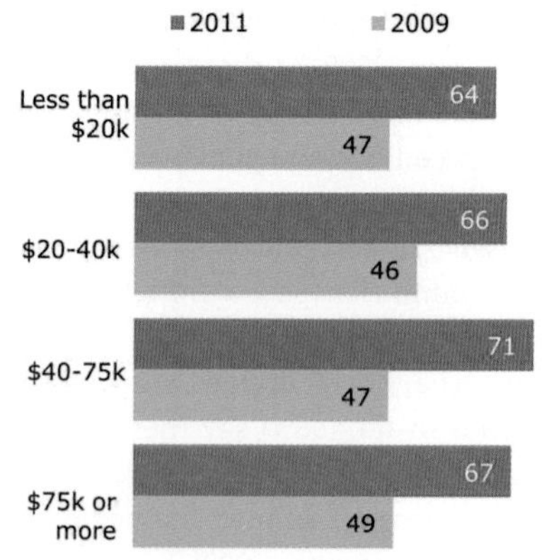


PEW RESEARCH CENTER

## Other Demographic Differences

Young people ages 18 to 34—the demographic group most closely associated with the Occupy movement—are more likely than those 35 or older to see "strong" conflicts between the rich and poor. According to the survey, more than seven-in-ten (71%) of these young adults say there are major disagreements between the most and least affluent, a 17 percentage point increase since 2009. 20

Baby Boomers ages 50 to 64—the mothers and fathers of the Occupy generation—are nearly as likely to say there are serious conflicts between the upper and lower classes; fully two-thirds (67%) say this, a 22-point increase in the past two years. Among those ages 35 to 49, more than six-in-ten (64%) see serious class conflicts.

While older adults are the least likely to see serious disagreements between the classes, the proportion who express this view increased from 36% two years ago to 55% in the current survey.

Women are more likely than men to say there are serious disagreements between the rich and poor (71% vs. 60%). In 2009, about half of all women (51%) and 43% of men said there was strong conflict between the classes.

**The Demographics of Class Conflict**

*% in each group who say there are "very strong" or "strong" conflicts between rich and poor*

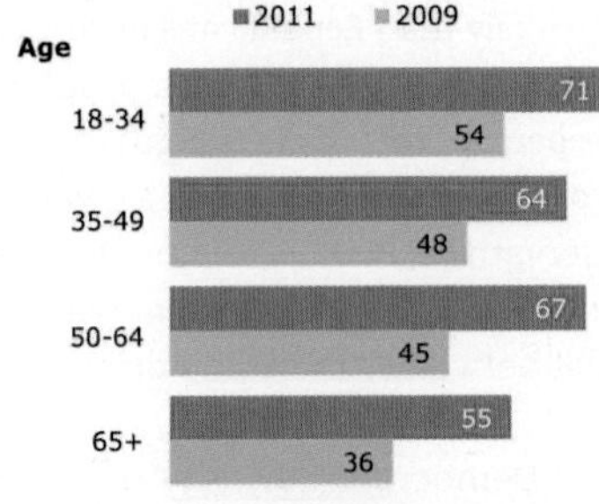


**Education**

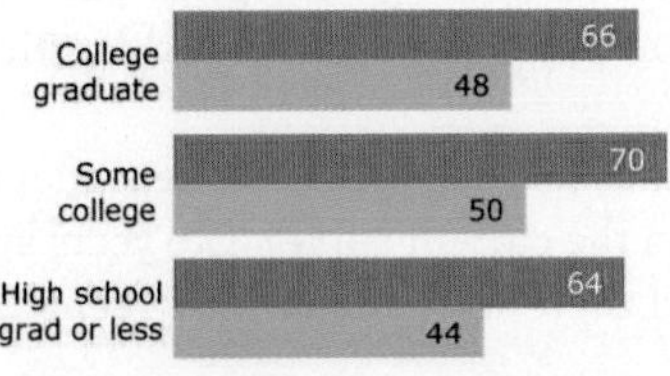


PEW RESEARCH CENTER

### PERCEPTIONS OF CLASS CONFLICT SURGE AMONG WHITES

In the past two years, the proportion of whites who say there are strong conflicts between the rich and the poor has grown by 22 percentage points to 65%. That is more than triple the increase among blacks or Hispanics. The result is that the "perceptions gap" between blacks and whites on class conflict has been cut in half, while among Hispanics the difference has disappeared and may have reversed.

25 In the latest survey, the difference in the share of blacks and whites who say there are strong conflicts between rich and poor stands at 9 percentage points (74% for blacks vs. 65% for whites). In 2009 the black-white divide on this question stood at 23 percentage points (66% vs. 43%).

Among Hispanics, the gap has closed and may have reversed: In 2009, the share of Hispanics who said there were serious conflicts between the economic classes was 12 points larger than the share of whites (55% vs. 43%). Today, the proportion of whites who say there are serious disagreements is 4 percentage points greater than the share of Hispanics who hold the same view (65% for whites vs. 61% for Hispanics), though this difference is not statistically significant.

**Political Orientation and Perceptions of Class Conflict**

*% in each group who say there are "very strong" or "strong" conflicts between rich and poor*

■ 2011 ■ 2009

**Party Identification**

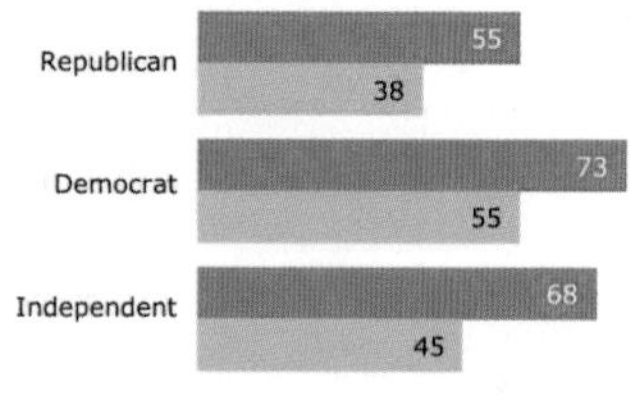


**Ideology**

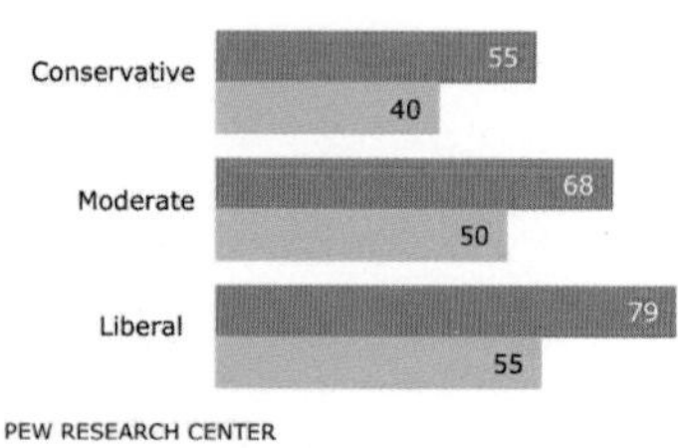


PEW RESEARCH CENTER

### THE POLITICS OF CLASS CONFLICT

Democrats and political liberals are far more likely than Republicans or conservatives to say there are major conflicts between rich people and poor people.

At the same time, in just two years the perceptions of class conflict have increased significantly among members of both political parties as well as among self-described independents, conservatives, liberals and moderates. The result is that majorities of each political party and ideological point of view now agree that serious disputes exist between Americans on the top and bottom of the income ladder.

Nearly three-quarters of self-described Democrats (73%) say there are serious class conflicts, an 18 percentage point increase over those who said that in 2009. The increase among Republicans was about as large (17 percentage points); currently a majority of GOP partisans see serious conflicts between rich and poor.

30 Views of class conflicts increased the most among political independents, swelling by 23 percentage points to 68% in the current survey. Two years ago, fewer than half of all independents said there were major disagreements between the classes.

Similarly, perceptions of class conflict among ideological liberals increased by 23 percentage points to 79% in the past two years while rising less quickly among conservatives (15 points) or moderates (18 points).

## How the Rich Got Wealthy

Americans divide nearly evenly when they are asked if the rich became wealthy mostly due to their own hard work or mainly because they were born into a wealthy family or had connections.

A narrow plurality° (46%) believes the rich are wealthy because they were born into money or "know the right people." But nearly as many (43%) say the rich got that way because of their own "hard work, ambition or education."

*plurality:* in situations where there are three or more groups, the largest group (in contrast to the majority, which must account for more than 50% of the population).

The latest result is virtually identical to the findings of a 2008 Pew survey. It found that 46% of the public believed that riches are mostly the result of having the right connections or being born into the right family, while 42% say hard work and individual characteristics are the main reason the rich are wealthy.[3]

These competing explanations of wealth are cited by roughly equal shares 35
of all income groups. According to the latest Pew survey, 46% of those with family incomes of less than $20,000 a year believe that luck and connections explain most wealth, a view shared by 47% of those with family incomes of $100,000 or more.

In contrast, attitudes of Republicans and Democrats on this issue are mirror opposites of each other. Nearly six-in-ten Democrats (58%) say wealth is mainly due to family money or knowing the right people. An identical proportion of Republicans say wealth is mainly a consequence of hard work, ambition, or having the necessary education to get ahead.

Political independents fall in between: slightly less than half (45%) credit personal effort, while an equal share believe family circumstances or connections is the most likely explanation.

African Americans (54%) are more likely than non-Hispanic whites (44%) to see wealth as a consequence of family money or connections, a view shared by 51% of Hispanics. Women in the survey are slightly more likely than men to say wealth is the result of family or connections, but these differences are not statistically significant.

Young people are significantly more likely than older adults to believe most wealth is due to family money or connections (51% for those ages 18–34 but 37% for adults 65 or older). However, the views of the "younger young"—those 18 to 25—differ significantly from those who are just a few years older.

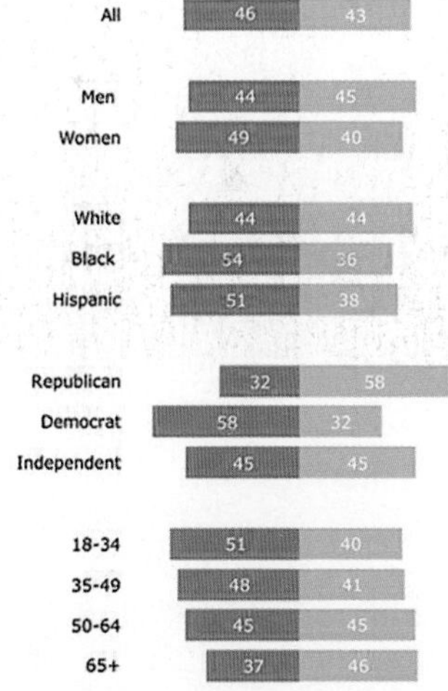

According to the survey, less than half (47%) of those 18 to 25 say the rich 40
are wealthy because of reasons other than personal effort or drive, or about equal to the proportion of those 35 or older who share this view. In contrast, a majority (55%) of those 26 to 34 say being born into a wealthy family or personal connections are the main reasons that people are rich.

### Views on Wealth, Class Conflict

Attitudes toward the wealthy—specifically, how the rich got that way—are somewhat correlated with views on class conflict.

According to the survey, those who believe the rich acquired their fortunes mainly through their own efforts are significantly less likely than those who hold the contrary view to say there are strong conflicts between the classes (60% vs. 72%).

**Attitudes toward Wealth Correlated With Views on Class Conflict**

*Perceptions of class conflict among those who say the rich are wealthy ...*

■ Strong conflicts between rich and poor
■ No strong conflicts between rich and poor

...because of own hard work, ambition or education

...because they know right people or were born into wealthy families

Note: Percentage who say "neither/other" or "both equally" not shown

PEW RESEARCH CENTER

## Pew Social & Demographic Trends

### December 2011 Youth and Economy Survey
### Topline for Selected Questions
### Dec 6–19, 2011
### Total N=2,048, Ages 18–34 N=808

**Note: All numbers are percentages. The percentages greater than zero but less than 0.5% are replaced by an asterisk (*). Columns/rows may not total 100% due to rounding. Unless otherwise noted, all trends reference surveys from Social & Demographic Trends and the Pew Research Center for the People & the Press.**

**Ask all:**

On a different topic . . .

Q.6 In all countries, there are differences or conflicts between different social groups. In your opinion, in AMERICA, how much conflict is there between . . . [READ AND RANDOMIZE°] . . . Very strong conflicts, strong conflicts, not very strong conflicts, there are not conflicts. [REPEAT CATEGORIES AS NECESSARY] In America, how much conflict is there between . . . [INSERT NEXT ITEM] READ IF NECESSARY: Very strong conflicts, strong conflicts, not very strong conflicts, there are not conflicts.

a. Young people and older people

| | | July 2009 | *GSS*° 2000[4] | *GSS* 1992[5] |
|---|---|---|---|---|
| 10 | Very strong conflicts | 6 | 10 | 11 |
| 24 | Strong conflicts | 19 | 31 | 31 |
| 50 | Not very strong conflicts | 56 | 48 | 43 |
| 12 | There are not conflicts | 14 | 7 | 10 |
| 1 | Can't choose (VOL.°) | 1 | 4 | 5 |
| 3 | Don't know/Refused (VOL.) | 4 | n/a | n/a |

b. Poor people and rich people

| | | July 2009 | *GSS* 2000 | *GSS* 1992 | *GSS* 1987 |
|---|---|---|---|---|---|
| 30 | Very strong conflicts | 15 | 14 | 20 | 15 |
| 36 | Strong conflicts | 32 | 41 | 46 | 44 |
| 23 | Not very strong conflicts | 34 | 37 | 26 | 33 |
| 7 | There are not conflicts | 10 | 3 | 3 | 3 |
| 1 | Can't choose (VOL.) | 3 | 6 | 5 | 5 |
| 4 | Don't know/Refused (VOL.) | 6 | n/a | n/a | n/a |

***randomize:*** here, an instruction to the interviewer to change the ordering of possible responses so as to minimize any influence that ordering might have on the answers respondents give. Thus, in one interview, the interviewer would offer the options as "Very strong conflicts, strong conflicts, not very strong conflicts, there are not conflicts" while the ordering would be reversed in the next interview. Researchers engage in such techniques to reduce bias created by the conditions under which the data are collected; hence, these techniques help create an ethos of trustworthiness for researchers.

***GSS:*** General Social Survey, a lengthy sociological survey conducted every other year on a random sample of Americans using face-to-face interviews to collect information on demographic characteristics, reported behaviors, and attitudes.

***VOL.:*** volunteered; in other words, the respondent said, "I can't choose," "I don't know," "I don't want to answer," or something similar.

c. Blacks and whites

| | | July 2009 |
|---|---|---|
| 10 | Very strong conflicts | 9 |
| 28 | Strong conflicts | 30 |
| 47 | Not very strong conflicts | 45 |
| 7 | There are not conflicts | 8 |
| 2 | Can't choose (VOL.) | 3 |
| 5 | Don't know/Refused (VOL.) | 6 |

d. Immigrants and people born in the United States

| | | July 2009 |
|---|---|---|
| 24 | Very strong conflicts | 18 |
| 38 | Strong conflicts | 36 |
| 26 | Not very strong conflicts | 30 |
| 6 | There are not conflicts | 8 |
| 1 | Can't choose (VOL.) | 3 |
| 4 | Don't know/Refused (VOL.) | 5 |

**Ask all:**

Q.8 Which of these statements comes closer to your own views—even if neither is exactly right? **[READ AND RANDOMIZE]**

| | | Jan 2008 |
|---|---|---|
| 43 | Most rich people today are wealthy mainly because of their own hard work, ambition or education | 42 |
| 46 | Most rich people today are wealthy mainly because they know the right people or were born into wealthy families | 46 |
| 8 | Neither/Both equally (VOL.) | 8 |
| * | Other (VOL.) | * |
| 3 | Don't know/Refused (VOL.) | 4 |

## Notes

1. See Pew Social & Demographic Trends, "Forty Years after Woodstock, a Gentler Generation Gap," August 12, 2009 (http://www.pewsocialtrends.org/2009/08/12/forty-years-after-woodstockbra-gentler-generation-gap/).
2. For a detailed look at one aspect of the wealth gap, see "The Rising Age Gap in Economic Well-Being," by Richard Fry et al., Pew Research Center, Nov. 11, 2011 (http://www.pewsocialtrends.org/2011/11/07/the-rising-age-gap-in-economic-well-being/).

3. See Pew Social & Demographic Trends, "Inside the Middle Class: Bad Times Hit the Good Life," April 9, 2008 (http://www.pewsocialtrends.org/2008/04/09/inside-the-middle-class-bad-times-hit-the-good-life/).
4. The GSS questions didn't include "Don't know/Refused" option.
5. The question wording is slightly different in the 1992 GSS: "In all countries there are differences or even conflicts between . . ."

## RESPOND •

1. What was your response to this information? Was it old news to you? Did any of the findings surprise you? If so, which ones and why? How aware were you of changes that have taken place in American attitudes toward these issues over the past decades?
2. Why do the authors of this report give the wording of the question that those interviewed responded to? (Pay special attention to endnotes 4 and 5 here.) In what other ways do the authors demonstrate that they are seeking to create an ethos of trustworthiness?
3. Evaluate the visual arguments in this report. How effective are they? Consider them from two perspectives that are often used to evaluate visual arguments. First, can each chart stand alone? (That is, can you understand each chart without reading the accompanying text?) Second, is the relationship between the chart and the text that comments on it clear and easy to follow? Finally, consider a third question: Would the figures and text have worked better together if the authors had labeled each figure with a number (e.g., Figure 1, Figure 2, etc.) and referred to the chart by number in the text, as is required by the style manual of the American Psychological Association? Why or why not?
4. In your college classes, odds are that you will be asked to read documents like this one with some frequency, especially in courses in the social sciences, and to summarize their main findings in a paragraph or two. **Write two healthy paragraphs** in which you do exactly that: summarize the major, most interesting, or most significant findings of this report from your perspective. As you write, take care to ensure that you report the findings with the qualifications and nuance that you find in the original. (Chapters 17–19 provide tips that will help you as you write your summary.)
5. Factual arguments like this one become the basis for much public debate. As careful readers note, the investigators who collected the data and wrote the report did not investigate *why* respondents held the attitudes they did; rather, they sought to report what current attitudes were at the time the data were collected; to analyze the

data by demographic categories like sex, race/ethnicity, age, and political affiliation; and to compare current data to data collected in earlier surveys. Choose one such factual finding from the report and **construct a causal argument**, trying to provide a coherent possible argument for why the data pattern as they do. (Here's an example to demonstrate: On page 889, we read, ". . . younger adults, women, Democrats, and African Americans are somewhat more likely than older people, men, Republicans, whites or Hispanics to say there are strong disagreements between rich and poor." Why might this be the case?) In planning your essay, you may well need to conduct some research of your own, whether talking to members of various groups to get their opinions or searching for information on the Internet. Whatever you do, don't lapse into unsupported claims, especially prejudice-filled ones, about members of various groups. (Chapter 11 discusses causal arguments while Chapters 18, 19, and 21 provide information on the appropriate use and documentation of sources.)

▼ *Rana Foroohar is the assistant managing editor of* Time; *she also appears on* MSNBC's Now with Alex Wagner *and writes for the* Daily Beast. *Earlier in her career, she was* Newsweek's *deputy editor for international business and economics and wrote for* Forbes. *She also spent six years in London, where she focused on coverage of these topics in Europe and the Middle East, and received an award from the German Marshall Fund for this trans-Atlantic reporting. As a Barnard undergrad, Foroohar was an English major. This selection appeared in the November 14, 2011, edition of* Time *as part of a series entitled "Opportunity Nation," itself the name of a nonpartisan coalition composed of some two hundred organizations with a focus on increasing social mobility in the United States. As you read this selection, note the ways that Foroohar contextualizes the situation in which America finds itself with respect to its history and with respect to other countries around the world.*

# What Ever Happened to Upward Mobility?

RANA FOROOHAR

America's story, our national mythology, is built on the idea of being an opportunity society. From the tales of Horatio Alger° to the real lives of Henry Ford° and Mark Zuckerberg,° we have defined our country as a place where everyone, if he or she works hard enough, can get ahead. As Alexis de

***Horatio Alger Jr. (1832–1899):*** author of over thirty juvenile novels and many other literary works with titles like *Ragged Dick; or, Street Life in New York with the Bootblacks* (1869), his best-selling novel, and *Luck and Pluck; or, John Oakley's Inheritance* (1869). The recurring didactic motif of his work is the poor protagonist, who, thanks to his virtuous hard work, rises to the edges of the lower middle class.

***Henry Ford (1863–1947):*** American industrialist and founder of the motor company that bears his name; Ford was the first to support the use of the assembly line as part of the mass production of consumer goods at lower prices.

***Mark Zuckerberg (1984– ):*** one of the creators of Facebook and its current chief executive.

*Lesley Perez, 24, is a New York City kindergarten teacher and earns just $23,000 a year. To save money, she lives with her parents. She is $35,000 in debt from college loans.*

© Joakim Eskildsen for *Time*

Tocqueville° argued more than 150 years ago, it's this dream that enables Americans to tolerate much social inequality—this coming from a French aristocrat—in exchange for what we perceive as great dynamism° and opportunity in our society. Modern surveys confirm what Tocqueville sensed back then: Americans care much more about being able to move up the socioeconomic ladder than where we stand on it. We may be poor today, but as long as there's a chance that we can be rich tomorrow, things are O.K.

But does America still work like that? The suspicion that the answer is no inspires not only the Occupy Wall Street (OWS) protests that have spread across the nation but also a movement as seemingly divergent as the Tea Party. While OWS may focus its anger on rapacious° bankers and the Tea Party on spendthrift politicians, both would probably agree that there's a cabal of entitled elites on Wall Street and in Washington who have somehow loaded the dice and made it impossible for average people to get ahead. The American Dream, like the rest of our economy, has become bifurcated.°

Certainly the numbers support the idea that for most people, it's harder to get ahead than it's ever been in the postwar era.° Inequality in the U.S., always high compared with that in other developed countries, is rising. The 1% decried by OWS takes home 21% of the country's income and accounts for 35% of its wealth.

***Alexis de Tocqueville (1805–1859):*** French historian, political thinker, and author of *Democracy in America* (1835, 1840), his reflections on the evolution of American democracy and market capitalism as they contrasted with the situation in Europe.

***dynamism:*** energy or vigor.

***rapacious:*** greedy or predatory.

***bifurcated:*** divided or forked into two branches.

***postwar era:*** the period since 1945, when World War II ended. The end of the war marked the beginning of a period of great economic growth; the population grew as well, giving rise to what is usually called the "baby boom."

**Evan, 22, Sophia, 50, and Brent Nagao, 54**

*Because his Selma, Calif., farm isn't profitable, Brent works for the USDA. Evan quit his job to work the farm, while Sophia cares for Brent's ailing parents.*

**Maria, 39, and Darren Sumner, 40**

*The New Orleans couple were laid off from design and architecture jobs in 2008. Steady work was scarce for years until Maria landed a job as a design director in September. Darren is still looking.*

Wages, which have stagnated in real terms since the 1970s, have been falling for much of the past year, in part because of pervasively high unemployment. For the first time in 20 years, the percentage of the population employed in the U.S. is lower than in the U.K., Germany and the Netherlands. "We like to think of America as the workingest nation on earth. But that's no longer the case," says Ron Haskins, a co-director, along with Isabel Sawhill, of the Brookings Institution's Center on Children and Families.

Nor are we the world's greatest opportunity society. The Pew Charitable Trusts' Economic Mobility Project has found that if you were born in 1970 in the bottom one-fifth of the socioeconomic spectrum in the U.S., you had only about a 17% chance of making it into the upper two-fifths. That's not good by international standards. A spate of new reports from groups such as Brookings, Pew and the Organization for Economic Co-operation and Development show

**Felecia Ogbodo, 37, and her daughter Ermaline, 18**

*Felecia, from Fresno, Calif., lost her job as a social worker and is filing for bankruptcy. Ermaline, a student at UC Santa Cruz, worries about needing to support her mom.*

that it's easier to climb the socioeconomic ladder in many parts of Europe than it is in the U.S. It's hard to imagine a bigger hit to the American Dream than that: you'd have an easier time getting a leg up in many parts of sclerotic,° debt-ridden, class-riven° old Europe than you would in the U.S.A. "The simple truth," says Sawhill, "is that we have a belief system about ourselves that no longer aligns with the facts."

5 The obvious question is, What happened? The answers, like social mobility itself, are nuanced and complex. You can argue about what kind of mobility really matters. Many conservatives, for example, would be inclined to focus on absolute mobility, which means the extent to which people are better off than their parents were at the same age. That's a measure that focuses mostly on how much economic growth has occurred, and by that measure, the U.S. does fine. Two-thirds of 40-year-old Americans live in households with larger incomes, adjusted for inflation, than their parents had at the same age (though the gains are smaller than they were in the previous generation).

But just as we don't feel grateful to have indoor plumbing or multichannel digital cable television, we don't necessarily feel grateful that we earn more than our parents did. That's because we don't peg ourselves to our parents; we peg ourselves to the Joneses. Behavioral economics tells us that our sense of well-being is tied not to the past but to how we are doing compared with our peers. Relative mobility matters. By that standard, we aren't doing very well at all. Having the right parents increases your chances of ending up middle to upper middle class by a factor of three or four. It's very different in many other countries, including Canada, Australia, the Nordic nations° and, to a lesser extent, Germany and France. While 42% of American men with fathers in the bottom fifth of the earning curve remain there, only a quarter of Danes and Swedes and only 30% of Britons do.

Yet it's important to understand that when you compare Europe and America, you are comparing very different societies. High-growth Nordic nations with good social safety nets, which have the greatest leads in social mobility over the U.S., are small and homogeneous.° On average, only about 7% of their populations are ethnic minorities (who are often poorer and thus less mobile than the overall population), compared with 28% in the U.S. Even bigger nations like Germany don't have to deal with populations as socially and economically diverse as America's.

Still, Europe does more to encourage equality. That's a key point because high inequality—meaning a large gap between the richest and poorest in society—has a strong correlation to lower mobility. As Sawhill puts it, "When the rungs on the ladder are farther apart, it's harder to climb up them." Indeed, in order to understand why social mobility in the U.S. is falling, it's

---

*sclerotic:* generally, hardened (as in sclerotic tissue or arteries); used here figuratively to mean "lacking innovation."

*class-riven:* split apart by social class differences.

*Nordic nations:* Denmark, Norway, and Sweden, all of which are characterized by governments that provide strong social services and citizenries that are willing to pay high taxes in comparison to those paid by Americans.

*homogeneous:* characterized by similarity; here, the reference is to similarity of ethnic background.

important to understand why inequality is rising, now reaching levels not seen since the Gilded Age.°

There are many reasons for the huge and growing wealth divide in our country. The rise of the money culture and bank deregulation° in the 1980s and '90s certainly contributed to it. As the financial sector grew in relation to the rest of the economy (it's now at historic highs of about 8%), a winner-take-all economy emerged. Wall Street was less about creating new businesses—entrepreneurship has stalled as finance has become a bigger industry—but it did help set a new pay band for top talent. In the 1970s, corporate chiefs earned about 40 times as much as their lowest-paid worker (still closer to the norm in many parts of Europe). Now they earn more than 400 times as much.

10 The most recent blows to economic equality, of course, have been the real estate and credit crises, which wiped out housing prices and thus erased the largest chunk of middle-class wealth, while stocks, where the rich hold much of their money, have largely recovered. It is telling that in the state-by-state Opportunity Index recently released by Opportunity Nation, a coalition of private and public institutions dedicated to increasing social mobility, many of the lowest-scoring states—including Nevada, Arizona and Florida—were those hardest hit by the housing crash and are places where credit continues to be most constrained.

But the causes of inequality and any resulting decrease in social mobility are also very much about two megatrends that have been reshaping the global economy since the 1970s: the effects of technology and the rise of the emerging markets.° Some 2 billion people have joined the global workforce since the 1970s. According to Goldman Sachs, the majority of them are middle class by global standards and can do many of the jobs that were once done by American workers, at lower labor costs. Goldman estimates that 70 million join that group every year.

While there's no clear formula for ascribing the rise in inequality (via wage compression) and subsequent loss of mobility to the rise of China and India, one key study stands out. Nobel laureate Michael Spence's recent examination of major U.S. multinationals for the Council on Foreign Relations found that since the 1980s, companies that operated in the tradable sector—meaning they made things or provided services that could be traded between nations—have created virtually no net new jobs. The study is especially illustrative of the hollowing out of the American manufacturing sector in that period as middle-wage jobs moved abroad. The only major job

***Gilded Age:*** the period in U.S. history between the end of the Civil War and the end of the nineteenth century, which was characterized by the extremely rapid growth of the population and the economy as well as an increase in income inequality as some industrialists and financiers, including John D. Rockefeller, Andrew Carnegie, J. P. Morgan, and Cornelius Vanderbilt—all names that continue to connote great wealth—made their fortunes.

***deregulation:*** a reduction in government regulatory control.

***emerging markets:*** countries whose economies are experiencing rapid growth and industrialization; currently, these would include Brazil, China, the Czech Republic, India, Russia, South Africa, and Turkey, among others.

creation was in more geographically protected categories like retail and health care (another reason wages are shrinking, since many of the fastest-growing jobs in the U.S., like home health care aide and sales clerk, are low-paying).

That so many of the jobs we now create are low end underscores a growing debate over technology and its role in increasing or decreasing opportunity. Many of the jobs that have disappeared from the U.S. economy have done so not only because they were outsourced but also because they are now done by computers or robots. Advocates of technology-driven economic growth, like the McKinsey Global Institute, would argue that the creative destruction wrought by such innovations creates more and better jobs in the future; microchip making employs just 0.6% of the U.S. workforce, but chips make all sorts of businesses more efficient so they can develop new products and services. The problem is that those jobs tend to be skewed toward the very top (software engineer) or the bottom (sales clerk). The jobs in the middle have disappeared. According to the New America Foundation, a public-policy think tank, the share of middle-income jobs in the U.S. fell from 52% in 1980 to 42% in 2010.

While there's no doubt that so far, technology has been a net° plus in terms of the number of jobs in our economy, a growing group of experts believe that link is being broken. Two economists at MIT, Erik Brynjolfsson and Andrew McAfee, have just published an influential book titled *Race against the Machine*, looking at how computers are increasingly able to perform tasks better than humans do, from driving (Google software recently took a self-driving Prius on a 1,000-mile trip) to sophisticated pattern recognition to writing creative essays and composing award-winning music. The result, they say, is that technology may soon be a net job destroyer.

15 The best hope in fighting the machines is to improve education, the factor that is more closely correlated with upward mobility than any other. Research has shown that as long as educational achievement keeps up with technological gains, more jobs are created. But in the late 1970s, that link was broken in the U.S. as educational gains slowed. That's likely an important reason that Europeans have passed the U.S. in various measures of mobility. They've been exposed to the same Malthusian forces° of globalization, but they've been better at using public money to buffer them. By funding postsecondary education and keeping public primary and secondary schools as good as if not better than private ones, Europeans have made sure that the best and brightest can rise.

There are many other lessons to be learned from the most mobile nations. Funding universal health care without tying it to jobs can increase labor flexibility and reduce the chance that people will fall into poverty because of medical emergencies—a common occurrence in the U.S., where such medical crises are a big reason a third of the population cycles in and out of poverty every year. Focusing more on less-expensive preventive care (including family planning, since high teen birthrates correlate with lack of mobility) rather than on expensive procedures can increase the general health levels in a society, which is also correlated to mobility.

Europe's higher spending on social safety nets has certainly bolstered the middle and working classes. (Indeed, you could argue that some of America's great

***net:*** total or final, remaining after any deductions; thus, here, jobs created after we subtract the jobs that have been lost.

***Malthusian forces:*** the claim that population grows exponentially (1, 2, 4, 16) while the food supply grows arithmetically (1, 2, 3, 4) unless there is outside intervention, an argument first made by Thomas Malthus (1766–1834), an English demographer and political economist.

social programs, including Social Security and Medicaid, enabled us to become a middle-class nation.) Countries like Germany and Denmark that have invested in youth-employment programs and technical schools where young people can learn a high-paying trade have done well, which is not surprising given that in many studies, including the Opportunity Nation index, there's a high correlation between the number of teenagers who are not in school or not working and lowered mobility.

Of course, the debt crisis in Europe and the protests over austerity cuts in places like Athens and London make it clear that the traditional European welfare systems are undergoing very profound changes that may reduce mobility throughout the continent. But there is still opportunity in efficiency. Germans, for example, made a command decision after the financial downturn in 2008 not to let unemployment rise because it would ultimately be more expensive to put people back to work than to pay to keep them in their jobs. The government subsidized companies to keep workers (as many as 1.4 million in 2009) on the payroll, even part time. Once the economy began to pick up, companies were ready to capitalize on it quickly. Unemployment is now 6%—lower than before the recession—and growth has stayed relatively high.

The Nordic nations, too, have figured out clever ways to combine strong economic growth with a decent amount of security. As in Germany, labor and corporate relations are collaborative rather than contentious. Union reps often sit on company boards, which makes it easier to curb excessive executive pay and negotiate compromises over working hours. Worker retraining is a high priority. Danish adults spend a lot of time in on-the-job training. That's one reason they also enjoy high real wages and relatively low unemployment.

20 The final lesson that might be learned is in tax policy. The more-mobile European nations have fewer corporate loopholes, more redistribution to the poor and middle class via consumption taxes° and far less complication. France's tax code, for example, is 12% as long as the U.S.'s. Tax levels are also higher, something that the enlightened rich in the U.S. are very publicly advocating.

No wonder. A large body of academic research shows that inequality and lack of social mobility hurt not just those at the bottom; they hurt everyone. Unequal societies have lower levels of trust, higher levels of anxiety and more illness. They have arguably less stable economies: International Monetary Fund research shows that countries like the U.S. and the U.K. are more prone to boom-and-bust cycles. And they are ultimately at risk for social instability.

That's the inflection point° that we are at right now. The mythology of the American Dream has made it difficult to start a serious conversation about how to create more opportunity in our society, since many of us still believe that our mobility is the result of our elbow grease° and nothing more.

---

***consumption taxes:*** taxes levied and paid at the time consumer goods or services are purchased; sales tax is a kind of consumption tax.

***inflection point:*** in a mathematical graph, the point at which a curve changes sign (that is, where a positive curve becomes negative or a negative curve becomes positive).

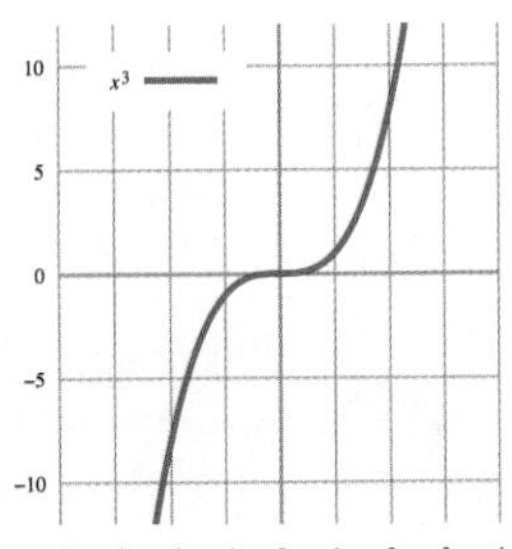


***elbow grease:*** hard work often involving physical exertion.

But there is a growing truth, seen in the numbers and in the protests that are spreading across our nation, that this isn't so. We can no longer blame the individual. We have to acknowledge that climbing the ladder often means getting some support and a boost.

**RESPOND•**

1. Clearly, Foroohar assumes that the situation Americans find themselves in is a complex one that is best understood by thinking historically and thinking comparatively, that is, by comparing the United States to other countries around the world. What does each perspective contribute to her causal argument? To your understanding of issues of inequality in the United States?
2. Among the things that Foroohar does well as a writer is give her readers background information in places where they might need it, whether in terms of definitions or short descriptions that give readers a context for interpreting claims she is making. In what specific ways does she define or describe each of the following terms or things?
   - absolute mobility (paragraph 5)
   - relative mobility (paragraph 6)
   - Opportunity Nation (paragraph 10)
   - McKinsey Global Institute (paragraph 13)
   - New America Foundation (paragraph 13)

   Why is this information useful and perhaps even necessary?
3. Another skill Foroohar has mastered is the ability to move between levels of generality within a paragraph. Thus, most paragraphs begin with a generalization or topic sentence and then become more specific before moving on to make a point in support of her argument. Analyze paragraphs 8 and 17 in this regard, explaining what Foroohar does to move from more general to more specific. In other words, how does she use specific forms of evidence to shift from general claim to more specific support for that claim? Choose a third paragraph you find interesting, and comment on it from this perspective.
4. Frequently in college writing, students are called upon to summarize a complex argument like Foroohar's in some detail. As noted in question 1, Foroohar is offering a causal argument. **Analyze and then summarize her argument** in three to five paragraphs (much as you might do on an essay exam), being sure to present your summary in terms of the appropriate kind of causal argument described in Chapter 11 in the section "Understanding Causal Arguments."

▼ *As Rana Foroohar noted in the previous selection, "What Ever Happened to Upward Mobility?" for all their differences, those who occupied Wall Street and many other cities in the United States and Canada and their supporters actually share some important assumptions with the Tea Party and its supporters. This posting from CATO@LIBERTY seeks to make explicit both what those similarities might be and what the differences are and to contextualize both. CATO@LIBERTY is the blog of the Cato Institute, a libertarian think tank located in Washington, D.C. Its stated goal is "to increase the understanding of public policies based on the principles of limited government, free markets, individual liberty, and peace." Jim Harper, who posted this selection, is the director of information policy studies for the Cato Institute, where he focuses on issues related to new technologies—intellectual property, privacy, security, and telecommunications. As you'll see, he is actually reposting and (re)contextualzing a visual argument created by James Sinclair, whose blog is entitled "How Conservatives Drove Me Away . . . from conservatism, as examined by a liberal-leaning libertarian who believes in tolerance, diversity, and compassion, and is offended way too easily." (Sinclair blogs at http://howconservativesdrovemeaway.blogspot.com/.) As you read this selection, focus on both Sinclair's visual argument itself and the way that Harper puts it in context.*

# Tea Party, Meet Occupy Wall Street. OWS, Tea Party.

JIM HARPER

Broad political movements are going to have none of the coherence that we demand of ourselves in ideological movements like libertarianism. The Tea Party has some people with views that libertarians reject and many that we embrace. Occupy Wall Street has a lot of people with views that libertarians reject and some that libertarians embrace—freedom from police abuse being one. (Such a favor the NYPD officer who pepper-sprayed female protesters did to OWS by driving attention and sympathy its way.)

That's all caveat to sharing an image created by James Sinclair that's making waves on Facebook. It makes a hopeful statement, I think, about the Occupy Wall Street movement and its potential or actual kinship with Tea Partyism. There's something wrong in the country, and this image suggests that there might be consensus on the framing of what's wrong: the unity of government and corporate power against people's freedom and prosperity.

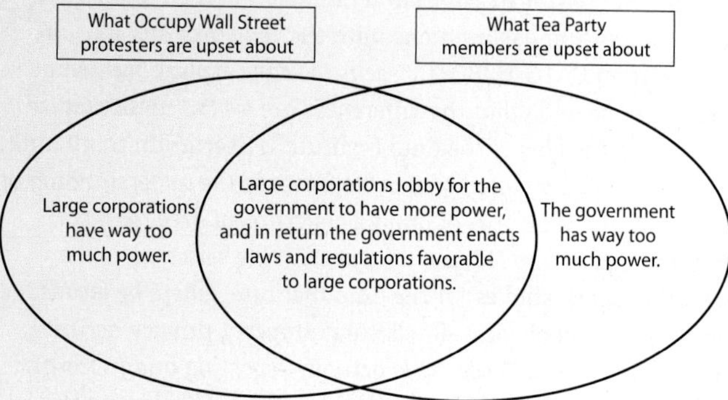


There are plenty of reasons to reject the possibility of alliance between Tea Partyism and OWS, but not necessarily good ones. The easiest out is to pour this new wine into old bottles° and characterize OWS as dirty hippies using retrograde° protest tactics. Many are kinda like that. But that stuff was a couple of decades ago. No, wait—four decades ago. These kids have no direct knowledge or experience of, say, Kent State,° and older observers might be too prone to fitting them into a pattern that doesn't exist for them.

To the extent the substance of their grievance is, or can be turned to, corporations' use of government power to win unjust power and profits for themselves, that's a grievance I can sit in a drum circle° for.

***new wine into old bottles:*** a common allusion to a parable told by Jesus of Nazareth and recorded in the New Testament. At the time of Jesus, wine was often stored in wineskins made from the skin of a goat. Because old wineskins (referred to as "old bottles" in this saying) stretched and became brittle as the wine fermented, they would break open if new, unfermented wine was put in them, causing the (new) wine to be lost. The parallel here is that if people, including libertarians, fall back on old metaphors—that of "dirty hippies" for example—in understanding the Occupy movement, they will miss what is new and valuable about the protestors of that movement.

***retrograde:*** backward.

## RESPOND

1. Summarize the argument James Sinclair is making in his visual argument, and summarize the argument Jim Harper, who is responsible for this reposting on the Cato Institute blog, is making in his contextualization of Sinclair's argument.
2. Who is Harper's intended audience? His invoked audience? How can you use specific comments in the text, including the items that we felt we needed to gloss, as evidence for claims about Harper's intended and invoked audiences? (See Chapter 1 for a discussion of audience.)
3. Examine the way that Sinclair contextualized his own visual argument by reading the blog posting in which it originally appeared in "Occupy Wall Street vs. the Tea Party" at http://bit.ly/oHPX6B as well as a later

posting about responses to the diagram reproduced here, "Bringing America Together, One Venn Diagram at a Time," at http://bit.ly/nANf74. (By the way, *cromulent* in the latter posting means "fine," and our online dictionary labels it as slang. We had to look it up, so we thought you might need to know its meaning too.) What was Sinclair trying to do with the original diagram? What was his motivation for creating the visual argument? Does it appear that he succeeded? Why or why not? Could we consider Sinclair's diagram a case of Rogerian argumentation? Why or why not? (Chapter 7 discusses Rogerian argumentation.)

4. As the title of one of his blog postings notes (see question 3), Sinclair contends that Venn diagrams are very useful in thinking through complex problems. What advantages can you see to using visual arguments like the one Sinclair presents? If you haven't read the posting "Bringing America Together, One Venn Diagram at a Time" at http://bit.ly/nANf74 (mentioned in question 3), do so now, and explain what Sinclair thinks the advantages of such diagrams are in understanding issues and creating arguments.

5. Take another aspect of the broad issue of inequality in America and seek to **construct a visual argument** about it using a Venn diagram as Sinclair has. Likely, the most successful arguments will be those that use the Venn diagrams to show areas of intersection in situations where most people think there are none. Once you've created your visual argument, contextualize it as you might if you were going to use it as part of a blog posting. (Chapter 14 discusses visual arguments.)

***Kent State:*** a public university in Kent, Ohio, where, in May 1970, the Ohio National Guard fired on students protesting the Vietnam War (specifically, the invasion of Cambodia as part of this war), wounding nine and killing four. (The Guard had been called in following several protests, some of which had become violent; the university's ROTC building was burnt down during one of these demonstrations.) Images of these events, called the "Kent State Massacre" by those sympathetic to the protesters, remain potent reminders of public contention over U.S. foreign policy at the time for those who were adults in the 1970s. Following the shootings, the university and hundreds of others across the country were closed because of growing student unrest.

***drum circle:*** a group of people, often men, who sit in a circle and play hand drums and other percussion instruments. The practice arose in the United States in the 1960s and 1970s and is often associated with counterculture groups including neopagans, shamanic groups, groups of people who are not Indians but who are influenced by Native American spiritual traditions, and the men's movement of the 1990s—all groups we would not expect libertarians to find appealing.

▼ *The author of this selection, John Marsh, is an assistant professor in the English department at Pennsylvania State University. The selection itself comes from Marsh's latest book,* Class Dismissed: Why We Cannot Teach or Learn Our Way Out of Inequality, *which was published in 2011. Marsh has two other books: an anthology of poetry written by workers and labor organizers and first published in U.S. labor newspapers in the 1930s and a book examining the role of workers and the poor in the creation of American modernist poetry. This selection originally appeared in the* Chronicle of Higher Education, *now an online newspaper focusing on all aspects of higher education that is widely read by college and university administrators, staff, and faculty. (It also appears in a print edition forty-two weeks out of the year.) In this essay, Marsh uses personal experience—both recent and distant—as the basis for his central argument. As you read, pay special attention to the territory Marsh stakes out for his argument and the ways in which he distinguishes it from arguments that on the surface may seem similar to it but that, as Marsh seeks to demonstrate, decidedly are not.*

# Why Education Is Not an Economic Panacea°

JOHN MARSH

Each May, the University of Illinois at Urbana-Champaign holds its commencement. So many students graduate from this flagship state university,° and so many families wish to attend the ceremonies, that not even the campus's basketball arena, Assembly Hall, which seats more than 16,000, can accommodate everyone. To handle the crowds, the university has two separate ceremonies, one in the morning and one in the afternoon. At both, students gamely° don caps and gowns; proud parents drive down from the suburbs of Chicago and snap digital picture after digital picture; a B-list intellectual, political, or cultural icon offers graduating seniors some warmed-over wisdom; and students march down the aisles to the strains of "Pomp and Circumstance."

As deadly boring as these commencements can be, they can also be quite charming. They celebrate a definitive moment in a young person's life, and they remind the community of the purpose and value of higher education.

Even though I taught some of those Illinois students who collected

*panacea:* a cure-all or solution to all problems. (Panacea was a goddess of healing in ancient Greek mythology.)

*flagship university:* within a state university system, the institution that is usually the oldest, the largest, the best financed, and the most prestigious of the schools in the system.

*gamely:* with pluck, spirit, or courage.

their diplomas on graduation day, I rarely attended those official ceremonies. Not because I feared being bored (or charmed) to death, but because across town, in a shabby multipurpose room of a branch library in Champaign-Urbana's only dodgy neighborhood, another sort of graduation ceremony was usually underway.

In the fall of 2005, I began to organize a class in the humanities for low-income adults in the community. The idea was simple. Faculty from the University of Illinois would offer night classes in their areas of expertise (literature, philosophy, art history, U.S. history, writing) for anyone in the community who was between the ages of 18 and 45 and lived at 150 percent of the poverty level° of income or lower. (Although you would not know it if you stuck to campus and its adjacent neighborhoods, Champaign-Urbana had a significant population of poor people.) Students who completed the nine-month course would receive six hours of college credit, which they could then transfer to other institutions of higher learning. Everything would be free: tuition, books, even child care at a nearby community center. We named it after a similar program in Chicago, the Odyssey° Project.

5 Classes met at night, on Tuesdays and Thursdays, in the same shabby multipurpose room that hosted our graduation. We sat around banquet tables. Although there were exceptions, most of the people who enrolled in Odyssey were women, usually in their 30s or 40s, a majority of them minority (African-American or Latino). Most of the women were mothers. Most had jobs. One or two had two jobs.

Those with two jobs did not last long. But then again, few people lasted long.

In signing up for the class, students signed on to a whirlwind introduction to the humanities. On any given night, they might have read—or skimmed, or not have read—and discussed Plato's "Allegory of the Cave,"° a Shakespeare sonnet, or the text of the 14th Amendment° to the Constitution. Or students would

---

***150 percent of the poverty level:*** in 2009, $16,742 for an individual and $32,634 for a family of four (two parents and two children).

***odyssey:*** a lengthy series of adventures, often involving wandering and hardship. *The Odyssey* is an ancient Greek epic poem by Homer that recounts the ten-year journey of Odysseus (called Ulysses in Latin) to return to Ithaca after the fall of Troy.

***"Allegory of the Cave":*** a section of Plato's *Republic* that seeks to demonstrate the liberatory potential of education and particularly the value of studying philosophy.

***14th Amendment:*** Adopted July 9, 1868, the 14th Amendment provided full citizenship for all Americans, including former slaves, thereby overruling the 1857 Supreme Court decision *Dred Scott v. Sandford*, which had held that blacks were not entitled to the right of U.S. citizenship. The amendment continues to be of great importance in legal debates because in addition to the "citizenship clause," which extended citizenship to all persons born or naturalized in the United States, it also contains the "due process" and the "equal protection" clauses. Section 1 of the amendment reads: "All persons born or naturalized in the United States, and subject to the jurisdiction thereof, are citizens of the United States and of the State wherein they reside. No State shall make or enforce any law which shall abridge the privileges or immunities of citizens of the United States; nor shall any State deprive any person of life, liberty, or property, without due process of law; nor deny to any person within its jurisdiction the equal protection of the laws."

sit in a darkened room and learn to distinguish Italian Renaissance° from Impressionist° paintings. Or they would learn how to make arguments about what they had read or studied: how to write a thesis statement, what counted as evidence, how to anticipate opposition to the argument they made.

Our first graduation took place in the spring of 2007. By comparison with the University of Illinois graduation ceremonies, ours, like the room itself, seemed a little threadbare. Earlier in the day, my spouse, a professor at the university whom I had enlisted to teach the philosophy course, helped me set up a podium and some stained chairs in neat rows. She stood at the door handing out a crudely designed program I had made on my computer. As graduates and their families filed in, I tried not to think about all the problems the course faced. We had started the year with close to 30 students. Within the first few weeks, we lost a dozen people. Over the next few months, we lost another half-dozen.

By the time May rolled around, our graduating class consisted of some 12 people, about half of whom had regularly attended classes, completed the assigned work, and thus deserved to graduate. The same gradual erosion of students from the class, occasionally worse, occurred year after year. On the first night of class in early September, I would put out 25 or 30 chairs. As the year proceeded, I would have to unfold fewer and fewer tables and drag out fewer and fewer chairs. For every student who made it, two or three would not. Needless to say, one graduation ceremony almost always sufficed—sometimes it seemed like one too many.

But if I wanted the program to 10
continue, in the hope that it would eventually succeed—and I did—I needed to keep up appearances, and that meant handing out diplomas to as many bodies as I could muster.

While I am sure he had other, more sincere motives, one of the reasons the chancellor° of the University of Illinois had supported the program is that for a pittance,° really, it would bring in extraordinarily good publicity.

And to the untrained eye, the class and the first graduation ceremony seemed like a success. Our valedictorian, a brilliant young African-American woman who had been chosen by her fellow students to represent the class, gave a moving speech, thanking each of the professors individually for their time and describing, in a marvelously pithy nutshell, what she had learned from each. Our official commencement speaker, a pro-

---

***Italian Renaissance:*** end of the thirteenth century until around 1600; a period of great cultural, artistic, and intellectual activity that began in Italy but spread across Europe. During this period, Europe, led by Italy, moved from the medieval period to the early modern period. The image reproduced here, Raphael's *School of Athens*, a fresco painted in 1510–11 in the Vatican, depicts twenty-one famous ancient thinkers, including Socrates, Plato, and Aristotle—a key feature of Renaissance art is its fondness for classical Greek and Roman culture. This fresco is considered one of the finest representations of Italian Renaissance art and thought.

***Impressionism:*** a late nineteenth-century French art movement; the painters who were part of the Impressionist school, including Monet, Renoir, Pissarro, Morisot, and Cassatt, sought to represent the shimmering quality of light as it hit landscapes or people who were outside, and they were often interested in capturing a sense of movement or the passing of time. In so doing, they rejected the dominant style of painting at the time that preferred realist depictions of historical events and still lifes painted indoors. The canvas reproduced here, Monet's *Impression, Soleil levant* ("Impression, Sunrise") (1872), gave the movement its name.

vost° from the university, thoughtfully congratulated the families of graduates, who deserved to be honored, she urged, for muddling through while the graduates, most of them women, and most of them mothers, had played a kind of reverse hooky from their homes to attend school at night.

After the speeches, I handed out diplomas, shook each graduate's hand, and, feeling better about the whole thing, comforted myself with the half-truth that even if the program had failed for most of our students, it had succeeded for some, and that if it worked for just one, it must have been worth doing.

After the ceremony, as graduates and their families enjoyed the sodas and deli trays my spouse and I had picked up for the reception, I spoke with the local media, which had turned out for the event. (The chancellor's investment had paid off.) Cutbacks must have hit the local news channel, though, because the cameraman who asked to interview me also turned out to be the interviewer. As he was setting up his camera, we chatted about the program, and he confessed that he and his wife talked about "this"—education—a lot. He praised the program and what I had done. "If only people could get an education," he added, "we wouldn't have all these problems." The interview began before I could ask what he meant by "all these problems," but I didn't need to ask. He meant what everyone means by "all these problems" when they come to neighborhoods like the one we found ourselves in that day: unemployment, crime, teenage pregnancy, single motherhood, and, as an embodiment of all those, poverty.

15 At which point, it hit me, as it had Victor Frankenstein°: I had created a monster. I had started the class with the hope that it would give poor adults a chance to start or—for those who had dropped out—to return to the world of higher education. But I never believed that it would solve "all these problems." Our graduating class represented a fraction of a fraction of the poor in Champaign County, and it was not even clear that the education they received in the program would help them all that much. Few had actually thrived in the course, and even fewer had any concrete plans about what to do after it was finished.

Yet to most people, as it had to the cameraman, an education like the one offered by the Odyssey Project would mean a solution to every social ill one could imagine. I had given false hopes to students but, even worse, false comfort to the community.

You could not blame the cameraman for thinking that education would solve the problems, especially if those problems were poverty and its less visible but no less pernicious° cousin, economic inequality. Indeed, he and his wife had impeccable company in their faith in education as diagnosis and cure. A few months before our first graduation, for example, President George W. Bush surprised journalists and observers by acknowledging the growing economic inequality in the United States. "The fact is that income inequality is real," Bush told an audience of Wall Street business executives. "It's been rising for more than 25 years." He added: "The reason is clear. We have an economy that

---

***chancellor:*** the highest-ranking administrative officer in some American colleges and universities.

***pittance:*** a meager amount of money. Etymologically, the word is related to *pity*; originally, a pittance was a small amount of money given to a monastery to help supply it with food.

***provost:*** one of the highest-ranking administrators at a college or university.

***Victor Frankenstein:*** the major character in Mary Shelley's 1818 novel, *Frankenstein; or, The Modern Prometheus.* Interested first in alchemy and later in chemistry, the scientist Frankenstein ultimately creates a living monster, which is given no name in the novel. (In Shelley's novel, Frankenstein is the scientist; in popular culture, "Frankenstein" is often used to refer to the monster.)

***pernicious:*** causing ruin, harm, or even death.

increasingly rewards education and skills because of that education." As the *Washington Post* noted in its coverage of the speech, "Bush's remarks were an unremarkable statement of what many economists accept as common wisdom."

That common wisdom consists not just of the fact that income inequality is real and rising—Bush is right, it is—but that income inequality results primarily from differences in education. Whereas someone with only a high-school diploma could once earn a middle-class living by, say, working in a factory, those days, or so the thinking goes, are over. In the new, postindustrial knowledge economy, the job market rewards those with an education and punishes those without one.

Remarkably, this faith in the power of education to make or break lives traverses the political spectrum. Indeed, a surprising consensus has grown up in the United States around the belief that what causes poverty and economic inequality is lack of education, and that what will fix those ills is more and better education. Crucially, the conventional wisdom explains not just why some people get ahead, but also justifies why some people are left behind. And though they may agree on little else, liberals, conservatives, and cameramen can nevertheless agree on this.

20 One could quote many authorities—and any number of ordinary people—who hold such views about the economic power of education. And these people are not wrong. Those who have advanced degrees earn more than those who have bachelor's degrees, who in turn earn more than those who have high-school degrees, on down the line. And the returns on education, as economists put it, have increased in recent years. In short, education pays, and pays more than ever. If so, it must seem as if the best way to get ahead is to get an education. Unsurprisingly, then, nothing dominates our thinking about poverty and economic inequality so much as the belief that education (or lack of it) causes these problems, and thus that education (and more of it) will fix them.

During the period when I started the Odyssey Project, part of me must have believed this conventional wisdom. After all, my prosperity was owed directly to education. I was born into a family that occasionally drifted near and once or twice fell below the poverty line. But I graduated from college, earned a Ph.D., eventually found a tenure-track job in academe, and now make more money than I ever imagined possible. (Let me hasten to assure you that this owes more to my limited imagination than it does to my high salary.) If education had worked for me, I told myself, shouldn't it work for others, too? Moreover, if it had worked for me, shouldn't everyone have a chance—or, for some of the people I sought to enroll in the Odyssey Project, a second chance—to make it work for them?

You did not need to look any further for answers to these questions than to the University of Illinois at Urbana-Champaign, which was one of the first land-grant colleges.° Their mission, according to the Morrill Act of 1862, which founded public higher education in the United States, was "to promote the liberal and practical education of the industrial classes in the several pursuits and professions in life." Although these land-grant institutions have changed quite a bit since 1862, and the terminology now feels dated, they still count promoting the education of the industrial classes—those previously excluded from higher education who nevertheless seek to improve their lives through it—among their many missions.

More so, arguably, than the University of Illinois at Urbana-Champaign itself—which now enrolls mostly well-to-do teenagers from the suburbs of Chicago—the Odyssey Project would embody these ideals of public higher education. If a college degree is what it takes to earn a decent living in the United States today, then everyone ought to have the opportu-

***land-grant college:*** institutions of higher education, nearly all public, in each state that were originally created with proceeds from the sale of land the federal government gave the state. Traditionally, land-grant institutions focused on the fields of agriculture and engineering, though today they can be known for excellence in any field.

nity to go to or go back to college. That is why I started the Odyssey Project. And that is what made rooting for it so easy, on the occasion of our first graduation ceremony, with our graduates and their families in their best clothes, also snapping digital picture after digital picture.

The interview with the local television news, however, changed my life. Although I continued to direct the Odyssey Project and to teach classes in it (usually literature or writing), from then on I had my doubts. These doubts only intensified as I watched Odyssey students drift away as the academic year wore on, victims of various crises, other claims on their time, or, less dramatically, the realization that the humanities and higher education left them cold. My doubts, I should add, were not about whether education should serve the industrial classes, the poor and low-income, but whether it really does, whether it is capable of doing so, and what good would come of it if it could. Even if every Odyssey student who enrolled in the fall graduated in the spring, and even if every Odyssey student who graduated in the spring enrolled in a real college that fall, I began to ask myself, would we be appreciably closer to solving the twin problems of poverty and economic inequality in the United States? Or forget about the United States. What about Champaign County?

25 To put it bluntly, can we teach our way out of poverty and economic inequality, as so many people in and out of power so fervently hope? Reluctantly, I have concluded that education bears far too much of the burden of our hopes for economic justice, and, moreover, that we ask education to accomplish things it simply cannot do.

While this thesis—that education alone will not change things—has occasionally surfaced, few writers have given it the extended treatment it requires. I know, because when I began to have my doubts about the Odyssey Project, I went looking for answers to my questions and had to look hard for anyone else even asking them. When did the belief in education as an economic panacea arise? Why? More empirically, is it true? If not, why has it proved so attractive? Why do so many people, especially those in power, so urgently want to believe it? And how has it influenced what teachers and students do or imagine what they do? Finally, if it is not true that education will solve poverty and inequality, what might?

Within the last few years, a number of critics have begun to challenge our unexamined faith in "college for all," as one economist has put it. Unlike those critics, mostly conservatives, I do not argue that too many students are going to college (Charles Murray), that the United States has overinvested in higher education (Richard Vedder), that more young people should enter the trades rather than attend college (Murray, Vedder, and Matthew B. Crawford), or that since college teaches "few useful job skills," a degree, as the economist Bryan Caplan puts it, merely signals "to employers that graduates are smart, hardworking, and conformist" (Murray, Vedder, Crawford, and others too numerous to mention). Nor, as other critics have begun to argue, do I believe that a college degree has ceased to offer a good return on a young person's investment of time and money. As nearly every economist and journalist who has studied this manufactured controversy° has shown, college continues to pay off. Even those like me foolish enough to major in English or some other supposedly irrelevant humanities or fine-arts discipline still earn, on average, more than those with only a high-school degree, and more than enough to offset the costs of tuition and forgone earnings needed to earn a degree. Indeed, today the *starting* salary for someone with a degree in English ($37,800) is higher than the *average* income of all those, including older and experienced workers, with only a high-school degree ($32,000).

Yet we find ourselves in an unusual position. The advice we would offer

***manufactured controversy:*** that is, a controversy that has been made up or falsely created.

every halfway intelligent young person with a pulse—go to college—is not, I argue, counsel we can offer a whole generation of young people, let alone adults like those who might have enrolled in the Odyssey Project. An is ("Education pays") is not an ought ("Everyone ought to get an education"). Some people may escape poverty and low incomes through education, but a problem arises when education becomes the only escape route from those conditions—because that road will very quickly become bottlenecked. As the political scientist Gordon Lafer has written, "It is appropriate for every parent to hope that their child becomes a professional; but it is not appropriate for federal policy makers to hope that every American becomes one." As Bryan Caplan has also put it, "Going to college is a lot like standing up at a concert to see better. Selfishly speaking, it works, but from a social point of view, we shouldn't encourage it."

Unlike others who argue this point, however, my concern is not with the inefficiencies that come from everyone standing up to see better but, rather, with the injustices that result. That is, my concern is with those who cannot stand up, those who, because of lack of ability, lack of interest, or other barriers to entry, do not or cannot earn a college degree. Insisting that they really should is neither a wise nor a particularly humane solution to the problem those workers will encounter in the labor market.

30 Nor is it a particularly feasible one. The U.S. economy, despite claims to the contrary, will continue to produce more jobs that do not require a college degree than jobs that do. A college degree will not make those jobs pay any more than the pittance they currently do. As some of my colleagues from graduate school could confirm, a Ph.D. working as a bartender earns bartender wages, not a professor's salary. What *will* make those bartending and other jobs outside the professions pay something closer to a living wage°—if not a living wage itself—constitutes, to my mind, one of the major public-policy challenges of the 21st century. Education, however, is not the answer.

In terms of educational and economic policy, we may have even put the cart in front of the horse. As it stands, we seek to decrease inequality and poverty by improving educational enrollment, performance, and attainment. A good deal of evidence, however, suggests that we should do just the opposite. Only by first decreasing inequality and poverty might we then improve educational outcomes.

To be quite honest, though I recognize the incongruity° of a professor, of all people, confessing this, I care less about educational outcomes than I do about economic ones. I admit that background may play a part in this attitude. As I have said, during one or two rough patches, our family dropped into the ranks of the poor. From what I remember, which is more than I would like, I still cannot decide what was worst about it. Was it the persistent feelings of inferiority? Or the terrifying sense of insecurity? Either way, I am convinced that poverty and economic insecurity are ruinous, wicked. No one, least of all children, should have to suffer that fate. Yet over the last 30 years, more and more do. Next to this fact, education, while I have committed my life to it, matters far less than it otherwise would.

In any event, we need to cultivate a new modesty regarding education: to stop believing that it is a magic potion for the poor or for anyone else. Only after we've cleared the deck of those mistaken beliefs can we embark on a serious effort to fix the problems.

I do not regret starting the Odyssey Project, or the better part of my life that it occupied for the five years I remained involved with it. I met some extraordinary individuals. I came to know the community I lived in better

---

***living wage:*** the minimum income necessary to meet basic needs, including shelter, clothing, and food. It is important to note that in some circumstances, earning the minimum wage is not equivalent to earning a living wage because the minimum wage fails to enable a worker to have adequate shelter, clothing, and food.

***incongruity:*** the state of being inconsistent, not harmonious, or inappropriate.

than most academics do. I had some fascinating discussions with students whom I would not have otherwise had the chance to teach. Reading *Native Son*° with people who grew up on the South Side of Chicago or who still have family there is a different, and in many ways more rewarding, experience than reading it with students who have spent their lives avoiding those neighborhoods.

35 So too is reading *A Doll's House*° with women who have had husbands or boyfriends far more patronizing, and occasionally far more violent, than Torvald Helmer. Despite my doubts, too, the program did work as intended for a few—too few, but still, a few—people.

My association with the Odyssey Project also gave me a better, though by no means thorough, understanding of the lives of the poor and low-income people who struggle to make ends meet, who struggle to be in two places at once. People who are one crisis away—a job loss, an illness, a missed rent check—from having their lives upended, and people for whom more often than not that crisis comes. People of stunning intelligence, and people completely unprepared to benefit from whatever educational opportunities they might encounter. More than anything, though, my association with the Odyssey Project taught me that programs like it are neither necessary nor sufficient responses to the problems of poverty and economic inequality in the United States.

---

**Native Son:** Richard Wright's 1940 novel about Bigger Thomas, who lives in abject poverty on the South Side of Chicago. This influential novel questions the relationship between free will and conditioned response to societal expectations as far as African Americans at the time were concerned; in so doing, it explained the black/white racial divide in the United States as resulting from the conditions the dominant society had imposed on African Americans.

**A Doll's House:** 1879 play by Norwegian Henrik Ibsen in which the marriage between Torvald and Nora Helmer unravels as she comes to realize that she has been treated as a doll in a dollhouse, first by her father and now by her husband. As the play ends, Nora has decided to leave her husband, and she tries to explain to him that she must do so in order to discover who she is. He begs her to stay lest his reputation be ruined. As she puts her keys and wedding ring on the table and turns to leave, he begins to sob, completely unable to comprehend what is happening—to *him*. Nora exits, slamming the door. Although the play has been a favorite of supporters of women's rights since its first performance, Ibsen argued that he had not set out to write a play about this issue, but rather to write about the human condition and the process of self-discovery everyone needs to experience.

## RESPOND •

1. What arguments is Marsh making about the relationship between inequality and education in the United States? How does he distinguish his position from other common arguments about the degree to which education, especially higher education, can or cannot serve as a panacea for social ills in this or other countries?
2. What evidence does Marsh offer for his argument? Can you restate his argument, including the evidence, in the form of a Toulmin argument, as discussed in Chapter 7?

3. How convincing is the evidence Marsh offers for his argument? Why? What criteria can you use in evaluating the evidence he offers? How might readers with different value commitments evaluate his evidence? Why? What are the advantages and disadvantages of relying heavily on personal experience as evidence in the way that Marsh does?
4. This essay, based largely on personal experience, employs a common trope or figure of speech not discussed in Chapter 6, specifically, *protrepticus*, or "turning," in other words, a change of one's path (see especially paragraphs 15–24). This trope is, of course, found in all conversion narratives, whether the change involves accepting a new religion or philosophy (even if the new one is atheism or agnosticism) or rejecting an old one. What triggers Marsh's turning? How reasonable is it that someone with his life experience would never have entertained the doubts he comes to entertain? What might the fact that he had not entertained these doubts tell us about the power of the set of beliefs he comes to question?
5. In paragraph 31, Marsh summarizes the current state of the thinking of most Americans and then presents his argument:

   > As it stands, we seek to decrease inequality and poverty by improving educational enrollment, performance, and attainment. A good deal of evidence, however, suggests that we should do just the opposite. Only by first decreasing inequality and poverty might we then improve educational outcomes.

   Obviously, either perspective offers a proposal argument of the sort discussed in Chapter 12. Take a side in this debate, and **write an essay** in which you argue for one of these alternatives or the other. (Of course, you may wish to select some third course of action.) Whatever you propose, be sure to acknowledge other perspectives on the issue. You will almost surely need to do research in order to construct sound arguments. (Remember to consult Chapters 18–21 so that you can choose and use the sources you consult appropriately.)

# Making a Visual Argument: Inequality and the Occupy Movement

*The daily news in America for at least two months beginning in September 2011 was dominated by Occupy Wall Street. The movement's Web site (http://occupywallst.org) characterized it in this way in May 2012:*

> *Occupy Wall Street is a people-powered movement that began on September 17, 2011, in Liberty Square in Manhattan's Financial District, and has spread to over 100 cities in the United States and actions in over 1,500 cities globally. #ows is fighting back against the corrosive power of major banks and multinational corporations over the democratic process and the role of Wall Street in creating an economic collapse that has caused the greatest recession in generations. The movement is inspired by popular uprisings in Egypt and Tunisia and aims to fight back against the richest 1% of people that are writing the rules of an unfair global economy that is foreclosing on our future.*

*This selection comprises six visual arguments associated with the movement. Before discussing them, however, we'd like to note that there were other images and texts related to images that we'd hoped to use but could not get permission for. This situation is instructive for what it teaches us about new media and the changing nature of intellectual property.*

*Because the Occupy Movement was grassroots in nature, individuals posted photos and wrote blogs about what they saw happening. Groups of people also created ephemeral documents—documents not meant to endure—containing no information about who had taken photos or who had written specific texts; therefore, it was impossible to determine who had the authority to give permission to reprint these texts or images.*

*One set that was especially interesting involved photos of individuals holding up sheets of paper (often torn from a notebook) on which they'd written narratives about their own dire economic situations and the extent to which they thought the American society was one that offered economic opportunities. In many cases, the photos didn't include a clear image of the writer but only of the handwritten text. These photos were then printed on one side of five-by-seven-inch cards that had information about the Occupy movement on the other.*

*Opponents of the movement soon used a similar strategy, posting handwritten personal responses to the movement in various places. One such posting sparked a blog response that went viral: Max Udargo's October 12, 2011, "Open Letter to That 53% Guy" (www.udargo.com) was picked up by Daily Kos, a liberal political blog, and became the top political article reposted on Facebook in 2011. Despite our best efforts, we were unable to contact Mr. Udargo to seek his permission to reprint the posting, which contained Udargo's response to the image of the nameless "53% guy" and his handwritten narrative, which reads:*

> *I am a former Marine.*
> *I work two jobs.*
> *I don't have health insurance.*
> *I worked 60–70 hours a week for 8 years to pay my way through college.*
> *I haven't had 4 consecutive days off in over 4 years.*
> *But I don't blame Wall Street.*

*Suck it up you whiners.*
*I am the 53%.*
*God bless the USA!*

*(If you want to find out who the 53% are and what they represent, you won't have to Google very long to discover the source of their name as well as their response to Occupy.) Such arguments conducted through images and words—and often words as parts of images—characterize the public conversations about inequality in the America that began in new ways in the last few months of 2011.*

*Here, we present images from that period of a protestor in Miami who has taped a dollar bill across his mouth, dollar bills that have been altered (some might claim defaced) by a group that calls itself "Occupy George" (http://occupygeorge.com), and several photos of demonstrators who are being or have been sprayed with pepper spray. The use of pepper spray and the ways police sought to deal with and contain Occupy demonstrations were often topics of debate during these months, and images like the ones reproduced here were frequently reproduced in various contexts where those debates occurred. Interestingly, there seem to be no comparably iconic images of demonstrations that took place without necessary permits or acts of vandalism committed by some who participated in these demonstrations. Individuals or groups who labeled themselves anarchists, or individuals who are opposed to the notion of nation-states and are frequently willing to use violence to oppose governments of any sort, certainly participated in some Occupy demonstrations, and the possible links between anarchism and the Occupy movement were hotly contested, especially among liberals.*

*As you examine these images, reflect not only on them but also on the images you recall from this period and what they tell us about the nature of public debate in the United States.*

A Miami protester has taped a dollar bill on which he's written OCCUPY over his mouth on October 15, 2011, the first day of protests in Occupy Miami.

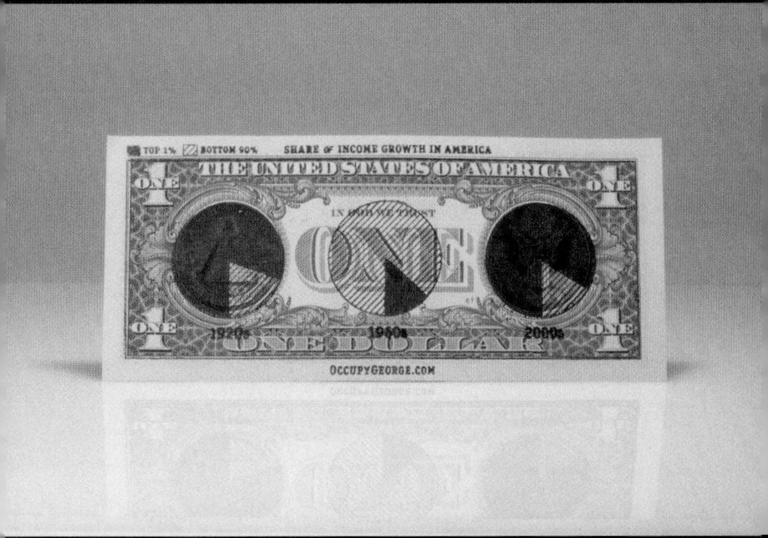

Occupy George is using a dollar bill to make a historical argument about inequality in the United States.

Here, Occupy George uses a dollar bill as the background for an argument about the relative pay for the average worker and the average CEO (chief executive officer) of a corporation.

Police in Portland, Oregon, using pepper spray against Elizabeth Nichols in the Occupy Portland "Day of Action" against the banks on November 17, 2011. In early 2012, charges against her were reduced, and much to her dismay and that of many of her supporters, her case was dismissed. Because the case was dismissed, arguments in court about what happened were precluded.

Seated demonstrators on the UC-Davis campus are sprayed with pepper spray by the campus police on November 19, 2011. Particularly because the demonstrators were seated, this incident gave rise to considerable debate.

Eighty-four-year-old Dorli Rainey, a longtime political activist and former mayoral candidate, was pepper-sprayed on November 15, 2011, while she participated in an Occupy Seattle demonstration. Following the event, Rainey was featured on several political talk shows.

## RESPOND •

1. What argument is each of the Occupy George dollar bills making? Why might supporters have chosen dollar bills as the medium with which to make their arguments?
2. Visit the Occupy George Web site (occupygeorge.com). How do the statements presented there help make the visual arguments printed in this section more concrete? How would you characterize the argument made by the Web site in terms of the arguments described in Chapters 8–12? In other words, what kinds of arguments are they? What evidence can you cite for your claims?
3. What are the similarities and differences in the images involving pepper spray? What arguments do these images make? Which is most effective in making its argument? Why? Why might such images provoke a great deal of debate in American society? Should they? Why or why not?
4. Visit the Web site of We Are the 99% (wearethe99percent.us). How would you characterize the arguments made by the Web site in terms of the arguments described in Chapters 8–12? What evidence can you cite for your claim? Do different parts of the Web site function as different kinds of argument? Why, in particular, might the site display such a large number of visual arguments? What does the Occupy movement assume about the power of such arguments?
5. **Write a rhetorical analysis** of a visual argument from the Occupy movement that you find especially powerful, perhaps because you experienced it as arresting, persuasive, or repugnant. (Remember that arguments you find repugnant are still succeeding in evoking a strong response, thereby demonstrating their power.) Obviously, you'll need to include a copy of your argument (or a link to it) in your analysis. (See Chapter 6 for a discussion of rhetorical analyses.)

▼ *Jonathan Chait (1972– ) writes for* New York *magazine, where this blog posting first appeared in early October 2011. Despite its title, the magazine's articles often focus on issues outside the city; its Web site is considered one of the most innovative of those associated with print publications. Chait describes himself as a "liberal hawk," that is, someone who is a fierce advocate of liberal positions. At the same time, he is quick to point out contradictions he sees among thinkers anywhere along the political spectrum. In this blog posting, he is doing just that. While he is critical of Kevin Williamson, deputy managing editor of the conservative* National Review, *he is likewise critical of the collective statement from the Occupy Wall Street protesters in Zuccotti Park in New York City. As you read this selection, pay attention to how Chait attacks those he accuses of making illogical claims.*

# Steve Jobs, Occupy Wall Street, and the Capitalist Ideal

JONATHAN CHAIT

The Occupy Wall Street movement has reopened a fundamental debate about capitalism and the role of government, and the death of Steve Jobs° clarifies some of the questions at stake. For the right, Jobs and Apple serve as the handiest metaphor for the genius of the private sector (and the failure of government). Mitt Romney likes to wave around his iPhone, a metaphor for capitalism, and accuse President Obama of employing a "pay phone strategy," a metaphor for government.

*National Review*° deputy managing editor Kevin Williamson likewise counterposes° the brilliance of Apple with the ugliness of government:

> I was down at the Occupy Wall Street protest today, and never has the divide between the iPhone world and the politics world been so clear: I saw a bunch of people very well-served by their computers and telephones (very often Apple products) but undeniably shortchanged by our government-run cartel° education system. And the tragedy for them—and for us—is that they will spend their energy trying to expand the sphere of the ineffective, hidebound,° rent-seeking, unproductive political world, giving the Barney Franks° and Tom DeLays° an even stronger whip hand over the Steve Jobses and Henry Fords.° And they—and we—will be poorer for it.

*Steve Jobs (1955–2011):* American inventor and businessman who is given credit for the personal computer revolution; he was co-founder, chairman, and CEO of Apple. He was known for his perfectionism; it is often said that he had an uncanny ability to imagine high-tech products that, once consumers saw them, they could not live without.

**National Review:** magazine published every two weeks and known for its conservative stance on issues related to politics and culture.

*counterpose:* to contrast or set up as opposites.

*cartel:* in business, an agreement among companies to control prices, marketing, and production; here, public education is being compared to a cartel that has no competition. The word almost always carries negative connotations.

*hidebound:* inflexible, conservative, oriented toward the past; another word that almost always carries negative connotations.

*Barney Frank (1940– ):* U.S. Democratic representative from Massachusetts from 1981 to 2013; in 1987, Frank announced that he was gay. Because of his seniority, intelligence, and quick wit, he was seen as wielding great power in the House.

*Tom DeLay (1947– ):* former U.S. Republican representative from Texas, serving from 1984 to 2006. He served as House majority leader from 2003 until 2005 but had to resign because of charges of criminal money laundering. He was convicted and sentenced to three years in prison in 2011, but in early 2012, at the time this book was written, he was out on bail.

*Henry Ford (1863–1947):* founder of the Ford Motor Company and creator of the automobile that bears his name. His innovations in auto manufacturing altered American industry in profound ways.

*absolutist:* here, someone who subscribes to the "purest" form of a way of thinking and who opposes any notion of compromise.

*Occupy Wall Street protesters in New York City uploading material after a march in early October 2011.*

> And to the kids camped out down on Wall Street: Look at the phone in your hand. Look at the rat-infested subway. Visit the Apple Store on Fifth Avenue, then visit a housing project in the South Bronx. Which world do you want to live in?

Personally, I want to live in a world in which it is possible to ride the subway down to the Apple Store. Preferably without stepping over the bodies of people dying of easily treatable diseases for lack of insurance.

Is that such a difficult concept? Apparently it is. The liberal vision of modified capitalism has always been flanked on both sides by a right and a left that agree that capitalism is indivisible. The socialists and the free market absolutists° agree that it's all or nothing—if you object to the worst features of capitalism, you object to all of capitalism, and we must keep it all or scrap it.

It's currently an open question whether Occupy Wall Street will ultimately 5
take the form of an anti-capitalist movement. There is a long, grim history of left-wing movements being hijacked by their most radical elements, which are usually the most organized and fanatical. For one example of this hijacking,

take a gander at this "collective statement" from the protestors in Zuccotti Park. It's filled with Marxist drivel.° ("They have used the military and police force to prevent freedom of the press. . . . They purposefully keep people misinformed and fearful through their control of the media. . . . They have perpetuated colonialism at home and abroad.") The point is that corporations are responsible for all the world's ills, and the only conclusion is that we must do away with them all.

***drivel:*** literally, saliva flowing from the side of the mouth; figuratively, as here, claims that are foolish or senseless.

On the other hand, the intellectual influences most apparent in the movement are those of advocates of regulated capitalism, like Joe Stiglitz.° There is a reason the movement is called "Occupy Wall Street," not "Occupy Main Street" or "Occupy Silicon Valley." It is no doubt because most of the participants, or sympathizers, understand that Wall Street is not the same thing as free enterprise°—that it is one element that, unlike Apple, poses a unique threat to the functioning of the free marketplace.

***Joe Stiglitz (1943– ):*** Nobel Prize–winning economist and professor at Columbia University. Stiglitz also served as cabinet member under President Bill Clinton and as senior vice president and chief economist of the World Bank. Stiglitz has often been critical of aspects of how globalization has been managed, including by institutions like his former employer, the World Bank, and the International Monetary Fund.

If you define the problem as "corporations," then you lose the capacity to make these distinctions. For an example of this same analytic trap on the right, return to another bit from Williamson's *National Review* essay:

> The beauty of capitalism—the beauty of the iPhone world as opposed to the world of politics—is that that question does not matter one little bit. Whatever drove Jobs, it drove him to create superior products, better stuff at better prices. Profits are not deductions from the sum of the public good, but the real measure of the social value a firm creates. Those who talk about the horror of putting profits over people make no sense at all. The phrase is without intellectual content. Perhaps you do not think that Apple, or Goldman Sachs,° or a professional sports enterprise, or an internet pornographer actually creates much social value; but markets are very democratic—everybody gets to decide for himself what he values.

***free enterprise:*** economic system dominant in the Western world and characterized by wage labor; competitive (and unfettered) markets; private ownership of goods, including the means of production; and the ability for individuals to accumulate capital.

Hold it right there. You see what he did? He made capitalism indivisible again. We were nodding our heads at the way Apple and sports teams and Internet porn fulfills the basic free-market model, offering consumers a wanted good for the market-supplied price, and Williamson snuck Goldman Sachs onto the list. The whole liberal argument is that Goldman Sachs is not like those other things. It is not a case of one person selling a gadget to another person, with nobody else impacted. It creates externalities.° One person sells a financial product to another person, and soon we have systemic risk° affecting hundreds of millions of people who are not party to the transaction.

***Goldman Sachs:*** American multinational banking and securities firm that has been the subject of great scrutiny and criticism since the beginning of the economic downturn in 2008.

*externalities:* In contrast to exchanges where both parties benefit and where all costs are calculated into pricing, externalities are costs or benefits that are not included in the price. They may be negative (a manufacturer who creates pollution causing problems for nearby neighbors may not be forced to compensate them or to include the costs of the pollution in the price of goods manufactured) or positive (when all children are vaccinated, the health of the community as a whole may improve).

*systemic risk:* that is, a risk to the entire economic system.

That is why we have millions of jobless, and millions more struggling to survive. There are measures to address that problem, which would also allow corporations to reap enormous profits. Will Occupy Wall Street, as a movement, understand this?

**RESPOND•**

1. What argument is Chait making about Occupy Wall Street at this point in the movement's history, that is, early October 2011? What argument is he making about conservative thinkers like Mitt Romney and Kevin Williamson? How would you summarize Chait's position with respect to the issues he discusses?
2. How does Chait carve out a space for his position by pointing out what he sees as the shortcomings of others' positions? Locate specific places in the text where he does this.
3. Chait mentions Romney's use of a metaphor involving iPhones and pay phones. Unpack this metaphor; that is, explain exactly what two things are being compared literally and metaphorically. Why might Romney speak of a "pay phone strategy" instead of, say, a "land-line strategy"? How effective do you find this metaphor? What are its limits or limitations? (Chapter 13 offers a discussion of metaphors.)
4. Like many bloggers, Chait is quick to employ lengthy quotations from other sources and to make his point by using sarcasm and humor. How effective are these practices in blogging? Why? Why are they generally less effective—or even impermissible—in academic writing? (Chapter 6 on rhetorical analysis and 16 on academic arguments may help you with this question.)
5. Building on question 4, respond to Chait's blog posting by **creating an academic argument** that engages the issues he raises in some way. You may wish to pick up the strand of his posting on the Occupy Wall Street movement, focusing on whether its supporters were initially or ultimately anti-capitalists. You could also accept or critique Chait's assessment of corporations and their ideal role in a capitalist society like our own. Finally, you may choose to treat some other aspect of Chait's argument. (Chapter 16 offers information on academic arguments.)

*Mac McClelland is an award-winning journalist who writes most frequently about issues of human rights for* Mother Jones, *where this selection first appeared in November/December 2011.* Mother Jones, *a magazine since 1970 named for Mary Harris Jones (1837–1930), an American community and labor organizer, and now a Web site, is likely the most widely read liberal publication in the country. In this lengthy essay, McClelland seeks to capture the consequences of the economic downturn for friends of hers and people she meets in Ohio. The introductory text of the essay, "Wherein I go home . . . ," cues readers into the fact that she is in some sense parodying novels of earlier periods that often had chapter subtitles reporting the events recounted therein and that presented daily life in great detail. As you read, try to determine McClelland's argument, which she does not state explicitly.*

# Goodbye, Columbus°: Ohio's War on the Middle Class

MAC McCLELLAND

*Wherein I go home, watch public servants get axed, visit the warehouse of unbearable sorrow, hang with jobless thirtysomethings living in abandoned homes, and consider whether my generation is flat-out screwed.*

The decor of Erin and Anthony Rodriguez's guest room could really only happen in the United States. In fact, a European did lay eyes on it one time, and his superior brow furrowed instantly with disbelief as he said, "What . . . is THAT?" It isn't just the powder-pinkness of the third bedroom in their Gahanna, Ohio, home. It's more the hot pink stars stenciled along the ceiling border, and that between them alternate the words "Katie" and "an American Girl." Erin, who's 30, Ohio born and raised, Ohio for life, can't

**Goodbye, Columbus:** title of a 1959 collection of stories by Philip Roth, which became the basis for a 1969 comedy movie starring Ali MacGraw and Richard Benjamin. In the movie, the character played by Benjamin, a college student from a working-class background, falls in love with a wealthier character played by MacGraw. Much of the film deals with issues of class differences and assimilation within the Jewish community since both are Jewish. In the end, the relationship doesn't work out, and some read the title as evidence that Benjamin's character has said good-bye to the world represented by MacGraw's character and her family—a world that is much more affluent and assimilated than the one he is from.

decide herself if she should be excited—I mean, it's not *not* funny—or mildly embarrassed to show it to people. Nobody named Katie lives here. This paint scheme was left by the previous owners. On the early June afternoon when I drop my suitcase by the bed, Erin exclaims, "You can be our Katie!"

We've been roommates before. But that was back when we went to Ohio State, from which we graduated almost 10 years ago. Now Erin has a grown-up job as a public school teacher and a husband who's a public information specialist for the Ohio agency that keeps tabs on local utilities and makes sure they don't go all Enron° on consumers. They have a baby, Jocelyn, who is extremely cute and well behaved, as well as a gray cat named Princess Vespa and a black cat named Barack Obama. For a long time, my contact with Erin has been limited mostly to occasional phone check-ins during which we brief each other on, like, how adulthood is going. Now I'm taking up temporary residence here not as a fun former roomie but as a reporter. I write Erin a rent check for a third of the mortgage—$430. She says she's really happy to see me, even though she knows the grown-up reporter reason I'm here is that she and her husband are state employees, so something bad is bound to happen to them in the next month. That $430, she tells me, might make an important difference in their finances soon.

If the sign at the edge of town is to be believed, Gahanna is one of the Top 100 Places to Live. The Columbus suburb is a lot like the Cleveland suburb I grew up in. Green. Sprawly. Solidly middle-class, chock-full of shopping centers. And Erin and Anthony's house is a lot like a lot of houses around it, a modest split-level with a big front yard and a deck in the back. In the wedding pictures on the walls, Erin's got short blond hair. Currently, her locks are chin length and closer in color to the chocolate corduroy couch on which we sit while, on the floor before us, Jocelyn makes herself the center of a four-foot radius of toys. Erin's beaming in the photos, and that's pretty much what she usually looks like, pretty teeth bared, shiny cheeks. She still feels warm and open even as her face creases with anxiety and she says, "When we bought our house, we basically wiped out our savings." The only reason there's any money left in the bank at all is because of the rebate from President Obama's first-time homebuyer's credit program. Because the house, like most people's houses, isn't paid for, and neither is Anthony's car, like many people's cars, the prospect that Anthony might have only three more paychecks coming is making Erin "not fine," though she's "trying to be fine." When we were in college, we all had these fabulous plans. Or at least plans to be supersecure once we found careers. To make a living and then . . . live. Erin blames the governor for her doubts now. She calls him some unsavory names.

A lot of people are doing that. A couple of weeks ago, a poll showed the approval ratings of John Kasich, the newly elected Republican governor, at 33 percent. Once upon a time Kasich was a United States congressman, before he left in 2001 to become a managing director at Lehman Brothers, where he worked until it imploded and destroyed a bunch of lives in 2008. On the side, he hosted his own show on Fox News, as well as frequently guest-hosting *The O'Reilly Factor* and appearing on the Sean Hannity vehicles.

***go all Enron:*** The allusion is to Enron, a Houston-based energy company that, prior to its bankruptcy in 2001 resulting from accounting fraud, was much beloved of investors and hailed as one of the country's most innovative and successful corporations. Today, Enron symbolizes the worst excesses of corporate corruption and fraud.

He took office in January, and his approval ratings have been abysmal since March, something to do, no doubt, with the release of his proposed budget for fiscal years 2012–13.

5 To Erin's specific dismay, the governor's plan slashes $3.1 billion from an estimated $58.8 billion state budget largely by cutting funding to city governments and services. Anthony's state agency, the Ohio Consumers' Counsel (OCC)—which advocates for customers in complaints, regulatory hearings, and court cases involving utility companies—is slated to lose 51 percent. The Department of Education loses 10.2 percent. A local think tank estimates that 51,000 state jobs are at stake. Local unions are panicking that the public employees who remain will have little control over their own futures, since Kasich effectively killed collective bargaining in a bill called SB 5 shortly after he took office. This is the manifestation of his campaign promise to "shine up the state." In one of his campaign videos, he says that his parents used to say, "Johnny, make sure the place that you were is a little better off because of the fact that you were there." He won the 2010 election, barely, on a job creation platform. His budget is called "The Jobs Budget."

But for the differing accents and college football allegiances, this could be Florida, or Michigan, or Wisconsin. They've all got their own new Republican governors facing protests over public-sector job cuts or voter ID bills or union dismantling or destruction of public transportation projects or unemployment benefits. And those governors all have plummeting approval ratings.

Erin and Jocelyn have been going to these protests in Columbus. Neither one of us was really an activist or even especially politically minded in college, but lately, a phone conversation that starts about these amazing ice cream bars ends with news about what Kasich is doing or some kind of fretting, like she's doing right now. With the news that Anthony will likely lose his job, she's panicked that she missed the open enrollment period for her health insurance plan because she assumed, with the faith that professionals tend to default to when they're employed, that no one in her family was about to be jobless. All three Rodriguezes are currently on Anthony's insurance, because it's much better, and cheaper. Luckily, it's not too late to switch. By the end of the week, she'll drive to the appropriate office to drop off the paperwork. And then she'll cry in the car for an hour while Jocelyn's asleep in the backseat, which she'll confess to me when I tell her she's handling her "freaking out" well.

Erin recognizes that she could do a lot worse; if her nightmare of losing her house ever did come close to a reality, her parents would likely rescue her, she knows, as much as she would hate to have to take their money. But her friend, for example, who had a baby at the same time, has been surviving with her husband on his teaching-assistant salary only because they fell into a situation with free rent. Now they have to move, and they have no idea what they're going to do. And a parent of several of Erin's former students had to choose between sending his kid to college and working, since the only job he could get didn't pay enough to cover tuition—and financial aid would be available only if he were unemployed. Erin acknowledges that having to downgrade to a less-great health insurance plan is the sort of thing the upwardly mobile liberals of our generation like to refer to on the internet as "white people problems." A layoff might knock her back an income class or two. But not everyone she knows has a spare income class to fall.

Now, Erin eyes her 11-month-old when she says, "Thank God I have a job. And a job with insurance. Anthony's applying for jobs like crazy, but he's not getting any bites."

That's what he does when he gets home. It's late, 10
almost dark out, at a time of year when the days are longest. There was a public meeting tonight about an impending rate hike from American Electric Power, the local utility, and he was there to look out for the OCC

and consumers. Still, after he arrives in a tie and glasses only to get back to work on his laptop, he continuously flashes a grin that demands to be described as toothy. At his work, people are getting ready to move their desks because the office is consolidating from two floors to one; the state Senate has proposed softening the OCC's cuts from 51 to 34 percent, but a lot of layoffs are still on the table. No one knows exactly what will happen when the budget is reconciled and signed at the end of the month, and right now Anthony is working on a freelance consulting project and looking for more of those and another job while the rest of us watch reality TV.

"We're in that mode," Anthony says of his 81 coworkers, shaking his head, "where we're like, 'What the hell are we going to do?'" And he can fit in only a few minutes of searching and overtime, because Jocelyn misses him and won't stop pointing at him, so he picks her up to pace the carpet with her head against his shoulder, singing a soothing little song.

At 4:41 in the morning, Barack Obama finds his cat-magic way through a closed door and enters my bedroom. The Rodriguez house is as dark as the sky. But within an hour, lights are on, Jocelyn's burbling, and Anthony's walking around in shorts. As I am somewhat unaccustomed to this waking time, I'm looking sad about it under the kitchen fluorescents, I guess, since Anthony walks in and laughs at me.

It's one of Erin's last days of teaching before school lets out for the summer. It's a 40-minute drive out to her rural district, plus a quick stop to drop Jocelyn off at day care. Out here, there are a lot of long, empty roads and farmland. Out here, the public schools spend nearly 20 percent less per student than the national average. It's so hot outside that a school in a city nearby actually had to shut down the other day when its air conditioning broke, but Erin's middle school never has had AC. Her seventh- and eighth-graders are restless, sweating. She spends even more time than usual vying for their attention, especially in the computer class that has access to internet games.

I'm exhausted just watching her by third period, but she loves, loves, loves her job as a writing teacher, she tells me when we lock the door between classes so she can pump breast milk. Still, she'd prefer to be a stay-at-home morn to Jocelyn for a while. She's heartbroken every time she leaves her at day care, maybe even more than she is over the prospect of becoming a single-income family.

Actually, she's not totally free from worrying about 15
becoming a no-income family; the Ohio Education Association says Kasich's budget will cost 10,000 public education jobs—nearly 5 percent of such jobs in the state. Already, Erin's school recently laid off a couple of teachers and cut a few more to half time. While her salary after eight years of teaching would normally be protected by a long-standing experience- and education-based pay schedule, a provision in the budget would require many schools—including hers—to move to a more merit-based pay system. Which sounds great and all, but what it means is this: Unless organizers get 231,147 signatures to put a repeal of anticollective-bargaining SB 5 on the ballot in November, and then voters indeed vote to repeal it, her union will have far less power to help her if her cash-strapped school district decides she should make some arbitrary number of thousands of dollars less.

It's not like she's in it for the money. American middle school teachers work more hours than those in any other leading industrialized nation except one, but they rank near the bottom in terms of pay. Erin knew that going in, but still.

"How many of you have summer jobs?" Erin asks her afternoon batch of about 30 eighth-graders. Lots of them put their hands up. When she asks them how many have jobs because they're working for family farms or businesses, most of those with their hands up keep them raised. Job growth in this county is −0.16 percent. One 14-year-old without those kinds of family connections explains he's been looking, he's looking, but no, he doesn't have a job. When I ask him why, he pauses, surprised for a second, then says, "No jobs to be had."

When Erin and I were in college, I worked summers for a moving company. Before and after jobs, my coworkers and I hung around the cavernous warehouse full of cardboard boxes, the smell of heavy paper landing in the back of our throats in a thick and lingering way.

My college girlfriend now works in a warehouse, too, as a supervisor—in a quieter, sadder warehouse, where people ship merchandise for big online companies everyone has heard of but that can't be named here. The company running it, which I also can't name, is a temp agency that provides staffing for a nationwide logistics contractor that handles getting those internet purchases from their origins—many of them Chinese factories—to people's doorsteps.

20 My ex's name is not Susie, but let's call her that so we don't get her in trouble. The first stop on the tour she gave me of her workplace: workers standing at tables, taking items out of a bulk box and putting them into smaller boxes with shipping labels on them. And . . . that's pretty much it. For efficiency purposes, every step of every process here has been broken down and separated out so that almost everyone does the exact same motion over and over. Like the people at the next stop, who are standing at tables and putting the labels on the boxes. Over and over. Sweating.

"It's hot in here," I say unhelpfully. It's 90 degrees outside, and the Midwestern humidity concentrates itself in this giant metal-and-cement cube. "Don't you guys have air conditioning?" "We do, but it's controlled by the big guys in the suits." It is not, Susie adds, equally unpleasant for everyone. We pass by the loading docks, where a semi is backed up to the open door. A guy standing inside the cramped metal trailer bed catches taped-up, ready-to-ship boxes off the conveyor belt and stacks them in the truck. "That job sucks," she says. She shakes her head. "There's no circulation in there." She says in the winter, everybody in the warehouse wears hats and coats because it's freezing inside.

The workers on this shift all make about $9 an hour. That's a dollar less than I made at the moving company when I started there in 1998, but it's a lot more than the state minimum wage of $7.40 and way more than nothing, which is what 8.6 percent of Ohio workers currently earn.

These workers are all hired as temps by Susie's company. If they make it 90 days, they have the opportunity, in theory, if there's an opening, to become full employees of the logistics company, which means better benefits and about an extra dollar an hour. It has been six months since the logistics company graduated someone here from temp to employee status. At one of the other locations Susie manages, no one has been hired as a real employee for two years. One of the workers in this warehouse has been a temp for a year and a half.

After we walk past workers stuffing inflated plastic air pockets in boxes and a guy continuously taping shut the bottoms of just-made cartons, we go to Susie's office. "Hold on, I gotta fire somebody real quick," she says, picking up the phone. She calls a man who's been working for her for two months. She's sorry, she tells him, but she has to let him go because one of the supervisors caught him talking on the floor. The man, who she thinks is in his late 40s or early 50s, protests that he only asked a new guy where he was from. That's just not the culture, Susie tells him. You know the rules. The logistics company sets them, and she has no choice but to enforce them.

25 It does say in the new-employee handout that there are no personal conversations allowed on the warehouse floor. Also, no cell phones are permitted. Like a high school teacher, Susie has a pile of phones she's confiscated in a plastic bowl on her desk. Two sick days are allotted per year, and workers must be excused to take them without penalty; after that, the temp is terminated, doctor's note or no. Every temp is

allowed one 30-minute break per day, and it must be taken on company premises. Every temp is required to have an ID badge. The cost of this badge, more than an hour's worth of wages, is deducted from the temp's first paycheck.

I haven't finished the orientation packet when Susie picks up the phone to hear instructions from another supervisor that I can tell are bad news for a worker. "You're not really about to fire somebody else, are you?" I ask.

"Yeah."

"You just fired somebody less than 10 minutes ago."

"Yeah, but he's been taking too many breaks."

"Are you kidding? Is anybody going to ask him 30
why he's taking breaks? Maybe he's sick."

"No, they said he's been doing it all week. He's a bigger dude, so they think he's doing it"—the break room and the bathroom are in the air-conditioned part of the warehouse where the suits have offices—"because it's too hot for him on the floor."

Later, when I tell my father about this, he groans. Coincidentally, he works with the CEOs of logistics companies sometimes.

"Somebody did studies and spreadsheets and crunched those numbers," he says, "and figured out that the cheapest way to get that job done is to treat people like that." Which is important, because "the profit margins on those contracts are razor thin." Naturally. A lot of the internet retailers' merchandise is nearly worthless—Ice Princess Star-Shaped Ice Cube Tray with Straws, anthropomorphic° stuffed bacon toys—and is sold for nearly nothing, often with free or reduced-price shipping.

"When I was a kid working in a warehouse, I made $10 an hour," my father says.

That can't be right, I tell him. As proof that he's 35
mistaken, I point out that that's the same wage warehouses pay now.

"Exactly," he says. "That's the problem. The cost of living has gone way up, but wages have just been"—and here he makes sort of a Tupperware-closing sound—"locked in." In 1980, he got his first professional job with a high school diploma in Cleveland for $28,000 a year. In 2007, I got my first professional job with a master's degree in San Francisco for $27,000. A hundred dollars in my pocket today was the equivalent of $274 in his then. "And wages are exactly the same." It's not always true, of course, that the actual wages for the same job are actually the same. But it is true that in 2010 the average full-time male worker earned $47,715. In 1980, after adjusting for inflation, he earned $46,889.

"When you were six, I was driving a brand new Chevy station wagon and paying $125 a month," he says. "I remember seeing Cadillac commercials on TV saying, 'Drive away today with little money down and $450 a month,' and I remember thinking, 'I'll never be able to afford that.' And today that's a totally common car payment. We lived in a three-bedroom condo with two full baths for $280 a month. Nothing"—except the kind of crap boxed up in Susie's warehouse—"is cheaper now than it was then."

My father did ultimately lease a string of Cadillacs when I was older. Now he drives a Lexus SUV. Now he works at a firm that companies hire to headhunt the managers and VPs and CEOS they need, generally people in the $130,000 range but often much more. At the moment, my father has been tapped by a company to find the right candidate for a position that pays $600,000. Last year he placed someone who made $1.4 million annually, and another who made $1.5 mil. He bills enough that at the office, where I've had occa-

***anthropomorphic:*** in the shape of humans.

sion to use the nap room, his is one of the faces etched in bronze on the plaques for people who've earned the firm a million or more.

"You know, you used to be able to survive blue collar," he says. "Now, the blue-collar guy, they just crush the life out of him. It's very depressing." Unemployment has doubled since the beginning of the recession, and home equity has fallen by more than a third, but Wall Street profits are up more than 700 percent. Profits at his firm, which is part of a global group with more than 4,000 employees, have remained steady. "Recessions," as my father sometimes puts it, "don't affect people like me."

40 It's June 16, the day after Erin's birthday, and even from inside my pink room, I can hear the stress in her voice as she says into the phone, "Why are you yelling at me?"

When she slumps to the floor in the hallway outside my door, she tells me Anthony lost his job. The budget is still being reconciled in committee, but even the best-case version slashes OCC funding by more than 30 percent. And the cut looks mostly like a favor to utility companies, rather than a money-saving measure; the OCC isn't funded out of the state's general revenue fund but rather via a surcharge on utility companies. It's one of several exciting bits of a non-cost-cutting agenda slipped into the cost-cutting budget, which also, for example, makes it extremely difficult to get an abortion. Anthony has been given two weeks' notice. After that, their income will be cut in half.

Erin and I frown quietly at each other for a while. "How are you doing?" I ask.

"I don't know."

Jocelyn crawls across her knees.

45 "What are we gonna do, monkey?" Erin asks her, then, with effort, puts on a googoo voice. "I'm going to have to start entering you in pageants."

When Anthony comes home, there's a save-the-date card on the dining room table. Erin calls his attention to it, says Kristi and Scott are getting married. The Rodriguezes wouldn't have to travel. But they'd have to bring a present, and Anthony begins to sigh heavily, and Erin says quickly, "We don't have to go; we don't have to talk about it now," at the same time that he says, "Now's not the time." Tonight, while he works on his portfolio, to use in interviews "if I ever get one," he dips into the bottle of Johnnie Walker Green Label someone bought them for their wedding.

At the Columbus Metropolitan Library a few days later, there's a career workshop courtesy of Ohio State University's Office of Continuing Education, which doesn't restrict its job services to recent alumni, or even to alumni at all. "A lot of the people I'm working with have been laid off or find their field is shrinking," adviser Jeff Robek tells the audience. In 2008, librarians became overwhelmed with requests for job search assistance. So now all of CML's 20 branches run assistance programs. For as long as is feasible, anyway: Ohio libraries are in line for a 5 percent cut in Kasich's budget, in addition to the 30 percent they lost under the previous governor, while demand for services went up more than 20 percent during the same period. CML's website is the second most visited in the whole county, and the Job Help Center page is one of the most visited within it. As Robek speaks, yet another presentation is going on in a different conference room, about LinkedIn. Just before that, there was a volunteer available to help guide people through online applications. "I work with a lot of older job seekers," Robek says to a crowd ranging from twenty-somethings to the AARP° set. He is most perfectly Midwestern, with clean manners and khakis. "Fifty-plus, sixty-plus."

***AARP (American Association of Retired Persons):*** an interest group with membership open to anyone over 50 who pays annual dues; it is one of the most powerful lobbying groups in the country.

In the middle of this Monday afternoon, Robek warns us that it's a hirer's market: "With the job market as tight as it is right now, employers are picky." He has a slide with statistics reinforcing the adage° that it's not what you know, but who you know: 70 percent of jobs come from networking. Only 11 percent of people land a position through staffing agencies, 5 percent through sending resumes, and 14 percent through advertised jobs. The latter is how Anthony has been applying with increased fervor. The other day he had an interview, his first after sending out dozens of applications. Though he was lucky to get that far with 150 total applicants, he's still up against 11 other interviewees. He put on a purple shirt, and I complimented him on it. "I don't like to be bland," he said.

The experienced laid-off like Anthony, plus the "encore career" crowd, which seems to be a euphemism for professionals who are old but can't afford to retire, are creating challenges for the branch of Ohio State's career offices that tries to place another huge population: OSU graduates. Stephanie Ford, the director of the university's Arts and Sciences Career Services Office, explains to me that the shrinking number of jobs and swelling number of applicants are "a double whammy" for Ohio State's 6,702 graduating seniors. "Overall," she says, "it's harder to find students employment in their field" than it was when I graduated 10 years ago. I can't tell if I feel worse for them, for myself and my fellow 2002 graduates who might be competing with them, for the warehouse workers whose jobs they might be forced to take because they can't get "real" jobs, or for the encore career people who are up against the lot of us but have more responsibilities, probably less energy, and the handicap of cultural ageism. Christ.

According to Robek, there used to be a general 50
rule in job searching: For every $10,000 in annual salary earned, it took one month of looking. I schedule an advising session with him, and he explains that nobody has fingered the standard for the new economic order yet, but anecdotally, what used to take 3 to 6 months often now takes 6 to 12. "Or even longer sometimes!" he says.

Given the state of the journalism industry, statistically it would surprise no one if I got laid off. Indeed, fairly recently, Robek advised a local journalist alum who was about my age. He had worked in media for years but lost his job due to cutbacks. He searched and searched for work. Committed to staying a reporter, in the end, Robek tells me, he moved to DC and took an unpaid internship. This is a terrible story, and at this point in the economy and the industry, I have concerns about whether I could even compete for that internship. If the most recent batch of interns at my own magazine is any indication, college graduates are listening to the advice people like Ford give them about going up against people like me: Build rock-solid resumes. Among them, *Mother Jones'* eight interns speak Farsi, French, Hebrew, Italian, Russian, Spanish, and Thai and have worked at PBS's *Frontline*—two of them—NPR, NBC, *New York Press*, the *Miami Herald, Washington Monthly,*° *The Nation,*° *Sierra,*° *Bangkok*

---

***adage:*** a common saying generally accepted as true.

**Washington Monthly:** bimonthly magazine devoted to politics and government that takes a moderate- to left-leaning stance.

**The Nation:** a left-leaning weekly magazine focusing on culture and politics.

**Sierra:** the magazine of the Sierra Club, a grassroots environmental organization.

*Post,*° the *American Prospect,*° the ACLU,° the Federal Trade Commission, and for the Special Inspector General for Iraq Reconstruction.

"If the field you're working in has no opportunities, it might be time to find something else you're passionate about," Robek tells me. A career compatibility chart shows me to have some important values for moving to France and becoming a goat farmer—tradition, practicality, common sense—but to be lacking in crucial skills like mechanical competence. Robek says that to find a job in a new field, I'd need to do a lot of information gathering, talking to current professionals about what it's really like before stalking sites like Monster and LinkedIn to try to find a way in on the ground level. Which, as it does for many of Robek's clients, would likely involve going back to school, especially since I very pragmatically° spent two years of my life obtaining a master's degree in fine arts. In an employer's market, Robek emphasizes, employers can demand exactly whatever they want.

Back at the Rodriguezes', I'm not sure how long I've been sitting on my bed staring down an encroaching panic when voices call up from the family room downstairs.

"Katie!" they are yelling. It's time for the weekly family tradition of watching *MasterChef.* Erin and I will gently attempt and fail to distract Jocelyn from pulling the cord out of Anthony's laptop ("Could you not, uh," Anthony will say, waving her baby fingers away, and when she makes a mad-baby face, apologize: "I know. I'm sorry. But I'm kinda trying to find a job.") or throwing pieces of his portfolio on the floor or taking pages of a job description he's studying in each hand and repeatedly slamming them together. Anthony announces he's just been rejected for a job he applied for—at Ohio State, as it happens—without even making it to the interview stage. Susie calls and says he can work for her if he gets desperate. She's hired five of her friends straight out of college to work that shit warehouse job while they struggle to find something they went to school for. Though it isn't much, it is still a favor. She has applications from hundreds of people who want it; "I could fire every person in here right now" without costing her bosses a dime of lost profits, she told me when I visited. There's no need for the logistics clients to invest in a better or more sustainable work culture. Quite literally, her workers are as disposable as the products they're shipping.

I'm not too young to remember Cleveland as a 55
place of industrial productivity. Or rather, I remember the transition between that time and now, when a lot of those factories were getting shut down, when a laid-off steel worker started yelling at me after I knocked on his door to collect for some nonprofit. Now when I come home my father shows me big blank spots on the bank of the Cuyahoga River where they tore down an entire entertainment district, a thriving strip of restaurants and bars where I used fake IDs. The population implosion that revved back up again a decade ago hasn't stopped. The city's down to its lowest number of people since 1900.

The Cleveland neighborhood my sister lives in has its own abandonment issues. After I drive north from

---

**Bangkok Post:** the English-language newspaper published daily in Bangkok, Thailand.

**American Prospect:** monthly political magazine that takes liberal perspectives on issues.

***ACLU (American Civil Liberties Union):*** a nonpartisan group dedicated to protecting the Constitution; though it is nonpartisan, many conservatives see it as having a liberal bias because of the causes it has traditionally supported.

***pragmatically:*** behaving in a practical manner.

Columbus to visit her in her new place, she tells me to look for the rusted-out couch frame on the porch. It's there to keep her pit bull from wandering out into the yard, Jessica says when I arrive. She's got less of an explanation for what exactly happened to the kitchen, with its walls all ripped up. It's not her house, after all. She just squats here with three other people since the owners were foreclosed on and walked away.

"There's not much to see," she says of the spacious two-story. In lieu of furniture, the family room has piles of discarded clothes and boxes along the walls and in the corners. Upstairs in the bedrooms there are mattresses on the floor, marker scrawlings on the walls (NIETZSCHE SUCKS), clothes hanging from a pull-up bar jerry-rigged out of wood and bolted to the ceiling. One of the downstairs rooms has a couch in it, and that's where Jessica's boyfriend, Randal, is sitting.

This house used to belong to his parents. They bought it 10 years ago. Now, though it's big and has nice albeit filthy wood floors, it's valued at $40,000, which is less than they still owed on it, so they packed up and moved out last year. By that time, Randal had been looking for jobs as a line cook for months with no luck. Some of the positions he applied for had more than 100 other applicants. Eventually he gave up on the prospect of using his skills and shot for low-paying jobs like dishwashing. He applied all over town, but gave up on that, too, shortly after he asked the person in charge of hiring for a $7.25-an-hour job if they'd gotten a lot of applicants, and the guy said, "Oh, yeah. Seventy."

Jess and Randal, 35 and 33, respectively, have been living here since September of last year. During the day, she puts on a nice white shirt and serves people $20 appetizers at a restaurant in Shaker Heights, one of the ritziest Cleveland suburbs and once the wealthiest city in the country. At night, she goes back home to an area she calls "the hood." Crime statistics seem to support this description; Cleveland is currently ranked one of the most dangerous cities in America.

While we're sitting around chatting, the back door 60
slams and footsteps approach. "Is someone HERE?" my sister asks, and there's so much edge in her voice that I instinctively brace myself, and we both start to get to our feet. There's the pit bull, but he's a pussycat. A 23-year-old unemployed and strong-looking Navy vet who was discharged for depression and anxiety also lives here, but he is very, very high. Anyway, it's just Randal's sister stopping by to say hello. "Do you want to see my gun?" my sister asks me, and she takes me upstairs to show me where she keeps it in her room and explains she's got throwing knives in her car.

Before this, they were renting half of a duplex at a reasonable $400 a month. But Randal has been out of work for a long time now, and there's not much point in paying rent when this house is just standing here empty. It's something of a trend to occupy abandoned homes in the post-housing-crash world, and Randal's sort of a pro at this point. His grandmother also lost her house a little while back. She was disabled; when she worked at an auto plant in her 30s, a piece of sheet metal that flew off a rack sliced off both her feet. She took out a mortgage on her paid-for house after her husband died; later, she couldn't keep up with the payments and had to leave. It was foreclosed on and emptied, but Randal stayed on. "They probably won't get around to coming and throwing anybody out for a long time," he says. "At the rate houses foreclose around here, they can't keep up."

It doesn't matter anyway. My sister and Randal and the vet are all talking about getting out of town, moving someplace where there might be opportunities—the West, Oregon. They'll become part of Ohio's population problem. Growth here over the last decade was 1.6 percent. Nationwide, it was 9.7 percent.

"We need people to stay here, and to come here," Kathleen Clyde tells me over coffee back in Columbus. This is a battleground state. It's the heart of the country, geographically—nay, spiritually—and the next presidential election probably won't be won without it. But, as Clyde says, "Who's gonna wanna move here?" At 32, Democratic state Rep. Clyde is the youngest elected woman in the Ohio legislature, charming, exceedingly tall, of the same age and politics as most of the people I know but actually working in politics. She's not just stressing over the recession. She's talking about a sea change. "It really feels like Ohio's at an important crossroads," she laments, "and we're headed in the wrong direction." The Ohio General Assembly is passing legislation that allows guns in bars. Drilling in state parks. Giveaways to big businesses. Privatization of the state's revenues from liquor sales. A 53 percent cut to the Alzheimer's Respite program and an 85 percent cut to the Department of Aging. And, simultaneous to the cuts, lawmakers have extended a $1 billion income tax break, 40 percent of which goes to the wealthiest 5 percent of Ohioans, and suspended an estate tax that only applied to the top 10 percent of estates. Ohio, which lost 600,000 private-sector jobs in the first decade of the millennium, where the percentage of working men is the lowest in its recorded history, and where median wages have declined more than in any other state since 2000, is about to seriously downsize its public sector too.

Because many of these policies are being pushed through the Ohio General Assembly by "70-year-olds," Clyde says, because the Ohio House was taken over by Republicans last year, when they were promising to fix the recession's problems with fiscal conservatism, Clyde urges me to move back to my home state and consider going into politics. Because engaging and energizing our generation and the one behind it might be Ohio's only shot.

65 This is just one more in a long series of highly depressing conversations I've had over the last month. I'm reporting from Ohio, for God's sake, not the Third World, yet still my interviewees are sweating over how they'll manage to survive despite living in the richest country in the history of the world. Because some politicians are passing some greedy and indecent and inhumanely neglectful and inconsiderate laws. "Is it really so dire?" I ask Clyde.

She hesitates. She opens her mouth and winces, before finally saying: "I think it is. Being in this legislature makes it hard to sleep at night."

On a Wednesday in late June, Wisconsin Gov. Scott Walker's Wisconsin Act 10, which stripped most public-sector unions of most of their collective-bargaining rights, went into effect. On the same hot day in Ohio, Erin almost runs down Columbus Mayor Michael Coleman with Jocelyn's stroller.

"I was just trying to shake his hand!" she says breathlessly after regaining control of the unwieldy carriage. And Mayor Coleman was trying to shake hers, and thousands of other people's, standing on the sidelines of a massive parade marching through the capital. Shirts and flags identify the participants as firefighters, transit workers, teachers, electricians, bikers, state troopers; residents of Columbus, Cleveland, Findlay, Toledo; members of the SEIU, UAW, AFL-CIO. A drum line accompanied their chanting: Hey hey. Ho ho. SB 5 has got to go. Workers' rights are human rights. This is what democracy looks like. This swell of people has a delivery for the secretary of state. To keep SB 5 from becoming law and get it on the ballot for repeal in November, they need 231,147 signatures. They are turning in 1.3 million.

"We can't guarantee anything," says a spokeswoman for We Are Ohio, the group driving the effort, "but we're confident with the amount of signatures we've collected that we have a lot of support on our side." In polls, Ohioans heavily favor the repeal, and most also say now, just months after the Republican majority they elected to the legislature took office, that if a congressional election took place today, they'd vote for the Democratic candidate—like angry constituents in Florida have hollered for the recall of Rick Scott, and in Michigan, of Rick Snyder. Wisconsin's Walker has an approval rate of 43 percent. Next year, Ohio will indeed be a battleground, one where the cop finds out how much it can get away with.

70 This year, anyway, SB 5 has the potential to be forestalled. Another one of our college friends, Lindsey, is also looking to that for job and wage and general security. She teaches middle school English in rural Logan, about an hour outside Columbus, and she stops by Erin's with her two-month-old one day. After she and Erin have a very lengthy discussion about breast-feeding, they worry together.

"I don't want to take any"—Lindsey's got this lovely southern Ohio drawl, so she says it a little bit like *ayny*—"money out of our savings" until the repeal passes, or doesn't, this fall. Her and her husband's livelihoods could both depend on the outcome, since he also teaches in the same school district. "We don't know what's gonna happen." Until she knows for sure how it will play out, she won't let her husband buy a couch though they've got two kids now and not enough places to sit.

White people problems. Like that. And that, like the rest of the Americans holding the $873 billion in outstanding student loans, Lindsey and her husband also have to figure student-loan debt into their monthly budget. There's $50,000 of it between them. "We joke that we have to pay $450 a month in loans just to make our crappy teacher pay," she says. Yes. Hilarious, for all of us. Rep. Clyde also mentioned that it's an effort to make her roughly $500-a-month loan payment on her $60,500 legislative salary. And the other day, another college roommate pointed to $120,000 in outstanding loans as the reason she can't leave her law firm, even though she's discovered she doesn't like her profession. When I asked her what she's going to do, she said, "What everybody does. Be a lawyer and hate it until I die."

Erin and Anthony owe $26,000. They both went to Ohio State, which raised tuition every year we were there, in all but one of the nine years since, and will again this year after its 15 percent cut in the final budget. This debt isn't insignificant for the Rodriguezes, especially coupled with the mortgage and the car payment, but it's quite manageable—if both of them are employed.

At home, the day of the parade, Erin pops into my room. "I'm shaking," she says. Anthony just called. The conference committee reconciling the House and Senate versions of the budget adopted the slightly smaller of the proposed massive cuts to the OCC. Kasich would sign it into law the next day. Anthony's boss has given him the news that he is very, very lucky. Forty OCC employees are being laid off. But Anthony's position is now in the 42 that remain.

75 "He's just really worried about what this year is gonna be like," Erin says, "because they have no money, no support staff." She's worked up, breathing shallow, talking fast. "But I was like, I don't care what your workload is—you have a job."

She sticks a finger into Jocelyn's diaper through the leg hole and, wetness confirmed, takes her to the baby's room next door. On my first day here, I heard Anthony call down from this room to Erin in the family room: "Come here. Fast." She went tearing up the stairs and, when she arrived to find he wanted only to show her how cute their baby was, started to chastise him for making it sound like an emergency, but then they were both looking at the baby on the changing table, and then nobody was mad. Jocelyn's on the table again now, in the jungle-themed room, and Erin is chatting her up like always as she changes her. "Jocelyn, are you so excited that Mommy doesn't have to force you into pageant work now?" she asks. Jocelyn stares at her, the two of them below the window valance printed with happy cartoon monkeys. "Now we can just do it for fun."

## RESPOND •

1. How would you summarize McClelland's argument? Can you likewise summarize the kinds of evidence she provides to support it? Do you believe that "[her] generation is flat-out screwed," a question raised in the selection's introduction?
2. Rather than stating an argument explicitly, McClelland tells a series of interlocking stories. Which of the stories (or strands of a story) do you find most effective? Why? Which do you find least compelling? Why? Are they all necessary? Why or why not?
3. As noted, McClelland recounts a series of stories rather than making an explicit argument. What are the advantages and disadvantages of using such a technique when constructing an argument? To what extent is the evidence for her argument the cumulative weight of all the stories she tells?
4. Examine this article as it originally appeared online at http://bit.ly/qrnrrG, paying special attention to the photos that are part of the layout as well as their captions. Choose two that you think are especially effective in supporting McClelland's argument. Be prepared to explain your choices to your classmates.
5. Although McClelland is an award-winning writer, this particular piece is not written in a style that most professors would find effective or acceptable. (Importantly, however, McClelland didn't set out to write an academic essay, and we must evaluate her stylistic choices in light of her goals.) Even professors who have no trouble with the ways McClelland constructs her argument implicitly by telling stories could easily object to the informality of her prose—both her word choice and her syntax, which is often quite conversational in nature. **Choose a paragraph of the selection** that you find especially effective as written, and **rewrite it in a more academic style.** You may tackle this assignment in two ways: you can simply rewrite the paragraph as if you were creating it in your own register of academic language, or you may want to write about the paragraph, summarizing and quoting it as you might in a research paper you would write for one of your courses. If you choose the latter option, be sure to consult Chapters 19–21 for help with incorporating quotations from other sources effectively and correctly.

6. To return to McClelland's introduction, is her generation flat-out screwed? And what about your generation (if you are not a thirty-something)? **Write an essay** in which you respond to one of these questions. In light of question 5, you'll first need to think about a way to formulate the topic in more academic terms since "flat-out screwed" is too informal for most college writing. Then, you'll need to decide exactly what you wish to claim about the likely future fate of your generation or of McClelland's. Notice that in a very real sense, you'll most likely be constructing an evaluative essay. (See Chapter 10 on evaluative essays.)

▼ *Andrew Kohut is president of the Pew Research Center, the organization that issued the report featured as the first selection in this chapter. One of the country's foremost experts on opinion polling, he is coauthor of four books, and he appears frequently on National Public Radio and PBS's* NewsHour, *where he discusses public opinion on various topics. Not surprisingly, he favors quantitative evidence—inartistic appeals, as discussed in Chapter 4—in constructing arguments, but as you'll also see, in interpreting these statistics, he is very aware of the power of artistic appeals, those that rely on logic and common sense. As you read this selection, which first appeared on the op-ed page of the* New York Times *in late January 2012, reflect on the ways that Kohut recontextualizes the opening selection of the chapter as well as the ways he interprets statistics in providing evidence for his claims.*

# Don't Mind the Gap°

**ANDREW KOHUT**

Income inequality has become a hot-button issue during this political campaign. A recent Pew Research Center poll, for example, attracted an extraordinary amount of attention when it found that 66 percent of Americans believed there were "very strong" or "strong" conflicts between the rich and the poor—an increase of 19 percentage points since 2009.

But while Americans are hearing more and more about class conflict, there is little indication that they are increasingly divided along these lines. People don't necessarily want to take money from the wealthy; they just want a better chance to get rich themselves. They care about policies that give everyone a fair shot—a distinction that candidates in both parties should understand as they head into the 2012 campaigns.

An awareness of economic inequality is not new. Pew surveys going back to 1987 have found an average of 75 percent of the American public thinking that the "rich are getting richer and the poor are getting poorer." As far back as 1941, 60 percent of respondents told the Gallup poll that there was too much power in the hands of a few rich people and large corporations in the United States.

Despite that longstanding sense of inequality, there is no more sentiment today for populist revolt° than there was then. A Gallup poll last month found 54 percent believing that income inequality was an "acceptable part of our economic system"—a slight increase, in fact, over the 45 percent that held that view back in 1998.

5 What's different these days is that a despondent public, struggling with difficult times and an uncertain future, is upset over a perceived lack of fairness in public policy. For example, 61 percent of Americans now say the economic system in this country unfairly favors the wealthy.

***"Mind the Gap":*** a phrase familiar to anyone who has ever visited London and taken the Tube, London's underground rapid transit system; "mind the gap" is a warning to passengers, reminding them to be aware of the gap, or space, between the edge of the platform and the door of the train car.

***populist revolt:*** revolt or revolution by the people.

*Do you think that the fact that some people in the United States are rich and others are poor represents a problem that needs to be fixed (or) is an acceptable part of our economic system?*

| | Problem that needs to be fixed | Acceptable part of economic system |
|---|---|---|
| | % | % |
| Nov 28–Dec 1, 2011 | 45 | 52 |
| Apr 23–May 31, 1998 | 52 | 45 |

GALLUP

Pew's surveys in recent years present a detailed picture of these frustrations. One major complaint is tax policy: Dissatisfaction with the tax system has grown over the past decade, but the focus is not on how much respondents themselves pay, but rather on the perception that the wealthy are simply not paying their fair share. Just 11 percent of Americans say they are bothered by the amount they pay, while 57 percent of respondents say they are bothered by what they believe are unfairly low amounts paid by the wealthy.

Reactions to the bailout programs of 2008 and 2009 got the unfairness ball rolling. Early on the public was divided over the fairness of government helping financial institutions, and overwhelmingly opposed loans to Detroit automakers. Much of the public was even put off by plans to help homeowners facing mortgage foreclosures. By 2010, 51 percent said the bailout of the banks was the wrong thing for the government to do, while just 40 percent thought it was right.

No doubt outrage over Wall Street bonuses played a large part in this trend: Pew Research Center surveys at the time found 86 percent disapproved of high bonuses reportedly given out by many financial institutions, with as many as 62 percent saying they were angered by them.

Even recent reforms to financial-sector regulation have not allayed public concerns. In a poll last month, 56 percent of Americans said the power and influence of banks and other financial institutions represented a major threat to the country.

But before candidates read this 10
frustration as a call for class warfare, they should recognize the limits of that approach. Americans are still confident that their society provides opportunities for economic mobility. In one recent Pew poll, 58 percent of respondents said they believed that people who wanted to get ahead could make it if they were willing to work hard.

The issue here is not about class envy. Rather, it's a perception that government policies are skewed toward helping the already wealthy and powerful. While a December Gallup poll found few respondents wanting the government to attempt to reduce the income gap between rich and poor, 70 percent said it was important for the government to increase opportunities for people to get ahead. What the public wants is not a war on the rich but more policies that promote opportunity.

**RESPOND•**

1. What is Kohut's argument in this selection? As Kohut notes, the Pew Research Center's poll on income inequality, which was the first selection in this chapter, "Rising Share of Americans See Conflict between Rich and Poor," received "an extraordinary amount of attention." Do you think Kohut believes the poll merited the attention it received? Why or why not?

2. How does Kohut go about contextualizing the findings of the poll that served as the first selection in the chapter? What can his essay teach us about the ways statistical information, including polls, can be used to support very different arguments?
3. Throughout this essay, Kohut relies most strongly on inartistic arguments, specifically, data from opinion surveys, as evidence. Choose two paragraphs that contain statistical data and analyze carefully how Kohut presents the information in such a way as to support his larger point. As you will note, he doesn't merely drop statistics in; he uses them strategically. What you're trying to get a feel for is how researchers who rely on quantitative data do so effectively.
4. Now take one of the paragraphs you analyzed in question 3 and present it as a Toulmin argument, as discussed in Chapter 7. Pay careful attention to the inartistic and artistic arguments (as discussed in Chapter 4) that Kohut uses in the paragraph you analyze.
5. As indicated in the headnote, this selection was published in late January 2012, only a few months after the Occupy Wall Street movements were at their height. During this period, terms like "income inequality" and "class warfare" as well as "vulture capitalism," a term used by Texas Governor Rick Perry during his failed presidential campaign, showed up frequently. Choose one of these terms or some other term used to talk about this constellation of issues that you find interesting and investigate its use in detail. Using the electronic version of a newspaper or the search function on the archives of its Web site, look for instances of the term in context. Try to find a dozen or more examples. You will likely want to limit your search to the period from late 2011 to early 2012, when the selections in this chapter appeared, or to a period closer to the present, that is, when you are using this textbook. Study these examples carefully to determine the contexts in which the term is used and the sorts of writers who use it (in terms of their own beliefs or ideological commitments). Once you've completed your analysis, **write an essay** that defines the term (see Chapter 9) but does so in a rhetorical way (see Chapter 6). In other words, your goal is to explain the meaning of the term to your readers, using the quotations you collected as evidence, and to make clear how those who use the term do so not merely to label a phenomenon but also to construct an argument. (Remember also to consult Chapters 20 and 21 on acknowledging and citing quotations correctly.)

# Fair Is Fair

STANLEY FISH

▶ *Since 2005, Stanley Fish (1938– ) has served as Davidson-Kahn Distinguished Professor of Humanities and Law at Florida International University, teaching in the College of Law there. Prior to becoming a law professor, Fish made his reputation as one of the most important literary theorists of this era with his work on the poet John Milton, the notion of interpretive communities, and special problems in the interpretation of literary texts. For the past few years, he has blogged for the* New York Times, *where this posting first appeared in late January 2011, a few days after President Obama's State of the Union address. As you read this selection, consider how framing questions relevant to inequality as matters of fairness rather than of equality or inequality changes the debates in significant ways.*

President Obama's choice to emphasize fairness rather than equality in the State of the Union address makes good political sense. Although equality is the central concern of the Occupy Wall Street movement, focused as it is on income disparities, Americans are at least ambivalent toward equality as a primary value. They think emphasizing equality was O.K. in the context of the Civil War and segregation because inequality was institutionalized in those days and it is a good thing those days are over.

But Americans also hear in the invocation° of equality an appeal to the redistribution of income. Americans don't mind if income is redistributed as long as it is done by market forces and not the government. Income equality is fine if it is "naturally" achieved, but if it is socially engineered° it can be perceived as class warfare, a plot against the well-to-do.

*The December 2011 "March for Jobs and Economic Fairness" in New York City. Participants included Occupy Wall Street demonstrators and members of over three hundred unions.*

***invocation:*** the act of invoking, or calling upon someone or something for assistance or support.

***social engineering:*** efforts to solve social problems by government intervention rather than by letting the market or other "natural" social processes solve them.

Fairness is a better mantra° than equality, for it rests on a notion of formal° equality—everyone should be treated alike—rather than a notion of substantive° equality—everyone should have the same stuff. Fairness, rather than undermining the American virtues of self-realization° and entrepreneurial advancement, establishes a framework within which these virtues can be exercised. Fairness doesn't tamper with the rules or skew° them in the direction of the unemployed or impoverished: it just insists that the rules be followed and that no one gets to go to the head of the line if it is not his turn.

The difference between equality and fairness can be illustrated by considering the issue of Mitt Romney's taxes.° In the eyes of most Americans, it is O.K. that Mitt Romney makes more money than they do; there's no demand for the equalizing of income so that he can be brought down to their level. But it is not O.K. (or at least the Democrats will argue) for Mitt Romney to be paying a lower tax rate than his housecleaner. It's unfair. So inequalities that arise from the unequal abilities of people and even from the unequal distribution of luck and birth are all right; but the kind of unfairness that occurs when someone plays by different rules than the rules you are held to isn't.

5 President Obama can take the fairness mantra all the way to the bank and a second term. He can make the same argument up and down the line. Is it fair that children who live in school districts with a poor tax base° because the residents of the district are poor should receive an inferior education? (Notice that this is not an argument against school districts made up of wealthy people; it is an argument against allowing wealth to skew the educational opportunities that should be fairly available to everyone.) Is it fair that Internet pirates in China can appropriate without paying for it the intellectual property of Americans who rely for their income on ideas they have copyrighted? Is it fair that those who fail to purchase health insurance take advantage of hospital emergency rooms at the expense of those who do the responsible thing? Is it fair that the voices of some citizens should be incredibly amplified because they have the money to buy a megaphone larger than the National Broadcasting Company? Is it fair that insurance companies that take premiums from us in return for taking risk make every effort possible to insulate themselves from risk, by refusing, as they long have, to cover pre-existing conditions?

Equality and freedom have often been trumpeted as the key words in the lexicon of liberal democracy.° But they are too abstract, and they won't play in the political arena. Everyone understands fair, and fair is the word Obama should be uttering again and again and again.

***mantra:*** an often-repeated word or phrase; originally, a line from the Veda chanted as a prayer among Hindus.

***formal:*** having the same shape.

***substantive:*** real or actual, here in reference to possessions.

***self-realization:*** achieving the goals one sets for oneself.

***skew:*** to distort, often unfairly.

***Mitt Romney's taxes:*** during the 2012 presidential campaign, Romney revealed that in 2010, his tax rate was 13.9%. For comparison, that of Gingrich was 32.2% while that of Obama had been 26.8%. The median taxpayer paid 7.4% in 2010.

***school districts with a poor tax base:*** the reference here is to the fact that in the United States, schools are paid for primarily with property taxes, so districts made up of expensive houses will likely have far more money to spend than those made up of inexpensive houses.

***liberal democracy:*** system of government like that of the United States where, ideally, decisions are made by a majority of voters voting directly on issues or voting to elect legislators who will represent the will of the voters. The will of the majority holds as long as the decisions made do not limit rights promised in a constitution.

## RESPOND •

1. Why does Fish argue that emphasizing fairness rather than equality is a more astute way to frame debates about social inequality in the United States? What evidence does he offer? To what extent do you agree or disagree with Fish? Why?
2. What distinction does Fish draw between "formal equality" and "substantive equality"? Why is it important to his argument? To what extent do you agree with this distinction? With the ways that Fish uses it?
3. In paragraph 4, Fish uses an extended example to illustrate the distinction between equality and fairness. How effective is this example? Why? What can you learn from this paragraph about how to provide effective examples that help clarify the definitions of terms? (Chapter 9 on arguments of definition may help you here.)
4. In many ways, Fish is offering a proposal argument (see Chapter 12), contending that one way of framing the issue—fairness—is ultimately more effective than framing the issue another way—equality. Which way of framing the issue(s) is more appropriate when the topic is the subject of this chapter—how we define inequality in this society? (You may wish to propose a third way of framing the issues.)
5. What are the similarities and differences between Fish's argument and the argument offered by Andrew Kohut in the previous selection, "Don't Mind the Gap"? Pay attention not only to the content of the argument but to the use of artistic and inartistic evidence, as discussed in Chapter 4, as well.
6. In paragraph 5, Fish mentions ". . . opportunities that should be fairly available to everyone" in reference to education in particular. Based on what you have learned in this chapter and perhaps other reading you have done, **write an essay** in which you define the "opportunities that should be fairly available to all Americans." Of course, you may wish to argue that there are no such opportunities. Whatever you argue for (or against), be sure to provide sound evidence for your claims. (Chapter 9 provides information on arguments of definition.)

# GLOSSARY

**academic argument** writing that is addressed to an audience well informed about the topic, that aims to convey a clear and compelling point in a somewhat formal style, and that follows agreed-upon conventions of usage, punctuation, and formats.

**accidental condition** in a definition, an element that helps to explain what's being defined but isn't essential to it. An accidental condition in defining a bird might be "ability to fly" because most, but not all, birds can fly. (See also *essential condition* and *sufficient condition*.)

***ad hominem* argument** a fallacy of argument in which a writer's claim is answered by irrelevant attacks on his or her character.

**analogy** an extended comparison between something unfamiliar and something more familiar for the purpose of illuminating or dramatizing the unfamiliar. An analogy might, say, compare nuclear fission (less familiar) to a pool player's opening break (more familiar).

**anaphora** a figure of speech involving repetition, particularly of the same word at the beginning of several clauses.

**antithesis** the use of parallel structures to call attention to contrasts or opposites, as in *Some like it hot; some like it cold.*

**antonomasia** use of a title, epithet, or description in place of a name, as in *Your Honor* for *Judge*.

**argument** (1) a spoken, written, or visual text that expresses a point of view; (2) the use of evidence and reason to discover some version of the truth, as distinct from *persuasion*, the attempt to change someone else's point of view.

**artistic appeal** support for an argument that a writer creates based on principles of reason and shared knowledge rather than on facts and evidence. (See also *inartistic appeal.*)

**assumption** a belief regarded as true, upon which other claims are based.

**assumption, cultural** a belief regarded as true or commonsensical within a particular culture, such as the belief in individual freedom in American culture.

**audience** the person or persons to whom an argument is directed.

**authority** the quality conveyed by a writer who is knowledgeable about his or her subject and confident in that knowledge.

**background** the information a writer provides to create the context for an argument.

**backing** in Toulmin argument, the evidence provided to support a *warrant*.

**bandwagon appeal** a fallacy of argument in which a course of action is recommended on the grounds that everyone else is following it.

**begging the question** a fallacy of argument in which a claim is based on the very grounds that are in doubt or dispute: *Rita can't be the bicycle thief; she's never stolen anything.*

**causal argument** an argument that seeks to explain the effect(s) of a cause, the cause(s) of an effect, or a causal chain in which A causes B, B causes C, C causes D, and so on.

**ceremonial argument** an argument that deals with current values and addresses questions of praise and blame. Also called *epideictic*, ceremonial arguments include eulogies and graduation speeches.

**character, appeal based on** a strategy in which a writer presents an authoritative or credible self-image to convince an audience to accept a claim.

**circumstantial evidence** in legal cases, evidence from which conclusions cannot be drawn directly but have to be inferred.

**claim** a statement that asserts a belief or truth. In arguments, most claims require supporting evidence. The claim is a key component in *Toulmin argument*.

**classical oration** a highly structured form of an argument developed in ancient Greece and Rome to defend or refute a thesis. The oration evolved to include six parts—*exordium, narratio, partitio, confirmatio, refutatio*, and *peroratio*.

***confirmatio*** the fourth part of a classical oration, in which a speaker or writer offers evidence for the claim.

**connotation** the suggestions or associations that surround most words and extend beyond their literal meaning, creating associational effects. *Slender* and *skinny* have similar meanings, for example, but carry different connotations, the former more positive than the latter.

**context** the entire situation in which a piece of writing takes place, including the writer's purpose(s) for writing; the intended audience; the time and place of writing; the institutional, social, personal, and other influences on the piece of writing; the material conditions of writing (whether it's, for instance, online or on paper, in handwriting or print); and the writer's attitude toward the subject and the audience.

**conviction** the belief that a claim or course of action is true or reasonable. In a proposal argument, a writer must move an audience beyond conviction to action.

**credibility** an impression of integrity, honesty, and trustworthiness conveyed by a writer in an argument.

**criterion** in evaluative arguments, the standard by which something is measured to determine its quality or value.

**deductive reasoning** a process of thought in which general principles are applied to particular cases.

**definition, argument of** an argument in which the claim specifies that something does or doesn't meet the conditions or features set forth in a definition: *Pluto is not a major planet.*

**deliberative argument** an argument that deals with action to be taken in the future, focusing on matters of policy. Deliberative arguments include parliamentary debates and campaign platforms.

**delivery** the presentation of a spoken argument.

**dogmatism** a fallacy of argument in which a claim is supported on the grounds that it's the only conclusion acceptable within a given community.

***either-or* choice** a fallacy of argument in which a complicated issue is misrepresented as offering only two possible alternatives, one of which is often made to seem vastly preferable to the other.

**emotional appeal** a strategy in which a writer tries to generate specific emotions (such as fear, envy, anger, or pity) in an audience to dispose it to accept a claim.

**enthymeme** in Toulmin argument, a statement that links a claim to a supporting reason: *The bank will fail* (claim) *because it has lost the support of its largest investors* (reason). In classical rhetoric, an enthymeme is a *syllogism* with one term understood but not stated: *Socrates is mortal because he is a human being.* (The understood term is: *All human beings are mortal.*)

**epideictic argument** see *ceremonial argument*.

**equivocation** a fallacy of argument in which a lie is given the appearance of truth, or in which the truth is misrepresented in deceptive language.

**essential condition** in a definition, an element that must be part of the definition but, by itself, isn't enough to define the term. An essential condition in defining a bird might be "winged": all birds have wings, yet wings alone don't define a bird since some insects and mammals also have wings. (See also *accidental condition* and *sufficient condition*.)

**ethical appeal** see *character, appeal based on*, and *ethos*.

**ethnographic observation** a form of field research involving close and extended observation of a group, event, or phenomenon; careful and detailed note-taking during the observation; analysis of the notes; and interpretation of that analysis.

**ethos** the self-image a writer creates to define a relationship with readers. In arguments, most writers try to establish an ethos that suggests authority and credibility.

**evaluation, argument of** an argument in which the claim specifies that something does or doesn't meet established criteria: *The Nikon D3X is the most sophisticated digital SLR camera currently available.*

**evidence** material offered to support an argument. See *artistic appeal* and *inartistic appeal*.

**example, definition by** a definition that operates by identifying individual examples of what's being defined: *sports car—Corvette, Viper, Miata, Boxster.*

***exordium*** the first part of a classical oration, in which a speaker or writer tries to win the attention and goodwill of an audience while introducing a subject.

**experimental evidence** evidence gathered through experimentation; often evidence that can be quantified (for example, a survey of students before and after an election might yield statistical evidence about changes in their attitudes toward the candidates). Experimental evidence is frequently crucial to scientific arguments.

**fact, argument of** an argument in which the claim can be proved or disproved with specific evidence or testimony: *The winter of 1998 was the warmest on record for the United States.*

**fallacy of argument** a flaw in the structure of an argument that renders its conclusion invalid or suspect. See ad hominem *argument*, *bandwagon appeal*, *begging the question*, *dogmatism*, either-or *choice*, *equivocation*, *false authority*, *faulty analogy*, *faulty causality*, *hasty generalization*, *non sequitur*, *scare tactic*, *sentimental appeal*, *slippery slope*, and *straw man*.

**false authority** a fallacy of argument in which a claim is based on the expertise of someone who lacks appropriate credentials.

**faulty analogy** a fallacy of argument in which a comparison between two objects or concepts is inaccurate or inconsequential.

**faulty causality** a fallacy of argument making the unwarranted assumption that because one event follows another, the first event causes the second. Also called *post hoc, ergo propter hoc*, faulty causality forms the basis of many superstitions.

**firsthand evidence** data—including surveys, observations, personal interviews, etc.—collected and personally examined by the writer. (See also *secondhand evidence*.)

**flashpoint** see *fallacy of argument*.

**forensic argument** an argument that deals with actions that have occurred in the past. Sometimes called judicial arguments, forensic arguments include legal cases involving judgments of guilt or innocence.

**formal definition** a definition that identifies something first by the general class to which it belongs (*genus*) and then by the characteristics that distinguish it from other members of that class (*species*): *Baseball is a game* (genus) *played on a diamond by opposing teams of nine players who score runs by circling bases after striking a ball with a bat* (species).

**genus** in a definition, the general class to which an object or concept belongs: *baseball is a* sport; *green is a* color.

**grounds** in Toulmin argument, the evidence provided to support a claim and reason—that is, an *enthymeme*.

**hard evidence** support for an argument using facts, statistics, testimony, or other evidence the writer finds.

**hasty generalization** a fallacy of argument in which an inference is drawn from insufficient data.

**hyperbole** use of overstatement for special effect.

**hypothesis** an expectation for the findings of one's research or the conclusion to one's argument. Hypotheses must be tested against evidence, opposing arguments, and so on.

**immediate reason** the cause that leads directly to an effect, such as an automobile accident that results in an injury to the driver. (See also *necessary reason* and *sufficient reason*.)

**inartistic appeal** support for an argument using facts, statistics, eyewitness testimony, or other evidence the writer finds rather than creates. (See also *artistic appeal*.)

**inductive reasoning** a process of thought in which particular cases lead to general principles.

**intended readers** the actual, real-life people whom a writer consciously wants to address in a piece of writing.

**invention** the process of finding and creating arguments to support a claim.

**inverted word order** moving grammatical elements of a sentence out of their usual order (subject-verb-object/complement) for special effect, as in *Tired I was; sleepy I was not*.

**invitational argument** a term used by Sonja Foss to describe arguments that are aimed not at vanquishing an opponent but at inviting others to collaborate in exploring mutually satisfying ways to solve problems.

**invoked readers** the readers directly addressed or implied in a text, which may include some that the writer didn't consciously intend to reach. An argument that refers to *those who have experienced a major trauma*, for example, invokes all readers who have undergone this experience.

**irony** use of language that suggests a meaning in contrast to the literal meaning of the words.

***kairos*** the opportune moment; in arguments, the timeliness of an argument and the most opportune ways to make it.

**line of argument** a strategy or approach used in an argument. Argumentative strategies include appeals to the heart (emotional appeals), to character (ethical appeals), and to facts and reason (logical appeals).

**logical appeal** a strategy in which a writer uses facts, evidence, and reason to make audience members accept a claim.

**metaphor** a figure of speech that makes a comparison, as in *The ship was a beacon of hope.*

***narratio*** the second part of a classical oration, in which a speaker or writer presents the facts of a case.

**necessary reason** a cause that must be present for an effect to occur; for example, infection with a particular virus is a necessary reason for the development of AIDS. (See also *immediate reason* and *sufficient reason.*)

**non sequitur** a fallacy of argument in which claims, reasons, or warrants fail to connect logically; one point doesn't follow from another: *If you're really my friend, you'll lend me five hundred dollars.*

**operational definition** a definition that identifies an object by what it does or by the conditions that create it: *A line is the shortest distance between two points.*

**parallelism** use of similar grammatical structures or forms for pleasing effect: *in the classroom, on the playground, and at the mall.*

**paraphrase** a restatement of the meaning of a piece of writing using different words from the original.

***partitio*** the third part of a classical oration, in which a speaker or writer divides up the subject and explains what the claim will be.

**patchwriting** a misuse of sources in which a writer's phrase, clause, or sentence stays too close to the original language or syntax of the source.

**pathos, appeal to** see *emotional appeal.*

***peroratio*** the sixth and final part of a classical oration, in which a speaker or writer summarizes the case and moves the audience to action.

**persuasion** the act of seeking to change someone else's point of view.

**plagiarism** the act of using the words, phrases, and expressions of others without proper citation or acknowledgment.

**precedents** actions or decisions in the past that have established a pattern or model for subsequent actions. Precedents are particularly important in legal cases.

**premise** a statement or position regarded as true and upon which other claims are based.

**propaganda** an argument advancing a point of view without regard to reason, fairness, or truth.

**proposal argument** an argument in which a claim is made in favor of or opposing a specific course of action: *Sport-utility vehicles should have to meet the same fuel economy standards as passenger cars.*

**purpose** the goal of an argument. Purposes include entertaining, informing, convincing, exploring, and deciding, among others.

**qualifiers** words or phrases that limit the scope of a claim: *usually; in a few cases; under these circumstances.*

**qualitative argument** an argument of evaluation that relies on nonnumerical criteria supported by reason, tradition, precedent, or logic.

**quantitative argument** an argument of evaluation that relies on criteria that can be measured, counted, or demonstrated objectively.

**reason** in writing, a statement that expands a claim by offering evidence to support it. The reason may be a statement of fact or another claim. In *Toulmin argument*, a *reason* is attached to a *claim* by a *warrant*, a statement that establishes the logical connection between claim and supporting reason.

**rebuttal** an answer that challenges or refutes a specific claim or charge. Rebuttals may also be offered by writers who anticipate objections to the claims or evidence they offer.

**rebuttal, conditions of** in Toulmin argument, potential objections to an argument. Writers need to anticipate such conditions in shaping their arguments.

**red herring** a fallacy of argument in which a writer abruptly changes the topic in order to distract readers from potentially objectionable claims.

***refutatio*** the fifth part of a classical oration, in which a speaker or writer acknowledges and refutes opposing claims or evidence.

**reversed structures** a figure of speech that involves the inversion of clauses: *What is good in your writing is not original; what is original is not good.*

**rhetoric** the art of persuasion. Western rhetoric originated in ancient Greece as a discipline to prepare citizens for arguing cases in court.

**rhetorical analysis** an examination of how well the components of an argument work together to persuade or move an audience.

**rhetorical questions** questions posed to raise an issue or create an effect rather than to get a response: *You may well wonder, "What's in a name?"*

**rhetorical situation** the relationship between topic, author, audience, and other contexts (social, cultural, political) that determine or evoke an appropriate spoken or written response.

**Rogerian argument** an approach to argumentation based on the principle, articulated by psychotherapist Carl Rogers, that audiences respond best when they don't feel threatened. Rogerian argument stresses trust and urges those who disagree to find common ground.

**scare tactic** a fallacy of argument presenting an issue in terms of exaggerated threats or dangers.

**scheme** a figure of speech that involves a special arrangement of words, such as inversion.

**secondhand evidence** any information taken from outside sources, including library research and online sources. (See also *firsthand evidence*.)

**sentimental appeal** a fallacy of argument in which an appeal is based on excessive emotion.

**simile** a comparison that uses *like* or *as*: *My love is like a red, red rose* or *I wandered lonely as a cloud.*

**slippery slope** a fallacy of argument exaggerating the possibility that a relatively inconsequential action or choice today will have serious adverse consequences in the future.

**species** in a definition, the particular features that distinguish one member of a *genus* from another: *Baseball is a sport* (genus) *played on a diamond by teams of nine players* (species).

**spin** a kind of political advocacy that makes any fact or event, however unfavorable, serve a political purpose.

**stacking the deck** a fallacy of argument in which the writer shows only one side of an argument.

**stance** the writer's attitude toward the topic and the audience.

**stasis theory** in classical rhetoric, a method for coming up with appropriate arguments by determining the nature of a given situation: *a question of fact*; *of definition*; *of quality*; or *of policy*.

**straw man** a fallacy of argument in which an opponent's position is misrepresented as being more extreme than it actually is, so that it's easier to refute.

**sufficient condition** in a definition, an element or set of elements adequate to define a term. A sufficient condition in defining God, for example, might be "supreme being" or "first cause." No other conditions are necessary, though many might be made. (See also *accidental condition* and *essential condition*.)

**sufficient reason** a cause that alone is enough to produce a particular effect; for example, a particular level of smoke in the air will set off a smoke alarm. (See also *immediate reason* and *necessary reason*.)

**summary** a presentation of the substance and main points of a piece of writing in very condensed form.

**syllogism** in formal logic, a structure of deductive logic in which correctly formed major and minor premises lead to a necessary conclusion:

| | |
|---|---|
| **Major premise** | All human beings are mortal. |
| **Minor premise** | Socrates is a human being. |
| **Conclusion** | Socrates is mortal. |

**testimony** a personal experience or observation used to support an argument.

**thesis** a sentence that succinctly states a writer's main point.

**Toulmin argument** a method of informal logic first described by Stephen Toulmin in *The Uses of Argument* (1958). Toulmin argument describes the key components of an argument as the *claim*, *reason*, *warrant*, *backing*, and *grounds*.

**trope** a figure of speech that involves a change in the usual meaning or signification of words, such as *metaphor*, *simile*, and *analogy*.

**understatement** a figure of speech that makes a weaker statement than a situation seems to call for. It can lead to powerful or to humorous effects.

**values, appeal to** a strategy in which a writer invokes shared principles and traditions of a society as a reason for accepting a claim.

**warrant** in *Toulmin argument*, the statement (expressed or implied) that establishes the logical connection between a claim and its supporting reason.

| | |
|---|---|
| **Claim** | Don't eat that mushroom; |
| **Reason** | it's poisonous. |
| **Warrant** | What is poisonous should not be eaten. |

# Acknowledgments

## Text

**Marjorie Agosín.** "Always Living in Spanish." Trans. by Celeste Kostopulos-Cooperman. "English." Trans. by Monica Bruno. Reprinted by permission of Marjorie Agosín.

**Mark Bauerlein.** "The Major and the Job Market, the Dream and the Reality." From the *Chronicle of Higher Education*, October 27, 2011. Reprinted by permission of the author.

**Anne E. Becker.** "Television, Disordered Eating, and Young Women in Fiji: Negotiating Body Image and Identity during Rapid Social Change." From *Culture, Medicine, and Psychiatry*, vol. 4, #28, December 2004. Copyright © 2004 Springer. Reprinted with permission of Springer Business Media via the Copyright Clearance Center.

**Daniel Ben-Ami.** "Why People Hate Fat Americans." From *Spiked*, September 9, 2005. Copyright © 2005. Reprinted by permission of the author.

**Mark Bittman.** "Is Junk Food Really Cheaper?" From the *New York Times*, September 24, 2011. Copyright © 2011 The New York Times. All rights reserved. Used by permission and protected by the Copyright Laws of the United States. The printing, copying, redistribution, or retransmission of this Content without express written permission is prohibited.

**Michele J. Bornert.** Three Postings from *Deaf Expressions*. Reprinted by permission of Michele J. Bornert.

**Jennifer Delahunty Britz.** "To All the Girls I've Rejected." From the *New York Times*, March 23, 2006. Copyright © 2006 by The New York Times. All rights reserved. Used by permission and protected by the Copyright Laws of the United States. The printing, copying, redistribution, or retransmission of this Content without express written permission is prohibited.

**David Brooks.** "It's Not about You." From the *New York Times*, July 26, 2011. Copyright © 2011 The New York Times. All rights reserved. Used by permission and protected by the Copyright Laws of the United States. The printing, copying, redistribution, or retransmission of this Content without express written permission is prohibited.

**Lan Cao.** "The Gift of Language." From *Monkey Bridge*. Copyright © 1997 by Lan Cao. Used by permission of Viking Penguin, a division of Penguin Group (USA), Inc.

**Jonathan Chait.** "Steve Jobs, Occupy Wall Street, and the Capitalist Ideal." From *New York* magazine, October 6, 2011. Reprinted by permission of New York Media LLC.

**Sandra Cisneros.** Excerpt from "Bien Pretty" in *Woman Hollering Creek*. Copyright © 1991 by Sandra Cisneros. Published by Vintage Books, a division of Random House Inc. and originally in hardcover by Random House Inc. By permission of Susan Bergholz Literary Services, New York, NY, and Lamy, NM. All rights reserved.

**Patricia Cohen.** "Professors' Liberalism Contagious? Maybe Not." From the *New York Times*, November 3, 2008. Copyright © 2008 by The New York Times. Reprinted by permission. All rights reserved. Used by permission and protected by the Copyright Laws of the United States. The printing, copying, redistribution, or retransmission of this Content without express written permission is prohibited.

**Mark Coleman.** Review of *Bottlemania: How Water Went on Sale and Why We Bought It*. From the *Los Angeles Times*, June 1, 2008. Copyright © 2008 Los Angeles Times. Reprinted by permission of the publisher.

**Jennifer Conlin.** "The Freedom to Choose Your Pronoun." From the *New York Times*, September 30, 2011. Copyright © 2011 The New York Times. All rights reserved. Used by permission and protected by the Copyright Laws of the United States. The printing, copying, redistribution, or retransmission of this Content without express written permission is prohibited.

***Cook's Country Magazine.*** "Ready-to-Bake Chocolate Chip Cookies." April 2005 issue. Copyright © 2005 Cook's Country Magazine.

***Cook's Illustrated Magazine.*** "Solving the Mystery of the Chewy Chocolate Chip Cookie." January 1996 issue. Copyright © 1996 Cook's Illustrated Magazine. Illustrations provided by America's Test Kitchen. Copyright © 2009 by America's Test Kitchen. Reprinted by permission. All rights reserved. www.americastestkitchen.com.

**N'Gai Croal.** "You Don't Have to Be a Nerd." From *Newsweek*, August 8, 2008. Copyright © 2008 The Newsweek/DailyBeast Company LLC. All rights reserved. Used by permission and protected by the Copyright Laws of the United States. The printing, copying, redistribution, or retransmission of the Material without express written permission is prohibited.

***Daily Californian.*** "Live Blog: Increase Diversity Bake Sale." September 27, 2011, by Jordan Bach-Lombardo. Reporting by Chloe Hunt, Nicholas Luther, Curan Mehra, J.D. Morris, Annie Sciacca, Alex Sklueff, Amruta Trivedi, Christopher Yee, and Mihiir Zaveri of the *Daily Californian*. Reprinted by permission of the publisher.

**Sam Dillon.** "Evictions at Sorority Raise Issue of Bias." From the *New York Times*, February 25, 2007. Copyright © 2007 The New York Times. All rights reserved. Used by permission and protected by the Copyright Laws of the United States. The printing, copying, redistribution, or retransmission of this Content without express written permission is prohibited.

**Rod Dreher.** "Poll's Shocking SOS for Texas GOP." From Dallasnews.com, December 3, 2008. Reprinted with permission of The Dallas Morning News.

**Firoozeh Dumas.** "The 'F Word.'" From *Funny in Farsi: A Memoir of Growing Up Iranian in America*. Copyright © 2003 by Firoozeh Dumas. Used by permission of Villard Books, a division of Random House, Inc.

**Clay Bonnyman Evans.** Letter to the Editor of the *New York Times*. July 13, 2011. Reprinted by permission of Clay Bonnyman Evans.

**Stanley Fish.** "Fair Is Fair." From the *New York Times*, January 26, 2012. Copyright © 2012 by The New York Times. All rights reserved. Used by permission and protected by the Copyright Laws of the United States. The printing, copying, redistribution, or retransmission of this Content without express written permission is prohibited.

**Lisa W. Foderaro.** "The Well-to-Do Get Less So, and Teenagers Feel the Crunch." From the *New York Times*, December 13, 2008. Copyright © 2008 by The New York Times. All rights reserved. Used by permission and protected by the Copyright

Laws of the United States. The printing, copying, redistribution, or retransmission of this Content without express written permission is prohibited.

**Rana Foroohar.** "What Ever Happened to Upward Mobility?" From *TIME*, November 14, 2011. Copyright © 2011 by TIME Inc. All rights reserved. TIME is a registered trademark of Time, Inc. Reprinted by permission.

**Stewart D. Friedman.** "The Fallacy of 'Work-Life Balance.'" Reprinted by permission of Harvard Business Publishing. "Take the Four-Way View." Excerpt from *Total Leadership: Be a Better Leader, Have a Richer Life*. Copyright © 2008 by Stewart D. Friedman.

**Thomas L. Friedman.** "The Start-Up of You." From the *New York Times*, July 13, 2011. Copyright © 2011 by The New York Times. All rights reserved. Used by permission and protected by the Copyright Laws of the United States. The printing, copying, redistribution, or retransmission of this Content without express written permission is prohibited.

**Ellen Goodman.** "The Culture of Thin Bites Fiji." From the *Boston Globe*, Op-Ed Section, May 27, 1999. Copyright © 1999 Boston Globe. All rights reserved. Used by permission and protected by the Copyright Laws of the United States. The printing, copying, redistribution, or retransmission of this Content without express written permission is prohibited.

**Daniel S. Hamermesh.** "Ugly? You May Have a Case." From the *New York Times*, August 27, 2011. Copyright © 2011 by The New York Times. All rights reserved. Used by permission and protected by the Copyright Laws of the United States. The printing, copying, redistribution, or retransmission of this Content without express written permission is prohibited.

**Stephanie Hanes.** "Little Girls or Little Women? The Disney Princess Effect." From the *Christian Science Monitor*, September 24, 2011. Reprinted by permission of the author.

**Lia Hardin.** "Cultural Stress Linked to Suicide." From the *Stanford Daily*, May 31, 2007. Copyright © 2007 The Stanford Daily, Inc. All rights reserved. Reprinted with permission of the publisher.

**Jim Harper.** "Tea Party, Meet Occupy Wall Street. OWS, Tea Party." Posted October 11, 2011. Text reprinted by permission of the Cato Institute. The diagram is reprinted by permission of James Sinclair.

**Adriene Hill.** "Eating Ethically—It's Complicated." From *Marketplace Money*, September 22, 2011. Copyright © 2011 American Public Media. Used with permission. All rights reserved.

**Skip Hollandsworth.** "Toddlers in Tiaras." www.goodhousekeeping.com, September 22, 2011. Reprinted by permission of the author.

**David Isay.** Dr. Monica Mayer Interview by Spencer Wilkinson Jr., and Ken Kobus Interview by Ron Baraff. From *Listening Is an Act of Love*, ed. by David Isay, StoryCorps project. Copyright © 2007 by Sound Portraits Productions, Inc. Used by permission of The Penguin Press, a division of Penguin Group (USA) Inc.

**Molly Ivins.** Excerpt from "Eloquent Barbara Jordan: A Great Spirit Has Left Us." From the *Seattle Times*, January 22, 1996. Reprinted by permission of Pom, Inc.

**Brooks Jackson.** "Democrats Deny Social Security's Red Ink." Posted February 25, 2011, on FactCheck.org, a project of the Annenberg Public Policy Center of the University of Pennsylvania. Reprinted by permission.

**Scott Jaschik.** "Affirmative Action for Men." From *Inside Higher Ed*, March 27, 2006. Reprinted by permission of the publisher.

**Porochista Khakpour.** "Reality TV Goes Where Football Meets the Hijab." From the *New York Times*, November 10, 2011. Copyright © 2011 by The New York Times. All rights reserved. Used by permission and protected by the Copyright Laws of the United States. The printing, copying, redistribution, or retransmission of this Content without express written permission is prohibited.

**Martin Luther King Jr.** Excerpt from "I Have a Dream." Reprinted by arrangement with The Heirs to the Estate of Martin Luther King Jr. c/o Writers House as agent for the proprietor, New York, NY.

**Andrew Kohut.** "Don't Mind the Gap." From the *New York Times*, January 27, 2012. Copyright © 2012 by The New York Times. All rights reserved. Used by permission and protected by the Copyright Laws of the United States. The printing, copying, redistribution, or retransmission of this Content without express written permission is prohibited.

**Tina Korbe.** "Remember the Racist Cupcakes? Fordham University Fights Back with Its Own Bake Sale." From HOTAIR.com, October 7, 2011. Reprinted by permission of the publisher and author.

**Michael Krasny.** "The Berkeley Bake Sale." Transcript from the radio series FORUM, September 27, 2011, with guests Andy Nevis and Vishalli Loomba. Reprinted by permission of KQED Public Radio and guests. Copyright © 2011 by KQED, Inc. All rights reserved.

**Paul Krugman.** Excerpt from "The Cult That Is Destroying America." From the *New York Times*, July 26, 2011. Copyright © 2011 The New York Times. All rights reserved. Used by permission and protected by the Copyright Laws of the United States. The printing, copying, redistribution, or retransmission of this Content without express written permission is prohibited.

**Adam Kuban.** Excerpt from "Martha, Martha, Martha." From *Serious Eats*, April 10, 2007. Copyright © 2007. Reprinted by permission of the author.

**Craig Lambert.** "Our Unpaid, Extra Shadow Work." From the *New York Times*, October 29, 2011. Copyright © 2011 by The New York Times. All rights reserved. Used by permission and protected by the Copyright Laws of the United States. The printing, copying, redistribution, or retransmission of this Content without express written permission is prohibited.

**Michael Lassell.** "How to Watch Your Brother Die." Copyright © 1985 by Michael Lassell. Reprinted by permission of the author.

**Heather Mac Donald.** "Half Baked: UC Berkeley's Diversity Machine Loses Its Mind over Cupcakes." From *City Journal*, September 28, 2011. Copyright © 2011 Manhattan Institute. Reprinted by permission. All rights reserved.

**Mack D. Mariani and Gordon J. Hewitt.** "Indoctrination U.? Faculty Ideology and Changes in Student Political Orientation." From *Political Science & Politics*, October 2008. Copyright © 2008 The American Political Science Association. Reprinted by permission of Cambridge University Press.

**John Marsh.** "Why Education Is Not an Economic Panacea." From *Class Dismissed*. Reprinted by permission of Monthly Review Press. Copyright © 2011 by Monthly Review Press.

**Mac McClelland.** "Goodbye, Columbus: Ohio's War on the Middle Class." From *Mother Jones*, November/December 2011. Copyright © 2012 by the Foundation for National Progress. Reprinted by permission of the publisher.

**Rebecca Mead.** "Learning by Degrees." Originally published in the *New Yorker*. Copyright © 2010 Condé Nast. Reprinted by permission of the publisher.

**Walter Benn Michaels.** "The Trouble with Diversity: How We Learned to Love Identity and Ignore Inequality." Copyright © 2006 by Walter Benn Michaels. Reprinted by arrangement with Henry Holt and Company, LLC.

**Andi Miller.** Review of *The Invention of Hugo Cabret*, by Brian Selznick. Reprinted by permission of Andi Miller.

**Moonlight Social.** Web posting from February 8, 2011. Reprinted by permission of Moonlight Social LLC.

**Richard Morin and the Pew Research Center.** "Rising Share of Americans See Conflict between Rich and Poor." Copyright © 2012 by Pew Research Center. Reprinted by permission.

**Eric Mortenson.** "A Diversified Farm Prospers in Oregon's Willamette Valley by Going Organic and Staying Local." From OregonLive.com, September 30, 2011. Copyright © 2011 by Oregonian Publishing Co. Reproduced with permission of the publisher via Copyright Clearance Center.

***New York Times.*** Excerpt from "Beijing's Bad Faith Olympics" (editorial). August 23, 2008. Copyright © 2008 by The New York Times. All rights reserved. Used by permission and protected by the Copyright Laws of the United States. The printing, copying, redistribution, or retransmission of this Content without express written permission is prohibited.

**Omar Offendum.** Excerpt from the lyrics to "#Jan25" by Omar Offendum, Freeway, The Narcicyst, Amri Sulaiman, and Ayah. Reprinted by permission of Advent Media Productions and Omar Offendum.

***Onion.*** Excerpt from "First-Ever Gay 'Dear John' Letters Begin Reaching U.S. Troops Overseas." Reprinted with permission of THE ONION. Copyright © 2011 by Onion, Inc., www.theonion.com.

**Edward F. Palm.** "The Veterans Are Coming! The Veterans Are Coming!" First published in *Inside Higher Ed*, September 19, 2008. Copyright © 2008. Reprinted by permission of the author.

**Alex Pattakos.** "The Meaning of Friendship in a Social-Networked World." Posted October 16, 2010, on HUFFPOST Healthy Living. Reprinted by permission of the author.

**Christophe Pelletier.** "The Locavore's Dilemma." From *The Food Futurist*, December 1, 2010. Copyright © 2010 The Happy Future Group Consulting Ltd. Reprinted by permission of Christophe Pelletier.

**Virginia Postrel.** "Why We Prize That Magical Mystery Pad." From the *Wall Street Journal*, March 12, 2011. Copyright © 2011 Dow Jones & Company. Used by permission.

**Charles A. Riley II.** "Disability and the Media: Prescriptions for Change." Copyright © 2005 by University Press of New England, Lebanon, NH. Reprinted with permission of the publisher and author.

**Elizabeth Royte.** Excerpt from *Bottlemania: How Water Went on Sale and Why We Bought It*. Copyright © 2005. Reprinted by permission of Bloomsbury Publishing PLC.

**Alan Salzberg.** Excerpt from his blog "What Are the Chances? Musings on Everyday Probability." http://what-are-the-chances.blogspot.com/2008/08/atlantic-monthly-indicted-for-criminal.html. Reprinted by permission of Alan Salzberg.

**Libby Sander.** "Blue-Collar Boomers Take Work Ethic to College." From the *Chronicle of Higher Education*, January 18, 2008. Copyright © 2008 The Chronicle of Higher Education. Reprinted by permission.

**Kirk Semple.** "Moving to U.S. and Amassing a Fortune, No English Needed." From the *New York Times*, November 8, 2011. Copyright © 2011 The New York Times. All rights reserved. Used by permission and protected by the Copyright Laws of the United States. The printing, copying, redistribution, or retransmission of this Content without express written permission is prohibited.

**Jack Shakley.** "Indian Mascots—You're Out!" From the *Los Angeles Times*, August 25, 2011. Reprinted by courtesy of the author.

**Laurence Shatkin.** "Education Pays, but Perhaps Less Than You Thought." Originally published on the blog *Career Laboratory*, October 20, 2008, on FastCompany.com. Reprinted by permission of the author.

**Amy Martinez Starke.** "Hmong Elder Didn't Forget the Old Ways." Copyright © 2008 by Oregonian Publishing Co. Reproduced with permission of Oregonian Publishing Co. via the Copyright Clearance Center.

**Claude M. Steele.** "An Introduction: At the Root of Identity." From *Whistling Vivaldi and Other Clues to How Stereotypes Affect Us*. Copyright © 2010 by Claude M. Steele. Used by permission of W.W. Norton & Company, Inc.

**Seth Stevenson.** Excerpt from "Tangled Up in Boobs." From *Slate*, April 12, 2004. Copyright © 2004 by Seth Stevenson. Reprinted by permission of the author.

**Margaret Talbot.** Excerpt from "Men Behaving Badly." Originally published in the *New York Times Magazine*. Copyright © 2002 by Margaret Talbot. Used by permission of The Wylie Agency LLC.

**Amy Tan.** "Mother Tongue." Copyright © 1990 by Amy Tan. First appeared in *The Threepenny Review*. Reprinted by permission of the author and the Sandra Dijsktra Literary Agency.

**Deborah Tannen.** "Why Is Compromise Now a Dirty Word?" From *Politico*, June 15, 2011. Reprinted by permission of the author.

**Stuart Taylor Jr. and K.C. Johnson.** Excerpt from "Guilty in the Duke Case." Published in the *Washington Post*, September 7, 2007. Reprinted by permission of the authors.

**John Tierney.** "Can a Playground Be Too Safe?" From the *New York Times*, July 18, 2011. Copyright © 2011 by The New York Times. All rights reserved. Used by permission and protected by the Copyright Laws of the United States. The printing, copying, redistribution, or retransmission of this Content without express written permission is prohibited.

**Kathryn H. Tunheim.** Letter to the Editor of the *New York Times*. July 13, 2011. Reprinted by permission of Kathryn H. Tunheim.

**Twin Cities Public Television.** "First Speakers: Restoring the Ojibwe Language." Produced by Twin Cities Public Television, Inc., and made possible by the Legacy Amendment's Arts and Cultural Heritage Fund. Used by permission.

**Neil Warner.** Excerpt from "The Anatomy of a Spring." From teaandtoast.ie, May 12, 2011. Reprinted by permission of Neil Warner.

**Wikipedia.** "Local Food" and "Farm-to-Table." From Wikipedia, the free encyclopedia: http://en.wikipedia.org/wiki/Local_food, http://en.wikipedia.org/wiki/Farm-to-table.

**Shirley J. Wilcher.** "Perspectives: Affirmative Action May Be Needed—for Men." From diverseeducation.com, November 1, 2010. Reprinted with permission from Diverse Issues in Higher Education, www.diverseeducation.com.

**Patricia J. Williams.** "Are We Worried about Storm's Identity—or Our Own?" From *The Nation*, June 1, 2011. Reprinted with permission of the publisher.

**Sean Wilsey.** "The Things They Buried." From the *New York Times* Book Review Section, June 18, 2006. Copyright © 2006 The New York Times. All rights reserved. Used by permission and protected by the Copyright Laws of the United States. The printing, copying, redistribution, or retransmission of this Content without express written permission is prohibited.

**Malia Wollan.** "Migration, on Ice: How Globalization Kills Chickens for Their Parts." From meatpaper.com, July 2008. Reprinted by permission of the author.

**Lan Xue.** "China: The Prizes and Pitfalls of Progress." From *Nature* magazine, vol. 454, July 24, 2008. Reprinted by permission from Macmillan Publishers Ltd. Copyright © 2008 by the Nature Publishing Group.

**Byron York.** Excerpt from "White House: Libya Fight Is Not War, It's 'Kinetic Military Action.'" From the *Washington Examiner*, March 23, 2011. Reprinted by permission of the author and publisher.

**Illustrations**

p. iv: (left to right) Courtesy of the Massachusetts Horticultural Society; *Sir Isaac Newton (1642–1723)* (oil on canvas) (detail) by Sir Godfrey Kneller (1646–1723), Academie des Sciences, Paris, France/Giraudon/The Bridgeman Art Library; AP/Wide World Photos; © Carlos Barria/Reuters/Corbis; © Lynn Johnson/Aurora/Getty Images; A. S. Alexander Collection of Ernest Hemingway. Department of Rare Books and Special Collections, Princeton University Library; The Ad Council, Discovering Nature Campaign in partnership with the USDA Forest Service; Bill Wight/Getty Images; Design copyright © 2010 Steven Barrymore; Ivan Cash & Any Dao; p. 3: (l-r) STR/Reuters/Landov; © Chappatte in *International Herald Tribune*, www.globecartoon.com; p. 4: AP/Wide World Photos; p. 7: © David Sipress/The New Yorker Collection/www.cartoonbank.com; p. 8: © Benjamin Hummel; p. 9: Justin Sullivan/Getty Images; p. 10: Kelly Woen/Zuma/Corbis; p. 12: (t) © Tribune Media Services, Inc. All rights reserved. Reprinted with permission; (b) Peter Macdiarmid/Getty Images; p. 14: AP Photo/Office de Tourisme de Chartres; p. 17: Michael N. Todaro/FilmMagic/Getty Images; p. 19: Robert Galbraith/Reuters/Landov; p. 21: Bettmann/Corbis; p. 23: (t + b) Courtesy of Mellcom.com; pp. 26–27: © Doctors Without Borders/Medecins Sans Frontieres; p. 29: www.bumperart.com; p. 30: (l-r) AP/Wide World Photos; © Tribune Media Services, Inc. All Rights Reserved. Reprinted with permission; p. 31: Pete Souza/The White House/Getty Images; p. 33: Chip Somodevilla/Getty Images; p. 35: © Robert Mankoff/The New Yorker Collection/www.cartoonbank.com; p. 37: Sara D. Davis/Getty Images; p. 40: (l) www.bumperart.com; (r) Courtesy of www.cafepress.com; p. 42: (l-r) John Arnold

Images Ltd/Alamy; Andy Kropa/Getty Images; Tony Avelar/Bloomberg via Getty Images; p. 43: Ezra Shaw/Getty Images; p. 44: Jim Spellman/WireImage/Getty Images; p. 46: Martin H. Simon/Pool via Bloomberg/Getty Images; p. 48: Used with permission of Volkswagen Group of America, Inc.; p. 49: Kim Ludbrook/epa/Corbis; p. 55: (l-r) CBS/Photofest; NBC/Photofest; Frank Cotham/www.cartoonbank.com; p. 57: AP/Wide World Photos; p. 58: Jake Fuller/Artizans.com; p. 59: (l + r) © Sepah News/Handout/Document Iran/Corbis; p. 63: www.CartoonStock.com; p. 64: From *USA Today* (Academic Permission), 2/1/2012 Issue, © 2012 Gannett. All rights reserved. Used by permission and protected by the Copyright Laws of the United States. The printing, copying, redistribution, or retransmission of this Content without express written permission is prohibited; p. 68: © Randy Glasbergen; p. 71: AP/Wide World Photos; p. 74: (l) Illustration by Rob Corley in "The Fallacy Detective"; (m) Scott Olson/Getty Images; p. 77: Tim Boyle/Getty Images; p. 78: © Roz Chast/ The New Yorker Collection/www.cartoonbank.com; p. 82: (t-b) Courtesy of Google, Inc. Reprinted with permission; p. 84: Al Messerschmidt/Getty Images; p. 85: V.J. Lovero/Sports Illustrated/Getty Images; p. 87: William Warren, Americans for Limited Government, 2009; p. 90: (l-r) Robert Galbraith/Reuters/Landov; David Becker/Getty Images; Junko Kimura/Getty Images; p. 94: Chris Maddaloni/CQ Roll Call/Getty Images; p. 95: Designed by Sean Geng (www.designspasm.net); p. 97: Beth Hall/Bloomberg News via Getty Images; p. 99: The Ad Council; p. 103: AP/Wide World Photos; p. 107: City of Munster, Germany; p. 108: David Levene/eyevine/ Redux; p. 129: World History Archive/Alamy; p. 130: AP/Wide World Photos; p. 135: © Charles Barsotti/The New Yorker Collection/www.cartoonbank.com; p. 137: PhotoLink/Getty Images; p. 141: Design copyright © 2010 Steven Barrymore; p. 144: NEA; p. 147: Photo © Stephen Voss; p. 152: (l-r) mediablitzimages (UK) Limited/ Alamy; Alfred Eisenstaedt/Pix Inc./Time & Life Pictures/Getty Images; David R. Frazier Photolibrary, Inc./Alamy; p. 154: Pat Bagley/CagleCartoons.com; p. 157: PolitiFact.com; p. 159: The Arthritis Foundation and the Ad Council. Young and Rubicam, NY; p. 187: (l-r) Eightfish/Alamy; Frederick M. Brown/Getty Images; Bill Wight/Getty Images; p. 189: Nate Beeler, politicalcartoons.com; p. 191: Jonathan Alcorn/Bloomberg via Getty Images; p. 193: www.cartoonstock.com; p. 194: © Discovr Music 2012; p. 199: Design by Shane Snow. Originally appeared on SixRevisions.com via Wix; p. 214: (l-r) Mario Tama/Getty Images; AP/Wide World Photos; Hulton Archive/Getty Images; p. 215: Jamie Sabau/Getty Images; p. 217: The Ad Council, Discovering Nature Campaign in partnership with the USDA Forest Service; p. 220: Gareth Cattermole/Getty Images for Netflix; p. 223: © Cho Taussig/Courtesy Everett Collection; p. 224: Chiaki Nozu/Wire Images/Getty Images; p. 226: Cover of *Fun Home: A Family Tragicomic* by Alison Bechdel. Jacket art copyright © 2006 by Alison Bechdel. Reprinted by permission of Houghton-Mifflin Harcourt Publishing Company. All rights reserved; p. 228: NHTSA; p. 242: (l-r) U.S. Fish and Wildlife Service via Bloomberg/Getty Images; Robyn Beck/AFP/Getty Images; Mario Tama/Getty Images; p. 243: Karen Kasmauski/National Geographic/ Getty Images; p. 246: Paresh Nath, www.politicalcartoons.com; p. 249: Ed Arno/The New Yorker Collection/www.cartoonbank.com; p. 258: Image Courtesy of PETA, www.peta2.com; p. 269: Dith Pran/The New York Times/Redux; p. 273: (l-r) Martin Bernetti/AFP/Getty Images; AP/Wide World Photos; Spencer Platt/Getty Images; p. 274: Dave Granlund, www.politicalcartoons.com; p. 277: Michael Williamson/

The Washington Post/Getty Images; p. 278: Joshua Roberts/Bloomberg/Getty Images; p. 279: Ron Sanford/Photo Researchers; p. 281: Mike Keefe, www.political cartoons.com; p. 283: Andy Singer, www.politicalcartoons.com; p. 285: (l) Chris Goodney/Bloomberg News/Getty Images; (r) Lucy Nicholson/Reuters/Landov; p. 289: AP/Wide World Photos; p. 296: Courtesy of Manasi Deshpande; p. 309: (l-r) Andrew D. Bernstein/NBAE via Getty Images; Lynda Barry/*Drawn & Quarterly*; Justin Sullivan/Getty Images; p. 310: *Sir Isaac Newton (1642–1723)* (oil on canvas) (detail) by Sir Godfrey Kneller (1646–1723), Academie des Sciences, Paris, France/Giraudon/ The Bridgeman Art Library; p. 313: Photofest; p. 318: Miluckovich Atlanta Journal-Constitution; p. 320: © 1999 Aaron McGruder. Reprinted by permission of Universal Press Syndicate. All rights reserved; p. 321: www.cartoonstock.com; p. 326: (l-r) AP/ Wide World Photos; National Institute of Mental Health, National Institutes of Health, Department of Health and Human Services; AP/Wide World Photos; p. 328: Bernard Gotfryd/Getty Images; p. 329: Poster Design: Woody Pirtle; p. 330: Khaled Desoaki/AFP/Getty Images; p. 331: © 2012 Paul Davis; p. 332: © Carlos Barria/ Reuters/Corbis; p. 333: Creative Commons/Wikipedia; p. 335: NASA; p. 336: (l-r) Used with permission of the American Red Cross; U.S. Deparment of Homeland Security; TM/MC © Used under license from the Canadian Olympic Committee, 2012; p. 338: Dave Granlund/politicalcartoons.com; p. 340: Ron Kimball Stock; p. 342: Bureau of Labor Statistics; p. 344: (l-r) AP/Wide World Photos; Phoebe Yu/ Cornell University; AP/Wide World Photos; p. 349: AP/Wide World Photos; p. 351: Fox Broadcasting/Photofest, © and ™ Fox; p. 352: AP/Wide World Photos; p. 356: (t + b) © Frank Miller; p. 360: © Moonlight Social LLC, 2012. Photography by Mark Rocha; p. 362: Courtesy of Max Cougar Oswald; p. 364: (clockwise from top l) Wonkette.com; Courtesy of Talking Points Memo; Courtesy of HotAir.com; p. 367: (l-r) Jonathan Oiley/Getty Images; Ryan Collerd/The NY Times/Redux; Juan Castillo/ AFP/Getty Images; p. 370: © 2008 Tolpa Studios, Inc.; p. 371: Jonathan Oiley/Getty Images; p. 378: © 2012 ITHAKA. Reprinted courtesy of JSTOR. All rights reserved; pp. 389, 391: Nature Publishing Group; p. 397: John Ditchburn/INKCINCT Cartoons; p. 401: Courtesy of Google, Inc. Reprinted with permission; p. 405: © George Price/ The New Yorker Collection/www.cartoonbank.com; p. 407: Ryan Collerd/The NY Times/Redux; p. 411: www.cartoonstock.com; p. 412: AP/Wide World Photos; p. 414: (l) Printed with permission from *Popular Science* ® Bonnier Corporation. Copyright 2009. All rights reserved; (r) Reprinted with permission from *American Journal of Physics*, vol. 6, no. 7, July 2008. American Association of Physics Teachers; p. 415: (clockwise from top l) NOAA; Discovery Channel; Courtesy of http://tornadochaser .net; p. 419: Joe Burbank/Orlando Sentinel/MCT via Getty Images; p. 421: Ed Fisher/ The New Yorker Collection/www.cartoonbank.com; p. 425: Juan Castillo/AFP/Getty Images; p. 428: Roz Chast/The New Yorker Collection/www.cartoonbank.com; p. 437: FBI; p. 438: Courtesy of the Massachusetts Horticultural Society; p. 441: Doonesbury Copyright © 2002 G. B. Trudeau. Reprinted with permission of Universal Press Syndicate. All rights reserved; p. 442: Creative Commons/ Wikipedia; pp. 482–85: Melanie Stetson Freeman/© 2011 The Christian Science Monitor (www.CSMonitor.com). Reprinted with permission; p. 487: Ben Hider/ Getty Images; p. 503: AP/Wide World Photos; p. 504: © Thomas Cockrem/Alamy; p. 508: © MAPS.com/Corbis; p. 511: Keith Bernstein/© HBO/Everett Collection; pp. 515, 517: Andrew Hancock; p. 521: (l) A. Ramey/PhotoEdit; (r) © Macduff Everton/

Corbis; p. 526: Frederick M. Brown/Getty Images; p. 528: Bill Pugliano/Getty Images; p. 535: Eugene Gologursky/WireImage/Getty Images; p. 536: AP/Wide World Photos; p. 537: (l) Film still from *The Miracle Worker*, Courtesy Everett Collection; (r) © Robert Pitts/Landov; p. 538: Mary Evans Picture Library/Everett Collection; p. 544: © Lynn Johnson/Aurora/Getty Images; p. 546: AP/Wide World Photos; p. 558: (l) *Portrait of Antonio Vivaldi (1678–1741)* (oil on canvas), Italian School (18th century)/Civico Museo Bibliografico Musicale, Bologna, Italy/Alinari/Bridgeman Art Library International; (r) Hedrich Blessing Collection/Chicago History Museum/Getty Images; p. 561: Jeff Siner/Charlotte Observer/MCT via Getty Images; pp. 572–87: U.S. Census Bureau; p. 597: Tony Vaccaro/Getty Images; p. 601: © Bernard Martinez/Roger Viollet/The Image Works; p. 602: © Bettmann/Corbis; p. 611: National Institute of Mental Health; p. 612: Hispanic Scholarship Fund; p. 617: © David Wells/The Image Works; p. 624: © Jim McHugh; p. 630: Brian Cassella/Chicago Tribune/MCT via Getty Images; p. 632: AP/Wide World Photos; p. 640: Lane Christiansen/Chicago Tribune/MCT via Getty Images; pp. 649–51: Richard Perry/The New York Times/Redux; pp. 654–55: Chang W. Lee/The New York Times; p. 659: Daniel Borris/The New York Times/Redux; p. 660: From the *New York Times*, September 24, 2011. All rights reserved. Used by permission and protected by the Copyright Laws of the United States. The printing, copying, redistribution, or retransmission of this Content without express written permission is prohibited; p. 662: AP/Wide World Photos; pp. 664–72: Creative Commons/Wikipedia; pp. 678–87: John Knetchtel, ed., "Food." *Alphabet City Magazine* 12, pp. 198–207, © 2007, Massachusetts Institute of Technology & Alphabet City Inc., by permission of The MIT Press and Claire Ironside. "The Big Apple, Colborne, Ontario" photograph by Adrian Black; p. 707: Malia Wollan; p. 713: Jon Furniss/Getty Images; p. 718: Romeo Gacad/Getty Images; pp. 721–22: From the *New York Times*, July 15, 2007. All rights reserved. Used by permission and protected by the Copyright Laws of the United States. The printing, copying, redistribution, or retransmission of this Content without express written permission is prohibited; p. 726: © Ned Frisk/Corbis; p. 735: Used with permission of Student Artist Joseph Wagner and Department of Residence Life, Western Washington University; p. 741: Used with permission of Student Artist Megan Stampfli and Department of Residence Life, Western Washington University; p. 757: (t) Carli Baker/The Daily Californian; (b) Ashley Chen/The Daily Californian; p. 759: (t) Shirin Ghaffary/The Daily Californian; (m) Kevin Hahn/The Daily Californian; (b) Randy Adam Romero/The Daily Californian; p. 760: (t) Derek Remsburg/The Daily Californian; (b) Giana Tansman/The Daily Californian; p. 761: (t) Randy Adam Romero/The Daily Californian; (m, b) Anna Vignet/The Daily Californian; p. 762: (t) Carli Baker/The Daily Californian; (b) Giana Tansman/The Daily Californian; p. 763: (t) Kevin Foote/The Daily Californian; (m) Jan Flatley-Feldman/The Daily Californian; (b) Randy Adam Romero/The Daily Californian; p. 772: Design: Gail Anderson and Sam Eckersley. Client: The New York Times; p. 783: © Chuck Savage/Corbis; p. 788: Mark Kauffman/Getty Images; p. 790: © Bettmann/Corbis; p. 793: Hulton Archive/Getty Images; p. 810: (t) A. S. Alexander Collection of Ernest Hemingway. Department of Rare Books and Special Collections, Princeton University Library; (b) The Kobal Collection at Art Resource, NY; pp. 818, 820: From *Listening Is an Act of Love*, ed. by David Isay. Copyright © 2007 by Sound Portraits Productions, Inc. Used by permission of The Penguin Press, a division of

Penguin Group (USA) Inc.; p. 824: From the *New York Times*, December 12, 2008. All rights reserved. Used by permission and protected by the Copyright Laws of the United States. The printing, copying, redistribution, or retransmission of this Content without express written permission is prohibited; p. 825: Michelle V. Agins/The New York Times; pp. 840–51: U.S. Bureau of Labor Statistics; p. 861: John Tlumaki/The Boston Globe via Getty Images; p. 872: Harvard Business School Publishing; p. 901: (r) David Paul-Morris/Bloomberg via Getty Images; pp. 902–3: Joakim Eskildsen; pp. 905–14: Creative Commons/Wikipedia; p. 923: Ivan Cash & Any Dao; p. 924: (t) Jay Readle/Getty Images; (b) Joshua Trujillo/Seattlepi.com; p. 925: (t) Randy L. Rasmussen/The Oregonian; (b) AP/Wide World Photos; p. 928: Mario Tama/Getty Images; p. 946: Gallup, 2011; p. 948: Spencer Platt/Getty Images.

**e-Pages**

**Gist.** "Rise of the Mobile Workstyle." Courtesy of Gist.

**Paula Lavigne.** "What's Lurking in Your Stadium Food?" Courtesy of Outside the Lines/ESPN.com.

**Jennifer Siebel Newsom.** "Trailer for *Miss Representation*." Courtesy of Missrepresentation.org.

***New York Times* (with photos by Ruth Fremson).** "After Iraq, a New Chapter at College." From the *New York Times*, January 9, 2010. Copyright © 2010 The New York Times. All rights reserved. Used by permission and protected by the Copyright Laws of the United States. The printing, copying, redistribution, or retransmission of this Content without express written permission is prohibited.

***New York Times* (with photos by Jim Wilson).** "An Education, Over the Border and Under the Radar." From the *New York Times*, January 12, 2012. Copyright © 2012 The New York Times. All rights reserved. Used by permission and protected by the Copyright Laws of the United States. The printing, copying, redistribution, or retransmission of this Content without express written permission is prohibited.

**Max Cougar Oswald.** "Progress." Courtesy of Max Cougar Oswald.

**Landon Thomas Jr.** "Young and Unemployed." From the *New York Times*, February 15, 2012. Copyright © 2012 The New York Times. All rights reserved. Used by permission and protected by the Copyright Laws of the United States. The printing, copying, redistribution, or retransmission of this Content without express written permission is prohibited.

# INDEX

Entries followed by a e symbol may be found online at **bedfordstmartins.com/everythingsanargument/epages**.

**Missing something?** To access the e-Pages that accompany this text, visit **bedfordstmartins.com/everythingsanargument/epages**. Students who do not buy a new print book can purchase access to e-Pages at this site.

## Inside the e-Pages for *Everything's an Argument with Readings*

Barack Obama, *President Obama on the Death of Osama bin Laden* [speech]

Max Cougar Oswald, *Progress* [multimedia presentation]

Jennifer Siebel Newsom, *Trailer for* Miss Representation [documentary film trailer]

*New York Times* (with photos by Jim Wilson), *An Education, Over the Border and Under the Radar* [slide show]

Paula Lavigne, ESPN, *What's Lurking in Your Stadium Food?* [online article]

Landon Thomas Jr., *Young and Unemployed* [video]

Gist, *Rise of the Mobile Workstyle* [infographic]

The White House, *The Buffett Rule* [video]

... and more!